P9-CQC-525

Adult Psychopathology
and Diagnosis

Adult Psychopathology and Diagnosis

Fifth Edition

Edited by

Michel Hersen

Samuel M. Turner

Deborah C. Beidel

John Wiley & Sons, Inc.

This book is printed on acid-free paper.

Copyright © 2007 by John Wiley & Sons, Inc. All rights reserved.

Published by John Wiley & Sons, Inc., Hoboken, New Jersey.
Published simultaneously in Canada.

Wiley Bicentennial Logo: Richard J. Pacifico.

No part of this publication may be reproduced, stored in a retrieval system, or transmitted in any form or by any means, electronic, mechanical, photocopying, recording, scanning, or otherwise, except as permitted under Section 107 or 108 of the 1976 United States Copyright Act, without either the prior written permission of the Publisher, or authorization through payment of the appropriate per-copy fee to the Copyright Clearance Center, Inc., 222 Rosewood Drive, Danvers, MA 01923, (978) 750–8400, fax (978) 646–8600, or on the web at www.copyright.com. Requests to the Publisher for permission should be addressed to the Permissions Department, John Wiley & Sons, Inc., 111 River Street, Hoboken, NJ 07030, (201) 748–6011, fax (201) 748–6008, or online at http://www.wiley.com/go/permissions.

Limit of Liability/Disclaimer of Warranty: While the publisher and author have used their best efforts in preparing this book, they make no representations or warranties with respect to the accuracy or completeness of the contents of this book and specifically disclaim any implied warranties of merchantability or fitness for a particular purpose. No warranty may be created or extended by sales representatives or written sales materials. The advice and strategies contained herein may not be suitable for your situation. You should consult with a professional where appropriate. Neither the publisher nor author shall be liable for any loss of profit or any other commercial damages, including but not limited to special, incidental, consequential, or other damages.

This publication is designed to provide accurate and authoritative information in regard to the subject matter covered. It is sold with the understanding that the publisher is not engaged in rendering professional services. If legal, accounting, medical, psychological or any other expert assistance is required, the services of a competent professional person should be sought.

Designations used by companies to distinguish their products are often claimed as trademarks. In all instances where John Wiley & Sons, Inc. is aware of a claim, the product names appear in initial capital or all capital letters. Readers, however, should contact the appropriate companies for more complete information regarding trademarks and registration.

For general information on our other products and services please contact our Customer Care Department within the United States at (800) 762-2974, outside the United States at (317) 572-3993 or fax (317) 572-4002.

Wiley also publishes its books in a variety of electronic formats. Some content that appears in print may not be available in electronic books. For more information about Wiley products, visit our web site at www.wiley.com.

Library of Congress Cataloging-in-Publication Data:

Adult psychopathology and diagnosis / [edited] by Michel Hersen, Samuel M. Turner, Deborah C. Beidel.—5th ed.
    p. ; cm.
  Includes bibliographical references and indexes.
  ISBN: 978-0-471-74584-6 (cloth : alk. paper)
 1. Psychology, Pathological. 2. Mental illness—Diagnosis. I. Hersen, Michel. II. Turner, Samuel M., 1944- III. Beidel, Deborah C.
  [DNLM: 1. Mental Disorders—diagnosis. 2. Mental Disorders. 3. Adult. WM 141 A244 2007]
  RC454.A324 2007
  616.89—dc22   2006025196

Printed in the United States of America.

10 9 8 7 6 5 4 3 2 1

Preface

This is the fifth edition of *Adult Psychopathology and Diagnosis*. Publication of this volume again was necessitated by the continued rapid advancement in the field of psychopathology as it relates to assessment and modification. Since the fourth edition many new data have been collected, and these have been documented across the 17 chapters herein. This volume originally was planned by Samuel M. Turner and Michel Hersen. However, with the untimely death of Sam, Deborah C. Beidel, a friend and close colleague of his, graciously agreed to take over the editorial duties. Thus, it is with very mixed emotions that I write this Preface. I was delighted once again to have the pleasure of working with Debbie. But it was very sad not to be able to get Sam's valued input on given issues as they manifested themselves. I missed those telephone conversations with him. Debbie and I therefore dedicate this volume to Sam's memory and to the wonderful work he accomplished in his much-too-short lifetime. He is indeed missed by his family, friends, and students alike.

The fifth edition contains 17 chapters divided into two parts (Part One: Overview; Part Two: Specific Disorders). Part One has four chapters by experts in the field: Dimensional versus Categorical Classification, Dual Diagnosis, Structured Interviewing and Semistructured Interviewing, and Impact of Race and Ethnicity. These four topics are at the cutting edge of assessing psychopathology and help make this volume truly contemporary both in substance and spirit. The fourth chapter dealing with race and ethnicity is especially important given that the cross-cultural impact has often been overlooked by those in the clinical world. Obviously we believe this to have been a very serious oversight.

Part Two on Specific Disorders includes 13 chapters that cover many of the major diagnostic entities and problems seen in daily clinical work by those in hospitals, clinics, and private practice. To the extent possible, we have asked our eminent contributors to follow a standard format. Exceptions were allowed as dictated by the data inherent in each chapter. Generally, however, each chapter has a Description of the Disorder, a Case Study, material about Epidemiology, Clinical Picture, Course and Prognosis, Diagnostic Considerations (including those of dual diagnoses), Psychological and Biological Assessment, and Etiological Considerations. In this latter category we have asked authors to talk about Familial and Genetic issues, Learning and Modeling, Life Events, Gender and Racial-Ethnic issues, and Biological and Physiological considerations.

Many individuals have contributed to the fifth edition of this textbook. First, we thank our experts who agreed to share contemporary knowledge about their respective areas. Second, we thank Carole Londerée for her most perspective editorial assistance. Once again, she has helped us to keep on track. Third, we thank

Cynthia Polance and Christopher Brown for their able technical assistance. And finally, we thank Patricia Rossi and her very able staff at John Wiley & Sons. We also need to acknowledge the fact that our students have kept all of us on our toes with respect to answering many of the difficult challenges posed by psychopathology and diagnosis.

MICHEL HERSEN

Hillsboro, Oregon

Contributors

Emily B. Ansell, PhD
School of Medicine
Yale University
New Haven, Connecticut

Patricia A. Areán, PhD
Department of Psychiatry
UC San Francisco
San Francisco, California

Deborah C. Beidel, PhD
Penn State College of Medicine
Milton S. Hershey Medical Center
Hershey, Pennsylvania

Melanie E. Bennett, PhD
School of Medicine
University of Maryland
Baltimore, Maryland

Marina A. Bornovalova, MA
Department of Psychology
University of Maryland
College Park, Maryland

Lori A. Brotto, PhD
Department of Obstetrics and
    Gynaecology
University of British Columbia
Vancouver, British Columbia, Canada

Etzel Cardeña, PhD
Department of Psychology
University of Lund
Lund, Sweden

Dennis R. Combs, PhD
Department of Psychology
University of Tulsa
Tulsa, Oklahoma

Frederick L. Coolidge, PhD
Department of Psychology
University of Colorado
Colorado Springs, Colorado

Christopher J. Correia, PhD
Department of Psychology
University of Maryland
College Park, Maryland

Stacey B. Daughters, PhD
Department of Psychology
University of Maryland
College Park, Maryland

Jack D. Edinger, PhD
Psychology Service
Veterans Affairs Medical Center
Durham, North Carolina

Leilani Feliciano, PhD
Department of Psychiatry
University of California, San Francisco
San Francisco, California

Selvija Gjonbalaj-Morovic, PhD
School of Medicine
University of Maryland
Baltimore, Maryland

David H. Gleaves, PhD
Department of Psychology
University of Canterbury
Christchurch, New Zealand

Gerald Goldstein, PhD
Psychology Service
Veterans Affairs Medical Center
Pittsburgh, Pennsylvania

Carlos M. Grilo, PhD
Department of Psychiatry
Yale University
New Haven, Connecticut

Sandra Jenkins, PhD
Psychological Service Center
Pacific University
Portland, Oregon

Sheri L. Johnson, PhD
Department of Psychology
University of Miami
Miami, Florida

Bill N. Kinder, PhD
Department of Psychology
University of South Florida
Tampa, Florida

Laurence J. Kirmayer, MD
Culture and Mental Health Research
   Unit
Sir Mortimer B. Davis–Jewish General
   Hospital
Montréal, Québec, Canada

Carolin Klein, PhD
Department of Psychology
University of British Columbia
Vancouver, British Columbia, Canada

C. W. Lejuez, PhD
Department of Psychology
University of Maryland
College Park, Maryland

Susan Tinsley Li, PhD
Psychological Service Center
Pacific University
Portland, Oregon

Karl J. Looper, MD
Culture and Mental Health Research
   Unit
Sir Mortimer B. Davis–Jewish General
   Hospital
Montréal, Québec, Canada

David J. Miklowitz, PhD
Department of Psychology
University of Colorado
Boulder, Colorado

Charles M. Morin, PhD
École de Psychologie
Université Laval
Sainte-Foy, Québec, Canada

Kim T. Mueser, PhD
Dartmouth Psychology Center
University of New Hampshire
Concord, New Hampshire

Stephanie Mullins-Sweatt, MA
Department of Psychology
University of Kentucky
Lexington, Kentucky

Megan Roehrig, PhD
Department of Psychology
University of South Florida
Tampa, Florida

Daniel L. Segal, PhD
Department of Psychology
University of Colorado
Colorado Springs, Colorado

Linda C. Sobell, PhD
Center for Psychological Studies
Nova Southeastern University
Fort Lauderdale, Florida

Mark B. Sobell, PhD
Center for Psychological Studies
Nova Southeastern University
Fort Lauderdale, Florida

Brooke Stipelman, MA
Department of Psychology
University of Maryland
College Park, Maryland

Alecia Sundsmo, MS
Psychological Service Center
Pacific University
Portland, Oregon

J. Kevin Thompson, PhD
Department of Psychology
University of South Florida
Tampa, Florida

Eric F. Wagner, PhD
Community-Based Intervention
    Reading Group
Florida International University
Miami, Florida

Thomas A. Widiger, PhD
Department of Psychology
University of Kentucky
Lexington, Kentucky

Contents

PART I OVERVIEW

1 Mental Disorders as Discrete Clinical Conditions:
   Dimensional versus Categorical Classification   3
   Thomas A. Widiger and Stephanie Mullins-Sweatt

2 The Problem of Dual Diagnosis   34
   Melanie E. Bennett and Selvija Gjonbalaj-Morovic

3 Structured and Semistructured Interviews for Differential
   Diagnosis: Issues and Applications   78
   Daniel L. Segal and Frederick L. Coolidge

4 Impact of Race and Ethnicity   101
   Susan Tinsley Li, Sandra Jenkins, and Alecia Sundsmo

PART II SPECIFIC DISORDERS

5 Delirium, Dementia, and Amnestic and
   Other Cognitive Disorders   125
   Gerald Goldstein

6 Substance-Related Disorders: Alcohol   166
   Eric F. Wagner, Mark B. Sobell, and Linda C. Sobell

7 Psychoactive Substance Use Disorders: Drugs   201
   *Stacey B. Daughters, Marina A. Bornovalova, Christopher J. Correia,
   and C. W. Lejuez*

8 Schizophrenia   234
   Dennis R. Combs and Kim T. Mueser

9 Mood Disorders: Depressive Disorders   286
   Leilani Feliciano and Patricia A. Areán

10 Bipolar Disorder   317
   David J. Miklowitz and Sheri L. Johnson

11 Anxiety Disorders   349
   Deborah C. Beidel and Brooke Stipelman

12 Somatoform Disorders   410
   Laurence J. Kirmayer and Karl J. Looper

13 Dissociative Disorders   473
   Etzel Cardeña and David H. Gleaves

14 Sexual and Gender Identity Disorders   504
   Lori A. Brotto and Carolin Klein

15 Eating Disorders 571
J. Kevin Thompson, Megan Roehrig, and Bill N. Kinder
16 Sleep Disorders 601
Charles M. Morin and Jack D. Edinger
17 Personality Disorders 633
Emily B. Ansell and Carlos M. Grilo

Author Index 679

Subject Index 721

PART I

OVERVIEW

CHAPTER 1

Mental Disorders as Discrete Clinical Conditions: Dimensional versus Categorical Classification

THOMAS A. WIDIGER AND STEPHANIE MULLINS-SWEATT

"In *DSM-IV*, there is no assumption that each category of mental disorder is a completely discrete entity with absolute boundaries dividing it from other mental disorders or from no mental disorder" (American Psychiatric Association [APA], 2000, p. xxxi). This carefully worded disclaimer, however, is somewhat hollow, as it is the case that "*DSM-IV* is a categorical classification that divides mental disorders into types based on criterion sets with defining features" (APA, 2000, p. xxxi). Researchers and clinicians, following this lead, diagnose and interpret the conditions presented in *DSM-IV* as disorders that are qualitatively distinct from normal functioning and from one another.

The question of whether mental disorders are discrete clinical conditions or arbitrary distinctions along dimensions of functioning is a long-standing issue (Kendell, 1975), but its significance is escalating with the growing recognition of the limitations of the categorical model (Widiger & Clark, 2000; Widiger & Samuel, 2005). "Indeed, in the last 20 years, the categorical approach has been increasingly questioned as evidence has accumulated that the so-called categorical disorders like major depressive disorder and anxiety disorders, and schizophrenia and bipolar disorder seem to merge imperceptibly both into one another and into normality . . . with no demonstrable natural boundaries" (First, 2003, p. 661). In 1999, a *DSM-V* Research Planning Conference was held under joint sponsorship of the APA and the National Institute of Mental Health (NIMH), the purpose of which was to set research priorities that would optimally inform future classifications. One impetus for this effort was the frustration with the existing nomenclature.

In the more than 30 years since the introduction of the Feighner criteria by Robins and Guze, which eventually led to *DSM-III*, the goal of validating these syndromes and discovering common etiologies has remained elusive. Despite many proposed candidates, not one laboratory marker has been found to be specific in identifying any of the *DSM*-defined syndromes. Epidemiologic and clinical studies have shown extremely high rates of comorbidities among the disorders, undermining the hypothesis that the syndromes represent distinct etiologies. Furthermore, epidemiologic studies have shown a high degree of short-term diagnostic instability for many disorders. With regard to treatment, lack of treatment specificity is the rule rather than the exception. (Kupfer, First, & Regier, 2002, p. xviii)

DSM-V Research Planning Work Groups were formed to develop white papers that would set an effective research agenda. The Nomenclature Work Group, charged with addressing fundamental assumptions of the diagnostic system, concluded that it will be "important that consideration be given to advantages and disadvantages of basing part or all of *DSM-V* on dimensions rather than categories" (Rounsaville et al., 2002, p. 12).

The purpose of this chapter is to review the *DSM-IV* categorical diagnosis. The chapter begins with a discussion of fundamental categorical distinctions, including the boundaries with normality and among the existing diagnoses (the boundary with physical disorders was discussed briefly in a prior version of this chapter; Widiger, 1997). Reasons for maintaining a categorical model will then be considered. The chapter concludes with a recommendation for an eventual conversion to a more quantitative, dimensional classification of mental disorders.

BOUNDARY WITH NORMALITY

"In *DSM-IV*, each of the mental disorders is conceptualized as a clinically significant behavioral or psychological syndrome or pattern that occurs in an individual and that is associated with present distress (e.g., a painful symptom) or disability (i.e., impairment in one or more important areas of functioning) or with a significantly increased risk of suffering death, pain, disability, or an important loss of freedom" (APA, 2000, p. xxxi). If one considers the fundamental, defining features of a mental disorder, it is perhaps apparent that it would not be realistic for a qualitative distinction between normal and abnormal functioning to exist. This will be illustrated with respect to dyscontrol, impairment, and pathology—fundamental components of most concepts of mental disorder (Bergner, 1997; Klein, 1978, 1999; Spitzer & Williams, 1982; Wakefield, 1992; Widiger & Sankis, 2000; Widiger & Trull, 1991).

DYSCONTROL

Central to the concept of a mental disorder is dyscontrol (Bergner, 1997; Klein, 1999; Widiger & Trull, 1991). A mental disorder as an "*involuntary* organismic impairment in psychological functioning" (Widiger & Trull, 1991, p. 112; our emphasis). "Involuntary impairment remains the key inference" (Klein, 1999, p. 424). Dyscontrol is not within the concept of a physical disorder, but it is fundamental to a mental disorder, as the latter concerns impairments to feelings, thoughts, and behaviors over which normal, healthy persons attempt to exert volitional or regulatory control.

Persons who freely choose to engage in harmful or impairing behaviors would not be said to have a mental disorder. Presumably, persons can choose to consume alcohol, take anabolic steroids, shoot heroin, gamble, steal, assault, or engage in deviant sexual acts without being compelled to do so by the presence of a mental disorder. Gambling, drug usage, theft, assaults, and deviant sexual acts can be harmful and maladaptive, but the occurrence of a harmful (or deviant) act would not itself constitute a mental disorder (Gorenstein, 1984; Wakefield, 1992; Widiger & Trull, 1991). Similarly, to the extent that a person can control, modulate, manage, or regulate painful or harmful feelings of sadness, anxiety, or anger, the person would not be considered to have a mood or anxiety disorder (Widiger & Sankis, 2000). "It is the ability to flexibly adjust the way one regulates one's emotions to environmental exigencies that is related to mental health" (Gross & Munoz, 1995, p. 151). It is when a person lacks sufficient control of mood, anxiety, or a harmful behavior pattern that a person might be diagnosed with a mental disorder (Frances, Widiger, & Sabshin, 1991).

There is, however, no qualitative distinction between the presence and absence of self-control. It is not even clear how much volitional or regulatory control a normal, healthy person has over adaptive, healthy behaviors (Bargh & Ferguson, 2000; Howard & Conway, 1986; Kirsch & Lynn, 2000; Wegner & Wheatley, 2000). Both normal and abnormal human functioning is, at best, the result of a complex interaction of apparent volitional choice with an array of biogenetic and environmental determinants.

A continuum (or ambiguity) of self-control is particularly evident in those disorders that involve behaviors that provide immediate benefits or pleasures to the person, such as pedophilia, intermittent explosive disorder, transvestic fetishism, kleptomania, antisocial personality, bulimia nervosa, anorexia nervosa, pathological gambling, and substance-related disorders such as alcohol abuse, cocaine abuse, anabolic steroid abuse, and nicotine dependence. These disorders are difficult to diagnose and are often controversial precisely because there is no distinct point at which dyscontrol occurs (Widiger & Smith, 1994). At one time, persons with alcohol dependence were thought to have a discrete pathology that rendered them entirely incapable of any control of their drinking. However, there is now sufficient research to indicate that persons vary in the extent to which they have inadequate control (Hyman, 2005; Kalivas & Volkow, 2005; Peele, 1984). Treatment for the purpose of controlled drinking is controversial because there is no absolute point of demarcation and persons who lack sufficient control will also lack an adequate awareness of their dyscontrol (Vaillant, 1995). In sum, determination of adequate versus inadequate self-control is fundamental to many social and clinical decisions, but the boundary is at best grossly ill-defined and poorly understood (Alper, 1998; Hyman, 2005; Kalivas & Volkow, 2005).

IMPAIRMENT

An additional fundamental feature of mental disorders is impairment (APA, 1994, 2000; Wakefield, 1992; Widiger & Trull, 1991). "The definition of mental disorder in the introduction to *DSM-IV* requires that there be clinically significant impairment" (APA, 2000, p. 8). The purpose of this requirement is to distinguish between a mental disorder and simply a problem in living. "The ever-increasing number of new categories meant to describe the less impaired outpatient population raises the question of where psychopathology ends and the wear and tear of everyday life begins" (Frances, First, & Pincus, 1995, p. 15).

> To highlight the importance of considering this issue, the criteria sets for most disorders include a clinical significance criterion (usually worded ". . . causes clinically significant . . . impairment in social, occupational, or other important areas of functioning"). This criterion helps establish the threshold for the diagnosis of a disorder in those situations in which the symptomatic presentation by itself (particularly in its milder forms) is not inherently pathological and may be encountered in individuals for whom a diagnosis of "mental disorder" would be inappropriate. (APA, 2000, p. 8)

DSM-III-R (APA, 1987) failed to include this requirement within the criterion sets for many of the disorders, contributing to a confusion of apparently harmless deviances, eccentricities, peculiarities, or annoyances with the presence of a mental disorder (Frances et al., 1991). For example, in DSM-III-R the attention-deficit hyperactivity and oppositional defiant disorders were diagnosed even if the behaviors resulted in "only minimal or no impairment in school and social functioning" (APA, 1987, pp. 53, 58). Similarly, transvestic fetishism could be diagnosed with DSM-III-R simply on the basis of intense sexual urges, fantasies, and behaviors involving cross-dressing that continued for more than six months (APA, 1987). A man who engaged in this behavior for longer than six months but experienced no impairment in functioning would still have been considered in DSM-III-R to have been mentally ill solely because he engaged in deviant sexual acts for longer than six months. It is possible that a six-month duration is a valid indicator for impairment (as well as dyscontrol) but (assuming that volitional behavior does exist) deviant sexual preferences could also be largely harmless. Therefore, DSM-IV required that "the fantasies, sexual urges, or behaviors cause clinically significant distress or impairment in social, occupational, or other important areas of functioning" (APA, 1994, p. 531).

However, nowhere in DSM-IV is a "clinically significant" impairment defined, not even within the section of the manual identified by the heading "Criteria for Clinical Significance" (APA, 2000, p. 8). It is only stated that this "is an inherently difficult clinical judgment" (APA, 2000, p. 8), and it is advised that the clinician consider information obtained from family members and other third parties. Frances et al. (1995) in fact stated that "the evaluation of clinical significance is likely to vary in different cultures and to depend on the availability and interests of clinicians" (p. 15). Absence of a clear basis for the judgment has also helped fuel the considerable controversy of premenstrual dysphoric disorder, a mental disorder that is diagnosed when normal premenstrual experiences (that occur in a substantial proportion of normal adult women) reach an ill-defined level of clinically significant impairment (Winstead & Sanchez, 2005).

Spitzer and Williams (1982), the original authors of the DSM-IV definition of mental disorder, defined a clinically significant impairment as that point at which the attention of a clinician is indicated. "There are many behavioral or psychological conditions that can be considered 'pathological' but the clinical manifestations of which are so mild that clinical attention is not indicated" (p. 166). They provided three examples: caffeine withdrawal, jet lag syndrome, and insomnia because of environmental noise. Impairments in each case were considered by Spitzer and Williams to be too small to be "justified as syndromes that were clinically significant to mental health professionals" (p. 166). These three examples, however, proved to be ironic, as jet lag syndrome was actually included within *DSM-III-R* as a variant of sleep-wake schedule disorder (APA, 1987, p. 306); caffeine withdrawal was subsequently included in the appendix to *DSM-IV* (APA, 1994); and a strong case has been made for the inclusion of caffeine dependence (Hughes, Oliveto, Helzer, Higgins, & Bickel, 1992).

What is considered to be a sufficient level of impairment to warrant treatment probably varies substantially across patients and across clinicians (Samuel & Widiger, in press) as well as often being below the threshold for many of the existing *DSM-IV* criterion sets. Clark, Watson, and Reynolds (1995) documented well the reliance of clinicians on the category of "not otherwise specified" (NOS) to diagnose subthreshold cases. Whenever this catchall diagnosis is included within a study, it is often the most frequent diagnosis, as in the case of mood disorders (Angst, 1992), dissociative disorders (Spiegel & Cardena, 1991), and personality disorders (Verheul & Widiger, 2004).

New additions to the diagnostic manual rarely concern newly discovered forms of psychopathology; instead, they are typically efforts to plug holes in between existing diagnosis and normal functioning (as well as filling gaps among the existing diagnoses). For example, acute stress disorder is essentially posttraumatic stress disorder with a shorter duration; recurrent brief depressive disorder is major depression with shorter episodes; mixed anxiety-depressive disorder concerns subthreshold cases of mood and anxiety disorders; binge eating disorder concerns subthreshold cases of bulimia nervosa; and mild neurocognitive disorder concerns subthreshold cases of dementia, delirium, or amnestic disorder (Frances et al., 1995). A fundamental difficulty shared by all of these diagnoses is the lack of a clear distinction with normal functioning. Two cases that illustrate well the absence of a clear boundary between normal and abnormal functioning are minor depressive disorder (which is considered to be a mental disorder, although not yet officially recognized) and age-related cognitive decline (which is not considered to be a mental disorder).

Minor depressive disorder was a new addition to *DSM-IV* that attempted to plug the gap between *DSM-III-R* mood disorder and normal sadness. There is considerable reluctance to add a new diagnosis for subthreshold depression (Pincus, McQueen, & Elinson, 2003), but it has been estimated that up to 50% of depressive symptomatology is currently being treated by primary care physicians without any consultation or involvement of a mental health clinician in part because the depression is below the threshold of a mood disorder diagnosis (Munoz, Hollon, McGrath, Rehm, & VandenBos, 1994). Many of these persons would meet the *DSM-IV* criteria for minor depressive disorder. However, it is acknowledged in *DSM-IV* that "symptoms meeting . . . criteria for minor depressive disorder can be difficult to distinguish from periods of sadness that are an inherent part of everyday life" (APA, 2000, p. 776). Only two distinctions are provided, one of which is a two-week duration. If a person is sad for less than two weeks, it is normal sadness. If it lasts longer than two weeks, it is a mental disorder. This is comparable to diagnosing cross-dressing as a transvestic fetishism if it is done longer than six months (APA, 1987). The second distinction is that "the depressive symptoms must cause clinically significant distress or impairment" (APA, 2000, p. 776) but, again, clinical significance is left undefined.

Age-related cognitive decline was a new addition to the section of the manual for conditions that are not mental disorders but might be the focus of clinical attention."Cognitive decline in the elderly can be considered dimensionally . . . , involving aging-associated cognitive decline, mild cognitive impairment, and dementia" (Caine, 1994, p. 335)."It may be very difficult to establish an arbitrary or numerical level where a disease state should be proclaimed"(Caine, 1994, p. 334). Age-related cognitive decline concerns "problems remembering names or appointments or . . . difficulty in solving complex problems" (APA, 2000, p. 740). Persons with this condition are often troubled by their cognitive deterioration and they seek the help of clinicians who specialize in the treatment of dementia, thereby meeting the threshold for a clinically significant level of impairment proposed by Spitzer and Williams (1982). However, the *DSM-IV* Task Force decided that age-related cognitive decline should not be classified as a mental disorder because the decline in cognitive functioning is the result of "the aging process that is within normal limits given the person's age" (APA, 2000, p. 740). The level of impairment is sufficient to warrant professional intervention but it is not considered to be a mental disorder because the level of impairment is normative for that time in life. One might question, however, whether being close to the norm is any more relevant for a diagnosis than being deviant from the norm (Frances et al., 1991; Gorenstein, 1984). The fact that age-related cognitive decline is the result of the normal (i.e., common) process of aging does not indicate that it is adaptive, healthy, or without an underlying neuropathology. The aging process is part of the explanation for the development of neuropathology. Fortunately, physicians do not apply the same reasoning by judging that deteriorations in the functioning of one's vision, liver, or bladder are not disorders because they are simply the result of aging and are common to persons within one's age group.

PATHOLOGY

Fundamental to many definitions of mental disorder is the presence of some form of pathology (Klein, 1978; Wakefield, 1992, 1997)."The necessary crucial inference is that something has gone wrong, not simply that something is undesirable or rare" (Klein, 1999, p. 421). Clinicians do not treat normal, healthy functioning; clinicians treat pathologies in cognitive, interpersonal, neurochemical, or psychodynamic functioning. Textbooks of psychopathology, such as this one, are largely efforts to identify and characterize pathologies that are the bases for each respective mental disorder. Presumably, there are persons who lack these pathologies. Such persons could be described as having normal, healthy psychological functioning. The boundary between normal and abnormal psychological functioning might then be identified by the presence versus absence of a respective pathology (Klein, 1978).

Missing from the diagnostic criterion sets in *DSM-IV,* however, are references to underlying pathologies (Wakefield, 1997). Explicit within the *DSM-IV* definition of mental disorder is that the condition "must currently be considered a manifestation of a behavioral, psychological, or biological dysfunction in the individual" (APA, 2000, p. xxxi) but few, if any, of the criterion sets refer explicitly to a behavioral, psychological, or biological dysfunction or abnormality. The diagnostic criterion sets emphasize instead the distress or impairment that is presumably the manifestations of an underlying pathology. Perhaps inclusion of the underlying pathology within a diagnostic criterion set would provide a scientifically and clinically meaningful distinction between a respective mental disorder and normal (nonpathological) functioning (Spitzer & Wakefield, 1999; Wakefield, 1997; Wakefield & Spitzer, 2002).

A limitation of this proposal, however, is the absence of consensus as to fundamental pathologies that should be required. Pathologies are not currently included within diagnostic criterion sets in part because there is insufficient empirical support favoring one particular cognitive, interpersonal, neurochemical, or psychodynamic model of pathology over another (Widiger, 2004). Wakefield (1997), for example, indicated that in order to provide a meaningful distinction between major depressive disorder and normal bereavement, it is "necessary to formulate some account ... of the evolutionary programming of the mechanisms with respect to what kinds of triggering circumstances are supposed to cause which kinds of responses (e.g., loss-response mechanisms are designed so that perceptions of major losses trigger roughly proportional sadness responses)" (p. 647). Wakefield's (1992) conceptualization of mental disorder is tied to evolutionary theory. Evolutionary theory has enriched current understanding of the etiology and pathology of many mental disorders but it is unclear whether the normal and pathologic behavioral response mechanisms from the perspective of evolutionary theory can be adequately specified for the purposes of a clinician's diagnosis. In addition, because it is a model of psychopathology that is derived from a particular theoretical perspective, it may not be capable of serving as a general definition of mental disorder that would be compatible with or suitable for alternative theoretical models (Bergner, 1997; Lilienfeld & Marino, 1999; Widiger & Sankis, 2000).

Even if clinicians and researchers agreed on a particular theoretical model of pathology, it is unclear whether qualitative distinctions between normal functioning and abnormal pathologies could be identified. Klein (1999) believes that there are qualitative distinctions between normal and abnormal neurochemical functioning that would provide a compelling basis for classification. As suggested by Klein, "currently, positive experience with psychopharmacological agents, which have little effect on normal people but have marked benefits on patients with chronic disorders, leads to the inference of something chronically but reversibly wrong" (p. 425). However, there has not in fact been much research on the effects of current psychopharmacological agents on normal neurochemical functioning, and what limited research there is contradicts Klein's assertion.

For example, Knutson et al. (1998) administered paroxetine, a selective serotonin reuptake inhibitor (SSRI), for four weeks in a double-blind study to 23 of 48 normal volunteers. None of the participants met currently, or throughout their lifetime, the *DSM-IV* diagnostic criteria for a mental disorder, as assessed with a semistructured interview. None of them had ever previously received a psychotropic medication, had ever abused drugs, or had ever been in treatment for a mental disorder, nor were any of them currently seeking or desiring treatment for a mental disorder. In sum, they were in many respects above normal in psychological functioning. The paroxetine and placebo treatments continued for four weeks. Knutson et al. reported that SSRI administration (relative to placebo) reduced negative effects and increased social facilitation. The magnitude of changes in functioning even correlated with the plasma levels of SSRI within the treatment group. "This is the first empirical demonstration that chronic administration of a selective serotonin reuptake blockade can have significant personality and behavioral effects in normal humans in the absence of baseline depression or other psychopathology" (p. 378). More generally, effectiveness of anxiolytics and antidepressants for clinical treatment might be their ability to impair, inhibit, or block normal neurochemical mechanisms of sadness and anxiousness rather than reversing or altering pathological neurochemical processes.

Mayberg et al. (1999) investigated with positron emission techniques two complementary alterations in mood: transient sadness provoked in healthy volunteers and treatment-induced resolution of dysphoria in clinically depressed patients. The results indicated "reciprocal changes involving nearly identical limbic-paralimbic and neocortical regions" (pp. 678–679). In other words, the neurophysiology of a mood disorder might be, at best, only quantitatively different from the neurophysiology of normal sadness. Kendler (2005) goes further to suggest for anxiety disorders that neurophysiologically "a panic attack during a near-fatal climbing accident in a psychiatrically healthy individual or in a crowded shopping mall in a patient with agoraphobia are probably the same" (p. 437).

No neurophysiological laboratory technique is currently able to identify the presence of psychopathology independent of or blind to a clinical diagnosis (Steffens & Krishnan, 2003). Substantial attention is being given to structural and functional brain imaging with the hope that these instruments could be used eventually to diagnose neurophysiological pathology (Drevets, 2002; Epstein, Isenberg, Stern, & Silbersweig, 2002). However, there is a virtual absence of research indicating their ability to provide independent, blind diagnoses. Despite enthusiasm for their potential diagnostic value, there are no studies that have assessed the sensitivity and specificity of neuroimaging techniques for the diagnosis or differential diagnosis of specific mental disorders (Steffens & Krishnan, 2003). The diagnosis of a mental disorder requires instead an assessment of the person's behavior within an environmental context, as "functional impairment or disability, not the presence of a lesion, is the essential element in the medical concept of disease" (Bergner, 1997, p. 245).

BOUNDARIES AMONG MENTAL DISORDERS

A concern that predominates attention of many clinicians and researchers is the excessive comorbidity among mental disorders (Caron & Rutter, 1991; Clark et al., 1995; Krueger & Markon, in press; Widiger & Clark, 2000). A fundamental question is whether this apparent comorbidity is the co-occurring presence of multiple mental disorders or the presence of one disorder that is being given multiple diagnoses.

DSM-IV provides diagnostic criterion sets to help guide the clinician toward a purportedly correct diagnosis and an additional section devoted to differential diagnosis that indicates "how to differentiate [the] disorder from other disorders that have similar presenting characteristics" (APA, 2000, p. 10). The intention of the diagnostic manual is to help the clinician determine which particular mental disorder is present, the selection of which would presumably indicate the presence of a specific pathology that will explain the occurrence of the symptoms and suggest a specific treatment that will ameliorate the patient's suffering (Frances et al., 1995; Kendell, 1975).

However, it is evident that *DSM-IV* routinely fails in the goal of guiding the clinician to the presence of one specific disorder. Despite the best efforts of the leading clinicians and researchers who have been the primary authors of each revision of the diagnostic manual, diagnostic comorbidity rather than specificity is the norm (Clark et al., 1995; Krueger & Markon, in press). The high rate of multiple diagnoses at the time of clinical treatment is problematic to the conceptualization of mental disorders as distinct clinical conditions, and the extent of this comorbidity is even higher when one includes lifetime as well as current comorbidity (Brown, Campbell, Lehman, Grisham, & Mancill, 2001). "The greatest challenge that the extensive comorbidity data pose to the current nosological system concerns the validity of the diagnostic categories themselves—do these disorders constitute distinct clinical entities?" (Mineka, Watson, & Clark, 1998, p. 380). "It is clear that the classic Kraepelinian model in which all psychopathology is comprised of discrete and mutually exclusive diseases must be modified or rejected" (Maser & Cloninger, 1990, p. 12). Diagnostic comorbidity has become so prevalent that some researchers argue for an abandonment of the term *comorbidity* in favor of a term (e.g., *co-occurrence*) that is more simply descriptive and does not imply the presence of distinct clinical entities (Lilienfeld, Waldman, & Israel, 1994). There are instances in which presence of multiple diagnoses does suggest presence of distinct yet comorbid psychopathologies, but in most instances presence of co-occurring diagnoses does appear to suggest the presence of a common, shared pathology (Clark, in press; Kendler, Prescott, Myers, & Neale, 2003; Krueger & Markon, in press; Watson, in press; Widiger & Clark, 2000). "Comorbidity may be trying to show us that many current treatments are not so much treatments for transient 'state' mental disorders of affect and anxiety as they are treatments for core processes, such as negative affectivity, that span normal and abnormal variation as well as undergird multiple mental disorders" (Krueger, 2002, p. 44).

DSM-IV appears to be replete with unresolvable boundary distinctions, and, as suggested earlier, the function of new diagnoses is generally to fill these problematic gaps, thereby making the problem even worse by adding to the nomenclature new problematic boundaries (Phillips, Price, Greenburg, & Rasmussen, 2003; Pincus et al., 2003). Notable examples include bipolar II (filling a gap between *DSM-III-R* bipolar and cyclothymic mood disorders), mixed anxiety-depressive disorder (anxiety and mood disorders), depressive personality disorder (personality and mood disorders), and postpsychotic depressive disorder of schizophrenia (schizophrenia and major depression). These new diagnostic categories are helpful in decreasing clinicians' reliance on the NOS diagnostic category to plug the holes among the existing categories, but they also have the effect of creating additional boundary confusions.

Problematic boundaries within *DSM-IV* include such well-known examples as the distinction between oppositional defiant, attention-deficit (with and without hyperactivity-impulsivity), and conduct disorder; anorexia and bulimia; trichotillomania and obsessive-compulsive anxiety disorder; depressive personality disorder and dysthymia; conversion and dissociative disorder; and body dysmorphic disorder and anxiety disorder (First, 2003; Frances et al., 1995). To illustrate, we will discuss briefly problematic boundaries for generalized social phobia, acute stress disorder, and schizoaffective disorder.

Generalized Social Phobia

Social phobia was a new addition to *DSM-III* (Spitzer, Williams, & Skodol, 1980; Turner & Beidel, 1989). It was considered to be a distinct, circumscribed condition, consistent with the definition of a phobia, or a "persistent, irrational fear of a *specific* object, activity, or situation" (APA, 1994, p. 770, our emphasis). However, it became apparent to anxiety disorder researchers and clinicians that the behavior of many of their patients was rarely so discrete and circumscribed (Spitzer & Williams, 1985). Therefore, authors of *DSM-III-R* developed a generalized subtype for when "the phobic situation includes most social situations" (APA, 1987, p. 243).

DSM-III-R generalized social phobia, however, merged into the *DSM-III* diagnosis of avoidant personality disorder. Both were concerned with a pervasive, generalized social insecurity, discomfort, and timidity. Efforts to distinguish them have indicated only that avoidant personality disorder tends to be, on average, relatively more dysfunctional than generalized social phobia (Turner, Beidel, & Townsley, 1992; Widiger, 1992).

DSM-IV provided no solution. In fact, it was acknowledged that generalized social phobia emerges "out of a childhood history of social inhibition or shyness" (APA, 1994, p. 414), consistent with the concept of a personality disorder. An argument for classifying this condition as an anxiety rather than a personality disorder is that many persons with the disorder benefit from pharmacologic interventions (Liebowitz, 1992). "One may have to rethink what the personality disorder concept means in an instance where 6 weeks of phenelzine therapy begins to reverse longstanding interpersonal hypersensitivity as well as discomfort in socializing" (p. 251). If so, one might have to rethink what the anxiety disorder concept means when an antidepressant is an effective form of treating an anxiety disorder. In any case, it is unclear why a maladaptive personality trait should not be responsive to a pharmacologic intervention (Knutson et al., 1998; Livesley, 2001b). *DSM-IV* concluded that these two conditions "may be alternative conceptualizations of the same or similar conditions" (APA, 2000, p. 720).

ACUTE STRESS DISORDER

Spiegel and his colleagues proposed a new diagnosis for *DSM-IV*, brief reactive dissociative disorder, for inclusion within the dissociative disorders section (Cardena, Lewis-Fernandez, Bear, Pakianathan, & Spiegel, 1996; Task Force, 1991). The predominant phenomenology consisted of symptoms of dissociation, including derealization, depersonalization, detachment, stupor, and amnesia. However, brief reactive dissociative disorder resembled closely posttraumatic stress disorder (PTSD), classified as an anxiety disorder (APA, 1987). The major distinction between them was simply that brief reactive dissociative disorder was of a shorter duration (2 days to 4 weeks, whereas PTSD requires a duration of longer than 4 weeks).

Compelling arguments were therefore made for moving PTSD to the dissociative disorders section (Cardena, Butler, & Spiegel, 2003; Spiegel & Cardena, 1991). The etiology and treatment of persons suffering from PTSD resembles more closely the etiology and treatment of dissociative disorders than most anxiety disorders (e.g., panic disorder, social phobia, obsessive-compulsive anxiety disorder, or specific phobia). Dissociative identity disorder and dissociative amnesia are almost invariably in response to having experienced, witnessed, or been confronted with a PTSD stressor. The cognitive pathology of PTSD and dissociative disorders concerns difficulties accepting or integrating a severe trauma (expressed dysfunctionally through gross denial, avoidance, and/or recurrent recollections). The theories, treatment techniques, and concerns of persons who specialize in crisis intervention, trauma, victimization, and abuse may overlap more with specialists in dissociative disorders than with specialists in anxiety disorders.

On the other hand, there are arguments to support the conceptualization of PTSD as an anxiety disorder (Davidson & Foa, 1991). Dissociative symptomatology is often seen in persons with PTSD but this dissociation could be understood as a cognitive avoidance of anxiety. In addition, dissociative symptoms are not as prevalent or predominant as anxious, avoidant symptoms in cases of PTSD. Finally, animal models can reproduce much of the PTSD symptomatology without invoking the notion that the animal is experiencing dissociation.

The final decision for *DSM-IV* was to classify brief reactive dissociative disorder within the anxiety disorders section and to rename it as acute stress disorder (i.e., subthreshold PTSD). The best solution might have been to classify it as both an anxiety and as a dissociative disorder so that clinicians would recognize the importance of considering the presence of both a dysregulation of anxiety and dissociation in their understanding of the pathology and treatment of the condition, but this option would be inconsistent with the categorical assumption of distinct conditions and was not available to the authors of *DSM-IV.*

SCHIZOAFFECTIVE DISORDER

Schizoaffective disorder might be the prototypic boundary condition. It had the unique distinction in *DSM-III* (APA, 1980) of being the only disorder that lacked the specific and explicit criterion set that was the major innovation of the diagnostic manual (Spitzer et al., 1980). A consensus could not be reached on its defining features in large part because it represented the grey area between schizophrenia and mood disorders. It was to be used in *DSM-III* "for those instances in which the clinician is unable to make a differential diagnosis with any degree of certainty" (APA, 1980, p. 202).

However, clinicians had difficulty identifying and researchers had difficulty studying a condition with no diagnostic criteria. Therefore, specific and explicit diagnostic criteria were developed for *DSM-III-R* (APA, 1987). The *DSM-III-R* diagnostic criteria, though, were notably complex and problematic (Frances et al., 1995). Proposed revisions therefore included the development of increasingly more narrow definitions, hoping to eventually identify a distinct clinical entity, or, alternatively, the delineation of new diagnoses, such as "mainly affective" and "mainly schizophrenic" subtypes (Aubert & Rush, 1996).

It is perhaps paradoxical to create a distinct clinical entity that demarcates the overlapping and nebulous area between two other disorders. Schizoaffective disorder might be best understood as an inherently ambiguous condition that occupies the overlapping boundary between the categories of schizophrenia and mood disorder (Blacker & Tsuang, 1992). It could be a phenotypic variation of either schizophrenia or mood disorder that over time crosses the boundaries between them or a genetic interform that occupies their border (Kendler, Neale, & Walsh, 1995). Schizoaffective disorder may not itself be a distinct condition; it may represent instead an inevitable point of confusion in the effort to demarcate a clear, unambiguous distinction between the overlapping schizophrenic, mood, and psychotic disorders (Fowles, 2003).

RATIONALE AND JUSTIFICATION
FOR CATEGORICAL MODEL

There are a number of reasons that diagnostic categories are used rather than clinical spectra or dimensions of functioning (Kendell, 1975), including simplicity, tradition, credibility, utility, and validity. Each of these will be considered in turn.

SIMPLICITY

It is human nature to categorize (De Boeck, Wilson, & Acton, 2005). It is difficult to be cognizant of all shades of gray. Typologies are created in large part to render information into simpler, more succinct formats, and proponents of categorical systems argue that dimensional models are too complex and confusing for clinical use (Frances et al., 1995).

However, as the diagnostic manual continues to expand, filling gaps among arbitrary boundaries of overlapping categories, the illusion of the simplicity of the categorical model may continue to weaken. Mental disorder categories are frustrating and troublesome to clinicians precisely because they suggest a uniformity of presentation and homogeneity of pathology that rarely seems to be present. Widiger, Costa, and McCrae (2002) suggest that dimensional classifications that offer more precise and accurate descriptions may in fact be less cumbersome and complex than the existing diagnostic categories that require the assessment of numerous diagnostic criteria in a frustratingly unsuccessful effort to make illusory categorical distinctions. For example, semistructured interviews for the *DSM-IV* personality disorders must evaluate 80 diagnostic criteria, which does not even include the 14 additional criteria for the two personality disorders included within the appendix to *DSM-IV*, the not-otherwise-specified diagnosis, nor the criteria for conduct disorder that are necessary for the diagnosis of antisocial personality disorder. In contrast, a semistructured interview for the five-factor model of personality that provides a more comprehensive dimensional description of normal and maladaptive personality functioning requires the assessment of only 30 facets of personality functioning (Trull & Widiger, 1997). A classification system that abandons the fruitless effort to make illusory distinctions among overlapping diagnostic categories in favor of a more straightforward description of each individual's unique profile of psychopathology will likely be much easier to use.

TRADITION AND CREDIBILITY

The diagnosis of mental disorders has been largely within the domain of medicine, which has used since the days of Hippocrates a categorical model of classification (Kendell, 1975). It might seem to be a major departure from this tradition to convert to a dimensional form of describing and diagnosing psychopathology. Many clinicians identify themselves as being within a branch of medicine, treating pathologies that are qualitatively distinct from normal functioning. A reformulation of mental disorders as shading imperceptibly into normal psychological functioning could complicate the identity of the profession (Guze, 1978; Guze & Helzer, 1987).

Advocates of categorical distinctions also suggest that dimensional models might trivialize the concept of mental disorder. If the distinction between mental disorders and normal psychological functioning is arbitrary, then perhaps there is no meaningful justification for differentiating persons as having versus not having a mental disorder. Perhaps there is a loss of credibility if mental disorders are not considered to be qualitatively distinct from normal psychological processes (Regier et al., 1998).

However, absence of a discrete, qualitative point of demarcation does not suggest the absence of meaningful distinctions. Mental retardation is currently defined dimensionally as a level of intelligence below an intelligence quotient (IQ) of approximately 70 (APA, 1980, 2000). This point of demarcation does not carve nature at a discrete joint. It is an arbitrary point of demarcation along a continuous distribution, but the arbitrariness of this point of demarcation does not suggest that the disorder of mental retardation is illusory, invalid, or trivial. Persons with IQs lower than 70 do suffer from a wide variety of quite significant and meaningful impairments secondary to their limited levels of intelligence, and it is very helpful and meaningful to identify a specific point of demarcation at which one would or should provide professional intervention to address these impairments (Zachar, 2000).

A related concern is that a dimensional model of psychopathology might trivialize or hinder the study of psychopathology by suggesting that it can be meaningfully or adequately studied within nonclinical populations, such as college students enrolled within introductory psychology courses (Coyne, 1994; Flett, Vredenburg, & Krames, 1997). However, absence of a qualitative point of demarcation between mild, moderate, or severe levels of depression does not necessarily suggest that research on mild levels of depression would generalize meaningfully to high levels of depression. Being extremely tall, introverted, or depressed is not equivalent to being somewhat tall, introverted, or depressed. The experiences, social impairments, treatment implications, and other important correlates of depression will vary with the severity of the disorder. Presence of a continuous distribution does not suggest that the psychopathology seen within clinical settings can always or fully be understood by studies of the psychopathology seen within college students.

Regier and Narrow (2002) suggest that the thresholds for diagnosis in *DSM-IV* should be raised because epidemiologic research has obtained prevalence rates that are beyond expectations. They question whether the diagnostic criterion sets are identifying instances of "true psychopathologic disorder" (p. 114). However, Regier et al. (1998) are forthright in their acknowledgment that their concern is based in part on the implications of high prevalence rates for health care policy. "In the current US climate of determining the medical necessity for care in managed health care plans, it is doubtful that 28% or 29% of the population would be judged to need mental health treatment" (p. 114). However, in order to protect the availability of treatment for the most severe variants of psychopathology, many additional persons in need of treatment are also being neglected. At the same time that Regier et al. suggest raising the bar of diagnosis to limit health care coverage, other clinicians and researchers are arguing for lowering the bar to help gain access to health care coverage for persons with subthreshold anxiety, mood, eating, and other forms of psychopathology (e.g., Magruder & Calderone, 2000; Shisslak, Crago, & Estes, 1995; Stein, Walker, Hazen, & Forde, 1997).

We suspect that a dimensional model might in fact increase the credibility of mental disorder classification by providing the means with which to identify more explicitly and reliably the precise points at which access to health care funding is optimally provided. The credibility of the profession is perhaps being undermined more by the substantial problems and errors generated by a model that claims to carve psychological or neurochemical functioning at discrete joints but fails to do so. A dimensional model of classification could be preferable to governmental, social, and professional agencies because it would provide more reliable, valid, and explicitly defined bases for making these important social and clinical decisions.

UTILITY

The first paragraph of the introduction to *DSM-IV* states that "our highest priority has been to provide a helpful guide to clinical practice" (APA, 2000, p. xxiii). Revisions to the diagnostic manual have usually emphasized matters of reliability and validity (Frances, Widiger, & Pincus, 1989; Spitzer et al., 1980), but it is possible that matters of clinical utility will be provided greater emphasis with *DSM-V* (First et al., 2004). A valid diagnostic manual that is not being used effectively within clinical practice is unlikely to realize its full potential. First et al. suggest that for *DSM-V* a "crucial target for evaluating the advantages and disadvantages of a particular change is its effect on clinical utility" (p. 953), and it is matters of clinical utility that concern many of those who argue against shifting to a dimensional model (Benjamin, 1993; Shedler & Westen, 2004; Sprock, 2003).

Consider, for example, the personality disorder diagnostic categories. There is currently a considerable amount of clinical literature concerning the treatment of each diagnostic category (e.g., Beck, Freeman, and Davis, 2003; Benjamin, 2002). The APA (2001) has even published an authoritative guideline for the treatment of borderline personality disorder. It is the concern of many clinicians that much of this experience and wisdom will be lost if the diagnostic manual shifted to a dimensional model of classification.

This concern, however, is addressed in a number of ways. First, many of the alternative dimensional models of personality disorder concern dimensions that are currently the explicit focus of treatment and treatment outcome research (e.g., dimensions of emotional dysregulation, self-harm, social avoidance, workaholism, and impulsivity). It would require very little, if any, additional training to have clinicians focus their clinical attention on these maladaptive personality traits rather than on the global personality disorder constructs. In fact, it is likely that clinicians already focus on these underlying components of a respective personality disorder rather than attempting to treat the entire diagnostic category as a single entity (e.g., the focus of dialectical behavior therapy is on emotion regulation, distress tolerance, and interpersonal effectiveness rather than on the global construct of borderline personality disorder; Linehan, 1993).

In addition, it is not in fact the case that the existing diagnostic categories have considerable treatment utility (Verheul, 2005). "Apologists for categorical diagnoses argue that the system has clinical utility being easy to use and valuable in formulating cases and planning treatment [but] there is little evidence for these assertions" (Livesley, 2001a, p. 278). Psychosocial and pharmacologic interventions, with few exceptions, target and have effects upon broad domains of symptomatology rather than being specific to individual diagnostic categories that describe a heterogenous constellation of symptoms and traits (Livesley, 2001b). In fact, a unique advantage of dimensional models of classification would be the ability to provide alternative cutoff points along dimensions of maladaptive personality functioning for different social and clinical decisions. Cutoff points can be placed along distribution of anxious, depressive, introverted, and other dimensions of functioning that will be more meaningful and specific to various social and clinical decisions. The optimal points along a distribution of aberrant cognitions (for instance) at which a particular medication, hospitalization, insurance coverage, and disability are optimally provided are unlikely to be equivalent (Kendler, 1990). A dimensional model of classification has considerably greater flexibility in setting alternative cutoff points than the categorical system; minimally, a dimensional model of classification can be readily converted to the categorical classification whereas the categorical diagnosis, once implemented, cannot recover the dimensional profile (Trull, 2005; Verheul, 2005). A classification system that provided different cutoff points specific to different clinical and social decisions would probably have greater utility than the existing diagnostic system that relies on a single diagnostic threshold.

Even if *DSM-V* shifted to a dimensional classification of general personality structure, we would argue that this classification system would still prove to have greater clinical utility for treatment decisions than the existing diagnostic categories. Widiger et al. (2002) have proposed a four-step procedure for clinicians to use to diagnose the presence of a personality disorder from the perspective of the five-factor model (FFM) of general personality structure. The FFM consists of five broad domains of personality: extraversion (or positive affectivity) versus introversion, antagonism versus agreeableness, conscientiousness (or constraint), emotional instability (or neuroticism), and unconventionality (or openness). Each of the five broad domains has been further differentiated by Costa and McCrae (1992) into more specific facets. For example, the facets of agreeableness versus antagonism are trust versus mistrust, straightforwardness versus deception, altruism versus exploitation, compliance versus opposition, modesty versus arrogance, and tender-mindedness versus tough-mindedness.

The first step in a diagnosis of personality disorder using the FFM is to obtain a comprehensive assessment of personality functioning with an existing measure of the FFM, of which there are many alternative options (De Raad & Perugini, 2002). The most commonly used self-report measure is the NEO Personality Inventory-Revised (Costa & McCrae, 1992). However, a semistructured interview that includes the maladaptive variants of each pole of each facet was developed by Trull and Widiger (1997), and Mullins-Sweatt, Jamerson, Samuel, Olson, and Widiger (in press) report good convergent and discriminant validity for a very brief, one-page assessment instrument. The second step is to identify the social and occupational impairments and distress associated with the individual's characteristic personality traits. Widiger et al. (2002) identify common impairments that are associated with each of the 60 poles of the 30 facets of the FFM, including (but not limited to) *DSM-IV* personality disorder symptomatology. The third step is to determine whether the dysfunction and distress reach a clinically significant level of impairment. The fourth step is a quantitative matching of the individual's personality profile to prototypic profiles of diagnostic constructs. This last step is provided for clinicians and researchers who wish to continue to provide single diagnostic labels to characterize a person's personality profile. To the extent that an individual's profile does match the FFM profile of a prototypic case, a single term (e.g., psychopathic) would provide a succinct means of communication (Lynam, 2002). However, prototypic profiles will be quite rare within clinical practice. In such cases, the matching can serve to indicate the extent to which any particular diagnostic category would be adequately descriptive.

Widiger et al. (2002) expect that an FFM diagnosis of personality disorder will in fact prove to have considerable clinical utility. A five-factor description of maladaptive personality functioning will facilitate the development of more specific treatment recommendations, as each domain has more differentiated implications for functioning and treatment planning than the existing diagnostic categories. For example, the extraversion and agreeableness domains concern disorders of interpersonal relatedness that would be of particular interest and concern to clinicians specializing in marital, family, or other forms of interpersonal dysfunction. The domain of conscientiousness involves, at the low end, disorders of impulse dysregulation and disinhibition for which there is again a considerable amount of specific treatment literature. Disorders within this realm would be particularly evident in behavior that affects work, career, and parenting, with laxness, irresponsibility, and negligence at one pole and a maladaptively excessive perfectionism and workaholism at the other pole. The domain of neuroticism or negative affectivity would be most suggestive of pharmacotherapy (as well as psychotherapeutic) interventions for the treatment of various forms of affective dysregulation that are currently spread across the diagnostic categories, including anxiousness, depressiveness, anger, and instability of mood. Finally, high levels of the domain of openness would have specific implications for impaired reality testing, magical thinking, and perceptual aberrations, whereas at the other pole, it includes alexithymia, prejudice, closed-mindedness, and a sterile absence of imagination.

VALIDITY

The major reason for retaining a categorical model should be its validity and there is the concern that dimensional models could mask underlying latent class taxons (Benjamin, 1993; Gunderson, Links, & Reich, 1991; Lenzenweger & Korfine, 1992; Meehl, 1995). A wide variety of statistical and methodological approaches for testing the validity of categorical and dimensional models of classification has been used, including (but not limited to) the search for evidence of incremental validity, bimodality, discrete breaks within distributions, and reproducibility of factor analytic solutions across groups, as well as taxometric, latent class, item response theory, and admixture analyses (De Boeck et al., 2005; Klein & Riso, 1993; Kraemer, Noda, & O'Hara, 2004; Ruscio & Ruscio, 2004; Trull & Durrett, 2005; Waller & Meehl, 1998). Researchers have at times obtained results that are more consistent with a categorical than a dimensional model of classification (e.g., Lenzenweger & Korfine, 1992; Santor & Coyne, 2001), but the body of research does appear to be more consistent with a dimensional model (Blacker & Tsuang, 1992; First et al., 2002; Flett et al., 1997; Klein & Riso, 1993; Widiger & Clark, 2000).

For the purpose of illustration, we will summarize some of the empirical support for a dimensional classification of personality disorder. We are confining this summary to personality disorders as the magnitude of this research across all areas of psychopathology has now grown so large that it is not feasible to do justice to any one of them. Quite extensive and compelling arguments regarding other areas of psychopathology are available elsewhere (e.g., Cloninger, 1998; Goldberg, 1996; Krueger and Markon, in press; Widiger & Samuel, 2005), including more specifically (but not limited to) depression (Flett et al., 1997), anxiety disorders (Watson, in press), mood and anxiety disorders (Clark, in press), alcoholism (Meyer, 2001; Widiger & Smith, 1994), and psychotic disorders (Peralta, Cuesta,

Giraldo, Cardenas, & Gonzales, 2002; Serreti, Macciardi, & Smeraldi, 1996; Van Os et al., 1999). It is perhaps appropriate though to confine this particular discussion to the personality disorders, as the *DSM-V* Research Planning Nomenclature Work Group highlighted the particular need and benefit of piloting a shift to a dimensional classification of psychopathology first with the personality disorders. "If a dimensional system of personality performs well and is acceptable to clinicians, it might then be appropriate to explore dimensional approaches in other domains" (Rounsaville et al., 2002, p. 13).

It is also important to appreciate at the outset that no single study, or method of study, will provide conclusive results. The conclusion that a dimensional model provides a more valid description and classification of personality disorders will be reached instead through the cumulative and converging impact of construct validation studies that address different assumptions and hypotheses of these alternative models.

An initial argument in favor of a dimensional classification of personality disorders is the repeated failure to obtain compelling empirical support for a categorical classification. Four concerns with respect to the categorical model of personality disorder diagnosis commonly cited are excessive diagnostic co-occurrence, heterogeneity among persons with the same diagnosis, absence of a nonarbitrary boundary with normal functioning (contributing to unstable prevalence estimates with each revision to the diagnostic manual), and inadequate coverage of maladaptive personality functioning (Livesley, 2003; Widiger & Mullins-Sweatt, 2005; Widiger & Sanderson, 1995). A dimensional model of personality disorder classification would address effectively all of these problems. Patients would be provided with specific, individualized descriptions of their profile of maladaptive personality traits rather than being placed within inadequate, overlapping, and arbitrary diagnostic categories. In addition, any dimensional model of personality disorder classification that is reasonably comprehensive would be able to cover a greater range of maladaptive personality functioning without requiring additional diagnostic categories by avoiding the inclusion of redundant, overlapping diagnoses, by organizing the traits within a hierarchical structure, by representing a broader range of maladaptive personality functioning along each particular dimension, and by allowing for the representation of relatively unique or atypical personality profiles.

In addition, integrating the APA classification of personality disorders with a dimensional model of general personality structure has a number of advantages, notably the incorporation of the considerable amount of basic science research on personality into our understanding of disorders of personality. Blashfield and Intoccia (2000) conducted a computer search of the personality disorder research literature and concluded that there were "five disorders (dependent, narcissistic, obsessive-compulsive, paranoid, and passive-aggressive) that had very small literatures" (p. 473). "The only personality disorder whose literature is clearly alive and growing is that of borderline personality disorder" (p. 473). They characterized the literature concerning the dependent, narcissistic, obsessive-compulsive, paranoid, passive-aggressive, schizoid, and histrionic personality disorders as being "dead" or "dying" (p. 473).

In contrast, dimensions of general personality structure, and the FFM in particular, have obtained considerable scientific support. The FFM was derived originally from factor analytic studies of extensive samples of trait terms within the English language (Ashton & Lee, 2001). The relative importance of a trait is indicated by the number of terms that have been developed within a language to describe the various degrees and nuances of that trait, and the structure of the traits is evident by the relationship among the trait terms. The five broad domains of the FFM have been replicated in lexical studies of the trait terms in a wide variety of languages (Ashton & Lee, 2001). The FFM is the predominant model of personality in a number of different fields, including health psychology, aging, and developmental research (McCrae & Costa, 1999; Mullins-Sweatt & Widiger, in press). Empirical support for the FFM has been extensive, including convergent-discriminant validity across self, peer, and spouses ratings (Costa & McCrae, 1992), etic and emic cross-cultural research (Allik, 2005; Ashton & Lee, 2001), temporal stability across the life span (Roberts & DelVecchio, 2000), behavioral and molecular genetic heritability (Livesley, 2005; Sen, Burmeister, & Ghosh, 2004), and integration with the fundamental child-hood temperaments (Mervielde, De Clercq, De Fruyt, & Van Leeuwen, 2005; Shiner & Caspi, 2003). This is a scientific foundation that is virtually nonexistent for the personality disorder diagnostic categories.

Research that has documented whether and how the existing personality disorder diagnostic categories can be understood in terms of the FFM is also extensive. Widiger and Costa (2002) identified more than 50 studies that have addressed explicitly an understanding of personality disorders from the perspective of the FFM. These studies have used a wide variety of measures and have sampled from a variety of clinical and nonclinical populations. All but a few of the authors concluded that the personality disorders are well understood from the perspective of the FFM. Saulsman and Page (2004) conducted a meta-analysis of FFM personality disorder studies and concluded that "the results showed that each [personality] disorder displays a five-factor model profile that is meaningful and predictable given its unique diagnostic criteria" (p. 1055). Livesley (2001b) concluded on the basis of his review of this research that "multiple studies provide convincing evidence that the *DSM* personality disorder diagnoses show a systematic relationship to the five-factor framework" (p. 24). We will briefly describe a few of these individual studies.

O'Connor and Dyce (1998) conducted independent principal-axes common factor analyses on the correlation matrices among the personality disorders using a variety of samples and assessment instruments reported in nine previously published studies. The personality disorder matrices were rotated to a least squares fit to the target matrices generated by alternative dimensional models. These analyses were not exploratory searches of data sets, obtaining whatever factor analytic solution might capitalize on the particular measures and samples that were used. The confirmatory analyses "were powerful, support-seeking attempts to find the view on a correlational structure that was most consistent with a given model" (O'Connor & Dyce, 1998, p. 14). They found consistent support for the ability of the FFM to account for the personality disorder symptomatology: "The highest and most consistent level of fit were obtained for the five-factor model" (O'Connor & Dyce, 1998, p. 14).

Livesley, Jang, and Vernon (1998) compared the phenotypic and genetic structure of a comprehensive set of personality disorder symptoms in samples of 656 personality disordered patients, 939 general community participants, and 686 twin pairs. Principal components analysis yielded four broad dimensions (emotional dysregulation, dissocial behavior, inhibitedness, and compulsivity) that were replicated across all three samples. Multivariate genetic analyses also yielded the same four factors. "The stable structure of traits across clinical and nonclinical samples is consistent with dimensional representations of personality disorders" (Livesley et al., 1998, p. 941). Livesley et al. noted as well how "the higher-order traits of personality disorder strongly resemble dimensions of normal personality" (p. 941). Emotional dysregulation corresponded to five-factor model (FFM) neuroticism (identified by others as negative affectivity, as it includes such traits as fearfulness, depressiveness, anxiousness, anger, guilt, and vulnerability); the dissocial domain (defined by interpersonal hostility, judgmental attitudes, callousness, criminal behavior, and conduct problems) corresponded to FFM antagonism (which includes such traits as deceptiveness, exploitation, aggression, oppositionality, arrogance, and callousness); inhibitedness (defined by intimacy problems and restricted affect) corresponded to FFM introversion (which includes such traits as placidity, withdrawal, reservation, aloofness, and passivity); and *DSM-IV* compulsivity corresponded to FFM conscientiousness (which includes such traits as perfectionism, dutifulness, industriousness, discipline, deliberation, and organization). It is "quite striking that an extensive history of research to develop a dimensional model of normal personality functioning that has been confined to community populations is so closely congruent with a model that was derived from an analysis confined to personality disorder symptoms" (Widiger, 1998, p. 865).

Joint factor analyses of measures of the FFM and comprehensive representations of personality disorder symptoms have consistently identified a common underlying structure (Clark & Livesley, 2002; Markon, Krueger, & Watson, 2005; Widiger & Costa, 2002). "The evidence suggests that personality disorders are not characterized by functioning that differs in quality from normal functioning; rather, personality disorder can be described with traits or dimensions that are descriptive of personality, both disordered and normal" (Schroeder, Wormworth, & Livesley, 1992, p. 52).

Quite a few studies not considered in the reviews of Livesley (2001b), Saulsman and Page (2004), and Widiger and Costa (2002) have since been published. We will provide a few illustrative examples. For example, although many studies have verified that FFM agreeableness is associated with dependent personality traits, conscientiousness with obsessive-compulsive personality traits, and openness with schizotypal traits (Mullins-Sweatt & Widiger, in press), some studies have failed to confirm these associations, the reason for which appears to be methodological rather than substantive. Most existing FFM instruments have been developed for the study of general personality functioning (De Raad & Perugini, 2002) rather than being concerned specifically with the maladaptive personality traits included within the FFM. As a result, they might not provide adequate fidelity for the assessment and description of the maladaptive variants of the FFM. Haigler and Widiger (2001) demonstrated empirically that the negative findings for agreeableness, extraversion, and openness are largely because of the absence of adequate representation of the maladaptive variants of these domains within the predominant measures of the FFM. Haigler and Widiger first replicated the insignificant to marginal correlations of NEO PI-R (Costa & McCae, 1992) agreeableness, conscientiousness, and openness scales with the dependent, obsessive-compulsive, and schizotypal personality disorders (each of the latter was assessed by three independent measures). They then revised existing NEO PI-R items by inserting words to indicate that the behavior described within each item was excessive, extreme, or maladaptive. The content of the items was not otherwise altered. This experimental manipulation of the NEO PI-R items resulted in quite substantial correlations of agreeableness with dependency, conscientiousness with the obsessive-compulsive personality disorder, and (to a somewhat lesser extent) openness with schizotypal personality disorder. Haigler and Widiger (2001) concluded that their findings "offer further support for the hypothesis that personality disorders are maladaptive variants of normal personality traits by indicating that correlations of NEO PI-R conscientiousness, agreeableness, and openness scales with obsessive-compulsive, dependent, and schizotypal symptomatology would . . . be obtained by simply altering existing NEO PI-R . . . items that describe desirable, adaptive behaviors or traits into items that describe undesirable, maladaptive variants of the same traits" (p. 356).

Lynam and Widiger (2001) explored whether the co-occurrence among the *DSM-IV* personality disorders could itself be explained by the FFM. They had personality disorder researchers describe prototypic cases of each *DSM-IV* personality disorder in terms of the 30 facets of the FFM. They then obtained the correlations among the personality disorders with respect to their FFM descriptions, and they found that the personality disorder diagnostic co-occurrence reported in 15 previous studies could be largely accounted for by the covariation among the FFM personality trait profiles. For example, the FFM understanding of the antisocial personality disorder accounted for 85% of its diagnostic occurrence reported in nine *DSM-III* (APA, 1980) studies and 76% of its diagnostic co-occurrence reported in the six *DSM-III-R* (APA, 1987) studies obtained for the authors of the *DSM-IV* criterion sets. "Under the FFM account, disorders appear comorbid to the extent that they are characterized by the same [FFM] facets" (Lynam & Widiger, 2001, p. 409).

O'Connor (2005) conducted a joint factor analysis of 33 previously published personality disorder studies to yield a consensus comorbidity structure. He then conducted a comparable interbattery factor analysis to yield a consensus model for the relationship of the FFM to the personality disorders, using results reported in 20 previously published studies. He then determined empirically whether the congruence between the consensus personality disorder and consensus FFM-personality disorder structure was consistent with the theoretically based descriptions of these personality disorders provided by Widiger, Trull, Clarkin, Sanderson, and Costa (2002). He concluded that "the obtained congruences for their model are . . . quite impressive, especially considering that no other . . . personality disorder configuration model receives comparable degrees of support" (p. 340). "The interbattery factor analytic technique, used in the present study, provided a more stringent test of the empirically based representation of the FFM, yet stronger support for the FFM nevertheless emerged" (O'Connor, 2005, p. 340).

Warner et al. (2004) considered the role of FFM personality traits in accounting for the temporal stability of personality disorder symptoms. Using data obtained from the Collaborative Longitudinal Study of Personality Disorders (Gunderson et al., 2000), they reported that "there is a specific temporal relationship between traits and disorder whereby changes in the [FFM] personality traits hypothesized to underlie personality disorders lead to subsequent changes in the disorder [but] this relationship does not seem to hold in the opposite direction, which supports the contention that personality disorders stem from particular constellations of personality traits" (Warner et al., 2004, pp. 222–223).

Miller and Lynam (2003) demonstrated that a quantitative measure of the extent to which a person's FFM personality trait profile matched the hypothesized FFM profile of psychopathy reproduced the findings commonly reported for psychopathy, including drug usage, delinquency, risky sex, aggression, and several laboratory assessments of associated pathologies, including willingness to delay gratification in a time discounting task and a preference for aggressive responses in a social-information processing paradigm. Trull, Widiger, Lynam, and Costa (2003) similarly demonstrated that the extent to which a person's FFM personality trait profile matched the hypothesized FFM profile of borderline personality disorder correlated as highly with measures of borderline personality disorder as the latter correlated with one another. The FFM borderline index even demonstrated incremental validity in accounting for borderline psychopathology beyond the variance that was explained by a two-hour, semistructured interview devoted to the assessment of this personality disorder. In sum, the extent to which a person's FFM profile of personality traits is consistent with hypothesized FFM profiles for a respective personality disorder reproduces the nomological net of predictions that have been hypothesized for that personality disorder (Miller & Lynam, 2003; Trull et al., 2003).

CONCLUSIONS

The modern effort to demarcate a taxonomy of distinct clinical conditions is often traced to Kraepelin (1917). Kraepelin, however, had himself acknowledged that "wherever we try to mark out the frontier between mental health and disease, we find a neutral territory, in which the imperceptible change from the realm of normal life to that of obvious derangement takes place" (p. 295). The *DSM-IV* diagnostic categories do provide valid and useful information (as indicated in the chapters included within this text). However, undermining their validity and clinical utility is the false assumption that they are qualitatively distinct conditions. An adequate understanding of the diagnosis, etiology, pathology, comorbidity, and treatment of all mental disorders may require an acknowledgment that they are not conditions qualitatively distinct from one another nor from the anxiety, depression, sexual functioning, sleep, cognitive aberrations, drug and alcohol usage, and personality traits evident within all persons.

Most mental disorders appear to be the result of a complex interaction of an array of interacting biological vulnerabilities and dispositions with an equally complex array of environmental, psychosocial events unfolding over time (Rutter, 2003). The symptoms and pathologies of mental disorders are highly responsive to a wide variety of neurochemical, interpersonal, cognitive, and other mediating and moderating variables that help to develop, shape, and form a particular individual's psychopathology profile (Andreasen, 1997; Rutter, 2003; Tsuang, Stone, & Faraone, 2000). This complex etiological history and individual psychopathology profile are unlikely to be well described by a single diagnostic category.

A model for the future might be provided by one of the more well-established diagnoses, mental retardation. A dimensional classification of mental disorders is viewed by some as a radical departure, but *DSM-IV* already includes a strong precedent. The point of demarcation for the diagnosis of mental retardation is an arbitrary, quantitative distinction along the normally distributed levels of hierarchically and multifactorially defined intelligence. The current point of demarcation is an intelligence quotient of 70, along with a clinically significant level of impairment. This point of demarcation is arbitrary in the sense that it does not carve nature at a discrete joint, but it was not randomly or mindlessly chosen (Haslam, 2002). It is a well-reasoned and defensible selection that was informed by the impairments in functioning commonly associated with an IQ of 70 or below (Zachar, 2000).

The *DSM-IV* classification of maladaptive levels of intelligence is also a useful model because it illustrates how categorical and dimensional diagnoses are not necessarily mutually exclusive. There are instances of mental retardation that have specific etiologies. Recognizing that psychopathology is generally best classified along continuous distributions does not imply that no instances of qualitatively distinct conditions would not exist or could not be recognized. On the other hand, the categorical diagnoses in the case of mental retardation are generally placed on Axis III as physical disorders (e.g., Down syndrome) that can be traced to a specific biological event (i.e., trisomy 21), and the mental retardation of persons with these categorically distinct disorders is still described well in terms of the continuously distributed cognitive impairments. A general factor of intelligence (ability to reason, plan, solve, learn, and comprehend information) saturates most to all measures of cognitive ability (as a temperament of neuroticism might be common to many anxiety disorders), but it can in turn be further differentiated with respect to particular facets (e.g., quantitative, spatial, and verbal intelligence) that can themselves be in turn further differentiated into more specific components (Lubinski, 2004). The domain of intelligence is distributed as a hierarchical, multifactorial continuous variable, as most persons' level of intelligence, including most of those with mental retardation, is the result of a complex interaction of multiple genetic, fetal and infant development, and environmental influences (Lubinski, 2004; Neisser et al., 1996). There are no discrete breaks in its distribution that would provide an absolute distinction between normal and abnormal intelligence. We suggest that the future classification of anxiety, sleep, sexual, substance, mood, psychotic, personality, and other mental disorders would do best to follow the lead provided by mental retardation.

REFERENCES

Allik, J. (2005). Personality dimensions across cultures. *Journal of Personality Disorders, 19,* 212–232.

Alper, J. S. (1998). Genes, free will, and criminal responsibility. *Social Science and Medicine, 46,* 1599–1611.

American Psychiatric Association. (1980). *Diagnostic and statistical manual of mental disorders* (3rd ed.). Washington, DC: Author.

American Psychiatric Association. (1987). *Diagnostic and statistical manual of mental disorders* (3rd ed., rev. ed.). Washington, DC: Author.

American Psychiatric Association. (1994). *Diagnostic and statistical manual of mental disorders* (4th ed.). Washington, DC: Author.

American Psychiatric Association. (2000). *Diagnostic and statistical manual of mental disorders. Text revision* (4th ed., rev. ed.). Washington, DC: Author.

American Psychiatric Association. (2001). *Practice guidelines for the treatment of patients with borderline personality disorder.* Washington, DC: Author.

Andreasen, N. C. (1997). Linking mind and brain in the study of mental illnesses: A project for a scientific psychopathology. *Science, 275,* 1586–1593.

Angst, J. (1992). Recurrent brief psychiatric syndromes of depression, hypomania, neurasthenia, and anxiety from an epidemiological point of view. *Neurological, Psychiatric, and Brain Research, 1,* 5–12.

Appelbaum, P. S., Robbins, P. C., & Roth, L. H. (1999). Dimensional approach to delusions: Comparison across types and diagnoses. *American Journal of Psychiatry, 156,* 1938–1943.

Ashton, M. C., & Lee, K. (2001). A theoretical basis for the major dimensions of personality. *European Journal of Personality, 15,* 327–353.

Aubert, J. L., & Rush, A. J. (1996). Schizoaffective disorder. In T. A. Widiger, A. J. Frances, H. A. Pincus, R. Ross, M. B. First, & W. W. Davis (Eds.), *DSM-IV sourcebook* (Vol. 2). Washington, DC: American Psychiatric Association.

Bargh, J. A., & M. J. Ferguson. (2000). Beyond behaviorism: On the automaticity of higher mental processes. *Psychological Bulletin, 126,* 925–945.

Beck, A. T., Freeman, A., & Davis, D. D. (2003). *Cognitive therapy of personality disorders* (2nd ed.). New York: Guilford.

Benjamin, L. S. (1993). Dimensional, categorical, or hybrid analyses of personality: A response to Widiger's proposal. *Psychological Inquiry, 4,* 91–95.

Benjamin, L. S. (2002). *Interpersonal diagnosis and treatment of personality disorders* (2nd ed.). New York: Guilford.

Bergner, R. M. (1997). What is psychopathology? And so what? *Clinical Psychology: Science and Practice, 4,* 235–248.

Blacker, D., & Tsuang, M. T. (1992). Contested boundaries of bipolar disorder and the limits of categorical diagnosis in psychiatry. *American Journal of Psychiatry, 149,* 1473–1483.

Blashfield, R. K, & Intoccia, V. (2000). Growth of the literature on the topic of personality disorders. *American Journal of Psychiatry, 157,* 472–473.

Brown, T. A., Campbell, L. A., Lehman, C. L., Grisham, J. R., & Mancill, R. B. (2001). Current and lifetime comorbidity of the *DSM-IV* anxiety and mood disorders in a large clinical sample. *Journal of Abnormal Psychology, 110,* 585–599.

Caine, E. D. (1994). Should aging-associated memory decline be included in *DSM-IV?* In T. A. Widiger, A. J. Frances, H. A. Pincus, M. B. First, R. Ross, & W. W. Davis (Eds.), *DSM-IV sourcebook* (Vol. 1, pp. 329–337). Washington, DC: American Psychiatric Association.

Cardena, E., Butler, L. D., & Spiegel, D. (2003). Stress disorders. In I. Weiner, G. Stricker, & T. A. Widiger (Eds.), *Handbook of psychology: Vol. 8. Clinical psychology* (pp. 229–249). New York: Wiley.

Cardena, E., Lewis-Fernandez, R., Bear, D., Pakianathan, I., & Spiegel, D. (1996). Dissociative disorders. In T. A. Widiger, A. J. Frances, H. A. Pincus, R. Ross, M. B. First, & W. W. Davis (Eds.), *DSM-IV sourcebook* (Vol. 2, pp. 973–1005). Washington, DC: American Psychiatric Association.

Caron, C., & Rutter, M. (1991). Comorbidity in child psychopathology: concepts, issues and research strategies. *Journal of Child Psychology and Psychiatry, 32,* 1063–1080.

Clark, L. A. (in press). Temperament as a unifying basis for personality and psychopathology. *Journal of Abnormal Psychology.*

Clark, L. A., & Livesley, W. J. (2002). Two approaches to identifying the dimensions of personality disorder: Convergence on the five-factor model. In P. T. Costa & T. A. Widiger (Eds.), *Personality disorders and the five-factor model of personality* (2nd ed., pp. 161–176). Washington, DC: American Psychological Association.

Clark, L. A., Watson, D., & Reynolds, S. (1995). Diagnosis and classification of psychopathology: challenges to the current system and future directions. *Annual Review of Psychology, 46,* 121–153.

Cloninger, C. R. (1998). A new conceptual paradigm from genetics and psychobiology for the science of mental health. *Australian and New Zealand Journal of Psychiatry, 33,* 174–186.

Cloninger, C. R., & Svrakic, D. M. (1994). Differentiating normal and deviant personality by the seven-factor personality model. In S. Strack & M. Lorr (Eds.), *Differentiating normal and abnormal personality* (pp. 40–64). New York: Springer.

Costa, P. T., & McCrae, R. R. (1992). *Revised NEO Personality Inventory (NEO-PI-R) and NEO Five-Factor Inventory (NEO-FFI) professional manual.* Odessa, FL: Psychological Assessment Resources.

Coyne, J. C. (1994). Self-reported distress: Analog or ersatz depression? *Psychological Bulletin, 116,* 29–45.

Davidson, J. R. T., & Foa, E. B. (1991). Diagnostic issues in posttraumatic stress disorder. *Journal of Abnormal Psychology, 100,* 346–355.

De Boeck, P., Wilson, M., & Acton, G. S. (2005). A Conceptual and Psychometric Framework for Distinguishing Categories and Dimensions. *Psychological Review, 112,* 129–158.

De Raad, B., & Perugini, M. (Eds.). (2002). *Big five assessment.* Bern, Switzerland: Hogrefe & Huber.

Drevets, W. C. (2002). Neuroimaging studies of mood disorders. In J. E. Helzer & J. J. Hudziak (Eds.), *Defining psychopathology in the 21st century: DSM-V and beyond* (pp. 71–105). Washington, DC: American Psychiatric Press.

Epstein, J., Isenberg, N., Stern, E., & Silbersweig, D. (2002). Toward a neuroanatomical understanding of psychiatric illness: The role of functional imaging. In J. E. Helzer & J. J. Hudziak (Eds.), *Defining psychopathology in the 21st century: DSM-V and beyond* (pp. 57–69). Washington, DC: American Psychiatric Press.

First, M. B. (2003). Psychiatric classification. In A. Tasman, J. Kay, & J. Lieberman (Eds.), *Psychiatry* (2nd ed., Vol. 1, pp. 659–676). New York: Wiley.

First, M. B., Bell, C. B., Cuthbert, B., Krystal, J. H., Malison, R., Offord, D. R., Reiss, D., Shea, M. T., Widiger, T. A., & Wisner, K. L. (2002). Personality disorders and relational disorders: A research agenda for addressing crucial gaps in *DSM*. In D. J. Kupfer, M. B. First, & D. A. Regier (Eds.), *A research agenda for DSM-V* (pp. 123–199). Washington, DC: American Psychiatric Association.

First, M. B., Pincus, H. A., Levine, J. B., Williams, J. B. W., Ustun, B., & Peele, R. (2004). Clinical utility as a criterion for revising psychiatric diagnoses. *American Journal of Psychiatry, 161,* 946–954.

Flett, G. L., Vredenburg, K., & Krames, L. (1997). The continuity of depression in clinical and nonclinical samples. *Psychological Bulletin, 121,* 395–416.

Fowles, D. C. (2003). Schizophrenia spectrum disorders. In I. Weiner, G. Stricker, & T. A. Widiger (Eds.), *Handbook of psychology: Vol. 8. Clinical psychology* (pp. 65–92). New York: Wiley.

Frances, A. J., First, M. B., & Pincus, H. A. (1995). *DSM-IV guidebook.* Washington, DC: American Psychiatric Press.

Frances, A. J., First, M. B., Widiger, T. A., Miele, G., Tilly, S., Davis, W. W., & Pincus, H. A. (1991). An A to Z guide to *DSM-IV* conundrums. *Journal of Abnormal Psychology, 100,* 407–412.

Frances, A. J., Widiger, T. A., & Pincus, H. A. (1989). The development of *DSM-IV. Archives of General Psychiatry, 46,* 373–375.

Frances, A. J., Widiger, T. A., & Sabshin, M. (1991). Psychiatric diagnosis and normality. In D. Offer & M. Sabshin (Eds.), *The diversity of normal behavior* (pp. 3–38). New York: Basic Books.

Goldberg, D. (1996). A dimensional model for common mental disorders. *British Journal of Psychiatry, 168,* 44–49.

Goodman, A. (1990). Addiction: Definition and implications. *British Journal of Addiction, 85,* 1403–1408.

Gorenstein, E. (1984). Debating mental illness. *American Psychologist, 39,* 50–56.

Gross, J. J., & Munoz, R. F. (1995). Emotion regulation and mental health. *Clinical Psychology: Science and Practice, 2,* 151–164.

Gunderson, J. G., Links, P. S., & Reich, J. H. (1991). Competing models of personality disorders. *Journal of Personality Disorders, 5,* 60–68.

Gunderson, J. G., Shea, M. T., Skodol, A. E., McGlashan, T. H., Morey, L. C., Stout, R. L., Zanarini, M. C., Grilo, C. M., Oldham, J. M., & Keller, M. B. (2000). The Collaborative Longitudinal Personality Disorders Study, I: Development, aims, design, and sample characteristics. *Journal of Personality Disorders, 14,* 300–315.

Guze, S. B. (1978). Nature of psychiatric illness: Why psychiatry is a branch of medicine. *Comprehensive Psychiatry, 19,* 295–307.

Guze, S. B., & Helzer, J. E. (1987). The medical model and psychiatric disorders. In R. Michels & J. Cavenar (Eds.), *Psychiatry* (Vol. 1, Chapt. 51, pp. 1–8). Philadelphia: Lippincott.

Haigler, E. D., & Widiger, T. A. (2001). Experimental manipulation of NEO PI-R items. *Journal of Personality Assessment, 77,* 339–358.

Haslam, N. (2002). Kinds of kinds: A conceptual taxonomy of psychiatric categories. *Philosophy, Psychiatry, & Psychology, 9,* 203–217.

Howard, G. S., & Conway, C. G. (1986). Can there be an empirical science of volitional action? *American Psychologist, 41,* 1241–1251.

Hughes, J. R., Oliveto, A. H., Helzer, J. E., Higgins, S. T., & Bickel, W. K. (1992). Should caffeine abuse, dependence, or withdrawal be added to *DSM-IV* or *ICD-10? American Journal of Psychiatry, 149,* 33–40.

Hyman, S. E. (2005). Addiction: A disease of learning and memory. *American Journal of Psychiatry, 162,* 1414–1422.

Kalivas, P. W., & Volkow, N. C. (2005). The neural basis of addiction: A pathology of motivation and choice. *American Journal of Psychiatry, 162,* 1403–1413.

Kendell, R. C. (1975). *The role of diagnosis in psychiatry.* Oxford, England: Blackwell Scientific.

Kendler, K. S. (1990). Toward a scientific psychiatric nosology: Strengths and limitations. *Archives of General Psychiatry, 47,* 969–973.

Kendler, K. S. (1998). Boundaries of major depression: An evaluation of *DSM-IV* criteria. *American Journal of Psychiatry, 155,* 172–177.

Kendler, K. S. (2005). Toward a philosophical structure for psychiatry. *American Journal of Psychiatry, 162,* 433–440.

Kendler, K. S., Neale, M. C., & Walsh, D. (1995). Evaluating the spectrum concept of schizophrenia in the Roscommon family study. *American Journal of Psychiatry, 152,* 749–754.

Kendler, K. S., Prescott, C. A., Myers, J., & Neale, M. C. (2003). The structure of genetic and environmental risk factors for common psychiatric and substance use disorders in men and women. *Archives of General Psychiatry, 60,* 929–937.

Kirsch, I., & Lynn, S. J. (2000). Automaticity in clinical psychology. *American Psychologist, 54,* 504–515.

Klein, D. F. (1978). A proposed definition of mental illness. In R. L. Spitzer & D. F. Klein (Eds.), *Critical issues in psychiatric diagnosis* (pp. 41–71). New York: Raven Press.

Klein, D. F. (1999). Harmful dysfunction, disorder, disease, illness, and evolution. *Journal of Abnormal Psychology, 108,* 421–429.

Klein, D. N., & Riso, L. P. (1993). Psychiatric disorders: Problems of boundaries and comorbidity. In C. G. Costello (Ed.), *Basic issues in psychopathology* (pp. 19–66). New York: Guilford.

Knutson, B. Wolkowitz, O. M., Cole, S. W., Chan, T., Moore, E. A., Johnson, R. C., Terpstra, J., Turner, R. A., & Reus, V. H. (1998). Selective alteration of personality and social behavior by serotonergic intervention. *American Journal of Psychiatry, 155,* 373–379.

Kraemer, H. C., Noda, A., & O'Hara, R. (2004). Categorical versus dimensional approaches to diagnosis: Methodological approaches. *Journal of Psychiatric Research, 38,* 17–25.

Kraepelin, E. (1917). *Lectures on clinical psychiatry* (3rd ed.). New York: William Wood.

Krueger, R. F. (2002). Psychometric perspectives on comorbidity. In J. E. Helzer & J. J. Hudziak (Eds.), *Defining psychopathology in the 21st century: DSM-V and beyond* (pp. 41–54). Washington, DC: American Psychiatric Publishing.

Krueger, R. F., & Markon, K. E. (in press). Reinterpreting comorbidity: A model-based approach to understanding and classifying psychopathology. *Annual Review of Clinical Psychology.*

Kupfer, D. J., First, M. B., & Regier, D. E. (2002). Introduction. In D. J. Kupfer, M. B. First, & D. E. Regier (Eds.), *A research agenda for DSM-V* (pp. xv-xxiii). Washington, DC: American Psychiatric Association.

Lenzenweger, M. F., & Korfine, L. (1992). Confirming the latent structure and base rate of schizotypy: A taxometric analysis. *Journal of Abnormal Psychology, 101,* 567–571.

Liebowitz, M. R. (1992). Diagnostic issues in anxiety disorders. In A. Tasman & M. B. Riba (Eds.), *Review of psychiatry* (Vol. 11, pp. 247–259). Washington, DC: American Psychiatric Press.

Lilienfeld, S. O., & Marino, L. (1995). Mental disorder as a Roschian concept: A critique of Wakefield's "harmful dysfunction" analysis. *Journal of Abnormal Psychology, 104,* 411–420.

Lilienfeld, S. O., & Marino, L. (1999). Essentialism revisited: Evolutionary theory and the concept of mental disorder. *Journal of Abnormal Psychology, 108,* 400–411.

Lilienfeld, S. O., Waldman, I. D., & Israel, A. C. (1994). A critical examination of the use of the term "comorbidity" in psychopathology research. *Clinical Psychology: Science and Practice, 1,* 71–83.

Linehan, M. M. (1993). *Cognitive-behavioral treatment of borderline personality disorder.* New York: Guilford.

Livesley, W. J. (2001a). Commentary on reconceptualizing personality disorder categories using trait dimensions. *Journal of Personality, 69,* 277–286.

Livesley, W. J. (2001b) (Ed.). *Handbook of personality disorders: Theory, research, and treatment.* New York: Guilford.

Livesley, W. J. (2003). Diagnostic dilemmas in classifying personality disorder. In K. A. Phillips, M. B. First, & H. A. Pincus (Eds.), *Advancing DSM: Dilemmas in psychiatric diagnosis* (pp. 153–190). Washington, DC: American Psychiatric Association.

Livesley, W. J. (2005). Behavioral and molecular genetic contributions to a dimensional classification of personality disorder. *Journal of Personality Disorders, 19,* 131–155.

Livesley, W. J., Jang, K. L., & Vernon, P. A. (1998). Phenotypic and genetic structure of traits delineating personality disorder. *Archives of General Psychiatry, 55,* 941–948.

Livesley, W. J., Schroeder, M. L., Jackson, D. N., & Jang, K. L. (1994). Categorical distinctions in the study of personality disorder: Implications for classification. *Journal of Abnormal Psychology, 103,* 6–17.

Lubinski, D. (2004). Introduction to the special section on cognitive abilities: 100 years after Spearman's (1904) "'General Intelligence,' Objectively Determined and Measured." *Journal of Personality and Social Psychology, 86,* 96–111.

Lynam, D. R. (2002). Psychopathy from the perspective of the five-factor model of personality. In P. T. Costa & T. A. Widiger (Eds.), *Personality disorders from the perspective of the five-factor model* (2nd ed., pp. 325–348). Washington, DC: American Psychological Association.

Lynam, D. R., & Widiger, T. A. (2001). Using the five factor model to represent the *DSM-IV* personality disorders: An expert consensus approach. *Journal of Abnormal Psychology, 110,* 401–412.

Magruder, K. M., & Calderone, G. E. (2000). Public health consequences of different thresholds for the diagnosis of mental disorders. *Comprehensive Psychiatry, 41,* 14–18.

March, J. S. (1990). The nosology of posttraumatic stress disorder. *Journal of Anxiety Disorders, 4,* 61–82.

Markon, K. E., Krueger, R. F., & Watson, D. (2005). Delineating the structure of normal and abnormal personality: An integrative hierarchical approach. *Journal of Personality and Social Psychology, 88,* 139–157.

Maser, J. D., & Cloninger, C. R. (1990). Comorbidity of anxiety and mood disorders: Introduction and overview. In J. D. Maser & C. R. Cloninger (Eds.), *Comorbidity of mood and anxiety disorders* (pp. 3–12). Washington, DC: American Psychiatric Press.

Mayberg, H. S., Liotti, M., Brannan, S. K., McGinnis, S., Mahurin, R. K., Jerabek, P. A., Silva, J. A., Tekell, J. L., Martin, C. C., Lancaster, J. L., & Fox, P. T. (1999). Reciprocal limbic-cortical function and negative mood: Converging PET findings in depression and normal sadness. *American Journal of Psychiatry, 156,* 675–682.

McCrae, R. R., & Costa, P. T. (1999). A five-factor theory of personality. In L. A. Pervin & O. P. John (Eds.), *Handbook of personality* (2nd ed., pp. 139–153). New York: Guilford.

McGlashan, T. H., & Fenton, W. S. (1994). Classical subtypes for schizophrenia. In T. A. Widiger, A. J. Frances, H. A. Pincus, M. B. First, R. Ross, & W. W. Davis (Eds.), *DSM-IV sourcebook* (Vol. 1, pp. 419–440). Washington, DC: American Psychiatric Association.

Meehl, P. E. (1995). Bootstraps taxometrics: Solving the classification problem in psychopathology. *American Psychologist, 50,* 266–275.

Mervielde, I., De Clercq, B., De Fruyt, F., & Van Leeuwen, K. (2005). Temperament, personality, and developmental psychopathology as childhood antecedents of personality disorders. *Journal of Personality Disorders, 19,* 171–201.

Meyer, R. (2001). Finding paradigms for the future of alcoholism research: An interdisciplinary perspective. *Alcoholism: Clinical and Experimental Research, 25,* 1393–1406.

Miller, J. D, & Lynam, D. R. (2003). Psychopathy and the five-factor model of personality: A replication and extension. *Journal of Personality Assessment, 81,* 168–178.

Mineka, S., Watson, D., & Clark, L. E. A. (1998). Comorbidity of anxiety and unipolar mood disorders. *Annual Review of Psychology, 49,* 377–412.

Morey, L. C. (1988). Personality disorders under *DSM-III* and *DSM-III-R*: An examination of convergence, coverage, and internal consistency. *American Journal of Psychiatry, 145,* 573–577.

Mullins-Sweatt, S. N., Jamerson, J. E., Samuel, D. B., Olson, D. R., & Widiger, T. A. (in press). Psychometric properties of an abbreviated instrument of the five-factor model. *Assessment.*

Mullins-Sweatt, S. N., & Widiger, T. A. (in press). The five-factor model of personality disorder: A translation across science and practice. In R. Krueger & J. Tackett (Eds.), *Personality and psychopathology: Building bridges.* New York: Guilford.

Munoz, R. F., Hollon, S. D., McGrath, E., Rehm, L. P., & VandenBos, G. P. (1994). On the AHCPR Depression in Primary Care guidelines. *American Psychologist, 49,* 42–61.

Neisser, U., Boodoo, G., Bouchard, T. J., Boykin, A. W., Brody, N., Ceci, S. J., Halpern, D. F., Loehlin, J. C., Perloff, R., Sternberg, R. J., & Urbina, S. (1996). Intelligence: Knowns and unknowns. *American Psychologist, 51,* 77–101.

O'Connor, B. P. (2005). A search for consensus on the dimensional structure of personality disorders. *Journal of Clinical Psychology, 61,* 323–345.

O'Connor, B. P., & Dyce, J. A. (1998). A test of models of personality disorder configuration. *Journal of Abnormal Psychology, 107,* 3–16.

Peele, S. (1984). The cultural context of psychological approaches to alcoholism. *American Psychologist, 39,* 1337–1351.

Peralta, V., Cuesta, M. J., Giraldo, C., Cardenas, A., & Gonzalez, F. (2002). Classifying psychotic disorders: Issues regarding categorical vs. dimensional approaches and time frame to assess symptoms. *European Archives of Psychiatry and Clinical Neuroscience, 252,* 12–18.

Phillips, K. A., Price, L. H., Greenburg, B. D., & Rasmussen, S. A. (2003). Should the *DSM* diagnostic groupings be changed? In K. A. Phillips, M. B. First, & H. A. Pincus (Eds.), *Advancing DSM: Dilemmas in psychiatric diagnosis* (pp. 57–84). Washington, DC: American Psychiatric Association.

Pincus, H. A., McQueen, L. E., & Elinson, L. (2003). Subthreshold mental disorders: Nosological and research recommendations. In K. A. Phillips, M. B. First, & H. A. Pincus (Eds.), *Advancing DSM: Dilemmas in psychiatric diagnosis* (pp. 129–144). Washington, DC: American Psychiatric Association.

Portin, P., & Alanen, Y. O. (1997). A critical review of genetic studies of schizophrenia. II. Molecular genetic studies. *Acta Psychiatrica Scandinavica, 95,* 73–80.

Regier, D. A., Kaelber, C. T., Rae, D. S., Farmer, M. E., Knauper, B., Kessler, R. C., & Norquist, G. S. (1998). Limitations of diagnostic criteria and assessment instruments for mental disorders: Implications for research and policy. *Archives of General Psychiatry, 55,* 109–115.

Regier, D. A., & Narrow, W. E. (2002). Defining clinically significant psychopathology with epidemiologic data. In J. E. Helzier & J. J. Hudziak (Eds.), *Defining psychopathology in the 21st century: DSM-V and beyond* (pp. 19–30). Washington, DC: American Psychiatric Publishing.

Roberts, B. W., & DelVecchio, W. F. (2000). The rank-order consistency of personality traits from childhood to old age: A quantitative review of longitudinal studies. *Psychological Bulletin, 126,* 3–25.

Rosenthal, R. J. (1989). Pathological gambling and problem gambling: Problems in definition and diagnosis. In H. Shaffer, S. A. Stein, & B. Gambino (Eds.), *Compulsive gambling: Theory, research, and practice* (pp. 101–125). Lexington, MA: Lexington Books.

Rounsaville, B. J., Alarcon, R. d., Andrews, G., Jackson, J. S., Kendell, R. E., & Kendler, K. (2002). Basic nomenclature issues for DSM-V. In D. J. Kupfer, M. B. First, & D. E. Regier (Eds,), *A research agenda for DSM-V* (pp. 1–29). Washington, DC: American Psychiatric Association.

Ruscio, J., & Ruscio, A. M. (2004). Clarifying boundary issues in psychopathology: The role of taxometrics in a comprehensive program of structural research. *Journal of Abnormal Psychology, 113,* 24–38.

Rutter, M. L. (1997). Implications of genetic research for child psychiatry. *Canadian Journal of Psychiatry, 42,* 569–576.

Rutter, M. (2003, October). *Pathways of genetic influences on psychopathology.* Zubin Award Address at the 18th Annual Meeting of the Society for Research in Psychopathology, Toronto, Ontario, Canada.

Samuel, D. B., & Widiger, T. A. (2004). Clinicians' personality descriptions of prototypic personality disorders. *Journal of Personality Disorders, 18,* 286–308.

Samuel, D., & Widiger, T. A. (in press). Normal versus abnormal personality from the perspective of the *DSM.* In S. Strack & M. Lorr (Eds.), *Differentiating normal and abnormal personality* (2nd ed.). New York: Springer.

Santor, D. A., & Coyne, J. C. (2001). Evaluating the continuity of symptomatology between depressed and nondepressed individuals. *Journal of Abnormal Psychology, 110,* 216–225.

Saulsman, L. M., & Page, A. C. (2004). The five-factor model and personality disorder empirical literature: A meta-analytic review. *Clinical Psychology Review, 23,* 1055–1085.

Schroeder, M. L., Wormworth, J. A., & Livesley, W. J. (1992). Dimensions of personality disorder and their relationship to the Big Five dimensions of personality. *Psychological Assessment, 4,* 47–53.

Sen, S., Burmeister, M., & Ghosh, D. (2004). Meta-analysis of the association between a serotonin transporter polymorphism (5-HTTLPR) and anxiety-related personality traits.
American Journal of Medical Genetics Part B, 127B, 85–89.

Serreti, A., Macciardi, F., & Smeraldi, E. (1996). Identification of symptomatologic patterns
concern in major psychoses: Proposal for a phenotypic definition. *American Journal of
Medical Genetics, 67,* 393–400.

Shedler J., & Westen, D. (2004). Dimensions of personality pathology: An alternative to the
five-factor model. *American Journal of Psychiatry, 161,* 1743–1754.

Shiner, R. L., & Caspi, A. (2003). Personality differences in childhood and adolescence: Measurement, development, and consequences. *Journal of Child Psychology and Psychiatry,
44,* 2–32.

Shisslak, C. M., Crago, M., & Estes, L. S. (1995). The spectrum of eating disturbances. *International Journal of Eating Disorders, 18,* 209–219.

Siever, L. J., & Davis, K. L. (1991). A psychobiological perspective on the personality disorders. *American Journal of Psychiatry, 148,* 1647–1658.

Spiegel, D., & Cardena, E. (1991). Disintegrated experience: The dissociative disorders revisited. *Journal of Abnormal Psychology, 100,* 366–378.

Spitzer, R. L., & Wakefield, J. C. (1999). The *DSM-IV* diagnostic criterion for clinical significance: Does it help solve the false positives problem? *American Journal of Psychiatry,
156,* 1856–1864.

Spitzer, R. L., & Williams, J. B. W. (1982). The definition and diagnosis of mental disorder. In
W. Gove (Ed.), *Deviance and mental illness* (pp. 15–31). Beverly Hills, CA: Sage.

Spitzer, R. L., & Williams, J. B. W. (1985). Proposed revisions in the *DSM-III* classification of
anxiety disorders based on research and clinical experience. In A. H. Tuma & J. Maser
(Eds.), *Anxiety and the anxiety disorders* (pp. 759–773). Hillsdale, NJ: Erlbaum.

Spitzer, R. L., Williams, J. B. W., & Skodol, A. E. (1980). *DSM-III:* The major achievements and
an overview. *American Journal of Psychiatry, 137,* 151–164.

Sprock, J. (2003). Dimensional versus categorical classification of prototypic and nonproto-
typic cases of personality disorder. *Journal of Clinical Psychology, 59,* 991–1014.

Steffens, D. C., & Krishnan, K. R. R. (2003). Laboratory testing and neuroimaging: implica-
tions for psychiatric diagnosis and practice. In K. A. Phillips, M. B. First, & H. A. Pincus
(Eds.), *Advancing DSM: Dilemmas in psychiatric diagnosis* (pp. 85–103). Washington,
DC: American Psychiatric Association.

Stein, M. B., Walker, J. R., Hazen, A. L., & Forde, D. R. (1997). Full and partial posttraumatic
stress disorder: Findings from a community survey. *American Journal of Psychiatry, 154,*
1114–1119.

Task Force on *DSM-IV.* (1991, September). *DSM-IV options book.* Work in progress.
Washington, DC: American Psychiatric Association.

Trull, T. J. (2005). Dimensional models of personality disorder: Coverage and cutoffs. *Journal
of Personality Disorders, 19,* 262–282.

Trull, T. J. , & Durrett, C. A. (2005).Categorical and dimensional models of personality disorder. *Annual Review of Clinical Psychology, 1,* 355–380.

Trull, T. J., & Widiger, T. A. (1997). *Structured Interview for the Five-Factor Model of Personality.* Odessa, FL: Psychological Assessment Resources.

Trull, T. J., Widiger, T. A., Lynam, D. R., & Costa, P. T. (2003). Borderline personality disorder
from the perspective of general personality functioning. *Journal of Abnormal Psychology,
112,* 193–202.

Tsuang, M. T., Stone, W. S., & Faraone, S. V. (2000). Toward reformulating the diagnosis of
schizophrenia. *American Journal of Psychiatry, 157,* 1041–1050.

Turner, S. M., & Beidel, D. C. (1989). Social phobia: Clinical syndrome, diagnosis, and comorbidity. *Clinical Psychology Review, 9,* 3–18.

Turner, S. M., Beidel, D. C., & Townsley, R. M. (1992). Social phobia: A comparison of specific and generalized subtypes and avoidant personality disorder. *Journal of Abnormal Psychology, 101,* 326–331.

Vaillant, G. E. (1995). *The natural history of alcoholism revisited.* Cambridge, MA: Harvard University Press.

Van Os, J., Gilvarry, C., Bale, E., Van Horn, E., Tattan, T., White, I., & Murray, R. (1999). A comparison of the utility of dimensional and categorical representations of psychosis. *Psychological Medicine, 29,* 595–606.

Verheul, R. (2005). Clinical utility of dimensional models for personality pathology. *Journal of Personality Disorders, 19,* 283–302.

Verheul, R., & Widiger, T. A. (2004). A meta-analysis of the prevalence and usage of the personality disorder not otherwise specified (PDNOS) diagnosis. *Journal of Personality Disorders, 18,* 309–319.

Wakefield, J. C. (1992). Disorder as harmful dysfunction: A conceptual critique of *DSM-III-R*'s definition of mental disorder. *Psychological Review, 99,* 232–247.

Wakefield, J. C. (1997). Diagnosing *DSM-IV*—Part I: *DSM-IV* and the concept of disorder. *Behavioral Research and Therapy, 35,* 633–649.

Wakefield, J. C., & Spitzer, R. L. (2002). Why requiring clinical significance does not solve epidemiology's and *DSM*'s validity problem: Response to Regier and Narrow. In J. E. Helzier & J. J. Hudziak (Eds.), *Defining psychopathology in the 21st century: DSM-V and beyond* (pp. 31–40). Washington, DC: American Psychiatric Publishing.

Waller, N. G., & Meehl, P. E. (1998). *Multivariate taxometric procedures: Distinguishing types from continua.* Thousands Oaks, CA: Sage.

Warner, M. B., Morey, L. C., Finch, J. F., Gunderson, J. G., Skodol, A. E., Sanislow, C. A., Shea, M. T., McGlashan, T. H., & Grilo, C. M. (2004). The longitudinal relationship of personality traits and disorders. *Journal of Abnormal Psychology, 113,* 217–227.

Watson, D. (in press). Rethinking the mood and anxiety disorders: A symptom-based hierarchical model. *Journal of Abnormal Psychology.*

Wegner, D. M., & Wheatley, T. (2000). Apparent mental causation: Sources of the experience of will. *American Psychologist, 54,* 480–492.

Widiger, T. A. (1992). Generalized social phobia versus avoidant personality disorder: A commentary on three studies. *Journal of Abnormal Psychology, 101,* 340–343.

Widiger, T. A. (1997). Mental disorders as discrete clinical conditions: Dimensional versus categorical classification. In S. M. Turner & M. Hersen (Eds.), *Adult psychopathology and diagnosis* (3rd ed., pp. 3–23). New York: Wiley.

Widiger, T. A. (1998). Four out of five ain't bad. *Archives of General Psychiatry, 55,* 865–866.

Widiger, T. A. (2004). Overview of models of psychopathology. In J. Thomas & M. Hersen (Eds.), *Psychopathology in the workplace: Recognition and adaptation* (pp. 9–24). New York: Brunner-Routledge.

Widiger, T. A., & Clark, L. A. (2000). Toward *DSM-V* and the classification of psychopathology. *Psychological Bulletin, 126,* 946–963.

Widiger, T. A., & Costa, P. T. (2002). FFM personality disorder research. In P. T. Costa & T. A. Widiger (Eds.), *Personality disorders and the five factor model of personality* (2nd ed., pp. 59–87). Washington, DC: American Psychological Association.

Widiger, T. A., Costa, P. T., & McCrae, R. R. (2002). Proposal for Axis II: Diagnosing personality disorders using the five factor model. In P. T. Costa & T. A. Widiger (Eds.), *Personality disorders and the five factor model of personality* (2nd ed., pp. 431–456). Washington, DC: American Psychological Association.

Widiger, T. A., & Mullins-Sweatt, S. (2005). Categorical and dimensional models of personality disorder. In J. Oldham, A. Skodol, & D. Bender (Eds.), *Textbook of Personality Disorders* (pp. 35–53). Washington, DC: American Psychiatric Press.

Widiger, T. A., & Samuel, D. (2005). Diagnostic categories or dimensions: A question for *DSM-V. Journal of Abnormal Psychology.*

Widiger, T. A., & Sanderson, C. J. (1995). Toward a dimensional model of personality disorders. In W. J. Livesley (Ed.), *The DSM-IV personality disorders* (pp. 433–458). New York: Guilford.

Widiger, T. A., & Sankis, L. (2000). Adult psychopathology: Issues and controversies. *Annual Review of Psychology, 51,* 377–404.

Widiger, T. A., & Smith, G. T. (1994). Substance use disorder: Abuse, dependence, and dyscontrol. *Addiction, 89,* 267–282.

Widiger, T. A., & Trull, T. J. (1991). Diagnosis and clinical assessment. *Annual Review of Psychology, 42,* 109–133.

Widiger, T. A., Trull, T. S., Clarkin, J. F., Sanderson, C., & Costa, P. T. (2002). A description of the *DSM-IV* personality disorders with the five-factor model of personality. In P. T. Costa & T. A. Widiger (Eds.), *Personality disorders and the five-factor model of personality* (pp. 89–99). Washington, DC: American Psychological Association.

Winstead, B. A., & Sanchez, J. (2005). Gender and psychopathology. In J. E. Maddux & B. A. Winstead (Eds.), *Psychopathology: Foundations for a contemporary understanding* (pp. 39–61). Mahwah, NJ: Erlbaum.

Zachar, P. (2000). Psychiatric disorders are not natural kinds. *Philosophy, Psychiatry, Psychology, 7,* 167–182.

CHAPTER 2

The Problem of Dual Diagnosis

MELANIE E. BENNETT AND SELVIJA GJONBALAJ-MOROVIC

In recent years, the issue of psychiatric comorbidity has gained increased attention. Research indicates that a substantial percentage of the general population with a lifetime psychiatric disorder has a history of some other disorder (Kessler, 1997; Kessler et al., 1994), and more than half of patients in psychiatric treatment meet criteria for more than one diagnosis (Wolf, Schubert, Patterson, Marion, & Grande, 1988). The issue of comorbidity broadly refers to combinations of any types of psychiatric disorders that co-occur in the same individual. A diagnostic pair that has received significant attention over the last two decades is that of mental illness and substance abuse. The term *dual diagnosis* describes individuals who meet diagnostic criteria for an Axis I or Axis II mental disorder (or disorders) along with one or more substance use disorders. Since the 1980s, rates of co-occurring mental illness and substance use disorders have been found to have increased sharply. This increase is likely owing to a range of factors including more specific diagnostic criteria for substance use disorders, as well as the development of standardized diagnostic interviews that allow for reliable and valid assessments of Axis I disorders in a range of patient populations (Wittchen, Perkonigg, & Reed, 1996). It is likely that these recently documented increases in rates of dual diagnosis reflect what was truly there all along—a frequent association between mental and substance use disorders that we have only now begun to measure accurately.

It is now clear that dual diagnosis impacts all aspects of psychopathology research and clinical practice, from service utilization, treatment entry, and treatment retention to assessment and diagnosis of psychological problems to research on psychopathology and treatment outcome. In this chapter, we will review current data on rates of dual diagnosis, both generally and for specific domains of disorders, as well as discuss some of the ways in which dual diagnosis impacts the course, prognosis, assessment, and treatment of adult psychopathology. Finally, we will review current research on the etiology of dual diagnosis, and highlight clinical and research directions.

EPIDEMIOLOGY

METHODOLOGICAL ISSUES

There are several methodological issues to consider when evaluating the literature on the epidemiology of dual diagnosis. First, data come from both epidemiological and clinical studies. Several large-scale epidemiological studies examining rates of dual diagnosis in general population samples have been carried out since the mid-1980s. These studies provide representative information on rates of mental illness and substance use disorders, use structured diagnostic interviews, and generate results that are reliable and relevant to the population as a whole. Most of the information on rates of dual diagnosis comes from studies of clinical populations. Although such studies are not representative of the general population, they provide valuable information on the types of problems that are faced by individuals in treatment, as well as on the links between dual diagnosis, service utilization, impact on illness, and treatment outcome. Importantly, individuals with multiple disorders are more likely to seek treatment, a condition known as "Berkson's fallacy" (Berkson, 1949), so that estimates of the prevalence of comorbid disorders will be higher in clinical samples. Relatedly, factors such as inpatient or outpatient status and chronicity of illness may affect rates of dual diagnosis. For example, research on patients with schizophrenia has found that more severely impaired inpatients are less likely to abuse substances than patients who are less ill (Mueser et al., 1990). Dual diagnosis rates have also been found to differ by setting, with hospital emergency rooms reflecting higher estimates than other settings (Barbee, Clark, Crapanzano, Heintz, & Kehoe, 1989; Galanter, Castaneda, & Ferman, 1988).

Second, definitions of what constitutes dual diagnosis are far from uniform. Studies of dual diagnosis often employ differing definitions of substance use disorders, making prevalence rates diverse and difficult to compare. For example, definitions of substance abuse vary, ranging from problem use of a substance, to abuse or dependence based on *DSM* criteria. This is a particularly important issue in terms of diagnostic criteria for both mental and substance use disorders. The publication of *DSM-IV* (American Psychiatric Association, 1994) and the changes in that system from its predecessor may affect dual diagnosis prevalence rates in both community and clinical samples. These changes include a greater focus on determining that a mental disorder is independent from a substance use disorder by determining that the mental disorder either predated the substance use disorder or persists for at least four weeks following cessation of alcohol or drug use. Others do not specify the exact nature of the substance use they are assessing. Among studies that define the type of substance use they are assessing, different diagnostic criteria are often used, making interpretation and comparison difficult. In addition, the methods used to determine psychiatric and substance use diagnoses can influence findings. The types of diagnostic measures used include structured research interviews, nonstructured clinical interviews, self-report ratings, and reviews of medical records. Although structured interviews are the most reliable method of diagnosis (Mueser, Bellack, & Blanchard, 1992), research with clinical samples will often employ less well-standardized assessments. Relatedly, studies measure different substances in their assessments of dual diagnosis, typically including alcohol, cocaine, heroin, hallucinogens, stimulants, and marijuana. Importantly, some substances are not typically considered in assessments of dual diagnosis. For example, nicotine is usually not considered a substance of abuse in dual diagnosis research, despite the high rates of use among individuals with both mental illness (Lasser et al., 2000) and substance abuse (Bien & Burge, 1990), as well as a growing literature that suggests that nicotine dependence has links, perhaps biological in nature, to both major depression (Quattrocki, Baird, & Yurgelun-Todd, 2000) and schizophrenia (Dalack & Meador-Woodruff, 1996; Ziedonis & George, 1997). Others have found elevated rates of psychiatric and substance use disorders in smokers (Keuthen et al., 2000). Taken together, factors such as the type of problematic substance use assessed, the measures that are used, and the specific substances that are included in an assessment all contribute to varying meanings of the term *dual diagnosis*.

A final methodological issue involves the split between the mental health treatment system and the substance abuse treatment system, and the impact that this separation has on dual diagnosis research. The literature on dual diagnosis really includes two largely separate areas of investigation: research on substance abuse in individuals with mental illness, as well as research on mental illness in primary substance abusers. In order to get an accurate picture of dual diagnosis and its full impact on clinical functioning and research in psychopathology, both aspects of this literature must be examined.

FINDINGS FROM MAJOR EPIDEMIOLOGICAL STUDIES

Over the last 25 years, there have been a number of large-scale epidemiological studies of mental illness that examine rates of dual diagnosis, including the Epidemiologic Catchment Area Study (ECA; Regier et al., 1990), the National Comorbidity Survey (NCS; Kessler et al., 1994), the National Comorbidity Survey Replication (NCS-R; Kessler & Merikangas, 2004), and the National Longitudinal Alcohol Epidemiology Study (NLAES; Grant et al., 1994). Although each study differs somewhat from the others in methodology, inclusion/exclusion criteria, and diagnostic categories assessed (see Table 2.1 for a brief description of methods for these studies), there are a number of points that we can take from this literature that can contribute to our thinking about and understanding of dual diagnosis.

Dual Diagnosis Is Highly Prevalent in Community Samples   First, epidemiological studies consistently show that dual diagnosis is highly prevalent in community samples. Each of these studies finds that people with mental illness are at greatly increased risk of having a co-occurring substance use disorder, and people with a substance use disorder are likewise much more likely to meet criteria for an Axis I mental disorder. For example, the Epidemiologic Catchment Area Study (ECA; Regier et al., 1990) was the first large-scale study of comorbidity of psychiatric and substance use disorders in the general population, and documented high rates of dual diagnosis among both individuals with primary mental disorders and those with primary substance use disorders. Overall, individuals with a lifetime history of a mental illness had an odds ratio of 2.3 for a lifetime history of alcohol use disorder and 4.5 for drug use disorder, a clear illustration of how those with mental illness are at substantially increased risk of having a comorbid substance use diagnosis. When examined by type of disorder, antisocial personality disorder (ASP) showed the highest comorbidity rate (83.6%), followed by bipolar disorder (60.7%), schizophrenia (47.0%), panic disorder (35.8%), obsessive-compulsive disorder (32.8%), and

Table 2.1
Methods of Several Major Epidemiological Studies on Dual Diagnosis

Study	Years	Methods
ECA (Regier et al., 1990)	1980–84	Surveyed more than 20,000 adults in 5 cities across the United States both in the community and in institutions. Trained interviewers used the Diagnostic Interview Schedule to determine *DSM-III* diagnoses. Included affective, anxiety, and schizophrenia-spectrum disorders.
NCS (Kessler et al., 1994)	1990–92	Assessed 12-month and lifetime prevalence rates for a range of psychiatric disorders in over 8,000 noninstitutionalized individuals ages 15–54 across 48 states using the Composite International Diagnostic Interview (CIDI) and based on *DSM-III-R* criteria.
NLAES (Grant et al., 1994)	1991–92	Examined rates of co-occurrence of alcohol and drug use disorders and affective disorders in a general population sample. The NLAES is a household survey of over 42,000 adults in the United States that utilized diagnostic interviews to assess *DSM-IV* diagnostic criteria for alcohol use disorders.
NCSR (Kessler et al., 2004)	2001–02	Nationally representative face-to-face household survey of over 9,000 noninstitutionalized people ages 18 years or older. Diagnoses based on *DSM-IV* criteria assessed via CIDI interviews.
NESARC (Grant et al., 2004)	2001–02	Nationally representative face-to-face survey of 43,093 noninstitutionalized respondents, 18 years of age or older, conducted by NIAAA. *DSM-IV* criteria for substance use disorders and 9 independent mood and anxiety disorders were assessed with the Alcohol Use Disorders and Associated Disabilities Interview Schedule-*DSM-IV* Version (AUDADIS-IV), a structured diagnostic interview administered by lay interviewers.

major depression (27.2%). Further analysis of ECA data (Helzer, Robbins, & McEvoy, 1987) found that men and women with posttraumatic stress disorder (PTSD) were 5 times and 1.4 times more likely, respectively, to have a drug use disorder as men and women without PTSD. Substantial rates of dual diagnosis were also found in primary substance abusers (Regier et al., 1990). Overall, 37% of individuals with an alcohol disorder and 53% of those with a drug use disorder had comorbid mental illness. Further analyses (Helzer & Pryzbeck, 1988) found that among those with alcohol use disorders, the strongest association was with ASP (odds ratio = 21.0), followed by mania (OR = 6.2) and schizophrenia (OR = 4.0).

Like the ECA study, the NCS and that NLAES found markedly high rates of dual diagnosis. NCS (Kessler et al., 1994) findings showed that respondents with mental illness had at least twice the risk of lifetime alcohol or drug use disorder, with even greater risk for individuals with certain types of mental illnesses. Findings were similar for primary substance abusers: The majority of respondents with an alcohol or drug use disorder had a history of some nonsubstance use psychiatric disorder (Kendler, Davis, & Kessler, 1997; Kessler, 1997). Overall,

56.8% of men and 72.4% of women with alcohol abuse met diagnostic criteria for at least one psychiatric disorder, as did 78.3% of men and 86.0% of women with alcohol dependence (Kendler et al., 1997). Moreover, 59% of those with a lifetime drug use disorder also met criteria for a lifetime psychiatric disorder (Kessler, 1997). Likewise the NLAES (Grant et al., 1994; Grant & Harford 1995) found that among respondents with major depression, 32.5% met criteria for alcohol dependence during their lifetime, as compared to 11.2% of those without major depression. Those with primary alcohol use disorders were almost four times more likely to be diagnosed with lifetime depression, and the associations were even stronger for drug use disorders: Individuals with drug dependence were nearly seven times more likely to report lifetime major depression than those without drug dependence (see Bucholz, 1999 for a review). Such findings clearly illustrate that rates of dual diagnosis are significant among individuals with mental illness and primary substance abusers, and that many types of psychiatric disorders confer an increased risk of substance use disorder. Overall these studies find that a psychiatric diagnosis yields at least double the risk of a lifetime alcohol or drug use disorder.

High Prevalence Rates of Dual Diagnosis Persist over Time   A second important feature of rates of dual diagnosis is that they appear to be persistent. Examining how rates persist or change over time is important for several reasons. When the ECA and NCS findings first were published, the findings of high rates of both single and dual disorders were significant because they illustrated the many ways in which the understanding, assessment, and treatment of mental illness and substance use disorders were incomplete. The NCS in particular came under increased scrutiny, given that the rates it found for mental illness were even higher than those found by the ECA. Replications of these studies can demonstrate whether the high rates found in the first studies persist over time. In addition, since the first epidemiologic studies were conducted, *DSM* criteria have changed, leading to questions of how these diagnostic changes might impact illness rates. Finally, seeking treatment for mental distress, as well as use of medications for symptoms of depression and anxiety, are now more widely discussed and accepted than they were 10 to 20 years ago, and it is unclear how changing attitudes might impact rates of dual disorders.

Findings from several replications of large epidemiologic studies indicate that even with changes in diagnostic criteria and attitudes about psychological distress, rates of dual disorders remain high. For example, the NCS was recently replicated in the NCS-R. The NCS-R (Kessler & Merikangas, 2004) shared much of the same methodology as the original NCS, repeated many questions from the original survey, and included additional questions to tap *DSM-IV* diagnostic criteria. Conducting these studies 10 years apart allows for an examination of the stability in rates of dual diagnosis, as well as how changes in assessment and diagnostic criteria impact the prevalence of dual diagnosis and other comorbid conditions. Comparisons of data from both studies illustrate the persistent nature of dual diagnosis. That is, while specific values have changes from one interview to another, the overall picture of dual diagnosis remains the same: Prevalence rates are high, and people with mental illness remain at greatly increased risk for developing substance use disorders. For example, for major depressive disorder (MDD; Kessler et al., 1996) found that 38.6% of respondents who met criteria for lifetime MDD also had a diagnosis of substance use disorder based on NCS data, while 18.5% of respondents who met criteria for 12-month MDD also had a diagnosis of substance use disorder. Results from the NCSR confirmed the high prevalence rates of dual diagnosis in people with MDD: 24.0% of those with lifetime MDD also met criteria for a substance use disorder, and 27.1% of those who met criteria for 12-month MDD also met criteria for a substance use disorder (Kessler et al., 2005). Although the exact percentages change over time, the rates for dual MDD and substance use diagnoses remain strikingly high over the 10 years between studies.

Similar comparisons can be made between the NLAES and a more recent NIAAA survey called the National Epidemiologic Survey on Alcohol and Related Conditions (NESARC; Grant et al., 2004). The NESARC stressed the need to assure that diagnoses of mood and anxiety disorders were independent from substance use disorders. A comparison of the two studies shows that dual mood/anxiety and substance use disorders continue to be highly prevalent in community samples. For example, in the NLAES (Grant & Harford, 1995), respondents with a past year diagnosis of major depression had a 21.36% rate of a co-occurring alcohol use disorder, compared with 6.92% of those without 12-month major depression (OR = 3.65). Similarly, high odds ratios were found for 12-month major depression and drug use disorders (Grant, 1995). Importantly, results of the NESARC confirm the persistent association of substance use disorders and affective disorders. People who met criteria for any 12-month mood disorder were 4.5 times more likely to meet criteria for substance dependence (range of 3.4 to 6.4 for the four mood disorders assessed). People who met criteria for any 12-month anxiety disorder were 2.8 times more likely to meet substance dependence criteria (range of 2.2 to 4.2 for the five anxiety disorders assessed). Examining the results in terms of prevalence rates is similar: 19.97% of those with any 12-month mood disorder had at least 1 substance use disorder (SUD), and 14.96% of those with any 12-month anxiety disorder had at least one SUD. Similarly, 19.67% of those with a 12-month SUD had at least one mood disorder, and 17.71% had at least one anxiety disorder. Overall, comparisons from replications of large epidemiologic studies illustrate the persistence of dual diagnosis over time.

Dual Diagnosis is Only One Part of the Comorbidity Puzzle A third issue that is highlighted in some epidemiological studies is the fact that the term and typical understanding of dual diagnosis may not accurately reflect the nature and complexity of the problem of co-occurring mental and substance use disorders. That is, co-occurring disorders can take many forms, and limiting attention to a particular number or combination of problems may restrict what we can learn about the links and interactions between mental illness and substance use disorders. As discussed previously, the term *dual diagnosis* has most often been used to refer to a combination of one mental illness and one substance use disorder. However, epidemiologic studies find high prevalence rates of 3 or more co-occurring disorders that include but are not limited to dual mental-SUD combinations. For example, Kessler and colleagues (1994) found that 14% of the NCS sample met criteria for three or more comorbid *DSM* disorders, and that these respondents accounted for well over half of the lifetime and 12-month diagnoses found in the sample. Moreover, these respondents accounted for 89.5% of the severe 12-month disorders, which included active mania, nonaffective psychosis, or other disorders requiring hospitalization or associated with severe role impairment. Other data from the NCS (Kessler et al., 1996) showed that 31.9% of respondents with lifetime MDD and 18.5% of those with 12-month MDD met criteria for three or more comorbid conditions. In the NCS-R, Kessler, Berglund, Demler, Jin, and Walters (2005) found that 17.3% of respondents met criteria for three or more lifetime disorders. In addition, in examining projected lifetime risk of developing different *DSM* disorders, these authors reported that 80% of projected new onsets were estimated to occur in people who already had disorders. In examining 12-month disorders in the NCS-R sample, Kessler, Chiu, Demler, and Walters (2005) found similar results: 23% of the sample met criteria for three or more diagnoses. As these authors state: "Although mental disorders are widespread, serious cases are concentrated among a relatively small proportion of cases with high comorbidity" (Kessler, Chiu, Demler, & Walters, 2005, p. 617). Taken together, these findings illustrate the importance of thinking about dual diagnosis in the context of the broader picture of comorbid conditions. People with "dual" mental and substance use disorders may in fact meet criteria for a combination of multiple mental and substance use disorders. Such aggregation of mental and substance use disorders in a small proportion of people should influence conceptualizations regarding the processes underlying dual and comorbid conditions.

In addition, comorbidity appears to be influenced by severity of mental illness. Using data from the NCS-R, Kessler and colleagues (2003) examined differences in rates of comorbid disorders (including but not limited to SUDs) in respondents with MDD of differing levels of severity. Specifically, respondents who met criteria for 12-month MDD were classified as showing mild, moderate, severe, or very severe symptoms, based on scores on the Quick Inventory of Depressive Symptomatology Self Report (QIDS-SR) for the worst month in the past year. As severity level increased, so did rates of comorbidity, defined as the percentage of respondents with 2 or more comorbid 12-month disorders, including substance use disorders. Specifically, 34.9% of mild, 58.0% of moderate, 77.3% of severe, and 82.1% of very severe MDD cases met criteria for 2 or more comorbid disorders. This finding of increased severity as number of disorders increases was also found for 12-month diagnoses (Kessler, Chiu, Demler, & Walters, 2005). This trend is another reminder that dual diagnosis and comorbidity labels represent heterogeneous groups of people that differ in meaningful ways that likely have significance in terms of assessment, treatment, and etiology of mental and substance use disorders.

In sum, epidemiological studies are now able to tell us not only that dual diagnosis is highly prevalent, but also that rates of dual disorders persist over time. In addition, we now have ample evidence to suggest that talking about "dual" disorders is actually a simplification of a complex problem in that patients often have more than two psychiatric disorders as well as use, abuse, or are dependent on multiple substances. Such findings suggest that thinking about the causes of dual disorders may need to be broadened in order to be able to explain this range of diversity among dual disordered patients.

FINDINGS FROM STUDIES OF CLINICAL SAMPLES

The fact that dual diagnosis is fairly common in the general population serves to highlight the even higher rates found in treatment settings. Clinical studies of dual diagnosis have assessed general psychiatric patients, patients with specific psychiatric disorders, and primary substance abusing patients.

Dual Diagnosis in General Psychiatric Patients   Clinical studies of dual diagnosis over the last 20 years indicate that one-third to three-quarters of general psychiatric patients may meet criteria for comorbid psychiatric and substance use disorders, depending on the diagnostic makeup of the sample and the level of chronicity represented (Ananth et al., 1989; Galanter, Castaneda, & Ferman, 1988; McLellan, Druley, & Carson, 1978; Mezzich, Ahn, Fabrega, & Pilkonis, 1990; Safer, 1987). Rates seem to fall in the higher end of this range for samples comprising more impaired patient populations. For example, Ananth and colleagues (1989) found that 72.0% of a sample of patients with schizophrenia, bipolar disorder, and atypical psychosis received a comorbid substance use diagnosis. Mezzich, Ahn, Fabrega, & Pilkonis (1990) conducted a large-scale assessment of dual diagnosis in more than 4,000 patients presenting for evaluation and referral for mental health problems over an 18-month period and found substantial rates of dual diagnosis among a number of diagnostic subsamples. The highest rates were seen among patients with severe mental illnesses such as bipolar disorder (45% diagnosed with an alcohol use disorder and 39% diagnosed with a drug use disorder) and schizophrenia or paranoid disorders (42% and 38% were diagnosed with alcohol and other substance use disorders, respectively). However, dual diagnosis was also pronounced in other patient groups. Specifically, 33% of patients with major depression were diagnosed with an alcohol use disorder, and 18% were diagnosed with a drug use disorder. Among patients with anxiety disorders, 19% and 11% were diagnosed with alcohol and other substance use disorders, respectively.

Dual Diagnosis in Samples of Patients with Specific Disorders   Rates of dual diagnosis have been extensively studied among patients with severe mental illness, including schizophrenia (Dixon, Haas, Weiden, Sweeney, & Frances, 1991; Mueser et al., 1990), bipolar disorder (Bauer et al., 2005; McElroy et al., 2001; Salloum & Thase, 2000; Vieta et al., 2000), and major depression (Goodwin & Jamison, 1990; Lynskey, 1998; Merikangas, Leckman, Prusoff, Pauls, & Weissman, 1985; Swendsen & Merikangas, 2000). Findings show that dual diagnosis is common in such samples. Mueser et al. (1990) evaluated 149 patients with schizophrenia spectrum disorders and found that 47% had a lifetime history of alcohol abuse, while many had abused stimulants (25%), cannabis (42%), and hallucinogens (18%). Dixon and colleagues (1991) found that 48% of a sample of schizophrenia patients met criteria for an alcohol or drug use disorder. Recently, Chengappa, Levine, Gershon, and Kupfer (2000) evaluated the prevalence of substance abuse and dependence in patients with bipolar disorder. Among patients with bipolar I, 58% met abuse or dependence criteria for at least one substance, and 11% abused or were dependent on three or more substances. In the bipolar II group, the rate of dual diagnosis was approximately 39%. Recently, Baethge and colleagues (2005) followed a group of first episode bipolar I patients and found that about one-third of the sample had a substance use disorder at the baseline assessment, and that patients using two or more substances showed poorer outcomes over the two years of the study. Hasin, Endicott, and Lewis (1985) examined rates of comorbidity in a sample of patients with affective disorder presenting for treatment as part of the National Institute of Mental Health Collaborative Study of Depression and found that 24% of these patients reported serious problems with alcohol and 18% met diagnostic criteria for an alcohol use disorder. In an examination of patients with major depression, bipolar disorder and controls participating in the National Institute of Mental

Health Collaborative Program on the Psychobiology of Depression, Winokur and colleagues (1998) found that affective disorder patients had substantially higher rates of dual substance use disorders than did controls.

Dual diagnosis is also common among patients with anxiety disorders. In their review of studies of dual anxiety and substance use disorders, Kushner, Sher, and Beitman (1990) found that rates differ by type of anxiety disorder, with social phobia (ranging from 20% to 36% rate of dual diagnosis) and agoraphobia (ranging from 7.0% to 27.0% rate of dual diagnosis) showing the highest rates of substance abuse comorbidity. Others have found a 22% rate of lifetime alcohol use disorder among patients with social phobia (Himle & Hill, 1991), a 10% to 20% rate for patients with agoraphobia (Bibb & Chambless, 1986), and up to 12% rate of lifetime alcohol dependence among patients with obsessive-compulsive disorder (Eisen & Rasmussen, 1989). In addition, more attention is being given recently to dual substance abuse and PTSD in clinical samples. A growing literature examining this diagnostic combination finds high rates of dual diagnosis among patients with PTSD, with some findings as high as 80% (Keane, Gerardi, Lyons, & Wolfe, 1988). Research both with samples of veterans with PTSD and samples of women with assault or trauma-related PTSD show strikingly high rates of comorbid substance abuse and dependence (see Stewart, Pihl, Conrol, & Dongier, 1998 for a review). Moreover, Breslau, Davis, Peterson, and Schultz (1997) interviewed a sample of 801 women and found that PTSD significantly increased the likelihood for later alcohol use disorder.

Importantly, the highest rates of comorbidity are found for patients with personality disorders, especially ASP. Studies show that comorbid ASP accelerates the development of alcoholism (Hesselbrock, Hesselbrock, & Workman-Daniels, 1986), and that 80% of patients with ASP have a history of problem use of alcohol (Schuckit, 1983). In a recent review of studies on dual substance use disorders and borderline personality disorder (BPD), Trull and colleagues (2000) found that, across studies, more than 48% of patients with BPD met criteria for alcohol use disorders, and 38% of those with BPD met criteria for a drug use disorder.

Dual Diagnosis in Patients with Primary Substance Use Disorders   Substance-abusing patients in treatment are a heterogeneous group, encompassing a range of substances and levels of severity. Nonetheless, researchers have found high rates of dual disorders across diverse samples of patients seeking substance abuse treatment (Arendt & Munk-Jorgensen, 2004; Falck, Wang, Siegal, & Carlson, 2004; Herz, Volicer, D'Angelo, & Gadish, 1990; Mirin, Weiss, Griffin, & Michael, 1991; Mirin, Weiss, & Michael, 1988; Penick et al., 1984; Powell, Penick, Othmer, Bingham, & Rice, 1982; Ross, Glaser, & Stiasny, 1988; Rounsaville, Weissman, Kleber, & Wilber, 1982; Watkins et al., 2004; Weissman & Meyers, 1980). Findings of lifetime rates of psychiatric disorder range from 73.5% of a sample of cocaine abusers (Rounsaville et al., 1991) to 77% of a sample of hospitalized alcoholics (Hesselbrock, Meyer, & Keener, 1985) to 78% of a sample of patients in an alcohol and drug treatment facility (Ross, Glaser, & Germanson, 1988). Findings of current psychiatric disorder are similarly high, ranging from 55.7% of a group of cocaine abusers (Rounsaville et al., 1991) to 65% in a general substance-abusing sample (Ross et al., 1988).

Further reflecting their diagnostic heterogeneity, substance abusers in treatment experience a range of comorbid psychiatric disorders. Among the most widely studied have been affective disorders, and treatment-seeking substance abusers show high rates of both major depression (Hasin, Grant, & Endicott, 1988;

Hesselbrock et al., 1985; Merikangas & Gelernter, 1990; Mezzich et al., 1990; Miller, Klamen, Hoffmann, & Flaherty, 1996; Rounsaville, Weissman, Wilber, Crits-Christoph, & Kleber, 1982; Weissman & Meyers, 1980) and bipolar disorder (Strakowski & DelBello, 2000). Miller and colleagues (1996) surveyed a sample of more than 6,000 substance abuse treatment patients from 41 sites and found that 44% had a lifetime history of major depression. In a review of comorbidity of affective and substance use disorders, Lynskey (1998) found that the prevalence of unipolar depression among patients receiving treatment for substance use disorders ranged from a low of 25.8% for lifetime depression in a sample of 93 alcohol-dependent men (Sellman & Joyce, 1996) to a high of 67% meeting a lifetime diagnosis of major depression among a sample of 120 inpatients (Grant et al., 1989). Busto, Romach, and Sellers (1996) evaluated rates of dual diagnosis in a sample of 30 patients admitted to a medical facility for benzodiazepine detoxification and found that 33% met *DSM-III-R* criteria for lifetime major depression. Results from large studies of treatment-seeking substance abusers find that these patients show 5 to 8 times the risk of having a comorbid bipolar diagnosis (see Strakowski & DelBello, 2000 for a review). The importance of dual mental illness in substance-abusing samples lies in its link to functioning and treatment outcome. Burns, Teesson, and O'Neill (2005) studied the impact of dual anxiety disorders and/or depression on outcome of 71 patients seeking outpatient alcohol treatment. Comorbid patients showed greater problems at baseline (more disabled, drank more heavily) than did substance abuse only patients, a difference that persisted at a follow-up assessment three months later.

An extensive literature documents high rates of comorbid personality disorders in primary substance abusers (Khantzian & Treece, 1985; Nace, 1990; Nace, Davis, & Gaspari, 1991), especially ASP (Herz et al., 1990; Hesselbrock et al., 1985; Liskow, Powell, Nickel, & Penick, 1991; Morgenstern, Langenbucher, Labouvie, & Miller, 1997; Penick et al., 1984; Powell et al., 1982). In their evaluation of a large sample of treatment-seeking substance abusers, Mezzich and colleagues (1990) found that 18% of those with alcohol use disorders and almost 25% of those with drug use disorders met criteria for an Axis II disorder. Busto and colleagues (1996) found that 42% of their sample of patients undergoing benzodiazepine detoxification met *DSM-III-R* criteria for ASP. Morgenstern, Langenbucher, Labouvie, and Miller (1997) assessed prevalence rates of personality disorders in a multisite sample of 366 substance abusers in treatment. Results showed that more than 57% of the sample met criteria for at least one personality disorder. ASP was the most prevalent (22.7% of the sample), followed by borderline (22.4%), paranoid (20.7%), and avoidant (18%) personality disorders. Moreover, the presence of a personality disorder doubled the likelihood of meeting criteria for a comorbid Axis I disorder. Brooner and colleagues (1997) assessed psychiatric disorders in 716 opioid abusers on methadone maintenance therapy and found that 47% of the sample met criteria for at least one disorder, with ASP and major depression being the most common co-occurring diagnoses. In addition, psychiatric comorbidity was associated with more severe substance use disorder. Kokkevi and colleagues (1998) surveyed 226 treatment-seeking individuals with drug dependence in Greece and found a 59.5% prevalence rate of personality disorder, with more than 60% of these patients meeting criteria for more than one personality disorder. Moreover, those with personality disorders were at twice the risk for meeting an additional Axis I diagnosis.

Findings are similar with anxiety disorders, with high rates of comorbid phobias (Bowen, Cipywnyk, D'Arcy, & Keegan, 1984; Hasin et al., 1988; Ross et al., 1988), panic disorder (Hasin et al., 1988; Penick et al., 1984), and obsessive-compulsive disorder (Eisen & Rasmussen, 1989) documented in substance-abusing populations. Thomas, Thevos, and Randall (1999) reported a 23% prevalence rate of social phobias in a large study of both inpatients and outpatients with alcohol dependence. Substance abusers also appear to be especially affected by PTSD (Cottler, Compton, Mager, Spitznagel, & Janca, 1992; Davis & Wood, 1999; Triffleman, Marmar, Delucchi, & Ronfeldt, 1995). In an analysis of cocaine-dependent patients in the National Institute on Drug Abuse Collaborative Cocaine Treatment Study, Najavits and colleagues (1998) found that 30.2% of women and 15.2% of men met *DSM-III-R* criteria for PTSD. Recently, Back and colleagues (2000) found that 42.9% of a sample of cocaine-dependent individuals met criteria for PTSD, and Bonin and colleagues (2000) found a 37.4% rate of PTSD in a sample of patients attending a community substance abuse treatment program.

In sum, the literature clearly documents high rates of dual substance abuse and psychiatric disorders for a variety of psychopathological conditions and in a range of patient populations. Findings from epidemiological studies show that dual diagnosis is relatively common in the general population, and results of clinical studies illustrate the frequency of dual diagnosis among individuals in treatment. That rates of dual diagnosis are similarly high in both mentally ill and in primary substance-abusing populations serves to highlight the serious difficulties in having two separate and independent systems of care for mental illness and substance abuse (Grella, 1996; Ridgely, Lambert, Goodman, Chichester, & Ralph, 1998), despite the fact that both populations of patients are quite likely to be suffering from both types of disorders.

CLINICAL IMPACT OF DUAL DISORDERS

The importance of dual diagnosis lies in its negative impact on the course and prognosis of both psychiatric and substance use disorders, as well as its influence on assessment, diagnosis, and treatment outcome. Individuals with dual disorders show more adverse social, health, economic, and psychiatric consequences than those with only one disorder, and they show more severe difficulties, often a more chronic course of psychiatric disorder, and a poorer response to both mental health and substance abuse treatment. In the next section we review the ways that dual diagnosis impacts three general areas: patient functioning, clinical care, and research.

IMPACT OF DUAL DIAGNOSIS ON PATIENT FUNCTIONING

Symptoms, Course of Illness, and Life Functioning   Dual diagnosis severely impacts the severity and course of many disorders, especially among patients with serious mental illnesses such as schizophrenia, bipolar disorder, and recurrent major depression. Often these dually diagnosed individuals show a poorer and more chaotic course of disorder, with more severe symptoms (Alterman, Erdlen, Laporte, & Erdlen, 1982; Barbee et al., 1989; Hays & Aidroos, 1986; Negrete and Knapp, 1986), more frequent hospitalizations (Carpenter, Heinrichs, & Alphs, 1985; Drake & Wallach, 1989; Sonne, Brady, & Morton, 1994), and more frequent relapses than patients without co-occurring substance abuse (Linszen, Dingemans, & Lenior, 1994; O'Connell, Mayo, Flatow, Cuthbertson, & O'Brien, 1991; Sokolski et al., 1994). Haywood et al. (1995) found that substance abuse, along with medication noncompliance, was the most important predictor of more frequent rehospitalization among schizophrenia patients. Recently, Margolese and colleagues (2004) compared three groups of schizophrenia patients: those with current SUD, those with lifetime but not current SUD, and those with no current or history of SUD. Patients with current SUD showed more positive symptoms than both other patient groups, higher scores on measures of depression as compared to the single diagnosis group, and were more likely to be noncompliant with their medications than the single diagnosis group. Winokur and colleagues (1998) found that patients with drug abuse and bipolar disorder had an earlier age of onset of bipolar disorder than those with bipolar disorder alone, as well as a stronger family history of mania. Nolan and colleagues (2004) rated patients with bipolar or schizoaffective disorder on severity of manic symptoms, severity of depressive symptoms, and number of illness episodes over a 1-year period (n = 258). Results showed that ratings for mania severity were associated with comorbid substance abuse. Lehman and colleagues (1993) compared individuals with dual mental illness and substance use diagnoses to those with just a primary mental illness and found that the dual diagnosis group had a higher rate of personality disorder and more legal problems. Hasin, Endicott, and Keller (1991) followed 135 individuals with dual mood and alcohol use disorders who were originally studied as part of the National Institute of Mental Health Collaborative Study on the Psychobiology of Depression. Although most had experienced at least one 6-month period of remission of the alcohol disorder at some point during the follow-up period, most had relapsed after 5 years. Mueller and colleagues (1994) examined the impact of alcohol dependence on the course of major depression over 10 years among individuals with depression who participated in the National Institute of Mental Health Collaborative Depression Study. Those who were alcohol dependent at baseline had a much lower rate of recovery from major depression than those with major depression alone, illustrating the negative impact of alcohol use disorders on the course of major depressive disorder.

Dual diagnosis is also a serious issue for patients with anxiety disorders such as PTSD (Najavitis, Weiss, & Shaw, 1997; Ouimette, Brown, & Najavitis, 1998). Overall, the combination of substance abuse and PTSD appears to be linked to higher rates of victimization, more severe PTSD symptoms in general, more severe subgroups of PTSD symptoms, and higher rates of Axis II comorbidity (Ouimette, Wolfe, & Chrestman, 1996). Saladin, Brady, Dansky, and Kilpatrick (1995) compared 28 women with both substance abuse and PTSD to 28 women with PTSD only and found that the dual diagnosis group reported more symptoms of avoidance and arousal, more sleep disturbance, and greater traumatic event exposure than the PTSD-only group. Back and colleagues (2000) similarly found higher rates of exposure to traumatic events, more severe symptomatology, and higher rates of Axis I and Axis II disorders among cocaine-dependent individuals with PTSD as compared to those without lifetime PTSD. Moreover, evidence suggests that the combination of PTSD and cocaine dependence remains harmful over several years, with patients showing a greater likelihood of continued PTSD as well as revictimization several years after an initial substance abuse treatment episode (Dansky, Brady, & Saladin, 1998).

Dual diagnosis also exerts a profound impact on overall life functioning. Patients with severe mental illnesses such as schizophrenia who abuse substances appear to be particularly hard hit in this regard (see Bradizza & Stasiewicz, 1997 for a review; Kozaric-Kovacic, Folnegovic-Smalc, Folnegovic, & Marusic, 1995). Drake and colleagues consistently have found that individuals with schizophrenia and comorbid substance abuse show substantially poorer life adjustment than do their nonsubstance-abusing counterparts, including poorer self-care, less stable living environments, and fewer regular meals (Drake, Osher, & Wallach, 1989; Drake & Wallach, 1989). Havassy and Arns (1998) surveyed 160 frequently hospitalized adult psychiatric patients and found not only high rates of dual disorders (48% of patients had at least one current substance use disorder; of these, 55.1% met criteria for polysubstance dependence), but also that dual diagnosis was related to increased depressive symptoms, poor life functioning, lower life satisfaction, and a greater likelihood of being arrested or in jail. Research similarly shows that patients with dual affective and alcohol use disorders show greater difficulties in overall functioning and social functioning than patients with depression (Hirschfeld, Hasin, Keller, Endicott, & Wunder, 1990) or bipolar disorder (Singh, Mattoo, Sharan, & Basu, 2005). Newman and colleagues (1998) examined the impact of different types of comorbidity (including but not limited to substance abuse-psychiatric disorder combinations) on life functioning in a large sample of young adults. Multiple disorder cases showed poorer functioning than single disordered cases in almost every area measured, including health status, suicide attempts, disruption in performance of daily activities, the number of months disabled because of psychiatric illness, greater life dissatisfaction, less social stability (more residence changes, greater use of welfare for support, greater rates of adult criminal conviction records), greater employment problems, lower levels of educational attainment, and greater reports of physical health problems. Weiss and colleagues (2005) examined the interplay between bipolar disorder and recovery from substance use disorders on a range of quality-of-life factors in a sample of 1,000 patients with current or lifetime bipolar disorder. Specifically, three groups were compared: those with no history of SUDs, those with past SUDs, and those with current SUDs. Results showed that the current SUD group had the poorest functioning, and both SUD groups reported lower quality of life and higher lifetime rates of suicide attempts than did the non-SUD group. Moreover, the toxic effects of psychoactive substances in individuals with schizophrenia and bipolar disorder may be present even at use levels that may not be problematic in the general population (Lehman, Myers, Dixon, & Johnson, 1994; Mueser et al., 1990).

Treatment Noncompliance and Violence   Substance abuse often interferes with compliance with both behavioral and psychopharmacological treatments. Lambert, Griffith, and Hendrickse (1996) surveyed patients on a general psychiatry unit in a Veterans Administration medical center and found that discharges against medical advice (AMA) were more likely to occur among patients with alcohol and/or substance use disorders. Pages and colleagues (1998) similarly assessed predictors of AMA discharge in psychiatric patients. The presence of a SUD and a greater quantity and frequency of substance use were among the most important predictors. Owen and colleagues (1996) followed a sample of 135 inpatients after discharge and found that medication noncompliance was related to substance abuse, and that this combination was significantly associated with lack of outpatient contact in the follow-up period. Specifically, those with dual diagnoses were more than eight times more likely to be noncompliant with their medication. In a large-scale study of factors related to medication adherence in schizophrenia patients, Gilmer and colleagues (2004) found that substance abusers were less likely to be adherent to antipsychotic medication regimens than were schizophrenia patients who did not abuse substances. Such findings are especially important when linked to functioning and service use. For example, schizophrenia patients who were nonadherent with their medications were more than 2.5 times more likely to be hospitalized than those that were adherent (Gilmer et al., 2004).

Verduin, Carter, Brady, Myrick, and Timmerman (2005) compared bipolar only, alcohol-dependent only, and comorbid bipolar and alcohol-dependent patients on several treatment variables, including number of outpatient psychiatric visits and length of psychiatric hospitalizations, in the year leading up to and including an index hospitalization at a veterans hospital from 1999 through 2003. The comorbid group had fewer outpatient psychiatric visits and shorter inpatient hospitalizations than did either of the single disorder groups.

For many disorders, substance abuse and its associated noncompliance with treatment is linked not only to poorer outcomes but also to greater risk for violence (Marzuk, 1996; Poldrugo, 1998; Sandberg, McNiel, & Binder, 1998; Scott et al., 1998; Soyka, 2000; Steadman et al., 1998; Swanson, Borum, Swartz, & Hiday, 1999; Swartz et al., 1998). Fulwiler, Grossman, Forbes, and Ruthazer (1997) compared differences between two groups of outpatients with chronic mental illness: those with and without a history of violence. The only significant differences between the two groups involved alcohol or drug use. McFall and colleagues (1999) examined 228 male Vietnam veterans seeking inpatient treatment for posttraumatic stress disorder and found levels of substance abuse were positively correlated with violence and aggression. The combination of schizophrenia and antisocial personality disorder appears to put people at high risk for violence, especially when drinking (Joyal, Putkonen, Paavola, & Tiihonen, 2004). Substance abuse is also associated with greater suicidal ideation and risk of suicide among patients with mental illness, including those with schizophrenia (Cohen, Test, & Brown, 1990; Karmali et al., 2000; Landmark, Cernovsky, & Merskey, 1987), depression (Pages et al., 1997), and bipolar disorder (reviewed in Goodwin & Jamison, 1990; Verduin et al., 2005). Pages and colleagues (1997) surveyed 891 psychiatric inpatients with major depressive disorder and found that both substance use and substance dependence were associated with higher levels of suicidal ideation. Potash and colleagues (2000) examined the relationship between alcohol use disorders and suicidality in bipolar patients and found that 38% of subjects with dual bipolar and alcohol use disorders had attempted suicide as compared to 22% of those with bipolar disorder only. Recently, McCloud, Barnaby, Omu, Drummond, and Aboud (2004) examined alcohol disorders and suicidality (defined as any record of self-harm or thoughts or plans of self-harm or suicide written in the medical record) in consecutive admissions to a psychiatric hospital. Problem drinking (as measured by the Alcohol Use Disorders Identification Test or AUDIT) was strongly related to suicidality, with higher AUDIT scores (representing greater severity of problems with alcohol) showing higher rates of suicidality.

IMPACT OF DUAL DIAGNOSIS ON CLINICAL CARE AND RELATED FACTORS

Service Utilization and Health Care Costs   The fact that clinical settings routinely demonstrate higher rates of dual diagnosis patients points to the fact that having both psychiatric and substance use disorders increases rates of treatment seeking.

Increased service utilization among the dually diagnosed has been borne out in both large-scale household surveys and clinical studies. For example, Helzer and Pryzbeck (1988) examined data from the ECA study and found that, for respondents of both sexes with alcohol use disorders, the number of additional nonsubstance use disorder diagnoses had a significant impact on treatment seeking: those with more diagnoses reported greater utilization of treatment services. Grant (1997) examined the influence of comorbid major depression and substance abuse on rates of seeking alcohol and drug treatment in data collected from the National Longitudinal Alcohol Epidemiological Survey (Grant et al., 1994). The percentage of individuals with alcohol use disorders seeking treatment practically doubled, from 7.8% to 16.9%, when a comorbid major depressive disorder was also present. Interestingly, the greatest rate of treatment seeking (35.3%) was found among respondents who met criteria for all three disorders—alcohol, drug, and depression—illustrating how the term *dual diagnosis* is somewhat misleading because some individuals have two or more substance use and psychiatric disorders and each might have an additive effect on negative outcomes. Similarly, Wu and colleagues (1999), analyzing data from the NCS, found that although 14.5% of patients with a pure alcohol disorder reported using mental health and substance abuse intervention services, more than 32% of patients with comorbid alcohol and mental disorders used such services. Menezes and colleagues (1996) studied the impact of substance use problems on service utilization over one year in a sample of 171 individuals with serious mental illness. Although the number of inpatient admissions was equivalent for those with dual disorders and those with mental illness only, the dual diagnosis group used psychiatric emergency services 1.3 times more frequently and spent 1.8 times as many days in the hospital than the single disorder group.

Given their increased rates of service utilization, it is not surprising that dual diagnosis patients generally accrue greater health care costs than do patients with a single diagnosis (Maynard & Cox, 1998; McCrone et al., 2000). Dickey and Azeni (1996) examined the costs of psychiatric treatment for more than 16,000 seriously mentally ill individuals with and without comorbid substance use disorders. Patients with dual diagnoses had psychiatric treatment costs that were nearly 60% higher than the costs of psychiatrically impaired individuals without substance abuse. Interestingly, most of the increased cost was owing to greater rates of inpatient psychiatric treatment, suggesting that the impact of substance abuse on psychiatric symptom and illness relapse is realized when patients require costly psychiatric hospitalization. Garnick, Hendricks, Comstock, and Horgan (1997) examined health insurance data files over three years from almost 40,000 employees and found that those with dual diagnoses routinely accrued substantially higher health care costs than those with substance abuse only. Such findings suggest that individuals with dual disorders access the most expensive treatment options (inpatient hospitalization, visits to emergency rooms) that are short-term in order to manage acute distress and fail to get the comprehensive and ongoing care they require.

These findings on rates of services use can be perplexing. For example, if dual diagnosis patients are accessing more and more expensive services, why do they consistently have more severe psychiatric symptoms, more substance-use related problems, and poorer outcomes than those with single disorders? As noted earlier, dual diagnosis patients appear to more often access expensive but short-term or acute treatment options while being noncompliant or not adhering to longer-term medication and outpatient treatment regiments. Other factors include lack of integrated care, as well as increased numbers of problems to treat associated with treating more than one disorder (Watkins, Burnam, Kung, & Paddock, 2001). In addition, researchers recently have begun to more closely examine the quality of services accessed by dual diagnosis patients. For example, in their study of patients with bipolar disorder with and without comorbid substance use disorders, Verduin and colleagues (2005) found that patients with bipolar disorder and comorbid substance abuse were less likely than patients with substance abuse alone to be referred to intensive substance abuse treatment. Watkins and colleagues (2001) looked at the delivery of appropriate care to probable dual diagnosis patients assessed as part of the Healthcare for Communities Survey (a study of a subset of respondents from the Community Tracking Study, a nationally representative study of the civilian, noninstitutionalized people in the United States [see Kemper et al., 1996 for details]). Appropriate care included medications for severe mental illness (a mood stabilizer for bipolar disorder, antipsychotic medication for a psychiatric disorder), medications and/or psychosocial interventions for anxiety disorders or major depression, and at least four sessions of any sort of treatment in the past year. In addition, variables addressed included whether patients are receiving integrated care for dual disorders (receiving both mental health and substance abuse treatment from one provider) or comprehensive substance abuse treatment (defined as including inpatient or outpatient substance use treatment that included a physical examination, a mental health evaluation, or job or relationship counseling). Results showed that 72% of dual diagnosis patients did not receive any specialty mental health or substance abuse services (i.e., services provided by a mental health or substance abuse professional rather than a primary care physician), 8% received both mental health and substance abuse treatment (either integrated or by different providers), 23% received appropriate mental health care, and 9% received comprehensive substance abuse treatment.

Other studies have found a disconnect between services accessed and services needed in dual diagnosis samples (Najavits, Sullivan, Schmitz, Weiss, & Lee, 2004). Such findings suggest that the complicated clinical picture presented by dual diagnosis patients makes it difficult for patients and providers to determine and administer appropriate care.

Other Societal Impacts
PHYSICAL ILLNESS   Dual diagnosis puts people at risk for different forms of illness and disease. One of the most significant health problems in this population is risk for HIV and AIDS. Individuals with dual diagnosis show greatly increased risk for HIV and AIDS. People with schizophrenia and other severe mental illness are now one of the highest-risk groups for HIV (Gottesman & Groome, 1997; Krakow, Galanter, Dermatis, & Westreich, 1998), and data indicate that substance use substantially increases the likelihood of unsafe sex practices (Carey, Carey, & Kalichman, 1997) and other high-risk behaviors in those with mental illness. For example, McKinnon and colleagues (1996) found that 17.5% of a sample of psychiatric patients had a history of injection drug use, 35% reported using drugs during sex, and 30% traded sex for drugs—all substance use behaviors that are highly risky in terms of the transmission of HIV and AIDS. In their sample of 145 psychiatric inpatients and outpatients in Australia, Thompson and colleagues (1997) found that 15.9% of dual diagnosis patients reported injection drug use, a figure that is

10 times higher than that found in the general population. Hoff, Beam-Goulet, and Rosenheck (1997) examined data from the 1992 National Survey of Veterans and found that the combination of PTSD and substance abuse increased the risk of HIV infection by almost 12 times over individuals with either disorder alone.

There is increasing evidence that other physical illnesses and high-risk health habits are also found more often in people with dual disorders. For example, Stuyt (2004) found that 29.7% of a dual diagnosis sample had hepatitis C, a rate that is 16 times higher than that found in the general population. Salloum, Douaihy, Ndimbie, and Kirisci (2004) examined physical health and disorders in three groups of psychiatric patients hospitalized on a dual diagnosis treatment unit: a group with both alcohol and cocaine dependence, a group with alcohol dependence only, and group with cocaine dependence only. Results showed that the group with both alcohol and cocaine dependence showed higher rates of a range of medical problems, including multiple hepatitis infections, than both single diagnosis groups. Recently Jones and colleagues (2004) examined physical health problems among people with severe mental illness and found that 74% of the sample was treated for one chronic health condition, and 50% was treated for two or more. The two most highly prevalent chronic health conditions—pulmonary disease and infectious disease—were both associated with substance use disorders in this sample. Moreover, results of regression analysis showed that substance abuse, along with age and obesity, was a significant predictor of health problem severity. Others have found high rates of mortality and other dangerous health conditions among those with dual diagnosis (Dickey, Dembling, Azeni & Normand, 2004; Lambert, LePage & Schmitt, 2003).

LEGAL PROBLEMS   There is also evidence that individuals with dual diagnoses have more frequent contacts with the legal system. Clark, Ricketts, and McHugo (1999) followed a sample of individuals with mental illness and substance use disorders over three years to longitudinally examine legal involvement and its correlates in this population. The sample consisted of 203 patients receiving treatment in a dual diagnosis treatment program. Cost and use data were collected from a range of sources, including police, defenders, prosecutors, and jails. Interestingly, while rates of arrest were certainly high, patients were four times more likely to have encounters with the legal system that did not result in arrest. This suggests that frequency of arrest, while significant, is an underrepresentation of the frequency of contact that dual diagnosis patients have with the legal system. In addition, continued substance abuse over the follow-up period was significantly associated with a greater likelihood of arrest.

HOMELESSNESS   The combination of mental illness and substance abuse also increases risk for homelessness. In a study of patients with schizophrenia, Dixon (1999) found that those who used substances experienced not only greater psychotic symptoms and relapses, a higher incidence of violent behavior and suicide, elevated rates of HIV infection, increased mortality, higher rates of treatment and medication noncompliance, but also were more likely to live in an unstable housing situation or be homeless. Caton and colleagues (1994) compared a sample of mentally ill homeless men to a sample of mentally ill men who were not homeless and found higher rates of drug use disorders among the homeless group. Leal and colleagues (1999) assessed homelessness in a sample of 147 patients with dual diagnosis and found that those in the group with so-called protracted homelessness (no residence for one year or more) were significantly more likely to report a history of injection drug use than those patients without protracted homelessness.

Recently Folsom et al. (2005) examined risk factors for homelessness and patterns of service use among those who are homeless in a large sample (n = 10,340) of patients with severe mental illness from a large public mental health system in southern California. Homelessness was associated with a range of variables, including substance abuse—60.5% of the homeless mentally ill group showed a substance use disorder as compared to 20.9% of the nonhomeless mentally ill group. Moreover, results of multivariate logistic regression showed that those with mental illness and substance abuse were more than four times as likely to be homeless than were patients who did not abuse substances.

ISSUES FOR WOMEN WITH SEVERE MENTAL ILLNESS AND SUBSTANCE ABUSE   Importantly, dual diagnosis is often particularly problematic for individuals who are also otherwise underserved. As noted, individuals with schizophrenia appear to be particularly hard hit by the additional difficulties of SUD. Another such population is women with severe mental illness and substance abuse. Research on women with dual diagnoses has shown that those with comorbid severe mental illness and substance abuse show poorer retention in treatment (Brown, Melchior, & Huba, 1999), and elevated levels of anxiety, depression, and medical illness (Brunette & Drake, 1998), as well as being more difficult to engage in treatment and more underrepresented in treatment overall (Comtois & Ries, 1995). In addition, women with dual diagnoses appear to have alarmingly higher rates of sexual and physical victimization that are substantially higher than those observed among women in the general population (Gearon & Bellack, 1999; Goodman, Rosenburg, Mueser, & Drake, 1997). Prevalence rates for physical victimization for women with serious mental illness range between 42% and 64% (Jacobson, 1989), and other research finds that 21% to 38% of women with serious mental illness report adult sexual abuse (Goodman, Dutton & Harris, 1995). Among women receiving treatment in a residential therapeutic community, 49% reported physical abuse and 40% reported sexual abuse (Palacios, Urmann, Newel, & Hamilton, 1999). Data from 28 women and 24 men with serious mental illness and SUDs indicated that, when compared with men, women were more likely to report being physically (60% of women vs. 29% of men) and sexually (47% of women vs. 17% of men) victimized (Gearon, Bellack, Nidecker, & Bennett, 2003). In addition, women with dual diagnosis are often affected by issues related to pregnancy and parenting. Grella (1997) summarized some of the many difficulties in terms of services for pregnant women with dual disorders, including receiving adequate prenatal care, use of substances and psychiatric medications while pregnant, and lack of coordinated treatment planning and provision among medical, psychiatric, and addictions professionals. Kelly and colleagues (1999) examined the medical records of all women delivering babies in California hospitals in 1994 and 1995 and found that women with both psychiatric and substance use diagnoses were at greatly elevated risk of receiving inadequate prenatal care. There are also substantial barriers to treatment and medical care for these women, including fears of losing custody of the unborn child or their other children, lack of medical insurance, and the often disjointed nature of available services for the medical and psychiatric care of these patients (Grella, 1997). Finally, when compared to men, women with dual diagnosis may have different treatment needs. Grella (2003) compared differences in substance use and treatment histories and perceptions of service needs between men and women diagnosed with severe mental illness (mood or psychotic disorders) on admission to inpatient drug treatment. Women reported greater needs for family and trauma-related services, and women with psychotic disorders had the greatest level of need of all the groups for basic services.

Assessment and Diagnosis

SYMPTOM OVERLAP   Symptom overlap is a significant complication in terms of assessment and diagnosis. The symptoms of many psychiatric disorders overlap with those of substance use disorders, making diagnosis of either class of disorders difficult. For example, *DSM* lists problems in social functioning as symptoms of both schizophrenia and substance use disorders. That some criteria can count toward multiple diagnoses can potentially increase comorbidity rates and can make diagnosis of substance abuse difficult. This overlap can work against identification of the psychiatric disorder in some cases. For example, high rates of dual substance use and bipolar disorders lead to an underdiagnosis of bipolar disorder, because of the often incorrect assumption that the behavioral manifestations of bipolar disorder are secondary to substance use (Evans, 2000). Others (Brady, Killeen, Brewerton, & Lucerini, 2000; Brunello et al., 2001) suggest that underdiagnosis can also be an issue with dual PTSD and substance use disorders.

MULTIPLE IMPAIRMENTS OWING TO DIFFERENT DISORDERS   Substance use disorders are often overlooked in mental health settings in which patients present with a range of acute impairments that exert a negative impact on overall functioning. There is often diagnostic confusion in terms of whether or not a given impairment is owing to substance abuse, psychiatric disorder, both, or neither. For example, it is exceedingly difficult to determine the impact of substance abuse when serious mental illness profoundly affects all areas of functioning. Patients with severe mental illness in particular have a range of impairments in social, cognitive, occupational, and psychological functioning, and evaluating the negative impact of substance abuse is difficult when the functioning of individuals in this patient population is so poor to begin with. Moreover, *DSM-IV* diagnoses of substance abuse and dependence are based for the most part on diagnostic criteria that reflect substance use becoming more pervasive in a person's life and interfering with normal functioning. For example, criteria involve substance use impairing one's ability to work, engage in relationships, complete responsibilities, and participate in activities. However, such factors often do not apply to many with mental illness—their already substantial level of impairment associated with the psychiatric disorder often precludes them from having a job, being in relationships, or engaging in other activities. It becomes unclear how to measure the negative impact of substance use when there are few competing demands, activities, or responsibilities to be disrupted.

SUBSTANCE-INDUCED DISORDERS RESEMBLE PSYCHIATRIC DISORDERS   Diagnosis of psychopathology in the presence of substance abuse and dependence is especially difficult because symptoms of substance use and withdrawal can resemble psychiatric disorders (Schuckit, 1983; Schuckit & Monteiro, 1988). Schuckit and Monteiro (1988) review several instances in which symptoms of substance abuse resemble or "mimic" psychiatric symptoms. For example, long-term alcohol use and withdrawal can lead to psychotic symptoms, and abuse of amphetamines often results in psychotic symptoms that are identical to schizophrenia. Alcohol abuse and withdrawal also resemble symptoms of anxiety disorders (Kushner, Sher, & Beitman, 1990). Panic and obsessive behavior are often found with stimulant use and withdrawal from depressant drugs (Schuckit, 1983). Because symptoms of substance use and withdrawal can resemble psychiatric symptoms, differential diagnosis may be confounded. The lack of clear rules for differential diagnosis has important implications. Rates of dual diagnosis might be inflated, with individuals experiencing psychiatric disorders concurrent with alcohol or drug dependence being counted among those with dual disorder, despite the fact that many of these symptoms will likely fade following a period of abstinence. Or, incorrect treatment decisions may be made if interventions are aimed at what appear to be acute symptoms of psychiatric disorder but are in fact substance-induced symptoms. For example, Rosenthal and Miner (1997) review the issue of differential diagnosis of substance-induced psychosis and schizophrenia and stress that medicating what appears to be acute psychosis due to schizophrenia but is actually substance-induced psychosis is not only incorrect but also ineffective treatment. Schuckit and colleagues (1997) suggest that too little attention has been paid to the "independent versus concurrent distinction" as it applies to dual diagnosis. Some alcoholics suffer from long-term psychiatric disorders that are present before, during, and after alcohol dependence and require treatment independent of that for their alcohol abuse or dependence. However, many individuals present with substance-induced disorders, including depression, anxiety, and psychosis, that will remit after several weeks of abstinence. They suggest that much dual diagnosis, while distressing and clinically relevant in the short-term, is temporary, likely to improve after several weeks, and thus holds different clinical and treatment implications from a true, independent psychiatric disorder. Their data, taken from the Collaborative Study on the Genetics of Alcoholism, shows that the majority of alcohol-dependent men and women did not meet diagnostic criteria for an "independent" mood or anxiety disorder that occurred outside of the context of the alcohol dependence. Specifically, there was no increased risk of a range of disorders in the alcohol-dependent sample, including major depression, obsessive-compulsive disorder, or agoraphobia. In contrast, there was an increased risk of independent bipolar, panic disorder, and social phobia.

Others have also found that a majority of dual diagnosis patients have concurrent psychiatric diagnoses that are likely owing to the effects of heavy substance use. Rosenblum and colleagues (1999) used an algorithm to determine whether individuals with co-occurring mood and cocaine use disorders have either an "autonomous" mood disorder, that is, one that either existed prior to the cocaine use disorder or persists during times of abstinence (similar to Schuckit's independent distinction), or a "nonautonomous" mood disorder that followed from the cocaine use disorder and would remit during cocaine abstinence. Results showed that 27% of subjects were rated as having an autonomous mood disorder, while 73% were rated as having a nonautonomous mood disorder. At this point, differentiating independent from concurrent dual disorders requires significant investment in training interviewers and in interviewing patients. Such requirements often cannot be met in the day-to-day operations of mental health treatment programs. Moreover, multiple assessments may be necessary. For example, Ramsey and colleagues (2004) examined changes in classifying depressive episodes in alcohol-dependent patients as either substance-induced depression or independent major depressive disorder. Patients in a partial hospital program for alcohol treatment were assessed 5 times over a year for symptoms of MDD. Results showed that many (more than 25%) of cases first categorized as substance-induced MDD were reclassified as independent MDD at some point during the year, owing to depressive symptoms that persisted once the patients had achieved a long period of abstinence.

IMPLICATIONS FOR NOSOLOGY   The fact that two disorders co-occur with great regularity raises the question of whether both categories actually represent two distinct disorders at all (Sher & Trull, 1996). For example, the literature regarding SUDS and ASP finds a high rate of comorbidity between the two disorders, one that is likely enhanced by the symptom overlap inherent in the ASP diagnosis. However, some suggest (Widiger & Shea, 1991) that such a high degree of co-occurrence between these two disorders may mean that these are not, in fact, unique diagnoses, but rather that such a pattern of comorbidity indicates the presence of a single disorder.

Provision of Treatment and Treatment Outcome   Co-occurring SUDs raise problems for interventions that have been designed to impact specific psychiatric symptoms, or ones that have been validated on samples that have excluded dual diagnosis patients. In addition, clinicians often experience difficulties in making referrals for dual diagnosis patients in the current system of single-disorder treatment that effectively separates the treatment systems for mental illness and substance abuse. The fact that patients must often be forced into single diagnostic categories no doubt results in SUDs being overlooked or ignored by treatment professionals who have expertise in treating only single conditions or in dual diagnosis patients not receiving both the psychiatric and the substance abuse treatment they require (Blanchard, 2000).

Patients with dual diagnosis are more difficult to treat and show poorer retention in treatment as well as poorer treatment outcomes as compared to single-disorder patients. Such findings tend to be true both for patients with primary mental illness and co-occurring substance abuse (see Drake et al., 1998 and Polcin, 1992 for reviews; Goldberg, Garno, Leon, Kocsis, & Portera, 1999), as well as for patients identified through substance abuse treatment programs with comorbid mental illness (Glenn & Parsons, 1991; Ouimette, Ahrens, Moos, & Finney, 1998; Rounsaville, Kosten, Weissman, & Kleber, 1986). An early study by McLellan et al. (1983) found that higher psychiatric severity was associated with poorer treatment outcome among alcohol and drug abuse treatment patients. Tomasson and Vaglum (1997) examined the impact of psychiatric comorbidity on 351 treatment-seeking substance abusers over a 28-month period and found that patients with comorbid psychiatric disorders at admission showed worse outcome in terms of mental health functioning at follow-up. More recently, Ouimette, Gima, Moos, and Finney (1999) reported findings of a 1-year follow-up of three groups of patients with dual substance use and psychiatric disorders (psychotic disorders, affective/anxiety disorders, and personality disorders) as compared to a group of substance abuse-only patients. Although all the groups showed comparable decreases in substance use at follow-up, patients with dual diagnoses showed greater levels of psychological distress and psychiatric symptoms and lower rates of employment than did patients with only SUDs. In a 3-year follow-up of a sample of patients with alcohol use disorders, Kranzler, Del Boca, and Rounsaville (1996) found that the presence of comorbid psychiatric disorders, including depression and ASP, is generally associated with worse 3-year outcomes. Thomas, Melchert, and Banken (1999) examined treatment outcome in 252 patients in substance abuse treatment and found the likelihood of relapse within the year following treatment was significantly increased in patients with dual personality disorders. Specifically, 6% of patients with personality disorders were abstinent 1-year posttreatment as compared with 44% of those with no diagnosed personality disorders. A study by Havassy, Shopshire, and Quigley (2000) examined the effects of substance dependence on treatment outcome in 268 psychiatric patients following two different case management programs. Regardless of program, dual diagnosis patients showed more negative outcomes than patients with only a psychiatric disorder. Such results illustrate that the dually diagnosed fare worse than patients with either SUDs or psychiatric disorders alone following treatment. Importantly, the fact that dual diagnosis patients are often found to still be adversely affected by psychiatric symptomatology following substance abuse treatment is a stark reminder that treatment strategies have yet to evolve that effectively address symptoms of both types of disorders.

IMPACT OF DUAL DIAGNOSIS ON PSYCHOPATHOLOGY RESEARCH

Dual diagnosis affects several areas that are critical to psychopathology research, including diagnosis, sample selection, and interpretation of research findings.

Diagnostic and Sample Selection Issues in Psychopathology Research   An accurate diagnosis is a necessary starting point for any psychopathology study, and dual diagnosis presents an abundance of diagnostic challenges. Individuals with dual diagnoses may provide unreliable diagnostic information, or their data may be inaccurate because of greater severity of impairments. Alternatively, they may minimize their substance use and associated consequences, especially if they have much to lose by admitting to or honestly discussing their substance use, such as services, benefits (Ridgely, Goldman, & Willenbring, 1990), or child custody. The timing of a research diagnostic interview can also impact results, as answers and resulting diagnostic decisions may vary depending on type of use, stage of treatment, and psychiatric stabilization. The method of assessment also can impact diagnostic findings (Regier et al., 1998), and diagnoses given in a clinical setting may vary with those obtained through more structured methods (Fennig, Craig, Tanenberg-Karant, & Bromet, 1994). As presented previously, establishing an accurate diagnosis in individuals with active substance use or withdrawal can be problematic, as the effects of substance use can imitate the symptoms of various psychiatric disorders. Most diagnostic systems used in psychopathology research contend with this difficulty by asking if psychiatric symptoms have been experienced solely during the course of substance use, and may recommend assessment only after a sustained period of abstinence. However, patient report may be inaccurate, and histories may be too extensive and complicated to allow for this level of precise understanding. Finally, the issue of overlapping diagnostic criteria can pose a significant difficulty for psychopathology research, as common diagnostic criteria may contribute to the diagnosis of multiple disorders when in fact the psychopathology is better understood as a single pathological process rather than two distinct disorders (Blashfield, 1990; Sher & Trull, 1996). The overlap of SUDs with ASP is notably problematic, and this frequent comorbidity has long been recognized (Widiger & Shea, 1991). Krueger (1999) examined 10 common mental disorders using structural equation modeling and found that ASP loads onto a common "externalizing" factor along with alcohol and drug dependence, suggesting that substance dependence and ASP may share certain underlying features. Whether this overlap is indeed because of common conceptual characteristics or is an artifact of similar diagnostic criteria is unknown.

All of these diagnostic issues impact research findings, in that poor diagnoses will necessarily lead to poor quality data. Researchers can improve diagnostic reliability by using structured interviews, using collateral information and behavioral observation to inform diagnostic decisions, and assessing the patient at multiple time points (Carey & Correia, 1998).

In terms of sample selection, psychopathology and treatment outcome research tends to focus on single or pure disorders, and routinely excludes dual diagnosis cases, a practice that has several implications for research. First, screening out dual diagnosis patients yields samples that are atypical. Most patients with one psychiatric disorder meet criteria for some other disorder. Eliminating patients with dual disorders means that the resulting sample is less impaired and less representative of patients who present for treatment, resulting in limited generalizability of research findings (Kruger, 1999). In addition, dual diagnosis patients often have other characteristics that are not adequately represented in the resultant study sample. For example, Partonen, Sihvo, and Lonnqvist (1996) report descriptive data on patients excluded from an antidepressant efficacy that screened out individuals with "chronic alcohol or drug misuse." As a result, younger male patients were likely to be excluded, with current substance abuse as the strongest excluding influence. Second, dual diagnosis impacts required sample sizes. In their examination of the impact of comorbid disorders on sample selection, Newman and colleagues (1998) discuss findings related to effect sizes of examining only single disorder cases versus the inclusion of dual disorder cases when analyzing group differences. Results showed that when dual disorder cases are excluded, larger sample sizes are required in order to detect small effect sizes. In contrast, retaining dual disorder cases yielded greater variance on study measures, resulting in larger effect sizes requiring smaller sample sizes. Third, psychopathology and treatment outcome research most often combines those with dual diagnoses together without classification by the specific type of drug use disorder. Whereas some might limit the scope of the study to alcohol only, most cast a wide net and include patients with alcohol, drug, and poly-substance use disorders. For example, research on substance abuse among patients with severe mental illness typically includes disorders of any number or combination of substances including alcohol, marijuana, cocaine, and heroin. The impact of grouping all substance use disorders together is unclear, but it certainly raises the possibility that research may miss important issues potentially particular to one substance. For example, it would not be surprising if interventions for patients with a greater number of drug use disorders or with both alcohol and drug use disorders required adaptations not necessary for patients with single-drug or alcohol-use disorders. Similarly, there are likely meaningful differences between patients who inject drugs and those who do not, patients who have long histories of substance dependence and those who do not, or patients who are dependent on cocaine or heroin versus those who are abusing marijuana.

Interpretation of Psychopathology and Treatment Outcome Research   The overall result of screening out those with substance use disorders from psychopathology and treatment outcome research is that there are very few data to inform treatment. For example, following completion of an antidepressant efficacy trial, Partonen and colleagues (1996) point out that they were left without information regarding the efficacy of antidepressants among patients with dual disorders. Given the significant rates of dual disorders found in clinical samples, such an omission is clearly problematic. In their discussion of the many complex issues surrounding comorbidity and psychopathology research, Sher and Trull (1996) question the advantage of studying pure cases when certain disorders occur together with such great frequency that there really may be no ultimate benefit of studying either one alone. It also is unclear how well findings from psychopathology and treatment outcome research will generalize to the larger population of individuals with a particular disorder if patients with dual diagnoses are not included. The epidemiological studies reviewed earlier clearly illustrate that a significant number of those with mental illness or substance abuse experience dual disorders. The relevance of single-disorder research to this substantial population of dually impaired individuals is highly suspect and excluding dual diagnosis cases yields samples that are not representative of those presenting for treatment.

However, routinely including dual diagnosis cases in psychopathology and treatment outcome research has its drawbacks. Sher and Trull (1996) and Kruger (1999) discuss the fact that if dual diagnosis cases are included in psychopathology research, understanding of both mental and substance use disorders is compromised, in that samples would be less well-defined. As a result, it would be unclear whether results could be attributed to the disorder under study or to comorbid disorders represented in the sample. In addition, comorbidity complicates longitudinal data because different patterns of comorbidity may emerge over time within individuals (Sher and Trull, 1996). One possible strategy for dealing with dual disorders in psychopathology and treatment outcome research is the use of samples that include comorbid cases in percentages found in the general population in order to increase the generalizability of findings (Newman et al., 1998; Sher and Trull, 1996). Widiger and Shea (1991) offer additional options including having one diagnosis take precedence over another, adding criteria in order to make a differential diagnosis, or removing criteria shared by disorders. Sher and Trull (1996) additionally suggest statistically controlling for comorbidity via regression techniques but acknowledge that this practice can serve to mask important common features of disorders.

THEORIES OF DUAL DIAGNOSIS

This review makes two points clear: Dual diagnosis is highly prevalent, and it has a pervasive impact on both clinical and research domains. There now is general agreement that the time has come to define more precisely the mechanisms underlying dual diagnosis, a complex task for several reasons. Most important, there is a great degree of heterogeneity found in dual diagnosis populations. The numerous types of psychopathological disorders and substances of abuse ensure a great number of dual diagnosis combinations. In addition, although the term *dual* is meant to describe cases with both mental illness and substance use problems, it can in actuality reflect more than two disorders (for example, an individual might meet criteria for an affective disorder, an anxiety disorder, and a substance use disorder). Thus it is unlikely that one explanation or causal model for dual diagnosis can explain the diversity of cases and experiences that are found.

Models to explain dual diagnoses tend to fall into one of four general categories (see Mueser, Drake, & Wallach, 1998 for a review). Third variable or common factors models suggest that some shared influence is responsible for the development of both psychiatric and substance use disorders. The two types of causal models—secondary substance use disorder models and secondary psychiatric disorder models—posit that either type of disorder causes the other. Bidirectional models suggest that either psychiatric or substance use disorders can increase risk for and exacerbate the impact of the other. These models have been more or less described depending on the particular area of psychopathology. Examination of this literature finds that models of dual diagnosis are typically organized by disorder, with research focused on specific combinations of dual disorders rather than at the issue of dual diagnosis across disorders. Extensive reviews of models in each of these categories can be found (Blanchard, 2000; Mueser et al., 1998). The following section provides a review of some models of dual diagnosis in their respective domains of psychopathology.

COMMON FACTORS MODELS

Common factors models suggest a shared etiological basis for psychiatric and substance use disorders. Most research has focused on genetics as the likely common factor. Results of numerous twin, adoption, and family studies clearly show that both mental illness and substance abuse run in families, and that familial aggregation of single disorders is substantial (Kushner, Sher, & Beitman, 1990; Kendler, Davis, & Kessler, 1997; Merikangas et al., 1985; Merikangas & Gelernter, 1990). Such findings have led to the hypothesis that commonly co-occurring disorders might be linked via common genetic factors. However, for genetics to serve as a viable common factor, family studies must show high rates of transmission of pure forms of both substance use and psychiatric disorders. For example, a proband with depression only should have an increased rate of alcoholism only in the individual's relatives in order to provide evidence of shared genetic etiology. Studies of familial transmission of a range of comorbid psychiatric and substance use disorders find that the evidence for a common genetic factor is lacking. Merikangas and Gelernter (1990) reviewed family, twin, and adoption studies of alcoholism and depression and concluded that familial transmission of pure forms of the disorders was not supported: "Depressed only" probands did not have increased rates of "alcoholism only" in their relatives, and "alcoholism only" probands did not have increased rates of "depression only" in their relatives. These authors stress that although familial aggregation of disorders is evident, the notion of a common genetic factor underlying the two is not supported and the disorders appear to be transmitted separately. In subsequent analyses of familial transmission of comorbid depression and substance use disorders using data from the Yale Family Study of Comorbidity of Substance Disorders, Swendsen and Merikangas (2000) similarly found that there was no support for a common factors model: Mood disorders in the proband were not associated with an increased risk of alcohol dependence in relatives. Similar results have been reported with schizophrenia (Kendler, 1985), ASP (Hesselbrock, 1986), and patients with schizoaffective and bipolar disorders (Gershon et al., 1982).

Importantly, common factors other than genetics may exist. Several possible common factors might link substance use disorders and severe mental illness, including comorbid ASP, low socioeconomic status, and poor cognitive functioning (Mueser, Drake, & Wallach, 1998). For example, ASP is associated with both substance use disorders and severe mental illness. Mueser and colleagues (1999) examined the links between conduct disorder, ASP, and substance use disorders in patients with severe mental illness and found that both childhood conduct disorder and adult ASP were significant risk factors for SUDs. However, the status of ASP as a risk factor is unclear, given that problem substance use is part of the diagnosis of ASP, raising the possibility that ASP may be a byproduct of substance use disorder. Also, ASP is based in large part on criminality and socioeconomic status, both of which are difficulties that often go along with both substance use disorder and severe mental illness (Mueser et al., 1998).

Other researchers are proposing multivariate approaches to identifying common factors of dual disorders. One such model is described by Trull and colleagues (2000) to explain the high prevalence of dual substance use disorders and borderline personality disorder. These authors suggest that a family history of psychopathology inspires both dysfunctional family interactions and the inheritance of deviant personality traits that are associated with the development of both borderline personality disorder and substance use disorders. Specifically, the personality traits of affective instability and impulsivity are central to both disorders, and are conceptualized as stemming from a combination of "constitutional and environmental factors" (Trull, Sher, Minks-Brown, Durbin, & Burr, 2000) that include inherited deficiencies in serotonergic functioning, in combination with a deviant family environment that may include associated childhood trauma. These factors in turn impact the development of borderline personality disorder and substance use disorder, both alone and in combination. These authors stress that while this model is currently speculative, more prospective, longitudinal studies with a developmental and multivariate focus will enable the pieces of the models to be evaluated simultaneously. This model provides an example of combining strategies from family studies and psychopathology research into a multivariate framework that provides rich details as to how two disorders could be developmentally related.

SECONDARY SUBSTANCE ABUSE MODELS

Secondary substance abuse models contend that mental illness increases vulnerability to substance use disorders. Probably the most widely discussed model of this type is the self-medication model, which asserts that individuals with psychiatric disorders use substances as a way to self-medicate psychopathological symptoms and relieve discomfort associated with the primary psychiatric disorder. There are several types of studies used to examine applicability of a self-medication model to different forms of psychopathology. Some determine the ages of onset of dual disorders, with the idea being that SUDs developing after other Axis I psychopathology support the self-medication hypothesis. Some examine subjective reasons for use among patients with different disorders, while others correlate levels of symptoms with levels of substance abuse (from a self-medication perspective, greater symptoms should correlate with greater substance abuse). Another line of self-medication research involves investigating the types of substances used by different patient groups. According to a self-medication hypothesis, patients with certain psychopathological conditions should preferentially seek out and use substances that will directly impact symptoms associated with their specific psychopathology.

Support for a self-medication model varies depending on the type of mental illness under investigation. For example, although the model is popular among treatment providers working with patients with severe mental illness, empirical support for a self-medication model has not been compelling (see Mueser, Drake, & Wallach, 1998 for a review). Although it has been suggested that schizophrenia patients preferen-tially abuse stimulants to self-medicate negative symptoms (Schneier & Siris, 1987), this finding has not been replicated in other studies (Mueser, Yarnold, & Bellack, 1992). Most important, studies fail to find evidence that specific substances are used in response to specific symptoms. Rather, patterns of drug use appear to be strongly associated with demographic factors and drug availability (Mueser, Yarnold, & Bellack, 1992). In addition, a self-medication model of SUDs in severe mental illness would predict that the more symptomatic patients would be at higher risk for sub-stance use disorders (Mueser, Bellack, & Blanchard, 1992). Several studies, however, have found the opposite to be true: More severely ill patients are less likely to abuse substances (Chen et al., 1992; Cohen & Klein, 1970; Mueser, Yarnold, & Bellack, 1992), and patients with SUDs have better premorbid social functioning (Dixon et al., 1991). Although individuals with schizophrenia and other severe mental illnesses report a range of reasons for substance use—to alleviate social problems, insomnia, or depression; to get high; to relieve boredom; and to increase energy—few endorse using specific substances to combat particular psychiatric symptoms (see Brunette, Mueser, Xie, & Drake, 1997 for a review). Moreover, many studies have found that patients with schizophrenia report worsening of symptoms with substance abuse, including increased hallucinations, delusions, and paranoia (Barbee et al., 1989; Cleghorn et al., 1991; Dixon et al., 1991; Drake et al., 1989), and others have found that more severe symptoms of schizophrenia are not linked to more severe substance abuse (Brunette et al., 1997). Similarly, findings of increased rates of cocaine use among patients with bipolar disorder, interpreted by some to indicate self-medication of de-pressive symptoms, have been found upon review to more likely reflect attempts to prolong euphoric feelings associated with mania (Goodwin & Jamison, 1990).

There are other secondary substance abuse models that may be more relevant to patients with severe mental illness. A social facilitation model suggests that patients with severe mental illness may have fewer available opportunities for social interac-tion, and that substance abuse helps smooth the process of social engagement in patients who lack appropriate social and interpersonal skills. Finding that a large portion of substance use/abuse by individuals with schizophrenia occurs in a pub-lic setting, Dixon, Haas, Weiden, Sweeney, & Frances (1990) suggest that drug use may provide "isolated, socially handicapped individuals with an identity and a social group" (p. 74) or to fulfill needs for contact and acceptance (Mueser, Bellack, & Blanchard, 1992). Others offer an alleviation of dysphoria model; substance abuse represents an attempt to alleviate these negative mood states.

Evidence for self-medication may be more relevant to dual diagnosis within other psychopathological disorders. For example, several reviews have found that self-medication may apply to dual PTSD and SUDs, especially among women with trauma-related PTSD. Three main theories (Chilcoat & Breslau, 1998) are (1) the self-medication hypothesis, which suggests that drugs are used to medicate PTSD symptoms; (2) the high-risk hypothesis, which suggests that drug use puts indi-viduals at heightened risk for trauma that can lead to PTSD; and (3) the suscepti-bility hypothesis, which suggests that drug users are more likely to develop PTSD following exposure to a traumatic event. They then use data from a sample of more than 1,000 young adults who were randomly selected from enrollees in a large health maintenance organization and were followed longitudinally over 5 years in order to examine the timing of the development of both PTSD and substance use disorders. Those with a history of PTSD at baseline were four times more likely to develop drug abuse or dependence at some point during the five years of the study than those without PTSD. In contrast, baseline drug abuse/dependence did not confer any increased risk of subsequent exposure to trauma or to developing PTSD in those who did experience some traumatic event during the follow-up period. Other data on dual SUD and PTSD (Stewart et al., 1998) that also lend support to a self-medication model include (1) development of substance abuse most often follows development of PTSD; (2) patients often report that they perceive substance use to be effective in controlling PTSD symptoms; (3) patients with both PTSD and substance use disorder report more severe trauma and a greater severity of PTSD symptoms, suggesting that substances are used in an effort to control greater psychiatric symptomatology; and (4) drugs of abuse may be related to different clusters of PTSD symptoms, suggesting that substance abuse may be linked to attempts to control intrusion or arousal symptoms of PTSD. These authors stress that although a self-medication model is likely too simplistic to explain all forms of PTSD-SUD comorbidity, at this point it provides a good fit for the current literature.

Recently there has been increased interest in neurobiological mechanisms that underlie dual diagnosis, particularly with respect to the ways in which mental illness and addiction share common neurological pathways. The foundation for this research is that neurobiological deficits and abnormalities that provide the basis for different forms of mental illness may predispose those with mental illness to substance abuse. This literature includes animal studies of dual diagnosis where brain lesions are produced to simulate different forms of psychopathology, and factors such as the ability to experience reinforcement from drug use, and differential patterns of use and/or cravings are examined.

A good summary of this approach to dual diagnosis in schizophrenia is presented by Chambers, Krystal, and Self (2001). Briefly, increased vulnerability to substance use disorders in schizophrenia results from impairment in brain systems that are central to schizophrenia—the most important of which may be the mesolimbic dopamine system (MDS). According to this model, the MDS is implicated in the reinforcing effects of drug use (drug use increases dopamine levels), as well as in the development of schizophrenia (high dopamine levels are implicated as a major factor in the development of schizophrenia). In other words, these authors suggest that "the neuropathology of schizophrenia may contribute to the vulnerability to addiction by facilitating neural substrates that mediate positive reinforcement. . . . The putative neuropathology underlying schizophrenia involves alterations in neuroanatomic circuitry that regulate positive reinforcement, incentive motivation, behavioral inhibition, and addictive behavior" (Chambers et al., 2001, p. 71).

Thus the neurobiological problems that give rise to schizophrenia also put the individual at heightened risk for developing SUDs. Several studies have found support for this sort of neurological linkage in schizophrenia. Chambers and Self (2002) studied rats with neonatal ventral hippocampal lesions (NVHL rats), a procedure that produces behavioral disturbances in rats that resemble the psychopathological behaviors seen in schizophrenia, including positive and negative symptoms and abnormal cognitive functioning (see Chambers & Self, 2002 and Chambers & Taylor, 2004 for details of the procedure and its effects). In comparison to controls (rats with sham lesions), NVHL rats showed faster rates of cocaine self-administration, higher degree of binge cocaine use, and faster relapse to cocaine use following a period of nonuse. Other studies using this and similar methodologies have generated similar findings (Chambers & Taylor, 2004).

Similar animal models are available for depression and substance use. In one model for depression, rats undergo bilateral olfactory bulbectomy (OBX), creating behavior that is biologically and behaviorally similar to depression in humans, including decreased pleasure seeking, disruptions in sleep, agitation, and other cognitive problems that respond only to chronic (and not acute) antidepressant treatment (see Holmes et al., 2002 for a thorough review). Importantly, this procedure also causes dopamine dysregulation in areas of the brain implicated in the reinforcing effects of drugs of abuse again similar to those found in humans. In comparison to rats with sham lesions (Holmes et al., 2002) those with OBX lesions were more sensitive to the reinforcing effects of amphetamine. Specifically, they learned to self-administer amphetamine more quickly and had higher levels of stable amphetamine administration. Other studies have used rats genetically bred for signs of learned helplessness as an operational definition of depression in rats. For example, Vengeliene and colleagues (2005) examined differences in alcohol intake between congenital learned helplessness rats (cLH) and congenital nonlearned helplessness rats (cNLH)—two lines of rats selectively bred for different escape reactions following inescapable shock (cLH rats do not try to escape the shock, even though they have not been exposed to it before, while cNLH rats will try to escape the shock). In this study, these two groups of rats were given access to alcohol and tap water for self-administration for 6 weeks, and then underwent 2 weeks of no alcohol access followed by renewed access to alcohol for 4 days. Although results showed no differences in males, female cLH rats consumed greater amounts of alcohol than cNLH rats during the self-administration portion of the study, and showed a more pronounced alcohol deprivation effect (greater consumption of alcohol following a period of time with no alcohol consumption). The authors suggest that inborn "depressive-like" behavior in female rats is associated with increase alcohol intake. These and other animal models of depression (Fagergren, Overstreet, Goiny, & Hurd, 2005) appear to be a useful avenue for the study of dual diagnosis involving depression and substance abuse. Such studies are finding that "depressed" animals respond differently to drugs and alcohol than other animals, providing interesting new leads in the search for biological mechanisms that lead to dual diagnosis.

SECONDARY PSYCHIATRIC DISORDER MODELS

With some specific differences, these models suggest that substance abuse causes psychopathology. Schuckit and Monteiro (1988; Schuckit, 1983) stress that the use of or withdrawal from many psychoactive substances causes reactions that appear indistinguishable from psychiatric disorder. As reviewed earlier, these authors contend that often substance use disorders are diagnosed mistakenly as psychiatric disorders because of similar symptomatology, and that while serious psychopathology can be expected in the course of substance use disorder, substance-induced disorders are likely to remit following several weeks of abstinence.

The case for substance-induced psychiatric disorder appears to be particularly relevant to dual substance use disorders and major depression. Raimo and Schuckit (1998) review the evidence in support of the idea that most cases of comorbid depression and alcohol dependence are substance-induced, including findings that (1) drinking can cause severe depressive symptoms; (2) treatment-seeking substance abusers show increased rates of depression that often remit following abstinence and in the absence of specific treatments for depression; (3) individuals with substance-induced depression do not show elevated rates of depression in family members; and (4) children of alcoholics show higher rates of alcohol use disorders but do not show elevated rates of major depression. These authors stress that while having independent depression in addition to alcohol abuse or dependence is certainly possible, most of the depression that is comorbid with alcohol use disorders is substance-induced and not independent in nature. Following this example, Swendson and Merikangas (2000) reviewed findings that are relevant to an etiological model of dual substance abuse and depression: (1) the onset of alcohol dependence typically precedes the onset of unipolar depression; (2) symptoms of depression often remit following several weeks of abstinence from alcohol; and (3) genetic studies do not support a shared genetic basis for comorbidity of depression and alcohol dependence. They suggest that the association between unipolar depression and alcohol dependence may best be described via a secondary psychiatric disorder model, in which chronic alcohol use causes unipolar depression, through either the considerable life stress that alcohol dependence promotes for the drinker in many important domains of functioning, or through the pharmacological properties of alcohol as a depressant substance.

BIDIRECTIONAL MODELS

Bidirectional models propose that ongoing, interactional effects account for increased rates of comorbidity. Support for a bidirectional model for anxiety and alcohol dependence (Kushner, Abrams, & Borchardt, 2000) includes the following: (1) most patients with anxiety and alcohol use disorders report drinking to control fears and reduce tension; (2) drinking can cause anxiety (i.e., anxiety can result from long-term alcohol use, patients report increased anxiety after drinking, withdrawal from alcohol can cause physiological symptoms of anxiety); (3) alcohol dependence can lead to anxiety disorders (i.e., alcohol dependence puts one at increased risk for later development of an anxiety disorder, chronic drinking can cause neurochemical changes that cause anxiety and panic); and (4) anxiety disorders can lead to alcohol dependence (i.e., having an anxiety disorder puts one at increased risk for later development of alcohol dependence, alcohol provides stress-response dampening and reduces the clinical symptoms of anxiety, many people use alcohol to self-medicate anxiety symptoms). The authors conclude that alcohol and anxiety interact to produce an exacerbation of both anxiety symptoms and drinking. Whereas initial use of alcohol provides short-term relief of anxiety symptoms, it negatively reinforces further drinking, leading to increased physiological symptoms of anxiety. They then propose a so-called "feed-forward" cycle wherein drinking is promoted by its short-term anxiety-reducing effects of alcohol, while at the same time anxiety symptoms are worsened by heavy drinking, leading to continued drinking in response to these worsened anxiety symptoms. Although several caveats and issues remain to be clarified (i.e., the model seems to best fit with comorbid alcohol dependence and its relevance to drug use disorders is unknown, those for whom the anxiety disorder begins first would not necessarily experience the anxiety-reducing properties of alcohol in a way that would initiate the feed-forward cycle), the authors suggest that a bidirectional model can best explain existing findings and can focus future research on comorbidity of anxiety and substance use disorders. Moreover, this sort of bidirectional model highlights the possibility that unidirectional causal models are likely too simplistic an approach in explaining comorbidity.

Rather, the relationship between psychiatric and substance use disorders is more likely characterized by complex interactions between two disorders.

SUMMARY AND FUTURE DIRECTIONS

We have learned much about the prevalence and impact of dual disorders from general population and clinical studies over the last several decades. Currently we can say with certainty that dual diagnosis is common, both in the general population and among clients in mental health and substance abuse treatment. Comorbid psychiatric and substance use disorders impact a large percentage of people, and dual disorders persist over time. Importantly, we are now beginning to see that patients who present with multiple diagnoses are the most difficult and complex patients to treat and understand. The notion of "dual" disorders may require reconceptualization as the frequency of individuals with two, three, or more comorbid psychiatric and substance use disorders continues to climb. Second, it is clear that dual diagnosis affects patient functioning, clinical service, and psychopathology research, and the services designed to assist patients with either mental illness or substance abuse are ill equipped to address comorbidity of these problems. Moreover, research on psychopathology and its treatments is complicated by questions of dual diagnosis, including how it impacts findings and how it can be handled in data collection and analysis. Third, there are a number of models to explain dual diagnosis that take into account the different types of psychopathology and substances of abuse, as well as the differences in disorder severity. Research linking neurobiological development of psychiatric disorders to substance abuse vulnerability highlights the need to incorporate biological and psychological constructs as we proceed in trying to understand dual diagnosis.

The next step is to further examine causal mechanisms and determine how these models work given the significant heterogeneity seen in the dual diagnosis population. Although a range of theories have been proposed, more specific work is required to fully examine the links between mental illness and substance use disorders. Moreover, many studies report that as the number of psychiatric disorders increases, the likelihood of co-occurring substance abuse increases as well. This means that research examining dual disorders must reflect the current reality—individuals with dual disorders often have multiple diagnoses, each of which might have different impacts on functioning and treatment needs. It is unclear how prevailing models of dual disorders that are organized around a pair of problems are going to be relevant to individuals with three or more diagnoses. A final challenge is treatment. We are only initiating efforts to treat those with dual disorders comprehensively. Efforts aimed at treatment development must be linked to research on underlying causal factors. Improving our understanding of the causes of dual disorders will provide insight into interventions for treating these complex and recurring problems.

REFERENCES

Alterman, A. I., Erdlen, D. L., Laporte, D. L., & Erdlen, F. R. (1982). Effects of illicit drug use in an inpatient psychiatric setting. *Addictive Behaviors, 7*(3), 231–242.

American Psychiatric Association. (1994). *Diagnostic and statistical manual of mental disorders* (4th ed.). Washington, DC: Author.

Anath, J., Vandewater, S., Kamal, M., Brodsky, A., Gamal, R., & Miller, M. (1989). Mixed diagnosis of substance abuse in psychiatric patients. *Hospital and Community Psychiatry, 40,* 297–299.

Arendt, M., & Munk-Jorgensen, P. (2004). Heavy cannabis users seeking treatment: Prevalence of psychiatric disorders. *Social Psychiatry and Psychiatric Epidemiology, 39*(2), 97–105.

Back, S., Dansky, B. S., Coffey, S. F., Saladin, M. E., Sonne, S., & Brady, K. T. (2000). Cocaine dependence with and without post-traumatic stress disorder: A comparison of substance use, trauma history, and psychiatric comorbidity. *American Journal on Addictions, 9*(1), 51–62.

Baethge, C., Baldessarini, R. J., Khalsa, H. M., Hennen, J., Salvatore, P., & Tohen, M. (2005). Substance abuse in first-episode bipolar I disorder: Indications for early intervention. *American Journal of Psychiatry, 162*(5), 1008–1010.

Barbee, J. G., Clark, P. D., Crapanzano, M. S., Heintz, G. C., & Kehoe, C. E. (1989). Alcohol and substance abuse among schizophrenic patients presenting to an emergency psychiatric service. *Journal of Nervous and Mental Disease, 177,* 400–407.

Bauer, M. S., Altshuler, L., Evans, D. R., Beresford, T., Williford, W. O., & Hauger, R. (2005). Prevalence and distinct correlates of anxiety, substance, and combined comorbidity in a multi-site public sector sample with bipolar disorder. *Journal of Affective Disorders, 85,* 301–315.

Berkson, J. (1949). Limitations of the application of four-fold tables to hospital data. *Biometric Bulletin, 2,* 47–53.

Bibb, J. L., & Chambless, D. L. (1986). Alcohol use and abuse among diagnosed agoraphobics. *Behavior Research and Therapy, 24*(1), 49–58.

Bien, T. H., & Burge, J. (1990). Smoking and drinking: A review of the literature. *International Journal of the Addictions, 25,* 1429–1454.

Blanchard, J. J. (2000). The co-occurrence of substance use in other mental disorders: Editor's introduction. *Clinical Psychology Review, 20*(2), 145–148.

Blashfield, R. K. (1990). Comorbidity and classification. In J. D. Master & C. R. Cloninger (Eds.), *Comorbidity of mood and anxiety disorders* (pp. 61–82). Washington, DC: American Psychiatric Association Press.

Bonin, M. F., Norton, G. R., Asmundson, G. J., Dicurzio, S., & Pidlubney, S. (2000). Drinking away the hurt: The nature and prevalence of posttraumatic stress disorder in substance abuse patient attending a community-based treatment program. *Journal of Behavior Therapy and Experimental Psychiatry, 31*(1), 55–66.

Bowen, R. C., Cipywnyk, D., D'Arcy, C., & Keegan, D. (1984). Alcoholism, anxiety disorders, and agoraphobia. *Alcoholism Clinical and Experimental Research, 8*(1), 48–50.

Bradizza, C. M., & Stasiewicz, P. R. (1997). Integrating substance abuse treatment for the seriously mentally ill into inpatient psychiatric treatment. *Journal of Substance Abuse Treatment, 14*(2), 103–111.

Brady, K. T., Killeen, T. K., Brewerton, T., & Lucerini, S. (2000). Comorbidity of psychiatric disorders and posttraumatic stress disorder. *Journal of Clinical Psychiatry, 61*(Suppl. 7), 22–32.

Breslau, N., Davis, G. C., Peterson, E. L., & Schultz, L. (1997). Psychiatric sequelae of posttraumatic stress disorder in women. *Archives of General Psychiatry, 54*(1), 81–87.

Brooner, R. K., King, V. L., Kidorf, M., Schmidt, C. W., & Bigelow, G. E. (1997). Psychiatric and substance use comorbidity among treatment-seeking opioid abusers. *Archives of General Psychiatry, 54*(1), 71–80.

Brown, V. B., Melchior, L. A., & Huba, G. J. (1999). Level of burden among women diagnosed with severe mental illness and substance abuse. *Journal of Psychoactive Drugs, 31*(1), 31–40.

Brunello, N., Davidson, J. R., Deahl, M., Kessler, R. C., Mendlewicz, J., Racagni, G., Shalev, A. Y., & Zohar, J. (2001). Posttraumatic stress disorder: Diagnosis and epidemiology, co-morbidity and social consequences, biology and treatment. *Neuropsychobiology, 43*(3), 150–162.

Brunette, M. F., & Drake, R. E. (1998). Gender differences in homeless persons with schizophrenia and substance abuse. *Community Mental Health Journal, 34,* 627–642.

Brunette, M. F., Mueser, K. T., Xie, H., & Drake, R. E. (1997). Relationships between symptoms of schizophrenia and substance abuse. *Journal of Nervous and Mental Disease, 185,* 13–20.

Bucholz, K. K. (1999). Nosology and epidemiology of addictive disorders and their comorbidity. *Psychiatric Clinics of North America, 22*(2), 221–239.

Burns, L., Teesson, M., & O'Neill, K. (2005). The impact of comorbid anxiety and depression on alcohol treatment outcomes. *Addiction, 100*(6), 787–796.

Busto, U. E., Romach, M. K., & Sellers, E. M. (1996). Multiple drug use and psychiatric comorbidity in patients admitted to the hospital with severe benzodiazepine dependence. *Journal of Clinical Psychopharmacology, 16*(1), 51–57.

Carey, K. B., & Correia, C. J. (1998). Severe mental illness and addictions: Assessment considerations. *Addictive Behaviors, 23*(6), 735–748.

Carey, M. P., Carey, K. B., & Kalichman, S. C. (1997). Risk for human immunodeficiency virus (HIV) infection among persons with severe mental illnesses. *Clinical Psychology Review, 17,* 271–291.

Carpenter, W. T. J., Heinrichs, D. W., & Alphs, L. D. (1985). Treatment of negative symptoms. *Schizophrenia Bulletin, 11,* 440–452.

Caton, C. L., Shrout, P. E., Eagle, P. F., Opler, L. A., Felix, A., & Dominguez, B. (1994). Risk factors for homelessness among schizophrenic men: A case-control study. *American Journal of Public Health, 84,* 265–270.

Chambers, R. A., Krystal, J. H., & Self, D. W. (2001). A neurobiological basis for substance abuse comorbidity in schizophrenia. *Biological Psychiatry, 50,* 71–83.

Chambers, R. A., & Self, D. W. (2002). Motivational responses to natural and drug rewards in rats with neonatal ventral hippocampal lesions: An animal model of dual diagnosis schizophrenia. *Neuropsychopharmacology, 27,* 889–905.

Chambers, R. A., & Taylor, J. R. (2004). Animal modeling dual diagnosis schizophrenia: Sensitization to cocaine in rats with neonatal ventral hippocampal lesions. *Biological Psychiatry, 56,* 308–316.

Chen, C., Balogh, R., Bathija, J., Howanitz, E., Plutchik, R., & Conte, H. R. (1992). Substance abuse among psychiatric inpatients. *Comprehensive Psychiatry, 33,* 60–64.

Chengappa, K. N., Levine, J., Gershon, S., & Kupfer, D. J. (2000). Lifetime prevalence of substance or alcohol abuse and dependence among subjects with bipolar I and II disorders in a voluntary registry. *Bipolar Disorder, 2*(3, Pt. 1), 191–195.

Chilcoat, H. D., & Breslau, N. (1998). Investigations of causal pathways between posttraumatic stress disorder and drug use disorders. *Addictive Behaviors, 23*(6), 827–840.

Clark, R. E., Ricketts, S. K., & McHugo, G. J. (1999). Legal system involvement and costs for persons in treatment for severe mental illness and substance use disorders. *Psychiatric Services, 50*(5), 641–647.

Cleghorn, J. M., Kaplan, R. D., Szechtman, B., Szechtman, H., Brown, G. M., & Franco, S. (1991). Substance abuse and schizophrenia: Effect on symptoms but not on neurocognitive function. *Journal of Clinical Psychiatry, 52,* 26–30.

Cohen, L. J., Test, M. A., & Brown, R. J. (1990). Suicide and schizophrenia: Data from a prospective community treatment study. *American Journal of Psychiatry, 147,* 602–607.

Cohen, M., & Klein, D. F. (1970). Drug abuse in a young psychiatric population. *American Journal of Orthopsychiatry, 40,* 448–455.

Comtois, K. A., & Ries, R. (1995). Sex differences in dually diagnosed severely mentally ill clients in dual diagnosis outpatient treatment. *American Journal on Addictions, 4,* 245–253.

Cottler, L. B., Compton, W. M. 3rd, Mager, D., Sptiznagel, E. L., & Janca, A. (1992). Posttraumatic stress disorder among substance users from the general population. *American Journal of Psychiatry, 149*(5), 664–670.

Dalack, G. W., & Meador-Woodruff, J. H. (1996). Smoking, smoking withdrawal and schizophrenia: Case reports and a review of the literature. *Schizophrenia Research, 22,* 133–141.

Dansky, B. S., Brady, K. T., & Saladin, M. E. (1998). Untreated symptoms of posttraumatic stress disorder among cocaine-dependent individuals: Changes over time. *Journal of Substance Abuse Treatment, 15*(6), 499–504.

Davis, T. M., & Wood, P. S. (1999). Substance abuse and sexual trauma in a female veteran population. *Journal of Substance Abuse Treatment, 16*(2), 123–127.

Dickey, B., & Azeni, H. (1996). Persons with dual diagnoses of substance abuse and major mental illness: Their excess costs of psychiatric care. *American Journal of Public Health, 86*(7), 973–977.

Dickey, B., Dembling, B., Azeni, H., & Normand, S. T. (2004). Externally caused deaths for adults with substance use and mental disorders. *Journal of Behavioral Health Services & Research, 31*(1), 75–85.

Dixon, L. (1999). Dual diagnosis of substance abuse in schizophrenia: Prevalence and impact on outcomes. *Schizophrenia Research, 35,* S93–S100.

Dixon, L., Haas, G., Weiden, P., Sweeney, J., & Frances, A. J. (1990). Acute effects of drug abuse in schizophrenic patients: Clinical observations and patients' self-reports. *Schizophrenia Bulletin, 16*(1), 69–79.

Dixon, L., Haas, G., Weiden, P., Sweeney, J., & Frances, A. J. (1991). Drug abuse in schizophrenic patients: Clinical correlates and reasons for use. *American Journal of Psychiatry, 149,* 231–234.

Drake, R. E., Mercer-McFadden, C., Mueser, K. T., McHugo, G. J., & Bond, G. R. (1998). Review of integrated mental health and substance abuse treatment for patients with dual disorders. *Schizophrenia Bulletin, 24*(4), 589–608.

Drake, R. E., Osher, F. C., & Wallach, M. A. (1989). Alcohol use and abuse in schizophrenia: A prospective community study. *Journal of Nervous and Mental Disease, 177,* 408–414.

Drake, R. E., & Wallach, M. A. (1989). Substance abuse among the chronically mentally ill. *Hospital and Community Psychiatry, 40,* 1041–1046.

Eisen, J. L., & Rasmussen, S. A. (1989). Coexisting obsessive compulsive disorder and alcoholism. *Journal of Clinical Psychiatry, 50*(3), 96-98.

Evans, D. L. (2000). Bipolar disorder: Diagnostic challenges and treatment consideration. *Journal of Clinical Psychiatry, 61*(Suppl. 13), 26–31.

Fagergren, P., Overstreet, D. H., Goiny, M., & Hurd, Y. L. (2005). Blunted response to cocaine in the Flinders hypercholinergic animal model of depression. *Neuroscience, 132,* 1159–1171.

Falck, R. S., Wang, J., Siegal, H. A., Carlson, & R. G. (2004). The prevalence of psychiatric disorder among a community sample of crack cocaine users: An exploratory study with practical implications. *Journal of Nervous and Mental Disease, 192*(7), 503–507.

Fennig, S., Craig, T. J., Tanenberg-Karant, M., & Bromet, E. J. (1994). Comparison of facility and research diagnoses in first-admission psychotic patients. *American Journal of Psychiatry, 151*(10), 1423–1429.

Folsom, D. P., Hawthorne, W., Lindamer, L., Gilmer, T., Bailey, A., Golshan, S., Garcia, P., Unutzer, J., Hough, R., & Jeste, D. V. (2005). Prevalence and risk factors for homelessness and utilization of mental health services among 10,340 patients with serious mental illness in a large public mental health system. *American Journal of Psychiatry, 162*(2), 370–376.

Fulwiler, C., Grossman, H., Forbes, C., & Ruthazer, R. (1997). Early-onset substance abuse and community violence by outpatient with chronic mental illness. *Psychiatric Services, 48*(9), 1181–1185.

Galanter, M., Castaneda, R., & Ferman, J. (1988). Substance abuse among general psychiatric patients: Place of presentation, diagnosis, and treatment. *American Journal of Drug and Alcohol Abuse, 14*(2), 211–235.

Garnick, D. W., Hendricks, A. M., Comstock, C., & Horgan, C. (1997). Do individuals with substance abuse diagnoses incur higher charges than individuals with other chronic conditions? *Journal of Substance Abuse Treatment, 14*(5), 457–465.

Gearon, J. S., & Bellack, A. S. (1999). Women with schizophrenia and co-occurring substance use disorders: An increased risk for violent victimization and HIV. *Journal of Community Mental Health, 35,* 401–419.

Gearon, J. S., Bellack, A. S., Nidecker, M., & Bennett, M. E. (2003). Gender differences in drug use behavior in people with serious mental illness. *American Journal on Addictions, 12*(3), 229–241.

Gershon, E. S., Hamovit, J., Guroff, J. J., Dibble, E., Leckman, J. F., Sceery, W., Nurnberger, J. I., Goldin, L. R., & Bunney, W. E. (1982). A family study of schizoaffective, bipolar I, bipolar II, and normal probands. *Archives of General Psychiatry, 39*(10), 1157–1167.

Gilmer, T. P., Dolder, C. R., Lacro, J. P., Folsom, D. P., Lindamer, L., Garcia, P., & Jeste, D. V. (2004). Adherence to treatment with antipsychotic medication and health care costs among Medicaid beneficiaries with schizophrenia. *American Journal of Psychiatry, 161,* 692–699.

Glenn, S. W., & Parsons, O. A. (1991). Prediction of resumption of drinking in posttreatment alcoholics. *International Journal of the Addictions, 26*(2), 237–254.

Goldberg, J. F., Garno, J. L., Leon, A. C., Kocsis, J. H., & Portera, L. (1999). A history of substance abuse complicates remission from acute mania in bipolar disorder. *Journal of Clinical Psychiatry, 60*(11), 733–740.

Goodman, L. A., Dutton, M. A., & Harris, M. (1995). The relationship between violence dimensions and symptom severity among homeless, mentally ill women. *Journal of Traumatic Stress, 10*(1), 51–70.

Goodman, L., Rosenburg, S., Mueser, K. T., & Drake, R. (1997). Physical and sexual assault history in women with SMI: Prevalence, correlates, treatment, and future research directions. *Schizophrenia Bulletin, 23,* 685–696.

Goodwin, F. K., & Jamison, K. R. (1990). *Manic-depressive illness.* New York: Oxford University Press.

Gottesman, I. I., & Groome, C. S. (1997). HIV/AIDS risks as a consequence of schizophrenia. *Schizophrenia Bulletin, 23,* 675–684.

Grant, B. F. (1995). Comorbidity between *DSM-IV* drug use disorders and major depression: Results of a national survey of adults. *Journal of Substance Abuse, 7*(4), 481–497.

Grant, B. F. (1997). The influence of comorbid major depression and substance use disorders on alcohol and drug treatment: Results of a national survey. *National Institute on Drug Abuse Research Monograph, 172,* 4–15.

Grant, B. F., & Harford, T. C. (1995). Comorbidity between *DSM-IV* alcohol use disorders and major depression: Results of a national survey. *Drug and Alcohol Dependence, 39,* 197–206.

Grant, B. F., Harford, T. C., Dawson, D. A., Chou, P., Dufour, M., & Pickering, R. (1994). Prevalence of *DSM-IV* alcohol abuse and dependence: United States, 1992. *Alcohol Health and Research World, 18*(3), 243–248.

Grant, B. F., Hasin, D. S., & Harford, T. C. (1989). Screening for major depression among alcoholics: An application of receiver operating characteristic analysis. *Drug and Alcohol Dependence, 23,* 123–131.

Grant, B. F., Stinson, F. S., Dawson, D. A., Chou, S. P., Dufour, M. C., Compton, W., Pickering, R. P., & Kaplan, K. (2004). Prevalence and co-occurrence of substance use disorders and independent mood and anxiety disorders: Results from the National Epidemiologic Survey on Alcohol and Related Conditions. *General Psychiatry, 61*(8), 807–816.

Grella, C. E. (1996). Background and overview of mental health and substance abuse treatment systems: Meeting the needs of women who are pregnant or parenting. *Journal of Psychoactive Drugs, 28*(4), 319–343.

Grella, C. E. (1997). Services for perinatal women with substance abuse and mental health disorders: The unmet need. *Journal of Psychoactive Drugs, 29*(1), 67–78.

Grella, C. E. (2003). Effects of gender and diagnosis on addiction history, treatment utilization, and psychosocial functioning among a dually-diagnosed sample in drug treatment. *Journal of Psychoactive Drugs 35* (Suppl. 1), 169–179.

Hasin, D. S., Endicott, J., & Keller, M. B. (1991). Alcohol problems in psychiatric patients: 5-year course. *Comprehensive Psychiatry, 32*(4), 303–316.

Hasin, D. S., Endicott, J., & Lewis, C. (1985). Alcohol and drug abuse in patients with affective syndromes. *Comprehensive Psychiatry, 26*(3), 283–295.

Hasin, D. S., Grant, B. F., & Endicott, J. (1988). Lifetime psychiatric comorbidity in hospitalized alcoholics: Subject and familial correlates. *International Journal of the Addictions, 23*(8), 827–850.

Havassy, B. E., & Arns, P. G. (1998). Relationship of cocaine and other substance dependence to well-being of high-risk psychiatric patients. *Psychiatric Services, 49*(7), 935–940.

Havassy, B. E., Shopshire, M. S., & Quigley, L. A. (2000). Effects of substance dependence on outcomes of patients in a randomized trial of two case management models. *Psychiatric Services, 51*(5), 639–644.

Hays, P., & Aidroos, N. (1986). Alcoholism followed by schizophrenia. *Acta Psychiatrica Scandinavica, 74*(2), 187–189.

Haywood, T. W., Kravitz, H. M., Grossman, L. S., Cavanaugh, J. L., Jr., Davis, J. M., & Lewis, D. A. (1995). Predicting the "revolving door" phenomenon among patients with schizophrenic, schizoaffective, and affective disorders. *American Journal of Psychiatry, 152,* 856–861.

Helzer, J. E., & Pryzbeck, T. R. (1988). The co-occurrence of alcoholism with other psychiatric disorders in the general population and its impact on treatment. *Journal of Studies on Alcohol, 49*(3), 219–224.

Helzer, J. E., Robbins, L. H., & McEvoy, L. (1987). Post-traumatic stress disorder in the general population. *New England Journal of Medicine, 317,* 1630–1634.

Herz, L. R., Volicer, L., D'Angelo, N., & Gadish, D. (1990). Additional psychiatric illness by Diagnostic Interview Schedule in male alcoholics. *Comprehensive Psychiatry, 30*(1), 72–79.

Hesselbrock, M. N., Meyer, R. E., & Keener, J. J. (1985). Psychopathology in hospitalized alcoholics. *Archives of General Psychiatry, 42,* 1050–1055.

Hesselbrock, V. M. (1986). Family history of psychopathology in alcoholics: A review and issues. In R. E. Meyer (Ed.), *Psychopathology and addictive disorders* (pp. 41–56). New York: Guilford Press.

Hesselbrock, V. M., Hesselbrock, M. N., & Workman-Daniels, K. L. (1986). Effect of major depression and antisocial personality on alcoholism: Course and motivational patterns. *Journal of Studies on Alcohol, 47*(3), 207–212.

Himle, J. A., & Hill, E. M. (1991). Alcohol abuse and anxiety disorders: Evidence from the Epidemiologic Catchment Area Survey. *Journal of Anxiety Disorders, 5,* 237–245.

Hirschfeld, R. M. A., Hasin, D., Keller, M. D., Endicott, J., & Wunder, J. (1990). Depression and alcoholism: Comorbidity in a longitudinal study. In J. D. Maser and C. R. Cloninger (Eds.), *Comorbidity of mood and anxiety disorders.* Washington, DC: American Psychiatric Association Press.

Hoff, R. A., Beam-Goulet, J., & Rosenheck, R. A. (1997). Mental disorder as a risk factor for human immunodeficiency virus infection in a sample of veterans. *Journal of Nervous and Mental Disease, 185*(9), 556–560.

Holmes, P. V., Masini, C. V., Primuaux, S. D., Garrett, J. L., Zellner, A., Stogner, K. S., Duncan, A. A., & Crystal, J. D. (2002). Intravenous self-administration of amphetamine is increased in a rat model of depression. *Synapse, 46*(4), 4–10.

Jacobson, A. (1989). Physical and sexual assault histories among psychiatric outpatients. *American Journal of Psychiatry, 146*(6), 755–758.

Jones, D. R., Macias, C., Barreira, P. J., Fisher, W. H., Hargreaves, W. A., & Harding, C. M. (2004). Prevalence, severity, and co-occurrence of chronic physical health problems of persons with severe mental illness. *Psychiatric Services, 55*(11), 1250–1257.

Joyal, C. C., Putkonen, A., Paavola, P., & Tiihonen, J. (2004). Characteristics and circumstances of homicidal acts committed by offenders with schizophrenia. *Psychological Medicine, 34*(3), 433–442.

Karmali, M., Kelly, L., Gervin, M., Browne, S., Larkin, C., & O'Calleghan, E. (2000). The prevalence of comorbid substance misuse and its influence on suicidal ideation among inpatients with schizophrenia. *Acta Psychiatrica Scandinavica, 101*(6), 452–456.

Keane, T. M., Gerardi, R. J., Lyons, J. A., & Wolfe, J. (1988). The interrelationship of substance abuse and posttraumatic stress disorder: Epidemiological and clinical considerations. In M. Galanter (Ed.), *Recent developments in alcoholism.* New York: Plenum Press.

Kelly, R. H., Danielsen, B. H., Golding, J. M., Anders, T. F., Gilbert, W. M., & Zatzick, D. F. (1999). Adequacy of prenatal care among women with psychiatric diagnoses giving birth in California in 1994 and 1995. *Psychiatric Services, 50*(12), 1584–1590.

Kemper, P., Blumenthal, D., Corrigan, J. M., Cunningham, P. J., Felt, S. M., Grossman, J. M., Kohn, L. T., Metcalf, C. E., St. Peter, R. F., Strouse, R. C., & Ginsburg, P. B. (1996). The design of the community tracking study: A longitudinal study of health system change and its effects on people. *Inquiry, 33*(2), 195–206.

Kendler, K. S. (1985). A twin study of individuals with both schizophrenia and alcoholism. *British Journal of Psychiatry, 147,* 48–53.

Kendler, K. S., Davis, C. G., & Kessler, R. C. (1997). The familial aggregation of common psychiatric and substance use disorders in the National Comorbidity Survey: A family history study. *British Journal of Psychiatry, 170,* 541–548.

Kessler, R. C. (1997). The prevalence of psychiatric comorbidity. In S. Wetzler & W. C. Sanderson (Eds.), *Treatment strategies for patients with psychiatric comorbidity* (pp. 23–48). New York: Wiley.

Kessler, R. C., Berglund, P., Demler, O., Jin, R., Koretz, D., Merikangas, K. R., Rush, A. J., Walters, E. E., & Wang, P. S. (2003). The epidemiology of major depressive disorder: Results from the National Comorbidity Survey Replication (NCS-R). *Journal of the American Medical Association, 289*(23), 3095–3105.

Kessler, R. C., Berglund, P., Demler, O., Jin, R., Merikangas, K. R., & Walters, E. E. (2005). Lifetime prevalence and age-of-onset distributions of *DSM-IV* disorders in the National Comorbidity Survey Replication. *Archives of General Psychiatry, 62,* 593–602.

Kessler, R. C., Chiu, W. T., Demler, O., & Walters, E. E. (2005). Prevalence, severity, and comorbidity of 12-month *DSM-IV* disorders in the National Comorbidity Survey Replication. *Archives of General Psychiatry, 62,* 617–627.

Kessler, R. C., McGonagle, K. A., Zhao, S., Nelson, C. B., Hughes, M., Eshleman, S., Wittchen, H., & Kendler, K. S. (1994). Lifetime and 12-month prevalence of *DSM-III-R* psychiatric disorders in the United States. *Archives of General Psychiatry, 51,* 8–19.

Kessler, R. C., & Merikangas, K. R. (2004). The National Comorbidity Survey Replicaton (NCS-R): Background and aims. *International Journal of Methods in Psychiatric Research, 13*(2), 60–68.

Kessler, R. C., Nelson, C. B., McGonagle, K. A., Liu, J., Swartz, M., & Blazer, D. G. (1996). Comorbidity of *DSM-III-R* major depressive disorder in the general population: Results from the US National Comorbidity Survey. *British Journal of Psychiatry, 168*(Suppl. 30), 17–30.

Keuthen, N. J., Niaura, R. S., Borrelli, B., Goldstein, M., DePue, J., Murphy, C., Gastfriend, D., Reiter, S. R., & Abrams, D. (2000). Comorbidity, smoking behavior, and treatment outcome. *Psychotherapy and Psychosomatics, 69,* 244–250.

Khantzian, E. J., & Treece, C. (1985). *DSM-III* psychiatric diagnoses of narcotic addicts. *Archives of General Psychiatry, 42,* 1067–1071.

Kokkevi, A., Stephanis, N., Anastasopoulou, E., & Kostogianni, C. (1998). Personality disorders in drug abusers: Prevalence and their association with Axis I disorders as predictors of treatment retention. *Addictive Behaviors, 23*(6), 841–853.

Kozaric-Kovacic, D., Folnegovic-Smalc, V., Folnegovic, Z., & Marusic, A. (1995). Influence of alcoholism on the prognosis of schizophrenia patients. *Journal of Studies on Alcohol, 56,* 622–627.

Krakow, D. S., Galanter, M., Dermatis, H., & Westreich, L. M. (1998). HIV risk factors in dually diagnosed patients. *American Journal of Addictions, 7*(1), 74–80.

Kranzler, H. R., Del Boca, F. K., & Rounsaville, B. J. (1996). Comorbid psychiatric diagnosis predicts three-year outcomes in alcoholics: A posttreatment natural history study. *Journal of Studies on Alcohol, 57,* 619–626.

Kruger, R. F. (1999). The structure of common mental disorders. *Archives of General Psychiatry, 56,* 921–926.

Kushner, M. G., Abrams, K., & Borchardt, C. (2000). The relationship between anxiety disorders and alcohol use disorders: A review of major perspectives and findings. *Clinical Psychology Review, 20*(2), 149–171.

Kushner, M. G., Sher, K. J., & Beitman, B. D. (1990). The relation between alcohol problems and the anxiety disorders. *American Journal of Psychiatry, 147*(6), 685–695.

Lambert, M. T., Griffith, J. M., & Hendrickse, W. (1996). Characteristics of patients with substance abuse diagnoses on a general psychiatry unit in a VA medical center. *Psychiatric Services, 47*(10), 1104–1107.

Lambert, M. T., LePage, J. P., & Schmitt, A. L. (2003). Five-year outcomes following psychiatric consultation to a tertiary care emergency room. *American Journal of Psychiatry, 160*(7), 1350–1353.

Landmark, J., Cernovsky, Z. Z., & Merskey, H. (1987). Correlates of suicide attempts and ideation in schizophrenia. *British Journal of Psychiatry, 151,* 18–20.

Lasser, K., Boyd, J. W., Woolhandler, S., Himmelstein, D. U., McCormick, D., & Bor, D. H. (2000). Smoking and mental illness: A population-based study. *Journal of the American Medical Association, 284*(2), 2606–2610.

Leal, D., Galanter, M., Dermatis, H., & Westreich, L. (1999). Correlates of protracted homelessness in a sample of dually diagnosed psychiatric inpatients. *Journal of Substance Abuse Treatment, 16*(2), 143–147.

Lehman, A. F., Myers, C. P., Dixon, L. B., & Johnson, J. L. (1994). Defining subgroups of dual diagnosis patients for service planning. *Hospital and Community Psychiatry, 45*(6), 556–561.

Lehman, A. F., Myers, C. P., Thompson, J. W., & Corty, E. (1993). Implications of mental and substance use disorders: A comparison of single and dual diagnosis patients. *Journal of Nervous and Mental Disease, 181*(6), 365–370.

Linszen, D. H., Dingemans, P. M., & Lenior, M. E. (1994). Cannabis abuse and the course of recent-onset schizophrenic disorders. *Archives of General Psychiatry, 51,* 273–279.

Liskow, B., Powell, B. J., Nickel, E. J., & Penick, E. (1991). Antisocial alcoholics: Are there clinically significant diagnostic subtypes? *Journal of Studies on Alcohol, 52*(1), 62–69.

Lynskey, M. T. (1998). The comorbidity of alcohol dependence and affective disorders: Treatment implications. *Drug and Alcohol Dependence, 52,* 201–209.

Margolese, H. C., Malchy, L., Negrete, J. C., Tempier, R., & Gill, K. (2004). Drug and alcohol use among patients with schizophrenia and related psychosis: Levels and consequences. *Schizophrenia Research, 67*(2–3), 157–166.

Marzuk, P. M. (1996). Violence, crime, and mental illness: How strong a link? *Archives of General Psychiatry, 53,* 481–486.

Maynard, C., & Cox, G. B. (1988). Psychiatric hospitalization of persons with dual diagnoses: estimates from two national surveys. *Psychiatric Services, 49*(12), 1615–1617.

McCloud, A., Barnaby, B., Omu, N., Drummond, C., & Aboud, A. (2004). Relationship between alcohol use disorders and suicidality in a psychiatric population: In-patient prevalence study. *British Journal of Psychiatry, 184,* 439–445.

McCrone, P., Menezes, P. R., Johnson, S., Scott, H., Thornicroft, G., Marshall, J., Bebbington, P., & Kuipers, E. (2000). Service use and costs of people with dual diagnosis in South London. *Acta Psychiatrica Scandinavica, 101*(6), 464–472.

McElroy, S. L., Altshuler, L. L., Suppes, T., Keck, P. E., Jr., Frye, M. A., Denicoff, K. D., Nolen, W., Kupka, R. W., Leverich, G. S., Rochussen, J. R., Rush, A. J., & Post, R. M. (2001). Axis I psychiatric comorbidity and its relationship to historical illness variables in 288 patients with bipolar disorder. *American Journal of Psychiatry, 158*(3), 420–426.

McFall, M., Fontana, A., Raskind, M., & Rosenheck, R. (1999). Analysis of violent behavior in Vietnam combat veteran psychiatric inpatients with posttraumatic stress disorder. *Journal of Traumatic Stress, 12*(3), 501–517.

McKinnon, K., Cournos, F., Sugden, R., Guido, J. R., & Herman, R. (1996). The relative contributions of psychiatric symptoms and AIDS knowledge to HIV risk behaviors among people with severe mental illness. *Journal of Clinical Psychiatry, 57*(11), 506–513.

McLellan, A. T., Druley, K. A., & Carson, J. E. (1978). Evaluation of substance abuse in a psychiatric hospital. *Journal of Clinical Psychiatry, 39*(5), 425–430.

McLellan, A. T., Luborsky, L., Woody, G. E., O'Brien, C. P., & Cruley, K. A. (1983). Predicting response to alcohol and drug abuse treatments: Role of psychiatric severity. *Archives of General Psychiatry, 40,* 620–625.

Menezes, P. R., Johnson, S., Thornicroft, G., Marshall, J., Prosser, D., Bebbington, P., & Kuipers, E. (1996). Drug and alcohol problems among individuals with severe mental illnesses in South London. *British Journal of Psychiatry, 168,* 612–619.

Merikangas, K. R. & Gelernter, C. S. (1990). Comorbidity for alcoholism and depression. *Psychiatric Clinics of North America, 13*(4), 613–633.

Merikangas, K. R., Leckman, J. F., Prusoff, B. A., Pauls, D. L., & Weissman, M. M. (1985). Familial transmission of depression and alcoholism. *Archives of General Psychiatry, 42,* 367–372.

Mezzich, J. E., Ahn, C. W., Fabrega, H., & Pilkonis, P. (1990). Patterns of psychiatric comorbidity in a large population presenting for care. In J. D. Maser & C. R. Cloninger (Eds.), *Comorbidity of mood and anxiety disorders* (pp. 189–204). Washington, DC: American Psychiatric Association Press.

Miller, N. S., Klamen, D., Hoffmann, N. G., & Flaherty, J. A. (1996). Prevalence of depression and alcohol and other drug dependence in addictions treatment populations. *Journal of Psychoactive Drugs, 28,* 111–124.

Mirin, S. M., Weiss, R. D., Griffin, M. L., & Michael, J. L. (1991). Psychopathology in drug abusers and their families. *Comprehensive Psychiatry, 32*(1), 36–51.

Mirin, S. M., Weiss, R. D., & Michael, J. L. (1988). Psychopathology in substance abusers: Diagnosis and treatment. *American Journal of Drug and Alcohol Abuse, 14,* 139–157.

Morgenstern, J., Langenbucher, J., Labouvie, E., & Miller, K. J. (1997). The comorbidity of alcoholism and personality disorders in a clinical population: Prevalence rates and relation to alcohol typology variables. *Journal of Abnormal Psychology, 106*(1), 74–84.

Mueller, T. I., Lavori, P. W., Keller, M. B., Swartz, A., Warshaw, M., Hasin, D., Coryell, W., Endicott, J., Rice, J., & Akiskal, H. (1994). Prognostic effect of the variable course of alcoholism on the 10-year course of depression. *American Journal of Psychiatry, 151*(5), 701–706.

Mueser, K. T., Bellack, A. S., & Blanchard, J. J. (1992). Comorbidity of schizophrenia and substance abuse: Implications for treatment. *Journal of Consulting and Clinical Psychology, 60*(6), 845–856.

Mueser, K. T., Drake, R. E., & Wallach, M. A. (1998). Dual diagnosis: A review of etiological theories. *Addictive Behaviors, 23*(6), 717–734.

Mueser, K. T., Rosenberg, S. D., Drake, R. E., Miles, K. M., Wolford, G., Vidaver, R., & Carrieri, K. (1999). Conduct disorder, antisocial personality disorder, and substance use disorders in schizophrenia and major affective disorders. *Journal of Studies on Alcohol, 60*(2), 278–284.

Mueser, K. T., Yarnold, P. R., & Bellack, A. S. (1992). Diagnostic and demographic correlates of substance abuse in schizophrenia and major affective disorder. *Acta Psychiatrica Scandinavica, 85,* 48–55.

Mueser, K. T., Yarnold, P. R., Levinson, D. F., Singh, H., Bellack, A. S., Kee, K., Morrison, R. L., & Yadalam, K. G. (1990). Prevalence of substance abuse in schizophrenia: Demographic and clinical correlates. *Schizophrenia Bulletin, 16*(1), 31–56.

Nace, E. P. (1990). Personality disorder in the alcoholic patient. *Psychiatric Annals, 19,* 256–260.

Nace, E. P., Davis, C. W., & Gaspari, J. P. (1991). Axis II comorbidity in substance abusers. *American Journal of Psychiatry, 148*(1), 118–120.

Najavitis, L. M., Gastfriend, D. R., Barber, J. P., Reif, S., Muenz, L. R., Blaine, J., Frank, A., Crits-Christoph, P., Thase, M., & Weiss, R. D. (1998). Cocaine dependence with and without posttraumatic stress disorder among subjects in the National Institute on Drug Abuse Collaborative Cocaine Treatment Study. *American Journal of Psychiatry, 155*(2), 214–219.

Najavitis, L. M., Sullivan, T. P., Schmitz, M., Weiss, R. D., & Lee, C. S. (2004). Treatment utilization by women with PTSD and substance dependence. *American Journal of Addictions, 13*(3), 215–224.

Najavitis, L. M., Weiss, R. D., & Shaw, S. R. (1997). The link between substance abuse and posttraumatic stress disorder in women: A review. *American Journal of Addiction, 6*(4), 273–283.

Negrete, J. C., & Knapp, W. P. (1986). The effects of cannabis use on the clinical condition of schizophrenics. *National Institute on Drug Abuse Research Monograph, 67,* 321–327.

Newman, D. L., Moffitt, T. E., Caspi, A., & Silva, P. (1998). Comorbid mental disorders: Implications for treatment and sample selection. *Journal of Abnormal Psychology, 107*(2), 305–311.

Nolan, W. A., Luckenbaugh, D. A., Altshuler, L. L., Suppes, T., McElroy, S. L., Frye, M. A., Kupka, R. W., Keck, P. E., Leverich, G. S., & Post, R. M. (2004). Correlates to 1-year prospective outcome in bipolar disorder: Results from the Stanley Foundation Bipolar Network. *American Journal of Psychiatry, 161*(8), 1447–1454.

O'Connell, R. A., Mayo, J. A., Flatow, L., Cuthbertson, B., & O'Brien, B. E. (1991). Outcome of bipolar disorder on long-term treatment with lithium. *British Journal of Psychiatry, 159,* 123–129.

Ouimette, P. C., Ahrens, C., Moos, R. H., & Finney, J. W. (1998). During treatment changes in substance abuse patients with posttraumatic stress disorder: The influence of specific interventions and program environments. *Journal of Substance Abuse Treatment, 15*(6), 555–564.

Ouimette, P. C., Brown, P. J., & Najavitis, L. M. (1998). Course and treatment of patients with both substance use and posttraumatic stress disorders. *Addictive Behaviors, 23*(6), 785–795.

Ouimette, P. C., Gima, K., Moos, R. H., & Finney, J. W. (1999). A comparative evaluation of substance abuse treatment IV: The effect of comorbid psychiatric diagnoses on amount of treatment, continuing care, and 1-year outcomes. *Alcoholism: Clinical and Experimental Research, 23*(3), 552–557.

Ouimette, P. C., Wolfe, J., & Chrestman, K. R. (1996). Characteristics of posttraumatic stress disorder–alcohol abuse comorbidity in women. *Journal of Substance Abuse, 8*(3), 335–346.

Owen, R. R., Fischer, E. P., Booth, B. M., & Cuffel, B. J. (1996). Medication noncompliance and substance abuse among persons with schizophrenia. *Psychiatric Services, 47*(8), 853–858.

Pages, K. P., Russo, J. E., Roy-Byrne, P. P., Ries, R. K., & Cowley, D. S. (1997). Determinants of suicidal ideation: The role of substance use disorders. *Journal of Clinical Psychiatry, 58*(11), 510–515.

Pages, K. P., Russo, J. E., Wingerson, D. K., Ries, R. K., Roy-Byrne, P. P., & Cowley, D. S. (1998). Predictors and outcome of discharge against medical advice from the psychiatric units of a general hospital. *Psychiatric Services, 49*(9), 1187–1192.

Palacios, S., Urmann, C. F., Newel, R., Hamilton, N. (1999). Developing a sociological framework for dually diagnosed women. *Journal of Substance Abuse Treatment, 17*(1–2), 91–102.

Partonen, T., Sihvo, S., & Lonnqvist, J. K. (1996). Patients excluded from an antidepressant efficacy trial. *Journal of Clinical Psychiatry, 57*(12), 572–575.

Penick, E. C., Powell, B. J., Othmer, E., Binghan, S. F., Rice, A. S., & Liese, B. S. (1984). Subtyping alcoholics by coexisting psychiatric syndromes: Course, family history, outcome. In D. W. Goodwin, K. T. Van Dusen, & S. A. Mednick (Eds.), *Longitudinal research in alcoholism.* Boston: Kluwer-Nijhoff.

Polcin, D. L. (1992). Issues in the treatment of dual diagnosis clients who have chronic mental illness. *Professional Psychology: Research and Practice, 23*(1), 30–37.

Poldrugo, F. (1998). Alcohol and criminal behavior. *Alcohol and Alcoholism, 33*(1), 12–15.

Potash, J. B., Kane, H. S., Chiu, Y. F., Simpson, S. G., MacKinnon, D. F., McInnis, M. G., McMahon, F. J., & DePaulo, J.R., Jr. (2000). Attempted suicide and alcoholism in bipolar disorder: Clinical and familial relationships. *American Journal of Psychiatry, 157*(12), 2048–2050.

Powell, B. J., Penick, E. C., Othmer, E., Bingham, S. F., & Rice, A. S. (1982). Prevalence of additional psychiatric syndromes among male alcoholics. *Journal of Clinical Psychiatry, 43*(10), 404–407.

Quattrocki, E., Baird, A., & Yurgelun-Todd, D. (2000). Biological aspects of the link between smoking and depression. *Harvard Review of Psychiatry, 8*(3), 99–110.

Raimo, E. B., & Schuckit, M. A. (1998). Alcohol dependence and mood disorders. *Addictive Behaviors, 23*(6), 933–946.

Ramsey, S. E., Kahler, C. W., Read, J. P., Stuart, G. L., & Brown, R. A. (2004). Discriminating between substance-induced and independent depressive episodes in alcohol dependent patients. *Journal of Studies on Alcohol, 65*(5), 672–676.

Regier, D. A., Farmer, M. E., Rae, D. S., Locke, B. Z., Keither, S. J., Judd, L. L., & Goodwin, F. K. (1990). Comorbidity of mental disorders with alcohol and other drug abuse. *Journal of the American Medical Association, 264,* 2511–2518.

Regier, D. A., Kaelber, C. T., Rae, D. S., Farmer, M. E., Knauper, B., Kessler, R. C., & Norquist, G. S. (1998). Limitations of diagnostic criteria and assessment instruments for mental disorders: Implications for research and policy. *Archives of General Psychiatry, 55,* 109–115.

Ridgely, M. S., Goldman, H. H., & Willenbring, M. (1990). Barriers to the case of persons with dual diagnoses: Organizational and financing issues. *Schizophrenia Bulletin, 16*(1), 123–132.

Ridgely, M. S., Lambert, D., Goodman, A., Chichester, C. S., & Ralph, R. (1998). Interagency collaboration in services for people with co-occurring mental illness and substance use disorder. *Psychiatric Services, 49,* 236–238.

Rosenblum, A., Fallon, B., Magura, S., Handelsman, L., Foote, J., & Bernstein, D. (1999). The autonomy of mood disorders among cocaine-using methadone patients. *American Journal of Drug and Alcohol Abuse, 25*(1), 67–80.

Rosenthal, R. N., & Miner, C. H. (1997). Differential diagnosis of substance-induced psychosis and schizophrenia in patients with substance use disorders. *Schizophrenia Bulletin, 23*(2), 187–193.

Ross, H. E., Glaser, F. B., & Germanson, T. (1988). The prevalence of psychiatric disorders in patients with alcohol and other drug problems. *Archives of General Psychiatry, 45,* 1023–1031.

Ross, H. E., Glaser, F. B., & Stiasny, S. (1988). Differences in the prevalence of psychiatric disorders in patients with alcohol and drug problems. *British Journal of Addiction, 83,* 1179–1192.

Rounsaville, B. J., Anton, S. F., Carroll, K., Budde, D., Prusoff, B. A., & Gawin, F. (1991). Psychiatric diagnoses of treatment seeking cocaine abusers. *Archives of General Psychiatry, 48,* 43–51.

Rounsaville, B. J., Kosten, T. R., Weissman, M. M., & Kleber, H. D. (1986). Prognostic significance of psychopathology in treated opiate addicts. *Archives of General Psychiatry, 43,* 739–745.

Rounsaville, B. J., Weissman, M. M., Kleber, H., & Wilber, C. (1982). Heterogeneity of psychiatric diagnosis in treated opiate addicts. *Archives of General Psychiatry, 39,* 161–166.

Rounsaville, B. J., Weissman, M. M., Wilber, C. H., Crits-Christoph, K., & Kleber, H. D. (1982). Diagnosis and symptoms of depression in opiate addicts: Course and relationship to treatment outcome. *Archives of General Psychiatry, 39,* 151–156.

Safer, D. J. (1987). Substance abuse by young adult chronic patients. *Hospital and Community Psychiatry, 38*(5), 511–514.

Saladin, M. E., Brady, K. T., Dansky, B. S., & Kilpatrick, D. G. (1995). Understanding comorbidity between posttraumatic stress disorder and substance use disorders: Two preliminary investigations. *Addictive Behaviors, 20*(5), 643–655.

Salloum, I. M., Douaihy, A., Ndimbie, O. K., & Kirisci, L. (2004). Concurrent alcohol and cocaine dependence impact on physical health among psychiatric patients. *Journal of Addictive Disorders, 23*(2) 71–81.

Salloum, I. M., & Thase, M. E. (2000). Impact of substance abuse on the course and treatment of bipolar disorder. *Bipolar Disorder, 2*(3, Pt. 2), 269–280.

Sandberg, D. A., McNiel, D. E., & Binder, R. L. (1998). Characteristics of psychiatric inpatients who stalk, threaten, or harass hospital staff after discharge. *American Journal of Psychiatry, 155*(8), 1102–1105.

Schneier, F. R., & Siris, S. G. (1987). A review of psychoactive substance use and abuse in schizophrenia: Patterns of drug choice. *Journal of Nervous and Mental Disease, 175,* 641–650.

Schuckit, M. A. (1983). Alcoholism and other psychiatric disorders. *Hospital and Community Psychiatry, 34*(11), 1022–1027.

Schuckit, M. A., & Monteiro, M. G. (1988). Alcoholism, anxiety, and depression. *British Journal of Addiction, 83,* 1373–1380.

Schuckit, M. A., Tipp, J. E., Bucholz, K. K., Nurnberger, J. I., Hesselbrock, V. M., Crowe, R. R., & Kramer, J. (1997). The life-time rates of three major mood disorder and four major anxiety disorders in alcoholics and controls. *Addiction, 92*(10), 1289–1304.

Scott, H., Johnson, S., Menezes, P., Thornicroft, G., Marshall, J., Bindman, J., Bebbington, P., & Kuipers, E. (1998). Substance misuse and risk of aggression and offending among the severely mentally ill. *British Journal of Psychiatry, 172,* 345–350.

Sellman, J. D., & Joyce, P. R. (1996). Does depression predict relapse in the 6 months following treatment for men with alcohol dependence? *Australian New Zealand Journal of Psychiatry, 30,* 573–578.

Sher, K. J., & Trull, T .J. (1996). Methodological issues in psychopathology research. *Annual Review of Psychology, 47,* 371–400.

Singh, J., Mattoo, S. K., Sharan, P., & Basu, D. (2005). Quality of life and its correlates in patients with dual diagnosis of bipolar affective disorder and substance dependence. *Bipolar Disorder, 7*(2), 187–191.

Sokolski, K. N., Cummings, J. L., Abrams, B. I., DeMet, E. M., Katz, L. S., & Costa, J. F. (1994). Effects of substance abuse on hallucination rates and treatment responses in chronic psychiatric patients. *Journal of Clinical Psychiatry, 55,* 380–387.

Sonne, S. C., Brady, K. T., & Morton, W. A. (1994). Substance abuse and bipolar affective disorder. *Journal of Nervous and Mental Disease, 182*(6), 349–352.

Soyka, M. (2000). Substance misuse, psychiatric disorder and violent and disturbed behaviour. *British Journal of Psychiatry, 176,* 345–350.

Steadman, H. J., Mulvey, E. P., Monoahan, J., Robbins, P. C., Appelbaum, P. S., Grisson, T., Roth, L. H., & Silver, E. (1998). Violence by people discharged from acute psychiatric inpatient facilities and by others in the same neighborhoods. *Archives of General Psychiatry, 55*(5), 393–401.

Stewart, S. H., Pihl, R. O., Conrod, P. J., & Dongier, M. (1998). Functional associations among trauma, posttraumatic stress disorder and substance-related disorders. *Addictive Behaviors, 23*(6), 797–812.

Strakowski, S. M., & DelBello, M. P. (2000). The co-occurrence of bipolar and substance use disorders. *Clinical Psychology Review, 20*(2), 191–206.

Stuyt, E. B. (2004). Hepatitis C in patients with co-occurring mental disorders and substance use disorders: Is tobacco use a possible risk factor? *American Journal of Addictions, 13*(1), 46–52.

Swanson, J., Borum, R., Swartz, M., & Hiday, V. (1999). Violent behavior preceding hospitalization among persons with severe mental illness. *Law and Human Behavior, 23*(2), 185–204.

Swartz, M. S., Swanson, J. W., Hiday, V. A., Borum, R., Wagner, H. R., & Burns, B. J. (1998). Violence and severe mental illness: The effects of substance abuse and nonadherence to medication. *American Journal of Psychiatry, 155*(2), 226–231.

Swendsen, J. D., & Merikangas, K. R. (2000). The comorbidity of depression and substance use disorders. *Clinical Psychology Review, 20*(2), 173–189.

Thomas, S. E., Thevos, A. K., & Randall, C. L. (1999). Alcoholics with and without social phobia: A comparison of substance use and psychiatric variables. *Journal of Studies on Alcohol, 60,* 472–479.

Thomas, V. H., Melchert, T. P., & Banken, J. A. (1999). Substance dependence and personality disorders: Comorbidity and treatment outcome in an inpatient treatment population. *Journal of Studies on Alcohol, 60*(2), 271–277.

Thompson, S. C., Checkley, G. E., Hocking, J. S., Crofts, N., Mijch, A. M., & Judd, F. K. (1997). HIV risk behavior and HIV testing of psychiatric patients in Melbourne. *Australia and New Zealand Journal of Psychiatry, 31*(4), 566–576.

Tomasson, K., & Vaglum, P. (1997). The 2-year course following detoxification treatment of substance abuse: The possible influence of psychiatric comorbidity. *European Archives of Psychiatry and Clinical Neuroscience, 247*(6), 320–327.

Triffleman, E. G., Marmar, C. R., Delucchi, K. L., & Ronfeldt, H. (1995). Childhood trauma and posttraumatic stress disorder in substance abuse inpatients. *Journal of Nervous and Mental Disease, 183*(3), 172–176.

Trull, T. J., Sher, K. J., Minks-Brown, C., Durbin, J., & Burr, R. (2000). Borderline personality disorder and substance use disorders: A review and integration. *Clinical Psychology Review, 20*(2), 235–253.

Vengeliene, V., Vollmayr, B., Henn, F. A., & Spanagel, R. (2005). Voluntary alcohol intake in two rat lines selectively bred for learned helpless and non-helpless behavior. *Psychopharmacology, 178*, 125–132.

Verduin, M. L., Carter, R. E., Brady, K. T., Myrick, H., & Timmerman, M. A. (2005). Health service use among persons with comorbid bipolar and substance use disorders. *Psychiatric Services, 56*(4), 475–480.

Vieta, E., Colom, F., Martinez-Aran, A., Benabarre, A., Reinares, M., & Gasto, C. (2000). Bipolar II disorder and comorbidity. *Comprehensive Psychiatry, 41*(5), 339–343.

Watkins, K. E., Burnam, A., Kung, F.Y., & Paddock, S. (2001). A national survey of care for persons with co-occurring mental and substance use disorders. *Psychiatric Services, 52*(8), 1062–1068.

Watkins, K. E., Hunter, S. B., Wenzel, S. L., Tu, W., Paddock, S. M., Griffin, A., & Ebener, P. (2004). Prevalence and characteristics of clients with co-occurring disorders in outpatient substance abuse treatment. *American Journal of Drug and Alcohol Abuse, 30*(4), 749–764.

Weiss, R. D., Ostacher, M. J., Otto, M. W., Calabrese, J. R. Fossey, M., Wisiewski, S. R., Bowden, C. L., Nierenberg, A. A., Pollack, M. H., Salloum, I. M., Simon, N. M., Thase, M. E., Sachs, G. S., & STEP-BD Investigators. (2005). Does recovery from substance use disorder matter in patients with bipolar disorder? *Journal of Clinical Psychiatry, 66*(6), 730–750.

Weissman, M. M., & Myers, J. K. (1980). Clinical depression in alcoholism. *American Journal of Psychiatry, 137*, 372–373.

Widiger, T. A., & Shea, T. (1991). Differentiation of Axis I and Axis II disorders. *Journal of Abnormal Psychology, 100*(3), 399–406.

Winokur, G., Turvey, C., Akiskal, H., Coryell, W., Solomon, D., Leon, A., Mueller, T., Endicott, J., Maser, J., & Keller, M. (1998). Alcoholism and drug abuse in three groups—bipolar I, unipolars, and their acquaintances. *Journal of Affective Disorders, 50*(2–3), 81–89.

Wittchen, H., Perkonigg, A., & Reed, V. (1996). Comorbidity of mental disorders and substance use disorders. *European Addiction Research, 2*, 36–47.

Wolf, A. W., Schubert, D. S. P., Patterson, M. B., Marion, B., & Grande, T. P. (1988). Associations among major psychiatric disorders. *Journal of Consulting and Clinical Psychology, 56*, 292–294.

Wu, L., Kouzis, A. C., & Leaf, P. J. (1999). Influence of comorbid alcohol and psychiatric disorders on utilization of mental health services in the National Comorbidity Survey. *American Journal of Psychiatry, 156*, 1230–1236.

Ziedonis, D. M., & George, T. P. (1997). Schizophrenia and nicotine use: Report of a pilot smoking cessation program and review of neurobiological and clinical issues. *Schizophrenia Bulletin, 23*, 247–254.

CHAPTER 3

Structured and Semistructured Interviews for Differential Diagnosis: Issues and Applications

DANIEL L. SEGAL AND FREDERICK L. COOLIDGE

Structured and semistructured interviews were borne out of a serious short-coming in the mental health field: Clinicians and researchers alike had tremendous difficulty agreeing about psychiatric diagnoses given to individuals. In the original *Diagnostic and Statistical Manual* (*DSM*; American Psychiatric Association [APA], 1952), the definition of mental illness was fuzzy at best and the criteria for the specific disorders were too general. At that time, because reliability of diagnosis (even for the common disorders) was so poor, validity of the entire classification system was called into serious question. The problem of inadequately specified criteria has been largely addressed in subsequent revisions of the *DSM* (the current version is the *DSM-IV-TR*, APA, 2000), which increasingly operationalized criteria in specific and explicit behavioral terms.

However, despite these improvements in the classification system, another barrier to accurate diagnosis became evident; namely, lack of uniformity or standardization of questions asked of respondents to evaluate the nature and extent of their psychiatric symptoms. Structured and semistructured interviews were designed largely in part to address this particular problem, and such instruments have become increasingly popular and effective. Indeed, since the 1970s, the ability of clinicians and researchers to accurately diagnose psychiatric disorders has improved in quantum leaps. Structured and semistructured interviews have played a major role in this advancement in diagnostic clarity and precision. The purpose of this chapter is to provide a basic introduction to structured and semistructured interviews. Topics include the major features, advantages, and drawbacks of structured and semistructured interviews and a discussion of several popular multidisorder instruments.

BASIC ISSUES REGARDING STRUCTURED AND SEMISTRUCTURED INTERVIEWS

The most common method to evaluate and diagnose individuals is the direct clinical interview. However, different types of interviews vary tremendously, especially as to the amount of "structure" that is imposed. Indeed, some important differences exist between unstructured interviews and structured ones. For starters, unstructured clinical interviews are heavily influenced by the individual patient's needs, the patient's responses, and the clinician's intuitions. With unstructured interviews, clinicians are entirely responsible for asking whatever questions they decide are necessary to reach a diagnostic conclusion. In fact, any type of question (relevant or not) can be asked in any way that fits the mood, preferences, training, specific interests, or philosophy of the clinician. The amount and specific kind of information gathered during an interview is largely determined by the clinician's theoretical model (e.g., psychoanalytic, behavioral, existential/humanistic, etc.), view of psychopathology, training, knowledge base, and interpersonal style. As a consequence, one can imagine the kind of variability in an interview from one clinician to another. A potential drawback to the unstructured approach is reduced reliability and validity of diagnosis whereas a potential benefit is the diversity of rich clinical information that can be gleaned.

Structured interviews, on the other hand, conform to a standardized list of questions (including follow-up questions), a standardized sequence of questioning, and systematized ratings of the patient's responses. In fact, impetus for the development of structured interviews was generated by the need to standardize questions and provide explicit guidelines for categorizing or coding responses. Adoption of such procedures serves to: (1) increase coverage of many disorders that otherwise might be overlooked, (2) enhance the diagnostician's ability to accurately determine whether particular symptoms are present or absent, and (3) reduce variability among interviewers, which improves reliability. These features of structured interviews add much in developing clinical psychology into a true science. For example, structured interviews are subject to evaluation and statistical analysis, and they are modified and improved based on the emerging database of the field.

It is also important to emphasize that the term *structured interview* is a broad one and that the actual amount of "structure" provided by an interview varies considerably. Basically, structured interviews can be divided into one of two types: fully structured or semistructured. In a fully structured interview, questions are asked verbatim to the respondent, the wording of probes used to follow up on initial questions is specified, and interviewers are trained to not deviate from this very rigid format. In a semistructured interview, although the initial questions for each symptom are specified and are typically asked verbatim to the respondent, the interviewer has substantial latitude to follow up on responses. For example, the interviewer can modify existing questions and augment standard inquiries with individualized and contextualized probes to more accurately rate specific symptoms. The amount of structure provided in an interview clearly impacts the extent of clinical experience and judgment needed to administer the interview appropriately: semistructured interviews require clinically experienced examiners to administer the interview and to make diagnoses, whereas fully structured interviews can be administered by nonclinicians who receive training on the specific instrument. This latter difference makes fully structured interviews popular and economical, especially in large-scale research studies in which an accurate diagnosis is essential.

Structured interviews are used in many different venues and for many different purposes. Application of structured interviews falls into three broad areas: research, clinical practice, and clinical training.

- The research domain is the most common application, in which an interview is used to diagnose participants for inclusion in a study so that etiology, comorbidity, and treatment approaches (among other topics) can be analyzed for a particular diagnosis or group of diagnoses. Certainly, good research requires that individuals assigned a diagnosis truly meet full criteria for that diagnosis. Another research application for structured interviews is to provide a standardized method for assessing change in one's clinical status over time. As noted by Rogers (2003), these types of longitudinal comparisons are essential for establishing outcome criteria, which is vital to diagnostic validity.
- In clinical settings, administration of a structured interview may be used as part of a comprehensive and standardized intake evaluation. However, routine and complete administration of a structured interview is uncommon at the present time, the primary barrier being the time required for full administration. A more palatable variation on this theme is that sections of a structured interview may be administered subsequent to a traditional unstructured interview to clarify and confirm the diagnostic impressions. Another thoughtful alternative has been proposed by Widiger and Samuel (2005), especially regarding assessment of personality disorders in clinical practice. They recommend the strategy of administering an objective self-report inventory first followed by a semistructured interview that focuses on the personality disorders that received elevated scores from the testing. This strategy is responsive to time constraints in clinical practice but also allows for collection of standardized, systematic, and objective data from the structured interview. Finally, we wish to emphasize that in clinical settings structured interviews will not (and in fact, should not) take the place of traditional interviews. Rather, the combination of the two approaches, integrated flexibly to meet the needs of the individual clinician and his or her patients, reflects the best of the scientist-practitioner model in which the science and art of assessment are both valued and valuable (Rogers, 2003).
- Lastly, use of structured interviews for training mental health professionals is an ideal application because interviewers have the opportunity to learn (through repeated administrations) specific questions and follow-up probes used to elicit information and evaluate specific diagnostic criteria provided by the *DSM-IV-TR*. Modeling one's own questions and flow of the interview from a well-developed structured interview can be an invaluable source of training for the beginning clinician.

Over the past several decades, proliferation of structured interviews has been steady. Structured interviews have been created to assist with the differential diagnosis of all major Axis I clinical disorders and all standard Axis II personality disorders. Interviews used for diagnosis are typically aligned with the *DSM* system and therefore assess the formal diagnostic criteria specified in the manual. But structured interviews for *DSM* differential diagnosis are not the only kind of structured interviews; other structured interviews are more narrow in focus, for example, to assess a specific problem or form of psychopathology (e.g., eating disorders, substance abuse, borderline personality disorder features) in great depth. An excellent resource for information about a host of specialized interviews is provided by Rogers (2001).

ADVANTAGES AND DISADVANTAGES OF STRUCTURED AND SEMISTRUCTURED INTERVIEWS

No assessment device in the mental health field is perfect—structured and semistructured interviews are no exception to this truism. In this section, the strengths and weaknesses of structured interviews are discussed. Our intention is to give the reader an appreciation of the major issues to be considered when deciding whether to use the structured interview approach to assessment. A brief summary of the advantages and disadvantages is presented in Table 3.1.

ADVANTAGES OF STRUCTURED AND SEMISTRUCTURED INTERVIEWS

Increased Reliability Perhaps the most important advantage of structured interviews centers on their ability to increase diagnostic reliability (reliability defined in this context refers to consistency or agreement about diagnoses assigned by different raters; Segal & Coolidge, 2006a). By systemizing and standardizing the questions interviewers ask and the way answers to those questions are recorded and interpreted, structured interviews decrease the amount of information variance in diagnostic evaluations (Rogers, 2001; Segal & Falk, 1998). That is, structured interviews decrease the chances that two different interviewers will elicit different information from the same patient, which may result in different diagnoses. Interviewers may arrive at different information from patients for a variety of reasons. For example, they may ask different questions, they may focus on different criteria for the same disorders, they may ask questions in different sequences, they may rate the intensity of the reported symptoms in different ways, or they may record the information patients give them differently (Rogers, 2001). Structured interviews help eliminate this variability by standardizing all of these aspects of a diagnostic evaluation. Thus, interrater reliability, or the likelihood that two different interviewers examining the same individual will arrive at the same diagnosis, is greatly increased.

Increased interrater reliability has broad implications in clinical and research settings. Because many methods of psychological treatment are intimately tied to specific diagnoses, it is imperative that those diagnoses are accurate (Segal & Coolidge, 2001). Thus, if different clinicians interviewing the same patient arrive at different diagnostic conclusions, it would be challenging at best to make a definitive decision about treatment. Similarly, accurate diagnosis is also essential for many types of clinical research, for example, studies that address causes and treatments of specific forms of psychopathology (Segal & Coolidge, 2001). Imagine a

Table 3.1
Advantages and Disadvantages of Structured and Semi-structured Interviews

Advantages	Disadvantages
Increased reliability: Because questions are standardized, structured interviews decrease variability among interviewers, which enhances interrater reliability. Structured interviews also increase the reliability of assessment for a patient's symptoms across time, as well as the reliability between patient report and collateral information.	**May hinder rapport:** Use of structured interviews may damage rapport because they are problem-centered, not person-centered, and poorly trained interviewers may neglect to use their basic clinical skills during the assessment.
Increased validity: Structured interviews assure that diagnostic criteria are covered systematically and completely. This is important because it serves to increase the validity of diagnosis.	**Limited by the validity of the classification system itself:** Structured interviews used for diagnosis are inherently tied to diagnostic systems. Thus, they are only as valid as the systems upon which they are based. Furthermore, it is difficult to establish the validity of particular structured interviews because there is no gold standard in psychiatric diagnosis.
Utility as training tools: Structured interviews are excellent training tools for clinicians-in-training because structured interviews promote the learning of specific diagnostic questions and probes used by experienced clinical interviewers. In addition, nonclinicians can easily be trained to administer fully structured interviews, which can be cost effective in both research and clinical settings.	**Tradeoff of breadth vs. depth:** Structured interviews are limited because they cannot cover all disorders or topic areas. When choosing a structured interview, one must think carefully about the tradeoffs of breadth versus depth of assessment.

study examining different treatments for bipolar disorder. In such a study, it would be imperative to be certain that those in the treatment groups actually suffer from bipolar disorder. Indeed, researchers must be able to accurately and definitively diagnose participants with the disorder being studied before researchers can even begin to examine theories of etiology or the effectiveness of treatment for that particular mental disorder.

In addition to increasing interrater reliability, structured interviews increase the likelihood that the diagnosis is reliable across time and across different sources of information (Rogers, 2001). In many clinical and research settings, individuals are in fact assessed on different occasions. The danger in making multiple assessments is that if an interviewer evaluates a patient in a different manner with different questions on different occasions, the patient's presentation may be substantially altered, not because the patient's symptoms or diagnosis has changed but rather because the way the patient is asked about those symptoms has changed. Using a standardized interview for multiple assessments helps ensure that if a patient's presentation has changed, it is because his or her symptoms are actually different, not because of variance in interviews (Rogers,

2001). Likewise, in many settings, clinicians conduct collateral interviews with important people in the patient's life to glean a broader picture of the patient's symptoms, problems, and experiences. Using a structured interview for both a patient and a collateral source will likely increase the chances that discrepancies between the patient and collateral informant are real, rather than a byproduct of different interviewing styles (Rogers, 2001).

Increased Validity   Validity of psychiatric diagnosis has to do with the meaningfulness or usefulness of the diagnosis (Segal & Coolidge, 2006b). A required prerequisite for validity is reliability. Thus, by virtue of the fact that structured interviews greatly increase reliability of diagnosis, they also increase the likelihood that the diagnosis is valid. Structured interviews also improve the validity of diagnoses in other ways. The systematic construction of structured interviews lends a methodological validity to these types of assessments compared to unstructured approaches. Because structured interviews are designed to thoroughly and accurately assess well-defined diagnostic criteria, they are often better assessments of those criteria than unstructured interviews (Rogers, 2001). According to Rogers, clinicians who use unstructured interviews sometimes diagnose too quickly, narrow their diagnostic options too early in the process, and miss comorbid diagnoses. Because structured interviews "force" clinicians to assess all of the specified criteria for a broad range of diagnoses, they offer a more thorough and valid assessment of many disorders compared to unstructured interviews.

To elaborate, some unstructured interviews may provide information about the presence or absence of only a few common mental disorders. Coverage of other disorders may be neglected during an unstructured interview if, for example, the interviewer is unfamiliar with the specific criteria of some disorders. Some unstructured interviews may also provide limited information about whether comorbid psychopathology exists as well as inconsistent information about the severity of the psychopathology. Structured interviews, because they incorporate systematic ratings, easily provide information that allows for the determination of the level of severity and the level of impairment associated with a particular diagnosis. Structured interviews provide the same information about comorbid conditions as well.

Utility as Training Tools   Structured interviews can be invaluable training tools for beginning mental health professionals as well as experienced clinicians who desire to enhance their diagnostic skills. Use of structured interviews in the training context may help clinicians develop or enhance their understanding of the flow, format, and questions inherent in a good diagnostic interview. With repeated administrations, much of a structured interview can be internalized by the clinician. In addition, use of structured interviews for training may reduce anxiety, especially among neophyte clinicians, because the format and flow of the interview is laid out for the interviewer. Structured interviews can also be a useful means of training those who make preliminary mental health assessments, for example, intake staff at hospitals, so that patients are thoroughly and accurately evaluated in preparation for treatment planning. In the case of nonclinician interviewers, fully structured interviews are advisable because they minimize the amount of clinical judgment needed for accurate administration. Use of these trained paraprofessionals can make large-scale research studies cost effective.

DISADVANTAGES OF STRUCTURED AND SEMISTRUCTURED INTERVIEWS

May Hinder Rapport   Despite advantages of structured interviews, their application is not without controversy. The most common criticism of structured interviews is that their use may damage rapport (Craig, 2005; Rogers, 2001) and, thus, the therapeutic alliance that is widely viewed as an essential component of good psychotherapy. Indeed, attaining a reliable and accurate diagnosis of a patient achieves a hollow victory if the process results in the failure of the therapeutic alliance to form; or, in a more dramatic example of clinical failure, the patient does not return for continued treatment. The well-known joke poking fun at medicine, "the operation was a success but the patient died," might be recast in terms of structured interviews as "the diagnosis was impeccable but the patient fled treatment."

How exactly might structured interviews damage rapport? Perhaps most important, structured interviews may impede the connection between patient and clinician because interviews are problem-centered rather than person-centered. There is a danger that interviewers may get so wrapped up in the protocol of their interview that they fail to demonstrate the warmth, empathy, and genuine regard necessary to form an alliance. Indeed, the standardization of the interview may play out as "routinization" (Rogers, 2003). In addition, interviewers who are overly focused on the questions they must "get through" in an interview may miss important behavioral cues or other information that could prove essential to the case.

Proponents of structured interviews point out that the problem of rapport-building during a structured interview can be overcome with training, experience, and flexibility (Rogers, 2001, 2003). We concur and emphasize the observation that "rapid inquiries or monotonous questioning represents clear misuses of structured interviews" (Rogers, 2003, p. 22). If interviewers make an effort to use their basic clinical skills, structured interviews can and should be conducted in such a way that serves to establish rapport and enhance understanding of the patient. To assure that this is the case, however, interviewers must be aware of the potential negative effects of structured interviews on rapport-building and make the nurturance of the therapeutic alliance a prominent goal during an interview, even when they are also focused on following the protocol. It behooves those who use structured interviews to engage their respondents in a meaningful way during the interview and to avoid a rotelike interviewing style that may serve to alienate them. On the other hand, it should be pointed out that not all patients have a negative perception of a structured interview that must be intentionally overcome. Some patients actually like the structured approach to assessment because it is perceived as thorough and detailed, and in these cases, rapport is easily attained.

Limited by the Validity of the Classification System Itself   Earlier, we noted that structured interviews frequently offer a more reliable and valid assessment of *DSM* diagnostic criteria than unstructured interviews. Thus, proponents of structured interviews claim, structured interviews are more valid in general. The assumption inherent in this argument is that the *DSM* diagnostic criteria are truly valid. Some would argue, however, that this assumption is a false one (Rogers, 2001). A point to consider is that *DSM* diagnostic criteria were developed to measure reified constructs (e.g., depression, schizophrenia) so there is no absolute basis on which criteria were created. Although successive editions of the *DSM* have been better grounded in empirical research, and the criteria for some disorders (e.g., major depression) have solid research support, other disorders (e.g., most of the personality disorders) and their criteria have not been examined as consistently or as completely, therefore leaving questions about their attendant validity (Segal & Coolidge, 2001). This point is also bolstered by the fact that the criteria for some disorders have changed significantly from one edition to another in the evolution of the *DSM*. Furthermore, some criteria for some disorders in the *DSM* are impacted by cultural and subcultural variations in the respondent. Thus, some criteria may be valid only for a particular group of individuals at a particular point in time. The way we conceptualize diagnoses, while improving, is far from perfect. And, because structured interviews are intimately tied to diagnostic criteria, they are, by definition, limited by the same inadequacies inherent in those criteria.

In addition to potential problems with *DSM* diagnostic criteria, another issue regarding structured interviews is that it is challenging to establish firmly the validity of any particular structured interview (Segal & Falk, 1998). The problem is that our best means of establishing the validity of a structured interview is to compare diagnoses obtained from such interviews to diagnoses obtained by expert clinicians or by other structured interviews. This is inherently problematic because we cannot be certain that diagnoses by experts or other structured interviews are in fact valid in the first place (Segal & Falk, 1998).

The Tradeoff of Breadth versus Depth   A final criticism of structured interviews centers on the fact that no one structured interview can be all things in all situations. A particular structured interview cannot cover all disorders and eventualities (Rogers, 2001). For example, if a structured interview has been designed to cover an entire diagnostic system (like the *DSM* that identifies over several hundred specific disorders), then the inquiries about each disorder must be limited to a few inclusion criteria. In this case, the fidelity of the official diagnostic criteria has been compromised for the sake of a comprehensive interview. If the fidelity of the criteria is not compromised, then the structured interview becomes unwieldy in terms of time and effort required for its full administration. Most structured interviews attempt some kind of compromise between these two approaches.

Thus, regarding breadth versus depth of approach, users of structured interviews are forced to make a choice about what is most useful in a given situation. Both choices have their limitations. If a clinician or researcher decides to use an interview that provides great breadth of information, he or she ensures that a wide range of disorders and a great many different areas of a respondent's life are assessed. However, one may not have the depth of information needed to fully conceptualize a case. On the other hand, deciding to use an interview focused on one or two specific areas will provide clinicians and researchers with a wealth of information about those specific areas but it may result in missing information that could lead to additional diagnoses or a different case conceptualization. It is essential to understand that when choosing a particular structured interview there are often tradeoffs regarding breadth and depth of information.

WEIGHING BOTH ADVANTAGES AND DISADVANTAGES

Our examination of the strengths and limitations of structured interviews highlights the importance of carefully contemplating what is needed in a particular clinical or research situation before choosing a structured interview. Structured interviews can be invaluable tools in both clinical and research work; however, it is essential that one does not make use of such tools without accounting for some of the problems inherent in their use. A helpful perspective voiced by Rogers (2001) is that it would be unwise to view the interviewing process as an either/or proposition (i.e., unstructured vs. structured interview). In certain situations, unstructured interviews may meet the objectives of a particular clinical inquiry more efficiently than a structured interview. For example, in a crisis situation, flexibility on the part of the clinician is required to meet the pressing demands of this fluid and potentially volatile interaction. However, in other cases, greater assurances that the diagnostic conclusions are valid and meaningful would take priority, for example, in clinical research or in the delivery of clearly defined psychotherapeutic intervention protocols. As we noted earlier, integration of a nonstandardized or clinical interview with a structured interview may also be an excellent option for the clinician or researcher.

In conclusion, introduction of operationalized and specified criteria for mental disorders in conjunction with the development of standardized structured diagnostic interviews has served to revolutionize the diagnostic process, vastly improving diagnostic reliability and validity. Specifically, structured interviews have greatly improved clinical and research endeavors by providing a more standardized, scientific, and quantitative approach to the evaluation of psychiatric symptoms and disorders. With this backdrop in mind, descriptions of several specific interviews are provided next.

STRUCTURED AND SEMISTRUCTURED INTERVIEWS FOR DIFFERENTIAL DIAGNOSIS

In this section, several popular structured interviews are examined. These interviews can be divided into those that focus on either Axis I clinical disorders or Axis II personality disorders. Axis I instruments include the Diagnostic Interview Schedule for *DSM-IV*, the Schedule for Affective Disorders and Schizophrenia, and the Structured Clinical Interview for *DSM-IV* Axis I Disorders. Axis II instruments include the Structured Clinical Interview for *DSM-IV* Axis II Personality Disorders, the Structured Interview for *DSM-IV* Personality, the International Personality Disorder Examination, the Personality Disorder Inventory-IV, and the Diagnostic Interview for Personality Disorders-IV. Each of these structured interviews for Axis I or Axis II assesses a variety of disorders and therefore can assist in the important task of differential diagnosis (i.e., a systematic way of discriminating among numerous possible disorders to identify specific ones for which the patient meets the diagnostic threshold). Each interview also allows for an assessment of comorbid mental disorders on the diagnostic axis on which it focuses. An important caveat is that this list is not an exhaustive one—other multidisorder structured interviews have been created and researched. The interested reader is referred to Rogers (2001) and Summerfeldt and Antony (2002) for coverage of instruments not reviewed in this chapter.

STRUCTURED AND SEMISTRUCTURED INTERVIEWS FOR AXIS I

Diagnostic Interview Schedule for DSM-IV   The Diagnostic Interview Schedule for *DSM-IV* (DIS-IV; Robins et al., 2000) is designed to ascertain the presence or absence of major psychiatric disorders of the *DSM-IV* (APA, 1994). It is unique among the multidisorder diagnostic interviews in that it is a *fully structured* interview specifically designed for use by nonclinician interviewers, whereas the other interviews are semistructured. By definition, a fully structured interview clearly specifies all questions and probes and does not permit deviations. Thus, the DIS-IV by virtue of its structure minimizes the amount of clinical judgment and experience required to administer it.

To ensure standardized administration of the DIS, the paper and pencil version of the instrument is no longer recommended because of the complicated format. Instead, a computerized version of the DIS-IV (C-DIS) is recommended. Computerized administration may be interviewer-administered or self-administered. In both formats, the exact wording of all questions and probes is presented to the respondent in a fixed order on a computer screen. Rephrasing of questions is discouraged, although DIS interviewers can repeat questions as necessary to ensure that they are understood by the respondent. All questions are closed-ended and replies are coded with a forced choice "yes" or "no" format that eliminates the need for clinical judgment to rate the responses. The DIS gathers all necessary information about the person from his or her self-report; collateral sources of information are not used. The DIS is self-contained and covers all necessary symptoms to make many *DSM-IV* diagnoses. The coded responses are directly entered into a database during the interview and the diagnosis is made according to the explicit rules of the *DSM-IV* diagnostic system.

In 1978, development of the original DIS was begun by researchers at the Washington University Department of Psychiatry in St. Louis at the request of the National Institute of Mental Health (NIMH). At that time, the NIMH Division of Biometry and Epidemiology was planning a set of large-scale, multicenter epidemiological investigations of mental illness in the general adult population in the United States as part of its Epidemiological Catchment Area Program. Variables under study included incidence and prevalence of many psychiatric disorders and utilization profiles of health and mental health services. With this impressive purpose in mind, development of a structured interview that could be administered by nonclinicians was imperative because of the prohibitive cost of using professional clinicians as interviewers. As a result, the DIS was designed as a fully structured diagnostic interview and it was explicitly crafted so that it can be administered and scored by nonclinician interviewers.

The DIS has undergone several major revisions since its inception. For example, the original DIS (Robins, Helzer, Croughan, & Ratcliff, 1981) covered criteria for *DSM-III* (APA, 1980) disorders. DIS questions and diagnostic algorithms were revamped to establish compatibility with *DSM-III-R* (APA, 1987) and this was called Version DIS-III-R (Robins, Helzer, Cottler, & Goldring, 1989). The current version of the DIS (Version IV; Robins et al., 2000) is closely tied to the *DSM-IV* system, and to this end, *DSM* diagnostic criteria for the disorders have been faithfully turned into specific questions on the DIS.

Because the DIS was designed for epidemiological research with normative samples, interviewers do not elicit a presenting problem from the respondent, as would be typical in unstructured clinical interviews. Rather, DIS interviews begin by asking questions about symptoms in a standardized order. Like most of the other structured interviews we examine, the DIS has sections that cover different disorders. Each diagnostic section is independent, except where one diagnosis preempts another. Once a symptom is reported to be present, further closed-ended questions are asked about diagnostically relevant information such as severity, frequency, time frame, and possibility of organic etiology of the symptom. The DIS includes a set of core questions that are asked of each respondent. Core questions are followed by contingent questions that are administered only if the preceding core question is endorsed. DIS interviewers use a "probe flow chart" that indicates which probes to use in which circumstances.

For each symptom, the respondent is asked to state whether it has ever been present and how recently. All data about presence or absence of symptoms and time frames of occurrence are coded and entered into the computer. Consistent with its use of nonclinician interviewers who may not be overly familiar with the *DSM-IV* or psychiatric diagnosis, the diagnostic output of the DIS is generated by a computer program that analyzes data from the completed interview. The output provides estimates of prevalence for two time periods: current and lifetime.

Owing to its highly structured format, full administration of the DIS-IV typically requires between 90 and 150 minutes. To shorten administration time, the modular format makes it possible to drop evaluation of disorders that are not of interest in a particular study. Another option is to drop further questioning for a particular disorder once it is clear that the threshold number of symptoms needed for diagnosis will not be met. Although designed for use by nonclinician administrators, training for competent administration of the DIS is necessary. Trainees typically attend a one-week training program at Washington University during which they review the DIS manual, listen to didactic presentations about the structure and conventions of the DIS, view videotaped vignettes, complete workbook exercises, and conduct several practice interviews followed by feedback and review. Additional supervised practice is also recommended.

The psychometric properties of the original DIS and its revisions are excellent and such data has been documented in an impressive array of studies. The interested reader is referred to Compton and Cottler (2004) for an excellent summary of the psychometric characteristics of the DIS. Overall, the DIS has proven to be a popular and useful diagnostic assessment tool, especially for large-scale epidemiological research. The DIS has been translated into more than a dozen languages. It is used in countries across the globe for epidemiological research and served as the basis for the Composite International Diagnostic Interview used by the World Health Organization. Like earlier versions, the DIS-IV can be expected to enjoy widespread application in psychiatric research, service, and training. For information on DIS materials, training, and developments, the interested reader may consult the DIS web site at http://epi.wustl.edu.

Schedule for Affective Disorders and Schizophrenia   The Schedule for Affective Disorders and Schizophrenia (SADS; Endicott & Spitzer, 1978) is a semistructured diagnostic interview designed to evaluate a range of Axis I clinical disorders, with a focus on mood and psychotic disorders. Ancillary coverage is provided for anxiety symptoms, substance abuse, psychosocial treatment history, and antisocial personality features. The SADS provides in-depth but focused coverage of the mood and psychotic disorders and also supplies meaningful distinctions of impairment in the clinical range for these disorders.

The original SADS focused on psychiatric symptoms as specified by the Research Diagnostic Criteria (RDC; Spitzer, Endicott, & Robins, 1978), which made available specific inclusion and exclusion criteria for many psychiatric disorders. The RDC predated publication of the *DSM-III* (APA, 1980) and was a significant predecessor of that system. Many of the specified criteria described in the RDC were adopted for inclusion in *DSM-III*. As such, much information derived from SADS interviews can be applied to make *DSM*-based diagnoses.

The SADS is intended to be used with adult respondents and to be administered by trained mental health professionals. It focuses heavily on the differential diagnosis of mood and psychotic disorders with great depth of assessment in these areas. In the beginning of the interview, a brief overview of the respondent's background and psychiatric problems is elicited in an open-ended inquiry. The SADS is then divided into two parts, each focusing on a different time period. Part I provides for a thorough evaluation of current psychiatric problems and concomitant functional impairment. A unique feature of the SADS is that for the current episode, symptoms are rated when they were at their worst levels to increase diagnostic sensitivity and validity. In contrast, Part II provides a broad overview of past episodes of psychopathology and treatment. Overall, the SADS covers more than 20 diagnoses in a systematic and comprehensive fashion and provides for diagnosis of both current and lifetime psychiatric disorders. Some examples include schizophrenia (with 6 subtypes), schizoaffective disorder, manic disorder, hypomanic disorder, major depressive disorder (with 11 subtypes), minor depressive disorder, panic disorder, obsessive compulsive disorder, phobic disorder, alcoholism, and antisocial personality disorder (Endicott & Spitzer, 1978).

In the SADS, questions are clustered according to specific diagnoses, which improves the flow of the interview. For each disorder, standard questions are specified to evaluate specific symptoms of that disorder. Questions are either dichotomous or rated on a Likert scale, which allows for uniform documentation of levels of severity, persistence, and functional impairment associated with each symptom. To supplement patient self-report and obtain the most accurate symptom picture, the SADS allows for consideration of all available sources of information (i.e., chart records, input from relatives). In addition to the standard questions asked of each respondent, optional probes may be selectively used to clarify responses, and unstructured questions may be generated by the interviewer to augment answers to the optional probes. Thus, considerable clinical experience and judgment is needed to administer the SADS. To reduce length of administration and evaluation of symptoms that are not diagnostically significant, many diagnostic sections begin with screening questions that provide for "skip-outs" to the next section if the respondent shows no evidence of having the disorder. Administration of the SADS typically takes between 1 1/2 and 2 1/2 hours. Formal diagnostic appraisals are made by the interviewer after the interview is completed. At present, no computer scoring applications have been designed because of the complex nature of the diagnostic process and the strong reliance on clinical judgment.

As noted earlier, the SADS was designed for use by trained clinicians. Considerable clinical judgment, interviewing skills, and familiarity with diagnostic criteria and psychiatric symptoms are requisite for competent administration. As such, it is recommended that the SADS only be administered by professionals with graduate degrees and clinical experience, such as clinical psychologists, psychiatrists, and psychiatric social workers (Endicott & Spitzer, 1978). Training in the SADS is intensive and can encompass several weeks. The process includes reviewing the most recent SADS manual and practice in rating written case vignettes and videotaped

SADS interviews. Additionally, trainees typically watch and score live interviews as if participating in a reliability study with a simultaneous-rating design. Throughout, discussion and clarification with expert interviewers regarding diagnostic disagreements or difficulties add to the experience. Finally, trainees conduct their own SADS interviews that are observed and critiqued by the expert trainers.

Numerous additional versions of the SADS have been devised, each with a distinct focus and purpose. Perhaps the most common is the SADS-L (Lifetime version), which can be used to make both current and lifetime diagnoses but has significantly less details about current psychopathology than the full SADS and results in a quicker administration time. The SADS-L generally is used with nonpsychiatric samples in which there is no assumption of a significant current psychiatric problem. The SADS-Change Version is also popular and consists of 45 key symptoms from the SADS Part 1. Extensive study of the SADS suggests that it possesses excellent psychometric characteristics. The interested reader is referred to Rogers, Jackson, and Cashel (2004) for a comprehensive review of these data.

The SADS has been translated into several languages but its primary use has been in North America. The SADS has been widely used in clinical research over the past three decades, and consequently has a large body of empirical data associated with it. As such, it is often the instrument of choice for clinical researchers desiring in-depth assessment of depression and schizophrenia. The extensive subtyping of disorders provided by the SADS is also highly valued by clinical researchers. However, owing to its length and complexity, the SADS is infrequently chosen for use in pure clinical settings.

Structured Clinical Interview for DSM-IV Axis I Disorders   The Structured Clinical Interview for *DSM-IV* Axis I Disorders (SCID-I) is a flexible, semistructured diagnostic interview designed for use by trained clinicians to diagnose many adult *DSM-IV* Axis I clinical disorders. The current version is the product of many prior editions that were updated and modified over time. With each revision, the SCID has been reworked to enhance accuracy and ease of use, culminating in the February 2001 revision when the SCID was updated to match the *DSM-IV-TR* (APA, 2000). The SCID-I has widespread popularity as an instrument to obtain reliable and valid psychiatric diagnoses for clinical, research, and training purposes, and it has been used in more than 1,000 studies.

The original SCID was designed for application in both research and clinical settings. Recently, the SCID has been split into two distinct versions: the Research Version and the Clinician Version. The Research Version covers more disorders, subtypes, and course specifiers than the Clinician Version and therefore takes longer to complete. The benefit, however, is that it provides for a wealth of diagnostic data that is particularly valued by clinical researchers. The research version is distributed by the Biometrics Research Department of the New York State Psychiatric Institute.

The Clinician Version of the SCID (SCID-CV; First, Spitzer, Gibbon, & Williams, 1997a) is designed for use in clinical settings. It has been trimmed to encompass only those *DSM-IV* disorders that are most typically seen in clinical practice and can further be abbreviated on a module-by-module basis. The SCID-CV contains 6 self-contained modules of major diagnostic categories (mood episodes, psychotic symptoms, psychotic disorders, mood disorders, substance use disorders, and anxiety and other disorders).

The modular design of the SCID is a major strength of the instrument because administration can be customized easily to meet the unique needs of the user. For example, the SCID can be shortened or lengthened to include only those categories of interest and the order of modules can be altered. The format and sequence of the SCID was designed to approximate the flow-chart and decision trees followed by experienced diagnostic interviewers. The SCID begins with an open-ended overview portion, during which the development and history of the present psychological disturbance are elicited and tentative diagnostic hypotheses are generated. Then the SCID systematically presents modules that allow for assessment of specific disorders and symptoms. Most disorders are evaluated for two time periods: current (meets criteria for the past month) and lifetime (ever met criteria).

Consistent with its linkage with *DSM-IV,* formal diagnostic criteria are included in the SCID booklet, thus permitting interviewers to see the exact criteria to which the SCID questions pertain. This unique feature makes the SCID an excellent training device for clinicians because it facilitates the learning of diagnostic criteria and good questions to assess the criteria. The SCID has many open-ended prompts that encourage respondents to elaborate freely about their symptoms. At times, open-ended prompts are followed by closed-ended questions to clarify fully a particular symptom. Although the SCID provides structure to cover criteria for each disorder, its semistructured format provides significant latitude for interviewers to restate questions, ask for further clarification, probe, and challenge if the initial prompt was misunderstood by the interviewee or clarification is needed to rate a symptom. SCID interviewers are encouraged to use all sources of information about a respondent, and gentle challenging of the respondent is encouraged if discrepant information is suspected.

During administration, each symptom is rated as either absent (or below threshold) or present (and clinically significant). A question mark (?) denotes that inadequate information was obtained to code the symptom. The SCID flow-chart instructs interviewers to "skip-out" of a particular diagnostic section when essential symptoms are judged to be below threshold or absent. These skip-outs result in decreased time of administration as well as the skipping of items with no diagnostic significance. Administration of the SCID is typically completed in one session and typically takes from 45 to 90 minutes. Once administration is completed, all current and past disorders for which criteria are met are listed on a Diagnostic Summary sheet.

The SCID is optimally administered by trained clinicians. Because of the semistructured format of the SCID, proper administration often requires that interviewers restate or clarify questions in ways that are sometimes not clearly outlined in the manual to judge accurately if a particular diagnostic criterion has been met. The task requires that SCID assessors have a working knowledge of psychopathology, *DSM-IV* diagnostic criteria, and basic interviewing skills. Standard procedures for training to use the SCID include carefully reading the SCID Users Guide (First, Spitzer, Gibbon, & Williams, 1997b), reviewing the SCID administration booklet and score sheet, viewing SCID videotape training materials that are available from the SCID authors, and conducting role-played practice administrations with extensive feedback discussions. Next, trainees may administer the SCID to representative participants who are jointly rated so that a discussion about sources of disagreements can ensue. In research settings, a formal reliability study is advantageous. Reliability and validity of the SCID in adult populations with diverse disorders has been evaluated in a number of investigations, with generally excellent results among widely varied participant samples and experimental designs (see First & Gibbon, 2004; also, Segal, Hersen, & Van Hasselt, 1994).

Overall, the SCID is a widely used and respected assessment tool. It has been translated into 12 languages and has been applied successfully in research studies and clinical practice in many countries. Computer-assisted clinician-administered versions of the SCID-CV and SCID Research Version are available. A self-administered computerized screening version of the SCID, called the SCID-Screen-PQ, is also available, but it does not produce final diagnoses. Rather, likely diagnoses are further evaluated by a full SCID interview or a clinical evaluation. For more information on the SCID, the interested reader may visit the SCID web site at www.scid4.org.

SEMISTRUCTURED INTERVIEWS FOR AXIS II

Structured Clinical Interview for DSM-IV Axis II Personality Disorders   To complement the Axis I version of the SCID, a version focusing on Axis II personality disorders according to *DSM-IV* has been developed, and it is called the Structured Clinical Interview for *DSM-IV* Axis II Personality Disorders (SCID-II; First, Gibbon, Spitzer, Williams, & Benjamin, 1997). Instruments such as the SCID-II are particularly important because clinicians and researchers alike have struggled with their ability to accurately diagnose personality disorders and distinguish one personality disorder from another (Coolidge & Segal, 1998; Westen & Shedler, 2000; Widiger, 2005). The SCID-II has a similar semistructured format as the SCID Axis I version but it covers the 10 standard *DSM-IV* Axis II personality disorders, as well as depressive personality disorder and passive-aggressive personality disorder (which are listed as disorders to be studied further in an appendix of the *DSM-IV*).

For comprehensive assessment, the SCID-II may be easily used in conjunction with the Axis I SCID that would be administered prior to personality disorder assessment. This is encouraged so that the respondent's present mental state can be considered when judging accuracy of self-reported personality traits. The basic structure and conventions of the SCID-II closely resemble those of the SCID-I. An additional feature of the SCID-II is that it includes a 119-item self-report screening component called the Personality Questionnaire that may be administered prior to the interview portion and takes about 20 minutes. The purpose of the Personality Questionnaire is to reduce overall administration time because only those items that are scored in the pathological direction are further evaluated during the structured interview portion.

During the structured interview component, the pathologically endorsed screening responses are further pursued to ascertain whether the symptoms are actually experienced at clinically significant levels. Here, the respondent is asked to elaborate about each suspected personality disorder criteria and specified prompts are provided. Like the Axis I SCID, the *DSM-IV* diagnostic criteria are printed on the interview page for easy review and responses are coded as follows: "?" indicates inadequate information, "1" indicates absent or false, "2" indicates subthreshold, and "3" indicates threshold or true. Each personality disorder is assessed completely, and diagnoses are made before proceeding to the next disorder. The modular format permits researchers and clinicians to tailor the SCID-II to their specific needs and reduce administration time. Clinicians who administer the SCID-II are expected to use their clinical judgment to clarify responses, gently challenge inconsistencies, and ask for additional information as required to rate accurately each criterion. Collection of diagnostic information from ancillary sources is permitted. Complete administration of the SCID-II typically takes less than 1 hour.

Training requirements and interviewer qualifications are similar to that of the Axis I SCID. There is no Clinician Version of the SCID-II. The psychometric properties of the SCID-II are strong, and the interested reader is referred to First and Gibbon (2004) for a comprehensive review. Given the extensive coverage of the personality disorders, modular approach, and strong operating characteristics, the SCID-II should remain a popular and effective tool for personality disorder assessment. The SCID-II web site is the same as for the Axis I SCID, and can be accessed at www.scid4.org.

Structured Interview for DSM-IV Personality   The Structured Interview for *DSM-IV* Personality (SIDP-IV; Pfohl, Blum, & Zimmerman, 1997) is a comprehensive semistructured diagnostic interview for *DSM-IV* personality disorders. It covers 14 *DSM-IV* Axis II diagnoses, including the 10 standard personality disorders, self-defeating personality disorder, depressive personality disorder, negativistic personality disorder, and mixed personality disorder. Prior to the SIDP-IV structured interview, a full evaluation of current mental state or Axis I conditions is required (Pfohl et al., 1997). This is not surprising given that self-report of enduring personality characteristics can be seriously compromised in a respondent who is experiencing acute psychopathology. Indeed, the aim of all personality assessment measures is to rate the respondent's typical, habitual, and lifelong personal functioning rather than acute or temporary states.

Interestingly, the SIDP-IV does not cover *DSM* personality categories on a disorder-by-disorder basis. Rather, *DSM-IV* personality disorder criteria are reflected in items that are grouped according to 10 "topical sections" that reflect a different dimension of personality functioning. These sections include interests and activities, work style, close relationships, social relationships, emotions, observational criteria, self-perception, perception of others, stress and anger, and social conformity. These categories are not scored; rather, they reflect broad areas of personal functioning under which personality disorder items can logically be subsumed (Pfohl et al., 1997).

Each SIDP-IV question corresponds to a unique *DSM-IV* Axis II criterion, except that one item addresses two criteria. An attractive feature is that the specific *DSM-IV* criterion associated with each question is provided for interviewers to easily see. All questions are administered, and there are no skip-out options. Most questions are conversational in tone and open-ended to encourage respondents to talk about their *usual* behaviors and long-term functioning. In fact, respondents are specifically instructed to focus on their typical or habitual behavior when addressing each item and are prompted to "remember what you are like when you are your usual self." Based on patient responses, each criterion is rated on a scale with four anchor points. A rating of "0" indicates that the criterion was not present, "1" corresponds to a subthreshold level where there is some evidence of the trait but it is not sufficiently prominent, "2" refers to the criterion being present for most of the last 5 years, and "3" signifies a strongly present and debilitating level. The SIDP-IV requires that a trait be prominent for most of the last 5 years to be considered a part of the respondent's personality. This "5 year rule" helps ensure that the particular personality characteristic is stable and of long duration as required by the General Diagnostic Criteria for a Personality Disorder described in *DSM-IV*.

A strong point of the organizational format by personality dimensions (rather than by disorders) is that data for specific diagnoses are minimized until final ratings have been collated on the summary sheet. This feature can potentially reduce interviewer biases, such as the halo effect or changing thresholds, if it is obvious that a subject needs to meet one additional criteria to make the diagnosis. This topical organization also makes the intent of the interview less transparent compared to the disorder-by-disorder approach of some other interviews.

Significant clinical judgment is required to properly administer the SIDP-IV because interviewers are expected to ask additional questions to clarify patient responses when necessary. Also, data are not limited to self-report; rather, chart records, and significant others such as relatives and friends who know the patient well should be consulted when available, and a standard informed consent is included for informant interviews. Such collateral information is particularly prized when evaluating personality disordered individuals who may lack insight into their own maladaptive personality traits and distort facts about their strengths and limitations. Moreover, informants can also provide diagnostic data that can help resolve the state/trait distinction about specific criterion behaviors.

If discrepancies between sources of information are noted, interviewers must consider all data and use their own judgment to determine veracity of each source. Making this distinction can be one of the challenges faced by SIDP-IV administrators. Given the multiple sources of diagnostic data, final ratings are made after all sources of information are considered. Such ratings are then transcribed onto a summary sheet that lists each criterion organized by personality disorder, and formal diagnoses are assigned. As required by the *DSM,* diagnoses are made only if the minimum number of criteria (or threshold) has been met for that particular disorder.

Minimum qualifications for competent administration consist of an interviewer with an undergraduate degree in the social sciences and six months experience with diagnostic interviewing. Moreover, an additional one month of specialized training and practice with the SIDP is required to become a competent interviewer (Pfohl et al., 1997). Administrators are required to possess an understanding of manifest psychopathology and the typical presentation and course of Axis I and Axis II disorders. Training tapes and workshop information are available from the instrument authors. The SIDP typically requires 60 to 90 minutes for the patient interview, 20 minutes for interview of significant informants, and approximately 20 minutes to fill out the summary score sheet. Studies documenting the strong psychometric properties of the SIDP are plentiful, and they are summarized in the manual for the instrument (Pfohl et al., 1997).

International Personality Disorder Examination The International Personality Disorder Examination (IPDE; Loranger, 1999) is an extensive, semistructured diagnostic interview administered by experienced clinicians to evaluate personality disorders for both the *DSM-IV* and the *International Classification of Diseases, 10th edition (ICD-10)* classification systems. The current instrument is an outgrowth of two earlier versions (see Loranger, Susman, Oldham, & Russakoff, 1987; also see Loranger, Hirschfeld, Sartorius, & Regier, 1991) that were tied to previous editions of the *DSM.* The IPDE was developed within the Joint Program for the Diagnosis and Classification of Mental Disorders of the World Health Organization and U.S.

National Institute of Health aimed at producing a standardized assessment instrument to measure personality disorders on a worldwide basis. As such, the IPDE is the only personality disorder interview based on worldwide field trials. The IPDE Manual contains the interview questions to assess either the 11 *DSM-IV* or the 10 *ICD-10* personality disorders. The two IPDE modules (*DSM-IV* and *ICD-10*) contain both a self-administered screening questionnaire and a semistructured interview booklet with scoring materials.

The Screening Questionnaire is a self-administered form that contains 77 *DSM-IV* or 59 *ICD-10* items written at a 4th grade reading level. Items are answered either True or False and the questionnaire is typically completed in about 15 minutes. The clinician can quickly score the questionnaire and identify those respondents whose scores suggest the presence of a personality disorder. Subsequently, the IPDE clinical interview is administered.

The IPDE Interview modules (for either the *DSM-IV* or *ICD-10* systems) contain questions, each reflecting a personality disorder criteria that are grouped into six thematic headings: work, self, interpersonal relationships, affects, reality testing, and impulse control (Loranger, 1999). Because disorders are not covered on a one-by-one basis, the intent of the evaluation is less transparent, similar to the SIDP-IV. At the beginning of each section, open-ended inquiries are provided to enable a smooth transition from the previous section and to encourage respondents to elaborate about themselves in a less structured fashion. Then, specific questions are asked to evaluate each personality disorder criterion. For each question, the corresponding personality disorder and the specific diagnostic criterion is identified with precise scoring guidelines.

Respondents are encouraged to report their typical or usual functioning, rather than their personality functioning during times of episodic psychiatric illness. The IPDE requires that a trait be prominent during the last 5 years to be considered a part of the respondent's personality. Information about age of onset of particular behaviors is explored to determine if a late-onset diagnosis (after age 25 years) is appropriate. When a respondent acknowledges a particular trait, interviewers follow up by asking for examples and anecdotes to clarify the trait or behavior, gauge impact of the trait on the person's functioning, and fully substantiate the rating. Such probing requires significant clinical judgment and knowledge on the part of interviewers about each criterion. Items may also be rated based on observation of the respondent's behavior during the session, and this too requires a certain level of clinical expertise. To supplement self-report, an interview of informants is encouraged. Clinical judgment is needed to ascertain which source is more reliable if inconsistencies arise.

Each criterion is rated on a scale with the following definitions: "0" indicates that the behavior or trait is absent or within normal limits, "1" refers to exaggerated or accentuated degree of the trait, "2" signifies criterion level or pathological, and "?" indicates the respondent refuses or is unable to answer. Comprehensive item-by-item scoring guidelines are provided in the manual (Loranger, 1999). At the end of the interview, the clinician records the scores for each response on the appropriate IPDE Answer Sheet. Ratings are then collated either by hand or computer. The ultimate output is quite extensive, including: presence or absence of each criterion, number of criteria met for each personality disorder, a dimensional score (sum of individual scores for each criteria for each disorder), and a categorical diagnosis (definite, probable, or negative) for each personality disorder (Loranger, 1999). Such comprehensive output is often of value to clinical researchers.

The IPDE is intended to be administered by experienced clinicians who have also received specific training in the use of the IPDE. Such training typically involves a workshop with demonstration videotapes, discussions, and practice. Average administration time is 90 minutes for the interview, which can be reduced by using the screening questionnaire (omitting interview items associated with unlikely personality disorders). Because the IPDE has been selected by the WHO for international application, it has been translated into numerous languages to facilitate transcultural research. Ample evidence of reliability and validity of the IPDE has been documented (Loranger et al., 1994; Loranger, 1999). Because of the instrument's ties to the *DSM-IV* and *ICD-10* classification systems and adoption by the WHO, the IPDE is widely used for international and cross-cultural investigations of personality pathology.

Personality Disorder Interview-IV   The Personality Disorder Interview-IV (PDI-IV; Widiger, Mangine, Corbitt, Ellis, & Thomas, 1995) is a semistructured interview for the assessment of the 10 standard personality disorders in the *DSM-IV* as well as the two personality disorders (depressive and passive-aggressive) in the *DSM-IV* appendix as criteria sets provided for further study. The PDI-IV is appropriate for respondents ages 18 years and older and administration time is about 90 to 120 minutes.

A unique feature of the PDI-IV is that it is available in two separate versions, each with its own interview booklet. The PDI-IV Personality Disorders Interview Booklet arranges the diagnostic criteria and corresponding questions by personality disorder. The Thematic Content Areas Interview Booklet organizes the criteria and questions by thematic content. The nine topical areas are attitudes toward self, attitudes toward others, security of comfort with others, friendships and relationships, conflicts and disagreements, work and leisure, social norms, mood, and appearance and perception. Notably, the questions for each diagnostic criterion are the same in each interview form, but the organization is different. The modular approach easily lends itself to focused and rapid assessment of particular personality disorders of interest to the researcher or clinician. A screening questionnaire is not provided for the PDI-IV.

In the PDI-IV administration book, questions for assessment of each of the 94 individual personality disorder diagnostic criteria are presented. Direct instructions to interviewers, as well as prompts and suggestions for follow-up questions, are included in each booklet. Space is provided for recording responses to each question. Each criterion is cross-referenced to the *DSM-IV*. During administration, each criterion is rated on the following three-point scale: "0" indicates not present, "1" indicates present at a clinically significant level, and "2" indicates present to a more severe or substantial degree. A particular strength of the PDI-IV is its comprehensive manual (Widiger et al., 1995), which extensively discusses the history and rationale for each diagnostic question as well as problems that often arise in the assessment of each criterion.

After the interview is completed, the clinician summarizes the responses to individual PDI-IV criteria and plots the overall dimensional profile in a booklet. According to the manual, this profile may help clinicians to rank multiple diagnoses by order of importance and to identify characteristics in the respondent that are relevant to psychopathology and treatment. Notably, the output provided is both a dimensional rating for each personality disorder as well as a categorical rating. Reliability and validity data, as summarized in the manual (Widiger et al., 1995), are solid although relatively few psychometric studies by independent researchers have been conducted. As further studies are conducted, it is expected that the PDI-IV will become increasingly popular in the coming decades.

Diagnostic Interview for DSM-IV Personality Disorders   The Diagnostic Interview for *DSM-IV* Personality Disorders (DIPD-IV; Zanarini, Frankenburg, Sickel, & Yong, 1996) is a semistructured interview designed to assess the presence or absence of the 10 standard *DSM-IV* personality disorders as well as depressive personality disorder and passive-aggressive personality disorder in the *DSM-IV* appendix. The DIPD-IV evolved from earlier versions of the measure (see Zanarini, Frankenburg, Chauncey, & Gunderson, 1987; Zanarini, Gunderson, Frankenburg, & Chauncey, 1989). Before personality assessment, a full screening for Axis I disorders is recommended. Additionally, an assessment of the respondent's general functioning (e.g., in the areas of work, school, and social life) is advised before administration of the DIPD-IV (Zanarini et al., 1996).

The interview is conducted on a disorder-by-disorder basis. The interview contains 108 sets of questions each designed to assess a specific *DSM-IV* personality disorder diagnostic criterion. The *DSM-IV* criterion is provided in bold below each set of questions for easy cross-reference. The initial question for each criterion typically has a yes-no format that is followed up by open-ended questions to explore more fully the experiences of the patients. Patients are informed that the interview pertains to the past two years of their life and that the interviewer wants to learn about the thoughts, feelings, and behaviors that have been typical for them during the two-year period. Whereas patients are the sole source of information for rating most of the diagnostic criteria, behavior exhibited during the interview is valued and may override patient self-report if there are contradictions. Probing on the part of the administrator is encouraged if responses appear incomplete or untrue.

Each diagnostic criterion is rated on the following scale: "0" indicates absent or clinically insignificant, "1" indicates present but of uncertain clinical significance, "2" indicates present and clinically significant, and "NA" indicates not applicable. After all 108 criteria are rated, final categorical diagnosis for each personality disorder is made based on the number of criteria met. The final output is recorded as "2" indicting "yes" or met full criteria, "1" indicating "subthreshold" (one less than required number of criteria), or "0" indicating "no."

Information about administration and scoring of the DIPD-IV is relatively sparse, at least compared to the other Axis II interviews. The training requirements include at minimum a bachelor's degree, at least one year of clinical experience with personality-disordered patients, and several training interviews in which the person observes skilled administrators and then administers the interview. Training tapes and workshops are available, as is a Spanish version. Administration time is typically about 90 minutes. Most notably, the DIPD-IV has been chosen as the primary diagnostic measure for personality disorders in the Collaborative Longitudinal Personality Disorders Study, which is a large, multisite, prospective naturalistic longitudinal study of personality disorders and comorbid mental health problems. For further information on the DIPD-IV, contact Dr. Mary C. Zanarini at McLean Hospital, 115 Mill Street, Belmont, MA 02478; e-mail: zanarini@mclean.harvard.edu.

SUMMARY

This chapter highlights the fact that structured and semistructured interviews have greatly facilitated psychiatric diagnosis, objective measurement of symptoms, *DSM-IV-TR* classification, and problem clarification in a diverse range of clinical and research settings. Reliability of diagnosis is much improved with the use of structured interviews compared to the nonstandardized approach common in clinical practice, and improved reliability provides the foundation for enhanced validity of diagnosis. Given the field's recent emphasis on empirically supported psychotherapeutic interventions and processes (e.g., Antony & Barlow, 2002; Castonguay & Beutler, 2005), we hope that a concomitant focus on clinically relevant, standardized, objective, and validated assessment procedures will be realized as well. Structured and semistructured interviews can and should play an important role in the advancement of the science of clinical psychology. This chapter provided a broad overview of the basic issues surrounding structured interviews and described many interviews available to clinicians and researchers. We hope that this information enables clinicians and researchers to choose instruments that will most appropriately suit their needs.

REFERENCES

American Psychiatric Association. (1952). *Diagnostic and statistical manual of mental disorders.* Washington, DC: Author.

American Psychiatric Association. (1980). *Diagnostic and statistical manual of mental disorders* (3rd ed.). Washington, DC: Author.

American Psychiatric Association. (1987). *Diagnostic and statistical manual of mental disorders* (3rd ed., rev.). Washington, DC: Author.

American Psychiatric Association. (1994). *Diagnostic and statistical manual of mental disorders* (4th ed.). Washington, DC: Author.

American Psychiatric Association. (2000). *Diagnostic and statistical manual of mental disorders* (4th ed. text revision). Washington, DC: Author.

Antony, M. M., & Barlow, D. H. (Eds.). (2002). *Handbook of assessment and treatment planning for psychological disorders.* New York: Guilford Press.

Castonguay, L. G., & Beutler, L. E. (Eds.). (2005). *Principles of therapeutic change that work.* New York: Oxford University Press.

Compton, W. M., & Cottler, L. B. (2004). The Diagnostic Interview Schedule (DIS). In M. Hersen (Ed.-in-Chief) & M. Hilsenroth & D. L. Segal (Vol. Eds.), *Comprehensive handbook of psychological assessment: Vol. 2. Personality assessment* (pp. 153–162). New York: Wiley.

Coolidge, F. L., & Segal, D. L. (1998). Evolution of the personality disorder diagnosis in the *Diagnostic and statistical manual of mental disorders. Clinical Psychology Review, 18,* 585–599.

Craig, R. J. (2005). The clinical process of interviewing. In R. J. Craig (Ed.), *Clinical and diagnostic interviewing* (2nd ed., pp. 21–41). Lanham, MD: Jason Aronson.

Endicott, J., & Spitzer, R. L. (1978). A diagnostic interview: The Schedule for Affective Disorders and Schizophrenia. *Archives of General Psychiatry, 35,* 837–844.

First, M. B., & Gibbon, M. (2004). The Structured Clinical Interview for *DSM-IV* Axis I Disorders (SCID-I) and the Structured Clinical Interview for *DSM-IV* Axis II Disorders (SCID-II). In M. Hersen (Ed.-in-Chief) & M. Hilsenroth & D. L. Segal (Vol. Eds.), *Comprehensive handbook of psychological assessment: Vol. 2. Personality assessment* (pp. 134–143). New York: Wiley.

First, M. B., Gibbon, M., Spitzer, R. L., Williams, J. B. W., & Benjamin, L. S. (1997). *Structured Clinical Interview for DSM-IV Axis II Personality Disorders (SCID-II).* Washington, DC: American Psychiatric Press.

First, M. B., Spitzer, R. L., Gibbon, M., & Williams, J. B. W. (1997a). *Structured Clinical Interview for DSM-IV Axis I Disorders—Clinician Version (SCID-CV)*. Washington, DC: American Psychiatric Press.

First, M. B., Spitzer, R. L., Gibbon, M., & Williams, J. B. W. (1997b). *User's guide to the Structured Clinical Interview for DSM-IV Axis I Disorders—Clinician Version (SCID-CV)*. Washington, DC: American Psychiatric Press.

Loranger, A. W. (1999). *International Personality Disorder Examination (IPDE)*. Odessa, FL: Psychological Assessment Resources.

Loranger, A. W., Hirschfeld, R. M., Sartorius, N., & Regier, D. A. (1991). The WHO/ADAMHA International Pilot Study of Personality Disorders: Background and purpose. *Journal of Personality Disorders, 5,* 296–306.

Loranger, A. W., Sartorius, N., Andreoli, A., Berger, P., Buchheim, P., Channabasavanna, S. M., Coid, B., Dahl, A., Diekstra, R. F. W., Ferguson, B., Jacobsberg, L. B., Mombour, W., Pull, C., Ono, Y., & Regier, D. A. (1994). The International Personality Disorder Examination: The World Health Organization/Alcohol, Drug Abuse, and Mental Health Administration International Pilot Study of Personality Disorders. *Archives of General Psychiatry, 51,* 215–224.

Loranger, A. W., Susman, V. L., Oldham, J. M., & Russakoff, L. M. (1987). The Personality Disorder Examination: A preliminary report. *Journal of Personality Disorders, 1,* 1–13.

Pfohl, B., Blum, N., & Zimmerman, M. (1997). *Structured Interview for DSM-IV Personality*. Washington, DC: American Psychiatric Press.

Robins, L. N., Cottler, L. B., Bucholz, K. K., Compton, W. M., North, C. S., & Rourke, K. (2000). *The Diagnostic Interview Schedule for DSM-IV (DIS-IV)*. St. Louis, MO: Washington University School of Medicine.

Robins, L. N., Helzer, J. E., Cottler, L. B., & Goldring, E. (1989). *The Diagnostic Interview Schedule, Version III-R*. St. Louis, MO: Washington University School of Medicine.

Robins, L. N., Helzer, J. E., Croughan, J., & Ratcliff, K. S. (1981). National Institute of Mental Health Diagnostic Interview Schedule: Its history, characteristics, and validity. *Archives of General Psychiatry, 38,* 381–389.

Rogers, R. (2001). *Handbook of diagnostic and structured interviewing*. New York: Guilford Press.

Rogers, R. (2003). Standardizing *DSM-IV* diagnoses: The clinical applications of structured interviews. *Journal of Personality Assessment, 81,* 220–225.

Rogers, R., Jackson, R. L., & Cashel, M. (2004). The Schedule for Affective Disorders and Schizophrenia (SADS). In M. Hersen (Ed.-in-Chief) & M. Hilsenroth & D. L. Segal (Vol. Eds.), *Comprehensive handbook of psychological assessment: Vol. 2. Personality assessment* (pp. 144–152). New York: Wiley.

Segal, D. L., & Coolidge, F. L. (2001). Diagnosis and classification. In M. Hersen & V. B. Van Hasselt (Eds.), *Advanced abnormal psychology* (2nd ed., pp. 5–22). New York: Kluwer Academic/Plenum.

Segal, D. L., & Coolidge, F. L. (2006a). Reliability. In N. J. Salkind (Ed.), *Encyclopedia of human development* (pp. 1073–1074). Thousand Oaks, CA: Sage.

Segal, D. L., & Coolidge, F. L. (2006b). Validity. In N. J. Salkind (Ed.), *Encyclopedia of human development* (pp. 1297–1298). Thousand Oaks, CA: Sage.

Segal, D. L., & Falk, B. (1998). Structured interviews and rating scales. In A. S. Bellack & M. Hersen (Eds.), *Behavioral assessment: A practical handbook* (4th ed., pp. 158–178). Boston: Allyn and Bacon.

Segal, D. L., Hersen, M., & Van Hasselt, V. B. (1994). Reliability of the Structured Clinical Interview for *DSM-III-R:* An evaluative review. *Comprehensive Psychiatry, 35,* 316–327.

Spitzer, R. L., Endicott, J., & Robins, E. (1978). Research diagnostic criteria. *Archives of General Psychiatry, 35,* 773–782.

Summerfeldt, L. J., & Antony, M. (2002). Structured and semistructured diagnostic interviews. In M. M. Antony & D. H. Barlow (Eds.), *Handbook of assessment and treatment planning for psychological disorders* (pp. 3–37). New York: Guilford Press.

Westen, D., & Shedler, J. (2000). A prototype matching approach to diagnosing personality disorders: Toward *DSM-V. Journal of Personality Disorders, 14,* 109–126.

Widiger, T. A. (2005). Personality disorders. In R. J. Craig (Ed.), *Clinical and diagnostic interviewing* (2nd ed., pp. 251–277). Lanham, MD: Jason Aronson.

Widiger, T. A., Mangine, S., Corbitt, E. M., Ellis, C. G., & Thomas, G. V. (1995). *Personality Disorder Interview-IV. A semistructured interview for the assessment of personality disorders. Professional manual.* Odessa, FL: Psychological Assessment Resources.

Widiger, T. A., & Samuel, D. B. (2005). Evidence based assessment of personality disorders. *Psychological Assessment, 17,* 278–287.

Zanarini, M. C., Frankenburg, F. R., Chauncey, D. L., & Gunderson, J. G. (1987). The Diagnostic Interview for Personality Disorders: Interrater and test-retest reliability. *Comprehensive Psychiatry, 28,* 467–480.

Zanarini, M. C., Frankenburg, F. R., Sickel, A. E., & Yong, L. (1996). *The Diagnostic Interview for DSM-IV Personality Disorders (DIPD-IV).* Belmont, MA: McLean Hospital.

Zanarini, M. C., Gunderson, J. G., Frankenburg, F. R., & Chauncey, D. L. (1989). The Revised Diagnostic Interview for Borderlines: Discriminating BPD from other Axis II disorders. *Journal of Personality Disorders, 3,* 10–18.

CHAPTER 4

Impact of Race and Ethnicity

SUSAN TINSLEY LI, SANDRA JENKINS, AND ALECIA SUNDSMO

IMPACT OF RACE AND ETHNICITY ON THE EXPRESSION, ASSESSMENT, AND DIAGNOSIS OF PSYCHOPATHOLOGY

This chapter is designed to provide an overview and framework for understanding race and ethnicity as factors that affect adult psychopathology. Of primary interest is the assessment and diagnosis of psychopathology in diverse individuals that is responsible, responsive, and knowledgeable with respect to the unique issues that nondominant individuals bring to the mental health arena.

The chapter is organized in three sections. In the first section, we address multicultural competency. The second section includes considerations for assessment with diverse individuals, and the final section focuses specifically on the process of diagnosis with ethnic minorities while attempting to identify common concerns and pitfalls.

Competent and ethical multicultural diagnosis continues to be a daunting and dubious endeavor even after three decades of changes in philosophy, instrumentation, and research methods. Starting in the 1950s and 1960s social forces such as the civil rights, women's, and gay/lesbian movements have exerted considerable pressure on mental health professionals to reexamine the state of fair, humane, competent, and equitable treatment practices. As a result of these influences there was a momentous increase in multicultural research in psychology. The early 2000s were marked by a significant increase in writings regarding multicultural/cross-cultural assessment in neuropsychology (Fletcher-Janzen, Strickland, & Reynolds, 2000), general multicultural assessment (Suzuki, Ponterotto, & Meller, 2001), and personality assessment (Dana, 2000).

Other forces, notably demographic and economic forces, have been major factors in the ongoing efforts to reevaluate the appropriateness of traditional mainstream standards for multicultural practice. The United States is rapidly undergoing a redistribution of racial and ethnic populations. By the middle of the current century it is projected that the composition of the United States will be 13.3% foreign-born; whites 52.8%; African Americans 14.7%; Hispanics 24.5%; Asians/Pacific Islanders 9.3%, and Native Americans 1.1%. Other projections suggest that visible "minority" groups will make up more than half of the U.S. population before mid-century (Dana, 1996; Stuart, 2004; Sue, Arredondo, & McDavis, 1992). These transitions are because of worldwide immigration patterns and differences in birth rates (Chui, 1996). Indeed, in some states such as California, New Mexico, Hawaii, and the District of Columbia, the transition has already occurred and minorities are no longer "minorities."

Demographic and social change pressures have propelled the philosophy that mental health has an inherent cultural component (Good, 1996). Cultural dimensions affect the expressions of different symptoms, the uniformity of psychological constructs, and the validity of assessment instruments. The main thrust of post-1960s mental health standards has been to identify the need for culturally sensitive and culturally relative diagnosis and treatment. In response to the addition of culture as a moderator variable, psychological and psychiatric associations revised their guidelines for practice to include competency and appropriate practice with ethnic minority groups.

MULTICULTURAL COMPETENCY

When considering the need for multicultural competency, the mandate has been made clear. Researchers and clinicians are called upon to work with and serve a variety of individuals, groups, and families that significantly differ from the population on which the prevailing measures and diagnostic systems used for identifying and categorizing psychopathology were developed. Recognizing the need for change, the American Psychological Association (APA) has issued a set of guidelines that outline the areas in which psychologists are called upon to gain cultural competency (APA, 2002b). The Guidelines on Multicultural Education, Training, Research, Practice, and Organizational Change for Psychologists build upon the work of authors such as Sue and Sue (2003) and Arredondo et al. (1996) who were instrumental in originally conceptualizing the components of multicultural competency, such as clinician awareness and attitudes, knowledge, and skills.

The six APA guidelines are designed to cover the broad array of roles and settings in which psychologists encounter diverse individuals. The guidelines are less restrictive than mandated requirements such as those provided in the APA ethics code (APA, 2002a), but are also expected to be viewed as "strongly encouraged" rather than as purely aspirational goals. It is incumbent on the professional to personally drive the movement toward greater competency in the domains in which the professional functions. Unlike previous clinical service-oriented guidelines, these guidelines also address research and organizational change in addition to clinical competency. Three guidelines specifically focus on the clinician, including clinician attitudes, beliefs, and biases (guideline 1), the clinician's recognition of the importance of cultural competency (guideline 2), and the clinician's responsibility to provide culturally competent services (guideline 5). Guidelines 4 and 6, respectively, address the importance of conducting culturally competent research and the importance of cultural competence within organizations and involvement in organizational policy. Guideline 3 is directed toward educators and focuses on the importance of diversity in a clinician's education. Together, these guidelines lay a foundation for responsible research and practice with ethnic and racial minorities.

MULTICULTURAL CONSIDERATIONS

Diagnosis and assessment with racial and ethnic minority individuals requires knowledge of key considerations that impact these processes. Multicultural considerations include ethnic identity of the individual, level of acculturation, psychological-mindedness, and willingness to access mental health services. Table 4.1 provides a list and examples of some cultural issues that can impact diagnosis and assessment. Although this list is not comprehensive, it includes many of the typical areas of content covered in general human diversity courses. In the move toward integrating diversity with courses on psychopathology and assessment, these areas must become part and parcel of competent diagnosis and assessment. For example, differences in the manifestation of symptoms for dominant and nondominant individuals can ultimately affect the selection of appropriate measures and the diagnoses given. Consider the following true scenario:

Ms. N is a 19-year-old Vietnamese immigrant who was admitted to the inpatient unit at the state hospital for psychotic symptoms. Upon entering the day room, the examiner (who was also of Asian descent) approached the patient and greeted her. The patient immediately fell to her knees, prostrated herself, and began praying to the examiner as if she were one of her ancestors. Ms. N would not return to her chair or stand as requested, but continued to remain on her knees throughout the encounter.

This situation raises a number of issues to be considered. Germane to accurate diagnosis of Ms. N is her level of acculturation, her beliefs about illness, and the way in which she is manifesting symptoms. The function of her behaviors and how normative these are within her cultural context will impact the severity of the diagnosis given and whether a diagnosis of psychosis is truly warranted.

ASSESSMENT

One of the major issues in effective assessment of racial and ethnic minorities is identifying the appropriate measures that should be used with a given individual or population (Wong, Strickland, Fletcher-Janzen, Ardila, & Reynolds, 2000). Standard 9.02 of the American Psychological Association Ethics Code (APA, 2002a) emphasizes using instruments whose validity and reliability have been established for use with members of the population tested. Although there is no doubt that using measures validated for a given population is appropriate and best practice, there are a number of difficulties in meeting this standard. Rarely are clinical instruments standardized on members of ethnic and racial groups with the same rigor applied to the dominant Caucasian group. Even when diverse individuals are included within the standardization sample, a careful review of the manual frequently reveals that the actual numbers within each grouping is small and unlikely to be representative. Although some authors have issued a call for test developers to provide better standardization (e.g., Okazaki & Sue, 2000), other authors have pointed out the unlikelihood of such a change occurring and the impossibility of

Table 4.1
Multicultural Considerations

Ethnic Identity
- Affirmation and belonging; ethnic pride; self, group, and other orientation as appreciating or deprecating; stages of development

Acculturation
- Immigration/generational status; behavioral vs. attitudinal acculturation; acculturative stress

Beliefs about illness
- Beliefs about the origin and cause of disease; amount of external control; acceptability of distress, pain, or mental illness

Manifestation of symptoms
- Emotional expressivity, somatization, and definition of pathology

Norms/Values within the culture and worldview
- Examples: collectivism, familism

Resiliency and natural sources of protection
- Examples: elicitation of individual, family, and cultural strengths/competencies

Need for systemic involvement
- Examples: information as viewed by the client, the family, the community, and by professionals; level of distress and perceived functioning as reported by multiple systems

Orientation to mental health services
- Cultural perception of outside intervention; familiarity with mental health services; issues of underutilization; trust, shame, stigma, and knowledge about potential treatments; use of traditional providers and alternative treatments

Nature of reporting
- Use of stories; brief vs. extended answers; cultural proscriptions against disclosure; verbal and nonverbal behaviors; other forms of expression such as art, poetry, music, play, drawings; cultural responses to Likert scales

---

ever standardizing a test on all of the myriad of ethnic groups on which the test will eventually be used (Hays, 2001). Thus, it becomes incumbent on the examiner to understand the limitations of assessment measures when used with ethnic and racial minorities and to be familiar with the areas of knowledge necessary for competency.

CROSS-CULTURAL MEASUREMENT EQUIVALENCE

Fundamental to the assessment enterprise are issues of validity and reliability. In the realm of diversity assessment, reliability and validity are linked to questions of cross-cultural measurement equivalence. The literature on cross-cultural measurement equivalence has grown substantially in the last 20 years such that a set of key terms and statistical techniques has been identified and associated with quality work in this area. At a fundamental level, the goal of measurement equivalence studies is to determine if a particular instrument is valid for use with a population on which the measure was not initially developed or standardized. Allen and Walsh

(2000) and Nichols, Padilla, and Gomez-Maqueo (2000) have defined a similar set of guidelines for determining measurement equivalence that include linguistic or translation equivalence, conceptual equivalence, and psychometric equivalence (see also Arnold & Matus, 2000).

Linguistic/translation equivalence involves the accuracy of the translation and whether diverse individuals have a similar understanding of words or phrases used in the instrument. There is a standard for appropriate translation of a measure that involves both forward and back translation (e.g., Butcher, 1996). A poor-quality translation is easily detected by the absence of back translation in the development process, or by using untrained translators who are not fully bilingual (i.e., are not fully proficient in both languages, but show limited or partial bilingualism). Despite the presence of this standard, there continue to be translations of measures by untrained individuals without adequate education in both languages.

Of greatest concern to assessment is the notion of conceptual equivalence or whether the underlying construct holds the same meaning across groups. Do dominant and nondominant individuals give equivalent meaning to the construct such that psychosis or psychotic thought processes are the same concept in both groups? A common example of difficulty is when one group defines specific behaviors as mental illness or psychopathology while another group views the same behaviors as normative and not associated with a cluster of diagnostic symptoms.

Once the translation phase is complete and there is reasonable certainty that the constructs are the same across groups, additional steps are required to determine whether there is psychometric equivalence between groups. Using configural invariance, scalar equivalence, metric equivalence, and item equivalence, psychometric equivalence addresses the issue of whether the instrument measures the same attribute among people from different groups. Statistical procedures for determining the psychometric equivalence of measures have been outlined by various authors and continue to be developed (Hui & Triandis, 1985; Knight & Hill, 1998; Vandenberg & Lance, 2000). Debate exists as to whether differences at the item level appear at the scale level (Bruno, 2003) and the best way to establish equivalence. However, the ultimate goal of psychometric equivalence studies is the same. A well-validated and reliable measure should manifest the same psychometric properties across groups so that conclusions based on the measure are not biased. For example, can a clinical cutoff score for one population be used in the second population without resulting in greater misclassification such as increased false positives and false negatives? Do dominant and nondominant individuals respond to a Likert scale in similar ways? As Orlando and Marshall (2002) found when evaluating a PTSD scale for use with Latinos, nondominant groups often do not use standard response categories in the same fashion as Caucasians on whom the scale was developed.

Examples of well-conducted measurement equivalence studies come from the depression literature. Cross-cultural measurement equivalence has been a focus of attention for researchers interested in measures of symptomatology and depression for Caucasians and Latinos (Crockett, Randall, Shen, Russell, & Driscoll, 2005; Knight, Virdin, Ocampo, & Roosa, 1994; Posner, Stewart, Marin, & Perez-Stable, 2001). Posner et al. (2001) found a lack of both configural and metric equivalence for the Center for Epidemiological Studies Depression Scale (CES-D) among Latino males. However, the measure was found to be more appropriate for Latino females. Crockett et al. (2005) reported mixed evidence for the equivalence of the

CES-D across Anglo, Mexican-American, Cuban, and Puerto Rican adolescents. Crockett et al.'s findings indicated that the CES-D would likely underestimate depression in 1% to 2% of youths and could result in greater risk of misclassification with particular Latino subgroups (i.e., Cuban and Puerto Rican) because of differences in the nature of symptoms expressed. Another depression instrument, the Beck Depression Inventory, has shown promising results in a college sample of acculturated Latino students, but has not been validated for use with older or less-acculturated samples who are likely to show greater differences (Contreras, Fernandez, Malcarne, Ingram, & Vaccarino, 2004). Furthermore, differential item functioning has been found for a Spanish translation of the Beck Depression Inventory when used with a Latino medical sample (Azocar, Arean, Miranda, & Munoz, 2001).

Measurement studies such as Posner et al. (2001) have important implications for the assessment of symptomatology and establishing the prevalence of psychopathology in racial and ethnic minorities. More research is needed to establish measurement equivalence for instruments most frequently used by psychologists for diagnostic purposes. For widely adopted psychopathology measures such as the MMPI-2, there is modest availability of writings with regard to the use of this measure across cultures (Carbonell, 2000; Nichols et al., 2000; Okazaki & Sue, 2000), but for most clinical assessment tools, the evidence is lacking.

Given the dearth of instruments for which equivalence has been established, researchers and clinicians are left to their own devices to determine how to proceed to ensure responsible and ethical assessment of racial and ethnic minorities. At a basic level, competent interpretation is emphasized. Standards 9.02 and 9.06 of the APA Ethics Code (APA, 2002a) state that if validity and reliability of a measure have not been established, strengths and limitations of the results and subsequent interpretations need to be described to account for cultural differences. However, these standards only address the outcome of the assessment and not the process. Guidance for how to modify the assessment process for diverse individuals exist in the multicultural assessment literature.

MODELS OF MULTICULTURAL ASSESSMENT

The proliferation of research has led to a number of multicultural assessment models to guide the evaluation of ethnic and racial minorities. These models build upon the multicultural considerations previously presented and attempt to outline the process of assessment with racial and ethnic minorities. For example, Dana (1998, 2000) developed an Assessment-Intervention Model for research and practice with multicultural populations. The model includes an elaborate flowchart in which the answers to seven questions lead the reader through a series of decision points to arrive at a diagnostic formulation and intervention appropriate to that individual. Through the process of answering the seven questions (see Table 4.2), the evaluator addresses the individual's cultural orientation, evaluates the availability of etic (i.e., universal) and emic (i.e., culture-specific) instruments, assesses the appropriateness of using standard norms, considers the need for a culture-specific orientation, and determines whether a diagnosis is truly necessary.

The final diagnostic formulation that results from the flowchart can range from a universal diagnostic formulation to a standard Anglo diagnostic formulation to a combined formulation with both standard Anglo and culture-specific elements. The formulation is considered to directly impact any interventions chosen. Interventions may be culture-universal, culture-general, a combination of culture-general

Table 4.2
Models of Multicultural Assessment

Grieger & Ponterotto's Six-Step Applied Assessment Framework (Ponterotto, Gretchen, & Chauhan, 2001)	Dana's Assessment-Intervention Model (Dana, 1998, 2000)	Morris's Culturally Sensitive Assessment and Treatment Model (Morris, 2000)
1. Client's level of psychological mindedness	1. Is an etic (universal) instrument available?	1. *Worldview:* predominant Eurocentric to predominantly ethnic
2. Family's level of psychological mindedness	2. What is the individual's cultural orientation?	2. *Racial identity*
3. Client's and family's attitudes toward helping and counseling	3. Is a clinical diagnosis necessary?	3. *Treatment goals:* individual goals vs. cultural goals or some balance of both
4. Client's level of acculturation	4. Is there an emic (culture-specific) instrument available?	4. *Assessment measures:* standard measures, modified measures, or culture-specific measures
5. Family's level of acculturation	5. Can Anglo or standard norms be used?	5. *Conceptual synthesis:* monocultural American to cross-cultural to monocultural ethnic
6. Family's attitude toward acculturation	6. Is there cross-cultural interaction stress such that a culture-specific conceptualization is required?	6. *Intervention strategies:* universal strategies, combined, or culture-specific strategies
	7. Is a diagnosis necessary?	7. *Diagnosis:* appropriate, appropriate with clarification, or inappropriate

and specific, culture-specific or identity-specific, depending on the answers to the seven questions.

The emphasis on the consideration of client characteristics found in Dana's (2000) model and the range of outcomes possible for each individual (i.e., specific to universal) is reflected in other models of cross-cultural assessment such as Grieger and Ponterotto's Six-Step Applied Assessment Framework (Ponterotto, Gretchen, & Chauhan, 2001) and Morris's (2000) Culturally Sensitive Assessment and Treatment Model. Detailed steps for each of these models are listed in Table 4.2. Other writers such as Gopaul-McNicol and Armour-Thomas (2002) have addressed topics such as report writing and testing the limits with diverse individuals in addition to considering individual aspects of cultural orientation.

SYMPTOM EXPRESSION AND DIAGNOSIS

The way in which an individual describes the experience of psychological distress varies from person to person. However, the current diagnostic system (APA, 2000) assumes some commonalities in clusters of symptoms reported. The problem with this assumption is that research defining those symptom clusters was largely based on Euro-American individuals. Consequently, experiences of psychological distress by individuals from nondominant cultures may not be captured in the diagnostic descriptions, and, conversely, symptoms linked to pathology in dominant individuals may not be indicative of pathology for some individuals from nondominant cultures. Draguns and Tanaka-Matsumi (2003) suggested that symptom expression may vary according to the cultural dimensions outlined by Hofstede (2001) such as an individualistic or collectivistic orientation. For example, people from more individualistic cultures may be more likely to express psychological distress and dysfunction through symptoms of "guilt, alienation, and loneliness" (p. 768), whereas people from more collectivistic cultures may be more likely to describe symptoms of "unrewarding personal relationships, social rejection, and shame" (p. 768). Looking for general themes such as these may be helpful in determining whether self-reported experiences are part of a pathological or culturally concordant process.

SOMATIZATION ACROSS CULTURES

According to the U.S. Department of Health and Human Services (U.S. DHHS) in *Mental Health: Culture, Race, and Ethnicity—A supplement to Mental Health: A Report of the Surgeon General* (2001), somatization is a common presentation of distress across all cultures; however, the type and frequency of bodily symptoms expressed may vary. For example, Latinos and whites may report abdominal problems (e.g., stomachache or chest pains), Asians may report vestibular problems (e.g., feeling dizzy or having trouble seeing clearly), and Africans may report burning sensations in their extremities (U.S. DHHS, 2001). Although there is a general tendency toward somatization across all cultures, ethnic minority individuals in the United States appear more likely to express distress through bodily symptoms for two primary reasons: as compared to whites, there is a higher level of stigma associated with mental illness and there is less of a distinction between mind and body among ethnic minorities (U.S. DHHS, 2001).

There are also specific instances under which the tendency to somaticize distress is more likely. For example, the context of talking to a mental health worker may increase the likelihood that a Chinese individual will express bodily symptoms rather than affective symptoms. African Americans tend to express mild somatic symptoms more frequently than whites. Specific subgroups of the Latino population are more likely than others to report bodily symptoms as an expression of mental distress. Puerto Ricans tend to somaticize more than Mexican Americans, and Mexican American women more than 40 years old tend to somaticize more than whites. In sum, somatization of psychological distress occurs across cultures and yet culture sets the parameters for how people report these bodily symptoms.

It is important to note that not all studies have noted the same patterns of increased somatization for ethnic minorities. Zhang and Snowden (1999) reported data from a multicity study of 18,152 community residents in which they did not find increased somatization among Hispanic and Asian Americans as compared to whites. In fact, they found that although Hispanic Americans reported similar rates of somatic symptoms as whites, Asian Americans actually reported significantly fewer somatic symptoms than whites. Consistent with the Surgeon General's report (U.S. DHHS, 2001), however, Zhang and Snowden found that African Americans reported more somatic symptoms than whites.

INFLUENCE OF LANGUAGE

Another influence on symptom expression is the language of discourse. Malgady and Constantino (1998) examined the influence of language by experimentally varying the language spoken during the interview using Hispanic clinicians. They found that severity of psychopathology (as measured by the Brief Psychiatric Rating Scale) was highest in the bilingual condition, followed by the Spanish-speaking condition, and then the English-speaking condition. According to the results of this study, there was a tendency for clinicians to rate Latino clients speaking Spanish or Spanish and English as having more severe psychopathology and as functioning less well than Latino clients speaking English only. Malgady and Constantino aptly noted that "what remains to be determined is whether or not this is bias in the form of overly pathologizing on the clinicians' part or whether they are more sensitive to patients' presenting symptoms" (p. 125). Regardless, there appears to be an important effect of language on diagnosis.

PATHOLOGICAL VERSUS NONPATHOLOGICAL "SYMPTOMS"

Classical training in diagnosis emphasizes certain behaviors and symptoms as indicators of pathological processes. However, cultural differences in belief systems, values, and experiences shape the extent to which behaviors are or are not part of a pathological process. The most obvious examples of this are paranoid ideation and hallucinations, which are often quickly labeled as part of psychosis in the dominant U.S. culture, and, therefore, part of a pathological process. However, this may not be the case for nondominant individuals for whom the specific symptoms may be more normative. Sharpley, Hutchinson, McKenzie, and Murray (2001) described how a paranoid attributional style among African and African-Caribbean individuals in the United Kingdom resulted not from an inherent biological pathology, but was based on "their experience of social disadvantage and racial discrimination in the United Kingdom." This experience results in (1) a need to question self-perception and identity, and (2) more threat in their everyday social life (Sharpley et al., 2001, p. 65). Researchers in the United States have come to similar conclusions regarding the relationship of paranoia to social disadvantage and attributional style among ethnic minorities. Whaley (1998) found that paranoia and mistrust were associated not only with African Americans but with many different groups who have experienced powerlessness, such as women, people of low socioeconomic status, and people with less education. He, like Sharpley et al., purported that this paranoia and mistrust were related to attributional style:

> If people live in an environment in which they experience powerlessness in the face of victimization, then paranoia serves a self-protective function. People can protect their self-esteem and prevent depression associated with experiences of failure, when they can attribute that failure to the power of external others. (p. 328)

He went on to state that psychotic disorders are being overdiagnosed among African Americans and others when a diagnosis of depression (or no diagnosis) may be more accurate. In other words, Whaley argued that paranoia among African Americans may be less often part of a psychotic, pathological spectrum and more often part of a normal experience of an oppressed individual. The explanations put forth by these authors further illustrate the tendency for an overemphasis on pathological explanations among dominant culture individuals when diagnosing and evaluating nondominant individuals.

Besides paranoia, another symptom that can often be mistaken as inherently pathological is hallucinations. Geltman and Chang (2004) interviewed Caribbean Latinos (85% of whom were from Puerto Rico or the Dominican Republic) receiving outpatient mental health treatment and found that 46% of them reported some experience of hallucinations. Furthermore, they found that "hallucinations were not associated with clinical variables including neurological illness, history of head trauma, mood disorders, and current or prior substance abuse" (Geltman & Chang, 2004, p. 154). Draguns and Tanaka-Matsumi (2003) reviewed the literature on hallucinations across cultures and stated that many aspects of hallucinations are culturally determined, such as the definition of the experience as pathological or not and the sensory modality through which they are most commonly experienced. These authors suggested that one must assess what was going on before and after the experience, along with the setting in which the hallucinations were experienced, to determine whether or not the hallucinations are indeed a symptom of pathology or if they are part of a culturally concordant experience. "Like any other behavior, hallucinations become a symptom when they are so labeled" (Draguns & Tanaka-Matsumi, 2003, p. 765). In summary, paranoid ideation and hallucinations are examples of two symptoms that may lead to misdiagnosis owing to differences in conceptualizations across cultures.

ROLE OF STEREOTYPES, BIASES, AND THE CLINICIAN'S CULTURE

Findings of different prevalence rates of symptom clusters among various ethnic groups create questions about the role of stereotypes, biases, and Eurocentric training of clinicians. For example, Minsky, Vega, Miskimen, Gara, and Escobar (2003) attributed the higher rates of depression in Latinos to "cultural variances in characteristic symptom clusters typically used by clinicians as a template for assigning a diagnosis in a treatment setting" (p. 643). Furthermore, Gonzales et al. (1997) stated that clinicians tended to restrict their diagnoses of Mexican Americans to a fraction of the disorders represented in the DSM. They hypothesized that this restriction may be based on clinicians' interpretation of the idiom of distress displayed by Mexican Americans or possibly the clinicians' stereotypes of Mexican American patients.

Evidence of how stereotypes can influence clinician judgments was presented by Abreu (1999). In this experimental study, stereotypes of African Americans, unrelated to psychopathology, were primed prior to giving clinicians a vignette. Abreu found an interaction between years of clinician experience and the race of the individual in the vignette, such that more experienced clinicians gave more pathological interpretations of the vignette when the individual in the vignette was revealed to be African American (as opposed to the other condition in which the race of the individual in the vignette was not disclosed). Abreu hypothesized that the potentially racially based "clinical schemas [of the experienced clinicians] may be the source of biases in clinical judgment" (p. 392).

In their article on the role of healthcare providers in maintaining racial and ethnic disparities in access to services, van Ryn and Fu (2003) summarized the impact of social cognition research for providers:

> It is both difficult and painful for many of us to accept the massive evidence that social categories automatically and unconsciously influence the way we perceive people and, in turn, influence the way in which we interpret their behavior and behave toward them. However, given that this type of strategy is common to all humans in all cultures and is more likely to be used in situations that tax cognitive resources (e.g., time pressure), the expectation that providers will be immune is unrealistic. (p. 250)

Consequently, extra care must be taken to improve diagnostic accuracy and how mental health professionals view themselves and the individuals they interview. Clinicians must consider which stereotypes they are using in categorization (e.g., a stereotype of what psychosis looks like, a stereotype of what a "normal" African American looks like, etc.) and the possible alternative explanations that exist for the observed behavior.

DIAGNOSIS

The purpose of diagnosis is to understand the cause or reasons for a behavior or syndrome of behaviors that are symptoms of disordered functioning. The causes and extent of pathology is at the center of effective and adequate treatment strategies. Diagnosis is essential for correctly identifying particular disorders and subsequently, selecting the proper treatment approaches. Because diagnosis precedes treatment, the diagnosis often determines the treatment, or lack of treatment, that will follow. It is, therefore, imperative for psychologists to accurately interpret and integrate cultural variables into diagnostic procedures in order to provide competent and ethical mental health services to minorities or nonmainstream clients.

In 1994 the American Psychiatric Association used a large and diverse group of mental health professionals who revised the *Diagnostic and Statistical Manual (DSM-IV)* to include cultural constructs as components of standard diagnostic practice. Axis V of the *DSM-IV* is used to incorporate social problems including racial discrimination. Appendix I of the *DSM-IV* provides a glossary of "culture-bound syndromes" that are common in specific cultural groups, but may be unknown in the mainstream culture.

For several decades psychologists and psychiatrists have debated the merits and pitfalls of the diagnostic process, including the use of diagnostic categories. After five revisions of the *DSM,* questions of reliability, utility, validity, empirical and theoretical underpinnings, etc., have been addressed to a suitable level of professional agreement. The debates, however, continue. Questions concerning biopsychosocial rather than medical models and nomenclature, plus indications that inclusion or exclusion of some diagnostic disorders are subject to the political views of the times, continue to be areas of dispute (Nathan, 1998).

Yet, despite these reforms and revisions, there is reason to believe that many clinicians are conducting cross-racial and cross-cultural assessments that arrive at diagnoses that are often inconsistent with the standards for ethical practice. Evidence shows that minorities are often misdiagnosed or diagnoses are often determined by mainstream cultural norms, rather than the appropriate cultural criteria for the individual client. Both Type I (diagnose presence of pathology when there is none) and Type II (diagnose no pathology when pathology is present) errors are cited in the literature (Gasquoine, 2001; Ridley, Li, & Hill, 1998).

Much of the research shows that blacks and Hispanics are misdiagnosed as schizophrenic, when the more probable diagnosis would be bipolar disorder. In particular, blacks are more often given the diagnosis of paranoid schizophrenia than are whites with similar symptoms. Some studies show that paranoid schizophrenia is the most frequent diagnosis given to blacks. For Hispanics the research results are mixed and contradictory. Solomon (1992) reports that more Puerto Ricans are diagnosed schizophrenic than any other group, including other Hispanics. Chui (1996) asserts that Hispanics receive a diagnosis of schizophrenia less often than blacks and whites, but more often receive diagnoses of other mental illnesses. In any case, when minorities are diagnosed with psychotic or affective disorders they are more likely to be viewed as chronic, rather than acute disorders as compared to whites with the same diagnoses. Likewise, assessments of dangerousness follow a racial bias pattern. Potential for violence and levels of dangerousness are repeatedly overestimated for black inpatients and black prison inmates (Good, 1996; Wood, Garb, Lilienfeld, & Nezworski, 2002).

Founded upon biased and culturally incompetent diagnoses, treatment discrepancies also follow distinct racial patterns. Minorities are typically overmedicated as compared to whites (Wood et al., 2002). Hispanics, however, are less likely to be medicated than blacks and whites. Black inpatients are less often referred for individual and group psychotherapy treatments, and are discharged earlier than whites.

Currently, 75% of persons entering the workforce are women and ethnic minorities (Sue et al., 1992). As the ethnic and racial composition of the United States changes, educational systems are under increasing pressure to conduct culturally fair academic assessments and cognitive diagnoses of minority individuals (Taylor, 1994). Since 1967, U.S. courts have had to deal with the problem of significant overrepresentation of minorities in classes designated for mentally retarded students. Out of these court decisions have come new requirements for testing and diagnosing of mental abilities, especially for individuals for whom English is a second language (Figueroa, 1979; Mercer, 1979). However, intellectual assessment and subsequent diagnosis of adult clients continues to be an area of concern and debate. Diagnosing cognitive impairment in ethnic and racial minorities is a tricky endeavor laden with social implications. It is further complicated by the lack of well-standardized intellectual assessment instruments with high validity across cultural groups. For example, Renteria (2005) conducted a standardization of the WAIS-TEA, the Spanish version of the WAIS-III normed in Spain, on an urban sample of Mexican Americans. Overall, internal-consistency reliabilities for the IQ scores were all lower than those reported in Caucasian samples, and level of acculturation had a significant effect on IQ scores. Furthermore, many of the individuals in this community-based sample scored in the borderline range of intellectual ability. Thus, differences in test scores, as a result of a less valid and reliable measure and inaccurate interpretation practices, could lead to potentially inaccurate cognitive diagnostic conclusions.

Another interesting finding of Renteria's (2005) study was that the participants performed equally on measures of performance and verbal abilities. This is in contrast to the common practice of using performance tests under the assumption that they are a better indicator of intellectual ability than verbal tests. In fact, the performance IQ score of an individual who is tested in English (when English is not the first language) may still underestimate the individual's true intellectual ability.

The previous sections have raised a myriad of issues with regard to accurate assessment, differences in symptom expression, and diagnostic considerations with ethnic and racial minorities. A case study is provided to illustrate some of the issues involved in multicultural assessment and diagnosis specifically with a Latino male client.

Case Study

Mr. A is a 47-year-old Mexican-American male referred for evaluation following a right cerebral vascular injury. Prior to his stroke, Mr. A was regularly employed as a maintenance worker in the local school district. Mr. A has not worked since the stroke and currently requires help from his wife with dressing and some self-care activities due to left-sided hemiparesis. Mr. A is only able to drive during daylight hours due to left-sided visual neglect.

Results from Mr. A's evaluation indicated general intellectual functioning in the low average range with significantly poorer visual-spatial than verbal skills. During the evaluation, Mr. A's mood was dysphoric and his affect was constricted. Mr. A was reported to have exhibited significant personality changes following the stroke and by his own report, he is experiencing a high degree of frustration with the recovery process.

Of significant consideration in the case of Mr. A is the impact of cultural values on his ability to cope with a disabling condition and the loss of masculine roles. Mr. A was the primary economic source for his family in a traditional household. Cultural values such as machismo and familism that are common Latino values affect his current views of his limitations (U.S. DHHS, 2001; Santiago-Rivera, Arredondo, & Gallardo-Cooper, 2002).

The evaluation of Mr. A requires an analysis of cultural elements. Using Dana's (2000) model, one would need to ascertain Mr. A's cultural orientation, determine what assessment measures were available, and decide whether a diagnosis was necessary. In Mr. A's case, a diagnosis was required in order for Mr. A to qualify for Social Security benefits due to his disability. Thus, it was important to complete a comprehensive evaluation and arrive at an accurate diagnosis.

In terms of his intellectual evaluation, Mr. A's intellectual test scores must be viewed with caution. A review of the literature has revealed that the WAIS-III has not been standardized with Spanish-speaking Mexican American individuals in the United States and may underestimate or produce unreliable intellectual ability estimates (Renteria, 2005). When evaluating Mr. A's emotional functioning, a number of difficulties are encountered. In terms of

(continued)

specific measures to assess personality and mood, several of the widely used measures have both strengths and limitations. Although the validity of the MMPI-2 has been investigated with Latino populations, Latino individuals often produce invalid profiles on the MMPI-2 (Carbonell, 2000). Carbonell (2000) notes that the MMPI-2 "continues to have great potential for clinical misuse" (p. 563) and should be used with caution with Latinos.

Mr. A was also reported to have personality changes following his stroke and is a likely candidate for depressive symptoms. However, as noted earlier, depression scales such as the CES-D are problematic when evaluating depression in Latino males (Posner et al. 2001). As Uomoto and Wong (2000) point out, "in the rehabilitation setting, cultural sensitivity to the evaluation of mood is necessary to fairly evaluate the efficacy of interventions for depression in the multicultural patient" (p. 180).

Overall, the assessment of Mr. A's cognitive and emotional functioning is complicated by the lack of well-validated, reliable measures for his ethnic group. As is often encountered in the assessment of ethnic and racial minorities, there is no "right" instrument available to best answer the question of interest. Alternatively, as noted in the APA guidelines, how the instrument is used and interpreted become primary concerns.

In summary, successful evaluation and diagnosis of Mr. A requires expertise in knowledge of multicultural considerations for Mr. A's cultural group and an awareness of the strengths and limitations of the evaluation measures and diagnostic systems available.

In the next sections we describe some of the common problems in diagnosis with ethnic and racial minorities and our recommendations for advancing the field to further address multicultural competency among mental health professionals.

COMMON PROBLEMS IN ASSESSMENT, DIAGNOSIS, AND TREATMENT WITH ETHNIC AND RACIAL MINORITIES

The reasons for deficiencies in diagnoses and treatment have been explored by a series of researchers. The following is a condensation and composite overview of the problems as presented by research findings.

1. *Flawed assessment strategies and procedures.* This list of problems includes test instruments that yield information that is often inadequate or misleading when used with cultural minorities because test validity and reliability were normed for the mainstream culture (Dana, 1996). Poor validity, poor equivalence of constructs (a construct does not have a shared meaning in the different cultures), and instrument bias have all been identified as factors contributing to flawed diagnostic results (Bhui, Mohamud, Warfa, Craig & Stansfeld, 2003; Constantine, 1998; Vijver & Phalet, 2004). In addition, language barriers, when not adequately accounted for, can lead to misinterpretations of test results. This can be especially true in cognitive evaluations and

neuropsychological testing and forensic work (Echemendia, 2004; Gasquoine, 2001; Wood et al., 2002). Other client variables such as income level, education levels, etc., will also affect test outcomes unless these variables are incorporated into the selection of test instruments and interviewing approaches. In addition, trends in managed care restrict the amount of time and money allotted for assessment services. This can lead to additional flaws because of a tendency to select tests for their time and effort utility rather than for their cultural appropriateness (Ridley et al., 1998; Wood et al., 2002).

2. *Symptoms are experienced and expressed differently in different cultures.* As previously discussed, different expressions and presentations can suggest different diagnostic impressions in different cultures. Symptoms of depression, dissociation, and somatic vs. affective presentations have been shown to be subject to learned cultural norms (Frey & Roysicar, 2004; Nelson-Jones, 2002). Mainstream clinicians, using mainstream cultural norms, can make assessment and diagnostic mistakes when observing and interviewing clients from different cultural groups.

3. *Lack of knowledge of different cultural norms, behaviors, and values, etc.* This problem is most often cited as the major obstruction to competent cross-cultural diagnosis. Many problems can be mitigated when clinicians have ample knowledge of the cultural norms as presented by the client being evaluated. Many minorities have little experience with mainstream professionals or how and why an evaluation is conducted. People who are knowledgeable about the professional norms will answer questions differently and provide different information, as well as establish different overall impressions, than will persons who lack this knowledge. Culture can also determine the client's responsiveness during an evaluation session (Parron, 1997). Many minorities, for example, blacks are taught to be wary of the motives and judgment calls of professionals, whereas Asian Americans are taught to be respectful and cooperative with authority figures. Because many clinicians are unfamiliar with these cultural patterns, mistaken notions about the client's diagnostic picture become commonplace.

4. *Clinician bias.* Many psychologists and psychiatrists do not take into account their own racial and cultural biases when conducting an assessment from which they derive a diagnostic conclusion. In effect, they can see what they already believe to be true, for example, blacks are socially prone to delinquent behavior rather than, this particular black individual is acting out deeper problems with symptoms of stress, depression, or PTSD, etc. Or, blacks and Hispanics are generally more disturbed and functioning at a lower level than most whites. The upshot is minorities receive more serious diagnoses and fewer referrals for psychotherapy treatments (Kwan, 2001; Solomon, 1992; Whaley, 1997).

5. *Different ethnic/racial/cultural groups are numerous and not homogenous.* Within-group differences can be greater than between-group differences. This can be especially true when other variables such as education, income, levels of acculturation, differences between subgroups (such as Asian Americans and Hispanic Americans), length of time in the second culture, amount of intercultural contact, etc., are taken into account. It can become daunting to acquire sufficient knowledge of all of the different cultural and subcultural groups to become a competent cross-cultural diagnostician. How

to sort through all of the variables, especially compounding variables of race, gender, age, education, sexuality, etc., in order to arrive at an accurate case formulation for the individual client has been an ongoing problem. Multiple variables notwithstanding, the aim of successful diagnosis is to derive a comprehensive portrayal of the nature of the problems and suggest an adequate treatment strategy. In order to do this successfully, clinicians need to master a comprehensive, systematic methodology to sort through and integrate the group vs. individual variables. Thus far, this methodology is in a formative stage and has not been applied consistently (Arbona, 1998).

6. *Lack of a sufficient scientific evidence base.* Much of the literature points to the need for further research to develop adequate models for cross-cultural assessment and diagnosis. Debates are ongoing about the nature of cultural variables and their impact on individual clients (Spengler, 1998). Questions of racial identity formation, political forces, and levels of acculturation continue to lack adequate empirically based norms that should be applied to the administration and interpretation procedures of diagnostic testing and interviewing.

7. *Lack of adequate training of professionals.* It is likely that most of the problems with competent multicultural diagnosis are because of inadequate training. Many degree programs now have a course or courses in cross-cultural or multicultural practice, but it is still not known how many schools include or do not include these training programs. Moreover, the quality of the existing training programs and the competency outcomes of the training have not been systematically investigated (Ponterotto, Rieger, Barrett, & Sparks, 1994).

SUMMARY

Much work is needed to bring multicultural diagnostic procedures into the twenty-first century. Trends in misdiagnosis and inadequate treatment decisions raise ethical concerns about unfair, as well as incompetent, professional practices. The mental health services needs of minorities are frequently mismanaged and these regrettable prevailing outcomes have been well documented for at least three decades. If these trends continue, we are essentially establishing separate and unequal mental health services systems in the United States.

What are some of the changes in professional practice that need to be in place before this century reaches the midpoint and demographic forces begin to exacerbate the situation? We suggest four possible changes that need to be implemented as soon as possible.

First, we suggest that a large-scale measurement equivalence undertaking supported by federal agencies such as NIMH is needed that could result in a set of robust measures recognized by the professional community as meeting the basic requirements of equivalency. This would be a significant advancement for the individual clinician or researcher to be able to rely on an established set of cross-culturally validated measures.

The fact that multicultural diagnosis is exceedingly hard to do, let alone do well, has been widely acknowledged. Competent and responsible cross-cultural diagnosis requires years of training to master the knowledge base and refined skills required. One or two courses in graduate school are simply not sufficient to meet the demands and standards of ethical practice. Given the wide range of diversity in our society,

Table 4.3

Establishing a Plan for Competent Assessment and Diagnosis

1. *Consult the literature*. Review recent literature in both specialty journals as well as established journals to determine tests with more or less evidence or particular diagnostic recommendations with the group of interest.

2. *Seek specialty training*. Investigate opportunities for specialty classes, workshops, and trainings in how profiles/scores or diagnostic symptoms vary in the group of interest.

3. *Gain direct knowledge and exposure to the culture*. Immerse in cultures and communities that are representative of the individuals with whom you are likely to encounter. By attending activities and celebrations within the community, reading local and community newspapers, and volunteering at local community agencies, you will develop better hypotheses of how assessments and diagnoses are likely to be affected.

4. *Seek consultation/supervision*. Consult with a recommended expert who is familiar with the community. Use professional networks to identify an expert in assessment and diagnosis for the particular group. Engage a mentor who is culturally competent.

our second suggestion asserts that it may be time to require additional postdoctoral training for all professionals conducting cross-cultural diagnostic evaluations. As such, professionals could receive certification verifying their competence levels by attending training seminars and CE workshops.

Third, responsible assessment allows for the fact that valid results are often hard to achieve. When the cultural gaps between clinician and client are broad and the client is not well educated or is from a low-income background, results can be particularly dubious. It should become allowable to make a diagnostic call that recognizes the possible long-term risks present in that situation. A diagnosis of "Due to the extent and degree of cultural differences, no reliable diagnosis is possible at this time" should be included in the *DSM-V*.

Fourth, at a minimum, individuals who work with racial and ethnic minorities should consider establishing a personal plan for competent assessment and diagnosis. Elements of that plan may include researching the literature and staying abreast of new developments. In Table 4.3 we describe some of the components of a plan for competency, including consultation, specialty training, and increased direct knowledge of the population.

Misdiagnosis of minorities can lead to biased distortions, mismanagement of treatment, poor predictive validity, and gross injustices in delivery of adequate mental health services. Competent assessment, diagnosis, and treatment for all individuals and groups should be the goal for mental health professionals across the field. By taking into account the considerations raised in this chapter, researchers and clinicians will view psychopathology among racial and ethnic minorities in a different light with fuller attention to the unique challenges inherent in multicultural assessment and diagnosis.

REFERENCES

Abreu, J. M. (1999). Conscious and nonconscious African American stereotypes: Impact on first impression and diagnostic ratings by therapists [Electronic version]. *Journal of Consulting & Clinical Psychology, 67*(3), 387–393.

Allen, J., & Walsh, J. A. (2000). A construct-based approach to equivalence: Methodologies for cross-cultural/multicultural personality assessment research. In R. H. Dana (Ed.), *Handbook of cross-cultural and multicultural personality assessment* (pp. 63–85). Mahwah, NJ: Erlbaum.

American Psychiatric Association. (2000). *Diagnostic and statistical manual of mental disorders* (4th ed. text revision). Washington, DC: Author.

American Psychological Association. (2002a). *Ethical principles of psychologists and code of conduct.* Washington, DC: Author.

American Psychological Association (2002b). *Guidelines on multicultural education, training, research, practice, and organization change for psychologists.* Washington, DC: Author.

Arbona, C. (1998). Psychological assessment: Multicultural or universal? *The Counseling Psychologist, 26,* 911–921.

Arnold, B. R., & Matus, Y. E. (2000). Test translation and cultural equivalence methodologies for use with diverse populations. In I. Cuellar & F. A. Paniagua (Eds.), *Handbook of multicultural mental health* (pp. 121–136). San Diego, CA: Academic Press.

Arredondo, P., Toporek, R., Pack Brown, S., Jones, J., Locke, D. C., Sanchez, J., & Stadler, H. (1996). Operationalization of the multicultural counseling competencies. *Journal of Multicultural Counseling and Development, 24,* 42–78.

Azocar, F., Arean, P., Miranda, J., & Munoz, R. F. (2001). Differential item functioning in a Spanish translation of the Beck Depression Inventory. *Journal of Clinical Psychology, 57,* 355–365.

Bhui, K., Mohamud, S., Warfa, N., Craig, T. J., & Stansfeld, S. A. (2003). Cultural adaptation of mental health measures: Improving the quality of clinical practice and research. *British Journal of Psychiatry, 183,* 184–186.

Bruno, Z. (2003). Does item-level DIF manifest itself in scale-level analyses? Implications for translating language tests. *Language Testing, 20,* 136–147.

Butcher, J. N. (1996). Translation and adaptation of the MMPI-2 for international use. In J. N. Butcher (Ed.), *International adaptations of the MMPI-2* (pp. 3–46). Minneapolis: University of Minnesota Press.

Carbonell, S. I. (2000). An assessment practice with Hispanics in Minnesota. In R. H. Dana (Ed.), *Handbook of cross-cultural and multicultural personality assessment* (pp. 547–572). Mahwah, NJ: Erlbaum.

Chui, T. L. (1996). Problems caused for mental health professionals worldwide by increasing multicultural populations and proposed solutions [Electronic version]. *Journal of Multicultural Counseling & Development, 24,* 129–140.

Constantine, M. G. (1998). *The Counseling Psychologist, 26,* 922–929.

Contreras, S., Fernandez, S., Malcarne, V. L., Ingram, R. E., & Vaccarino, V. R. (2004). Reliability and validity of the Beck Depression and Anxiety inventories in Caucasian Americans and Latinos. *Hispanic Journal of Behavioral Sciences, 26,* 446–462.

Crockett, L. J., Randall, B. A., Shen, Y-L., Russell, S. T., & Driscoll, A. K. (2005). Measurement equivalence of the center for epidemiological studies depression scale for Latino and Anglo adolescents: A national study. *Journal of Consulting and Clinical Psychology, 73,* 47–58.

Dana, R. H. (1996). Culturally competent assessment practice in the United States. *Journal of Personality Assessment, 66,* 472–487.

Dana, R. H. (1998). *Understanding cultural identity in intervention and assessment.* Thousand Oaks, CA: Sage.

Dana, R. H. (2000). *Handbook of cross-cultural and multicultural personality assessment.* Mahwah, NJ: Erlbaum.

Draguns, J. G., & Tanaka-Matsumi, J. (2003). Assessment of psychopathology across and within cultures: Issues and findings [Electronic version]. *Behaviour Research and Therapy, 41,* 755–776.

Echemendia, R. J. (2004). Cultural diversity and neuropsychology: An uneasy relationship in a time of change. *Applied Neuropsychology, 11,* 1–3.

Figueroa, R. A. (1979). The system of multicultural pluralistic assessment. *School Psychology Digest, 8,* 28–36.

Fletcher-Janzen, Strickland, T. L., & Reynolds, C. R. (2000). *Handbook of cross-cultural neuropsychology.* New York: Kluwer.

Frey, L., & Roysicar, G. (2004). Effects of acculturation and worldview for white American, South American, South Asian, and Southeast Asian students. *International Journal for the Advancement of Counseling, 26,* 229–248.

Gasquoine, P. G. (2001). Research in clinical neuropsychology with Hispanic and American participants: A review. *The Clinical Neuropsychologist, 15,* 2–12.

Geltman, D., & Chang, G. (2004). Hallucinations in Latino psychiatric outpatients: A preliminary investigation [Electronic version]. *General Hospital Psychiatry, 26*(2), 152–157.

Gonzales, M., Castillo-Canez, I., Tarke, H., Soriano, F., Garcia, P., Velasquez, R. J. (1997). Promoting the culturally sensitive diagnosis of Mexican Americans: Some personal insights. *Journal of Multicultural Counseling & Development, 25*(2), 156–161.

Good, B. J. (1996). Culture and *DSM-IV*: Diagnosis, knowledge and power. *Culture, Medicine and Psychiatry, 20,* 127–132.

Gopaul-McNicol, S., & Armour-Thomas, E. (2002). *Assessment and culture: Psychological tests with minority populations* San Diego, CA: Academic Press.

Hays, P. A. (2001). *Addressing cultural complexities in practice: A framework for clinicians and counselors.* Washington, DC: American Psychological Association.

Hofstede, G. (2001). *Culture's consequences: Comparing values, institutions, and organizations across nations* (2nd ed.). Thousand Oaks, CA: Sage.

Hui, C. H., & Triandis, H. C. (1985). Measurement in cross-cultural psychology. *Journal of Cross-Cultural Psychology, 16,* 131–152.

Knight, G. P., & Hill, N. (1998). Measurement equivalence in research involving minority adolescents. In V. C. McLoyd & L. Steinberg, (Eds.), *Studying minority adolescents: Conceptual, methodological, and theoretical issues* (pp. 183–210). Mahwah, NJ: Erlbaum.

Knight, G. P., Virdin, L. M., Ocampo, K. A., & Roosa, M. (1994). An examination of the cross-ethnic equivalence of measures of negative life events and mental health among Hispanic and Anglo American children. *American Journal of Community Psychology, 22,* 767–783.

Kwan, K. K. (2001). Models of racial and ethnic identity development: Delineation of practice implications. *Journal of Mental Health Counseling, 23,* 269–277.

Malgady, R. G., & Constantino, G. (1998). Symptom severity in bilingual Hispanics as a function of clinician ethnicity and language of interview [Electronic version]. *Psychological Assessment, 10*(2), 120–127.

Mercer, J. R. (1979). In defense of racially and culturally non-discriminatory assessment. *School Psychology Digest, 8,* 89–115.

Minsky, S., Vega, W., Miskimen, T., Gara, M., & Escobar, J. (2003). Diagnostic patterns in Latino, African American, and European American psychiatric patients. *Archives of General Psychiatry, 60*(6), 637–644.

Morris, E. F. (2000). Assessment practices with African Americans: Combining standard assessment measures within an Africentric orientation. In R. H. Dana (Ed.), *Handbook of cross-cultural and multicultural personality assessment* (pp. 573–603). Mahwah, NJ: Erlbaum.

Nathan, P. E. (1998). The *DSM-IV* and its antecedents: Enhancing syndromal diagnosis. In J. Barron (Ed.), *Making diagnosis meaningful: Enhancing evaluation and treatment of psychological disorders* (pp. 2–27). Washington, DC: American Psychological Association.

Nelson-Jones, R. (2002). Diverse goals for multicultural counseling and therapy. *Counseling Psychology Quarterly, 15,* 133–143.

Nichols, D. S., Padilla, J., & Gomez-Maqueo, E. L. (2000). Issues in the cross-cultural adaptation and use of the MMPI-2. In R. H. Dana (Ed.), *Handbook of cross-cultural and multicultural personality assessment.* Mahwah, NJ: Erlbaum.

Okazaki, S., & Sue, S. (2000). Implications of test revisions for assessment with Asian Americans. *Psychological Assessment, 12,* 272–280.

Orlando, M., & Marshall, G. N. (2002). Differential item functioning in a Spanish translation of the PTSD checklist: Detection and evaluation of impact. *Psychological Assessment, 14,* 50–59.

Parron, D. L. (1997). The fusion of cultural horizons: Cultural influences on the assessment of psychopathology on children. *Applied Development Science, 1,* 156–159.

Ponterotto, J. G., Gretchen, D., & Chauhan, R. V. (2001). Cultural identity and multicultural assessment: Quantitative and qualitative tools for the clinician. In L. A. Suzuki, J. G. Ponterotto, & P. J. Meller (Eds.), *Handbook of multicultural assessment: Clinical psychological and education applications* (2nd ed., pp. 67–99). Thousand Oaks, CA: Sage.

Ponterotto, J. G., Rieger, B. P., Barrett, A., & Sparks, R. (1994). Assessing multicultural counseling competence: A review of instrumentation. *Journal of Counseling & Development, 72,* 316–322.

Posner, S. F., Stewart, A. L., Marin, G., & Perez-Stable, E. J. (2001). Factor variability of the Center for Epidemiological Studies Depression Scale (CES-D) among urban Latinos. *Ethnicity & Health, 6,* 137–144.

Renteria, L. (2005). *Validation of the Spanish language Wechsler Adult Intelligence Scale (3rd Edition) in a sample of American, urban, Spanish speaking Hispanics.* Unpublished doctoral dissertation. Loyola University, Chicago.

Ridley, C. R., Li, L. C., & Hill, C. L. (1998). Multicultural assessment: Reexamination, reconceptualization, and practical application. *The Counseling Psychologist, 26,* 827–910.

Santiago-Rivera, A. L., Arredondo, P., & Gallardo-Cooper, M. (2002). *Counseling Latinos and la familia: A practical guide.* Thousand Oaks, CA: Sage.

Sharpley, M., Hutchinson, G., McKenzie, K., & Murray, R. M. (2001). Understanding the excess of psychosis among the African-Caribbean population in England [Electronic version]. *British Journal of Psychiatry, 178* (Suppl. 40), 60–68.

Solomon, A. (1992). Clinical diagnosis among diverse populations: A multicultural perspective. *Families in Society: The Journal of Contemporary Human Services, 73,* 371–377.

Spengler, P. M. (1998). Multicultural assessment and a scientist-practitioner model of psychological assessment. *The Counseling Psychologist, 26,* 930–938.

Stuart, R. B. (2004). Twelve practical suggestions for achieving multicultural competence. *Professional Psychology: Research and Practice, 35,* 3–9.

Sue, D. W., Arredondo, P., & McDavis, R. J. (1992). Multicultural counseling competencies and standards: A call to the profession. *Journal of Multicultural Counseling & Development, 20,* 64–88.

Sue, D. W., & Sue, D. (2003). *Counseling the culturally diverse: Theory and practice* (4th ed.). New York: Wiley.

Suzuki, L. A., Ponterotto, J. G., & Meller, P. J. (2001). *Handbook of multicultural assessment: Clinical psychological and education applications* (2nd ed.). Thousand Oaks, CA: Sage.

Taylor, T. R. (1994). A review of three approaches to cognitive assessment, and a proposed integrated approach based on a unifying theoretical framework [Electronic version]. *South African Journal of Psychology, 24,* 184–207.

Uomoto, J. M., & Wong, T. M. (2000). Multicultural perspectives on the neuropsychology of brain injury assessment and rehabilitation. In E. Fletcher-Janzen, T. L. Strickland, & C. R. Reynolds (Eds.), *Handbook of cross-cultural neuropsychology* (pp. 169–184). New York: Kluwer.

U.S. Department of Health and Human Services (2001). *Mental health: Culture, race, and ethnicity—A supplement to mental health: A report of the Surgeon General.* Substance Abuse and Mental Health Services Administration, Center for Mental Health Services. Rockville, MD.

Vandenberg, R. J., & Lance, C. E., (2000). A review and synthesis of the measurement invariance literature: Suggestions, practices, and recommendations for organizational research. *Organizational Research Methods, 3,* 4–70.

van Ryn, M., & Fu, S. S. (2003). Paved with good intentions: Do public health and human service providers contribute to racial/ethnic disparities in health? [Electronic version]. *American Journal of Public Health, 93*(2), 248–255.

Vijver, F., & Phalet, K. (2004). Assessment in multicultural groups: The role of acculturation. *Applied Psychology: An International Review, 53,* 215–236.

Whaley, A. L. (1997). Ethnicity/race, paranoia, and psychiatric diagnoses: Clinician bias versus sociocultural differences. *Journal of Psychopathology and Behavioral Assessment, 19,* 1–20.

Whaley, A. L. (1998). Cross-cultural perspective on paranoia: A focus on the black American experience [Electronic version]. *Psychiatric Quarterly, 69*(4), 325–343.

Wong, T. M., Strickland, T. L., Fletcher-Janzen, E., Ardila, A., & Reynolds, C. R. (2000). Theoretical and practical issues in the neuropsychological assessment and treatment of culturally dissimilar patients. (pp. 3–18). In E. Fletcher-Janzen, T. L., Strickland, & C. R. Reynolds (Eds.), *Handbook of cross-cultural neuropsychology.* New York: Kluwer.

Wood, J. M., Garb, H. N., Lilienfeld, S. O,. & Nezworski, M. T. (2002). Clinical assessment. *Annual Review of Psychology, 53,* 519–543.

Zhang, A. Y., & Snowden, L. R. (1999). Ethnic characteristics of mental disorders in five U. S. communities. *Cultural Diversity and Ethnic Minority Psychology, 5,* 134–146.

PART II
SPECIFIC DISORDERS

CHAPTER 5

Delirium, Dementia, and Amnestic and Other Cognitive Disorders

GERALD GOLDSTEIN

Most of the neurological disorders of mankind are ancient diseases, and developments in treatment and cure have been painfully slow. However, we continue to learn more about these disorders, and in a previous version of this chapter (Goldstein, 1997) we commented on two major new events that took place during recent years that represented highly substantive developments. A new disorder, AIDS dementia, had appeared, and the marker for the Huntington's disease gene had been discovered. Since the time of that writing, there are, fortunately, no new diseases, with the possible exception of a still mysterious and controversial disorder sustained by military personnel during the war with Iraq in the Persian Gulf area, popularly known as the "Gulf War Syndrome." An aspect of this syndrome has been said to involve impaired brain function (Goldstein, Beers, Morrow, Shemansky, & Steinhauer, 1996). We also commented on the substantial change in how the organic mental disorders are classified by psychiatry, reflected in the most recent diagnostic and statistical manual (*DSM-IV;* American Psychiatric Association [APA], 1994). In this author's judgment, the major developments over the past 10 years have been technological in nature. Increasingly sophisticated techniques have been developed to image the brain, not only structurally as in an X-ray, but also functionally. We now have very advanced capacities to image brain activity while the individual is engaging in some form of behavior. At present functional magnetic resonance imaging (fMRI) is the most widely used of these procedures. It involves performing magnetic resonance imaging while the individual is given tasks to perform and recording changes in brain activity. Thus, for example, it is possible to observe increased activity in the language area of the brain while the person is performing a language task.

Since the last writing there have been no changes in the formal classification system, as *DSM-V* has not arrived as yet. There continue to be substantial technological advances. Perhaps the major one is the development of a technique to make a pathological diagnosis of Alzheimer's disease in a living person. Previously, the diagnosis could only be made at autopsy. Now there is a neuroimaging procedure that can visualize neurochemical changes in the brain that can make a specific diagnosis. It involves an amyloid-imaging positron emission tomography (PET) tracer that detects amyloid in the brain. Amyloid is known to be central to the pathogenesis of Alzheimer's disease (Fagan et al., 2005; Klunk et al., 2004). Other developments have been more incremental, with increases in our understanding of the Gulf War Syndrome and neurodevelopmental disorders, notably autism.

The changes in *DSM-IV* have essentially codified the abandonment of the traditional distinction made in psychopathology between the so-called organic and functional disorders. The latter type of disorder was generally viewed as a reaction to some environmental or psychosocial stress, or as a condition in which the presence of a specific organic etiological factor is strongly suspected, but not proven. The anxiety disorders would be an example of the first alternative, and schizophrenia would be an example of the second. The organic mental disorders are those conditions that can be more or less definitively associated with temporary or permanent dysfunction of the brain. Thus, individuals with these illnesses are frequently described as "brain damaged" patients or patients with "organic brain syndromes." It is clear that recent developments in psychopathological research and theory have gone a long way toward breaking down this distinction, and it is becoming increasingly clear that many of the schizophrenic, mood, and attentional disorders have their bases in some alteration of brain function. Perhaps most recently, the significance of brain function for a number of developmental disorders, notably autism and related pervasive developmental disorders, has been recognized and emphasized. Psychiatric classification has therefore dropped use of the word *organic* to describe what was formerly called the organic mental disorders. The word has been replaced by several terms: delirium, dementia, amnesia, cognitive disorders, and mental disorders due to a general medical condition. Nevertheless, the clinical phenomenology, assessment methods, and treatment management procedures associated with patients generally described as brain damaged are sufficiently unique that the traditional functional versus organic distinction is probably worth retaining for certain purposes. Brain damaged patients have clinical phenomenologies, symptoms, courses, and outcomes that are quite different from those of patients with other psychopathological disorders. However, in order to delineate the subject matter of this chapter as precisely as possible, we would nevertheless prefer to say that we will be concerned with individuals having structural brain damage rather than with "organic patients."

The theoretical approach taken here will be neuropsychological in orientation, in that it will be based on the assumption that clinical problems associated with brain damage can be understood best in the context of what is known about the relationships between brain function and behavior. Thus, attempts will be made to expand our presentation beyond the descriptive psychopathology of *DSM-IV* (APA, 1994) in the direction of attempting to provide some material related to basic brain-behavior mechanisms. There are many sources of brain dysfunction, and the nature of the source has a great deal to do with determining behavioral consequences: morbidity and mortality. Thus, a basic grasp of key neuropathological processes is crucial to understanding the differential consequences of brain damage. Furthermore, it is important to have some conceptualization of how the brain functions. Despite great advances in neuroscience we still do not know a great deal about this matter yet, and so it remains necessary to think in terms of brain models or conceptual schema concerning brain function. However, we have learned a great deal about the genetics and neurochemistry of how memories are preserved in brain tissue. There are several neuropsychological models and hypotheses concerning memory, portions of which have been supported by neurochemical and neurophysiological research. In recent years, however, knowledge of the neurological systems important for such areas as memory and language has been substantially expanded. For example, it seems clear now that there are several separate memory systems located in different areas of the brain, notably the hippocampus, the amygdala, neocortex, and the cerebellum. Each system interacts with the others, but supports a different form of memory such as immediate recall, remote recall, and the brief storage of information during ongoing cognitive activity known as working memory (Baddeley, 1986).

In recognition of the complexities involved in relating structural brain damage to behavioral consequences, the field of clinical neuropsychology has emerged as a specialty area within psychology. Clinical neuropsychological research has provided a number of specialized instruments for assessment of brain damaged patients, and a variety of rehabilitation methods aimed at remediation of neuropsychological deficits. This research has also pointed out that *brain damage,* far from being a single clinical entity, actually represents a wide variety of disorders. Initially, neuropsychologists were strongly interested in the relationship between localization of the brain damage and behavioral outcome. In recent years, however, localization has come to be seen as only one determinant of outcome, albeit often a very important one. Other considerations include such matters as the age of the individual, the individual's age when the brain damage was acquired, the premorbid personality and level of achievement, and the type of pathological process producing the brain dysfunction. Furthermore, neuropsychologists are now cognizant of the possible influence of various "nonorganic" factors on their assessment methods, such as educational level, socioeconomic status, and mood states. There has been an increasing interest in sociocultural aspects of neuropsychological assessment, particularly with reference to research and testing in cultures throughout the world that are experiencing significant effects of some brain disease, such as AIDS dementia (Heaton, 2006). Thus, this chapter will concern itself with concepts of brain dysfunction in historical and contemporary perspectives, the various causes of brain dysfunction, and the clinical phenomenology of a number of syndromes associated with brain damage in relation to such factors as localization, age of the individual, age of the lesion, and pathological process.

CHANGING VIEWS OF BRAIN FUNCTION AND DYSFUNCTION

Concepts of how mental events are mediated have evolved from vague philosophical speculations concerning the "mind-body problem" to rigorous scientific theories supported by objective experimental evidence. We may recall from studies of the history of science that it was not always understood that the "mind" was in the brain and mental events were thought to be mediated by other organs of the body. Boring (1950) indicates that Aristotle thought that the mind was in the heart.

Once the discovery was made that it was in the brain, scientists turned their interest to how the brain mediates behavior, thus ushering in a line of investigation that to this day is far from complete. Two major methodologies were used in this research: direct investigations of brain function through lesion generation or brain stimulation in animal subjects, and studies of patients who had sustained brain damage, particularly localized brain damage. The latter method, with which we will be mainly concerned here, can be reasonably dated back to 1861 when Paul Broca produced his report (1861) on the case of a patient who had suddenly developed speech loss. An autopsy done on this patient revealed that he had sustained an extensive infarct in the area of the third frontal convolution of the left cerebral hemisphere. Thus, an important center in the brain for speech had been discovered, but perhaps more significantly, this case produced what many would view as the first reported example of a neuropsychological or brain-behavior relationship in a human. Indeed, to this day, the third frontal convolution of the left hemisphere is known as Broca's area, and the type of speech impairment demonstrated by the patient is known as Broca's aphasia. Following Broca's discovery, much effort was devoted to relating specific behaviors to discrete areas of the brain. Wernicke made the important discovery that the area that mediates the comprehension as opposed to the expression of speech is not the Broca area but in a more posterior region in the left temporal lobe: the superior temporal gyrus. Other investigators sought to localize other language, cognitive, sensory, and motor abilities in the tradition of Broca and Wernicke, some using animal lesion and stimulation methods, and others clinical autopsy investigations of human brain damaged patients. Various syndromes were described, and centers or pathways whose damage or disconnection produced these syndromes were suggested. These early neuropsychological investigations not only provided data concerning specific brain-behavior relationships, but also explicitly or implicitly evolved a theory of brain function, now commonly known as classical localization theory. In essence, the brain was viewed as consisting of centers for various functions connected by neural pathways. In human subjects, the presence of these centers and pathways was documented through studies of individuals who had sustained damage to either a center or the connecting links between one center and another such that they became disconnected. To this day, the behavioral consequences of this latter kind of tissue destruction is referred to as a *disconnection syndrome* (Geschwind, 1965). For example, there are patients who can speak and understand, but who cannot repeat what was just said to them. In such cases, it is postulated that there is a disconnection between the speech and auditory comprehension centers.

From the beginnings of the scientific investigation of brain function, not all investigators advocated localization theory. The alternative view is that rather than functioning through centers and pathways the brain functions as a whole in an integrated manner. Views of this type are currently known as mass action, holistic, or organismic theories of brain function. Although we generally think of holistic theory as a reaction to localization theory, it actually can be seen as preceding localization theory, in that the very early concepts of brain function proposed by Galen and Descartes can be understood as holistic in nature. However, what is viewed as the first scientific presentation of holistic theory was made in 1824 by Flourens. Flourens (1824) proposed that the brain might have centers for special functions (action propre). But there is a unity to the system as a whole (action commune), and this unity dominates the entire system. Boring (1950) quotes Flourens's statement, "Unity is the great principle that reigns; it is everywhere, it dominates everything." The legacy of holistic theory has come down to us from Flourens through the neurologist Hughlings Jackson. Jackson proposed a distinction between primary and secondary symptoms of brain damage. The primary symptoms are the direct consequences of the insult to the brain itself, while the secondary symptoms are the changes that take place in the unimpaired stratum. Thus, a lesion produces changes not only at its site, but also throughout the brain. In contemporary neuropsychology the strongest advocates of holistic theory were Kurt Goldstein, Martin Scheerer, and Heinz Werner. Goldstein and Scheerer (1941) are best known for their distinction between abstract and concrete behavior, their description of the "abstract attitude," and the tests they devised to study abstract and concrete functioning in brain damaged patients. Their major proposition was that many of the symptoms of brain damage could be viewed not as specific manifestations of damage to centers or connecting pathways but as some form of impairment of the abstract attitude. The abstract attitude is not localized in any region of the brain but depends upon the functional integrity of the brain as a whole. Goldstein (1959) describes the abstract attitude as the capacity to transcend immediate sensory impressions and consider situations from a conceptual standpoint. Generally, it is viewed as underlying such functions as planning, forming intentions, developing concepts, and separating ourselves from immediate sensory experience. The abstract attitude is evaluated objectively primarily through the use of concept formation tests that involve sorting or related categorical abilities. In language it is evaluated by testing the patient's ability to use speech symbolically. Often this testing is accomplished by asking the patient to produce a narrative about some object that is not present in the immediate situation.

Heinz Werner and various collaborators applied many of Goldstein's concepts to studies of brain injured and mentally retarded children (e.g., Werner & Strauss, 1942). His analyses and conceptualizations reflected an orientation toward Gestalt psychology and holistic concepts, dealing with such matters as figure-ground relationships and rigidity. Halstead (1947) made use of the concept of the abstract attitude in his conceptualizations of brain function, but in a modified form. Like most contemporary neuropsychologists, Halstead viewed abstraction as one component or factor in cognitive function among many, and did not give it the central role attributed to it by Goldstein and his followers. Correspondingly, rather than adhering to an extreme position concerning the absence of localization, Halstead provided evidence to suggest that the frontal lobes were of greater importance in regard to mediation of abstract behavior than were other regions of the brain. Goldstein (1936) also came to accept the view that the frontal lobes were particularly important in regard to mediation of the abstract attitude.

The notion of a nonlocalized generalized deficit underlying many of the specific behavioral phenomena associated with brain damage has survived to some extent in contemporary neuropsychology, but in a greatly modified form. Similarly, some aspects of classical localization theory are still with us, but also with major changes (Mesulam, 1985). None of the current theories accepts the view that there is no localization of function in the brain, and correspondingly, none of them would deny that there are some behaviors that cannot be localized to some structure or group of structures. This synthesis is reflected in a number of modern concepts of brain function, the most explicit one probably being that of Luria (1973). Luria has developed the concept of functional systems as an alternative to both strict localization and mass action theories. Basically, a functional system consists of a number of elements involved in the mediation of some complex behavior. For example, there may be a functional system for auditory comprehension of language. The concept of pluripotentiality is substituted for Lashley's (1960) older concept of equipotentiality. Equipotentiality theory suggests that any tissue in a functional area can carry out the functions previously mediated by destroyed tissue. Pluripotentiality is a more limited concept suggesting that one particular structure or element may be involved in many functional systems. Thus, no structure in the brain is only involved in a single function. Depending upon varying conditions, the same structure may play a role in several functional systems.

Current neuropsychological thought reflects some elements of all of the general theories of brain function briefly outlined in the preceding paragraphs. In essence, it is thought that the brain is capable of highly localized activity directed toward control of certain behaviors, but also of mediating other behaviors through means other than geographically localized centers. Indeed, since the discovery of the neurotransmitters (chemical substances that appear to play an important role in brain function), there appears to have been a marked change in how localization of function is viewed. To some authorities at least, localization is important only because the receptor sites for specific neurotransmitters appear to be selectively distributed in the brain. Neuroscientists now tend to think not only in terms of geographical localization but of neurochemical localization as well. With regard to clinical neuropsychology, however, the main point seems to be that there are both specific and nonspecific effects of brain damage. Evidence for this point of view has been presented most clearly by Teuber and his associates (Teuber, 1959) and by Satz (1966). The Teuber group was able to show that patients with penetrating brain wounds that produced very focal damage had symptoms that could be directly attributed to the lesion site, but they also had other symptoms that were shared by all patients studied, regardless of their specific lesion sites. For example, a patient with a posterior lesion might have an area of cortical blindness associated with the specific lesion site in the visual projection areas, but he or she might also have difficulties in performing complex nonvisual tasks such as placing blocks into a formboard while blindfolded. Most of Teuber's patients had difficulty with formboard type and other complex tasks regardless of specific lesion site. In clinical settings we may see brain damaged patients with this combination of specific and nonspecific symptoms as well as patients with only nonspecific symptoms. One of the difficulties with early localization theory is that investigators tended to be unaware of the problem of nonspecific symptoms and so only reported the often more dramatic specific symptoms.

An old principle of brain function in higher organisms that has held up well and that is commonly employed in clinical neuropsychology involves contralateral control; the right half of the brain controls the left side of the body and vice versa. Motor, auditory, and somatosensory fibers cross over at the base of the brain and thus control the contralateral side of the body. In the case of vision the crossover is atypical. The optic nerve enters a structure called the optic chiasm, at which point fibers coming from the outer or temporal halves of the retinas go to the ipsilateral side of the brain, while fibers from the inner or nasal halves cross over and go the contralateral cerebral hemispheres. However, the pattern is thought to be complete and all fibers coming from a particular hemiretina take the same course. In the case of somesthesis, hearing, and motor function, the crossover is not complete, but the majority of fibers do cross over. Thus, for example, most of the fibers from the right auditory nerve find their way to the left cerebral hemisphere. The contralateral control principle is important for clinical neuropsychology because it explains why patients with damage to one side of the brain only may become paralyzed on the opposite side of their body or may develop sensory disturbances on that side. We see this condition most commonly in individuals who have had strokes, but it is also seen in some patients who have head injuries or who have brain tumors.

Although aphasia, or impaired communicative abilities as a result of brain damage, was recognized before Broca (Benton & Joynt, 1960), it was not recognized that it was associated with destruction of a particular area of one side of the brain. Thus, the basic significance of Broca's discovery was not the discovery of aphasia, but of cerebral dominance. *Cerebral dominance* is the term that is commonly employed to denote the fact that the human brain has a hemisphere that is dominant for language and a nondominant hemisphere. In most people, the left hemisphere is dominant, and left hemisphere brain damage may lead to aphasia. However, some individuals have dominant right hemispheres, while others do not appear to have a dominant hemisphere. What was once viewed as a strong relationship between handedness and choice of dominant hemisphere has not held up in recent studies. But the answers to questions regarding why the left hemisphere is dominant in most people and why some people are right dominant or have no apparent dominance remain unknown. In any event, it seems clear that for individuals who sustain left hemisphere brain damage, aphasia is a common symptom, while aphasia is a rare consequence of damage to the right hemisphere. Following Broca's discovery, other neuroscientists discovered that just as the left hemisphere has specialized functions in the area of language, the right hemisphere also has its own specialized functions. These functions all seem to relate to nonverbal abilities such as visual-spatial skills, perception of complex visual configurations, and, to some extent, appreciation of nonverbal auditory stimuli such as music. Some investigators have conceptualized the problem in terms of sequential as opposed to simultaneous abilities. The left hemisphere is said to deal with material in a sequential, analytic manner, while the right hemisphere functions more as a detector of patterns or configurations (Dean, 1986). Thus, while patients with left hemisphere brain damage tend to have difficulty with language and other activities that involve sequencing, patients with right hemisphere brain damage have difficulties with such tasks as copying figures and producing constructions, because such tasks involve either perception or synthesis of patterns. In view of these findings regarding specialized functions of the right hemisphere, many neuropsychologists now prefer to use the expression *functional asymmetries of the cerebral hemispheres* rather than *cerebral dominance*. The former terminology suggests that one hemisphere does not really dominate or lead the other. Rather, each hemisphere has its own specialized functions.

Since the appearance of the last version of this chapter it would probably be fair to say that a third major methodology has been added to the study of brain function, in addition to animal and human lesion studies. It derives from neuroradiology, but has become far more advanced than the films of the skull that we looked at in the past, and even beyond the earlier development of the CT scan. It is now possible to directly observe numerous aspects of brain function in living individuals while they are engaged in some targeted activity. The two most widely used procedures to do this are positron emission tomography (PET) and functional magnetic resonance imaging (*f*MRI). Using different technologies, these procedures can detect changes when the brain is behaviorally activated. It has become possible to elicit very specific activity in relation to specific stimuli. Language tasks might activate areas in the language zone of the brain in the left temporal lobe. Conceptual activities, such as doing a sorting test, will activate portions of the frontal lobes. These methods are known as *on-line* procedures because the individual is having recordings made at the same time as the behavior is performed.

A second new development is magnetic resonance spectroscopy (MRS). MRS uses MRI technology, but instead of producing a visualization of brain structure or activity it generates a chemical profile of the brain. While the individual lies under the magnet, a surface coil placed around the head generates various chemical spectra that provide data about underlying tissue at a microbiological level. In the brain, the phosphorous spectrum produces information about brain metabolism based on the activity of phospholipids that exist in cell membranes. The hydrogen spectrum is most often used to determine the level of a substance called N-Acetyl Aspartate (NAA). NAA level has been found to be associated with integrity of neurons and thus provides an index of neuronal loss, deterioration, or maldevelopment. We therefore have a way of examining brain tissue at a molecular biological level in a living individual. PET, fMRI, and MRS have substantially advanced our capability of assessing brain function.

DESCRIPTION OF THE DISORDER

NEUROPATHOLOGICAL CONSIDERATIONS

As indicated previously, localization alone is not the sole determinant of the behavioral outcomes of brain damage. Although age, sociocultural, and personality factors make their contributions, perhaps the most important consideration is the type of brain damage. Some would argue that neuropsychological assessment is rarely the best method of determining type of brain damage because other techniques such as the CT scan, cerebral blood flow studies, and magnetic resonance imaging (MRI) are more adequate for that purpose. The point may be well taken, but the problem remains that different types of lesions produce different behavioral outcomes even when they involve precisely the same areas of the brain. Thus, the clinician should be aware that the assessment methodology he or she uses may not be the best one to meet some specific diagnostic goal, and it is often necessary to use a variety of methods coming from different disciplines to arrive at an adequate description of the patient's condition. In the present context, an adequate description generally involves identification of the kind of brain damage the patient has as well as its location. In order to point out the implications of this principle, it is necessary to provide a brief outline of the types of pathology that involve the brain and their physical and behavioral consequences.

The brain may incur many of the illnesses that afflict other organs and organ systems. It may be damaged by trauma or it may become infected. The brain can become cancerous or can lose adequate oxygen through occlusion of the blood vessels that supply it. The brain can be affected through acute or chronic exposure to toxins, such as carbon monoxide or other poisonous substances. Nutritional deficiencies can alter brain function just as they alter the function of other organs and organ systems. Aside from these general systemic and exogenous factors, there are diseases that more or less specifically have the central nervous system as their target. These conditions, generally known as degenerative and demyelinating diseases, include Huntington's disease, multiple sclerosis, Parkinson's disease, and a number of disorders associated with aging. From the point of view of neuropsychological considerations, it is useful to categorize the various disorders according to temporal and topographical parameters. Thus, certain neuropathological conditions are static and do not change substantially; others are slowly progressive; and some are rapidly progressive. With regard to topography, certain conditions tend to involve focal, localized disease, others multifocal lesions, and still others diffuse brain damage without specific localization. Another very important consideration has to do with morbidity and mortality. Some brain disorders are more or less reversible, some are static and do not produce marked change in the patient over lengthy periods of time, while some are rapidly or slowly progressive, producing increasing morbidity and eventually leading to death. Thus, some types of brain damage produce a stable condition with minimal changes, some types permit substantial recovery, while other types are in actuality terminal illnesses. It is therefore apparent that the kind of brain disorder the patient suffers from is a crucial clinical consideration in that it has major implications for treatment, management, and planning.

HEAD TRAUMA

Although the skull affords the brain a great deal of protection, severe blows to the head can produce temporary brain dysfunction or permanent brain injury. The temporary conditions, popularly known as concussions, are generally self-limiting and involve a period of confusion, dizziness, and perhaps double vision. However, there seems to be complete recovery. In these cases, the brain is not thought to be permanently damaged. More serious trauma is generally classified as closed or open head injury. In closed head injury, which is more common, the vault of the skull is not penetrated, but the impact of the blow crashes the brain against the skull and thus may create permanent structural damage. A commonly occurring type of closed head injury is the subdural hematoma in which a clot of blood forms under the dura: one of the protective layers on the external surface of the brain. These clots produce pressure on the brain that may be associated with clear-cut neurological symptoms. They may be removed surgically, but even when that is done there may be persistent residual symptoms of a localized nature, such as weakness of one side of the body. In the case of open head injury, the skull is penetrated by a missile of some kind. Open head injuries occur most commonly during wartime as a result of bullet wounds. They sometimes occur as a result of vehicular or industrial accidents, if some rapidly moving object penetrates the skull. Open head injuries are characterized by the destruction of brain tissue in a localized area. There are generally thought to be more remote effects as well, but usually, the most severe symptoms are likely to be associated with the track of the missile through the brain. Thus, an open head injury involving the left temporal lobe could produce an aphasia, while similar injury to the back of the head could produce a visual disturbance. A major neuropsychological difference between open and closed head injury is that while the open injury typically produces specific, localized symptoms, the closed head injury, with the possible exception of subdural hematoma, produces diffuse dysfunction without specific focal symptoms. In both cases, some of these symptoms may disappear with time, while others may persist.

There is generally a sequence of phases that applies to the course of both closed and open head injury. Often, the patient is initially unconscious and may remain that way for an extremely varying amount of time, ranging from minutes to weeks or months. After consciousness is regained, the patient generally goes through a so-called acute phase during which there may be confusion and disorientation.

Very often a condition called posttraumatic amnesia is present, in which the patient cannot recall events that immediately preceded the trauma up to the present time. Research has shown that the length of time spent unconscious as well as the length of posttraumatic amnesia are reasonably accurate prognostic signs; the longer either persists, the worse the prognosis. During this stage seizures are common, and treatment with anticonvulsant drugs is often necessary. When the patient emerges from this acute phase, the confusion diminishes, amnesia may persist but may not be severe as previously, the seizures may abate, and one gets a better picture of what the long-term outcome will be. The range of variability here is extremely wide, extending from patients remaining in persistent vegetative states to essentially complete recovery of function. In general, the residual difficulties of the head trauma patient, when they are significant, represent a combination of cognitive and physical symptoms. With regard to the latter, these patients are often more or less permanently confined to wheelchairs because of partial paralysis. Frequently there are sensory handicaps such as partial loss of vision or hearing.

Trauma to the head not only can do damage to the brain but to other parts of the head as well, such as the eyes and ears. Additionally, there is sometimes substantial disfigurement in the form of scars, some of which can be treated with cosmetic surgery. The cognitive residual symptoms of head trauma are extremely varied because they are associated with whether the injury was open head or closed head and if there was clear tissue destruction. Most often, patients with closed head injury have generalized intellectual deficits involving abstract reasoning ability, memory, and judgment. Sometimes, marked personality changes are noted, often having the characteristic of increased impulsiveness and exaggerated affective responsivity. Patients suffering from the residual of open head injury may have classic neuropsychological syndromes such as aphasia, visual-spatial disorders, and specific types of memory or perceptual disorders. In these cases, the symptoms tend to be strongly associated with the lesion site. For example, a patient with left hemisphere brain damage may have an impaired memory for verbal material such as names of objects, while the right hemisphere patient may have an impaired memory for nonverbal material such as pictures or musical compositions. In these cases there is said to be both modality (e.g., memory) and material (e.g., verbal stimuli) specificity. Head trauma is generally thought to be the most frequently seen type of brain damage in adolescents and young adults. It therefore generally occurs in a reasonably healthy brain. When the combination of a young person with a healthy brain exists, the prognosis for recovery is generally good if the wound itself is not devastating in terms of its extent or the area of the brain involved. For practical purposes, residual brain damage is a static condition that does not generate progressive changes for the worse. Although there is some research evidence (Walker et al., 1969) that following a long quiescent phase, head injured individuals may begin to deteriorate more rapidly than normal when they become elderly, and there is some evidence that brain injury may be a risk factor for Alzheimer's disease (Lye & Shores, 2000), head injured individuals may nevertheless have many years of productive functioning.

There has been a strong interest in outcome following mild head injury (Levin, Eisenberg, & Benton, 1989), as well as in the specific problems associated with head injury in children (Goethe & Levin, 1986). It has been frequently pointed out in recent years that trauma is the major cause of death in children, and head trauma among children is not uncommon. Most recently, a marked interest has developed in sports injuries (e.g., Schatz et al., 2006) with most studies assessing athletes shortly after sustaining a concussion and evaluating future outcome.

BRAIN TUMORS

Cancer of the brain is a complex area, particularly as cancer in general continues to be incompletely understood. However, the conventional distinction between malignant and nonmalignant tumors is a useful one for the brain as it is for other organs and organ systems. Thus, some brain tumors are destructive, rapidly progressive, and essentially untreatable. Generally, these tissue structures are known as intrinsic tumors because they directly infiltrate the parenchyma of the brain. The most common type is a class of tumor that is known as glioma. Other types of tumors grow on the external surface of the brain and produce symptoms through the exertion of pressure on brain tissue. This type of tumor is described as being extrinsic, and the most common type is called a meningioma. Aside from these two types, there are metastases in which tumors have spread to the brain from some other organ of the body, often the lung. The extrinsic tumors are often treatable surgically, but metastases are essentially untreatable. The clinical symptoms of tumor include headache that frequently occurs at night or on awakening, seizures, and vomiting. There are often progressive cognitive changes, perhaps beginning with some degree of confusion and poor comprehension and progressing to severe dementia during the terminal stages. Because tumors often begin in quite localized areas of the brain, the symptoms associated with them tend to be dependent upon the particular location affected. For example, there is a large literature on frontal lobe tumors in which impairment of judgment, apathy, and general loss of the ability to regulate and modulate behavior are the major symptoms (Berg, 1998). As in the case of head injury, patients with left hemisphere tumors may develop aphasia, while patients with right hemisphere tumors may have visual-spatial disorders as their most prominent symptoms. The difference from head injury is that short of surgical intervention, the severity of symptoms increases with time, sometimes at a very slow and sometimes at a very rapid rate, depending upon the type of tumor. On rare occasions, the clinical psychologist or psychiatrist may see patients with tumors that affect particular structures in the brain, thereby generating characteristic syndromes. Among the most common of these are the cranial pharyngiomas, the pituitary adenomas, and the acoustic neuromas.

The cranial pharyngiomas are cystic growths that lie near the pituitary gland and often depress the optic chiasm so that the primary symptoms may involve delayed development in children and waning libido and amenorrhea in adults, in combination with weakening of vision. The pituitary adenomas are similar in location but the visual loss is often more prominent, frequently taking the form of what is called a bitemporal hemianopia: a loss of vision in both peripheral fields. The acoustic neuromas are tumors of the auditory nerve and thereby produce hearing loss as the earliest symptom. However, because the auditory nerve also has a vestibular component, there may be progressive unsteadiness of gait and dizziness. Clinicians may also see patients who have had surgically treated tumors. When these patients demonstrate residual neuropsychological symptoms, they look like patients with histories of open head injury. Perhaps that is because the brain lesion has, in a manner of speaking, been converted from a mass of abnormal tissue to a stable, nonmalignant wound. When neurosurgery has been successful, the changes are often rapid and very substantial. One is normally concerned about recurrence, and these patients should remain under continued medical care. However, successful surgical treatment may leave the patient with many years of productive life.

BRAIN MALFORMATIONS AND EARLY LIFE BRAIN DAMAGE

Perhaps nowhere in the organic mental disorders is the type of lesion issue as significant as it is in the case of the developmental disorders of brain function. The crux of the matter here is that there is a great deal of difference between destruction of a function already acquired and destruction of the brain mechanisms needed to acquire that function before it has been developed. Thus, the consequences of being born with an abnormal brain or acquiring brain damage during the early years of life may be quite different from the consequences of acquiring brain damage as an adult. On the positive side, the young brain generally has greater plasticity than the older brain, and it is somewhat easier for preserved structures to take over functions of impaired structures. On the negative side, however, when the brain mechanisms usually involved in the acquisition of some function are absent or impaired, that function is often not learned or not learned at a normal level. Although the relationship between age and consequences of brain damage remains an intensively researched area (Baron & Gioia, 1998; Johnson & Almi, 1978), for practical purposes it can be said that there is a population of individuals born with abnormal brain function, or who have sustained structural brain damage at or shortly after birth, who go on to have developmental histories of either generalized or specific cognitive subnormality. Those with generalized deficit, when it is sufficiently severe, are frequently described with a variety of terms such as minimal brain damage, learning disability, and attention deficit disorder.

One common subclass of this specific group consists of children who fail to learn to read normally despite adequate educational opportunity and average intelligence. These children are described as having dyslexia or developmental dyslexia. A related recently described rare condition is developmental amnesia, or global anterograde amnesia, in which there is exceptionally poor development of episodic memory in the context of otherwise normal cognitive abilities (Vargha-Khadem et al., 1997). With regard to neuropathological considerations, there are several types of brain disorder that may occur during the prenatal period. Some of them are developmental in nature in the sense that either the brain itself or the skull does not grow normally during gestation. When the skull is involved, the brain is damaged through the effects of pressure on it. Sometimes a genetic factor is present as is clearly the case with Down syndrome. Sometimes poor prenatal care is the responsible agent, the fetal alcohol syndrome perhaps being an extreme case of this condition. Sometimes an infection acquired during pregnancy, notably rubella (German measles), can produce severe mental retardation in the embryo. Probably most often, however, the causes of the developmental abnormality are unknown.

Damage to the brain can also occur as the result of a traumatic birth. Such conditions as cerebral anoxia, infection, and brain dysfunction associated with such ongoing conditions as malnutrition or exposure to toxic substances are the major agents. Children have strokes and brain tumors, but they are quite rare. In essence, brain damage can occur in the very young before, during, and after birth. Although the neuropathological distinction among the various disorders is quite important, the life span development of individuals from all three categories shares some common characteristics. And retrospectively, it is often difficult to identify the responsible agent in the school-age child or adult. Thus, it is sometimes useful to think in terms of some general concept, such as perinatal or early life brain damage, rather than to attempt to specifically relate a particular developmental course or pattern of functioning to a single entity.

Early life brain damage is usually a static condition in the sense that the lesion itself does not change, but it may have varying consequences throughout life. During the preschool years, the child may not achieve the generally accepted landmarks such as walking and talking at the average times. In school, these children often do not do well academically and may be either poor learners in general or have specific disabilities in such areas as reading, arithmetic, or visual-spatial skills. These academic difficulties may be accompanied by some form of behavior disorder, often manifested in the form of hyperactivity or diminished attentional capacity. During adulthood, it is often found that these individuals do not make satisfactory vocational adjustments, and many researchers now feel that they are particularly vulnerable to certain psychiatric disorders, notably alcoholism (Tarter, 1976) or schizophrenia (Green, 1998).

We would note that, although this volume does not address itself to child psychopathology, there are several disorders that would now be classed as organic mental, or neurobehavioral, disorders that begin during childhood, but persist into adulthood. There is growing evidence (Katz, Goldstein, & Beers, 2001; Spreen, 1987) that learning disability frequently persists into adulthood. Autism, which is now generally viewed as a neurobehavioral disorder (Minshew, 1996) also generally persists into adulthood. A study (Rumsey & Hamburger, 1988) that followed up some of Kanner's (1943) original cases demonstrated the persistence of neuropsychological deficit in these autistic adults. Since the pioneering study of Rumsey and Hamburger there has been a rapidly growing literature concerning neuropsychological aspects of autism using a wide variety of tests, experimental procedures, and theoretical frameworks (Katz, Goldstein, & Beers, 2001).

Diseases of the Circulatory System

Current thinking about the significance of vascular disease has changed from the time when it was felt that cerebral arteriosclerosis or "hardening of the arteries" was the major cause of generalized brain dysfunction in the middle-aged and elderly. Although this condition is much less common than was once thought, the status of the heart and the blood vessels are significantly related to the intactness of brain function. Basically, the brain requires oxygen to function and oxygen is distributed to the brain through the cerebral blood vessels. When these vessels become occluded, circulation is compromised and brain function is correspondingly impaired. This impairment occurs in a number of ways, perhaps the most serious and abrupt way being stroke. A stroke is a sudden total blockage of a cerebral artery caused by blood clot or a hemorrhage. The clot may be a thrombosis formed out of atherosclerotic plaque at branches and curves in the cerebral arteries or an embolism, which is a fragment that has broken away from a thrombus in the heart that has migrated to the brain. Cerebral hemorrhages are generally fatal, but survival from thrombosis or embolism is not at all uncommon. Following a period of stupor or unconsciousness, the most common and apparent postacute symptom is hemiplegia: paralysis of one side of the body. There is also a milder form of stroke known as a transient ischemic attack (TIA), which is basically a temporary, self-reversing stroke that does not produce severe syndromes, or may be essentially asymptomatic.

A somewhat different picture emerges in another cerebral vascular disorder called vascular dementia in APA (1994). As opposed to the abruptly rapid onset seen in stroke, vascular dementia is a progressive condition based on a history of small strokes associated with hypertension. Patients with vascular dementia experience a stepwise deterioration of function, with each small stroke making the dementia worse in some way. There are parallels between vascular dementia and the older concept of cerebral arteriosclerosis in that they both relate to the role of generalized cerebral vascular disease in producing progressive brain dysfunction. However, vascular dementia is actually a much more precisely defined syndrome that, while not rare, is not extremely common either. Many of the patients that used to be diagnosed as having cerebral arteriosclerosis would now be diagnosed as having one of the degenerative diseases associated with the presenile or senile period of life. Other relatively common cerebrovascular disorders are associated with aneurysms and other vascular malformations in the brain. An aneurysm is an area of weak structure in a blood vessel that may not produce symptoms until it balloons out to the extent that it creates pressure effects or it ruptures. A ruptured aneurysm is an extremely serious medical condition in that it may lead to sudden death. However, surgical intervention in which the aneurysm is ligated is often effective.

Arteriovenous malformations are congenitally acquired tangles of blood vessels. They may be asymptomatic for many years, but can eventually rupture and hemorrhage. They may appear anywhere in the brain, but commonly they occur in the posterior half. The symptoms produced, when they occur, may include headache and neurological signs associated with the particular site.

There are major neuropsychological differences between the individual with a focal vascular lesion, most commonly associated with stroke, and the patient with generalized vascular disease such as vascular dementia. The stroke patient is not only characterized by the hemiplegia or hemiparesis, but sometimes by an area of blindness in the right or left visual fields and commonly by a pattern of behavioral deficits associated with the hemisphere of the brain affected and the locus within that hemisphere. If the stroke involves a blood vessel in the left hemisphere, the patient will be paralyzed or weak on the right side of the body, the area of blindness, if present, will involve the right field of vision and there will frequently be an aphasia. Right hemisphere strokes may produce left-sided weakness or paralysis and left visual fields defects but no aphasia. Instead, a variety of phenomena may occur. The patient may acquire a severe difficulty with spatial relations; a condition known as constructional apraxia. The ability to recognize faces or to appreciate music may be affected. A phenomenon known as unilateral neglect may develop in which the patient does not attend to stimuli in the left visual field, although it may be demonstrated that basic vision is intact. Sometimes affective changes occur in which the patient denies that he or she is ill, and may even develop euphoria. In contrast with this specific, localized symptom picture seen in the stroke patient, the individual with vascular dementia or other generalized cerebral vascular disease has quite a different set of symptoms. Generally, there is no unilateral paralysis, no visual field deficit, no gross aphasia, and none of the symptoms characteristic of patients with right hemisphere strokes. Rather there is a picture of generalized intellectual, and to some extent physical, deterioration. If weakness is present, it is likely to affect both sides of the body, and typically there is general diminution of intellectual functions including memory, abstraction ability, problem solving ability, and speed of thought and action. In the case of the patient with vascular dementia, there may be localizing signs, but there would tend to be several of them, and they would not point to a single lesion in one specific site.

The more common forms of cerebral vascular disease are generally not seen until at least middle age, and for the most part are diseases of the elderly. Clinically significant cerebral vascular disease is often associated with a history of generalized cardiovascular or other systemic diseases, notably hypertension and diabetes. There are some genetic or metabolic conditions that promote greater production of atheromatous material than is normal, and some people are born with arteriovenous malformations or aneurysms, placing them at higher than usual risk for serious cerebral vascular disease. When a stroke is seen in a young adult it is usually because of an aneurysm or other vascular malformation. Most authorities agree that stroke is basically caused by atherosclerosis, and so genetic and acquired conditions that promote atherosclerotic changes in blood vessels generate risk of stroke. With modern medical treatment there is a good deal of recovery from stroke with substantial restoration of function. However, in the case of the diffuse disorders, there is really no concept of recovery because they tend to be slowly progressive. The major hope is to minimize the risk of future strokes, through such means as controlling blood pressure and weight.

An area of particular interest is the long-term effects of hypertension on cerebral function, as well as the long-term effects of antihypertensive medication. Reviews (Elias & Streeten, 1980; King & Miller, 1990) have demonstrated that hypertension in itself, as well as antihypertensive medication, can impair cognitive function, but there are no definite conclusions in this area as yet, with studies reporting mixed as well as benign outcomes associated with prudent use of the newer antihypertensive medications (Goldstein, 1986).

DEGENERATIVE AND DEMYELINATING DISEASES

The degenerative and demyelinating diseases constitute a variety of disorders that have a number of characteristics in common, but that are also widely different from each other in many ways. What they have in common is that they specifically attack the central nervous system, they are slowly progressive and incurable, and while they are not all hereditary diseases, they appear to stem from some often unknown but endogenous defect in physiology. Certain diseases, once thought to be degenerative, have been found not to be so, or are thought not to be so at present. For example, certain dementias have been shown to be caused by a so-called slow virus, while multiple sclerosis, the major demyelinating disease, is strongly suspected of having a viral etiology. Thus, in these two examples, the classification would change from degenerative to infectious disease.

The term *degenerative disease* means that for some unknown reason the brain or the entire central nervous system gradually wastes away. In some cases this wasting, or atrophy, resembles what happens to the nervous system in very old people, but substantially earlier than the senile period, perhaps as early as the late forties. The previously made distinction between presenile and senile dementia is not currently used much, apparently based upon the understanding that it is the same disease, most often Alzheimer's disease, but the research literature continues to be controversial, showing some important neurobiological differences between those who demonstrate presence of the disease before or during late life. *DSM-IV* does make a distinction within dementia of the Alzheimer's type between early onset (65 years or under) and late onset (after age 65) subtypes. Senile dementia is generally diagnosed in elderly individuals when the degree of cognitive deficit is substantially greater than one would expect with normal aging. In other words, not all old people become significantly demented before death. Most of those who do, but do not have another identifiable disease of the central nervous system, are generally thought to have Alzheimer's disease. Indeed, Alzheimer's disease is now thought to account for more senile dementia than does vascular disease.

There is another disorder related to Alzheimer's disease call Pick's disease, but it is difficult to distinguish from Alzheimer's disease in living individuals. The distinction only becomes apparent on autopsy, as the neuropathological changes in the brain are different. Within psychiatry, there is no longer an attempt to differentiate clinically among Alzheimer's, Pick's, and some rarer degenerative diseases. *DSM-IV* describes them with the single term *dementia of the Alzheimer's type*. However, efforts have been made to refine the diagnosis of dementia.

Another frequently occurring degenerative disease found in younger adults is called Huntington's chorea or Huntington's disease. The disease is characterized by progressive intellectual deterioration and a motor disorder involving gait disturbance and involuntary jerky, spasmodic movements. It has definitely been established as a hereditary disorder, and there is a 50% chance of acquiring the disease if born to a carrier of the gene for it. Symptoms may begin to appear during the second or third decade, and survival from the time of appearance of symptoms is generally about eight years. The intellectual deterioration is characterized by progressively profound impairment of memory with most cognitive functions eventually becoming involved. There is often a speech articulation difficulty because of the loss of control of the musculature involved in speech.

Although much is still not known about the degenerative disorders, much has been discovered in recent years. The major discovery was that Alzheimer's and Huntington's disease are apparently based on neurochemical deficiencies. In the case of Alzheimer's disease, the deficiency is thought to be primarily the group of substances related to choline, one of the neurotransmitters. The disease process itself is characterized by progressive death of the choline neurons; the cells that serve as receptor sites for cholinergic agents. Huntington's disease is more neurochemically complex because three neurotransmitters are involved: choline, GABA, and substance P. The reasons for these neurochemical deficiency states remain unknown, but the states themselves have been described and treatment efforts have been initiated based on this information. For example, some Alzheimer's patients have been given choline or lecithin, a substance related to choline, and other newer drugs such as Aricept, in the hope of slowing down the progression of the illness. As indicated previously, the genetic marker for Huntington's disease has been discovered.

Most recently, an extensive literature has developed around progressive dementias that resemble but are pathologically or behaviorally different from Alzheimer's disease. One group is now known as prion diseases. Prions are proteins that are infectious and can transmit biological information. They are apparently associated with Creutzfeldt-Jakob disease, a progressive dementia. A condition has been identified known as frontotemporal dementia in which there is specific impairment of social judgment, decision making, and particular language and memory skills. There is a related condition called semantic dementia in which there is specific impairment of semantic memory. Lewy body dementia is a condition that has a different pathology from Alzheimer's disease, being associated more with Parkinson's disease (McKeith et al., 2004). The major symptoms are variations in alertness, recurrent hallucinations, and Parkinsonian symptoms (e.g., tremor, rigidity). Lewy bodies are intraneuron inclusion bodies first identified in the substantia nigra of patients with Parkinson's disease.

Multiple sclerosis is the most common of the demyelinating diseases, and is described as such because its pathology involves progressive erosion of the myelin sheaths that surround fibers in the central nervous system. Both the brain and the spinal cord are involved in this illness. Nerve conduction takes place along the myelin sheaths and therefore cannot occur normally when these sheaths erode. This abnormality leads to motor symptoms such as paralysis, tremor, and loss of coordination, but there are characteristic changes in vision if the optic nerve is involved, and in cognitive function. Obviously, cognitive skills that involve motor function tend to be more impaired than those that do not. Until its final stages, multiple sclerosis does not have nearly as devastating an effect on cognitive function as do the degenerative diseases. The crippling motor disorder may be the only apparent and significantly disabling symptom for many years. Less often, but not infrequently, progressive loss of vision also occurs. Multiple sclerosis acts much like an infectious disease, and some authorities feel that it is, in fact, caused by some unknown viral agent. Symptoms generally appear during young adulthood and may be rapidly or slowly progressive, leading some authorities to differentiate between acute and chronic multiple sclerosis. Individuals with this disorder may live long lives; there are sometimes lengthy periods during which no deterioration takes place. Sometimes temporary remission of particular symptoms is seen in the so-called relapsing-remitting form of multiple sclerosis. There have been extensive neuropsychological studies of multiple sclerosis (reviewed in Allen et al., 1998), and a particular interest in differences between relapsing-remitting and chronic-progressive forms of the disease (Heaton et al., 1985).

ALCOHOLISM

The term *alcoholism* in the context of central nervous system function involves not only the matter of excessive consumption of alcoholic beverages, but a complex set of considerations involving nutritional status, related disorders such as head trauma, physiological alterations associated with the combination of excessive alcohol consumption and malnutrition, and possible genetic factors. What is frequently observed in long-term chronic alcoholism is a pattern of deterioration of intellectual function not unlike what is seen in patients with degenerative dementia of the Alzheimer's type. However, it is not clear that the deteriorative process is specifically associated with alcohol consumption per se. Thus, while some clinicians use the term *alcoholic dementia*, this characterization lacks sufficient specificity, as it is rarely at all clear that the observed dementia is in fact solely a product of excessive use of alcohol. Looking at the matter in temporal perspective, there first of all may be a genetic propensity for the acquisition of alcoholism that might ultimately have implications for central nervous system function (Goodwin, 1979). Second, Tarter (1976) has suggested that there may be an association between having minimal brain damage or a hyperactivity syndrome as a child and the acquisition of alcoholism as an adult. These two considerations suggest the possibility that at least some individuals who eventually become alcoholics may not have completely normal brain function anteceding the development of alcoholism. Third, during the course of becoming chronically alcoholic, dietary habits tend to become poor and multiple head injuries may be sustained as a result of fights or accidents. As the combination of excessive alcohol abuse and poor nutrition progresses, major physiological changes may occur particularly in the liver, and to some extent in the pancreas and gastrointestinal system. Thus, the dementia seen in long-term alcoholic patients may well involve a combination of all of these factors in addition to the always present possibility of other neurological complications.

The majority of alcoholics who develop central nervous system complications manifest it in the form of general deterioration of intellectual abilities, but some develop specific syndromes. The most common of these is the Wernicke-Korsakoff syndrome. The Wernicke-Korsakoff disorder begins with the patient going into a confusional state accompanied by difficulty in walking and controlling eye movements, and by polyneuritis, a condition marked by pain or loss of sensation in the arms and legs. The latter symptoms may gradually disappear, but the confusional state may evolve into a permanent, severe amnesia. When this transition has taken place, the patient is generally described as having Korsakoff's syndrome or alcohol amnestic disorder, and is treated with large dosages of thiamine, because the etiology of the disorder appears to be a thiamine deficiency rather than a direct consequence of alcohol ingestion. There is now evidence (Blass & Gibson, 1977) that the thiamine deficiency must be accompanied by an inborn metabolic defect related to an enzyme that metabolizes thiamine. It should be noted that the amnesic and intellectual disorders found in chronic alcoholics are permanent and present even when the patient is not intoxicated. The acute effects of intoxication or withdrawal (e.g., delirium tremens [DTs]) are superimposed on these permanent conditions. These disorders are also progressive as long as the abuse of alcohol and malnutrition persist. Other than abstinence and improved nutrition, there is no specific treatment. Even thiamine treatment for the Korsakoff patient does not restore memory; it is used primarily to prevent additional brain damage.

It is probably fair to say that a major interest in recent years has been the genetics of alcoholism. Findings have been impressive thus far, and there is a growing, probably well justified, belief that the presence in an individual of a positive family history of alcoholism puts that individual at increased risk for becoming alcoholic, if exposed to alcoholic beverages. The research done has been broad-ranging, including extensive family adoption studies (Goodwin et al., 1973); neuropsychological studies of relatives (Schaeffer, Parsons & Yohman, 1984) and children of alcoholics (Tarter et al., 1984); psychophysiological studies, emphasizing brain event–related potentials in siblings (Steinhauer, Hill, & Zubin, 1987) and children (Begleiter et al.,

1984) of alcoholics; and laboratory genetic studies. In summary, there is an extensive effort being made to find biological markers of alcoholism (Hill, Steinhauer, & Zubin, 1987), and to determine the transmission of alcoholism in families. At this point in research, several susceptibility genes have been identified (Hill et al., 2004). One reasonable assumption is that alcoholism is a heterogeneous disorder and there may be both hereditary and nonhereditary forms of it (Cloninger, Bohman, & Sigvardsson, 1981).

TOXIC, INFECTIOUS, AND METABOLIC ILLNESSES

The brain may be poisoned by exogenous or endogenous agents or it may become infected. Sometimes these events occur with such severity that the person dies, but more often, the individual survives with a greater or lesser degree of neurological dysfunction. Beginning with the exogenous toxins, we have already discussed the major one: alcohol. However, excessive use of drugs such as bromides and barbiturates may produce at least temporary brain dysfunction. This temporary condition, called delirium in *DSM-IV,* is basically a loss of capacity to maintain attention with corresponding reduced awareness of the environment. Tremors and lethargy may be accompanying symptoms. Delirium is reversible in most cases, but may evolve into a permanent dementia or other neurological disorder.

In psychiatric settings a fairly frequently seen type of toxic disorder is carbon monoxide poisoning. This disorder and its treatment are quite complex because it usually occurs in an individual with a major mood or psychotic disorder who attempted to commit suicide by inhaling car fumes in a closed garage. The brain damage sustained during the episode may often be permanent, resulting in significant intellectual and physical dysfunction in addition to the previously existing psychiatric disorder. Other toxic substances that may affect central nervous system function include certain sedative and hypnotic drugs, plant poisons, heavy metals, and toxins produced by certain bacteria leading to such conditions as tetanus and botulism. The specific effects of these substances themselves, as well as of whether exposure is acute (as in the case of tetanus or arsenic poisoning) or chronic (as in the case of addiction to opiates and related drugs), are often crucial.

There is a very large number of brain disorders associated with inborn errors of metabolism. In some way a fault in metabolism produces a detrimental effect on the nervous system, generally beginning in early life. There are so many of these disorders that we will only mention two of the more well-known ones as illustrations. The first is phenylketonuria (PKU). PKU is an amino acid uria, a disorder that involves excessive excretion of an amino acid into the urine. It is genetic, and, if untreated, can produce mental retardation accompanied by poor psychomotor development and hyperactivity. The treatment involves a diet low in a substance called phenylalanine. The second disorder is Tay-Sach's disease. The enzyme abnormality here is a deficiency in a substance called hexasaminidase A, which is important for the metabolism of protein and polysaccharides. It is hereditary, occurs mainly in Jewish children, and is present from birth. The symptoms are initially poor motor development and progressive loss of vision, followed by dementia, with death usually occurring before age five. These two examples illustrate similarity in process, which is basically an inherited enzyme deficiency, but variability in outcome. PKU is treatable, with a relatively favorable prognosis, while Tay-Sachs is a rapidly progressive, incurable terminal illness.

Bacterial infections of the brain are generally associated with epidemics, but sometimes are seen when there are no epidemics at large. They are generally referred to as encephalitis, when the brain itself is infected, or meningitis, when the infection is in the membranous tissue that lines the brain, known as the meninges. Infections, of course, are produced by microorganisms that invade tissue and produce inflammation. During the acute phase of the bacterial infections, the patient may be quite ill and survival is an important issue. Headaches, fever, and a stiff neck are major symptoms. There may be delirium, confusion, and alterations in state of consciousness ranging from drowsiness, through excessive sleeping, to coma. Some forms of encephalitis were popularly known as "sleeping sickness." Following the acute phase of bacterial infection, the patient may be left with residual neurological and neuropsychological disabilities and personality changes. Sometimes infections are local, and the patient is left with neurological deficits that correspond with the lesion site. The irritability, restlessness, and aggressiveness of postencephalitic children are mentioned in the literature. Jervis (1959) described them as overactive, restless, impulsive, assaultive, and wantonly destructive.

Neurosyphylis is another type of infection that has a relatively unique course. Most interesting, aside from the progressive dementia that characterizes this disorder, there are major personality changes involving the acquisition of delusions and a tendency toward uncritical self-aggrandizement. Although neurosyphilis or general paresis played a major role in the development of psychiatry, it is now a relatively rare disease and is seldom seen in clinical practice. Similarly, the related neurosyphilitic symptoms, such as tabes dorsalis and syphilitic deafness, are also rarely seen. The incidence and perhaps the interest in the bacterial infections and neurosyphilis have diminished, but interest in viral infections has increased substantially during recent years. There are perhaps four reasons for this phenomenon: Jonas Salk's discovery that poliomyelitis was caused by virus and could be prevented by vaccination; the recent increase in the incidence of Herpes simplex, which is a viral disorder; the appearance of AIDS; and the discovery of the "slow viruses." The latter two reasons are probably of greatest interest in the present context. With regard to the slow viruses, it has been discovered that certain viruses have a long incubation period and may cause chronic degenerative disease, resembling Alzheimer's disease in many ways. Thus, some forms of dementia may be produced by a transmittable agent. One of these dementias appears to be a disease known as kuru, and another is known as Creutzfeldt-Jakab disease. Recently, there has been an outbreak of a related disorder called "mad cow disease" or bovine spongiform encephalopathy (Balter, 2001). The importance of the finding is that the discovery of infection as the cause of disease opens the possibility of the development of preventive treatment in the form of a vaccine. AIDS dementia is another form of viral encephalopathy. It is a consequence of human immunovirus infection and apparently represents an illness that has not appeared on the planet previously. It has been characterized as a progressive "subcortical dementia" of the type seen in patients with Huntington's disease and other neurological disorders in which the major neuropathology is in the subcortex. The syndrome itself has not been completely described, but there is substantial evidence of neuropsychological abnormalities. The first papers in this area appeared circa 1987, with the best known study being that of Grant et al. (1987). A review is contained in Bornstein,

Nasrallah, Para, and Whitacre (1993) and a recent update has been provided by Heaton (2006).

EPILEPSY

Despite the usual manner in which this condition is described, epilepsy is really a symptom of many diseases and not really a disease in itself. Patients are generally diagnosed as "epileptics" when seizures are the major or only presenting symptoms and the cause cannot be determined. However, seizures are commonly associated with diagnosable disorders such as brain tumors, alcoholism, or head trauma. Furthermore, the view that epilepsy means that the patient has "fits" or episodes of falling and engaging in uncontrolled, spasmodic movements is also not completely accurate. These fits or convulsions do represent one form of epilepsy, but there are other forms as well. There have been several attempts made to classify epilepsy into subtypes, and we will mention only the most recent one generally accepted by neurologists (Gastaut, 1970).

The major distinction made is between generalized and partial seizures. In the case of the generalized seizures there is a bilaterally symmetrical abnormality of brain function, with one of two things generally happening. One is a massive convulsion with a sequence of spasmodic movements and jerking, while the other is a brief abrupt loss of consciousness with little in the way of abnormal motor activity. There may be some lip smacking or involuntary movements of the eyelids. The former type used to be called a grand mal seizure, while the latter type was called a petit mal seizure or absence. The partial seizures may have what is described as a simple or complex symptomatology. In the simple case, the seizure may be confined to a single limb and may involve either motor or sensory function. When motor function is involved, there is often a turning movement of the head, accompanied by contractions of the trunk and limbs. There is a relatively rare form of this disorder called a Jacksonian motor seizure, in which there is a spread of the spasmodic movements from the original site to the entire side of the body. The phenomenon is referred to as a march. In the case of sensory seizures, the epileptic activity may consist of a variety of sensory disorders such as sudden numbness, "pins and needles" feeling, seeing spits of light, or even a buzzing or roaring in the ears.

The complex partial seizures involve confused but purposeful-appearing behavior followed by amnesia for the episode. In this condition, sometimes known as temporal lobe or psychomotor epilepsy, the patient may walk around in a daze, engage in inappropriate behavior, or have visual or auditory hallucinations. From this description, it is clear that not all seizures involve massive motor convulsions. What all of these phenomena have in common is that they are based on a sudden, abrupt alteration of brain function. The alteration is produced by an excessive, disorganized discharge of neurons. Thus, if one were looking at an epileptic individual's brain waves on an electroencephalograph (EEG), if a seizure occurred, there would be a sudden and dramatic alteration in the characteristics of the EEG. The presence and particular pattern of these alterations are often used to identify and diagnose various forms of epilepsy.

The question of whether there is an association between epilepsy and intellectual impairment is a complex one. According to Klove and Matthews (1974), individuals having complex partial (temporal lobe) seizures demonstrate little in the way of intellectual impairment. However, individuals with generalized seizures of unknown etiology that appear early in life are likely to have significant intellectual deficit. The matter is also complicated by the cause of the seizure. If an individual has seizures related to a brain tumor, it is likely that the neuropsychological deficits generally associated with the lesion sites involved can be expected to appear as well as the seizures. The question of intellectual deficit seems to arise primarily in the case of individuals who are just epileptic and have no other apparent neurological signs of symptoms. This condition is known as recurrent seizures of unknown cause or as idiopathic epilepsy. Our tentative answer to the question appears to be that there is a higher probability of significant intellectual deficit when the disorder involves generalized seizures and appears early in life.

The mental health practitioner should be aware that, although epilepsy is an eminently treatable disorder through the use of a variety of anticonvulsant medications, the epileptic patient might have many difficulties of various types. There still appears to be some degree of social stigma attached to the disorder, either in the form of superstitious beliefs or the inaccurate stereotype that epileptics tend to be violent or impulsive people. More realistically, epileptics do have difficulties with such matters as obtaining driver's licenses or insurance coverage that allows them to work around potentially hazardous equipment. It is possible that during a complex partial seizure an individual can perform an antisocial act over which he or she honestly has no control and cannot remember. Epileptic seizures may be symptoms of some life-threatening illness. Children with petit mal epilepsy may have school difficulties because of their momentary lapses of consciousness. Individuals with motor seizures may injure their heads during the seizure and produce additional brain dysfunction through trauma. Thus, the epileptic may have many problems in living that are not experienced by the nonepileptic, and frequently may be assisted through an understanding of the nature of the condition, and counseling and support in coping with it.

Myslobodsky and Mirsky (1988) have edited an extensive work on petit mal epilepsy that covers its genetic, neurophysiological, neuropsychological, metabolic, and electrophysiological aspects. There is a growing interest in psychosocial aspects of epilepsy. Having seizures clearly produces an impact on one's environment, and people in the environment may maintain the older superstitions and false beliefs about epilepsy. Furthermore, modifications of behavior in epileptics may be largely biologically determined because of the cerebral dysfunction associated with the disorder. Dodrill (1986) has reviewed the extensive literature on psychosocial consequences of epilepsy, providing a useful outline of the types of psychosocial difficulties epileptics commonly experience, the relationship between psychosocial and neuropsychological function, and treatment-related issues.

SOME COMMON SYNDROMES

In this section we will provide descriptions of the more commonly occurring disorders associated with structural brain damage. It is clear that what is common in one setting may be rare in another. Thus, we will focus on what is common in an adult neuropsychiatric setting. The neuropsychological syndromes found in childhood are often quite different from what is seen in adults and deserve separate treatment. Furthermore, the emphasis will be placed on chronic rather than acute syndromes because, with relatively rare exceptions, the psychologist and psychiatrist encounter the former type far more frequently than the latter. However, initially acute conditions such as stroke that evolve into chronic conditions will be dealt with in some detail.

Thus far, we have viewed matters from the standpoints of general concepts of brain function and of neuropathological processes. Now we will be looking at the behavioral manifestations of the interaction between various brain mechanisms and different types of pathology. It is useful to view these manifestations in the form of identified patterns of behavioral characteristics that might be described as neuropsychological syndromes. Although there are admittedly other ways of describing and classifying neuropsychological deficit, the syndrome approach has the advantage of providing rather graphic phenomenological descriptions of different kinds of brain damaged patients. However, it runs the risk of suggesting that every brain damaged patient can be classified as having some specific, identifiable syndrome—something that is not at all true. It is therefore important to keep in mind that we are discussing classic types of various disorders that are in fact seen in some actual patients. However, there are many brain damaged patients who do not have classic-type syndromes, their symptomatology reflecting an often complex combination of portions of several syndromes.

Heilman and Valenstein (1993), in the way in which they outlined their clinical neuropsychology text, have suggested a useful and workable classification of syndromes. There are first of all the communicative disorders that may be subdivided into aphasia and the specialized language or language-related disorders, including reading impairment (alexia), writing disorders (agraphia), and calculation disorders (acalculia). Second, there are the syndromes associated with some aspect of perception or motility. These include the perception of one's body (the body schema disturbances), the various visual-spatial disorders (which may involve perception, constructional abilities, or both), the gnostic disorders (impairment of visual, auditory, and tactile recognition), the neglect syndromes, and the disorders of skilled and purposeful movement, called apraxias. Third, there are the syndromes that primarily involve general intelligence and memory-dementia and the amnesic disorders. Associated with this latter type are the relatively unique syndromes associated with damage to the frontal lobes. These three general categories account for most of the syndromes seen in adults, and our discussion here will be limited to them.

The Communicative Disorders   In general, aphasia and related language disorders are associated with unilateral brain damage to the dominant hemisphere, which in most individuals is the left hemisphere. Most aphasias result from stroke, but it can be acquired on the basis of left hemisphere head trauma or from brain tumor. Whereas the definition has changed over the years, the most current one requires the presence of impairment of communicative ability associated with focal, structural brain damage. Thus, the term is not coextensive with all disorders of communicative ability and does not include, for example, the language disorders commonly seen in demented individuals with diffuse brain damage. The study of aphasia has in essence become a separate area of scientific inquiry, having its own literature and several theoretical frameworks. The term *aphasia* itself does not convey a great deal of clinically significant information because the various subtypes are quite different from each other. Numerous attempts have been made to classify the aphasias, and there is no universally accepted system.

Contemporary theory indicates that perhaps the most useful major distinction is between fluent and nonfluent aphasias. To many authorities, this distinction is more accurate than the previously more commonly made one between expressive and receptive aphasias. The problem is that aphasics with primarily expressive problems do not generally have normal language comprehension, and it is almost always true that aphasics with major speech comprehension disturbances do not express themselves normally. However, there are aphasics who talk fluently and aphasics whose speech is labored, very limited, and halting, if present at all in a meaningful sense. In the case of the former group, while speech is fluent, it is generally more or less incomprehensible because of a tendency to substitute incorrect words for correct ones; a condition known as verbal paraphasia. However, the primary disturbance in these patients involves profoundly impaired auditory comprehension. This combination of impaired comprehension and paraphasia is generally known as Wernicke's aphasia. The responsible lesion is generally in the superior gyrus of the left temporal lobe. In nonfluent aphasia, comprehension is generally somewhat better, but speech is accomplished with great difficulty, and is quite limited. This condition is generally known as Broca's aphasia, the responsible lesion being in the lower, posterior portion of the left frontal lobe (i.e., Broca's area).

There are several other types of aphasia that are relatively rare and will not be described here. However, it is important to point out that most aphasias are mixed, having components of the various pure types. Furthermore, the type of aphasia may change in the same patient particularly during the course of recovery. The disorders of reading, writing, and calculation may also be divided into subtypes. In the case of reading, our interest here is in the so-called acquired alexias in which an individual formerly able to read has lost that ability because of focal, structural brain damage. The ability to read letters, words, or sentences may be lost. Handwriting disturbances or agraphia might involve a disability in writing words from dictation or a basic disability in forming letters. Thus, some agraphic patients can write, but with omissions and distortions relative to what was dictated. However, some can no longer engage in the purposive movements needed to form letters. Calculation disturbances or acalculias are also of several types. The patient may lose the ability to read numbers, to calculate even if the numbers can be read, or to arrange numbers in a proper spatial sequence for calculation. The various syndromes associated with communicative disorders, while sometimes existing in pure forms, often merge together. For example, alexia is frequently associated with Broca's aphasia, and difficulty with handwriting is commonly seen in patients with Wernicke's aphasia. However, there is generally a pattern in which there is a clear primary disorder, such as impaired auditory comprehension, with other disorders, such as difficulty with reading or writing, occurring as associated defects. Sometimes rather unusual combinations occur, as in the case of the syndrome of alexia without agraphia. In this case, the patient can write but cannot read, often to the extent that he or she cannot read what was just written. Based upon recent research, we would add that academic deficits are frequently seen in adults that are not the product of brain damage acquired during adulthood, nor of inadequate educational opportunity. Rather, people with these deficits have developmentally based learning disabilities that they never outgrew. The view that learning disability is commonly outgrown has been rejected by most students of this area (Katz, Goldstein, & Beers, 2001).

Disorders of Perception and Motility   The disorders of perception can involve perception of one's body as well as perception of the external world. In the case of the external world, the disorder can involve some class of objects or some geographical location. The disorders of motility to be discussed here will not be primary losses of motor function as in the cases of paralysis or paresis, but losses in the area of the capacity to perform skilled, purposive acts. The set of impairments found in this area is called apraxia. There is also the borderline area in which the neuropsychological defect has to do with the coordination of a sense modality, usually vision, and purposive movement. These disorders are sometimes described as impairment of constructional or visual-spatial relations ability. In some patients the primary difficulty is perceptual, while in others it is mainly motoric. The body schema disturbances most commonly seen are of three types. The first has to do with the patient's inability to point to his or her own body parts on command. The syndrome is called autotopognosia, meaning lack of awareness of the surface of one's body. A more localized disorder of this type is finger agnosia in which, while identification of body parts is otherwise intact, the patient cannot identify the fingers of his or her own hands, or the hands of another person. Finger agnosia has been conceptualized as a partial dissolution of the body schema. The third type of body schema disturbance is right-left disorientation, in which the patient cannot identify body parts in regard to whether they are on the right or left side. For example, when the patient is asked to show the right hand, he or she may become confused or show the left hand. More commonly, however, a more complex command is required to elicit this deficit, such as asking the patient to place the left hand on the right shoulder. The traditional thinking about this disorder is that both finger agnosia and right-left disorientation are part of a syndrome, the responsible brain damage being in the region of the left angular gyrus. However, Benton (1985) has pointed out that the matter is more complicated than that, and the issue of localization involves the specific nature of these defects in terms of the underlying cognitive and perceptual processes affected.

The perceptual disorders in which the difficulty is in recognition of some class of external objects are called gnostic disorders or agnosias. These disorders may be classified with regard to modality and verbal or nonverbal content. Thus, one form of the disorder might involve visual perception of nonverbal stimuli, and would be called visual agnosia. By definition, an agnosia is present when primary function of the affected modality is intact, but the patient cannot recognize or identify the stimulus. For example, in visual agnosia, the patient can see but cannot recognize what he or she has seen. In order to assure oneself that visual agnosia is present, it should be determined that the patient can recognize and name the object in question when it is placed in his or her hand, so that it can be recognized by touch, or when it produces some characteristic sound, so that it can be recognized by audition. The brain lesions involved in the agnosias are generally in the association areas for the various perceptual modalities. Thus, visual agnosia is generally produced by damage to association areas in the occipital lobes. When language is involved, there is obviously a great deal of overlap between the agnosias and the aphasias. For example, visual-verbal agnosia can really be viewed as a form of alexia. In these cases, it is often important to determine through detailed testing whether the deficit is primarily a disturbance of perceptual recognition or a higher level conceptual disturbance involving language comprehension. There is a wide variety of gnostic disorders reported in the literature involving such phenomena as the inability to recognize faces, colors, or spoken works. However, they are relatively rare conditions, and when present may only persist during the acute phase of the illness. In general, agnosia has been described as "perception without meaning" and it is important to remember that it is quite a different phenomenon from what we usually think of as blindness or deafness.

Sometimes a perceptual disorder does not involve a class of objects but a portion of geographical space. The phenomenon itself is described by many terms; the most frequently used ones being neglect and inattention. It is seen most dramatically in vision, where the patient may neglect the entire right or left side of the visual world. It also occurs in the somatosensory modality, in which case the patient may neglect one side or the other of his or her body. Neglect can occur on either side, but it is more common on the left side, because it is generally associated with right hemisphere brain damage. In testing for neglect, it is often useful to employ the method of double stimulation, for example, in the form of simultaneous finger wiggles in the areas of the right and left visual fields. Typically, the patient may report seeing the wiggle in the right field but not in the left. Similarly, when the patient with neglect is touched lightly on the right and left hand at the same time, he or she may report feeling the touch in only one hand or the other. As in the case of the gnostic disorders, neglect is defined in terms of the assumption of intactness of the primary sensory modalities. Thus, the patient with visual neglect should have otherwise normal vision in the neglected half field, while the patient with tactile neglect should have normal somatosensory function. Clinically, neglect may be a symptom of some acute process and should diminish in severity or disappear as the neuropathological condition stabilizes. For example, visual neglect of the left field is often seen in individuals who have recently sustained right hemisphere strokes, but can be expected to disappear as the patient recovers.

The apraxias constitute a group of syndromes in which the basic deficit involves impairment of purposive movement occurring in the absence of paralysis, weakness, or unsteadiness. For some time, the distinction has been made among three major types of apraxia: ideomotor, limb-kinetic, and ideational. In ideomotor apraxia, the patient has difficulty in performing a movement to verbal command. In the case of limb-kinetic apraxia, movement is clumsy when performed on command or when the patient is asked to imitate a movement. In ideational apraxia, the difficulty is with organizing the correct motor sequences in response to language. In other words, it may be viewed as a disability in regard to carrying out a series of acts. In addition there are facial apraxias in which the patient cannot carry out facial movements to command. These four types are thought to involve different brain regions and different pathways. However, they are all generally conceptualized as a destruction or disconnection of motor engrams or traces that control skilled, purposive movement. Certain of the visual-spatial disorders are referred to as apraxias, such as constructional or dressing apraxia, but they are different in nature from the purer motor apraxias described above.

The basic difficulty the patient with a visual-spatial disorder has relates to comprehension of spatial relationships, and in most cases, coordination between visual perception and movement. In extreme cases, the patient may readily become disoriented and lose his or her way when going from one location to another. However, in most cases the difficulty appears to be at the cognitive level and may be examined by asking the patient to copy figures or solve jigsaw or block design type puzzles. Patients with primarily perceptual difficulties have problems in localizing points in space, judging direction, and maintaining geographical orientation, as tested by asking the patient to describe a route or use a map. Patients with constructional difficulties have problems with copying and block building. So-called dressing apraxia may be seen as a form of constructional disability in which the patient cannot deal effectively with the visual-spatial demands involved in suck tasks as buttoning clothing. Whereas visual-spatial disorders can arise from lesions found in most parts of the brain, they are most frequently seen, and seen with the greatest severity, in patients with right hemisphere brain damage. Generally, the area that will most consistently produce the severest deficit is the posterior portion of the right hemisphere. In general, while some patients show a dissociation between visual-spatial and visual-motor or constructional aspects of the syndrome of constructional apraxia, most patients have difficulties on both purely perceptual and constructional tasks.

Dementia   Dementia is probably the most common form of organic mental disorder. There are several types of dementia but they all involve usually slowly progressive deterioration of intellectual function. The deterioration is frequently patterned, with loss of memory generally being the first function to decline, and other abilities deteriorating at later stages of the illness. One major class of dementia consists of those disorders that arise during late life, either during late middle age or old age. *DSM-IV* makes this distinction with the terms *early onset* and *late onset* in place of the previously used terms *presenile* and *senile.* As the terms are used now, dementia may occur at any age. In children it is differentiated from mental retardation on the basis of the presence of deterioration from a formerly higher level. Dementia may result from head trauma or essentially any of the neuropathological conditions discussed previously. One common cause of dementia appears to be alcoholism and the nutritional disorders that typically accompany it. A specific type of dementia that generally appears before the presenile period is Huntington's disease. The term *dementia,* when defined in the broad way suggested here, is not particularly useful and does not really provide more information than do such terms as *organic brain syndrome* or *chronic brain syndrome.* However, when the term is used in a more specific way, it becomes possible to point out specific characteristics that may be described as syndromes. This specificity may be achieved by defining the dementias as those disorders in which for no exogenous reason, the brain begins to deteriorate and continues to do so until death. *DSM-IV* describes these conditions as dementia of the Alzheimer's type because the most common type of progressive degenerative dementia is Alzheimer's disease. As indicated earlier, a diagnostic method has recently become available to specifically diagnose Alzheimer's disease in the living patient. Its presence also becomes apparent on examination of the brain at autopsy. Clinically, the course of the illness generally begins with signs of impairment of memory for recent events, followed by deficits in judgment, visual-spatial skills, and language. The language deficit has become a matter of particular interest, perhaps because the communicative difficulties of dementia patients are becoming increasingly recognized. Generally, the language difficulty does not resemble aphasia, but can perhaps be best characterized as an impoverishment of speech, with word-finding difficulties and progressive inability to produce extended and comprehensible narrative speech. Basically the same finding was noted in the descriptive writing of Alzheimer's disease patients (Neils, Boller, Gerdeman, & Cole, 1989). The patients wrote shorter descriptive paragraphs than age-matched controls, and also made more handwriting errors of various types.

The end state of dementia is generalized, severe intellectual impairment involving all areas, with the patient sometimes surviving for various lengths of time in a persistent vegetative state. The progressive dementia seen in Huntington's disease also involves significant impairment of memory, with other abilities becoming gradually affected through the course of the illness. However, it differs from Alzheimer's disease in that it is accompanied by the choreic movements described earlier and by the fact that the age of onset is substantially earlier than is the case for Alzheimer's disease. Because of the chorea, there is also a difficulty in speech articulation frequently seen, which is not the case for Alzheimer's patients. A form of dementia that does not have an unknown etiology but that is slowly progressive is vascular dementia. This disorder is known to be associated with hypertension and a series of strokes, with the end result being substantial deterioration. However, the course of the deterioration is not thought to be as uniform as is the case in Alzheimer's disease, but rather is generally described as stepwise and patchy. The patient may remain relatively stable between strokes, and the symptomatology produced may be associated with the site of the strokes. It may be mentioned that whereas these distinctions between vascular and Alzheimer's type dementia are clearly described, in individual patients it is not always possible to make a definitive differential diagnosis. Even such sophisticated radiological methods as the CT scan and MRI do not always contribute to the diagnosis. During the bulk of the course of the illness, the dementia patient will typically appear as confused, possibly disoriented, and lacking in the ability to recall recent events. Speech may be very limited, and if fluent, likely to be incomprehensible. Thus, these patients do not have the specific syndromes of the type described previously surrounded by otherwise intact function. Instead, the deficit pattern tends to be global in nature with all functions more or less involved. Some investigators have attempted to identify syndromal subtypes, with some having more deficit in the area of abstraction and judgment, some in the area of memory, and some in regard to affect and personality changes. This typology has recently received support from studies delineating frontotemporal dementia, semantic dementia, and Lewy body dementia as separate entities, but most patients have difficulties with all three areas. Although there are some treatable dementias, particularly dementias associated with endocrine disorders or normal pressure hydrocephalus, there is no curative treatment for Alzheimer's type dementia. Current research offers the hope that pharmacological treatment may eventually be able to ameliorate the course of Alzheimer's disease, but thus far no such effective treatment is available.

As indicated, frontal lobe or frontotemporal dementia has been proposed as a separate disorder. It is only diagnosed when Alzheimer's disease has been ruled out, and the patient must have symptoms that can be characterized as forming a "frontal lobe syndrome" (Rosenstein, 1998). The generic term commonly used to characterize the behaviors associated with this syndrome is *executive dysfunction,* a concept originally introduced by Luria (1966). Executive function is progressively impaired, and personality changes involving either apathy and indifference or childishness and euphoria occur. Compared with patients with Alzheimer's disease, frontal dementia patients have greater impairment of executive function but relatively better memory and visuoconstructional abilities. The outstanding features all may be viewed as relating to impaired ability to control, regulate, and program behavior. This impairment is manifested in numerous ways, including poor abstraction ability, impaired judgment, apathy, and loss of impulse control.

Language is sometimes impaired, but in a rather unique way. Rather than having a formal language disorder, the patient loses the ability to control behavior through language. There is also often a difficulty with narrative speech that has been interpreted as a problem in forming the intention to speak or in formulating a plan for a narrative. Such terms as lack of insight or of the ability to produce goal-oriented behavior are used to describe the frontal lobe patient. In many cases, these activating, regulatory, and programming functions are so impaired that the outcome looks like a generalized dementia with implications for many forms of cognitive, perceptual, and motor activities. Frontal dementia may occur as a result of a number of processes such as head trauma, tumor, or stroke, but the syndrome produced is more or less the same.

Amnesia

Whereas some degree of impairment of memory is a part of many brain disorders, there are some conditions in which loss of memory is clearly the most outstanding deficit. When the loss of memory is particularly severe and persistent, and other cognitive and perceptual functions are relatively intact, the patient can be described as having an amnesic syndrome. Dementia patients are often amnesic, but their memory disturbance is embedded in significant generalized impairment of intellectual and communicative abilities. The amnesic patient generally has normal language and may be of average intelligence. As in the case of aphasia and several of the other disorders, there is more than one amnesic syndrome. The differences among them revolve around what the patient can and cannot remember. The structures in the brain that are particularly important for memory are the limbic system, especially the hippocampus, and certain brain stem structures, including the mammilary bodies and the dorsomedial nucleus of the thalamus. There are many systems described in the literature for distinguishing among types of amnesia and types of memory. With regard to the amnesias, perhaps the most basic distinction is between anterograde and retrograde amnesia. Anterograde amnesia involves the inability to form new memories from the time of the onset of the illness producing the amnesia, while retrograde amnesia refers to the inability to recall events that took place before the onset of the illness. This distinction dovetails with the distinction between recent and remote memory. It is also in some correspondence with the distinction made between short-term and long-term memory in the experimental literature. However, various theories define these terms somewhat differently and perhaps it is best to use the more purely descriptive terms *recent* and *remote* memory in describing the amnesic disorders. It then can be stated that the most commonly appearing amnesic disorders involve dramatic impairment of recent memory with relative sparing of remote memory. This sparing becomes greater as the events to be remembered become more remote. Thus, most amnesic patients can recall their early lives, but may totally forget what occurred during the last several hours. This distinction between recent and remote memory possibly aids in explaining why most amnesic patients maintain normal language function and average intelligence. In this respect, an amnesic disorder is not so much an obliteration of the past as it is an inability to learn new material.

Probably the most common type of relatively pure amnesic disorder is alcoholic Korsakoff's syndrome. These patients, while often maintaining average levels in a number of areas of cognitive function, demonstrate a dense amnesia for recent events with relatively well-preserved remote memory. Alcoholic Korsakoff's syndrome has been conceptualized by Butters and Cermak (1980) as an information-processing defect in which new material is encoded in a highly degraded manner leading to high susceptibility to interference. Butters and Cermak (1980), as well as numerous other investigators, have accomplished detailed experimental studies of alcoholic Korsakoff's patients in which the nature of their perceptual, memory, and learning difficulties has been described in detail. The results of this research aid in explaining numerous clinical phenomena noted in Korsakoff's patients, such as their capacity to perform learned behaviors without recall of when or if those behaviors were previously executed, or their tendency to confabulate or "fill in" for the events of the past day that they do not recall. It may be noted that while confabulation was once thought to be a cardinal symptom of Korsakoff's syndrome, it is only seen in some patients. Another type of amnesic disorder is seen when there is direct, focal damage to the temporal lobes, and most important, to the hippocampus. These temporal lobe or limbic system amnesias are less common than Korsakoff's syndrome, but have been well studied because of the light they shed on the neuropathology of memory. These patients share many of the characteristics of Korsakoff's patients but have a much more profound deficit in regard to basic consolidation and storage of new material. When Korsakoff's patients are sufficiently cued and given enough time, they can learn. Indeed, sometimes they can demonstrate normal recognition memory. However, patients with temporal lobe amnesias may find it almost impossible to learn new material under any circumstances.

In some cases, amnesic disorders are modality specific. If one distinguishes between verbal and nonverbal memory, the translation can be made from the distinction between language and nonverbal abilities associated with the specialized functions of each cerebral hemisphere. It has in fact been reported that patients with unilateral lesions involving the left temporal lobe may have memory deficits for verbal material only, while right temporal patients have corresponding deficits for nonverbal material. Thus, the left temporal patient may have difficulty with learning word lists, while the right temporal patient may have difficulty with geometric forms. In summary, whereas there are several amnesic syndromes, they all have in common the symptom of lack of ability to learn new material following the onset of the illness. Sometimes the symptom is modality specific, involving only verbal or nonverbal material, but more often than not it involves both modalities. There are several relatively pure types of amnesia, notably Korsakoff's syndrome, but memory difficulties are cardinal symptoms of many other brain disorders, notably the progressive dementias and certain disorders associated with infection. For example, people with Herpes encephalitis frequently have severely impaired memories, but they have other cognitive deficits as well.

ALTERNATIVE DESCRIPTIVE SYSTEMS

As has been indicated, not all clinicians or researchers associated with brain damaged patients have adopted the neuropsychologically oriented syndrome approach briefly described in the preceding sections. There are many reasons for the existence of these differing views, some of them methodological and some substantive in nature. The methodological issues largely revolve around the operations used by investigators to establish the existence of a syndrome. Critics suggest that syndromes may be established on the basis of overly subjective inferences as well as on incomplete examinations. The alternative method proposed is generally described as a dimensional approach in which rather than attempting to assign patients to categories, they are measured on a variety of neuropsychologically relevant dimensions such as intellectual function, language ability, and memory. Advocates of this approach are less concerned with determining whether the patient has a recognizable syndrome and more involved with profiling the patient along a number of continuous dimensions and relating that profile to underlying brain mechanisms. Rourke and Brown (1986) have clarified this issue in a full discussion of similarities and differences between behavioral neurology and clinical neuropsychology.

Using a dimensional philosophy, there is no need to develop a classification system except perhaps in terms of certain characteristic profiles. For purposes of providing an overview of the descriptive phenomenology of structural brain damage, however, the substantive matters probably are of more relevance. In essence, the disciplines of neurology, neuropsychology, and psychiatry have all developed descriptive classificatory systems that differ in many respects. We have already discussed the ways in which brain damage is described and classified by neurologists and neuropsychologists. However, the psychiatric descriptions are also quite important, because they point to problems not uncommonly seen in brain damaged patients that are not always clearly identifiable in the neurological and neuropsychological systems. There is an area of overlap in regard to dementia and the amnesias, but *DSM-III, DSM-III-R,* and *DSM-IV* contain a number of categories that are not clearly defined neurologically or neuropsychologically. However, there has been a major reorganization of the categorization of these disorders in *DSM-IV,* largely revolving around an abandonment of the term *organic.* In general, what was previously characterized as an *organic disorder,* such as *organic delusional syndrome,* is now characterized as a mental disorder due to a general medical condition. Thus, the closest diagnosis to "organic delusional syndrome" would be "psychotic disorder due to a general medical condition," and the diagnostic criteria are listed under the heading "Schizophrenia and Other Psychotic Disorders." Patients with this disorder have delusional beliefs or hallucinations while in a normal state of consciousness as the primary symptoms. It must be established that the delusions have an organic basis and the patient is not actually delusional because of a paranoid or schizophrenic disorder. The neurological basis for this syndrome is varied, and may involve drug abuse, right hemisphere brain damage, or in some cases Huntington's disease or other dementias. This diagnosis incorporates what was previously described as organic hallucinosis. Delusions or hallucinations are specified as the predominant symptom. Other mental disorders due to a general medical condition include disorders of mood, anxiety, sexual dysfunction, sleep, and catatonic disorder. *DSM-IV* also contains a category of personality change due to a general medical condition. Such changes may be classified as disinhibited, aggressive, paranoid, other, or combined. The personality changes noted often involve increased impulsiveness, emotional lability, or apathy. Perhaps these are really mainly frontal lobes syndromes, but the syndrome may also be seen in conjunction with temporal lobe epilepsy. In *DSM-IV,* the specific medical condition, if known, becomes a part of the diagnosis.

DSM-IV also classifies under the organic mental disorders substance-induced delirium and persisting dementia. Delirium may be associated with intoxication or withdrawal. If cognitive symptoms persist beyond the period of delirium, intoxication, or withdrawal, the diagnosis of substance-induced persisting dementia is made. The specific substance or substance combination is indicated if known. Thus, for example, one can make the diagnosis of alcohol-induced persisting dementia. Typically, delirium is an acute phenomenon and does not persist beyond a matter of days. However, delirium, notably when it is associated with alcohol abuse, may eventually evolve into permanent disorders in the form of persistent dementia. The behavioral correlates of delirium generally involve personality changes such as euphoria, agitation, anxiety, hallucinations, and depersonalization. The more permanent cognitive changes might include impairment of memory and inability to concentrate. Within the context of psychopathology, the commonality between these conditions and those related to more permanent, structural brain damage is that they all have an identified or presumed organic basis and are therefore distinct from the functional psychiatric disorders. The phraseology used throughout the organic mental disorders section of *DSM-IV* is, "There is evidence, from the history, physical examination, or laboratory findings of" the presence of the disorder under consideration; for example, "that the deficits are etiologically related to the persisting effects of substance abuse."

Psychiatrically based categorization can perhaps be most productively viewed as supplemental to the type of neuropsychological system used by Heilman and Valenstein (1993), rather than as an alternative to it. It plays a major role in describing the noncognitive kinds of symptomatology that are often associated with structural brain damage, particularly for those cases in which these personality, mood, and affective changes are the predominant symptoms. These considerations are of the utmost clinical importance because the failure to recognize the organic basis for some apparently functional symptom such as a personality change may lead to the initiation of totally inappropriate treatment or the failure to recognize a life-threatening physical illness.

Although alterations in brain function can give rise to symptoms that look like functional personality changes, the reverse can also occur. That is, a nonorganic personality change, notably the acquisition of a depression, can produce symptoms that look like they have been produced by alterations in brain function. The term generally applied to this situation is *pseudodementia,* and is most frequently seen in elderly people who become depressed. The concept of pseudodementia or depressive pseudodementia is not universally accepted, but it is not uncommon to find elderly patients diagnosed as demented when in fact the symptoms of dementia are actually produced by depression. The point is proven when the symptoms disappear or diminish substantially after the depression has run its course, or the patient is treated with antidepressant medication. Wells (1979, 1980) has pointed out that this differential diagnosis is a difficult one to make, and cannot be accomplished satisfactorily with the usual examinational, laboratory, and psychometric methods. He suggests that perhaps the most useful diagnostic criteria are clinical features. For example, patients with pseudodementia tend to complain about their cognitive losses, while patients with dementia tend not to complain. In a more recent formulation, Caine (1986) pointed to the many complexities of differential diagnosis in the elderly, referring in particular to the abundant evidence for neuropsychological deficits in younger depressed patients, and to the not uncommon coexistence of neurological and psychiatric impairments in the elderly.

In recent years there has been substantial rethinking about the concept of pseudodementia in the direction of characterizing it as a neurobiological disorder associated with demonstrable changes in brain structure. Clinicians have observed that depression may sometimes be the first indicator of Alzheimer's disease, and Nussbaum (1994), based on an extensive review of the literature, concluded that pseudodementia or late-life depression has a neurological substrate involving subcortical structures and the frontal lobes. He indicated that the probable pathology is leukoaraiosis, diminution in the density of white matter, which particularly involves the subcortex in this disorder. Leukoaraiosis is frequently seen in the MRIs of elderly depressed individuals.

EPIDEMIOLOGY

The epidemiology of delirium, dementia, and amnestic and other cognitive disorders varies with the underlying disorder, and so is unlike what is the case for most of the other diagnostic categories in *DSM-IV*. Here, we will only sample from those disorders in which epidemiological considerations are of particular interest. There are some exceptionally interesting and well-documented findings for multiple sclerosis, in which prevalence is directly related to latitude in which one resides; the farther from the equator, the higher the prevalence. Further study of this phenomenon has tended to implicate an environmental rather than an ethnic factor.

The epidemiology of head trauma has been extensively studied, with gender, age, and social class turning out to be important considerations. Head trauma has a higher incidence in males than in females (274 per 100,000 in males and 116 per 100,000 in females in one study) (Levin, Benton, & Grossman, 1982). It is related to age, with risk peaking between ages 15 and 24, and occurs more frequently in individuals from lower social classes. Alcohol is a major risk factor, but marital status, preexisting psychiatric disorder, and previous history of head injury have also been implicated. The major causes of head injury are motor vehicle accidents, falls, assaults, and recreational or work activities, with motor vehicle accidents clearly being the major cause (50% to 60%) (Smith, Barth, Diamond, & Giuliano, 1998).

The epidemiology of Huntington's disease has also been extensively studied. The disease is transmitted as an autosomal dominant trait, and the marker for the gene has been located on the short arm of chromosome 4 (Gusella et al., 1983). Prevalence estimates vary between 5 and 7 per 100,000. There are no known risk factors for acquiring the disorder, the only consideration being having a parent with the disease. If that is the case, the risk of acquiring the disorder is 50%. A test is now available to detect carriers of the defective gene, and its availability and usage may eventually reduce the prevalence of Huntington's disease.

There is a great interest in the epidemiology of Alzheimer's disease because the specific cause of the disease is not fully understood and prevention of exposure to risk factors for Alzheimer's disease and related disorders remains a possibility. General health status considerations do not appear to constitute risk factors, but some time ago there were beliefs that a transmissible infective agent existed, and that exposure to aluminum might be a risk factor. The aluminum hypothesis has largely been discarded. It now seems well established that an infective agent is responsible in the case of a rare form of dementia called Creutzfeldt-Jakob disease, but Alzheimer's disease is apparently not associated with infection. Recently, it has been reported that Creutzfeldt-Jakob disease resembles mad cow disease, and it is thought that a risk factor may be eating beef from cattle possibly exposed to mad cow disease. Recently, episodes of head trauma have been implicated as a possible risk factor for Alzheimer's disease (Lye & Shores, 2000). A reasonably solid genetic association involving chromosome 21 trisomy has been formed between what appears to be an inherited form of Alzheimer's disease and Down syndrome.

Much of the epidemiology of the organic mental disorders merges with general considerations regarding health status. Cardiovascular risk factors such as obesity and hypertension put one at greater than usual risk for stroke. Smoking is apparently a direct or indirect risk factor for several disorders that eventuate in brain dysfunction. The diagnosis of dementia associated with alcoholism is now relatively widely accepted, although it was controversial at one time. Alcohol most clearly, and perhaps several other abused substances, make for significant risk factors. In some cases, the crucial risk factor is provided not by the individual, but by the mother of the individual during pregnancy. Existence of fetal alcohol syndrome is well established, and the evidence for association between birth defects and other forms of substance abuse during pregnancy is increasing. Up until recently, risk of acquiring brain disease by infection had diminished substantially, but that situation has changed markedly with the appearance of human immunodeficiency virus, or HIV-1 infection, or acquired immunodeficiency syndrome (AIDS) dementia (Bornstein et al., 1993; Grant et al., 1987; van Gorp et al., 1989). It has become increasingly clear that AIDS is frequently transmitted to children during pregnancy or in association with breast feeding. New anti-infection medication is in actual use or in the process of going through extensive clinical trials, and there is great promise of effectiveness.

In summary, the prevalence and incidence of the organic mental disorders vary substantially, ranging from very rare to common diseases. Number of risk factors also varies, ranging from complete absence to a substantial number of them. The genetic and degenerative diseases, notably Huntington's and Alzheimer's disease, possess little in the way of risk factors, and there is not much that can be done to prevent their occurrence. The development of a test for risk of transmitting Huntington's disease has opened up the admittedly controversial and complex matter of genetic counseling. On the other hand, such disorders as dementia associated with alcoholism, and perhaps stroke, are preventable by good health maintenance. Indeed, the incidence of major stroke has declined in recent years.

COURSE AND PROGNOSIS

Course and prognosis for delirium, dementia, and amnestic and other cognitive disorders also vary with the underlying disorder. We will review the basic considerations here by first introducing some stages of acceleration and development. Then we will provide examples of disorders that have courses and prognoses consistent with various acceleration and developmental combinations. The acceleration stages are steady state, slow, moderate, and rapid. The developmental stages are the perinatal period, early childhood, late childhood and adolescence, early adulthood, middle age, and old age. The acceleration stages have to do with the rate of progression of the disorder, while the developmental stages characterize the age of onset of symptoms.

Mental retardation would be a disorder with a course involving onset during the perinatal period and steady-state acceleration. Mental retardation is one of those disorders in which there is little if any progression of neuropathology, but there may be a slowly progressive disability because of increasing environmental demands for cognitive abilities that the individual does not possess. Other developmental disorders, such as specific learning disability, do not have their onsets during the perinatal period but rather during early childhood when academic skills are first expected to be acquired.

In contrast to these disorders, stroke is typically characterized by onset during middle age. The acceleration of the disorder is first extremely rapid and then slows down, gradually reaching steady state. Thus, the stroke patient, at the time of the stroke, becomes seriously ill very rapidly, and this is followed by additional destructive processes in the brain. Assuming a good outcome, a gradual recovery period follows, and there is restoration of the brain to a relatively normal steady state. On the other hand, malignant brain tumors that also tend to appear during middle age progress rapidly and do not decelerate unless they are successfully surgically removed.

The progressive dementias generally appear during middle or old age and accelerate slowly or moderately. Huntington's disease generally progresses less rapidly than Alzheimer's disease, and so the Huntington's patient may live a long life with his or her symptoms. Head trauma is a disorder that may occur at any age, but once the acute phase of the disorder is over, the brain typically returns to a steady state. Thus, the head trauma patient, if recovery from the acute condition is satisfactory, may have a normal life expectancy with an often dramatic picture of deterioration immediately following the trauma until completion of resolution of the acute phase followed by substantial recovery. However, the degree of residual disability may vary widely.

Briefly summarizing these considerations from a developmental standpoint, the most common organic mental disorder associated with the perinatal period is mental retardation and its variants. During early childhood, the specific and pervasive developmental disorders begin to appear. Head trauma typically begins to appear during late childhood and adolescence, and incidence peaks during young adulthood. Systemic illnesses, notably cardiovascular, cardiopulmonary, and neoplastic disease, most commonly impact negatively on brain functions during middle age. Dementia associated with alcoholism also begins to appear during early middle age. The progressive degenerative dementias are largely associated with old age. With regard to acceleration, following the time period surrounding the acquisition of the disorder, developmental, vascular, and traumatic disorders tend to be relatively stable. Malignant tumors and certain infectious disorders may be rapidly progressive, and the degenerative disorders progress at a slow to moderate pace.

Although the connotation of the term *progressive* is progressively worse, not all of the organic mental disorders remain stable or get worse. There is recovery of certain disorders as a natural process or with the aid of treatment. In the case of head trauma, there is a rather typical history of initial unconsciousness, lapsing into coma for a varying length of time, awakening, a period of memory loss and incomplete orientation called posttraumatic amnesia, and resolution of the amnesia. Rehabilitation is often initiated as some point in this progression; sometimes beginning while the patient is still in a coma. The outcome of this combination of spontaneous recovery and rehabilitation is rarely, if ever, complete return to preinjury status, but often allows for a return to productive living in the community. Recovery from stroke is also common, and many poststroke patients can return to community living. Among the most important prognostic indicators for head trauma are length of time in coma and length of posttraumatic amnesia. General health status is a good predictor for stroke outcome and potential for recurrence. Patients who maintain poor cardiac status, hypertension, inappropriate dietary habits, or substance abuse are poorer candidates for recovery than are poststroke patients who do not have these difficulties. Some patients, particularly those with chronic, severe hypertension, may have multiple strokes, resolving into a vascular dementia.

There is increasing evidence that rehabilitation of head trauma may often have beneficial effects over and above spontaneous recovery. With regard to the developmental disorders, enormous efforts have been made in institutional and school settings to provide appropriate educational remediation for developmentally disabled children, often with some success. Effective treatment at the time of onset of acute disorder also has obvious implications for prognosis. Use of appropriate medications and management following trauma or stroke, and the feasibility and availability of neurosurgery, are major considerations. Tumors can be removed, aneurysms can be repaired, and increased pressure can be relieved by neurosurgeons. These interventions during the acute phase of a disorder are often mainly directed toward preservation of life, but also have important implications for the outcomes of surviving patients.

FAMILIAL AND GENETIC PATTERNS

The organic mental disorders are based on some diseases of known genetic origin, some diseases in which a genetic or familial component is suspected, and some that are clearly acquired disorders. It is well established that Huntington's disease and certain forms of mental retardation, notably Down syndrome, are genetic disorders. There appears to be evidence that there is a hereditary form of Alzheimer's disease, although the genetic contribution to Alzheimer's disease in general is not fully understood. A relatively rare genetic subtype has been identified. The great majority of individuals with this subtype have a gene on chromosome 14 called Apolipoprotein E that promotes development of the amyloid plaques that constitute the major brain pathology associated with the disease. Whether multiple sclerosis has a genetic component remains under investigation, although it is clearly not a hereditary disorder like Huntington's disease.

Of great recent interest is the role of genetics in the acquisition of alcoholism, and subsequently dementia associated with alcoholism or alcohol amnestic disorder. Evidence suggests that having an alcoholic parent places one at higher than average risk for developing alcoholism. The specific genetic factors are far from understood, but the association in families appears to be present. Whether having a family history of alcoholism increases the risk of acquiring dementia associated with alcoholism is not clear, but it has been shown that nonalcoholic sons of alcoholic fathers do more poorly on some cognitive tests than do matched controls. The matter is substantially clearer in the case of alcohol amnestic disorder of Korsakoff's syndrome. A widely cited study by Blass and Gibson (1977) showed the acquisition of Korsakoff's syndrome is dependent upon the existence of a genetic defect in a liver enzyme called transketolase in combination with a thiamine deficiency.

Other genetic and familial factors associated with the organic mental disorders relate largely to the genetics of underlying systemic disorders. Thus, the genetics of cancer might have some bearing on the likelihood of acquiring a brain tumor, while the genetics of the cardiovascular system might have some bearing on the risk for stroke. Disorders such as hypertension and diabetes appear to run in families and have varying incidences in different ethnic groups. Ethnic specificity is sometimes quite precise (but this is rare), as in the case of Tay-Sachs disease, a degenerative disorder of early childhood that is found almost exclusively in eastern European Jews.

SUMMARY

The diagnostic category of delirium, dementia, and amnestic and other cognitive disorders, formerly known as organic mental disorders, comprises a large number of conditions in which behavioral changes may be directly associated with some basis in altered brain function. Although the general diagnostic term *organic brain syndrome* has commonly been used to describe these conditions, the wide variability in the manifestations of brain dysfunction makes this term insufficiently precise in reference to clinical relevance, and it has been abandoned. It was pointed out that the variability is attributable to a number of factors, including the following considerations: (1) the location of the damage in the brain, (2) the neuropathological process producing the damage, (3) the length of time the brain damage has been present, (4) the age and health status of the individual at the time the damage is sustained, and (5) the individual's premorbid personality and level of function.

The neuropsychological approach to the conceptualization of the organic mental disorders has identified a number of behavioral parameters along which the manifestations of brain dysfunction can be described and classified. The most frequently considered dimensions are intellectual function, language, memory, visual-spatial skills, perceptual skills, and motor function. Some important concepts related to brain function and brain disorders include the principle of contralateral control of perceptual and motor functions and functional hemisphere asymmetries. In addition, studies of brain damaged patients have shown that particular structures in the brain mediate relatively discrete behaviors. Neurologists and neuropsychologists have identified a number of syndromes in such areas as language dysfunction, memory disorder, and general intellectual impairment. It was pointed out that there also are major variations in the courses of the organic mental disorders. Some are transient, leaving little or no residual; some are permanent but not progressive; others are either slowly or rapidly progressive. Whereas these disorders most profoundly and commonly involve impairment of cognitive, perceptual, and motor skills, sometimes personality changes of various types are the most prominent symptoms. More often than not, personality and affective changes appear in brain damaged patients along with their cognitive, perceptual, and motor disorders. Thus, a mood disorder or such symptoms as delusions and hallucinations may be sequelae of brain damage for various reasons.

During the years spanning the writing of the various editions of this chapter, there have been several major developments in the area of what was originally called the organic mental disorders. There has been the appearance of at least one new disorder, AIDS dementia; major discoveries in the genetics of Huntington's disease and alcoholism; enormous developments in the technology of neuroimaging; and a reconceptualization by psychiatry of the previously held distinction between functional and organic disorders. The work in neuroimaging is particularly exciting because it goes beyond obtaining more refined pictures of the brain and now allows us to observe the working of the brain during ongoing behavior through fMRI, and to examine the molecular biology of brain function through MRS.

REFERENCES

Allen, D. N., Sprenkel, D. G., Heyman, R A., Schramke, C. J., & Heffron, N. E. (1998). Evaluation of demyelinating and degenerative disorders. In G. Goldstein, P. D. Nussbaum & S. R. Beers (Eds.) *Neuropsychology*, New York: Plenum Press.

American Psychiatric Association. (1994). *Diagnostic and statistical manual of mental disorders* (4th ed.). Washington, DC: Author.

Baddeley, A. (1986). *Working memory.* New York: Oxford University Press.

Balter, M. (2001). Genes and disease: Immune gene linked to vCJD susceptibility. *Science, 294,* 1438–1439.

Baron, I. S., & Gioia, G. A. (1998). Neuropsychology of infants and young children. In G. Goldstein, P. D. Nussbaum, & S. R. Beers (Eds.), *Neuropsychology* (pp. 9–34). New York: Plenum Press.

Begleiter, H., Porjesz, B., Bihari, B., & Kissin, B. (1984). Event-related potentials in boys at high risk for alcoholism. *Science, 225,* 1493–1496.

Benton, A. (1985). Body schema disturbances: Finger agnosia and right-left disorientation. In K M. Heilman & E. Valenstein (Eds.), *Clinical neuropsychology* (2nd ed., pp. 115–129). New York: Oxford University Press.

Benton, A. L., & Joynt, R. J. (1960). Early descriptions of aphasia. *Archives of Neurology, 3,* 205–222.

Berg, R. A. (1998). Evaluation of neoplastic processes. In G. Goldstein, P. D. Nussbaum, & S. R. Beers (Eds.), *Neuropsychology* (pp. 248–269). New York: Plenum Press.

Blass, J. P., & Gibson, G. E. (1977). Abnormality of a thiamine-requiring enzyme in patients with Wernicke-Korsakoff syndrome. *The New England Journal of Medicine, 297,* 1367–1370.

Boring, E. G. (1950). *A history of experimental psychology* (2nd ed.). New York: Appleton-Century-Crofts.

Bornstein, R. A., Nasrallah, H. A., Para, M. F., & Whitacre, C. C. (1993). Neuropsychological performance in symptomatic and asymptomatic HIV infection. *AIDS, 7,* 519–524.

Broca, P. (1861). Perte de la parole. Ramollissement chronique et destruction partielle du lobe anterieur gauche du cerveau. [Loss of the word. Chronic softening and partial destruction of the left frontal lobe of the brain.] *Bulletin de la Société Anthropologique, 2,* 235–238.

Butters, N., & Cermak, L. S. (1980). *Alcoholic Korsakoff's syndrome.* New York: Academic Press.

Caine, E. D. (1986). The neuropsychology of depression: The pseudodementia syndrome. In I. Grant & K. M. Adams (Eds.), *Neuropsychological assessment of neuropsychiatric disorders* (pp. 221–243). New York: Oxford University Press.

Cloninger, C. R., Bohman, M., & Sigvardsson, S. (1981). Inheritance of alcohol abuse: Cross-fostering analysis of adopted men. *Archives of General Psychiatry, 38,* 861–868.

Dean, R. S. (1986). Lateralization of cerebral functions. In D. Wedding, A. M. Horton Jr., & J. Webster (Eds.), *The neuropsychology handbook: Behavioral and clinical perspectives* (pp. 80–102). New York: Springer.

Dodrill, C. B. (1986). Psychosocial consequences of epilepsy. In S. B. Filskov & T. J. Boll (Eds.), *Handbook of clinical neuropsychology: Vol. 2* (pp. 338–363). New York: Wiley.

Elias, M. F., & Streeten, D. H. P. (1980). *Hypertension and cognitive processes.* Mount Desert, ME: Beech Hill.

Fagan, A. M., Mintun, M. A., Mach, R. H., Lee, S. Y., Dence, C. S., Shah, A. R., Larossa, G. N., Spinner, M. L., Klunk, W. E., Mathis, C. A. Dekosky, S. T., Morris, J. C., Holtzman, D. M. (2005). Inverse relation between in vivo amyloid imaging load and cerebrospinal fluid Abets in humans. *Annals of Neurology, 59,* 512–519.

Flourens, M. J. P. (1824). Recherches experimentales sur les proprietes et les fonctions du systeme nerveux dans les animaux vertebres. [Experimental research on the properties and functions of the nervous system in vertebrate animals.] Paris: Crevot.

Gastaut, H. (1970). Clinical and electroencephalographical classification of epileptic seizures. *Epilepsia, 11,* 102–103.

Geschwind, N. (1965). Disconnection syndromes in animals and man. *Brain, 88,* 237–294.

Goethe, K. E., & Levin, H. S. (1986). Neuropsychological consequences of head injury in children. In G. Goldstein & R. E. Tarter (Eds.), *Advances in clinical neuropsychology: Vol. 3* (pp. 213–242). New York: Plenum Press.

Goldstein, G. (1986, February). *Neuropsychological effects of five antihypertensive agents.* Poster session presented at the annual meeting of the International Neuropsychological Society, Denver, CO.

Goldstein, G., Beers, S. R., Morrow, L. A., Shemansky, W. J., Steinhauer, S. R. (1996). A preliminary neuropsychological study of Persian Gulf veterans. *Journal of the International Neuropsychological Society, 2,* 368–371.

Goldstein, K. (1936). The significance of the frontal lobes for mental performance. *Journal of Neurology and Psychopathology, 17,* 27–40.

Goldstein, K. (1959). Functional disturbances in brain damage. In S. Arieti (Ed.), *American handbook of psychiatry.* New York: Basic Books.

Goldstein, K., & Scheerer, M. (1941). Abstract and concrete behavior: An experimental study with special tests. *Psychological Monographs, 53*(2, Whole No. 239).

Goodwin, D. W. (1979). Alcoholism and heredity: A review and hypothesis. *Archives of General Psychiatry, 36,* 57–61.

Goodwin, D. W., Schulsinger, F., Hermansen, L., Guze, S. B., & Winokur, G. (1973). Alcohol problems in adoptees raised apart from alcoholic biological parents. *Archives of General Psychiatry, 28,* 238–243.

Grant, I., Atkinson, J. H., Hesselink, J. R., Kennedy, C. J., Richman, D. D., Spector, S. A., & McCutchan, J. A. (1987). Evidence for early central nervous system involvement in the acquired immunodeficiency syndrome (AIDS) and other human immunodeficiency virus (HIV) infections. *Annals of Internal Medicine, 107,* 828–836.

Green, M. F. (1998). *Schizophrenia from a neurocognitive perspective.* Boston: Allyn and Bacon.

Gusella, J. F., Wexler, N. S., Conneally, P. M., Naylor, S. L., Anderson, M. A., Tanzi, R. E., Watkins, P. C., Ottina, K., Wallace, M. R., Sakaguchi, A. Y., Young, A. B., Shoulson, I., Bonilla, E., & Martin, J. B. (1983). A polymorphic DNA marker genetically linked to Huntington's disease. *Nature, 306,* 234–238.

Halstead, W. C. (1947). *Brain and intelligence.* Chicago: University of Chicago Press.

Heaton, R. K. (2006, February 1–4). Presidential address given at the annual meeting of the International Neuropsychological Society, Boston.

Heaton, R. K., Nelson, L. M., Thompson, D. S., Burks, J. S., & Franklin, G. M. (1985). Neuropsychological findings in relapsing-remitting and chronic-progressive multiple sclerosis. *Journal of Consulting and Clinical Psychology, 53,* 103–110.

Heilman, K. M., & Valenstein, E. (Eds.). (1993). *Clinical neuropsychology* (3rd ed.). New York: Oxford University Press.

Hill, S. Y., Shen, S., Zezza, N., Hoffman, E. K., Perlin, M., & Alan, W. (2004). A genome wide search for alcoholism susceptibility genes. *American Journal of Medical Genetics B: Neuropsychiatric Genetics, 128,* 102–113.

Hill, S. Y., Steinhauer, S. R., & Zubin, J. (1987). Biological markers for alcoholism: A vulnerability model conceptualization. In C. Rivers (Ed.), *Nebraska symposium on motivation: Vol. 34. Alcohol and addictive behavior* (pp. 207–256). Lincoln: University of Nebraska Press.

Jervis, G. A. (1959). The mental deficiencies. In S. Arieti (Ed.), *American handbook of psychiatry: Vol. 4.* New York: Basic Books.

Johnson, D., & Almi, C. R. (1978). Age, brain damage and performance. In S. Finger (Ed.), *Recovery from brain damage: Research and theory.* New York: Plenum Press.

Kanner, L. (1943). Autistic disturbances of affective contact. *Nervous Child, 2,* 217–250.

Katz, L. J., Goldstein, G., & Beers, S. R. (2001). *Learning disabilities in older adolescents and adults.* New York: Kluwer Academic/Plenum.

King, H. E., & Miller, R. E. (1990). Hypertension: Cognitive and behavioral considerations. *Neuropsychology Review, 1,* 31–73.

Klove, H., & Matthews, C. G. (1974). Neuropsychological studies of patients with epilepsy. In R. M. Reitan & L. A. Davison (Eds.), *Clinical neuropsychology: Current status and applications.* New York: Winston-Wiley.

Klunk, W. E., Engler, H., Nordberg, A., Wang, Y., Blomqvist, G., Holt, D. P., et al. (2004). Imaging brain amyloid in Alzheimer's disease with Pittsburgh Compound-B. *Annals of Neurology, 5,* 306–319.

Lashley, K. S. (1960). In search of the engram. In F. A. Beach, D. O. Hebb, C. T. Morgan, & H. W. Nissen (Eds.), *The neuropsychology of Lashley.* New York: McGraw-Hill. (Originally published in 1950)

Levin, H. S., Benton, A. L. & Grossman, R. G. (1982). *Neurobehavioral consequences of closed head injury.* New York: Oxford University Press.

Levin, H. S., Eisenberg, H. M., & Benton, A. L. (1989). *Mild head injury.* New York: Oxford University Press.

Luria, A. R. (1966). *Higher cortical functions in man.* (B. Haigh, Trans.) New York: Basic Books.

Luria, A. R. (1973). *The working brain.* New York: Basic Books.

Lye, T. C., & Shores, E. A. (2000). Traumatic brain injury as a risk factor for Alzheimer's disease: A review. *Neuropsychology Review, 10,* 115–129.

McKeith, I., Mintzer, J., Aarsland, D., Burn, D., Chiu, H., Cohen-Mansfield, J., et al. (2004). Dementia with Lewy bodies. *Lancet Neurology, 3,* 19–28.

Mesulam, M. M. (1985). *Principles of behavioral neurology.* Philadelphia: F. A. Davis.

Minshew, N. J. (1996). Autism. In B. O. Berg (Ed.), *Principles of child neurology* (pp. 1713–1730). New York: McGraw-Hill.

Myslobodsky, M. S., & Mirsky, A. F. (1988). *Elements of petit mal epilepsy.* New York: Peter Lang.

Neils, J., Boller, F., Gerdeman, B., & Cole, M. (1989). Descriptive writing abilities in Alzheimer's disease. *Journal of Clinical and Experimental Neuropsychology, 11,* 692–698.

Nussbaum, P. D. (1994). Pseudodementia: A slow death. *Neuropsychology Review, 4,* 71–90.

Rosenstein, L. D. (1998). Differential diagnosis of the major progressive dementias and depression in middle and late adulthood: A summary of the literature of the early 1990s. *Neuropsychology Review, 8,* 109–167.

Rourke, B. P., & Brown, G. G. (1986). Clinical neuropsychology and behavioral neurology: Similarities and differences. In S. B. Filskov & T. J. Boll (Eds.), *Handbook of clinical neuropsychology: Vol. 2* (pp. 3–18). New York: Wiley.

Rumsey, J. M., & Hamburger, S. D. (1988). Neuropsychological findings in high-functioning men with infantile autism, residual state. *Journal of Clinical and Experimental Neuropsychology, 10,* 201–221.

Satz, P. (1966). Specific and nonspecific effects of brain lesions in man. *Journal of Abnormal Psychology, 71,* 65–70.

Schaeffer, K. W., Parsons, O. A., & Yohman, J. R. (1984). Neuropsychological differences between male familial and nonfamilial alcoholics and nonalcoholics. *Alcoholism: Clinical and Experimental Research, 8,* 347–351.

Schatz, P., Pardini, J. F., Lovell, M. R., Collins, M. W. & Podell, K. (2006). Sensitivity and specificity of the ImPACT Test Battery for concussion in athletes. *Archives of Clinical Neuropsychology, 21,* 91–99.

Smith, R. J., Barth, J. T., Diamond, R., & Giuliano, A. J. (1998). Evaluation of head trauma. In G. Goldstein, P. D. Nussbaum, & S. R. Beers (Eds.), *Neuropsychology* (pp. 135–170). New York: Plenum Press.

Spreen, O. (1987). *Learning disabled children growing up: A follow-up into adulthood.* Lisse, the Netherlands: Swets & Zeitlinger.

Steinhauer, S. R., Hill, S. Y., & Zubin, J. (1987). Event related potentials in alcoholics and their first-degree relatives. *Alcoholism, 4,* 307–314.

Tarter, R. E. (1976). Neuropsychological investigations of alcoholism. In G. Goldstein & C. Neuringer (Eds.), *Empirical studies of alcoholism.* Cambridge, MA: Ballinger.

Tarter, R. E., Hegedus, A., Goldstein, G., Shelly, C., & Alterman, A. I. (1984). Adolescent sons of alcoholics: Neuropsychological and personality characteristics. *Alcoholism: Clinical and Experimental Research, 8,* 216–222.

Teuber, H.-L. (1959). Some alterations in behavior after cerebral lesions in man. In A. D. Bass (Eds.), *Evolution of nervous control from primitive organisms to man.* Washington, DC: American Association for the Advancement of Science.

Van Gorp, W. G., Miller, E. N., Satz, P., & Visscher, B. (1989). Neuropsychological performance in HIV-1 immunocompromised patients: A preliminary report. *Journal of Clinical and Experimental Neuropsychology, 11,* 763–773.

Vargha-Khadem, F., Gadian, D. G., Watkins, K. E., Connelly, A., Van Paesschen, W. P., & Mishkin, M. (1997). Differential effects of early hippocampal pathology on episodic and semantic memory. *Science, 277,* 376–380.

Walker, A. E., Caveness, W. F., & Critchley, M. (Eds.). (1969). *Late effects of head injury.* Springfield, IL: Charles C. Thomas.

Wells, C. E. (1979). Pseudodementia. *American Journal of Psychiatry, 136,* 895–900.

Wells, C. E. (1980). The differential diagnosis of psychiatric disorders in the elderly. In J. O. Cole & J. E. Barrett (Eds.), *Psychopathology in the aged.* New York: Raven Press.

Werner, H., & Strauss, A. (1942). Experimental analysis of the clinical symptom "perseveration" in mentally retarded children. *American Journal of Mental Deficiency, 47,* 185–188.

CHAPTER 6

Substance-Related Disorders: Alcohol

ERIC F. WAGNER, MARK B. SOBELL, AND LINDA C. SOBELL

DESCRIPTION OF THE DISORDER

Historically, the scientific study of alcohol abuse has focused almost exclusively on individuals who have been severely dependent on alcohol. The relatively recent recognition that such persons constitute a minority of the alcohol-abusing population has led to increased attention to individuals with less severe alcohol problems. This chapter addresses diagnostic and assessment issues related to alcohol abusers all along the problem continuum, ranging from those who are "misusers" or abusers to those who are severely dependent.

Views about alcohol use disorders are a mix of concepts derived from research and from clinical anecdote. To understand present views about alcohol problems, it is necessary to understand how views have changed. Over the years, public opinion has ranged from viewing alcohol abusers as being moral reprobates to being victims of a disease. Regardless of public opinion, however, the focus was on individuals who were severely dependent on alcohol. Such individuals are highly visible and typically have experienced multiple serious consequences, making them easy to identify and a serious public health problem. In the United States, the view that alcohol problems are a disorder became dominant in the mid-1900s with the rise of Alcoholics Anonymous (AA) and the proclamation that alcoholism was a disease by the American Medical Association (Pattison, Sobell, & Sobell, 1977). The embracing of a disease concept, however, was not based on biological evidence. Rather, it was intended to shift responsibility for dealing with alcohol problems from the criminal justice system to the health care system. These views, referred to as traditional conceptualizations of alcohol problems (Pattison et al., 1977), stemmed primarily from AA (Bacon, 1973) and Jellinek (1960).

Alcoholics Anonymous viewed alcoholics as suffering from a biological aberration—an "allergy" to alcohol (i.e., with repeated exposure to alcohol, alcoholics would change to quickly become physically dependent upon alcohol if they started to drink), and once dependent they would continue to drink to avoid withdrawal symptoms. This, however, does not explain why people who had been drinking for some time would return to drinking. To explain relapse, AA stated that alcoholics had an "obsession" to drink like normal drinkers. In addition, alcoholism was thought to be a progressive disorder (i.e., if alcoholics continued to drink, their problem would inevitably worsen, even following a long abstinence period).

E. M. Jellinek, a scientist, attempted to bridge the gap between lay views and the little scientific knowledge available by postulating a disease concept of alcoholism. He and others felt that the medical profession should be responsible for treating alcohol abusers (Bacon, 1973). Although he alluded to genetic components, he did not speculate as to why some drinkers develop alcohol problems and others do not. Jellinek postulated that alcoholics (1) use alcohol to cope with emotional problems, (2) over time develop tolerance to alcohol thereby leading to increased consumption to achieve desired effects, and (3) eventually develop "loss of control." By loss of control, he hypothesized that consumption of even small amounts of alcohol would initiate physical dependence that would trigger continued drinking (Jellinek, 1960). Jellinek proposed that there were many types of alcohol problems. The type previously described he called *gamma* alcoholism, which he felt was most common in the United States and was a progressive disorder.

Since these early views, considerable research has yielded findings that refute traditional conceptualizations. Although the research literature suggests that some individuals may be genetically predisposed to develop alcohol problems, a large proportion of individuals with alcohol problems do not have a positive family history for alcohol use disorders (Dahl et al., 2005; Fingarette, 1988). Research also shows that social and cultural factors play a large role in the development of alcohol problems (Hendershot, MacPherson, Myers, Carr, & Wall, 2005; Miles, Silberg, Pickens, & Eaves, 2005; Penninkilampi-Kerola, Kaprio, Moilanen, & Rose, 2005; Sigvardsson, Cloninger, & Bohman, 1985) and in most cases, the natural history of the disorder is not progressive (Dawson, 1996; Institute of Medicine, 1990). Rather, it includes periods of alcohol problems of varying severity separated by periods of either nondrinking or of drinking limited quantities without problems (Cahalan, 1970; King & Tucker, 2000).

Epidemiological studies have demonstrated that individuals with less serious alcohol problems outnumber those who have severe problems (Institute of Medicine, 1990). As will be discussed, because alcohol use patterns lie along a continuum ranging from no problems to severe problems, conceptualizations must explain the entire continuum of cases. The treatment implications of the epidemiological findings are profound. Traditional conceptualizations view alcohol problems as a progressive disorder and persons who are mildly dependent on alcohol as in the "early stages" of the development of alcoholism. Consequently, even those with mild problems are viewed as needing the same treatment as those who are severely dependent. That is, everyone who experiences problems with alcohol is labeled an "alcoholic" and told they can never drink again. Considerable research, however, shows that mildly dependent alcohol abusers not only respond well to brief interventions, but also often recover by moderating rather than ceasing their drinking (Bien, Miller, & Tonigan, 1993; Sobell & Sobell, 1993a; Sobell & Sobell, 1995b).

With regard to loss of control, research has demonstrated that even in very severe cases, physical dependence is not initiated by a small amount of drinking (Marlatt, 1978; Pattison et al., 1977). This suggests that other factors, such as conditioned cues

(Niaura et al., 1988) and positive consequences of drinking (Orford, 2001) are neces-sary to explain why some people continue drinking despite having repeatedly suf-fered adverse consequences.

Another area of research that has relevance to treatment is natural recoveries. Recent studies indicate that recovery from alcohol problems in the absence of treat-ment is more prevalent than once thought (Dawson et al., 2005; Klingemann et al., 2001; Sobell, Cunningham, & Sobell, 1996a; Sobell, Ellingstad, & Sobell, 2000). From a public health standpoint, this body of research suggests that community interven-tions might facilitate the self-change process by motivating people to identify their problem sooner than would otherwise have occurred and to attempt to recover on their own (Sobell et al., 1996b). The following case study provides an example of a typical client presenting for outpatient treatment of alcohol use problems.

Case Study

The patient is a 27-year-old white, single male who voluntarily entered treat-ment at the Guided Self-Change (GSC) Clinic at the Addiction Research Foundation (Toronto, Canada). Guided Self-Change treatment, a motivation-ally based cognitive-behavioral intervention, emphasizes helping clients help themselves (Sobell & Sobell, 1993a). The intervention includes an assessment, four semistructured sessions, and an aftercare component. In addition, clients are given an opportunity to request additional sessions. The GSC treatment in-tervention has been evaluated in several clinical trials (Sobell & Sobell, 1998).

The patient was in his last year of graduate school and was planning to pursue a postdoctoral fellowship in the coming year. He reported seeking treatment because of "hitting a personal rock bottom," and an "ultimatum from my girlfriend." The client reported that two years prior to treatment the frequency and quantity of his drinking had increased and that he had tried to cut down and stop without success. He also reported that his university friends and colleagues drank heavily after seminars, and that he perceived there was a "stigma" attached to people who left after a few drinks. He also reported that he felt pressured to drink when others around him drank.

At treatment entry, he reported he was "extremely ready" to take action to change his drinking, and at the assessment he stated, "I've started working on my problem, but I need some help." When asked why he decided to seek treatment he stated:

A series of events which started with increased drinking, behavioral change, fights when I was intoxicated, or drunk for a better word, breakups with friends, stupid arguments with friends, arguments with girlfriends— Just a lot of bad times and a lot of problems. I usually go for maybe two or three weeks and say "I'm positively not going to have anything to drink," but when I would say "Okay, well I can handle this now," it seemed to get worse, so I thought it's time to talk to somebody about it.

Although he reported drinking heavily for 8 years, he felt that his drinking had only been a problem for the last 4 years. His score on the Alcohol De-pendence Scale (ADS; Skinner & Allen, 1982) was 11 and on the Drug Abuse

Screening Test (DAST-20; Skinner, 1982) was 1. An ADS score of 11 is in the first quartile for ADS norms and is reflective of someone who has a mild alcohol problem. A DAST-20 score of 1 suggests no current drug problem. The patient also reported no current use of prescription medications or other psychoactive substances, including nicotine. He reported no current health problems or past treatment for mental health or substance use problems. He also reported never having attended self-help group meetings (e.g., AA) and had no prior alcohol-related hospitalizations or arrests. He reported no morning drinking in the past year, and in terms of family history, reported that his father had had a problem with alcohol.

He reported experiencing several alcohol-related consequences in the 6 months prior to the assessment (e.g., fights in bars, personal problems, verbally abusive, spending too much money on alcohol). He reported that his highest risk situations for problem drinking were when home alone, bored and stressed, and when with friends after work at seminars. He also reported that on about half the days when he drank alcohol, it was when he was alone. Although this was his first treatment experience, he reported several prior attempts to quit or reduce his alcohol use. At the assessment, his subjective evaluation of the severity of his alcohol problem was "major," and he rated the overall quality of his life as "very unsatisfactory."

Self-report of his drinking in the past year using the Timeline Followback assessment (LaBrie, Pedersen, & Earleywine, 2005; Sobell & Sobell, 1992) was: (1) *abstinence:* 59% of the days; (2) *drinks per drinking day:* 4.5 standard drinks (SDs; 1 SD = 13.6 g of absolute ethanol); (3) *average weekly consumption:* 13 SDs; (4) *highest single drinking day in the past year:* 14 SDs; (5) *low consumption days (1–3 SDs):* 42% of all days; (6) *heavy consumption:* 22% of all days (20% = 4–9 SDs, 2% were ≥ 10 SDs). When shown the personalized feedback based on his self-reports of drinking (Sobell & Sobell, 1996; Sobell & Sobell, 1998; Substance Abuse and Mental Health Administration, 1999), he said: "I'm a little alarmed. More than a little alarmed, but I'm alarmed that I'm at the high end, but I know, I, that's why I'm here. The other part that alarms me is that most of the people I know, I would put them in that."

Based on the assessment interview, this patient met the criteria for a *DSM-IV* diagnosis of alcohol dependence (American Psychiatric Association, 2000a); however, on a continuum of alcohol problems (Sobell & Sobell, 1993b), like most GSC clients (Sobell & Sobell, 1993a), the severity of his problem would be evaluated as mild. With such patients, a brief cognitive-behavioral motivational intervention is a good first treatment in a stepped care model (Sobell & Sobell, 2000b).

At the assessment, the patient was given an explanation about the treatment (i.e., helping clients help themselves). Shortly into treatment when he was asked what he thought of the intervention., he replied: "I like it so far. It's making me think and I guess I, before I always thought I was too busy to sit down and think about some of these things, and that's why I never had any success in curbing the problem. This is good because it puts the onus on me."

EPIDEMIOLOGY

General population surveys provide information on rates of alcohol consumption as well as the prevalence of problem drinking. Next to caffeine, alcohol is the second most used psychoactive substance (American Psychiatric Association [APA], 1994). In North America, per capita consumption generally has been declining since the early 1980s (RWJF, 2001). This decline is consistent with patterns observed in other developed countries (Smart, 1989) and is thought to be owing either to an aging population (i.e., older people decrease use) or increased adoption of healthy lifestyles (National Institute on Alcohol Abuse and Alcoholism, 1993).

Drinking problems typically have been defined as either diagnosis-based or symptom-based. Reporting the prevalence of abuse and dependence using current *DSM* definitions has the advantage that those definitions generally are accepted by researchers and clinicians. However, a symptom-based approach where rates of specific types of problems (e.g., physiological vs. psychosocial) are reported would be more congruent with a conceptualization of alcohol problems as lying along a severity continuum (Institute of Medicine, 1990).

The National Institute on Alcohol Abuse and Alcoholism (NIAAA) surveyed a representative sample of 42,862 American individuals ages 18 and older in the National Longitudinal Alcohol Epidemiologic Survey (Grant, 1997). It was found that the lifetime prevalence of alcohol dependence was 13.3%, and the past year prevalence was 4.4%. Men were more likely than women to use alcohol and to have alcohol use disorders. The NIAAA conducted a second survey of a representative sample of 43,093 Americans in the National Epidemiologic Survey on Alcohol and Related Conditions (Stinson et al., 2005), and found the 12-month prevalence of alcohol use disorders only to be 7.35% and of comorbid alcohol and substance use disorders to be 1.10%. In terms of the stability of diagnoses, Hasin, Grant, & Endicott (1990) found that of those individuals originally diagnosed as alcohol dependent, 46% were still classified as dependent four years later, 15% were classified as having alcohol abuse, and 39% could not be diagnosed with an alcohol problem. Similarly, in a national survey Dawson (1996) found that of 4,585 adults who previously had met criteria for a *DSM-IV* diagnosis of alcohol dependence, 28% still met the criteria for alcohol abuse or dependence, 22% were abstinent, and 50% could not be diagnosed as having an alcohol problem. As compared to those who had not been in treatment, treated individuals were more likely to be abstinent (39% vs. 16%), while those who had not been treated were more likely to be drinking asymptomatically (58% vs. 28%). These findings underscore that alcohol problems are not necessarily progressive. In another national survey, Dawson (2000) reported that frequency of intoxication had the strongest association with the probability of having a diagnosable alcohol use disorder, followed by the frequency of drinking ≥ five drinks per day.

From the standpoint of symptom-based prevalence, the ratio of problem drinkers to severely dependent drinkers is a function of the definitions used and the populations sampled. Regardless of the definitions, on a problem severity continuum the population of persons with identifiable problems but no severe signs of dependence is much larger than the population with severe dependence (Sobell & Sobell, 1993a). Problem drinkers constitute 15% to 35% of individuals in the adult population, whereas severely dependent drinkers account for 3% to 7% (Hilton, 1991; Institute of Medicine, 1990). Moreover, the prevalence of alcohol abuse is approximately twice the prevalence of alcohol dependence (Harford, Grant, Yi, & Chen, 2005).

Drinking problems are not distributed equally across sociodemographic groups. Males greatly outnumber females (Fillmore, 1988; Hilton, 1987), but the gap has been narrowing since the Vietnam War (Grant, 1997). Besides gender differences in prevalence, problem drinking tends to occur later in life for women (Fillmore, 1987). In addition, women appear to be more vulnerable to the adverse physical consequences of heavy alcohol use (Dawson & Grant, 1993). For example, alcohol dependent women may be at higher risk of dying of alcohol-related problems such as hypertension and liver disease (Ashley & Rankin, 1979; Hill, 1984). Compared to women without alcohol problems, women with alcohol problems have a higher incidence of menstrual irregularities, have more difficulty becoming pregnant, have more prenatal complications, and have more gynecological and obstetric problems (Beckman, 1979; Collins, 1993b; Wilsnack & Wilsnack, 1995). This increased vulnerability may result from gender differences in body composition resulin that lead women to experience higher blood alcohol levels after consuming an equivalent amount of alcohol. Alcohol-related problems also appear to be inversely related to age, with the highest problem rates occurring for those 18 to 29 years of age (Fillmore, 1988; National Institute on Alcohol Abuse and Alcoholism, 2000; Robins & Regier, 1991). Marital status is similarly related to problem drinking, with single individuals experiencing more physiological symptoms of dependence and more psychosocial problems than those who are married (Hilton, 1991).

Even though epidemiological studies provide information on ethnic and racial differences in relation to alcohol use and abuse, the methods for categorizing respondents' cultural/ethnic backgrounds have been rudimentary. Consequently, data on ethnic differences must be considered preliminary. Across ethnic/racial groups, heavy drinking patterns occur at different points in the lifespan (Caetano & Kaskutas, 1995; National Institute on Alcohol Abuse and Alcoholism, 1993; Robins, 1991). Among white males, frequency of heavy drinking typically peaks in one's 20s and decreases in one's late 30s to 40s, while heavy drinking among young African American males is low at first (Caetano, 1984; Herd, 1989) but then increases during middle age. For example, African Americans before the age of 40 demonstrate a lower in incidence of heavy drinking (i.e., $\geq$ 4 drinks in a day) than whites and Hispanics/Latinos (National Institute on Alcohol Abuse and Alcoholism, 2000). This late heavy drinking onset may explain why, despite similar heavy drinking rates among African American and white males, alcohol-related health problems (e.g., liver cirrhosis) were more common among African American males. Such age-related differences have not been observed between African American and white females.

The Hispanics/Latinos population in the United States is very heterogeneous (e.g., Mexicans, Puerto Ricans, Cubans). Some studies show Hispanics/Latinos with lower rates of heavy drinking than other Americans (National Institute on Drug Abuse, 1991; Welte & Barnes, 1995), while other studies show Hispanics/ Latinos with higher rates (Caetano, 1989; Caetano & Kaskutas, 1995). These latter studies have found increased prevalence of alcohol-related problems among Hispanic/Latino males, especially those who are young to middle-aged. This is consistent with research showing that acculturation appears to be associated with increased rates of heavy drinking among Hispanics/Latinos (Caetano, 1985; Cahalan & Room, 1974).

Among Asian Americans alcohol problem rates are generally lower than the U.S. norms (National Institute on Alcohol Abuse and Alcoholism, 1993). As with other ethnic groups there is marked variation in drinking patterns and problems among different Asian groups. Surveys of Hawaiians found that whites report drinking significantly more alcohol than Japanese, Chinese, or Filipinos, and reports of alcohol problems paralleled use patterns (Ahern, 1985; Murakami, 1985). Across several studies, Chinese men and women report the lowest levels of alcohol use and abuse, with a large proportion reporting no drinking (Ahern, 1985; Yu, Liu, Xia, & Zhang, 1989). Low use has been attributed both to cultural norms and to physiological sensitivity to alcohol (Clark & Hesselbrock, 1988).

CLINICAL PICTURE

When someone is considering abandoning a valued behavior, unless the reasons for stopping are extremely compelling, ambivalence would be expected. For individuals whose alcohol problems are not severe, ambivalence can be very pronounced as the decision to stop or reduce drinking may be largely based on risks rather than actual consequences. Failure to recognize this ambivalence can have serious consequences during the assessment process and can affect how clients are perceived by clinicians.

Traditional conceptualizations assert that individuals with alcohol problems will present in denial; that is, they will fail to recognize that their drinking is a problem (Nowinski, Baker, & Carroll, 1992; Substance Abuse and Mental Health Administration, 1999). In this regard, traditional assessments attempt to confront and break through the denial. The rationale is that this procedure is consistent with the first step of AA (i.e., recognizing that one is powerless over alcohol; Nowinski et al., 1992). However, when individuals feel attacked, such as being labeled as alcoholic, they typically resist the label and its implications. In other words, a confrontational interviewing style can result in a client denying or not adopting the label. An alternative approach considers the individual ambivalent and avoids the use of confrontation, labeling, or other tactics that provoke defensiveness and resistance. This alternative nonthreatening, nonconfrontational style of interviewing is called motivational interviewing (Miller & Rollnick, 1991, 2002; Substance Abuse and Mental Health Administration, 1999). Because individuals who present with alcohol problems in clinical settings can show impairment ranging from very mild symptoms (e.g., repeated hangovers) to severe symptoms (e.g., major withdrawal symptoms), use of a motivational interviewing style is recommended.

Because traditional views are based on a model that emphasizes severe dependence, many individuals who have less severe alcohol problems may not be identified. It is important, therefore, for clinicians to learn to recognize individuals with mild alcohol problems. Such individuals respond well to brief interventions that allow reduced drinking as a goal (Bien et al., 1993; Copeland, Blow, & Barry, 2003; Heather, 1990; Sobell & Sobell, 1993a).

COURSE AND PROGNOSIS

Traditional concepts of alcohol problems, based on Jellinek's work on progressivity (Jellinek, 1952), postulated that such problems develop in early adulthood (i.e., 20 to

30 years of age) and increase in severity over the course of several years. As noted earlier, the notion of progressivity has not been supported by research, although some alcohol problems do worsen over time. Research also shows that alcohol problems can occur at any age (Atkinson, 1994; Schonfeld & Dupree, 1991; Wilsnack, Klassen, Schur, & Wilsnack, 1991). The temporal pattern can be variable, with problems sometimes remitting, worsening, or improving (Cahalan & Room, 1974; Dawson, 1996; Hasin et al., 1990; Mandell, 1983). If an individual is experiencing alcohol problems at one point, it is not possible to predict that in the absence of treatment the problem will worsen. It has been found, however, that men whose alcohol problems are severe are likely to continue to worsen over time if they continue to drink (Fillmore & Midanik, 1984).

Alcohol problems have been characterized as a recurrent disorder (Polich, Armor, & Braiker, 1981). This characteristic has given the disorder a reputation as difficult to treat and seldom cured. Recent research, however, has found that the probability of relapse in persons who have been in remission for several years is low (De Soto, O'Donnell, & De Soto, 1989; Finney & Moos, 2001; Sobell & Sobell, 1992 July; Sobell, Sobell, & Kozlowksi, 1995). Clinically, the high likelihood of recurrence has led to relapse prevention procedures (Marlatt & Gordon, 1985). Such procedures include advising clients that setbacks may occur during recovery from the disorder, and that they should use these setbacks as learning experiences to prevent future relapses, rather than as evidence that recovery is impossible. Finally, the presence of psychiatric comorbidity is associated with a more guarded prognosis for recovery (Baigent, 2005; Le Fauve et al., 2004; Modesto-Lowe & Kranzler, 1999).

DIAGNOSTIC CONSIDERATIONS

The classification of alcohol problems has evolved considerably. The two major diagnostic classifications of mental disorders are the *Diagnostic and Statistical Manual of Mental Disorders (DSM)* and the *Mental Disorder Section of the International Classification of Diseases (ICD)*. The first *DSM (DSM-I)* was published in 1952 by the American Psychiatric Association and was a variant of the *ICD-6*. Today, the terms in the *DSM-IV* are compatible with both the *ICD-9* and *ICD-10* (American Psychiatric Association, 1994). Although the *DSM* and *ICD* diagnostic schema are highly similar, nevertheless "agreement between *DSM-IV* and *ICD-10* on whether subjects were dependent or not is less than optimal" (Caetano & Tam, 1995). According to these authors (Caetano & Tam, 1995), the *ICD-10* finds a higher prevalence of dependence among young males. This is thought to be related to identifying consequences of episodic heavy drinking as signs of dependence. Because the primary diagnostic classification schema used in the United States is the *DSM*, this section will focus on *DSM* classifications.

Over the years, changes in the *DSM* classification criteria have reflected both the state of knowledge and contemporary attitudes. The most recent *DSM* is the *DSM-IV* (APA, 1994). Although a text revision of the *DSM-IV* (i.e., *DSM-IV-TR*) was recently published (APA, 2000a), the criteria for alcohol use disorders are unchanged. Whereas the *DSM-III-R* viewed alcohol dependence as a graded phenomenon ranging from mild (enough consequences to meet criteria but no major withdrawal symptoms) to severe (several negative consequences and withdrawal symptoms), the *DSM-IV* separates psychological from physiological dependence by making physical dependence a specifier rather than a central criterion. In other words, using the *DSM-IV* it is possible to diagnose an individual as severely alcohol dependent "without physiological dependence."

The major difference between an alcohol dependence and an alcohol abuse diagnosis is that abuse is for less serious alcohol problems. A diagnosis of alcohol abuse is preempted by the diagnosis of alcohol dependence if the person's drinking pattern has *ever* met the criteria for dependence. Such a criterion implies that the disorder is progressive and that the condition will worsen unless an individual stops drinking. As reviewed earlier, several studies have failed to support the progressivity concept. Other problems relating to the lack of a sufficient empirical basis for the *DSM-IV* have been noted by Grant (1995).

A high prevalence of comorbidity of psychiatric disorders among alcohol abusers has been well documented (Anthony, Warner, & Kessler, 1994; Berglund & Ojehagen, 1998; Cox, Norton, Swinson, & Endler, 1990; Drake et al., 1990; Kessler et al., 1996; Le Fauve et al., 2004; Modesto-Lowe & Kranzler, 1999; Regier et al., 1990). Psychiatric disorders reported as having exceptionally high co-occurrence with alcohol problems include mood disorders such as depression (Swendsen & Merikangas, 2000) and bipolar disorders (Drake & Mueser, 1996; Strakowski & DelBello, 2000), anxiety disorders (Kushner, Abrams, & Borchardt, 2000; Oei & Loveday, 1997), schizophrenia (Blanchard, Brown, Horan, & Sherwood, 2000; Drake & Mueser, 1996), and personality disorders such as antisocial personality disorder (Clark & Bukstein, 1998; Morgenstern, Langenbucher, Labouvie, & Miller, 1997) and borderline personality disorder (Trull, Sher, MinksBrown, Durbin, & Burr, 2000). Although it is common to advocate using an integrated treatment approach with clients who have co-occurring disorders (Drake & Mueser, 1996; Woody, 1996) and such an approach has intuitive appeal, there is a lack of studies demonstrating the development and evaluation of such treatments (Baigent, 2005; Le Fauve et al., 2004; Modesto-Lowe & Kranzler, 1999).

Because of the high comorbidity rates among alcohol abusers, diagnostic formulations are a two-step process. First, the extent and nature of the problem must be assessed. This can be done with instruments reviewed in the assessment section of this chapter. The second step is to establish whether other psychiatric disorders (i.e., anxiety, depression) are present, and, if so, to determine whether the alcohol problem is the primary or secondary disorder.

Diagnostic formulations have clinical utility beyond insurance and clinical recording requirements (Sobell, Sobell, Toneatto, & Shillingford, 1994a; Sobell, Wilkinson, & Sobell, 1990; Sokolow, Welte, Hynes, & Lyons, 1981; Toneatto, Sobell, Sobell, & Leo, 1991). An accurate diagnosis is important because it defines the problem in a way that can be communicated and understood by clinicians and researchers. A diagnostic formulation coupled with an assessment provides an initial understanding of the problem as well as a foundation for initial treatment planning. Diagnostic formulations play an important role in decisions about treatment goals and intensities.

Over the past decade there have been several significant developments in the alcohol field that call for differential treatment planning. Among these developments are a growing recognition of the importance of assessing and treating alcohol abusers with dual diagnoses, whether the second disorder is a psychiatric disorder or another substance use disorder. The *DSM-IV* provides a general discussion of the differential diagnoses of alcohol-induced disorders that resemble primary mental disorders (e.g., major depressive disorder vs. alcohol-induced mood disorder with depressive features, with onset during intoxication). There are significant prognostic implications for alcohol abusers with comorbid psychiatric problems. Several studies have shown that alcohol abusers who have serious psychiatric problems generally have poorer treatment outcomes than alcohol abusers without major psychiatric symptoms (Berglund & Ojehagen, 1998; Le Fauve et al., 2004; Meyer & Kranzler, 1988; Modesto-Lowe & Kranzler, 1999; Rounsaville, Dolinsky, Babor, & Meyer, 1987). Although it has been suggested that patients with serious psychiatric problems and a primary alcohol disorder should receive additional counseling, there is a lack of empirical data suggesting whether treatment of the comorbid problem reliably improves treatment outcomes. Although evidence is also lacking regarding whether treatment for alcohol and other psychiatric problems should be concurrent or sequential and in separate or similar settings, currently most dually diagnosed clients with alcohol problems are treated in the mental health system (Carey, 1996). An important issue is the extent to which substance use may interfere with assessing psychiatric comorbidity. Thus, it has been suggested that individuals should be alcohol free for several weeks before comorbidity can be accurately assessed (Schuckit, 1995).

For alcohol abusers who use or abuse other drugs including nicotine, it is important to gather a comprehensive profile of psychoactive substance use. Over the course of an intervention, drug use patterns may change (e.g., decreased alcohol use, increased smoking; decreased alcohol use, increased cannabis use). Furthermore, alcohol abusers who use other drugs raise the possibility of pharmacological synergism (i.e., a multiplicative effect of similarly acting drugs taken concurrently). Cross-tolerance (i.e., lessened drug effect because of past heavy use of pharmacologically similar drugs) should also be considered when assessing alcohol abusers who use other drugs. Finally, the treatment of alcohol abusers who abuse other drugs may not parallel that for individuals who only abuse alcohol (Battjes, 1988; Burglass & Shaffer, 1983; Burling & Ziff, 1988; Kaufman, 1982).

For alcohol abusers, diagnostic formulations may also play an important role in decisions about treatment goals and treatment intensity (Sobell & Sobell, 1987). Some research suggests that severity of alcohol dependence may interact with response to treatment goals, that is, abstinence or nonproblem drinking (Institute of Medicine, 1990; Miller, Leckman, Delaney, & Tinkcom, 1992; Sobell & Sobell, 1993a), and different treatment intensities (Annis, 1986; Orford & Keddie, 1986). Considering the most appropriate treatment for alcohol abusers with different levels of dependence (e.g., mild vs. severe) is consistent with client-treatment matching (DiClemente, Carroll, Connors, & Kadden, 1994; Donovan et al., 1994; Mattson et al., 1994).

Because alcohol withdrawal symptoms are defining features for an alcohol dependence diagnosis, a careful history of past withdrawals is necessary. Thus, it is important that clients understand what is meant by withdrawal symptoms. For example, a critical term that often causes alcohol abusers confusion is *delirium tremens* or DTs (Sobell, Toneatto, & Sobell, 1994b). This term, which is frequently confused with minor withdrawal symptoms (e.g., psychomotor agitation), refers to actual delirium and implies severe dependence on alcohol. A history of past withdrawal symptoms coupled with reports of recent heavy ethanol consumption can alert clinicians that withdrawal symptoms are likely to occur upon cessation of drinking and require medical interventions.

PSYCHOLOGICAL AND BIOLOGICAL ASSESSMENT

A thorough and careful assessment is an important part of the treatment process for individuals with all types of alcohol problems. The assessment is critical to the development of meaningful treatment plans. Accurate diagnosis of alcohol and other concurrent disorders is integral to the assessment process. The assessment can serve several critical functions: (1) it provides clinicians with an in-depth picture of a person's alcohol use and related consequences, particularly the severity of the disorder; this picture can be used to develop treatment plans tailored to the needs of each client; (2) if change is not evident during treatment, ongoing assessment information can be used to make systematic changes in the treatment plan; and (3) progress during treatment can be compared with the initial assessment to evaluate the extent and types of changes that have occurred, and to suggest where further interventions are needed. The depth and intensity of an assessment will be related to problem severity and the complexity of the presenting case as well as the individual needs of the clinician and/or researcher. Ultimately, assessments should be determined based on clinical judgment and current clinical needs. The instruments and methods described in this chapter can be used clinically to gather information relevant to the assessment and treatment planning process. The implications of assessment data for treatment issues, such as drinking goals and treatment intensity, show how the clinical interview can significantly impact on treatment. Critical issues in assessment (e.g., self-reports, convergent data sources) are discussed as well.

Critical Issues in Assessment

In the alcohol field most research and clinical information is obtained through retrospective self-reports (Babor, Brown, & Del Boca, 1990; Sobell & Sobell, 1990). Despite widespread skepticism among practitioners, several major reviews of the scientific literature have concluded that alcohol abusers' self-reports are generally accurate if clients are interviewed in clinical or research settings, when they are alcohol free, and when they are given assurances of confidentiality (Babor et al., 1990; Babor, Steinberg, Anton, & Del Boca, 2000; Brown, Kranzler, & Del Boca, 1992; Del Boca & Noll, 2000; Sobell & Sobell, 1990). The one condition when alcohol abusers' self-reports have been found to be inaccurate is when they are interviewed with any alcohol in their system (Leigh & Skinner, 1988; Sobell, Sobell, & VanderSpek, 1979). However, because all studies find some proportion, albeit small, of self-reports to be inaccurate, one way of identifying inaccurate self-reports is to obtain information from multiple sources (e.g., chemical tests, self-reports, collateral reports, official records). Data from different sources are then compared and conclusions are based on a convergence of information (Maisto, McKay, & Connors, 1990; Sobell & Sobell, 1990). When the measures converge, one can have confidence in the accuracy of the reports.

Information gathered through the assessment process can be used to provide feedback to clients to enhance their commitment to change. The feedback should be delivered in a nonconfrontational manner using principles of motivational interviewing. Readers desiring a comprehensive description of how to do motivational interviewing and how to use advice/feedback from an assessment are referred to excellent publications by the Substance Abuse and Mental Health Administration (1999) and the National Institute on Alcohol Abuse and Alcoholism (2003, 2005).

With respect to the length of an assessment, intense and in-depth assessments are no longer justified for all clients. Because persons with less severe alcohol problems often respond well to a brief intervention (Bien et al., 1993; Sobell & Sobell, 1993a), an assessment that is longer than the intervention makes little sense. In contrast, severely dependent alcohol abusers may require a more intensive assessment covering such areas as organic brain dysfunction, psychiatric comorbidity, and social needs. Ultimately, an assessment should be based on clinical judgment and the client's needs.

The next section describes different assessment areas and reviews relevant assessment instruments, scales, and questionnaires that can be used for assessing alcohol use and abuse. Readers interested in a comprehensive listing of assessment tools for alcohol use and abuse are referred to several published directories (Allen & Columbus, 1995; APA, 2000b). In this chapter, only instruments that have sound psychometric properties and clinical utility are discussed. With respect to selecting an appropriate instrument it is helpful to ask, "What will I learn from using the instrument that I would not otherwise know from a routine clinical interview?" (Sobell et al., 1994b).

ASSESSING ALCOHOL USE

Assessing alcohol consumption involves measuring the quantity and frequency of past and present use. When choosing an instrument to assess drinking, a decision must be made about the type of information desired, that is, level of precision and time frame (Sobell & Sobell, 1995a; Sobell et al., 1994b). Two major dimensions along which measures differ is whether they gather summarized information (e.g., "How many days per week on average do you drink any alcohol?") versus specific information (e.g., "How many drinks did you have on each day of the following interval?"), and whether the information was recalled retrospectively or recorded when it occurred. Specific measures are preferred over summary measures for pretreatment and within-treatment assessments because they provide information about patterns of drinking and opportunities to inquire about events associated with problem drinking that are not possible using summary data (e.g., "What was happening on Friday when you had 12 drinks?").

In terms of key instruments, there are four established methods for assessing past alcohol consumption: (1) Lifetime Drinking History, LDH (Skinner & Sheu, 1982; Sobell & Sobell, 1995a; Sobell et al., 1994b); (2) Quantity-Frequency methods, QF (Room, 1990; Skinner & Sheu, 1982; Sobell & Sobell, 1995a); (3) Timeline Followback, TLFB (APA, 2000b; Sobell & Sobell, 1992; Sobell & Sobell, 1995a; Sobell & Sobell, 2000a); and (4) Self-Monitoring, SM (Sobell & Sobell, 1995a; Sobell, Bogardis, Schuller, Leo, & Sobell, 1989). The first three are retrospective estimation methods (i.e., they obtain information about alcohol use after it has occurred). The TLFB can also be used in treatment as an advice-feedback tool to help increase clients' motivation to change (Sobell & Sobell, 1995a). The fourth method, Self-Monitoring, asks clients to record their drinking at or about the same time that it occurred, and it has several clinical advantages: (1) it provides feedback about treatment effectiveness; (2) it identifies situations that pose a high-risk of relapse; and (3) it gives outpatient clients an opportunity to discuss their drinking since the previous session (Sobell et al., 1994b). Because several reviews have detailed the advantages and disadvantages of these drinking instruments they will not be reviewed here. Readers interested in the use of these instruments are referred to the source articles previously cited for each method.

CONSEQUENCES OF ALCOHOL USE

One of the key defining characteristics of a *DSM-IV* diagnosis is alcohol-related consequences. Several short self-administered scales have been developed to assess alcohol-related psychosocial consequences and dependence symptoms: (1) Alcohol Use Disorders Identification Test, AUDIT (Saunders, Aasland, Babor, De La Fuente, & Grant, 1993), (2) Severity of Alcohol Dependence Questionnaire, SADQ (Stockwell, Murphy, & Hodgson, 1983; Stockwell, Sitharthan, McGrath, & Lang, 1994); (3) Alcohol Dependence Scale, ADS (Skinner & Allen, 1982); and (4) Short Alcohol Dependence Data Questionnaire, SADD (Raistrick, Dunbar, & Davidson, 1983). These scales take about five minutes to administer and range from 10 to 25 items in length.

Although several scales are used for brief screening and identification of harmful and hazardous alcohol use, the AUDIT stands out for its psychometric characteristics, convenience, and cross-cultural validation. The AUDIT, developed as a multinational World Health Organization project, is a brief screening test for the early detection of harmful and hazardous alcohol use in primary health care settings (Saunders et al., 1993). The 10 questions are scored based on the frequency of the experience (i.e., from 0 = never to 4 = daily use, maximum score = 40). The AUDIT has been shown to be as good as or better than other screening tests (e.g., CAGE, MAST, ADS) in identifying individuals with probable alcohol problems when a cutoff score of ≥ 8 is used (Barry & Fleming, 1993; Fleming, Barry, & MacDonald, 1991). According to the authors the differences between the AUDIT and most other screening tests are that it: (1) detects drinkers along the entire severity continuum from mild to severe; (2) emphasizes hazardous consumption and frequency of intoxication compared with drinking behavior and adverse consequences; (3) uses a time frame that asks questions about current (i.e., past year) and lifetime use; and (4) avoids using a "yes/no" format and instead uses Likert rating scales to reduce face validity.

ASSESSING RISK SITUATIONS AND SELF-EFFICACY

Because relapse rates among treated alcohol abusers are extremely high, assessment of high-risk situations for problem drinking is important at assessment and during treatment (Marlatt & Gordon, 1985; Sobell & Sobell, 1993a). The Situational Confidence Questionnaire (SCQ-39) assesses situational (i.e., present time) self-efficacy by measuring how confident clients are that they will be able to resist the urge to drink heavily in particular situations. Clients are asked to imagine themselves in each situation and to rate their confidence on a 6-point scale (100% confident to 0% confident) that they would be able to resist urges to drink heavily or use drugs in that situation. The SCQ-39 takes about 10 to 20 minutes to complete and contains 8 subscales (e.g., unpleasant emotions, pleasant emotions, testing personal control) based on research by Marlatt and Gordon (Marlatt & Gordon, 1985). For clinical purposes, an easy-to-score and interpret variant of the SCQ, the Brief SCQ (BSCQ), was developed and consists of the original 8 items that represent the 8 subscales (Breslin, Sobell, Sobell, & Agrawal, 2000). Although the BSCQ can be used clinically to enhance treatment planning, it only identifies generic situations/ problem areas. To examine clients' individual high-risk situations or areas where they lack self-confidence, clinicians should explore specific situations with clients. For example, clients can be asked to describe their two or three highest-risk situations for alcohol use in the past year (Sobell & Sobell, 1993a).

Another recently introduced instrument to measure situational self-efficacy is the Drug-Taking Confidence Questionnaire-8 (DTCQ-8; Sklar & Turner, 1999). The DTCQ-8 is an 8-item questionnaire similar to the BSCQ but developed to be used across a variety of different substance use disorders.

ASSESSMENT OF PSYCHIATRIC COMORBIDITY WITH ALCOHOL ABUSERS

As reviewed earlier, a substantial number of alcohol abusers have psychiatric problems (Le Fauve et al., 2004; Modesto-Lowe & Kranzler, 1999; Woody, 1996). Such problems need to be evaluated. Although several diagnostic interviews and scales exist for assessing comorbidity with alcohol abusers, the comprehensiveness of assessments of individuals with comorbid disorders will depend on the resources available, specificity of the information required, the treatment setting, and most important, the assessor's skill level (Sobell et al., 1994b). Several brief instruments, while not yielding formal diagnoses, can serve to evaluate comorbidity: (1) Beck Depression Inventory (Beck, Steer, & Garbin, 1988); (2) Beck Anxiety Inventory (Beck, Epstein, Brown, & Steer, 1988); (3) Hamilton Rating Scale for Depression (Hamilton, 1960); and (4) Symptom Checklist-90-R (Derogatis, 1983). For brief descriptions of the clinical utility of these instruments, the reader is referred to two recent reviews (Carey & Correia, 1998; Sobell et al., 1994b).

NEUROPSYCHOLOGICAL ASSESSMENT

Screening for organic brain damage related to alcohol abuse is important for treatment planning. The Trail Making Test (Davies, 1968) and the Digit Symbol subscale of the WAIS, are recommended as brief screening tests for assessing probable organic brain dysfunction due to alcohol consumption (Lezak, 1976; Miller & Saucedo, 1983; Wilkinson & Carlen, 1980). Both tests are relatively easy and quick to administer (e.g., ≤5 minutes) and are highly sensitive to alcohol-related brain dysfunction. Readers interested in the application and interpretation of assessing neuropsychological impairment and functioning related to alcohol problems are referred to reviews of this literature (Bates & Convit, 1999; Miller & Saucedo, 1983; Neiman, 1998; Parsons, 1987; Parsons & Farr, 1981).

BARRIERS OR POTENTIAL BARRIERS TO CHANGE

In developing a treatment plan it is helpful to anticipate possible barriers that clients might encounter with respect to changing their behavior. Barriers can be both motivational and practical. If an individual is not motivated to change, then there is little reason to expect that change will occur. Because many alcohol abusers are coerced into treatment (e.g., courts, significant others), such individuals might not have a serious interest in changing (Cunningham, Sobell, Sobell, & Gaskin, 1994). Thus, it is important to evaluate a client's motivation for and commitment to change. According to Miller and Rollnick (1991), "motivation is a *state* of readiness or eagerness to change, which may fluctuate from one time or situation to another. This state is one that can be influenced"(p. 14). Thus, rather than a trait, motivation is a state that can be influenced by several variables, one of which is the therapist. An easy way to assess readiness to change is to use a Readiness Ruler (see p. 139; Substance Abuse and Mental Health Administration, 1999). The Readiness Ruler asks clients to indicate their readiness to change using a 5-point scale ranging from "not ready to change" to "unsure" to "very ready to change." The ruler has face validity, is user friendly, and takes only a few seconds to complete. For a detailed description of methods for increasing motivation for change, readers are referred to two excellent resources (Miller & Rollnick, 1991; Substance Abuse and Mental Health Administration, 1999).

Environmental factors can also present formidable obstacles to change. For example, individuals in an environment where alcohol is readily available and where there are many cues to drink might find it difficult to abstain. For some individuals social avoidance strategies (e.g., avoiding bars, no alcohol in the house) might be the only effective alternative. Finally, clinicians should attend to individual barriers that can also affect a person's ability to enter and complete treatment (e.g., child care, transportation, inability to take time off from work, unwillingness to adopt an abstinence goal) (Schmidt & Weisner, 1995).

BIOCHEMICAL MEASURES

Because no self-report measure is error free, the use of measures complementary to self-reports is recommended with the set of measures yielding a convergent validity approach to assessment (Sobell & Sobell, 1980). Although there has been a tendency to consider biochemical measures as "gold standards" and superior to self-report, several reviews have found that even biochemical measures suffer from validity problems (Bernadt, Mumford, Taylor, Smith, & Murray, 1982; Leigh & Skinner, 1988; Levine, 1990; Maisto & Connors, 1992; O'Farrell & Maisto, 1987). In fact, some reviews have found self-reports to be superior to certain biochemical measures (Petersson, Trell, & Kristensson, 1983; Salaspuro, 1986).

Issues of self-report accuracy take on different meanings for clinical versus research purposes, where different levels of reporting precision are required (Baker & Brandon, 1990; Litten & Fertig, 2003; Rankin, 1990). For example, clinicians do not routinely have to obtain information to confirm their clients' alcohol use unless the situation warrants it. However, in clinical trials researchers typically need to verify their clients' self-reports using an alternative measure (e.g., collateral reports).

The use of alcohol, tobacco, and other drugs can be detected in different bodily fluids (e.g., breath, blood, urine, hair, saliva) and by several detection methods. Biochemical measures can be classified into two categories: (1) recent/current (i.e., past 24 hours) use, and (2) use over an extended time period. For an in-depth review of the advantages and disadvantages of different testing methods, readers are referred to several reviews (Phelps & Field, 1992; Shute, 1988; Verebey & Turner, 1991).

BREATH ALCOHOL TESTS

Because of the phenomenon of tolerance, clinical judgment is not adequate to determine when clients are under the influence of alcohol (Sobell et al., 1994b). Furthermore, there is evidence that when individuals have a detectable BAC their self-reports of drinking may be invalid (Sobell et al., 1994b). Thus, at least in the case of alcohol abusers, breath alcohol testers should be used routinely in assessments. A breath analyzer will yield accurate readings of a person's blood alcohol concentration (BAC). Several portable testers differing in cost and precision are commercially available. Breath alcohol testers are noninvasive, inexpensive (a few dollars per test), easy to use, portable, and provide an immediate determination of BAC. To avoid false positives, clients should not smoke or drink anything for about 15 minutes prior to the test.

Urine Tests

Urinalysis can provide qualitative (i.e., different types of drugs including alcohol and prescription medications) as well as quantitative (i.e., amount of the substance or the substance's metabolite currently in the body) information on drug use. However, all urine tests have limitations. Urinalyses cannot specify when a drug was taken. Rather, they provide evidence of whether consumption occurred and the amount of drug or the drug's metabolite in the system at the time of testing. For some drugs that have long half-lives (e.g., marijuana) the individual being tested might not have used for several weeks or even months, but still tests positive. It is not uncommon for urine tests to yield both false positive and false negative results (Dilts, Gendel, & Williams, 1996; Sellers, Kadlec, Kaplan, & Naranjo, 1988).

Hair Analysis

Although hair analysis can detect drug use over several years and is highly accurate (Cook, Bernstein, & Andrews, 1997; Gibson & Manley, 1991; Magura, Freeman, Siddiqi, & Lipton, 1992; Strang, Black, Marsh, & Smith, 1993), it is also very costly. Presently, the clinical utility of hair analysis is undetermined.

Liver Function Tests

Blood tests to assess acute hepatic dysfunction are routinely used by physicians. Liver function tests, if elevated, can be used as an advice feedback tool to help motivate clients to consider changing their drinking (Romelsjö et al., 1989). Such tests have limited utility with drinkers whose problems are not severe and who do not drink daily. In fact, a sizeable percentage of problem drinkers, those who are not severely dependent on alcohol, show no elevations on liver function tests at assessment (Sobell, Agrawal, & Sobell, 1999). Clinicians who are not physicians and want to use liver function tests will need to arrange for physicians to order and evaluate such tests.

Cirrhosis, which is permanent and nonreversible cellular liver damage (Maher, 1997), occurs in a small percentage of alcohol abusers (Klatsky & Armstrong, 1992), usually those with heavier drinking patterns (Sørensen et al., 1984; Wodak, Saunders, Ewusi-Mensah, Davis, & Williams, 1983). Unlike assessment of acute hepatic dysfunction, cirrhosis must be diagnosed through a liver biopsy.

Carbon Monoxide

Many clients with alcohol problems also smoke cigarettes, and several biochemical measures can be used to verify tobacco use (e.g., cotinine, thiocyanate, carbon monoxide). Carbon monoxide (CO), a byproduct present in tobacco smoke, is rapidly absorbed through the lungs into the bloodstream. It has a very short half–life (3 to 5 hours) that can be affected by various factors (e.g., exercise, pollutants). Compared to other tests of nicotine use, CO tests have major advantages (e.g., easily administered, highly correlated with exposure to cigarette smoke, portable testers) and disadvantages (e.g., short half-life).

ETIOLOGICAL CONSIDERATIONS

FAMILIAL AND GENETIC

It is well documented that close relatives of individuals with alcohol problems have an increased risk of demonstrating drinking problems, and both environmental and genetic explanations exist for this phenomenon. In regard to environmental factors, family issues are prominent in both the theoretical and empirical literature on the etiology of alcohol problems. Familial factors (e.g., children's perception of their parents' and siblings' drinking, instability of family rituals because of parental drinking, poor parenting, impaired family communication and problem solving) have been found to increase the risk for alcohol problems (O'Farrell & Fals-Stewart, 1999). Currently, three models of familial influence are predominant (Hesselbrock, Hesselbrock, & Epstein, 1999). The first, the "family disease" model, assumes a biological etiology of alcohol problems, with family members assuming roles of either alcoholic or codependent and these roles perpetuating drinking problems within the family. The second model, the "family systems" model, assumes that alcohol stabilizes family equilibrium, and that families organize themselves to maintain alcohol problems despite its inherent repercussions. The third model, the "behavioral family" model, examines families' behaviors as antecedents to and reinforcing consequences of alcohol use.

In regard to genetic explanations, recent studies indicate that genes explain 40% to 60% of the variance in alcohol abuse and dependence; these findings support the importance of both genetic and environmental contributions to the etiology of alcohol problems (Knopik et al., 2004; Schuckit, 2000). Close relatives of persons with alcohol problems, adopted away children of men and women with alcohol problems, and identical twins whose parents had alcohol problems all have been found to demonstrate a much higher likelihood of demonstrating alcohol use problems than the general population. Although genetic studies have documented genetic influences on the risk of alcohol problems in men, this has occurred less so with women (McGue, 1999).

Although many specific genes have been and continue to be evaluated as possible contributors to the risk of alcohol problems, variations of genetic material across a variety of genes likely contribute to the risk of drinking problems. Several endophenotypes, or subconditions that increase the risk for a disorder, have been identified in regard to alcohol problems, and these endophenotypes appear to have strong genetic influences (Schuckit, 2000). The absence or limited production of alcohol-metabolizing enzymes (most common among Asians), low response level to alcohol (i.e., needing a greater number of drinks to have an effect), low amplitude of the P300 wave component of event-related potentials, and low alpha activity and voltage on electroencephalograms all are associated with an increased risk of drinking problems, and all have strong genetic influences.

Learning and Modeling

Learning theory, as applied to alcohol use and abuse, assumes that drinking is largely learned, and that basic learning principles guide the acquisition, maintenance, and modification of drinking behavior (Carroll, 1999). Classical conditioning models posit that the development of a drinking problem occurs largely through the pairing of conditioned stimuli, such as locations or people, with the unconditioned stimulus of alcohol (Hesselbrock et al., 1999). Through repeated pairings with alcohol, the conditioned stimuli come to elicit a conditioned response, which is manifested in craving for alcohol. Tolerance to alcohol also has been explained using a classical conditioning model, where the conditioned stimuli come to elicit a conditioned compensatory response (i.e., an opposite reaction to the initial drug effects) that resembles the unconditioned compensatory response elicited by alcohol consumption (Sherman, Jorenby, & Baker, 1988; Wikler, 1973). Operant conditioning models assume that alcohol consumption is governed by its reinforcing effects, including physiological and phenomenological changes in response to drinking, the social consequences of drinking, and/or the avoidance or cessation of withdrawal symptoms (Hesselbrock et al., 1999). In summary, learning models have been used to explain how drinking problems may develop, and have provided guidance in the design of interventions designed to modify drinking.

An especially influential variable in alcohol use and abuse that appears to be governed by basic learning principles is alcohol expectancies. Alcohol expectancies are the effects (positive and negative) attributed to alcohol that an individual anticipates experiencing when drinking (Goldman, Del Boca, & Darkes, 1999). Expectancies appear to develop early in life, are consistent across gender, and are learned according to social learning principles, including classical conditioning, operant conditioning, and modeling (Hesselbrock, Hesselbrock, & Epstein, 1999). In several different studies, alcohol expectancies have been shown to be highly related to adult and adolescent drinking practices, including drinking problems and relapse to drinking following a period of abstinence (Goldman et al., 1999; Quigley & Marlatt, 1999).

Research on the modeling of alcohol consumption emerged from Bandura's (1969) social learning theory, which posits that modeling influences the acquisition and performance of a variety of social behaviors. Caudill and Marlatt (1975) were among the first to experimentally study the influence of social modeling on drinking behavior, and found that participants exposed to a heavy drinking model (a research confederate) consumed significantly more wine than participants exposed to a light drinking or no model. Collins and Marlatt (1981) reviewed the research in 1981 and concluded that modeling was a powerful influence on drinking that occurred regardless of study setting or moderating variables (e.g., gender, age). More recently, Quigley and Collins (1999) performed a meta-analysis on published studies concerning the modeling of alcohol consumption and found "a definitive effect" of modeling on drinking behavior. Large effect sizes for both amount of alcohol consumed and BAC were documented.

Life Events

For centuries, stressful situations have been thought to be related to alcohol consumption, and drinking has been seen as relieving stress (Sayette, 1999). The relationship between drinking and stress can be traced to the sociological literature of the 1940s and the emergence of the tension-reduction hypothesis in the 1950s (Pohorecky, 1991). The tension-reduction hypothesis proposes that (1) alcohol consumption will reduce stress under most circumstances, and (2) people will be motivated to drink in times of stress. This hypothesis forms the basis of current research about the relationship between drinking and stress (Sayette, 1999). Although studies indicate that drinking can reduce stress in certain people and under certain circumstances, the relationship between drinking and stress is far more complex than originally thought. Individual differences, including a family history of alcohol problems, certain personality traits, extent of self-consciousness, level of cognitive functioning, gender, and situational factors including distraction and the timing of drinking and stress, have all been shown to be important moderators of the degree to which alcohol will reduce the subjective, behavioral, neurochemical, and immunological consequences of stress (Sayette, 1999).

In alcohol-abusing populations, the relationship between alcohol use and stress has been difficult to establish, and studies vary widely in the strength and directionality of documented pathways (Johnson & Pandina, 2000). Some researchers have noted that the stress-relieving effects of alcohol are "neither robust or reliable" (Cooper, Russell, Skinner, Frone, & Mudar, 1992, p. 139), while others have concluded that alcohol is "a two-edged sword" because it can be both a response to stress and a cause of stress (Johnstone, Garrity, & Straus, 1997, p. 258). In a recent longitudinal study, Johnson and Pandina (2000) found that levels of stress, and especially stress related to life events, did not differentiate nonproblem and problem users during adolescence. Moreover, stress at ages 12 or 15 years was unrelated to drinking outcomes at age 25. Nonetheless, adults with alcohol problems do appear to experience more frequent, more severe, and more prolonged stress than those without alcohol problems (Pohorecky, 1991). Johnson and Pandina's (2000) study, however, suggests this may be more a consequence than a cause of drinking problems. Moreover, de Wit (1996) found that stressful life events may increase desire to drink and relapse to drinking among abstinent alcohol abusers. In summary, it appears that drinking and drinking problems are related to stress, at least among certain groups of people and under certain circumstances (Johnstone et al., 1997; Sayette, 1999).

Gender and Racial-Ethnic

Whenever and wherever women's and men's alcohol use has been measured, results show that women drink less than men, and women's drinking leads to fewer social problems than their male counterparts (Wilsnack et al., 2000). However, few studies have gone beyond demonstrating that men use and abuse alcohol more than women do, and currently both biological and social-structural theoretical explanations exist for these gender differences (Wilsnack et al., 2000). The biological explanations emphasize gender differences in the metabolism of alcohol, and the social-structural explanations emphasize gender differences in social roles, and how these differences may influence drinking behavior.

In regard to biological explanations, a number of animal studies have documented gender differences in alcohol metabolism, and it appears that hormonal differences between the sexes may modulate these differences (Smith & Lin, 1996). Moreover, women are more susceptible to alcoholic liver injury than are men, and this appears to be the result of less metabolism of alcohol in the stomach, and thus greater exposure to high alcohol concentrations (Frezza et al., 1990; Moack & Anton, 1999; Morgan, 1994; Schenker, 1997). Whereas research has suggested that women's reproductive functioning influences alcohol metabolism, evidence is mixed regarding how menstrual cycle phase may effect alcohol consumption, metabolism, and self-estimates of blood alcohol levels (Jensvold, 1996). Although one study has suggested that the use of oral contraceptives results in decreased alcohol metabolism, and thus increased alcohol effects (Jones & Jones, 1976), another study found no effect of oral contraceptives on alcohol metabolism (Hobbes, Boutagy, & Shenfield, 1985).

In regard to social-structural explanations, a number of investigators have examined how women's social roles vis-à-vis alcohol may explain lower rates of alcohol use and abuse among women than men. Cross-culturally, women's drinking has been more socially restricted than their male counterparts, primarily because it may negatively affect women's social behavior and responsibilities (Wilsnack et al., 2000). Consistent with this perspective, there is evidence that social influences play a greater role in women's than men's drinking. For example, partners' heavy drinking has a greater influence on female problem drinking than on male problem drinking (Gomberg, 1994), and there is more marital disruption (i.e., never married, divorced or separated, widowed) among females (Gomberg, 1995).

It appears that both biological and social-structural explanations may be needed to account for gender differences in alcohol use and abuse. Wilsnack et al. (2000) recently conducted an in-depth review of international studies concerning gender differences in drinking and concluded "that gender differences in drinking are too consistent in direction for explanations based solely on variable social or cultural influences, but are too variable in size for explanations based solely on biological influences" (p. 261). Thus, conceptualizations of gender differences in alcohol use and misuse should include biological and social-structural considerations.

Several studies have examined personality factors as they relate to gender differences in the clinical presentations of men and women with alcohol problems. Although there is evidence that male alcohol abusers may be more psychopathic, aggressive, and impulsive than women, and women may be more affectively affected than men (e.g., Hesselbrock, 1991), unfortunately this literature is plagued with methodological problems. Recent studies have suggested that factors such as differential base rates of psychopathology among men and women, and differences in the age of onset of alcohol problems, may explain gender differences in personality factors associated with alcohol problems (Sher, Trull, Bartholow, & Vieth, 1999). It should be noted that suicide attempts are almost twice as common among females than male alcohol abusers, with 41% of women and 21% of men reporting at least one suicide attempt (Hesselbrock, Hesselbrock, Syzmanski, & Weidenman, 1988).

Epidemiological studies show that alcohol use, morbidity, and mortality vary by race/ethnicity in seemingly paradoxical ways. For example, African Americans and some Hispanic/Latino groups have lower overall rates of alcohol involvement than non-Latino whites (Vega & Gil, 1998). However, these groups demonstrate higher rates of alcohol- and other drug-related morbidity and mortality than non-Latino whites (Gilliland, Becker, Samet, & Key, 1995; Lee, Markides, & Ray, 1997). This paradox may result from ethnic/racial variations in the processes by which alcohol use can lead to alcohol problems. For example, the accelerated progression from use to problem use seen among these minority populations could result from socioeconomic polarization, criminal justice problems, or the lack of appropriate treatment options. Moreover, both African American and Hispanic/Latino populations have been shown to chronically underutilize substance abuse treatment services (Giachello, 1994; Longshore, Hsieh, Anglin, & Annon, 1992; Molina & Aguirre-Molina, 1994; Neal & Turner, 1991; Neighbors, 1985), which also may contribute to the accelerated development of alcohol and other drug problems among these groups. Additional factors that may affect the progression to alcohol problems, as well as response to alcohol abuse treatment, include perceived discrimination and cultural mistrust for African Americans, and acculturation stress, nativity, and immigration history for Hispanics/Latinos.

Although it has long been recognized that race/ethnicity is likely to impact multiple aspects of the alcohol abuse treatment process (Collins, 1993a), and several face valid explanations exist as to how race/ethnicity may influence alcohol use trajectories and responses to alcohol abuse treatment, little empirical research has examined the effectiveness of alcohol abuse treatment for ethnic minorities. Despite the recognition of problems related to alcohol use in the African American community, ranging from shorter life expectancy (U.S. Department of Health and Human Services, 1985) to perinatal substance use problems (Ernest & Sokoll, 1987; Roman, 1986), there is a paucity of knowledge about how to effectively intervene (Biafora & Zimmerman, 1998; Dawkins, 1996; Herd, 1985). Similar issues exist with Hispanics/Latinos. Whereas alcohol problems are common in Hispanic/Latino communities, very little is known about how to address alcohol and other drug use problems in a culturally sensitive manner among Hispanics/Latinos (Gil, Wagner, & Vega, 2000; Vega & Gil, 1998). Although it appears that cultural sensitivity may enhance the degree to which a specific intervention may address alcohol problems among clients from specific racial/ethnic groups (Longshore & Grills, 2000; Longshore, Grills, & Annon, 1999; Perez-Arce, Carr, & Sorensen, 1993), how race/ethnicity may moderate treatment processes and outcomes, and how interventions may be modified to improve cultural congruency, remains an area in need of considerable research.

BIOLOGICAL AND PHYSIOLOGICAL

Multiple biological and physiological systems are impacted by and appear to influence alcohol consumption. As reviewed earlier, biological factors found to be associated with the development of alcohol problems include the absence or limited production of alcohol-metabolizing enzymes, low level of response to alcohol (i.e., needing more drinks to have an effect), low amplitude of the P300 wave component of event-related potentials, and low alpha activity and voltage on electroencephalograms. These factors all substantially raise the likelihood that an individual will develop alcohol problems, but none, alone or in combination, is a sufficient or necessary determinant of alcohol abuse or dependence.

In addition, two other biological systems are currently receiving considerable research attention. The hypothalamic-pituitary-adrenal (HPA) axis is a hormone system that plays a central role in the body's response to stress. Alcohol consumption has been shown to stimulate the HPA axis system, and several studies suggest that individuals who demonstrate greater HPA activity in response to various stimuli may find alcohol consumption more reinforcing than individuals who demonstrate lower HPA activity (Gianoulakis, 1998; Kiefer, Jahn, Schick, & Wiedemann, 2002).

The endogenous opioid system plays a central role in various physiological processes including pain relief, euphoria, and the rewarding and reinforcing effect of psychoactive substances. Alcohol consumption also stimulates the endogenous opioid system, and it appears that endogenous opioids help mediate the reinforcing effects of alcohol (Gianoulakis, 1998). Moreover, individuals at high risk for developing alcohol problems have been found to exhibit greater endogenous opioid system activity in response to alcohol consumption than low-risk individuals (Gianoulakis, Krishnan, & Thavundayil, 1996).

SUMMARY

Conceptualizations of alcohol problems have changed markedly over the past three decades, affecting thought about alcohol problems and their treatment. In particular, it is now recognized that severely dependent alcohol abusers represent only a small percentage of those of who have alcohol problems. A one-size-fits-all approach is no longer seen as appropriate for all individuals with alcohol problems, and inpatient treatment has fallen out of favor. The concept that alcohol problems can be scaled along a continuum of severity has major implications for assessment and treatment. For example, less severely dependent alcohol abusers can benefit from brief treatment, accompanied by a brief assessment. The idea of a continuum of severity suggests that treatment for alcohol problems should be provided using a stepped-care model where the first treatment is the least intensive, least costly, least invasive, has demonstrated effectiveness and consumer appeal. If treatment is not successful, then it can be stepped up to include longer, more intensive, or different components.

Assessment of alcohol problems is critical to good treatment planning and is a process that carries on throughout treatment. Besides using sound psychometric assessments instruments, the instruments should be clinically useful. There are also are a number of important issues that need to be addressed at assessment. Tantamount among these is the assessment of other comorbidity, including psychiatric disorders and other drug and nicotine use.

Although many alcohol abusers voluntarily seek treatment, many are coerced to seek treatment (e.g., by the courts, significant others, employers). In this regard, they often exhibit resistance and a lack of commitment to change. Motivational enhancement techniques and a motivational interviewing style can be used to decrease resistance and increase commitment to change. Lastly, although alcohol problems can be treated successfully, there is still a high rate of relapse that must be addressed in treatment, but recurrence of problems should not be taken as an indication that the disorder is worsening as there is now abundant data showing that alcohol problems are not necessarily progressive.

REFERENCES

Ahern, F. M. (1985). *Alcohol use and abuse among four ethnic groups in Hawaii: Native Hawaiians, Japanese, Filipinos, and Caucasians* (DHHS Publication No. [ADM] 89–1435). Rockville, MD: National Institute on Alcohol Abuse and Alcoholism.

Allen, J. P., & Columbus, M. (1995). *Assessing alcohol problems: A guide for clinicians and researchers.* Rockville, MD: National Institute on Alcohol Abuse and Alcoholism.

American Psychiatric Association. (1994). *Diagnostic and statistical manual of mental disorders* (4th ed.). Washington, DC: Author.

American Psychiatric Association. (2000a). *Diagnostic and statistical manual of mental disorders* (4th ed., rev.). Washington, DC: Author.

American Psychiatric Association. (2000b). *Handbook of psychiatric measures.* Washington, DC: Author.

Annis, H. A. (1986). Is inpatient rehabilitation of the alcoholic cost effective? Con position. *Advances in Alcohol and Substance Abuse, 5,* 175–190.

Anthony, J. C., Warner, L. A., & Kessler, R. C. (1994). Comparative epidemiology of dependence on tobacco, alcohol, controlled substances, and inhalants: Basic findings from the National Comorbidity Survey. *Experimental and Clinical Psychopharmacology, 2,* 244–268.

Ashley, M. J., & Rankin, J. G. (1979). Alcohol consumption and hypertension: The evidence from hazardous drinking and alcoholic populations. *Australian and New Zealand Journal of Medicine, 9,* 201–206.

Atkinson, R. M. (1994). Late onset problem drinking in older adults. *International Journal of Geriatric Psychiatry, 9,* 321–326.

Babor, T. F., Brown, J., & Del Boca, F. K. (1990). Validity of self-reports in applied research on addictive behaviors: Fact or fiction? *Addictive Behaviors, 12,* 5–32.

Babor, T. F., Steinberg, K., Anton, R., & Del Boca, F. K. (2000). Talk is cheap: Measuring drinking outcomes in clinical trials. *Journal of Studies on Alcohol, 61,* 55–63.

Bacon, S. D. (1973). The process of addiction to alcohol: Social aspects. *Quarterly Journal of Studies on Alcohol, 34,* 1–27.

Baigent, M. F. (2005). Understanding alcohol misuse and comorbid psychiatric disorders. *Current Opinion in Psychiatry, 18,* 223–228.

Baker, T. B., & Brandon, T. H. (1990). Validity of self-reports in basic research. *Behavioral Assessment, 12,* 33–52.

Bandura, A. (1969). *Principles of behavior modification.* New York: Holt, Rinehart & Winston.

Barry, K. L., & Fleming, M. F. (1993). The Alcohol Use Disorders Identification Test (AUDIT) and the SMAST-13: Predictive validity in a rural primary care sample. *Alcohol and Alcoholism, 28,* 33–42.

Bates, M. E., & Convit, A. (1999). Neuropsychology and neuroimaging of alcohol and illicit drug abuse. In C. Avraham (Ed.), *Assessment of neuropsychological functions in psychiatric disorders* (pp. 373–445). Washington, DC: American Psychiatric Association.

Battjes, R. J. (1988). Smoking as an issue in alcohol and drug abuse treatment. *Addictive Behaviors, 13,* 225–230.

Beck, A. T., Epstein, N., Brown, G., & Steer, R. A. (1988). An inventory for measuring clinical anxiety: Psychometric properties. *Journal of Consulting and Clinical Psychology, 56,* 893–897.

Beck, A. T., Steer, R. A., & Garbin, M. G. (1988). Psychometric properties of the Beck Depression Inventory: Twenty-five years of evaluation. *Clinical Psychology Review, 8,* 77–100.

Beckman, L. J. (1979). Reported effects of alcohol on the sexual feelings and behavior of women alcoholics and nonalcoholics. *Journal of Studies on Alcohol, 40,* 272–282.

Berglund, M., & Ojehagen, A. (1998). The influence of alcohol drinking and alcohol use disorders on psychiatric disorders and suicidal behavior. *Alcoholism: Clinical and Experimental Research, 22,* 333S-345S.

Bernadt, M. R., Mumford, J., Taylor, C., Smith, B., & Murray, R. M. (1982). Comparison of questionnaire and laboratory tests in the detection of excessive drinking and alcoholism. *Lancet, I,* 325–328.

Biafora, F., & Zimmerman, R. S. (1998). Developmental patterns of African American adolescent drug use. In W. Vega & A. G. Gil (Eds.), *Drug use and ethnicity in early adolescence* (pp. 149–175). New York: Plenum Press.

Bien, T. H., Miller, W. R., & Tonigan, J. S. (1993). Brief interventions for alcohol problems: A review. *Addiction, 88,* 315–336.

Blanchard, J. J., Brown, S. A., Horan, W. P., & Sherwood, A. R. (2000). Substance use disorders in schizophrenia: Review, integration, and a proposed model. *Clinical Psychology Review, 20,* 207–234.

Breslin, F. C., Sobell, L. C., Sobell, M. B., & Agrawal, S. (2000). A comparison of a brief and long version of the Situational Confidence Questionnaire. *Behaviour Research and Therapy, 38,* 1211–1220.

Brown, J., Kranzler, H. R., & Del Boca, F. K. (1992). Self-reports by alcohol and drug abuse inpatients: Factors affecting reliability and validity. *British Journal of Addiction, 87,* 1013–1024.

Burglass, M. E., & Shaffer, H. (1983). Diagnosis in the addictions I: Conceptual problems. *Advances in Alcohol and Substance Abuse, 3,* 19–34.

Burling, T. A., & Ziff, D. C. (1988). Tobacco smoking: A comparison between alcohol and drug inpatients. *Addictive Behaviors, 13,* 185–190.

Caetano, R. (1984). Ethnicity and drinking in northern California: A comparison among whites, blacks, and Hispanics. *Alcohol and Alcoholism, 19,* 31–44.

Caetano, R. (1985). Two versions of dependence: *DSM-III* and the alcohol dependence syndrome. *Drug and Alcohol Dependence, 15,* 81–103.

Caetano, R. (1989). *Drinking patterns and alcohol problems in a national sample of U.S. Hispanics* (NIAAA Research Monograph No. 18). Rockville, MD: National Institute on Alcohol Abuse and Alcoholism.

Caetano, R., & Kaskutas, L. A. (1995). Changes in drinking patterns among whites, blacks and Hispanics, 1984–1992. *Journal of Studies on Alcohol, 56,* 558–565.

Caetano, R., & Tam, T. W. (1995). Prevalence and correlates of *DSM-IV* and *ICD-10* alcohol dependence: 1990 US national alcohol survey. *Alcohol and Alcoholism, 30,* 177–186.

Cahalan, D. (1970). *Problem drinkers: A national survey.* San Francisco: Jossey-Bass.

Cahalan, D., & Room, R. (1974). *Problem drinking among American men.* Piscataway, NJ: Rutgers University, Rutgers Center of Alcohol Studies.

Carey, K. B. (1996). Substance use reduction in the context of outpatient psychiatric treatment: A collaborative, motivational, harm reduction approach. *Community Mental Health Journal, 32,* 291–306.

Carey, K. B., & Correia, C. J. (1998). Severe mental illness and addictions: Assessment considerations. *Addictive Behaviors, 23,* 735–748.

Carroll, K. M. (1999). Behavioral and cognitive behavioral treatments. In B. S. McCrady & E. E. Epstein (Eds.), *Addictions: A comprehensive guidebook* (pp. 250–267). New York: Oxford University Press.

Caudill, B. D., & Marlatt, G. A. (1975). Modeling influences in social drinking: An experimental analogue. *Journal of Clinical & Consulting Psychology, 43,* 405–415.

Clark, D. B., & Bukstein, O. G. (1998). Psychopathology in adolescent alcohol abuse and dependence. *Alcohol Health & Research World, 22,* 117–121.

Clark, W. B., & Hesselbrock, M. A. (1988). *A comparative analysis of U.S. and Japanese drinking patterns.* In T. Harford & L. Towle (Eds.), *Cultural influences and drinking patterns: A focus on Hispanic and Japanese populations* (pp. 79–98) (NIAAA Research Monograph No. 19). Washington DC: U.S. Government Printing Office.

Collins, R. L. (1993a). Sociocultural aspects of alcohol use and abuse: Ethnicity and gender. *Drugs and Society, 8,* 89–116.

Collins, R. L. (Ed.). (1993b). *Women's issues in alcohol use and smoking.* New York: Sage.

Collins, R. L., & Marlatt, G. A. (1981). Social modeling as a determinant of drinking behavior: Implications for prevention and treatment. *Addictive Behaviors, 6,* 233–239.

Cook, R. F., Bernstein, A. D., & Andrews, C. M. (1997). Assessing drug use in the workplace: A comparison of self-report, urinalysis, and hair analysis. In L. Harrison & A. Hughes (Eds.), *The validity of self-reported drug use: Improving the accuracy of survey estimates* (NIDA Research Monograph No. 167, pp. 247–272). Washington, DC: National Institute on Drug Abuse.

Cooper, M. L., Russell, M., Skinner, J. B., Frone, M. R., & Mudar, P. (1992). Stress and alcohol use: Moderating effects of gender, coping, and alcohol expectancies. *Journal of Abnormal Psychology, 101,* 139–152.

Copeland, L. A., Blow, F. C., & Barry, K. L. (2003). Health care utilization by older alcohol-using veterans: Effects of a brief intervention to reduce at-risk drinking. *Health Education and Behavior, 30,* 305–321.

Cox, B. M., Norton, R. G., Swinson, R. P., & Endler, N. S. (1990). Substance abuse and panic-related anxiety: A critical review. *Behaviour Research and Therapy, 28,* 385–393.

Cunningham, J. A., Sobell, L. C., Sobell, M. B., & Gaskin, J. (1994). Alcohol and drug abusers' reasons for seeking treatment. *Addictive Behaviors, 19,* 691–696.

Dahl, J. P., Doyle, G. A., Oslin, D. W., Buono, R. J., Ferraro, T. N., Lohoff, F. W., & Berrettini, W. H. (2005). Lack of association between single nucleotide polymorphisms in the corticotropin releasing hormone receptor 1 (CRHR1) gene and alcohol dependence. *Journal of Psychiatric Research, 39,* 475–479.

Davies, A. D. M. (1968). The influence of age on trail making test performance. *Journal of Clinical Psychology, 24,* 96–98.

Dawkins, M. P. (1996). The social context of substance use among African American youth: Rural, urban, and suburban comparisons. *Journal of Alcohol and Drug Education, 41,* 68–86.

Dawson, D. A. (1996). Correlates of past-year status among treated and untreated persons with former alcohol dependence: United States, 1992. *Alcoholism: Clinical and Experimental Research, 20,* 771–779.

Dawson, D. A. (2000). Drinking patterns among individuals with and without *DSM-IV* alcohol use disorders. *Journal of Studies on Alcohol, 61,* 111–120.

Dawson, D. A., & Grant, B. F. (1993). Gender effects in diagnosing alcohol abuse and dependence. *Journal of Clinical Psychology, 49,* 298–307.

Dawson, D. A., Grant, B. F., Stinson, F. S., Chou, P. S., Huang, B., & Ruan, W. J. (2005). Recovery from *DSM-IV* alcohol dependence: United States, 2001–2002. *Addiction, 100,* 281–292.

De Soto, C. B., O'Donnell, W. E., & De Soto, J. L. (1989). Long-term recovery in alcoholics. *Alcoholism: Clinical and Experimental Research, 13,* 693–697.

de Wit, H. (1996). Priming effects with drugs and other reinforcers. *Experimental and Clinical Psychopharmacology, 4,* 5–10.

Del Boca, F. K., & Noll, J. A. (2000). Truth or consequences: The validity of self-report data in health services research on addictions. *Addiction, 95,* S347-S360.

Derogatis, L. R. (1983). *SCL-90 Revised Version Manual-1.* Baltimore, MD: Johns Hopkins University School of Medicine.

DiClemente, C. C., Carroll, K. M., Connors, G. J., & Kadden, R. M. (1994). Process assessment in treatment matching research. *Journal of Studies on Alcohol* (Suppl. 12), 156–162.

Dilts, S. L., Gendel, M. H., & Williams, M. (1996). False positives in urine monitoring of substance abusers: The importance of clinical context. *American Journal on Addictions, 5,* 66–68.

Donovan, D. M., Kadden, R. M., DiClemente, C. C., Longabaugh, R., Zweben, A., & Rychtarik, R. (1994). Issues in the selection and development of therapies in alcoholism treatment matching research. *Journal of Studies on Alcohol* (Suppl. 12), 138–148.

Drake, R. E., & Mueser, K. T. (1996). Alcohol-use disorder and severe mental illness. *Alcohol Health and Research World, 20,* 87–93.

Drake, R. E., Osher, F. C., Noordsy, D. L., Hurlbut, S. C., Teague, G. B., & Beaudett, M. S. (1990). Diagnosis of alcohol use in schizophrenia. *Schizophrenia Bulletin, 16,* 57–67.

Ernest, A., & Sokoll, R. (1987). Incidence of fetal alcohol syndrome and economic impact of FAS-related anomalies. *Drug and Alcohol Dependence, 19,* 53–55.

Fillmore, K. M. (1987). Prevalence, incidence and chronicity of drinking patterns and problems among men as a function of age: A longitudinal and cohort analysis. *British Journal of Addiction, 82,* 77–83.

Fillmore, K. M. (1988). *Alcohol use across the life course: A critical review of 70 years of international longitudinal research.* Toronto, Ontario: Addiction Research Foundation.

Fillmore, K. M., & Midanik, L. (1984). Chronicity of drinking problems among men: A longitudinal study. *Journal of Studies on Alcohol, 45,* 228–236.

Fingarette, H. (1988). *Heavy drinking: The myth of alcoholism as a disease.* Berkeley, CA: University of California Press.

Finney, J. W., & Moos, R. H. (1991). The long-term course of treated alcoholism: I. Mortality, relapse and remission rates and comparisons with community controls. *Journal of Studies on Alcohol, 52,* 44–54.

Fleming, M. F., Barry, K. L., & MacDonald, R. (1991). The Alcohol Use Disorders Identification Test (AUDIT) in a college sample. *International Journal of Addictions, 26,* 1173–1185.

Frezza, M., di Padova, C., Pozzato, G., Terpin, M., Baraona, E., & Lieber, C. S. (1990). High blood alcohol levels in women: The role of decreased gastric alcohol dehydrogenase activity and first-pass metabolism. [see comments]. [erratum appears in N Engl J Med 1990 Aug 23;323(8):553; N Engl J Med 1990 May 24;322(21):1540]. *New England Journal of Medicine, 322,* 95–99.

Giachello, A. L. M. (1994). Issues of access and use. In C. W. Molina & M. Aguirre-Molina (Eds.), *Latino health in the US: A growing challenge* (pp. 83–111). Washington, DC: American Public Health Association.

Gianoulakis, C. (1998). Alcohol seeking behavior: The roles of the hypothalamic-pituitary-adrenal axis and the endogenous opioid system. *Alcohol Health and Research World, 22,* 202–210.

Gianoulakis, C., Krishnan, B., & Thavundayil, J. (1996). Enhanced sensitivity of pituitary beta-endorphin to ethanol in subjects at high risk of alcoholism. [erratum appears in Arch Gen Psychiatry 1996 Jun;53(6):555]. *Archives of General Psychiatry, 53,* 250–257.

Gibson, G. S., & Manley, S. (1991). Alternative approaches to urinalysis in the detection of drugs. *Social Behavior and Personality, 19,* 195–204.

Gil, A. G., Wagner, E. F., & Vega, W. A. (2000). Acculturation, familism, and alcohol use among Latino adolescent males: Longitudinal relations. *Journal of Community Psychology, 28,* 443-458.

Gilliland, F. D., Becker, T. M., Samet, J. M., & Key, C. R. (1995). Trends in alcohol-related mortality among New Mexico's American Indians, Hispanics, and non-Hispanic whites. *Alcoholism: Clinical and Experimental Research, 19,* 1572–1577.

Goldman, M. S., Del Boca, F. K., & Darkes, J. (1999). Alcohol expectancy theory: The application of cognitive neuroscience. In K. E. Leonard & H. T. Blane (Eds.), *Psychological theories of drinking and alcoholism* (2nd ed., pp. 203–246). New York: Guilford Press.

Gomberg, E. S. L. (1994). Risk factors for drinking over a woman's life span. *Alcohol Health and Research World, 18,* 220–227.

Gomberg, E. S. L. (1995). Older women and alcohol. In M. Galanter (Ed.), *Recent developments in alcoholism: Vol. 12* (pp. 61–70). New York: Plenum Press.

Grant, B. F. (1995). The *DSM-IV* field trial for substance use disorders: Major results. *Drug and Alcohol Dependence, 38,* 71–75.

Grant, B. F. (1997). Prevalence and correlates of alcohol use and *DSM-IV* alcohol dependence in the United States: Results of the National Longitudinal Alcohol Epidemiologic Survey. *Journal of Studies on Alcohol, 58,* 464–473.

Hamilton, M. (1960). A rating scale for depression. *Journal of Neurology, Neurosurgery and Psychiatry, 23,* 56–62.

Harford, T. C., Grant, B. F., Yi, H., & Chen, C. M. (2005). Patterns of *DSM-IV* alcohol abuse and dependence criteria among adolescents and adults: Results from the 2001 National Household Survey on Drug Abuse. *Alcoholism: Clinical and Experimental Research, 29,* 810–828.

Hasin, D. S., Grant, B., & Endicott, J. (1990). The natural history of alcohol abuse: Implications for definitions of alcohol use disorders. *American Journal of Psychiatry, 147,* 1537–1541.

Heather, N. (1990). *Brief intervention strategies.* New York: Pergamon Press.

Hendershot, C. S., MacPherson, L., Myers, M. G., Carr, L. G., & Wall, T. L. (2005). Psychosocial, cultural and genetic influences on alcohol use in Asian American youth. *Journal of Studies on Alcohol, 66,* 185–195.

Herd, D. (1985). Rethinking black drinking. *British Journal of Addiction, 82,* 219–223.

Herd, D. (1989). The epidemiology of drinking patterns and alcohol-related problems among U.S. blacks. In *Alcohol use among ethnic minorities* (pp. 3–50) (NIAAA Research Monograph No. 18. DHHS Pub. No. [ADM] 89–1435). Washington, DC: Supt. of Docs., U.S. Government Printing Office.

Hesselbrock, M. N. (1991). Gender comparison of antisocial personality disorder and depression in alcoholism. *Journal of Substance Abuse, 3,* 205–219.

Hesselbrock, M. N., Hesselbrock, V. M., & Epstein, E. E. (1999). Theories of etiology of alcohol and other drug use disorders. In B. S. McCrady & E. E. Epstein (Eds.), *Addictions: A comprehensive guidebook* (pp. 50–72). New York: Oxford University Press.

Hesselbrock, M. N., Hesselbrock, V. M., Syzmanski, K., & Weidenman, M. (1988). Suicide attempts and alcoholism. *Journal of Studies on Alcohol, 49,* 436–442.

Hill, S. Y. (Ed.). (1984). Vulnerability to the biomedical consequences of alcoholism and alcohol-related problems among women. New York: Guilford Press.

Hilton, M. (1987). Drinking patterns and drinking problems in 1984: Results from a general population survey. *Alcoholism: Clinical and Experimental Research, 11,* 167–175.

Hilton, M. E. (1991). Trends in U.S. drinking patterns: Further evidence from the past twenty years. In W. B. Clark & M. E. Hilton (Eds.), *Alcohol in America* (pp. 121–138). Albany: State University of New York Press.

Hobbes, J., Boutagy, J., & Shenfield, G. M. (1985). Interactions between ethanol and oral contraceptive steroids. *Clinical Pharmacology & Therapeutics, 38,* 371–80.

Institute of Medicine. (1990). *Broadening the base of treatment for alcohol problems.* Washington, DC: National Academy Press.

Jellinek, E. M. (1952). Phases of alcohol addiction. *Quarterly Journal of Studies on Alcohol, 13,* 673–684.

Jellinek, E. M. (1960). *The disease concept of alcoholism.* New Brunswick, NJ: Hillhouse Press.

Jensvold, M. F. (1996). Nonpregnant reproductive age women, Part I: The menstrual cycle and psychopharmacology. In M. F. Jensvold, U. Halbreich, & J. A. Hamilton (Eds.),

Psychopharmacology and women: Sex, gender, and hormones (pp. 139–169). Washington, DC: American Psychiatric Press.

Johnson, V., & Pandina, R. J. (2000). Alcohol problems among a community sample: Longitudinal influences of stress, coping, and gender. *Substance Use & Misuse, 35,* 669–686.

Johnstone, B. M., Garrity, T. F., & Straus, R. (1997). The relationship between alcohol and life stress. In T. W. Miller (Ed.), *Clinical disorders and stressful life events* (pp. 247–279). Madison, CT: International Universities Press.

Jones, B. M., & Jones, M. K. (1976). Male and female intoxication levels for three alcohol doses, or do women really get higher than men? *Alcohol Technical Reports, 5,* 11–14.

Kaufman, E. (1982). The relationship of alcoholism and alcohol abuse to the abuse of other drugs. *American Journal of Drug and Alcohol Abuse, 9,* 1–17.

Kessler, R. C., Nelson, C. B., McGonagle, K. A., Edlund, M. J., Frank, R. G., & Leaf, P. J. (1996). The epidemiology of co-occurring addictive and mental disorders: Implications for prevention and service utilization. *American Journal of Orthopsychiatry, 66,* 17–31.

Kiefer, F., Jahn, H., Schick, M., & Wiedemann, K. (2002). Alcohol self-administration, craving and HPA-axis activity: An intriguing relationship. *Psychopharmacology, 164,* 239–240.

King, M. P., & Tucker, J. A. (2000). Behavior change patterns and strategies distinguishing moderation drinking and abstinence during the natural resolution of alcohol problems without treatment. *Psychology of Addictive Behaviors, 14,* 48–55.

Klatsky, A. L., & Armstrong, M. A. (1992). Alcohol, smoking, coffee, and cirrhosis. *American Journal of Epidemiology, 136,* 1248–1257.

Klingemann, H. K., Sobell, L. C., Barker, J., Blomquist, J., Cloud, W., Ellinstad, D., et al. (2001). *Promoting self-change from problem substance use: Practical implications for policy, prevention and treatment.* Boston: Kluwer Academic.

Knopik, V. S., Heath, A. C., Madden, P. A. F., Bucholz, K. K., Slutske, W. S., Nelson, E. C., Statham, D., Whitfield, J. B., & Martin, N. G. (2004). Genetic effects on alcohol dependence risk: Re-evaluating the importance of psychiatric and other heritable risk factors. *Psychological Medicine, 34,* 1519–1530.

Kushner, M. G., Abrams, K., & Borchardt, C. (2000). The relationship between anxiety disorders and alcohol use disorders: A review of major perspectives and findings. *Clinical Psychology Review, 20,* 149–171.

LaBrie, J., Pedersen, E., & Earleywine, M. (2005). A group-administered timeline followback assessment of alcohol use. *Journal of Studies on Alcohol, 66,* 693–697.

Lee, D. J., Markides, K. S., & Ray, L. A. (1997). Epidemiology of self-reported past heavy drinking in Hispanic adults. *Ethnicity & Health, 2,* 77–88.

Le Fauve, C. E., Litten, R. Z., Randall, C. L., Moak, D. H., Salloum, I. M., & Green, A. I. (2004). Pharmacological treatment of alcohol abuse/dependence with psychiatric comorbidity. *Alcoholism: Clinical and Experimental Research, 28,* 302–312.

Leigh, G. L., & Skinner, H. A. (1988). *Physiological assessment.* New York: Guilford Press.

Levine, J. (1990). The relative value of consultation, questionnaires, and laboratory investigation in the identification of excessive alcohol consumption. *Alcohol and Alcoholism, 25,* 539–553.

Lezak, M. D. (1976). *Neuropsychological assessment.* New York: Oxford University Press.

Litten, R. Z., & Fertig, J. (2003). Self-report and biochemical measures of alcohol consumption. *Addiction, 98* (Suppl. 2), iii–iv.

Longshore, D., & Grills, C. (2000). Motivating illegal drug use recovery: Evidence for a culturally congruent intervention. *Journal of Black Psychology, 26,* 288–301.

Longshore, D., Grills, C., & Annon, K. (1999). Effects of a culturally congruent intervention on cognitive factors related to drug-use recovery. *Substance Use and Misuse, 34,* 1223–1241.

Longshore, D., Hsieh, S. C., Anglin, M. D., & Annon, T. A. (1992). Ethnic patterns in drug abuse treatment utilization. *Journal of Mental Health Administration, 19,* 268–277.

Magura, S., Freeman, R. C., Siddiqi, Q., & Lipton, D. S. (1992). The validity of hair analysis for detecting cocaine and heroin use among addicts. *International Journal of the Addictions, 27,* 51–69.

Maher, J. J. (1997). Exploring alcohol's effects on liver function. *Alcohol Health and Research World, 21,* 5–12.

Maisto, S. A., & Connors, G. J. (1992). Using subject and collateral reports to measure alcohol consumption. In R. Z. Litten & J. Allen (Eds.), *Measuring alcohol consumption: Psychosocial and biological methods* (pp. 73–96). Totowa, NJ: Humana Press.

Maisto, S. A., McKay, J. R., & Connors, G. J. (1990). Self-report issues in substance abuse: State of the art and future directions. *Behavioral Assessment, 12,* 117–134.

Mandell, W. (1983). Types and phases of alcohol dependence. In M. Galanter (Ed.), *Recent developments in alcoholism: Vol. 3* (pp. 415–448). New York: Plenum Press.

Marlatt, G. A. (1978). *Craving for alcohol, loss of control, and relapse.* New York: Plenum Press.

Marlatt, G. A., & Gordon, J. R. (1985). *Relapse prevention.* New York: Guilford Press.

Mattson, M. E., Allen, J. P., Longabaugh, R., Nickless, C. J., Connors, G. J., & Kadden, R. M. (1994). A chronological review of empirical studies matching alcoholic clients to treatment. *Journal of Studies on Alcohol* (Suppl. 12), 16–29.

McGue, M. (1999). Behavioral genetic models of alcoholism and drinking. In K. E. Leonard & H. T. Blane (Eds.), *Psychological theories of drinking and alcoholism* (2nd ed., pp. 372–421). New York: Guilford Press.

Meyer, R. E., & Kranzler, H. R. (1988). Alcoholism: Clinical implications of recent research. *Journal of Clinical Psychiatry, 49,* 8–12.

Miles, D. R., Silberg, J. L., Pickens, R. W., & Eaves, L. J. (2005). Familial influences on alcohol use in adolescent female twins: Testing for genetic and environmental interactions. *Journal of Studies on Alcohol, 66,* 445–451.

Miller, W. R., Leckman, A. L., Delaney, H. D., & Tinkcom, M. (1992). Long-term follow-up of behavioral self-control training. *Journal of Studies on Alcohol, 53,* 249–261.

Miller, W. R., & Rollnick, S. (1991). *Motivational interviewing: Preparing people to change addictive behavior.* New York: Guilford Press.

Miller, W. R., & Rollnick, S. (2002). *Motivational interviewing: Preparing people for change* (2nd ed.). New York: Guilford Press.

Miller, W. R., & Saucedo, C. F. (1983). *Assessment of neuropsychological impairment and brain damage in problem drinkers.* New York: Grune & Stratton.

Moack, D. H., & Anton, R. F. (1999). Alcohol. In B. S. McCrady & E. E. Epstein (Eds.), *Addictions: A comprehensive guidebook* (pp. 75–94). New York: Oxford University Press.

Modesto-Lowe, V., & Kranzler, H. R. (1999). Diagnosis and treatment of alcohol-dependent patients with comorbid psychiatric disorders. *Alcohol Health and Research World, 23,* 144–149.

Molina, C. W., & Aguirre-Molina, M. (1994). *Latino health in the US: A growing challenge.* Washington, DC: American Public Health Association.

Morgan, M. Y. (1994). The prognosis and outcome of alcoholic liver disease. *Alcohol and Alcoholism* (Suppl. 2), 335–343.

Morgenstern, J., Langenbucher, J., Labouvie, E., & Miller, K. J. (1997). The comorbidity of alcoholism and personality disorders in a clinical population: Prevalence rates and relation to alcohol typology variables. *Journal of Abnormal Psychology, 106,* 74–84.

Murakami, S. R. (1985). An epidemiological survey of alcohol, drug, and mental health problems in Hawaii. In *Alcohol use among U.S. ethnic minorities.* (Research monograph 18.

DHHS Pub. No. [ADM] 89–1435). Rockville, MD: National Institute on Alcohol Abuse and Alcoholism.

National Institute on Alcohol Abuse and Alcoholism. (1993). *Eighth special report to the U.S. Congress on alcohol and health.* NIH Pub. No. 94–3699. Washington, DC: U.S. Government Printing Office.

National Institute on Alcohol Abuse and Alcoholism. (2000). *Tenth special report to the U.S. Congress on alcohol and health.* REP 023 Washington, DC: U.S. Government Printing Office.

National Institute on Drug Abuse. (1991). *National household survey on drug abuse.* DHHS Pub. No. ADM 91–1788. Rockville, MD: U.S. Department of Health and Human Services.

Neal, A. M., & Turner, S. M. (1991). Anxiety disorders research with African Americans: Current status. *Psychological Bulletin, 109,* 400–410.

Neighbors, H. W. (1985). Seeking professional help for personal problems: Black Americans' use of health and mental health services. *Community Mental Health Journal, 21,* 156–166.

Neiman, J. (1998). Alcohol as a risk factor for brain damage: Neurological aspects. *Alcoholism: Clinical and Experimental Research, 22,* 346S–351S.

Niaura, R. S., Rohsenow, D. J., Binkoff, J. A., Monti, P. M., Abrams, D. A., & Pedraza, M. (1988). Relevance of cue reactivity to understanding alcohol and smoking relapse. *Journal of Abnormal Psychology, 97,* 133–152.

Nowinski, J., Baker, S. C., & Carroll, K. (1992). *Twelve step facilitation therapy manual* (Project MATCH Monograph Vol. 1). Rockville, MD: National Institute on Alcohol Abuse and Alcoholism.

Oei, T. P. S., & Loveday, W. A. L. (1997). Management of co-morbid anxiety and alcohol disorders: Parallel treatment of disorders. *Drug and Alcohol Review, 16,* 261–274.

O'Farrell, T. J., & Fals-Stewart, W. (1999). Treatment models and methods: Family methods. In B. S. McCrady & E. E. Epstein (Eds.), *Addictions: A comprehensive guidebook* (pp. 287–305). New York: Oxford University Press.

O'Farrell, T. J., & Maisto, S. A. (1987). The utility of self-report and biological measures of alcohol consumption in alcoholism treatment outcome studies. *Advances in Behaviour Research and Therapy, 9,* 91–125.

Orford, J. (2001). Addiction as excessive appetite. *Addiction, 96,* 15–31.

Orford, J., & Keddie, A. (1986). Abstinence or controlled drinking in clinical practice: Indications at initial assessment. *Addictive Behaviors, 11,* 71–86.

Parsons, O. A. (1987). *Neuropsychological consequences of alcohol problems: Many questions—some answers.* New York: Guilford Press.

Parsons, O. A., & Farr, S. P. (1981). *The neuropsychology of alcohol and drug use.* New York: Wiley.

Pattison, E. M., Sobell, M. B., & Sobell, L. C. (1977). *Emerging concepts of alcohol dependence.* New York: Springer.

Penninkilampi-Kerola, V., Kaprio, J., Moilanen, I., & Rose, R. J. (2005). Co-twin dependence modifies heritability of abstinence and alcohol use: A population-based study of Finnish twins. *Twin Research and Human Genetics, 8,* 232–244.

Perez-Arce, P., Carr, K. D., & Sorensen, J. L. (1993). Cultural issues in an outpatient program for stimulant abusers. *Journal of Psychoactive Drugs, 25,* 35–44.

Petersson, B., Trell, E., & Kristensson, H. (1983). Comparison of g-glutamyltransferase and questionnaire test as alcohol indicators in different risk groups. *Drug and Alcohol Dependence, 11,* 279–286.

Phelps, G., & Field, P. (1992). Drug testing: Clinical and workplace issues. In M. F. Fleming & K. L. Barry (Eds.), *Addictive disorders* (pp. 125–142). St. Louis, MO: Mosby.

Pohorecky, L. A. (1991). Stress and alcohol interaction: An update of human research. *Alcoholism: Clinical and Experimental Research, 15,* 438–459.

Polich, J. M., Armor, D. J., & Braiker, H. B. (1981). *The course of alcoholism: Four years after treatment.* New York: Wiley.

Quigley, B. M., & Collins, R. L. (1999). The modeling of alcohol consumption: A meta-analytic review. *Journal of Studies on Alcohol, 60,* 90–98.

Quigley, L. A., & Marlatt, G. A. (1999). Relapse prevention: Maintenance of change after initial treatment. In K. E. Leonard & H. T. Blane (Eds.), *Psychological theories of drinking and alcoholism* (2nd ed., pp. 370–384). New York: Guilford Press.

Raistrick, D., Dunbar, G., & Davidson, R. (1983). Development of a questionnaire to measure alcohol dependence. *British Journal of Addiction, 78,* 89–95.

Rankin, H. (1990). Validity of self-reports in clinical settings. *Behavioral Assessment, 12,* 107–116.

Regier, D. A., Farmer, M. D., Rae, D. S., Locke, B. Z., Keith, S. J., Judd, L. L., et al. (1990). Comorbidity of mental disorders with alcohol and other drug abuse. *Journal of the American Medical Association, 264,* 2511–2518.

Robert Wood Johnson Foundation (2001). *Substance abuse: The nation's number one health problem.* Princeton, NJ: The Robert Wood Johnson Foundation.

Robins, L. (1991). Assessing substance abuse and psychiatric disorders: History of problems, state of affairs. In L. Harris (Ed.), *Problems of drug dependence 1990: Proceeding of the 52nd Annual Scientific Meeting—The Committee on Problems of Drug Dependence* (NIDA Research Monograph No. 105, pp. 203–212). Washington, DC: National Institute on Drug Abuse.

Robins, L. N., & Regier, D. A. (1991). *Psychiatric disorders in America: The Epidemiologic Catchment Area study.* New York: Free Press.

Roman, L. (1986). Alcohol-related health risks among black Americans. *Alcohol Health and Research World,* 36–39.

Romelsjö, A., Andersson, L., Barrner, H., Borg, S., Grandstrand, C., Hultman, O., et al. (1989). A randomized study of secondary prevention of early stage problem drinkers in primary health care. *British Journal of Addiction, 84,* 1319–1327.

Room, R. (1990). *Measuring alcohol consumption in the United States: Methods and rationales.* New York: Plenum Press.

Rounsaville, B. J., Dolinsky, Z. S., Babor, T. F., & Meyer, R. E. (1987). Psychopathology as a predictor of treatment outcome in alcoholics. *Archives of General Psychiatry, 44,* 505–513.

Salaspuro, M. (1986). Conventional and coming laboratory markers of alcoholism and heavy drinking. *Alcoholism: Clinical and Experimental Research, 10,* 5S–10S.

Saunders, J. B., Aasland, O. G., Babor, T. F., De La Fuente, J. R., & Grant, M. (1993). Development of the Alcohol Use Disorders Identification Test (AUDIT): WHO collaborative project on early detection of persons with harmful alcohol consumption—II. *Addiction, 88,* 791–804.

Sayette, M. A. (1999). Does drinking reduce stress? *Alcohol Health and Research World, 23,* 250–255.

Schenker, S. (1997). Medical consequences of alcohol abuse: Is gender a factor? *Alcoholism: Clinical and Experimental Research, 21,* 179–181.

Schmidt, L., & Weisner, C. (1995). *The emergence of problem-drinking women as a special population in need of treatment.* New York: Plenum Press.

Schonfeld, L., & Dupree, L. W. (1991). Antecedents of drinking for early-onset and late-onset elderly alcohol abusers. *Journal of Studies on Alcohol, 52,* 587–592.

Schuckit, M. A. (1995). *Drug and alcohol abuse: A clinical guide to diagnosis and treatment* (4th ed.). New York: Plenum Press.

Schuckit, M. A. (2000). Genetics of the risk for alcoholism. *American Journal on Addictions, 9,* 103–112.

Sellers, E. M., Kadlec, K. E., Kaplan, H. L., & Naranjo, C. A. (1988). Limitations in the measurement of urine ethanol in clinical trials to monitor ethanol consumption. *Journal of Studies on Alcohol, 49,* 567–570.

Sher, K. J., Trull, T. J., Bartholow, B. D., & Vieth, A. (1999). Personality and alcoholism: Issues, methods, and etiological processes. In K. E. Leonard & H. T. Blane (Eds.), *Psychological theories of drinking and alcoholism* (2nd ed., pp. 54–105). New York: Guilford Press.

Sherman, J. E., Jorenby, D. E., & Baker, T. B. (1988). Classical conditioning with alcohol: Acquired preferences and aversions, tolerance, and urges/cravings. In C. D. Chaudron & D. A. Wilkinson (Eds.), *Theories on alcoholism* (pp. 173–237). Toronto, Canada: Addiction Research Foundation.

Shute, P. A. (1988). Patients' alcohol drinking habits in general practice: Prevention and education. *Journal of the Royal Society of Medicine, 81,* 450–451.

Sigvardsson, S., Cloninger, C. R., & Bohman, M. (1985). Prevention and treatment of alcohol abuse: Uses and limitations of the high risk paradigm. *Social Biology, 32,* 185–193.

Skinner, H. A. (1982). The Drug Abuse Screening Test. *Addictive Behaviors, 7,* 363–371.

Skinner, H. A., & Allen, B. A. (1982). Alcohol dependence syndrome: Measurement and validation. *Journal of Abnormal Psychology, 91,* 199–209.

Skinner, H. A., & Sheu, W. J. (1982). Reliability of alcohol use indices: The Lifetime Drinking History and the MAST. *Journal of Studies on Alcohol, 43,* 1157–1170.

Sklar, S. M., & Turner, N. E. (1999). A brief measure for the assessment of coping self-efficacy among alcohol and other drug users. *Addiction, 94,* 723–729.

Smart, R. G. (1989). Is the postwar drinking binge ending? Cross-national trends in per capita alcohol consumption. *British Journal of Addictions, 84*(7), 743–748.

Smith, M., & Lin, K.-M. (1996). Gender and ethics differences in the pharmacogenetics of psychotropics. In M. F. Jensvold, U. Halbreich, & J. A. Hamilton (Eds.), *Psychopharmacology and women: Sex, gender, and hormones* (pp. 121–136). Washington, DC: American Psychiatric Press.

Sobell, L. C., Agrawal, S., & Sobell, M. B. (1999). Utility of liver function tests for screening "alcohol abusers" who are not severely dependent on alcohol. *Substance Use & Misuse, 34,* 1723–1732.

Sobell, L. C., Cunningham, J. A., & Sobell, M. B. (1996a). Recovery from alcohol problems with and without treatment: Prevalence in two population surveys. *American Journal of Public Health, 86,* 966–972.

Sobell, L. C., Cunningham, J. A., Sobell, M. B., Agrawal, S., Gavin, D. R., Leo, G. I., et al. (1996b). Fostering self-change among problem drinkers: A proactive community intervention. *Addictive Behaviors, 21,* 817–833.

Sobell, L. C., Ellingstad, T. P., & Sobell, M. B. (2000). Natural recovery from alcohol and drug problems: Methodological review of the research with suggestions for future directions. *Addiction, 95,* 749–764.

Sobell, L. C., & Sobell, M. B. (1980). *Convergent validity: An approach to increasing confidence in treatment outcome conclusions with alcohol and drug abusers.* New York: Pergamon Press.

Sobell, L. C., & Sobell, M. B. (1990). Self-report issues in alcohol abuse: State of the art and future directions. *Behavioral Assessment, 12,* 91–106.

Sobell, L. C., & Sobell, M. B. (1992). Timeline follow-back: A technique for assessing self-reported alcohol consumption. In R. Z. Litten & J. Allen (Eds.), *Measuring alcohol consumption: Psychosocial and biological methods* (pp. 41–72). Totowa, NJ: Humana Press.

Sobell, L. C., & Sobell, M. B. (1992, July). *Stability of natural recoveries from alcohol problems.* Paper presented at the Second International Conference on Behavioural Medicine, Hamburg, Germany.

Sobell, L. C., & Sobell, M. B. (1995a). Alcohol consumption measures. In J. P. Allen & M. Columbus (Eds.), *Assessing alcohol problems: A guide for clinicians and researchers* (pp. 55–73). Rockville, MD: National Institute on Alcohol Abuse and Alcoholism.

Sobell, L. C., & Sobell, M. B. (1996). *Alcohol Timeline Followback (TLFB) Users' Manual.* Toronto, Canada: Addiction Research Foundation.

Sobell, L. C., & Sobell, M. B. (2000a). Alcohol Timeline Followback (TLFB). In American Psychiatric Association (Ed.), *Handbook of psychiatric measures* (pp. 477–479). Washington, DC: Author.

Sobell, L. C., Sobell, M. B., Toneatto, T., & Shillingford, J. A. (1994a). Alcohol problems. In M. Hersen & S. M. Turner (Eds.), *Diagnostic interviewing* (2nd ed., pp. 155–188). New York: Plenum Press.

Sobell, L. C., Toneatto, T., & Sobell, M. B. (1994b). Behavioral assessment and treatment planning for alcohol, tobacco, and other drug problems: Current status with an emphasis on clinical applications. *Behavior Therapy, 25,* 533–580.

Sobell, M. B., Bogardis, J., Schuller, R., Leo, G. I., & Sobell, L. C. (1989). Is self-monitoring of alcohol consumption reactive? *Behavioral Assessment, 11,* 447–458.

Sobell, M. B., & Sobell, L. C. (1987). *Conceptual issues regarding goals in the treatment of alcohol problems.* New York: Haworth Press.

Sobell, M. B., & Sobell, L. C. (1993a). *Problem drinkers: Guided self-change treatment.* New York: Guilford Press.

Sobell, M. B., & Sobell, L. C. (1993b). Treatment for problem drinkers: A public health priority. In J. S. Baer, G. A. Marlatt, & R. J. McMahon (Eds.), *Addictive behaviors across the lifespan: Prevention, treatment, and policy issues* (pp. 138–157). Beverly Hills, CA: Sage.

Sobell, M. B., & Sobell, L. C. (1995b). Controlled drinking after 25 years: How important was the great debate? *Addiction, 90,* 1149–1153.

Sobell, M. B., & Sobell, L. C. (1998). Guiding self-change. In W. R. Miller & N. Heather (Eds.), *Treating addictive behaviors* (2nd ed., pp. 189–202). New York: Plenum Press.

Sobell, M. B., & Sobell, L. C. (2000b). Stepped care as a heuristic approach to the treatment of alcohol problems. *Journal of Consulting and Clinical Psychology, 68,* 573–579.

Sobell, M. B., Sobell, L. C., & Kozlowksi, L. T. (1995). Dual recoveries from alcohol and smoking problems. In J. B. Fertig & J. A. Allen (Eds.), *Alcohol and tobacco: From basic science to clinical practice* (NIAAA Research Monograph No. 30, pp. 207–224). Rockville, MD: National Institute on Alcohol Abuse and Alcoholism.

Sobell, M. B., Sobell, L. C., & VanderSpek, R. (1979). Relationships between clinical judgment, self-report and breath analysis measures of intoxication in alcoholics. *Journal of Consulting and Clinical Psychology, 47,* 204–206.

Sobell, M. B., Wilkinson, D. A., & Sobell, L. C. (1990). Alcohol and drug problems. In A. S. Bellack, M. Hersen, & A. E. Kazdin (Eds.), *International handbook of behavior modification and therapy* (2nd ed., pp. 415–435). New York: Plenum Press.

Sokolow, L., Welte, J., Hynes, G., & Lyons, J. (1981). Multiple substance use by alcoholics. *British Journal of Addiction, 76,* 147–158.

Sørensen, T., Bentsen, K., Eghøje, K., & Christoffersen, P. (1984). Prospective evaluation of alcohol abuse and alcoholic liver injury in men as predictors of development of cirrhosis. *Lancet, August* 4;2(8397), 241–244.

Stinson, F. S., Grant, B. F., Dawson, D. A., Ruan, W. J., Huang, B., & Saha, T. (2005). Comorbidity between *DSM-IV* alcohol and specific drug use disorders in the United States: Results from the National Epidemiologic Survey on Alcohol and Related Conditions. *Drug and Alcohol Dependence, 80,* 105–116.

Stockwell, T., Murphy, D., & Hodgson, R. (1983). The Severity of Alcohol Dependence Questionnaire: Its use, reliability and validity. *British Journal of Addiction, 78,* 145–155.

Stockwell, T., Sitharthan, T., McGrath, D., & Lang, E. (1994). The measurement of alcohol dependence and impaired control in community samples. *Addiction, 89,* 167–174.

Strakowski, S. M., & DelBello, M. P. (2000). The co-occurrence of bipolar and substance use disorders. *Clinicial Psychology Review, 20,* 191–206.

Strang, J., Black, J., Marsh, A., & Smith, B. (1993). Hair analysis for drugs: Technological breakthrough or ethical quagmire? *Addictions, 88,* 163–166.

Substance Abuse and Mental Health Administration. (1999). *Enhancing motivation for change in substance abuse treatment (Treatment Improvement Protocol Series).* Rockville, MD: U.S. Department of Health and Human Services.

Swendsen, J. D., & Merikangas, K. R. (2000). The comorbidity of depression and substance use disorders. *Clinicial Psychology Review, 20,* 173–189.

Toneatto, T., Sobell, L. C., Sobell, M. B., & Leo, G. I. (1991). *Psychoactive substance use disorder (Alcohol).* New York: Wiley.

Trull, T. J., Sher, K. J., MinksBrown, C., Durbin, J., & Burr, R. (2000). Borderline personality disorder and substance use disorders: A review and integration. *Clinicial Psychology Review, 20,* 235–253.

U.S. Department of Health and Human Services. (1985). *Report of the Secretary's task force on black & minority chemical dependency and diabetes: Vol. VII.* Washington, DC: Author.

U.S. Department of Health and Human Services (2005 [revised 2007]). *Helping patients who drink too much: A clinician's guide.* DHHS Pub. No. 07–3769. Rockville, MD: National Institute on Alcohol Abuse and Alcoholism.

Vega, W., & Gil, A. G. (1998). *Drug use and ethnicity in early adolescence.* New York: Plenum Press.

Verebey, K., & Turner, C. E. (1991). Laboratory testing. In R. J. Frances & S. I. Miller (Eds.), *Clinical textbook of addictive disorders* (pp. 221–236). New York: Guilford Press.

Welte, J. W., & Barnes, G. M. (1995). Alcohol and other drug use among Hispanics in New York state. *Alcoholism: Clinical and Experimental Research, 19,* 1061–1066.

Wikler, A. (1973). Dynamics of drug dependence. *Archives of General Psychiatry, 28,* 611–616.

Wilkinson, D. A., & Carlen, P. L. (1980). Neuropsychological and neurological assessment of alcoholism: Discrimination between groups of alcoholics. *Journal of Studies on Alcohol, 41,* 129–139.

Wilsnack, R. W., Vogeltanz, N. D., Wilsnack, S. C., & Harris, T. R. (2000). Gender differences in alcohol consumption and adverse drinking consequences: Cross-cultural patterns. *Addiction, 95,* 251–265.

Wilsnack, S. C., Klassen, A.D., Schur, B. E., & Wilsnack, R. W. (1991). Predicting onset and chronicity of women's problem drinking: A five-year longitudinal analysis. *American Journal of Public Health, 81,* 305–318.

Wilsnack, S. C., & Wilsnack, R. W. (1995). *Drinking and problem drinking in US women: Patterns and recent trends.* New York: Plenum Press.

Wodak, A. D., Saunders, J. B., Ewusi-Mensah, I., Davis, M., & Williams, R. (1983). Severity of alcohol dependence in patients with alcoholic liver disease. *British Medical Journal, 287,* 1420–1422.

Woody, G. (1996). The challenge of dual diagnosis. *Alcohol Health and Research World, 20,* 76–80.

Yu, E. S. H., Liu, W. T., Xia, Z., & Zhang, M. (1989). *Alcohol use, abuse, and alcoholism among Chinese Americans: A review of the epidemiologic data.* DHHS Pub. No. (ADM) 89–1435. Rockville, MD: National Institute on Alcohol Abuse and Alcoholism.

CHAPTER 7

Psychoactive Substance Use Disorders: Drugs

STACEY B. DAUGHTERS, MARINA A. BORNOVALOVA,
CHRISTOPHER J. CORREIA, AND C. W. LEJUEZ

DESCRIPTION OF THE DISORDER

The incidence and prevalence of substance use disorders (SUDs) continue to present major costs to individuals, families, and society at large. The *DSM-IV* (APA, 1994) diagnostic criteria for substance dependence specifies a maladaptive pattern of substance use leading to clinically significant impairment or distress as manifested by three (or more) problems occurring at any time in the same 12-month period. An estimated 19.1 million (7.9%) Americans aged 12 or older were current (past month) illicit drug users in 2004. It has been estimated that $484 billion is spent each year on substance abuse–related costs, including treatment and prevention, health care expenditures, lost wages, reduced job production, accidents, and crime, with more than 60% of these costs linked to drug-related incidents. Aside from the troubling public cost statistics, and as illustrated in the case study below, SUDs are associated with engagement in multiple health-compromising behaviors (e.g., condom nonuse, multiple partners, exchange of sex for money or drugs) resulting in numerous adverse physical, social, and emotional consequences (Office of National Drug Control Policy [ONDCP], 2002; Substance Abuse and Mental Health Services Administration [SAMHSA], 2005).

Case Study

The patient (Carole) is a 38-year-old African American female who was court-mandated to 30 days of treatment at a community residential substance use

(continued)

---

treatment center. At the time of treatment entry, she reported living with her boyfriend of 5 years and their 2-year-old son, as well as a son (aged 16) and two daughters (aged 14 and 17) from her previous marriage. Carole completed high school and had worked for 15 years as an administrative assistant at a small paint company. About 3 years ago she was fired largely because of substance-induced impairment at work and she has not worked since this time. She reported financial dependence on her boyfriend, but refused to provide details regarding his employment. She displayed psychomotor agitation and her thought process was somewhat clouded; however, no obvious perceptual abnormalities were evident. Her speech volume and tone were within normal limits, yet her speech rate was somewhat faster than normal.

At intake, the SCID-IV and Addiction Severity Index were administered to determine substance dependence, substance use history and severity, environmental strengths and stressors, legal issues, and psychiatric symptoms. Based on this assessment, she met criteria for current crack/cocaine dependence and alcohol abuse. She reported past heroin dependence more than 5 years ago when she first began using drugs regularly, but crack/cocaine had become her sole drug of choice over the last 3 to 4 years. She reported an extensive family history of substance use, including heroin and crack/cocaine dependence in her father who passed away about 5 years ago. In her current environment, her boyfriend uses crack/cocaine and alcohol regularly. She reported that he is unwilling to seek treatment for his substance use, and has interfered with her past abstinence attempts. Although she was unsure, she suspected that her oldest son might be using drugs and engaging in criminal activity, which was a source of great worry for her. She reported no substance use concerns regarding her other children.

The assessment of legal issues indicated that she was mandated to treatment following her participation in the robbery of a local convenience store. She was the only one apprehended and she refused to reveal the identity of the others involved. This was her only interaction with the legal system, with the exception of being arrested with her boyfriend about two months ago for a domestic disturbance; charges against both parties were eventually dropped. She denied any other criminal activity on the part of her or her boyfriend. When questioned further about domestic violence, she reported that the relationship sometimes "gets physical," but she was unwilling to provide any details or acknowledge any abuse or imminent danger to herself or her children. Carole evidenced difficulty in identifying strengths; however, with some additional probing she was able to acknowledge potential support from her sister and the importance of her spirituality.

The assessment of psychiatric symptoms indicated elevated depressive symptoms and difficulty controlling violent behavior. She reported a long history of emotional sensitivity with frequent "ups and downs" in her relationships with friends, family, and significant others. Because of time and resource constraints at the center, the SCID-IV or any other more elaborate measure of Axis-I and II psychiatric comorbidity was not administered. Such assessment may have been useful in this case for further exploring the extent of her depression (including its independence from substance use), the likely presence of borderline personality disorder, and for ruling out antisocial personality disorder.

Especially given that she was court-mandated and not self-referred, additional assessment of her motivation and treatment readiness included the Stages of Change Readiness and Treatment Eagerness Scale (SOCRATES) and a brief history of past drug treatment efforts and self-initiated abstinence attempts. The SOCRATES indicated that she was in the contemplation stage, suggesting awareness of her problem but ambivalence about seeking treatment. Although not an extensive functional analysis (again because of time and resource constraints), further targeted questioning was used to identify barriers to change and the extent to which these barriers were negatively influencing her motivation for treatment. First, given her boyfriend's substance use problems she was concerned about the care of her 2-year-old child while she was to complete her 30 days of mandated treatment. Further, she reported serious concern with treatment interference she might receive from her boyfriend, as well as difficulties that their volatile relationship might produce once she returned home. Finally, she reported intensifying feelings of sadness and shame that she had used crack/cocaine and how this had affected her children, as well as the potential legal consequences of her criminal behavior.

Following review of her initial assessment, a preliminary treatment plan was developed to treat her crack/cocaine dependence. Specific attention was focused on addressing environmental factors maintaining her substance use including coping with triggers identified in the initial assessment. Efforts to enhance her motivation to change also were planned through the targeting of barriers identified above, including childcare and potential interference from her boyfriend, as well as greater attention to potential strengths and supports that might be used in treatment. Ongoing assessment of mood and psychiatric consultation also was planned to assess the impact of substance use treatment on overall well-being and to identify the need for more explicit and specific treatment of other co-morbid conditions. Finally, a posttreatment ASI was planned to identify treatment gains and additional areas for further attention in aftercare following her discharge.

EPIDEMIOLOGY

An estimated 22.5 million persons (9.4%) aged 12 or older in 2004 were classified with substance dependence or abuse in the past year, with only 3.8 million (1.6%) having received some kind of treatment for a problem related to substance use (SAMHSA, 2005). Marijuana is the most commonly used illicit drug, closely followed by cocaine, hallucinogens, and heroin. Specifically, 7.9% of persons 12 or older reported past-month use of any illicit drug, with 54.6% of these individuals using only marijuana, 20.6% using marijuana and some other drug, and 24.8% using only drugs other than marijuana. Finally, more then 2 million people used cocaine within the past 30 days (0.8%) and that over 5.6 million people used it within the past year (2.4%). With regard to heroin, 166,000 (0.1%) individuals used it in the past month, and 398,000 (0.1%) in the past year.

Young adults are especially vulnerable to the initiation and continued use of illicit drugs. For instance, data from the Monitoring the Future Study (an ongoing study of the behaviors, attitudes, and values of American secondary school students, college students, and young adults) indicates that although the use of several drugs (including marijuana, ecstasy, and amphetamines) is beginning to decline, the rates are still relatively high. Up to 15% of adolescents have used amphetamines and up to 46% have used marijuana. Moreover, there is a recent increase in prescription drug and inhalant use, with 17% of high school students having used inhalants at least once (Johnson, O'Malley, Bachman, & Schulenberg, 2005).

As one may expect, SUD prevalence rates are considerably higher when examining inpatient and psychiatric centers. Data indicate that among psychiatric outpatients, current and lifetime rates of SUDs range from 20% to 40%, and among psychiatric inpatients, current and lifetime rates of SUDs range from 40% to 60%. Among incarcerated individuals, rates of SUDs are the highest, from 45% to 70%. These elevated rates are not surprising, given that the risk factors that lead to psychiatric hospitalization or incarceration (i.e., psychiatric disorders, risky behavior) also leave one vulnerable to substance abuse and dependence (de Lima, Lorea, & Carpena, 2002).

CLINICAL PICTURE

Drugs of abuse are often categorized into specific drug classes that differ in their physiological and behavioral effects on the individual. These include cannabinoids (i.e., marijuana), CNS depressants (i.e., benzodiazepines), dissociative anesthetics (i.e., ketamine), entactogens (i.e., ecstacy), hallucinogens (i.e., LSD), inhalants (i.e., nitrous oxide), opioid analgesics (i.e., heroin), and stimulants (i.e., cocaine). Table 7.1 lists information on the most commonly used and abused substances along with their behavioral and physiological effects. This is not meant to be an exhaustive list; thus the interested reader is referred to Julien (2004) for a more extensive discussion of this topic.

COURSE AND PROGNOSIS

Although many adolescents may experiment with drugs, the majority do not progress to abuse or dependence (Newcomb and Richardson, 1995). As such, it is important to understand the risk factors for the development of substance dependence. Evidence indicates that earlier age of substance use initiation and heavy use during adolescence are two risk factors (Kandel & Davis, 1992). In addition, drug-related problems (i.e., some symptoms of an SUD without meeting full diagnostic criteria) in adolescence significantly predicts a future substance use disorder, elevated levels of depression, and antisocial and borderline personality disorder symptoms by age 24 (Rohde, Lewinsohn, Kahler, Seeley, & Brown, 2001). Finally, for adolescents who later develop a substance use disorder, drug involvement is typically progressive, beginning with substances legal for adults, followed by marijuana, and then other illicit drugs (e.g., Anthony & Petronis, 1995). Gender differences have been noted in this progression, such that for males, progression to illicit drug use was dependent on prior use of alcohol, whereas for females either cigarette or alcohol use was sufficient for progression to illicit drug use (Kandel & Davis, 1992).

Table 7.1

Common Drugs of Abuse: Summary of Routes of Administration and Behavioral Effects

Drugs, Commercial and Slang Name(s)	Routes of Administration	Acute Effects of Intoxication	Possible Adverse Effects	Tolerance and Dependence
Cannabinoids				
Hashish boom, hash, hash oil, hemp Marijuana Marinol, pot, grass, weed, reefer, blunt	Smoked via cigarette, pipe, or water-filtered pipe (i.e., bong). Can also be administered orally.	Effects include increased pulse and appetite, dry mouth, enhanced sensory perception, mild euphoria, relaxation, sedation, and psychomotor impairment. Higher doses can produce dizziness, illusions, and hallucinations in some users.	Risk of toxic overdose is minimal, although some users experience brief paranoid reactions and panic at high doses. Chronic use of smoked THC associated with pulmonary damage; deficits in learning, cognition, and motivation; immunosupression; precipitation of psychotic episode among those with latent potential.	Tolerance occurs with repeated use. Withdrawal symptoms are typically mild and can include restlessness, anxiety, depression, irritability/aggression, insomnia, tremor, and chills. Withdrawal does not pose medical risk.
CNS Depressants				
Alcohol Barbiturates Amytal, Seconal, Phenobarbital, barbs, reds, yellows Benzodiazepines Diazepam (Valium), Lorazepam (Ativan), Clonazepam (Klonopin), Alprazolam (Xanax), candy, downers, sleeping pills	Benzodiazepines and alcohol are orally administered.	Effects of CNS depressants can be context dependent and "biphasic." Euphoria and disinhibition are common at low to moderate doses. High doses produce clouded sensorium, sedation, impaired judgment and motor ability, amnesia/blackouts, affect lability, aggression, delusions, and hallucinations. Benzodiazepines are	Dangerous levels of respiratory depression are possible at high doses or when CNS depressants are taken in combination with one another. Other effects include sedation, impaired judgment and cognitive performance, amnesia, and psychomotor impairment. High doses of alcohol can lead to asphyxiation from vomiting. Chronic heavy use of alcohol can lead to irreversible	Tolerance occurs with long-term use. Withdrawal symptoms include agitation and increased anxiety, insomnia, muscle tension and nausea with vomiting. Severe withdrawal symptoms include tremors and seizures (e.g., deliriums tremens) hallucinations, and psychotic symptoms. These symptoms can be fatal and often require medical attention.

(continued)

Table 7.1 *(Continued)*

Drugs, Commercial and Slang Name(s)	Routes of Administration	Acute Effects of Intoxication	Possible Adverse Effects	Tolerance and Dependence
		intended for short-term relief of anxiety and insomnia; higher doses produce lightheadedness, vertigo, and muscle incoordination.	liver damage, dementia, pancreatitis, gastritis, peptic ulcers, and cancers.	
Dissociative Anesthetic				
Ketamine cat, K, special K, vitamin K, date rape drug Phencyclidine PCP, angel dust, boat, hog, love boat, peace pill, rocket fuel, sherms	Ketamine can be injected, snorted, or smoked. PCP can also be swallowed.	Dream-like disorientation, euphoria, and analgesia are among the most commonly reported effects. Additional effects include impaired motor functioning, slurred speech, and detachment from environment, as well as increased heart rate, blood pressure, and temperature.	PCP can cause potentially lethal seizures and coma. Possible acute and prolonged psychotic states leading to bizarre or dangerous behaviors have also been observed. Ketamine produces more extreme CNS depression, numbness, nausea and vomiting, amnesia and dissociation.	Tolerance rises quickly, and chronic users will experience permanent tolerance after several months of use. These drugs do not appear to produce withdrawal symptoms or physical addiction.
Entactogens				
Methylenedioxy-amphetamine MDA Methylenedioxy-ethlylamphetamine	Usually swallowed in the form of a pill, although pure powder forms are sometimes injected, and tablets	MDMA produced mild hallucinogenic effects, increased tactile sensitivity, empathic feelings, mental alertness, and sympathetic	MDMA can be fatal when combined with high levels of physical activity, leading to hyperthermia, hypertension, and kidney failure. MDMA	Tolerance develops, but there is no evidence of physical withdrawal. Aftereffects can include fatigue, depression, and anxiety.

Drug / street names	Route	Effects	Tolerance and dependence
MDEA, Eve Methylenedioxy-methamphetamine MDMA, Ecstasy, X, XTC, Adam, lover's speed, peace, STP. Trail mix and sex-tasy used to denote combination of MDMA and Viagra (sildenafil citrate).	can be inserted into the anus.	nervous system stimulation. MDEA effects resemble those of MDMA, but without the empathic qualities. MDA produces stronger hallucinogenic effects.	appears to lead to short and potentially long-term changes in the serotonergic system, which may result in residual anxiety, depression, and cognitive impairment. Flashbacks following repeated use have been reported.
Hallucinogens			
Dimethyltrypyamine DMT, business man's trip Lysergic acid diethylamide LSD, acid, blotter, cubes, microdot	Oral administration is typical. LSD can also be absorbed through mouth tissue; DMT and mescaline can be smoked.	Altered states of perception and bodily sensations, intense emotions, detachment from self and environment, and, for some users, feelings of insight with mystical or religious significance. Mescaline also has some amphetamine-like effects.	Psychological symptoms such as emotional lability, panic, and paranoia can lead to bizarre or dangerous behavior. Persisting mental disorders, including panic attacks and psychosis, can be precipitated by use in those with latent potential. Hallucinogenic persisting perception disorder ("flashbacks") can occur, particularly during periods of stress or fatigue, or as a result of subsequent drug intoxication.
Mescaline peyote, buttons, cactus Psilocybin psychedelic or magic mushrooms, shrooms			Tolerance builds up rapidly but fades after a few days. Hallucinogens do not produce withdrawal and are not physically addictive.

(continued)

Table 7.1 (*Continued*)

Drugs, Commercial and Slang Name(s)	Routes of Administration	Acute Effects of Intoxication	Possible Adverse Effects	Tolerance and Dependence
Inhalants				
Anesthetics nitrous oxide Solvents paint thinner, glue, correction fluid, marker pens Gases butane, propane Aerosols paint, hair spray Nitrites "poppers" from heart medications	Inhalation	Rapid onset of sedation, euphoria, and disinhibition. Acute effects can include loss of consciousness, blackout, muscle weakness, impaired coordination, and slurred speech. Nitrates dilate blood vessels and produce sensation of heat and excitement believed to enhance sexual pleasure.	Use of inhalants can lead to lack of oxygen, ischemia of heart tissue, life-threatening cardiac arrhythmias, cardiac collapse, peripheral nerve damage, liver or kidney damage, and suffocation. Regular use can produce irreversible brain and peripheral nerve damage.	Tolerance and withdrawal are possible with prolonged use of nitrates. Tolerance to nitrous oxide is possible but unlikely with recreational use. Little is know about the tolerance and withdrawal profile of other inhalants.
Opioid Analgesics				
Heroin black tar, smack, junk, dope Prescription Analgesics Morphine, Codeine, Demerol, Oxycodone Oxycontin, Percocet, Vicodin	Heroin is injected, smoked, and used intranasally. Oral medications are misused by crushing tablet and snorting or injecting.	Analgesia, euphoria, sedation, reduced anxiety, tranquility, respiratory depression, and cough suppression.	Respiratory depression can be fatal at high doses, or when regular users use in novel environments. Other side effects include nausea, vomiting, constipation and intestinal cramping, severe itching, and	Tolerance occurs with prolonged use. Withdrawal includes flu-like symptoms, craving, sweating, anxiety, depression, irritability, vomiting, diarrhea, and pain. Compulsive use to avoid withdrawal is common.

Stimulants

Drug	Administration	Effects	Health Risks	Dependence/Withdrawal
Amphetamines Adderall, Dexedrine; bennies, speed, Cocaine Cooke, blow, crack, Methamphetamine crank, crystal fire, ice, meth, speed Methylphenidate Ritalin; vitamin R Nicotine Chew, cigars, cigarettes, smokeless tobacco, snuff, spit tobacco	Injected, smoked, and snorted. Stimulant medication can be swallowed, or crushed and then snorted or injected.	Commonly reported effects include feelings of euphoria, increased energy, mental alertness, and rapid speech. Signs of sympathetic nervous system stimulation include increased, heart rate, blood pressure, temperature, and both purposeful and compulsive movements.	Rapid or irregular heart beat, heart failure, respiratory failure, strokes, seizures, headaches, abdominal pain, nausea. With prolonged exposure to high doses, a psychotic state of hostility and paranoia can emerge that is similar to acute paranoid schizophrenia. Specific effects of prolonged exposure to nicotine products include chronic lung disease, cardiovascular disease, stroke, and cancer. asthma-like symptoms. HIV, Hepatitis C, and bacterial infections are spread through injecting.	Tolerance builds quickly. Users typically experience fatigue and dysphoria after intoxication. Withdrawal symptoms can be severe but are dangerous and include fatigue, anxiety, sleeplessness, nightmares, irritability, anhedonia, and depression.

Once a substance use disorder is present, recovery is notoriously difficult, even with exceptional treatment resources. These difficulties extend beyond treatment-seeking individuals, and begin with those who do not enter treatment at all. National Comorbidity Survey (NCS) data indicate that a majority of people with substance use disorders receive no professional treatment for their substance use (Kessler, Blazer, McGonagle, & Swartz, 1994). Individuals who do not seek treatment services are traditionally expected to have poor outcomes. In support of this, Öjesjö (2000) examined data from a 40-year follow-up study of substance-related problems among substance users who did and did not receive treatment. Compared to the treated substance abusers, untreated substance abusers reported significantly more medical (64% vs. 25%), mental (45% vs. 17%), family (27% vs. 0%), and work (18% vs. 8%) problems.

Many clients who do eventually seek treatment wait until they are well into a drug-using lifestyle. For instance, the NIDA-supported Drug Abuse Treatment Outcome Study (DATOS) indicates that on average, treatment entry lags 6 to 10 years after the initiation of drug use, despite the clear negative lifestyle, health, and emotional consequences of drug use. In a study of 276 treatment-seeking drug users who were provided referrals to local drug treatment programs, 38% did not enter treatment, with nearly half (48%) reporting that they had decided they did not need treatment after all; 25% said that it was too difficult to make the necessary arrangements to go to treatment; and 20% were dissuaded by the latency to treatment initiation by the mental health provider (i.e., waiting list; Hser, Maglione, Polinsky, & Anglin, 1997). Among other reasons were program admission eligibility problems (23%), financial difficulty (21%), and scheduling conflicts (8%). Together, these results are consistent with previous studies suggesting that the desire for treatment among many drug users may change prior to their first treatment session.

Once treatment is initiated, the next challenge is staying in treatment. Treatment dropout rates range up to 50% (SAMHSA, 2005). Such high rates of premature treatment termination are of concern, because length of time in treatment is significantly related to positive outcomes (e.g., Simpson, Joe, & Brown, 1997). For clients who remain in treatment, relapse and eventual readmission are fairly common and particularly likely when addiction is accompanied by one or more psychiatric problems. Indeed, estimates suggest that 90% of heroin- and cocaine-dependent users experience at least one relapse within the 4 years after treatment, with many relapsing considerably sooner. Further, of the patients admitted to the U.S. public treatment system in 1999, 60% were reentering treatment, including 23% for the second time, 13% for the third time, 7% for the fourth time, 4% for the fifth time, and 13% for sixth or subsequent times (Office of Applied Studies, 2000). Retrospective and prospective treatment studies report that most participants initiate three to four episodes of treatment over multiple years before reaching a stable state of abstinence (Hser, Grella, Chou, & Anglin, 1998).

At first glance, the high rates of dropout and relapse may seem rather disappointing. Interestingly, however, a recent review by Hser and colleagues (1999) suggests that, given the chronic, relapsing course of drug dependence, multiple treatment episodes may be better understood as parts of a cyclical process of recovery than as categorical failures. The rationale is that treatment for drug dependence may require an extended intervention involving staged recovery efforts that are not usually possible in a single treatment episode. Further, recent research has begun to report some encouraging findings indicating that treatment effects may be cumulative—that is, they accumulate across multiple treatment episodes (Powers & Anglin, 1993). Despite these findings, the continued investigation of a "first-time" effective treatment for substance dependence is needed, given that many individuals suffering from substance use disorders lack the financial resources or motivation to attempt multiple treatment episodes.

DIAGNOSTIC CONSIDERATIONS

The *Diagnostic and Statistical Manual* (*DSM-IV-TR*; APA, 2000) provides a comprehensive classification system for the assessment and subsequent diagnosis of substance abuse and dependence. The *DSM-IV-TR* diagnostic criteria for substance *abuse* require evidence of a maladaptive pattern of substance use with clinically significant levels of impairment or distress. Impairment in this case is defined as an inability to meet major role obligations, leading to reduced functioning in one or more major life areas, risk-taking behavior, an increase in the likelihood of legal problems because of possession, and exposure to hazardous situations. Within the *DSM*, substance abuse is treated as a residual category, such that it can only be met without the presence of current substance dependence.

The *DSM-IV-TR* diagnostic criteria for substance *dependence* specifies a maladaptive pattern of substance use leading to clinically significant impairment or distress as manifested by three (or more) problems occurring at any time in the same 12-month period. These problems include (1) taking the substance in larger amounts or over a longer period than intended; (2) a persistent desire or unsuccessful efforts to cut down or control substance use; (3) spending a great deal of time in activities necessary to obtain (e.g., visiting multiple doctors or driving long distances), use (e.g., chain smoking), or recover (e.g., recovering from a hangover) from the effects of substance use; (4) reduction in important social, occupational, or recreational activities; and (5) continued use despite knowledge of having a persistent or recurrent psychological or physical problem that is caused or exacerbated by use of the substance. Additional symptoms of dependence are tolerance, defined as either a need for increasing amounts of the substance in order to achieve intoxication or desired effect or markedly diminished effect with continued use of the same amount; and withdrawal that is manifested by physical or psychological symptoms characteristic for a particular substance (APA, 2000). For instance, in the case of heroin, withdrawal symptoms may include flulike symptoms, nausea, stomachaches, and cramps. In contrast, withdrawal from crack/cocaine usually includes severe but transient dysphoria, nightmares, and fatigue. Interestingly, anecdotal and empirical evidence suggest that when an individual is dependent on two or more drugs (e.g., cocaine and heroin), withdrawal from one drug (heroin) might "mask" the relatively less severe withdrawal from its counterpart (cocaine), suggesting a need for careful screening and questioning in diagnostic interviews. Additional information on the withdrawal symptoms associated with specific drugs is included in Table 7.1.

Another system, the *International Classification of Diseases, Tenth Revision* (*ICD-10*; World Health Organization [WHO], 1994) is considered the international standard diagnostic classification for all general epidemiological and many health management purposes, including the analysis of the general health situation of population groups and monitoring of the incidence and prevalence of diseases in relation to social, biological, and interpersonal variables. Although the *DSM* and

ICD have very similar definitions of substance dependence, the two systems have had different paradigms for less severe forms of maladaptive substance use that overlap only partially. Consider the example of a diagnosis of substance abuse (in the *DSM-IV*) and the corresponding diagnosis of harmful use (in the *ICD-10*). As pointed out previously, the *DSM-IV* defines substance abuse as a residual category; simply stated, the diagnosis of substance abuse cannot be made in the presence of substance dependence, as one category subsumes the other. In contrast, this is not the case for harmful use in the *ICD-10.* Further, the *DSM-IV* characterizes substance abuse by negative *legal* and *social* consequences of recurrent or continued use. In contrast, the *ICD-10* includes a category for harmful use (a nonresidual category) that requires demonstrable *physical* or *psychological* harm. The emphasis on physical or psychological harm (rather than legal and social) in the *ICD-10* stems from a need for developing criteria that can be applied uniformly across different countries and cultures. Although agreement between and reliability of *ICD* and *DSM-IV* substance dependence diagnoses is high across classes of drugs and across different settings and countries, agreement between *ICD-10* harmful use and *DSM-IV* abuse is generally low, and test-retest reliability of *ICD-10* harmful use and *DSM-IV* abuse falls in the low to moderate range (Üstün et al., 1997). Finally, *DSM* and *ICD* differ in their criteria for remission from substance dependence and in their definitions of substance-induced disorders. Although no current data support the adoption of one system over the other, the preceding studies do point to a need for a careful interpretation of empirical results, at least in regard to abuse and harmful use.

Evidence indicates that substance use disorders co-occur with the majority of adult *DSM-IV-TR* Axis I and II disorders. Community epidemiological studies suggest that among individuals with SUDs, 53% to 76% have at least one other co-occurring psychiatric disorder (Zilberman, Cao, & Jacobsen, 2003), with mood and anxiety disorders being the most commonly occurring, followed by schizophrenia-spectrum disorders (Kushner, Abrams, & Borchardt, 2000). In addition to Axis-I comorbidity, SUDs often co-occur with Axis II disorders. Specifically, borderline and antisocial personality disorders have the highest rates of comorbidity; with estimates ranging from 5% to 32% and 14% to 69%, respectively (e.g., Trull, Sher, Minks-Brown, Durbin, & Burr, 2000). In fact, estimates from the ECA study suggest that SUDs are more strongly associated with antisocial personality disorder than with any other Axis I disorder (Regier et al., 1993).

Rates of comorbidity within psychiatric inpatient and residential substance abuse treatment facilities are considerably higher than within the general community. A recent study (Mowbray, Collins, Plum, Masterton, & Mulder, 1997) of an inpatient unit suggested that for those with an SUD, the most common co-occurring diagnoses were schizophrenia-spectrum disorders (42%), affective disorders (29%), personality or adjustment disorders (26%), and organic mood disorders (21%); percentages add up to more than 100 because participants could receive more than one diagnosis.

Although comprehensive coverage of comorbidity is beyond the scope of this chapter, a brief discussion of causal direction is warranted (for a comprehensive discussion, the interested reader is referred to Kessler & Price, 1993), as each indicates different prevention and intervention strategies. The first directional model involves a simple linear pathway in which substance use may lead to mental health problems, or conversely, psychiatric distress may cause substance abuse and/or dependence (with the latter often referred to as the "self-medication hypothesis"). As one example, panic attacks may result from cocaine use and persist even after cocaine abstinence has been achieved, with the latter possibly increasing the likelihood of relapse back to cocaine or another drug to cope with these panic attacks. As a second example, patients with eating disorders may progress from using amphetamine-containing diet pills to using another CNS stimulant (e.g., cocaine), in turn, leading to dependence on the substance in question. Similarly, a persistent affective disorder may lead to illicit drug use, serving as a maladaptive yet reinforcing coping strategy. The second potential directional model suggests that biological factors (including neurotransmitter function and genetic effects) could contribute to the development of both disorders (Trull et al., 2000). In the case of neurotransmitter function, there is considerable evidence that both substance use disorders and many other psychiatric disorders are characterized by disturbances in serotonergic functioning (e.g., Brown, Korn, & Van Praag, 1990). Similarly, research has focused on deficiencies in dopamine (a neurotransmitter that plays a crucial role in the mechanism of reward and reinforcement) as a unifying mechanism between substance use disorders and psychiatric comorbidity. Specifically, a number of studies have indicated that those with comparatively lower levels of dopamine are likely to repeat behaviors that increase dopamine release to compensate for a chronic low reward state (Blum et al., 2000), and a parallel line of evidence has implicated reduced dopamine in a number of disorders and maladaptive behaviors that commonly co-occur with substance abuse and dependence (e.g., Heinz, 2002). In support of a genetic link, using a twin study design it was reported that the heritable factor of disinhibition may underlie the development of both substance use and impulse-control disorders (Krueger et al., 2002). As a final directional model, social and environmental factors, such as a chaotic household, childhood trauma, poverty, or family history of psychopathology may lead to either SUD, psychiatric disorders, or the comorbidity between the two (Fergusson, Horwood, & Lynskey, 1994). Of course these directional models are not mutually exclusive, but understanding the role of each may indicate the most effective targets for intervention.

PSYCHOLOGICAL AND BIOLOGICAL ASSESSMENT

There are a number of variables to consider when determining the best method of assessment for patients with substance use problems. It is important to determine if the goal of the assessment is to screen for potential substance use problems, determine if an individual meets diagnostic criteria for SUD, develop treatment goals and a treatment plan, or to assess treatment outcome. Also, variation in assessment environments (i.e., primary care vs. treatment setting) will play a role in determining the most appropriate assessment measure. The following section describes the options for each assessment level.

SCREENING AND DIAGNOSIS

Screening Instruments   Given the high rate of comorbidity between SUD and other Axis-I disorders, patients often present to treatment for problems other than drug dependence. As such, screening measures are often useful means for identifying individuals with a drug use problem. Modeled after the Alcohol Use Disorders Identification Test (AUDIT; Saunders, Aasland, Babor, et al., 1993), the Drug Use Disorder

Identification Test (DUDIT; Stuart, Moore, & Kahler, 2003) is an 11-item self-report measure to screen for drug-related problems across the following drug classes: cannabis, cocaine, hallucinogens, stimulants, sedatives, and opiates. The DUDIT has demonstrated strong reliability (.80) and has predicted drug dependence in accordance with the *DSM-IV* and ICD-10 at 78% and 88%, respectively (Berman, Bergman, Palmstierna, & Schlyter, 2005).

The CAGE is a mnemonic that uses the following four questions for assessing four areas related to lifetime alcohol use: (1, C) Have you ever felt the need to Cut down on your drinking? (2, A) Have you ever felt Annoyed by someone criticizing your drinking? (3, G) Have you ever felt bad or Guilty about your drinking? (4, E) Have you ever had a drink first thing in the morning to steady your nerves and get rid of a hangover? (Eye-opener) (Cooney, Zweben, & Fleming, 1995). Each "have you ever" question can be answered either Yes or No and each positive response gets 1 point. A score of 1 of 4 indicates "possible," and 2 detects most cases of substance misuse. Because it requires less than one minute for administration, it is a useful bedside clinical desk instrument for family practice physicians, general internists, and nurses. The CAGE has a sensitivity and specificity of 86% and 78%, respectively. It is of note that because many false positives have been reported among women when using the CAGE (because of the question about guilt), the TACE mnemonic, which uses similar but not identical questions, was developed as a gender appropriate version for women. The Drug Abuse Screening Test (DAST; Skinner, 1982) consists of 20 items focused on lifetime severity of drug abuse and its consequences and provides an index of drug-use severity. The DAST covers a variety of consequences related to drug use without specifying drug type, alleviating the necessity of using different instruments specific to each drug. It has a demonstrated internal consistency of .92.

The MCMI-III (Millon & Meagher, 2004) has a 14-item drug-dependence scale. High scores on this scale suggest a recurrent or recent history of drug abuse, a tendency to have poor impulse control, and an inability to manage the consequences of drug use and impulsive behavior. (The scale has coefficients of .82 and .92 for internal consistency and test-retest reliability, respectively). The questions on the MCMI-III are subtle and indirect in asking about drug use, which has been argued as advantageous by some because it can detect individuals reluctant to discuss their drug use openly. However, this advantage also brings disadvantages. For example, one study found that only 49% of known drug abusers were identified with the MCMI-III drug-dependence scale, questioning the clinical utility of the measure as an effective drug screening tool (Bryer, Martines, & Dignan, 1990).

An additional measure that does not directly assess substance use behavior, but was designed to identify personality characteristics and lifestyle patterns that are associated with substance abuse is the Addiction Potential Scale (APS) of the MMPI-2 (Weed, Butcher, & McKenna, 1992). The APS is a self-report scale consisting of 39 true/false items with internal consistency and test-retest reliability of .77 and .69, respectively.

The Simple Screening Instrument for Substance Abuse (SSI-SA; SAMHSA, 2005) is a 16-item measure in both interview and self-administered formats that was developed to assess a broad spectrum of signs and symptoms for substance use disorders. The SSI-SA screens for five domains of substance use, including substance consumption, preoccupation and loss of control, adverse consequences, problem recognition, and tolerance and withdrawal. The SSI-SA has demonstrated high sensitivity and excellent test-retest reliability.

The Alcohol, Smoking, and Substance Involvement Screening Test (ASSIST; Ali et al., 2002) is an 8-item interview questionnaire developed to detect psychoactive substance use and related problems among primary care patients. The ASSIST provides information about the specific substances patients have used including tobacco, alcohol, cannabis, cocaine, amphetamines, stimulants, sedatives, hallucinogens, inhalants, opioids, and other drugs, as well as the time period of use including lifetime and past three months. Additional items assess problems related to substance use, the risk of current or future harm, level of dependence, and method of use (e.g., needle injection). The ASSIST is especially designed for use by health care workers in a range of health care settings.

The Prescription Drug Use Questionnaire (PDUQ; Compton, Darakjian, & Miotto, 1998) is a 20-minute semistructured interview that was developed to identify pain patients who are likely to become either nonaddicted, a substance abuser, or substance dependent on pain medication. The PDUQ has demonstrated an acceptable internal consistency of .79. Similarly, the Screener and Opioid Assessment for Patients with Pain (SOAPP; Butler, Budman, Fernandez, & Jamison, 2004) is a 14-item self-report tool to determine which chronic pain patients are at risk for long-term addiction to opioid medication. It has an internal consistency of .74 and test-retest reliability of .71.

Diagnostic Instruments   A number of diagnostic instruments are available for use in both research and clinical settings, with advantages and disadvantages inherent in each instrument with regard to administration, cost, and interviewer qualification and training requirements. A recent study evaluated five of the most widely used diagnostic instruments for SUD to determine the most pragmatic and scientifically sound instrument (the interested reader is referred to Forman, Svikis, Montoya, & Blaine, 2004 for more detail). A brief description of each follows.

Although time-consuming and rarely implemented in treatment settings, the Structured Clinical Interview for *DSM-IV-TR* (SCID; First, Spitzer, Gibbon, & Williams, 1997) provides a precise method for identifying substance dependence and abuse and is the most frequently used instrument in clinical trials. In addition to guidelines for general substance dependence and abuse, the interview assesses for dependence and abuse of 11 classes of drugs including alcohol, amphetamines, caffeine, cannabis, cocaine, hallucinogens, inhalants, nicotine, opioids, phencyclidine (PCP), and sedatives, hypnotics, or anxiolytics. The SCID has demonstrated good reliability and validity in clinical research studies. It typically requires 20 to 30 minutes to administer the substance-use module, and computer programs are available for data entry and scoring. Training for clinicians typically requires two to three days.

The Substance Dependence Severity Scale (SDSS; Miele et al., 2000) is a semistructured, clinician-administered interview that assesses *DSM-IV* dependence and abuse, as well as *ICD-10* harmful use across 11 drug classes. The SDSS also is unique in that it assesses both the frequency and severity of symptoms. For each symptom, the SDSS assesses total number of days a symptom occurred, usual severity of the symptom, and worst severity of the symptom over a 30-day time frame. In contrast, other measures are limited because they assess only one substance (e.g., alcohol or opiates) or one dimension, such as how often a symptom occurred or how intense or severe a symptom was. In studies of substance abusers the test-retest reliability and internal consistency of the SDSS has ranged from good to excellent across drug classes. It can be administered by a clinician in 30 to 45 minutes and typically requires two to three days of training.

The Diagnostic Interview Schedule for *DSM-IV* (DIS-IV; Robins, Helzer, Croughan, & Ratcliff, 1981) is a fully structured interview that assesses for the presence of *DSM-IV* lifetime and past-12-month history of symptoms across 11 drug classes. The DIS-IV has demonstrated good reliability and validity and can be administered by a lay interviewer, which greatly reduces training and supervision costs. The interview itself takes 15 to 25 minutes; a computerized version is also available.

The Composite International Diagnostic Interview—Second Edition (CIDI-2; Kessler & Üstün, 2004) Substance Abuse Module is a fully structured interview that provides lifetime diagnoses for past and current substance use disorders according to both the *DSM-IV* and *ICD-10*. An SUD diagnosis from the CIDI has demonstrated good reliability and validity and can be administered by a lay interviewer in approximately 20 to 30 minutes. Computerized and paper-and-pencil versions are also available, as well as data entry and scoring software.

TREATMENT PLANNING ASSESSMENTS

Measures of the Severity and Consequence of Substance Use   Once a substance use problem or diagnosis is established, it is important to assess how the patient's level of substance use has affected other life areas (e.g., social and occupational functioning) in order to develop appropriate treatment goals and a treatment plan. A variety of measures is available to aid with this process. The most comprehensive and widely used measure is the Addiction Severity Index (ASI; McLellan et al., 1992), which can be administered either as a self-report questionnaire or by a trained clinician in an hour-long interview. The ASI assesses drug and alcohol use, medical status, employment status, family history, legal status, psychiatric status, and family and social relationships. Because it identifies problem areas in need of targeted intervention, it has been used extensively in clinical settings for treatment planning and outcome evaluation. The ASI has consistently demonstrated strong internal consistency and test-retest reliability among treatment populations and homeless substance abusers. There is a total of 200 items within 7 subscales, and it takes approximately 50 minutes to 1 hour to administer. It is available in three different formats: pencil-and-paper self-administered, clinician interview, or computer-based.

If an in-depth clinical interview is not feasible, the Drug Use Screening Inventory (DUSI; Tarter & Hegedus, 1991) is a 149-item measure in either a paper-and-pencil or computerized format that identifies 10 domains of functioning, including severity of alcohol and drug use, physical and mental health status, and level of psychosocial adjustment. Internal consistencies have been reported at .74 for males and .78 for females and test-retest reliability has averaged .95 for males and .88 for females, respectively. In addition to the DUSI, the Inventory of Drug Use Consequences (InDUC; Tonigan & Miller, 2002) is a 50-item self-report inventory of adverse consequences related to drug use that was developed based upon the Drinker Inventory of Consequences (DrInC; Miller, Tonigan, & Longabaugh, 1995), a measure of alcohol-related consequences. The InDUC is distinct from screening instruments in that it measures adverse consequences of substance use including items referring to pathological use practices (e.g., rapid use), items reflecting dependence symptoms (e.g., craving), and items concerning help-seeking (e.g., Narcotics Anonymous). The InDUC includes five scales including impulse control, social responsibility, and physical, interpersonal, and intrapersonal domains. Four of the five scales have demonstrated good to excellent test-retest reliability.

Motivation and Treatment Readiness Additional assessment techniques are used prior to and during treatment to target processes such as treatment planning, use of services, and goal attainment. It has been suggested that, once an individual has been screened and a substance-use problem identified, assessing the person's readiness for change prior to developing a treatment plan will improve treatment outcomes (DiClemente & Prochaska; 1998). Accordingly, the transtheoretical model (TTM) argues that the individual moves through five stages when changing behaviors: precontemplation, contemplation, preparation, action, and maintenance. Individuals in the *precontemplation* stage are the most resistant to change and are characterized as processing less information about their problems, engaging in less personal evaluation, and experiencing fewer emotional reactions to their substance use. Individuals who are aware of their problem and weigh the positive and negative consequences of their actions are in the *contemplation* stage. Individuals in the *preparation* stage have made a decision to take action within the next month, while individuals in the *action* stage are currently taking steps such as changing their behavior, environment, or experiences. Finally, individuals in the *maintenance* stage are learning and engaging in behaviors that will prevent relapse.

Three well-known assessment measures have been used to assess a patient's level of readiness: The 32-item University of Rhode Island Change Assessment (URICA; McConnaughy, Prochaska, &Velicer, 1983), the 20-item Stages of Change Readiness and Treatment Eagerness Scale (SOCRATES; Miller & Tonigan, 1996), and the 12-item Readiness to Change Questionnaire (RCQ; Rollnick, Heather, Gold, & Hall, 1992). Although the TTM has received a great deal of empirical and clinical support since its inception, it has also been met with some criticism. In a detailed review, Sutton (2001) provides evidence suggesting that the transtheoretical model does not adequately implement the theory behind the model. Specifically, he argues that the staging algorithms are based on arbitrary time periods, the questionnaires (above) demonstrate strong correlations between stages suggesting that they are not measuring discrete stages of change, and that evidence for the use of the TTM among drug users is small and inconsistent. Thus, while assessing patients' motivation and readiness for change may indeed provide useful in guiding treatment planning, caution should be taken in making treatment-outcome predictions based upon the discrete categories that were developed based upon the TTM until further, more specific evidence is provided.

Functional Analysis A functional analysis approach often is used in the context of treatment for substance use to help patients effectively problem solve ways to reduce the probability of future drug use. Within this model, an analysis of the antecedents and consequences of drug use is used to develop alternative cognitive and behavioral skills to reduce the risk of future drug use. Working together, the therapist and patient identify high-risk situations and the (1) trigger for that situation, (2) thoughts during that situation, (3) feelings experienced in response to the trigger and thoughts, (4) drug use behavior, and (5) positive and negative consequences of drug use. After analyzing this behavior chain, the therapist and patient then develop strategies for altering the thoughts, feelings, and behaviors when the patient is faced with those same situations. Keeping with the focus here on assessment as opposed to treatment, those interested in the use of functional analysis in treatment are directed to Monti et al. (2002) or the National Institute for Drug Abuse online publication *A Community Reinforcement Approach: Treating Cocaine Addiction.*

POSTTREATMENT ASSESSMENT

Outcome assessments should include a wide range of dimensions beyond substance use behavior, including changes in social, occupational, and psychological functioning. As such, it is ideal to readminister comprehensive measures such as the Addiction Severity Index, Drug Use Screening Inventory, and Inventory of Drug Use Consequences. In addition, the following self-report and biological indicators can be used to determine return to drug use, drug use behavior, and psychiatric symptoms.

Self-Report   The Timeline Followback (TLFB; Fals-Stewart, O'Farrell, & Freitas, 2000) is a semistructured clinical interview used to obtain self-report retrospective estimates of substance use. The TLFB uses a calendar method and other recall-enhancing techniques to assist individuals with their descriptions of their daily substance use over a targeted time interval and has been successfully used to obtain information on illicit drugs. The TLFB has demonstrated high test-retest reliability, convergent and discriminant validity, agreement with collateral informants' reports of patients' substance use, and agreement with results from patients' urine analysis. The TLFB also may be useful for assessing other events and mood over this time period to assess the relationship between these variables and substance use.

Similarly, Form 90D (Westerberg, Tonigan, & Miller, 1998) is a semistructured interview with intake and follow-up versions that assesses lifetime and past 90-day drug use of 12 drug categories. The assessment instrument uses a calendar format in which the patient first fills in days of complete abstinence followed by days of drug use. In addition, quantity of use and routes of administration are assessed for each day. Thus for every drug class the 90D format estimates age at first use, lifetime weeks of use, frequency of use in the current period, intensity of that use (by categorization), and relative use of various routes of administration. In addition, a strength of Form 90D is that it also assesses history of psychosocial and environmental variables such as treatment services received, living experiences, incarceration, work, and education experiences. The interview takes approximately 40 to 60 minutes and computerized scoring and interpretation is available. The measure has demonstrated strong test-retest reliability, internal consistency, and criterion and construct validity. As with the TLFB, Form 90D also may be useful for assessing other events and mood over this time period to assess the relationship between these variables and substance use.

Biological Indicators   The following is a brief overview of recent trends in the biological assessment of substance use. The interested reader is referred to Wolff et al. (1999) for a more comprehensive review. Although recent work has been conducted to identify cutting-edge technologies for the biological testing of substance use, urinalysis remains the most preferred method of detection of illicit drug use. First, because urinalysis procedures have been used historically, it is well known and many of the problems associated with it have been addressed. Second, urine contains high concentrations of the target drug or its metabolites (e.g., benzoylecgonine in the case of cocaine). Third, it is inexpensive and may be acquired in a minimally invasive manner compared other biological approaches. Self-contained urine-based testing kits that can reliably detect the most commonly used psychoactive substances are becoming increasingly available, which allow practitioners and researchers to conduct on-site testing across a much wider range of settings. Finally, recently developed quantitative and semiquantitative tests are more sensitive to changes in the pattern, frequency, and amount of use (Preston, Silverman, Schuster, & Charles, 2002). Thus, in addition to indicating the presence or absence of a drug, quantitative urinalysis can be useful in detecting initial efforts to reduce drug use and monitoring the effects of treatments.

Although urinalysis has several advantages and obvious clinical utility, there are several limitations. Urine can only indicate drug use in the past 3 days (except for cannabis, methadone, and diazepam), thereby increasing the reliance on self-report for longer-term follow-up periods. In addition, urine is easily adulterated by using chemicals such as bleach, vinegar, or liquid soap and can be easily diluted by using old urine or someone else's urine. Conversely, over-the-counter medications and certain foods can produce positive test results in the absence of illicit drug use. As such, careful attention to detail and procedures are needed to ensure accurate collection, and positive tests may need additional confirmation.

Blood collection is another method that can detect very recent drug use and is considered an ideal method for assessing quantitative levels when accuracy is the primary criterion for measure selection. However, blood often is not collected because of the invasive nature of collection, reliance on trained personnel, and the potential risks of spreading infections such as HIV and hepatitis. Saliva is the only body fluid that can be used as a substitute for blood, as drug concentration levels are comparable. Saliva collection has the advantage of being easy to obtain and is cost-effective because, similar to urinalysis, self-contained testing kits that eliminate the need for trained personnel and of on-site testing have become widely available. One collection procedure often used is the sallivete-sampling device. It consists of a cotton wool swab, which is placed in the patient's buccal cavity for saliva collection by absorption. Drawbacks to saliva collection include difficulty collecting an adequate amount for drug detection, and the possible contamination of the oral cavity as a result of oral, intranasal, and smoking drug use. Hair testing has recently been developed and theorized to have the potential benefits of drug detection over a longer period of time than is possible with the other methods. However, quality-control criteria and standard laboratory methods have yet to be established. In addition, evidence indicates that drug detection may differentially appear in darker hair, leading to a bias toward missing drug use in blonde-headed whites and differentially detecting it in people with black hair. In addition, hair is sensitive to smoke in the air, resulting in a false positive for individuals who abstain yet are surrounded by people who have smoked drugs.

ETIOLOGICAL CONSIDERATIONS

FAMILIAL AND GENETIC

Recent work suggests that substance dependence has a familial and genetic basis. Heritability estimates for liability of SUD based upon twin, adoption, and family studies have been as high as 0.78 for alcohol and tobacco dependence (e.g., Kendler & Prescott, 1998), yet less evidence has been provided for the heritability of illicit drug use (Comings, 1996). For instance, Tsuang et al. (1998) examined the genetic factors accounting for substance use disorder among male twin veterans and reported significantly greater MZ than DZ twin concordance, with genetic factors and shared environmental factors accounting for 34% and 28% of the total liability variance, respectively. However, Gynther, Carey, Gottesman, & Vogler (1995) assessed the genetic and environmental contribution to drug use liability among twins and reported that both factors accounted for less than one-fourth of the variance, and that, either one, but not both, could be removed from the model without a statistically significant decrease in fit. In addition, among adolescent twins, genetic factors and environmental factors accounted for 45% and 47% respectively, of the variance in liability for ever using an illicit drug.

Several studies have examined differences in genetic influence across specific drug classes. In the Tsuang et al. (1998) study, heritability was discriminated between drug classes with estimates ranging from a low of 0.25 for PCP/psychedelics to a high of 0.44 for stimulants. Van den Bree, Johnson, Neale, and Pickens (1998) reported mixed findings for estimates of genetic, common environmental, and specific environmental influences among twins enrolled in drug treatment programs for illicit drug use. For cannabis use in males, a low heritability estimate (0.17) was found along with a substantial common environmental influence (0.61). Yet for cannabis abuse and/or dependence, the heritability estimate was 0.68 with an additional 0.24 attributable to common environmental influences. Interestingly, for sedative use among males, a heritability estimate of 0.74 was found, with minimal common environmental influences (0.02). Yet for sedative abuse and/or dependence in males, the heritability estimate was 0.58 with no evidence of common environmental factors. Thus, it is suggested that variability in genetic and environmental origins exist across drug type, severity of use, and gender.

Beyond studies using a global twin and family design, several investigations have focused on a more molecular level of analysis in heritability research; namely, if genetic polymorphisms (variations in DNA structure) contribute to one's vulnerability for an SUD. The majority of research to date has investigated the polymorphisms in the dopamine receptor genes that may play a critical role in the mechanism of reward and reinforcement behavior (Blum et al., 2000). Indeed, a recent meta-analysis including 55 studies and approximately 10,000 participants examining the association between the A1[+] allele of the DRD2 gene and substance abuse confirmed the A1[+] allele of the DRD2 as a marker of substance use and severe substance misuse (Young, Lawford, Nutting, & Noble, 2004). The mechanisms by which substance use affects the dopaminergic system are discussed by Schultz (2000), who suggests that substances of abuse may (1) amplify existing dopaminergic responses to natural rewards, (2) signal an artificial reward in the absence of natural rewards, or (3) activate the neuronal mechanisms that recognize natural rewards. As such, drug addiction may be conceptualized as a disorder of associative learning where substances and environmental cues associated with their use continue to activate the dopamine system (Young et al., 2004).

Beyond examining genetic factors in isolation, many contextual variables are hypothesized to interact with genes in contributing to the development of SUD. In the Van den Bree et al. (1998) study, with the exception of sedatives and opiates, heritability estimates were greater for drug abuse/dependence than for drug use, whereas environmental factors contributed more to drug use, suggesting that environmental influences shared by family members are more important to drug use than to becoming drug dependent, which is more genetically influenced. In addition, Han, McGue, and Iacono (1999) assessed MZ and DZ twins on illicit drug use and reported that the adolescent initiation of substance use, a powerful predictor of adult SUD (Grant & Dawson, 1997), is influenced more by environmental than by genetic factors. Family, peer, and socioeconomic variables have all been researched extensively as environmental contributors to the development of SUD. In adolescent and adult samples, conflictual family environments (Wills, Sandy, Yaeger, & Shinar, 2001); amount and quality of parental supervision (Jacob & Johnson, 1999); religiosity (Kendler, Gardner, & Prescott, 1997); parenting skills (Clark, Neighbors, & Lesnick, 1998); trauma (Clark, Lesnick, & Hegedus, 1997); sibling relationship (McGue, Sharma, & Benson, 1996); peer influence, emotional support (Wills & Cleary, 1996); and economic factors (Warner, Kessler, Hughes, & Anthony, 1995) have all demonstrated an association with increased substance use and abuse. Although these relationships highlight the importance of environmental variables, it remains unclear how they interact with one's genotype in the development of SUD.

Learning and Modeling

Theories of learning and conditioning have been used to understand the development and maintenance of SUD, and as a result a number of studies have been conducted in laboratory animals and humans that support the notion of drugs as reinforcers (for a review, see Higgins, Heil, & Lussier, 2004), with drug use theorized to be a form of operant behavior influenced by antecedents and consequences.

Much of the work supporting behavioral perspectives involved nonhuman animals. In an early study by Spragg (1940), a chimpanzee that had been made dependent on morphine learned to open a box with a wooden stick to retrieve a syringe loaded with morphine, which the experimenter then injected intramuscularly. The likelihood of opening the box increased with time since the last injection, suggesting that the behavior of opening the box was negatively reinforced by reductions in early signs of morphine withdrawal symptoms. Years later, Headlee, Coppock, and Nichols (1955) showed that restrained rats would move their heads to one side if it resulted in administration of morphine or codeine. When the development of reliable and long-lasting intravenous cannulae allowed the study of drug self-administration in monkeys (Thompson, Schuster, Dockens, & Lee, 1964) and rats (Weeks, 1962), the study of drugs of abuse as reinforcers began to flourish. Subsequently it was shown that rats and monkeys would self-administer most of the drugs commonly administered by humans (e.g., Carroll, 1985). Furthermore, it has been shown that physical dependence on the drug is not necessary for drugs to serve as reinforcers.

Drug self-administration studies with humans have examined the influence of nondrug reinforcers on heroin and cocaine use (Comer, Collins, & Fischman, 1997; Higgens et al., 1994). In each study, the choice of using either cocaine or heroin decreased in an orderly and graded function of increasing value of a monetary option. Specifically, as the nondrug reinforcer increased in value, the value of drug use decreased, suggesting the power of alternative reinforcers in affecting drug use. In addition, evidence suggests that associated environmental consequences occurring while under the influence of drug use may also affect future use. For instance, Alessi, Roll, Reilly, & Johanson (2002) reported that when drug use was associated with increased earning on a performance task, future preference for drug use was increased, and when drug use was associated with a decrease in earnings while completing the same task, future drug preference was decreased. Taken together, these results provide support for the influence of environmental reinforcers on drug use.

Taking this approach a step further, the behavioral economics perspective proposes that the reinforcing value of drug use is critically influenced by the environmental context of other available reinforcers. Accordingly, research has revealed a relationship between degree of substance use and the engagement in substance-free activities. Specifically, high rates of drug use are most likely in contexts without substance-free sources of reinforcement, and drug use will generally decrease if access to alternative reinforcers is increased (Higgins et al., 2004). Indeed, in a comprehensive review of the literature, Carroll (1996) concludes that the availability of nondrug alternative reinforcers reliably reduces drug use in animals and humans and across a variety of drug types, routes of administration, and types of alternative reinforcers. Although the majority of research in this area has focused on alcohol use (e.g., Correia, Benson, & Carey, 2005), findings have also been demonstrated among illicit drug users (Van Etten, Higgins, & Budney, 1998).

It has been suggested that drug users' susceptibility to the immediate effects of environmental reinforcers can be conceptualized under a specific behavioral economics process, namely delay discounting (Bickel & Marsch, 2001). Specifically, delay discounting theory suggests that individuals with SUD discount the value of delayed reinforcement more so than individuals without SUD, such that they prefer immediate reinforcements of smaller magnitude over delayed reinforcements of larger magnitude as well as delayed losses of greater magnitude over immediate losses of a smaller magnitude. A great deal of empirical research with substance abusers supports this theory (e.g., Giordano, Bickel, & Lowenstein, 2002).

Taken together, these findings suggest a strong environmental influence on the reinforcing effects of drug use. In the development of SUD, it follows that individuals with fewer alternative behavioral choices aside from drug use will be more likely to develop an SUD. Accordingly, evidence indicates that college graduates are significantly less likely to engage in illicit drug use than noncollege graduates (SAMHSA, 2005), and lower annual income, education level, and unemployment are all risk factors for SUD (Anthony & Petronis, 1995). Additionally, clinical research has reported positive outcomes for treatments developed based upon reinforcement theories such as contingency management (e.g., Correia, Sigmon, & Silverman, 2005) and a community reinforcement approach (e.g., Higgins et al., 2004), further supporting a behavior approach to understanding the etiology and maintenance of substance dependence.

Cognition   Turning to research emphasizing the role of cognition, social learning theories (Bandura, 1977) emphasize the role of a biased belief system in maintaining addictive behavior. At a basic level these theories posit that positive outcome expectancies for engaging in drug use, coupled with minimal negative expectancies and poor self-efficacy beliefs regarding one's ability to cope without drugs, lead to the development and maintenance of SUDs. Accordingly, empirical evidence indicates that there is a relationship between positive outcome expectancies and substance use (for a detailed review, see McCusker, 2001). However, many of these studies rely on self-reported cognition, which has been argued to be incomplete and subject to bias.

To address the self-report bias, cognitive research in addiction in the past decade has begun to develop methods of assessing cognition by making inferences about cognitive processes and structures based on behavioral responses, or implicit cognition. Studies have used a modified version of the Stroop task to demonstrate that substance users are quicker to name the colors of drug-related words than control words, suggesting an attentional bias for drug-related words (McCusker & Gettings, 1997). Additionally, the visual probe task involves the presentation of pairs of words or picture stimuli, followed by the presentation of a small probe in the location of one of the stimuli. The participant is instructed to respond as quickly as possible to the probe. As such, it is theorized that individuals will respond more quickly (reaction time) to stimuli that appear in an attended, rather than unattended, region of visual display. Accordingly, attentional bias has been demonstrated for drug-related stimuli in opiate (Lubman, Peters, Mogg, Bradley, & Deakin, 2000) and cocaine addicts (Franken & Hendriks, 2000). Finally, the implicit association task (IAT; Greenwald, McGhee, & Schwartz, 1998) assesses the existence of an attentional bias for substance-related words. Specifically, the speed with which an individual can link two concepts reflects how strongly associated these concepts are in memory. Participants should categorize the stimuli faster when the paired categories are matched versus when they are mismatched. The dependent variable is the average response time between matched and mismatched classifications, which is interpreted as the degree of automatic association between the paired categories. Whereas most of the evidence for this relationship has been provided in alcohol abusers and smokers (e.g., Palfai & Ostafin, 2003), recent evidence suggests an attentional bias among illicit drug users (Field, Mogg, & Bradley, 2004).

Taken as a whole, the preceding evidence suggests an etiology of addictive behavior in which long-term memory links one's representation of drug use with specific outcomes (i.e., stress reduction, euphoria). Not only are these representations a direct result of drug use, but they are also derived from information in the environment. The early stages in the development of an addiction are characterized by positive experiences, which are strengthened with repeated behavior, creating an accessibility bias for positive information regarding drug use (McCusker, 2001). Drug dependence thus results as automatic processes override purposeful mental efforts required to cope with high-risk situations when attempting abstinence. In particular, Tiffany and Carter (1998) suggest that craving occurs when one attempts to block these automatic cognitions, often resulting in a lapse, and thus continuing to reinforce the positive expectancy bias.

Gender and Racial-Ethnic

There exists a striking absence of empirical attention to gender and ethnic differences among individuals with an SUD. To address this issue, greater attention and funding has been allocated to research on the distinct problems faced by underserved populations; however, there is still a paucity of literature detailing the unique circumstances encountered by women and minorities. In particular, these groups face unique challenges because of differing psychological effects of drugs and differing environments for drug use. The following section attempts to provide an overview of the unique challenges experienced by women and minorities with SUDs, and future directions for addressing these challenges.

Research has demonstrated that women differ significantly from men in terms of their pathways into drug addiction. Compared to men, women are less likely to be substance abusers and the onset of their substance abuse tends to be later in life, yet women become dependent at a quicker rate and experience more severe consequences of drug use over shorter periods of time (e.g., Hser, Huang, Teruga, & Anglin, 2004). Often for women, the pathway into drug use and misuse is relationship-based; for instance, women with SUDs are more likely than men with SUDs to have a partner who uses illegal drugs (Westermeyer & Boedicker, 2000); similarly, women are more likely to cope with emotional distress resulting from the ending of a relationship via drugs (Amaro, 1995). Beyond relationship-related pathways, substance-using women suffer from higher rates and different types of psychiatric comorbidity compared to male substance users. Data from the ECA and NCS studies suggest that the rate of psychiatric comorbidity in women with SUDs is at least 20% greater than in men (Kessler et al., 1997). In support of the self-medication pathway, these data have indicated that the comorbid diagnoses more often precede the substance-related disorder in women, whereas the opposite pattern is seen with men. With regard to particular comorbid diagnoses, women suffering from SUDs report a higher rate of anxiety and mood disorders than men (Brooner, King, Kidorf, Schmidt, & Bigelow, 1997). In addition, compared to men, women with an SUD are more likely to suffer from PTSD (Cottler, Nishith, & Compton, 2001) and BPD (Trull et al., 2000).

Clearly, women face unique barriers to treatment entry and engagement, which may account for findings suggesting that women are less likely to enter treatment than men. For instance, responsibility for children including limited access to child care services, as well as society's punitive attitude toward substance abuse by women as childbearers present just some of the major treatment barriers for women suffering from SUDs (e.g., Allen, 1995). Further, the lack of attention to the interplay of gender-specific drug use patterns and sex-related risk behaviors and consequent HIV risk may create an environment within the treatment community where women's major concerns are not met (e.g., Hodgins, El-Guebaly, & Addington, 1997). Perhaps for these reasons, research indicates that women differ from men in their response to treatment. Detailed data on this topic have proven to be somewhat conflicting: whereas some researchers have reported that women are more likely than men to drop out of substance abuse treatment (Bride, 2001), others have proposed a complex interaction of gender and treatment modality (e.g., methadone vs. drug-free programs; Joe, Simpson, & Broome, 1999; McCaul, Svikis, & Moore, 2001; Simpson, Joe, Rowan-Szal, & Greener, 1997). The causes underlying this interaction are unknown, but suggest a fruitful avenue for future research.

Little SUD research explicitly focused on minority samples has been conducted. An even larger potential problem is that much of the research that has been conducted has targeted individuals in low socio-economic settings (SES). As such it is important to recognize this confound when reviewing the literature on SUDs and race/ethnicity. With that caveat in mind, existing studies have suggested unique risks and needs among many minority individuals who misuse drugs. For instance, several reports have indicated that ethnic/racial minorities who often reside in inner-city areas are particularly vulnerable to drug use and risky sexual behavior (RSB) as a result of higher levels of poverty, violence, general risk practices, and availability of street drugs (e.g., Avants, Marcotte, Arnold, & Margolin, 2003). Indeed, certain minorities such as Native American and African American populations evidence prevalence rates somewhat above those of Caucasian samples. Specifically, illicit drug use in the past month among persons aged 12 or older in 2004 was highest among persons reporting two or more races (13.3%), followed by Native Americans (12.3%), African Americans (8.7%), Caucasians (8.1%), and Hispanics (7.2%) (SAMHSA, 2005). Mechanisms such as the exchange of sex for drugs or money, frequent sexual contact within a population at an elevated risk for seropositivity (i.e., IV drug users), and engagement in RSB as a result of drug use play a potent role in the spread of HIV/AIDS among minorities (e.g., Avants et al., 2003).

Beyond risk factors, treatment outcome studies suggest that ethnic and racial minorities are less likely to complete and/or seek treatment, receive fewer treatment services, and are less likely to achieve recovery (Jerrell & Wilson, 1997; Rebach, 1992). However, a number of research reports indicate that minority clients do not differ from nonminority clients in their response to treatment (e.g., Pickens & Fletcher, 1991). Clearly, additional research is needed to clarify which factors predict poor or favorable treatment outcomes among minority individuals; however, two recent studies do indeed address this issue. Lundgren, Amodeo, Ferguson, and Davis (2001) found that different racial and ethnic groups enter different types of drug treatment; specifically, Latino drug users were a third less likely than Caucasian drug users to enter residential treatment and African American drug users were half as likely as Caucasian drug users to enter methadone maintenance treatment.

SUMMARY

It has become increasingly clear that understanding the development and maintenance of SUDs is a complex problem. Toward this goal, this chapter provides an overview of current practices and cutting-edge advancements for understanding and assessing drug-specific SUDs. Although much work is still needed, great progress has been made in understanding the development of SUDs as a function of biological, genetic, behavioral, and cognitive factors, with greatest promise evident in approaches that consider the interactive influence of these factors. Additionally, clear advancements have been made in both initial as well as ongoing assessment using self-report, interview, behavioral, and biological methods. Also of great promise is the greater attention to gender and minority issues when considering vulnerabilities to developing SUDs, as well as barriers to assessment and proper treatment. In summary, although the challenges of understanding and assessing SUDs continue to grow, it is clear that the field has evidenced important advancements aimed at addressing these challenges.

REFERENCES

Alessi, S. M., Roll, J. M., Reilly, M. P., & Johanson, C. E. (2002). Establishment of a diazepam preference in human volunteers following a differential-conditioning history of placebo versus diazepam choice. *Experimental and Clinical Psychopharmacology, 10* (2), 77–83.

Ali, R., Awward, E., Babor, T., Bradley, F., Butau, T., Farrell, M., et al. (2002). The Alcohol, Smoking and Substance Involvement Screening Test (ASSIST): Development, reliability and feasibility. *Addiction, 97,* 1183–1194.

Allen, K. A. (1995). Barriers to treatment for addicted African American women. *Journal of the National Medical Association, 87,* 751–756.

Amaro, H. (1995). Love, sex and power: Considering women's needs in HIV prevention. *American Psychologist, 50* (6), 437–447.

American Psychiatric Association. (1994). *Diagnostic and statistical manual of mental disorders* (4th ed.). Washington, DC: Author.

American Psychiatric Association (2000). *Diagnostic and statistical manual of mental disorders* (4th ed., tx. rev.). Washington, DC: Author.

Anthony, J. C., & Petronis, K. R. (1995). Early-onset drug use and risk of later drug problems. *Drug and Alcohol Dependence, 40* (1), 9–15.

Avants, S. K., Marcotte, D., Arnold, R., & Margolin, A. (2003). Spiritual beliefs, world assumptions, and HIV risk behavior among heroin and cocaine users. *Psychology of Addictive Behaviors, 17* (2), 159–162.

Bandura, A. (1977). *Social learning theory.* Oxford, England: Prentice-Hall.

Berman, A. H., Bergman, H., Palmstierna, T., & Schlyter, F. (2005). Evaluation of the Drug Use Disorders Identification Test (DUDIT) in criminal justice and detoxification settings and in a Swedish population sample. *European Addiction Research, 11* (1), 22–31.

Bickel, W. K., & Marsch, L. A. (2001). Toward a behavioral economic understanding of drug dependence: Delay discounting processes. *Addiction, 96* (1), 73–86.

Blum, K., Braverman, E. R., Holder, J. M., Lubar, J. F., Monastra, V. J., Miller, D., Lubar, J. O., Chen, T. J. H., & Comings, D. E. (2000). Reward deficiency syndrome: A biogenetic model for the diagnosis and treatment of impulsive, addictive, and compulsive behaviors. *Journal of Psychoactive Drugs, 32* (Suppl. 1), 1–68.

Bride, B. E. (2001). Single-gender treatment of substance abuse: Effect on treatment retention and completion. *Social Work Research, 25*(4), 223–232.

Brooner, R. K., King, V. L., Kidorf, M., Schmidt, C. W., & Bigelow, G. E. (1997). Psychiatric and substance use comorbidity among treatment-seeking opioid abusers. *Archives of General Psychiatry, 54* (1), 71–80.

Brown, S. L., Korn, M. L., Van Praag, H. M. (1990). Serotonin in depression and anxiety. In R. Paoletti, P. M. Wanhoutte, N. Brunello, & F. M. Maggi (Eds.), *Serotonin. From Cell Biology to Pharmacology and Therapeutics* (pp. 487–491). Dordrecht, The Netherlands: Kluwer Academic Publishers.

Bryer, J. B., Martines, K. A., & Dignan, M. A. (1990). Millon Clinical Multiaxial Inventory Alcohol Abuse and Drug Abuse scales and the identification of substance-abuse patients. *Psychological Assessment, 2* (4), 438–441.

Butler, S. F., Budman, S. H., Fernandez, K., & Jamison, R. N. (2004). Validation of a screener and opioid assessment measure for patients with chronic pain. *Pain, 112* (1–2), 65–75.

Carroll, M. E. (1985). Concurrent phencyclidine and saccharin access: Presentation of an alternative reinforcer reduces drug intake. *Journal of the Experimental Analysis of Behavior, 43* (1), 131–144.

Carroll, M. E. (1996). Reducing drug abuse by enriching the environment with alternative nondrug reinforcers. In L. Green & J. H. Kagel (Eds.), *Advances in behavioral economics: Vol. 3. Substance use and abuse.* Westport, CT: Ablex.

Clark, D. B., Lesnick, L. A., & Hegedus, A. M. (1997). Traumas and other adverse life events in adolescents with alcohol abuse and dependence. *Journal of the American Academy of Child & Adolescent Psychiatry, 36* (12), 1744–1751.

Clark, D. B., Neighbors, B. D., & Lesnick, L. A. (1998). Family functioning and adolescent alcohol use disorders. *Journal of Family Psychology, 12* (1), 81–92.

Comer, S. D., Collins, E. D., & Fischman, M. W. (1997). Choice between money and intranasal heroin in morphine-maintained humans. *Behavioural Pharmacology, 8* (8), 677–690.

Comings, D. E. (1996). *The gene bomb: Does higher education and advanced technology accelerate the selection of genes for learning disorders, ADHD, addictive, and disruptive behaviors?* Duarte, CA: Hope Press.

Compton, P., Darakjian, J., & Miotto, K. (1998). Screening for addiction in patients with chronic pain and "problematic" substance use: Evaluation of a pilot assessment tool. *Journal of Pain and Symptom Management, 16* (6), 355–363.

Cooney, N. L., Zweben, A., & Fleming, M. F. (1995). Screening for alcohol problems and at-risk drinking in health-care settings. In R. K. Hester & W. R. Miller (Eds.), *Handbook of alcoholism treatment approaches: Effective alternatives* (2nd ed., pp. 45–60). Needham Heights, MA: Allyn & Bacon.

Correia, C. J., Benson, T. A., & Carey, K. B. (2005). Decreased substance use following increases in alternative behaviors: A preliminary investigation. *Psychology of Addictive Behaviors, 30* (1), 19–27.

Correia, C. J., Sigmon, S. C., & Silverman, K. (2005). A comparison of voucher-delivery schedules for the iitiation of cocaine abstinence. *Experimental and Clinical Psychopharmacology, 13* (3), 253–258.

Cottler, L. B., Nishith, P., & Compton, W. M. (2001). Gender differences in risk factors for trauma exposure and post-traumatic stress disorder among inner-city drug abusers in and out of treatment. *Comprehensive Psychiatry, 42,* 11–117.

de Lima, M. S., Lorea, C. F., & Carpena, M. P. (2002). Dual diagnosis on "substance abuse." *Substance Use & Misuse, 37*(8–10) Special issue: The Middle Eastern Summer Institute on Drug Use Proceedings: 1997–1999, pp. 1179–1184.

DiClemente, C. C., & Prochaska, J. O. (1998). Toward a comprehensive, transtheoretical model of change: Stages of change and addictive behaviors. In W. R. Miller & N. Heather (Eds.), *Treating addictive behaviors* (2nd ed., pp. 3–24). New York: Plenum Press.

Fals-Stewart, W., O'Farrell, T. J., & Freitas, T. T. (2000). The Timeline Followback reports of psychoactive substance use by drug-abusing patients: Psychometric properties. *Journal of Consulting and Clinical Psychology, 68* (1), 134–144.

Fergusson, D. M., Horwood, L. J., & Lynskey, M. T. (1994). The childhoods of multiple problem adolescents: A 15-year longitudinal study. *Journal of Child Psychology & Psychiatry & Allied Disciplines, 35,* 1123–1140.

Field, M., Mogg, K., & Bradley, B. P. (2004). Cognitive bias and drug craving in recreational cannabis users. *Drug and Alcohol Dependence, 74* (1), 105–111.

First, M. B., Spitzer, R. I., Gibbon, M., & Williams, J. B. W. (1997). Structured Clinical Interview for *DSM-IV* Axis I Disorders—Clinician Version (SCID-CV). Washington, DC: American Psychiatric Press.

Forman, R. F., Svikis, D., Montoya, I. D., & Blaine, J. (2004). Selection of a substance use disorder diagnostic instrument by the National Drug Abuse Treatment Clinical Trials Network. *Journal of Substance Abuse Treatment, 27,* 1–8.

Franken, I. H. A., & Hendriks, V. M. (2000). Early-onset of illicit substance use is associated with greater Axis-II comorbidity, not with Axis-I comorbidity. *Drug and Alcohol Dependence, 59* (3), 305–308.

Giordano, L. A., Bickel, W. K., & Lowenstein, G. (2002). Mild opioid deprivation increases the degree that opioid-dependent outpatients discount delayed heroin and money. *Psychopharmacology, 163* (2), 174–182.

Grant, B. F., & Dawson, D. A. (1997). Age at onset of alcohol use and its association with *DSM-IV* alcohol abuse and dependence: Results from the National Longitudinal Alcohol Epidemiologic Survey. *Journal of Substance Abuse, 9,* 103–110.

Greenwald, A. G., McGhee, D. E., & Schwartz, J. L. K. (1998). Measuring individual differences in implicit cognition: The implicit association test. *Journal of Personality and Social Psychology, 74*(6), 1464–1480.

Gynther, L. M., Carey, G., Gottesman, I. I., & Vogler, G. P. (1995). A twin study of non-alcohol substance abuse. *Journal of Psychiatry Research, 56* (3), 213–220.

Han, C., McGue, M. K., & Iacono, W. G. (1999). Lifetime tobacco, alcohol and other substance use in adolescent Minnesota twins: Univariate and multivariate behavioral genetic analyses. *Addiction, 94* (7), 981.

Headlee, C. P., Coppock, H. W., & Nichols, J. R. (1955). Apparatus and technique involved in a laboratory method of detecting the addictiveness of drugs. *Journal of the American Pharmaceutical Association, Scientific Edition, 44* (4), 229–231.

Heinz, A. (2002). Dopaminergic dysfunction in alcoholism and schizophrenia—Psychological and behavioral correlates. *European Psychiatry, 17*(1), 9–16.

Higgins, S. T., Budney, A. J., Bickel, W. K., Foerg, F. E., Donham R., & Badger, G. J. (1994). Incentives improve outcome in outpatient behavioral treatment of cocaine dependence. *Archives of General Psychiatry, 51* (7), 568–576.

Higgins, S. T., Heil, S. H., & Lussier, J. P. (2004). Clinical implications of reinforcement as a determinant of substance use disorders. *Annual Review of Psychology, 55,* 431–461.

Hodgins, D. C., El-Guebaly, N., & Addington, J. (1997). Treatment of substance abusers: Single or mixed gender programs. *Addictions, 92* (7), 805-812.

Hser, Y. I., Grella, C. E., Chou, C. P., & Anglin, M. D. (1998). Relationships between drug treatment careers and outcomes: Findings from the National Drug Abuse Treatment Outcome Study. *Evaluation Review, 22,* 496–519.

Hser, Y., Huang, Y., Teruga, C., & Anglin, M. D. (2004). Gender differences in treatment outcomes over a three-year period: A path model analysis. *Journal of Drug Issues, 34,* 419–440.

Hser, Y., Maglione, M. A., Polinsky, M. L., & Anglin, M. D. (1997). Predicting treatment entry among treatment-seeking drug abusers. *Journal of Substance Abuse Treatment, 15,* 213–220.

Hser, Y., Polinsky, M. L., Maglione, M. A., & Anglin, M. D. (1999). Matching patients' needs with drug treatment services. *Journal of Substance Abuse Treatment, 16,* 299–305.

Jacob, T., & Johnson, S. L. (1999). Family influences on alcohol and substance abuse. In P. J. Ott, R. E. Tarter, & R. T. Ammerman (Eds.), *Sourcebook on substance abuse: Etiology, epidemiology, assessment, and treatment* (pp. 166-174). Needham Heights, MA: Allyn & Bacon.

Jerrell, J. M., & Wilson, J. L. (1997). Ethnic differences in the treatment of dual mental and substance disorders. *Journal of Substance Abuse Treatment, 14*(2), 133.

Joe, G. W., Simpson, D. D., & Broome, K. M. (1999). Retention and patient engagement models for different treatment modalities in DATOS. *Drug and Alcohol Dependence, 57,* 113–125.

Johnson, L. D., O'Malley, P. M., Bachman, J. G., & Schulenberg, J. E. (2005). *Monitoring the future national results on adolescent drug use: Overview of key findings, 2004* (NIH Publication No. 05-5726). Bethesda, MD: National Institute of Drug Abuse.

Julien, R. M. (2004). *A primer of drug action* (10th ed.). New York: Worth Publishers.

Kandel, D. B., & Davies, M. (1992). Progression to regular marijuana involvement: Phenomenology and risk factors for near-daily use. In M. D. Glantz & R. W. Pickens (Eds.), *Vulnerability to drug abuse* (pp. 211–253). Washington, DC: American Psychological Association.

Kendler, K. S., Gardner, C. O., & Prescott, C. A. (1997). Religion, psychopathology, and substance use and abuse: A multimeasure, genetic-epidemiologic study. *American Journal of Psychiatry, 154* (3), 322–329.

Kendler, K. S., & Prescott, C. A. (1998). Cannabis use, abuse, and dependence in a population-based sample of female twins. *American Journal of Psychiatry, 155* (8), 1016–1022.

Kessler, R. C., Blazer, D. G., McGonagle, K. A., & Swartz, M. S. (1994). The prevalence and distribution of major depression in a national community sample: The National Comorbidity Survey. *American Journal of Psychiatry, 151,* 979–986.

Kessler, R. C., Crum, R. M., Warner, L. A., Nelson, C. B., Schulenberg, J., & Anthony, J. C. (1997). The lifetime co-occurrence of *DSM-III-R* alcohol abuse and dependence with other psychiatric disorders in the National Comorbidity Survey. *Archives of General Psychiatry, 54,* 313–321.

Kessler, R. C., & Price, R. H. (1993). Primary prevention of secondary disorders: A proposal and agenda. *American Journal of Community Psychology, 21,* 607–633.

Kessler, R. C., & Üstün, T. B. (2004). The World Mental Health (WMH) Survey Initiative Version of the World Health Organization (WHO) Composite International Diagnostic Interview (CIDI). *International Journal of Methods in Psychiatric Research, 13* (2), 93–121.

Krueger, R. F., Hicks, B. M., Patrick, C. J., Carlson, S. R., Iacono, W. G., & McGue, M. (2002). Etiologic connections among substance dependence, antisocial behavior, and personality: Modeling the externalizing spectrum. *Journal of Abnormal Psychology, 111,* 411–424.

Kushner, M. G., Abrams, K., & Borchardt, C. (2000). The relationship between anxiety disorders and alcohol use disorders: A review of major perspectives and findings. *Clinical Psychology Review, 20,* 149–171.

Lubman, D. I., Peters, L. A., Mogg, K., Bradley, B. P., & Deakin, J. F. W. (2000). Attentional bias for drug cues in opiate dependence. *Psychological Medicine, 30* (1), 169–175.

Lundgren, L. M., Amodeo, M., Ferguson, F., & Davis, K. (2001). Racial and ethnic differences in drug treatment entry of injection drug users in Massachusetts. *Journal of Substance Abuse Treatment, 21,* 145–153.

McCaul, M. E., Svikis, D. S., & Moore, R. D. (2001). Predictors of outpatient treatment retention: Patient versus substance use characteristics. *Drug and Alcohol Dependence, 62,* 9–17.

McConnaughy, E. A., Prochaska, J. O., & Velicer, W. F. (1983). Stages of change in psychother-apy: Measurement and sample profiles. *Psychotherapy: Theory, Research & Practice, 20* (3), 368–375.

McCusker, C. G. (2001). Cognitive biases and addiction: An evolution in theory and method. *Addiction, 96* (1), 47–56.

McCusker, C. G., & Gettings, B. (1997). Automaticity of cognitive biases in addictive be-haviours: Further evidence with gamblers. *British Journal of Clinical Psychology, 36* (4), 543–554.

McGue, M., Sharma, A., & Bensen, P. (1996). The effect of common rearing on adolescent ad-justment: Evidence from a U.S. adoption cohort. *Developmental Psychology, 32,* 94–613.

McLellan, A. T., Kushner, H., Metzger, D., Peters, R., Smith, I., & Grissom, G. (1992). The fifth edition of the Addiction Severity Index. *Journal of Substance Abuse Treatment, 9* (3), 199–213.

Miele, G. M., Carpenter, K. M., Cockerham, M. S., Trautman, K. D., Blaine, J. D., & Hasin, D. S. (2000). Concurrent and predictive validity of the Substance Dependence Severity Scale (SDSS). *Drug and Alcohol Dependence, 59,* 77–88.

Miller, W. R., & Tonigan, J. S. (1996). Assessing drinkers' motivations for change: The Stages of Change Readiness and Treatment Eagerness Scale (SOCRATES). *Psychology of Ad-dictive Behaviors, 10* (2), 81–89.

Miller, W. R., Tonigan, J. S., & Longabaugh, R. (1995). *The Drinker Inventory of Consequences (DrInC): An instrument for assessing adverse consequences of alcohol abuse.* Albuquerque, NM: Center on Alcoholism, Substance Abuse and Addictions.

Millon, T., & Meagher, S. E. (2004). The Millon Clinical Multiaxial Inventory-III (MCMI-III). In M. J. Hilsenroth & D. L. Segal (Eds.), *Comprehensive handbook of psychological as-sessment: Vol. 2. Personality assessment* (pp. 109–121). Hoboken, NJ: Wiley.

Monti, P. M., Kadden, R. M., Rohsenhow, D. J., Cooney, N. L., & Abrams, D. B. (2002). *Treating alcohol dependence: A coping skills training guide* (2nd ed.). New York: Guilford Press.

Mowbray, C. T., Collins, M. E., Plum, T. B., Masterton, T., & Mulder, R. (1997). Harbinger. I: The development and evaluation of the First PACT replication. *Administration and Policy in Mental Health, 25,* 105–123.

Newcomb, M. D., & Richardson, M. A. (1995). In M. Hersen & R. T. Ammerman (Eds.), *Ad-vanced abnormal child psychology* (pp. 411–431). Hillsdale, NJ: Erlbaum.

Office of Applied Studies (2000). *National Household Survey on Drug Abuse, 1999.* Rockville, MD: Substance Abuse and Mental Health Services Administration, U.S. Department of Health and Human Services.

Office of National Drug Control Policy. (October, 2002). *Drug Policy Information Clearing-house Fact Sheet.* Retrieved, July 9, 2006, from www.whitehousedrugpolicy.gov.

Öjesjö, L. (2000). The recovery from alcohol problems over the life course: The Lundby longitudinal study, Sweden. *Alcohol, 22* (1), 1–5.

Palfai, T. P., & Ostafin, D. B. (2003). Alcohol-related motivational tendencies in hazardous drinkers: Assessing implicit response tendencies using the modified-IAT. *Behaviour Research and Therapy, 41* (10), 1149–1162.

Pickens, R., & Fletcher, B. (1991). Overview of treatment issues. In R. Pickens, C. Leukefeld, & C. Schuster (Eds.), *Improving drug abuse treatment* (pp. 1–19) (NIDA Research Monograph No. 106). Rockville, MD: National Institute on Drug Abuse.

Powers, K. I., & Anglin, M. D. (1993). Cumulative versus stabilizing effects of methadone maintenance: A quasi-experimental study using longitudinal self-report data. *Evalua-tion Review, 17* (3), 243–270.

Preston, K. L., Silverman, K., & Schuster, C. R. (2002). Assessment of cocaine use with quantitative urinalysis and estimation of new uses. *Addiction, 92* (6), 717–727.

Rebach, H. (1992). Alcohol and drug use among ethnic minorities. In J. Trimble, C. Bolek, & S. Niemcryk (Eds.), *Ethnic and multicultural drug abuse: Perspective on current research* (pp. 23–57). New York: Haworth.

Regier, D. A., Farmer, M. E., Rae, D. S., Myers, J. K., & Ratcliff, K. S. (1993). One-month prevalence of mental disorders in the United States and sociodemographic characteristics: The Epidemiologic Catchment Area program. *Acta Psychiatrica Scandinavica, 88,* 35–47.

Robins, L. N., Helzer, J. E., & Croughan, J. L. (1981). National Institute of Mental Health diagnostic interview schedule: Its history, characteristics, and validity. *Archives of General Psychiatry, 38* (4), 381–389.

Rohde, P., Lewinsohn, P. M., Kahler, C. W., Seeley, J. R., & Brown, R. A. (2001). Natural course of alcohol use disorders from adolescence to young adulthood. *Journal of the American Academy of Child & Adolescent Psychiatry, 40* (1), 83–90.

Rollnick, S., Heather, N., Gold, R., & Hall, W. (1992). Development of a short 'readiness to change' questionnaire for use in brief, opportunistic interventions among excessive drinkers. *British Journal of Addiction, 87* (5), 743–754.

Saunders, J. B., Aasland, O. G., Babor, T. F., de la Fuente, J. R., & Grant, M. (1993). Development of the Alcohol Use Disorders Identification Test (AUDIT): WHO collaborative project on early detection of persons with harmful alcohol consumption: II. *Addiction, 88* (6), 791–804.

Schacter, D. L. (1992). Priming and multiple memory systems: Perceptual mechanisms of implicit memory. *Journal of Cognitive Neuroscience, 4* (3), 244–256.

Schafer, J., & Brown, S. A. (1991). Marijuana and cocaine effect expectancies and drug use patterns. *Journal of Consulting and Clinical Psychology, 59* (4), 558–565.

Schultz, W., Tremblay, L., & Hollerman, J. R. (2000). Reward processing in primate orbitofrontal cortex and basal ganglia. Cerebral Cortex, *10* (3), 272–283.

Simpson, D. D., Joe, G. W., & Brown, B. S. (1997). Treatment retention and follow-up outcomes in the drug abuse treatment outcome study (DATOS). *Psychology of Addictive Behaviors, 11* (4), 294–307.

Simpson, D. D., Joe, G. W., Rowan-Szal, G. R., & Greener, J. (1997). Drug abuse treatment process components that improve retention. *Journal of Substance Abuse Treatment, 14* (6), 565–572.

Skinner, H. A. (1982). The Drug Abuse Screening Test. *Addictive Behaviors, 7* (4), 363–371.

Spragg, S. D. S. (1940). Morphine addiction in chimpanzees. *Journal of Comparative Psychology Monographs, 15* (7), 132.

Stuart, G. L., Moore, T. M., Kahler, C. W. & Ramsey, S. E. (2003). Substance abuse and relationship violence among men court-referred to batterers' intervention programs. *Substance Abuse, 24* (2), 107–122.

Substance Abuse and Mental Health Services Administration, U.S. Department of Health and Human Services. (2005). *Results from the 2004 National Survey on Drug Use and Health: National Findings* (NSDUH Series H-28, DHHS Publication No. SMA 05-4062). Rockville, MD: Author.

Sutton, S. (2001). Back to the drawing board? A review of applications of the transtheoretical model to substance use. *Addiction, 96*(1), 175–186.

Tarter, R., & Hegedus, A. M. (1991). The Drug Use Screening Inventory: Its applications in the evaluation and treatment of alcohol and other drug abuse. *Alcohol Health and Research World, 15,* 65.

Thompson, T., Schuster, C. R., Dockens, W., & Lee, R. (1964). Mouth-operated food and water manipulanda for use with monkeys. *Journal of the Experimental Analysis of Behavior, 7* (2), 171–172.

Tiffany, S. T., & Carter, B. L. (1998). Is craving the source of compulsive drug use? *Journal of Psychopharmacology, 12*(1), 23–30.

Tonigan, J. S., & Miller, W. R. (2002). The inventory of drug use consequences (InDUC): Test-retest stability and sensitivity to detect change. *Psychologically Addictive Behavior, 16* (2), 165–168.

Trull, T. J., Sher, K. J., Minks-Brown, C., Durbin, J., & Burr, R. (2000). Borderline personality disorder and substance use disorders: A review and integration. *Clinical Psychology Review, 20,* 235–253.

Tsuang, M. T., & Faraone, S. V. (1996). The inheritance of mood disorders. In L. L. Hall (Ed.), *Genetics and mental illness: Evolving issues for research and society* (pp. 79–109). New York: Plenum Press.

Tsuang, M. T., Lyons, M. J., Meyer, J. M., Doyle, T., Eisen, S. A., Goldberg, J., et al. (1998). Co-occurrence of abuse of different drugs in men: The role of drug-specific and shared vulnerabilities. *Archives of General Psychiatry, 55,* 967–972.

Üstün, B., Compton, W., Mager, D., Babor, T., Baiyewu, O., Chatterji, S., et al. (1997). WHO study on the reliability and validity of the alcohol and drug use disorder instruments: Overview of methods and results. *Drug and Alcohol Dependence, 47,* 161–169.

Van den Bree, M. B. M., Johnson, E. O., Neale, M. C., & Pickens, R. R. W. (1998). Genetic and environmental influences on drug use and abuse/dependence in male and female twins. *Journal of Drug and Alcohol Dependence, 52* (3), 231–241.

Van Etten, M. L., Higgins, S. T., Budney, A. J. (1998). Comparison of the frequency and enjoyability of pleasant events in cocaine abusers vs. non-abusers using a standardized behavioral inventory. *Addiction, 93* (11), 1669–1680.

Warner, L. A., Kessler, R. C., Hughes, M., & Anthony, J. C. (1995). Prevalence and correlates of drug use and dependence in the United States: Results from the National Comorbidity Survey. *Archives of General Psychiatry, 52* (3), 219–229.

Weed, N.C., Butcher, J. N., & McKenna, T. (1992). New measures for assessing alcohol and drug abuse with the MMPI-2: The APS and AAS. *Journal of Personality Assessment, 58* (2), 389–404.

Weeks, J. M. (1962). Experimental morphine addiction: Method for automatic intravenous injections in unrestrained rats. *Science, 138,* 143–144.

Westerberg, V. S., Tonigan, J. S., & Miller, W. R. (1998). Reliability of Form 90D: An instrument for quantifying drug use. *Substance Abuse, 19,* 179–189.

Westermeyer, J., & Boedicker, A. E. (2000). Course, severity, and treatment of substance abuse among women verses men. *American Journal of Drug Alcohol Abuse, 26* (4), 523–535.

Wills, T. A., & Cleary, S. D. (1996). How are social support effects mediated? A test with parental support and adolescent substance use. *Journal of Personality and Social Psychology, 71*(5), 937–952.

Wills, T. A., Sandy, J. M., Yaeger, A., & Shinar, O. (2001). Family risk factors and adolescent substance use: Moderation effects for temperament dimensions. *Journal of Developmental Psychology, 37* (3), 283–297.

Wolff, K., Farrell, M., Marsden, J., Monteiro, M. G., Ali, R., Welch, S., et al. (1999). A review of biological indicators of illicit drug use, practical considerations and clinical usefulness. *Addiction, 94,* 1279–1298.

World Health Organization. (1992). *International Classification of Diseases and Related Health.* Geneva, Switzerland: World Health Organization.

Young, R., Lawford, B. R., Nutting, A., & Noble, E. P. (2004). Advances in molecular genetics and the prevention and treatment of substance misuse: Implications of association studies of the A-sub-1 allele of the D-sub-2 dopamine receptor gene. *Journal of* Addictive Behaviors, *29* (7), 1275–1294.

Zilberman, D., Cao, X., & Jacobsen, S. E. (2003). Comorbidity of mental disorders with alcohol and other drug abuse: Results from the Epidemiologic Catchment Area (ECA) Study. *Journal of the American Medical Association, 264,* 2511–2518.

CHAPTER 8

Schizophrenia

DENNIS R. COMBS AND KIM T. MUESER

Schizophrenia is the most debilitating and costly of all adult psychiatric illnesses. Despite the recent trend toward community-oriented treatment, about 25% of all psychiatric hospital beds are occupied by persons with schizophrenia. The costs of treating schizophrenia are significant in terms of both financial and personal costs. It was estimated that the fiscal cost of schizophrenia in the United States was $62.7 billion in 2002 (Wu et al., 2005) and $6.85 billion in Canada in 2004 (Goerre et al., 2005). About one-third (roughly 22.7 billion) of the U.S. dollars spent on schizophrenia is directed to the treatment and medical needs of this population. Despite the economic costs, the impact on the person's social and occupational functioning over their lifetime may be even more devastating (Knapp, Mangalore, & Simon, 2004). In fact, the largest indirect cost associated with schizophrenia is the loss of productivity over the lifetime. The burden of schizophrenia places the disorder as one of the top 10 most disabling conditions in the world in terms of illness-adjusted life years (Mueser & McGurk, 2004; Murray & Lopez, 1996). Even when persons with schizophrenia receive optimal treatments, many continue to experience substantial impairments throughout most of their lives.

Since schizophrenia was first described more than 100 years ago, the nature of the disorder has been hotly debated, and public misconceptions about it have been commonplace. In recent years, there has been a growing consensus among clinicians and researchers to more rigorously define the psychopathology and diagnostic features of this disorder. Once referred to as a "wastebasket diagnosis," the term *schizophrenia* is now used to describe a specific clinical syndrome. Current arguments about the disorder have focused on the validity of the diagnostic category of schizophrenia and alternative models argue that is more beneficial to focus on psychotic symptoms (e.g., paranoia, hallucinations, and delusions) (Bentall, Jackson, & Pilgrim, 1988). Nonetheless, an understanding of the core clinical features of schizophrenia is necessary for diagnosis and treatment planning. After many years of struggling to improve the long-term course of schizophrenia, there is now abundant evidence that combined pharmacological and psychosocial interventions can have a major impact on improving functioning. This chapter provides an up-to-date review of schizophrenia, with a particular focus on the psychopathology of the illness and its impact on other domains of functioning.

DESCRIPTION OF THE DISORDER

Schizophrenia is characterized by impairments in social functioning, including difficulty establishing and maintaining interpersonal relationships, problems working or fulfilling other instrumental roles (e.g., student, homemaker, employee), and difficulties caring for oneself (e.g., poor grooming and hygiene). These problems in daily living, in the absence of significant impairment in intellectual functioning, are the most distinguishing characteristics of schizophrenia, and are a necessary criterion for its diagnosis according to most diagnostic systems (e.g., American Psychiatric Association [APA], 2000). Consequently, many individuals with the illness depend on others to meet their daily living needs. For example, estimates suggest that between 25% and 60% of persons with schizophrenia live with relatives, and an even higher percentage rely on relatives for caregiving (Goldman, 1982; Torrey, 2001). Time spent providing support and care for a person with schizophrenia can be substantial (with reports as high as 6 to 9 hours per day; Magliano et al., 1998). Individuals without family support typically rely on mental health, residential, and case management services to get their basic needs met. In the worst-case scenario, persons with schizophrenia who have insufficient contact with relatives and who fall between the cracks of the social service delivery system end up in jail (Torrey et al., 1992) or become homeless, with between 10% and 20% of homeless persons having schizophrenia (Susser, Stuening, & Conover, 1989).

In addition to the problems in daily living, which characterize schizophrenia, individuals with the illness experience a range of different symptoms. As the following case study illustrates, the most common symptoms include positive symptoms (e.g., hallucinations, delusions, disorganization), negative symptoms (e.g., social withdrawal, apathy, anhedonia, poverty of speech), cognitive impairments (e.g., memory difficulties, planning ability, abstract thinking), and problems with mood (e.g., depression, anxiety, anger). The specific nature of these symptoms is described in greater detail in the section titled "Clinical Picture." The symptoms of schizophrenia appear to account for some, but not all of the problems in social functioning (Glynn, 1998).

The various impairments associated with schizophrenia tend to be long-term, punctuated by fluctuations in severity (i.e., relapse) over time. For this reason, schizophrenia has a broad impact on the family, and individuals are often impeded from pursuing personal life goals. Despite the severity of the disorder, advances in the treatment of schizophrenia provide solid hope for improving the outcome.

Case Study

Jamie is a 25-year-old man who was diagnosed with schizophrenia 5 years ago. During the summer prior to his junior year in college, he was working in a busy office. He became increasingly concerned that his office mates

(continued)

were "out to get him" and that there was an intricate plot to discredit him. He also believed that his coworkers were secretly communicating with each other about him through certain facial expressions, choice of clothing, and the configuration of items on their desks. As his paranoia escalated, he became more disorganized in his thinking and behavior, he was less able to take care of his daily activities, and he could no longer come to work. He began to believe he was dying, and attributed a variety of factors that were playing a role in his demise, including being poisoned by indoor air pollution. These symptoms led to a psychiatric hospitalization where he was first diagnosed with provisional schizophreniform disorder and treated with antipsychotic medication. At that time, he had to leave his job, quit school, and move back home with his parents. After 6 months of impairment, his diagnosis was changed to schizophrenia.

Jamie benefited from his treatment, and his most flagrant symptoms improved substantially, including his belief that others were plotting against him. Nevertheless, Jamie continues to struggle with schizophrenia today, 5 years later. Even in the absence of psychotic symptoms, he maintains poor eye contact and shows little facial expression. For example, he rarely smiles spontaneously. His hygiene is generally good, but when his psychotic symptoms increase he becomes more disheveled, smokes more cigarettes, and becomes agitated. He is prescribed medications that he says help him feel better, less paranoid, and decrease his ideas of reference (i.e., beliefs that things around him have special meaning for him). However, Jamie lacks basic insight into his psychiatric disorder, and he does not believe he has a mental illness. Jamie also does not like having to take medications, partly because of the weight gain he has experienced from his antipsychotic medication. He periodically stops taking his medications when he feels better. These breaks from taking medication often lead to relapses in his symptoms, a deterioration in functioning, and sometimes rehospitalization.

Although Jamie continues to have symptoms and impairments of schizophrenia, he has also made some positive steps toward improving the quality of his life, with the help of his treatment team and his family. After several years of living at home, Jamie moved out 2 years ago to his own apartment. Jamie has been able to live on his own with the support of his family members and his case manager, who coordinates his care with Jamie's treatment team. At first when Jamie moved back home there was a significant amount of tension in the household, as Jamie's parents and younger sisters did not understand the nature of his illness, and were upset by his occasionally disruptive living habits, such as staying up much of the night. With the help of a clinician who worked with Jamie and his family for 15 months after Jamie returned home, his family was able to learn more about schizophrenia, the principles of its treatment, and strategies for solving problems together. Last, after attending a local day treatment program Jamie became interested in working. The mental health center where he receives his treatment had a supported employment program in which an employment specialist was assigned to Jamie to help him find a job in his area of interest, and to stay on the job through support and help with his employer. Jamie said he liked working with animals, and was able to get a job working part-time at a local pet store, where he cares for the animals, feeds them, and cleans their cages. Jamie has kept this job for almost 2 years; on two occasions he has had to take some time off when he had a relapse of his symptoms and had to return to the hospital. His employment specialist arranged with his employer for him to be able to return to his job when he had recovered from his relapse.

Many of the symptoms described in this vignette are highlighted in *DSM-IV-TR* criteria (See "Diagnostic Considerations" and Table 8.1). Jamie experienced at least two "characteristic symptoms," including delusions (e.g., his beliefs about his coworkers) and negative symptoms (e.g., flat facial expression). He experienced clear impairments in social/occupational functioning—at the time of diagnosis, he was no longer able to care for himself or to come to work. The duration criteria of *DSM-IV-TR* were met because these difficulties lasted longer than 6 months. In addition, other diagnoses were ruled out (e.g., mood disorders, substance abuse, developmental disorders). In addition to describing some of the symptoms of schizophrenia, this vignette illustrates that people with this illness are often able to lead rewarding and productive lives, usually with help of pharmacological and psychological treatment, as well as social supports, despite continued symptoms and impairment due to the illness.

EPIDEMIOLOGY

It is estimated that approximately 2.2 million persons in the United States have schizophrenia at any given time (Narrow, Rae, Robins, & Regier, 2002; Torrey, 2001). The annual incidence rate of new cases of schizophrenia has ranged from 16 to 40 per 100,000 persons (Jablensky, 2000). One-year prevalence rates of schizophrenia have ranged from 1% to 4.6% per 1,000 persons (Goldner, Hsu, Waraich, & Somers, 2002; Jablensky, 2000; Narrow, Rae, Robins, & Regier, 2002). The lifetime prevalence (proportion of persons who meet criteria for schizophrenia at any point in their lifetime) of schizophrenia (including the closely related disorders of schizoaffective disorder and schizophreniform disorder) lies between 0.55% and 1% per 100 persons (Goldner, Hsu, Waraich, & Somers, 2002; Keith, Regier, & Rae, 1991; Saha, Chant, Welham, & McGrath, 2005).

In general, the prevalence of schizophrenia is believed to be remarkably stable across a wide range of different populations and cultures. There has been little difference in the rates of schizophrenia according to gender, race, religion, or level of industrialization (Jablensky, 1999). Similar incidence rates and symptom patterns were found across 10 countries in a study sponsored by the World Health Organization (WHO; Jablensky et al., 1992). However, a more recent review of prevalence studies showed considerable heterogeneity in the rates of schizophrenia between different countries that may be partly owing to variations in diagnostic criteria (Goldner et al., 2002). Furthermore, there is evidence that schizophrenia is more heavily concentrated in urban areas of industrialized countries and, in fact, persons from developing countries may have a better prognosis and course of illness (Jablensky, 2000; Jablensky et al., 2000; Peen & Dekker, 1997; Takai, Sham, O'Callaghan, Glover, & Murray, 1995; Torrey, Bowler, & Clark, 1997). This increased risk appears to be related not only to the likelihood of people with schizophrenia drifting to urban areas, but to being born in urban areas as well (Torrey et al., 1997).

As schizophrenia frequently has an onset during early adulthood when important educational, social, and occupational milestones are often achieved, persons with the illness are especially affected in that they are less likely to marry or remain married, particularly males (Eaton, 1975; Munk-Jørgensen, 1987), and are less likely to complete higher levels of education (Kessler, Foster, Saunders, & Stang, 1995), and have problems in occupational performance (Marwaha & Johnson, 2004). In terms of employment rates, only 14% to 20% of persons with schizophrenia hold competitive employment despite reporting a desire to work (Mueser, Slayers, & Mueser, 2001; Rosenheck et al., 2006). It has long been known that there is an association between poverty and schizophrenia, with people belonging to lower socioeconomic classes more likely to develop the disorder (Hollingshead & Redlich, 1958; Salokangas, 1978). Historically, two theories have been advanced to account for this association. The *social drift* hypothesis postulates that the debilitating effects of schizophrenia on capacity to work result in a lowering of socioeconomic means, and hence poverty (Aro, Aro, & Keskimäki, 1995). The *environmental stress* hypothesis proposes that the high levels of stress associated with poverty precipitate schizophrenia in some individuals who would not otherwise develop the illness (Bruce, Takeuchi, & Leaf, 1991). Recently, attention has been aimed at different ethnic and migratory groups such as second-generation Afro-Caribbeans living in the United Kingdom who show higher incidence rates of schizophrenia (Boydell et al., 2001; Cantor-Graae & Selten, 2005). It is believed that being a minority in a potentially hostile social environment where racism and discrimination are present may lead to increased stress and potentially higher rates of symptoms (Clark et al., 1999; Combs et al., 2006). Both of these explanations may be partly true, and longitudinal research on changes in socioeconomic class status (SES) and schizophrenia provide conflicting results. For example, Fox (1990) reanalyzed data from several longitudinal studies and found that after controlling for initial levels of socioeconomic class, downward drift was not evident. Furthermore, Samele et al. (2001) found that a downward drift in occupational functioning over a 2-year period was not linked to illness course or prognosis. However, Dohrenwend et al. (1992) did find evidence for social drift, even after controlling for socioeconomic class. Also, it is possible that SES level may interact with gender as males from higher SES homes show poorer clinical outcomes (Parrott & Lewine, 2005). Thus, more work is needed to sort out the relationships between socioeconomic status and schizophrenia.

CLINICAL PICTURE

Most studies on the dimensions of schizophrenia agree on at least three major groups of symptoms (Liddle, 1987; Mueser, Curran, & McHugo, 1997; Van Der Does, Dingemans, Linszen, Nugter, & Scholte, 1993), including positive symptoms, negative symptoms, and cognitive impairments. *Positive symptoms* refer to thoughts, sensory experiences, and behaviors that are present in persons with the disorder, but are ordinarily absent in persons without the illness. Common examples of positive symptoms include hallucinations (e.g., hearing voices, seeing visions), delusions (e.g., believing that people are persecuting the person), and bizarre, disorganized behavior (e.g., maintaining a peculiar posture for no apparent reason, wearing multiple layers of clothes). Persecutory delusions (i.e., belief that some entity, group, or person has clear ongoing or future intentions to harm the person) are the most common type of delusion found in schizophrenia (Appelbaum, Robbins, & Roth 1999; as reviewed in Bentall et al., 2001). About 75% of persons with schizophrenia report hallucinations (Cutting, 1995). Auditory hallucinations are the most common form and are frequently derogatory, negative, or abusive, although some can be benevolent, comforting, and kind (Chadwick & Birchwood, 1995; Copolov, Mackinnon, & Trauer, 2004; Cutting, 1995). Less frequent, but more specific to schizophrenia, are voices that keep a running commentary on the person's actions or consist of two or more voices having a conversation. Auditory hallucinations can range from inaudible sounds (buzzing sounds, noises, muffled speech) or clearly perceived voices of either gender and can occur intermittently or on a continuous basis. It has been assumed that visual hallucinations were infrequent in schizophrenia and more reflective of a medical condition (prevalence of 10% to 15% in schizophrenia), but recent evidence suggests that these symptoms are more common than initially believed, especially in more severe forms of the disorder (Bracha, Wolkowitz, Lohr, Karson, & Bigelow, 1989; Mueser, Bellack, & Brady, 1990). *Negative symptoms,* on the other hand, refer to the absence or diminution of cognitions, feelings, or behaviors, which are ordinarily present in persons without the illness. Common negative symptoms include blunted or flattened affect (e.g., diminished facial expressiveness), poverty of speech (i.e., diminished verbal communication), anhedonia (i.e., inability to experience pleasure), apathy, psychomotor retardation (e.g., slow rate of speech), and physical inertia. *Cognitive impairments* refer to difficulties in verbal and visual learning and memory, working memory, attention/vigilance, abstract reasoning/executive functioning (i.e., understanding a concept, planning, organizing), and speed of information processing (Green et al., 2004). These cognitive deficits have been observed in unmedicated, medicated, first-episode, remitted, and high-risk children prior to developing the disorder. Thus, cognitive impairments are so commonplace that they are now considered a core feature of schizophrenia (Palmer et al., 1997; Wilk et al., 2005). A recent meta-analysis of cognitive performance found that normal controls without a history of schizophrenia perform consistently better (about 1 standard deviation) than persons with schizophrenia on most cognitive tasks, which suggests that a generalized cognitive deficit is present (Heinrichs, 2005). These deficits also appear to be relatively stable over time and do not reflect a progressive deterioration (Heaton et al., 2001). These cognitive impairments may interfere with the person's ability to focus for sustained periods on work or recreational pursuits, interact effectively with others, perform basic activities of daily living, or participate in conventional psychotherapeutic interventions (Bellack, Gold, & Buchanan, 1999; Brekke, Raine, Ansel, Lencz, & Bird, 1997; Green et al., 2000; Sevy & Davidson, 1995; Velligan et al., 1997). Cognitive impairments also result in difficulties generalizing training or knowledge to other areas (i.e., transfer of training problems) (Mueser, Bellack, Douglas, & Wade, 1991; Smith, Hull, Romanelli, Fertuck, & Weiss, 1999). Thus, many rehabilitative efforts focus on teaching persons with schizophrenia directly in the environment in which skills will be used or involve specialized teaching methods, such as errorless learning procedures (Kern, Liberman, Kopelowicz, Mintz, & Green, 2002).

In addition to cognitive deficits, it has become apparent that impairments in social cognition (defined as the way people perceive, interpret, and understand social information) are also found in schizophrenia (Penn, Corrigan, Bentall, Racenstein, & Newman, 1997). Deficits in emotion and social cue perception, problems inferring the intentions and motivations of others (Theory of Mind), and impairments in social knowledge and schemata have all been found in schizophrenia (Brune, 2005; Edwards, Jackson, & Pattison, 2002; Penn & Corrigan, 2001). More specifically, persons with persecutory delusions exhibit an attributional style in which they tend to blame others rather than situations for negative events (e.g., personalizing attributional style; see Garety & Freeman, 1999). Deficits in social cognition appear to be independent from nonsocial cognition (e.g., memory, attention) in that they predict incremental variance in social functioning and may arise from distinct brain structures involved in social information processing (Penn, Combs, & Mohamed, 2001; Penn et al., 1997; Pinkham, Penn, Perkins, & Lieberman, 2003). The exact nature of the relationship between social cognition and cognition is unclear, but social cognition appears to be important in the social functioning in schizophrenia (Green, Oliver, Crawley, Penn, & Silverstein, 2005).

The positive symptoms of schizophrenia tend to fluctuate over the course of the disorder and are often in remission between episodes of the illness. In addition, positive symptoms tend to be responsive to the effects of antipsychotic medication (Kane & Marder, 1993). In contrast, negative symptoms and cognitive impairments tend to be stable over time and are less responsive to antipsychotic medications (Greden & Tandon, 1991). However, there is some evidence that atypical antipsychotic medications, such as clozapine, risperidone, and olanzapine have a beneficial impact on negative symptoms and cognitive functioning (Breier, 2005; Green et al., 1997; Tollefson & Sanger, 1997; Wahlbeck, Cheine, Essali, & Adams, 1999).

Aside from the core symptoms of schizophrenia, many persons with schizophrenia experience negative emotions (e.g., depression, anxiety, and anger) as a consequence of their illness (Freeman & Garety, 2003). Depression is quite common (estimated co-morbidity rate of 45%; Leff, Tress, & Edwards, 1988) among people with schizophrenia and has been associated with poor outcomes (e.g., increased hospital use, lower employment rates) and suicidal tendencies (Sands & Harrow, 1999). Depressive symptoms can occur during all phases of the illness (prepsychotic, prodrome, acute, and remission), but tends to attenuate as the active psychotic symptoms remit (Birchwood, Iqbal, Chadwick, & Trower, 2000). In addition, it is generally estimated that approximately 10% of the persons with this illness die from suicide (Bromet, Fochtmann, Carlson, & Tanenberg-Karant, 2005; Drake, Gates, Whitaker, & Cotton, 1985; Jobe & Harrow, 2005; Roy, 1986), but recent research examining suicide rates has lowered this estimate to around 4.0% to 5.6% (Palmer, Pankratz, & Bostwick, 2005; Inskip, Harris, & Barraclough, 1998). Risk of suicide is greater in the presence of mood symptoms and substance use, if previous suicide attempts were made, during the initial onset of the disorder (Hawton, Sutton, Haw, Sinclair, & Deeks, 2005; first psychotic episode; rates 11% to 26%, as reviewed in Malla & Payne, 2005), and in time immediately preceding and following inpatient hospitalization (Qin & Nordentoft, 2005). Anxiety is also common in schizophrenia (estimated comorbidity rate of 43%) and is a frequent precursor to psychosis (Argyle, 1990; Braga, Mendlowicz, Marrocos, & Figueria, 2005; Cosoff & Hafner, 1998; Penn, Hope, Spaulding, & Kucera, 1994; Tien & Eaton, 1992). Specifically, there is evidence for the role of anxiety in both the formation and maintenance of persecutory delusions (threat beliefs) as well as hallucinations (Freeman et al., 2002;

Freeman & Garety, 2003). Finally, anger, hostility, and social avoidance may also be present, especially when the person is paranoid (Bartels, Drake, Wallach, & Freeman, 1991; Freeman, Garety, & Kuipers, 2001; Gay & Combs, 2005). Interestingly, as paranoia increases so does the tendency to perceive ambiguous interactions in a negative, threatening manner (Combs & Penn, 2004; Freeman et al., 2005).

In addition to the symptoms and negative emotions commonly present in schizophrenia, individuals with this diagnosis often have comorbid substance-use disorders. Epidemiological surveys have repeatedly found that persons with psychiatric disorders are at increased risk for alcohol and drug abuse (Mueser et al., 1990; Mueser, Yarnold, & Bellack, 1992). This risk is highest for persons with the most severe psychiatric disorders, including schizophrenia and bipolar disorder. For example, individuals with schizophrenia are more than four times as likely to have a substance abuse disorder than individuals in the general population (Regier et al., 1990). In general, approximately 50% of all persons with schizophrenia have a lifetime history of substance use disorder, and 25% to 35% have a recent history of such a disorder (Mueser, Bennett, & Kushner, 1995).

The presence of comorbid substance-use disorders in schizophrenia has consistently been found to be associated with a worse course of the illness, including increased vulnerability to relapses and hospitalizations, housing instability and homelessness, violence, economic family burden, and treatment noncompliance (Drake & Brunette, 1998). For these reasons, the recognition and treatment of substance-use disorders in persons with schizophrenia is crucial to the overall management of the illness.

Another important clinical feature of schizophrenia is lack of insight and compliance with treatment (Amador & Gorman, 1998; Amador, Strauss, Yale, & Gorman, 1991). Many individuals with schizophrenia have little or no insight into the fact that they have a psychiatric illness, or even that they have any problems at all. This denial of illness can lead to noncompliance with recommended treatments, such as psychotropic medications and psychosocial therapies (McEvoy et al., 1989). Furthermore, fostering insight into the illness is a difficult and often impossible task with these persons.

Noncompliance with treatment is a related problem, but can also occur because of the severe negativity often present in the illness, independent of poor insight. Problems with paranoia and distrust may contribute to noncompliance, in that some persons may believe medications or treatment providers are dangerous to them. Further, side effects of some medications (sedation, dry mouth, motor side effects), particularly the conventional antipsychotics, are unpleasant and can also lead to noncompliance. Medication noncompliance increases the risk of relapse, and between 50% to 75% of individuals who discontinue their medication will relapse within one year. Therefore, treatment compliance is a major concern to clinical treatment providers (Buchanan, 1992). It has been argued that the newer atypical antipsychotics may lead to higher rates of compliance owing to better side effect profiles (Breier, 2005). However, a recent study of 63,000 individuals with schizophrenia in the Veteran's Affairs medical system found widespread noncompliance (compliance measured in terms of filling needed prescriptions) across both conventional and atypical antipsychotics (Valenstein et al., 2004). Strategies for enhancing compliance involve helping the person become a more active participant in his or her treatment, identifying personal goals of treatment that have high relevance for that individual, and helping develop strategies for taking medications into the daily routines (Azrin & Teichner, 1998; Corrigan, Liberman, & Engle, 1990; Kemp, Hayward, Applewhaite, Everitt, & David, 1996; Kemp, Kirov, Everitt, Hayward, & David, 1998).

People with schizophrenia are sometimes assumed to be violent or otherwise dangerous. Indeed, rates of violence have been found to be relatively higher in people with schizophrenia and other severe mental illnesses compared to the general population (Hodgins, Mednick, Brennan, Schulsinger, & Engberg, 1996; Swanson, Holzer, Ganju, & Jono, 1990). However, a more accurate comparison may be to examine the rates of violence between schizophrenia with other psychiatric disorders. Data from the MacArthur Risk Assessment Study found that the actual rates of violence for persons with schizophrenia was 8% for the first 20 weeks following discharge (most violent events occur in the first 20 weeks) and 14% over the course of a 1-year period (Monahan et al., 2001). In comparison, the rates of violence for persons with schizophrenia were actually lower than those persons with depression and bipolar disorder for the same time period. A prospective study of violent behaviors in females with severe mental illness reported a prevalence rate of 17% over a 2-year period (Dean et al., 2006). Rates vary widely depending upon source of information (e.g., self-report vs. collateral reports), definition of violence, population studied (e.g., inpatients vs. outpatients), and where the research takes place (e.g., country). However, it should be emphasized that the majority of people with schizophrenia and other mental illnesses are not violent (Swanson, 1994). When violence does occur, it is often associated with substance abuse (Steadman et al., 1998) or the combination of substance abuse and medication noncompliance (Swartz et al., 1998). Other factors such as psychopathy (Nolan, Volavka, Mohr, & Czobor, 1999) or antisocial personality disorder (Hodgins & Côté, 1993, 1996) also have been implicated. Finally, targets of violence tend to be family members or friends rather than strangers, which is not unexpected given that most persons with schizophrenia rely heavily on family members for support (Steadman et al., 1998).

Although there is an increased rate of violence in schizophrenia, people with schizophrenia are much more likely to be the victims of violence and violent crime (Hiday, Swartz, Swanson, Borum, & Wagner, 1999). About 34% to 53% of individuals with severe mental illness report childhood sexual or physical abuse (Greenfield, Strakowski, Tohen, Batson, & Kolbrener, 1994; Jacobson & Herald, 1990; Rose, Peabody, & Stratigeas, 1991; Ross, Anderson, & Clark, 1994), and 43% to 81% report some type of victimization over their lives (Carmen, Rieker, & Mills, 1984; Hutchings & Dutton, 1993; Jacobson, 1989; Jacobson & Richardson, 1987; Lipschitz et al., 1996). Two recent surveys of a large number of people with severe mental illness found high rates of severe physical or sexual assault in the past year (Goodman et al., 2001; Silver, Arseneault, Langley, Caspi, & Moffitt, 2005). These numbers are striking compared to estimates of the general population, in which 0.3% of women and 3.5% of men reported assault in the past year (Tjaden & Thoennes, 1998). Studies of the prevalence of interpersonal trauma in women with severe mental illness indicate especially high vulnerability to victimization, with rates ranging as high as 77% to 97% for episodically homeless women (Davies-Netzley, Hurlburt, & Hough, 1996; Goodman, Dutton, & Harris, 1995). The prevalence of PTSD among people with schizophrenia and other severe mental illnesses in various samples has ranged from 29% to 43% (Cascardi, Mueser, DeGirolomo, & Murrin, 1996; Craine, Henson, Colliver, & MacLean, 1988; Mueser et al., 1998; Mueser et al., 2004; Switzer et al., 1999), but has been as low as 3.8% (Braga, Mendlowicz, Marrocos, & Figueira, 2005). These *current* rates of PTSD are far in excess of the *lifetime* prevalence of PTSD in the general population, with range from estimates ranging between 8% and 12% (Breslau, Davis, Andreski, & Peterson, 1991; Kessler, Sonnega, Bromet, Hughes, & Nelson, 1995; Resnick, Kilpatrick, Dansky, Saunders, & Best, 1993). Thus, interpersonal violence is so common in the serious mental illness (SMI) population that it must sadly be considered a normative experience (Goodman, Dutton, & Harris, 1997).

COURSE AND PROGNOSIS

Schizophrenia usually has an onset in late adolescence or early adulthood, most often between the ages of 16 and 25. However, there is evidence that signs of the disorder are present long before the clinical symptoms of psychosis appear. Children who later develop schizophrenia show impairments in sociability, emotional expressiveness (less positive and more negative facial expressions), and neuromotor functioning (Schiffman et al., 2004; Walker, Grimes, Davis, & Smith, 1993). Data from the New York High Risk Project, which followed a cohort of children at high risk for schizophrenia, found that deficits in verbal memory, attentional vigilance, and gross motor skills in childhood (ages 7 to 12) predicted the development of schizophrenia later in life (Erlenmeyer-Kimling et al., 2000). Some individuals display a maladaptive pattern of behaviors, including disruptive behavior, problems in school, poor interpersonal relationships, and impulsivity (Amminger et al., 1999; Baum & Walker, 1995; Fuller et al., 2002; Hans, Marcus, Henson, Auerbach, & Mirsky, 1992). Similarly, symptoms of conduct disorder in childhood, such as repeated fighting, truancy, and lying, have been found to be predictive of the later development of schizophrenia (Asarnow, 1988; Cannon et al., 1993; Neumann, Grimes, Walker, & Baum, 1995; Robins, 1966; Robins & Price, 1991; Rutter, 1984; Watt, 1978). However, other persons with schizophrenia display no unusual characteristics in their premorbid functioning or competence (Zigler & Glick, 1986). The signs of schizophrenia in childhood may be subtle, irregular, and gradual in onset, but become increasingly more apparent as adolescence approaches (Dworkin et al., 1991).

Prior to the emergence of schizophrenia, many persons enter a prodromal period of the illness, which is characterized by changes in mood and behavior (Yung & McGorry, 1996). The prodrome is an intensification of the core features of the disorder that can last up to 5 years. Prodromal symptoms are subclinical or attenuated symptoms that fail to reach the threshold for an clinical diagnosis, but become increasingly apparent to others. Disruptions in sleep, anxiety, depression, aggression/irritability, paranoia, and odd beliefs are common in the prodromal phase (Hafner, Maurer, Trendler, an der Heiden, & Schmidt, 2005; Norman, Scholten, Malla, & Ballageer, 2005; Malla & Payne, 2005; Yung & McGorry, 1996). Social isolation, withdrawal, changes in role functioning, and avolition may be present during this stage as well.

The initial emergence of clinical symptoms (first-episode or first break) is a crucial time for treatment and intervention (Lincoln & McGorry, 1995). It is widely believed that the earlier antipsychotic medications are initiated, the better the long-term outcome becomes (Penn, Waldheter, Perkins, Mueser, & Lieberman, 2005). In fact, a critical time for treatment appears to be during the first 5 years of the disorder (Malla, Norman, & Joober, 2005). This finding combined with the efficacy of antipsychotic medications (50% show remission after 3 months and 80% show remission at 1 year; as reviewed in Penn et al., 2005) in first-episode individuals makes early intervention programs a crucial aspect of treatment. Unfortunately, even after symptom remission is attained, a majority still has deficits in social, vocational, and community functioning (Tohen et al., 2000). Negative symptoms in first-episode individuals have been linked to poor cognitive functioning and longer durations of untreated psychosis (Malla & Payne, 2005).

It is extremely rare for the first onset of schizophrenia to occur before adolescence (e.g., before the age of 12), with most diagnostic systems considering childhood-onset schizophrenia to be a different disorder than adolescent or adult onset (APA, 2000). More common than childhood schizophrenia, but nevertheless rare in the total population of persons with schizophrenia, are individuals who develop the illness later in life, such as after the age of 40 (late-onset schizophrenia) or after the age of 60 (very late onset schizophrenia) (Cohen, 1990; Howard, Rabins, Seeman, Jeste, & the International Late-Onset Schizophrenia Group, 2000). It is estimated that approximately 23% of individuals with schizophrenia develop symptoms after the age of 40 (Harris & Jeste, 1988). Late-onset schizophrenia is more common in women, and there is evidence of better social, educational, and occupational functioning as compared to early-onset schizophrenia (Howard et al., 2000). Late-onset schizophrenia is more likely to involve positive symptoms (visual, tactile, and olfactory hallucinations; persecutory delusions) and less likely to involve formal thought disorder or negative symptoms (Bartels, Mueser, & Miles, 1998). Late-onset schizophrenia is further complicated by the lack of clear-cut distinguishing characteristics that discriminate this disorder from a variety of other disorders that develop later in old age such as dementia (Howard, Almeida, & Levy, 1994). Thus, it is important to emphasize that the symptoms of schizophrenia can arise at any point in life and are a developmental phenomenon.

The onset, course, and prognosis of the illness are closely tied to gender (Haas & Garratt, 1998). Women tend to have later age of onset of the illness (average onset is between 25 to 29 years), spend less time in hospitals, have fewer negative symptoms, demonstrate less cognitive impairment, and have better social competence and social functioning than men with the illness (Goldstein, 1988; Häfner et al., 1993; Leung & Chue, 2000; Mueser, Bellack, Morrison, & Wade, 1990; Salem & Kring, 1998). The benefits experienced by women do not appear to be explained by societal differences in tolerance for deviant behavior. A variety of different hypotheses have been advanced to account for the superior outcome of women with schizophrenia (e.g., role of estrogen on dopamine receptors, more adaptive coping with socioenvironmental stressors, improved social networks and competence (Castle & Murray, 1991; Flor-Henry, 1985; Halari et al., 2004), but no single theory has received strong support.

In general, the onset of schizophrenia can be described as either gradual or acute. The gradual onset of schizophrenia can take place over many months or years, and it may be difficult for family members and others to clearly distinguish onset of the illness (prepsychotic and prodromal signs). In other cases, the symptoms develop rapidly over a period of a few weeks with dramatic and easily observed changes occurring over this time. People with acute onset of schizophrenia have a somewhat better prognosis than those with a more insidious illness (Fenton & McGlashan, 1991; Kay & Lindenmayer, 1987).

Although schizophrenia is a long-term and severe psychiatric illness, there is considerable interindividual variability in the course and outcome of the illness over time (Marengo, 1994). Generally, though, once schizophrenia has developed, the illness usually continues to be present at varying degrees of severity throughout most of the person's life. Schizophrenia is usually an episodic illness with periods of acute symptom exacerbation (i.e., relapse) requiring more intensive, often inpatient, treatment interspersed by periods of higher functioning between episodes (i.e., remission). Preventing relapse is a significant clinical concern because each relapse leads to more persistent symptoms and greater cognitive and psychosocial impairment. Despite the fact that most persons with schizophrenia live in the community, it is comparatively rare, at least in the short-term, for individuals to return to their premorbid levels of functioning between episodes. Remission is the reduction of active symptoms to nonproblematic, less severe levels (Andreasen et al., 2005). Recovery is much broader and includes both symptom remission and an improvement in social, community, occupational, and adaptive functioning. Recovery is also largely based on consumer perceptions of improvement. A recent review of 10 longitudinal studies on outcome in schizophrenia, some of which followed individuals for more than 20 years, reported that between 21% and 57% of persons with schizophrenia showed periodic episodes of recovery (improved symptoms; greater social, educational, and occupational functioning; Jobe & Harrow, 2005). In fact, some of these individuals showed extended periods of recovery without mental health treatment (Harrow, Grossman, Jobe, & Herbener, 2005; Jobe & Harrow, 2005).

Some general predictors of the course and outcome of schizophrenia have been identified, such as premorbid functioning, but overall, the ability to predict outcome is rather poor (Avison & Speechley, 1987; Tsuang, 1986). The primary reason for this is that symptom severity and functioning are determined by the dynamic interplay between biological vulnerability, environmental factors, and coping skills (Nuechterlein & Dawson, 1984; Liberman et al., 1986). Factors such as compliance with medication (Buchanan, 1992), substance abuse (Drake, Osher, & Wallach, 1989), exposure to a hostile or critical environment (Butzlaff & Hooley, 1998), the availability of psychosocial programming (Bellack & Mueser, 1993), and assertive case management and outreach (Mueser, Bond, Drake, & Resnick, 1998; Mueser, Drake, & Bond, 1997; Phillips et al., 2001; Quinlivan et al., 1995) are all environmental factors that in combination play a large role in determining outcome.

The importance of environmental factors and rehabilitation programs in determining the outcome of schizophrenia is illustrated by two long-term outcome studies conducted by Harding and her associates (DeSisto, Harding, McCormick, Ashikaga, & Brooks, 1995; Harding, Brooks, Ashikaga, Strauss, & Breier, 1987a, 1987b). The first study was conducted in Vermont, which had a highly developed system of community-based rehabilitation programs for persons with severe mental illness. Persons with schizophrenia in this study demonstrated surprisingly positive outcomes (60% recovery rate) over the 20- to 40-year follow-up period. In contrast, similar individuals in Maine, where more traditional hospital-based treatment programs existed, fared substantially worse over the long-term course of their illness. Thus, the outcome of most cases of schizophrenia is not predetermined by specific biological factors, but rather is influenced by the interaction between biological and environmental factors.

In summary, the prognosis of schizophrenia is usually considered poor to fair, and there is general agreement that it is worse than for other major psychiatric disorders, such as bipolar disorder or major depression (Jobe & Harrow, 2005). Despite the widespread acceptance that schizophrenia is usually a lifelong disability, recent research on the long-term outcome of schizophrenia has challenged this assumption. Many persons with schizophrenia can attain symptom remission and recovery with the appropriate pharmacological and psychosocial treatment (Ciompi, 1980; Harding et al., 1987a, 1987b; Harrow, Grossman, Jobe, & Herbener, 2005).

DIAGNOSTIC CONSIDERATIONS

The diagnostic criteria for schizophrenia are fairly similar across a variety of different diagnostic systems. In general, the diagnostic criteria specify some degree of social impairment, combined with positive and negative symptoms lasting a significant duration (e.g., 6 months or more). The diagnostic criteria for schizophrenia according to *DSM-IV-TR* (APA, 2000) are summarized in Table 8.1.

Table 8.1
DSM-IV-TR Criteria for the Diagnosis of Schizophrenia

A. Presence of at least two or the following characteristic symptoms in the active phase for at least 1 month (unless the symptoms are successfully treated).

   1. Delusions.

   2. Hallucinations.

   3. Disorganized speech (e.g., frequent derailment or incoherence).

   4. Grossly disorganized or catatonic behavior.

   5. Negative symptoms (i.e., affect flattening, alogia, or avolition).

   Note: Only one of these symptoms is required if delusions are bizarre or hallucinations consist of a voice keeping up a running commentary on the person's behavior or thoughts, or two or more voices conversing with each other:

B. Social/occupational dysfunction: For a significant proportion of the time from the onset of the disturbance, one or more areas of functioning, such as work, interpersonal relations, or self-care, is markedly below the level achieved prior to the onset (or, when the onset is in childhood or adolescence, failure to achieve expected level of interpersonal, academic, or occupational achievement).

C. Duration: Continuous signs of the disturbance persist for at least 6 months. This 6-month period must include at least 1 month of symptoms that meet criterion A (i.e., active-phase symptoms) and may include periods of prodromal or residual symptoms. During these prodromal or residual periods, the signs of the disturbance may be manifested by only negative symptoms or by two or more symptoms listed in criterion A present in an attenuated form (e.g., odd beliefs, unusual perceptual experiences).

D. Schizoaffective and mood disorders exclusion: Schizoaffective disorder and mood disorder with psychotic features have been ruled out because either (1) no major depressive or manic episodes have occurred concurrently with the active-phase symptoms, or (2) if mood episodes have occurred during active-phase symptoms, their total duration has been brief relative to the duration of the active and residual periods.

E. Substance/general medical condition exclusion: The disturbance is not owing to the direct effects of a substance (e.g., drugs of abuse, medication) or a general medical condition.

The diagnosis of schizophrenia requires a clinical interview with the patient, a thorough review of all available records, and standard medical evaluations to rule out the possible role of organic factors (e.g., CAT scan to rule out a brain tumor). In addition, because many persons with schizophrenia are poor historians or may not provide accurate accounts of their behavior, information from significant others, such as family members, is often critical to establish a diagnosis of schizophrenia. The use of family and other informants is especially important in the assessment of prodromal and prepsychotic states. Because of the wide variety of symptoms characteristic of schizophrenia and variations in interviewing style and format across different clinical interviewers, the use of structured clinical interviews, such as the Structured Clinical Interview for *DSM-IV* (SCID; First, Spitzer, Gibbon, & Williams, 1996) can greatly enhance the reliability and validity of psychiatric diagnosis.

Structured clinical interviews have two main advantages over more open clinical interviews. First, structured interviews provide definitions of the key symptoms, agreed upon by experts, thus making explicit the specific symptoms required for diagnosis. Second, by conducting the interview in a standardized format, including a specific sequence of asking questions, variations in interviewing style are minimized, thus enhancing the comparability of diagnostic assessments across different clinicians. The second point is especially crucial considering that most research studies of schizophrenia employ structured interviews to establish diagnoses. It is important that interviewers are properly trained and interrater reliability with a criterion-trained or expert rater is established before the use of structured interviews are initiated. If the findings of clinical research studies are to be generalized into clinical practice, efforts must be taken to ensure the comparability of the patient populations and the assessment techniques employed.

The symptoms of schizophrenia overlap with many other psychiatric disorders. Establishing a diagnosis of schizophrenia requires particularly close consideration of four other overlapping disorders: substance-use disorders, affective disorders, schizoaffective disorder, and delusional disorder. We discuss issues related to each of these disorders and the diagnosis of schizophrenia in the following sections.

SUBSTANCE-USE DISORDERS

Substance-use disorder, such as alcohol dependence or drug abuse, can either be a differential diagnosis to schizophrenia or a comorbid disorder (i.e., the individual can have both schizophrenia *and* a substance use disorder). With respect to differential diagnosis, substance-use disorders can interfere with a clinician's ability to diagnosis schizophrenia, and can lead to misdiagnosis if the substance abuse is covert, denied, or not reported accurately (Corty, Lehman, & Myers, 1993; Kranzler et al., 1995). Psychoactive substances, such as alcohol, marijuana, cocaine, and amphetamine, can produce symptoms that mimic those found in schizophrenia, such as hallucinations, delusions, and social withdrawal (Schuckit, 1995). In those cases in which the substance is involved in the etiology of psychosis, a diagnosis of substance-induced psychotic disorder would be appropriate. Further complicating matters, the use of these substances can exacerbate psychotic symptoms and in many cases lead to a return of acute psychosis. Because the diagnosis of schizophrenia requires the presence of specific symptoms in the absence of identifiable organic factors, schizophrenia can only be diagnosed in persons with a history of substance use disorder by examining the individual's functioning during sustained periods of abstinence from drugs or alcohol. When such periods of abstinence can be identified, a reliable diagnosis of schizophrenia can be made. However, persons with schizophrenia who have a long history of substance abuse, with few or no periods of abstinence, are more difficult to assess. For example, in a sample of 461 individuals admitted to a psychiatric hospital, a psychiatric diagnosis could not be confirmed nor ruled out because of history of substance abuse in 71 persons (15%; Lehman, Myers, Dixon, & Johnson, 1994).

Substance use disorder is the most common comorbid diagnosis for persons with schizophrenia. As substance abuse can worsen the course and outcome of schizophrenia, recognition and treatment of substance abuse in schizophrenia is a critical goal of treatment. The diagnosis of substance abuse in schizophrenia is complicated by several factors. Substance abuse, as in the general population, is often denied because of social and legal sanctions (Stone, Greenstein, Gamble, & McLellan, 1993; Galletly, Field, & Prior, 1993)—a problem that may be worsened in this population because of a fear of losing benefits. Denial of problems associated with substance abuse, a core feature of primary substance-use disorders, may be further heightened by psychotic distortions and cognitive impairments present in schizophrenia. Furthermore, the criteria used to establish a substance-use disorder in the general population are less useful for diagnosis in schizophrenia (Corse, Hirschinger, & Zanis, 1995). For example, the common consequences of substance abuse in the general population of loss of employment, driving under the influence of alcohol, and relationship problems are less often experienced by people with schizophrenia, who are often unemployed, do not own cars, and have limited interpersonal relationships. Rather, persons with schizophrenia more often experience increased symptoms and rehospitalizations, legal problems, and housing instability because of substance abuse (Drake & Brunette, 1998).

Individuals with schizophrenia tend to use smaller quantities of drugs and alcohol (Cohen & Klein, 1970; Crowley, Chesluk, Dilts, & Hart, 1974; Lehman et al., 1994) and rarely develop the full physical dependence syndrome that is often present in persons with a primary substance-use disorder (Corse et al., 1995; Drake et al., 1990; Test, Wallisch, Allness, & Ripp, 1989) or show other physical consequences of alcohol such as stigmata (Mueser et al., 1999). Even very low scores on instruments developed for the primary substance-use disorder population, such as the Addiction Severity Inventory, may be indicative of substance-use disorder in persons with schizophrenia (Appleby, Dyson, Altman, & Luchins, 1997; Corse et al., 1995; Lehman, Myers, Dixon, & Johnson, 1996). Because of the difficulties in using existing measures of substance abuse for people with schizophrenia and other severe mental illnesses, a screening tool was developed specifically for these populations: the Dartmouth Assessment of Lifestyle Instrument (DALI; Rosenberg et al., 1998). The DALI is an 18-item questionnaire that has high classification accuracy for current substance-use disorders of alcohol, cannabis, and cocaine for people with severe mental illness.

Despite the difficulties involved in assessing comorbid substance abuse in persons with schizophrenia, recent developments in this area indicate that if appropriate steps are taken, reliable diagnoses can be made (Drake, Rosenberg, & Mueser, 1996; Maisto et al., 2000). The most critical recommendations for diagnosing substance abuse in schizophrenia include: (1) maintain a high index of suspicion of current substance abuse, especially if a person has a past history of substance abuse; (2) use multiple assessment techniques, including self-report instruments, interviews, clinician reports, reports of significant others, and biological assays for the presence of substances, which are routinely collected on admission to inpatient treatment; and (3) be alert to signs that may be subtle indicators of the presence of a substance-use disorder, such as unexplained symptom relapses, familial conflict, money management problems, and sudden depression or suicidality. Once a substance-use disorder has been diagnosed, integrated treatment that addresses both the schizophrenia and the substance-use disorder (co-occurring disorders) is necessary to achieve a favorable clinical outcome (Drake, Mercer-McFadden, Mueser, McHugo, & Bond, 1998).

MOOD DISORDERS

Schizophrenia overlaps more prominently with the major mood disorders than any other psychiatric disorder. The differential diagnosis of schizophrenia from mood disorders is critical because the disorders respond to different treatments, particularly pharmacological interventions. Two different mood disorders can be especially difficult to distinguish from schizophrenia, bipolar disorder and major depression. The differential diagnosis of these disorders from schizophrenia is complicated by the fact that mood symptoms are frequently present in all phases of schizophrenia (prodrome, acute, and remission), and psychotic symptoms (e.g., hallucinations, delusions) may be present in persons with severe mood disorders (APA, 2000; Pope & Lipinski, 1978).

The crux of making a differential diagnosis between schizophrenia and a major mood disorder is determining whether psychotic symptoms are present *in the absence of* mood symptoms. If there is strong evidence that psychotic symptoms persist even when the person is not experiencing symptoms of mania or depression, then the diagnosis is either schizophrenia or the closely related disorder of schizoaffective disorder (discussed in the following section). If, on the other hand, symptoms of psychosis are present only during an mood episode, but disappear when the person's mood is stable, the appropriate diagnosis is either major depression or bipolar disorder. For example, it is common for people with bipolar disorder to have hallucinations and delusions during the height of a manic episode, but for these psychotic symptoms to remit when the person's mood becomes stable again. Similarly, persons with major depression often experience hallucinations or delusions during a severe depressive episode, which subside as their mood improves. If the patient experiences chronic mood problems, meeting criteria for manic, depressive, or mixed episodes, it may be difficult or impossible to establish a diagnosis of schizophrenia, because there are no sustained periods of stable mood.

SCHIZOAFFECTIVE DISORDER

Schizoaffective disorder is a diagnostic entity that overlaps with both the mood disorders and schizophrenia (APA, 2000). Three conditions must be met for a person to be diagnosed with schizoaffective disorder: (1) the person must meet criteria for a mood episode (i.e., a 2-week period in which manic, depressive, or mixed mood features are present to a significant degree); (2) the person must also meet criteria for the symptoms of schizophrenia during a period when that person is not experiencing a mood syndrome (e.g., hallucinations or delusions in the absence of manic or depressive symptoms); and (3) the mood episode must be present for

Table 8.2

DSM-IV-TR Criteria for the Diagnosis of Schizoaffective Disorder

A. An uninterrupted period of illness during which at some time there is either a major depressive episode (which must include depressed mood) or manic episode concurrent with symptoms that meet criterion A of schizophrenia.

B. During the same period of illness, there have been delusions or hallucinations for at least 2 weeks in the absence of prominent mood symptoms.

C. Symptoms meeting the criteria for a mood disorder are present for a substantial portion of the total duration of the active and residual periods of the illness.

D. The disturbance is not owing to the direct effects of a substance (e.g., drugs of abuse, medication) or a general medical condition.

a substantial period of the person's psychiatric illness (i.e., a person who experiences brief, transient mood states and who is chronically psychotic and has other long-standing impairments would be diagnosed with schizophrenia, rather than schizoaffective disorder); see Table 8.2.

Schizoaffective disorder and major mood disorder are frequently mistaken for one another because it is incorrectly assumed that schizoaffective disorder simply requires the presence of both psychotic and mood symptoms at the same time. Rather, as described in the preceding section, if psychotic symptoms always coincide with mood symptoms, the person has a mood disorder, whereas if psychotic symptoms are present in the absence of a mood episode, the person meets criteria for either schizoaffective disorder or schizophrenia. Thus, schizoaffective disorder requires longitudinal information about the relationship between mood and psychosis to make a diagnosis. Oftentimes, this information is obtained from the individual, but is subject to memory and self-reporting biases (poor insight, or lack of awareness of mood states). The distinction between schizophrenia and schizoaffective disorder can be more difficult to make, because judgment must be made as to whether the affective symptoms have been present for a substantial part of the person's illness. Decision rules for determining the extent to which mood symptoms must be present to diagnose a schizoaffective disorder have not been clearly established.

Although the differential diagnosis between schizophrenia and schizoaffective disorder is difficult to make, the clinical implications of this distinction are less important than between the mood disorders and either schizophrenia or schizoaffective disorder. Research on family history and treatment response suggest that schizophrenia and schizoaffective disorder are similar disorders and respond to the same interventions (Kramer, et al., 1989; Levinson & Levitt, 1987; Levinson & Mowry, 1991; Mattes & Nayak, 1984). In fact, many studies of schizophrenia routinely include persons with schizoaffective disorder and find few differences. Therefore, the information provided in this chapter on schizophrenia also pertains to schizoaffective disorder, and the differential diagnosis between the two disorders is not of major importance from a clinical perspective.

DELUSIONAL DISORDER

Delusions can be found in schizophrenia, schizoaffective disorder, severe mood disorders, organic conditions, and delusional disorder and are a nonspecific symptom in many cases. Persons with delusional disorder develop fixed, non-bizarre delusions and do not show the other symptoms of schizophrenia (auditory hallucinations, disorganization, negative symptoms). The delusion may lead to problems with others, but in general the person has good social, educational, and occupational functioning. Tactile and olfactory hallucinations can be present and will usually be incorporated into the delusional belief. Delusional disorder is more common in females (3:1 female to male ratio) and has a later age of onset (mean age of 40; Evans, Paulsen, Harris, Heaton, & Jeste, 1996; Manschreck, 1996; Yamanda, Nakajima, & Noguchi, 1998). Delusional disorder accounts for 1% to 4% of all inpatient admissions and is relatively rare in clinical practice (Kendler, 1982). The differential diagnosis between delusional disorder and schizophrenia is based on the presence of nonbizarre delusions and absence of other symptoms of schizophrenia. Nonbizarre delusions are based on events or situations that could occur in the real life, but are highly improbable and lack supporting evidence (Sedler, 1995). Examples of nonbizarre delusions include being watched, followed, spied upon, harassed, loved, or poisoned. In contrast, bizarre delusions involve mechanisms not believed to exist in an individual's culture, such as beliefs of thought insertion, control, and broadcasting. In reality, the distinction between nonbizarre and bizarre beliefs is highly subjective and difficult (Junginger, Barker, & Coe, 1992; Sammons, 2005). Many persons with delusions will provide convincing arguments that their beliefs are true and a decision on whether the belief is plausible must often be made with very little corroborating evidence (Flaum, Arndt, & Andreasen, 1991; Jones, 1999). An examination of the person's history, premorbid and current functioning, and symptom profile can be useful in distinguishing delusional disorder from schizophrenia. A structured interview, such as the SCID, can be useful in assessing delusional beliefs along with the other symptoms of schizophrenia.

PSYCHOLOGICAL AND BIOLOGICAL ASSESSMENT

Diagnostic assessment provides important information about the potential utility of interventions for schizophrenia (e.g., antipsychotic medications). However, assessment does not end with a diagnosis. It must be supplemented with additional psychological and biological assessments.

PSYCHOLOGICAL ASSESSMENT

A wide range of different psychological formulations have been proposed for understanding schizophrenia. For example, there are extensive writings about psychodynamic and psychoanalytic interpretations of schizophrenia. Although this work has made contributions to the further development of these theories, these formulations do not appear to have improved the ability of clinicians to understand persons with this disorder or led to more effective interventions (Mueser & Berenbaum, 1990). Therefore, the use of projective assessment techniques based on psychodynamic concepts of personality, such as the Rorschach and Thematic Apperception Test, is not considered here.

One of the primary areas to assess is severity of psychotic symptoms as treatment progression is mainly judged by a reduction of symptoms (Andreasen et al., 2005). This includes an assessment of positive and negative symptoms and general psychopathology due to the high co-morbidity with anxiety and mood disorders. Measures such as the Positive and Negative Syndrome Scale (PANNS; Kay, Fiszbein, & Opler, 1987), the Brief Psychiatric Rating Scale (BPRS; Overall & Gorham, 1962), and the Psychotic Rating Scale (PSYRATS; Haddock et al., 1999) have been frequently used in schizophrenia research and have good psychometric properties. Scales specific to positive (Scale for the Assessment of Positive Symptoms; Andreasen & Olsen, 1982) and negative symptoms (Scale for the Assessment of Negative Symptoms; Andreasen, 1982) can be used for a more in-depth and detailed assessment of these areas. There are also self-report and interview-based measures of insight available as well (see Amador & David, 2004). Commonly, these symptom measures are used in conjunction with a structured diagnostic interview in the assessment of schizophrenia.

As noted earlier, schizophrenia is often associated with a variety of neuropsychological impairments. Core areas to assess in terms of cognitive functioning are verbal and visual learning and memory, working memory, attention/vigilance, abstract reasoning/executive functioning, speed of information processing, and social cognition. These areas are part of the National Institute of Mental Health-Measurement and Treatment Research to Improve Cognition in Schizophrenia cognitive battery (NIMH-MATRICS; Green et al., 2004). Having information on cognitive functioning in these areas will aid in examining the beneficial effects of antipsychotic medication on cognition. It also is important to consider the generalization of these impairments to different situations (i.e., transfer of training problems). Thus, assessment needs to be conducted in the environments in which the skills are to be used in order to provide a more ecologically valid assessment. For example, successful employment interventions incorporate assessment on the job on an ongoing basis rather than extensive prevocational testing batteries that do not generalize to real-world settings (Bond, 1998; Drake & Becker, 1996). Similarly, when assessing independent living skills, it is important that these to be measured directly in the living environment of the patient or in simulated tests (Wallace, Liberman, Tauber, & Wallace, 2000).

A great deal of research has been done on the functional assessment of social skills in people with schizophrenia. Social skills refer to the individual behavioral components, such as eye contact, voice loudness, and the specific choice of words, which in combination are necessary for effective communication with others (Mueser & Bellack, 1998). As previously described, poor social competence is a hallmark of schizophrenia. Although not all problems in social functioning are the consequence of poor social skill, many social impairments appear to be related to skill deficits (Bellack, Morrison, Wixted, & Mueser, 1990).

A number of different strategies can be used to assess social competence. Clinical interviews can be a good starting place for identifying broad areas of social dysfunction. These interviews can focus on answering questions such as: Is the patient lonely?, Would the patient like more or closer friends?, Is the patient able to stand up for his or her rights?, and Is the patient able to get others to respond positively to him or her? Patient interviews are most informative when combined with interviews with significant others, such as family members and clinicians who are familiar with the nature and quality of the patient's social interactions, as well as naturalistic observations of the patient's social interactions. The combination of these sources of information is useful for identifying specific areas in need of social skills training.

One strategy for assessing social skills that yields the most specific type of information is role play assessments. Role plays usually involve brief simulated social interactions between the person and a confederate taking the role of an interactive partner. During role plays individuals are instructed to act as though the situation were actually happening in real life. Role plays can be as brief as 15 to 30 seconds, to assess skill areas such as initiating conversations, or can be as long as several minutes, to assess skills such as problem-solving ability. Role plays can be audiotaped or videotaped and later rated on specific dimensions of social skill. Alternatively, role playing can be embedded into the procedures of social skills training, in which persons with schizophrenia practice targeted social skills in role plays, followed by positive and corrective feedback and additional role play rehearsal. In the latter instance, the assessment of social skills is integrated into the training of new skills, rather than preceding skills training. A commonly used assessment measure for social skill is the Maryland Assessment of Social Competence (MASC; Bellack & Thomas-Lohrman, 2003). The MASC is a structured role play assessment that consists of four 3-minute interactions. Following each role play, ratings on verbal and nonverbal skill and effectiveness are made, thus allowing the clinician to examine social skill across different situations and contexts.

Recent research on the reliability and validity of social skill assessments, and the benefits of social skills training for persons with schizophrenia, has demonstrated the utility of the social skills construct. Persons with schizophrenia have consistently been found to have worse social skills than persons with other psychiatric disorders (Bellack, Morrison, Wixted, & Mueser, 1990; Bellack, Mueser, Wade, Sayers, & Morrison, 1992; Mueser, Bellack, Douglas, & Wade, 1991), and approximately half of the persons with schizophrenia demonstrate stable deficits in basic social skills compared to the nonpsychiatric population (Mueser, Bellack, Douglas, & Morrison, 1991). In the absence of skills training, social skills tend to be stable over periods of time as long as 6 months to 1 year (Mueser, Bellack, Douglas, & Morrison, 1991). Social skill in persons with schizophrenia is moderately correlated with level of premorbid social functioning, current role functioning, and quality of life (Mueser, Bellack, Morrison, & Wixted, 1990). Social skills tend to be associated with negative symptoms (Appelo et al., 1992; Bellack, Morrison, Wixted, & Mueser, 1990; Lysaker, Bell, Zito, & Bioty, 1995; Penn, Mueser, Spaulding, Hope, & Reed, 1995), but not with positive symptoms (Mueser, Douglas, Bellack, & Morrison, 1991; Penn et al., 1995). Furthermore, role play assessments of social skill are also strongly related with social skill in more natural contexts, such as interactions with significant others (Bellack, Morrison, Mueser, Wade, & Sayers, 1990). Persons with schizophrenia show a wide range of impairments in social skills, including areas such as conversational skill, conflict resolution, assertiveness, and problem solving (Bellack, Sayers, Mueser, & Bennett, 1994; Douglas & Mueser, 1990). Thus, ample research demonstrates that social skills are impaired with persons with schizophrenia, tend to be stable over time in the absence of intervention, and are strongly related to other measures of social functioning. Furthermore, there is growing evidence supporting the efficacy of social skills training for schizophrenia (Bellack, 2004; Heinssen, Liberman, & Kopelowicz, 2000).

The broadest area of psychological assessment is community functioning, and improvement in this area is linked to the concept of recovery (see "Course and

Prognosis"). Persons with schizophrenia not only show poor social skills, but also poor adaptive functioning in the community. Ideally, treatment programs should aim to improve the person's quality of life and satisfaction. Independent living skills, quality of life, and social functioning may be need to be assessed in order to examine the person's current functional capacity level. The Social Functioning Scale (Birchwood, Smith, Cochrane, Wetton, & Copstake, 1990) and UCSD Performance-Based Skills Assessment (Patterson, Goldman, McKibbin, Hughs, & Jeste, 2001) are widely used measures of adaptive and community functioning.

FAMILY ASSESSMENT

The assessment of family functioning has high relevance in schizophrenia for two reasons. First, Expressed Emotion (EE), which refers to the presence of hostile, critical, or emotionally overinvolved attitudes and behaviors on the part of close relatives of persons with schizophrenia, is an important stressor that can increase the chance of relapse and rehospitalization (Butzlaff & Hooley, 1998). Second, caring for an individual with a psychiatric illness can lead to a significant burden on relatives (Webb et al., 1998), which ultimately can threaten their ability to continue to provide emotional and material support to the individual. Family burden has its own negative consequences, and can be related to EE and the ability of the family to care for the person with schizophrenia. Thus, a thorough assessment of these family factors is important in order to identify targets for family intervention.

A number of specific methods can be used to assess a negative emotional climate in the family and burden of the illness. Interviews with individual family members, including the person with schizophrenia, as well as with the entire family, coupled with observation of more naturalistic family interactions, can provide invaluable information about the quality of family functioning. The vast majority of research on family EE has employed a semistructured interview with individual family members, the Camberwell Family Interview (Leff & Vaughn, 1985). This instrument is primarily a research instrument, and it is too time-consuming to be used in clinical practice. Alternatives to the Camberwell Family Interview have been proposed (e.g., Magaña et al., 1986), although none have gained widespread acceptance yet. Several studies have successfully employed the Family Environment Scale (Moos & Moos, 1981), a self-report instrument completed by family members, which has been found to be related to symptoms and outcome in patients with schizophrenia (Halford, Schweitzer, & Varghese, 1991).

Many instruments have been developed for the assessment of family burden. The most comprehensive instrument, with well-established psychometric properties, is the Family Experiences Interview Schedule (Tessler & Gamache, 1995). This measure provides information regarding both dimensions of subjective burden (e.g., emotional strain) and objective burden (e.g., economic impact), as well as specific areas in which the burden is most severe (e.g., household tasks).

The importance of evaluating family functioning is supported by research demonstrating clinical benefits of family intervention for schizophrenia. Numerous controlled studies of family treatment for schizophrenia have shown that family intervention has a significant impact on reducing relapse rates and rehospitalizations (Dixon et al., 2001; Pitschel-Walz et al., 2001). The critical elements shared across different models of family intervention are education about schizophrenia, the provision of ongoing support, improved communication skills, and a focus on helping all family members improve the quality of their lives (Dixon & Lehman, 1995; Glynn, 1992; Lam, 1991).

BIOLOGICAL ASSESSMENT

Biological assessments are becoming more common in the clinical management of schizophrenia. For diagnosis, biological assessments may be used to rule out possible organic factors such as a tumor, stroke, or covert substance abuse. Urine and blood specimens are sometimes obtained in order to evaluate the presence of substance abuse. Similarly, blood samples may be obtained in order to determine whether the person is compliant with the prescribed antipsychotic medication, although the specific level of medication in the blood has not been conclusively linked to clinical response. Blood levels may also be monitored to ensure appropriate levels of mood stabilizers (e.g., lithium). Some newer medications (e.g., Clozaril) also require ongoing blood tests to detect very rare, but potentially lethal, blood disorders (Alvir, Lieberman, & Safferman, 1995; Young, Bowers, & Mazure, 1998). Client participant in this type of medical monitoring is crucial in using these medications.

Biological measures are sometimes used to characterize impairments in brain functioning associated with schizophrenia, although these assessments do not have clear implications for treatment of the illness at this time and are expensive. In addition, many clinicians do not have access to imaging technology and its use has been specific to research settings. In terms of brain function and structure, CAT scans indicate that between one-half and two-thirds of all persons with schizophrenia display enlarged cerebral ventricles, particularly the lateral and third ventricles, which is indicative of cortical atrophy (Liddle, 1995). MRI studies have found structural changes and a reduction in gray matter volumes in the prefrontal, superior temporal, amygdala, hippocampus, and thalamus (Lawrie & Abukmeil, 1998; Wright et al., 2000). These findings have also been found in first-episode and nonill relatives as well and may be a pathophysiological marker for the disorder (Fannon et al., 2000; McDonald et al., 2002). These gross structural impairments in brain functioning, such as enlarged ventricles, tend to be associated with a wide range of neuropsychological impairments and negative symptoms often present in schizophrenia (Andreasen, Flaum, Swayze, Tyrrell, & Arndt, 1990; Buchanan et al., 1993; Merriam, Kay, Opler, Kushner, & van Praag, 1990). In addition, positron emission tomography (PET) and single photon emission computerized tomography (SPECT) have shown reduced metabolism and blood flow in several of the prefrontal and temporal cortex and abnormal activation of the thalamus (Kindermann, Karimi, Symonds, Brown, & Jeste, 1997; Liddle, 1997; McClure, Keshavan, & Pettegrew, 1998; Miyamoto et al., 2003). Functional MRI (fMRI) studies have found less activation in the prefrontal cortex and anterior cingulate cortex during working memory tasks (Carter et al., 2001; Perlstein, Carter, Noll, & Cohen, 2001). Finally, diffuse tensor imaging methods, which assess the integrity of white matter pathways in the brain, have found problems in myleinated neurons in the prefrontal lobes specifically and in the connections between the frontal, temporal, and parietal lobes (Burns et al., 2003; Lim et al., 1998).

To date, most of the advances in the treatment of schizophrenia have been in psychopharmacology. Biological assessments are still not useful for diagnosing the illness or for guiding treatment. However, the clinical utility of biological assessment is likely to increase in the years to come as advances continue to be made in the understanding of the biological roots of schizophrenia.

ETIOLOGICAL CONSIDERATIONS

FAMILIAL AND GENETIC

The etiology of schizophrenia has been a topic of much debate over the past 100 years. Kraepelin (1919/1971) and Bleuler (1911/1950) clearly viewed the illness as having a biological origin. However, from the 1920s to the 1960s alternative theories gained prominence, speculating that the disease was the result of disturbed family interactions (Bateson, Jackson, Haley, & Weakland, 1956). Psychogenic theories of the etiology of schizophrenia, positing that the illness was psychological in nature rather than biological, played a dominant role in shaping the attitudes and behavior of professionals toward persons with schizophrenia and their relatives (Fromm-Reichmann, 1950; Searles, 1965). These theories have not been supported empirically (Jacob, 1975; Waxler & Mishler, 1971). Moreover, in many cases, psychogenic theories fostered poor relationships between mental health professionals and relatives (Terkelsen, 1983), which have only begun to mend in recent years (Mueser & Glynn, 1999).

For more than a century, clinicians have often noted that schizophrenia tends to "run in families." However, the clustering of schizophrenia in family members could reflect learned behavior that is passed on from one generation to the next, rather than predisposing biological factors. In the 1950s and 1960s, two paradigms were developed for evaluating the genetic contributions to the illness. The first approach, the *high risk* paradigm involves examining the rate of schizophrenia in adopted-away or biological offspring of mothers with schizophrenia. If the rate of schizophrenia in children of biological parents with schizophrenia is higher than in the general population, even in the absence of contact with those parents, a role for genetic factors in developing the illness is supported. The second approach, the *monozygotic/dizygotic twin* paradigm involves comparing the concordance rate of schizophrenia in identical twins (monozygotic) compared to fraternal twins (dizygotic). Because monozygotic twins share the exact same gene pool, whereas dizygotic twins only share approximately half their genes, a higher concordance rate of schizophrenia among monozygotic twins than dizygotic twins, even reared in the same environment, would support a role for genetic factors in the etiology of schizophrenia.

Over the past 30 years, numerous studies employing either the high risk or twin paradigm have been conducted examining the role of genetic factors in schizophrenia. There has been almost uniform agreement across studies indicating that the risk of developing schizophrenia in biological relatives of persons with schizophrenia is greater than in the general population, even in the absence of any contact between the relatives (Kendler & Diehl, 1993). Thus, support exists for the role of genetic factors in the etiology of at least some cases of schizophrenia. For example, the odds of developing schizophrenia if one parent has the disorder is 13% and rises to about 50% if both parents have the disorder, compared to only 1% risk in the general population (Gottesman, 1991; 2001; McGuffin, Owen, & Farmer, 1995). Similarly, the concordance rate of one identical twin developing schizophrenia if his or her co-twin also has schizophrenia is between 25% and 50%, compared to about 6% and 15% for fraternal twins (Cardno et al., 1999; Faraone & Tsuang, 1985; Torrey, 1992; Walker, Downey, & Caspi, 1991). It also appears that the risk of developing schizophrenia is greater in more severe types of schizophrenia (average 20% for disorgranized and catatonic types; see Gottesman & Shields, 1982).

The fact that identical twins do not have a 100% concordance rate of schizophrenia (heritability rates = 0.80 on average), as might be expected if the disorder were purely genetic, has raised intriguing questions about the etiology of schizophrenia. In a review of 40 studies on genetic risk it was found that 80% of persons with psychotic symptoms do not have a single parent with the disorder and 60% have a negative family history (Gottesman, 2001). It is likely that the development of schizophrenia results from an interaction between genetic and environmental factors. The results of a series of longitudinal studies support this case. Tienari (1991; Tienari et al., 1987, 2004) compared the likelihood of developing schizophrenia in three groups of children raised by adoptive families. Two groups of children had biological mothers with schizophrenia, the third group had biological mothers with no psychiatric disorder. The researchers divided the adoptive families of the children into two broad groups based on the level of disturbance present in the family: healthy adoptive families and disturbed adoptive families. Follow-up assessments were conducted to determine the presence of schizophrenia and other severe psychiatric disorders in the adopted children raised in all three groups. The researchers found that biological children of mothers with schizophrenia who were raised by adoptive families with high levels of disturbance were significantly more likely to develop schizophrenia or another psychotic disorder (46%) than either similarly vulnerable children raised in families with low levels of disturbance (5%), or children with no biological vulnerability raised in either disturbed (24%) or healthy (3%) adoptive families. This study raises the intriguing possibility that some cases of schizophrenia develop as a result of the interaction between biological vulnerability and environmental stress.

Although families do not cause schizophrenia, there are important interactions between the family and person with schizophrenia that deserve consideration. First, as previously mentioned, it has repeatedly been found that critical attitudes and high levels of emotional overinvolvement (Expressed Emotion [EE]) on the part of the relatives toward the individual with schizophrenia are strong predictors of the likelihood that persons with schizophrenia will relapse and be rehospitalized (Butzlaff & Hooley, 1998). The importance of family factors is underscored by the fact that the severity of persons' psychiatric illness or their social skill impairments is not related to family EE (Mueser et al., 1993). Rather, family EE seems to act as a stressor, increasing the vulnerability of persons with schizophrenia to relapse.

A second important family consideration is the amount of burden on relatives caring for a mentally ill person. Family members of persons with schizophrenia typically experience a wide range of negative emotions related to coping with the illness, such as anxiety, depression, guilt, and anger (Hatfield & Lefley, 1987, 1993; Oldridge, & Hughes, 1992). Burden is even associated with negative health consequences for relatives (Dyck, Short, & Vitaliano, 1999). Family burden may be related to levels of EE, ability to cope with the illness, and ultimately the ability of the family to successfully monitor and manage the schizophrenia in a family member (Mueser & Glynn, 1999). Thus, EE and family burden are important areas for assessment and intervention.

Finally, researchers have been interested in discovering genes and chromosomal areas involved in schizophrenia. Current research has focused on 9 chromosomes (i.e., 8p and 22q) and 7 candidate genes, which may be important in schizophrenia (see Harrison & Owen, 2003). In particular, researchers are particularly interested in identifying genes found across family members with the disorder (linkage studies) or directly related to the underlying pathophysiology of schizophrenia (e.g., genes that affect neurotransmitter functioning such as dopamine, serotonin, or glutamate). This area of research has been hampered by the lack of independent replication of these genetic markers. The exact mechanism for genetic transmission of the disorder is unknown, but it appears that schizophrenia does not follow a Mendelian single gene pattern of inheritance. It is more likely that schizophrenia is a polygenetic condition or arises from an interaction of multiple genes, which increase the susceptibility to the disorder (Craddock, O'Donovan, & Owen, 2006; Miyamoto et al., 2003).

LEARNING AND MODELING

Although schizophrenia is broadly accepted to be a biologically based disorder, and not a learned one, learning and modeling may play a role in the course, outcome, and symptom expression of the disorder. In terms of symptom expression, there is empirical support for the role of operant conditioning in delusions and hallucinations (e.g., hallucinations increase when reinforced). Furthermore, research has shown that that psychotic behavior can be modified using differential reinforcement (i.e., attention for any other behavior besides the expression of delusional statements) or punishment principles (Schock, Clay & Cipani, 1998; Jimenez, Todman, Perez, Godoy, & Landon-Jimenez, 1996). However, these processes are probably more relevant for the maintenance of psychotic symptoms than etiology. Haynes (1986) proposed a behavioral model of paranoia in which suspiciousness partially stems from the reinforcement of paranoid statements and parental modeling, but this theory has been largely untested. As described in the following section, the stress-vulnerability model of schizophrenia posits that coping skills mediate the noxious effects of stress on psychobiological vulnerability on symptoms and relapses (Liberman et al., 1986; Nuechterlein & Dawson, 1984). Coping skills, such social skills for developing and maintaining close relationships with others and strategies for managing negative emotions and distorted thinking processes, can be acquired either naturalistically through access to good role models (e.g., family, friends) or through social learning-based programs, such as social skills training (Bellack, Mueser, Gingerich, & Agresta, 1997) or cognitive-behavior therapy (Chadwick & Birchwood, 1995; Fowler, Garety, & Kuipers, 1995). Thus, improving coping skills, as well as other life skills, through the systematic application of social learning methods is a common treatment goal in schizophrenia.

LIFE EVENTS

Although stressful life events alone are not the cause of schizophrenia, some theories hypothesize that life events may contribute to the development of the disorder and can play an important role in the course of schizophrenia. The stress-vulnerability model (Liberman et al., 1986; Zubin & Spring, 1977), assumes that symptom severity and related impairments of psychiatric disorders such as schizophrenia have a biological basis (*psychobiological vulnerability*) determined by a combination of genetic and early environmental factors. This vulnerability can be decreased by medications and worsened by substance use disorder. *Stress,* including discrete events such as traumas and exposure to ongoing conditions such as a hostile environment, can impinge on vulnerability, precipitating relapses and worse outcomes. Finally, *coping* resources, such as coping skills or the ability to obtain social support, can minimize the effects of stress on relapse and the need for acute care.

As described above, Expressed Emotion represents a stressful environment that may increase relapse and hospitalization in people with schizophrenia. In addition, in the "Clinical Picture" section, we discussed that people with schizophrenia are often the targets of violence and have frequently been exposed to physical and/or sexual assault. Exposure to traumatic events may lead to posttraumatic stress disorder (PTSD), a condition characterized by reliving the traumatic experience (e.g., nightmares, intrusive memories), avoidance of people, places, and things that remind the person of the event, and increased arousal symptoms (e.g., irritability, sleep problems). Exposure to trauma and the presence of PTSD are likely to worsen the course of schizophrenia and complicate treatment (Mueser, Rosenberg, Goodman, & Trumbetta, 2002). For example, research shows that both discrete stressors (e.g., life events) and exposure to a stressful environment can worsen psychotic disorders (Butzlaff & Hooley, 1998). PTSD is also associated with substance abuse (Chilcoat & Breslau, 1998), which, as described earlier, can have severe consequences for people with schizophrenia.

GENDER AND RACIAL-ETHNIC

A number of issues related to gender are important for understanding the psychopathology in the course of schizophrenia. As described in the section on course and prognosis, women tend to have a milder overall course and later onset of schizophrenia than men. The net consequence of this is that, although similar numbers of men and women have schizophrenia, men are more likely to receive treatment for the disorder. In fact, most research on the treatment of schizophrenia is conducted on samples ranging from 60% to 100% male.

Because treatment studies usually sample persons with schizophrenia who are currently receiving treatment, often inpatient treatment, the efficacy of widely studied psychosocial interventions, such as social skills training and family therapy, has been less adequately demonstrated in women. For example, some research suggests that social skills training may be more helpful to men than to women (Mueser, Levine, Bellack, Douglas, & Brady, 1990; Schaub, Behrendt, Brenner, Mueser, & Liberman, 1998; Smith et al., 1997). There is a need for more research on the effects of treatments for women with schizophrenia. At the same time, further consideration needs to be given to the different needs of women with this illness. For example, women with schizophrenia are much more likely to marry and have children than are men. It is crucial, therefore, that psychosocial interventions be developed to address the relationship, family planning, and parenting needs of women with schizophrenia (Apfel & Handel, 1993; Brunette & Dean, 2002; Coverdale & Grunebaum, 1998).

Another issue related to gender in need of further consideration is exposure to trauma. As described earlier, people with schizophrenia are at risk for being the victims of violence. Although both men and women with schizophrenia report histories of abuse and assault, women report more sexual assault (Goodman et al., 2001; Mueser et al., 1998). Further, in the general population, women are more likely to be abused than men, are more likely to sustain injuries, and are more likely to be economically dependent upon perpetrators of domestic violence. Thus, there is particular need to recognize and address trauma in the lives of women with schizophrenia. Accurate detection of trauma is further complicated by the fact that most severely mentally ill persons who have been physically or sexually assaulted deny that they have been abused (Cascardi et al., 1996). The development of programs that both address the cause of domestic violence and their sequelae, especially for women with schizophrenia, is a priority in this area (Harris, 1996; Rosenberg et al., 2001).

Research on the relationships between race, ethnicity, and severe psychiatric disorders demonstrates that cultural factors are critical to understanding how persons with schizophrenia are perceived by others in their social milieu, as well as the course of the illness. Although the prevalence of schizophrenia is comparable across different cultures, several studies have shown that course of the illness is more benign in developing countries compared to industrialized nations (Lo & Lo, 1977; Murphy & Raman, 1971; Sartorius et al., 1986). Westermeyer (1989) has raised questions about the comparability of clinical samples in cross-cultural studies, but a consensus remains that the course of schizophrenia tends to be milder in nonindustrialized countries (Jablensky, 1989).

A variety of different interpretations has been offered to account for the better prognosis of schizophrenia in some cultures (Lefley, 1990). It is possible that the strong stigma and social rejection that results from serious mental illness and poses an obstacle to the ability of persons with schizophrenia to cope effectively with their disorder and assimilate into society (Fink & Tasman, 1992) is less prominent in some cultures (Parra, 1985). Greater cultural and societal acceptance of the social deviations present in schizophrenia may enable these persons to live less stressful and more productive lives. Family ties, in particular, may be stronger in developing countries or in certain ethnic minorities, and less vulnerable to the disorganizing effects of mental illness (Lin & Kleinman, 1988). For example, Liberman (1994) has described how the strong functional ties of seriously mentally ill persons to their families and work foster the reintegration of persons with schizophrenia back into Chinese society following psychiatric hospitalization. In contrast, until recently, families of persons with schizophrenia in many Western societies were viewed by mental health professionals as either irrelevant, or worse, as causal agents in the development of the illness (Lefley, 1990; Mueser & Glynn, 1999), thus precluding them from a role in psychiatric rehabilitation. Furthermore, the use of other social supports may vary across different ethnic groups or cultures, such as importance of the church to the African American community and its potential therapeutic benefits (Griffith, Young, & Smith, 1984; Lincoln & Mamiya, 1990).

Some have hypothesized that different cultural interpretations of the individual's role in society and of the causes of mental illness may interact to determine course and outcome. Estroff (1989) has suggested that the emphasis on the "self" in Western countries, compared to a more family or societally based identification, has an especially disabling effect on persons with schizophrenia, whose sense of self is often fragile or fragmented. Another important consideration is the availability of adaptive concepts for understanding mental illness. For example, *espiritismo* in Puerto Rican culture is a system of beliefs involving the interactions between the invisible spirit world and the visible world in which spirits can attach themselves to persons (Comas-Díaz, 1981; Morales-Dorta, 1976). Spirits are hierarchically ordered in terms of their moral perfection, and the practice of espiritismo is guided by helping individuals who are spiritually ill achieve higher levels of this perfection. Troubled persons are not identified as "sick" nor are they blamed for their difficulties; in some cases, symptoms such as hallucinations may be interpreted favorably as signs that the person is advanced in his or her spiritual development, resulting in some prestige (Comas-Díaz, 1981). Thus, certain cultural interpretations of schizophrenia may promote more acceptance of persons who display the symptoms of schizophrenia, as well as avoiding the common assumption that these phenomenological experiences are the consequence of a chronic, unremitting condition.

Understanding different cultural beliefs, values, and social structures can have important implications for the diagnosis of schizophrenia. Religious practices and beliefs may complicate diagnosis. For example, high levels of religiosity have been found in people with schizophrenia (Brewerton, 1994). Without a clear understanding of the religious and cultural background, patients may be misdiagnosed (May, 1997). Ethnic groups may differ in their willingness to report symptoms, as illustrated by one study that reported that African American persons were less likely to report symptoms than Hispanics or non-Hispanic whites (Skilbeck, Acosta, Yamamoto, & Evans, 1984). Several studies have shown that ethnic differences in diagnosis vary as a function of both the client's and the interviewer's ethnicity (Baskin, Bluestone, & Nelson, 1981; Loring & Powell, 1988). Misdiagnosis of mood disorders as schizophrenia is the most common problem with the diagnosis of ethnic minorities in the United States (e.g., Jones, Gray, & Parsons, 1983; Jones, Gray, & Parsons, 1981). Other studies have found that African Americans are more likely to be diagnosed with paranoid schizophrenia than other ethnic groups, which has been viewed as a clinician-bias in the interpretation of mistrust (Adams, Dworkin, & Rosenberg, 1984; Combs, Penn, & Fenigstein, 2002; Combs et al., 2006; Whaley, 1997, 2001). Alternatively, this finding may also represent the effects of stress and poverty in the development of schizophrenia (Bruce, Takeuchi, & Leaf, 1991; as discussed in "Epidemiology"). Knowledge of cultural norms appears critical to avoid the possible misinterpretation of culturally bound beliefs, experiences, and practices when arriving at a diagnosis.

Cultural differences are also critical in the treatment of schizophrenia, both with respect to service utilization and the nature of treatment provided. There is a growing body of information documenting that ethnic groups differ in their use of psychiatric services. A number of studies have indicated that Hispanics and Asian Americans use fewer psychiatric services than non-Hispanic whites, whereas blacks use more emergency and inpatient services (Cheung & Snowden, 1990; Hough et al., 1987; Hu, Snowden, Jerrell, & Nguyen, 1991; Padgett, Patrick, Burns, & Schlesinger, 1994; Sue, Fujino, Hu, Takeuchi, & Zane, 1991). Aside from cultural-based practices that may cause some individuals to seek assistance outside the mental health system (e.g., practitioners of *santeria;* González-Wippler, 1992), access to and retention in mental health services may be influenced by the proximity of mental health services (Dworkin & Adams, 1987) and by the ethnicity of treatment providers. Sue et al. (1991) reported that matching clinician and client ethnicity resulted in higher retention of ethnic minorities in mental health services. Increasing access to needed services for racial/ethnic minorities may require a range of strategies, including ensuring that services are available in the communities where clients live, working with the natural social supports in the community, awareness of relevant cultural norms, and adequate representation of ethnic minorities as treatment providers.

Cultural factors may have an important bearing on psychotherapeutic treatments provided for schizophrenia. Sue and Sue (1990) have described the importance of providing psychotherapy driven by goals that are compatible with clients' cultural norms. This requires both knowledge of subcultural norms and familiarity with the other social support mechanisms typically available to those individuals. Interventions developed for one cultural group may need substantial modification to be effective in other groups. For example, Telles et al. (1995) reported that behavioral family therapy, which has been found to be effective at reducing relapse in schizophrenia for samples of non-Hispanic white and African American individuals (Mueser & Glynn, 1999), was significantly less effective for Hispanic Americans (of Mexican, Guatemalan, and Salvadoran descent) with low levels of acculturation than more acculturated individuals. In addition, behavioral family therapy has been found to be effective when implemented in Spain and China (Montero et al., 2001; Xiong et al., 1994; Zhang, Wang, Li, & Phillips, 1994). These findings underscore the importance of tailoring psychosocial interventions to meet the unique needs of clients from different cultural backgrounds.

A final cultural factor is stigma, that is, negative attitudes that lead to prejudice and discrimination against people with schizophrenia. Although stigma can be present for a variety of disabilities, attitudes toward people with serious mental illness tend to be more negative (Corrigan & Penn, 1999). Stigma may stem from characteristics of the disorder itself, such as poor social skills, bizarre behavior, and unkempt appearance, and stigma may develop and be maintained through negative media portrayals and myths (e.g., dangerousness, unpredictability) (Farina, 1998). Stigma and discrimination can greatly undermine the person's ability to recover from the effects of schizophrenia and integrate into society. For example, people with serious mental illness identify role functioning, such as employment, developing and maintaining friendships and intimate relationships, and regular activities as critical to their recovery (Uttaro & Mechanic, 1994). However, many studies have shown that these are the very areas most affected by stigma (Farina, 1998). Much is being done to try to reduce stigma associated with schizophrenia and other mental illness. In particular, strategies that involve active education and increased contact with people with mental illness may be most effective for eradicating this serious problem (Corrigan & Penn, 1999).

BIOLOGICAL AND PHYSIOLOGICAL

Although there is clear evidence that genetic factors can play a role in the development of schizophrenia, there is also a growing body of evidence pointing to the influence of other biological, nongenetic factors playing a critical role. For example, obstetric complications, maternal exposure to the influenza virus, and other environmental-based insults to developing fetus (e.g., maternal starvation) are all associated with an increased risk of developing schizophrenia (Geddes & Lawrie, 1995; Kirch, 1993; Rodrigo, Lusiardo, Briggs, & Ulmer, 1991; Susser & Lin, 1992; Susser et al., 1996; Takei et al., 1996; Thomas et al., 2001; Torrey, Bowler, Rawlings, & Terrazas, 1993). Thus, there is a growing consensus that the etiology of schizophrenia may be heterogeneous, with genetic factors playing a role in the development of some cases, and early environmental-based factors playing a role in the development of other cases. This heterogeneity may account for the fact that the genetic contribution to schizophrenia has consistently been found to be lower than the genetic contribution to bipolar disorder (Goodwin & Jamison, 1990). Other biological and physiological factors include alterations in brain chemistry and structure.

Pharmacological research has identified many neurochemical changes associated with schizophrenia. By far, the neurotransmitter most commonly implicated in the onset of schizophrenia is dopamine. The dopamine hypothesis proposes that alterations in levels of dopamine are responsible for the symptoms of schizophrenia. Originally, this hypothesis was based on findings that substances that increase dopamine (e.g., levadopa used to treat Parkinson's disease) increase psychotic symptoms and substances that decrease dopamine reduce psychotic symptoms. Current versions of this hypothesis suggest that an overabundance of dopamine in certain limbic areas of the brain may be responsible for positive symptoms while a lack of dopamine in cortical areas may be responsible for negative symptoms (Davis, Kahn, Ko, & Davidson, 1991; Moore, West, & Grace, 1999). Other neurochemicals also appear to be implicated in schizophrenia. In particular, serotontin may directly or indirectly (e.g., by mediating dopamine) affect symptoms of schizophrenia as several of the newer antipsychotic medications impact serotonin levels (Lieberman et al., 1998). In addition, glutamate and GABA may be altered in schizophrenia (Pearlson, 2000).

As discussed in "Biological Assessment," abnormalities in several brain structures also have been identified. In particular, enlarged ventricles and decreased brain volume and blood flow to cortical areas have been associated with a wide range of cognitive impairments and negative symptoms of schizophrenia (Andreasen et al., 1990; Buchanan et al., 1993; Merriam et al., 1990).

SUMMARY

Schizophrenia is a severe, long-term psychiatric illness characterized by impairments in social functioning, the ability to work, self-care skills, positive symptoms (hallucinations, delusions), negative symptoms (social withdrawal, apathy), and cognitive impairments. Schizophrenia is a relatively common illness, afflicting approximately 1% of the population, and tends to have an episodic course over the lifetime, with symptoms gradually improving over the long term. Most evidence indicates that schizophrenia is a biological illness that may be caused by a variety of factors, such as genetic contributions and early environmental influences (e.g., insults to the developing fetus). Despite the biological nature of schizophrenia, environmental stress can either precipitate the onset of the illness or symptom relapses. Schizophrenia can be reliably diagnosed with structured clinical interviews, with particular attention paid to the differential diagnosis of affective disorders. There is a high comorbidity of substance-use disorders in persons with schizophrenia, which must be treated if positive outcomes are to accrue. Psychological assessment of schizophrenia is most useful when it focuses on behavioral, rather than dynamic, dimensions of the illness. Thus, assessments and interventions focused on social skill deficits and family functioning have yielded promising treatment results. Biological assessments are useful at this time primarily for descriptive rather than clinical purposes. Finally, there are a great many issues related to gender and racial or ethnic factors that remain unexplored. Although schizophrenia remains one of the most challenging psychiatric illnesses to treat, substantial advances have been made in recent years in developing reliable diagnostic systems, understanding the role of various etiological factors, development of effective pharmacological and psychosocial treatments, and the identification of factors that mediate the long-term outcome of the illness, such as stress and substance abuse. These developments bode well for the ability of researchers and clinicians to continue to make headway in treating this serious illness.

REFERENCES

Adams, G. L., Dworkin, R. J., & Rosenberg, S. D. (1984). Diagnosis and pharmacotherapy issues in the care of Hispanics in the public sector. *The American Journal of Psychiatry, 141,* 970–974.

Alvir, J. M. J., Lieberman, J. A., & Safferman, A. Z. (1995). Do white-cell count spikes predict agranulocytosis in clozapine recipients? *Psychopharmacology Bulletin, 31,* 311–314.

Amador, X. F., & David, A. (2004). *Insight and psychosis: Awareness of illness in schizophrenia and related disorders.* New York: Oxford University Press.

Amador, X. F., & Gorman, J. M. (1998). Psychopathologic domains and insight in schizophrenia. *The Psychiatric Clinics of North America, 21,* 27–42.

Amador, X. F., Strauss, D., Yale, S., & Gorman, J. M. (1991). Awareness of illness in schizophrenia. *Schizophrenia Bulletin, 17,* 113–132.

American Psychiatric Association. (2000). *Diagnostic and statistical manual of mental disorders* (4th ed.). *Text revision.* Washington, DC: Author.

American Psychiatric Association. (2000). *Diagnostic and statistical manual of mental disorders: Text revision.* Washington, DC: Author.

Amminger, G. P., Pape, S., Rock, D., Roberts, S. A., Ott, S. L., Squires-Wheeler, E., Kestenbaum, C., & Erlenmeyer-Kimling, L. (1999). Relationship between childhood behavioral disturbance and later schizophrenia in the New York high-risk project. *The American Journal of Psychiatry, 156,* 525–530.

Andreasen, N. C. (1982). Negative symptoms in schizophrenia: Definition and reliability. *Archives of General Psychiatry, 39,* 784–788.

Andreasen, N. C., Carpenter, W. T., Kane, J. M., Lasser, R. A., Marder, S. R., & Weinberger, D. R. (2005). Remission in schizophrenia: Proposed criteria and rational for consensus. *The American Journal of Psychiatry, 162,* 441–449.

Andreasen, N. C., Flaum, M., Swayze, II, V. W., Tyrrell, G., & Arndt, S. (1990). Positive and negative symptoms in schizophrenia: A critical reappraisal. *Archives of General Psychiatry, 47,* 615–621.

Andreasen, N. C., & Olsen, S. (1982). Negative versus positive schizophrenia: Definition and validation. *Archives of General Psychiatry, 39,* 784–788.

Apfel, R. J., & Handel, M. H. (1993). *Madness and loss of motherhood: Sexuality, reproduction, and long-term mental illness.* Washington, DC: American Psychiatric Press.

Appelbaum, P. S., Robbins, P. C., & Roth, L. H. (1999). Dimensional approach to delusions: Comparison across types and diagnoses. *American Journal of Psychiatry, 156,* 1938–1943.

Appelo, M. T., Woonings, F. M. J., van Nieuwenhuizen, C. J., Emmelkamp, P. M. G., Sloof, C. J., & Louwerens, J. W. (1992). Specific skills and social competence in schizophrenia. *Acta Psychiatrica Scandinavica, 85,* 419–422.

Appleby, L., Dyson, V., Altman, E., & Luchins, D. (1997). Assessing substance use in multi-problem patients: Reliability and validity of the Addiction Severity Index in a mental hospital population. *Journal of Nervous and Mental Disease, 185,* 159–165.

Argyle, N. (1990). Panic attacks in chronic schizophrenia. *British Journal of Psychiatry, 157,* 430–433.

Aro, S., Aro, H., & Keskimäki, I. (1995). Socio-economic mobility among patients with schizophrenia or major affective disorder: A 17-year retrospective follow-up. *British Journal of Psychiatry, 166,* 759–767.

Asarnow, J. R. (1988). Children at risk for schizophrenia. Converging lines of evidence. *Schizophrenia Bulletin, 14,* 613–631.

Avison, W. R., & Speechley, K. N. (1987). The discharged psychiatric patient: A review of social, social-psychological, and psychiatric correlates of outcome. *American Journal of Psychiatry, 144,* 10–18.

Azrin, N. H., & Teichner, G. (1998). Evaluation of an instructional program for improving medication compliance for chronically mentally ill outpatients. *Behaviour Research and Therapy, 36,* 849–861.

Bartels, S. J., Drake, R. E., Wallach, M. A., & Freeman, D. H. (1991). Characteristic hostility in schizophrenic outpatients. *Schizophrenia Bulletin, 17,* 163–171.

Bartels, S. J., Mueser, K. T., & Miles, K. M. (1998). Schizophrenia. In M. Hersen and V. B. Van Hasselt (Eds.), *Handbook of clinical geropsychology* (pp. 173–194). New York: Plenum.

Baskin, D., Bluestone, H., & Nelson, M. (1981). Ethnicity and psychiatric diagnosis. *Journal of Clinical Psychology, 37,* 529–537.

Bateson, G., Jackson, D. D., Haley, J., & Weakland, J. (1956). Toward a theory of schizophrenia. *Behavioral Science, 1,* 251–264.

Baum, K. M., & Walker, E. F. (1995). Childhood behavioral precursors of adult symptom dimensions in schizophrenia. *Schizophrenia Research, 16,* 111–120.

Bellack, A. S. (2004). Skills training for people with severe mental illness. *Psychiatric Rehabilitation Journal, 27,* 375–391.

Bellack, A. S., Gold, J. M., & Buchanan, R. W. (1999). Cognitive rehabilitation for schizophrenia: problems, prospects, and strategies. *Schizophrenia Bulletin, 25,* 257–74.

Bellack, A. S., Morrison, R. L., Mueser, K. T., Wade, J. H., & Sayers, S. L. (1990). Role play for assessing the social competence of psychiatric patients. *Psychological Assessment, 2,* 248–255.

Bellack, A. S., Morrison, R. L., Wixted, J. T., & Mueser, K. T. (1990). An analysis of social competence in schizophrenia. *British Journal of Psychiatry, 156,* 809–818.

Bellack, A. S., & Mueser, K. T. (1993). Psychosocial treatment for schizophrenia. *Schizophrenia Bulletin, 19,* 317–336.

Bellack, A. S., Mueser, K. T., Gingerich, S., & Agresta, J. (1997). *Social skills training for schizophrenia: A step-by-step guide.* New York: Guilford.

Bellack, A. S., Mueser, K. T., Wade, J. H., Sayers, S. L., & Morrison, R. L. (1992). The ability of schizophrenics to perceive and cope with negative affect. *British Journal of Psychiatry, 160,* 473–480.

Bellack, A. S., Sayers, M., Mueser, K. T., & Bennett, M. (1994). An evaluation of social problem solving in schizophrenia. *Journal of Abnormal Psychology, 103,* 371–378.

Bellack, A. S., & Thomas-Lohrman, S. (2003). *Maryland assessment of social competence.* Unpublished assessment manual, Baltimore.

Bentall, R. P., Corcoran, R., Howard, R., Blackwood, N., & Kinderman, P. (2001). Persecutory delusions: A review and theoretical integration. *Clinical Psychology Review, 21,* 1143–1192.

Bentall, R. P., Jackson, H. F., & Pilgrim D. (1988). Abandoning the concept of schizophrenia: Some implications of validity arguments for psychological research into psychotic phenomena. *British Journal of Clinical Psychology, 27,* 156–169.

Birchwood, M., Iqbal, Z., Chadwick, P., & Trower, P. (2000). Cognitive approach to depression and suicidal thinking in psychosis I: Ontogeny of post-psychotic depression. *British Journal of Psychiatry, 177,* 516–521.

Birchwood, M., Smith, J., Cochrane, R., Wetton, S., & Copstake, S. (1990). The social functioning scale: The development and validation of a new scale of social adjustment for the use in family intervention programmes with schizophrenic patients. *British Journal of Psychiatry, 157,* 853–859.

Bond, G. R. (1998). Principles of the individual placement and support model: Empirical support. *Psychiatric Rehabilitation Journal, 22,* 11–23.

Boydell, J., van Os, J., McKenzie, K., Allardyce, J., Goel, R., McCreadie, R. G., & Murray, R. M. (2001). Incidence of schizophrenia in ethnic minorities in London: Ecological study into interactions with environment. *BMJ, 323,* 1336–1338.

Bracha, H. S., Wolkowitz, O. M., Lohr, J. B., Karson, C. N., & Bigelow, L. B. (1989). High prevalence of visual hallucinations in research subjects with chronic schizophrenia. *The American Journal of Psychiatry, 146,* 526–528.

Braga, R. J., Mendlowicz, M. V., Marrocos, R. P., & Figueria, I. L. (2005). Anxiety disorders in outpatients with schizophrenia: Prevalence and impact on the subjective quality of life. *Journal of Psychiatric Research, 39,* 409–414.

Breier, A. (2005). Developing drugs for cognitive impairment in schizophrenia. *Schizophrenia Bulletin, 31,* 816–822.

Brekke, J. S., Raine, A., Ansel, M., Lencz, T., & Bird, L. (1997). Neuropsychological and psychophysiological correlates of psychosocial functioning in schizophrenia. *Schizophrenia Bulletin, 23,* 19–28.

Breslau, N., Davis, G. C., Andreski, P., & Peterson, E. (1991). Traumatic events and post-traumatic stress disorder in an urban population of young adults. *Archives of General Psychiatry, 48,* 216–222.

Brewerton, T. D. (1994). Hyperreligiosity in psychotic disorders. *Journal of Nervous and Mental Disease, 182,* 302–304.

Bromet, E. J., Naz, B., Fochtmann, L. J., Carlson, G. A., & Tanenberg-Karant, M. (2005). Long-term diagnostic stability and outcome in recent first-episode cohort studies of schizophrenia. *Schizophrenia Bulletin, 31,* 639–649.

Bruce, M. L., Takeuchi, D. T., & Leaf, P. J. (1991). Poverty and psychiatric status: Longitudinal evidence from the New Haven Epidemiologic Catchment Area Study. *Archives of General Psychiatry, 48,* 470–474.

Brune, M. (2005). "Theory of mind" in schizophrenia: A review of the literature. *Schizophrenia Bulletin, 31,* 21–42.

Brunette, M. F., & Dean, W. (2002). Community mental health care of women with severe mental illness who are parents. *Community Mental Health Journal, 38,* 153–165.

Buchanan, A. (1992). A two-year prospective study of treatment compliance in patients with schizophrenia. *Psychological Medicine, 22,* 787–797.

Buchanan, R. W., Breier, A., Kirkpatrick, B., Elkashef, A., Munson, R. C., Gellad, F., & Carpenter, W. T. (1993). Structural abnormalities in deficit and nondeficit schizophrenia. *American Journal of Psychiatry, 150,* 59–65.

Burns, H., Job, M., Bastin, M. E., Whalley, H., Macgillivray, T., Johnstone, E. C., & Lawrie, S. M. (2003). *British Journal of Psychiatry, 182,* 439–443.

Butzlaff, R. L., & Hooley, J. M. (1998). Expressed emotion and psychiatric relapse: A meta-analysis. *Archives of General Psychiatry, 55,* 547–552.

Cannon, T. D., Mednick, S. A., Parnas, J., Schulsinger, F., Praestholm, J., & Vestergaard, A. (1993). Developmental brain abnormalities in the offspring of schizophrenic mothers. *Archives of General Psychiatry, 50,* 551–564.

Cantor-Graae, E., & Selten, J. P. (2005). Schizophrenia and migration: A meta-analysis and review. *American Journal of Psychiatry, 162,* 12–24.

Cardno, A., Marshall, E. J., Coid, B., Macdonald, A. M., Ribchester, T. R., Davies, N. J., Venturi, P., Jones, L. A., Lewis, S. W., Sham, P. C., Gottesman, I. I., Farmer, A. E., McGuffin, P., Rveley, A. M., & Murray, R. M. (1999). Heritability estimates for psychotic disorders: The Maudsley twin psychosis series. *Archives of General Psychiatry, 56,* 162–168.

Carmen, E., Rieker, P. P., & Mills, T. (1984). Victims of violence and psychiatric illness. *American Journal of Psychiatry, 141,* 378–383.

Carter, C. S., MacDonald, A. W., Ross, L. L., & Stenger, V. A. (2001). Anterior cingulated cortex activity and impaired self-monitoring of performance in patients with schizophrenia: An event related f MRI study. *American Journal of Psychiatry, 158,* 1423–1428.

Cascardi, M., Mueser, K. T., DeGirolomo, J., & Murrin, M. (1996). Physical aggression against psychiatric inpatients by family members and partners: A descriptive study. *Psychiatric Services, 47,* 531–533.

Castle, D. J., & Murray, R. M. (1991). The neurodevelopmental basis of sex differences in schizophrenia [Editorial]. *Psychological Medicine, 21,* 565–575.

Chadwick, P., & Birchwood, M. (1995). The omnipotence of voices II: The beliefs about voices questionnaire. *British Journal of Psychiatry, 166,* 773–776.

Chadwick, P., Birchwood, M., & Trower, P. (1996). *Cognitive therapy for delusions, voices and paranoia.* Chichester, England: Wiley.

Cheung, F. K., & Snowden, L. R. (1990). Community mental health and ethnic minority populations. *Community Mental Health Journal, 26,* 277–289.

Chilcoat, H. D., & Breslau, N. (1998). Posttraumatic stress disorder and drug disorders: Testing causal pathways. *Archives of General Psychiatry, 55,* 913–917.

Ciompi, L. (1980). Catamnestic long-term study of life and aging in chronic schizophrenic patients. *Schizophrenia Bulletin, 6,* 606–618.

Clark, R., Anderson, N. B., Clark, V. R., & Williams, D. R. (1999). Racism as a stressor for African Americans. *American Psychologist, 54,* 805–816.

Cohen, C. I. (1990). Outcome of schizophrenia into later life: An overview. *The Gerontologist, 30,* 790–797.

Cohen, M., & Klein, D. F. (1970). Drug abuse in a young psychiatric population. *American Journal of Orthopsychiatry, 40,* 448–455.

Comas-Díaz, L. (1981). Puerto Rican *espiritismo* and psychotherapy. *American Journal of Orthopsychiatry, 51,* 636–645.

Combs, D. R., & Penn, D. L. (2004). The role of sub-clinical paranoia on social perception and behavior. *Schizophrenia Research, 69,* 93–104.

Combs, D. R., Penn, D. L., Cassisi, J., Michael, C. O., Wood, T. D., Wanner, J., & Adams, S. D. (2006). Perceived racism as a predictor of paranoia among African Americans. *Journal of Black Psychology, 32*(1), 87–104.

Combs, D. R., Penn, D. L., & Fenigstein, A. (2002). Ethnic differences in sub-clinical paranoia: An expansion of norms of the paranoia scale. *Cultural Diversity & Ethnic Minority Psychology, 8,* 248–256.

Copolov, D. L., Mackinnon, A., & Trauer, T. (2004). Correlates of the affective impact of auditory hallucinations in psychotic disorders. *Schizophrenia Bulletin, 30,* 163–171.

Corrigan, P. W., Liberman, R. P., & Engle, J. D. (1990). From noncompliance to collaboration in the treatment of schizophrenia. *Hospital and Community Psychiatry, 41,* 1203–1211.

Corrigan, P. W., & Penn, D. L. (1999). Lessons from social psychology on discrediting psychiatric stigma. *American Psychologist, 54,* 765–776.

Corrigan, P. W. & Penn, D. L. (2001). *Social cognition in schizophrenia.* Washington: American Psychological Association.

Corse, S. J., Hirschinger, N. B., & Zanis, D. (1995). The use of the Addiction Severity Index with people with severe mental illness. *Psychiatric Rehabilitation Journal, 19,* 9–18.

Corty, E., Lehman, A. F., & Myers, C. P. (1993). Influence of psychoactive substance use on the reliability of psychiatric diagnosis. *Journal of Consulting and Clinical Psychology, 61,* 165–170.

Cosoff, S. J., & Hafner, R. J. (1998). The prevalence of comorbid anxiety in schizophrenia, schizoaffective disorder, and bipolar disorder. *Australian and New Zealand Journal of Psychiatry, 32,* 67–72.

Coverdale, J. H., & Grunebaum, H. (1998). Sexuality and family planning. In K. T. Mueser and N. Tarrier (Eds.), *Social functioning in schizophrenia* (pp. 224–237). Boston: Allyn and Bacon.

Craddock, N., O'Donovan, M. C., & Owen, M. J. (2006). Genes for schizophrenia and bipolar disorder? Implications for psychiatric nosology. *Schizophrenia Bulletin, 32,* 9–16.

Craine, L. S., Henson, C. E., Colliver, J. A., & MacLean, D. G. (1988). Prevalence of a history of sexual abuse among female psychiatric patients in a state hospital system. *Hospital and Community Psychiatry, 39,* 300–304.

Crowley, T. J., Chesluk, D., Dilts, S., & Hart, R. (1974). Drug and alcohol abuse among psychiatric admissions. *Archives of General Psychiatry, 30,* 13–20.

Cutting, J. (1995). Descriptive psychopathology. In S. R. Hirsch & D. R. Weinberger (Eds.), *Schizophrenia.* New York: Cambridge University Press.

Davies-Netzley, S., Hurlburt, M. S., & Hough, R. (1996). Childhood abuse as a precursor to homelessness for homeless women with severe mental illness. *Violence and Victims, 11,* 129–142.

Davis, K. L., Kahn, R. S., Ko, G., & Davidson, M. (1991). Dopamine in schizophrenia: A review and reconceptualization. *American Journal of Psychiatry, 148,* 1474–1486.

Dean, K., Walsh, E., Moran, P., Tyrer, P., Creed, F., Byford, S., Burns, T., Murray, R., & Fahy, T. (2006). Violence in women with psychosis in the community: A prospective study. *British Journal of Psychiatry, 188,* 264–270.

DeSisto, M. J., Harding, C. M., McCormick, R. V., Ashikaga, T., & Brooks, G. W. (1995). The Maine and Vermont three-decade studies of serious mental illness: I. Matched comparison of cross-sectional outcome. *British Journal of Psychiatry, 167,* 331–342.

Dixon, L. B., & Lehman, A. F. (1995). Family interventions for schizophrenia. *Schizophrenia Bulletin, 21,* 631–643.

Dixon, L. B., McFarlane, W., Lefley, H., Lucksted, A., Cohen, C., Falloon, I., Mueser, K. T., Miklowitz, D., Solomon, P., & Sondheimer, D. (2001). Evidence-based practices for services to family members of people with psychiatric disabilities. *Psychiatric Services, 52,* 903–910.

Dohrenwend, B. R., Levav, I., Shrout, P. E., Schwartz, S., Naveh, G., Link, B. G., Skodol, A. E., & Stueve, A. (1992). Socioeconomic status and psychiatric disorders: The causation-selection issue. *Science, 255,* 946–952.

Douglas, M. S., & Mueser, K. T. (1990). Teaching conflict resolution skills to the chronically mentally ill: Social skills training groups for briefly hospitalized patients. *Behavior Modification, 14,* 519–547.

Drake, R. E., & Becker, D. R. (1996). The individual placement and support model of supported employment. *Psychiatric Services, 47,* 473–475.

Drake, R. E., & Brunette, M. F. (1998). Complications of severe mental illness related to alcohol and drug use disorders. In M. Galanter (Ed.), *Recent developments in alcoholism: Vol. 14. The consequences of alcoholism* (pp. 285–299). New York: Plenum Press.

Drake, R. E., Gates, C., Whitaker, A., & Cotton, P. G. (1985). Suicide among schizophrenics: A review. *Comprehensive Psychiatry, 26,* 90–100.

Drake, R. E., Mercer-McFadden, C., Mueser, K. T., McHugo, G. J., & Bond, G. R. (1998). Review of integrated mental health and substance abuse treatment for patients with dual disorders. *Schizophrenia Bulletin, 24,* 589–608.

Drake, R. E., Osher, F. C., Noordsy, D. L., Hurlbut, S. C., Teague, G. B., & Beaudett, M. S. (1990). Diagnosis of alcohol use disorders in schizophrenia. *Schizophrenia Bulletin, 16,* 57–67.

Drake, R. E., Osher, F. C., & Wallach, M. A. (1989). Alcohol use and abuse in schizophrenia: A prospective community study. *Journal of Nervous and Mental Disease, 177,* 408–414.

Drake, R. E., Rosenberg, S. D., & Mueser, K. T. (1996). Assessment of substance use disorder in persons with severe mental illness. In R. E. Drake & K. T. Mueser (Eds.), *Dual diagnosis of major mental illness and substance abuse disorder II: Recent research and clinical implications: Vol. 70. New Directions in Mental Health Services* (pp. 3–17). San Francisco: Jossey-Bass.

Dworkin, R. J., & Adams, G. L. (1987). Retention of Hispanics in public sector mental health services. *Community Mental Health Journal, 23,* 204–216.

Dworkin, R. H., Bernstein, G., Kaplansky, L. M., Lipsitz, J. D., Rinaldi, A., Slater, S. L., Cornblatt, B. A., & Erlenmeyer-Kimling, L. (1991). Social competence and positive and negative symptoms: A longitudinal study of children and adolescents at risk for schizophrenia and affective disorder. *American Journal of Psychiatry, 148,* 1182–1188.

Dyck, D. G., Short, R., & Vitaliano, P. P. (1999). Predictors of burden and infectious illness in schizophrenia caregivers. *Psychosomatic Medicine, 61,* 411–419.

Eaton, W. W. (1975). Marital status and schizophrenia. *Acta Psychiatrica Scandinavica, 52,* 320–329.

Edwards, J., Jackson, H. J., & Pattison, P. E. (2002). Emotion recognition via facial expression and affective prosody in schizophrenia: A methodological review. *Clinical Psychology Review, 22,* 789–832.

Erlenmeyer-Kimling, L., Rock, D., Roberts, S. A., Janal, M., Kestenbaum, C., Cornblatt, B., Adamo, U. H., & Gottesman, I. I. (2000). Attention, memory, and motor skills as childhood predictors of schizophrenia-related psychoses: The New York High-Risk project. *American Journal of Psychiatry, 157,* 1416–1422.

Estroff, S. E. (1989). Self, identity, and subjective experiences of schizophrenia: In search of the subject. *Schizophrenia Bulletin, 15,* 189–196.

Evans, J. D., Paulsen, J. S., Harris, M. J., Heaton, R. K., & Jeste, D. V. (1996). A clinical and neuropsychological comparison of delusional disorder and schizophrenia. *The Journal of Neuropsychiatry and Clinical Neurosciences, 8,* 281–286.

Fannon, D., Chitnis, X, Doku, V., Tennakoon, L., Ó'Ceallaigh, S., Soni, W., Sumich, A., Lowe, J., Santamaria, M., & Sharma, T. (2000). Features of structural brain abnormality detected in early first episode psychosis. *American Journal of Psychiatry, 157,* 1829–1834.

Faraone, S. V., & Tsuang, M. T. (1985). Quantitative models of the genetic transmission of schizophrenia. *Psychological Bulletin, 98,* 41–66.

Farina, A. (1998). Stigma. In K. T. Mueser & N. Tarrier (Eds.), *Handbook of social functioning in schizophrenia* (pp. 247–279). Boston: Allyn and Bacon.

Fenton, W. S., & McGlashan, T. H. (1991). Natural history of schizophrenia subtypes: II. Positive and negative symptoms and long term course. *Archives of General Psychiatry, 48,* 978–986.

Fink, P. J., & Tasman, A. (Eds.). (1992). *Stigma and mental illness.* Washington, DC: American Psychiatric Press.

First, M. B., Spitzer, R. L., Gibbon, M., & Williams, J. B. W. (1996). *Structured clinical interview for Axes I and II DSM-IV Disorders—Patient Edition (SCID-I/P).* New York: Biometrics Research Department, New York State Psychiatric Institute.

Flaum, M., Arndt, S., & Andreasen, N. C. (1991). The reliability of "bizarre" delusions. *Comparative Psychiatry, 32,* 59–65.

Flor-Henry, P. (1985). Schizophrenia: Sex differences. *Canadian Journal of Psychiatry, 30,* 319–322.

Fowler, D., Garety, P., & Kuipers, E. (1995). *Cognitive behaviour therapy for psychosis: Theory and practice.* Chichester, England: Wiley.

Fox, J. W. (1990). Social class, mental illness, and social mobility: The social selection-drift hypothesis for serious mental illness. *Journal of Health and Social Behavior, 31,* 344–353.

Freeman, D., & Garety, P. A. (2003). Connecting neurosis and psychosis: The direct influence of emotion on delusions and hallucinations. *Behaviour Research and Therapy, 41,* 923–947.

Freeman, D., Garety, P. A., Bebbington, P. E., Slater, M., Kuipers, E., Fowler, D., Green, C., Jordan, J., Ray, K., & Dunn, G., (2005). The psychology of persecutory ideation II: A virtual reality experimental study. *Journal of Nervous and Mental Disease, 193,* 309–315.

Freeman, D., Garety, P. A., & Kuipers, E. (2001). Persecutory delusions: Developing the understanding of belief maintenance and emotional distress. *Psychological Medicine, 31,* 1293–1306.

Freeman, D., Garety, P. A., Kuipers, E., Fowler, D., & Bebbington, P. E. (2002). A cognitive model of persecutory delusions. *British Journal of Clinical Psychology, 41,* 331–347.

Fromm-Reichmann, F. (1950). *Principles of intensive psychotherapy.* Chicago: University of Chicago Press.

Fuller, R., Nopoulos, P., Arndt, S., O'Leary, D., Ho, B., & Andreasen, N. C. (2002). Longitudinal assessment of premorbid cognitive functioning in patients with schizophrenia through examination of standardized scholastic test performance. *The American Journal of Psychiatry, 159,* 1183–1189.

Galletly, C. A., Field, C. D., & Prior, M. (1993). Urine drug screening of patients admitted to a state psychiatric hospital. *Hospital and Community Psychiatry, 44,* 587–589.

Garety, P. A., & Freeman, D. (1999). Cognitive approaches to delusions: A critical review of theories and evidence. *British Journal of Clinical Psychology, 38,* 113–154.

Gay, N. W., & Combs, D. R. (2005). Social behaviors in persons with and without persecutory delusions. *Schizophrenia Research, 80,* 2–3.

Geddes, J. R., & Lawrie, S. M. (1995). Obstetric complications and schizophrenia: A meta-analysis. *British Journal of Psychiatry, 167,* 786–793.

Glynn, S. M. (1992). Family-based treatment for major mental illness: A new role for psychologists. *The California Psychologist, 25,* 22–23.

Glynn, S. M. (1998). Psychopathology and social functioning in schizophrenia. In K. T. Mueser & N. Tarrier (Eds.), *Handbook of social functioning in schizophrenia* (pp. 66–78). Boston: Allyn and Bacon.

Goere, R., Farahati, F., Burke, N., Blackhouse, G., O'Reilly, D., Pyne, J., & Tarride, J. E. (2005). The economic burden of schizophrenia in Canada in 2004. *Current Medical Research & Opinion, 21,* 2017–2028.

Goldman, H. H. (1982). Mental illness and family burden: A public health perspective. *Hospital and Community Psychiatry, 33,* 557–560.

Goldner, E. M., Hsu, L., Waraich, P., & Somers, J. M. (2002). Prevalence and incidence studies of schizophrenic disorders: A systematic review of the literature. *Canadian Journal of Psychiatry, 47,* 833–843.

Goldstein, J. M. (1988). Gender differences in the course of schizophrenia. *American Journal of Psychiatry, 146,* 684–689.

González-Wippler, M. (1992). *Powers of the orishas: Santeria and the worship of saints.* New York: Original Publications.

Goodman, L. A., Dutton, M. A., & Harris, M. (1995). Physical and sexual assault prevalence among episodically homeless women with serious mental illness. *American Journal of Orthopsychiatry, 65,* 468–478.

Goodman, L. A., Dutton, M. A., & Harris, M. (1997). The relationship between violence dimensions and symptom severity among homeless, mentally ill women. *Journal of Traumatic Stress, 10,* 51–70.

Goodman, L. A., Salyers, M. P., Mueser, K. T., Rosenberg, S. D., Swartz, M., Essock, S. M., Butterfield, M. I., & the 5 Site Health and Risk Study Research Committee. (2001). Recent victimization in women and men with severe mental illness: Prevalence and correlates. *Journal of Traumatic Stress, 14,* 615–632.

Goodwin, F. K., & Jamison, K. R. (1990). *Manic-depressive illness.* New York: Oxford University Press.

Gottesman, I. I. (1991). *Schizophrenia genesis: The origins of madness.* New York: Freeman.

Gottesman, I. I. (2001). Psychopathology through a life span-genetic prism. *American Psychologist, 56,* 867–878.

Gottesman, I. I., & Shields, J. (1982). *Schizophrenia: The epigenetic puzzle.* New York: Cambridge University Press.

Greden, J. F., & Tandon, R. (Eds.). (1991). *Negative schizophrenic symptoms: Pathophysiology and clinical implications.* Washington, DC: American Psychiatric Press.

Green, M. F., Kern, R. S., Braff, D. L., & Mintz, J. (2000). Neurocognitive deficits and functional outcome in schizophrenia: Are we measuring the "right stuff"? *Schizophrenia Bulletin, 26,* 119–136.

Green, M. F., Marshall, B. D., Jr., Wirshing, W. C., Ames, D., Marder, S. R., McGurk, S., Kern, R. S., & Mintz, J. (1997). Does Risperidone improve verbal working memory in treatment-resistant schizophrenia? *American Journal of Psychiatry, 154,* 799–804.

Green, M. F., Nuechterlein, K. H., Gold, J. M., Barch, D. M., Cohen, J., Essock, S., Fenton, W. S., Frese, F., Goldberg, T. E., Heaton, R. K., Keefe, R. S. E., Kern, R. S., Kraemer, H., Stover, E., Weinberger, D. R., Zalcman, S., & Marder, S. R. (2004). Approaching a consensus battery for clinical trials in schizophrenia: The NIMH-MATRICS conference to select cognitive domains and test criteria. *Biological Psychiatry, 56,* 301–307.

Green, M. F., Olivier, B., Crawley, J. N., Penn, D. L., & Silverstein, S. (2005). Social cognition in schizophrenia: Recommendations from the measurement and treatment research to improve cognition in schizophrenia new approaches conference. *Schizophrenia Bulletin, 31,* 882–887.

Greenfield, S. F., Strakowski, S. M., Tohen, M., Batson, S. C., & Kolbrener, M. L. (1994). Childhood abuse in first-episode psychosis. *British Journal of Psychiatry, 164,* 831–834.

Griffith, E. E. H., Young, J. L., & Smith, D. L. (1984). An analysis of the therapeutic elements in a black church service. *Hospital and Community Psychiatry, 35,* 464–469.

Haas, G. L., & Garratt, L. S. (1998). Gender differences in social functioning. In K. T. Mueser & N. Tarrier (Eds.), *Handbook of social functioning in schizophrenia* (pp. 149–180). Boston: Allyn and Bacon.

Haddock, G., McCarron, J., Tarrier, N., & Faragher, E. B. (1999). Scales to measure dimensions of hallucinations and delusions: The psychotic symptom rating scales (PSYRATS). *Psychological Medicine, 29*(4), 879-89.

Häfner, H., Maurer, K., Trendler, G., an der Heiden, W., & Schmidt, M. (2005). The early course of schizophrenia and depression. *European Archives of Psychiatry and Clinical Neuroscience, 255,* 167–173.

Häfner, H., Riecher-Rössler, A., an der Heiden, W., Maurer, K., Fätkenheuer, B., & Löffler, W. (1993). Generating and testing a causal explanation of the gender difference in age at first onset of schizophrenia. *Psychological Medicine, 23,* 925–940.

Halari, R., Kumari, V., Mehorotra, R., Wheeler, M., Hines, M., & Sharma, T. (2004). The relationship of sex hormones and cortisol with cognitive functioning in schizophrenia. *Journal of Pharmacology, 18,* 366–374.

Halford, W. K., Schweitzer, R. D., & Varghese, F. N. (1991). Effects of family environment on negative symptoms and quality of life on psychotic patients. *Hospital and Community Psychiatry, 42,* 1241–1247.

Hans, S. L., Marcus, J., Henson, L., Auerbach, J. G., & Mirsky, A. F. (1992). Interpersonal behavior of children at risk for schizophrenia. *Psychiatry, 55,* 314–335.

Harding, C. M., Brooks, G. W., Ashikaga, T., Strauss, J. S., & Breier, A. (1987a). The Vermont longitudinal study of persons with severe mental illness, I: Methodology, study sample, and overall status 32 years later. *American Journal of Psychiatry, 144,* 718–726.

Harding, C. M., Brooks, G. W., Ashikaga, T., Strauss, J. S., & Breier, A. (1987b). The Vermont longitudinal study of persons with severe mental illness, II: Long-term outcome of subjects who retrospectively met *DSM-III* criteria for schizophrenia. *American Journal of Psychiatry, 144,* 727–735.

Harris, M. (1996). Treating sexual abuse trauma with dually diagnosed women. *Community Mental Health Journal, 32,* 371–385.

Harris, M. J., & Jeste, D. V. (1988). Late-onset schizophrenia: An overview. *Schizophrenia Bulletin, 14,* 39–45.

Harrison, P. J., & Owen, M. J. (2003). Genes for schizophrenia: Recent findings and their pathophysiological implications. *The Lancet, 361,* 417–419.

Harrow, M., Grossman, L. S., Jobe, T. H., & Herbener, E. S. (2005). Do patients with schizophrenia ever show periods of recovery? A 15-year multi-follow-up study. *Schizophrenia Bulletin, 31,* 723–734.

Hatfield, A. B., & Lefley, H. P. (Eds.). (1987). *Families of the mentally ill: Coping and adaptation.* New York: Guilford Press.

Hatfield, A. B., & Lefley, H. P. (Eds.). (1993). *Surviving mental illness: Stress, coping, and adaptation.* New York: Guilford Press.

Hawton, K., Sutton, L., Haw, C., Sinclair, J., & Deeks, J. J. (2005). Schizophrenia and suicide: Systematic review of risk factors. *British Journal of Psychiatry, 187,* 9–20.

Haynes, S. (1986). Behavioral Model of Paranoid Behaviors. *Behavior Therapy, 17,* 266–287.

Heaton, R. K., Gladsjo, J. A., Palmer, B. W., Kuck, J., Marcotte, T. D., & Jeste, D.V. (2001). Stability and course of neuropsychological deficits in schizophrenia. *Archives of General Psychiatry, 58,* 24–32.

Heinrichs, R. W. (2005). The primacy of cognition in schizophrenia. *American Psychologist, 60,* 229–242.

Heinssen, R. K., Liberman, R. P., & Kopelowicz, A. (2000). Psychosocial skills training for schizophrenia: Lessons from the laboratory. *Schizophrenia Bulletin, 26,* 21–46.

Hiday, V. A., Swartz, M. S., Swanson, J. W., Borum, R., & Wagner, H. R. (1999). Criminal victimization of persons with severe mental illness. *Psychiatric Services, 50,* 62–68.

Hodgins, S., & Côté, G. (1993). Major mental disorder and antisocial personality disorder: A criminal combination. *Bulletin of the American Academy of Psychiatry Law, 21,* 155–160.

Hodgins, S., & Côté, G. (1996). Schizophrenia and antisocial personality disorder: A criminal combination. In L. B. Schlesinger (Ed.), *Explorations in criminal psychopathology: Clincal syndromes with forensic implications* (pp. 217–237). Springfield, IL: Charles C. Thomas.

Hodgins, S., Mednick, S. A., Brennan, P. A., Schulsinger, F., & Engberg, M (1996). Mental disorder and crime: Evidence from a Danish birth cohort. *Archives of General Psychiatry, 53,* 489–496.

Hollingshead, A. B., & Redlich, F. C. (1958). *Social class and mental illness: A community study.* New York: Wiley.

Hough, R. L., Landsverk, J. A., Karno, M., Burnam, A., Timbers, D. M., Escobar, J. I., & Regier, D. A. (1987). Utilization of health and mental health services by Los Angeles Mexican Americans and non-Hispanic whites. *Archives of General Psychiatry, 44,* 702–709.

Howard, R., Almeida, O., & Levy R. (1994). Phenomenology, demography and diagnosis in late paraphrenia. *Psychological Medicine, 24,* 397–410.

Howard, R., Rabins, P. V., Seeman, M. V., Jeste, D. V., & the International Late-Onset Schizophrenia Group (2000). Late-onset schizophrenia and very-late-onset schizophrenia-like psychosis: An international consensus. *American Journal of Psychiatry, 157,* 172–178.

Hu, T., Snowden, L. R., Jerrell, J. M., & Nguyen, T. D. (1991). Ethnic populations in public mental health: Services choices and level of use. *American Journal of Public Health, 81,* 1429–1434.

Hutchings, P. S., & Dutton, M. A. (1993). Sexual assault history in a community mental health center clinical population. *Community Mental Health Journal, 29,* 59–63.

Inskip, H. M., Harris, E. C., & Barraclough, B. (1998). Lifetime risk of suicide for affective disorder, alcoholism, and schizophrenia. *British Journal of Psychiatry, 172,* 35–37.

Jablensky, A. (1989). Epidemiology and cross-cultural aspects of schizophrenia. *Psychiatric Annals, 19,* 516–524.

Jablensky, A. (1999). Schizophrenia: Epidemiology. *Current Opinion in Psychiatry, 12,* 19–28.

Jablensky, A. (2000). Epidemiology of schizophrenia: The global burden of disease and disability. *European Archives of Psychiatry and Clinical Neuroscience, 250,* 274–285.

Jablensky, A., McGrath, J., Herman, H., Castle, D., Gureje, O., Evans, M., Carr,V., Morgan, V., Korten, A., & Harvey, C. (2000). Psychotic disorders in urban areas: An overview of the study on low prevalence disorders. *Australian and New Zealand Journal of Psychiatry, 34,* 221–236.

Jablensky, A., Sartorius, N., Ernberg, G., Anker, M., Korten, A., & Cooper, J. E. (1992). Schizophrenia: Manifestations, incidence, and course in different cultures—A World Health Organization ten country study. *Psychological Medical Monograph Supplement, 20,* 1–97.

Jacob, T. (1975). Family interaction in disturbed and normal families: A methodological and substantive review. *Psychological Bulletin, 82,* 33–65.

Jacobson, A. (1989). Physical and sexual assault histories among psychiatric outpatients. *American Journal of Psychiatry, 146,* 755–758.

Jacobson, A., & Herald, C. (1990). The relevance of childhood sexual abuse to adult psychiatric inpatient care. *Hospital and Community Psychiatry, 41,* 154–158.

Jacobson, A., & Richardson, B. (1987). Assault experiences of 100 psychiatric inpatients: Evidence of the need for routine inquiry. *American Journal of Psychiatry, 144,* 508–513.

Jimenez, J. M., Todman, M., Perez, M., Godoy, J. F., & Landon-Jimenez, D. V. (1996). The behavioral treatment of auditory hallucinatory responding of a schizophrenic patient. *Journal of Behavioral Therapy and Experimental Psychiatry, 27,* 299–310.

Jobe, T. H., & Harrow, M. (2005). Long-term outcome of patients with schizophrenia: A review. *Canadian Journal of Psychiatry, 50,* 892–900.

Jones, B. E., Gray, B. A., & Parsons, E. B. (1981). Manic-depressive illness among poor urban blacks. *American Journal of Psychiatry, 138,* 654–657.

Jones, B. E., Gray, B. A., & Parsons, E. B. (1983). Manic-depressive illness among poor urban Hispanics. *American Journal of Psychiatry, 140,* 1208–1210.

Jones, E. (1999). The phenomenology of abnormal belief. *Philosophy, Psychiatry, and Psychology, 6,* 1–16.

Junginger, J., Barker, S., & Coe, D. (1992). Mood theme and bizarreness of delusions in schizophrenia and mood psychosis. *Journal of Abnormal Psychology, 101,* 287–292.

Kane, J. M., & Marder, S. R. (1993). Psychopharmacologic treatment of schizophrenia. *Schizophrenia Bulletin, 19,* 287–302.

Kay, S. R., Fiszbein, A., & Opler, L. A. (1987). The positive and negative syndrome scale (PANSS) for schizophrenia. *Schizophrenia Bulletin, 13,* 261–276.

Kay, S. R., & Lindenmayer, J. (1987). Outcome predictors in acute schizophrenia: Prospective significance of background and clinical dimensions. *Journal of Nervous and Mental Disease, 175,* 152–160.

Keith, S. J., Regier, D. A., & Rae, D. S. (1991). Schizophrenic disorders. In L. N. Robins & D. A. Regier (Eds.), *Psychiatric disorders in America: The Epidemiologic Catchment Area Study* (pp. 33–52). New York: The Free Press.

Kemp, R., Hayward, P., Applewhaite, G., Everitt, B., & David, A. (1996). Compliance therapy in psychotic patients: Randomised controlled trial. *British Medical Journal, 312,* 345–349.

Kemp, R., Kirov, G., Everitt, B., Hayward, P., & David, A. (1998). Randomised controlled trial of compliance therapy. 18-month follow-up. *British Journal of Psychiatry, 173,* 271–272.

Kendler, K. S. (1982). Demography of paranoid psychosis (delusional disorder): A review and comparison with schizophrenia and affective illness. *Archives of General Psychiatry, 39,* 890–902.

Kendler, K. S., & Diehl, S. R. (1993). The genetics of schizophrenia. *Schizophrenia Bulletin, 19,* 261–285.

Kern, R. S., Liberman, R. P., Kopelowicz, A., Mintz, J., & Green, M. F. (2002). Applications of errorless learning for improving work performance in persons with schizophrenia. *American Journal of Psychiatry, 159,* 1921–1926.

Kessler, R. C., Foster, C. L., Saunders, W. B., & Stang, P. E. (1995). Social consequences of psychiatric disorders, I: Educational attainment. *American Journal of Psychiatry, 152,* 1026–1032.

Kessler, R. C., Sonnega, A., Bromet, E., Hughes, M., & Nelson, C. B. (1995). Posttraumatic stress disorder in the national comorbidity survey. *Archives of General Psychiatry, 52,* 1048–1060.

Kindermann, S. S., Karimi, A., Symonds, L., Brown, G. G., & Jeste, D. V. (1997). Review of functional magnetic resonance imaging in schizophrenia. *Schizophrenia Research, 27,* 143–156.

Kirch, D. G. (1993). Infection and autoimmunity as etiologic factors in schizophrenia: A review and reappraisal. *Schizophrenia Bulletin, 19,* 355–370.

Knapp, M., Mangalore, R., & Simon, J. (2004). The global costs of schizophrenia. *Schizophrenia Bulletin, 30,* 279–293.

Kraepelin, E. (1971). *Dementia praecox and paraphrenia* (R. M. Barclay, Trans.). New York: Robert E. Krieger. (Original work published 1919)

Kramer, M. S., Vogel, W. H., DiJohnson, C., Dewey, D. A., Sheves, P., Cavicchia, S., Litle, P., Schmidt, R., & Kimes, I. (1989). Antidepressants in "depressed" schizophrenic inpatients. *Archives of General Psychiatry, 46,* 922–928.

Kranzler, H. R., Kadden, R. M., Burleson, J. A., Babor, T. F., Apter, A., & Rounsaville, B. J. (1995). Validity of psychiatric diagnoses in patients with substance use disorders: Is the interview more important than the interviewer? *Comprehensive Psychiatry, 36,* 278–288.

Lam, D. H. (1991). Psychosocial family intervention in schizophrenia: A review of empirical studies. *Psychological Medicine, 21,* 423–441.

Lawrie, S. M., & Abukmeil S. S. (1998). Brain abnormality in schizophrenia: A systematic and quantitative review of volumetric magnetic resonance imaging studies. *British Journal of Psychiatry, 172,* 110–120.

Leff, J., Tress, K., & Edwards, B. (1988). The clinical course of depressive symptoms in schizophrenia. *Schizophrenia Research, 1,* 25–30.

Leff, J., & Vaughn, C. (1985). *Expressed emotion in families: Its significance for mental illness.* New York: Guilford Press.

Lefley, H. P. (1990). Culture and chronic mental illness. *Hospital and Community Psychiatry, 41,* 277–286.

Lehman, A. F., Myers, C. P., Dixon, L. B., & Johnson, J. L. (1994). Defining subgroups of dual diagnosis patients for service planning. *Hospital and Community Psychiatry, 45,* 556–561.

Lehman, A. F., Myers, C. P., Dixon, L. B., & Johnson, J. L. (1996). Detection of substance use disorders among psychiatric inpatients. *The Journal of Nervous and Mental Disease, 184,* 228–233.

Leung, A., & Chue, P. (2000). Sex differences in schizophrenia: A review of the literature. *Acta Psychiatrica Scandinavica, 401,* 3–38.

Levinson, D. F., & Levitt, M. M. (1987). Schizoaffective mania reconsidered. *The American Journal of Psychiatry, 144,* 415–425.

Levinson, D. F., & Mowry, B. J. (1991). Defining the schizophrenia spectrum: Issues for genetic linkage studies. *Schizophrenia Bulletin, 17,* 491–514.

Liberman, R. P. (1994). Treatment and rehabilitation of the seriously mentally ill in China: Impressions of a society in transition. *American Journal of Orthopsychiatry, 64,* 68–77.

Liberman, R. P., Mueser, K. T., Wallace, C. J., Jacobs, H. E., Eckman, T., & Massel, H. K. (1986). Training skills in the psychiatrically disabled: Learning coping and competence. *Schizophrenia Bulletin, 12,* 631–647.

Liddle, P. F. (1987). Schizophrenic syndromes, cognitive performance and neurological dysfunction. *Psychological Medicine, 17,* 49–57.

Liddle, P. F. (1995). Brain Imaging. In S. R. Hirsch & D. R. Weinberger (Eds.), *Schizophrenia* (pp. 425–439). Cambridge, MA: Blackwell Science.

Liddle, P. F. (1997). Dynamic neuroimaging with PET, SPET or fMRI. *International Review of Psychiatry, 9,* 331–337.

Lieberman, J. A., Mailman, R. B., Duncan, G., Sikich, L., Chakos, M., Nichols, D. E., & Kraus, J. E. (1998). A decade of serotonin research: Role of serotonin in treatment of psychosis. *Biological Psychiatry, 44,* 1099–1117.

Lim, K. O., Hedehus, M., de Crespigny, A., Menon, V., & Moseley, M. (1998). Diffusion tensor imaging of white matter tracts in schizophrenia. *Biological Psychiatry, 43* (Suppl. 8S), 11S.

Lin, K-M., & Kleinman, A. M. (1988). Psychopathology and clinical course of schizophrenia: A cross-cultural perspective. *Schizophrenia Bulletin, 14,* 555–567.

Lincoln, E. C., & Mamiya, L. H. (1990). *The black church in the African American experience.* Durham, NC: Duke University Press.

Lincoln, C. V., & McGorry, P. (1995). Who cares? Pathways to psychiatric care for young people experiencing a first episode of psychosis. *Psychiatric Services, 46,* 1166–1171.

Lipschitz, D. S., Kaplan, M. L., Sorkenn, J. B., Faedda, G. L., Chorney, P., & Asnis, G. M. (1996). Prevalence and characteristics of physical and sexual abuse among psychiatric outpatients. *Psychiatric Services, 47,* 189–191.

Lo, W. H., & Lo, T. (1977). A ten-year follow-up study of Chinese schizophrenics in Hong Kong. *British Journal of Psychiatry, 131,* 63–66.

Loring, M., & Powell, B. (1988). Gender, race, and *DSM-III:* A study of the objectivity of psychiatric diagnostic behavior. *Journal of Health and Social Behavior, 29,* 1–22.

Lysaker, P. H., Bell, M. D., Zito, W. S., & Bioty, S. M. (1995). Social skills at work: Deficits and predictors of improvement in schizophrenia. *Journal of Nervous and Mental Disease, 183,* 688–692.

Magaña, A. B., Goldstein, M. J., Karno, M., Miklowitz, D. J., Jenkins, J., & Falloon, I. R. H. (1986). A brief method for assessing expressed emotion in relatives of psychiatric patients. *Psychiatry Research, 17,* 203–212.

Magliano, L., Fadden, G., Madianos, M., de Almeida, J. M., Held, T., Guarneri, M., Marasco, Tosini, P., & Maj, M. (1998). Burden on the families of patients with schizophrenia: Results of the BIOMED I study. *Social Psychiatry and Psychiatric Epidemiology, 33,* 405–412.

Maisto, S. A., Carey, M. P., Carey, K. B., Gordon, C. M., & Gleason, J. R. (2000). Use of the AUDIT and the DAST-10 to identify alcohol and drug use disorders among adults with a severe and persistent mental illness. *Psychological Assessment, 12,* 186–192.

Malla, A. K., Norman, R. M. G., & Joober, R. (2005). First-episode psychosis, early intervention, and outcome: What haven't we learned? *Canadian Journal of Psychiatry, 50,* 881–891.

Malla, A., & Payne, J. (2005). First-episode psychosis: Psychopathology, quality of life, and functional outcome. *Schizophrenia Bulletin, 31,* 650–671.

Manschreck, T. C. (1996). Delusional disorder: The recognition and management of paranoia. *The Journal of Clinical Psychiatry, 57,* 32–38.

Marengo, J. (1994). Classifying the courses of schizophrenia. *Schizophrenia Bulletin, 20,* 519–536.

Marwaha, S., & Johnson, S. (2004). Schizophrenia and employment: A review. *Social Psychiatry and Psychiatric Epidemiology, 39,* 337–349.

Mattes, J. A., & Nayak, D. (1984). Lithium versus fluphenazine for prophylaxis in mainly schizophrenic schizoaffectives. *Biological Psychiatry, 19,* 445–449.

May, A. (1997). Psychopathology and religion in the era of "enlightened science": A case report. *European Journal of Psychiatry, 11,* 14–20.

McClure, R. J., Keshavan, M. S., & Pettegrew, J. W. (1998). Chemical and physiologic brain imaging in schizophrenia. *Psychiatric Clinics of North America, 21,* 93–122.

McDonald, C., Grech, A., Toulopoulou, T., Schulze, K., Chapple, B., Sham, P., Walshe, M., Sharma, T., Sigmundsson, T., Chitnis, X., & Murray, R. M. (2002). Brain volumes in familial and non-familial schizophrenic probands and their unaffected relatives. *American Journal of Medical Genetics Neuropsychiatric Genetics, 114,* 616–625.

McEvoy, J. P., Freter, S., Everett, G., Geller, J. L., Appelbaum, P., Apperson, L. J., & Roth, L. (1989). Insight and the clinical outcome of schizophrenic patients. *The Journal of Nervous and Mental Disease, 177,* 48–51.

McGuffin, P., Owen, M. J., & Farmer, A. E. (1995). Genetic basis of schizophrenia. *The Lancet, 346,* 678–682.

Merriam, A. E., Kay, S. R., Opler, L. A., Kushner, S. F., & van Praag, H. M. (1990). Neurological signs and the positive-negative dimension in schizophrenia. *Biological Psychiatry, 28,* 181–192.

Miyamoto, S., LaMantia, A. S., Duncan, G. E., Sullivan, P., Gilmore, J. H., & Lieberman, A. (2003). Recent advances in the neurobiology of schizophrenia. *Molecular Interventions, 3,* 27–39.

Monahan, J., Steadman, H. J., Silver, E., Appelbaum, P. S., Robbins, P. C., Mulvey, E. P., Roth, L. H., Grisso, T., & Banks, S. (2001). *Rethinking risk assessment: The MacArthur study of mental disorder and violence.* New York: Oxford University Press.

Montero, I., Asencio, A., Hernádez, I., Masanet, M. J., Lacruz, M., Bellver, F., Iborra, M., & Ruiz, I. (2001). Two strategies for family intervention in schizophrenia. A randomized trial in a Mediterranean environment. *Schizophrenia Bulletin, 27,* 661–670.

Moore, H., West, A. R., & Grace, A. A. (1999). The regulation of forebrain dopamine transmission: Relevance to the pathophysiology and psychopathology of schizophrenia. *Biological Psychiatry, 46,* 40–55.

Moos, R. H., & Moos, B. S. (1981). *Family environment scale manual.* Palo Alto, CA: Consulting Psychologists Press.

Morales-Dorta, J. (1976). *Puerto Rican espiritismo: Religion and psychotherapy.* New York: Vantage Press.

Mueser, K. T., & Bellack, A. S. (1998). Social skills and social functioning. In K. T. Mueser and N. Tarrier (Eds.) *Handbook of social functioning in schizophrenia* (pp. 79–96). Boston: Allyn and Bacon.

Mueser, K. T., Bellack, A. S., & Brady, E. U. (1990). Hallucinations in schizophrenia. *Acta Psychiatrica Scandinavica, 82,* 26–29.

Mueser, K. T., Bellack, A. S., Douglas, M. S., & Morrison, R. L. (1991). Prevalence and stability of social skill deficits in schizophrenia. *Schizophrenia Research, 5,* 167–176.

Mueser, K. T., Bellack, A. S., Douglas, M. S., & Wade, J. H. (1991). Prediction of social skill acquisition in schizophrenic and major affective disorder patients from memory and symptomatology. *Psychiatry Research, 37,* 281–296.

Mueser, K. T., Bellack, A. S., Morrison, R. L., & Wade, J. H. (1990). Gender, social competence, and symptomatology in schizophrenia: A longitudinal analysis. *Journal of Abnormal Psychology, 99,* 138–147.

Mueser, K. T., Bellack, A. S., Morrison, R. L., & Wixted, J. T. (1990). Social competence in schizophrenia: Premorbid adjustment, social skill, and domains of functioning. *Journal of Psychiatric Research, 24,* 51–63.

Mueser, K. T., Bellack, A. S., Wade, J. H., Sayers, S. L., Tierney, A., & Haas, G. (1993). Expressed emotion, social skill, and response to negative affect in schizophrenia. *Journal of Abnormal Psychology, 102,* 339–351.

Mueser, K. T., Bennett, M., & Kushner, M. G. (1995). Epidemiology of substance use disorders among persons with chronic mental illnesses. In A. Lehman & L. Dixon (Eds.), *Double jeopardy: Chronic mental illness and substance abuse* (pp. 9–25). Chur, Switzerland: Harwood Academic.

Mueser, K. T., & Berenbaum, H. (1990). Psychodynamic treatment of schizophrenia: Is there a future? *Psychological Medicine, 20,* 253–262.

Mueser, K. T., Bond, G. R., Drake, R. E., & Resnick, S. G. (1998). Models of community care for severe mental illness: A review of research on case management. *Schizophrenia Bulletin, 24,* 37–74.

Mueser, K. T., Curran, P. J., & McHugo, G. J. (1997). Factor structure of the Brief Psychiatric Rating Scale in schizophrenia. *Psychological Assessment, 9,* 196–204.

Mueser, K. T., Douglas, M. S., Bellack, A. S., & Morrison, R. L. (1991). Assessment of enduring deficit and negative symptom subtypes in schizophrenia. *Schizophrenia Bulletin, 17,* 565–582.

Mueser, K. T., Drake, R. E., & Bond, G. R. (1997). Recent advances in psychiatric rehabilitation for patients with severe mental illness. *Harvard Review of Psychiatry, 5,* 123–137.

Mueser, K. T., & Glynn, S. M. (1999). *Behavioral family therapy for psychiatric disorders* (2nd ed.). Oakland, CA: New Harbinger.

Mueser, K. T., Goodman, L. B., Trumbetta, S. L., Rosenberg, S. D., Osher, F. C., Vidaver, R., Aucielo, P., & Foy, D. W. (1998). Trauma and posttraumatic stress disorder in severe mental illness. *Journal of Consulting and Clinical Psychology, 66,* 493–499.

Mueser, K. T., Levine, S., Bellack, A. S., Douglas, M. S., & Brady, E. U. (1990). Social skills training for acute psychiatric patients. *Hospital and Community Psychiatry, 41,* 1249–1251.

Mueser, K. T., & McGurk, S. R. (2004). Schizophrenia. *The Lancet, 363,* 2063–2072.

Mueser, K. T., Rosenberg, S. D., Drake, R. E., Miles, K. M., Wolford, G., Vidaver, R., & Carrieri, K. (1999). Conduct disorder, antisocial personality disorder, and substance use disorders in schizophrenia and major affective disorders. *Journal of Studies on Alcohol, 60,* 278–284.

Mueser, K. T., Rosenberg, S. D., Goodman, L. A., & Trumbetta, S. L. (2002). Trauma, PTSD, and the course of schizophrenia: An interactive model. *Schizophrenia Research, 53,* 123–143.

Mueser, K. T., Salyers, M. P., & Mueser, P. R. (2001). A prospective analysis of work in schizophrenia. *Schizophrenia Bulletin, 27,* 281–296.

Mueser, K. T., Salyers, M. P., Rosenberg, S. D., Goodman, L. A., Essock, S. M., Osher, F. C., Swartz, M. S., Butterfield, M. I., & the 5 Site Health & Risk Study Research Committee (2004). Interpersonal trauma and posttraumatic stress disorder in patients with severe mental illness: Demographic, clinical, and health correlates. *Schizophrenia Bulletin, 30,* 45–57.

Mueser, K. T., Yarnold, P. R., & Bellack, A. S. (1992). Diagnostic and demographic correlates of substance abuse in schizophrenia and major affective disorder. *Acta Psychiatrica Scandinavica, 85,* 48–55.

Mueser, K. T., Yarnold, P. R., Levinson, D. F., Singh, H., Bellack, A. S., Kee, K., Morrison, R. L., & Yadalam, K. Y. (1990). Prevalence of substance abuse in schizophrenia: Demographic and clinical correlates. *Schizophrenia Bulletin, 16,* 31–56.

Munk-Jørgensen, P. (1987). First-admission rates and marital status of schizophrenics. *Acta Psychiatrica Scandinavica, 76,* 210–216.

Murphy, H. B. M., & Raman, A. C. (1971). The chronicity of schizophrenia in indigenous tropical peoples. *British Journal of Psychiatry, 118,* 489–497.

Murray, C. J. L, & Lopez, A.D. (Eds.). (1996). *The global burden of disease and injury series: Vol. I. A comprehensive assessment of mortality and disability from diseases, injuries, and risk factors in 1990 and projected to 2020.* Cambridge, MA: Harvard University Press.

Narrow, W. E., Rae, D. S., Robins, L. N., & Regier, D. A. (2002). Revised prevalence estimates of mental disorders in the United States. *Archives of General Psychiatry, 59,* 115–123.

Neumann, C. S., Grimes, K., Walker, E., & Baum, K. (1995). Developmental pathways to schizophrenia: Behavioral subtypes. *Journal of Abnormal Psychology, 104,* 558–566.

Nolan, K. A., Volavka, J., Mohr, P., & Czobor, P. (1999). Psychopathy and violent behavior among patients with schizophrenia or schizoaffective disorder. *Psychiatric Services, 50,* 787–792.

Norman, R. M., Scholten, D. J., Malla, A. K., & Ballageer, T. (2005). Early signs in schizophrenia spectrum disorders. *The Journal of Nervous and Mental Disease, 193,* 17–23.

Nuechterlein, K. H., & Dawson, M. E. (1984). A heuristic vulnerability/stress model of schizophrenic episodes. *Schizophrenia Bulletin, 10,* 300–312.

Oldridge, M. L., & Hughes, I. C. T. (1992). Psychological well-being in families with a member suffering from schizophrenia. *British Journal of Psychiatry, 161,* 249–251.

Overall, J. E., & Gorham, D. R. (1962). The brief psychiatric rating scale. *Psychological Reports, 10,* 799–812.

Padgett, D. K., Patrick, C., Burns, B. J., & Schlesinger, H. J. (1994). Women and outpatient mental health services: Use by black, Hispanic, and white women in a national insured population. *The Journal of Mental Health Administration, 21,* 347–360.

Palmer, B. W., Heaton, R. K., Paulsen, J. S., Kuck, J., Braff, D., Harris, M. J., Zisook, S., & Jeste, D.V. (1997). Is it possible to be schizophrenic yet neuropsychologically normal? *Neuropsychology, 11,* 437–446.

Palmer, B. A., Pankratz, V. S., & Bostwick, J. M. (2005). The lifetime risk of suicide in schizophrenia: A reexamination. *Archives of General Psychiatry, 62,* 247–253.

Parra, F. (1985). Social tolerance of the mentally ill in the Mexican American community. *International Journal of Social Psychiatry, 31,* 37–47.

Parrott, B., & Lewine, R. (2005). Socioeconomic status of origin and the clinical expression of schizophrenia. *Schizophrenia Research, 75,* 417–424.

Patterson, T. L., Goldman, S., McKibbin, C. L., Hughs, T., & Jeste, D. (2001). UCSD performance-based skills assessment: Development of a new measure of everyday functioning for severely mentally ill adults. *Schizophrenia Bulletin, 27,* 235–245.

Pearlson, G. D. (2000). Neurobiology of schizophrenia. *Annals of Neurology, 48,* 556–566.

Peen, J. & Dekker, J. (1997). Admission rates for schizophrenia in the Netherlands: An urban/rural comparison. *Acta Psychiatrica Scandinavica, 96,* 301–305.

Penn, D. L., Combs, D. R., & Mohamed, S. (2001). Social cognition and social functioning in schizophrenia. In P. W. Corrigan & D. L. Penn (Eds.), *Social cognition and schizophrenia* (pp. 97–122). Washington, DC: American Psychological Association.

Penn, D. L., Corrigan, P. W., Bentall, R. P., Racenstein, J. M., & Newman, L. (1997). Social cognition in schizophrenia. *Psychological Bulletin, 121,* 114–132.

Penn, D., Hope, D. A., Spaulding, W. D., & Kucera, J. (1994). Social anxiety in schizophrenia. *Schizophrenia Research, 11,* 277–284.

Penn, D. L., Mueser, K. T., Spaulding, W. D., Hope, D. A., & Reed, D. (1995). Information processing and social competence in chronic schizophrenia. *Schizophrenia Bulletin, 21,* 269–281.

Penn, D. L., Waldheter, E. J., Perkins, D. O., Mueser, K. T., & Lieberman, J. A. (2005). Psychosocial treatment for first-episode psychosis: A research update. *American Journal of Psychiatry, 162,* 2220–2232.

Perlstein, W. M., Carter, C. S., Noll, D.C., & Cohen, J. D. (2001). Relation of prefrontal cortex dysfunction to working memory and symptoms of schizophrenia. *American Journal of Psychiatry, 158,* 1105–1113.

Phillips, S. D., Burns, B. J., Edgar, E. R., Mueser, K. T., Linkins, K. W., Rosenheck, R. A., Drake, R. E., & Herr, E. C. M. (2001). Moving Assertive Community Treatment into standard practice. *Psychiatric Services, 52,* 771–779.

Pinkham, A., Penn, D., Perkins, D., & Lieberman, J. (2003). Implications for the neural basis of social cognition for the study of schizophrenia. *The American Journal of Psychiatry, 160,* 815–824.

Pitschel-Walz, G., Leucht, S., Bäuml, J., Kissling, W., & Engel, R. R. (2001). The effect of family interventions on relapse and rehospitalization in schizophrenia: A meta-analysis. *Schizophrenia Bulletin, 27,* 73–92.

Pope, H. G., & Lipinski, J. F. (1978). Diagnosis in schizophrenia and manic-depressive illness. *Archives of General Psychiatry, 35,* 811–828.

Qin, P., & Nordentoft, M. (2005). Suicide risk in relation to psychiatric hospitalization: Evidence based on longitudinal registers. *Archives of General Psychiatry, 62,* 427–432.

Quinlivan, R., Hough, R., Crowell, A., Beach, C., Hofstetter, R., & Kenworthy, K. (1995). Service utilization and costs of care for severely mentally ill clients in an intensive case management program. *Psychiatric Services, 46,* 365–371.

Regier, D. A., Farmer, M. E., Rae, D. S., Locke, B. Z., Keith, S. J., Judd, L. L., & Goodwin, F. K. (1990). Comorbidity of mental disorders with alcohol and other drug abuse. *Journal of the American Medical Association, 264,* 2511–2518.

Resnick, H. S., Kilpatrick, D. G., Dansky, B. S., Saunders, B. E., & Best, C. L. (1993). Prevalence of civilian trauma and post-traumatic stress disorder in a representative national sample of women. *Journal of Consulting and Clinical Psychology, 61,* 984–991.

Robins, L. N. (1966). *Deviant children grown up.* Huntington, NY: Krieger.

Robins, L. N., & Price, R. K. (1991). Adult disorders predicted by childhood conduct problems: Results from the NIMH Epidemiologic Catchment Area project. *Psychiatry, 54,* 116–132.

Rodrigo, G., Lusiardo, M., Briggs, G., & Ulmer, A. (1991). Differences between schizophrenics born in winter and summer. *Acta Psychiatrica Scandinavica, 84,* 320–322.

Rose, S. M., Peabody, C. G., & Stratigeas, B. (1991). Undetected abuse among intensive case management clients. *Hospital and Community Psychiatry, 42,* 499–503.

Rosenberg, S. D., Drake, R. E., Wolford, G. L., Mueser, K. T., Oxman, T. E., Vidaver, R. M., Carrieri, K. L., & Luckoor, R. (1998). Dartmouth assessment of lifestyle instrument (DALI): A substance use disorder screen for people with severe mental illness. *The American Journal of Psychiatry, 155,* 232–238.

Rosenberg, S. D., Mueser, K. T., Friedman, M. J., Gorman, P. G., Drake, R. E., Vidaver, R. M., Torrey, W. C., & Jankowski, M. K. (2001). Developing effective treatments for posttraumatic disorders: A review and proposal. *Psychiatric Services, 52,* 1453–1461.

Rosenheck, R., Leslie, D., Keefe, R., McEvoy, J., Swartz, M., Perkins, D., Stroup, S., Hsiao, J. K., & Lieberman, J. (2006). Barriers to employment for people with schizophrenia. *The American Journal of Psychiatry, 163,* 411–417.

Ross, C. A., Anderson, G., & Clark, P. (1994). Childhood abuse and the positive symptoms of schizophrenia. *Hospital and Community Psychiatry, 45,* 489–491.

Roy, A. (Ed.) (1986). *Suicide.* Baltimore: Williams and Wilkins.

Rutter, M. (1984). Psychopathology and development: I. Childhood antecedents of adult psychiatric disorder. *Australian and New Zealand Journal of Psychiatry, 18,* 225–234.

Saha, S., Chant, D., Welham, J., & McGrath, J. (2005). A systematic review of the prevalence of schizophrenia. *Public Library of Science, 2,* e141.

Salem, J. E., & Kring, A. M. (1998). The role of gender in the reduction of etiologic heterogeneity in schizophrenia. *Clinical Psychology Review, 18,* 795–819.

Salokangas, R. K. R. (1978). Socioeconomic development and schizophrenia. *Psychiatria Fennica, 103–112.*

Samele, C., van Os, J., McKenzie, K., Wright, A., Gilvarry, C., Manley, C., Tattan, T., & Murray, R. (2001). Does socioeconomic status predict course and outcome in patients with psychosis? *Social Psychiatry and Psychiatric Epidemiology, 36,* 573- 581.

Sammons, M. T. (2005). Pharmacotherapy for delusional disorder and associated conditions. *Professional Psychology: Research and Practice, 36,* 476–479.

Sands, J. R., & Harrow, M. (1999). Depression during the longitudinal course of schizophrenia. *Schizophrenia Bulletin, 25,* 157–171.

Sartorius, N., Jablensky, A., Korten, A., Ernberg, G., Anker, M., Cooper, J. E., & Day, R. (1986). Early manifestations and first-contact incidence of schizophrenia in different cultures. *Psychological Medicine, 16,* 909–928.

Schaub, A., Behrendt, B., Brenner, H. D., Mueser, K. T., & Liberman, R. P. (1998). Training schizophrenic patients to manage their symptoms: Predictors of treatment response to the German Version of the Symptom Management Module. *Schizophrenia Research, 31,* 121–130.

Schiffman, J., Walker, E., Ekstrom, M., Schulsinger, F., Sorensen, H., & Mednick, S. (2004). Childhood videotaped social and neuromotor precursors of schizophrenia: A prospective investigation. *The American Journal of Psychiatry, 161,* 2021–2027.

Schock, K., Clay, C., & Cipani, E. (1998). Making sense of schizophrenic symptoms: Delusional statements and behavior may be functional in purpose. *Journal of Behavior Therapy and Experimental Psychiatry, 29,* 131–141.

Schuckit, M. A. (1995). *Drug and alcohol abuse: A clinical guide to diagnosis and treatment (Critical issues in psychiatry)* (4th ed.). New York: Plenum Press.

Searles, H. (1965). *Collected papers on schizophrenia and related subjects.* New York: International Universities Press.

Sedler, M. J. (1995). Understanding delusions. *The Psychiatric Clinics of North America, 18,* 251–262.

Sevy, S., & Davidson, M. (1995). The cost of cognitive impairment in schizophrenia. *Schizophrenia Research, 17,* 1–3.

Silver, E., Arseneault, L., Langley, J., Caspi, A., & Moffitt, T. E. (2005). Mental disorder and violent victimization in a total birth cohort. *American Journal of Public Health, 95,* 2015–2021.

Skilbeck, W. M., Acosta, F. X., Yamamoto, J., & Evans, L. A. (1984). Self-reported psychiatric symptoms among black, Hispanic, and white outpatients. *Journal of Clinical Psychology, 40,* 1184–1189.

Smith, T. E., Hull, J. W., Anthony, D. T., Goodman, M., Hedayat-Harris, A., Felger, T., Kentros, M. K., MacKain, S. J., & Romanelli, S. (1997). Post-hospitalization treatment adherence of schizophrenic patients: Gender differences in skill acquisition. *Psychiatry Research, 69,* 123–129.

Smith, T. E., Hull, J. W., Romanelli, S., Fertuck, E., & Weiss, K. A. (1999). Symptoms and neu-rocognition as rate limiters in skills training for psychotic patients. *The American Journal of Psychiatry, 156,* 1817–1818.

Steadman, H. J., Mulvey, E. P., Monahan, J., Robbins, P. C., Appelbaum, P. S., Grisso, T., Roth, L. H., & Silver, E. (1998). Violence by people discharged from acute psychiatric inpatient facilities and by others in the same neighborhoods. *Archives of General Psychiatry, 55,* 393–401.

Stone, A., Greenstein, R., Gamble, G., & McLellan, A. T. (1993). Cocaine use in chronic schizo-phrenic outpatients receiving depot neuroleptic medications. *Hospital and Community Psychiatry, 44,* 176–177.

Sue, D. W., & Sue, D. C. (1990). *Counseling the culturally different: Theory and practice* (2nd ed.). New York: Wiley.

Sue, S., Fujino, D. C., Hu, L-T., Takeuchi, D. T., & Zane, N. W. S. (1991). Community mental health services for ethnic minority groups: A test of the cultural responsiveness hypothesis. *Journal of Consulting and Clinical Psychology, 59,* 533–540.

Susser, E., & Lin, S. (1992). Schizophrenia after prenatal exposure to the Dutch Hunger Winter of 1944–1945. *Archives of General Psychiatry, 49,* 983–988.

Susser, E., Neugebauer, R., Hoek, H. W., Brown, A. S., Lin, S., Labovitz, D., & Gorman, J. M. (1996). Schizophrenia after prenatal famine: Further evidence. *Archives of General Psychiatry, 53,* 25–31.

Susser, E., Struening, E. L., & Conover, S. (1989). Psychiatric problems in homeless men: Lifetime psychosis, substance use, and current distress in new arrivals at New York City shelters. *Archives of General Psychiatry, 46,* 845–850.

Swanson, J. W. (1994). Mental disorder, substance abuse, and community violence: An epide-miological approach. In J. Monahan & H. Steadman (Eds.), *Violence and mental disorder: Developments in risk assessment* (pp. 101–136). Chicago: University of Chicago Press.

Swanson, J. W., Holzer, C. E., Ganju, V. K., & Jono, R. T. (1990). Violence and psychiatric disorder in the community: Evidence from the Epidemiologic Catchment Area Surveys. *Hospital and Community Psychiatry, 41,* 761–770.

Swartz, M. S., Swanson, J. W., Hiday, V. A., Borum, R., Wagner, H. R., & Burns, B. J. (1998). Violence and severe mental illness: The effects of substance abuse and nonadherence to medication. *The American Journal of Psychiatry, 155,* 226–231.

Switzer, G. E., Dew, M. A., Thompson, K., Goycoolea, J. M., Derricott, T., & Mullins, S. D. (1999). Posttraumatic stress disorder and service utilization among urban mental health center clients. *Journal of Traumatic Stress, 12,* 25–39.

Takei, N., Mortensen, P. B., Klaening, U., Murray, R. M., Sham, P. C., O'Callaghan, E., & Munk-Jorgensen, P. (1996). Relationship between in utero exposure to influenza epidemics and risk of schizophrenia in Denmark. *Biological Psychiatry, 40,* 817–824.

Takei, N., Sham, P. C., O'Callaghan, E., Glover, G., & Murray, R. M. (1995). Schizophrenia: Increased risk associated with winter and city birth—a case-control study in 12 regions within England and Wales. *Journal of Epidemiology and Community Health, 49,* 106–109.

Telles, C., Karno, M., Mintz, J., Paz, G., Arias, M., Tucker, D., & Lopez, S. (1995). Immigrant families coping with schizophrenia: Behavioral family intervention v. case manage-ment with a low-income Spanish-speaking population. *British Journal of Psychiatry, 167,* 473–479.

Terkelsen, K. G. (1983) Schizophrenia and the family: II. Adverse effects of family therapy. *Family Process, 22,* 191–200.

Tessler, R., & Gamache, G. (1995). *Evaluating family experiences with severe mental illness: To be used in conjunction with the Family Experiences Interview Schedule*

(FEIS): The Evaluation Center @ HSRI toolkit. Cambridge, MA: The Evaluation Center @ HSRI.

Test, M. A., Wallisch, L. S., Allness, D. J., & Ripp, K. (1989). Substance use in young adults with schizophrenic disorders. *Schizophrenia Bulletin, 15,* 465–476.

Thomas, H. V., Dalman, C., David, A. S., Gentz, J., Lewis, G., & Allebeck, P. (2001). Obstetric complications and risk of schizophrenia: Effect of gender, age at diagnosis and maternal history of psychosis. *British Journal of Psychiatry, 179,* 409–414.

Tien, A. Y., & Eaton, W. W. (1992). Psychopathologic precursors and sociodemographic risk factors for the schizophrenia syndrome. *Archives of General Psychiatry, 49,* 37–46.

Tienari, P. (1991). Interaction between genetic vulnerability and family environment: The Finnish Adoptive Family Study of schizophrenia. *Acta Psychiatrica Scandinavica, 84,* 460–465.

Tienari, P., Sorri, A., Lahti, I., Naarala, M., Wahlberg, K., Moring, J., Pohjola, J., & Wynne, L. C. (1987). Genetic and psychosocial factors in schizophrenia: The Finnish Adoptive Family Study. *Schizophrenia Bulletin, 13,* 477–484.

Tienari, P., Wynne, L. C., Sorri, A., Lahti, I., Lasky, K., Moring, J., Naarala, M., Nieminen, P., & Wahlberg, K. (2004). Genotype-environment interaction in schizophrenia spectrum disorder. *British Journal of Psychiatry, 184,* 216–222.

Tjaden, P., & Thoennes, N. (1998, November). *Prevalence, incidence, and consequences of violence against women: Findings from the National Violence against Women Survey* (Research in Brief). Washington, DC: U.S. Department of Justice, National Institute of Justice.

Tohen, M., Strakowski, S. M., Zarate, C., Hennen, J., Stoll, A. L., Suppes, T., Faedda, G., Cohen, B. M., Gebre-Medhin, P., & Baldessarinis, R. J. (2000). The Mclean-Harvard first episode project: Six month symptomatic and functional outcome in affective and nonaffective psychosis. *Biological Psychiatry, 48,* 467–476.

Tollefson, G. D., & Sanger, T. M. (1997). Negative symptoms: A path analytic approach to a double-blind, placebo- and haloperidol-controlled clinical trial with olanzapine. *American Journal of Psychiatry, 154,* 466–474.

Torrey, E. F. (1992). Are we overestimating the genetic contribution to schizophrenia? *Schizophrenia Bulletin, 18,* 159–170.

Torrey, E. F. (2001). *Surviving schizophrenia* (4th ed.). New York: HarperCollins.

Torrey, E. F., Bowler, A. E., & Clark, K. (1997). Urban birth and residence as risk factors for psychoses: An analysis of 1880 data. *Schizophrenia Research, 25,* 169–176.

Torrey, E. F., Bowler, A. E., Rawlings, R., & Terrazas, A. (1993). Seasonality of schizophrenia and stillbirths. *Schizophrenia Bulletin, 19,* 557–562.

Torrey, E. F., Stieber, J., Ezekiel, J., Wolfe, S. M., Sharfstein, J., Noble, J. H., & Flynn, L. M. (1992). *Criminalizing the seriously mentally ill: The abuse of jails as mental hospitals. Joint Report of the National Alliance of the Mentally Ill.* Washington, DC: Public Citizen's Health Research Group.

Tsuang, M. T. (1986). Predictors of poor and good outcome in schizophrenia. In L. Erlenmeyer-Kimling & N. E. Miller (Eds.), *Life-span research on the prediction of psychopathology.* Hillsdale, NJ: Erlbaum.

Uttaro, T., & Mechanic, D. (1994). The NAMI consumer survey analysis of unmet needs. *Hospital and Community Psychiatry, 45,* 372–374.

Valenstein, M., Blow, F. C., Copeland, L. A., McCarthy, J. F., Zeber, J. E., Gillon, L., Bingham, C. R., & Stavenger, T. (2004). Poor antipsychotic adherence among patients with schizophrenia: Medication and patient factors. *Schizophrenia Bulletin, 30,* 255–264.

Van Der Does, A. J. W., Dingemans, P. M. A. J., Linszen, D. H., Nugter, M. A., & Scholte, W. F. (1993). Symptom dimensions and cognitive and social functioning in recent-onset schizophrenia. *Psychological Medicine, 23,* 745–753.

Velligan, D. I., Mahurin, R. K., Diamond, P. L., Hazleton, B. C., Eckert, S. L., & Miller, A. L. (1997). The functional significance of symptomatology and cognitive function in schizophrenia. *Schizophrenia Research, 25,* 21–31.

Wahlbeck, K., Cheine, M., Essali, A., & Adams, C. (1999). Evidence of clozapine's effectiveness in schizophrenia: A systematic review and meta-analysis of randomized trials. *The American Journal of Psychiatry, 156,* 990–999.

Walker, E., Downey, G., & Caspi, A. (1991). Twin studies of psychopathology: Why do the concordance rates vary? *Schizophrenia Research, 5,* 211–221.

Walker, E. F., Grimes, K. E., Davis, D. M., & Smith, A. J. (1993). Childhood precursors of schizophrenia: Facial expressions of emotion. *The American Journal of Psychiatry, 150,* 1654–1660.

Wallace, C. J., Liberman, R. P., Tauber, R., & Wallace, J. (2000). The Independent Living Skills Survey: A comprehensive measure of the community functioning of severely and persistently mentally ill individuals. *Schizophrenia Bulletin, 26,* 631–658.

Watt, N. F. (1978). Patterns of childhood social development in adult schizophrenics. *Archives of General Psychiatry, 35,* 160–165.

Waxler, N. E., & Mishler, E. G. (1971). Parental interaction with schizophrenic children and well siblings. *Archives of General Psychiatry, 25,* 223–231.

Webb, C., Pfeiffer, M., Mueser, K. T., Mensch, E., DeGirolamo, J., & Levenson, D. F. (1998). Burden and well-being of caregivers for the severely mentally ill: The role of coping style and social support. *Schizophrenia Research, 34,* 169–180.

Westermeyer, J. (1989). Psychiatric epidemiology across cultures: Current issues and trends. *Transcultural Psychiatric Research Review, 26,* 5–25.

Whaley, A. L. (1997). Ethnicity, race, paranoia, and psychiatric diagnoses: Clinician bias versus socio-cultural differences. *Journal of Psychopathology and Behavioral Assessment, 19,* 1–20.

Whaley, A. L. (2001). Cultural mistrust: An important psychological construct for diagnosis and treatment of African-Americans. *Professional Psychology: Research and Practice, 32,* 555–562.

Wilk, C. M., Gold, J. M., McMahon, R. P., Humber, K., Iannone, V. N., & Buchanan, R. W. (2005). No, it is not possible to be schizophrenic yet neuropsychologically normal. *Neuropsychology, 6,* 778–786.

Wright, I. C., Rabe-Hesketh, S., Woodruff, P. W. R., David, A. S., Murrary, R. M., & Bullmore, E. T. (2000). Meta-analysis of regional brain volumes in schizophrenia. *The American Journal of Psychiatry, 157,* 16–25.

Wu, E. Q., Birnbaum, H. G., Shi, L., Ball, D. E., Kessler R. C., Moulis, M., & Aggarwal, J. (2005). The economic burden of schizophrenia in the United States in 2002. *The Journal of Clinical Psychiatry, 66,* 1122–1129.

Xiong, W., Phillips, M. R., Hu, X., Ruiwen, W., Dai, Q., Kleinman, J., & Kleinman, A. (1994). Family-based intervention for schizophrenic patients in China: A randomised controlled trial. *British Journal of Psychiatry, 165,* 239–247.

Yamada, N., Nakajima, S., & Noguchi, T. (1998). Age at onset of delusional disorder is dependent on the delusional theme. *Acta Psychiatrica Scandinavica, 97,* 122–124.

Young, C. R., Bowers, M. B., & Mazure, C. M. (1998). Management of the adverse effects of clozapine. *Schizophrenia Bulletin, 24,* 381–390.

Yung, A. R., & McGorry, P. D. (1996). The initial prodrome in psychosis: Descriptive and qualitative aspects. *The Australian and New Zealand Journal of Psychiatry, 30,* 587–599.

Zhang, M., Wang, M., Li, J., & Phillips, M. R. (1994). Randomised-control trial of family intervention for 78 first-episode male schizophrenic patients: An 18-month study in Suzhou, Jiangsu. *British Journal of Psychiatry, 165,* 96–102.

Zigler, E., & Glick, M. (1986). *A developmental approach to adult psychopathology.* New York: Wiley.

Zubin, J., & Spring, B. (1977). Vulnerability: A new view of schizophrenia. *Journal of Abnormal Psychology, 86,* 103–123.

CHAPTER 9

Mood Disorders: Depressive Disorders

LEILANI FELICIANO AND PATRICIA A. AREÁN

DESCRIPTION OF THE DISORDERS

Depressive disorders are among the most common psychiatric disorders occurring in both younger and older adults. They are characterized by feelings of sadness, lack of interest in formerly enjoyable pursuits, sleep and appetite disturbances, feelings of worthlessness, and at times thoughts of death and dying. In older adults, depressive disorders may present differently, with less reported sadness and depression and more somatic complaints.

All depressive disorders are extremely disabling, second only to heart disease as the illness most responsible for poor quality of life and disability (Pincus & Pettit, 2001). Depression is also associated with increased suicide risk. Statistics show that 15% of people with major depression complete suicide (Satcher, 2000). Fortunately, depressive disorders can be treated successfully with psychotherapy, antidepressant medication, or both (Moore & Bona, 2001). The research on these disorders continues to grow, and we know quite a bit about how depressive disorders are presented, their etiology, and their course and prognosis. The purpose of this chapter is to describe the depressive disorders, discuss their prevalence and effects on people who have these disorders, examine best methods for assessing depressive disorders, and present the latest research on their etiology.

According to the fourth edition of the *Diagnostic and Statistical Manual of Mental Disorders (DSM-IV;* American Psychiatric Association, 1994), depressive disorders include three categories of illnesses: *major depression (MDD), dysthymia,* and *depressive disorder not otherwise specified (depression NOS).* As outlined in Table 9.1, all three categories share common symptoms and clinical features. First, all three disorders consist of mood symptoms, which include feeling sad, empty, worried, and irritable. Second, these disorders are characterized by vegetative symptoms, which include fatigue, social withdrawal, and agitation. Disturbances

Table 9.1

DSM-IV Symptoms Required for Major Depressive Disorder and Dysthymia

Major Depressive Disorder	Dysthymia
5 of 9 symptoms must be present most of the day, nearly every day, for at least 2 weeks:	Depressed mood most days, for most of the week, for 2 years. Plus 2 or more of 6 symptoms:
1. Depressed mood	1. Poor appetite or overeating
2. Diminished interest or pleasure in all, or almost all, activities (One of the above is required.)	2. Insomnia or hypersomnia
	3. Low energy or fatigue
3. Significant weight loss or weight gain or a decrease or increase in appetite	4. Low self-esteem
	5. Poor concentration or difficulty making decisions
4. Insomnia or hypersomnia	6. Feelings of hopelessness
5. Psychomotor agitation or retardation	
6. Fatigue or loss of energy	
7. Feelings of worthless or excessive or inappropriate guilt	
8. Diminished ability to think or concentrate, or to make decisions	
9. Recurrent thoughts of death, suicidal ideation, plans, or attempts	

in sleep and appetite are also common, with lack of sleep and appetite being more typical in depression, although patients with an atypical presentation (discussed later) will complain of hypersomnia (increased sleep) or weight gain caused by frequent eating. Finally, all three disorders consist of cognitive symptoms. These include trouble concentrating; difficulty making decisions; low self-esteem; negative thoughts about oneself, the world, and others; guilt; and suicidal ideation. In its most severe forms, hallucinations and delusions are also seen (more common in individuals over the age of 50). The degree to which these features occur and the number of symptoms present will determine which type of depressive disorder a person may be experiencing. Next we discuss each disorder to clarify how it can be distinguished from the others.

MAJOR DEPRESSIVE DISORDER

Major depressive disorder (MDD) is the most serious and most widely studied depressive disorder. It is characterized by at least one major depressive episode, with no history of mania (period of intense energy, euphoria, distorted thinking, and behavioral excesses). To qualify for a major depressive episode, either depressed mood or lack of interest or pleasure in usual activities (anhedonia) must be present, most of the day, nearly every day, and the episode must last at least 2 weeks. In addition, at least five out of nine possible symptoms (listed in Table 9.1) present during that same period. The symptoms must be severe enough to interfere with the individual's social or occupational functioning. Major depressive disorder is further qualified as to its severity, chronicity, and remission status. Severity is generally determined by the degree of disability experienced by the affected person. If the person can continue to pursue obligations (work, family, and social activities) the depression is ranked as mild. If the person has trouble getting out of bed and can no longer engage in any obligated activities, the depression is ranked as moderate. If a person is thinking of death or dying; is so vegetative that he or she has not gotten out of bed, eaten, or engaged in any self-management activities; or is exhibiting psychotic behavior, then the depression is ranked as severe. Although rare, a depressed person can exhibit symptoms of catatonia, which is characterized by immobility, excessive motor activity, extreme negativism or mutism, and bizarre posturing. A person will be diagnosed as having MDD, recurrent type if there has been more than one episode of MDD. Chronic MDD is characterized by symptoms of MDD that can last for as long as 2 or more years. Because research has found MDD to be a recurrent disorder (single episodes are rare), if a person has had an episode of MDD but is no longer experiencing any depressive symptoms, that person is considered to be in remission.

MDD can be further delineated by type. The *DSM-IV* describes the concept of endogenous depression, which is subsumed under the category of melancholic depression. This category is characterized by lack of reactivity to pleasurable stimuli, experiencing more severe depression in the morning, and excessive guilt. Some researchers have suggested that this subtype is more typically associated with biological etiology and that it may be more responsive to psychopharmacological intervention than to psychotherapies (Simons & Thase, 1992). Typical features of depression include temporary brightening of mood in response to actual or potential positive events, weight gain, hypersomnia, a heavy feeling in arms or legs, and interpersonal sensitivity to rejection. These symptoms tend to be interpreted as suggesting a depressive disorder that is more likely to respond to psychosocial interventions than to medications and may be more stress related (Beck, 1961; Klerman, 1986).

DYSTHYMIA

Dysthymic disorder is typically thought to be a chronic depression (lasting 2 years or more) but one that is not as severe as major depression. Unlike MDD, dysthymia has only one typical presentation. Because of its chronicity and its lack of responsiveness to existing treatments, some feel that dysthymia may more accurately be considered a personality disorder rather than an acute illness like MDD. This opinion, however, is hotly contested.

The symptoms of dysthymia (listed in Table 9.1) must be present for 2 years, during which time there should be no more than a 2-month period in which the person is symptom free. Additionally, no major depressive episode during the first 2 years of dysthymia should have been present, although one could occur after the 2-year period. If MDD occurs after the 2-year period, it is commonly described as double depression. Symptoms of dysthymia must not be due exclusively to other disorders (including medical conditions) or to the direct physiological effects of a substance (including medication). As in MDD, the person must not ever have met criteria for manic episode, hypomanic episode, or cyclothymic disorder. If dysthymia occurs before age 21, it is described as having early onset; otherwise it is described as having late onset.

DEPRESSIVE DISORDER NOT OTHERWISE SPECIFIED

This category is a catchall for depressive conditions that are provisionary and have yet to be studied in depth. This category includes *premenstrual dysphoric disorder,* a mood disorder thought to be caused by hormonal fluctuations in the female menstrual cycle (with symptoms more severe than what is typically seen with premenstrual syndrome); *minor depressive disorder,* depressive episodes lasting for at least 2 weeks but with fewer than the five items needed to meet criteria for major depressive episode; *recurrent brief depressive disorder,* which is characterized by repeated episodes of depression that last for less than 2 weeks; *postpsychotic depressive disorder of schizophrenia,* a depression that follows a psychotic episode; *major depressive episode superimposed on psychotic or delusional disorders,* depression that co-occurs with a psychotic disorder; and *depression due to general medical conditions,* which is depression thought to be present but not able to be determined to be primary because of medical conditions or substance use.

DISCRETE VERSUS CONTINUOUS CONCEPTUALIZATIONS OF DEPRESSION

There has been considerable debate about whether depression types are best thought of as discrete illnesses or if depression is one illness along a severity continuum. As knowledge on depression advances, there is a strong movement toward considering both arguments in diagnosing and treating patients. As an example, most clinicians consider MDD to be a different disorder from dysthymia, requiring different treatment choices. However, clinicians also believe that within each disorder, there will be considerable variation in the degree to which the illness affects each patient. Moreover, it is very likely that minor depression is a precursor to a major depressive episode and thus may be important to treat to prevent clinical episodes of depression (Munoz, 1993).

WHEN DEPRESSION IS NOT A DEPRESSIVE DISORDER

Sometimes symptoms of depression may be present but may not be diagnosed as one of the depressive disorders. It is important to note that depressive disorders are different than sadness brought on by grief or the loss of a loved one. If bereavement accounts for symptoms of depression, and if these symptoms have not persisted longer than 2 months after such loss, then the episode is not major depression. People who become depressed after a significant life stressor for a short time are more likely to be suffering from an adjustment disorder rather than a mood disorder. Furthermore, a previous manic episode will also exclude a diagnosis of MDD. Finally, if the depressed person has a medical disorder known to cause symptoms of depression (e.g., hyperthyroidism), then the symptoms are classified as depression due to a general medical condition.

Everyone experiences feelings of sadness from time to time. This is a normal experience that should not be pathologized. Depressive symptoms are considered problematic when the symptoms persist for 2 weeks or more and are accompanied by considerable difficulty coping with day-to-day activities. In the next section, we provide examples of these disorders.

Case Studies

To illustrate the disorders just discussed, we will present three cases: one that describes the presentation of MDD, the second, dysthymia, and the third, depression NOS.

Major Depression

R.J. was a single 32-year-old African American woman seeking mental health services for what she called depression. R.J. was the younger of two female siblings from the northwestern section of the United States. As a child she did not have time for friends, as she was often caring for her sick mother. She was a good student but had dropped out of high school to care for her mother. Her father had left her mother and moved out of state shortly before her mother became ill. R.J. had a large extended family but acutely felt the loss of a father figure. Her uncle had problems with drugs and was incarcerated. Subsequently she had taken on the care of her younger niece and nephews.

As an adult, R.J. had success in school (she was able to achieve her GED and was successfully taking college courses) and in her work. She believed that she had suffered from depression twice before in her adult life but had always been able to overcome the depression on her own. However, she had often turned to food for comfort and was suffering from obesity. She explained that she had never sought help for her depression before because she was busy caring for her family and did not take time for herself. Further, she indicated that it was not like her to talk with someone about her feelings. She indicated that her family tended to "make light of everything" and rarely shared their feelings. She believed her mother was depressed following the loss of her husband and subsequent medical problems but was unsure of these facts, since these issues were never discussed.

Before seeking services, R.J. had contemplated getting gastric bypass surgery and was extremely unhappy with her employment. She was managing several large projects for the company and felt that she was the only member of her staff who was doing any work. She felt that she was not trusted to do her job, was not respected for the work she did, and was being taken for granted. She was also concerned about getting the surgery because she would need recovery time and would be unable to care for her family members. Her symptoms included feeling depressed nearly all day, every day for the last 12 months; feeling a lack of interest in her usual activities (in this case walking and attending a weight-loss program); and increased irritability. For the last 12 months, she reported insomnia, increased appetite, and feelings of worthlessness and hopelessness about the future. She reported feelings of guilt, believed that she was being punished, and constantly worried that she was not doing enough for her family. In addition, she reported having difficulty concentrating and making decisions. Although she had occasionally felt that she would be better off dead, she was not suicidal. She did not feel that suicide was an option and had no plan to harm herself. She wanted help, was interested in nonpharmacological treatment for her depression, but struggled with the belief that therapy was an indulgence.

Dysthymia

B.G. was a 55-year-old retired Caucasian man who sought services for depression after a doctor recommended he talk to a mental health professional. B.G. was the oldest of five in his family and was currently married with three children, all of whom were grown and living in other parts of the country. He completed high school and trade school afterward. He had been employed with one construction company his entire adult life. He was living with his wife at the time of his intake. He had no serious health problems other than chronic pain resulting from a back injury. B.G. retired because of a back injury that prevented him from performing his job. Three years ago, his wife took on a part-time job to make extra money, and B.G. began looking after the house. Prior to this visit, he had never sought mental health services, nor had he ever felt depressed. B.G. stated that for the last 3 years, he occasionally felt worthless, depressed, and irritable. He reported that some days he often found it difficult to get himself going to complete his chores for the day but would somehow manage to do so. He indicated that he was unsure of treatment, because he had "good days," but upon further probing he reported that these days were infrequent (no more than 1 or 2 days a week). Although he said he and his wife did not have marital problems, he felt guilty that she worked and he did not. The primary symptoms he complained about were occasional sadness, lack of energy, irritability, feelings of worthlessness, and guilt.

Depression NOS

T.J. was a 40-year-old woman who was referred by her physician for treatment of depression. She was an only child who was living with her mother at the time of referral. She had a college education and had been employed as an administrative assistant for 10 years. She was divorced with no children. According to the physician, T.J. was struggling with placing her elderly mother in a nursing home, and this struggle made her quite depressed. The provider indicated that T.J. had a recent diagnosis of hyperthyroidism and was being treated with medication. T.J. stated that she had been feeling depressed for a number of months, ever since her mother had become more seriously ill and T.J. began trying to find a nursing home for her. T.J. had indicated that she had been her mother's caregiver for most of her life and that they had a "love-hate" relationship. Her mother was being verbally abusive to T.J. regarding the placement, making T.J. feel guilty. T.J. indicated that she would normally be able to let her mother's abuse roll off her back, having long ago accepted that her mother was a difficult person. However, the last 4 months were hard to cope with, even though she had a good caseworker helping her and that

(continued)

her mother would be placed in a pleasant assisted-living facility within the next month. Her primary complaints were depression and sadness nearly all day, every day; feeling slowed down; and trouble with concentration. She also indicated that having had a recent diagnosis of hyperthyroidism complicated matters for her and that she had been unable to take her medication regularly. T.J. was encouraged to start taking her medication for hyperthyroidism and was educated about the link between the illness and depressive symptoms. T.J. and her therapist agreed to meet again in 2 weeks. At that meeting, T.J. reported that her mother had been placed in the assisted-living facility and that while she felt guilty for a few days, she found that her mother was actually quite happy at the facility. She also reported taking the medication regularly and stated she already felt much better ("like my old self"), although she was still somewhat symptomatic of depression (occasional sadness and poor energy). Now that her mother had been successfully placed, T.J. indicated that she would like to work on rebuilding her social life.

EPIDEMIOLOGY

The patients described in this chapter are representative of a growing number of people in the United States suffering from depressive disorders. Several large-scale epidemiological studies on mental illness have taken place in the United States. The Epidemiological Catchment Area Study (ECA) was conducted in the 1980s (Regier, 1988) and was the first to definitively determine the prevalence of psychiatric problems in the United States. The second study, called the National Comorbidity Study (NCS; Kessler, McGonagle, Zhao, et al., 1994) focused specifically on English-speaking adults between the ages of 18 and 65 and was mostly concerned with prevalence of co-occurring *DSM-III-R* psychiatric disorders in the United States. The NCS study was recently replicated in 2005 to examine the prevalence for the updated *DSM-IV* and the *International Classification of Disease, version 10 (ICD-10)* psychiatric disorders and provide age of onset estimates for mental health disorders in a representative U.S. sample (Kessler et al., 2005).

The data from these studies demonstrate that the prevalence of depressive disorders varies from population to population. The following discussion will therefore present the prevalence of depressive disorders by the different populations.

COMMUNITY SAMPLES

The lifetime prevalence rate, or the number of persons who have ever experienced any type of mood disorder, is 20.8% (Kessler et al., 2005), whereas the prevalence rate for an episode of major depression ranges from 5.8% (Regier, 1988) to 12% (Kessler, McGonagle, Zhao, et al., 1994), in community-dwelling individuals using *DSM-III* and *DSM-III-R* diagnostic criteria. When using the *DSM-IV* criteria, the lifetime prevalence rates of MDD increase to 16.6% (Kessler et al., 2005). These studies also indicate that in a given 6-month period, approximately 3% to 9% of the general population will experience an episode of major depression (Kessler, McGonagle, Zhao, et al., 1994; Regier, 1988). The lifetime prevalence rates for dysthymia are lower than the rates for major depression. According to the NCS and the NCS-R, between 2.5% and 6% of the general population has had a period of dysthymia in their lifetimes. Rates for bipolar I and II disorder were 3.9%, and rates of other depressive disorders were not available.

Prevalence by Gender

The ECA and the NCS show differential prevalence rates by gender. In the ECA studies, lifetime prevalence rates of affective disorders for adult women average 6.6% whereas in the NCS, rates are significantly higher, at 21.3% (Kessler, McGonagle, Nelson, et al., 1994; Regier, 1988). The lifetime rates for men, on the other hand, were 8.2% in the ECA, and 12.7% in the NCS. While the rates for depression varied between these two studies, a consistent theme emerges: that is, more women report having depressive episodes than men. Differences in rates between men and women have been found repeatedly throughout the world and thus appear to be accurate reflections of true differences in the prevalence of the disorder between men and women (Angold, Weissman, John, Wickramaratne, & Prusoff, 1991; Kessler, McGonagle, Nelson, et al., 1994). Although the reasons for these differences are relatively unknown, some speculate that biological differences, differences in cognitive and behavioral patterns of mood control (Nolen-Hoeksema, 2000), and social influences, including differential expectations for the two genders, account for the difference in prevalence.

Prevalence by Age Cohort

It has been nearly 30 years since there has been a national survey of the prevalence of psychiatric disorders in older adults. The NCS purposely excluded people aged 65 and older because the ECA data had indicated that psychiatric comorbidity was an uncommon problem in this population. The NCS-R included individuals over the age of 60 and up to the age of 75, which is an improvement over the previous sample (Kessler & Merikangas, 2004). However, the information on the differential prevalence rates of depression between younger and older people is limited and does not include our fastest-growing segment of the population, the old old, age 85 and older. As Burke, Burke, Rae, and Regier (1991) pointed out, the rates for all psychiatric disorders are increasing with each decade, indicating that disorders like depression may be influenced by cohort effects. Thus the rates of depressive disorders in older people in the ECA studies are thought to be underestimates.

With the preceding caveat in mind, it is important to highlight what is known about the prevalence of depression in older adults. The prevalence of depression among elderly populations exceeds that of any other mental disorder (Baldwin, 2000). According to the ECA, the rates for major depression in people over the age of 65 is 0.7% (Regier, 1988), whereas the rates for subsyndromal depressions, such as minor depression and dysthymia, are greater, approximately 10% to 20% (Koenig & Blazer, 1992). The NCS-R reports rates of major depression for individuals over the age of 60 to be much higher (10.6%) and dysthymia to be much lower at 1.3% (Kessler et al., 2005). The prevalence rate of depression in the United States appears to have been increasing steadily since the end of World War II: each 10-year cohort reports earlier onset of depression and a higher rate throughout the life span (Klerman, 1986). These apparent increases have been examined carefully and are found in several epidemiological databases.

PREVALENCE IN MINORITIES

Rates of depression also vary by ethnic group. According to the NCS data, African Americans have rates of depression similar to those of the Caucasian population. Approximately 3.1% of African Americans have had an MDD episode, and 3.2% have had dysthymia (Jackson-Triche et al., 2000). However, Asian Americans have the lowest rates, with only 0.8% saying they had experienced a major depression and 0.8% experiencing dysthymia (Jackson-Triche et al., 2000). Hispanics were found to have an interesting presentation of prevalence that depended on immigration status. According to Alderete, Vega, Kolody, and Aguilar-Gaxiola (1999), Hispanics who recently immigrated from Latin America were less likely to be depressed than Hispanics who were born and raised in the United States. Hispanics who were U.S.-born had prevalence rates of depression much like the rates of Caucasians (3.5% for MDD and 5% for dysthymia), whereas immigrants reported only half the prevalence rates of U.S.-born Hispanics. Although unconfirmed empirically, Vega, Kolody, Valle, and Hough (1986) believe that lower rates in immigrants result from a heartiness factor; those who are able to withstand the stress related to immigration are more likely to cope with stress related to depression.

PREVALENCE IN SPECIAL SETTINGS

Prevalence of depression in certain settings is greater than what has been found in the general community. For instance, people who are depressed are more likely to seek help in primary care settings (Wagner et al., 2000). Estimates as to the prevalence of depressive disorders vary, but most studies indicate that minor depression is the most common depressive disorder, with as many as 25% of patients meeting criteria for that disorder (Judd et al., 1998; Wagner et al., 2000). Although the prevalence of depressive disorders may be high, the recurrence rate is lower in these settings than in the community. According to van Weel-Baumgarten, Schers, van den Bosch, van den Hoogen, and Zitma (2000), patients treated in primary care medicine are less likely to suffer a relapse or remission than those treated in psychiatric settings. However, psychiatry tends to manage more severely depressed patients, and thus this findings is likely an artifact of the populations served in each setting.

Another setting with high rates for depression is the skilled nursing facility. According to Masand (1995), as many as 15% to 25% of people residing in these settings suffer from major depression. Some researchers have cited this number to have an even greater range, from 6% to 32% (Waraich, Goldner, Somers, & Hsu, 2004). The prevalence of depressive symptomatology is noted to be even higher, between 30% and 40% (Mulsant & Ganguli, 1999), with new episodes occurring in 13% of residents each year (National Institutes of Health, 1992). The causes for higher prevalence of depressive disorders in nursing home facilities may vary but most likely include loss of functional independence, loss of familiar surroundings, decreased access to pleasant activities or loved ones, and comorbid physical illnesses. Given the impact that depressive disorders have on rehabilitation, the high rate of these disorders in these settings is cause for concern and argues for more vigilant and proactive treatment of depression in skilled nursing facilities.

CLINICAL PICTURE

Major depression, dysthymia, and depression NOS all vary to a degree in their presentation but share several features that distinguish these disorders from other mental illnesses. People with depressive disorders can be identified by their pessimism and negativistic thinking, difficulty solving even everyday problems, and lack of initiative. People with depressive disorders are also quite disabled by the illness and often report having multiple somatic symptoms.

Most people with a depressive disorder exhibit what is called *negativistic thinking*. This term was coined by Aaron Beck (Beck, 1961) and has since been used extensively to describe the cognitive style of people suffering from depressive disorders. Negativistic thinking is best described as a style of thinking that is overly pessimistic and critical. People with depression tend to expect failure and disappointment at every turn and will focus only on their past failures as a way to confirm these beliefs (Alloy et al., 2000). As an example, in the first case study, R.J.'s faith in herself and others was impaired by her pessimism. Her problems with work-related stress were caused in part by the belief that no one at her place of employment was working hard enough, and her coworkers were not inclined to help her. She would take on extra work rather than delegate to her staff because she was afraid to ask them to do it, or she felt that they would do it poorly.

People with negativistic thinking also have poor self-esteem and are passive when difficulty arises (Lewinsohn, Hoberman, & Rosenbaum, 1988). In the second case study presented, B.G. often felt that because he was no longer working, he was a failure and feared that his wife saw him in the same way. When faced with a problem to solve at home, B.G. often doubted his decisions and would then avoid the problem, feeling that he was incapable of dealing with even small, mundane tasks. Even in the face of success, someone who is depressed will downplay a successful experience as an unusual event or an event that occurred despite the odds against it. In the last case example, whereas T.J. was glad to have found a residential facility for her mother, she was also cautious about this success, believing that her mother's good mood was likely to be short-lived and that she would probably be ejected from the new home.

The presence of negativistic thinking in depression is a bit of a "chicken or egg" problem: does depression cause negativistic thinking, or does negativistic thinking cause depression? Recent research suggests that the cause of depression is more likely an imbalanced thinking style and that negativistic thinking may have a clearer association with repeated exposure to failure and disappointment. In a study by Issacowitz and Seligman (2001), in fact, people with pessimistic thinking as well as those with optimistic thinking were both at risk for developing depressive symptoms after exposure to stressful life events. In fact, optimists were at higher risk for depression than pessimists were, although pessimists tended to have more persistent depression. Therefore, objective perceptions of one's abilities, of one's environment, and of other people are likely to be more protective than overly optimistic or pessimistic styles of thinking.

Negativistic thinking is primarily responsible for why depressed people find it difficult to engage in and enjoy activities that once gave them pleasure, and thus *social isolation* is a common feature of depressive disorders (Brugha et al., 1987). Many people with a depressive disorder will report that they have stopped socializing or engaging in pleasant activities, largely because they anticipate no enjoyment from the activity (Vinokur, Schul, & Caplan, 1987). R.J., for example, often reported that she did not feel "up to" going out with friends, particularly on days when she felt most depressed. She felt that when her mood was low, she was more likely to have a bad time, even though when probed about past outings with her friends she could not recall a time that was not enjoyable. It is important that people who are depressed try to reengage in social activities. Increased social isolation puts the depressed person at greater risk of severe depression. Several studies show that social support can offset occurrence or worsening of depression, and thus increasing exposure to socialization is an important process in recovering from depression (Brugha et al., 1987).

People with a depressive disorder also tend to use passive coping skills, or they avoid solving problems (Nolen-Hoeksema, Larson, & Grayson, 1999). This is sometimes due to a preexisting skills deficit or to *learned helplessness,* a condition caused by repeated attempts and failures to cope with problems (Folkman & Lazarus, 1986). Most often, after people become depressed, they avoid proactive attempts to solve problems because they anticipate that they are not capable of implementing a successful solution (Nezu, 1986). This avoidance often results in more problems; for instance, avoiding marital problems potentially results in divorce. B.G.'s marriage, while not in trouble yet, was certainly strained. He felt guilty about his wife having to work, yet he never spoke to her about this problem. Instead, he withdrew from her completely, which resulted in her feeling unsupported by him. Similarly, T.J.'s nonadherence to her new medication was a result of her avoiding "yet another problem." She was already struggling to cope with her mother's demands and had said, "I really felt like, if I ignored my illness, it was no big deal. I'd been sick a while; what's a little more time?" Unfortunately for T.J., not treating her illness most likely exacerbated her depressive symptoms.

A relatively recent movement, *positive psychology,* focuses on an individual's strengths (virtues) as well as skills deficits in the treatment of depression. Seligman and Csikszentmihalyi (2000) discuss positive psychology as an adjunct to treatment of mental health problems to provide treatment to the whole person rather than a focus on the depressive symptoms only. The main tenets involve putting our strengths to work in achieving a balance of three lives: the pleasant life, the good life, and the meaningful life. Seligman and colleagues have designed and researched a series of Internet exercises designed to increase happiness and decrease suffering. For a more detailed review see Seligman, Steen, Park, and Peterson (2005).

Many people are often surprised to discover how disabling depression is. People who are depressed will complain of somatic problems, such as fatigue, stomach upset, headaches, and joint pain (Davidson, Krishnan, France, & Pelton, 1985; Viinamaeki et al., 2000). These symptoms, coupled with the pessimism and avoidant style associated with depression, are related to the increased number of disability days reported by people with depressive disorders (Pincus & Pettit, 2001). In the NCS (Kessler & Frank, 1997), people with depression reported a fivefold increase in time lost from work than did nondepressed people. In fact, patients treated for depression incurred greater disability costs to employers than did people needing treatment for hypertension and had costs comparable to those with more severe chronic illness like diabetes (Conti & Burton, 1995; Druss, Rosenheck, & Sledge, 2000). Interestingly, costs related to treating depression are almost as great as the costs due to disability days from depression (Kessler et al., 1999), and some studies have found the treatment of depression to decrease disability days (Simon et al., 2000).

COURSE AND PROGNOSIS

Research has begun to identify variables that can predict toward better or worse course and outcome, but a great deal of uncertainty still exists. Here we present the descriptive data regarding length, severity, and prognosis of depressive disorders.

COURSE

Beyond the basic diagnostic criteria, MDD has several delineating features. Early-onset depression tends to appear before age 20 and has a more malignant course than late-onset depression. It is also associated with a family history of depression and other mood disorders. Late-onset depression, on the other hand, tends to emerge in the mid-30s and is associated with fewer recurrent episodes, comorbid personality disorders, and substance abuse disorders relative to early-onset depression (Klein et al., 1999). However, there is a much greater variation in the age of onset than in disorders such as schizophrenia. Second, the course of MDD tends to be time limited. The average episode lasts 6 months, although this varies greatly from person to person. Third, MDD tends to be a recurrent disorder. Patients who have one major depressive episode have a 36.7% chance of experiencing a second; those who have two previous episodes have a 48% chance of developing a third episode. With each additional episode, chances for another additional episode increase by approximately 15% (Kessing & Andersen, 1999).

Dysthymia, on the other hand, is a more chronic, long-lasting illness. The mean duration of dysthymia is 30 years, and almost half of those patients who have dysthymia will develop a major depressive episode in their lifetimes (Shelton et al., 1997; Wells, Burnam, Rogers, Hays, & Camp, 1992). Those with dysthymia have been found to have worse clinical prognosis than people with either major depression or depression NOS and are as disabled as those with major depression (Griffiths, Ravindran, Merali, & Anisman, 2000). Thankfully, dysthymia is responsive to both psychotherapy and medication treatment, at least in the short term (Kocsis et al., 1997), with some studies suggesting that the most robust intervention is a combination of psychotherapy and medication (Barrett et al., 2001). Unfortunately, few people with dysthymia ever receive treatment. Fewer than half will ever receive any kind of mental health treatment, and those do usually do so only after having experienced a major depressive episode (Shelton et al., 1997).

PROGNOSIS

Early diagnosis and treatment with therapy, medication, or both result in a better chance of recovery from MDD, dysthymia, and depression NOS (Wells et al., 1992). The ease of recovery from depression, however, is related to several factors. Prognosis is best when the patient is facing few stressful life events (Keitner, Ryan, Miller, & Zlotnick, 1997; Sherrington, Hawton, Fagg, Andrew, & Smith, 2001) and has a solid support network on which to rely (Keitner et al., 1997). Furthermore, individuals with an initial early recovery are less likely to develop recurring symptoms. Early improvements indicate that the patient has access to coping mechanisms that allow for a quick recovery, and this often suggests an overall positive long-term prognosis. The prognosis for dysthymia is less certain. Recently Ciechanowski and colleagues (Ciechanowski et al., 2004) demonstrated a 50% reduction at the end of a 12-month period in depressive symptoms and functional improvement using problem-solving therapy in home-based intervention for older adults with medical illnesses, minor depression, and dysthymia. As of this writing, few treatment studies have demonstrated any long-lasting positive effect for any intervention, although this literature is emerging.

Another factor involved in the prognosis for both MDD and dysthymia are levels of self-esteem. A higher self-esteem predicts an increasingly positive prognosis (Sherrington et al., 2001). Poor self-esteem, on the other hand, predicts a longer and more delayed recovery. The prognosis of depressive disorders is poor when they have an early onset, a premorbid personality disorder exists, and there has been a previous episode (Brodaty et al., 1993). More intensive and extended treatment can improve the remission and maintenance of remission from MDD episodes, even with high severity of the depression, although the evidence on dysthymia is limited. Longevity in the use of treatment is predictive of an improved long-term course of the appearance of symptoms. In a study by Dawson, Lavori, Coryell, Endicott, and Keller (1998), evidence showed that extended use of psychopharmacology past recovery resulted in fewer recurrent depressive episodes. Thus, though symptoms may have abated, prognosis can be significantly improved when treatment continues for a more extended period. This evidence shows that despite seemingly greater costs for continued treatment, the benefits from prolonged treatment are a worthwhile long-term investment.

DIAGNOSTIC CONSIDERATIONS

Although the *DSM-IV* provides a guideline for the diagnosis of depressive disorders, the comorbidity of other medical and psychiatric disorders can complicate a diagnostic decision. To make an accurate diagnosis of depression, the provider must consider physical health, medications, family and personal history, and medical history.

Medical Illness

The first important step in diagnosing depressive disorders is to have the patient get a complete physical. Many medical illnesses are related to the onset of a depressive episode, and at times, treating both the illness and the depression is a more efficient way to affect symptom change (Areán & Miranda, 1996; Zubenko et al., 1997). In endocrinological disorders like hyperthyroidism and hypothyroidism, one of the diagnostic signs is a change in affect and mood. People who are treated for these disorders experience radical changes in mood. Moreover, people with chronic illnesses like diabetes mellitus have high rates of depressive disorder (de Groot, Jacobson, Samson, & Welch, 1999; Wilkinson et al., 1988). Acute medical illnesses such as stroke (Starkstein et al., 1991), Parkinson's disease (Caap-Ahlgren & Dehlin, 2001; Starkstein, Berthier, Bolduc, Preziosi, & Robinson, 1989), pancreatic cancer (Holland et al., 1986), coronary heart disease (Kubzansky & Kawachi, 2000), and myocardial infarction (Fielding, 1991) are associated with depressive symptoms. Recent neurological findings suggest that cerebrovascular disease (particularly ischemic small-vessel disease) may be related to the onset of late-life depression (Rapp et al., 2005). Although it is unclear whether these illnesses directly cause depression or the depression is the result of the life changes brought on by the illness, recovery from these diseases (when possible) will help to alleviate depressive symptoms.

DRUG AND ALCOHOL ABUSE

The next step in establishing a diagnosis is to determine to what extent the person drinks or uses drugs. Often substance abuse or dependence disorders are strongly associated with depressive symptoms (Gunnarsdottir et al., 2000; Kessler, McGonagle, Zhao, et al., 1994; Merikangas & Avenevoli, 2000). Currently, scientists are debating whether depressive symptoms are a consequence of substance abuse and the problems related to this disorder, or the substance use is a means of "self-medicating" depressive symptoms. Whatever the true relationship, to obtain a clearer picture of the person's affective state, it is important for patients to abstain from using substances.

It is also crucial to get a list of all medications (both prescribed and over-the-counter) the person uses given that the side effects of many medications can cause or contribute to the depressive symptoms observed. This is particularly true with older adults, who are more vulnerable to the side effects of medication. For example, in a review of late-life depression Dick, Gallagher-Thompson, & Thompson (1996) note that medications such as antihistamines, antihypertensives, some antiparkinsonian drugs, and some pain medications commonly cause symptoms of depression. In addition, diuretics, synthetic hormones, and benzodiazepines have also been noted to contribute to depressive symptomatology (Cooper, Peters, & Andrews, 1998). The higher the number of drugs the person takes, the higher the risk for medications' side effects and drug-drug interactions.

GRIEF AND BEREAVEMENT

Grief over the loss of a special person or the presence of a major life stress or change can also complicate attempts to diagnose depressive disorders. Both uncomplicated bereavement and adjustment disorder have many of the symptoms of depression, but neither is considered a mood disorder. People with these problems are best helped by an understanding that their symptoms are common reactions to their recent stress. Although it is possible that those with uncomplicated bereavement or adjustment disorder can develop a depressive disorder, little is known about the extent to which grief can develop into depression.

DEPRESSION DUE TO OTHER PSYCHIATRIC DISORDERS

People with other psychiatric disorders can have co-occurring depressive symptoms, and thus a differential rule-out for these other disorders is often important. For instance, people with anxiety disorders, particularly generalized anxiety disorder, report feelings of sadness and hopelessness (Hopko et al., 2000). When under stress, people with Axis II disorders will also report significant symptoms of depression. In fact, they can become quite acutely depressed. Specifically, depressive episodes are most prevalent with avoidant, borderline, and obsessive-compulsive personality disorders (Rossi et al., 2001). Furthermore, personality disorders have an association with a longer remission onset from a depressive episode (O'Leary & Costello, 2001).

In addition, depression is common in prodromal phases of schizophrenia and is a recurrent feature in bipolar disorder.

DEPRESSION IN OLDER ADULTS

Depression, while not a natural consequence of aging, is one of the most common mental health disorders our elders experience. According to the American Psychological Association (1998), depression may present differently in older adults. Older adults are less likely to report feeling sad or depressed (American Psychological Association, 1998) or symptoms of guilt (Wallace & Pfohl, 1995) and may report more memory problems (in the absence of dementia) and somatic symptoms such as fatigue, decreased appetite, and muscle pain (Kim, Shin, Yoon, & Stewart, 2002). In addition, because older adults are more likely to have chronic illnesses, the presence of physical illness as well as the side effects of medications taken to treat these conditions can overshadow or worsen symptoms of depression (Areán & Reynolds, 2005), which can further complicate diagnosis. In older populations, depression is also associated with increased mortality and health service usage. This association highlights the importance of early recognition, differential diagnosis, and treatment of this disabling illness.

PSYCHOLOGICAL AND BIOLOGICAL ASSESSMENT

The assessment of depression has evolved over the decades, but many issues and controversies about the most adequate means of detecting this disorder still remain. Controversies over cultural differences, age differences, and the setting in which a client is being evaluated are still under investigation. This section focuses on the strengths and weaknesses of different methods for assessing depression, ranging from screening instruments to structured clinical interviews.

ASSESSING THE DEPRESSED PERSON

The most common way to assess for depressive disorders is by conducting an in-person interview with the patient. The interviewer, usually a mental health professional or trained clinic worker, asks the patient a number of questions regarding the current episode of depression, including the symptoms the patient is experiencing, how long they have been depressed, what they think caused the depression, and what they would like to do about the depressive episode. In addition, intake clinicians will also ask about family and personal history, past and current medical history, previous psychiatric history, and the impact the depression has had on their day-to-day functioning. All this information is compiled to determine whether the patient has a depressive disorder, the type of disorder they have, and the degree to which they are suffering. This information is then used to determine the appropriate treatment.

Most mental health professionals use their own methods of assessment. Some will conduct an open-ended interview that is guided not by any instrumentation, but only by the patient's responses to questions. Although this method is most commonly practiced, it also carries the greatest risk of misdiagnosis, particularly if the interviewer is not an expert in depressive disorders. Because of this risk, many mental health organizations prefer to use a combination of an open-ended interview with a screening instrument or a guide, such as a semistructured interview form, to help remind the clinician to ask for all relevant information. In using a screening instrument or semistructured interview, it is imperative that the instruments chosen be highly reliable and valid. Other than a medical examination to rule out physical causes for depressive symptoms, there is no biological test to diagnose depression, so accurate diagnosis rests with the clinician and the instrumentation used to confirm a diagnosis.

SCREENING INSTRUMENTS

In many health settings, practitioners are concerned with identifying as many people as possible who have the disorder so that quick and effective interventions can take place. This tradition comes from medical practice, where physicians routinely conduct medical tests when they suspect a particular illness. These screening tests help the doctor determine whether further tests are needed to make a specific diagnosis. For instance, when a patient sees a doctor about symptoms of fatigue, the physician will likely order blood and urine screens to determine whether the fatigue is due to anemia, diabetes, or mononucleosis. Standardized screening instruments are used for similar purposes in mental health. Screening instruments should be highly sensitive, that is, they should detect depression in everyone with the disorder. Otherwise, their utility is limited. Once someone screens positive for depression, further assessment is required to confirm a diagnosis.

The most common mechanism for diagnosing depression in adults is through self-report measures, such as the Beck Depression Inventory (BDI; Beck, 1961), the Center for Epidemiological Studies—Depression Scale (CES-D; (Radloff, 1977), the Zung Depression Scale (Zung, 1972), the Montgomery Asberg Depression Rating Scale (MADRS-S; Montgomery & Asberg, 1979), and the Profile of Mood States (POMS; Plutchik, Platman, & Fieve, 1968). Because some of these measures contain items that are related to somatic symptoms (e.g., fatigue) and are frequently scored in a depressed direction by older adults with acute physical or chronic illnesses (Gatz & Hurwicz, 1990), some self-report measures have been designed specifically for diagnosing depression in older adults, such as the Nine-Item Patient Health Questionnaire (PHQ-9; Spitzer, Williams, Kroenke, Hornyak, & McMurray, 2000) and the Geriatric Depression Scale (GDS; Yesavage et al., 1982). All of these instruments are completed by the patient, who indicates the degree to which he or she has experienced symptoms over a specified period (e.g., 1 week, 2 weeks), and then the instrument is hand scored by the person administering the scale. A patient's score on the instrument reflects the severity of depression. These instruments are considered cost-effective and efficient. They are useful in primary care settings in making quick diagnoses, especially when followed with a second-stage interview (Schmitz, Kruse, Heckrath, Alberti, & Tress, 1999). However, they are often too inclusive in that they tend to identify some people as depressed who are not. They also differ in their assessments of depression and specifications within the diagnosis. For example, the BDI and the MADRS-S are equivalent in their assessment of depression, but the MADRS-S has a greater focus on core depressive symptoms than does the BDI (Svanborg & Asberg, 2001). Additionally, and of late, many health care providers are using these instruments for determining a diagnosis. An issue that arises here is that these instruments are designed to be screening devices and not diagnostic tools. Furthering the problem, research indicates that such scales may be efficient in identifying psychological distress that might then be erroneously identified as major depression (Areán & Miranda, 1997; Schein & Koenig, 1997).

Because of the prevalence of depression in primary care medicine, a number of instruments have been created specifically for that environment. These instruments are meant to raise a red flag to the provider so that a more thorough depression assessment can be done. The Primary Care Evaluation of Mental Disorders (PRIME-MD; Spitzer et al., 1994) is a good example of such an instrument. The patient completes a brief questionnaire in which two questions are red flags for depression. If the patient endorses one of the two red-flag questions, then the provider asks more specific questions to finalize the diagnosis. The PRIME-MD has satisfactory reliability and validity (Spitzer, Kroenke, & Williams, 1999). Another brief self-report questionnaire for medical patients is the Beck Depression Inventory—Primary Care (BDI-PC; Beck, Guth, Steer, & Ball, 1997). This is a seven-item questionnaire consisting of some of the same items from the full BDI and instructs the patient to rate symptoms occurring over the last 2 weeks on a 4-point scale. In research examining the BDI-PC as a screening measure for MDD, it has been shown to have high internal consistency in primary care outpatient settings (Cronbach's alpha = 0.85; Steer, Cavalieri, Leonard, & Beck, 1999) and in medical inpatients as well (Cronbach's alpha = 0.86; Beck et al., 1997). When using a cut score of 4 and greater, it yielded excellent sensitivity (97%) and specificity (99%; Steer et al., 1999). Researchers noted that an advantage of the BDI-PC is that it has not been found to be correlated with age, sex, or ethnicity/racial status (Beck et al., 1997; Winter, Steer, Jones-Hicks, & Beck, 1999).

Another structured screening instrument designed for primary care is the Mini-International Neuropsychiatric Interview-Screen (MINI-Screen), a shorter version of the MINI, described in more detail in the following section. No data exist supporting its psychometric properties.

STRUCTURED AND SEMISTRUCTURED CLINICAL INTERVIEWS

Once a person screens positive for a depressive disorder, the next step is to confirm the diagnosis. This is best done by using a structured or semistructured interview. As stated earlier, most people who are expert in the diagnosis of depression disorders do not need the assistance of a structured instrument. However, because these experts are not always available and employing them can be quite costly, structured and semistructured interviews have been developed for use by less-experienced personnel. To address the concerns of managed-care systems these interviews have utility in that they increase standardization in service delivery, increase consistency in diagnosis, and allow for tracking outcomes (Sheehan et al., 1998). The best-known instruments are the Structured Clinical Interview for *DSM-IV* and the Composite International Diagnostic Interview. Another short structured diagnostic interview that has recently become more popular is the Mini-International Neuropsychiatric Interview. The Diagnostic Interview for *DSM* (DIS) has also been used widely but has been largely replaced by the CIDI and so will not be discussed in this chapter.

THE STRUCTURED CLINICAL INTERVIEW FOR *DSM-IV*

The Structured Clinical Interview for *DSM-IV* (SCID) was developed for clinical research to determine the presence of *DSM-IV* disorders. It is a semistructured interview to be used by formally trained staff. Although interviewers use the instrument as a guide to structure the interview, the interviewer can also rely on his or her judgment in interpreting a patient's answers to questions. Because there is a reliance on clinical judgment, the SCID functions best when administered by a mental health professional.

The SCID interview is divided into a number of sections: a historical overview of the presenting complaint, a screening list to determine beforehand whether the patient has symptoms of MDD, alcohol or substance abuse, obsessive-compulsive disorder and anxiety disorders, and the different diagnostic modules to reflect all the Axis I diagnoses of *DSM-IV*. Although the SCID has been used extensively in research studies, it has only fair validity and reliability. According to the SCID's creators, this instrument has a kappa coefficient of agreement equal to only 0.31 in nonpatient samples, indicating poor validity.

The main advantage to using the SCID is its structured nature, which thus decreases the amount of variation of diagnosis from clinician to clinician. However, it is still a costly instrument in that staff administering the SCID must be trained in its use and must be of a professional level. However, costs can be lowered while maintaining the effectiveness of the assessment by the use of trained research assistants rather than senior investigators to administer the test (Miller et al., 1999).

COMPOSITE INTERNATIONAL DIAGNOSTIC INTERVIEW

The Composite International Diagnostic Interview (CIDI) was developed by the World Health Organization for the purpose of providing a variety of diagnoses that are in accord with definitions from the *DSM-IV*. This structured clinical interview is a fully computerized interview and so is able to attain a complexity and depth of diagnosis with carefully programmed skip patterns and flowcharts. Its great advantage is that it does not require a mental health professional to administer the instrument—in fact, the CIDI can be used as a patient-only-administered instrument, although it is also common for a researcher to administer it. Because the program makes the diagnosis, the researcher giving the interview does not need to make any independent clinical judgments (Cooper et al., 1998).

The obvious benefits of the CIDI are that it is computerized and thus cuts down on costs of training interviewers and of using health practitioners to make diagnoses. There are, however, simultaneous negative aspects to the CIDI. One important one is that since it is computerized, certain disorders may be more difficult to diagnose because of individuals' desire to maintain secrecy or denial of mental disorders (Thornton, Russell, & Hudson, 1998). Additionally, since it is computerized, differences between individuals that the program does not account for cannot be adjusted within the interview. However, the CIDI can be a useful tool provided that it is used with a follow-up interview with a clinician.

THE MINI-INTERNATIONAL NEUROPSYCHIATRIC INTERVIEW

The Mini-International Neuropsychiatric Interview (MINI) was developed by Sheehan and colleagues (1998) to assess the most common *DSM-IV* and *ICD-10* psychiatric disorders. The MINI is purported to be shorter than typical interviews used in research settings but more thorough than screening tests with a 15-minute administration time. Like the CIDI, it is advantageous in that it does not require a mental health professional to administer the instrument, thus freeing time for the mental health professional to focus on other critical issues. The interview items focus on current symptoms (except for bipolar disorder), those most routinely asked about by clinicians. This allows for a shorter administration time than other interviews, such as the SCID, that probe for past symptomatology as well.

Research testing the validity of the clinician-rated MINI has shown good to very good concordance with other clinician-rated diagnostic interviews (SCID and the CIDI), and it has excellent interrater reliability (kappa > 0.79) for all diagnostic categories and good test/retest reliability (kappa > 0.63) for all diagnostic categories except simple phobia and current mania. The MINI also demonstrated very good specificity (>0.86 with SCID; >0.72 with CIDI) and very good positive and negative predictive values for most diagnostic categories. For more details see Sheehan et al., 1998.

The MINI is also available in other formats, including a longer version for the academic researcher called the MINI-Plus that includes 23 psychiatric disorders (as opposed to 19); a patient-rated version for use in outpatient settings (the MINI-PR); a version for children and adolescents (the MINI-Kid); and a shorter screening instrument, the MINI-Screen (as previously discussed) for primary care. There are also multiple translated-language versions and a computerized version now available whose properties are currently being investigated.

COMMENT

Determining the presence of a depressive disorder requires skill and effort in gathering information about the depression and its potential causes. The most efficient method to determine the presence of a depressive disorder is to first screen the patient, and, if the screening is positive, to perform an in-depth interview.

ETIOLOGICAL CONSIDERATIONS

The most debated topic in depression research is the area of causality. To date the majority of research in this area has focused on the etiology of MDD, with very little research studying the etiology of dysthymia. Depression NOS appears to be related to whatever is thought to be the comorbid cause. Most scientists now believe that depressive disorders are multifaceted, with causes resulting from the interactions of psychological, social, and biological factors (Kendler, Thornton, & Prescott, 2001; O'Keane, 2000). For example, stressful life events have been found to increase the risk for developing depression. However, the person's coping style, social support, and genetic makeup all mediate the impact that stress has on depression. A person who loses their job but has good social support and coping skills will be less likely to develop depression than another unemployed person who has weak coping skills and no social support. Though depression is related to many variables, their intermingling can most clearly predict the development of depression, rather than any single factor determining the onset. Genetics, learning, and life experiences all work together to cause depression.

FAMILIAL AND GENETIC

The most fascinating research on the etiology of depression has been the recent work on the role of genetics in mental health. With the mapping of the human genome, the prospect of clearly identifying the influence of genetics on mental health is within our reach. However, with depressive disorders, the contribution of genetics may take longer to uncover than for other disorders that have already demonstrated a clear genetic and biological cause (i.e., schizophrenia). Although past evidence from twin studies has been able to demonstrate some genetic involvement in depressive disorders, those links have thus far been weak.

Historically, the principal method for studying the influence of genetics on psychopathology was to compare the concordance of depression in identical twins (MZ; monozygotic twins) to that of fraternal twins (DZ; dizygotic). Because the frequency of twin births is low, genetic researchers also observe the rates of depressive disorder in first-degree relatives (often parents and children). According to the twin studies, MZ twins have greater concordance rates for depressive disorders than do DZ twins (Englund & Klein, 1990). The correlation between MZ twins is .46, compared to DZ twins, whose concordance rates are .20, although this concordance is lower than what is found in schizophrenia studies (McGuffin, Katz, Watkins, & Rutherford, 1996). Family studies also find that onset of depression is more likely in people with depressed relatives than in those who do not have depressed family members. Again, the rates are not that compelling, with relatives having only a 21% risk for developing depression (Kupfer, Frank, Carpenter, & Neiswanger, 1989).

Direct genetic comparisons are becoming a more popular method for determining genetic links to mood. These methods are considered superior to the methods discussed previously, because DNA is a specific measure that is unlikely to be modified by environmental influences. The results from twin and family studies cannot account for the impact of learning on development of depression, whereas DNA is less likely to be influenced by personal experience. DNA studies are able to compare depressed with nondepressed controls on characteristics of certain genes that are associated with neurotransmitters related to depressive disorder (see "Biological and Physiological" section following). Although still in its infancy, this research has been very helpful in confirming the role of genetics in the development of depressive disorders. For instance, Dikeos and colleagues (1999) studied whether the genetic location of the D3 dopamine receptor differed in patients with MDD as compared to those with no history or current MDD. The investigators observed that genotypes carrying the allele (DNA structure) associated with D3 polymorphisms were found in 75% of the MDD patients and in 50% of the controls, suggesting genetic influences in MDD. Other studies, however, have not found such robust effects (Frisch et al., 1999; Neiswanger et al., 1998; Qian et al., 1999). At best, the literature on the genetics of depressive disorders suggests a propensity to develop these disorders but that this propensity can be offset by learning and environmental influences.

LEARNING AND MODELING

Depressive disorders also appear to be related to three psychological variables:

1. People's cognitive appraisals of themselves, their lives, and others (Alloy et al., 2000)
2. Whether people proactively solve problems or avoid them (D'Zurilla & Nezu, 1999)
3. The degree to which proactive attempts to cope with stress have been successful (Folkman & Lazarus, 1988)

In this paradigm, people who have negative expectations about their ability to cope with problems generally acquire these expectations through past learning experience. Repeated failed attempts to solve problems, for instance, leaves a person feeling hopeless and helpless, abandoning his or her usual methods for solving problems, and becoming depressed (Seligman, Weiss, Weinraub, & Schulman, 1980). These factors—cognitive attributions, coping skills, and learned helplessness—have all been found to be predictive of depression.

People with negative expectations or cognitive vulnerabilities are more likely to become depressed when faced with a stressor than people who do not possess cognitive vulnerabilities. Grazioli and Terry (2000) found that in women with postpartum depression, both general and maternal-specific dysfunctional attitudes were associated with self-reported depression, particularly in women who had children found to be temperamentally difficult. Another study found that individuals with negative cognitive styles had higher lifetime prevalence of depression than people who were not cognitively vulnerable (Alloy et al., 2000). Therefore, people with negative perceptions of themselves and their environment are at risk for becoming depressed.

Coping skills have also been found to be related to depression. Most research has found that people who use active forms of coping, such as problem solving, are less likely to become depressed than are people who use passive forms of coping, such as avoidance. In fact, one study found that the prevalence of major depression was 59.4% in people with avoidant coping styles (Garcia, Valdes, Jodar, Riesco, & de Flores, 1994; Welch & Austin, 2001). Studies show that when faced with a problem to solve, depressed people are more likely to produce less effective solutions than nondepressed people, such as using distraction to cope with a stressor rather than trying to solve it (Marx, Williams, & Claridge, 1992).

Although coping skills deficits and cognitive style contribute to depression, the interaction of these two factors seems to have the biggest impact on the development of depression. Several studies have supported this interaction in learned helplessness. Originally, these theories were tested in animal models, where unsolvable problems were presented to animals and all attempts to solve the problem were met with unpleasant consequences, such as an electric shock. After repeated attempts to solve the problem failed, these animals would exhibit depressogenic behavior—withdrawal, acting as if they were in pain—and, even after a solution was presented to them, the animals would refuse to try the solution (Altenor, Volpicelli, & Seligman, 1979). Scientists have been able to draw a relationship between learned helplessness and depression in research. For instance, Swendsen (1997) found that people with high-risk attributional styles were more likely to experience depressed mood after exposure to negative stressful events. Kapci and Cramer (2000) also found that people were more likely to become depressed when they were exposed to numerous negative life events, but only if their faith in their ability to solve problems was impaired. Thus, the interaction of negative life events, coping skills, and attributions about coping skills influences whether a person will experience depression.

LIFE EVENTS

The literature is replete with data indicating that stressful life events contribute to the development of a depressive episode. Although not everyone who faces difficult problems becomes depressed, it is evident that prolonged exposure to psychosocial stress can precipitate a depressive episode (Brown, Bifulco, & Harris, 1987). A number of studies have found that most depressive episodes are preceded by a severe life event or difficulty in the 6 months before onset of the episode (Brown et al., 1987). In addition, patients with more long-term or chronic depression were more likely to report past abuse, though the causal relationship is unclear (Keitner et al., 1997).

Because depression is a multifaceted disorder, it is difficult to pinpoint the specific role life events have on the development of a depressive disorder. Most people at some point in their lives will have to face severe life stress, yet not everyone becomes depressed. How an individual views severe life events and the perceived control he or she feels over the situation both play an important role in determining one's vulnerability to depression. For instance, several studies find that the relationship of life events to depression is mediated by other factors such as social support, cognitive style, and coping abilities (Alloy et al., 2000; Brugha et al., 1987). Severe life events are significantly more likely to provoke a major depressive episode in individuals without social support (Bifulco, Brown, & Harris, 1987; Keitner et al., 1997). Support systems give an individual external support when internal coping skills are put to the test. Without the external support, however, an individual must rely exclusively on his or her own internal resources, which under severe duress might not be entirely effective. Therefore, although negative life events do influence the occurrence of depressive disorders, the social and psychological resources available to the person facing the stressful life event generally mediate the impact on mood.

GENDER AND RACIAL-ETHNIC

We have already reported that the prevalence of depression is higher among women and some minority populations as compared to white males. Many researchers have been trying to determine the reasons for the discrepant rates of depressive disorders in these populations. Are the reasons genetic or biological? Is it that these populations are exposed to more stress and have fewer resources to cope with stress and therefore are more vulnerable than men and nonminority groups? Or is depression presented differently across these groups, and therefore the estimates in the prevalence for depressive disorders in these populations are inaccurate? Mental health researchers are still struggling with these questions and have only been able to give a partial explanation of why the discrepancy exists.

Some theorists believe that the reason minorities have differing rates of depressive disorder is that they present their symptoms of depression differently than do Caucasians. Many researchers have spent years trying to discern the most appropriate way to assess depression in different cultures. Although research from the World Health Organization indicates that depression is similar across cultures, how one culture reports the symptoms and their cultural attitude about mental health (and its treatment) can cloud diagnoses. Screening instruments and scales that were developed for Anglo populations can be problematic if they are simply translated without regard for translation bias. Additionally, many studies have found that the factor structures and reliabilities of these instruments tend to differ across ethnic groups, indicating that groups vary in their reports of depressive symptoms (Areán & Miranda, 1997; Azocar, Areán, Miranda, & Munoz, 2001). For instance, lower rates of depression in Asians may be attributable to their tendency to underreport affective symptoms of depression and rely more on somatic presentation (Iwamasa, 1993).

Others have hypothesized that the different rates of depression in ethnic groups are associated with the fact that in this country, minorities such as African Americans and Hispanics are more likely to be impoverished and have to cope with financial and urban stress. Studies have demonstrated that socioeconomic status and exposure to trauma related to racism, urban living, and financial strain are correlated with depression and other mental illnesses such as anxiety and substance abuse. Other studies have found that the rates for depression in middle-class and affluent minorities are more similar to the national rates of depression as compared to middle class and affluent Caucasians. These studies seem to argue that in the case of minority populations, increased exposure to stress is the reason for the differing rates of depressive disorder (Olfson et al., 2000).

The differing rates of depressive disorders between men and women is an interesting yet complicated finding. Researchers initially thought that the different prevalence rates resulted from reluctance on the part of men to admit feelings of depression as well as men's tendency to cope with stress through substance use. Others suggest that the increased prevalence of depression in women is because women tend to be victims of sexual abuse and therefore suffer a significant psychosocial stressor that is not as common in men. And yet others suggest that the willingness of women to seek treatment services over men might account for the difference in prevalence. However, because the discrepancy between men and women seems to be universal, others claim that hormonal and biological differences account for the differential prevalence rates. Whatever the differential effect, the fact remains that depression is more commonly reported in women than in men, and this issue still needs to be resolved.

BIOLOGICAL AND PHYSIOLOGICAL

Much research effort has gone into determining biological determinants of depression. The literature shows evidence not only of the effects from both neurotransmitters and hormones, but also of physiological changes arising from stress that can also increase susceptibility to depression (Maes, Maes, & Suy, 1990).

First, the role of neurotransmitters in mood regulation is an area of ongoing research. Clinicians initially believed that depression was caused in part by lack of the two neurotransmitters norepinephrine and serotonin. Now, however, it is known that the dysregulation rather than the deficiency of these neurotransmitters causes depression (Moore & Bona, 2001). Antidepressants to regulate the production and distribution of norepinephrine and serotonin are effective in their ability to increase the availability of receptor sites rather than increase the production of the neurotransmitters (Veenstra-VanderWeele, Anderson, & Cook, 2000). Neurotransmitters provide an important but still only partial picture of the biological origin of depression because abnormalities in neurotransmitter regulation do not necessarily lead to a depressed mood.

Neuroendocrinology also adds to a more complete understanding of the biological causes of depression. Evidence points to an overabundance of cortisol in the systems of depressed patients. Additionally, abnormalities in thyroid functions are often related to symptoms of depression, further indicating an important role for the neuroendocrine system in depression. In a study by Ghaziuddin and colleagues (2000), neuroendocrine imbalances in adolescents with MDD as compared to their nondepressed counterparts demonstrated that depression is associated with abnormal baseline levels of prolactin as well as sharper prolactin and cortisol responses to serotonergic challenges. Evidence for such abnormalities not only yields a more complete understanding of causation but also aids in the development of more effective drug treatments.

Finally, physiological changes in the brain structure of depressed individuals support the hypotheses that MDD is related to structural changes in the brain. In a recent study by Sheline (2000), brain changes in early-onset depression were localized in the hippocampus, amygdala, caudate nucleus, putamen, and frontal cortex, whereas late-onset depression was noted to frequently occur with comorbid physical illnesses that often affect brain structures involved in emotion regulation. In addition, some researchers suggest that dysfunction in the mesial temporal lobe may be related to recurrent MDD (Rapp et al., 2005). These physical changes that can occur during stress and illness and that are associated so closely with depression give a more comprehensive picture and explanation of the causes of depression.

SUMMARY

Depressive disorders are common and widely studied. Given the extent of our knowledge of MDD and dysthymia, however, research continues to address the best means of recognizing depression, how to treat depression in different settings and in different cultures, and further clarification of the etiology of these disorders. The causes and symptoms of depressive disorders are extremely variable and intermingled. The causes include both physiological to environmental factors and the expressions of depression vary from short, severe episodes to chronic symptomatology. Because of the immense complexity of the depressive disorders, further research will aid in the ability to tailor diagnosis and therapy to each particular manifestation.

REFERENCES

Alderete, E., Vega, W. A., Kolody, B., & Aguilar-Gaxiola, S. (1999). Depressive symptomatology: Prevalence and psychosocial risk factors among Mexican migrant farmworkers in California. *Journal of Community Psychology, 27* (4), 457–471.

Alloy, L. B., Abramson, L. Y., Whitehouse, W. G., Hogan, M. E., Tashman, N. A., Steinberg D. L., Rose, D. T., & Donovan, P. (2000). The Temple-Wisconsin Cognitive Vulnerability to Depression Project: Lifetime history of axis I psychopathology in individuals at high and low cognitive risk for depression. *Journal of Abnormal Psychology, 109* (3), 403–418.

Altenor, A., Volpicelli, J. R., & Seligman, M. E. (1979). Debilitated shock escape is produced by both short- and long-duration inescapable shock: Learned helplessness versus learned inactivity. *Bulletin of the Psychomonic Society, 14* (5), 337–339.

American Psychiatric Association. (1994). *Diagnostic and Statistical Manual of Mental Disorders* (4th ed.). Washington, DC: Author.

American Psychological Association. (1998). What practitioners should know about working with older adults. *Professional Psychology—Research and Practice, 29,* 413–427.

Angold, A., Weissman, M. M., John, K., Wickramaratne, P., & Prusoff, B. (1991). The effects of age and sex on depression ratings in children and adolescents. *Journal of the American Academy of Child and Adolescent Psychiatry, 30* (1), 67–74.

Areán, P. A., & Miranda, J. (1996). Do primary care patients accept psychological treatments? *General Hospital Psychiatry, 18* (1), 22–27.

Areán, P. A., & Miranda, J. (1997). The utility of the Center of Epidemiological Studies-Depression Scale in older primary care patients. *Aging and Mental Health, 1*(1), 47–56.

Areán, P. A., & Reynolds, C.F., 3rd (2005). The impact of psychosocial factors on late-life depression. *Biological Psychiatry,* 58 (4):277-282.

Azocar, F., Areán, P., Miranda, J., & Munoz, R. F. (2001). Differential item functioning in a Spanish translation of the Beck Depression Inventory. *Journal of Clinical Psychology, 57* (3), 355–365.

Baldwin, R. C. (2000). Poor prognosis of depression in elderly people: Causes and actions. *Annals of Medicine, 32* (4), 252–256.

Barrett, J. E., Williams, J. W., Jr., Oxman, T. E., Frank, E., Katon, W., Sullivan, M., Hegel, M. T., Cornell, J.E., & Sengupta, A.S. (2001). Treatment of dysthymia and minor depression in primary care: A randomized trial in patients aged 18 to 59 years. *Journal of Family Practice, 50* (5), 405–412.

Beck, A. T. (1961). A systematic investigation of depression. *Comprehensive Psychiatry, 2,* 163–170.

Beck, A. T., Guth, D., Steer, R. A., & Ball, R. (1997). Screening for major depression disorders in medical inpatients with the Beck Depression Inventory for Primary Care. *Behaviour Research and Therapy, 35* (8), 785–791.

Bifulco, A. T., Brown, G. W., & Harris, T. O. (1987). Childhood loss of parent, lack of adequate parental care and adult depression: A replication. *Journal of Affective Disorders, 12* (2), 115–128.

Brodaty, H., Harris, L., Peters, K., Wilhelm, K., Hickie, I., Boyce, P., Mitchell, P., Parker, G., Eyers, K. (1993). Prognosis of depression in the elderly. A comparison with younger patients. *British Journal of Psychiatry, 163,* 589–596.

Brown, G. W., Bifulco, A., & Harris, T. O. (1987). Life events, vulnerability and onset of depression: Some refinements. *British Journal of Psychiatry, 150,* 30–42.

Brugha, T., Bebbington, P. E., MacCarthy, B., Potter, J., Sturt, E., & Wykes, T. (1987). Social networks, social support and the type of depressive illness. *Acta Psychiatrica Scandinavica, 76* (6), 664–673.

Burke, K. C., Burke, J. D., Jr., Rae, D. S., & Regier, D. A. (1991). Comparing age at onset of major depression and other psychiatric disorders by birth cohorts in five US community populations. *Archives of General Psychiatry, 48* (9), 789–795.

Caap-Ahlgren, M., & Dehlin, O. (2001). Insomnia and depressive symptoms in patients with Parkinson's disease. Relationship to health-related quality of life. An interview study of patients living at home. *Archives of Gerontology and Geriatrics, 32* (1), 23–33.

Ciechanowski, P., Wagner, E., Schmaling, K., Schwartz, S., Williams, B., Diehr, P., Kulzer, J., Gray, S., Collier, C., & LoGerfo, J. (2004). Community-integrated home-based depression treatment in older adults: A randomized controlled trial. *Journal of the American Medical Association, 291* (13), 1569–1577.

Conti, D. J., & Burton, W. N. (1995). The cost of depression in the workplace. *Behavioral Health Care Tomorrow, 4* (4), 25–27.

Cooper, L., Peters, L., & Andrews, G. (1998). Validity of the Composite International Diagnostic Interview (CIDI) psychosis module in a psychiatric setting. *Journal of Psychiatric Research, 32* (6), 361–368.

Davidson, J., Krishnan, R., France, R., & Pelton, S. (1985). Neurovegetative symptoms in chronic pain and depression. *Journal of Affective Disorders, 9* (3), 213–218.

Dawson, R., Lavori, P. W., Coryell, W. H., Endicott, J., & Keller, M. B. (1998). Maintenance strategies for unipolar depression: an observational study of levels of treatment and recurrence. *Journal of Affective Disorders, 49* (1), 31–44.

de Groot, M., Jacobson, A. M., Samson, J. A., & Welch, G. (1999). Glycemic control and major depression in patients with type 1 and type 2 diabetes mellitus. *Journal of Psychosomatic Research, 46* (5), 425–435.

Dick, L. P., Gallagher-Thompson, D., & Thompson, L. W. (1996). Cognitive-behavioral therapy. In R. T. Woods (Ed.), *Handbook of the clinical psychology of ageing* (pp. 509–544). Oxford, England: John Wiley & Sons.

Dikeos, D. G., Papadimitriou, G. N., Avramopoulos, D., Karadima, G., Daskalopoulou, E. G., Souery, D., Mendlewicz, J., Vassilopoulos, D., Stefanis, C. N. (1999). Association between the dopamine D3 receptor gene locus (DRD3) and unipolar affective disorder. *Psychiatric Genetics, 9* (4), 189–195.

Druss, B. G., Rosenheck, R. A., & Sledge, W. H. (2000). Health and disability costs of depressive illness in a major U.S. corporation. *American Journal of Psychiatry, 157* (8), 1274–1278.

D'Zurilla, T. J., & Nezu, A. M. (1999). *Problem-solving therapy: A social competence approach to clinical intervention.* New York: Springer.

Englund, S. A., & Klein, D. N. (1990). The genetics of neurotic-reactive depression: A reanalysis of Shapiro's (1970) twin study using diagnostic criteria. *Journal of Affective Disorders, 18* (4), 247–252.

Fielding, R. (1991). Depression and acute myocardial infarction: A review and reinterpretation. *Social Science and Medicine, 32* (9), 1017–1028.

Folkman, S., & Lazarus, R. S. (1986). Stress-processes and depressive symptomatology. *Journal of Abnormal Psychology, 95* (2), 107–113.

Folkman, S., & Lazarus, R. S. (1988). The relationship between coping and emotion: Implications for theory and research. *Social Science and Medicine, 26* (3), 309–317.

Frisch, A., Postilnick, D., Rockah, R., Michaelovsky, E., Postilnick, S., Birman, E., Laor, N., Rauchverger, B., Kreinin, A., Poyurovsky, M., Schneidman, M., Modai, I., Weizman, R. (1999). Association of unipolar major depressive disorder with genes of the serotonergic and dopaminergic pathways. *Molecular Psychiatry, 4* (4), 389–392.

Garcia, L., Valdes, M., Jodar, I., Riesco, N., & de Flores, T. (1994). Psychological factors and vulnerability to psychiatric morbidity after myocardial infarction. *Psychotherapy and Psychosomatics, 61* (3–4), 187–194.

Gatz, M., & Hurwicz, M. L. (1990). Are old people more depressed? Cross-sectional data on Center for Epidemiological Studies Depression Scale factors. *Psychology and Aging, 5* (2), 284–290.

Ghaziuddin, N., King, C. A., Welch, K. B., Zaccagnini, J., Weidmer-Mikhail, E., Mellow, A. M., Ghaziuddin, M., & Greden, J. F. (2000). Serotonin dysregulation in adolescents with major depression: Hormone response to meta-chlorophenylpiperazine (mCPP) infusion. *Psychiatry Research, 95* (3), 183–194.

Grazioli, R., & Terry, D. J. (2000). The role of cognitive vulnerability and stress in the prediction of postpartum depressive symptomatology. *British Journal of Clinical Psychology, 39* (Pt. 4), 329–347.

Griffiths, J., Ravindran, A. V., Merali, Z., & Anisman, H. (2000). Dysthymia: A review of pharmacological and behavioral factors. *Molecular Psychiatry, 5* (3), 242–261.

Gunnarsdottir, E. D., Pingitore, R. A., Spring, B. J., Konopka, L. M., Crayton, J. W., Milo, T., & Shirazi, P. (2000). Individual differences among cocaine users. *Addictive Behaviors, 25* (5), 641–652.

Holland, J. C., Korzun, A. H., Tross, S., Silberfarb, P., Perry, M., & Comis, R. (1986). Comparative psychological disturbance in patients with pancreatic and gastric cancer. *American Journal of Psychiatry, 143* (8), 982–986.

Hopko, D. R., Bourland, S. L., Stanley, M. A., Beck, J. G., Novy, D. M., Averill, P. M., & Swann, A. C. (2000). Generalized anxiety disorder in older adults: Examining the relation between clinician severity ratings and patient self-report measures. *Depression and Anxiety, 12* (4), 217–225.

Isaacowitz, D. M., & Seligman, M. E. (2001). Is pessimism a risk factor for depressive mood among community-dwelling older adults? *Behavior Research and Therapy, 39* (3), 255–272.

Iwamasa, G. Y. (1993). Asian Americans and cognitive behavioral therapy. *Behavior Therapist, 16* (9), 233–235.

Jackson-Triche, M. E., Greer Sullivan, J., Wells, K. B., Rogers, W., Camp, P., & Mazel, R. (2000). Depression and health-related quality of life in ethnic minorities seeking care in general medical settings. *Journal of Affective Disorders, 58* (2), 89–97.

Judd, L. L., Akiskal, H. S., Maser, J. D., Zeller, P. J., Endicott, J., Coryell, W., M. P., Kunovac, J. L, Leon, A. C., Mueller, T. I., Rice, J. A., & Keller, M. B. (1998). A prospective 12-year study of subsyndromal and syndromal depressive symptoms in unipolar major depressive disorders. *Archives of General Psychiatry, 55* (8), 694–700.

Kapci, E. G., & Cramer, D. (2000). The mediation component of the hopelessness depression in relation to negative life events. *Counseling Psychology Quarterly, 13* (4), 413–423.

Keitner, G. I., Ryan, C. E., Miller, I. W., & Zlotnick, C. (1997). Psychosocial factors and the long-term course of major depression. *Journal of Affective Disorders, 44* (1), 57–67.

Kendler, K. S., Thornton, L. M., & Prescott, C. A. (2001). Gender differences in the rates of exposure to stressful life events and sensitivity to their depressogenic effects. *American Journal of Psychiatry, 158* (4), 587–593.

Kessing, L. V., & Andersen, P. K. (1999). The effect of episodes on recurrence in affective disorder: A case register study. *Journal of Affective Disorders, 53* (3), 225–231.

Kessler, R. C., Barber, C., Birnbaum, H. G., Frank, R. G., Greenberg, P. E., Rose, R. M., Simon, G. E., & Wang, P. (1999). Depression in the workplace: Effects on short-term disability. *Health Affairs (Millwood), 18* (5), 163–171.

Kessler, R. C., Berglund, P., Demler, O., Jin, R., Merikangas, K. R., & Walters, E. E. (2005). Lifetime prevalence and age-of-onset distributions of DSM-IV disorders in the National Comorbidity Survey Replication. *Archives of General Psychiatry, 62* (6), 593–602.

Kessler, R. C., & Frank, R. G. (1997). The impact of psychiatric disorders on work loss days. *Psychological Medicine, 27* (4), 861–873.

Kessler, R. C., McGonagle, K. A., Nelson, C. B., Hughes, M., Swartz, M., & Blazer, D. G. (1994). Sex and depression in the National Comorbidity Survey. II: Cohort effects. *Journal of Affective Disorders, 30* (1), 15–26.

Kessler, R. C., McGonagle, K. A., Zhao, S., Nelson, C. B., Hughes, M., Eshleman, S., Wittchen, H. U., & Kendler, K. S. (1994). Lifetime and 12-month prevalence of DSM-III-R psychiatric disorders in the United States. Results from the National Comorbidity Survey. *Archives of General Psychiatry, 51* (1), 8–19.

Kessler R. C, & Merikangas K. R. (2004). The National Comorbidity Survey Replication (NCS-R): background and aims. *International Journal of Methods in Psychiatric Research, 13* (2), 60-68.

Kim, J. M., Shin, I. S., Yoon, J. S., & Stewart, R. (2002). Prevalence and correlates of late-life depression compared between urban and rural populations in Korea. *International Journal of Geriatric Psychiatry, 17* (5), 409–415.

Klein, D. N., Schatzberg, A. F., McCullough, J. P., Keller, M. B., Dowling, F., Goodman, D., Howland, R. H., Markowitz, J. C., Smith, C., Miceli, R., & Harrison, W. M. (1999). Early-versus late-onset dysthymic disorder: Comparison in out-patients with superimposed major depressive episodes. *Journal of Affective Disorders, 52* (1–3), 187–196.

Klerman, G. L. (1986). The National Institute of Mental Health—Epidemiologic Catchment Area (NIMH-ECA) program: Background, preliminary findings and implications. *Journal of Social Psychiatry, 21*(4), 159–166.

Kocsis, J. H., Zisook, S., Davidson, J., Shelton, R., Yonkers, K., Hellerstein, D. J., Rosenbaum, J., & Halbreich, U. (1997). Double-blind comparison of sertraline, imipramine, and placebo in the treatment of dysthymia: Psychosocial outcomes. *American Journal of Psychiatry, 154* (3), 390–395.

Koenig, H. G., & Blazer, D. G. (1992). Epidemiology of geriatric affective disorders. *Clinics in Geriatric Medicine, 8* (2), 235–251.

Kubzansky, L. D., & Kawachi, I. (2000). Going to the heart of the matter: Do negative emotions cause coronary heart disease? *Journal of Psychosomatic Research, 48* (4/5), 323–337.

Kupfer, D. J., Frank, E., Carpenter, L. L., & Neiswanger, K. (1989). Family history in recurrent depression. *Journal of Affective Disorders, 17* (2), 113–119.

Lewinsohn, P. M., Hoberman, H. M., & Rosenbaum, M. (1988). A prospective study of risk factors for unipolar depression. *Journal of Abnormal Psychology, 97* (3), 251–264.

Maes, M., Maes, L., & Suy, E. (1990). Symptom profiles of biological markers in depression: A multivariate study. *Psychoneuroendocrinology, 15* (1), 29–37.

Marx, E. M., Williams, J. M., & Claridge, G. C. (1992). Depression and social problem solving. *Journal of Abnormal Psychology, 101* (1), 78–86.

Masand, P. S. (1995). Depression in long-term care facilities. *Geriatrics, 50* (Suppl. 1), S16–S24.

McGuffin, P., Katz, R., Watkins, S., & Rutherford, J. (1996). A hospital-based twin register of the heritability of DSM-IV unipolar depression. *Archives of General Psychiatry, 53* (2), 129–136.

Merikangas, K. R., & Avenevoli, S. (2000). Implications of genetic epidemiology for the prevention of substance use disorders. *Addictive Behaviors, 25* (6), 807–820.

Miller, N. L., Markowitz, J. C., Kocsis, J. H., Leon, A. C., Brisco, S. T., & Garno, J. L. (1999). Cost effectiveness of screening for clinical trials by research assistants versus senior investigators. *Journal of Psychiatric Research, 33* (2), 81–85.

Montgomery, S. A., & Asberg, M. (1979). A new depression scale designed to be sensitive to change. *British Journal of Psychiatry, 134,* 382–389.

Moore, J. D., & Bona, J. R. (2001). Depression and dysthymia. *Medical Clinics of North America, 85* (3), 631–644.

Mulsant, B. H., & Ganguli, M. (1999). Epidemiology and diagnosis of depression in late life. *Journal of Clinical Psychiatry, 60* (Suppl. 20), 9–15.

Munoz, R. F. (1993). The prevention of depression: Current research and practice. *Applied and Preventive Psychology, 2* (1), 21–33.

Lebowitz B. D., Pearson J. L., Schneider L. S., Reynolds C. F. 3rd, Alexopoulos G. S., Bruce M. L., Conwell Y., Katz I. R., Meyers B. S., Morrison M. F., Mossey J., Niederehe G., & Parmelee P. (1997). Diagnosis and treatment of depression in late life. Consensus statement update. *Journal of the American Medical Association, 278* (14),1186-1190.

Neiswanger, K., Zubenko, G. S., Giles, D. E., Frank, E., Kupfer, D. J., & Kaplan, B. B. (1998). Linkage and association analysis of chromosomal regions containing genes related to neuroendocrine or serotonin function in families with early-onset, recurrent major depression. *American Journal of Medical Genetics, 81* (5), 443–449.

Nezu, A. M. (1986). Cognitive appraisal of problem solving effectiveness: Relation to depression and depressive symptoms. *Journal of Clinical Psychology, 42* (1), 42–48.

Nolen-Hoeksema, S. (2000). Further evidence for the role of psychosocial factors in depression chronicity. *Clinical Psychology: Science and Practice, 7* (2), 224–227.

Nolen-Hoeksema, S., Larson, J., & Grayson, C. (1999). Explaining the gender difference in depressive symptoms. *Journal of Personality and Social Psychology, 77* (5), 1061–1072.

O'Keane, V. (2000). Evolving model of depression as an expression of multiple interacting risk factors. *British Journal of Psychiatry, 177,* 482–483.

O'Leary, D., & Costello, F. (2001). Personality and outcome in depression: An 18-month prospective follow-up study. *Journal of Affective Disorders, 63* (1–3), 67–78.

Olfson, M., Shea, S., Feder, A., Fuentes, M., Nomura, Y., Gameroff, M., & Weissman, M.M. (2000). Prevalence of anxiety, depression, and substance use disorders in an urban general medicine practice. *Archives of Family Medicine, 9* (9), 876–883.

Pincus, H. A., & Pettit, A. R. (2001). The societal costs of chronic major depression. *Journal of Clinical Psychiatry, 62*(Suppl. 6), 5–9.

Plutchik, R., Platman, S. R., & Fieve, R. R. (1968). Repeated measurements in the manic-depressive illness: Some methodological problems. *Journal of Psychology, 70,* 131–137.

Qian, Y., Lin, S., Jiang, S., Jiang, K., Wu, X., Tang, G., & Wang, D. (1999). Studies of the DXS7 polymorphism at the MAO loci in unipolar depression. *American Journal of Medical Genetics, 88* (6), 598–600.

Radloff, L. S. (1977). The CES-D Scale: A self-report depression scale for research in the general population. *Applied Psychological Measurement, 1* (3), 385–401.

Rapp, M. A., Dahlman, K., Sano, M., Grossman, H. T., Haroutunian, V., & Gorman, J. M. (2005). Neuropsychological differences between late-onset and recurrent geriatric major depression. *American Journal of Psychiatry, 162* (4), 691–698.

Regier, D. A. (1988). The NIMH Depression Awareness, Recognition, and Treatment Program: Structure, aims, and scientific basis. *American Journal of Psychiatry, 145* (11), 1351–1357.

Rossi, A., Marinangeli, M. G., Butti, G., Scinto, A., Di Cicco, L., Kalyvoka, A., & Petruzzi, C. (2001). Personality disorders in bipolar and depressive disorders. *Journal of Affective Disorders, 65* (1), 3–8.

Satcher, D. (2000). Mental health: A report of the Surgeon General—executive summary. *Professional Psychology: Research and Practice, 31* (1), 5–13.

Schein, R. L., & Koenig, H. G. (1997). The Center for Epidemiological Studies—Depression (CES-D) Scale: Assessment of depression in the medically ill elderly. *International Journal of Geriatric Psychiatry, 12* (4), 436–446.

Schmitz, N., Kruse, J., Heckrath, C., Alberti, L., & Tress, W. (1999). Diagnosing mental disorders in primary care: The General Health Questionnaire (GHQ) and the Symptom Check List (SCL-90-R) as screening instruments. *Social Psychiatry and Psychiatric Epidemiology, 34* (7), 360–366.

Seligman, M. E., & Csikszentmihalyi, M. (2000). Positive psychology. An introduction. *American Psychology, 55* (1), 5–14.

Seligman, M. E., Steen, T. A., Park, N., & Peterson, C. (2005). Positive psychology progress: Empirical validation of interventions. *American Psychology, 60* (5), 410–421.

Seligman, M. E., Weiss, J., Weinraub, M., & Schulman, A. (1980). Coping behavior: Learned helplessness, physiological change and learned inactivity. *Behavior Research and Therapy, 18* (5), 459–512.

Sheehan, D. V., Lecrubier, Y., Sheehan, K. H., Amorim, P., Janavs, J., & Weiller, E. (1998). The Mini-International Neuropsychiatric Interview (MINI): The development and validation of a structured diagnostic psychiatric interview for DSM-IV and ICD-10. *Journal of Clinical Psychiatry, 59* (Suppl. 20), 22–33; quiz 34–57.

Sheline, Y. I. (2000). 3D MRI studies of neuroanatomic changes in unipolar major depression: The role of stress and medical comorbidity. *Biological Psychiatry, 48* (8), 791–800.

Shelton, R. C., Davidson, J., Yonkers, K. A., Koran, L., Thase, M. E., Pearlstein, T., & Halbreich, U. (1997). The undertreatment of dysthymia. *Journal of Clinical Psychiatry, 58* (2), 59–65.

Sherrington, J. M., Hawton, K., Fagg, J., Andrew, B., & Smith, D. (2001). Outcome of women admitted to hospital for depressive illness: Factors in the prognosis of severe depression. *Psychological Medicine, 31* (1), 115–125.

Simon, G. E., Revicki, D., Heiligenstein, J., Grothaus, L., VonKorff, M., Katon, W. J., & Hylan, T. R. (2000). Recovery from depression, work productivity, and health care costs among primary care patients. *General Hospital Psychiatry, 22* (3), 153–162.

Simons, A. D., & Thase, M. E. (1992). Biological markers, treatment outcome, and 1-year follow-up in endogenous depression: Electroencephalographic sleep studies and response to cognitive therapy. *Journal of Consulting and Clinical Psychology, 60* (3), 392–401.

Spitzer, R. L., Kroenke, K., & Williams, J. B. (1999). Validation and utility of a self-report version of PRIME-MD: The PHQ primary care study. Primary Care Evaluation of Mental Disorders. Patient Health Questionnaire. *Journal of the American Medical Association, 282* (18), 1737–1744.

Spitzer, R. L., Williams, J. B., Kroenke, K., Hornyak, R., & McMurray, J. (2000). Validity and utility of the PRIME-MD patient health questionnaire in assessment of 3000 obstetric-gynecologic patients: The PRIME-MD Patient Health Questionnaire Obstetrics-Gynecology Study. *American Journal of Obstetrics and Gynecology, 183* (3), 759–769.

Spitzer, R. L., Williams, J. B., Kroenke, K., Linzer, M., deGruy, F. V., 3rd, Hahn, S. R., Brody, D., & Johnson, J. G. (1994). Utility of a new procedure for diagnosing mental disorders in primary care. The PRIME-MD 1000 study. *Journal of the American Medical Association, 272* (22), 1749–1756.

Starkstein, S. E., Berthier, M. L., Bolduc, P. L., Preziosi, T. J., & Robinson, R. G. (1989). Depression in patients with early versus late onset of Parkinson's disease. *Neurology, 39* (11), 1441–1445.

Starkstein, S. E., Bryer, J. B., Berthier, M. L., Cohen, B., Price, T. R., & Robinson, R. G. (1991). Depression after stroke: The importance of cerebral hemisphere asymmetries. *Journal of Neuropsychiatry and Clinical Neuroscience, 3* (3), 276–285.

Steer, R. A., Cavalieri, T. A., Leonard, D. M., & Beck, A. T. (1999). Use of the Beck Depression Inventory for Primary Care to screen for major depression disorders. *General Hospital Psychiatry, 21* (2), 106–111.

Svanborg, P., & Asberg, M. (2001). A comparison between the Beck Depression Inventory (BDI) and the self-rating version of the Montgomery Asberg Depression Rating Scale (MADRS). *Journal of Affective Disorders, 64* (2–3), 203–216.

Swendsen, J. D. (1997). Anxiety, depression, and their comorbidity: An experience sampling test of the Helplessness-Hopelessness Theory. *Cognitive Therapy and Research, 21* (1), 97–114.

Thornton, C., Russell, J., & Hudson, J. (1998). Does the Composite International Diagnostic Interview underdiagnose the eating disorders? *International Journal of Eating Disorders, 23* (3), 341–345.

van Weel-Baumgarten, E. M., Schers, H. J., van den Bosch, W. J., van den Hoogen, H. J., & Zitma, F. G. (2000). Long-term follow-up of depression among patients in the community and in family practice settings. *Journal of Family Practice, 49* (12), 1113–1120.

Veenstra-VanderWeele, J., Anderson, G. M., & Cook, E. H., Jr. (2000). Pharmacogenetics and the serotonin system: Initial studies and future directions. *European Journal of Pharmacology, 410* (2–3), 165–181.

Vega, W. A., Kolody, B., Valle, R., & Hough, R. (1986). Depressive symptoms and their correlates among immigrant Mexican women in the United States. *Social Science and Medicine, 22* (6), 645–652.

Viinamaki, H., Tanskanen, A., Honkalampi, K., Koivumaa-Honkanen, H., Antikainen, R., Haatainen, K., & Hintikka, J. (2000). Effect of somatic comorbidity on alleviation of depressive symptoms. *Australian and New Zealand Journal of Psychiatry, 34* (5), 755–761.

Vinokur, A., Schul, Y., & Caplan, R. D. (1987). Determinants of perceived social support: Interpersonal transactions, personal outlook, and transient affective states. *Journal of Personality and Social Psychology, 53* (6), 1137–1145.

Wagner, H. R., Burns, B. J., Broadhead, W. E., Yarnall, K. S., Sigmon, A., & Gaynes, B. N. (2000). Minor depression in family practice: Functional morbidity, co-morbidity, service utilization and outcomes. *Psychological Medicine, 30* (6), 1377–1390.

Wallace, J., & Pfohl, B. (1995). Age-related differences in the symptomatic expression of major depression. *Journal of Nervous and Mental Disease, 183* (2), 99–102.

Waraich, P., Goldner, E. M., Somers, J. M., & Hsu, L. (2004). Prevalence and incidence studies of mood disorders: A systematic review of the literature. *Canadian Journal of Psychiatry, 49* (2), 124–138.

Welch, J. L., & Austin, J. K. (2001). Stressors, coping and depression in haemodialysis patients. *Journal of Advanced Nursing, 33* (2), 200–207.

Wells, K. B., Burnam, M. A., Rogers, W., Hays, R., & Camp, P. (1992). The course of depression in adult outpatients. Results from the Medical Outcomes Study. *Archives of General Psychiatry, 49* (10), 788–794.

Wilkinson, G., Borsey, D. Q., Leslie, P., Newton, R. W., Lind, C., & Ballinger, C. B. (1988). Psychiatric morbidity and social problems in patients with insulin-dependent diabetes mellitus. *British Journal of Psychiatry, 153,* 38–43.

Winter, L. B., Steer, R. A., Jones-Hicks, L., & Beck, A. T. (1999). Screening for major depression disorders in adolescent medical outpatients with the Beck Depression Inventory for Primary Care. *Journal of Adolescent Health, 24* (6), 389–394.

Yesavage, J. A., Brink, T. L., Rose, T. L., Lum, O., Huang, V., Adey, M., & Leirer, V. O. (1982). Development and validation of a geriatric depression screening scale: A preliminary report. *Journal of Psychiatric Research, 17* (1), 37–49.

Zubenko, G. S., Marino, L. J., Jr., Sweet, R. A., Rifai, A. H., Mulsant, B. H., & Pasternak, R. E. (1997). Medical comorbidity in elderly psychiatric inpatients. *Biological Psychiatry, 41* (6), 724–736.

Zung, W. W. (1972). The Depression Status Inventory: An adjunct to the Self-Rating Depression Scale. *Journal of Clinical Psychology, 28* (4), 539–543.

CHAPTER 10

Bipolar Disorder

DAVID J. MIKLOWITZ AND SHERI L. JOHNSON

O ver the past two decades, there has been a considerable resurgence of interest in bipolar affective disorder. This resurgence is attributable in part to the availability of new pharmacological agents, disorder-specific psychosocial treatments, and data on genetic mechanisms and neurophysiological and neuroanatomical correlates. It has also been driven by the increasing recognition that the onset of the disorder is often in childhood or adolescence.

In this chapter we review the current status of literature on bipolar disorder. In the initial sections we describe the disorder from the vantage points of diagnostic criteria, diagnostic controversies, epidemiology, and course and prognosis, with particular attention to developmental considerations pertinent to early-onset bipolar illness. A case study illustrates these issues.

We discuss the etiology and prognosis of bipolar disorder from both a genetic and a psychosocial viewpoint. Current models of the etiology of the disorder view bipolar disorder as a primarily genetic illness whose onset can be elicited by environmental stressors. Although few studies have examined psychosocial stressors relevant to the onset of bipolar disorder, there is now a considerable literature on psychosocial stressors that affect the course and outcome of the disease. In the final sections, we summarize the major recent findings concerning the treatment of the disorder and offer directions for further research.

DESCRIPTION OF THE DISORDER

MANIC, HYPOMANIC, DEPRESSIVE, AND MIXED EPISODES

Bipolar disorder (BD), formerly known as manic-depressive illness, is defined by manic symptoms. By the *Diagnostic and Statistical Manual of Mental Disorders,* fourth edition (American Psychiatric Association, 2000), people with bipolar, manic episodes experience elated, expansive, or irritable mood (or any combination of these) plus at least three (four if the mood is only irritable) of the following symptoms: decreased need for sleep; racing thoughts or flight of ideas; rapid speech; inflated self-esteem (also called grandiosity); impulsive, reckless behavior (e.g., spending sprees, hypersexuality); increased energy and activity; and distractibility. These symptoms must be present for at least 1 week or interrupted by hospitalization or emergency treatment. They must also cause functional impairment. Hypomania is characterized by parallel symptoms, but the criteria specify only that the symptoms last at least 4 days and result in a distinct, observable change in functioning rather than severe impairment. Bipolar II disorder is defined by hypomanic episodes as well as depressive episodes.

Depressive episodes last for at least 2 weeks and are characterized by sad mood, loss of interest or pleasure in daily activities, and at least five of the following: insomnia or hypersomnia, psychomotor agitation or retardation, increases or decreases in weight or appetite, loss of energy, difficulty concentrating or making decisions, feelings of worthlessness, and suicidal ideation or behavior. Depression must also be associated with functional impairment. Manic or depressive episodes that are clearly related to an ingested substance or to biological treatments—including antidepressant medications or light therapy—are classified as substance-induced mood disorders.

Manic and depressive episodes can occur simultaneously in a mixed episode. For example, patients can have irritable mood, distractibility, decreased need for sleep, and racing thoughts along with loss of interests, suicidal thinking, feelings of worthlessness, and psychomotor agitation. A mixed episode must last at least 1 week and patients must fulfill the criteria for a major depressive episode and a manic episode simultaneously. As many as 40% of patients with bipolar disorder have mixed episodes at some point in their illness (Calabrese, Fatemi, Kujawa, & Woyshville, 1996).

BIPOLAR SUBTYPES

Bipolar I disorder is defined by the presence of a single manic or mixed episode that is not substance-induced (see the following case study). In other words, patients need not have experienced a major depressive episode to be called bipolar. Rates of unipolar mania are between 25% and 33% in community samples but only about 10% in clinical samples (Depue & Monroe, 1978; Karkowski & Kendler, 1997; Kessler, Chiu, Demler, & Walters, 2005; Weissman & Myers, 1978). It would appear, however, that most patients with unipolar mania eventually develop depressive episodes. In a 20-year study of unipolar mania, 20 of 27 patients had episodes of depression at follow-up (Solomon et al., 2003).

Bipolar II disorder is characterized by major depressive episodes alternating with hypomanic episodes. About 1 in 10 bipolar II patients eventually develops a full manic or mixed episode over a 10-year follow-up, and thus converts to bipolar I disorder (Coryell et al., 1995).

Cyclothymia is a variant of bipolar disorder characterized by two or more years of alterations between hypomanic and depressive symptoms, but none of these alterations meet the full *DSM-IV* criteria for a hypomanic or major depressive episode. Bipolar disorder not otherwise specified (NOS) is reserved for patients whose disorder meets the minimum number of required symptoms but not the duration requirements for a full manic, hypomanic, mixed, or depressive episode. Many childhood-onset patients receive this diagnosis (National Institute of Mental Health, 2001).

Case Study

Case Identification and Presenting Complaints

Leonard, a 57-year-old White male, lived with his wife, Helen, and 15-year-old son in a rented house in the suburbs of a major metropolitan area. His wife requested treatment because of his anger outbursts, sleep disturbance, and bizarre preoccupations. He had become preoccupied with kickboxing and was spending hours on the Internet examining relevant web sites and writing about it. She discovered that he had written a 500-page manuscript describing the mechanics of kickboxing, containing sections that were rambling, philosophical, and at times incoherent. She explained that he was frequently awake until 4 A.M. and went to bed smelling of alcohol. He often slept until noon or later. For nearly 5 years he had been unable to hold a job.

Leonard presented in his first interview as combative and oppositional. He admitted that he had been feeling "revved" over the past 2 weeks, that he felt full of energy and ideas, and that he needed little sleep, but he denied any negative effects of his symptoms. He described an incident that appeared to be related to his recent manic behavior. He had made contact with a kickboxing champion in another state and had started writing to this man about setting up a new television network devoted to kickboxing. He also claimed he was going to start his own studio. The plans seemed unrealistic given that he had had little formal training in this sport and had no money to rent a studio. The kickboxing champion had stopped responding to Leonard's emails, which, Leonard claimed, might be because "he's raising money and wants to surprise me."

History

Leonard had one manic episode accompanied by hospitalization when he was in college. He had become entranced by a female professor and believed that she was related to him by blood. He began calling her continually and finally followed her out to a parking lot and tried to block her from getting into her car. A passerby called the police and Leonard was taken to the hospital. He was admitted with the diagnosis of bipolar I, manic episode.

Since this time Leonard had functioned poorly. His work had been intermittent, and he had been fired a number of times because, as he explained, "My bosses are always idiots and I'm more than happy to tell them so." He had tried to set up a web-based business selling auto window shields but had made little money. He met Helen during a meditation retreat in the mountains. They had married approximately 1 year after they met (a period of relative stability for Leonard) and had a child a year later.

Leonard had begun medication shortly after his son was born, explaining that he wanted to become a stable father. His psychiatrist recommended lithium carbonate 1,200 mg and divalproex sodium (Depakote) at 2,000 mg. Although he did not have further manic episodes, he had several hypomanic periods and complained of an ongoing depression that never fully remitted.

(continued)

He had thought of suicide several times, and these fantasies usually had a grandiose quality. For example, he fantasized about setting himself on fire and then jumping from a tall building. He never made an attempt.

Assessment

The clinician who evaluated Leonard administered the Structured Clinical Interview for *DSM-IV* (First, Spitzer, Gibbon, & Williams, 1995), which involved an individual interview with him followed by a separate interview with his wife. The interview confirmed the presence of elated and irritable mood for the past 2 weeks, along with inflated self-esteem, increased activity, decreased need for sleep, flight of ideas and racing thoughts, pressure of speech, and increased spending. His behavior did not require hospitalization but clearly interfered with his functioning. He was given a diagnosis of bipolar disorder I, manic episode and started on a regimen of lithium; divalproex; and an atypical antipsychotic agent, quetiapine (Seroquel).

EPIDEMIOLOGY

PREVALENCE OF BIPOLAR DISORDER

According to the National Comorbidity Survey replication, approximately 4% of the general population has bipolar I or II disorder (Kessler et al., 2005). Cyclothymia affects as much as 4.2% of the general population (Regeer et al., 2004). Major depressive illness is about four times more prevalent than bipolar disorder (Kessler et al., 2005). Notably, the onset of mood disorders appears to be getting younger in successive birth cohorts (Rice et al., 1987; Ryan et al., 1992; Wickramaratne, Weissman, Leaf, & Holford, 1989). For example, Kessler et al. (2005) reported that the lifetime risk of bipolar I or II disorders in 18- to 29-year-olds was 22 times higher than in persons over 60. It is possible, however, that younger persons are more likely to report mood disorder (notably manic) symptoms than older persons.

In a large representative sample of adolescents, Lewinsohn, Klein, and Seeley (Lewinsohn, Klein, & Seeley, 2000) reported that approximately 1% of high school students met diagnostic criteria for bipolar I or II, or cyclothymic disorder. Other estimates of bipolar disorder in children or adolescents are as high as 2% (Kessler, Avenevoli, & Ries-Merikangas, 2001).

AGE AT ONSET

The median age of onset of bipolar disorder is 25 years (Kessler et al., 2005), but there is substantial variability. In the National Comorbidity Survey replication, 25% of patients had onset by age 17 (Kessler et al., 2005). A review of studies prior to 1990 revealed that the peak age at onset is between 15 and 19 years (Goodwin & Jamison, 1990). Earlier age at onset is associated with rapid cycling and other negative outcomes in adulthood (Coryell et al., 2003; Schneck et al., 2004).

GENDER AND RACIAL-ETHNIC ISSUES

Women and men are equally likely to develop bipolar I disorder. Women, however, report more depressive episodes than men and, correspondingly, are more likely to be diagnosed with bipolar II disorder (e.g., Leibenluft, 1997; Schneck et al., 2004). Women are also more likely to meet the *DSM-IV* criteria for rapid cycling BD, especially with repeated episodes of depression (Schneck et al., 2004).

There may be racial and ethnic biases in the diagnosis and treatment of BD. Evidence exists that, compared to White patients, African American and Puerto Rican patients are less likely to be diagnosed with psychotic forms of affective disorder and more likely to be diagnosed with schizophrenia (Garb, 1997). Many patients with psychotic affective disorder are patients with bipolar disorder.

The course of BD illness may be worse among African American patients, who are more likely to have attempted suicide and been hospitalized than White patients. One study found that adult African American patients were less likely than Caucasians to be prescribed mood stabilizers or benzodiazepines and more likely to have been given antipsychotic medications (Kupfer, Frank, Grochocinski, Houck, & Brown, 2005). African American adolescents with bipolar disorder are treated for longer periods with atypical antipsychotics than Caucasian adolescents, even after adjusting for the severity of psychotic symptoms (Patel, DelBello, Keck, & Strakowski, 2005). Moreover, African American bipolar patients are less likely than Caucasian patients to have an outpatient follow-up visit within 3 months of the initial diagnosis (Kilbourne et al., 2005). The reasons for these racial disparities are unclear.

CLINICAL PICTURE

PHENOMENOLOGICAL STUDIES OF THE MANIC SYNDROME

Recent studies have examined the factor structure of the manic syndrome and whether there are differences between euphoric or pure mania and irritable or aggressive mania. A principal component analysis of data from 576 diagnosed manic patients identified seven stable underlying factors: depressive mood, irritable aggression, insomnia, depressive inhibition, pure manic symptoms, emotional lability/agitation, and psychosis (Sato, Bottlender, Kleindienst, & Moller, 2002). Through cluster analysis, Sato et al. identified four phenomenological subtypes of acute mania: pure, aggressive, psychotic, and depressive-mixed mania.

The pattern of manic symptoms has been investigated in youths with bipolar disorder. A meta-analysis of seven studies examining the phenomenological characteristics of mania among children and adolescents (aged 5–18; Kowatch, Youngstrom, Danielyan, & Findling, 2005); the most common symptoms during manic episodes were increased energy, distractibility, and pressure of speech. Approximately 80% showed irritability and grandiosity, whereas 70% had the cardinal manic symptoms of elated mood, decreased need for sleep, or racing thoughts. Less common symptoms included hypersexuality and psychotic symptoms. Thus, most manic children showed symptoms that also characterize adult mania.

SUICIDE

Bipolar disorder is associated with a number of threats to health and livelihood, but the most fundamental concern is the risk of suicide. Rates of completed suicide in bipolar disorder are at least 15 times higher than in the general population (Harris & Barraclough, 1997; Jamison & Baldessarini, 1999) and four times higher than rates among patients with recurrent major depression (Brown, Beck, Steer, & Grisham, 2000). Approximately 50% of patients attempt suicide during their lifetimes, and between 15% and 20% die by suicide (Harris & Barraclough, 1997; Jamison & Baldessarini, 1999). Rates are especially high among younger, recent-onset male patients, and those who have comorbid alcohol or substance abuse, social isolation, depression, significant anxiety, aggression, impulsiveness, a family history of suicide, or any combination of these (Angst, Angst, Gerber-Werder, & Gamma, 2005; Fawcett, Golden, & Rosenfeld, 2000; Jamison, 2000).

FUNCTIONAL IMPAIRMENT

Patients with bipolar disorder experience ongoing impairments in social, occupational, and familial functioning even between episodes, especially if they have unresolved depressive symptoms (Fagiolini et al., 2005). Within the first year after hospitalization, only half the patients who recover from a manic or mixed episode demonstrate full recovery (Keck et al., 1998). Diminished work, social, and family functioning persists for up to 5 years after a manic episode (Coryell et al., 1993). Goldberg, Harrow, and Grossman (1995) found that only about one in three patients with bipolar disorder taking lithium had good functioning over a 4.5-year follow-up.

In a survey of 253 patients with bipolar I and II disorder, only 33% worked full-time and 9% worked part-time outside of the home. Fully 57% reported being unable to work or working only in sheltered settings (Suppes et al., 2001). Only 42% of bipolar I, manic patients showed "steady" work performance an average of 1.7 years after hospital discharge (Harrow, Goldberg, Grossman, & Meltzer, 1990). In the 6 months after a hospitalization, one-third of patients were unable to work at all, and only one in five worked at their expected level (Dion, Tohen, Anthony, & Waternaux, 1988). The disorder is also associated with high rates of family or marital distress, dysfunction, separation, divorce, and problems in the adjustment of patients' offspring (Coryell et al., 1993; Hodgins, Faucher, Zarac, & Ellenbogen, 2002; Simoneau, Miklowitz, & Saleem, 1998).

On the positive side, there appears to be a link between bipolar disorder and creativity or productivity: many famous artists, musicians, writers, and politicians probably had the disorder (Jamison, 1993). Patients with bipolar disorder and highly creative persons without psychiatric disorder appear to have temperamental commonalities, such as openness to new experiences and novelty seeking (Nowakowska, Strong, Santosa, Wang, & Ketter, 2005). One study showed that children diagnosed with bipolar disorder and children who were the offspring of bipolar parents scored higher on a creativity index than healthy control children (Simeonova, Chang, Strong, & Ketter, 2005). Interestingly, the unaffected family members of patients with bipolar disorder demonstrate higher accomplishment and creativity than do their affected relatives (Johnson, 2005b; Richards, Kinney, Lunde, Benet, & Merzel, 1988).

COURSE AND PROGNOSIS

Virtually all patients with bipolar disorder have illness recurrences. The rates of recurrence, even when patients are treated with mood stabilizers, average 37% in 1 year, 60% over 2 years, and 73% over 5 years (Gitlin, Swendsen, Heller, & Hammen, 1995). Approximately one in five patients can be characterized as a rapid cycler, meaning they have four or more distinct episodes of mania, hypomania, mixed, or depressive disorder within 1 year (Calabrese et al., 1996; Schneck et al., 2004). Biological and psychosocial factors that predict illness recurrences are discussed further in the next section.

Even more significant are the persistent, mild-to-moderate residual symptoms that most patients experience between episodes, even when undergoing pharmacotherapy (Judd et al., 2002; Keller, Lavori, Coryell, Endicott, & Mueller, 1993; Post et al., 2003). Over a 13-year follow-up, subsyndromal symptoms were present during approximately half the weeks of follow-up (Judd et al., 2002). These symptoms were almost exclusively depressive rather than manic. A study of children with bipolar I, II, and NOS disorders observed similar patterns of residual symptoms over a 15-month follow-up (Birmaher et al., 2006). These findings have led to the recognition (e.g., Perlis et al., 2006) that one of the most challenging issues in the treatment of the disorder is the stabilization of depressive symptoms.

PSYCHOSOCIAL PREDICTORS OF THE COURSE OF BIPOLAR DISORDER

By the end of the 1980s, researchers began to acknowledge that biological and genetic models of BD did not explain the enormous heterogeneity in the course of the illness over time (Prien & Potter, 1990). This recognition contributed to a renewed emphasis on psychosocial predictors in the course of the disorder. For example, Ellicott, Hammen, Gitlin, Brown, and Jamison (1990) found that BD patients with high life-events-stress scores were at 4.5 times greater risk for relapse in a 2-year follow-up than patients with medium or low life-events-stress scores. Miklowitz, Goldstein, Nuechterlein, Snyder, and Mintz (1988) found that BD I manic patients who returned after a hospitalization to families rated high on expressed emotion (EE) attitudes (criticism, hostility, or emotional overinvolvement) or who showed high levels of caregiver-to-patient affective negativity (criticism, hostility, or guilt induction) during face-to-face interactions were at high risk for relapse. Those whose families had both high EE and high affective negativity were highly likely to relapse within 9 months (94%), whereas those whose families rated low on both attributes were unlikely to relapse within this time frame (17%). More recently, Hillegers et al. (2004) found that negative life events predicted the onset of mood disorders among children of bipolar parents.

Although these first-generation studies established the prognostic role of psychosocial factors, they did not address how psychosocial variables influence depression versus mania. A second generation of research has examined which psychosocial variables influence the course of BD depression and which influence the course of mania.

PSYCHOSOCIAL PREDICTORS OF DEPRESSION WITHIN BIPOLAR DISORDER

The symptomatology and neurobiology of unipolar and BD depression have many strong parallels (Cuellar, Johnson, & Winters, 2005). Given these parallels, one might expect that psychosocial predictors of unipolar depression would influence BD depression. Here, we focus on well-established predictors of unipolar depression, including negative life events (Monroe, Harkness, Simons, & Thase, 2001), low social support (Brown & Andrews, 1986), EE (Butzlaff & Hooley, 1998), neuroticism (Gunderson, Triebwasser, Phillips, & Sullivan, 1999), and negative cognitive styles (Alloy, Reilly-Harrington, Fresco, Whitehouse, & Zechmeister, 1999).

Negative life events have been perhaps the most examined predictors of bipolar depression. Fortunately, a set of BD studies have now used interview-based measures of life events. As reviewed by Johnson (2005a), three of these cross-sectional studies found that negative life events are equally common before episodes of BD depression and unipolar depression (Malkoff-Schwartz et al., 2000; Pardoen et al., 1996; Perris, 1984). Findings of prospective studies with interview-based measures also indicate that stressful life events are correlated with slow recoveries from depression (Johnson & Miller, 1997) and predict increases in BD depression over several months (Johnson, Kizer, Ruggero, Goodnick, & Miller, under review). Thus, the most methodologically rigorous studies suggest that negative life events are precipitants of bipolar depression.

Other variables involved in unipolar depression also appear to have validity as predictors of bipolar depression. For example, neuroticism (Heerlein, Richter, Gonzalez, & Santander, 1998; Lozano & Johnson, 2001), low social support (Johnson, Winett, Meyer, Greenhouse, & Miller, 1999), and family EE (Kim & Miklowitz, 2004; Yan, Hammen, Cohen, Daley, & Henry, 2004) have been found to predict increases in depressive symptoms but not manic symptoms over time. Although negative cognitive styles are often documented in BD (see Cuellar et al., 2005, for review), they (a) are most likely to be found during depression compared with well periods (Johnson & Kizer, 2002), (b) predict depression but not mania in some (Johnson & Fingerhut, 2004; Johnson, Meyer, Winett, & Small, 2000) but not all studies (Reilly-Harrington et al., 1999), and (c) can be explained by the presence of depressive history rather than manic history (Alloy et al., 1999).

In sum, variables that influence the course of unipolar depression also influence BD depression, including negative life events, poor social support, family EE, negative cognitive styles, and low self-esteem. It is worth noting, though, that relatively few prospective studies are available to help disentangle which symptoms are predicted by various risk factors.

Psychosocial Predictors of Mania

Compared with BD depression, less is known about the psychosocial predictors of mania. Available models highlight three sets of potential predictors: negative threats (the manic-defense model), goal engagement, and sleep/schedule disruption.

The Manic Defense Model   Psychodynamic models have long conceptualized mania as a defense against loss experiences and painful awareness of negative feelings about the self (Adler, 1964). Consistent with this idea, people with BD will show many negative cognitive patterns, such as blaming themselves for negative events and attending more to negative stimuli as compared to healthy controls. Nonetheless, they endorse relatively high levels of self-esteem compared to healthy controls (Lyon, Startup, & Bentall, 1999; Winters & Neale, 1985). A set of studies have focused on the idea that mania might occur in response to threats, as a way of trying to ward off negative feelings about the self.

Most studies that have used life event interviews have failed to find that negative life events trigger manic episodes (Johnson, 2005a). Nonetheless, a few recent studies suggest that BD may be characterized by uniquely activated and sensation-seeking responses to threats. For example, when asked to write an essay about their own mortality (one way to experimentally manipulate threat), people with high vulnerability to hypomania report more desire to engage in materialistic and defensive activities than people with low vulnerability to mania (Johnson, 2005a). People with BD also report that they are more likely to pursue highly stimulating, sensation-seeking activities during periods of stress (Thomas & Bentall, 2002). Thus, people with BD may show a specific profile of sensation-seeking behavior in response to threat. No research has been conducted to examine whether this specific defensive style spirals into mania in the context of negative life events.

Goal Dysregulation   Drawing on biological models of overly sensitive reward pathways, the goal dysregulation model suggests that people with BD may show more extreme responses to rewarding stimuli (Johnson, 2005b). People with a history of mania and students vulnerable to mania describe themselves as more sensitive to rewards (Meyer, Johnson, & Carver, 1999; Meyer, Johnson, & Winters, 2001). People with BD place a stably high emphasis on goal pursuit, even when not in an episode (Johnson & Carver, in press). This reward sensitivity would be expected to influence reactions to life events that involve major successes. Consistent with this idea, life events involving goal attainments (such as new relationships, births of children, or career successes) predicted increases in manic symptoms but not depressive symptoms (Johnson, Sandrow, et al., 2000). Such effects were apparent even after controlling for baseline levels of manic symptoms and excluding life events that could have been caused by the patients' symptoms.

Why might attaining an important goal trigger manic symptoms? A set of studies suggest that for people with BD, cognition becomes much more positive during good moods than it does for other people. Available evidence suggests that mood states are associated with distinct positive shifts in confidence (Johnson, 2005b; Stern & Berrenberg, 1979), autobiographical recall (Eich, Macaulay, & Lam, 1997), and attention to valenced stimuli (Murphy et al., 1999). Impulsivity, or the tendency to pursue rewards without awareness of potential negative consequences, also becomes elevated as people become manic (Swann, Dougherty, Pazzaglia, Pham, & Moeller, 2004). Mood-state-dependent shifts in confidence may contribute to increased goal setting (Johnson, 2005b). In turn, investment in goal pursuit predicts increases in manic symptoms over several months (Lozano & Johnson, 2001). Building on these findings, it has been hypothesized that goal attainments may trigger increased goal engagement, and this excess goal engagement may trigger manic symptoms (Johnson, 2005b).

SLEEP AND SCHEDULE DISRUPTION

Experimental studies (Barbini et al., 1998) as well as longitudinal studies (Leibenluft et al., 1996) suggest that sleep deprivation is an important trigger of manic symptoms. Wehr, Sack, and Rosenthal (1987) hypothesized that sleep disruption might be one way in which life events trigger episodes of BD, noting that illness episodes are often preceded by life events interfering with the ability to sleep (e.g., transmeridian flights, childbearing). This theory was broadened by Ehlers and colleagues (Ehlers, Frank, & Kupfer, 1988; Ehlers, Kupfer, Frank, & Monk, 1993), who suggested that social disruptions to other aspects of circadian rhythms could trigger symptoms (the "social zeitgebers model"). In two studies, Malkoff-Schwartz et al. (1998; Malkoff-Schwartz et al., 2000) found that bipolar patients reported more life events involving social-rhythm disruption (events that affect sleep or wake times, patterns of social stimulation, or daily routines) in the weeks preceding manic episodes compared to the weeks preceding depressive episodes. Thus, sleep disruptions and possibly broader schedule disruptions are important to the course of mania.

In sum, the variables hypothesized to influence the onset of mania include the use of sensation-seeking coping in response to threats, goal dysregulation, and sleep or schedule disruption. As with research on the predictors of bipolar depression, very few longitudinal studies are available. As discussed next, some of these risk factors are amenable to modification through psychosocial intervention.

TREATMENT OF BIPOLAR DISORDER: CURRENT TRENDS

Optimally, treatments for BD should involve combinations of pharmacological and psychosocial interventions. Unfortunately, in the era of managed care cost containment, drug treatments are often the only treatment provided. Perhaps as a result, the average duration of lithium treatment for patients in community settings is only 76 days (Johnson & McFarland, 1996).

PHARMACOLOGICAL TREATMENTS

Distinctions are usually made between acute pharmacological treatment and maintenance treatment. The goal of acute treatment is to stabilize an existing manic or depressive episode (for recent and thorough reviews of acute pharmacotherapy studies of adult and pediatric patients, see Goldberg, 2004, and Kowatch, Sethuraman, Hume, Kromelis, & Weinberg, 2003). Adjunctive psychotherapy is usually introduced during the postepisode stabilization phase and continued throughout maintenance treatment. The goals of adjunctive psychotherapy are to minimize residual symptoms and prevent recurrences. Untreated residual symptoms of mania or depression are prospectively associated with illness recurrences (Perlis et al., 2006).

Current pharmacotherapy algorithms for mania for adult and childhood-onset patients (e.g., Kowatch, Fristad, et al., 2005; McAllister-Williams, 2006) combine mood stabilizers (lithium carbonate, divalproex sodium, carbamazepine) with atypical antipsychotic medications (olanzapine, quetiapine, risperidone, aripiprazole, ziprasidone, and less frequently, clozapine). Adjunctive antidepressant agents are often recommended for bipolar depression, although antidepressant medications cause manic switching and acceleration of cycles in a significant number of patients (Ghaemi, Lenox, & Baldessarini, 2001). The anticonvulsant lamotrigine is an option for many patients given its antidepressant properties and lower propensity to cause cycle acceleration (Bowden et al., 2003; Calabrese et al., 1999; Calabrese et al., 2000).

Despite the clear effectiveness of many forms of pharmacotherapy, patients with BD are prone to discontinuing their medications, with as many as 60% being fully or partially noncompliant after a major episode of illness (Keck et al., 1998; Strakowski et al., 1998). Patients who discontinue their pharmacotherapy abruptly are at a high risk for recurrence and suicide attempts (Keck, McElroy, Strakowski, Bourne, & West, 1997; Strober, Morrell, Lampert, & Burroughs, 1990; Suppes, Baldessarini, Faedda, Tondo, & Tohen, 1993; Tondo & Baldessarini, 2000). For example, in a naturalistic study of adolescent BD patients followed 18 months after a hospitalization, relapse was three times more likely among patients who discontinued lithium than among patients who remained on it. Patients describe barriers to compliance that include missing high periods, objecting to having one's moods controlled by medications, lack of information about the disorder, or lack of social or familial supports (for review, see Colom et al., 2000).

PSYCHOTHERAPY AS AN ADJUNCT TO MEDICATION MAINTENANCE

Randomized controlled trials of psychotherapy indicate positive benefits for psychoeducational, skill-oriented, and interpersonal treatments. The modalities investigated in the trials have included individual, family, and group formats. Table 10.1 lists the key components of empirically supported treatments for BD, including individual or group psychoeducation, family psychoeducational therapy, cognitive-behavioral therapy (CBT), and interpersonal and social rhythm therapy (for review, see Miklowitz, 2006).

These treatments have a number of elements in common. First, all include an active psychoeducational component, which often involves teaching patients (and in some cases, family members) to recognize and obtain early treatment for manic episodes before they develop fully. All emphasize medication adherence, avoiding alcohol and street drugs, and the use of skills to cope more effectively with stress triggers. They differ in the emphasis on specific strategies, including involvement of family members in psychoeducation (family-focused therapy), stabilizing sleep/wake rhythms (interpersonal and social rhythm therapy), and cognitive restructuring (cognitive-behavioral therapy).

Table 10.1
Empirically Supported Adjunctive Psychotherapy for Bipolar Disorder

Modality	Main Techniques	References to Randomized Trials
Individual or group psychoeducation	Educating patients about coping with the disorder and its cycling; use of emergency services to prevent recurrence; setting appropriate life goals	Colom et al., 2003; Perry, Tarrier, Morriss, McCarthy, & Limb, 1999; Simon et al., 2005
Family psychoeducational therapy	Educating patients and family members about coping with bipolar disorder; enhancing communication and problem-solving skills	Clarkin et al., 1990; Clarkin, Carpenter, Hull, Wilner, & Glick, 1998; Miklowitz, George, Richards, Simoneau, & Suddath, 2003; Rea et al., 2003; Fristad, Gavazzi, & Mackinaw-Koons, 2003
Cognitive-behavioral therapy	Activity management, cognitive restructuring, problem-solving	Cochran, 1984; Lam et al., 2003; Scott et al., 2006
Interpersonal and social rhythm therapy	Stabilizing sleep/wake cycles and daily routines; resolving key interpersonal problems	Frank et al., 2005

The treatments listed in Table 10.1 have all been found in at least one study to delay relapses of BD when combined with pharmacotherapy. The control conditions vary and have included treatment as usual, individual supportive therapy, unstructured group support, and active clinical management. There are nonreplications as well: in a large-scale multicenter study, Scott et al. (2006) found that CBT was no more effective than treatment as usual in delaying recurrences. Post-hoc analyses, however, revealed that CBT was associated with longer time to recurrence among patients who had had fewer than 12 lifetime episodes.

There are still many gaps in research on psychosocial treatment. For example, it is not clear which treatments are most effective for preventing symptoms of mania versus depression, or whether particular subgroups of patients respond more completely to individual, family, or group treatment. Few studies have identified the mechanisms of action of psychosocial interventions (for example, whether they enhance medication adherence, improve the patient's ability to recognize prodromal symptoms of recurrence, or increase self-efficacy). The applicability of psychosocial interventions to early-onset BD, or children at risk for developing the illness, has just begun to be systematically investigated (Fristad et al., 2003; Miklowitz, Biuckians, & Richards, in press).

DIAGNOSTIC CONSIDERATIONS

The Bipolar Spectrum

Controversy exists over how to draw the boundaries of BD. Although it has traditionally been conceptualized as a disease involving shifts between the dramatic poles of mania and depression, there is increasing recognition that many patients have bipolar spectrum disorders, which, depending on the definition, may include subsyndromal manic episodes, manic or hypomanic episodes triggered by antidepressants, subsyndromal mixed episodes, or agitated depression (Akiskal, 1996; Akiskal, Benazzi, Perugi, & Rihmer, 2005; Akiskal et al., 2000). For example, Smith, Harrison, Muir, and Blackwood (2005) observed that many young adults with recurrent depression have symptoms that would be best considered within the bipolar spectrum. In a sample of young adults treated for recurrent depression at a university health service, only 16% met the *DSM-IV* criteria for bipolar disorder and 83% for recurrent major depressive illness. When broader definitions of the bipolar spectrum were used, between 47% and 77% received bipolar diagnoses. When broad (and often questionnaire-based) measures of the bipolar spectrum are used, lifetime prevalence rates for the disorder increase to 6.4% to 10% (Akiskal et al., 2000; Judd & Akiskal, 2003; McIntyre & Konarski, 2004).

What is the evidence that spectrum patients are really bipolar in the classic sense? Although they do not necessarily follow the same course of illness patterns as patients with bipolar I or II disorder, patients with subsyndromal forms of BD are more likely to have family histories of BD and higher rates of hypomania induced by antidepressants than people without subsyndromal BD symptoms. They also have high rates of suicide, marital disruption, and mental health service utilization (Akiskal, 1996; Judd & Akiskal, 2003; Smith et al., 2005).

Some researchers have examined the bipolar spectrum as a risk factor for the development of fully syndromal BD. Assessment instruments designed to identify persons at risk include the Temperament Evaluation of Memphis, Pisa, Paris, and San Diego—autoquestionnaire version (TEMPS-A; Akiskal et al., 2005). The TEMPS-A is a self- or parent-rated assessment of temperaments believed to precede the onset of full BD and to persist during the euthymic states. Five factors emerge from the TEMPS-A, each of which has high internal consistency: cyclothymic (0.91), depressive (0.81), irritable (0.77), hyperthymic (0.76), and anxious (0.67; Akiskal et al., 2005). A 2-year prospective follow-up of 80 clinically depressed children and adolescents found that high baseline cyclothymic-hypersensitive TEMPS-A scores predicted the later onset of BD (Kochman et al., 2005).

The 79-item General Behavior Inventory (Depue, Kleinman, Davis, Hutchinson, & Krauss, 1985) evaluates lifetime experiences of depressive and manic symptoms, as well as mood variability, on one to four scales of frequency. High scores during adolescence are associated with psychosocial impairment in adulthood (Klein & Depue, 1984), and a childhood version rated by parents discriminated pediatric BD from attention deficit hyperactivity disorder (ADHD; Danielson, Youngstrom, Findling, & Calabrese, 2003). Among adolescents with depression, higher scores on the General Behavior Inventory depression subscale predicted BD onset at 5-year follow-up (Reichart et al., 2005).

Finally, the Hypomanic Personality Scale (Eckblad & Chapman, 1986) has been used to assess hypomanic temperament in college-age individuals. Kwapil et al. (2000) found that high scores on this scale predicted the onset of bipolar spectrum disorders over a 13-year follow-up. Thus, self-report measures of spectrum symptoms and temperamental characteristics predict the onset of BDs in longitudinal studies.

DIAGNOSIS IN CHILDREN AND ADOLESCENTS

Perhaps the most controversial diagnostic dilemma is where to draw the boundaries of the bipolar diagnosis in children. Before about 1980, belief was widespread that neither mania nor depression could occur before puberty, although individual case reports of the phenomenon existed (e.g., Anthony & Scott, 1960; Strecker, 1921). This belief has changed significantly in the past two decades; for review, see Pavuluri, Birmaher, and Naylor (2005). Unfortunately, no separate diagnostic criteria exist for juvenile BD patients, and as a result there is little agreement on the operational definition of a manic or mixed episode, whether well-demarcated episodes of mania and depression must occur or whether the symptoms can be chronic and unremitting, the minimum duration of episodes, and what constitutes a symptom (Biederman et al., 2003; Leibenluft, Charney, Towbin, Bhangoo, & Pine, 2003; McClellan, 2005; McClellan & Werry, 2000). The reliability of the diagnosis appears to decrease with age (Carlson, 2005).

One research group, led by Geller and colleagues (2002), has recommended that BD not be diagnosed in children unless elevated mood and grandiosity are present. Another group, led by Biederman, Wozniak, and colleagues (Biederman, Faraone, Chu, & Wozniak, 1999; Wozniak, Biederman, & Richards, 2001) emphasizes the roles of irritability, aggression, and mixed symptoms as core illness features. A third group (Leibenluft et al., 2003) has recommended that BD in children be divided into three phenotypes: a narrow phenotype (meets *DSM-IV* criteria for mania or hypomania with elated mood and grandiosity), an intermediate phenotype (meets *DSM-IV* criteria but with irritable mood only), and a broad phenotype (e.g., mania that does not meet the duration criteria for bipolar I or II or is one symptom short).

Does childhood-onset BD develop into adult BD, or are they separate conditions? One long-term study found developmental continuity for a narrow BD phenotype from late adolescence to early adulthood, but not for a broader BD phenotype marked by irritability and euphoria without the associated manic symptoms (Lewinsohn, Seeley, Buckley, & Klein, 2002). In a multisite study of 263 children and adolescents, 25% with subsyndromal symptoms of mania (designated as bipolar NOS) developed bipolar I or bipolar II disorders during a 1.5-year follow-up (Birmaher et al., 2006). A 4-year follow-up of manic children (mean age 11) who met strict *DSM-IV* criteria revealed that the average duration of manic episodes was 79 weeks, and only 36% recovered fully within 1 year. At 4-year follow-up, 64% had a recurrence of mania. Follow-up into adulthood has not yet been accomplished (Geller, Tillman, Craney, & Bolhofner, 2004).

In a reanalysis of a large-scale longitudinal study of youths in semirural parts of New York (N = 776, mean age 13.8), two categories of risk were defined: episodic irritability (based on the parents' and child's answer to questions such as "Are there times when [the child] feels irritable or jumpy?" and "Do these times last for a week or more?") and "chronic irritability" (persistent arguing and temper tantrums across the home and school settings). Females exhibited higher levels of episodic and chronic irritability than males. Moreover, episodic irritability in adolescence predicted the onset of a mania by age 16 (Leibenluft, Cohen, Gorrindo, Brook, & Pine, 2006). In contrast, chronic irritability was associated with ADHD by midadolescence and major depressive illness in early adulthood. Episodic irritability was a unique predictor of mania by age 22, although this relationship was mediated by the cross-sectional correlation between episodic irritability and depression in early adolescence. Thus, the episodicity of symptoms is an important feature to assess when attempting to distinguish risk for BD from risk for other psychiatric syndromes among youths.

DUAL DIAGNOSIS

BD patients are highly likely to be diagnosed with one or more comorbid disorders. When 12-month prevalence rates in a community epidemiological sample are considered, the highest associations are found between mania/hypomania and ADHD, followed by oppositional defiant disorder, agoraphobia, panic disorder, generalized anxiety disorder, alcohol dependence, and drug abuse (Kessler et al., 2005). The prevalence of anxiety disorders in clinical and epidemiologic studies ranges from 10.6% to 62.5% for panic disorder, 7.8% to 47.2% for social anxiety disorder, 7% to 40% for posttraumatic stress disorder, 3.2% to 35% for obsessive-compulsive disorder, and 7% to 32% for generalized anxiety disorder (Simon et al., 2004).

In the Epidemiological Catchment Area Study, 6 of 10 patients with bipolar disorder had a lifetime history of alcohol or drug abuse (Regier et al., 1990). Other community and clinical population studies (Brady, Casto, Lydiard, Malcolm, & Arana, 1991; Goldberg, Garno, Leon, Kocsis, & Portera, 1999; Kessler et al., 1997) have documented rates of lifetime substance use disorder ranging from 21% to 45%. This represents a sixfold increase in substance use disorders among patients with BD relative to the general population. One study found that patients were more likely to use alcohol during depressive episodes and more likely to use cocaine and marijuana during manic episodes (Strakowski, DelBello, Fleck, & Arndt, 2000).

Comorbid diagnoses—and even subsyndromal symptoms of comorbid disorders—are associated with a poor prognosis of child and adult BD (Feske et al., 2000; Frank et al., 2002; Masi et al., 2004; Otto et al., 2006; Tohen, Waternaux, & Tsuang, 1990). For example, anxiety comorbidity has been linked with younger onset of BD, lower likelihood of recovery, poorer role functioning and quality of life, a greater likelihood of suicide attempts, and poorer response to medications (Henry et al., 2003; Simon et al., 2004). Studies have also documented lower recovery rates among patients with BD with a comorbid substance use disorder (Keller et al., 1986; Tohen et al., 1990), and a greater likelihood of rehospitalization (Brady et al., 1991; Reich, Davies, & Himmelhoch, 1974).

A separate issue is how to distinguish BD from comorbid disorders. A case in point is ADHD. In a sample of children, Geller et al. (1998) compared the frequency of symptoms that are considered classic or pathognomonic of mania versus those typically seen in either mania or ADHD. Elated mood, grandiosity, hypersexuality, decreased need for sleep, daredevil acts, and uninhibited people seeking were far more common in mania than ADHD. Distractibility, increased activity, and increased energy were observed in both disorders (see also Kim & Miklowitz, 2002). It is rare to see major depressive episodes in children with ADHD, and when the two do co-occur, the child is at high risk for developing BD (Chang, Steiner, & Ketter, 2000; Faraone, Biederman, Mennin, Wozniak, & Spencer, 1997a; Faraone et al., 1997b; Leibenluft et al., 2006).

DIAGNOSTIC ASSESSMENT METHODS

Most patients with BD are diagnosed by a clinical interview; there are no biological tests that verify the diagnosis. The most prominent is the Structured Diagnostic Interview for *DSM-IV* (SCID; First et al., 1995). Despite impressive reliability and validity statistics, the SCID and the Kiddie Schedule for Affective Disorders and Schizophrenia (KSADS) are not always sensitive in identifying the milder forms of BD (Chambers et al., 1985; Kaufman et al., 1997). For example, the SCID may underestimate identification of hypomanic episodes when comparing with diagnoses based on interviews by experienced clinicians (Dunner & Tay, 1993). Current thinking about diagnostic assessments is that instruments like the SCID should be supplemented by data from self-report questionnaires (especially those that examine subsyndromal forms of mania) as well as a thorough history of prior episodes involving an episode timeline, such as the National Institute of Mental Health Life Charting method (Leverich & Post, 1998). Life charting enables the clinician to investigate the frequency, severity, and timing of prior episodes; whether depressive, mixed, or manic episodes have dominated the clinical picture; and whether other disorders (e.g., substance dependence) preceded, coincided with, or developed after the onset of the mood disorder.

ETIOLOGICAL CONSIDERATIONS

Heritability

Estimates of the heritability of BD range from 59% to 87% (McGuffin et al., 2003). A review of studies by Alda (1997) indicated that the concordance rates for monozygotic twins averages 57%, whereas the concordance rate for dizygotic twins averages

14%. One twin study found that the heritability for depression was correlated with the heritability of mania, but not so highly that these genetic vulnerabilities should be considered as overlapping (McGuffin et al., 2003).

The risk of BD among children of bipolar parents is four times greater than the risk among children of healthy parents. Children of bipolar parents, however, are also at approximately 2.7 times higher risk for developing nonaffective disorders (including ADHD and conduct disorder) than are the children of well parents. Thus, a proportion of the familial risk is not specific to bipolar illness (Hodgins et al., 2002; LaPalme, Hodgins, & LaRoche, 1997).

Several genomic regions relevant to BD have been identified, including 13q32, 22q11, 8p22, and 10p14 (Badner & Gershon, 2002; Berrettini, 2003), but effects have generally been small and findings have not been entirely consistent from study to study. One model (Murray et al., 2004) emphasizes the genetic overlap between BD and schizophrenia and common susceptibility genes that predispose individuals to dopamine dysregulation and psychosis. In addition to common susceptibilities, there are probably other genes whose expression affects neuro-development, illness-specific neurological changes, the likelihood of exposure to certain types of environments, and the eventual outcome of BD, schizoaffective disorder, or schizophrenia (Murray et al., 2004).

NEUROTRANSMITTER DYSREGULATION

Traditional neurotransmitter models of mood disorders have focused on norepinephrine, dopamine, and serotonin (Charney, Menkes, & Heninger, 1981; Thase, Jindal, & Howland, 2002). It is now widely believed that dysregulations in these systems interact with deficits in other neurotransmitter systems, such as gamma-aminobutyric acid (GABA) and Substance P, to produce symptoms of mood disorders (Stockmeier, 2003). Given these complex interactions, current research focuses on the functioning of neurotransmitter systems rather than simple models of neurotransmitter levels being either high or low. Current paradigms include measuring sensitivity of the postsynaptic receptors through pharmacological challenges, neuroimaging, or molecular genetic research. This type of research has progressed particularly rapidly in understanding dysregulation in serotonin and dopamine systems.

DOPAMINE

Among people without BD, several different dopamine agonists, including stimulants, have been found to trigger manic symptoms, including increases in mood, energy, and talkativeness (Willner, 1995). People with BD show pronounced behavioral effects to stimulants (Anand et al., 2000). A number of paradigms have been used to challenge the dopamine system, including behavioral sensitization (the study of how repeated administration of dopamine agonists changes the sensitivity of dopaminergic reward pathways (Kalivas, Duffy, DuMars, & Skinner, 1988; Robinson & Becker, 1986) and sleep deprivation (which appears to interfere with normalizing the sensitivity of dopamine receptors; Ebert, Feistel, Barocks, Kaschka, & Pirner, 1994). Results obtained using these paradigms are consistent with the idea that BD is characterized by hypersensitivity of the dopamine system (Strakowski, Sax, Setters, & Keck, 1996; Strakowski, Sax, Setters, Stanton, & Keck, 1997; Winters, Johnson, & Cuellar, in press).

Molecular genetic studies have not yet identified polymorphisms that could explain these effects. For example, BD has not been found to consistently relate to polymorphisms in the d1, d2, d3, and d4 receptor genes or the dopamine transporter genes (Chiaroni et al., 2000; Georgieva et al., 2002; Gorwood, Bellivier, Ades, & Leboyer, 2000; Lopez et al., 2005; Manki, Kanba, Muramatsu, & Higuchi, 1996; Muglia et al., 2002). In animal models, though, a set of candidate genes for BD have been identified that relate to modulating dopamine signaling within reward pathways (Ogden et al., 2004).

Serotonin

Neuroimaging studies indicate that mood disorders are generally associated with decreased sensitivity of the serotonin receptors (Stockmeier, 2003). The functioning of the serotonin system can also be tested by manipulating levels of tryptophan, the precursor to serotonin (Staley, Malison, & Innis, 1998). Findings of tryptophan-manipulation studies are consistent with the idea of serotonin receptor dysfunction among persons with a family history of BD (Sobcazk, Honig, Schmitt, & Riedel, 2003; Sobczak et al., 2002). Meta-analyses, however, find that BD is not consistently related to genes regulating serotonin receptors (Anguelova, Benkelfat, & Turecki, 2003) or to serotonin transporter genes (Lotrich & Pollock, 2004).

Brain Regions Involved in Bipolar Disorder

Although findings are not entirely consistent, neuroimaging studies implicate a set of structures in the pathophysiology of BD. Many of these regions overlap substantially with those involved in emotional reactivity and regulation, and as such, many parallels are present with the brain correlates of unipolar depression (Davidson, Pizzagalli, & Nitschke, 2002; Mayberg, Keightley, Mahurin, & Brannan, 2004). Key structures include the amygdala, which is involved in the detection of the significance of emotionally salient stimuli, and a set of other regions involved in effective cognitive regulation of emotions and goal pursuit, such as the prefrontal cortex, anterior cingulate, and hippocampus. One model suggests that mood disorders are characterized by increased activity in regions involved in emotional sensitivity, combined with diminished activity in regions involved in effective thinking and planning in response to emotional cues (Phillips, Drevets, Rauch, & Lane, 2003).

More specifically, several Positron Emission Tomography (PET) and functional Magnetic Resonance Imaging (fMRI) studies of neural activity during cognitive or emotional tasks have shown a pattern of amygdala hyperactivity among people with bipolar I disorder (Altshuler et al., 2005; Chang et al., 2004; Kruger, Seminowicz, Goldapple, Kennedy, & Mayberg, 2003; Lawrence et al., 2004). Although some adult studies correspondingly suggest above-average volume of the amygdala (Phillips et al., 2003), early studies of juvenile BD suggest smaller volumes of the amygdala (Caetano et al., 2005). Thus, abnormalities in amygdalar volume may change as the disorder progresses.

Given that the neural regions involved in BD appear particularly tied to emotion reactivity and regulation, a central paradigm involves studying brain activity in response to positive and negative stimuli. Among such studies, increased neural activity has been particularly consistently documented in reactions to positive stimuli as opposed to negative stimuli (Johnson, Gruber, & Eisner, in press).

People with BD also appear to demonstrate diminished activity of the hippocampus and prefrontal cortex (Kruger et al., 2003). In parallel with the findings of functional studies, structural studies have found that BD is associated with a smaller-than-average volume in the prefrontal cortex, basal ganglia, hippocampus, and anterior cingulate (Phillips et al., 2003). Findings regarding diminished volume of the hippocampus have been identified in juvenile BD (Frazier et al., 2005). Diminished function of the prefrontal cortex and related circuits might interfere with effective planning and goal pursuit in the context of emotion, leading to a low capacity to regulate emotion. Although prefrontal cortical deficits have been implicated in schizophrenia as well (Barch, 2005), recent research suggests that the prefrontal deficits in BD compared to schizophrenia may be more specific to the orbitofrontal cortex (Altshuler et al., 2005; Cotter, Hudson, & Landau, 2005).

Evidence exists that patterns of neural activation shift with mood episodes. During depression, diminished activity in the anterior cingulate is observed (Mayberg et al., 2004). During mania, persons with BD may show diminished reactivity to negative stimuli compared with healthy or euthymic persons. For example, after viewing faces with different negative emotional expressions, Lennox, Jacob, Calder, Lupson, and Bullmore (2004) found decreased amygdala and subgenul anterior cingulate cortex activation in manic patients compared with controls. Hence, brain regions involved in identifying the importance of negative stimuli appear to become less active during manic episodes.

Finally, given models of reward sensitivity in BD, the role of structures within the basal ganglia, including the nucleus accumbens (Knutson, Adams, Fong, & Hommer, 2001), has become an important focus of research. Both at rest and during motor tasks, the level of activity in the basal ganglia is positively correlated with the concurrent level of manic symptoms (Blumberg et al., 1999; Caligiuri et al., 2003).

Hence, one theory is that BD is related to dysregulation in brain regions relevant to emotional reactivity, such as the amygdala, as well as regions in the prefrontal cortex involved in the regulation of emotion and cognitive control. Much of this research demonstrates strong parallels with unipolar depression. Evidence suggests that neural activation is somewhat mood-state dependent. Regions involved in reward motivation are an important focus for research.

SUMMARY

Much progress has been made in clarifying the diagnostic boundaries, genetic pathways, and neurobiological mechanisms relevant to bipolar illness. New studies recognize the strong influence of psychosocial variables against this background of biological and genetic vulnerability. Psychotherapy is an effective adjunct to pharmacotherapy in the long-term maintenance treatment of the illness, notably interventions that focus on enhancing the patient's understanding of the disorder and effectiveness in coping with its cycling.

Major focal areas for future studies include clarifying the validity of the bipolar spectrum. It is unclear whether bipolar illness should include only *DSM IV*-defined bipolar I or bipolar II disorder or whether it should also include subsyndromal mixed presentations (e.g., depression with significant anxious-agitation), cyclothymia, or episodes of mania, hypomania, or depression that do not meet the full severity or duration criteria. Nowhere are these questions more critical than in defining childhood-onset BD, which is being diagnosed with increasing frequency. In the future, it may be that fMRI or other imaging techniques will identify brain changes uniquely associated with bipolar illness, but until that time we must rely on clinical interviews and supplemental questionnaires to diagnose these conditions. Research that improves the reliability, clinical utility, and consumer acceptance of existing diagnostic methods is therefore critical.

The interface between psychosocial and biological risk factors deserves considerable study, especially as these factors relate to different poles of the disorder. As we have summarized, life events involving goal attainment and factors that disrupt sleep are strongly correlated with the onset of manic episodes, although their role in predicting illness onset has not been established in longitudinal studies. High intrafamilial EE and negative life events stress are most consistently associated with depressive episodes. Laboratory-based translational research may help clarify the avenues from specific stressors to biological changes to manic versus depressive symptom exacerbations.

The optimal combinations of psychotherapy and pharmacotherapy must be identified in trials that sample populations of diverse ethnicity, socioeconomic status, psychiatric and medical comorbidity, and chronicity. Large-scale studies such as the Systematic Treatment Enhancement Study for Bipolar Disorder (Sachs et al., 2003) are a move in this direction, but even studies of this size can be underpowered for examining treatment effects within specific subgroups (e.g., patients with comorbid substance dependence, rapid cycling patients, patients of African American or Latino heritage). Studies that adapt treatment methods to the cultural needs of specific populations are essential to moving the field forward.

Last, treatment studies should consider the synergy between biological and psychosocial interventions, and under what conditions combining one with the other will produce the most enduring effects. For example, drugs that stabilize mood symptoms may also energize patients to the extent that they become more amenable to the skill-oriented tasks of cognitive-behavioral treatment. Psychoeducational treatments may increase medication adherence, which in turn may allow patients to remain stable on fewer medications or on lower dosages. Interpersonal or family interventions that increase social support and decrease the impact of family or life stressors may decrease the need for adjunctive antidepressants in long-term maintenance. Ideally, the next generation of clinical research in BD will address these questions.

REFERENCES

Adler, A. (1964). *Problems of neurosis.* New York: Harper & Row.

Akiskal, H. S. (1996). The prevalent clinical spectrum of bipolar disorders: Beyond DSM-IV. *Journal of Clinical Psychopharmacology, 16*(Suppl. 1), 4–14.

Akiskal, H. S., Benazzi, F., Perugi, G., & Rihmer, Z. (2005). Agitated "unipolar" depression reconceptualized as a depressive mixed state: Implications for the antidepressant-suicide controversy. *Journal of Affective Disorders, 85,* 245–258.

Akiskal, H. S., Bourgeois, M. L., Angst, J., Post, R., Moller, H., & Hirschfeld, R. (2000). Reevaluating the prevalence of and diagnostic composition within the broad clinical spectrum of bipolar disorders. *Journal of Affective Disorders, 59*(Suppl. 1), S5–S30.

Akiskal, H. S., Mendlowicz, M. V., Jean-Louis, G., Rapaport, M. H., Kelsoe, J. R., Gillin, J. C., & Smith, T. L. (2005). TEMPS-A: Validation of a short version of a self-rated instrument designed to measure variations in temperament. *Journal of Affective Disorders, 85*(1–2), 45–52.

Alda, M. (1997). Bipolar disorder: From families to genes. *Canadian Journal of Psychiatry, 42,* 378–387.

Alloy, L. B., Reilly-Harrington, N., Fresco, D. M., Whitehouse, W. G., & Zechmeister, J. S. (1999). Cognitive styles and life events in subsyndromal unipolar and bipolar disorders: Stability and prospective prediction of depressive and hypomanic mood swings. *Journal of Cognitive Psychotherapy, 13,* 21–40.

Altshuler, L., Bookheimer, S., Proenza, M. A., Townsend, J., Sabb, F., Firestine, A., Bartzokis, G., Mintz, J., Mazziota, J., & Cohen, M. S. (2005). Increased amygdala activation during mania: A functional magnetic resonance imaging study. *American Journal of Psychiatry, 162,* 1211–1213.

Altshuler, L. L., Bookheimer, S. Y., Townsend, J., Proenza, M. A., Eisenberger, N., Sabb, F., Mintz, J., & Cohen, M. S. (2005). Blunted activation in orbitofrontal cortex during mania: A functional magnetic resonance imaging study. *Biological Psychiatry, 58*(10), 763–769.

American Psychiatric Association. (2000). *Diagnostic and statistical manual of mental disorders* (4th ed., text rev.). Washington, DC: American Psychiatric Press.

Anand, A., Verhoeff, P., Seneca, N., Zoghbi, S. S., Seibyl, J. P., Charney, D. S., Mintz, J., & Cohen, M. S. (2000). Brain SPECT imaging of amphetamine-induced dopamine release in euthymic bipolar disorder patients. *American Journal of Psychiatry, 157,* 1109–1114.

Angst, J., Angst, F., Gerber-Werder, R., & Gamma, A. (2005). Suicide in 406 mood-disordered patients with and without long-term medication: A 40 to 44 years' follow-up. *Archives of Suicide Research, 9*(3), 279–300.

Anguelova, M., Benkelfat, C., & Turecki, G. (2003). A systematic review of association studies investigating genes coding for serotonin receptors and the serotonin transporter: I. Affective disorders. *Molecular Psychiatry, 8,* 574–591.

Anthony, E. J., & Scott, P. (1960). Manic-depressive psychosis in childhood. *Child Psychology and Psychiatry, 1,* 53–72.

Badner, J. A., & Gershon, E. S. (2002). Meta-analysis of whole-genome linkage scans of bipolar disorder and schizophrenia. *Molecular Psychiatry, 7,* 405–411.

Barbini, B., Colombo, C., Benedetti, F., Campori, C., Bellodi, L., & Smeraldi, E. (1998). The unipolar-bipolar dichotomy and the response to sleep deprivation. *Psychiatry Research, 79,* 43–50.

Barch, D. M. (2005). The cognitive neuroscience of schizophrenia. *Annual Review of Clinical Psychology, 1,* 321–353.

Berrettini, W. (2003). Evidence for shared susceptibility in bipolar disorder and schizophrenia. *American Journal of Medical Genetics, Part C, 123C,* 59–64.

Biederman, J., Faraone, S. V., Chu, M. P., & Wozniak, J. (1999). Further evidence of a bidirectional overlap between juvenile mania and conduct disorder in children. *Journal of the American Academy of Child and Adolescent Psychiatry, 38,* 468–476.

Biederman, J., Mick, E., Faraone, S. V., Spencer, T., Wilens, T. E., & Wozniak, J. (2003). Current concepts in the validity, diagnosis and treatment of paediatric bipolar disorder. *International Journal of Neuropsychopharmacology, 6,* 293–300.

Birmaher, B., Axelson, D., Strober, M., Gill, M. K., Valeri, S., Chiappetta, L., Ryan, N., Leonard, H., Hunt, J., Iyengar, S., & Keller, M. (2006). Clinical course of children and adolescents with bipolar spectrum disorders. *Archives of General Psychiatry, 63*(2), 175–183.

Blumberg, H. P., Stern, E., Ricketts, S., Martinez, D., de Asis, J., White, T., Epstein, J., Isenberg, N., McBride, P. A., Kemperman, I., Emmerich, S., Dhawan, V., Eidelberg, D., Kocsis, J. H., &

Silbersweig, D.A. (1999). Rostral and orbital prefrontal cortex dysfunction in the manic state of bipolar disorder. *American Journal of Psychiatry, 156,* 1986–1988.

Bowden, C. L., Calabrese, J. R., Sachs, G., Yatham, L. N., Asghar, S. A., Hompland, M., Montgomery, P., Earl, N., Smoot, T. M., & DeVeaugh-Geiss, J. (2003). A placebo-controlled 18-month trial of lamotrigine and lithium maintenance treatment in recently manic or hypomanic patients with bipolar I disorder. *Archives of General Psychiatry, 60,* 392–400.

Brady, K. T., Casto, S., Lydiard, R. B., Malcolm, R., & Arana, G. (1991). Substance abuse in an inpatient psychiatric sample. *American Journal of Drug and Alcohol Abuse, 17,* 389–397.

Brown, G. K., Beck, A. T., Steer, R. A., & Grisham, J. R. (2000). Risk factors for suicide in psychiatric outpatients: A 20-year prospective study. *Journal of Consulting and Clinical Psychology, 68,* 371–377.

Brown, G. W., & Andrews, B. (1986). Social support and depression. In R. Trumbull & M. H. Appley (Eds.), *Dynamics of stress: Physiological, psychological, and social perspectives* (pp. 257–282). New York: Plenum Press.

Butzlaff, R. L., & Hooley, J. M. (1998). Expressed emotion and psychiatric relapse: A meta-analysis. *Archives of General Psychiatry, 55,* 547–552.

Caetano, S. C., Olvera, R. L., Glahn, D., Fonseca, M., Pliszka, S., & Soares, J. C. (2005). Fronto-limbic brain abnormalities in juvenile onset bipolar disorder. *Biological Psychiatry, 58,* 525–531.

Calabrese, J. R., Bowden, C. L., Sachs, G. S., Ascher, J. A., Monoaghan, E., & Rudd, G. D. (1999). A double-blind placebo-controlled study of lamotrigine monotherapy in outpatients with bipolar I depression. Lamictal 602 Study Group. *Journal of Clinical Psychiatry, 60,* 79–88.

Calabrese, J. R., Fatemi, S. H., Kujawa, M., & Woyshville, M. J. (1996). Predictors of response to mood stabilizers. *Journal of Clinical Psychopharmacology, 16*(Suppl. 1), 24–31.

Calabrese, J. R., Suppes, T., Bowden, C. L., Sachs, G. S., Swann, A. C., McElroy, S. L., Kusumakar, V., Ascher, J. A., Earl, N. L., Greene, P. L., & Monaghan, E. T. (2000). A double-blind, placebo-controlled, prophylaxis study of lamotrigine in rapid-cycling bipolar disorder. Lamictal 614 Study Group. *Journal of Clinical Psychiatry, 61,* 841–850.

Caligiuri, M. P., Brown, G. G., Meloy, M. J., Eberson, S. C., Kindermann, S. S., Frank, L. R., Zorrilla, L. E., & Lohr, J. B. (2003). An fMRI study of affective state and medication on cortical and subcortial regions during motor performance in bipolar disorder. *Psychiatry Research: Neuroimaging, 123,* 171–182.

Carlson, G. A. (2005). Early onset bipolar disorder: Clinical and research considerations. *Journal of Clinical Child and Adolescent Psychology, 34*(2), 335–345.

Chambers, W. J., Puig-Antich, J., Hirsch, M., Paez, P., Ambrosini, P. J., Tabrizi, M. A., et al. (1985). The assessment of affective disorders in children and adolescents by semi-structured interview: Test-retest reliability. *Archives of General Psychiatry, 42,* 696–702.

Chang, K., Adleman, N. E., Dienes, K., Simeonova, D. J., Menon, V., & Reiss, A. (2004). Anomalous prefrontal-subcortical activation in familial pediatric bipolar disorder: A functional magnetic resonance imaging investigation. *Archives of General Psychiatry, 61*(8), 781–792.

Chang, K. D., Steiner, H., & Ketter, T. A. (2000). Psychiatric phenomenology of child and adolescent bipolar offspring. *Journal of the American Academy of Child and Adolescent Psychiatry, 39,* 453–460.

Charney, D. S., Menkes, D. B., & Heninger, G. R. (1981). Receptor sensitivity and the mechanism of action of antidepressants. *Archives of General Psychiatry, 38,* 1160–1180.

Chiaroni, P., Azorin, J. M., Dassa, D., Henry, J. M., Giudicelli, S., Malthiery, Y., & Planells, R. (2000). Possible involvement of the dopamine D3 receptor locus in subtypes of bipolar affective disorder. *Psychiatric Genetics, 10,* 43–49.

Clarkin, J. F., Carpenter, D., Hull, J., Wilner, P., & Glick, I. (1998). Effects of psychoeducational intervention for married patients with bipolar disorder and their spouses. *Psychiatric Services, 49,* 531–533.

Clarkin, J. F., Glick, I. D., Haas, G. L., Spencer, J. H., Lewis, A. B., Peyser, J., DeMane, N., Good-Ellis, M., Harris, E., & Lestelle, V. (1990). A randomized clinical trial of inpatient family intervention: V. Results for affective disorders. *Journal of Affective Disorders, 18,* 17–28.

Cochran, S. D. (1984). Preventing medical noncompliance in the outpatient treatment of bipolar affective disorders. *Journal of Consulting and Clinical Psychology, 52,* 873–878.

Colom, F., Vieta, E., Martinez-Aran, A., Reinares, M., Benabarre, A., & Gasto, C. (2000). Clinical factors associated with treatment noncompliance in euthymic bipolar patients. *Journal of Clinical Psychiatry, 61,* 549–555.

Colom, F., Vieta, E., Martinez-Aran, A., Reinares, M., Goikolea, J. M., Benabarre, A., Torrent, C., Comes, M., Corbella, B., Parramon, G., & Corominas, J. (2003). A randomized trial on the efficacy of group psychoeducation in the prophylaxis of recurrences in bipolar patients whose disease is in remission. *Archives of General Psychiatry, 60,* 402–407.

Coryell, W. D. S., Turvey, C., Keller, M., Leon, A. C., Endicott, J., Schettler, P., Judd, L., & Mueller, T. (2003). The long-term course of rapid-cycling bipolar disorder. *Archives of General Psychiatry, 60,* 914–920.

Coryell, W., Endicott, J., Maser, J. D., Keller, M. B., Leon, A. C., & Akiskal, H. S. (1995). Long-term stability of polarity distinctions in the affective disorders. *American Journal of Psychiatry, 152,* 385–390.

Coryell, W., Scheftner, W., Keller, M., Endicott, J., Maser, J., & Klerman, G. L. (1993). The enduring psychosocial consequences of mania and depression. *American Journal of Psychiatry, 150,* 720–727.

Cotter, D., Hudson, L., & Landau, S. (2005). Evidence for orbitofrontal pathology in bipolar disorder and major depression, but not in schizophrenia. *Bipolar Disorders, 7,* 358–369.

Cuellar, A., Johnson, S. L., & Winters, R. (2005). Distinctions between bipolar and unipolar depression. *Clinical Psychology Review, 25,* 307–339.

Danielson, C. K., Youngstrom, E. A., Findling, R. L., & Calabrese, J. R. (2003). Discriminative validity of the general behavior inventory using youth report. *Journal of Abnormal Child Psychology, 31,* 29–39.

Davidson, R. J., Pizzagalli, D., & Nitschke, J. B. (2002). The representation and regulation of emotion in depression: Perspectives from affective neuroscience. In C. L. Hammen & I. H. Gotlib (Eds.), *Handbook of depression* (pp. 219–244). New York: Guilford Press.

Depue, R. A., Kleinman, R. M., Davis, P., Hutchinson, M., & Krauss, S. P. (1985). The behavioral high-risk paradigm and bipolar affective disorder: VII. Serum free cortisol in nonpatient cyclothymic subjects selected by the General Behavior Inventory. *American Journal of Psychiatry, 142,* 175–181.

Depue, R. A., & Monroe, S. M. (1978). The unipolar-bipolar distinction in the depressive disorders. *Psychological Bulletin, 85,* 1001–1029.

Dion, G., Tohen, M., Anthony, W., & Waternaux, C. (1988). Symptoms and functioning of patients with bipolar disorder six months after hospitalization. *Hospital and Community Psychiatry, 39,* 652–656.

Dunner, D. L., & Tay, L. K. (1993). Diagnostic reliability of the history of hypomania in bipolar II patients and patients with major depression. *Comprehensive Psychiatry, 34*(5), 303–307.

Ebert, D., Feistel, H., Barocks, A., Kaschka, W. P., & Pirner, A. (1994). SPECT assessment of cerebral dopamine D2 receptor blockade in depression before and after sleep deprivation. *Biological Psychiatry, 35,* 880–885.

Eckblad, M., & Chapman, L. J. (1986). Development and validation of a scale for hypomanic personality. *Journal of Abnormal Psychology, 95,* 214–222.

Ehlers, C. L., Frank, E., & Kupfer, D. J. (1988). Social zeitgebers and biological rhythms: A unified approach to understanding the etiology of depression. *Archives of General Psychiatry, 45,* 948–952.

Ehlers, C. L., Kupfer, D. J., Frank, E., & Monk, T. H. (1993). Biological rhythms and depression: The role of zeitgebers and zeitstorers. *Depression, 1,* 285–293.

Eich, E., Macaulay, D., & Lam, R. W. (1997). Mania, depression, and mood dependent memory. *Cognition and Emotion, 11,* 607–618.

Ellicott, A., Hammen, C., Gitlin, M., Brown, G., & Jamison, K. (1990). Life events and the course of bipolar disorder. *American Journal of Psychiatry, 147,* 1194–1198.

Fagiolini, A., Kupfer, D. J., Masalehdan, A., Scott, J. A., Houck, P. R., & Frank, E. (2005). Functional impairment in the remission phase of bipolar disorder. *Bipolar Disorders, 7*(281–285).

Faraone, S. V., Biederman, J., Mennin, D., Wozniak, J., & Spencer, T. (1997a). Attention-deficit hyperactivity disorder with bipolar disorder: A familial subtype? *Journal of the American Academy of Child and Adolescent Psychiatry, 36,* 1378–1387.

Faraone, S. V., Biederman, J., Wozniak, J., Mundy, E., Mennin, D., & O'Donnell, D. (1997b). Is comorbidity with ADHD a marker for juvenile-onset mania? *Journal of the American Academy of Child and Adolescent Psychiatry, 36,* 1046–1055.

Fawcett, J., Golden, B., & Rosenfeld, N. (2000). *New hope for people with bipolar disorder.* Roseville, CA: Prima Health.

Feske, U., Frank, E., Mallinger, A. G., Houck, P. R., Fagiolini, A., Shear, M. K., Grochocinski, V. J., & Kupfer, D. J. (2000). Anxiety as a correlate of response to the acute treatment of bipolar I disorder. *American Journal of Psychiatry, 157,* 956–962.

First, M. B., Spitzer, R. L., Gibbon, M., & Williams, J. B. W. (1995). *Structured clinical interview for DSM-IV axis I disorders.* New York: Biometrics Research Department, New York State Psychiatric Institute.

Frank, E., Cyranowski, J. M., Rucci, P., Shear, M. K., Fagiolini, A., Thase, M. E., Cassano, G. B., Grochocinski, V. J., Kostelnik, B., & Kupfer, D. J. (2002). Clinical significance of lifetime panic spectrum symptoms in the treatment of patients with bipolar I disorder. *Archives of General Psychiatry, 59,* 905–911.

Frank, E., Kupfer, D. J., Thase, M. E., Mallinger, A. G., Swartz, H. A., Fagiolini, A. M., Grochocinski, V., Houck, P., Scott, J., Thompson, W., & Monk, T. (2005). Two-year outcomes for interpersonal and social rhythm therapy in individuals with bipolar I disorder. *Archives of General Psychiatry, 62*(9), 996–1004.

Frazier, J. A., Chiu, S., Breeze, J. L., Makris, N., Lange, N., & Kennedy, D. N., Herbert, M. R., Bent, E. K., Koneru, V. K., Dieterich, M. E., Hodge, S. M., Rauch, S. L., Grant, P. E., Cohen, B. M., Seidman, L. J., Caviness, V. S., & Biederman, J. (2005). Structural brain magnetic resonance imaging of limbic and thalamic volumes in pediatric bipolar disorder. *American Journal of Psychiatry, 162,* 1256–1265.

Fristad, M. A., Gavazzi, S. M., & Mackinaw-Koons, B. (2003). Family psychoeducation: An adjunctive intervention for children with bipolar disorder. *Biological Psychiatry, 53,* 1000–1009.

Garb, H. N. (1997). Racial bias, social class bias, and gender bias in clinical judgment. *Clinical Psychology: Science and Practice, 4,* 99–120.

Geller, B., Tillman, R., Craney, J. L., & Bolhofner, K. (2004). Four-year prospective outcome and natural history of mania in children with a prepubertal and early adolescent bipolar disorder phenotype. *Archives of General Psychiatry, 61,* 459–467.

340   Bipolar Disorder

Geller, B., Williams, M., Zimerman, B., Frazier, J., Beringer, I., & Warner, K. L. (1998). Prepubertal and early adolescent bipolarity differentiated from ADHD by manic symptoms, grandiose delusions, ultra-rapid or ultraradian cycling. *Journal of Affective Disorders, 51,* 81–91.

Geller, B., Zimerman, B., Williams, M., Bolhofner, K., Craney, J. L., Frazier, J., Beringer, L., & Nickelsburg, M. J. (2002). DSM-IV mania symptoms in a prepubertal and early adolescent bipolar disorder phenotype compared to attention deficit hyperactive and normal controls. *Journal of the American Academy of Child and Adolescent Psychopharmacology, 12,* 11–25.

Georgieva, L., Dimitrova, A., Nikolov, I., Koleva, S., Tsvetkova, R., Owen, M. J., Toncheva, D., & Kirov, G. (2002). Dopamine transporter gene (DAT1) VNTR polymorphism in major psychiatric disorders: Family-based association study in the Bulgarian population. *Acta Psychiatrica Scandinavica, 105,* 396–399.

Ghaemi, S. N., Lenox, M. S., & Baldessarini, R. J. (2001). Effectiveness and safety of long-term antidepressant treatment in bipolar disorder. *Journal of Clinical Psychiatry, 62,* 565–569.

Gitlin, M. J., Swendsen, J., Heller, T. L., & Hammen, C. (1995). Relapse and impairment in bipolar disorder. *American Journal of Psychiatry, 152*(11), 1635–1640.

Goldberg, J., Garno, J., Leon, A., Kocsis, J., & Portera, L. (1999). A history of substance abuse complicates remission from acute mania in bipolar disorder. *Journal of Clinical Psychiatry, 60*(11), 733–740.

Goldberg, J. F. (2004). The changing landscape of psychopharmacology. In S. L. Johnson & R. L. Leahy (Eds.), *Psychological treatment of bipolar disorder* (pp. 109–138). New York: Guilford.

Goldberg, J. F., Harrow, M., & Grossman, L. S. (1995). Course and outcome in bipolar affective disorder: A longitudinal follow-up study. *American Journal of Psychiatry, 152,* 379–385.

Goodwin, F. K., & Jamison, K. R. (1990). *Manic-depressive illness.* New York: Oxford University Press.

Gorwood, P., Bellivier, F., Ades, J., & Leboyer, M. (2000). The DRD2 gene and the risk for alcohol dependence in bipolar patients. *European Psychiatry, 15,* 103–108.

Gunderson, J. G., Triebwasser, J., Phillips, K. A., & Sullivan, C. N. (1999). Personality and vulnerability to affective disorders. In R. C. Cloninger (Ed.), *Personality and psychopathology* (pp. 3–32). Washington, DC: American Psychiatric Press.

Harris, E. C., & Barraclough, B. (1997). Suicide as an outcome for mental disorders: A meta-analysis. *British Journal of Psychiatry, 170,* 205–208.

Harrow, M., Goldberg, J. F., Grossman, L. S., & Meltzer, H. Y. (1990). Outcome in manic disorders: A naturalistic follow-up study. *Archives of General Psychiatry, 47,* 665–671.

Heerlein, A., Richter, P., Gonzalez, M., & Santander, J. (1998). Personality patterns and outcome in depressive and bipolar disorders. *Psychopathology, 31,* 15–22.

Henry, C., Van den Bulke, D., Bellivier, F., Etain, B., Rouillon, F., & Leboyer, M. (2003). Anxiety disorders in 318 bipolar patients: Prevalence and impact on illness severity and response to mood stabilizer. *Journal of Clinical Psychiatry, 64,* 331–335.

Hillegers, M. H., Burger, H., Wals, M., Reichart, C. G., Verhulst, F. C., Nolen, W. A., & Ormel, J. (2004). Impact of stressful life events, familial loading and their interaction on the onset of mood disorders. *British Journal of Psychiatry, 185,* 97–101.

Hodgins, S., Faucher, B., Zarac, A., & Ellenbogen, M. (2002). Children of parents with bipolar disorder: A population at high risk for major affective disorders. *Child and Adolescent Psychiatric Clinics of North America, 11,* 533–553.

Jamison, K. R. (1993). *Touched with fire: Manic-depressive illness and the artistic temperament.* New York: Maxwell Macmillan International.

Jamison, K. R. (2000). Suicide and bipolar disorder. *Journal of Clinical Psychiatry, 61*(Suppl. 9), 47–56.

Jamison, K. R., & Baldessarini, R. J. (1999). Effects of medical interventions on suicial behavior. *Journal of Clinical Psychiatry, 60*(Suppl. 2), 4–6.

Johnson, R. E., & McFarland, B. H. (1996). Lithium use and discontinuation in a health maintenance organization. *American Journal of Psychiatry, 153,* 993–1000.

Johnson, S. L. (2005a). Life events in bipolar disorder: Towards more specific models. *Clinical Psychology Review, 25,* 1008–1027.

Johnson, S. L. (2005b). Mania and dysregulation in goal pursuit. *Clinical Psychology Review, 25,* 241–262.

Johnson, S. L., & Carver, C. (in press). Extreme goal setting and vulnerability to mania among undiagnosed young adults. *Cognitive Therapy and Research.*

Johnson, S. L., & Fingerhut, R. (2004). Negative cognitions predict the course of bipolar depression, not mania. *Journal of Cognitive Psychotherapy, 18,* 149–162.

Johnson, S. L., Gruber, J. L., & Eisner, L. R. (in press). Emotion and bipolar disorder. In J. Rottenberg & S. L. Johnson (Eds.), *Emotion and psychopathology.* Washington, DC: American Psychological Association.

Johnson, S. L., & Kizer, A. (2002). Bipolar and unipolar depression: A comparison of clinical phenomenology and psychosocial predictors. In I. H. Gotlib & C. Hammen (Eds.), *Handbook of depression* (pp. 141–165). New York: Guilford Press.

Johnson, S. L., Kizer, A., Ruggero, C., Goodnick, P., & Miller, I. (under review). Negative and goal-attainment life events: Predicting the course of mania and depression.

Johnson, S. L., Meyer, B., Winett, C., & Small, J. (2000). Social support and self-esteem predict changes in bipolar depression but not mania. *Journal of Affective Disorders, 58,* 79–86.

Johnson, S. L., & Miller, I. (1997). Negative life events and time to recovery from episodes of bipolar disorder. *Journal of Abnormal Psychology, 106,* 449–457.

Johnson, S. L., Sandrow, D., Meyer, B., Winters, R., Miller, I., Solomon, D., & Keitner, G. (2000). Increases in manic symptoms following life events involving goal-attainment. *Journal of Abnormal Psychology, 109,* 721–727.

Johnson, S. L., Winett, C. A., Meyer, B., Greenhouse, W. J., & Miller, I. (1999). Social support and the course of bipolar disorder. *Journal of Abnormal Psychology, 108,* 558–566.

Judd, L. L., & Akiskal, H. S. (2003). The prevalence and disability of bipolar spectrum disorders in the US population: Re-analysis of the ECA database taking into account subthreshold cases. *Journal of Affective Disorders, 73*(1–2), 123–131.

Judd, L. L., Akiskal, H. S., Schettler, P. J., Endicott, J., Maser, J., Solomon, D. A., Leon, A.C., Rice, J.A., & Keller, M.B. (2002). The long-term natural history of the weekly symptomatic status of bipolar I disorder. *Archives of General Psychiatry, 59,* 530–537.

Kalivas, P. W., Duffy, P., DuMars, L. A., & Skinner, C. (1988). Behavioral and neurochemical effects of acute and daily cocaine administration in rats. *Journal of Pharmacology and Experimental Therapeutics, 245*(2), 485–492.

Karkowski, L. M., & Kendler, K. S. (1997). An examination of the genetic relationship between bipolar and unipolar illness in an epidemiological sample. *Psychiatric Genetics, 7,* 159–163.

Kaufman, J., Birmaher, B., Brent, D., Rao, U., Flynn, C., Moreci, P., Williamson, D., & Ryan, N. (1997). Schedule for Affective Disorders and Schizophrenia for School-Age Children—Present and Lifetime Version (K-SADS-PL): Initial reliability and validity data. *Journal of the American Academy of Child and Adolescent Psychiatry, 36,* 98–988.

Keck, P. E. J., McElroy, S. L., Strakowski, S. M., Bourne, M. L., & West, S. A. (1997). Compliance with maintenance treatment in bipolar disorder. *Psychopharmacology Bulletin, 33,* 87–91.

Keck, P. E. J., McElroy, S. L., Strakowski, S. M., West, S. A., Sax, K. W., Hawkins, J. M., Bourne, M.L., & Haggard, P. (1998). Twelve-month outcome of patients with bipolar disorder following hospitalization for a manic or mixed episode. *American Journal of Psychiatry, 155*, 646–652.

Keller, M. B., Lavori, P. W., Coryell, W., Andreasen, N. C., Endicott, J., Clayton, P. J., Klerman, G.L., & Hirschfeld, R.M. (1986). Differential outcome of pure manic, mixed/cycling, and pure depressive episodes in patients with bipolar illness. *Journal of the American Medical Association, 255*, 3138–3142.

Keller, M. B., Lavori, P. W., Coryell, W., Endicott, J., & Mueller, T. I. (1993). Bipolar I: A five-year prospective follow-up. *Journal of Nervous and Mental Disease, 181*, 238–245.

Kessler, R. C., Avenevoli, S., & Ries-Merikangas, K. (2001). Mood disorders in children and adolescents: An epidemiologic perspective. *Biological Psychiatry, 49*, 1002–1014.

Kessler, R. C., Chiu, W. T., Demler, O., & Walters, E. E. (2005). Prevalence, severity, and comorbidity of 12-month DSM-IV disorders in the National Comorbidity Survey Replication. *Archives of General Psychiatry, 62*, 617–627.

Kessler, R. C., Crum, R. C., Warner, L. A., Nelson, C. B., Schulenberg, J., & Anthony, J. C. (1997). Lifetime co-occurrence of DSM-III-R alcohol abuse and dependence with other psychiatric disorders in the National Comorbidity Survey. *Archives of General Psychiatry, 54*, 313–321.

Kilbourne, A. M., Bauer, M. S., Han, X., Haas, G. L., Elder, P., Good, C. B., Shad, M., Conigliaro, J., & Pincus, H. (2005). Racial differences in the treatment of veterans with bipolar disorder. *Psychiatric Services, 56*, 1549–1555.

Kim, E. Y., & Miklowitz, D. J. (2002). Childhood mania, attention deficit hyperactivity disorder, and conduct disorder: A critical review of diagnostic dilemmas. *Bipolar Disorders, 4*, 215–225.

Kim, E. Y., & Miklowitz, D. J. (2004). Expressed emotion as a predictor of outcome among bipolar patients undergoing family therapy. *Journal of Affective Disorders, 82*, 343–352.

Klein, D. N., & Depue, R. A. (1984). Continued impairment in persons at risk for bipolar disorder: Results of a 19-month follow-up. *Journal of Abnormal Psychology, 93*, 345–347.

Knutson, B., Adams, C. M., Fong, G. W., & Hommer, D. (2001). Anticipation of increasing monetary reward selectively recruits nucleus accumbens. *Journal of Neuroscience, 21*(16), RC159.

Kochman, F. J., Hantouche, E. G., Ferrari, P., Lancrenon, S., Bayart, D., & Akiskal, H. S. (2005). Cyclothymic temperament as a prospective predictor of bipolarity and suicidality in children and adolescents with major depressive disorder. *Journal of Affective Disorders, 85*(1–2), 181–189.

Kowatch, R. A., Fristad, M., Birmaher, B., Wagner, K. D., Findling, R. L., Hellander, M., & the Child Psychiatric Workgroup on Bipolar Disorder. (2005). Treatment guidelines for children and adolescents with bipolar disorder. *Journal of the American Academy of Child and Adolescent Psychiatry, 44*(3), 213–235.

Kowatch, R. A., Sethuraman, G., Hume, J. H., Kromelis, M., & Weinberg, W. A. (2003). Combination pharmacotherapy in children and adolescents with bipolar disorder. *Biological Psychiatry, 53*, 978–984.

Kowatch, R. A., Youngstrom, E. A., Danielyan, A., & Findling, R. L. (2005). Review and meta-analysis of the phenomenology and clinical characteristics of mania in children and adolescents. *Bipolar Disorders, 7*(6), 483–496.

Kruger, S., Seminowicz, S., Goldapple, K., Kennedy, S. H., & Mayberg, H. S. (2003). State and trait influences on mood regulation in bipolar disorder: Blood flow differences with an acute mood challenge. *Biological Psychiatry, 54*, 1274–1283.

Kupfer, D. J., Frank, E., Grochocinski, V. J., Houck, P. R., & Brown, C. (2005). African-American participants in a bipolar disorder registry: clinical and treatment characteristics. *Bipolar Disorders, 7*(82–88).

Kwapil, T. R., Miller, M. B., Zinser, M. C., Chapman, L. J., Chapman, J., & Eckblad, M. (2000). A longitudinal study of high scorers on the hypomanic personality scale. *Journal of Abnormal Psychology, 109*, 222–226.

Lam, D. H., Watkins, E. R., Hayward, P., Bright, J., Wright, K., Kerr, N., Parr-Davis, G., & Sham, P. (2003). A randomized controlled study of cognitive therapy of relapse prevention for bipolar affective disorder: Outcome of the first year. *Archives of General Psychiatry, 60*, 145–152.

LaPalme, M., Hodgins, S., & LaRoche, C. (1997). Children of parents with bipolar disorder: A meta-analysis of risk for mental disorders. *Canadian Journal of Psychiatry, 42*, 623–631.

Lawrence, N. S., Williams, A. M., Surguladze, S., Giampietro, V., Brammer, M. J., Andrew, C., Frangou, S., Ecker, C., & Phillips, M.L. (2004). Subcortical and ventral prefrontal responses to facial expressions distinguish patients with BPD and major depression. *Biological Psychiatry, 55*, 578–587.

Leibenluft, E. (1997). Issues in the treatment of women with bipolar illness. *Journal of Clinical Psychiatry, 58*(Suppl. 15), 5–11.

Leibenluft, E., Charney, D. S., Towbin, K. E., Bhangoo, R. K., & Pine, D. S. (2003). Defining clinical phenotypes of juvenile mania. *American Journal of Psychiatry, 160*, 430–437.

Leibenluft, E., Cohen, P., Gorrindo, T., Brook, J. S., & Pine, D. S. (2006). Chronic vs. episodic irritability in youth: A community-based, longitudinal study of clinical and diagnostic associations. *Journal of Child and Adolescent Psychopharmacology, 16*, 456–466.

Lennox, R., Jacob, R., Calder, A. J., Lupson, V., & Bullmore, E. T. (2004). Behavioral and neurocognitive responses to sad facial affect are attenuated in patients with mania. *Psychological Medicine, 34*, 795–802.

Leverich, G. S., & Post, R. M. (1998). Life charting of affective disorders. *CNS Spectrums, 3*, 21–37.

Lewinsohn, P. M., Klein, D. N., & Seeley, J. R. (2000). Bipolar disorder during adolescence and young adulthood in a community sample. *Bipolar Disorders, 2*, 281–293.

Lewinsohn, P. M., Seeley, J. R., Buckley, M. E., & Klein, D. N. (2002). Bipolar disorder in adolescence and young adulthood. *Child and Adolescent Psychiatric Clinics of North America, 11*, 461–475.

Lopez, L. S., Croes, E. A., Sayed-Tabatabaei, F. A., Stephan, C., Van Broeckhoven, C., & Van Duijn, C. M. (2005). The dopamine D4 receptor gene 48-base-pair-repeat polymorphism and mood disorders: A meta-analysis. *Biological Psychiatry, 57*, 999–1003.

Lotrich, F. E., & Pollock, B. G. (2004). Meta-analysis of serotonin transporter polymorphisms and affective disorders. *Psychiatric Genetics, 14*, 121–129.

Lozano, B. L., & Johnson, S. L. (2001). Can personality traits predict increases in manic and depressive symptoms? *Journal of Affective Disorders, 63*, 103–111.

Lyon, H. M., Startup, M., & Bentall, R. P. (1999). Social cognition and the manic defense: Attributions, selective attention, and self-schema in bipolar affective disorder. *Journal of Abnormal Psychology, 108*, 273–282.

Malkoff-Schwartz, S., Frank, E., Anderson, B., Sherrill, J. T., Siegel, L., Patterson, D., & Kupfer, D. J. (1998). Stressful life events and social rhythm disruption in the onset of manic and depressive bipolar episodes: A preliminary investigation. *Archives of General Psychiatry, 55*, 702–707.

Malkoff-Schwartz, S., Frank, E., Anderson, B. P., Hlastala, S. A., Luther, J. F., Sherrill, J. T., Houck, P. R., & Kupfer, D. J. (2000). Social rhythm disruption and stressful life events in the onset of bipolar and unipolar episodes. *Psychological Medicine, 30*, 1005–1016.

Manki, H., Kanba, S., Muramatsu, T., & Higuchi, S. (1996). Dopamine D2, D3 and D4 receptor and transporter gene polymorphisms and mood disorders. *Journal of Affective Disorders, 40,* 7–13.

Masi, G., Perugi, G., Toni, C., Millepiedi, S., Mucci, M., Bertini, N., & Akiskal, H. S. (2004). Obsessive-compulsive bipolar comorbidity: Focus on children and adolescents. *Journal of Affective Disorders, 78,* 175–183.

Mayberg, H. S., Keightley, M., Mahurin, R. K., & Brannan, S. K. (2004). Neuropsychiatric aspects of mood and affective disorders. In R. E. Hales & S. C. Yudofsky (Eds.), *Essentials of neuropsychiatry and clinical neurosciences* (pp. 489–517). Washington, DC: American Psychiatric Publishing.

McAllister-Williams, R. H. (2006). Relapse prevention in bipolar disorder: A critical review of current guidelines. *Journal of Psychopharmacology, 20* (2 Suppl.), 12–16.

McClellan, J. (2005). Commentary: Treatment guidelines for child and adolescent bipolar disorder. *Journal of the American Academy of Child and Adolescent Psychiatry, 44,* 236–239.

McClellan, J., & Werry, J. (2000). Introduction—research psychiatric diagnostic interviews for children and adolescents. *Journal of the American Academy of Child and Adolescent Psychiatry, 39,* 19–27.

McGuffin, P., Rijsdijk, F., Andrew, M., Sham, P., Katz, R., & Cardno, A. (2003). The heritability of bipolar affective disorder and the genetic relationship to unipolar depression. *Archives of General Psychiatry, 60,* 497–502.

McIntyre, R. S., & Konarski, J. Z. (2004). Bipolar disorder: A national health concern. *CNS Spectrums, 9* (11 Suppl. 12), 6–15.

Meyer, B., Johnson, S. L., & Carver, C. S. (1999). Exploring behavioral activation and inhibition sensitivities among college students at-risk for bipolar-spectrum symptomatology. *Journal of Psychopathology and Behavioral Assessment, 21,* 275–292.

Meyer, B., Johnson, S. L., & Winters, R. (2001). Responsiveness to threat and incentive in bipolar disorder: Relations of the BIS/BAS scales with symptoms. *Journal of Psychopathology and Behavioral Assessment, 23,* 133–143.

Miklowitz, D. J. (2006). A review of evidence-based psychosocial interventions for bipolar disorder. *Journal of Clinical Psychiatry, 67* (Suppl. 11), 28-33.

Miklowitz, D. J., Biuckians, A., & Richards, J. A. (in press). Early-onset bipolar disorder: A family treatment perspective. *Development and Psychopathology.*

Miklowitz, D. J., George, E. L., Richards, J. A., Simoneau, T. L., & Suddath, R. L. (2003). A randomized study of family-focused psychoeducation and pharmacotherapy in the outpatient management of bipolar disorder. *Archives of General Psychiatry, 60,* 904–912.

Miklowitz, D. J., Goldstein, M. J., Nuechterlein, K. H., Snyder, K. S., & Mintz, J. (1988). Family factors and the course of bipolar affective disorder. *Archives of General Psychiatry, 45,* 225–231.

Monroe, S. M., Harkness, K., Simons, A., & Thase, M. (2001). Life stress and the symptoms of major depression. *Journal of Nervous and Mental Disease, 189,* 168–175.

Muglia, P., Petronis, A., Mundo, E., Lander, S., Cate, T., & Kennedy, J. L. (2002). Dopamine D4 receptor and tyrosine hydroxylase genes in bipolar disorder: Evidence for a role of DRD4. *Molecular Psychiatry, 7,* 860–866.

Murphy, F. C., Sahakian, B. J., Rubinsztein, J. S., Michael, A., Rogers, R. D., Robbins, T. W., & Paykel, E. S. (1999). Emotional bias and inhibitory control processes in mania and depression. *Psychological Medicine, 29,* 1307–1321.

Murray, R. M., Sham, P., Van Os, J., Zanelli, J., Cannon, M., & McDonald, C. (2004). A developmental model for similarities and dissimilarities between schizophrenia and bipolar disorder. *Schizophrenia Research, 71,* 405–416.

National Institute of Mental Health. (2001). Research Roundtable on Prepubertal Bipolar Disorder. *Journal of the American Academy of Child and Adolescent Psychiatry, 40,* 871–878.

Nowakowska, C., Strong, C. M., Santosa, C. M., Wang, P. W., & Ketter, T. A. (2005). Temperamental commonalities and differences in euthymic mood disorder patients, creative controls, and healthy controls. *Journal of Affective Disorders, 85,* 207–215.

Ogden, C. A., Rich, M. E., Schork, N. J., Paulus, M. P., Geyer, M. A., Lohr, J. B., Kuczenski, R., & Niculescu, A.B. (2004). Candidate genes, pathways, and mechanisms for bipolar (manic-depressive) and related disorders: An expanded convergent functional genomics approach. *Molecular Psychiatry, 9,* 1007–1029.

Otto, M.W., Simon, N.M., Wisniewski, S.R., Miklowitz, D.J., Kogan, J.N. Reilly-Harrington, N.A., Frank, E., Nierenberg, A. A., Marangell, L. B., Sagduyu, K., Weiss, R. D., Miyahara, S., Thas, M. E., Sachs, G. S., Pollack, M. H., & STEP-BD Investigators (2006). Prospective 12-month course of bipolar disorder in outpatients with and without anxiety comorbidity. *British Journal of Psychiatry, 189,* 20–25.

Pardoen, D., Bauewens, F., Dramaix, M., Tracy, A., Genevrois, C., Staner, L., & Mendlewicz, J. (1996). Life events and primary affective disorders: A one-year prospective study. *British Journal of Psychiatry, 169,* 160–166.

Patel, N. C., DelBello, M. P., Keck, P. E. J., & Strakowski, S. M. (2005). Ethnic differences in maintenance antipsychotic prescription among adolescents with bipolar disorder. *Journal of Child and Adolescent Psychopharmacology, 15*(6), 938–946.

Pavuluri, M. N., Birmaher, B., & Naylor, M. W. (2005). Pediatric bipolar disorder: A review of the past 10 years. *Journal of the American Academy of Child and Adolescent Psychiatry, 44*(9), 846–871.

Perlis, R. H., Ostacher, M. J., Patel, J., Marangell, L. B., Zhang, H., Wisniewski, S. R., Ketter, T.A., Miklowitz, D. J., Otto, M. W., Gyulai, L., Reilly-Harrington, N. A., Nierenberg, A. A., Sachs, S., & Thase, M.E. (2006). Predictors of recurrence in bipolar disorder: Primary outcomes from the Systematic Treatment Enhancement Program for Bipolar Disorder (STEP-BD). *American Journal of Psychiatry, 163*(2), 217–224.

Perris, H. (1984). Life events and depression: Part 2. Results in diagnostic subgroups and in relation to the recurrence of depression. *Journal of Affective Disorders, 7,* 25–36.

Perry, A., Tarrier, N., Morriss, R., McCarthy, E., & Limb, K. (1999). Randomised controlled trial of efficacy of teaching patients with bipolar disorder to identify early symptoms of relapse and obtain treatment. *British Medical Journal, 16,* 149–153.

Phillips, M. L., Drevets, W. C., Rauch, S. L., & Lane, R. (2003). Neurobiology of emotion perception II: Implications for major psychiatric disorders. *Biological Psychiatry, 54,* 515–528.

Post, R. M., Denicoff, K. D., Leverich, G. S., Altshuler, L. L., Frye, M. A., Suppes, T. M., Rush, A. J., Keck, P. E. Jr, McElroy, S. L., Luckenbaugh, D. A., Pollio, C., Kupka, R., & Nolen, W. A. (2003). Morbidity in 258 bipolar outpatients followed for 1 year with daily prospective ratings on the NIMH life chart method. *Journal of Clinical Psychiatry, 64,* 680–690.

Prien, R. F., & Potter, W. Z. (1990). NIMH Workshop report on treatment of bipolar disorder. *Psychopharmacology Bulletin, 26,* 409–427.

Rea, M. M., Tompson, M., Miklowitz, D. J., Goldstein, M. J., Hwang, S., & Mintz, J. (2003). Family focused treatment vs. individual treatment for bipolar disorder: Results of a randomized clinical trial. *Journal of Consulting and Clinical Psychology, 71,* 482–492.

Regeer, E. J., ten Have, M., Rosso, M. L., Hakkaart-van Roijen, L., Vollebergh, W., & Nolen, W. A. (2004). Prevalence of bipolar disorder in the general population: A reappraisal study of the Netherlands Mental Health Survey and Incidence Study. *Acta Psychiatrica Scandinavaca, 110,* 374–382.

Regier, D. A., Farmer, M. E., Rae, D. S., Locke, B. Z., Keith, S. J., Judd, L. L., & Goodwin, F.K. (1990). Comorbidity of mental disorders with alcohol and other drug abuse: Results from the Epidemiologic Catchment Area (ECA) Study. *Journal of the American Medical Association, 264,* 2511–2518.

Reich, L. H., Davies, R. K., & Himmelhoch, J. M. (1974). Excessive alcohol use in manic-depressive illness. *American Journal of Psychiatry, 131*(1), 83–86.

Reichart, C. G., van der Ende, J., Wals, M., Hillegers, M. H., Nolen, W. A., Ormel, J., & Verhulst, F. C. (2005). The use of the GBI as predictor of bipolar disorder in a population of adolescent offspring of parents with a bipolar disorder. *Journal of Affective Disorders, 89*(1–3), 147–155.

Reilly-Harrington, N. A., Alloy, L. B., Fresco, D. M., & Whitehouse, W. G. (1999). Cognitive styles and life events interact to predict bipolar and unipolar symptomatology. *Journal of Abnormal Psychology, 108,* 567–578.

Rice, J., Reich, T., Andreasen, N. C., Endicott, J., Van Eerdewegh, M., Fishman, R., Hirschfeld, R.M., & Klerman, G.L. (1987). The familial transmission of bipolar illness. *Archives of General Psychiatry, 44,* 441–447.

Richards, R., Kinney, D. K., Lunde, I., Benet, M., & Merzel, A. P. (1988). Creativity in manic-depressives, cyclothymes, their normal relatives, and control subjects. *Journal of Abnormal Psychology, 97,* 281–288.

Robinson, T. E., & Becker, J. B. (1986). Enduring changes in brain and behavior produced by chronic amphetamine administration: A review and evaluation of animal models of amphetamine psychosis. *Brain Research Review, 11,* 157–198.

Ryan, N. D., Williamson, D. E., Iyengar, S., Orvaschel, H., Reich, T., Dahl, R. E., & Puig-Antich, J. (1992). A secular increase in child and adolescent onset affective disorder. *Journal of the American Academy of Child and Adolescent Psychiatry, 31,* 600–605.

Sachs, G. S., Thase, M. E., Otto, M. W., Bauer, M., Miklowitz, D., Wisniewski, S. R., Lavori, P., Lebowitz, B., Rudorfer, M., Frank, E., Nierenberg, A.A., Fava, M., Bowden, C., Ketter, T., Marangell, L., Calabrese, J., Kupfer, D., & Rosenbaum, J.F. (2003). Rationale, design, and methods of the systematic treatment enhancement program for bipolar disorder (STEP-BD). *Biological Psychiatry, 53,* 1028–1042.

Sato, T., Bottlender, R., Kleindienst, N., & Moller, H. J. (2002). Syndromes and phenomenological subtypes underlying acute mania: A factor analytic study of 576 manic patients. *American Journal of Psychiatry, 159*(6), 968–974.

Schneck, C. D., Miklowitz, D. J., Calabrese, J. R., Allen, M. H., Thomas, M. R., Wisniewski, S. R., Miyahara, S., Shelton, M.D., Ketter, T. A., Goldberg, J.F., Bowden, C.L., & Sachs, G.S. (2004). Phenomenology of rapid cycling bipolar disorder: Data from the first 500 participants in the Systematic Treatment Enhancement Program for Bipolar Disorder. *American Journal of Psychiatry, 161,* 1902–1908.

Scott, J., Paykel, E., Morriss, R., Bentall, R., Kinderman, P., Johnson, T., Abbott, R., & Hayhurst, H. (2006). Cognitive behaviour therapy for severe and recurrent bipolar disorders: A randomised controlled trial. *British Journal of Psychiatry, 188,* 313–320.

Simeonova, D. I., Chang, K. D., Strong, C., & Ketter, T. A. (2005). Creativity in familial bipolar disorder. *Journal of Psychiatric Research, 39*(6), 623–631.

Simon, G. E., Ludman, E. J., Unutzer, J., Bauer, M. S., Operskalski, B., & Rutter, C. (2005). Randomized trial of a population-based care program for people with bipolar disorder. *Psychological Medicine, 35*(1), 13–24.

Simon, N. M., Otto, M. W., Weiss, R., Bauer, M. S., Miyahara, S., Wisniewski, S. R., Thase, M.E., Kogan, J., Frank, E., Nierenberg, A.A., Calabrese, J.R., Sachs, G.S., & Pollack, M.H.; STEP-BD Investigators. (2004). Pharmacotherapy for bipolar disorder and comorbid conditions: Baseline data from STEP-BD. *Journal of Clinical Psychopharmacology, 24,* 512–520.

Simoneau, T. L., Miklowitz, D. J., & Saleem, R. (1998). Expressed emotion and interactional patterns in the families of bipolar patients. *Journal of Abnormal Psychology, 107,* 497–507.

Smith, D. J., Harrison, N., Muir, W., & Blackwood, D. H. (2005). The high prevalence of bipolar spectrum disorders in young adults with recurrent depression: Toward an innovative diagnostic framework. *Journal of Affective Disorders, 84,* 167–178.

Sobcazk, S., Honig, A., Schmitt, J. A. J., & Riedel, W. J. (2003). Pronounced cognitive deficits following an intravenous L-tryptophan challenge in first-degree relatives of bipolar patients compared to healthy controls. *Neuropsychopharmacology, 28,* 711–719.

Sobczak, S., Riedel, W. J., Booij, L., Aan het Rot, M., Deutz, N. E. P., & Honig, A. (2002). Cognition following acute tryptophan depletion: Differences between first-degree relatives of bipolar disorder patients and matched healthy control volunteers. *Psychological Medicine, 32,* 503–515.

Solomon, D. A., Leon, A. C., Endicott, J., Coryell, W. H., Mueller, T. I., Posternak, M. A., & Keller, M. B. (2003). Unipolar mania over the course of a 20-year follow-up study. *American Journal of Psychiatry, 160,* 2049–2051.

Staley, J. K., Malison, R. T., & Innis, R. B. (1998). Imaging of the serotonergic system: Interactions of neuroanatomical and functional abnormalities of depression. *Biological Psychiatry, 44*(534–549).

Stern, G. S., & Berrenberg, J. L. (1979). Skill-set, success outcome, and mania as determinants of the illusion of control. *Journal of Research in Personality, 13,* 206–220.

Stockmeier, C. A. (2003). Involvement of serotonin in depression: Evidence from postmortem and imaging studies of serotonin receptors and the serotonin transporter. *Journal of Psychiatric Research, 37,* 357–373.

Strakowski, S. M., DelBello, M. P., Fleck, D. E., & Arndt, S. (2000). The impact of substance abuse on the course of bipolar disorder. *Biological Psychiatry, 48,* 477–485.

Strakowski, S. M., Keck, P. E., McElroy, S. L., West, S. A., Sax, K. W., Hawkins, J. M., Kmetz, G. F., Upadhyaya, V. H., Tugrul, K. C., & Bourne, M. L. (1998). Twelve-month outcome after a first hospitalization for affective psychosis. *Archives of General Psychiatry, 55,* 49–55.

Strakowski, S. M., Sax, K. W., Setters, M. J., & Keck, P. E. J. (1996). Enhanced response to repeated d-amphetamine challenge: Evidence for behavioral sensitization in humans. *Biological Psychiatry, 40,* 827–880.

Strakowski, S. M., Sax, K. W., Setters, M. J., Stanton, S. P., & Keck Jr., P. E. (1997). Lack of enhanced behavioral response to repeated d-amphetamine challenge in first-episode psychosis: Implications for a sensitization model of psychosis in humans. *Biological Psychiatry, 42,* 749–755.

Strecker, E. A. (1921). The prognosis in manic-depressive psychosis. *New York Medical Journal, 114,* 209–211.

Strober, M., Morrell, W., Lampert, C., & Burroughs, J. (1990). Relapse following discontinuation of lithium maintenance therapy in adolescents with bipolar I illness: A naturalistic study. *American Journal of Psychiatry, 147,* 457–461.

Suppes, T., Baldessarini, R. J., Faedda, G. L., Tondo, L., & Tohen, M. (1993, September/October). Discontinuation of maintenance treatment in bipolar disorder: Risks and implications. *Harvard Review of Psychiatry, 1,* 131–144.

Suppes, T., Leverich, G. S., Keck, P. E., Nolen, W. A., Denicoff, K. D., Altshuler, L. L., McElroy, S. L., Rush, A. J., Kupka, R., Frye, M. A., Bickel, M., & Post, R. M. (2001). The Stanley Foundation Bipolar Treatment Outcome Network. II. Demographics and illness characteristics of the first 261 patients. *Journal of Affective Disorders, 67,* 45–59.

Swann, A. C., Dougherty, D. M., Pazzaglia, P. J., Pham, M., & Moeller, F. G. (2004). Impulsivity: A link between bipolar disorder and substance abuse. *Bipolar Disorders, 6*, 204–212.

Thase, M. E., Jindal, R., & Howland, R. H. (2002). Biological aspects of depression. In I. H. Gotlib & C. L. Hammen (Eds.), *Handbook of Depression* (pp. 192-218). New York: Guilford Press.

Thomas, J., & Bentall, R. P. (2002). Hypomanic traits and response styles to depression. *British Journal of Clinical Psychology, 41*(3), 309–313.

Tohen, M., Waternaux, C. M., & Tsuang, M. T. (1990). Outcome in mania: A 4-year prospective follow-up of 75 patients utilizing survival analysis. *Archives of General Psychiatry, 47*, 1106–1111.

Tondo, L., & Baldessarini, R. J. (2000). Reducing suicide risk during lithium maintenance treatment. *Journal of Clinical Psychiatry, 61*(Suppl. 9), 97–104.

Wehr, T. A., Sack, D. A., & Rosenthal, N. E. (1987). Sleep reduction as a final common pathway in the genesis of mania. *American Journal of Psychiatry, 144*, 210–214.

Weissman, M. M., & Myers, J. K. (1978). Affective disorders in a U.S. urban community: The use of research diagnostic criteria in an epidemiological survey. *Archives of General Psychiatry, 35*, 1304–1311.

Wickramaratne, P. J., Weissman, M. M., Leaf, J. P., & Holford, T. R. (1989). Age, period and cohort effects on the risk of major depression: Results from five United States communities. *Journal of Clinical Epidemiology, 42*, 333–343.

Willner, P. (1995). Sensitization of dopamine D-sub-2- or D-sub-3-type receptors as a final common pathway in antidepressant drug action. *Clinical Neuropharmacology, 18*(Suppl. 1), S49–S56.

Winters, K. C., & Neale, J. M. (1985). Mania and low self-esteem. *Journal of Abnormal Psychology, 94*, 282–290.

Winters, R., Johnson, S. L., & Cuellar, A. (under review). Regulatory deficits in bipolar and unipolar disorders.

Wozniak, J., Biederman, J., & Richards, J. A. (2001). Diagnostic and therapeutic dilemmas in the management of pediatric-onset bipolar disorder. *Journal of Clinical Psychiatry, 62*(Suppl. 14), 10–15.

Yan, L. J., Hammen, C., Cohen, A. N., Daley, S. E., & Henry, R. M. (2004). Expressed emotion versus relationship quality variables in the prediction of recurrence in bipolar patients. *Journal of Affective Disorders, 83*, 199–206.

CHAPTER 11

Anxiety Disorders

DEBORAH C. BEIDEL AND BROOKE STIPELMAN

DESCRIPTION OF THE DISORDERS

Except for substance abuse, anxiety disorders constitute the most common psychiatric problem in the United States (Aalto-Setaelae, Marttunen, Tuulio-Henriksson, & Loennqvist, 2001; Beekman et al., 1998; Kessler et al., 1994), with lifetime prevalence rates of 31% in the general population. With increased recognition comes an extensive literature addressing all aspects of psychopathology. It is now clear that anxiety disorders result in significant distress and exert a significant toll on academic, occupational, social, and emotional functioning. Because of the numerous individual disorders that constitute the category of anxiety disorders, in this section we highlight the most relevant areas for each of the individual disorders.

Panic Attacks

Panic attacks constitute a discrete period of intense fear or discomfort that develops abruptly and peaks within 10 minutes of onset (*DSM-IV*; American Psychiatric Association [APA], 1994, p. 395). Cognitive and physical symptoms (four or more are necessary) include palpitations; pounding heart or accelerated heart rate; sweating; trembling or shaking; sensations of shortness of breath or smothering; feelings of choking; chest pain or discomfort; nausea or abdominal distress; feeling dizzy, unsteady, lightheaded, or faint; derealization or depersonalization; fear of losing control or going crazy; fear of dying; paresthesias; and chills or hot flushes. Panic attacks may be a component of the anxiety disorder but exist independently as well. About 15% of the general population report panic symptoms at some time in their lives (Eaton, Kessler, Wittchen, & Magee, 1994; Reed & Wittchen, 1998).

There are three types of panic attacks: (1) unexpected (uncued)—onset is not associated with a situational trigger; (2) situationally bound (cued)—the attack occurs immediately upon exposure to or in anticipation of exposure to the anxiety-producing stimulus; or (3) situationally predisposed—the attack is more likely to occur upon exposure although not immediately and not every time. Uncued attacks are more common in panic disorder (PD) and generalized anxiety disorder (GAD), whereas situationally bound attacks are more characteristic of specific and social phobia and obsessive-compulsive disorder. However, there is no specific relationship between type of attack and particular disorder.

PANIC DISORDER WITHOUT AGORAPHOBIA

When panic attacks are recurrent and unexpected, and at least one attack is followed by 1 month's concern about (1) additional attacks, (2) the implications of the attack, or (3) changes in behavior, a diagnosis of PD is warranted. Initially, antidepressants were effective in decreasing phobic inpatients' episodic anxiety or panic attacks but were ineffective for anticipatory anxiety or avoidance (Klein & Fink, 1962), whereas benzodiazepines were effective for anticipatory anxiety. Through semantic drift, anticipatory anxiety became synonymous with generalized anxiety (Turner, Beidel, & Jacob, 1988). Although this pharmacological dissection strategy was thought to have delineated two distinct types of anxiety, further intervention trials did not confirm this early theory of psychopathology (e.g., Kahn et al., 1981; Lydiard, Roy-Byrne, & Ballenger, 1988; Rickels et al., 2003).

PANIC DISORDER WITH AGORAPHOBIA

Agoraphobia, considered to be a complication of PD, is a fear of being in public places or situations where escape might be difficult or where help may be unavailable should a panic attack occur. Patients with agoraphobia avoid (or endure with marked distress) certain situations, and in its most severe form may refuse to leave the house. Thus, this disorder encompasses panic attacks plus behavioral avoidance. Commonly feared situations include being in crowded places, such as supermarkets, shopping malls, restaurants, churches, and theaters; riding in buses, cars, or planes; and traveling over bridges or through tunnels. Some individuals with agoraphobia will enter these situations but only with a trusted companion or while carrying certain items that serve as a safety signal.

AGORAPHOBIA WITHOUT HISTORY OF PANIC

Some individuals fear and/or avoid public places but deny panic attacks. Their behavioral avoidance does not appear to be triggered by fear of panic. Instead, they fear the occurrence of incapacitating or extremely embarrassing physical symptoms or limited symptom attacks (anxiety that consists of no more than three panic symptoms), dizziness or falling, loss of bowel or bladder control, or vomiting (APA, 1994). For some patients, the feared event has never occurred, at least not in public places, differentiating this diagnosis from PD with agoraphobia, where the sudden onset of panic constitutes the first stage of the disorder. Agoraphobia without history of panic is rarely seen in clinics and has not been the subject of much empirical study. Some patients with this diagnosis (for example, those who fear losing control of bodily functions) possess clinical characteristics reminiscent of obsessive-compulsive disorder and may actually fall within the obsessional realm

(Beidel & Bulik, 1990; Jenike, Vitagliano, Rabinowitz, Goff, & Baer, 1987). Furthermore, when individuals in the community originally diagnosed with agoraphobia without panic were reassessed by clinicians using standard interview schedules, most met diagnostic criteria for specific phobias instead (APA, 1994). Therefore, the nature and proper classification of this condition must await further study.

SOCIAL ANXIETY DISORDER

The third most common psychiatric disorder in the United States (Keller, 2003), social anxiety disorder (SAD; also known as social phobia) is a marked and persistent fear of social or performance situations in which embarrassment may occur (APA, 1994). Exposure almost invariably provokes anxiety, which can result in situationally bound or predisposed panic attacks. Situations are either avoided or endured with significant distress and include performing certain activities in the presence of others, such as speaking, eating, drinking, or writing, or fearing that one may do something that will cause humiliation or embarrassment, such as forgetting a speech, mispronouncing a word, or shaking uncontrollably. When the fear encompasses most social interactions, the individual is assigned the generalized subtype, which is associated with more severe anxiety, depression, social inhibition, fear of negative evaluation, avoidance, fearfulness, and self-consciousness (Herbert, Hope, & Bellack, 1992; Holt, Heimberg, & Hope, 1992; Turner, Beidel, & Townsley, 1992; Wittchen, Stein, & Kessler, 1999). This subtype also is associated with an earlier age of onset (Herbert et al., 1992; Holt et al., 1992; Wittchen et al., 1999) and greater levels of neuroticism, shyness during childhood, and introversion than the specific subtype (Stemberger, Turner, Beidel, & Calhoun, 1995).

SPECIFIC PHOBIA

Specific phobia is a marked and persistent fear of clearly discernible, circumscribed objects or situations (APA, 1994). When confronted with the feared situation, the individual experiences intense emotional distress that may reach the levels of situationally bound or situationally predisposed panic attacks. As a result, the situations are either avoided or endured with significant distress. Common specific phobias include fear of animals as well as of blood/injury, heights, and enclosed spaces (Agras, Sylvester, & Oliveau, 1969; APA, 1994; Curtis, Magee, Eaton, Wittchen, & Kessler, 1998). In clinical settings, claustrophobia (fear of closed spaces) and acrophobia (fear of heights) are most common (Emmelkamp, 1988). Specific phobias are not minor abreactions. Although a significant percentage of the general population suffers from a specific phobia, very few seek treatment (Barlow, DiNardo, Vermilyea, Vermilyea, & Blanchard, 1986). Those who do often present with additional Axis I or II conditions, or both (Barlow, 1988). In fact, the greater the number of specific phobias, the greater the predisposition toward other types of psychopathology (Curtis et al., 1998).

There are four specific phobia subtypes: animal (cued by animals or insects); natural environment (cued by objects or events such as storms, heights, or water); blood, injection, or injury (cued by blood, needles, or injuries); and situational (cued by situations such as using public transportation; traveling in tunnels, on bridges, or in elevators; flying; driving; or being in enclosed places; APA, 1994). There is also an "other" type for fears related to any other stimuli. In clinical settings, the situational subtype is most frequent, followed by natural environment; blood, injection, or injury; and animal.

OBSESSIVE-COMPULSIVE DISORDER

Obsessive-compulsive disorder (OCD) is characterized by intrusive thoughts, often coupled with repetitive behaviors that are elaborate, time-consuming, and distressful (APA, 1994). Obsessions are recurrent and persistent thoughts, impulses, or images that are intrusive and inappropriate and cause marked anxiety or distress. Obsessions are recognized as a product of one's own mind and not imposed externally—an important distinction that separates obsessions from delusions. Common forms of obsessions include doubts, thoughts, impulses, fears, images, and urges. Common content areas include dirt and contamination, aggression, inanimate-interpersonal objects or behaviors (e.g., locks, bolts, other safety devices, and orderliness), sex, and religion (Khanna & Channabasavanna, 1988; Kolada, Bland, & Newman, 1994). In most cases, the person recognizes the irrationality and attempts to ignore, suppress, or neutralize the thoughts with other thoughts or actions.

Compulsions are repetitive behaviors or mental acts that the person feels driven to perform in response to obsessions or according to rigid rules (APA, 1994). Compulsions are designed to prevent occurrence of a future event, or to neutralize a prior event, such as coming into contact with germs. They are similar to obsessions and the individual often recognizes their purposelessness, but the compulsion to complete the ritual remains. Completion may be negatively reinforcing; it temporarily decreases anxiety, although a few individuals report increased anxiety (e.g., Walker & Beech, 1969). Common forms of compulsions are hand washing and bathing, cleaning, checking, counting, and ordering. Repetitive cleaning behaviors often coexist with contamination fears, while checking behaviors are common among those experiencing self-doubt or future dread (Turner & Beidel, 1988). However, more than one type of obsession or compulsion, or both, is common. Patients often develop elaborate strategies to avoid feared objects or situations, thereby lessening daily distress and limiting the necessity to engage in ritualistic behaviors. OCD has the most chronic course among the anxiety disorders.

POSTTRAUMATIC STRESS DISORDER

When individuals are exposed to a traumatic event in which (1) the person experienced, witnessed, or was confronted with actual or threatened death or serious injury, or a threat to the physical integrity of self or others, and (2) the response involved intense fear, helplessness, or horror, they may meet *DSM-IV* criteria for posttraumatic stress disorder (PTSD). Traumatic events may include combat experiences, assault, rape, or observing the serious injury or violent death of another person. Patients with PTSD report "reexperiencing" the event through recurrent and intrusive recollections or dreams, or both; suddenly acting or feeling as if the event were recurring; intense psychological or physical reactivity; and distress when exposed to events that symbolize or resemble some aspect of the trauma. As a result, they attempt to avoid associated stimuli, including thoughts, feelings, activities, or situations, and they may have difficulty recalling important aspects of the event. Patients describe numbing of general emotions, including diminished interest in activities, a feeling of detachment or estrangement, restricted range of affect, and a sense of a foreshortened future. General and persistent autonomic arousal also exists and may include difficulty sleeping, irritability or anger, difficulty concentrating, hypervigilance, exaggerated startle responses, and physiologic reactivity when exposed to event-related stimuli (APA, 1994).

There are two subtypes of PTSD: acute (symptom duration less than 3 months), and chronic (symptom duration is 3 months or more). There is also a delayed onset specifier, if onset occurs at least 6 months after the event. Historically, PTSD was assigned to persons who had participated in combat, but now it is also used for those who experience natural disasters, assault or rape (Kilpatrick et al., 1989), or a host of other non-combat-related events. Rates for civilian PTSD range from 1% to 14%, depending on the method of assessment and the population (APA, 1994; Davidson, Hughes, Blazer, & George, 1991). Rates of combat-related PTSD vary, but most estimates range between 15% and 30% of combat veterans (Center for Disease Control, 1988; Kulka et al., 1988). Some suggest that many civilian forms of PTSD do not meet the classic criteria for combat-related PTSD, thus questioning whether some of these disorders are more likely stress reactions than classic PTSD (Blanchard et al., 1996; Norris & Kaniasty, 1994; Rothbaum et al., 1992). Furthermore, changing gender roles are likely to affect future rates of combat PTSD. Historically, for female veterans diagnosed with PTSD, the precipitating event was predominantly sexual assault or sexual harassment, not combat exposure (Butterfield, Forneris, Feldman, & Beckham, 2000; King & King, 1996; Wolfe et al., 1998), although this situation is changing rapidly as a result of recent international conflicts.

ACUTE STRESS DISORDER

The criterion for acute stress disorder (ASD) includes the same stress-inducing event and possible reactions listed for PTSD; only the duration requirement distinguishes the two disorders. Individuals with ASD experience emotional numbing, detachment, or absence of emotion; reduced awareness of surroundings; derealization; depersonalization; or dissociative amnesia. Symptoms of reexperiencing, avoidance, and anxiety or arousal are identical to those symptoms of PTSD. There must be clinically significant distress or functional impairment for the diagnosis to be assigned. The disturbance lasts for a minimum of 2 days and a maximum of 4 weeks. The short symptom duration (maximum of 4 weeks) makes it unclear if treatment is necessary. If the symptoms persist for longer than 4 weeks, a diagnosis of PTSD is warranted. The prevalence of this disorder in the general population remains unstudied.

GENERALIZED ANXIETY DISORDER

The essential feature of GAD is excessive anxiety and worry occurring more days than not for a period of at least 6 months about a number of events or activities (APA, 1994). The worry is difficult to control and is associated with somatic and cognitive symptoms: muscle tension, restlessness or feeling keyed up or on edge, being easily fatigued, difficulty concentrating or mind going blank, sleep disturbance, and irritability. Six out of 18 cognitive and somatic complaints are necessary for the diagnosis. The focus of the anxiety is not confined to the features of any other Axis I disorder, and the anxiety, worry, or physical symptoms cause clinically significant distress or functional impairment. In general, intolerance of uncertainty appears to be a hallmark feature of GAD (Ladouceur, Talbot, & Dugas, 1997). Individuals tend to believe that worrying may be an effective means of avoidance or preventing negative consequences, or both. One-month and lifetime prevalence rates are estimated at 5% to 10% in community and clinic samples (Maier et al., 2000; Weiller, Bisserbe, Boyer, Lepine, & Lecrubier, 1996; Wittchen & Hoyer, 2001), making it one of the most prevalent anxiety disorders in the primary care setting. However, studies examining GAD generally report unacceptable levels of interrater reliability; raising questions as to whether GAD is an independent syndrome.

Other Anxiety Disorders

Panic attacks, worry, obsessions, compulsions, or phobias can result from medical conditions (anxiety disorder due to a general medical condition). Thus, it is necessary to rule out medical disorders such as mitral valve prolapse, other cardiovascular conditions, vestibular abnormalities, hyperthyroidism, hypothyroidism, hypoglycemia, partial complex seizures, phenochromocytoma, hypoparathyroidism, hyperparathyroidism, and Cushing's syndrome (Jacob & Turner, 1988). Temporal order of the disease onset may assist in differential diagnosis. Similarly, presence of anxiety symptoms only during an episode of physical illness or an atypical age of onset may suggest an etiological role for a medical condition (APA, 1994).

Anxiety symptoms also can be induced by ingestion of or withdrawal from various substances including alcohol, caffeine, amphetamines, cannabis, cocaine, hallucinogens, inhalants, phencyclidine, sedatives, hypnotics, or anxiolytics. Also, medications such as anesthetics, analgesics, sympathomimetics, anticholinergics, insulin, thyroid preparations, oral contraceptives, antihistamines, antiparkinsonian medications, corticosteroids, antihypertensive and cardiovascular medications, anticonvulsants, lithium carbonate, antipsychotic medications, and antidepressant medications may produce anxious symptomatology. Another class of anxiety precipitants includes heavy metals and toxins (e.g., gasoline, organophosphate insecticides, and carbon monoxide). If anxiety is caused by any one of these conditions, treatment for the medical disorder should result in a remediation of the anxiety symptoms.

Case Studies

Anxiety disorders are complex, often chronic conditions that significantly impact many aspects of daily functioning. The cases studies in this chapter illustrate the severe and debilitating nature of these disorders. These vignettes clearly illustrate that anxiety disorders affect individuals of all ages, from all socioeconomic status (SES) groups, and across all racial and ethnic categories. Clearly, the symptoms are severe and affect all aspects of psychosocial functioning.

Posttraumatic Stress Disorder

Ron was a 27-year-old Ethiopian male who immigrated to the United States 3 years ago. He was currently employed in a traveling singing group. While in Ethiopia, he had been imprisoned numerous times for political reasons, beginning at age 16. Although unable to recall the specifics of his imprisonment, he believed that he was jailed three to five times, with each confinement lasting for several months. While in prison, he was repeatedly tortured and interrogated; during this time he reported feeling helpless and out of control. Currently, he had intrusive memories and recurrent dreams about the events, and a sense of reliving the events to the point where he was unsure if it were actually happening again. He was experiencing extreme emotional distress and physical reactivity to internal and external reminders of his incarceration and torture, including physiological distress when he saw police officers or soldiers. He had lost interest and decreased his participation in significant activities, and felt severely detached and emotionally distant from others. He also reported a restricted range of emotions, a sense of a foreshortened future, moderate difficulty sleeping, irritability, poor concentration, and an exaggerated startle response.

Social Phobia

Marcie, a 27-year-old Malaysian female who was married with four children, reported feeling shy and anxious in social situations since childhood. In elementary school, she received a failing grade in English because she hid in the bathroom, too afraid to give her book report in front of the class. Her symptoms continued without remission into adulthood. In addition to her lack of friendships, she was unable to attend college, fearing negative evaluation by the instructor or classmates. Working as a nurse's aide, she felt socially isolated at work and too anxious to ask questions of her coworkers. On several occasions, she had to do several hours of extra work as a result of her inability to ask for clarification and extra help. When in social situations, her physiological responses included severe heart palpitations, sweating, trembling hands and voice, and hot flashes.

Generalized Anxiety Disorder

Becky was a 35-year-old single Caucasian female working as a church secretary. She described excessive and uncontrollable worry about a number of everyday matters related to work, family, personal health, and world affairs. She spent about 75% of her day ruminating over these issues, which caused significant distress. As a result, Becky experienced severe restlessness, fatigue, and difficulty concentrating. Her worries were so intrusive that she could not "turn off her mind at night," resulting in sleep delay onset of 1 to 2 hours. She constantly felt exhausted and had little motivation to leave her apartment. In addition, her inability to concentrate made it difficult to focus and get work done efficiently.

Panic Disorder with Agoraphobia

Lydia was a 33-year-old single Caucasian female working as a communications director for a nonprofit organization. Since age 7, she had experienced unexpected panic attacks. Currently, she reported approximately 100-plus panic attacks per year, with each attack lasting approximately 15 to 20 minutes.

(continued)

Despite some variability, her physical symptoms included shortness of breath, heart palpitations, sweating, voice trembling, hot flashes, and fear of loss of control. She worried about future attacks. The attacks caused significant distress, despite the fact that she had been confronted with them almost her entire life, and she worried about future attacks. She avoided public places such as grocery stores, malls, doctors' offices, and large crowds. She felt trapped by her disorder and was "unable to live life to the fullest."

Obsessive-Compulsive Disorder

Tom was a divorced 51-year-old African American male working as a shipping manager. He reported obsessive thinking related to germs and contamination. To avoid contamination, he cleaned his office three times daily (45 minutes a day) with alcohol, including his doorknob, telephone receiver, desk, and other areas to avoid contamination. He also was concerned about contamination by paper money, finding it disgusting and smelly. Although he lived alone, he would not use his own toilet unless it was cleaned to his specific standards. He refused to use public restrooms. Thoughts about contamination consumed approximately 60% of his day, which significantly impacted his time, mental energy, and productivity. The thoughts and rituals had caused him to be late for work and negatively impacted his productivity.

EPIDEMIOLOGY

According to the National Comorbidity Survey Replication (NCSR; Kessler et al., 2005), which represents the most recent epidemiological data for mental disorders, 31.2% of the general population reported the lifetime occurrence of an anxiety disorder, and 18.7% of the sample endorsed the presence of an anxiety disorder in the past 12 months. This 12-month prevalence rate was higher than for any other diagnostic category, and the lifetime prevalence rate was second only to that for substance use and abuse disorders. Data for lifetime and 12-month prevalence rates are presented in Table 11.1.

Table 11.1
Lifetime and 12-Month Prevalence Rates for Anxiety Disorders

Disorder	Lifetime	12 Month
Panic disorder	4.7	2.7
Agoraphobia without panic	1.3	0.8
Social phobia	12.1	6.8
Specific phobia	12.5	8.7
Generalized anxiety disorder	5.7	2.7
Obsessive-compulsive disorder	1.8	1.1
Posttraumatic stress disorder	6.8	3.6
Any anxiety disorder	31.2	18.7

CLINICAL PICTURE

Differentiation of so-called normal anxiety from the clinical syndromes discussed previously is based on symptom severity and functional interference. Impairment is probably the most important criterion in determining whether symptoms actually are disorders. For example, 61% of a telephone survey sample reported being much more or somewhat more anxious than others in social situations, but only 18.7% reported at least moderate interference or distress. This percentage dropped to 7.1% when strict diagnostic criteria were applied and was further reduced to 1.9% when only "at least moderate impairment" was considered (Stein, Walker, & Forde, 1994).

Anxiety is a multidimensional construct and symptoms usually are divided into three categories: subjective distress (self-report), physiological response, and avoidance or escape behavior (overt behavioral; Lang, 1977). Somatic complaints are characterized primarily by sympathetic nervous system activation and include tachycardia, tremulousness, dizziness, light-headedness, paresthesias, and dyspnea, which may differ by the specific disorder. Those with SAD were significantly more likely to endorse blushing and muscle twitching (Amies, Gelder, & Shaw, 1983). Dizziness, difficulty breathing, choking or smothering sensations, weakness in limbs, fainting episodes, and buzzing or ringing in the ears were endorsed significantly more often by patients with PD with or without agoraphobia (Amies et al., 1983; Page, 1994). For GAD, gastrointestinal distress is common, including indigestion, nausea, constipation, diarrhea, and urinary urgency and frequency (Brown, Marten, & Barlow, 1995), with a predominance of muscle tension, irritability, and fatigue or a predominant central nervous system hyperarousal (Noyes et al., 1992). Finally, the reaction of blood, injection, or injury phobics is defined by parasympathetic (rather than sympathetic) activation manifested by bradycardia and hypotension (Ost, 1996), which may result in fainting and clearly differentiates this response from that in other phobic states.

Subjective distress (cognitive symptoms) entails worry about specific events involving danger or harm to oneself or others. Most often taking the form of specific thoughts, cognitive symptoms also may occur as ideas, images, or impulses. Knowledge that occurrence of the fearful event is usually of very low probability does little to assuage the overly aroused emotional state. In specific phobia or SAD, the thoughts are most often triggered by actual or anticipated contact with the feared stimulus. In contrast, those with GAD have a broader constellation of anxious cognitions, termed "worry," that encompass several thematic areas, have the characteristics of mental problem solving, and have the possibility of at least one negative outcome (Borkovec, Robinson, Pruzinsky, & DePress, 1983, p. 10). A final category of cognitive symptoms are obsessions that consist of intrusive unwanted thoughts, images, or impulses that are often horrific and perceived as uncontrollable, yet always as a product of one's own mind. An attempt to differentiate worry from obsessionality (Turner, Beidel, & Stanley, 1992) highlighted several distinguishing characteristics, including thematic content (GAD patients do not often report excessive concern with dirt, contamination, aggressive impulses, or horrific images), cognition form (GAD patients do not report images or impulses but primarily conceptual, verbal linguistic activity; Borkovec & Shadick, 1989), and intrusive quality (worry is perceived as less intrusive and less ego-dystonic). Intrusive quality (i.e., the egodystonic/egosyntonic distinction) appears to be a key dimension in distinguishing obsessive thought from worry (Langlois, Freeston, & Ladouceur, 2000).

The characteristic behavior of anxiety patients is escape from or avoidance of the feared stimulus, even to the point of becoming housebound. Many patients devise elaborate avoidance strategies, often engaging the cooperation of others. In the case of OCD, avoidance is usually accompanied by ritualistic behaviors, which serve to "undo" or prevent the feared event. Although almost always present, escape or avoidance is not required for a diagnosis. Behavioral avoidance can be manifested in subtle ways not always apparent to the patient but able to be detected by a clinician.

Other aspects of the clinical presentation include appetite or sleep disturbances, and concentration and memory difficulties. Suicidal ideation and suicide attempts have been reported in some anxiety patients but appear to be associated with the presence of comorbid conditions such as depression, eating disorders, and personality disorders (Cox, Direnfeld, Swinson, & Norton, 1994; Khan, Leventhal, Khan, & Brown, 2002; Warshaw, Dolan, & Keller, 2000). Even if not significantly depressed, anxiety patients often present with secondary dysphoric mood, affecting approximately 70% of patients with SAD (Lecrubier & Weiller, 1997). Interestingly, only 11% of patients with SAD (and comorbid depression) who presented to general practitioners were diagnosed with SAD, highlighting the fact that when patients present with a mixed symptom picture, anxiety disorders can be overlooked (see Diagnostic Considerations section).

COURSE AND PROGNOSIS

AGE OF ONSET

Specific phobias have the earliest age of onset, usually during early childhood. Phobias of animals first appear between the ages of 4.4 and 10 years (Marks & Gelder, 1966; McNally & Steketee, 1985; Ost, 1987). For other phobias, the average age of onset was 11.9 years for thunderstorm phobias, 5.5 to 8.8 years for blood phobias, and 10.8 years for dental phobias (Bienvenu & Eaton, 1998; Liddell & Lyons, 1978). Claustrophobia has a later average age of onset, ranging from 16.1 to 22.7 years (Marks & Gelder, 1966; Ost, 1987; Sheehan, Sheehan, & Minichiello, 1981; Thyer, Parrish, Curtis, Nesse, & Cameron, 1985). Due to the similarity to the age of onset for PD (see next paragraph), some (Klein, 1981; Ost, 1987) have hypothesized that claustrophobia may be a restricted but functional and descriptive equivalent of PD with agoraphobia.

The generally accepted age of onset for PD is early adulthood (McNally, 2001; Ost, 1987), ranging from 19.7 to 32 years of age, with a mean of 26.5 years. Three unpredictable and uncontrollable events (that threaten or result in physical harm) appear to be uniquely related to agoraphobia onset: life-threatening accidents; combat in war (for men); and fire, flood, or other natural disaster (Magee, 1999). Although uniquely related, they are not necessary or specific for the development of agoraphobia. For SAD, age of onset ranges from 15.7 to 20.0 years (Amies et al., 1983; Liebowitz et al., 1985; Marks & Gelder, 1966; Turner, Beidel, Dancu, & Keys, 1986). However, age of onset can be lower (11.6 years) in those with comorbid depression (Magee, 1999) and may occur in children as young as age 8 (Beidel, Turner, & Morris, 1999).

For OCD, typical age of onset ranges from late adolescence to early adulthood (e.g., Nestadt, Bienvenu, Cai, Samuels, & Eaton, 1998; Rasmussen & Tsuang, 1986) but can occur as young as age 4 (Turner & Beidel, 1988). Even when the frank onset is early adulthood, elements of OCD often are present at a much earlier age (Turner & Beidel, 1988). Prior to age 18, OCD is characterized by a greater number of obsessions and compulsions and greater levels of clinical impairment than cases of adult onset (Sobin, Blundell, & Karayiorgou, 2000). Finally, there are no available figures for a "typical" age of onset for GAD or PTSD. Overall, prevalence rates of GAD are low in adolescents and young adults but increase significantly with age (Wittchen & Hoyer, 2001). In the case of PTSD, given that the disorder is triggered by a traumatic event, onset can occur at any age (see McNally, 2001).

COURSE AND COMPLICATIONS

Without treatment, anxiety disorders tend to have a chronic course (e.g., Breier, Charney, & Heninger, 1986). For example, once established, fear intensity for OCD and specific phobia remained constant or gradually increased over subsequent years (McNally & Steketee, 1985; Rasmussen & Tsuang, 1986), although for a subset of OCD cases with a later age of onset, the course may be best described as episodic (Perugi et al., 1998). Along these lines, Eaton et al. (1998) reported that panic with agoraphobia is associated with a less intense onset but slower recovery than panic disorder without agoraphobia.

For patients with PD, probability of a symptom-free 8-week period was .42 (Goisman et al., 1994), whereas the probability for patients with agoraphobia was .15, indicating symptom-free periods were unlikely. Similar figures were reported by Keller et al. (1994); a .39 probability of full remission (8 weeks symptom-free) at 1-year follow-up for uncomplicated PD and a .17 probability of full remission for PD with agoraphobia. At 18 months, the probabilities increased to .49 and .20, respectively. However, there was a high probability of relapse (within 1 year) after remission; .31 for PD patients and .35 for PD with agoraphobia. Comorbidity of Axis II disorders may play a role in chronicity as 59% of those without a personality disorder had a 2-month period of remission compared to 29% of those with a comorbid personality disorder (Pollack, Otto, Rosenbaum, & Sachs, 1992), even though more than 80% of the patients received pharmacological treatment and 75% received psychological (nonspecific dynamic) intervention. In contrast, a 5-year follow-up of patients receiving pharmacological treatment found that 85% no longer met criteria for PD, although 62% still reported occasional panic attacks (Andersch, Hanson, & Haellstroem, 1997).

Onset of SAD prior to age 11 predicts nonrecovery in adulthood (Davidson, 1993). Among adults, neither demographic (gender or age) nor clinical variables (age of onset, duration of illness, comorbidity, or level of functioning) accurately predicted outcome 65 weeks after intake (Reich, Goldenberg, Goisman, Vasile, & Keller, 1994), although with psychological treatment, 85% of patients with SAD had remitted 10 years later (Fava et al., 2001). Typically, GAD has a gradual onset and an unremitting course (Noyes et al., 1992). At 5-year follow-up, significantly fewer GAD patients were fully remitted (18%) as compared to PD patients (45%; Woodman, Noyes, Black, Schlosser, & Yagla, 1999). Even with drug treatment, 50% continued to meet criteria for GAD (Mancuso, Townsend, & Mercante, 1993), and those who continued to have GAD symptoms were more likely to have concurrent diagnoses of dysthymia, SAD, or both, as well as more Axis II cluster B and C personality disorders.

The few empirical data that exist, along with our clinical experience, lead to the following tentative conclusions. First, symptom exacerbation is often correlated with onset of significant life stressors (Klein & Fink, 1962; Kukleta & Franc, 2000; Magee, 1999; Turner & Beidel, 1988). Second, once the disorder is established, behavioral avoidance often functions to reduce general emotional distress but results in social impairment, and symptoms tend to reemerge or worsen when there is contact with the phobic environment. Third, some patients likely overcome their disorder without professional intervention, but characteristics associated with these successful outcomes are unknown.

Anxiety disorders result in significant life complications. Among those with SAD, inability to work, incomplete educational attainment, lack of career advancement, lost work productivity, and severe social restrictions are common features (Liebowitz, Gorman, Fyer, & Klein, 1985; Turner et al., 1986; Van Amerigen, Mancini, & Streiner, 1993; Wittchen & Beloch, 1996; Zhang, Ross, & Davidson, 2004). Among patients with PD, agoraphobia, or both, 50% were receiving some form of financial assistance (unemployment, disability, welfare, or social security payments; Goisman et al., 1994). Failure to complete high school was positively and significantly associated with anxiety disorders or conduct disorders in females, whereas only anxiety disorders were positively related to failure to enter college and failure to complete college (Kessler, Foster, Saunders, & Stang, 1995). Among men, these transitions were significantly related only to conduct disorders. Furthermore, the economic burden of anxiety disorders is quite severe, with an annual cost of approximately $42.3 billion, or $1,542 per sufferer (Greenberg et al., 1999), including $23 billion in nonpsychiatric medical treatment costs, $13.3 billion in psychiatric medical costs, $4.1 billion in indirect workplace costs, $1.2 billion in mortality costs, and $0.8 billion in prescription pharmaceutical costs. It is clear that anxiety disorders exert a substantial cost on American society.

TREATMENT OUTCOME

Although it is clear that anxiety disorders are chronic conditions and rarely spontaneously remit, they also are disorders that are treatable. In fact, both pharmacological and behavioral or cognitive-behavioral interventions are efficacious treatments. It is beyond the scope of this chapter to provide a thorough review for each intervention with each disorder. Thus, we will comment on the efficacy of the various classes of agents, interventions, and factors that may predict treatment outcome.

PHARMACOLOGICAL TREATMENTS

Historically, the tricyclic antidepressants were among the first pharmacological treatments, being used successfully for PD and PD with agoraphobia (Ballenger, 1986; Barlow, Gorman, Shear, & Woods, 2000; Liebowitz, 1985), GAD (Rickels, Downing, Schweizer, & Hassman, 1993), and PTSD (Davidson, 1992, 2000). Phenelzine, a monoamine oxidase inhibitor (MAOI), was the first efficacious agent for generalized SAD (Liebowitz et al., 1988) but its side-effect profile and dietary restrictions limit its use as a first-line treatment. For patients with PTSD, nefazodone also may be efficacious (Zisook et al., 2000).

The benzodiazepine alprazolam appears efficacious for PD and PD with agoraphobia (Ballenger, 1990; Ballenger et al., 1988; Cross-National Collaborative Panic Study Second Phase Investigation, 1992; Curtis et al., 1993; Sheikh & Swales, 1999) and for GAD (Rickels, Downing, Schweizer, & Hassman, 1993). For SAD, clonazepam (another benzodiazepine) is efficacious (Davidson et al., 1993), but the beta-blocker atenolol is not (Liebowitz et al., 1988; Turner, Beidel, & Jacob, 1994).

Clearly, the drug class known as selective serotonin reuptake inhibitors (SSRIs) is now the treatment of choice for anxiety disorders (with the exception of specific phobia, for which there is no drug efficacy; Lydiard et al., 1988). SSRIs are efficacious for PD and PD with agoraphobia (Hoehn-Saric, McLeod, & Hipsley, 1993; Palatnik, Frolov, Fux, & Benjamin, 2001; Pohl, Wolkow, & Clary, 1998; Rapaport, Pollack, Clary, Mardekian, & Wolkow, 2001), SAD (Baldwin, Bobes, Stein, Schwarwächter, & Faure, 1999; den Boer, van Vliet, & Westenberg, 1994; D. Stein, Westenberg, Yang, Li, & Barbato, 2003; D. Stein et al., 1999; M. Stein et al., 1998; M. Stein, Fyer, Davidson, Pollack, & Wiita, 1999), OCD (Goodman, McDougle, & Price, 1992; Marazziti et al., 2001; Rivas-Vazquez, 2001; Stanley & Turner, 1995), and PTSD (van der Kolk et al., 1994). However, there are several caveats to bear in mind with respect to SSRI outcome. First, for OCD, antidepressant drugs that are less serotonergic than clomipramine are generally not effective, and as a result clomipramine remains the treatment of choice in refractory OCD (Todorov, Freeston, & Borgeat, 2000). Second, there has been a shift in the pharmacotherapy of GAD (Salzman, Goldenberg, Bruce, & Keller, 2001), with benzodiazepines being combined with or replaced by SSRIs (Rickels et al., 2000) to heighten treatment efficacy.

Positive outcome for all classes of pharmacological agents must be tempered by acknowledgment of moderate to high relapse rates (23% to 86%; Fontaine & Chouinard, 1986; Pato, Zohar-Kadouch, Zohor, & Murphy, 1988; Versiani, Amrein, & Montgomery, 1997). Many studies suffer from methodological confounds, with almost total reliance upon clinician and patient rating scales. Furthermore, the impact of comorbid disorders upon treatment response is unclear. Among PD patients, panic-free periods were more likely in patients without comorbid Axis I or II disorders (Pollack et al., 1992), whereas no clear predictors of treatment outcome have been reported for those with OCD (Stanley & Turner, 1995).

BEHAVIORAL AND COGNITIVE-BEHAVIORAL TREATMENTS

More than 30 years of compelling empirical data leave no doubt that behavioral and cognitive-behavioral interventions, or treatments (CBT), are the psychosocial treatments of choice (Beidel, Turner, & Ballenger, 1997; Butler, Chapman, Forman, & Beck, 2006). Although engineered differently, all of the interventions incorporate exposure procedures (e.g., Hoffart, 1993; Turner, Cooley-Quille, & Beidel, 1996). After briefly reviewing the literature, we will examine patient factors that affect treatment outcome.

In vivo exposure (with or without the concomitant use of medication or cognitive interventions) is efficacious for PD with agoraphobia (Barlow & Lehman, 1996; Clum, 1989; Craske, Lang, Aikins, & Mystkowski, 2005; Craske, Rapee, & Barlow, 1992;), producing improvement in the 60% to 70% range (Ballenger, Lydiard, & Turner, 1995), with remission rates of 93% after 2 years and 62% after 10 years (Fava et al., 2001).

SAD has been successfully treated by behavior therapy procedures including exposure, social skills training, and Social Effectiveness Therapy (Beidel & Turner, in press; Newman, Hofann, Trabert, Roth, & Taylor, 1994; Turner, Beidel, & Cooley, 1994; van Dam-Baggen & Kraaimaat, 2000; Wlazlo, Schroeder-Hartwig, Hand, Kaiser, & Munchau, 1990), with effects maintained for several years posttreatment (Fava et al., 2001). Behavioral interventions (systematic desensitization, imaginal and in vivo flooding, graduated in vivo exposure, and participant modeling) also result in positive treatment outcome for GAD (Butler, Fennell, Robson, & Gelder, 1991; Craske et al., 1992; Durham & Allan, 1993) and for specific phobias. With respect to specific phobia, successful outcome rates are quite high (averaging about 80% improvement) with very minimal treatment lengths (1.9–9.0 hours depending upon the particular phobia; Ost, 1996). Applied tension, developed specifically to address the biphasic physiological response of blood, injection, or injury phobias (i.e., the tendency to faint upon exposure to the fearful stimulus) has been markedly successful in the treatment of phobias (see Ost, 1996, for details).

Exposure combined with response prevention (ERP) is the treatment of choice for OCD. Even after adjusting for dropout and refusal rates that account for about 20% of treatment seekers, 72% of patients benefit from ERP and outcome is maintained up to 6 years later (Stanley & Turner, 1995). Graduated exposure is less efficacious than intensive procedures (Turner & Beidel, 1988) but more efficacious than cognitive-behavior therapy (McLean et al., 2001) or general anxiety management (Lindsay, Crino, & Andrews, 1997). When relapse prevention strategies are added (Hiss, Foa, & Kozak, 1994), relapse and recurrence rates were lower at 6-month follow-up when compared to psychological placebo. There is now an established literature supporting the use of prolonged or massed exposure for civilian populations with PTSD (Echeburua, de Corral, Zubizarreta, & Sarasua, 1997; Foa, Rothbaum, Riggs, & Murdock, 1991; Foa et al., 1999; Marks, Lovell, Noshirvani, Livanou, & Thrasher, 1998; Tarrier, Sommerfield, Pilgrim, & Humphreys, 1999).

Among combat veterans, exposure treatments are partially efficacious, but the data are less compelling. Intensive exposure (imaginal or in vivo) reduces anxiety, depression, startle responses, memory disturbance, sleep, nightmares, and intrusive thoughts (Boudewyns & Hyer, 1990; Cooper & Clum, 1989; Frueh, Turner, Beidel, Mirabella, & Jones, 1996; Keane, Fairbank, Caddell, & Zimering, 1989) but not negative symptoms (behavioral avoidance, social withdrawal, interpersonal difficulties, occupational maladjustment, and emotional numbing) or emotion management (anger control; see Frueh, Turner, & Beidel, 1995). Recently, added additional interventions in the form of behavioral family therapy (Glynn et al., 1999) and trauma management therapy (Turner, Beidel, & Frueh, 2005) have been used to enhance treatment outcome. Initial data appear promising, but more controlled trials are necessary.

CBT (e.g., cognitive restructuring, respiratory training) is efficacious for those with uncomplicated PD (Beck, 1988; Clark, Salkovskis, & Chalkley, 1985). Focused Cognitive Therapy (Beck, Sokol, & Clark, 1992) and Panic Control Therapy (PCT) (Barlow, Craske, Cerney, & Klosko, 1989; Craske, Maidenberg, & Bystritsky, 1995) incorporate exposure to somatic symptoms as well as cognitive restructuring. After these interventions, approximately 80% of patients describe themselves as panic-free, a rate superior to that of no-treatment control groups or alternative psychological interventions (Barlow & Lehman, 1996). Adding coping or cognitive strategies to exposure-based procedures may reduce treatment dropout for those with PD or

PD with agoraphobia but does not enhance treatment outcome (Clum, 1989). Traditional CBT is efficacious for GAD (Butler, Fennell, Robson, & Gelder, 1991; Craske et al., 1992; Durham & Allan, 1993), with higher response rates than for applied relaxation and nondirective treatment (Borkovec & Costello, 1993). A newer CBT strategy using (1) correction of erroneous beliefs and effective problem-solving strategies, and (2) cognitive exposure for worries not amenable to problem solving results in 77% improvement, with gains maintained 1 year later (Ladouceur et al., 2000).

Cognitive-behavioral Group Therapy (Heimberg et al., 1990) also is efficacious for SAD, and the effects are maintained for up to 5 years posttreatment (Heimberg, Salzman, Holt, & Blendell, 1993). Substantive reviews (Fairbrother, 2002; Rodebaugh, Holaway, & Heimberg, 2004; Zaider & Heimberg, 2003), dismantling studies (Hope, Heimberg, & Bruch, 1995; Salaberria & Echeburua, 1998), and meta-analyses (Feske & Chambless, 1995; Gould, Buckminster, Pollack, Otto, & Yap, 1997; Taylor, 1996; Wentzel, Statler-Cowen, Patton, & Holt, 1998) indicate clearly that the key ingredient is exposure; other interventions may be used but do not increase response rates. Finally, cognitive processing therapy (CPT; Resick, Nishith, Weaver, Astin, & Feuer, 2002) consists of cognitive therapy and exposure in the form of writing and reading about the event and is efficacious for civilian-related PTSD. A controlled trial of group CBT for OCD was no more efficacious than relaxation therapy alone (Fineberg, Hughes, Gale, & Roberts, 2005), although, consistent with the literature on panic disorder, group CBT resulted in a lower dropout rate than relaxation training (35% vs. 4%, respectively).

COMBINED OR COMPARATIVE PHARMACOLOGICAL AND PSYCHOSOCIAL TREATMENTS

A comparison of PCT and alprazolam (Klosko, Barlow, Tassinari, & Cerny, 1990) resulted in the following percentage of patients with PD who were panic-free at posttreatment: PCT (87%), alprazolam (50%), placebo (36%), and wait-list (33%). Combining both active interventions does not seem to produce a synergistic effect (Hegel, Ravaris, & Ahles, 1994), and 1 year after CBT and alprazolam withdrawal, 76% of patients were medication-free, and 85% remained panic-free. Combining fluvoxamine and psychological panic management (DeBeurs, van Balkom, Lange, Koele, & van Dyck, 1995) decreased self-reported agoraphobic avoidance when compared to psychological panic management plus exposure in vivo, placebo plus exposure in vivo, or exposure in vivo alone, but similar results were not found for the other variables included in the investigation.

For SAD, comparative trials suggest some superior efficacy for behavioral interventions. Intensive exposure was more effective than atenolol (Turner, Beidel, & Jacob, 1994), whereas the addition of propranolol did not result in superior outcome over exposure alone (Falloon, Lloyd, & Harpin, 1981). Two large comparative trials—phenelzine, placebo, cognitive-behavioral group treatment, and educational support (Heimberg et al., 1998) and fluoxetine, comprehensive cognitive behavioral therapy (CCBT), placebo, combined CCBT plus fluoxetine, and CCBT plus placebo (Davidson et al., 2004)—suggest that combining both medication and CBT results in significant improvement for 60% to 75% of the samples. After an untreated follow-up period, only 17% of those previously treated with cognitive-behavioral group therapy relapsed compared to 50% of those previously treated with phenelzine (Liebowitz, Heimberg, Schneier et al., 1999), suggesting longer-lasting effects for CBT.

For OCD, an initial meta-analysis indicated that both serotonergic antidepressants (clomipramine, fluoxetine, and fluvoxamine) and behavioral therapy were significantly superior to placebo (Christensen, Hadzi-Pavlovic, Andrews, & Mattick, 1987), with no differences between active treatments based on effect sizes. Examining the relative and combined efficacy of clomipramine and exposure and response prevention (EX/RP) using a double-blind, randomized, placebo-controlled trial (Foa et al., 2005), all active treatments were superior to placebo. EX/RP was superior to clomipramine but there was no increased benefit for the combination of clomipramine and EX/RP. Similar conclusions were reached by a meta-analysis examining five serotonin reuptake inhibitors SRIs (clomipramine, fluoxetine, sertraline, paroxetine, and fluvoxamine) and EX/RP (Kobak, Greist, Jefferson, Katzelnick, & Henk, 1998). After controlling for methodological variables, clomipramine was slightly more efficacious compared to the other SRIs but not significantly different from the effect size obtained by EX/RP and EX/RP plus SRI. In one of the few comparative trials, CBT or CBT plus an SRI (clomipramine, fluoxetine or fluvoxamine) resulted in equivalent improvement (Kordon et al., 2005). Two years later, as a result of the combined intervention strategy, discontinuation of the SRI did not result in a return of symptoms.

For disorders other than OCD, the combination of CBT and pharmacotherapy indicate that high-potency benzodiazepines exert a detrimental effect on outcome of CBT (Westra & Stewart, 1998), whereas low-potency benzodiazepines and antidepressants neither enhance nor attenuate CBT outcome. However, few outcome studies exist and further data are necessary. Behavior therapy and CBT have been used successfully to aid in benzodiazepine withdrawal for patients with PD (Otto et al., 1993), and the addition of CBT to medication alone improves treatment outcome for those with PD who are treated in the primary care setting (Craske, Golinelli, et al., 2005).

PREDICTORS OF TREATMENT OUTCOME

Across all disorders (except specific phobia), poorer treatment outcome is predicted by more severe psychopathology, in the form of either the primary anxiety disorder (Basoglu et al., 1994; Castle et al., 1994; Keijsers, Hoogduin, & Schaap, 1994; Steketee & Shapiro, 1995; Turner, Beidel, Wolff, Spaulding, & Jacob, 1996), comorbid affective and anxiety states (Albus & Scheibe, 1993; Brown, Antony, & Barlow, 1995; Keijsers, Hoogduin, & Schaap, 1994; Steketee & Shapiro, 1995; Turner, Beidel, Wolff, Spaulding & Jacob, 1996), or comorbid Axis II disorders (AuBuchon & Malatesta, 1994; Stanley & Turner, 1995; Turner, Beidel, Wolff, Spaulding & Jacob, 1996). One recent investigation suggested that the particular type of negative thought may predict successful treatment outcome (Hicks et al., 2005). Whereas cognitions related to physical or mental catastrophes did not predict treatment outcome, negative thoughts related to social catastrophes (e.g., "People will think I'm weird") did predict a more negative treatment outcome. No other clinical or demographic variables appear to predict future outcome.

In summary, pharmacological, behavioral, and cognitive-behavioral interventions have proven efficacious for the treatment of anxiety disorders, perhaps with the exception of combat-related PTSD, for which much more work is necessary. The challenge now, particularly for behavioral and cognitive-behavioral interventions, is to devise dissemination strategies so that those in need of these services have ready access to them. For example, there has been increasing interest in the area of virtual reality therapy as a tool for enhancing exposure opportunities for patients with various types of anxiety disorders (e.g., Klinger et al., 2005; Rothbaum, Hodges, Anderson, Price, & Smith, 2002). Furthermore, additional efforts to predict who will respond positively to a specific intervention are necessary. Current predictors such as illness severity or presence of a comorbid disorder are useful but do not provide the information needed to enhance treatment outcome for those individuals most in need of the services.

DIAGNOSTIC CONSIDERATIONS

Thorough diagnostic interviews are necessary to establish an accurate clinical presentation because a patient's presenting complaint can be misleading. In some instances, complaints of fears of knives (Barlow, 1988) or thunderstorms (Turner & Beidel, 1988) may indicate the presence of a more pervasive anxiety disorder, such as OCD, and not a specific phobia. Patients with extensive washing rituals often present at dermatology clinics with contact dermatitis, whereas those with the OCD-related condition of body dysmorphic disorder (BDD) seek services in the plastic surgeon's office (Rasmussen & Eisen, 1992). Among patients with BDD, 12% had SAD, which had its onset prior to the onset of BDD (Wilhelm, Otto, Zucker, & Pollack, 1997). In addition to increasing clinical complexity, differential diagnosis often is difficult because of actual substantial comorbidity among the anxiety disorders. Among those with a primary anxiety disorder, 50% had at least one other clinically significant anxiety or depressive disorder (Brown & Barlow, 1992).

Secondary comorbid anxiety disorders are quite common among those with a primary anxiety disorder. Among PD patients, 20% had secondary GAD, as did 36% of PD patients with mild agoraphobia. Similarly, 65% of PD patients in one study also met criteria for specific phobia (Starcevic & Bogojevic, 1997). Among those with SAD, 9% had secondary PD, and 29% of patients with primary GAD had SAD. Among patients with OCD, 24% had secondary GAD and 17% had a lifetime history of eating disorders (Rasmussen & Eisen, 1992). Finally, even patients presenting at specialty clinics typically do not have a singular diagnosis; in one study only 26% of patients had GAD as the sole diagnosis (Brawman-Mintzer et al., 1993). Common comorbid diagnoses included SAD (23%), specific phobia (21%), and major depression (42%), and this high degree of overlap has led some to hypothesize that GAD and depression may share genetic factors (Kendler et al., 1992a and 1992b; Kendler, 1996). Furthermore, the prevalence of comorbid GAD has led some investigators to suggest that it may be not a distinct disorder, but perhaps the basis from which other disorders arise, and the residual state often remaining following treatment for other specific disorders (Turner & Beidel, 1989a, 1989b). Brown, Barlow, and Liebowitz (1994) provided some evidence for the validity of GAD, but diagnostic unreliability and high rates of comorbidity continue to plague this diagnostic category.

Although anxiety and depressive states share many symptoms, the bulk of the evidence (actual symptoms, childhood characteristics and childhood events, differential predictors of outcome, personality characteristics, and analysis of genetic models), clearly indicates that they are different disorders. In an unselected sample of twins (3,798 pairs; Kendler, Heath, Martin, & Eaves, 1987), symptoms of anxiety and depression formed separate symptom clusters (depression-distress and general anxiety), and data indicated that it was the environment rather than any specific genetic influence that was depressogenic or anxiogenic. Even though they are distinct disorders, there is still the challenge of distinguishing between affective states with a high rate of concordance. Using epidemiological data, 2.1% of the general population were comorbid for panic attacks and major depression (Andrade, Eaton, & Chilcoat, 1994). However, 62% of those with panic attacks reported presence of a dysphoric mood. One method is to examine the disorder's etiology and designate as primary the one with the earliest onset. Thus, secondary depression (occurring after the onset of the anxiety disorder) is common, with estimates ranging from 17.5% to 60%, and averaging approximately 30% to 35% for PD and PD with agoraphobia (Barlow et al., 1986; Breier, Charney, & Heninger, 1984; Lesser et al., 1988; Uhde et al., 1985; Van Valkenberg, Akiskal, Puzantian, & Rosenthal, 1984).

Another approach to determining primacy is to examine longitudinal course. Among 60 patients with agoraphobia or PD, 70% had an episode of depression, with 43% reporting that depression occurred before the first panic attack (Breier et al., 1984). The average time between remission of depression and the subsequent onset of the panic attack was 4 years. Among the 57% of patients with both anxiety and depressive disorders, depression occurred following the onset of panic. For those patients, symptoms of panic, anticipatory anxiety, and generalized anxiety were chronic and unremitting, while symptoms of depression were episodic in nature, with 63% having remissions that lasted for 1 year or more (Breier et al., 1986). Among those with major depression, comorbid anxiety disorders were present in 50% of the patients with SAD (27%), specific phobia (17%), PD (14.5%), and GAD (10%) as the most common diagnoses (Fava et al., 2000). SAD and GAD preceded the first major depressive episode in approximately 65% of cases, while PD (21%) and agoraphobia (14%) were much less likely to precede the first major depressive episode than to emerge subsequently. These findings also indicate different temporal relationships between major depression and comorbid anxiety disorders.

Based on the Epidemiological Catchment Area data (ECA; Regier et al., 1998), 47% of those with major depression also had at least one comorbid anxiety disorder. Among those with comorbid conditions, SAD had an earlier age of onset (11.5 years) when compared to PD patients (23 years). Thus, certain anxiety disorders (e.g., SAD) may pose specific risk factors for the onset of major depression, while depression may represent a specific predisposing factor for other anxiety disorders (e.g., PD). Finally, the majority of patients with OCD may experience at least some dysphoric mood (Barlow et al., 1986). Depression that occurs after the onset of OCD is considered secondary but even so could have important treatment implications.

Often it is necessary to differentiate between patients with anxiety that is but one symptom of a primary Axis II personality disorder, and those who truly manifest comorbid Axis I and II disorders. Individuals with paranoid personality disorder are often anxious when in the company of others, but their anxiety is due to concern about the motives of others, not fear of doing something to humiliate or embarrass themselves. However, even with careful diagnosis and the use of hierarchical diagnostic rules, some individuals have both anxiety disorders and personality disorders (Mavissakalian & Hamann, 1986, 1988; Pollack et al., 1992; Reich & Noyes, 1987; Rennenberg, Chambless, & Gracely, 1992). Approximately 30% to 56% of PD patients have an Axis II disorder, primarily histrionic, dependent, avoidant, and obsessive-compulsive subtypes. Among those with SAD, 41%

met criteria for a personality disorder (Turner, Beidel, Borden, Stanley, & Jacob, 1991), most commonly avoidant personality disorder or obsessive-compulsive personality disorder. Introversion and depressive symptoms correctly predicted the presence (or absence) of avoidant personality disorder in 85% of those with SAD (van Velzen, Emmelkamp, & Scholing, 2000). Cluster C (anxious) personality disorders were identified in 17% of patients with GAD, whereas 2% of GAD patients had cluster B (unstable) personality disorder. The most common Axis II disorder in patients with OCD are avoidant, histrionic, and paranoid personality disorders (Sciuto et al., 1991), and there is evidence that those with OCD and comorbid schizotypal symptoms have a significantly poorer prognosis (Jenike, Baer, Minichiello, Schwartz, & Carey, 1986; Stanley, Turner, & Borden, 1990). Those with OCD and schizotypal symptoms represent a specific subgroup, distinguished by earlier age of onset of OCD, a higher number of comorbid diagnoses, and higher rates of learning disabilities (Sobin et al., 2000).

In summary, differential diagnosis is necessary to fully understand the disorder's clinical presentation and for proper treatment implementation. Although possible, differential diagnosis is complicated because a substantial percentage of anxiety patients are comorbid for an additional anxiety disorder, a depressive disorder, or a personality disorder. Overall, patients with comorbid diagnoses appear to be more symptomatic (Curtis et al., 1998; Jenike et al., 1986; Mavissakalian & Hamann, 1988; Turner & Beidel, 1989a, 1989b) and have a poorer treatment prognosis (Brown, Antony, & Barlow, 1995; Mavissakalian & Hamann, 1988).

PSYCHOLOGICAL AND BIOLOGICAL ASSESSMENT

Clinical interviews, self-report, and behavioral observation all provide useful data for the assessment of anxiety disorders. Each approach also has limitations; therefore, a multidimensional strategy will result in the most comprehensive clinical presentation.

CLINICAL INTERVIEW

The clinical interview provides a detailed analysis of the individual's psychiatric history and current behavioral functioning. Formats range from a highly structured and directive approach to a more unstructured, free-flowing conversation. Regardless of the structure, the goals of the clinical interview include (1) building rapport; (2) making an accurate diagnosis; and (3) establishing a detailed assessment of symptoms, stimuli, and functional impairment (Herbert, Rheingold, & Brandsma, 2000).

Although unstructured interviews are common in clinical settings, structured and semistructured interviews allow for enhanced standardization and reliability. The Anxiety Disorders Interview Schedule for *DSM-IV*—Lifetime (ADIS-IV-L; DiNardo, Brown, & Barlow, 1994) is a semistructured clinician-administered interview used to assess lifetime anxiety and mood, with additional screeners for somatoform, substance use, and psychotic disorders. The ADIS-IV-L maps onto current *DSM-IV* criteria and includes a diagnostic timeline to accurately identify onset, remission, and temporal order of current and past disorders, and also allows for rating the severity of the disorder. In addition, the ADIS-IV-L allows for dimensional ratings of symptom severity (0–8). For example, the SAD section rates fear and avoidance for 13 potentially fearful situations. These dimensional ratings provide important information on the frequency and severity of specific symptoms and subthreshold manifestations that a categorical format would typically overlook. The psychometric properties of the ADIS-IV-L include good to excellent interrater agreement for both current and lifetime diagnoses (Brown, DiNardo, Lehman, & Campbell, 2001), although interrater reliability must be continuously established as it is completely dependent upon the particular interviewer administering the interview. The interview also has good convergent and discriminant validity, particularly at the dimensional level (Brown, Chorpita, & Barlow, 1998).

Other structured interview schedules such as the Structured Clinical Interview for *DSM-IV* (SCID-IV; First, Spitzer, Gibbon, and Williams, 1994) and the Schedule for Affective Disorders and Schizophrenia (SADS; Spitzer & Endicott, 1978) are broader in scope, allowing for a more comprehensive assessment of psychopathology. Chapter limitations do not allow for an extensive discussion of these interview schedules and the reader is referred to other sources (Basco et al., 2000; Kranzler, Kadden, Babor, Tenne, & Rounsaville, 1996; Zanarini et al., 2000) for a review of their psychometric properties. However, the inclusion of more diagnostic categories is at the expense of a thorough assessment to determine the presence of anxiety disorders. One general strategy (followed in our clinic) is to conduct a general unstructured clinical interview. If anxiety appears to be the primary presenting complaint, a follow-up interview, using the ADIS-IV-L, is conducted.

SELF-REPORT MEASURES AND CLINICAL RATING SCALES

Questionnaires are an efficient and cost-effective method to assess anxiety disorders and related symptoms. There are a myriad of well-validated self-report measures, only a few of which can be mentioned here (see Antony & Barlow, 2002; Beidel & Nay, 2003; Everly & Lating, 2004; Herbert, Rheingold, & Brandsma, 2001; Steketee & Neziroglu, 2003). Some self-report measures assess more general levels of trait anxiety, such as the Spielberger State-Trait Anxiety Inventory (STAI; Speilberger, 1983) and the Beck Anxiety Inventory (BAI; Beck & Steer, 1993), whereas others assess specific disorders. Well-validated and frequently used instruments for SAD include the Social Phobia and Anxiety Inventory (SPAI; Turner, Beidel, Dancu, & Stanley, 1989), the Social Interaction Anxiety Scale (SIAS; Mattick & Clark, 1998), and the Social Phobia Scale (SPS; Mattick & Clark, 1998). For OCD, the Maudsley Obsessive Compulsive Inventory (MOCI; Rachman & Hodgson, 1980) and to a lesser extent the Obsessive-Compulsive Inventory (OCI; Foa, Kozak, Salkovskis, Coles & Amir, 1998) are often used. The Fear Questionnaire (FQ; Marks & Matthews, 1979) assesses several types of phobia, whereas for GAD, the Penn State Worry Questionnaire (PSWQ; Meyer, Miller, Metzger, & Borkovec, 1990), and the Generalized Anxiety Disorder Questionnaire (GADQ-IV; Newman et al., 2002) are both validated measures of general worry. The Panic Attack Questionnaire (PAQ; Norton, Dorward, & Cox, 1986) assesses panic attack symptoms, while the Anxiety Sensitivity Index (ASI; Reiss et al., 1986) is a trait measure of threatening beliefs about bodily sensations. Finally, there are a number of reliable and valid measures for PTSD and related symptomatology, including the PTSD Symptom Scale Self-Report (Falsetti, Resnick, Resick, & Kilpatrick, 1993), the PTSD checklist (Weathers, Litz, Herman, Huska, & Keane, 1993), and the Posttraumatic Stress Diagnostic Scale (PDS; Foa, 1995).

Clinician rating scales are an important tool in the assessment of anxiety disorders and are often used as a primary measure of treatment outcome. The most well established is the Hamilton Anxiety Scale (HAM-A; Hamilton, 1969), a 14-item measure that uses a Likert scale to provide a general assessment of anxiety. Other commonly used rating scales include the Yale-Brown Obsessive Compulsive Scale (YBOCS; Goodman & Price et al., 1989), the Liebowitz Social Anxiety Scale (LSAS; Liebowitz, 1987), the Brief Social Phobia Scale (BSPS; Davidson et al., 1991), and Clinician Assisted PTSD Scale (CAPS; Blake et al., 1995).

Behavioral Assessment and Self-Monitoring

Though rarely used in clinical settings, behavioral assessment strategies offer unique insights into the nature and expression of an individual's anxiety.

Behavioral Avoidance Tests Behavioral avoidance tests (BATs) expose the individual to a feared stimulus under controlled conditions in order to provide direct observation of their behavioral response. For example, a patient might be instructed to approach a feared stimulus (e.g., a dog or spider) and the distance between the patient and the object functions as a measure of avoidance. In addition, self-ratings of distress are obtained throughout the task. While the BAT was originally developed to assess fear and avoidance in specific phobia, SAD and agoraphobia, it has also been used more recently in OCD, SAD, and PTSD. Overall, BATs have good test-retest reliability and concurrent and criterion validity for specific phobia and agoraphobia (e.g., Beidel, Turner, Jacob, & Cooley, 1989; Bernstein & Nietzel, 1973; DeBeurs, Lange, Van Dyck, Blonk, & Koele, 1991; Mavissakalian & Hamann, 1986; McGlynn, 1988; Trudel, 1978). The single-task BAT has been criticized as limited in its ability to capture the full extent of the client's fear and avoidance pattern. Therefore, multiple-task BATs require the patient to complete a number of fear-related tasks (e.g., touching the toilet, leaving the room without checking, leaving a set of objects out of order). Independent observers record ratings of both distress and avoidance. Several BATs developed for OCD (e.g., Foa, Steketee, & Ozarow, 1985; Rachman et al., 1979; Steketee et al., 1996) have demonstrated modest concurrent validity for single-step tasks (Freund, 1987) and moderate convergent and good discriminant validity with the multiple steps/multiple tasks (Steketee et al., 1996; Woody, Steketee, & Chambless, 1995). Moreover, a meta-analysis found BATs to be a sensitive measure for detecting treatment effects for OCD (Taylor, 1995).

Behavioral Observation of Social Interactions Behavioral observation is an underutilized strategy that can be particularly informative for the assessment of SAD. Observations can be in vivo, allowing assessment in an actual social context with natural reinforcers and consequences. Although offering the highest degree of validity, it is not always pragmatic (Bellack, Hersen, & Turner, 1979). Therefore, as an alternative, analogue assessment strategies are often used, with the expectation that behavior in this setting will somewhat reflect actual functioning. Commonly used examples of standardized role-play assessments include the Behavioral Assertiveness Test—Revised (BAT-R; Eisler, Hersen, Miller, & Blanchard, 1975) and the Simulated Social Interaction Test (SSIT; Curran, 1982). Studies examining the validity of using role-play tasks in the assessment of social skills has been equivocal (e.g., Bellack, Hersen, &Lamparski, 1979; Bellack, Hersen, &Turner, 1979; Kern, 1991; Merluzzi and Biever, 1987; St. Lawrence, Kirksey, and Moore, 1983; Wessberg, Marriotta, Conger, Conger, & Farrel, 1979), but they can still provide unique and important clinical information that more traditional assessment modalities (e.g., clinical interview, self-report) are unable to capture.

Self-Monitoring   Self-monitoring refers to recording one's thoughts or behavior and is an important tool in the assessment and treatment of anxiety disorders. Self-monitoring forms can be developed to assess various dimensions of a disorder. For PD, monitoring typically occurs through event recording and includes important information such as the time of onset, intensity, symptoms, situation, and location (e.g., Barlow, Craske, Cerny, and Klosko, 1989; Craske, Rowe, Lewin, & Noriega-Dimitri, 1997; Rapee, Craske, & Barlow, 1990). For agoraphobia, patients might record the frequency and duration of excursions from home, distance traveled, whether they were alone, escape behaviors, and level of anxiety (e.g., Barlow, O'Brien, & Last, 1984; Margraf, Taylor, Ehlers, Roth, & Agras, 1987; Murphy, Michelson, Marchione, Marchione, & Testa, 1998). For SAD, self-monitoring could include frequency and duration of social contacts, the antecedents and consequences of these interactions, level of anxiety experienced, and self-reported skill (e.g., Dow, Biglan, & Glaser, 1985; Heimberg, Madsen, Montgomery, & McNab, 1980; Twentyman & McFall, 1975). For GAD, patients might rate their anxiety at discrete points during the day for a period of 2 weeks (e.g., Barlow, Rapee, & Brown, 1992), including information about the type of event, precipitating factors, level of control over worrying, and the extent to which the worry is realistic (e.g., Craske, Rapee, Jackel, & Barlow, 1989). For OCD, monitoring can include frequency and duration of obsessions and rituals as well as general levels of distress (e.g., Sternberger & Burns, 1991; Trinder & Salkovskis, 1994). Finally, for PTSD, monitoring can encompass specific PTSD symptoms (e.g., flashbacks, nightmares, hours of sleep, and severity of distress; Mueser, Yarnold, & Foy, 1991). In summary, although there is some evidence to suggest that self-monitoring can be subject to a variety of biases in the area of attention, judgment, and memory (e.g., Clark & Purdon, 1995; Rapee & Lim, 1992; Stopa & Clark, 1993; Taylor et al., 1986), it still provides valuable information regarding the nature of the client's anxiety and otherwise unavailable process data regarding treatment response and treatment outcome.

BIOLOGICAL ASSESSMENT

Biological assessment of anxiety disorders includes studies of neurochemistry, neurobiology, and neuroanatomy. High-technology imaging devices now used to determine the neuroanatomical substrates of anxiety include computerized tomography (CT) and magnetic resonance imaging (MRI). MRI, when compared to CT, results in enhanced views in several areas: spatial resolution, distinction between gray and white matter, and visualization of neuroanatomic structures (Saxena, Brody, Schwartz, & Baxter, 1998). Functional magnetic resonance imaging (*f*MRI) assesses brain activity, not just brain structure. CT and *f*MRI are used to assess steady-state (baseline) assessment in untreated patients and comparisons to normal controls, pharmacological challenge studies in untreated patients, and changes in neurochemistry after pharmacological treatment.

Using these same three challenge paradigms, functional imaging techniques assess brain activity (rather than neuroanatomical structure) or changes in brain activity using either single photon emission computed tomography (SPECT) or positron emission tomography (PET). SPECT and PET use trace amounts of ligands that are "labeled" with radioactive isotopes, which in turn allow measurement of cerebral metabolism or cerebral blood flow (Saxena et al., 1998). This radioactive "dye" is injected into the bloodstream, and the PET or SPECT scanners detect the radiation emitted by the isotopes, allowing measurement of their concentration in various brain regions. SPECT uses single photon emitters, whereas PET uses double signals (i.e., positrons and two gamma protons; see Saxena et al., 1998), giving PET a higher spatial resolution when compared to SPECT.

Investigations assessing neuroanatomy and neuroanatomical functioning offer exciting new avenues for anxiety disorders. As with the other assessment strategies, several limitations exist. Among patients with OCD, CT and MRI scans document structural brain abnormalities only among those with a concurrent neurological disorder (Insel & Winslow, 1992). Furthermore, variations in research methodologies, illness chronicity, and previous medication use all may contribute to the inconclusive data (Rosenberg & Keshavan, 1998). Also, there is the issue of anatomical ambiguity; the orbitofrontal cortex can be (and is) defined differently by various investigators. Even though some areas represent topographically contiguous brain regions, they also represent "cyboarchitecturally and functionally distinct" areas (Insel & Winslow, 1992, p. 740). Finally, abnormality is not equivalent to causality. Increases in metabolic activity in some areas of the brain may be compensating for decreased functioning in other areas, as happens for neurodegenerative disorders (Insel & Winslow, 1992).

ETIOLOGICAL CONSIDERATIONS

FAMILIAL AND GENETIC

Overall, family and family history studies reveal an increased morbidity rate among first-degree relatives of patients with an anxiety disorder. Data consistently demonstrate higher lifetime prevalence rates of PD among relatives of patient probands (7.7 to 20.5/100) compared to relatives of normal controls (0.8 to 7.7/100; Weissman, 1993). Similarly, rates of SAD in first-degree relatives of SAD probands were higher than in first-degree relatives of normal controls (16% vs. 5%; Fyer, 1993), whereas rates for other disorders were not significantly different. Also, rates for relatives of patient probands with specific phobia were higher than relatives of normal controls (31% vs. 11%; Fyer et al., 1990). When more broadly defined to include subclinical symptom presentation, OCD was more prevalent among parents of OCD probands compared to normal controls (16% vs. 3%). Rates of OCD and subthreshold OCD were significantly higher among OCD probands than normal controls (10.3% vs. 1.9% for OCD and 7.9% vs. 2.0% for subthreshold OCD; Pauls, Alsobrock, Goodman, Rasmussen, & Leckman, 1995). Nestadt et al. (2000) also reported a higher lifetime prevalence of OCD in OCD probands, although another study did not find this familial relationship (Black, Noyes, Goldstein, & Blum, 1992). Age of onset of OCD symptoms was strongly associated with familiality. Adults with early onset (prior to age 18) were much more likely to have a relative with OCD than adults with late onset (after age 18). For an overview of family and genetic studies of OCD, see Hanna (2000).

Often, conflictual findings may result from different methodologies (family studies vs. family history studies) or patient characteristics. Age of onset may affect familial rates; first-degree relatives of early-onset panic patients had significantly higher rates of PD than first-degree relatives of later-onset panic (Goldstein, Wickramaratne, Horwath, & Weissman, 1997). If earlier age of onset indicates more severe psychopathology (as appears to be the case for SAD), then those with greater severity are more likely to have the type that runs in families.

Some family data support the validity of GAD as a distinctive diagnosis. Three family studies indicated that (1) rates of PD were not different among relatives of GAD patients compared to normal controls, (2) rates of GAD were not different among relatives of PD patients versus controls, and (3) rates of GAD were higher among relatives of GAD patients (19.5/100) compared to relatives of PD patients (5.4/100) or normal controls (5.3/100; Weissman, 1990). Similarly, there was a higher frequency of GAD in families of GAD patients when compared to families of PD patients (Noyes et al., 1992). In contrast, there was more PD in families of PD patients than in families of GAD patients.

Studies of Children of Patients with Anxiety Disorders   In addition to the assessment of all available first-degree relatives, other investigations focus specifically on the parent-child relationship. These studies are one of two types: (1) those where the child is the proband and rates of anxiety disorders in the parents are assessed, and (2) those where the adult is the proband and the investigator seeks to establish the presence of anxiety disorders in the children.

Among studies assessing children of patients with an anxiety disorder, children of normal controls were significantly less anxious and depressed when compared to offspring of patients with PD or depression, whereas there were few differences between offspring of the two patient groups (Sylvester, Hyde, & Reichler, 1988). Two findings did suggest some symptom specificity. First, offspring of patients with PD reported higher trait anxiety than any other group. Second, children of parents with depression reported fewer pleasurable experiences and more depression than normal controls. In another study, children of patients with PD had significantly more severe diagnoses and a greater number of diagnoses than children of patients with animal phobia or no mental disorder (Unnewehr, Schneider, Florin, & Margraf, 1998). They also had significantly higher rates of separation anxiety disorder than the other two groups. Currently, equivocal evidence exists regarding the relationship between parental PD and childhood separation anxiety disorder. Specifically, although some studies have supported a specific transmission (e.g., Martin, Cabrol, Bouvard, Lepine, & Mouren-Siméoni, 1999; Unnewehr et al., 1998), other studies have not identified separation anxiety disorder as a specific risk factor for adult PD (e.g., Biederman et al., 2001). In general, there was mixed support for familial transmission of general anxiety proneness, with some evidence for the specific transmission of PD and agoraphobia. Overall, children of parents with both anxiety and depressive disorders were at greatest risk for multiple diagnoses.

When compared to children of parents with no disorder, children of parents with both depression and an anxiety disorder were at greater risk for a psychiatric disorder and more likely to be referred for treatment (Weissman, Leckman, Merikangas, Gammon, & Prusoff, 1984). Although this initial study did not include anxious parents without comorbid depression, more recent studies included patients with only PD (Warner, Mufson, & Weissman, 1995). Anxiety disorders were more common in children of parents with early-onset major depression disorder than in children of normal controls, and rates were similar among offspring of parents with PD and depression, PD without depression, and no disorder. Risk of anxiety disorder in the offspring was increased by recurrent early-onset major depression in the index parent and impaired functioning in the coparent. Furthermore, the relationship between major depression in the parent and panic spectrum disorders in the offspring was largely due to the family's chaotic environment. In this investigation, anxiety disorders included subthreshold conditions such as limited symptom attacks, near panic attacks, and situational panic attacks. When rates for *DSM-IV* anxiety disorders were compared, only those offspring of probands with PD plus major depression had higher rates of separation anxiety disorder than offspring of normal controls. Thus, although findings from this study potentially are important, they must be interpreted cautiously.

Offspring of anxiety disorders patients have been reported to be (1) almost three times as likely to have a psychiatric disorder as the children of dysthymic patients, (2) twice as likely as the children of dysthymic parents to have an anxiety disorder, and (3) over nine times as likely to have a psychiatric disorder as the children of normal parents (Turner, Beidel, & Costello, 1987). Results were replicated using a larger sample (Beidel & Turner, 1997). Rates of anxiety disorders among offspring were 33% for children of anxious parents, 21% for children of depressed parents, 33% for children of anxious and depressed parents, and 8% for children of normal control parents. Furthermore, offspring of anxious parents were significantly more likely to have only anxiety disorders, whereas offspring of depressed or mixed anxious and depressed parents had a broader range of disorders and higher rates of comorbidity, suggesting that rates of anxiety disorders are higher in offspring of parents with emotional disorders but not specifically just parents with anxiety disorders. In one controlled investigation specifically addressing the relationship of SAD among offspring of adults with the same disorder, 9.6% of the offspring of parents with SAD also had the disorder, compared to a 2.1% prevalence rate among the offspring of parents with no psychiatric disorder (Lieb et al., 2000).

Studies of the Relatives of Children Who Have Anxiety Disorders   Last and her colleagues (Last, Hersen, Kazdin, Francis, & Grubb, 1987; Last, Hersen, Kazdin, Orvaschel, & Ye, 1990) conducted extensive family studies of the presence of anxiety disorders in first- and second-degree relatives of children with an anxiety disorder. There was increased risk for anxiety disorders in the first- and second-degree relatives of children with anxiety disorders when compared to relatives of normal control children. Similarly, there was a trend for increased risk of anxiety disorders in the first- and second-degree relatives of children with anxiety disorders when compared to relatives of children with attention deficit disorder.

Behavioral Inhibition and Anxiety Disorders   The term behavioral inhibition (BI; Kagan, 1982) describes a child's sociability as displayed by behaviors ranging along an approach-withdrawal dimension. Briefly, inhibited children consistently emit few spontaneous vocalizations when in the presence of a stranger and cry and cling to their mothers rather than approach other children in play settings. Among behaviorally inhibited young children, 17% met diagnostic criteria for SAD compared to 5% of uninhibited children (Biederman et al., 2001). Furthermore, childhood BI was associated with the later development of generalized social anxiety (Schwartz,

Snidman, & Kagan, 1999) and SAD (Hayward, Killen, Kraemer, & Taylor, 1998), with a stronger relationship among girls (Schwartz et al., 1999), was stronger in girls than in boys. Most importantly, BI appears to be a specific risk factor for social anxiety, as there was no association between BI and specific fears, separation anxiety, or performance anxiety. In a series of studies (Biederman et al., 1990; Hirshfeld, Biederman, Brody, Faraone, & Rosenbaum, 1997; Rosenbaum et al., 1991; Rosenbaum et al., 1992) it was found that there are higher rates of parental anxiety disorders among behaviorally inhibited children, but primarily among those children who also had an anxiety disorder. Rates of parental pathology were not higher among children who had only BI (e.g., Rosenbaum et al., 1992). Methodological limitations to each of these investigations require cautious interpretation of the findings. For an extended review and discussion of these studies, the interested reader is referred to Turner, Beidel, and Wolff (1996).

Twin Studies   Twin studies also address potential genetic contributions. An early investigation (Torgersen, 1983) found that the proband-wise concordance rate for any anxiety disorders category, with the exception of GAD, was higher for monozygotic (MZ; 34%) than dizygotic (DZ; 17%) twins, but no co-twin had the same anxiety disorder as the proband. Thus, the data did not support a specific genetic transmission. Another study (Andrews, Stewart, Allen, & Henderson, 1990) reached similar conclusions. Among twin pairs, concordance rates for GAD range from 12% to 30%, indicating only moderate heritability (Hettema, Prescott & Kendler, 2001; Kendler, Neale, Kessler, Heath, & Eaves, 1992a, 1992b). Twin studies of OCD patients also support the heritability of a neurotic anxiety factor, but not necessarily the specific heritability of OCD (Rasmussen, 1993). Using 4,042 twin pairs from the Vietnam Era Twin registry (True et al., 1993), heritability appears to play a substantial role in the susceptibility for PTSD symptoms. Based on 2,163 personally interviewed female twins (Kendler et al., 1992a, 1992b), familial aggregation of agoraphobia, social phobia, situational phobics, and specific phobia was consistent with "phobia proneness," with heritability estimates indicating that "genetic factors play a significant but by no means overwhelming role in the etiology of phobias" (1992b, p. 279). Individual-specific environmental effects accounted for twice as much variance in liability as genetic factors. For PD, concordance rates were higher among MZ rather than DZ twins (73% vs. 0%), but rates for sporadic panic attacks did not show the same association (57% vs. 43%).

In summary, significantly higher rates of anxiety disorders appear in the families of anxiety probands when compared to families of normal controls. However, when families of probands with other types of psychopathology are included in the investigation (e.g., a psychiatric control group), the outcome is less clear. Twin studies do not support the direct transmission of a particular anxiety disorder, and several other factors warrant consideration in explaining the observed familial pattern. For example, the increased prevalence rate among probands' families could reflect the familial stress of coping with a psychiatrically ill relative, or some underlying vulnerability is manifested in different fashions dependent upon environmental circumstances.

Learning and Modeling

Behavioral Theories of Etiology   Substantive data confirm that conditioning experiences are instrumental in the onset of agoraphobia (76.7%–84%), claustrophobia

(66.7%), and dental phobias (68.4%; Ost, 1987; Ost & Hugdahl, 1983) and, although still present, less influential in the onset of SAD (58%), animal phobias (48%), and blood phobias (45%; Ost, 1987). In the case of animal and blood phobias, vicarious conditioning accounts for onset in approximately 25% of the cases. Although conditioning plays a prominent role, it is clear that no single theory can adequately account for the onset of these disorders. In the ensuing paragraphs, we will discuss various behavioral theories. In light of the voluminous literature, in this review we will touch briefly on important perspectives and highlight some of the more recent formulations.

The earliest accounts, exemplified by the case of Little Albert (Watson & Rayner, 1920), were based on a strict Pavlovian model, and at least 25 additional studies support conditioning as a mechanism for fear acquisition (Delprato & McGlynn, 1984). Also, a combination of classical and operant conditioning is inherent in the classic two-factor theory (e.g., Mowrer, 1947), a model frequently used to explain anxiety. However, traditional conditioning models are subject to a variety of criticisms. First, although conditioning is evident in the case histories of anxiety patients, there are an equivalent number of instances where no direct conditioning experiences exist. Second, even under the most ideal conditioning circumstances, some individuals fail to acquire fear (Rachman, 1990). Third, types of learning other than classical conditioning can effectively explain fear acquisition (Bandura, 1969). Rachman (1977) proposed "three-pathways" to the development of fear. Classical conditioning is one method through which fear is acquired. Other mechanisms include vicarious learning and transmission via information, instruction, or both.

Another problem for traditional conditioning models is their inability to adequately explain the unequal distribution of fears in the general population (Agras et al., 1969). For example, a significant proportion of individuals fear heights and snakes, yet few have direct conditioning experiences. To account for this, Seligman (1971) proposed the notion of preparedness. In this model, the unequal distribution of fears stems from a biological bias; certain fears are more easily acquired because they enhance species' survival. Nonhuman primate studies provided some support for preparedness theory. Fearful reactions were more easily acquired when laboratory-reared monkeys observed other monkeys behaving fearfully in the presence of fear-relevant stimuli such as snakes or lizards than when they behaved fearfully in the presence of rabbits or flowers (Cook & Mineka, 1989).

Seligman (1971) argued that biological preparedness accounts for phobia characteristics such as rapid acquisition, irrationality, belongingness, and high resistance to extinction. Initial laboratory studies (e.g., Ohman, 1986; Ohman, Eriksson, & Olafsson, 1975; Ohman, Fredrikson, Hugdahl, & Rimmo, 1976) provided some support, but McNally's (1987) comprehensive and thoughtful review argued persuasively that the body of experimental evidence for preparedness is equivocal. Only enhanced resistance to extinction of laboratory-conditioned electrodermal responses has been demonstrated consistently, whereas data supporting ease of acquisition, belongingness, and irrationality have received only minimal support (McNally, 1987).

Conditioning theories also must address the issue of previously acquired information. Observer monkeys in the Cook and Mineka (1989) study had no prior information about any of the stimuli as dangerous or safe, yet conditioning was more evident for those objects feared "naturally" by wild-bred monkeys. Other studies also indicated that prior information and experience may be significant mediating factors. Also, monkeys can be immunized against snake fear by prior observational learning (Mineka & Cook, 1986). Laboratory-bred monkeys first observed other monkeys behaving nonfearfully in the presence of a toy snake, then monkeys who behaved fearfully when confronted with the same snake. When the observer monkeys were exposed to the toy snake, they did not react fearfully, suggesting that prior exposure to nonfearful models "immunized" them against later fear acquisition. Thus, prior positive environmental experiences may explain why only some individuals acquire fear after a traumatic event. Also, conditioning experiences can be cumulative (Mineka, Davidson, Cook, & Heir, 1985), and there are factors before, within, and following the conditioning experience that are relevant for the onset of fear (Mineka & Zinbarg, 1991).

In summary, behavioral theories have evolved from simple, straightforward classical conditioning theories toward more complex conceptualizations. In fact, fear may be acquired as a result of vicarious conditioning, information transmission, or classical conditioning (Rachman, 1977). Vicarious conditioning may be a particularly powerful mechanism, as learning occurred within a very brief time (8 minutes) and produced strong emotional responses that were easily observable and approximately equivalent in intensity to those of the models (Cook & Mineka, 1989). Although extant family studies often have attributed strong familial prevalence rates to a biological etiology, the vicarious conditioning literature clearly indicates that other pathways may be equally important, or that some combination of biological and psychological-environmental parameters might provide a more robust explanation. Although behavioral theories may never fully account for the acquisition or maintenance of fear, the contemporary model of learning theory holds significant promise (Mineka & Zinbarg, 2006). It includes attention to both biological (genetics and temperament) and environmental (conditioning and social/cultural learning history, both direct and vicarious; perception of controllability/uncontrollability) vulnerabilities and stress factors (controllability and predictability of stressful events; direct/vicarious conditioning experiences; properties of the conditioned stimulus, or CS), all of which lead to the quality and intensity of conditioned associations. In turn, these factors are affected by postconditioning factors such as unconditioned stimulus (US) inflation and reevaluation and the presence of inhibitory or excitatory CSs. See the excellent review paper by Mineka and Zinbarg (2006).

Cognitive Theories of Etiology   Cognitive theories (e.g., Beck & Emery, 1985) use an information-processing model to explain maladaptive anxiety. Specifically, cognitive schemas are organized into cognitive constellations (cognitive sets). When a set is activated, the content directly influences the person's perceptions, interpretations, associations, and memories, which in turn assign meaning to the stimuli. Cognitive sets contain rules. For the anxiety disorders, rules relate to the estimations of danger, vulnerability, and capacity for coping. If there is a perception of high vulnerability, the rules result in conclusions that one is incapable of dealing with the situation. Unlike the rules for depression that are absolute, rules for anxiety disorders are conditional: If A happens, it *may* (rather than *will*) have a negative result. Thus, the crux of an anxiety disorder is "a cognitive process that may take the form of an automatic thought or image that appears rapidly, as if by reflex, after the initial stimulus that seems plausible (e.g., shortness of breath), and that is followed by a wave of anxiety" (Beck & Emery, 1985, pp. 5–6). If a specific thought or image cannot be identified, it still is possible to infer that a cognitive set with a meaning relevant to danger has been activated. However, the schema themselves appear to develop as a result of behavioral or environmental experiences. Because the cognitive schemata are the result of other experiences, this would appear to remove maladaptive cognition from a primary etiological function to one that might function to maintain the disorder. Thus, cognitive theory does not appear to have a unique explanatory role in illuminating etiology or in treatment outcome (Beidel & Turner, 1986; Brewin, 1985; Hughes, 2002).

Other cognitive theories include the "fear of fear" model (Goldstein & Chambless, 1978) and an expectancy model (e.g., Reiss, 1991; Reiss & McNally, 1985). Fear of fear posits that an individual who has panic attacks may, through the process of interoceptive conditioning, learn to fear any change in physiological state that could signal the onset of panic. Low-level bodily sensations become a conditioned stimulus that triggers worry regarding the onset of panic. Of course, this is not a purely cognitive model because interoceptive conditioning has a central role. Fear of fear may be particularly important for PD, and interventions built on this model typically involve exposure to the physical sensations as well as to the places where panic might occur. Building upon the fear of fear hypothesis, Reiss and his colleagues introduced the construct of "anxiety sensitivity," defined as a belief that the experience of anxiety causes illness, embarrassment, or additional anxiety (Reiss & McNally, 1985; Reiss, Peterson, Gursky, & McNally, 1986). However, whereas fear of fear was considered a consequence of panic attacks (Goldstein & Chambless, 1978), Reiss and McNally (1985) considered fear of fear to result from several factors: panic attacks, biological predisposition, and personality needs to avoid embarrassment or illness or maintain control (see Reiss, 1991). Anxiety sensitivity is the quantification of belief that anxiety causes illness or embarrassment and, like fear of fear, is considered as more prevalent in patients with agoraphobia.

Salkovskis, Clark, & Gelder (1996) proposed a cognitive model for OCD that begins with the concept that intrusive thoughts occur often and are experienced by everyone. However, in some individuals, intrusive thoughts activate preexisting cognitive schemata, and the thought is evaluated negatively (i.e., "It is bad to have a thought about killing my child"); emotional distress may result. These individuals also believe that they have the pivotal power to bring about or prevent negative consequences (i.e., actually killing the child). Such beliefs and cognitive schemata create distress that leads to attempts to control or undo the thoughts, which in turn increase thought saliency and frequency and emotional distress. There also is a feedback loop; beliefs about pivotal power (responsibility) are reinforced because rituals that eliminate the thoughts prevent disconfirmation of the belief. In a recent review of the OCD literature, Turner and colleagues (Turner, Beidel, Stanley, & Heiser, 2001) used existing empirical data to evaluate the veracity of this model, and we refer the reader there for a full discussion. To provide one example of the analysis, the current literature does not support the notion of unitary overresponsibility among patients with OCD. In fact, inflated responsibility associated with OCD appears to be situation-specific, connected primarily to checking (and not washing or hoarding, for example), and fails to prevent an individual with OCD from accepting other forms of responsibility (Rachman, Thordarson, Shafran, & Woody, 1995).

In the past 15 years, cognitive theories have dominated etiological explanations of anxiety disorders. A core assumption of this approach is that those with anxiety disorders process threat information differently (McNally, 1995). Furthermore, the assumption is that cognitive biases play a role in the maintenance, and perhaps the etiology, of anxiety disorders. To fit this theory, thoughts must fit the definition of automatic; that is, they must be capacity-free, unconscious, and involuntary. Capacity-free means that the information processing does not consume resources (i.e., the thoughts are produced effortlessly). However, cognitive biases are involuntary, may sometimes be unconscious, but are not capacity-free (McNally, 1995). Therefore, the most parsimonious explanation is that cognitions must be driven by some other function. In summary, cognitive theories directly examine the role of beliefs and cognitions in the etiology and maintenance of anxiety disorders. Although they are important syndromal phenomena and perhaps important in maintaining fear and avoidance, their role as primary etiological catalysts remains uncertain. High-risk studies may well be necessary to resolve the issue of primacy or secondary status for cognitive features of anxiety.

LIFE EVENTS

Although the literature examining the link between negative life events and the development and maintenance of anxiety disorders is small, data suggest that life events can play a role in the onset of PD, OCD, PTSD, and GAD (e.g., Blazer, Hughes, & George, 1987; Friedman, Smith, & Fogel, 2002; Keller, 2002; Magee, 1999; Venturello, Barzega, Maina, & Bogetto, 2002). Among individuals with PD, there was an increased number of life events in the 12-month period before the onset of the first panic attack when compared to controls, and also a greater frequency and severity of events deemed beyond their control (Faravelli & Pallanti, 1989). Similarly, those with OCD endorsed significantly more life events 6 months prior to their illness compared to controls, particularly undesirable and uncontrollable events regarding health and bereavement (Khanna, Rajendra, & Channabasavanna, 1988). With respect to GAD, men reporting four or more life events had an 8.5 times higher risk of developing the disorder compared to men reporting zero to three life events (Blazer, Hughes, & George, 1987). Furthermore, males and females who reported experiencing one or more unexpected, negative, very important life events had a threefold increased risk of developing GAD.

Although some researchers suggest specificity between negative life events and a particular anxiety disorder, others argue that increased frequency of negative life events may be associated merely with the development of anxiety in general (DeLoof, Zandbergen, Lousberg, Pols, & Griez, 1989; Rapee, Litwin, & Barlow, 1990). When the impact of life events over 6 months was examined in patients with panic disorder, other anxiety disorders, and nonanxious controls, there was no significant group difference in the number of events reported; however, all of those with an anxiety disorder rated these events as having a significantly greater negative impact compared to controls.

Negative or stressful life events are also associated with other disorders (e.g., depression, substance use, schizophrenia); thus, several studies have attempted to link specific life events with specific psychopathology. For anxiety disorders, uncontrollable or threatening events may be more likely to lead to anxiety (Barret, 1979; Brown, 1993; Eley & Stevenson, 2000; Finlay-Jones, 1989). In contrast to depression or hypochondriasis, onset of anxiety disorders was most often associated with life stressors related to threat (e.g., being involved in an accident, being assaulted), whereas major depression and hypochondriasis were associated with loss and health, respectively (Sandin, Chorot, Sante, & Valiente, 2004). Using a twin sample, threat and loss events were differentially associated with anxiety and depression, respectively (Eley & Stevenson, 2000). However, not all studies support this distinction. Some patients with PD endorsed more life events relating to loss in the year and months before the onset of their PD compared to controls (Faravelli & Pallanti, 1989; Horesh, Amir, Kedem, Goldberger, & Kotler, 1997). Therefore, although some evidence suggests specificity between type of life events and resulting psychopathology, no definitive conclusion is possible at this time.

GENDER AND RACIAL-ETHNIC

With respect to gender, PD (without agoraphobia) occurs twice as often in women (Eaton et al., 1998; Eaton et al., 1994; Reed & Wittchen, 1998), and PD with agoraphobia occurs three times as often in women (APA, 1994). Epidemiological data suggest that social phobia is more common in women, but both sexes are represented equally in clinic samples (Turner & Beidel, 1989a). Among individuals with situational, animal, and natural environment phobia types, 75% to 90% are female (except for heights, where 55%–70% are female). In one study, animal fears were most prevalent among women, while fear of heights was most common among men (Curtis et al., 1998). Among blood, injection, and injury subtypes, 55% to 70% are female (Bienvenu & Eaton, 1998). OCD affects men and women in equal proportions (Turner & Beidel, 1989b). In epidemiological samples, about 3% of the population meets criteria for GAD, two-thirds of whom are women (Wittchen & Hoyer, 2001). In clinical samples, approximately 55% to 60% of patients are women.

The Epidemiological Catchment Area Survey (ECA), the first modern comprehensive epidemiological survey of psychopathology in the United States, reported that African Americans had a higher lifetime prevalence than whites for simple phobia and agoraphobia (Blazer et al., 1985; Robins et al., 1984). However, the sampling strategy at two sites overincluded severely disadvantaged African Americans and elderly African Americans, underincluded low-income African American males, and virtually excluded middle-class African Americans. The more recent National Comorbidity Study (NCS; Kessler, 1994) reported that African Americans had anxiety disorder prevalence rates equivalent to that of whites. Neither study found differences in prevalence rates between Hispanics and whites for any anxiety disorder.

There are few differences in rates of anxiety disorders across racial and ethnic groups. Differences may exist, however, in the symptomatic expression of these disorders or in covarying conditions. Among Hispanics, *ataque de nervios* ("attack of nerves") describes symptoms bearing some similarities to PD. In addition to the typical features of panic, *ataque de nervios* includes becoming hysterical, screaming, hitting oneself or others, breaking things, and nervousness. These episodes occur in stressful situations such as funerals or family disputes (Kirmayer, Young, & Hayton, 1995). Among 156 Hispanic patients seeking treatment for anxiety disorders, 70% reported at least one episode of *ataque de nervios* in their lifetime; 80% of those were female and 41.3% had PD as their primary diagnosis (Liebowitz et al., 1994). Within this subgroup, 80% referred to their panic attacks as *ataque de nervios*. However, as with panic attacks, *ataque de nervios* occurred in individuals with other anxiety disorders as well as major depression, where common symptoms included increased rates of sweating, depersonalization, fear of going crazy, and fear of losing control. Therefore, *ataque de nervios* appears to be a condition that is broader than just PD. It remains unclear if it is a separate condition or whether it is a culturally specific manifestation of the same vulnerabilities associated with panic.

Another cultural difference in the expression of anxiety is *Taijin Kyofusho,* a form of SAD found in Asian cultures. *Taijin Kyofusho* differs from SAD in terms of the underlying (or core) fear (Kirmayer, 2001). In SAD, individuals fear public evaluation, scrutiny, or humiliation. *Taijin Kyofusho,* however, is a core fear of offending others or making others feel uncomfortable because of inappropriate social behavior or by having a physical blemish or deformity. Kirmayer et al. (1995) described this fear in terms of the importance of presenting oneself positively within the Japanese culture, and the importance of harmonious relationships and successful negotiation.

In their seminal article, Neal and Turner (1991) noted the paucity of empirical data regarding anxiety disorders in African Americans. There has been some improvement since that review, and the best epidemiological data suggest that prevalence rates are about the same for African Americans and Whites. Likewise, the clinical presentation of the anxiety disorders appears to be similar in African Americans as compared to White patients.

Although the core features of anxiety disorders appear to be essentially the same across racial and ethnic groups, secondary features or other syndromes may covary with them and complicate the diagnostic process, as in the case of isolated sleep paralysis (Bell & Jenkins, 1994). As described by these investigators, sleep paralysis, lasting from several seconds to a few minutes, is a state of consciousness that occurs while falling asleep or upon awakening, during which time the individual is unable to move. The individual is fully conscious of the experience, which can be accompanied by terrifying hallucinations (hypnopompic or hypnagogic) and a sense of acute danger. After the paralysis passes, the individual may experience panic symptoms and the realization that the distorted perceptions were false. Sleep paralysis that occurs in the absence of narcolepsy is referred to as isolated sleep paralysis (ISP). ISP appears to be far more common and recurrent among African Americans than among White Americans or Nigerian Blacks (Bell, Hildreth, Jenkins, & Carter, 1988; Neal-Barnett & Crowther, 2000). Among African American patients seeking treatment at a local health center, 41% reported at least one episode of ISP (Bell & Jenkins, 1994) in comparison to a 15% rate among Whites (Hufford, 1982). Furthermore, among African Americans who experienced episodes of ISP, 36% reported panic attacks and 16% met criteria for PD (Bell, Dixie-Bell, & Thompson, 1986). Bell and his colleagues have hypothesized that PD in African Americans may be manifested differently than in White Americans, with recurrent ISP and increased frequency of panic attacks as the core features. Alternatively, ISP could be a culturally specific manifestation of the same underlying vulnerability responsible for panic. In fact, Bell and Jenkins (1994) have proposed a stress-response hypothesis to explain the relationship of panic, ISP, and high rates of essential hypertension in African Americans.

With respect to racial and ethnic differences in treatment-seeking behaviors, 87% of a sample of African Americans sought help from some informal network (Neighbors, 1985). Among the 48% who sought out a professional, 22% went to emergency rooms, 22% went to a general physician, and 19% went to ministers. Only 9% sought help from a mental health clinician. Because of this low rate, treatment outcome data are limited (Paradis, Hatch, & Friedman, 1994). In one investigation, African American and White patients with agoraphobia improved equally from an in vivo exposure program (Chambless & Williams, 1995). However, because African Americans were more severely phobic at pretreatment, they were still more symptomatic at posttreatment. At follow-up, differences based on ethnicity were less evident. It is unclear from these data, however, if these differences could reflect symptom severity rather than racial group differences.

Culturally sensitive factors were important in the treatment outcome of an African American patient with SAD treated with Social Effectiveness Therapy (Fink, Turner, & Beidel, 1996). The treatment was efficacious, but only when racial factors, central to the development of the disorder, were specifically included in the exposure program, suggesting that incorporating ethnicity or racial factors might be critical for a positive treatment outcome.

Relatively few pharmacological trials report efficacy data for ethnic and racial groups (Turner & Cooley-Quille, 1996). Those that do indicate that various racial and ethnic groups respond differently to these drugs (Lin, Smith, & Ortiz, 2001; Lin, Poland, & Silver, 1993). Asians consistently require smaller doses of tricyclic antidepressants (TCAs; Lin, Poland, & Lesser, 1986; Yamamoto, Fung, Lo, & Reece, 1979), lithium, and benzodiazepines than Whites to achieve the same results. Similarly, African Americans and Hispanics positively respond to lower doses of TCAs than do Whites (Marcos & Cancro, 1982; Ziegler & Biggs, 1977).

Emerging data indicate that Hispanics and African Americans experience greater pharmacological side effects than Caucasians, suggesting a difference in pharmacokinetics among various racial and ethnic groups (Lin et al., 1986; Matsuda, Cho, Lin, & Smith, 1995; Sellwood & Tarrier, 1994). It appears, then, that ethnicity and racial factors need to be considered when various psychotropic drugs are used in treatment, and the control of these factors is essential to allowing unambiguous interpretation of outcome and making treatment recommendations. Additionally, because cultural differences may exist in terms of the patient's expectation of pharmacological treatment and compliance, it is also important to consider patient attitudes toward psychotropic drugs (Kirmayer, 2001).

BIOLOGICAL AND PHYSIOLOGICAL

Numerous investigators have attempted to shed light on potential biological vulnerabilities. Although not a perfect model, nonhuman primate studies have significant implications for understanding vulnerability in humans. Overall, substantial individual differences exist in both the intensity and extent of anxiety-like behaviors in infant and juvenile rhesus monkeys (Suomi, 1986). When in novel situations or separated from familiar surroundings, some infant monkeys show evidence of behavioral, autonomic, and endocrinological signs of fearfulness, whereas others respond with exploratory or play behaviors (Suomi, Kraemer, Baysinger, & Delizio, 1981), and these characteristics remain stable through young adulthood. Furthermore, environmental conditions do not completely alter constitutional vulnerability. When faced with challenging situations, biological monkey siblings "adopted away" at birth and raised in adoptive families continued to show greater similarity in both cortisol levels and behavioral fear scores than the similarity between adopted siblings (Suomi, 1986).

Kagan and his associates (Kagan, 1982; Kagan, Reznick, & Snidman, 1987; Kagan, Reznick, Snidman, Gibbons, & Johnson, 1988; Reznick et al., 1986) conducted a series of studies on behavioral inhibition (BI) and its relationship to anxiety disorders. From an initial pool of 300 children, 60 children consistently displayed inhibited or uninhibited behaviors in the presence of novel events (Kagan, 1982). Inhibited children cried, clung to their mothers when approached by a stranger, were reluctant to interact with their peers in a play situation, and emitted few spontaneous vocalizations when in the presence of an unknown investigator. When in these situations, these children had higher heart rates and less heart-rate variability than noninhibited children. Although BI is a stable behavioral pattern for some children, others become less inhibited with increasing age. Thus, the specific behaviors defining the BI construct are not immutable, even if they have a biological basis (Turner, Beidel, & Wolff, 1996). However, the *tendency* to react in an inhibited fashion under particular environmental circumstances might be biologically based (see Turner, Beidel, & Wolff, 1996, for an extended discussion of BI and its relationship to anxiety disorders).

Individuals high on BI may be more prone or vulnerable to anxiety reactions. A long-term outcome study indicated that those who maintained a stable pattern of BI (over a 5- to 6-year period) were significantly more likely to have anxiety disorders, and in particular, phobic disorders (Hirshfeld et al., 1992), a finding that has been confirmed by others (e.g., Gladstone, Parker, Mitchell, Wilhelm, & Malhi, 2005; Hayward et al., 1998). As noted previously, childhood BI predicted later SAD (Hayward et al., 1998). Furthermore, those who scored high on both social avoidance and fearfulness had a four times greater risk of developing SAD in high school compared to those with neither of these BI components. In addition, a 21-year longitudinal study reported that anxious or withdrawn behavior at age 8 led to an increased risk for both anxiety and depression at ages 16 to 21 (Goodwin, Fergusson, & Horwood, 2004). However, none of these studies provided any indication about the exact nature of the vulnerability.

Physiological reactivity may represent another aspect of biological vulnerability. In one paradigm, skin conductance variables of children with an anxiety disorder were compared to normal controls when presented with a 100 db tone and a picture of a snake appearing ready to strike (for specific details and the exact assessment protocol, see Turner, Beidel, & Epstein, 1991). Anxious children had a significantly higher mean response amplitude, indicative of increased arousal; a fivefold increase in spontaneous fluctuations during baseline and tone condition; and twice the number of spontaneous fluctuations during the snake condition. Furthermore, habituation rates were significantly lower among the anxious children than in normal controls. A more recent investigation (Turner, Beidel, Roberson-Nay, & Tervo, 2003) replicated these results in children who did not have an anxiety disorder but were the offspring of a patient with an anxiety disorder (i.e., a high-risk sample). These offspring had significantly more spontaneous fluctuations than children of normal controls or children of depressed parents. In addition, they were less likely to habituate to repeated presentations of the same stimulus (offspring of normal control parents habituated rapidly). Unlike the initial study, where these differences may have been attributed to the child's psychopathology, this second study suggested that when exposed to fearful or novel stimuli, even children of anxious parents who do not have an anxiety disorder have psychophysiological characteristics similar to those who do, indicating that these children might have "vulnerability" features that could predispose them to develop maladaptive anxiety at a later date.

Biological (Neuropsychiatric) Considerations   Historically, most studies examining biological etiology addressed peripheral symptomatology. During the late 1970s and early 1980s, the cardiovascular and vestibular systems were the objects of assessment in an effort to establish a biological etiology for PD. Although some studies established abnormalities in certain diagnostic groups (e.g., Gorman, Fyer, Glicklich, King, & Klein, 1981; Jacob, Moller, Turner, & Wall, 1985), subsequent studies did not necessarily confirm earlier findings (e.g., Kathol et al., 1980; Shear, Devereaux, Kranier-Fox, Mann, & Frances, 1984) or found biological differences only in a subgroup of patients (Jacob, Furman, Durrant, & Turner, 1996). In the early 1990s, there was substantial interest in the role of basal ganglia dysfunction in OCD. Specifically, dysfunction of the basal ganglia–thalamic frontal cortical loops produced excessive grooming, checking, and doubting behaviors (Rapoport, 1991). Clomipramine remediated trichotillomania, nail biting, and canine acral lick dermatitis, and fluoxetine reduced canine grooming behaviors, suggesting that the basal ganglia as a repository for species-typical behavior and the frontal cortex–basal ganglia–thalamic circuit as the center for phylogenetic self-protective behaviors (grooming or checking). This theory hypothesized that in those with OCD, trichotillomania, or nail biting, or dogs with acral lick dermatitis, this system has gone awry (see Rapoport, 1991, for an extensive discussion of this issue). Although intriguing, this hypothesis had several difficulties. First, no specific dysregulation or neuroanatomical abnormality has been identified (although newer neuroimaging studies described later suggest some possibilities), and this model cannot account for the efficacy of behavioral treatment (Rapoport, 1991). Second, anatomically, existence of these basal ganglia "loops" is still undetermined. However, as enhanced technology allows for more direct measures of the central nervous system, attention shifted to studies addressing the neuropsychiatric aspects of these disorders. Conceptually, this extensive body of data can be divided into the following subcategories: neuroanatomy, neurochemistry, neuroendocrinology, and neuroimmunology. Each of these categories will be reviewed briefly, and the reader will be directed to original sources for more details.

Neuroanatomy   For patients with PD, areas of the brain identified as important for pathology include the amygdala, a site of fear activation and fear processing, and the hippocampus and its adjacent cortex, where decreased blood flow and changes in metabolism might result from hyperventilation-induced decreases in carbon dioxide (Uhde & Singareddy, 2002). Although fewer data are available, those that do exist highlight the important role of the limbic, paralimbic, and prefrontal regions for patients with GAD, with higher activity detected in these regions when compared to normal controls (Stein & Hugo, 2004). Smaller hippocampal volumes (sometimes left hippocampal, sometimes right hippocampal, sometimes both sides) have been consistently demonstrated for combat veterans with PTSD and children who were sexually abused (Bremner et al., 1995; Bremner et al., 1997; Gurvits et al., 1996; Stein, Koverola, Hanna, Torchia, & McClarty, 1997), again suggesting a role for hippocampal regions. In contrast to these limited literatures, a plethora of structural and functional neuroimaging studies address OCD (see Turner et al., 2001, for a review). In brief, PET and SPECT only weakly support a basal ganglia dysfunction. The preponderance of the data suggest abnormalities in the orbital prefrontal cortex, and perhaps the caudate nucleus (Baxter, 1992). Psychological challenge studies (i.e., exposing OCD patients to feared contaminants during PET or SPECT scans) appear to implicate the orbitofrontal cortex, anterior cingulate, striatum, and thalamus (Trivedi, 1996). Treatment of OCD (either with medication or behavior therapy) reduced these abnormalities, although not always in the same regions. In an examination of treatment outcome, the left orbitofrontal cortex predicted response in those treated with behavior therapy but not those treated with fluoxetine (Brody et al., 1998). Similar activation results have been reported in nontreated OCD patients (Adler et al., 2000). Few data have addressed issues of neuroanatomy among those with social phobia, although preliminary data suggest that, as in the case for PD, there is some activation of the amygdala when in the presence of fear-producing stimuli (Birbaumer et al., 1998; Tillfors et al., 2001).

Neurochemistry   For all of the anxiety disorders, the serotonergic hypothesis is the most consistently reported, in part based on the response of these disorders to SSRIs. Among GAD patients, reduced cerebrospinal fluid and reduced platelet paroxetine binding have been noted (Iny et al., 1994; Stein & Hugo, 2004). A key role for serotonin has been documented for patients with panic disorder, PTSD, and OCD (Stein & Hugo, 2004). For patients with PD, pharmacological challenges with fenfluramine (a serotonin-releasing agent) and sometimes m-CPP (a postsynaptic receptor agonist) produce panic (Coplan, Gorman, & Klein, 1992; Targum & Marshall, 1989), whereas studies with L-tryptophan were not able to establish a role for serotonin in panic disorder (see Uhde & Singareddy, 2002). Similarly, m-CPP challenges in OCD have produced mixed results (Goodman et al., 1995; Hollander et al., 1992; Pigott et al., 1993; Smeraldi et al., 1996; Zohar, Mueller, Insel, Zohar-Kadouch, & Murphy, 1987), whereas m-CPP challenges have been supportive of a role for serotonin for PTSD (e.g., Connor & Davidson, 1998). Other neurochemical systems such as glutamate, gamma-aminobutyric acid (GABA), cholecystokinin (CCK), and dopamine also have been studied with some positive relationships for some of the anxiety disorders, although the evidence is less consistent than for serotonin (see Stein & Hugo, 2004; Uhde & Singareddy, 2002).

Neuroendocrinology   Corticotropin-releasing factor (CRF) is a product of the hypothalamus that stimulates a portion of the pituitary to produce the adrenocorticotropic hormone (ACTH) and other substances such as beta-endorphins. Among other sites, CRF neurons exist in the hypothalamus (mediating behavioral stress responses and cognitive appraisal of stress situations) and the amygdala (which is involved in the processing of emotions; Heim & Nemeroff, 1999). In animals, central administration of CRF produces somatic and behavioral reactions that mimic depression and anxiety. Furthermore, animal models of separation and loss, abuse or neglect, and social deprivation provide preclinical data that early life stress may result in persistent CRF hyperactivity in the hypothalamus and the amygdala and associated increased stress reactivity in adulthood (Heim & Nemeroff, 1999; Sanchez, Ladd, & Plotsky, 2001). If confirmed by additional research, these findings support a model where early life experiences produce vulnerability that in turn may put an individual at risk for the development of emotional disorders including anxiety, depression, or both.

With respect to specific disorders, plasma and urinary cortisol levels have been used to examine differences in the hypothalamic-pituitary-adrenal (HPA) axis system in patients with PD. Whereas free cortisol levels have been inconsistent, challenge tasks sometimes result in greater plasma cortisol increases in PD patients as compared to normal controls (see Uhde & Singareddy, 2002, for a review). In contrast, lower urinary and plasma cortisol has been found among PTSD patients (e.g., Yehuda, 2000). Few data are available addressing neuroendocrinology in other anxiety disorders.

Neuroimmunology   Some children exhibit a sudden onset or acute exacerbation of OCD symptoms following a beta-hemolytic streptococcal infection, a condition known as pediatric autoimmune neuropsychiatric disorder associated with strep (PANDAS; Leonard & Swedo, 2001). This interesting hypothesis begins with the premise that behaviors reminiscent of OCD often occur in children with Sydenham's chorea, a variant of rheumatic fever. Sydenham's chorea is triggered by anti-streptococcal antibodies, resulting in an autoimmune inflammation of the basal ganglia (hypothesized as a site of OCD). Because antineuronal antibodies formed after a strep infection cross-react with tissue in the caudate nucleus and initiate OC symptoms, PANDAS has been proposed as a form of OCD with a biological etiology (March, Franklin, Leonard, & Foa, 2004; Swedo et al., 1998). This is an interesting hypothesis, but much more research is necessary before we can draw a firm conclusion (see Beidel & Turner, 2005; Uhde & Singareddy, 2002). One limitation of the model is that the percentage of children with OCD whose symptoms follow a strep infection is quite small (22% of an initial screening sample responding to ads recruiting children with *sudden* onset of OCD). Therefore, although it may explain etiology in a few cases, at this time, it does not appear to account for the vast majority of children with OCD.

In summary, the contributions of neuroscience to furthering our understanding of anxiety disorders have dramatically changed our conceptualization of these disorders. It is likely that continued efforts in this area will inform and clarify current discrepancies in the extant literature. For example, although pharmacological challenges often indicate differences between a diagnostic group and one without a disorder, they do not implicate any one particular site, even within a disorder (see Turner et al., 2001, for a review). Others (Insel & Winslow, 1992; Trivedi, 1996) highlight a number of limitations, including the use of different technologies (CT, fMRI, SPECT, PET), and result in different outcomes, different scanning environments (which can result in different outcomes), different methods for analyzing and comparing regions, small sample sizes coupled with multiple comparisons, anatomical ambiguity, and the issue of epiphenomenon versus causality. Furthermore, to date, when attempting to determine whether specific anatomical regions are related to a specific disorder, few studies have included an anxious control group (Turner et al., 2001), leaving open the possibility that the findings are related to the presence of any anxiety state rather than one specific disorder.

SUMMARY

Conceptualization of the anxiety disorders has evolved radically over the past three decades. Increased attention to classification and diagnostic differentiation, along with high prevalence of these conditions in the general population, has contributed to a burgeoning interest in the area. Questions of etiology remain central to our further understanding of these disorders and will no doubt continue to occupy the attention of researchers over the next decade. It is clear that anxiety disorders are familial, but the exact nature of this familial factor is poorly understood. Emerging human and nonhuman primate data suggest that the high likelihood of early temperamental factors are related to increased vulnerability to anxiety disorders. To fully address the issue of vulnerability, longitudinal high-risk studies are necessary. However, based on the extant literature, the nature of this vulnerability is likely to be complex, encompassing biological, psychological, and environmental parameters.

Although many questions remain, there are now a number of treatment interventions (behavioral and drug) with demonstrated efficacy. Questions of efficacy for ethnic minority groups, however, are beginning to be addressed but still are largely unknown. Although the treatment for some of the anxiety disorders is better understood than for others, in our opinion, such treatment of these disorders has evolved to the point where few additional advances are likely possible without increased understanding of the basic psychopathology and the further elucidation of the mechanisms of change.

REFERENCES

Aalto-Setalae, T., Marttunen, M., Tuulio-Henriksson, A., & Loennqvist, J. (2001). One month prevalence of depression and other *DSM-IV* disorders among young adults. *Psychological Medicine, 31,* 791–801.

Adler, C., McDonough-Ryan, P., Sax, K., Holland, S., Arndt, S., & Strakowski, S. (2000). FMRI of neuronal activation with symptom provocation in unmedicated patients with obsessive compulsive disorder. *Journal of Psychiatric Research, 34,* 317–324.

Agras, W. S., Sylvester, D., & Oliveau, D. (1969). The epidemiology of common fear and phobia. *Comprehensive Psychiatry, 10,* 151–156.

Albus, M., & Scheibe, G. (1993). Outcome of panic disorder with or without concomitant depression: A two-year prospective follow-up study. *American Journal of Psychiatry, 150,* 1878–1880.

American Psychiatric Association. (1994). *Diagnostic and statistical manual of mental disorders* (4th ed.). Washington, DC: Author.

Amies, P. L., Gelder, M. G., & Shaw, P. M. (1983). Social phobia: A comparative clinical study. *British Journal of Psychiatry, 142,* 174–179.

Andersch, S., Hanson, L., & Haellstroem, T. (1997). Panic disorder: A five-year follow-up study of 52 patients. *European Journal of Psychiatry, 11,* 145–156.

Andrade, L., Eaton, W. W., & Chilcoat, H. (1994). Lifetime comorbidity of panic attacks and major depression in a population-based study: Symptom profiles. *British Journal of Psychiatry, 165,* 363–369.

Andrews, G., Stewart, G., Allen, R., & Henderson, A. S. (1990). The genetics of six anxiety disorders: A twin study. *Journal of Affective Disorders, 19,* 23–29.

Antony, M. M., & Barlow, D. H. (2002). *Handbook of assessment and treatment planning for psychological disorders.* New York: Guilford Press.

AuBuchon, P. G., & Malatesta, V. J. (1994). Obsessive-compulsive patients with comorbid personality disorder: Associated problems and response to a comprehensive behavior therapy. *Journal of Clinical Psychiatry, 55,* 448–453.

Baldwin, D., Bobes, J., Stein, D. J., Scharwachter, I., & Faure, M. (1999). Paroxetine in social phobia/social anxiety disorder. Randomised, double-blind, placebo-controlled study. Paroxetine study group. *British Journal of Psychiatry, 175,* 120–126.

Ballenger, J. C. (1986). Pharmacotherapy of the panic disorders. *Journal of Clinical Psychiatry, 47*(Suppl. 6), 27–32.

Ballenger, J. C. (1990). Efficacy of benzodiazepines in panic disorder and agoraphobia. *Journal of Psychiatric Research, 24*(Suppl. 2), 15–25.

Ballenger, J. C., Burrows, G. D., DuPont, R. L., Lesser, I. M., Noyes, R., Jr., Pecknold, J. C., Rifkin, A., & Swinson, R. P. (1988). Alprazolam in panic disorder and agoraphobia: Results from a multicenter trial. *Archives of General Psychiatry, 45*, 413–422.

Ballenger, J. C., Lydiard, R. B., & Turner, S. M. (1995). The treatment of panic disorder and agoraphobia. In G. O. Gabbard (Ed.), *Treatment of psychiatric disorders* (2nd ed., pp. 1422–1452). Washington, DC: American Psychiatric Press.

Bandura, A. (1969). *Principles of behavior modification.* New York: Holt, Rinehart, and Winston.

Barlow, D. H. (1988). *Anxiety and its disorders.* New York: Guilford.

Barlow, D. H., Craske, M. G., Cerny, J. A., & Klosko, J. S. (1989). Behavioral treatment of panic disorder. *Behavior Therapy, 20*, 261–282.

Barlow, D. H., DiNardo, P. A., Vermilyea, B. B., Vermilyea, J. A., & Blanchard, E. B. (1986). Comorbidity and depression among the anxiety disorders: Issues in diagnosis and classification. *Journal of Nervous and Mental Disease, 174*, 63–72.

Barlow, D. H., Gorman, J. M., Shear, M. K., & Woods, S. W. (2000). Cognitive-behavioral therapy, imipramine, or their combination for panic disorder. *Journal of the American Medical Association, 283*, 2529–2537.

Barlow, D. H., & Lehman, C. L. (1996). Advances in the psychosocial treatment of anxiety disorders. Implications for national health care. *Archives of General Psychiatry, 53*, 727–735.

Barlow, D. H., O'Brien, G. T., & Last, C. G. (1984). Couples treatment of agoraphobia. *Behavior Therapy, 15*, 41–58.

Barlow, D. H., Rapee, R. M., & Brown, T. A. (1992). Behavioral treatment of generalized anxiety disorder. *Behavior Therapy, 23*, 551–570.

Barret, J. E. (1979). The relationship of life events to the onset of neurotic disorders. In I. E. Barret (Ed.), *Stress and mental misorders* (pp. 87–109). New York: Raven Press.

Basco, M. R., Bostic, J. Q., Davies, D., Rush J., Witte, B., Hendrickse, W., & Barnett, V. (2000). Methods to improve diagnostic accuracy in a community mental health setting. *American Journal of Psychiatry, 157*, 1599–1605.

Basoglu, M., Marks, I. M., Kilic, C., Swinson, R. P., Noshirvani, H., Kuch, K., & O'Sullivan, G. (1994). Relationship of panic, anticipatory anxiety, agoraphobia, and global improvement in panic disorder with agoraphobia treated with alprazolam and exposure. *British Journal of Psychiatry, 164*, 647–652.

Baxter, L. R. (1992). Neuroimaging studies of obsessive-compulsive disorder. *Psychiatric Clinics of North America, 15*, 871–884.

Beck, A. T. (1988). Cognitive approaches to panic disorder: Theory and therapy. In S. Rachman & J. D. Maser (Eds.), *Panic: Psychological perspectives.* Hillsdale, NJ: Erlbaum.

Beck, A. T., & Emery, G. (1985). *Anxiety disorders and phobias: A cognitive perspective.* New York: Basic Books.

Beck, A. T., Sokol, D., & Clark, D. A. (1992). A crossover study of focused cognitive therapy for panic disorder. *American Journal of Psychiatry, 149*, 778–783.

Beck, A. T., & Steer, R. A. (1993). *Manual for the Revised Beck Depression Inventory.* San Antonio, TX: Psychological Corporation.

Beekman, A. T., Bremmer, M. A., Deeg, D. J., van Balkom, A. J., Smith, J. H., de Beurs, E., van Dyck, R., & Tilburg, W. (1998). Anxiety disorders in later life: A report from the Longitudinal Aging Study Amsterdam. *International Journal of Geriatric Psychiatry, 13*, 717–726.

Beidel, D. C., & Bulick, C. M. (1990). Flooding and response prevention as a treatment for bowel obsessions. *Journal of Anxiety Disorders, 4,* 247–256.

Beidel, D. C., & Nay, W. T. (2003). Anxiety disorders. In Michel Hersen and Samuel M. Turner (Eds.), *Diagnostic interviewing* (3rd ed.) (pp. 85–110). New York: Kluwer Academic/Plenum.

Beidel, D. C., & Turner, S. M. (1986). A critique of the theoretical bases of cognitive behavior theories and therapies. *Clinical Psychology Review, 6,* 177–197.

Beidel, D. C., & Turner, S. M. (1997). At risk for anxiety: I. Psychopathology in the offspring of anxious parents. *Journal of the American Academy of Child and Adolescent Psychiatry, 36,* 918–924.

Beidel, D. C., & Turner, S. M. (2005). *Childhood anxiety disorders: A guide to research and treatment.* New York: Routledge.

Beidel, D. C., & Turner, S. M. (in press). *Shy children, phobic adults: The nature and treatment of social anxiety disorder* (2nd ed.). Washington, DC: American Psychological Association Books.

Beidel, D. C., Turner, S. M., & Ballenger, J. C. (1997). A review of psychosocial treatments for anxiety disorders. In D. Dunner (Ed.), *Current psychiatric therapy II* (pp. 339–345). New York: W. B. Saunders.

Beidel, D. C., Turner, S. M., Jacob, R. G., & Cooley, M. R. (1989). Assessment of social phobia: Reliability of an impromptu speech task. *Journal of Anxiety Disorders, 3,* 149–158.

Beidel, D. C., Turner, S. M., & Morris, T. L. (1999). Psychopathology of childhood social phobia. *Journal of the American Academy of Child and Adolescent Psychiatry, 36,* 643–540.

Bell, C. C., Dixie-Bell, D. D., & Thompson, B. (1986). Further studies on the prevalence of isolated sleep paralysis in black subjects. *Journal of the National Medical Association, 78,* 649–659.

Bell, C. C., Hildreth, C., Jenkins, E. J., & Carter, C. (1988). The relationship of isolated sleep paralysis and panic disorder to hypertension. *Journal of the National Medical Assocation, 80,* 289–294.

Bell, C. C., & Jenkins, E. J. (1994). Isolated sleep paralysis and anxiety disorders. In S. Friedman (Ed.), *Anxiety disorders in African Americans* (pp. 117–127). New York: Springer.

Bellack, A. S., Hersen, M., & Lamparski, D. (1979). Role-play tests for assessing social skills: Are they valid? Are they useful? *Journal of Consulting and Clinical Psychology, 47,* 335–342.

Bellack, A. S., Hersen, S., & Turner, S. M. (1979). The relationship of role playing and knowledge of appropriate behavior to assertion in the natural environment. *Journal of Consulting and Clinical Psychology, 47,* 670–678.

Bernstein, D. A., & Nietzel, M. T. (1973). Procedural avoidance in behavioral avoidance tests. *Journal of Consulting and Clinical Psychology, 7,* 165–174.

Biederman, J., Faraone, S., Hirshfeld-Becker, D., Friedman, D., Robin, J., & Rosenbaum, J. (2001). Patterns of psychopathology and dysfunction in high-risk children of parents with panic disorder and major depression. *American Journal of Psychiatry, 158,* 49–57.

Biederman, J., Rosenbaum, J. F., Hirshfeld, D. R., Faraone, S. V., Bolduc, E. A., Gersten, M., Meminger, S. R., Kagan, J., Snidman, N., & Reznick, J. S. (1990) Psychiatric correlates of behavior inhibition in young children of parents with and without psychiatric disorders. *Archives of General Psychiatry, 47,* 21–26.

Bienvenu, O. J., & Eaton, W. W. (1998). The epidemiology of blood-injection-injury phobia. *Psychological Medicine, 18,* 1129–1136.

Birbaumer, N., Grodd, W., Diedrich, O., Klose, U., Erb, M., Lotze, M., Schneider, F., Weiss, U., & Flor, H. (1998). FMRI reveals amygdala activation to human faces in social phobics. *Neuroreport, 9,* 1223–1226.

Black, D. B., Noyes, R., Goldstein, R. B., & Blum, N. (1992). A family study of obsessive-compulsive disorder. *Archives of General Psychiatry, 49,* 362–368.

Blake, D. D., Weathers, F. W., Nagy, L. M., Kaloupek, D. G., Gusman, F. D., Charney, D. S., & Keane, T. M. (1995). The development of a clinician administered PTSD scale. *Journal of Traumatic Stress, 8,* 75–90.

Blanchard, E. B., Hickling, E. J., Taylor, A. E., Loos, W. R., Forneris, C. A., & Jaccard, J. (1996). Who develops PTSD from motor vehicle accidents? *Behaviour Research and Therapy, 34,* 1–10.

Blazer, D., George, L. K., Landerman, R., Pennybacker, M., Melville, M. L., Woodbury, M., Manton, K. G., Jordan, K., & Locke, B. (1985). Psychiatric disorders: A rural-urban comparison. *Archives of General Psychiatry, 42,* 652–656.

Blazer, D., Hughes, D., & George, L. K. (1987). Stressful life events and the onset of a generalized anxiety syndrome. *American Journal of Psychiatry, 144,* 1178–1183.

Borkovec, T. D., & Costello, E. (1993). Efficacy of applied relaxation and cognitive-behavioral therapy in the treatment of generalized anxiety disorder. *Journal of Consulting and Clinical Psychology, 61,* 611–620.

Borkovec, T. D., Robinson, E., Pruzinsky, T., & DePress, J. A. (1983). Preliminary exploration of worry: Some characteristics and processes. *Behaviour Research and Therapy, 21,* 9–16.

Borkovec, T. D., & Shadick, R. (1989). *The nature of normal versus pathological worry.* Paper prepared for the DSM-IV Task Force.

Boudewyns, P., & Hyer, L. (1990). Physiological response to combat memories and preliminary treatment outcome in Vietnam veteran PTSD patients treated with direct therapeutic exposure. *Behavior Therapy, 21,* 63–87.

Brawman-Mintzer, O., Lydiard, R. B., Emmamuel, N., Payeur, R., Johnson, M., Roberts, J., Jarrell, M. P., & Ballenger, J. C. (1993). Psychiatric comorbidity in patients with generalized anxiety disorder. *American Journal of Psychiatry, 150,* 1216–1218.

Breier, A., Charney, D. S., & Heninger, G. R. (1984). Major depression in patients with agoraphobia and panic disorder. *Archives of General Psychology, 41,* 1129–1135.

Breier, A., Charney, D. S., & Heninger, G. R. (1986). Agoraphobia with panic attacks. *Archives of General Psychology, 43,* 1029–1036.

Bremner, J. D., Randall, P., Scott, T. M., Bronen, R. A., Seibyl, J. P., Southwick, S. M., Delaney, R. C., McCarthy, G., Charney, D. S., & Innis, R. B. (1995). MRI-based measurement of hippocampal volume in patients with combat-related posttraumatic stress disorder. *American Journal of Psychiatry, 152,* 973–981.

Bremner, J. D., Randall, P., Vermetten, E., Staib, L., Bronen, R. A., Mazure, C., Capelli, S., McCarthy, G., Innis, R. B., & Charney, D. S. (1997). Magnetic resonance imaging-based measurement of hippocampal volume in posttraumatic stress disorder related to childhood physical and sexual abuse—a preliminary report. *Biological Psychiatry, 41,* 23–32.

Brewin, C. R. (1985). Depression and causal attributions: What is their relation? *Psychological Bulletin, 98,* 297–309.

Brody, A. L., Saxena, S., Schwartz, J. M., Stoessel, P. W., Maidment, K., Phelps, M. E., & Baxter, L. R. (1998). FDG-PET predictors of response to behavioral therapy and pharmacotherapy in obsessive compulsive disorder. *Psychiatry Research: Neuroimaging, 84,* 1–6.

Brown, G. W. (1993). Life events and affective disorder: Replications and limitations. *Psychosomatic Medicine, 55,* 248–259.

Brown, T. A., Antony, M. M., & Barlow, D. H. (1995). Diagnostic comorbidity in panic disorder: Effect on treatment outcome and course of comorbid diagnoses following treatment. *Journal of Consulting and Clinical Psychology, 63,* 408–418.

Brown, T. A., & Barlow, D. H. (1992). Comorbidity among anxiety disorders: Implications for treatment and DSM-IV. *Journal of Consulting and Clinical Psychology, 60,* 835–844.

Brown, T. A., Barlow, D. H., & Liebowitz, M. R. (1994). The empirical basis of generalized anxiety disorder. *American Journal of Psychiatry, 151,* 1272–1280.

Brown, T. A., Chorpita, B. F., & Barlow, D. H. (1998). Structure relationships among dimensions of the DSM-IV anxiety and mood disorders and dimensions of negative affect, positive affect, and autonomic arousal. *Journal of Abnormal Psychology, 107,* 179–192.

Brown, T. A., DiNardo, P. A., Lehman, C. L., & Campbell, L. A. (2001). Reliability of DSM-IV anxiety and mood disorders: Implications for the classification of emotional disorders. *Journal of Abnormal Psychology, 110,* 49–58.

Brown, T. A., Marten, P. A., & Barlow, D. H. (1995). Discriminant validity of the symptoms constituting the DSM-III-R and DSM-IV associated symptom criterion of generalized anxiety disorder. *Journal of Anxiety Disorders, 9,* 317–328.

Butler, A. C., Chapman, J. E., Forman, E. M., & Beck, A. T. (2006). The empirical status of cognitive-behavioral therapy: A review of meta-analyses. *Clinical Psychology Review, 26,* 17–31.

Butler, G., Fennell, M., Robson, P., & Gelder, M. (1991). Comparison of behavior therapy and cognitive behavior therapy in the treatment of generalized anxiety disorder. *Journal of Consulting and Clinical Psychology, 59,* 167–175.

Butterfield, M. I., Forneris, C. A., Feldman, M. E., & Beckham, J. C. (2000). Hostility and functional health status in women veterans with and without posttraumatic stress disorders: A preliminary study. *Journal of Traumatic Stress, 13,* 735–741.

Castle, D. J., Deale, A., Marks, I. M., Cutts, E., Chadhoury, Y., & Stewart, A. (1994). Obsessive-compulsive disorder: Prediction of outcome from behavioural psychotherapy. *Acta Psychiatrica Scandinavica, 89,* 393–398.

Center for Disease Control. (1988). Health status of Vietnam veterans. *Journal of the American Medical Association, 259,* 2701–2724.

Chambless, D. L., & Williams, K. E. (1995). A preliminary study of African Americans with agoraphobia: Symptom severity and outcome of treatment with in vivo exposure. *Behavior Therapy, 26,* 501–515.

Christensen, H., Hadzi-Pavlovic, D., Andrews, G., & Mattick, R. (1987). Behavior therapy and tricyclic medication in the treatment of obsessive-compulsive disorder: a quantitative review. *Journal of Consulting and Clinical Psychology, 55,* 701–711.

Clark, D. A., & Purdon, C. L. (1995). The assessment of unwanted intrusive thoughts: A review and critique of the literature. *Behaviour Research and Therapy, 33,* 967–976.

Clark, D. A., Salkovskis, P., & Chalkley, A. (1985). Respiratory control as a treatment for panic attacks. *Journal of Behavior Therapy and Experimental Psychiatry, 16,* 23–30.

Clum, G. (1989). Psychological interventions versus drugs in the treatment of panic disorder. *Behavior Therapy, 20,* 429–457.

Conner, K. M., & Davidson, J. R. T. (1998). The role of serotonin in posttraumatic stress disorder: Neurobiology and pharmacotherapy. *CNS Spectrums, 3,* 43–51.

Cook, M., & Mineka, S. (1989). Observational conditioning of fear to fear-relevant versus fear-irrelevant stimuli in rhesus monkeys. *Journal of Abnormal Psychology, 98,* 448–459.

Cooper, N., & Clum, G. (1989). Imaginal flooding as a supplementary treatment for PTSD in combat veterans: A controlled study. *Behavior Therapy, 20*(3), 381–391.

Coplan, J. D., Gorman, J. M., & Klein, D. F. (1992). Serotonin related functions in panic anxiety: A critical overview. *Neuropsychopharmacology, 6,* 189–200.

Cox, B. J., Direnfeld, D. M., Swinson, R. P., & Norton, G. R. (1994). Suicidal ideation and suicide attempts in panic disorder and social phobia. *American Journal of Psychiatry, 151,* 882–887.

Craske, M. G., Golinelli, D., Stein, M. B., Roy-Byrne, P., Bystritsky, A., & Sherbourne, C. (2005). Does the addition of cognitive behavioral therapy improve panic disorder treatment outcome relative to medication alone in the primary-care setting? *Psychological Medicine, 35,* 1645–1654.

Craske, M. G., Lang, A. J., Aikins, D., & Mystkowski, J. L. (2005). Cognitive behavioral therapy for nocturnal panic. *Behavior Therapy, 36,* 43–54.

Craske, M. G., Maidenberg, E., & Bystritsky, A. (1995). Brief cognitive-behavioral versus nondirective therapy for panic disorder. *Journal of Behavior Therapy and Experimental Psychiatry, 26,* 113–120.

Craske, M. G., Rapee, R. M., & Barlow, D. H. (1992). Cognitive-behavior treatment of panic disorder, agoraphobia and generalized panic disorder. In S. M. Turner, K. S. Calhoun, & H. E. Adams (Eds.), *Handbook of clinical behavior therapy* (2d ed., pp. 39–66). New York: Wiley.

Craske, M. G., Rapee, R. M., Jackel, L. & Barlow, D. H (1989). Qualitative dimensions of worry in DSM-III-R generalized anxiety disorder subjects and nonanxious controls. *Behaviour Research and Therapy, 27,* 397–402.

Craske, M. G., Rowe, M., Lewin, M., & Noriega-Dimitri, R. (1997). Interoceptive exposure versus breathing retraining within cognitive-behavioural therapy for panic disorder with agoraphobia. *British Journal of Clinical Psychology, 36,* 85–99.

Cross-National Collaborative Panic Study Second Phase Investigation. (1992). Drug treatment of panic disorder: Comparative efficacy of alprazolam, imipramine, and placebo. *British Journal of Psychiatry, 160,* 191–202.

Curran, J. P. (1982). A procedure for the assessment of social skills: The simulated social skills interaction test. In J. P. Curran & P. M. Monti (Eds.), *Social skills training: A practical handbook for assessment and treatment* (pp. 348–373). New York: Guilford Press.

Curtis, G. C., Magee, W. J., Eaton, W. W., Wittchen, H. U., & Kessler, R. C. (1998). Specific fears and phobias. Epidemiology and classification. *British Journal of Psychiatry, 173,* 212–217.

Curtis, G. C., Massena, J., Edina, C., Ayes, J. L., Casinos, G. B., & Perugi, G. (1993). Maintenance drug therapy of panic disorder. *Journal of Psychiatric Research, 27,* 127–142.

Davidson, J. R. T. (1992). Drug therapy of posttraumatic stress disorder. *British Journal of Psychiatry, 160,* 309–314.

Davidson, J. R. T. (2000). Pharmacotherapy of posttraumatic stress disorder: Treatment options, long-term follow-up, and predictors of outcome. *Journal of Clinical Psychiatry, 61*(Suppl. 5), 52–56.

Davidson, J. R. T. (1993, March). *Childhood histories of adult social phobics.* Paper presented at the Anxiety Disorders Association of America Annual Convention, Charleston, SC.

Davidson, J. R. T., Foa, E. B., Huppert, J. D., Keefe, F. J., Franklin, M. E., Compton, J. S., Zhao, N., Connor, K. M., Lynch, T. R., & Gadded, K. M. (2004). Fluoxetine, comprehensive cognitive behavioral therapy, and placebo in generalized social phobia. *Archives of General Psychiatry, 61,* 1005–1013.

Davidson, J. R. T., Hughes, D., Blazer, D. G., & George, L. K. (1991). Posttraumatic stress disorder in the community: An epidemiological study. *Psychological Medicine, 21,* 713–721.

Davidson, J. R. T., Potts, N. L. S., Richichi, E. A., Ford, S. M., Krishnan, R. R., Smith, R. D., & Wilson, W. (1991). The Brief Social Phobia Scale. *Journal of Clinical Psychiatry, 52,* 48–51.

Davidson, J. R. T., Potts, N., Richichi, E., Krishnan, R., Ford, S. M., Smith, R., & Wilson, W. (1993). Treatment of social phobia with clonazepam and placebo. *Journal of Clinical Psychopharmacology, 13,* 423–428.

DeBeurs, E., Lange, A., Van Dyck, R., Blonk, R., & Koele, P. (1991) Behavioral assessment of avoidance in agoraphobics. *Journal of Psychopathology and Behavioral Assessment, 13,* 285–300.

DeBeurs, E., van Balkom, A. J. L. M., Lange, A., Koele, P., & van Dyck, R. (1995). Treatment of panic disorder with agoraphobia: Comparison of fluvoxamine, placebo, and psychological panic management combined with exposure and of exposure in vivo alone. *American Journal of Psychiatry, 152,* 683–691.

De Loof, C., Zandbergen, J., Lousberg, H., Pols, H., & Griez, E. J. (1989). The role of life events in the onset of panic disorder. *Behaviour Research and Therapy, 27,* 461–463.

Delprato, D. J., & McGlynn, F. D. (1984). Behavioral theories of anxiety disorders. In S. M. Turner (Ed.), *Behavioral theories and treatment of anxiety* (pp. 1–49). New York: Plenum.

den Boer, J. A., van Vliet, I. M., & Westenberg, H. G. (1994). Recent advances in the psycho-pharmacology of social phobia. *Progress in Neuro-Psychopharmacology and Biological Psychiatry, 18,* 625–645.

DiNardo, P. A., Brown, T. A., & Barlow, D. H. (1994). *Anxiety disorders interview schedule for DSM-IV (ADIS-IV).* San Antonio, TX: Psychological Corporation.

Dow, M. G., Biglan, A., & Glaser, S. R. (1985). Multimethod assessment of socially anxious and socially nonanxious women. *Behavioral Assessment, 7,* 273–282.

Durham, R., & Allan, T. (1993). Psychological treatments of generalized anxiety disorder: A review of the clinical significance of results in outcome studies since 1980. *British Journal of Psychiatry, 156,* 19–26.

Eaton, W. W., Anthony, J. C., Romanoski, A., Tien, A., Gallo, J., Cai, G., Neufeld, K., Schlaepfer, T., Laugharne, J., & Chen, L. S. (1998). Onset and recovery from panic disorder in the Baltimore Epidemiologic Catchment Area follow-up. *British Journal of Psychiatry, 173,* 501–507.

Eaton, W. W., Kessler, R. C., Wittchen, H. U., & Magee, W. J. (1994). Panic and panic disorder in the United States. *American Journal of Psychiatry, 151,* 413–420.

Echeburúa, E., de Corral, P., Zubizarreta, I., & Sarasua, B. (1997). Psychological treatment of chronic posttraumatic stress disorder in victims of sexual aggression. *Behavior Modification, 21,* 433–456.

Eisen, J. L., Leonard, H. L., Swedo, S. E., Price, L. H., Zabriskie, J. B., Chiang, S. Y., Karitani, M., & Rasmussen, S. A. (2001). The use of antibody D8/17 to identify B cells in adults with obsessive-compulsive disorder. *Psychiatry Research, 104,* 221–225.

Eisler, R. M., Hersen, M., Miller, P. M., & Blanchard, E. B. (1975). Situational determinants of assertive behaviors. *Journal of Consulting and Clinical Psychology, 43,* 330–340.

Eley, T. C., & Stevenson, J. (2000). Specific life events and chronic experiences differen-tially associated with depression and anxiety in young twins. *Journal of Abnormal Child Psychology, 28,* 383–394.

Emmelkamp, P. M. G. (1988). Phobic disorders. In C. G. Last & M. Hersen (Eds.), *Handbook of anxiety disorders* (pp. 66–86). New York: Pergamon.

Everly, G. S., & Lating, J. M. (2004). Psychological and psychophysiological assessment of posttraumatic stress. In G. S. Everly & J. M. Lating (Eds.), *Personality-guided therapy for posttraumatic stress disorder* (pp. 73–88). Washington, DC: American Psychological Association.

Fairbrother, N. (2002). The treatment of social phobia—100 years ago. *Behaviour Research and Therapy, 40,* 1291–1305.

Falloon, I. R. H., Lloyd, G. G., & Harpin, R. E. (1981). The treatment of social phobia: Real life rehearsal with nonprofessional therapists. *Journal of Nervous and Mental Disease, 169,* 180–184.

Falsetti, S., Resnick, H., Resick, P., & Kilpatrick, D. (1993). The modified PTSD symptom scale: A brief self-report measure of posttraumatic stress disorder. *Behavior Therapist, 16,* 161–162.

Faravelli, C., & Pallanti, S.1989. Recent life events and panic disorder. *American Journal of Psychiatry, 146,* 622–626.

Fava, G. A., Grandi, S., Rafanelli, C., Ruini, C., Conti, S., & Belluardo, P. (2001). Long-term outcome of social phobia treated by exposure. *Psychological Medicine, 31,* 899–905.

Fava, M., Rankin, M. A., Wright, E. C., Alpert, J. E., Nierenberg, A. A., Pava, J., & Rosenbaum, J. F. (2000). Anxiety disorders in major depression. *Comprehensive Psychiatry, 41*, 97–102.

Feske, U., & Chambless, D. (1995). Cognitive-behavioral versus exposure treatment for social phobia: A meta-analysis. *Behavior Therapy, 26*, 695–720.

Fineberg, N. A., Hughes, A., Gale, T. M., & Roberts, A. (2005). Group cognitive behaviour therapy in obsessive-compulsive disorder (OCD): A controlled study. *International Journal of Psychiatry in Clinical Practice, 9*, 257–263.

Fink, C. M., Turner, S. M., & Beidel, D. C. (1996). Culturally relevant factors in the behavioral treatment of social phobia: A case study. *Journal of Anxiety Disorders, 10*, 201–209.

Finlay-Jones, R. (1989). Anxiety. In G. W. Brown & T. O. Harris (Eds.), Life events and illness (pp. 95–112). London: Unwin Hyman.

First, M. B., Spitzer, R. L., Gibbon, M., & Williams, J. B. W. (1994). *Structured Clinical Interview for Axis I DSM-IV Disorders—Patient Edition.* New York: Biometrics Research Department.

Foa, E. B. (1995). Posttraumatic Stress Diagnostic Scale (manual). Minneapolis, MN: National Computer Systems.

Foa, E. B., Dancu, C., Hembree, E., Jaycox, L., Meadows, E., & Street, G. (1999). A comparison of exposure therapy, stress inoculation training, and their combination for reducing post-traumatic stress disorder in female assault victims. *Journal of Consulting and Clinical Psychology, 67*, 194–200.

Foa, E. B., Kozak, M. J., Salkovskis, P. M., Coles, M. E., and Amir, N. (1998). The validation of a new obsessive-compulsive disorder scale: The Obsessive-Compulsive Inventory. *Psychological Assessment, 10*, 206–214.

Foa, E. B., Liebowitz, M. R., Kozak, M. J., Davies, S., Campeas, R., Franklin, M. E., Huppert, J. D., Kjernisted, K., Rowan, V., Schmidt, A. B., Simpson, H. B., & Tu, X. (2005). Randomized, placebo-controlled trial of exposure and ritual prevention, clomipramine, and their combination in the treatment of obsessive-compulsive disorder. *American Journal of Psychiatry, 162*, 151–161.

Foa, E. B., Rothbaum, B. O., Riggs, D. S., & Murdock, T. B. (1991). Treatment of posttraumatic stress disorder in rape victims: A comparison between cognitive-behavioral procedures and counseling. *Journal of Consulting and Clinical Psychology, 59*, 715–723.

Foa, E. B., Steketee, G. A., & Ozarow, B. J. (1985). Behavior therapy with obsessive-compulsives: From theory to treatment. In M. Mavissakalian, S. M. Turner, & L. Michelson (Eds.), *Obsessive-compulsive disorder—psychological and pharmacological treatments* (pp. 49–120). New York: Plenum.

Fontaine, R., & Chouinard, G. (1986). An open clinical trial of fluoxetine in the treatment of obsessive-compulsive disorder. *Journal of Clinical Psychopharmacology, 6*, 98–101.

Freund, B. V. (1987). Comparison of measures of obsessive-compulsive symptomatology: Rating scals of symptomatology and standardized, assessor- and self-rated. *Dissertation Abstracts International, 47 (9-A)*, 3365–3366.

Friedman, S., Smith, L., & Fogel, D. (2002). The incidence and influence of early traumatic life events in patients with panic disorder: A comparison with other psychiatric outpatients. *Journal of Anxiety Disorders, 16*, 259–272.

Frueh, B. C., Turner, S. M., & Beidel, D. C. (1995). Exposure therapy for combat-related PTSD: A critical review. *Clinical Psychology Review, 15*, 799–818.

Frueh, B. C., Turner, S. M., Beidel, D. C., Mirabella, R., & Jones, W. (1996). Trauma management therapy: A preliminary evaluation of a multicomponent behavioral treatment for chronic combat-related PTSD. *Behaviour Research and Therapy, 34*, 533–543.

Fyer, A. J. (1993). Heritability of social anxiety: A brief review. *Journal of Clinical Psychiatry, 54*, 10–12.

Fyer, A. J., Mannuzza, S., Gallops, M. S., Martin, L. Y., Aaronson, C., Gorman, J. M., Liebowitz, M. R., & Klein, D. E. (1990). Familial transmission of simple phobias and fears: A preliminary report. *Archives of General Psychiatry, 47,* 252–256.

Gladstone, G., Parker, G., Mitchell, P., Wilhelm, K., & Malhi, G. (2005). Relationship between self-reported childhood behavioral inhibition and lifetime anxiety disorders in a clinical sample. *Depression and Anxiety, 22,* 103–113.

Glynn, S. M., Eth, S., Randolph, E. T., Foy, D. W., Urbaitis, M., Boxer, L., Paz, G. G., Leong, G. B., Firman, G., Salk, J. D., Katzman, J. W., & Crothers, J. (1999). A test of behavioral family therapy to augment exposure for combat-related posttraumatic stress disorder. *Journal of Consulting and Clinical Psychology, 67,* 243–251.

Goisman, R. M., Warshaw, M. G., Peterson, L. G., Rogers, M. P., Cuneo, P., Hunt, M. E., Tomlin-Albanese, I. M., Kazim, A., Gollan, J. K., Epstein-Kaye, T., Reich, J. H., & Kellar, M. B. (1994). Panic, agoraphobia, and panic disorder with agoraphobia: Data from a multicenter anxiety disorders study. *Journal of Nervous and Mental Disease, 182,* 72–79.

Goldstein, A. J., & Chambless, D. L. (1978). A reanalysis of agoraphobia. *Behavior Therapy, 9,* 47–59.

Goldstein, R., Wickramaratne, P., Horwath, E., & Weissman, M. (1997). Familial aggregation and phenomenology of "early"-onset (at or before age 20 years) panic disorder. *Archives of General Psychiatry, 54,* 271–278.

Goodman, W. K., McDougle, C. J., & Price, L. H. (1992). Pharmacotherapy of obsessive-compulsive disorder. *Journal of Clinical Psychiatry, 53,* 29–37.

Goodman, W. K., McDougle, C. J., Price, L. H., Barr, L. C., Hills, O. F., Caplik, J. F., Charney, D. S., & Heninger, G. R. (1995). m-Chlorophenylpiperazine in patients with obsessive-compulsive disorder: Absence of symptom exacerbation. *Biological Psychiatry, 40,* 138–149.

Goodman, W. K., Prince, L. H., Rasmussen, S. A., Mazure, C., Fleischmann, R. L., Hill, C. L., Heninger, G. R., & Charney, D. S. (1989). The Yale-Brown Obsessive Compulsive Scale. I. Development, use, and reliability. *Archives of General Psychiatry, 46,* 1006–1011.

Goodwin, R., Fergusson, D., & Horwood, L. (2004). Early anxious/withdrawn behaviours predict later internalising disorders. *Journal of Child Psychology and Psychiatry, 45,* 874–883.

Gorman, J., Fyer, A. F., Glicklich, J., King, D., & Klein, D. E. (1981). Effect of imipramine on prolapsed mitral valves of patients with panic disorder. *American Journal of Psychiatry, 138,* 977–978.

Gould, R., Buckminster, S., Pollack, M., Otto, M., & Yap, L. (1997). Cognitive-behavioral and pharmacological treatment for social phobia: A meta-analysis. *Clinical Psychology: Science and Practice, 4,* 291–306.

Greenberg, P. E., Sisitsky, T., Kessler, R. C., Finkelstein, S. N., Berndt, E. R., Davidson, J. R., Ballenger, J. C., & Fyer, A. J. (1999). The economic burden of anxiety disorders in the 1990's. *Journal of Clinical Psychiatry, 60,* 427–435.

Gurvits, T. V., Shenton, M. E., Hokama, H., Hirokazu, O., Lasko, N. B., Gildertson, M. W., Orr, S. P., Kikinis, R., Jolesz, F. A., McCarley, R. W., & Pitman, R. K. (1996). Magnetic resonance imaging study of hippocampal volume in chronic, combat-related posttraumatic stress disorder. *Biological Psychiatry, 40,* 1091–1099.

Hamilton, M. (1969). Diagnosis and rating of anxiety. *British Journal of Psychiatry, 3,* 76–79.

Hanna, G. H. (2000). Clinical and family-genetic studies of childhood obsessive-compulsive disorder. *Obsessive-compulsive disorder: Contemporary issues in treatment* (pp. 87–103). Mahwah, NJ: Erlbaum.

Hayward, C., Killen, J., Kraemer, H., & Taylor, C. (1998). Linking self-reported childhood behavioral inhibition to adolescent social phobia. *Journal of the American Academy of Child and Adolescent Psychiatry, 37,* 1308–1316.

Hegel, M. T., Ravaris, C. L., & Ahles, T. A. (1994). Combined cognitive-behavioral and time-limited alprazolam treatment of panic disorder. *Behavior Therapy, 25,* 183–195.

Heim, C., & Nemeroff, C. (1999). The impact of early adverse experiences on brain systems involved in the pathophysiology of anxiety and affective disorders. *Biological Psychiatry, 46,* 1509–1522.

Heimberg, R. G., Dodge, C. S., Hope, D. A., Kennedy, C. R., Zollo, L., & Becker, R. E. (1990). Cognitive behavioral treatment of social phobia: Comparison to a credible placebo control. *Cognitive Therapy and Research, 14,* 1–23.

Heimberg, R. G., Liebowitz, M. R., Hope, D. A., Schneier, F. R., Holt, C. S., Welkowitz, L. A., Juster, H. R., Campeas, R., Bruch, M. A., Cloitre, M., Fallon, B., & Klein, D. F. (1998). Cognitive behavioral group therapy vs phenelzine therapy for social phobia: 12-week outcome. *Archives of General Psychiatry, 55,* 1133–1141.

Heimberg, R. G., Madsen, C. H., Montgomery, D., & McNabb, C. E. (1980). Behavioral treatments for heterosocial problems: Effects on daily self-monitored and role played interactions. *Behavior Modification, 4,* 147–172.

Heimberg, R. G., Salzman, D. G., Holt, C. S., & Blendell, K. A. (1993). Cognitive-behavioral group treatment of social phobia: Effectiveness at five-year follow-up. *Cognitive Therapy and Research, 17,* 325–339.

Herbert, J. D., Hope, D. A., & Bellack, A. S. (1992). Validity of the distinction between generalized social phobia and avoidant personality disorder. *Journal of Abnormal Psychology, 104,* 332–339.

Herbert, J., Rheingold, A., & Brandsma, L. (2001). Assessment of social anxiety and social phobia. In S.G. Hofmann & P. M. DiBartolo (Eds.), *From social anxiety to social phobia: Multiple perspectives* (pp. 20–45). New York: Allyn & Bacon.

Hettema, J., Prescott, C., & Kendler, K. (2001). A population-based twin study of generalized anxiety disorder in men and women. *Journal of Nervous and Mental Disease, 189,* 413–420.

Hicks, T. V., Leitenberg, H., Barlow, D. H., Gorman, J. M., Shear, M. K., & Woods, S. W. (2005). Physical, mental, and social catastrophic cognitions as prognostic factors in cognitive-behavioral and pharmacological treatment for panic disorder. *Journal of Consulting and Clinical Psychology, 73,* 506–514.

Hirshfeld, D., Biederman, J., Brody, L., Faraone, S., & Rosenbaum, J. (1997). Expressed emotion toward children with behavioral inhibition: Associations with maternal anxiety disorder. *Journal of the American Academy of Child and Adolescent Psychiatry, 36,* 910–917.

Hirshfeld, D. R., Rosenbaum, J. F., Biederman, J., Bolduc, E. A., Faraone, S. V., Snidman, N., Reznick, J. S., & Kagan, J. (1992). Stable behavioral inhibition and its association with anxiety disorder. *Journal of the American Academy of Child and Adolescent Psychiatry, 31,* 301–311.

Hiss, H., Foa, E., & Kozak, M. (1994). Relapse Prevention Program for treatment of obsessive-compulsive disorder. *Journal of Consulting and Clinical Psychology, 62,* 801–808.

Hoehn-Saric, R., McLeod, D. R., & Hipsley, P. A. (1993). Effect of fluvoxamine on panic disorder. *Journal of Clinical Psychopharmacology, 13,* 321–326.

Hoffart, A. (1993). Cognitive treatments of agoraphobia: A critical evaluation of theoretical bases and outcome evidence. *Journal of Anxiety Disorders, 7,* 75–91.

Hollander, E., DeCaria, C. M., Nitescu, A., Gully, R., Suckow, R. F., Cooper, T. B., Gorman, J. M., Klein, D. F., & Liebowitz, M. R. (1992). Serotonergic function in obsessive-compulsive disorder. Behavioral neuroendocrine responses to oral m-chlorophenylpiperazine and fenfluramine in patients and healthy volunteers. *Archives of General Psychiatry, 49,* 21–28.

Holt, C. S., Heimberg, R. G., & Hope, D. A. (1992). Avoidant personality disorder and the generalized subtype of social phobia. *Journal of Abnormal Psychology, 101,* 318–325.

Hope, D. A., Heimberg, R. G., & Bruch, M. A. (1995). Dismantling cognitive-behavioral therapy for social phobia. *Behaviour Research and Therapy, 33,* 637–650.

Horesh, N., Amir, M., Kedem, P., Goldberger, Y., & Kotler, M. (1997). Life events in childhood, adolescence and adulthood and the relationship to panic disorder. *Acta Psychiatrica Scandinavica, 96,* 373–378.

Hufford, D. (1982). *The terror that comes in the night.* Philadelphia: University of Pennsylvania Press.

Hughes, I. (2002). A cognitive therapy model of social anxiety problems: Potential limits on its effectiveness? *Psychology and Psychotherapy: Theory, Research and Practice, 75,* 411–435.

Insel, T. R., & Winslow, J. T. (1992). Neurobiology of obsessive-compulsive disorder. *Psychiatric Clinics of North America, 15,* 813–824.

Iny, L. J., Pecknold, J., Suranyi-Cadotte, B. E., Bernier, B., Luther, L., Nair, N. P. V., & Meaney, M. J. (1994). Studies of a neurochemical link between depression, anxiety, and stress from [3H] imipramine and [3H] paroxetine binding on human platelets. *Biological Psychiatry, 36,* 251–291.

Jacob, R. G., Furman, J. M., Durrant, J. D., & Turner, S. M. (1996). Panic, agoraphobia, and vestibular dysfunction. *American Journal of Psychiatry, 153,* 503–512.

Jacob, R. G., Moller, M. B., Turner, S. M., & Wall, C. (1985). Otoneurological examination in panic disorders and agoraphobia with panic attacks: A pilot study. *American Journal of Psychiatry, 142,* 715–720.

Jacob, R. G., & Turner, S. M. (1988). Panic disorder: Diagnosis and assessment. In A. J. Frances & R. E. Hales (Eds.), *Review of Psychiatry* (pp. 67–87). Washington, DC: American Psychiatric Press.

Jenike, M. A., Baer, L., Minichiello, W. E., Schwartz, C. E., & Carey, R. J., Jr. (1986). Concomitant obsessive-compulsive disorders and schizotypal personality disorder. *American Journal of Psychiatry, 143,* 530–532.

Jenike, M. A., Vitagliano, H. L., Rabinowitz, J., Goff, D. C., & Baer, L. (1987). Bowel obsessions responsive to tricyclic antidepressants in four patients. *American Journal of Psychiatry, 144,* 1347–1348.

Kagan, J. (1982). Heart rate and heart rate variability as signs of a temperamental dimension in infants. In C. E. Izard (Ed.), *Measuring emotions in infants and children* (pp. 38–66). Cambridge, England: Cambridge University Press.

Kagan, J., Reznick, J. S., & Snidman, N. (1987). The physiology and psychology of behavioral inhibition in children. *Child Development, 58,* 1459–1473.

Kagan, J., Reznick, J. S., Snidman, N., Gibbons, J., & Johnson, M. O. (1988). Childhood derivatives of inhibition and lack of inhibition to the unfamiliar. *Child Development, 59,* 1580–1589.

Kahn, R. J., McNair, D. M., Covi, L., Downing, R. W., Fisher, S., Lipman, R. S., Rickels, K., & Smith, V. (1981). Effects of psychotropic agents on high anxiety subjects. *Psychopharmacology Bulletin, 17,* 97–100.

Kathol, R. G., Noyes, R., Slyman, D. J., Crowe, R. R., Clancy, J., & Kerber, R. E. (1980). Propranolol in chronic anxiety disorders. *Archives of General Psychiatry, 37,* 1361–1365.

Keane, T., Fairbank, J., Caddell, J., & Zimering, R. (1989). Implosive (flooding) therapy reduces symptoms of PTSD in Vietnam combat veterans. *Behavior Therapy, 20,* 245–260.

Keijsers, G., Hoogduin, C., & Schaap, C. (1994). Predictors of treatment outcome in the behavioural treatment of obsessive-compulsive disorder. *British Journal of Psychiatry, 16,* 781–786.

Keller, M. B. (2002). The long-term clinical course of generalized anxiety disorder. *Journal of Clinical Psychiatry, 63*(Suppl. 8), 11–16.

Keller, M. B. (2003). The lifelong course of social anxiety disorder: A clinical perspective. *Acta Psychiatrica Scandinavica, 108,* 85–95.

Keller, M. B., Yonkers, K. A., Warshaw, M. G., Pratt, L. A., Gollan, J. K., Massion, A. O., White, K., Swartz, A. R., Reich, J., & Lavori, P. W. (1994). Remission and relapse in subjects with panic disorder and panic with agoraphobia. *Journal of Nervous and Mental Disease, 182,* 290–296.

Kendler, K. (1996). Major depression and generalised anxiety disorder same genes, (partly) different environments—revisited. *British Journal of Psychiatry, 16,* 68–75.

Kendler, K. S., Heath, A. C., Martin, N. G., & Eaves, L. J. (1987). Symptoms of anxiety and symptoms of depression: Same genes, different environments. *Archives of General Psychiatry, 44,* 451–457.

Kendler, K. S., Neale, M. C., Kessler, R. C., Heath, A. C., & Eaves, L. J. (1992a). Generalized anxiety disorder in women: A population-based twin study. *Archives of General Psychiatry, 49,* 267–272.

Kendler, K. S., Neale, M. C., Kessler, R. C., Heath, A. C., & Eaves, L. J. (1992b). The genetic epidemiology of phobias in women: The interrelationship of agoraphobia, social phobia, situational phobia, and simple phobia. *Archives of General Psychiatry, 49,* 273–281.

Kern, J. M. (1991). An evaluation of a novel role-play methodology: The standardized idiographic approach. *Behavior Therapy 22,* 13–29.

Kessler, R. (1994). The National Comorbidity Survey of the United States. *International Review of Psychiatry, 6,* 365.

Kessler, R. C., Berglund, P., Demier, O., Jin, R., Merikangas, K. R., & Walters, E. E. (2005). Lifetime prevalence and age-of-onset distributions of DSM-IV disorders in the National Comrobidity Survey Replication. *Archives of General Psychiatry, 62,* 593–602.

Kessler, R. C., Foster, C. L., Saunders, W. B., & Stang, P. E. (1995). Social consequences of psychiatric disorders, I: Education attainment. *American Journal of Psychiatry, 152,* 1026–1032.

Kessler, R. C., McGonagle, K. A., Zhao, S., Nelson, C. B., Hughes, M., Eshleman, S., Wittchen, H. U., & Kendler, K. S. (1994). Lifetime and 12-month prevalence of DSM-III-R psychiatric disorders in the United States. Results from the National Comorbidity Survey. *Archives of General Psychiatry, 51,* 8–19.

Khan, A., Leventhal, R. M., Kahn, S., & Brown, W. A. (2002). Suicide risk in patients with anxiety disorders: A meta-analysis of the FDA database. *Journal of Affective Disorders, 63,* 183–191.

Khanna, S., & Channabasavanna, S. M. (1988). Phenomenology of obsessions in obsessive-compulsive neurosis. *Psychopathology, 21,* 12–18.

Khanna, S., Rajendra, P. N., & Channabasavanna, S. M. (1988). Life events and onset of obsessive compulsive disorder. *International Journal of Social Psychiatry, 34,* 305–309.

Kilpatrick, D. G., Saunders, B. E., Amick-McMullan, A., Best, C. L., Veronen, L. J., & Resnick, H. S. (1989). Victim and crime factors associated with the development of crime-related posttraumatic stress disorder. *Behavior Therapy, 20,* 199–214.

King, D. W., & King, L. A. (1996). Prewar factors in combat-related posttraumatic stress disorder: Structural equation modeling with a national sample of female and male Vietnam veterans. *Journal of Consulting and Clinical Psychology, 3,* 520–532.

Kirmayer, L. (2001). Cultural variations in the clinical presentation of depression and anxiety: Implications for diagnosis and treatment. *Journal of Clinical Psychiatry, 62,* 22–28.

Kirmayer, L., Young, A., & Hayton, B. (1995). The cultural context of anxiety disorders. *Psychiatric Clinics of North America, 18,* 503–521.

Klein, D. F. (1981). Anxiety reconceptualized. In D. R Klein & J. R. Rabkin (Eds.), *Anxiety— new research and changing concepts* (pp. 235–263). New York: Raven.

Klein, D. F., & Fink, M. (1962). Psychiatric reaction patterns to imipramine. *American Journal of Psychiatry, 119,* 432–438.

Klinger, E., Vouchard, S., Legeron, P., Roy, S., Lauer, F., Chemin, I., & Nugues, P. (2005). Virtual reality therapy versus cognitive behavior therapy for social phobia: A preliminary controlled study. *CyberPsychology and Behavior, 8,* 76–88.

Klosko, J. S., Barlow, D. H., Tassinari, R., & Cerney, J. A. (1990). A comparison of alprazolam and behavior therapy in treatment of panic disorder. *Journal of Consulting and Clinical Psychology, 58,* 77–84.

Kobak, K., Greist, J., Jefferson, J., Katzelnick, D., & Henk, H. (1998). Behavioral versus pharmacological treatments of obsessive compulsive disorder: A meta-analysis. *Psychopharmacology, 136,* 205–216.

Kolada, J. L, Bland, R. C., & Newman, S. C. (1994). Epidemiology of psychiatric disorders in Edmonton. Obsessive-compulsive disorder. *Acta Psychiatrica Scandinavica Supplementum, 376,* 24–35.

Kordon, A., Kahl, K. G., Broocks, A., Voderholzer, U., Rasche-Räuchle, H., & Hohagen, F. (2005). Clinical outcome in patients with obsessive-compulsive disorder after discontinuation of SRI treatment: Results from a two-year follow-up. *European Archives of Psychiatry and Clinical Neuroscience, 255,* 48–50.

Kranzler, H. R., Kadden, R. M., Babor, T. F., Tennen, H., & Rounsaville, B. J. (1996). Validity of the SCID in substance abuse patients. *Addiction, 91,* 859–868.

Kukleta, M., & Franc, Z. (2000). Anxiety, depressive symptoms and psychosocial stress in general population. *Homeostasis in Health and Disease, 40,* 14–19.

Kulka, R. A., Schlenger, W. E., Fairbank, J. A., Hough, R. L., Jordan, B. K., Marmar, C. R., & Weiss, D. S. (1988). National Vietnam Veterans Readjustment Study (NVVRS): Description, current status, and initial PTSD prevalence estimates, final report. Washington, DC: Veterans Administration.

Ladouceur, R., Dugas, M. J., & Freeston, M. H. (2000). Efficacy of a cognitive-behavioral treatment for generalized anxiety disorder: Evaluation in a controlled clinical trial. *Journal of Consulting and Clinical Psychology, 68,* 957–964.

Ladouceur, R., Talbot, F., & Dugas, M. J. (1997). Behavioral expressions of intolerance of uncertainty in worry. *Behavior Medification, 21,* 355–371.

Lang, P. J. (1977). Physiological assessment of anxiety and fear. In J. D. Cone & R. P. Hawkins (Eds.), *Behavioral assessment: New directions in clinical psychology* (pp. 178–195). Brummer/Mazel.

Langlois, F., Freeston, M. H., & Ladouceur, R. (2000). Differences and similarities between obsessive and intrusive thoughts and worry in a non-clinical population: Study 1. *Behaviour Research and Therapy, 38,* 157–174.

Last, C. G., Hersen, M., Kazdin, A. E., Francis, G., & Grubb, H. J. (1987). Psychiatric illness in the mothers of anxious children. *American Journal of Psychiatry, 144,* 1580–1583.

Last, C. G., Hersen, M., Kazdin, A. E., Orvaschel, H., & Ye, W. (1990). *Anxiety disorders in children and their families.* Unpublished manuscript. Fort Lauderdale, FL: Nova University.

Lecrubier, Y., & Weiller, E. (1997). Comorbidities in social phobia. *International Clinical Psychopharmacology, 12*(Suppl. 6), 17–21.

Leonard, H. L., & Swedo, S. E. (2001). Paediatric autoimmune neuropsychiatric disorders associated with streptococcal infection (PANDAS). *International Journal of Neuropsychopharmacology, 4,* 191-198.

Lesser, I. M., Rubin, R. T., Pecknold, J. C., Rifkin, A., Swinson, R. P., Lydiard, R. B., Burrows, G. D., Noyes, R., Jr., & DuPont, R. L. (1988). Secondary depression in panic disorder and agoraphobia. *Archives of General Psychiatry, 45,* 437–443.

Liddell, A., & Lyons, M. (1978). Thunderstorm phobias. *Behaviour Research and Therapy, 16,* 306–308.

Lieb, R., Wittchen, H., Höfler, M., Fuetsch, M., Stein, M., & Merikangas, K. (2000). Parental psychopathology, parenting styles, and the risk of social phobia in offspring: A prospective-longitudinal community study. *Archives of General Psychiatry, 57,* 859–866.

Liebowitz, M. R. (1985). Imipramine in the treatment of panic disorder and its complications. *The Psychiatric Clinics of North America, 8,* 37–47.

Liebowitz, M. R. (1987). Social phobia. *Modern problems in pharmacopsychiatry, 22,* 141–173.

Liebowitz, M. R., Gorman, J. M., Fyer, A. J., Campeas, R., Levin, A. P., Sandberg, D., Hollander, E., Papp, L., & Goetz, D. (1988). Pharmacotherapy of social phobia: A placebo-controlled comparison of phenelzine and atenolol. *Journal of Clinical Psychiatry, 49,* 252–257.

Liebowitz, M. R., Gorman, J. M., Fyer, A. J., & Klein, D. R. (1985). Social phobia. *Archives of General Psychiatry, 42,* 729–736.

Liebowitz, M. R., Heimberg, R. G., Schneier, F. R., Hope, D. A., Davies, S., Holt, C. S., Goetz, D., Juster, H. R., Shu-Hsing Lin, H. R., Bruch, M. A., Marshall, R. D., & Klein, D. F. (1999). Cognitive-behavioral group therapy versus phenelzine in social phobia: Long term outcome. *Depression and Anxiety, 10,* 89–98.

Liebowitz, M. R., Salman, E., Jusino, C. M., Garfinkel, R., Street, L., Cardenas, D. L., Silvestre, J., Fyer, A. J., Carrasco, J. L., Davies, S., Guarnaccia, P., & Klein, D. F. (1994). *Ataque de nervios* and panic disorder. *American Journal of Psychiatry, 151,* 871–875.

Lin, K. M., Poland, R. E., & Lesser, I. M. (1986). Ethnicity and psychopharmacology. *Culture, Medicine, and Psychiatry, 10,* 151–165.

Lin, K. M., Poland, R. E., & Silver, B. (1993). The interface between psychobiology and ethnicity. In K. M. Lin, R. E. Poland, and G. Nakasaki (Eds.), *Psychopharmacology and psychobiology of ethnicity* (pp. 11–35). Washington, DC: American Psychiatric Press.

Lin, K., Smith, M., & Ortiz, V. (2001). Culture and psychopharmacology. *Psychiatric Clinics of North America, 24,* 523–538.

Lindsay, M., Crino, R., & Andrews, G. (1997). Controlled trial of exposure and response prevention in obsessive-compulsive disorder. *British Journal of Psychiatry, 171,* 135–139.

Lydiard, R. B., Roy-Byrne, P. P., & Ballenger, J. C. (1988). Recent advances in psychopharmacological treatment of anxiety disorders. *Hospital and Community Psychiatry, 39,* 1157–1165.

Magee, W. J. (1999). Effects of negative life experiences on phobia onset. *Social Psychiatry and Psychiatric Epidemiology, 34,* 343–351.

Maier, W., Gansicke, M., Freyberger, H. J., Linz, M., Heun, R., & Lecrubier, Y. (2000). *Acta Psychiatrica Scandinavica, 101,* 29–36.

Mancuso, D. M., Townsend, M. H., & Mercante, D. E. (1993). Long-term follow-up of generalized anxiety disorder. *Comprehensive Psychiatry, 34,* 441–446.

Marazziti, D., Dell'Osso, L., Gemignani, A., Ciapparellli, A., Presta, S., DiNasso, E., Pfanner, C., & Cassano, G. B. (2001). Citalapram in refractory obsessive-compulsive disorder: An open study. *International Clinical Psychopharmacology, 16,* 215–219.

March, J., Franklin, M., Leonard, H., & Foa, E. (2004). Obsessive-compulsive disorder. In J.S. March (Ed.), *Anxiety disorders in children and adolescents* (2nd ed., pp. 212–240). New York: Guilford Press.

Marcos, L. R., & Cancro, R. (1982). Pharmacotherapy of Hispanic depressed patients: Clinical observations. *American Journal of Psychotherapy, 36,* 505–512.

Margraf, J., Taylor, C. B., Ehlers, A., Roth, W. T., & Agras, W. S. (1987). Panic attacks in the natural environment (special issue). Mental disorders in their natural settings: The application of time allocation and experience-sampling techniques in psychiatry. *Journal of Nervous and Mental Disease, 175,* 558–565.

Marks, I. M., & Gelder, M. G. (1966). Different onset ages in varieties of phobias. *American Journal of Psychiatry, 123,* 218–221.

Marks, I. M., Lovell, K., Noshirvani, H., Livanou, M., & Thrasher, S. (1998). Treatment of posttraumatic stress disorder by exposure and/or cognitive restructuring: A controlled study. *Archives of General Psychiatry, 55,* 317–325.

Marks, I. M., & Mathews, A. M. (1979). Brief standard self-rating for phobic patients. *Behavior Research and Therapy, 17,* 263–267.

Martin, C., Cabrol, S., Bouvard, M., Lepine, J., & Mouren-Siméoni, M. (1999). Anxiety and depressive disorders in fathers and mothers of anxious school-refusing children. *Journal of the American Academy of Child and Adolescent Psychiatry, 38,* 916–922.

Matsuda, K. T., Cho, M. C., Lin, K. M., & Smith, M. W (1995, May). *Clozapine dosage, efficacy, side-effect profiles: A comparison of Asian and Caucasian patients.* Presented at the New Clinical Drug Evaluation Unit (NCDEU) Annual Meeting, Orlando, FL.

Mattick, R. P., & Clark, J. C. (1998). Development and validation of measure of social phobia scrutiny fear and social interaction anxiety. *Behavior Research and Therapy, 36,* 455–470.

Mavissakalian, M., & Hamann, S. (1986). DSM-III personality disorder in agoraphobia. *Comprehensive Psychiatry, 27,* 471–479.

Mavissakalian, M., & Hamann, M. S. (1988). Correlates of DSM-III personality disorder in panic disorder and agoraphobia. *Comprehensive Psychiatry, 29,* 535–544.

McGlynn, F. D. (1988). Behavioral avoidance tests. In M. Hersen and A. Bellack (Eds.), *Dictionary of behavioral assessment techniques* (pp. 59–60). Oxford, England: Pergamon.

McLean, P. D., Whittal, M. L., Thordarson, D. S., Taylor, S., Sochting, I., Koch, W. J., Paterson, R., & Anderson, K. W. (2001). Cognitive versus behavior therapy in the group treatment of obsessive-compulsive disorder. *Journal of Consulting and Clinical Psychology, 69,* 205–214.

McNally, R. J. (1987). Preparedness and phobias: A review. *Psychological Bulletin, 101,* 283–303.

McNally, R. J. (1995). Automaticity and the anxiety disorders. *Behaviour Research and Therapy, 33,* 747–754.

McNally, R. J. (2001). Vulnerability to anxiety disorders in adulthood. In R. E. Ingram & J. M. Price (Eds.), *Vulnerability to psychopathology: Risk across the lifespan* (pp. 304–321). New York: Guilford Press.

McNally, R. J., & Steketee, G. S. (1985). The etiology and maintenance of severe animal phobias. *Behaviour Research and Therapy, 23,* 431–435.

Merluzzi, T. V., & Biever, J. (1987). Role-playing procedures for the behavioral assessment of social skill: A validity study. *Behavioral Assessment, 9,* 361–377.

Meyer, T. J., Miller, M. L., Metzger, R. L., & Borkovec, T. D. (1990). Development and validation of the Penn State worry questionnaire. *Behavior Research and Therapy, 28,* 487–495.

Mineka, S., & Cook, M. (1986). Immunization against the observational conditioning of snake fear in rhesus monkeys. *Journal of Abnormal Psychology, 95,* 307–318.

Mineka, S., Davidson, M., Cook, M., & Heir, R. (1985). Observational conditioning of snake fear in rhesus monkeys. *Journal of Abnormal Psychology, 93,* 355–372.

Mineka, S., & Zinbarg, R. (1991). Animal models of psychopathology. In C. E. Walker (Ed.), *Clinical psychology: Historical and research foundations* (pp. 51–86). New York: Plenum.

Mineka, S., & Zinbarg, R. (2006). A contemporary learning theory perspective on the etiology of anxiety disorders: It's not what you thought it was. *American Psychologist, 61,* 10–26.

Mowrer, O. H. (1947). On the dual nature of learning: A reinterpretation of "conditioning" and "problem-solving." *Harvard Education Review, 17,* 102–148.

Mueser, K. T., Yarnold, P. R. & Foy, D. W. (1991). Statistical analysis for single-case designs: Evaluating outcome of imaginal exposure treatment of chronic PTSD. *Behavior Modification, 15,* 134–155.

Murphy, M. T., Michelson, L. K., Marchione, K., Marchione, N., & Testa, S. (1998). The role of self-directed in vivo exposure in combination with cognitive therapy, relaxation training, or therapist-assisted exposure in the treatment of panic disorder with agoraphobia. *Journal of Anxiety Disorders, 12,* 117–138.

Neal, A. M., & Turner, S. M. (1991). Anxiety disorders research with African Americans: Current status. *Psychological Bulletin, 109,* 400–410.

Neal-Barnett, A., & Crowther, J. (2000). To be female, middle class, anxious, and black. *Psychology of Women Quarterly, 24,* 129.

Neighbors, H. W. (1985). Seeking help for personal problems: Black Americans' use of health and mental health services. *Community Mental Health Journal, 21,* 156–166.

Nestadt, G., Bienvenu, O. J., Cai, G., Samuels, J., & Eaton, W. W. (1998). Incidence of obsessive-compulsive disorder in adults. *Journal of Nervous and Mental Disease, 186,* 401–406.

Nestadt, G., Lan, T., Samuels, J., Riddle, M., Bienvenu, O. J., Liang, K. Y., Hoehn-Saric, R., Cullen, B., Grados, M., Beaty, T. H., & Shugart, Y. Y. (2000). Complex segregation analysis provides compelling evidence for a major gene underlying obsessive-compulsive disorder and for heterogeneity by sex. *American Journal of Human Genetics, 67,* 1611–1616.

Newman, M. G., Hofann, S. G., Trabert, W., Roth, W. T., & Taylor, C. B. (1994). Does behavioral treatment of social phobia lead to cognitive changes? *Behavior Therapy, 25,* 503–517.

Newman, M. G., Zuellig, A. R., Kachin, K. E., Constantino, M. J., Przeworski, A., Erickson, T., Cashman-McGrath, L. (2002). Preliminary reliability and validity of the Generalized Anxiety Disorder Questionnaire-IV: A revised self-report diagnostic measure of generalized anxiety disorder. *Behavior Therapy, 33,* 215–233.

Norris, F. H., & Kaniasty, K. (1994). Psychological distress following criminal victimization in the general population: Cross-sectional, longitudinal , and prospective analysis. *Journal of Consulting and Clinical Psychology, 62,* 111–124.

Norton, G. R., Dorward, J., & Cox, B. J. (1986). Factors associated with panic attacks in nonclinical subjects. *Behaviour Research and Therapy, 17,* 239–252.

Noyes, R., Woodman, C., Garvey, M. J., Cook, B. L., Suelzer, M., Clancy, J., & Anderson, D. J. (1992). Generalized anxiety disorder versus panic disorder: Distinguishing characteristics and patterns of comorbidity. *Journal of Nervous and Mental Disease, 180,* 369–378.

Ohman, A. (1986). Face the beast and fear the face: Animal and social fears as prototypes for evolutionary analyses of emotion. *Psychophysiology, 23,* 123–145.

Ohman, A., Eriksson, A., & Olafsson, C. (1975). One-trial learning and superior resistance to extinction of autonomic responses conditioned to potentially phobic stimuli. *Journal of Comparative and Physiological Psychology, 88,* 619–627.

Ohman, A., Fredrikson, M., Hugdahl, K., & Rimmo, P. A. (1976). The premise of equipotentiality in human classical conditioning: Conditioned electrodermal responses to potentially phobic stimuli. *Journal of Experimental Psychology: General, 105,* 313–337.

Ost, L. G. (1987). Age of onset in different phobias. *Journal of Abnormal Psychology, 96,* 223–229.

Ost, L. G. (1996). Long-term effects of behavior therapy for specific phobia. In M. Mavissakalian and R. R Prien (Eds.), *Long-term treatments of anxiety disorders* (pp. 121–170). Washington, DC: American Psychiatric Association.

Ost, L. G., & Hugdahl, K. (1983). Acquisition of phobias and anxiety response patterns in clinical patients. *Behaviour Research and Therapy, 21,* 623–631.

Otto, M. W., Pollack, M. H., Sachs, G. S., Reiter, S. R., Meltzer-Brody, S., & Rosenbaum, J. R. (1993). Discontinuation of benzodiazepine treatment: Efficacy of cognitive-behavioral therapy for patients with panic disorder. *American Journal of Psychiatry, 150,* 1485–1490.

Page, A. C. (1994). Distinguishing panic disorder and agoraphobia from social phobia. *Journal of Nervous and Mental Disease, 182,* 611–617.

Palatnik, A., Frolov, K., Fux, M., & Benjamin, J. (2001). Double-blind, controlled, crossover trial of inositol versus fluvoxamine for the treatment of panic disorder. *Journal of Clinical Psychopharmacology, 21,* 335–339.

Paradis, C., Hatch, M., & Friedman, S. (1994). Anxiety disorders in African Americans: An update. *Journal of the National Medical Association, 86,* 609–612.

Pato, M. T., Zohar-Kadouch, R., Zohar, J., & Murphy, D. L. (1988). Return of symptoms after discontinuation of clomipramine in patients with obsessive-compulsive disorder. *American Journal of Psychiatry, 145,* 1521–1525.

Pauls, D. L., Alsobrook, J. P., Goodman, W., Rasmussen, S., & Leckman, J. F. (1995). A family study of obsessive-compulsive disorder. *American Journal of Psychiatry, 152,* 76–84.

Perugi, G., Akiskal, H. S., Gemingnani, A., Pfanner, C., Presto, S., Milanfranchi, A., Lensi, P., Ravagli, S., Maremmani, I., & Cassano, G. B. (1998). Episodic course in obsessive-compulsive disorder. *European Archives of Psychiatry and Clinical Neuroscience, 248,* 240–245.

Pigott, T. A., Hill, J. L., Grady, T. A., L'Heureux, F., Bernstein, S., Rubenstein, C. S., & Murphy, D. L. (1993). A comparison of the behavioral effects of oral versus intravenous mCPP administration in OCD patients and the effect of metergoline prior to i.v. mCPP. *Biological Psychiatry, 33,* 3–14.

Pohl, R. B., Wolkow, R. M., & Clary, C. M. (1998). Sertraline more than placebo for panic. *Brown University Psychopharmacology Update, 9,* 3–5.

Pollack, M. H., Otto, M. W., Rosenbaum, J. F., & Sachs, G. S. (1992). Personality disorders in patients with panic disorder: Association with childhood anxiety disorders, early trauma, comorbidity, and chronicity. *Comprehensive Psychiatry, 33,* 78–83.

Rachman, S. J. (1977). The conditioning theory of fear-acquisition. A critical examination. *Behaviour Research and Therapy, 15,* 375–387.

Rachman, S. J. (1990). *Fear and courage* (2nd ed.) New York: Freeman.

Rachman, S. J., Cobb, J., MacDonald, B., Mawson, D., Sartory, G., & Stern, R. (1979). The behavioral treatment of obsessive-compulsive disorders with and without clomipramine. *Behavior Research and Therapy, 17,* 467–478.

Rachman, S. J., & Hodgson, R. J. (1980). *Obsessions and compulsions.* Englewood Cliffs, NJ: Prentice Hall.

Rachman, S. J., Thordarson, D., Shafran, R., & Woody, S. (1995). Perceived responsibility: Structure and significance. *Behaviour Research and Therapy, 33,* 779–784.

Rapaport, M. H., Pollack, M. H., Clary, C. M., Mardekian, J., & Wolkow, R. (2001). Panic disorder and response to sertraline: The effect of previous treatment with benzodiazepines. *Journal of Clinical Psychopharmacology, 21,* 104–107.

Rapee, R. M., Craske, M. G., & Barlow, D. H. (1990). Subject described features of panic attacks using a new self-monitoring form. *Journal of Anxiety Disorders, 4,* 171–181.

Rapee, R. M., & Lim, L. (1992). Discrepancy between self- and observer ratings of performance in social phobics. *Journal of Abnormal Psychology, 101,* 728–731.

Rapee, R. M., Litwin, E. M., & Barlow, D. H. (1990). Impact of life events on subjects with panic disorder and on comparison subjects. *American Journal of Psychiatry, 147,* 640–644.

Rapoport, J. L. (1991). Recent advances in obsessive-compulsive disorder. *Neuropsychopharmacology, 5,* 1–10.

Rasmussen, S. (1993). Genetic studies of obsessive-compulsive disorder. *Annals of Clinical Psychiatry, 5,* 241–248.

Rasmussen, S., & Eisen, J. L. (1992). The epidemiology and differential diagnosis of obsessive compulsive disorder. *Journal of Clinical Psychiatry, 53,* 4–10.

Rasmussen, S. A., & Tsuang, M. T. (1986). Clinical characteristics and family history in DSM-III obsessive-compulsive disorder. *American Journal of Psychiatry, 143,* 317–322.

Reed, V., & Wittchen, H. U. (1998). DSM-IV panic attacks and panic disorder in a community sample of adolescents and young adults: How specific are panic attacks? *Journal of Psychiatric Research, 32,* 335–345.

Regier, D., Rae, D., Narrow, W., Kaelber, C., & Schatzberg, A. (1998). Prevalence of anxiety disorders and their comorbidity with mood and addictive disorders. *British Journal of Psychiatry, 173,* 24–28.

Reich, J., Goldenberg, I., Goisman, R., Vasile, R., & Keller, M. (1994). A prospective, follow-along study of the course of social phobia: II. Testing for basic predictors of course. *Journal of Nervous and Mental Disease, 182,* 297–301.

Reich, J. H., & Noyes, R., Jr. (1987). A comparison of DSM-III personality disorders in acutely ill panic and depressed patients. *Journal of Anxiety Disorders, 1,* 123–131.

Reiss, S. (1991). Expectancy theory of fear, anxiety, and panic. *Clinical Psychology Review, 11,* 141–153.

Reiss, S., & McNally, R. J. (1985). The expectancy model of fear. In S. Reiss & R. R. Bootzin (Eds.), *Theoretical issues in behavior therapy* (pp. 107–121). New York: Academic Press.

Reiss, S., Peterson, R. A., Gursky, D. M., & McNally, R. J. (1986). Anxiety sensitivity, anxiety frequency, and the prediction of fearfulness. *Behaviour Research and Therapy, 24,* 1–8.

Rennenberg, B., Chambless, D. L., & Gracely, E. J. (1992). Prevalence of SCID diagnosed personality disorders in agoraphobic outpatients. *Journal of Anxiety Disorders, 6,* 111–118.

Resick, P. A., Nishith, P., Weaver, T. L., Astin, M. C., & Feuer, C. A. (2002). A comparison of cognitive-processing therapy with prolonged exposure and a waiting list condition for the treatment of chronic posttraumatic stress disorder in female rape victims. *Journal of Consulting and Clinical Psychology, 70,* 867–879.

Reznick, J. S., Kagan, J., Sniderman, N., Gersten, M., Boak, K., & Rosenberg, A. (1986). Inhibited and uninhibited children: A follow-up study. *Child Development, 57,* 660–680.

Rickels, K., Downing, R., Schweizer, E., & Hassman, H. (1993). Antidepressants for the treatment of generalized anxiety disorder: A placebo-controlled comparison of imipramine, trazodone, and diazepam. *Archives of General Psychiatry, 50,* 884–895.

Rickels, K., Zaninelli, R., McCafferty, J., Bellew, K., Iyengar, M., & Sheehan, D. (2003). Paroxetine treatment of generalized anxiety disorder: A double-blind, placebo-controlled study. *American Journal of Psychiatry, 160,* 749–756.

Rivas-Vazquez, R. A. (2001). Antidepressants as first-line agents in the current pharmacotherapy of anxiety disorders. *Professional Psychology, 32,* 101–104.

Robins, L. N., Helzer, J. E., Weissman, M. M., Orvaschel, H., Greenberg, E., Burke, J. D., Jr., & Regier, D. A. (1984). Lifetime prevalence of specific psychiatric disorders at three sites. *Archives of General Psychiatry, 41,* 949–958.

Rodebaugh, T. L., Holaway, R. M., & Heimberg, R. G. (2004). The treatment of social anxiety disorder. *Clinical Psychology Review, 24,* 883–909.

Rothbaum, B. O., Foa, E. B., Riggs, D. S., Murdock, T., et al. (1992). A prospective examination of post-traumatic stress disorderin rape victims. *Journal of Traumatic Stress, 5*, 455–475.

Rosenbaum, J. F., Biederman, J., Bolduc, E. A., Faraone, S. V., Hirshfeld, D. R., & Kagan, J. (1992). Comorbidity of parental anxiety disorders at risk for childhood-onset anxiety in inhibited children. *American Journal of Psychiatry, 149*, 475–481.

Rosenbaum, J. F., Biederman, J., Hirshfeld, D. R., Bolduc, E. A., Kagan, J., Snidman, N., & Reznick, J. S. (1991). Further evidence of an association between behavioral inhibition and anxiety disorders: Results from a family study of children from a nonclinical sample. *Journal of Psychiatric Research, 25*, 49–65.

Rosenberg, D., & Keshavan, M. (1998). Toward a neurodevelopmental model of obsessive-compulsive disorder. *Biological Psychiatry, 43*, 623–640.

Rothbaum, B. O., Hodges, L., Anderson, P. L., Price, L., & Smith, S. (2002). Twelve-month follow-up of virtual reality and standard exposure therapies for fear of flying. *Journal of Consulting and Clinical Psychology, 70*, 428–432.

Salaberria, K., & Echeburua, E. (1998). Long-term outcome of cognitive therapy's contribution to self-exposure in vivo to the treatment of generalized social phobia. *Behavior Modification, 22*, 262–284.

Salkovskis, P., Clark, D., & Gelder, M. (1996). Cognition-behaviour links in the persistence of panic. *Behaviour Research and Therapy, 34*, 453–458.

Salzman, C., Goldenberg, I., Bruce, S. E., & Keller, M. B. (2001). Pharmacologic treatment of anxiety disorders in 1989 versus 1996: results from the Harvard/Brown anxiety disorders research program. *Journal of Clinical Psychiatry, 62*, 149–152.

Sánchez, M., Ladd, C., & Plotsky, P. (2001). Early adverse experience as a developmental risk factor for later psychopathology: Evidence from rodent and primate models. *Development and Psychopathology, 13*, 419–449.

Sandin, B., Chorot, P., Sante, M., & Valiente, R. (2004). Differences in negative life events between patients with anxiety disorders, depression and hypochondriasis. *Anxiety, Stress and Coping, 17*, 37–47.

Saxena, S., Brody, A., Schwartz, J., & Baxter, L. (1998). Neuroimaging and frontal-subcortical circuitry in obsessive-compulsive disorder. *British Journal of Psychiatry, 173*, 26–37.

Schwartz, C., Snidman, N., & Kagan, J. (1999). Adolescent social anxiety as an outcome of inhibited temperament in childhood. *Journal of the American Academy of Child and Adolescent Psychiatry, 38*, 1008–1015.

Sciuto, G., Diaferia, G., Battaglia, M., Perna, G., Gabriele, A., & Bellodi, L. (1991). DSM-III-R personality disorders in panic and obsessive-compulsive disorder: A comparison study. *Comprehensive Psychiatry, 32*, 450–457.

Seligman, M. (1971). Phobias and preparedness. *Behavior Therapy, 2*, 307–320.

Sellwood, W., & Tarrier, N. (1994). Demographic factors associated with extreme non-compliance in schizophrenia. *Social Psychiatry and Epidemiology, 29*, 172–177.

Shear, M. K., Devereux, R. B., Kranier-Fox, R., Mann, J. J., & Frances, A. (1984). Low prevalence of mitral valve prolapse in patients with panic disorder. *American Journal of Psychiatry, 141*, 302–303.

Sheehan, D. V., Sheehan, K. E., & Minichiello, W. E. (1981). Age of onset of phobic disorders. *Comprehensive Psychiatry, 22*, 544–553.

Sheikh, J. I., & Swales, P. J. (1999). Treatment of panic disorder in older adults: A pilot study comparison of alprazolam, imipramine, and placebo. *International Journal of Psychiatry in Medicine, 29*, 107–129.

Smeraldi, E., Diaferia, G., Erzegovsi, S., Lucca, A., Bellodi, L., & Moja, E. A. (1996). Tryptophan depletion in obsessive-compulsive patients. *Biological Psychiatry, 40*, 398–402.

Sobin, C., Blundell, M. L., & Karayiorgou, M. (2000). Phenotypic differences in early- and late-onset obsessive-compulsive disorder. *Comprehensive Psychiatry, 41,* 373–379.

Spielberger, C. D. (1983). *Manual for the State-Trait Anxiety Inventory (STAI).* Palo Alto, CA: Consulting Psychologists Press.

Spitzer, R. L., & Endicott, J. (1978). *Schedule for Affective Disorders and Schizophrenia* (3rd ed). New York: Biometrics Research.

St. Lawrence, J. S., Kirksey, W. A., & Moore, T. (1983). External validity of role play assessment of assertive behavior. *Journal of Behavioral Assessment, 5,* 25–34.

Stanley, M. A., & Turner, S. M. (1995). Current status of pharmacological and behavioral treatment of obsessive-compulsive disorder. *Behavior Therapy, 26,* 163–186.

Stanley, M., Turner, S., & Borden, J. (1990). Schizotypal features in obsessive-compulsive disorder. *Comprehensive Psychiatry, 31,* 511–518.

Starcevic, V., & Bogojevic, G. (1997). Comorbidity of panic disorder with agoraphobia and specific phobia: Relationship with the subtypes of specific phobia. *Comprehensive Psychiatry, 38,* 315–320.

Stein, D. J., Berk, M., Els, C., Emsley, R. A., Gittelson, L., Wilson, D., Oakes, R., & Hunter, B. (1999). A double-blind placebo-controlled trial of paroxetine in the management of social phobia (social anxiety disorder) in South Africa. *South African Medical Journal, 89,* 402–406.

Stein, D. J., & Hugo, F. J. (2004). Neuropsychiatric aspects of anxiety disorders. In S. C. Yudofsky and R. E. Hales (Eds.), *Essentials of neuropsychiatry and clinical neurosciences* (pp. 1049–1068). Washington, DC: American Psychiatric Association.

Stein, D. J., Westenberg, H. G. M., Yang, H., Li, D., & Barbato, L. M. (2003). Fluvoxamine CR in the long-term treatment of social anxiety disorder: The 12- to 24-week extension phase of a multicentre, randomized, placebo-controlled trial. *International Journal of Neuropsychopharmacology, 6,* 317–325.

Stein, M. B., Fyer, A. J., Davidson, J. R., Pollack, M. H., & Wiita, B. (1999). Fluvoxamine treatment of social phobia (social anxiety disorder): A double-blind, placebo-controlled study. *American Journal of Psychiatry, 156,* 756–760.

Stein, M. B., Koverola, C., Hanna, C., Torchia, M. G., & McClarty, B. (1997). Hippocampal volume in women victimized by childhood sexual abuse. *Psychological Medicine, 27,* 951–960.

Stein, M. B., Liebowitz, M. R., Lydiard, R. B., Pitts, C. D., Bushnell, W., & Gergel, I. (1998). Paroxetine treatment of generalized social phobia (social anxiety disorder): A randomized controlled trial. *Journal of the American Medical Association, 280,* 708–713.

Stein, M. B., Walker, J. R., & Forde, D. R. (1994). Setting diagnostic thresholds for social phobia: Considerations from a community survey of social anxiety. *American Journal of Psychiatry, 151,* 408–412.

Steketee, G., Chambless, D., Tran, G. Q., Worden, H., & Gillis, M. M. (1996). Behavioral Avoidance Test for obsessive-compulsive disorder. *Behavior Research and Therapy, 34,* 73–83.

Steketee, G., & Neziroglu, F. (2003). Assessment of obsessive-compulsive disorder and spectrum disorders. *Brief Treatment and Crisis Intervention. 3,* 169–185.

Steketee, G., & Shapiro, L. J. (1995). Predicting behavioral treatment outcome for agoraphobia and obsessive-compulsive disorder. *Clinical Psychology Review, 15,* 317–346.

Stemberger, R. I, Turner, S. M., Beidel, D. C., & Calhoun, K. (1995). Social phobia: An analysis of possible developmental factors. *Journal of Abnormal Psychology, 104,* 526–531.

Sternberger, L. G., & Burns, G. L. (1991). Obsessive compulsive disorder: Symptoms and diagnosis in a college sample. *Behavior Therapy, 22,* 569–576.

Stopa, L., & Clark, D. M. (1993). Cognitive processes in social phobia. *Behaviour Research and Therapy, 31,* 255–267.

Suomi, S. J. (1986). Anxiety in young nonhuman primates. In R. Gittelman (Ed.), *Anxiety disorders of childhood* (pp. 1–23). New York: Guilford.

Suomi, S. I., Kraemer, G. U., Baysinger, C. M., & Delizio, R. D. (1981). Inherited and experiential factors associated with individual differences in anxious behavior displayed by rhesus monkeys. In D. Klein & J. Rabkin (Eds.), *Anxiety: New research and changing concepts* (pp. 179–200). New York: Raven.

Swedo, S. E., Leonard, H. L., Garvey, M., Mittleman, B., Allen, A. J., Perlmutter, S., Lougee, S., Dow, S., Zamkoff, J., Dubbert, B. K. (1998). Pediatric autoimmune neuropsychiatric disorders associated with streptococcal infections: clinical description of the first 50 cases. *American Journal of Psychiatry, 155,* 264–271.

Sylvester, C. E., Hyde, T. S., & Reichler, R. J. (1988). Clinical psychopathology among children of adults with panic disorder. In D. L. Dunner, E. S. Gershon, & J. E. Barrett (Eds.), *Relatives at risk for mental disorder* (pp. 87–98). New York: Raven.

Targum, S. D., & Marshall, L. E. (1989). Fenfluramine provocation of anxiety in patients with panic disorder. *Psychiatry Research, 28,* 295–306.

Tarrier, N., Sommerfield, C., Pilgrim, H., & Humphreys, L. (1999). Cognitive therapy or imaginal exposure in the treatment of post-traumatic stress disorder. Twelve-month follow-up. *British Journal of Psychiatry, 175,* 571–575.

Taylor, C. B., Sheikh, J., Agras, W. S., Roth, W. T., Margraf, J., Ehlers, A., Madock, R. J., & Gossard, D. (1986). Ambulatory heart rate changes in clients with panic attacks. *American Journal of Psychiatry, 143,* 478–482.

Taylor, S. (1996). Meta-analysis of cognitive-behavioral treatments for social phobia. *Journal of Behavior Therapy and Experimental Psychiatry, 27,* 1–9.

Taylor, S. (1995). Assessment of obsessions and compulsions: Reliability, validity and sensitivity to treatment effects. *Clinical Psychology Review, 15,* 261–296.

Thyer, B. A., Parrish, R. T., Curtis, G. E., Nesse, R. M., & Cameron, O. G. (1985). Age of onset of DSM-III anxiety disorders. *Comprehensive Psychiatry, 26,* 113–121.

Tillfors, M., Furmark, T., Martinsdottir, I., Fischer, H., Pissiota, A., Langstrom, B., & Fredrikson, M. (2001). Cerebral blood flow in subjects with social phobia during stressful speaking tasks: A PET study. *American Journal of Psychiatry, 158,* 1220–1226.

Todorov, C., Freeston, M. H., & Borgeat, F. (2000). On the pharmacotherapy of obsessive-compulsive disorder: Is a consensus possible? *Canadian Journal of Psychiatry, 45,* 257–263.

Torgersen, S. (1983). Genetic factors in anxiety disorders. *Archives of General Psychiatry, 40,* 1085–1089.

Trinder, H., & Salkovskis, P. M. (1994). Personally relevant intrusions outside the laboratory: Long-term suppression increases intrusion. *Behaviour Research and Therapy, 32,* 833–842.

Trivedi, M. (1996). Functional neuroanatomy of obsessive-compulsive disorder. *Journal of Clinical Psychiatry, 57,* 26–36.

Trudel, G. (1978). The effects of instructions, level of fear, duration of exposure and repeated measures on the Behavioral Avoidance Test. *Behaviour Research and Therapy, 17,* 113–118.

True, W. R., Rice, J., Eisen, S. A., Heath, A. C., Goldberg, J., Lyons, M. J., & Nowak, J. (1993). A twin study of genetic and environmental contributions to liability for posttraumatic stress symptoms. *Archives of General Psychiatry, 50,* 257–264.

Turner, S. M., & Beidel, D. C. (1988). *Treating obsessive-compulsive disorder* New York: Pergamon.

Turner, S. M., & Beidel, D. C. (1989a). Social phobia: Clinical syndrome, diagnosis, and comorbidity. *Clinical Psychology Review, 9,* 3–18.

Turner, S. M., & Beidel, D. C. (1989b). *On the nature of obsessional thoughts and worry: Similarities and dissimilarities.* Paper prepared for the DSM-IV Task Force.

Turner, S. M., Beidel, D. C., Borden, J. W, Stanley, M. A., & Jacob, R. G. (1991). Social phobia: Axis I and 11 correlates. *Journal of Abnormal Psychology, 100,* 102–106.

Turner, S. M., Beidel, D. C., & Cooley, M. R. (1994). *Social effectiveness therapy: A program for overcoming social anxiety and phobia.* Toronto, Ontario: Multi-Health Systems.

Turner, S. M., Beidel, D. C., & Costello, A. (1987). Psychopathology in the offspring of anxiety disorders patients. *Journal of Consulting and Clinical Psychology, 55,* 229–235.

Turner, S. M., Beidel, D. C., Dancu, C. V., & Keys, D. J. (1986). Psychopathology of social phobia and comparison to avoidant personality disorder. *Journal of Abnormal Psychology, 95,* 389–394.

Turner, S. M., Beidel, D. C., Dancu, C. V., & Stanley, M. A. (1989). An empirically derived inventory to measure social fears and anxiety: The Social Phobia and Anxiety Inventory. *Psychological Assessment, 1,* 35–40.

Turner, S. M., Beidel, D. C., & Epstein, L. H. (1991). Vulnerability and risk for anxiety disorders. *Journal of Anxiety Disorders, 5,* 151–166.

Turner, S. M., Beidel, D. C., & Frueh, B. (2005). Multicomponent behavioral treatment for chronic combat-related posttraumatic stress disorder: Trauma management therapy. *Behavior Modification, 29,* 39–69.

Turner, S. M., Beidel, D. C., & Jacob, R. G. (1988). Assessment of panic. In S. Rachman & J. D. Maser (Eds.), *Panic: Psychological perspectives* (pp. 37–50). Hillsdale, NJ: Erlbaum.

Turner, S. M., Beidel, D. C., & Jacob, R. G. (1994). Behavioral and pharmacological treatment of social phobia. *Journal of Consulting and Clinical Psychology, 62,* 350–358.

Turner, S. M., Beidel, D. C., Roberson-Nay, R., & Tervo, K. E. (2003). Parenting behaviors in parents with anxiety disorders. *Behaviour Research and Therapy, 41,* 541–554.

Turner, S. M., Beidel, D. C., & Stanley, M. A. (1992). Are obsessional thoughts and worry different cognitive phenomena? *Clinical Psychology Review, 12,* 257–270.

Turner, S. M., Beidel, D. C., Stanley, M. A., & Heiser, N. (2001). *Obsessive-compulsive disorder. Comprehensive handbook of psychopathology* (3rd ed., pp. 155–182). New York: Kluwer Academic/Plenum Publishers.

Turner, S. M., Beidel, D. C., & Townsley, R. M. (1992). Social phobia: A comparison of specific and generalized subtypes and avoidant personality disorder. *Journal of Abnormal Psychology, 101,* 326–331.

Turner, S. M., Beidel, D. C., & Wolff, P. (1996). Behavioral inhibition: Relationship to anxiety disorders. *Clinical Psychology Review, 16,* 157–172.

Turner, S. M., Beidel, D. C., Wolff, P., Spaulding, S., & Jacob, R. (1996). Clinical features affecting treatment outcome in social phobia. *Behaviour Research and Therapy, 34,* 795–804.

Turner, S. M., & Cooley-Quille, M. R. (1996). Socioecological and sociocultural variables in psychopharmacological research: Methodological considerations. *Psychopharmacology Bulletin, 32,* 183–192.

Turner, S. M., Cooley-Quille, M. R., & Beidel, D. C. (1996). Behavioral and pharmacological treatment of social phobia: Long-term outcome. In M. Mavissakalian & R. Prien (Eds.), *Anxiety disorders: Psychological and pharmacological treatments* (pp. 291–300). Washington, DC: American Psychiatric Press.

Twentyman, C. T., & McFall, R. M. (1975). Behavioral training of social skills in shy males. *Journal of Consulting and Clinical Psychology, 43,* 384–395.

Uhde, T. W., Boulenger, J. P., Roy-Byrne, P. P., Geraci, M. E., Vittone, B. I., & Post, R. M. (1985). Longitudinal course of panic disorder: Clinical and biological considerations. *Progress in Neuro-Psychopharmacology and Biological Psychiatry, 9,* 39–51.

Uhde, T. W., & Singareddy, R. (2002). Biological research in anxiety disorders. In M. Maj (Ed.), *Psychiatry as a neuroscience* (pp. 237–285). New York: Wiley.

Unnewehr, S., Schneider, S., Florin, I., & Margraf, J. (1998). Psychopathology in children of patients with panic disorder or animal phobia. *Psychopathology, 31,* 69–84.

Van Amerigan, M., Mancini, C., & Streiner, D. (1993). Fluoxetine efficacy in social phobia. *Journal of Clinical Psychiatry, 54,* 27–32.

van Dam-Baggen, R., & Kraaimaat, F. (2000). Group social skills training or cognitive group therapy as the clinical treatment of choice for generalized social phobia? *Journal of Anxiety Disorders, 14,* 437–511.

van der Kolk, B. A., Dreyfuss, D., Michaels, M., Shera, D., Berkowitz, R., Fisler, R., & Saxe, G. (1994). Fluoxetine in posttraumatic stress disorder. *Journal of Clinical Psychiatry, 55,* 517–523.

Van Valkenberg, C., Akiskal, H. G., Puzantian, V., & Rosenthal, I. (1984). Anxious depressions: Clinical, family history, and naturalistic outcome—comparisons with panic and major depressive disorders. *Journal of Affective Disorders, 6,* 67–82.

van Velzen, C., Emmelkamp, P., & Scholing, A. (2000). Generalized social phobia versus avoidant personality disorder: Differences in psychopathology, personality traits, and social and occupational functioning. *Journal of Anxiety Disorders, 14,* 395–411.

Venturello, S., Barzega, G., Maina, G., & Bogetto, F. (2002). Premorbid conditions and precipitating events in early-onset panic disorder. *Comprehensive Psychiatry, 43,* 28–36.

Versiani, M., Amrein, R., & Montgomery, S. A. (1997). Social phobia: Long-term treatment outcome and prediction of response—moclobemide study. *International Clinical Psychopharmacology, 12,* 239–254.

Walker, V. J., & Beech, H. R. (1969). Mood states and the ritualistic behavior of obsessional patients. *British Journal of Psychiatry, 150,* 1261–1268.

Warner, V., Mufson, L., & Weissman, M. M. (1995). Offspring at high and low risk for depression and anxiety: Mechanisms of psychiatric disorder. *Journal of the American Academy of Child and Adolescent Psychiatry, 34,* 786–797.

Warshaw, M. G., Dolan, R. T., & Keller, M. B. (2000). Suicidal behavior in patients with current or past panic disorder: Five years of prospective data from the Harvard/Brown Anxiety Research Program. *American Journal of Psychiatry, 157,* 1876–1879.

Watson, I. B., & Rayner, R. (1920). Conditional emotional reactions. *Journal of Experimental Psychology, 3,* 1–14.

Weathers, F. W., Litz, B. T., Herman, D. S., Huska, J. A., & Keane, T. M. (1993). *The PTSD Checklist (PCL): Reliability, validity, and diagnostic utility.* Paper presented at the annual meeting of the International Society for Traumatic Stress Studies, San Antonio, TX.

Weiller, E., Bisserbe, J. C., Boyer, P., Lepine, J. P., & Lecrubier, Y. (1996). Social phobia in primary care: Level of recognition and drug use. *British Journal of Psychiatry, 168,* 169–74.

Weissman, M. M. (1990). Panic and generalized anxiety: Are they separate disorders? *Journal of Psychiatric Research, 24,* 157–162.

Weissman, M. M. (1993). Family genetic studies of panic disorder. *Journal of Psychiatric Research, 27,* 69–78.

Weissman, M. M., Leckman, J. F., Merikangas, K. R., Gammon, G. D., & Prusoff, B. A. (1984). Depression and anxiety disorders in parents and children. *Archives of General Psychiatry, 41,* 845–852.

Wentzel, A., Statler-Cowen, T., Patton, G. K., & Holt, C. S. (1998). *A comprehensive meta-analysis of psychosocial and pharmacological interventions for social phobia and social anxiety.* Poster presented at the 19th Annual Conference of the Anxiety Disorders Association of America, San Diego, CA.

Wessberg, H. W., Marriotta, M. J., Conger, A. J., Conger, J. C., & Farrel, A. D. (1979). The ecological validity of role-plays for assessing heterosocial anxiety and skill of male college students. *Journal of Consulting and Clinical Psychology, 47,* 525–535.

Westra, H., & Stewart, S. (1998). Cognitive behavioural therapy and pharmacotherapy: Complementary or contradictory approaches to the treatment of anxiety? *Clinical Psychology Review, 18,* 307–340.

Wilhelm, S., Otto, M., Zucker, B., & Pollack, M. (1997). Prevalence of body dysmorphic disorder in patients with anxiety disorders. *Journal of Anxiety Disorders, 11,* 499–502.

Wittchen, H. U., & Beloch, E. (1996). The impact of social phobia on quality of life. *International Clinical Psychopharmacology, 11*(Suppl. 3), 15–23.

Wittchen, H. U., & Hoyer, J. (2001). Generalized anxiety disorder: Nature and course. *Journal of Clinical Psychology, 62*(Suppl. 11), 15–19.

Wittchen, H. U., Stein, M. B., & Kessler, R. C. (1999). Social fears and social phobia in a community sample of adolescents and young adults: Prevalence, risk factors and co-morbidity. *Psychological Medicine, 29,* 309–323.

Wlazlo, A., Schroeder-Hartwig, K., Hand, I., Kaiser, G., & Munchau, N. (1990). Exposure in vivo versus social skills training for social phobia: Long-term outcome and differential effects. *Behaviour Research and Therapy, 28,* 181–193.

Wolfe, J., Sharkansky, E. J, Read, J. P., Dawson, R., Martin, J. A., & Ouimette, P. C. (1998). Sexual harassment and assault as predictors of PTSD symptomatology among U.S. female Persian Gulf War military personnel. *Journal of Interpersonal Violence, 13,* 40–58.

Woodman, C. L., Noyes, R., Black, D. W., Schlosser, S., & Yagla, S. J. (1999). A 5-year follow-up study of generalized anxiety disorder and panic disorder. *Journal of Nervous and Mental Disease, 187,* 3–10.

Woody, S., Steketee, G., & Chambless, D.L. (1995). The reliability of the Yale-Brown Obsessive-Compulsive Scale. *Behavior Research and Therapy, 33,* 597–605.

Yamamoto, J., Fung, D., Lo, S., & Reece, S. (1979). Psychopharmacology for Asian Americans and Pacific Islanders. *Psychopharmacology Bulletin, 15,* 29–31.

Yehuda, R. (2000). Biology of posttraumatic stress disorder. *Journal of Clinical Psychiatry, 61* (Suppl. 7), 14–21.

Zaider, T. I., & Heimberg, R. G. (2003). Non-pharmacologic treatments for social anxiety disorder. *Acta Psychiatrica Scandinavica, 108*(Suppl. 417), 72–85.

Zanarini, M. C., Skodol, A. E., Bender, D., Dolan, R., Sanislow, C., Schaefer, E., Morey, L. C., Grilo, C. M., Shea, M. T., McGlashan, T. H., & Gunderson, J. G. (2000). The Collaborative Longitudinal Personality Disorders Study: Reliability of Axis I and II diagnoses. *Journal of Personality Disorders, 14,* 291–299.

Zhang, W., Ross, J., & Davidson, J. R.T. (2004). Social anxiety disorder in callers to the Anxiety Disorders Association of America. *Depression and Anxiety, 20,* 101–107.

Ziegler, V. E., & Biggs, J. T. (1977). Tricyclic pasma levels. Effects of age, race, sex, and smoking. *Journal of the American Medical Association, 14,* 67–69.

Zisook, S., Chentsova-Dutton, Y. E., Smith-Vaniz, A., Kline, N. A., Ellenor, G. L., Kodsi, A. B., & Gillin, J. C. (2000). Nefazodone in patients with treatment-refractory posttraumatic stress disorder. *Journal of Clinical Psychiatry, 61,* 203–208.

Zohar, J., Mueller, E. A., Insel, T. R., Zohar-Kadouch, R. C., & Murphy, D. L. (1987). Serotonergic responsively in obsessive-compulsive disorder. Comparison of patients and healthy controls. *Archives of General Psychiatry, 44,* 964–951.

CHAPTER 12

Somatoform Disorders

LAURENCE J. KIRMAYER AND KARL J. LOOPER

T he somatoform disorders are a group of problems in which people suffer from somatic symptoms or worry about bodily illness or deformity that cannot be accounted for by an organic medical condition or another psychiatric disorder such as depression or anxiety. Although psychosomatic diseases are no longer recognized as distinct disorders—since psychological and behavioral factors may affect any medical condition—the somatoform disorders retain the implication of being wholly or predominantly caused by psychological processes that influence symptom perception and illness behavior. As we shall see, in some cases this presumption may be unwarranted.

The *DSM-IV* category of somatoform disorders emerged out of earlier notions of hysteria (Hyler & Spitzer, 1978) and includes seven related disorders: *somatization disorder* (formerly Briquet's syndrome or hysteria); *conversion disorder; pain disorder* (formerly psychogenic or somatoform pain disorder); *hypochondriasis; body dysmorphic disorder;* and two residual categories for patients who do not meet full criteria for any of the previously mentioned disorders, *undifferentiated somatoform disorder* and *somatoform disorder not otherwise specified.*

Despite many conceptual problems, the somatoform disorders survive as a set of diagnoses in the *DSM-IV* largely because of their relevance to Western health care systems, where patients with medically unexplained somatic symptoms and illness worry present a common and costly clinical problem (Barsky, Orav, & Bates, 2005). The diagnosis of a somatoform disorder serves to label and assign responsibility for patients who would otherwise fall through the cracks of a diagnostic system increasingly oriented around laboratory tests and biological treatments for specific pathophysiology.

The diagnostic category of somatoform disorders reproduces two fundamental dualisms that are deeply embedded in Western medicine, health psychology, and indeed, in the everyday concept of the person (Kirmayer, 1988). The first is that mind and body are distinct realms, so there is something noteworthy or even exceptional about people who express problems in somatic terms that a clinician

410

would situate in the psychological or social realm. The second is that what is physical is somehow more real, more substantial, and ultimately more legitimate as illness than what is purely psychological. Somatoform disorders emerge from this dualistic conception, contribute to it, and, in consequence, are part and parcel of social processes that challenge the legitimacy and reality of people's suffering. The obverse of somatization might be considered psychologization: the tendency to attribute to psychological factors symptoms that others see as fundamentally somatic in nature. Many mental health practitioners tend to be psychologizers, confidently attributing somatic distress to psychological conflicts, personality traits, or social stressors even when physiological explanations are available (Kirmayer, 2000).

Keeping in mind this cultural construction of the category, in this chapter we will review what is known about the somatoform disorders. We will argue that, just as the notion of "psychophysiological disorder" has been replaced by that of "psychological factors affecting physical condition"—a shift from a categorical, disorder-based scheme to one of diagnosing specific clinical situations—so too should the somatoform disorders be reconceptualized as symptoms or patterns of illness behavior that interact with other medical and psychiatric conditions. As illness behavior, somatoform disorders can be best typified and understood in terms of dimensions rather than categories, processes rather than symptoms and signs, and social contexts rather than isolated behaviors. We think this dimensional and contextual approach to somatization not only fits the research data better than the individual psychopathology-oriented perspective, it also has useful implications for clinical assessment and treatment. Rethinking the category of somatoform disorders from a social and cultural perspective will allow us to avoid some of the negative attitudes and stigmatization that plague patients who receive these diagnoses (Kirmayer, 1999).

DESCRIPTION OF THE DISORDERS

The *DSM-IV* somatoform disorders share two features: (1) They involve predominately somatic symptoms or bodily preoccupation, and (2) the focus on the body cannot be fully explained by any known medical disease or substance use. In addition to these features, the diagnostic criteria generally stipulate that symptoms are not caused by faking or malingering or by another psychiatric disorder. Although not a specific diagnostic criterion for each diagnosis, the use of a somatoform diagnosis to describe a patient's condition reflects the clinician's assessment that psychological factors are a large contributor to the symptom's onset, severity, and duration. To warrant diagnosis, these symptoms must result in significant distress, medical help seeking, impairment of functioning in work or other social roles, or any combination of these.

Somatization disorder (SD) is characterized by a pattern of multiple somatic symptoms recurring over a period of several years. Criterion A stipulates that symptoms must begin before age 30 and result in medical help seeking or lead to significant social or occupational impairment. Based on clinical reports and a field trial, *DSM-IV* has simplified the B criteria found in *DSM-III-R* to require four different types of symptoms: (1) a history of pain related to at least four different anatomical sites or functions, (2) a history of at least two gastrointestinal symptoms other than pain (e.g., nausea, bloating, vomiting other than during pregnancy, diarrhea or multiple food intolerance), (3) at least one sexual or reproductive symptom other than pain, and (4) at least one pseudoneurological (conversion) symptom not related to pain (American Psychiatric Association, 1994). A third criterion (C) requires either that there be no medical condition that can fully explain the symptoms or that the distress and disability are in excess of what can be medically explained. The simplified *DSM-IV* criteria show high concordance with the *DSM-III* and *DSM-III-R* diagnostic criteria based on longer explicit symptom lists (Yutsy et al., 1995).

Undifferentiated somatoform disorder is a broad category that includes patients who do not reach criteria for SD because their symptoms are fewer in number or less severe (Katon et al., 1991). Undifferentiated SD simply requires one or more medically unexplained physical complaints lasting at least 6 months and resulting in clinically significant distress or impairment of functioning. This category includes specific constellations of somatic symptoms for which there is no medical explanation. These syndromes are collectively referred to as functional somatic syndromes and are found in most areas of medicine (see Table 12.1). Examples include neurasthenia or chronic fatigue syndrome, fibromyalgia, and irritable bowel syndrome.

The status of the common functional somatic syndromes remains ambiguous in *DSM-IV* because of continuing controversy over the validity of medical diagnoses (Barsky & Borus, 1999; Wessely et al., 1999). Thus, irritable bowel syndrome (abdominal symptoms such as pain, bloating, and distension associated with alteration of bowel habits) is presumed to reflect disturbed gut motility and is widely viewed as a valid medical disorder. Fibromyalgia syndrome (widespread bodily pain with tenderness at specific anatomical sites called tender points) has steadily gained acceptance as a discrete rheumatologic disease, while chronic fatigue syndrome (the persistence of debilitating fatigue for at least 6 months associated with symptoms of malaise) continues to be a contested diagnosis. In spite of many years of medical research, and the growing acceptance of some functional somatic syndromes as medical diagnoses, their underlying organic pathology has not been demonstrated. The pressure to label these syndromes as medical diseases and to identify underlying medical causes is driven as much by patient groups and the popular media as it is by the process of scientific development and the medical community (Barsky & Borus, 1999). This may reflect the greater acceptance of medical diagnoses over psychological or ambiguous diagnoses and the resulting desire to avoid stigmatizing labels (Raguram et al., 1996). For these and other functional somatic syndromes, the diagnostic process requires excluding other organic medical explanations, and inferring the relevance of psychological mechanisms. Since this process of exclusion is never complete, uncertainty about diagnosis remains. Indeed, uncertainty about diagnosis, and the self-doubt and social ambiguity that ensue, are central to patients' experience of somatoform disorders.

Conversion disorder involves one or more symptoms that affect the voluntary motor or sensory systems and that mimic a neurological or other medical condition. The diagnostic criteria stipulate that psychological factors (i.e., conflicts or other stressors) are judged to be associated with the symptom because they antecede its onset or exacerbation. Conversion disorder may be subtyped as *with motor symptom or deficit* (e.g., paralyses, ataxia, aphonia, difficulty swallowing or globus hystericus [lump in throat]), *with sensory symptom or deficit* (e.g., paresthesias, diplopia, blindness, deafness, or hallucinations), *with seizures or convulsions* (pseudoepilepsy), or *with mixed presentation*.

Table 12.1
Symptoms and Syndromes of Uncertain Etiology in Medical Specialties

Ear, nose, and throat

Burning tongue or mouth	(Van Houdenhove & Joostens, 1995)
Intractable sneezing	(Fochtmann, 1995)
Stridor	(Lacy & McManis, 1994)
Tinnitus	(Sullivan et al., 1988)

Cardiology

Chest pain with normal angiogram	(Eifert, 1991)

Endocrinology

Pseudocyesis	(Starkman et al., 1985)

Gastroenterology

Dysphagia (difficulty swallowing)	(Kim et al., 1996)
Irritable bowel	(Thompson & Pigeon-Reesor, 1990)
Nonulcer dyspepsia	(Wilhelmsen, Haug, Ursin, & Berstad, 1995)

Gynecology

Chronic pelvic pain	(Walker et al., 1988)
Dysmenorrhea	(Whitehead et al., 1986)
Dyspareunia	(Meana & Binik, 1994)
Hyperemesis gravidarum	(Katon, Ries, Bokan, & Kleinman, 1980)
Premenstrual tension	(Kuczmierczyk, Labrum, & Johnson, 1995)
Vaginismus	
Vulvidynia	(McKay & Farrington, 1995)

Infectious disease and immunology

Chronic fatigue	(Abbey & Garfinkel, 1991)
Environmental sensitivity	(Göthe, Molin, & Nilsson, 1995)
Multiple or "total" allergy	(Simon, Katon, & Sparks, 1990)

Neurology

Conversion	(Toone, 1990)
Pseudoseizures	(Savard, 1990)
Paralysis	(Fishbain & Goldberg, 1991)
Paresthesias	
Sensory loss	(Rada, Meyer, & Kellner, 1978)
Dizziness	(O'Connor, Hallam, Beyts, & Hinclife, 1988)
Headache	(Blanchard, 1992)
Postconcussion syndrome	(Lishman, 1988)
Syncope	(Kapoor, Fortunato, Hanusa, & Schulberg, 1995)

(continued)

Table 12.1 *(Continued)*

Pulmonology	
Dyspnea (shortness of breath)	(Bass, 1992)
Rheumatology	
Fibromyalgia	(Bennett, 1981)
Myofascial pain syndromes	(Merskey, 1993)
Repetitive strain injury	(Sinclair, 1988)
Urology	
Interstitial cystitis	(Ratliff, Klutke, & McDougall, 1994)

Pain disorder involves any clinically significant pain that causes distress or impaired functioning for which psychological factors are judged to have an important role in the onset, severity, exacerbation, or maintenance of the pain. Pain due to mood, anxiety, or psychotic disorders and dyspareunia (painful intercourse in women) are specifically excluded from the category. Pain disorder is subtyped as associated exclusively with psychological factors or with both psychological factors and a medical condition. In each case it may be acute or chronic. If no psychological factors are associated with the pain, it is not given a somatoform diagnosis.

Hypochondriasis is characterized by at least 6 months of preoccupation with fears of having, or the idea that one has, a serious disease based on the person's misinterpretation of bodily symptoms. This preoccupation, fear, or idea must persist despite appropriate medical evaluation and reassurance. Hypochondriasis is distinguished from delusional disorder and other somatoform and anxiety disorders. If the person generally does not recognize the excessive or unreasonable nature of their illness worry but the disease conviction does not reach delusional intensity, the diagnosis may be qualified as with poor insight.

Body dysmorphic disorder (BDD) involves a preoccupation with an imagined defect in appearance or, if a mild physical anomaly is present, a preoccupation markedly in excess of what is reasonable or appropriate. Dissatisfaction with overall body shape and anorexia nervosa are explicitly excluded.

Somatoform disorder not otherwise specified is a residual category for people with clusters of symptoms that do not meet full criteria for any specific somatoform disorder. The illustrative examples given in *DSM-IV* are (1) pseudocyesis (hysterical pregnancy), (2) nonpsychotic hypochondriacal symptoms of less than 6 months' duration (i.e., acute or transient hypochondriacal worry), and (3) unexplained physical symptoms of less than 6 months' duration.

The International Classification of Diseases (*ICD-10*; World Health Organization [WHO], 1992) uses a very similar nosology. One distinction is that it classifies conversion as a dissociative disorder in recognition of the mechanism through which the symptoms may arise. Dissociation refers to the disruption of the usual integration of motor and sensory function with awareness and conscious control. The *ICD-10* also has the additional category of somatoform autonomic dysfunction, which involves psychogenic bodily symptoms in organs regulated by the autonomic nervous system. These autonomic syndromes are subdivided by system into heart and cardiovascular (e.g., cardiac neurosis), upper gastrointestinal tract (functional dyspepsia, aerophagia), lower gastrointestinal tract (irritable bowel syndrome), respiratory system (psychogenic hyperventilation, hiccup, cough), genitourinary system (frequent micturation, dysuria), and other organ or system. *ICD-10* also includes neurasthenia (chronic mental or physical fatigue, or both) as a distinct diagnosis under the rubric of other neurotic disorders; many isolated functional somatic symptoms and culture-related somatic syndromes would also be classified under this rubric. To a greater degree than *DSM-IV*, the *ICD* criteria conflate symptoms and somatic preoccupation, thus making hypochondriacal anxiety more closely related to functional symptoms.

EPIDEMIOLOGY

Defining and measuring somatoform disorders is particularly challenging. The diagnoses are based on the absence of medical pathology, which in many cases is very difficult to demonstrate, and standards of medical assessment vary widely depending on geography and clinical setting. Reporting the prevalence of somatoform disorders is also complicated by the task of defining meaningful clinical syndromes, particularly when the symptoms (when present in mild severity) are part of the daily physical experience of healthy individuals. This broad spectrum of severity is a recurring issue in the epidemiological literature on somatoform disorders. In their less severe forms somatoform disorders tend to be very common, whereas when the more restrictive diagnostic criteria are applied they are quite uncommon. Meanwhile the middle ground of the severity spectrum is poorly characterized but remains a common focus of clinical care (Creed & Barksy, 2004).

Somatoform disorders constitute the single most frequent class of problem in primary care medicine. Medically unexplained symptoms—especially pain, fatigue, and generalized malaise—comprise from 25% to 60% of family medicine practice visits (Barsky & Borus, 1995; Katon & Walker, 1998; Kirkwood et al., 1982). A study of patients presenting with common physical symptoms to a general medical clinic found that only 16% could be identified as having a clear medical origin, whereas the large majority of cases remained "medically unexplained" (Kroenke & Mangelsdorff, 1989). There are also a large number of medically unexplained syndromes, or constellations of physical symptoms that tend to co-occur (see Table 12.1). Every medical specialty has its own collection of idiopathic (unexplained) or functional somatic syndromes that overlap to varying degrees in clinical presentation and associated characteristics. The relationship among these syndromes remains controversial, with evidence for a general tendency to experience high levels of somatic distress as well as a variety of specific functional syndromes (Robbins, Kirmayer & Hemami, 1997; Wessely, Nimnuan, & Sharpe, 1999). In some cases, patients with multiple symptoms may be given different diagnoses by medical specialists focused on only one aspect of their distress. These syndromes occupy a large portion of clinicians' time and effort and account for substantial health care costs. Still, patients who present to the clinic with somatoform disorders represent a fraction of those in the general population with functional somatic symptoms.

Symptoms relating to fatigue or to the gastrointestinal or musculoskeletal systems are common experiences and overlap with what is considered normal physiological functions that are a part of daily experience. For example, approximately 54% of individuals surveyed from a community population responded that they were troubled by at least one abdominal symptom in the previous 3 months (Agreus,

Svardsudd, Nyren, & Tibbin, 1994). Similarly, 18% of individuals in a community setting reported persistent fatigue of 6 months or longer, and this was associated with psychological distress (Pawlikowska et al., 1994). Many people cope with these problems without medical help. Patients who do come to the clinic often are prompted by coexisting problems like depression, anxiety, or life stresses that may intensify symptoms and impair coping. Studies then find much higher rates of psychiatric comorbidity among patients with somatoform disorders in clinical settings compared to community samples. This comorbidity may partially reflect the cumulative effect of multiple problems on help seeking rather than an intrinsic connection between the mood and anxiety disorders and common functional symptoms. This tendency for clinical studies to overestimate the strength of the association in the general population (a form of what is called Berkson's bias in epidemiology) points to the need for community studies to establish the causes of somatoform disorders. Unfortunately, community epidemiological studies are hampered by the necessity for medical evaluation to rule out organic explanations before the diagnosis of somatoform disorders can be made with confidence.

Several epidemiological studies have assessed the prevalence of somatization disorder, which is perhaps the most severe and persistent of somatoform disorders. The Epidemiologic Catchment Area (ECA) studies in the United States assessed the prevalence of SD in the general population (Robins & Regier, 1991), using the Diagnostic Interview Schedule, a structured interview that lists 38 somatic symptoms and establishes the severity and lack of medical explanation for each symptom. The prevalence of SD varied from 0% to 0.44% across the five ECA sites, with a mean prevalence of 0.13% (Swartz, Landerman, George, Blazer, & Escobar, 1991). Another large community population study assessed the prevalence of SD using the Composite International Diagnostic Inventory, a structured diagnostic interview for establishing both *DSM-IV* and *ICD-10* diagnoses (WHO, 1992). In this study, SD was diagnosed in only one of 4,075 participants (Grabe et al., 2003). Other studies of community populations of SD have also identified only small numbers of individuals meeting diagnostic criteria, with rates varying from 0.03% to 0.84% (Creed & Barsky, 2004).

SD is more common among women than men, with a ratio of approximately 10:1 in the ECA study and 5:1 in the study by Rief and colleagues (Reif, Hessel, & Braehler, 2001). Prevalence rates also varied across ethnic groups in the ECA study, ranging from 0.08% of Hispanics to 0.1% of non-Hispanic Whites and 0.45% of Blacks. All participants with SD also met criteria for at least one other psychiatric disorder, including phobias (in 69% of SD individuals), major depression (55%), panic disorder (38%), alcohol abuse (23%), schizophrenia (21%), and dysthymia (19%). People with SD in the ECA study were equally divided among those with onset of SD before or after a coexisting psychiatric disorder, implying that SD cannot be understood as simply caused by an underlying affective or anxiety disorder. However, the development of major depression tended to follow SD, while the development of panic disorder was more closely associated with the onset of SD, suggesting that it may be implicated in the evolution of SD, possibly by increasing health anxiety.

SD has also been investigated in primary care settings. The WHO Study of Mental Illness in Primary Care (Gureje, Simon, Ustun, & Goldberg, 1997) surveyed 5,438 patients drawn from primary care clinics in 14 countries, using the Composite International Diagnostic Inventory (CIDI; WHO, 1992). The study found that SD was relatively uncommon, ranging from 0.1% to 3.0% in 13 of 15 sites. The prevalence rates were much higher in two South American sites, which may be due to cultural differences in symptom reporting, but no other geographical differences were reported. The mean age of patients diagnosed with SD was 43.3 years. Female gender, older age, and lower education were associated with the diagnosis, but no patterns of cultural differences (other than in the two South American sites) were observed. Somatizing patients reported more disease burden, negative health perception, higher rates of comorbid depression and generalized anxiety disorder, and greater occupational and social disability.

Most patients presenting to physicians with unexplained physical symptoms do not meet the full criteria for SD and fall into the category of undifferentiated somatoform disorder. Common medically unexplained symptoms involve pain in various parts of the body (head, back, chest, abdomen, joints), fatigue, dizziness, palpitations, shortness of breath, insomnia, numbness, bloating, and nausea (Kroenke & Price, 1993; Rief et al., 2001; Simon, Gater, Kisely, & Piccinelly, 1996). Although few studies have explicitly addressed the epidemiology of undifferentiated somatoform disorder, one study found that almost 20% of respondents from a general population survey reported the persistence of a distressing physical symptom for at least 6 months (Grabe et al., 2003). Only 1.3% in this study reported a severe impairment in their life as a result of a persistent physical symptom.

Numerous surveys have examined alternative criteria for subthreshold somatization in which individuals have significant unexplained physical distress but do not meet the complete criteria for SD. Escobar and colleagues (Escobar, Rubio-Stipec, Canino, & Karno, 1989) proposed an abridged somatization syndrome (SS) that involves a lifetime occurrence of four medically unexplained symptoms for men and six for women. SS approximates the combined prevalence of undifferentiated somatoform disorder and somatoform disorder NOS. In two large community samples from Los Angeles and Puerto Rico, the lifetime rate of SS identified by these criteria was 11.6%, with 4% of the sample having active SS based on symptoms within the past year. Other surveys in the general population have reported rates of SS from 4.4% to 19% (Creed & Barsky, 2004). In the primary care setting, the same criteria for abridged SD yield prevalences from 7.3% to 35% (Creed & Barsky, 2004).

As an alternative to the proposal of an abridged SS based on the lifetime occurrence of symptoms listed in the Diagnostic Interview Schedule, Kroenke et al. (1997) proposed multisomatoform disorder (MSD), which requires three or more currently bothersome unexplained physical complaints from a symptom checklist and a history of chronic somatization. In a primary care study of almost 3,000 patients, 19% met criteria for MSD, compared to 23% for abridged SD and 5.4% for full SD (Dickinson et al., 2003).

The classical presentations of conversion disorder, including paralysis and sensory loss (e.g., so-called hysterical blindness or deafness), are relatively uncommon in Western North American primary care settings; as a result, most studies have relied on clinical samples of patients referred to psychiatry or neurology (Akagi & House, 2001). The prevalence of conversion disorder among psychiatric patients is reported to be in the range of 0.87% to 7% (Guze, Woodruff, & Clayton, 1971; Stefansson, Messina, & Meyerowitz, 1976), and 1% to 9 % among neurology patients (Smith, Clarke, Handrinos, Dunsis, & McKenzie, 2000; Toone, 1990). Studies of community populations have reported the point prevalence to be 33 and 55 per 100,000 (Singh & Lee, 1997; Watts, Cawte, & Kuenssberg, 1964) and yearly prevalence of 0.3% and 0.7% (Faravelli et al., 1997; Nandi et al., 1980). Although the dramatic nature of many conversion symptoms ensures they come to medical attention, referral samples may nonetheless underestimate both community and primary care prevalence. In general, conversion symptoms are thought to be more common in rural regions, and in those of lower socioeconomic class and with less formal Western-style education, although elevated rates have also been found in some urban populations (Swartz, Landerman, Blazer, & George, 1989). Cultural differences are clearly important and may explain elevated rates and specific symptoms reported in various parts of the world (Kirmayer & Santhanam, 2001). Several authors have described a decline in the prevalence of conversion disorder in Britain and the United States over the last half century (Leff, 1988). However, since most studies are based on referral populations, it remains unclear to what extent this apparent decrease simply represents changes in symptoms and patterns of help seeking (Akagi & House, 2001).

The prevalence of hypochondriasis in the community population is not well established, with rates varying from 0.02% to 7.7% (Creed & Barsky, 2004). These differences may be due to the recruitment of patients through primary care registries (Faravelli et al., 1997), less stringent diagnostic criteria (Rief et al., 2001), and other methodological issues. Illness phobia, reported in 5% of subjects in a community survey (Noyes et al., 2000), is distinguished from hypochondriacal fear in that the individual has a fear or discomfort when exposed to thoughts of illness without necessarily having the fear of being ill themselves.

The prevalence of hypochondriasis in primary care patients was assessed by a large multinational study carried out by the WHO (Gureje et al., 1997). They found the full disorder to be relatively uncommon, affecting 0.8% of the sample, and reported a less restrictively defined syndrome in 2.2%. Other studies have identified clinically relevant levels of hypochondriacal symptoms in 4% to 8% of primary care patients (Barsky, Wyshak, Klerman, & Latham, 1990; Kirmayer & Robbins, 1991b). Patients with hypochondriasis have high rates of other Axis I disorders, in particular, mood and anxiety disorders (Barsky, Wyshak & Klerman, 1992; Gureje et al., 1997). Studies of both clinical and community samples demonstrate that hypochondriasis is associated with psychological distress, help seeking, and impaired functioning (Barsky, Wyshak, Klerman, & Latham, 1990; Gureje et al., 1997; Looper & Kirmayer, 2001; Simon, Gureje, & Claudio, 2001).

The epidemiology of pain disorder has not been well studied. One community survey reported the prevalence of pain disorder as 0.6% in the general population. Other reports indicate that 15% to 33% of the community population between the ages of 25 and 74 reported some form of sustained musculoskeletal pain (Magni, Caldieron, Rigatti-Luchini, & Merskey, 1990; Magni, Marchetti, Moreschi, Merskey, & Rigatti-Luchini, 1993), and up to 10% to 15% of adults in the United States have some degree of work disability from back pain alone (Von Korff, Dworkin, LeResche, & Kruger, 1990). The discrepancy between these findings and the relatively low rate reported for somatoform pain disorder may be due to the diagnostic criteria that require psychological factors to be clearly associated with the onset, course, or outcome of the pain symptom for the diagnosis to be made.

The prevalence of BDD has been reported by two independent studies to be 0.7% in the community (Faravelli et al., 1997; Otto, Wilhelm, Cohen, & Harlow, 2001). This may be an underestimate because patients are reluctant to acknowledge their symptoms and to seek psychological or psychiatric treatment (Cororve & Gleaves, 2001). Although the rate of BDD in clinical samples has not been thoroughly assessed, one would expect it to be considerably higher in medical specialties such as dermatology and plastic surgery, where patients with BDD tend to seek help to correct what they perceive as physical abnormalities. The broader issue of body image concerns and preoccupations may apply to a large proportion of the population as seen in two studies of college students that found similar rates of about 28% (Bohne, Keuthen, Wilhelm, Deckersbach, & Jenike, 2002; Fitts, Gibson, Redding, & Deister, 1989). The focus of concern in BDD is usually an aspect of the face or head but may involve any area of the body, multiple body parts, or the overall shape and size of the body (Phillips, McElroy, Keck, Pope, & Hudson, 1993). Mood, anxiety, and personality disorders are common comorbid diagnoses in patients with BDD (Veale et al., 1996). BDD has been associated with obsessive-compulsive disorder (Phillips et al., 1993; Simeon, Hollander, Stein, Cohen, & Aronowitz, 1995), but the two are distinguished by the restricted focus of concern regarding bodily appearance in BDD. The degree of insight into the excessive concern of patients with BDD is variable and includes an extreme at which the additional diagnosis of delusional disorder may be applied (Phillips & McElroy, 1993). Patients with BDD tend not to present spontaneously to mental health professionals but are occasionally referred by primary care physicians, surgeons, and specialists who identify excessive distress and treatment for relatively minor physical problems.

Somatoform disorder NOS is an ill-defined residual category intended to identify clinically relevant cases that do not meet the criteria of the other somatoform diagnoses. No global prevalence can be given for this diagnosis, because the vague diagnostic criteria collect a vast array of disparate symptoms and syndromes. One example is a transient form of hypochondriasis that tends to resolve spontaneously or with a doctor's reassurance, which is found in approximately 4% of primary care patients (Barsky, Cleary, Sarnie, & Klerman, 1993; Robbins & Kirmayer, 1996). Other types of problems categorized as somatoform disorder NOS may be rare, such as pseudocyesis (a persistent false conviction of being pregnant), or very common, as in various functional somatic symptoms.

CLINICAL PICTURE

The clinical picture of the somatoform disorders varies with the social and cultural background of patients, their specific somatic symptoms, and the clinical context in which patients are seen. Most patients with somatoform disorders seek medical care and are referred to mental health practitioners when medical diagnosis and treatment prove ineffective. As a result of this failure of conventional treatment, patients may seek many alternative forms of care (Kirmayer, 1999). By the time the mental health practitioner sees these patients, they may be frustrated and angry about the care they have received. Patients are often made to feel its "all in their heads." Clinicians, in turn, feel frustrated that ordinary reassurances or symptomatic treatments have been ineffective. The mutual disappointment and blaming of patient and physician sometimes erupt into hostility. In this context, it is easy for the consultant to misattribute anxious, hostile, or paranoid thoughts and behavior in the patient to personality traits when such behavior is, at least in part, a response to circumstances.

SOMATIZATION DISORDER

Though the age of onset of SD is required to be before age 30 by definition, in the ECA study 55% of participants reported an onset before age 15 (Swartz, 1991,

p. 231). This points to a development of SD in early adolescence or childhood. The most common symptoms in SD include chest pain, palpitations, abdominal bloating, depressed feelings, dizziness, weakness, quitting work because of poor health, shortness of breath without exertion, headache, and fatigue (Smith, Monson, & Ray, 1986b). This list, however, does not capture the richness of patients' language of suffering, as seen in Case Study 1.

In addition to their somatic complaints, patients with SD commonly experience the gamut of psychological symptoms and often meet criteria for mood and anxiety disorders (Wetzel, Guze, Cloninger, & Martin, 1994). It is misleading, therefore, to view SD patients as having predominately somatic problems. More than 70% of patients with SD also meet criteria for personality disorder (Stern, Murphy, & Bass, 1993). Although SD was classically related to histrionic personality (Slavney, 1990), the most commonly associated personality disorders are avoidant, paranoid, self-defeating, and obsessive-compulsive (Smith, Golding, Kashner, & Rost, 1991).

UNDIFFERENTIATED SOMATOFORM DISORDER

The number and diversity of functional somatic symptoms may identify subgroups of patients with undifferentiated somatoform disorder: (1) a diversiform group reports many different symptoms in different systems, particularly pain complaints that approximate SD; and (2) an asthenic group that reports fewer and less diverse

---

Case Study 1

A 31-year-old man was referred to a behavioral medicine clinic by an internist for treatment of abdominal pain. He arrived with a carefully written list of his current symptoms ranked by the degree of distress they caused him (from most to least): "constant ringing in the ears; dizziness/light-headedness; headaches with numbness in the face, squeezing at the temples with bands of pressure and fuzzy head; pain in the lower right abdomen; jerking sensations in the throat, chest, and stomach; rapid, steady throbbing throughout the entire body; pains in the middle back, left shoulder, and arm; numbness in the left forearm and hand (right forearm and hand less often); spots before eyes—occasionally; hard-to-breathe feeling; rapid, irregular heartbeat and pounding slow heartbeat, both usually accompanied by nausea and lasting several hours." He denied any personal or emotional problems and said that all was well with his work and home life, save that his wife and daughter were upset that his many illnesses prevented them from ever having a family vacation. Treatment focused on developing coping strategies for the four most distressing symptoms with the goal of his being able to take a vacation with his family. He was able to accomplish this after six sessions of cognitive-behavioral therapy with hypnosis for relaxation and symptom management. Three months later, he went to another hospital's emergency room, where his recurrent abdominal pain was diagnosed as irritable bowel syndrome. He felt relieved to have a "definite" diagnosis and embarked on a program to control his symptoms through dietary changes (Kirmayer, 1986).

symptoms, mainly fatigue, weakness, and minor illnesses such as upper respiratory tract infections, and resembles neurasthenia or chronic fatigue syndrome (Bohman, Cloninger, von Knorring, & Sigvardsson, 1984; Cloninger, Sigvardsson, von Knorring, & Bohman, 1984; Sigvardsson, Bohman, von Knorring, & Cloninger, 1986). There is evidence for both discrete somatic syndromes, which are common and hence often co-occur, and a general tendency to report many somatic symptoms across diverse physiological systems due to the generalized effects of somatic amplification (Barsky & Borus, 1999; Deary, 1999; Wessely et al., 1999). In general, patients with isolated functional symptoms or functional somatic syndromes resemble patients with other medical disorders in having elevated rates of depression, anxiety, and other psychological problems that may be both contributors to and consequences of their somatic illness (Kirmayer & Robbins, 1991a).

CONVERSION DISORDER

Conversion disorder occurs across the life span and tends to affect women more frequently than men (Akagi & House, 2001). By definition, patients with conversion disorder have symptoms resembling those of a neurological disorder. The most common symptoms include gait disturbances; pseudoseizures; episodes of fainting (syncope) or loss of consciousness; muscle tremors, spasms, weakness, or paralysis; and sensory changes, including paresthesias or anesthesia, speech disturbances (aphonia), and visual disturbances (blindness, diplopia; Tomasson, Dent, & Coryell, 1991; Toone, 1990; Watson & Buranen, 1979a). Among the symptoms classically described as hysterical conversion, the main exception to these pseudoneurological symptoms is pseudocyesis (hysterical pregnancy) which, in *DSM-IV*, is classified as somatoform disorder NOS (Martin, 1996). Pseudocyesis may be associated with endocrine disturbances, which sets it apart from other conversion symptoms (Small, 1986; Starkman, Marshall, La Ferla, & Kelch, 1985).

Case Study 2

A 52-year-old woman presented to the general hospital emergency room with sudden-onset paralysis of her left arm and the inability to straighten her torso; she walked and sat bent over at the waist (a symptom termed *camptocormia*). She described the symptoms as having started abruptly while she was working at her typewriter in the office where she was employed as a secretary. She feared she had had a stroke. Initially, she could give no precipitating stressful event. On later questioning by her regular family physician, she revealed that she had discovered that morning that her employer had promoted a coworker with less seniority, with whom he was having an affair, to a more senior position. She recalled that she initially felt shocked, angry, and betrayed, but these feelings were forgotten when her alarming paralysis suddenly developed. She accepted an explanation from this trusted family physician that her symptoms were a stress reaction, and she connected the intensity of her reaction to her having witnessed the sexual abuse of a sibling when she was a child. Her symptoms gradually resolved over the next 2 weeks, with two sessions of counseling in her doctor's office to validate her feelings, identify other stressors, and plan an appropriate response to her predicament at work.

Although patients with conversion symptoms were classically described as blandly indifferent to their symptoms, showing *la belle indifférence,* clinical experience suggests they are more often concerned and distressed. This distress, however, may be mitigated by the intimation that there are other even more distressing recent events from which the conversion symptoms serve as a distraction. The form of conversion symptoms may have symbolic meaning in some situations but usually is more readily attributed to available models of illness (Slavney, 1994). For example, patients with epilepsy may develop pseudoseizures (Savard, 1990). About 70% of unilateral conversion symptoms affect the left side of the body (Axelrod, Noonan, & Atanacio, 1980).

HYPOCHONDRIASIS

Patients with hypochondriasis show varying degrees of concern, worry, fear, and preoccupation with the notion that they have an illness. They remain concerned or convinced that something is wrong despite medical reassurance. At times this conviction may reach near delusional intensity. More typically, patients have anxieties that they view as irrational but find they cannot rid themselves of bodily preoccupation, rumination, and catastrophizing thoughts.

Hypochondriacal fears commonly accompany depression and anxiety disorders but may arise and persist even when mood and other anxiety symptoms are not present (Noyes et al., 1994a and 1994b). Hypochondriacal preoccupation often has an obsessional quality and may occur with other symptoms of obsessive-compulsive disorder (Starcevic, 1990). Indeed, obsessive rumination may distinguish hypochondriasis from other milder and more prevalent forms of illness

---

Case Study 3

A 24-year-old man presented to the mental health clinic with depression and the persistent fear that he had cancer or another mortal illness. Since the age of 12, when he learned of the sudden death of a cousin, he had suffered from constant worries about his health. His parents had responded to his fears by taking him on frequent visits to a pediatrician, where his hyperventilation was misdiagnosed at first as asthma. He viewed himself as vulnerable to illness and was preoccupied with symptoms of weakness, malaise, and a chronically stuffy nose for which he had become dependent on decongestant spray. He described sporadic panic attacks, usually triggered by events that should have made him angry. During these attacks he feared that he would lose his mind or die of a heart attack. Afterward, he was left feeling still more worried that he had a physical illness. Over many sessions of cognitive-behavioral therapy, it became apparent that he misidentified the bodily concomitants of strong emotions like anger, fear, or even intense happiness as possible symptoms of illness. Learning to reattribute these somatic symptoms to specific emotions and to the effects of physiological arousal resolved his hypochondriacal worries but did not entirely eliminate his panic attacks.

worry (Fink et al., 2004). A sense of bodily vulnerability may be associated with more pervasive feelings of fragility of the self or with fears of loss of control.

Body Dysmorphic Disorder

Patients with BDD are preoccupied with the notion that some aspect of their body is misshapen and ugly. This bodily defect is imagined or grossly exaggerated. The most common complaints involve the face (e.g., wrinkles, complexion, facial hair, asymmetric or disproportionate features), hair, nose, and skin, but any body part can be the focus of preoccupation (Phillips, 2005). Patients engage in frequent checking in the mirror to monitor their so-called defect and may attempt to camouflage it, usually without success. They are convinced that others are reacting negatively to them, and they commonly have ideas or delusions of reference. They fear embarrassment and avoid social situations, sometimes to the point of being housebound. As a result, the condition may result in severe social disability.

In a series of 30 cases of BDD referred to psychiatry, all but two cases had mood disorders, mainly major depression (Phillips et al., 1993). Anxiety disorders were the next most common current and lifetime diagnoses, including 50% with social phobia and 37% with obsessive-compulsive disorder. Fully 77% had a history of psychotic symptoms either associated with a mood disorder (43%) or as a primary psychotic disorder (33%). Given the predominance of obsessive thinking and compulsive behaviors, BDD may be related to obsessive-compulsive disorder and respond to similar pharmacological and behavioral treatments (Hollander, Neville,

---

Case Study 4

A 34-year-old married mother of four was referred to the mental health clinic by a concerned friend. She complained of a 5-year history of increasing social isolation caused by an intense fear of offending others with her physical appearance. She believed that her nose had been gradually growing and her eyes shrinking in size, leading to such profound ugliness that no one could stand to look at her. She had isolated herself from neighbors and family. She shopped only in stores on the other side of town, where she would not encounter people who knew her. She parked her car outside her children's school but would not go inside to pick them up. She never left her home unless she had a specific errand to run.

She dated the onset of her "physical change" to the birth of her youngest child, at which time the family moved to a new city so that she could care for her elderly parents. Over the 3 months before she consulted the clinic, she had become increasingly distressed and hopeless about her appearance. When others reassured her that her appearance was, in fact, attractive, she thanked them for their kindness but was left completely unconvinced. She asked for therapy to be conducted by telephone so that the therapist would not be offended by her appearance and so that she would not have to travel in public to get to appointments.

Frenkel, Josephson, & Liebowitz, 1992). As with obsessive-compulsive disorder, BDD patients' symptoms range along a spectrum of severity from obsession to delusion (Phillips, Kim, & Hudson, 1995).

Somatic Presentations of Other Psychiatric Disorders

The *DSM-IV* somatoform disorders leave out a group of patients sometimes described as somatizing who have underlying psychiatric disorders (mainly depression, anxiety, or personality disorders but sometimes also psychotic disorders) but who make exclusively somatic clinical presentations. The majority of these patients are willing to acknowledge a psychosocial contribution to their distress provided it is not presented as an explanation that excludes somatic factors (Kirmayer, Robbins, Dworkind, & Yaffe, 1993). As a group, presenting somatizers tend to be less depressed than patients who psychologize, show less social dissatisfaction, have a more negative attitude toward mental illness, and are more likely to have been a medical inpatient (Bridges, Goldberg, Evams, & Sharpe, 1991). They make more normalizing and fewer psychologizing attributions for common somatic symptoms, are less introspective, and are less likely to seek help if they are anxious or depressed (Kirmayer & Robbins, 1996).

COURSE AND PROGNOSIS

There is wide variation in course, disability, and outcome across the somatoform disorders. Patients who meet the relatively stringent diagnostic criteria of SD or hypochondriasis have a more severe and chronic course of illness. However, the majority of patients with a somatoform disorder, and in particular those with fewer somatic symptoms of shorter duration, usually classified as undifferentiated or NOS, have a much better prognosis, improving either spontaneously or with relatively brief interventions. In general, psychiatric comorbidity is one of the most important factors contributing to chronicity for the range of somatoform disorders (Rief, Hiller, Geissner, & Fichter, 1995). Nevertheless, recent research demonstrates that cognitive-behavioral interventions can significantly reduce symptomatology, distress, disability, and excessive or inappropriate health care utilization (Looper & Kirmayer, 2002; Sharpe et al., 1996; Speckens et al., 1995). Psychopharmacological management of somatoform disorders has not been rigorously studied, although antidepressants have been reported to be effective in treating functional somatic syndromes (Kroenke et al., 2002).

SD is defined as a chronic condition and patients generally accrue the requisite number of symptoms over a period of several years. The ECA study found that of patients with a lifetime diagnosis of SD, fully 90% had symptoms in the past year, yielding a remission rate of less than 8% (Swartz et al., 1991, p. 227). This high rate of diagnostic stability was also found in a study in which patients were reassessed after 4.5 years of the original diagnosis (Kent et al., 1995). Patients with SD are liable to continue to experience multiple somatic symptoms in shifting functional systems. They are at risk for iatrogenic illness due to complications of invasive diagnostic procedures, and for unnecessary medication or surgery. In contrast, patients with subthreshold SD have a much better outcome. In one study, 76% improved, including 30% recovered after a mean of 15.2 months (Specken, Van Hemert, Bolk, Rooijmans, & Hengeveld, 1996).

For patients with SD, a simple intervention consisting of a consultation letter to the patient's primary care physician has been shown to significantly reduce expenditures for health care and improve health outcomes (Rost, Kashner, & Smith, 1994; Smith et al., 1986a). The letter includes information on the diagnosis of SD and suggestions for the frequency of scheduled visits, reduction of investigations of new symptoms, and avoidance of hospitalization and surgery unless clearly indicated. Similar benefits have been demonstrated for psychiatric consultations with primary care patients with undifferentiated somatoform disorder or subsyndromal somatization (Smith, Rost, & Kashner, 1995).

Bass and Benjamin (1993) have outlined a general approach to the clinical management of the chronic somatizing patient geared to general practitioners. They include the following strategies: (1) In the initial interview identify psychosocial issues but avoid direct confrontation, (2) provide unambiguous information about medical findings, (3) plan time for gradual discussion of psychosocial issues, (4) work out a problem list and negotiate an agenda with the patient, and (5) set limits for diagnostic investigations. Additional efforts at psychological support and reattribution training may further improve outcome (Kashner, Rost, Cohen, Anderson, & Smith, 1995; Lidbeck, 2003; McLeod, Budd, & McClelland, 1997; Speckens et al., 1995; Sumathipala, Hewege, Hanwella, & Mann, 2000).

Conversion disorder tends to be an acute, self-limited condition, with approximately 50% to 90% improved or recovered in studies that reassessed patients after 2 to 6 years (Binzer & Kullgren, 1998; Crimlisk et al., 1998; Kent et al., 1995). Conversion symptoms usually have an abrupt onset in relation to some acute stressor, cause substantial impairment, and resolve spontaneously or respond to a wide variety of suggestive therapeutics. Patients who progress to chronicity have less recent onset of symptoms, greater psychiatric comorbidity, intractable social circumstances, and a broader propensity to experience and report multiple somatic symptoms through which they eventually reach criteria for SD (Couprie, Wijdicks, Rooijmans, & van Gijn, 1995; Kent, Tomasson, & Coryell, 1995). Longitudinal studies of patients with conversion disorders have found that 10% to 50% are eventually diagnosed with an organic disease that may have accounted for their conversion symptoms (Cloninger, 1987; Slater, 1965; Watson & Buranen, 1979b); however, the results of recent studies are in the lower end of this range of outcomes (Binzer & Kullgren, 1998; Crimlisk et al., 1998; Kent et al., 1995). The development of SD was found in about 20% of patients with conversion disorder followed for 2 years in a general hospital (Kent et al., 1995; Tomasson et al., 1991). The link between conversion disorder and SD is overstated in *DSM-IV,* however, given that in the general population, sporadic conversion symptoms are much more common than SD. The few recent studies of the treatment of conversion disorder have emphasized cognitive-behavioral therapy, the use of physical rehabilitation methods, and the use of hypnosis (Halligan, Bass, & Marshall, 2001).

Although hypochondriasis is defined as a chronic condition, about 50% of patients with high levels of hypochondriacal worry in primary care have their anxiety at least temporarily resolved with standard reassurance and so have transient hypochondriasis (Barsky, Wyshak, & Klerman, 1990b). Medical illness or other life events may give rise to transient hypochondriasis (Barsky et al., 1993). Previous or coexisting psychiatric disorders, including Axis I disorders and personality disorders, predispose a person to the development of persistent hypochondriasis (Barsky, Wyshak, & Klerman, 1992; Robbins & Kirmayer, 1996). Psychoeducational and cognitive-behavioral approaches to reduce hypochondriacal anxiety can improve the prognosis in this group with persistent worry (Barsky, 1996; Warwick & Salkovskis, 1990). Similar results have been reported for patients with BDD (Rosen, Reiter, & Orosan, 1995b).

As noted previously, up to 33% of the adult population in the United States suffer from some form of chronic pain. An 8-year follow-up study suggests that about one-third of people with chronic musculoskeletal pain will recover while two-thirds continue to be symptomatic (Magni et al., 1993). Patients with multiple, anatomically unrelated pains differ from those with discrete, localized chronic pain in having greater psychiatric comorbidity. Data from the ECA study suggest the total number of pain complaints is more predictive of associated psychopathology and utilization of health care services than the specific location, duration, severity, or medical explanation of the pain complaints (Dworkin, Von Korff, & LeResche, 1990; Von Korff, Wagner, Dworkin, & Saunders, 1991). People with single pain complaints did not differ from those with no history of pain in rates of psychiatric disorders and health service utilization. Psychological factors contribute to the risk of acute pain becoming a chronic condition. In a study of patients with acute herpes zoster (shingles), patients who went on to develop chronic pain had higher state and trait anxiety, more depressive symptoms, lower life satisfaction, and greater disease conviction at the time of their initial assessment (Dworkin et al., 1992).

ETIOLOGICAL CONSIDERATIONS

Studies of somatoform disorders have considered the role of personality, psychodynamic, cognitive, and social factors in shaping symptom experience. In this section we will consider putative etiological factors in terms of temperamental differences, personality and psychiatric comorbidity, sensory-perceptual mechanisms, cognitive-evaluative processes, emotion suppression or inhibition, and social-interactional factors. Finally, we will discuss the role of specific development experiences including trauma and present an integrative model of somatization.

PERSONALITY AND PSYCHIATRIC COMORBIDITY

The tendency to experience high levels of both somatic symptoms and emotional distress may reflect underlying temperamental traits, particularly the trait that has been termed neuroticism or negative affectivity in factorial studies of the dimensions of personality (Pennebaker & Watson, 1991). Individuals high on negative affectivity are more prone to experience affective and anxiety disorders that give rise to somatic symptoms. Health anxiety and hypochondriacal worry are strongly associated with neuroticism (Cox, Borger, Asmundson, & Taylor, 2000). Lower levels of dysphoria may also give rise to significant somatic symptoms through physiological mechanisms like hyperventilation or sleep disturbance (Sharpe & Bass, 1992). Individuals with high levels of negative affectivity may also experience more frequent, intense, and distressing bodily sensations caused by the dysregulation of autonomic or pain control systems even in the absence of dysphoric mood.

The majority of patients with SD meet criteria for personality disorders (Stern et al., 1993). Indeed, it has been suggested that SD itself is best conceptualized as a personality disorder based on an interaction between temperamental traits of negative affectivity and family experiences modeling and reinforcing the sick role (Kirmayer, Robbins, & Paris, 1994). First-degree relatives of patients with SD have elevated rates of SD, antisocial personality disorder, major depression, and alcoholism (Cloninger, Martin, Guze, & Clayton, 1986). Cross-fostering adoption studies of SD provides evidence for both heritable pathophysiological mechanisms and family environment in somatization (Bohman et al., 1984; Sigvardsson et al., 1986).

In a classic paper, Engel (1959) introduced the notion of the "pain-prone personality," characterized by perfectionistic striving and minimization or denial of emotional distress. Blumer and Heilbronn (1982) later expanded this notion to include "ergomania" or "workaholism" and a familial tendency toward depression. Personality factors may play a role in aggravating pain, whatever its origins, but do not reliably distinguish patients with clear-cut medical explanations for the pain from those whose problems are more complicated and obscure. Turk and Melzack (1992) concluded that "the search for a 'pain prone personality'... or psychogenic pain has proved futile" (p. 9).

Fully two-thirds of people with major depressive disorder in primary care have chronic pain, and in about 25% of those with depression the pain is disabling (Arnow et al., 2006). Studies of clinical populations with pain show high levels of comorbid Axis I disorders. Depression is the most common diagnosis and is found in 25% to 50% of hospital patients with acute pain referred to psychiatric evaluation, and from 10% to 100% of patients with chronic pain (Blumer & Heilbronn, 1982; Romano & Turner, 1985). However, earlier claims that chronic pain was essentially a variant of major depressive disorder (Blumer & Heilbronn, 1982) have not been borne out by more recent studies showing that many chronic pain patients have little or no evidence of depressed mood and that major depression is somewhat more likely to be a consequence of chronic pain than an antecedent (Brown, 1990; Magni, Moreschi, Rigatti-Luchini, & Merskey, 1994; Thieme, Turk, & Flor, 2004). Specific types of pain may be associated with other specific psychiatric disorders; for example, up to one-third of patients with noncardiac chest pain have concurrent panic disorder (Beitman, Mukerji, Flaker, & Basha, 1988).

SOMATIC PERCEPTION, ATTENTION, AND AMPLIFICATION

One obvious potential cause of increased symptom reporting is sensory or perceptual sensitivity to bodily sensations. Sensitivity to specific body sensations may increase in individuals who suffer from chronic health problems affecting that part of the body; for example, patients with asthma may become more aware of experimentally induced changes in their breathing (Rietveld & Houtveen, 2004). There is some evidence for greater sensitivity to specific bodily sensations in patients with irritable bowel syndrome (Kwan, Diamant, Mikula, & Davis, 2005), functional dyspepsia (Jones, Roth, & Crowell, 2005), and some chronic pain syndromes (Wahlund, List, & Ohrbach, 2005). Individuals with somatoform disorders may be more sensitive to a range of sensations (Houtveen, Rietveld, & de Greus, 2003).

Mechanic and others have studied the effect of introspectiveness on the increased reporting of both psychological and somatic symptoms (Hansell & Mechanic, 1986; Mechanic, 1979). Individual differences in the tendency to focus attention on the self and on bodily sensations are associated with elevated symptom reporting in the laboratory and in epidemiological studies (Kolk, Hanewald, Schagen, & van Wijk, 2003; Pennebaker, 1982; Robbins & Kirmayer, 1986, 1991b). Whereas self-focused patients tend to report both somatic and psychological symptoms, patients who preferentially attend to the body may be more likely to report somatic rather than cognitive or emotional symptoms.

Barsky and Klerman (1983) introduced the notion of somatic amplification: a hypothesized tendency for individuals to experience bodily sensations as intense, noxious, and disturbing. Related concepts include augmenting-reducing and perceptual sensitivity. Amplification may involve sensory, perceptual, and cognitive-evaluative processes. Some individuals may selectively focus on and amplify the background level of everyday bodily discomfort (a sort of bodily "white noise") as well as the higher levels of distress that ordinarily accompany illness or injury, giving rise to more varied and intense symptom reports and hypochondriacal worry.

To test this hypothesis, Barsky and colleagues (1990a) developed the Somato-sensory Amplification Scale (SSAS), an 11-item self-report questionnaire with adequate internal consistency and test-retest reliability. Higher levels on the SSAS were found in hypochondriacal patients as well as in patients making frequent use of medical care (Barsky, 1992; Barsky, Cleary, & Klerman, 1992). Unfortunately, despite its name, the SSAS does not really tap underlying perceptual processes of amplification. It includes many symptom experience items that represent the outcome of hypochondriacal cognitions rather than a mediating process (Aronson, Barrett, & Quigly, 2001). There is a need for measures of amplification that tap specific cognitive and perceptual processes and for longitudinal studies to determine the direction of causality between amplification and symptom experience.

Though selective attention and preoccupation with the body may lead to amplified somatic sensations, conversion symptoms seem to involve a different deployment of attention in which the affected body part, function, or sensory system is selectively ignored. This form of selective inattention or alternate control is usually subsumed under the construct of dissociation (Kihlstrom, 1992). Evidence that conversion disorders are related to dissociative mechanisms comes from observations of their frequent occurrence in patients with dissociative identity disorder (Putnam, Guroff, Silberman, Barban, & Post, 1986), high levels of hypnotic susceptibility in patients with conversion symptoms (Bliss, 1984), the ability to create laboratory models of conversion symptoms with hypnosis (Sackeim, Nordlie, & Gur, 1979), and a dramatic therapeutic response to hypnosis (Williams, Spiegel, & Mostofsky, 1978).

Dissociative mechanisms may also contribute to other somatic symptoms to the extent that individuals high on hypnotizability or openness to absorbing experiences may be more likely to become intensely focused on and absorbed by bodily sensations. Wickramasekera (1995) has suggested that there are two groups of somatizing patients: one with high levels of hypnotizability and the tendency to be absorbed by their symptoms, and the other with unusually low levels of hypnotizability and the inability to block out noxious sensations. Brown (2004) suggested that in response to traumatic events some individuals may develop "rogue representations" that are dissociated from consciousness and that give rise to persistent somatic symptoms.

COGNITIVE EVALUATION, ATTRIBUTION, AND COPING

Attention is guided by cognitive schemas that indicate potential sources of threat (Cioffi, 1991; Lazarus & Folkman, 1984). Somatizers may be primed by preexisting schemas or beliefs about their own vulnerability to disease to interpret the generalized malaise and symptoms that accompany affective or anxiety disorders as indicating serious physical illness. The literature on hypochondriasis and abnormal illness behavior has demonstrated the role of worry, fear, disease conviction, and self-rated bodily sensitivity or intolerance to noxious stimuli as important correlates of somatic symptom reporting (Barsky, Goodson, Lane, & Cleary, 1988; Barsky & Klerman, 1983; Pilowsky, 1967). Hypochondriacal worry often accompanies depression and anxiety disorders and, when sufficiently intense, may overshadow other symptoms (Barsky, Wyshak, & Klerman, 1992).

A lack of effective coping with common bodily symptoms or illnesses may result in greater anxiety about the body, increased body focus, persistent symptoms, and hypochondriacal worry. Hypochondriacal college women (as indicated by high scores on the Minnesota Multiphasic Personality Inventory [MMPI] hypochondriasis scale) tend to spend more time on health-related pursuits than those who are less symptomatic (Karoly & Lecci, 1993). This preoccupation with efforts to assess and maintain one's health interacts with more specific thoughts linking bodily sensations to illness. Hypochondriacal patients are prone to catastrophizing thoughts in which they equate specific bodily sensations or events with the idea that they are sick (Salkovskis, 1989). For example, a patient may think, "This tightness in my chest is not normal. It's probably from my heart. Maybe I'm going to have a heart attack." These thoughts create more anxiety and focus attention on the chest area. Both the anxiety and the attentional focus may increase muscle tension in the chest wall, leading to more symptoms that, in turn, increase the conviction that one is ill. The more dire the symptom interpretation, the greater the anxiety, tension, and distress.

Somatic amplification affects both somatic and emotional distress and so cannot account for the denial of coexisting emotional problems found in some somatizing patients. The selective emphasis on somatic symptoms and explanations for distress may have more to do with attributional style, defense style, or structural factors influencing help seeking and stigmatization. An unwillingness or inability to attribute the bodily concomitants of emotional arousal or affective disorder to psychosocial causes may lead patients to present clinically with somatic symptoms while minimizing underlying emotional distress (Robbins & Kirmayer, 1986).

Robbins and Kirmayer (1991a) developed the Symptom Interpretation Questionnaire (SIQ), a self-report measure that asks respondents to rate the extent to which they would attribute common somatic symptoms to each of three types of hypothetical causes: *somatic* (physical disorder or disease); *psychological* (emotional distress or problem), and *normalizing* (environmental or other ordinary external event; e.g., "If I felt fatigued, I would probably think that it is because [1] I'm emotionally exhausted or discouraged; [2] I'm anemic or my blood is weak; or [3] I've been overexerting myself or not exercising enough"). Among family medicine patients, the SIQ has been found to predict somatizing or psychologizing clinical presentations of depression and anxiety (Kirmayer & Robbins, 1996; Robbins & Kirmayer, 1991a). Patients with psychiatric disorders are more likely to attribute common somatic symptoms to psychological causes on the SIQ (Wise & Mann, 1995). A subset of items on the SIQ predicted the tendency for primary care patients with fatigue associated with an acute viral illness to subsequently develop chronic fatigue (Cope, David, Pelosi, & Mann, 1994). Patients who are high-frequency users of medical care are less able to generate normalizing explanations for common somatic symptoms (Sensky, MacLeod & Rigby, 1993).

Bridges and colleagues (1991) found that patients who make somatized presentations of depression or anxiety in primary care have more hostile attitudes toward mental illness than those who make psychosocial presentations. Somatizers may live in familial or cultural contexts where mental illness is stigmatized. These negative attitudes toward mental illness extend to a greater hesitancy among somatizers to talk to a doctor about any emotional problem and a greater reluctance to seek specialty mental health care (Kirmayer & Robbins, 1996).

Attributions of distress to physical illness may also act to limit the dysphoria and loss of self-esteem that would otherwise result when distress is attributed to personal character or emotional weakness. Bridges and colleagues (1991) suggested that insisting on a physical illness explanation for symptoms and holding the doctor responsible for missing the correct organic diagnosis removes personal blame from the somatizer. The blame-avoidance function of somatization may explain why patients who make somatic presentations of depression or anxiety in primary care tend to report lower levels of dysphoria than do psychosocial presenters (Bridges et al., 1991; Powell, Dolan, & Wessely, 1990; Verhaak & Tijhuis, 1994).

The interaction between anxiety, attention, and attributions is demonstrated very clearly in the phenomenon of "medical students' disease" (Mechanic, 1972). A substantial proportion of medical students experience transient hypochondriasis. The pressures of study, sleep loss, and apprehension about examinations lead to anxiety. Inundated by information about pathophysiology, students scan their bodies and misinterpret benign sensations as signs and symptoms of disease. The hypochondriacal worry that results usually resolves when the stress of examinations passes and when students acquire additional information to clarify that their unusual sensations do not fit the pattern of any disease. To the extent that this is a useful model of transient hypochondriasis, what must be added to explain clinical hypochondriasis are the factors that lead to chronicity.

Emotion Suppression, Inhibition, and Denial

There is limited empirical support for an earlier generation of psychodynamic hypotheses about the relationship of intrapsychic conflict, personality, and defense mechanisms to somatization. Much of this literature assumed an either/or relationship between somatization and psychological-mindedness in which distress was either adequately cognized and expressed in symbolic terms through the language of psychology or suppressed, repressed, and converted into physiological distress. This either/or theory has not been borne out in large-scale epidemiological studies where somatic and emotional distress are found to be highly positively correlated rather than inversely correlated as psychodynamic theory might suggest (Simon & Von Korff, 1991). However, these epidemiological studies have not attempted to separate out a subgroup for whom emotional and somatic distress might be inversely correlated, nor can they deal with the possibility that self-reports are not accurate reflections of underlying distress or physiological disturbance. It is possible that epidemiological studies based on self-report questionnaires or lay interviewers incorrectly classify as healthy some people who deny both emotional distress and somatic symptoms (Shedler, Mayman, & Manis, 1993). Study of the consequences of this type of illusory mental health requires careful clinical assessments and measures of dysfunction that are independent of self-report.

A group of related concepts—including *repression-sensitization, alexithymia, levels of emotional awareness,* and *level of thinking*—involve the tendency to suppress emotional expression or the inability to cognitively elaborate emotional conflict. The relevance of these concepts for somatization derives from the theory that suppression or hypocognition of strong emotions will lead to more prolonged emotional arousal, which in turn may result in higher levels of somatic symptoms and distress (Pennebaker, 1995).

Some support for the notion of somatization versus verbalization as either/or phenomena comes from studies of repressive coping style (Schwartz, 1990). There is evidence that although individuals who are repressors initially report less emotional distress in response to an acute stressor, they show more prolonged levels of physiological arousal and increased depressive and somatic symptomatology over the long term (Bonanno & Singer, 1990). Similarly, suppressing or not telling one's story of stress or trauma may lead to persistent somatic symptoms. Conversely, telling one's story can relieve symptoms (Pennebaker, 1990).

It often has been claimed that somatizing patients lack psychological-mindedness—that is, the ability to label, symbolize, and describe their emotions, fantasies, conflicts, or other aspects of their inner life. Efforts have been made to operationalize this deficit in the concept of alexithymia—a term coined by Sifneos (1973) from Greek roots to mean "no words for feeling." Alexithymic individuals are said to lack the ability to discriminate feelings and bodily sensations, tend not to express their psychological states, think in a concrete and action-oriented rather than a reflective way about the world, and lack a rich fantasy life. The Toronto Alexithymia Scale (TAS) is currently the most psychometrically sound self-report measure of alexithymia (Taylor, Bagby, Ryan, & Parker, 1990). The most recent version of the TAS has three distinct dimensions that correlate differently with symptom and personality measures (Hendryx, Haviland, Gibbons, & Clark, 1992; Hendryx, Haviland, & Shaw, 1991; Kirmayer & Robbins, 1993). Scores on the TAS are also significantly affected by level of education (Kauhanen, Kaplan, Julkunen, Wilson, & Salonen, 1993; Kirmayer & Robbins, 1993).

Some studies have found that individuals with somatoform disorders have elevated scores on the TAS (De Gucht, Fischler, & Heiser, 2004; Waller & Scheidt, 2004), while others have found no association between alexithymia and the prevalence or course of medically unexplained symptoms (Kooiman, Bolk, Brand, Trijsburg, & Rooijmans, 2000; Kooiman, Bolk, Rooijmans, & Trijsburg, 2004). A community study found no relationship between alexithymia and somatic symptom reporting when anxiety and neuroticism were controlled (Lundh & Simonsson-Sarnecki, 2001). In fact, alexithymia is more closely related to measures of depressive symptoms than to somatization (Cohen, Auld, & Brooker, 1994; Honkalampi, Hintikka, Tanskanen, Lehtonen, & Viinamaki, 2000). Depression or dysphoria may be associated with a range of confusing sensations that cannot be clearly separated into emotions and bodily symptoms, and this is the dimension of the TAS that is most strongly associated with medically unexplained symptoms. Cultural differences in expressive style may be mistaken for alexithymia (Kirmayer, 1997; Kirmayer, Dao, & Smith, 1998). At present the TAS has little utility in clinical settings (Kooiman, Spinhoven, & Trijsburg, 2002) and, in particular, should not be used to exclude patients from psychotherapy because they are deemed not psychologically minded, since this is likely to be a state secondary to preoccupation with somatic symptoms that can change as these symptoms are directly addressed through techniques of behavioral medicine (Looper & Kirmayer, 2002; Wise, Mann, Mitchell, Hryniak, & Hill, 1990).

FAMILY, SOCIAL, AND DEVELOPMENTAL FACTORS

Developmental experiences of reinforcement and modeling of illness behavior shape adult patterns of symptom reporting and health care utilization (Wilkinson, 1988). For example, childhood reinforcement of illness behavior in response to menstruation correlates with adult premenstrual symptoms and associated disability; similarly, reinforcement of illness behavior in response to colds predicts adult levels of symptomatology and disability with colds (Whitehead et al., 1994). Exaggerated parental concerns with illness, pathologizing of normal sensations (or misattribution of bodily concomitants of emotional distress), and medical help seeking may predispose children to develop bodily preoccupation and anxiety as adults (Benjamin & Eminson, 1992; Watt, Stewart, & Cox, 1998). Compared to mothers with a history of stomach ulcers, mothers with irritable bowel symptoms were more likely to take their infants for treatment, providing evidence of early social reinforcement of illness behavior (Crane & Martin, 2004). This early infant experience might increase the child's vulnerability to a range of functional disorders, including irritable bowel syndrome, by modeling and reinforcing symptom reporting, help seeking, or sickness behavior. For example, childhood reinforcement of illness behavior in response to menstruation correlates with adult premenstrual symptoms and associated disability; similarly, reinforcement of illness behavior in response to colds predicts adult levels of symptomatology and disability with colds (Whitehead et al., 1994). These effects are specific to illness and independent of the effects of life stress and neuroticism. A lack of parental protection in childhood may also increase the likelihood of high rates of health care utilization for somatoform symptoms in adulthood (Craig, Drake, Mills, & Boardman, 1994). A study in an experimental setting found some tendency for mothers with somatoform disorders to pay less attention than nonsomatizing mothers to their children's play but to show greater interest when their children played with a toy doctor's kit (Craig, Bialas, Hodson, & Cox, 2004). This suggests a pathway in the intergenerational transmission of bodily preoccupation and symptom reporting.

There has been increasing interest in the role of trauma in medically unexplained symptoms (Walker, Gelfand, Gelfand, Koss, & Katon, 1995; Walker, Katon, Neraas, Jemelka, & Massoth, 1992). Traumatic experiences in adulthood, such as domestic violence or state violence experienced by refugees, may also lead to persistent somatic problems (McCauley et al., 1995; Westermeyer, Bouafuely, Neider, & Callies, 1989).

There has been some suggestion that SD and conversion symptoms, in particular, may be associated with childhood sexual abuse (Alper, Devinsky, Perrine, Vazquez, & Luciano, 1993; Coryell & Norten, 1981; Morrison, 1989). However, the association is nonspecific in that histories of trauma and abuse are found among patients with a wide range of psychological disorders. Most studies find that somatoform disorders are associated not with sexual abuse, but with childhood emotional abuse and parental rejection or neglect (Brown, Schrag, & Trimble, 2005; Lackner, Gudleski, & Blanchard, 2004). The impact of childhood psychological abuse is mediated by poor family functioning (Salmon, Al-Marzooqi, Baker, & Reilly, 2003). A lack of parental protection in childhood may increase the likelihood of high rates of health care utilization for somatoform symptoms in adulthood (Craig et al., 1994). Evidence exists that adults with somatoform disorders tend to display insecure attachment styles (Waller, Scheidt, & Hartmann, 2004). Childhood trauma may lead to insecure attachment as an adult, which in turn may contribute to the tendency to report multiple somatic symptoms and high levels of medical service utilization (Waldinger, Schulz, Barsky, & Ahern, 2006). Insecure attachment may also play a role in hypochondriasis. Hypochondriacal patients attending a medical clinical have evidence of interpersonal problems and an insecure attachment style, characterized by fear of rejection (Noyes et al., 2003). This may lead them to seek medical care, but their anxious efforts to obtain reassurance eventually may provoke the very rejection they fear.

Psychophysiological Processes

By definition, psychological and social processes are a central component in the development of physical distress in somatoform disorders. However, this does not imply that the physical symptoms are feigned or otherwise imaginary. Medically unexplained symptoms are often referred to as functional, in that they are a result of an alteration or disturbance of a physiological function rather than an abnormal structure. This provides a possible biological link in the development of somatoform symptoms, through the many interactions between psychological processes and physiological systems. Although these interactions are not yet well understood, some of the interfaces between psychological and physical systems have been identified.

Sickness behavior is a term that refers to a constellation of nonspecific physical symptoms and behaviors manifested during the acute phase of illness. This may include decreased activity, appetite, and interest and malaise, which are symptoms common to both medical and emotional distress. Sickness behavior has a physiological basis, mediated by centrally acting proinflammatory cytokines such as interleukin and tumor necrosis factor (Kelley et al., 2003). Among patients with viral infections, proinflammatory cytokines released from peripheral blood mononuclear cell cultures have been associated with reported manifestations of acute sickness behavior (Vollmer-Conna et al., 2004). Although infection is the classical example of acute phase illness reaction, the release of cytokines can be triggered by an exogenous danger signal such as a physical or emotional threat in the environment (Fleshner, Campisi, Amiri, & Diamond, 2004). The responsiveness of the brain cytokine system may be modified by sensitization during early stages of development, repeated activation, and prior exposure to environmental stressors (Dantzer, 2005).

The hypothalamic-pituitary-adrenal (HPA) axis has long been a focus of investigation of psychophysiological effects. Emotional distress has been linked with HPA alterations causing elevated cortisol levels and the failure of dexamethasone suppression of cortisol (McEwen, 2000). Although the sudden release of cortisol is part of the "fight-or-flight" response characterized by physiological and behavioral activation, chronic stimulation or dysregulation of the HPA axis may have damaging physical effects. HPA dysregulation may be an underlying process in the development of functional syndromes characterized by fatigue and pain. Decreased adrenocorticotropic hormone (ACTH) levels were associated with the duration and severity of fatigue in a study of chronic fatigue syndrome (Gaab et al., 2004).

HPA dysfunction may be an acquired phenomenon resulting from biological triggers such as infection or secondary factors such as prolonged inactivity, physical deconditioning, and sleep abnormalities. The body's stress response system has immunological effects through two basic mechanisms. Glucocorticoids such as cortisol have an immunosuppressant effect, while other neuroimmune modulation may occur through direct sympathetic innervation of lymphoid organs (Felten, Madden, Bellinger, et al., 1998). The HPA stress response system and immune system have complex interactions that may contribute to persistent feelings of sickness and a wide range of somatic symptoms (Dinan et al., 2006).

The most common physical symptoms identified as a source of physical distress are pain symptoms including joint pain, back pain, headache, chest pain, and abdominal pain (Kroenke & Price, 1993). Theories of pain perception in functional gastrointestinal disorders have been well developed and provide an example relevant to other somatic pain syndromes. The function of the gastrointestinal tract is controlled by a complex neuronal network including the intrinsic enteric nervous system, which spans the entire length of the gastrointestinal system, and the extrinsic nervous system, which includes both central and peripheral (spinal and autonomic) components (Ringel & Drossman, 1999). This bidirectional system allows both physical and emotional factors to initiate and moderate sensations of gastrointestinal pain. Early theories of pain conceptualized a unidirectional flow of pain signals from peripheral nerves to the central nervous system that would be a passive recipient of sensory input (Benini & DeLeo, 1999). Current theories attribute an active role for the central nervous system in the experience of pain through sensory, affective, and cognitive processing as well as several descending pathways involved in peripheral pain modulation (Fields, 2000; Petrovic, Kalso, Petersson, & Ingvar, 2002).

A growing literature indicates that multiple interacting systems are involved in the development of somatic symptoms including initiating, modulating, and perceiving these sensory experiences. Theoretical models of somatoform symptoms must include the interaction of psychological processes with physiological systems including the nervous system, the HPA axis, and the immune system in explaining symptom formation.

AN INTEGRATIVE MODEL

The physiological, psychological, and social factors discussed previously may interact in a series of nested vicious cycles to give rise to persistent somatoform disorders. Figure 12.1 depicts just some of these loops that may explain the emergence, persistence, and outcome of somatoform disorders.

Bodily sensations arise from everyday physiological disturbances or common illness, such as viral infections, or from emotional arousal or major mood or anxiety disorders. These sensations may be more or less insistent, capturing attention despite efforts to ignore them, but even mild sensations can become magnified once attention is focused on the affected region of the body. Selective attention to the body or to specific sensations is guided by cognitive-interpretive processes that make use of symptom and illness schemas. These include attributional processes by which sensations may be interpreted as symptoms or signs of an illness. Once an illness schema is accessed, it may guide subsequent attention to identify further symptoms confirmatory of the illness out of the background noise of bodily

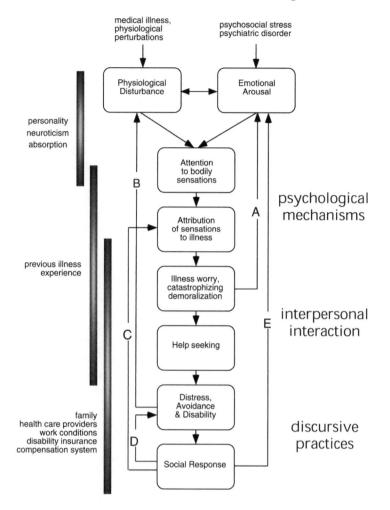

medical illness, physiological perturbations

psychosocial stress psychiatric disorder

Physiological Disturbance

Emotional Arousal

personality neuroticism absorption

Attention to bodily sensations

B

Attribution of sensations to illness

A

psychological mechanisms

previous illness experience

Illness worry, catastrophizing demoralization

C

Help seeking

E

interpersonal interaction

Distress, Avoidance & Disability

family health care providers work conditions disability insurance compensation system

D

Social Response

discursive practices

Figure 12.1 *An Integrative Model of Somatization.* Physiological, psychological, inter-personal, and sociocultural processes all contribute to vicious cycles of symptom ampli-fication that can result in disabling medically unexplained somatic symptoms. Only a few of these potential cycles are depicted: (A) illness worry and catastrophizing thoughts result in increased emotional arousal and anxiety, which in turn give rise to somatic symptoms associated with autonomic arousal and hyperventilation; (B) avoidance of activity and sick role behavior lead to physical deconditioning, sleep disturbance, and other forms of physi-ological dysregulation; (C & D) cultural interpretations of symptoms and sick role behavior reinforce pathologizing attributions for new sensations as well as distress and disablement; (E) sick role behavior may lead to interpersonal conflict, which in turn increases emotional arousal, leading to more somatic symptoms. Each of these processes may be targeted by specific clinical interventions aimed at interrupting the vicious cycles.

sensations (Arkes & Harkness, 1980). More or less neutral sensations may also be reevaluated as uncomfortable and threatening. To the extent that the ensuing thoughts and images represent the putative illness as serious, cognitive evaluation will lead to illness worry, catastrophizing, and demoralization. The identification of a potentially worrisome symptom leads to the search for a remedy and, if it persists, to adoption of the sick role with restrictions in activity. The response of care providers may validate the sick role or question the reality of the person's symptoms and suffering.

Specific traits and external factors may act at many levels in this evolution of illness cognition and behavior. Constitutional or acquired differences in autonomic and emotional reactivity may make some individuals more prone to experience uncomfortable bodily sensations due to physiological dysregulation or dysphoric mood. Differences in attentional set, attributional style, and coping will influence the tendency to minimize, ignore, or explain away symptoms on the one hand, or, on the other, to become absorbed in sensations and convince oneself that they are symptoms of a serious illness.

All of these processes are normal aspects of the response to any illness. They may reach disabling levels for some individuals either because of the intensity of specific factors or because of runaway feedback loops. Only some of these potential loops have been drawn in Figure 12.1. One loop involves feedback from illness worry and catastrophizing to emotional arousal, which in turn generates more symptoms. This loop is the focus of the cognitive assessment and treatment of hypochondriasis (Warwick & Salkovskis, 1990). A second loop runs from the social responses to help seeking, expressions of distress, disability and other aspects of sick role behavior back to physiological disturbance; this occurs, for example, when restriction or avoidance of activity leads to physical deconditioning with consequent feelings of fatigue, weakness, and muscular discomfort. This loop has been postulated to play a key role in the genesis of chronic fatigue syndrome, and cognitive-behavioral interventions aimed at modifying this cycle have proven therapeutically efficacious (Wessely & Sharpe, 1995).

Finally, two loops are drawn to suggest the importance of social processes in exacerbating and maintaining somatization. There is much evidence that the response of family members, employers, health care professionals, and the larger society to a person's illness behavior may either aggravate or resolve somatoform disorders (McDaniel, Hepworth, & Doherty, 1992). Many of these studies involve patients with chronic pain. Couple and family response is known to influence the intensity and disability associated with chronic pain (Block, Kremer, & Gaylor, 1980).

Several studies have measured multiple levels of this model to examine the interaction of factors and demonstrate the independent contributions and interactions of processes including attentional focus, symptom attribution, and coping (Kolk, Hanewald, Schagen, & van Wijk, 2002, 2003; Kolk, Schagen, & Hanewald, 2004; Robbins & Kirmayer, 1991b). The model is quite general in that similar processes are at work in individuals' adaptation to symptoms of any illness. As such, the model lends itself to attempts to reformulate the somatoform disorders in terms of dimensions of illness behavior and to relocate these problems under the diagnostic rubric of "psychosocial factors affecting physical condition" (Mayou, Kirmayer, Simon, Kroenke, & Sharp, 2005). Each of the identified processes would constitute a dimension of illness behavior that could be unpacked to develop a more refined nosology that would include assessments of attentional focus, attributional bias, symptom meanings, and coping strategies.

The model goes beyond psychological processes within the individual to consider the impact of social context. The course of somatoform disorders is strongly influenced by the response of care providers and the health care system. Excessive and invasive diagnostic investigations may increase patients' worry and conviction that they are ill, heighten body consciousness, and lead to the reporting of more somatic symptoms. Conversely, realistic reassurance and opportunities to receive support and clinical care without the need to present fresh somatic symptoms as a "ticket" to see the doctor can reduce the intensity of somatic distresss, health care utilization and costs, and the risk of iatrogenic illness (Smith, Monson, & Ray, 1986a). The single best predictor of return to work after back injury is preinjury level of job satisfaction (Kleinman, Brodwin, Good, & Good, 1992).

Wider societal attitudes and cultural notions about specific illnesses and vulnerabilities may also contribute to the emergence of specific syndromes. This was observed in the sudden rise in repetitive strain injury syndrome in Australia in response to insurance and disability coverage (Hall & Morrow, 1988). Similar stories could be told about environmental sensitivity syndrome, hypoglycemia, chronic candidiasis, and other historically popular diagnoses that may be promoted by mass media (Shorter, 1994). Chronic fatigue syndrome may be an example of an enduring problem that underwent a renaissance due, in part, to media coverage (Abbey & Garfinkel, 1991). In the case of chronic fatigue, the influence from social responses also runs back to attributions. Patients who find their illness doubted or discounted by health care providers may become more insistent on a disease explanation for their distress in an effort to gain legitimacy and counteract the stigma associated with psychological and psychiatric problems (Wessely, 1994). Clinicians' power to ratify illness is a double-edged sword. There is evidence, for example, that primary care patients with an acute viral illness who are intensively investigated are more likely to go on to develop chronic fatigue (Cope et al., 1994). It is particularly important to reassess these social loops when problems do not respond to interventions focused exclusively at an individual level.

DIAGNOSTIC CONSIDERATIONS

The category of somatoform disorders arises from the assumption that medically unexplained somatic distress and worry can be attributed to psychopathology. In fact, this determination is often difficult to make (Kirmayer, 1994). The diagnostic criteria for somatoform disorders raise a number of thorny diagnostic problems, including the questions of (1) when a symptom is medically unexplained; (2) when worry or distress is excessive; and (3) when a symptom can be said to be psychogenic, that is, predominately caused by psychological factors.

The notion that a symptom is medically unexplained is based on efforts to rule out identifiable organic causes. The extent of the medical investigation depends on available technology and clinical practices. The offering of a plausible explanation for symptoms, even in the absence of definite laboratory confirmation, depends on current medical knowledge. New theories and technology allow further investigations and provide new explanations for previously obscure symptoms. To some extent, the decision that a symptom or syndrome is idiopathic or unexplained reflects diagnostic conventions within the medical community that are, in turn, influenced by larger social forces. For many patients and practitioners, calling a syndrome unexplained is tantamount to saying that symptoms are imaginary. However, many types of physiological perturbation can give rise to significant somatic distress (Sharpe & Bass, 1992). For example, unnoticed hyperventilation can give rise to feelings of faintness, shortness of breath, paresthesias, and other unusual sensations. Our ability to measure abnormalities in the functioning of many physiological systems is still quite rudimentary. It is likely that many functional symptoms and syndromes are caused by disturbances of physiological process rather than gross structural abnormalities and hence will lie beyond the power of clinical and laboratory measures to resolve for some time to come.

In the case of hypochondriasis, there is an assumption that worry and emotional distress are greater than appropriate for the severity or likelihood of organic disease. However, there are no established norms for how much distress is appropriate to a given condition, so clinical judgments that distress is exaggerated may be influenced by factors other than the relative level of patients' worry. The diagnostic criteria for hypochondriasis also include the notion that the patient's illness worry does not respond to appropriate medical reassurance. But how much reassurance is enough? Do most patients given the label hypochondriacal actually receive adequate reassurance? When assessed in primary care, each laboratory investigation the clinician conducts causes apprehension and uncertainty, so the clinician's ultimate declaration that nothing is wrong may be met with some doubt. When hypochondriacal patients are evaluated and treated by mental health practitioners, they may find that a sudden shift to focus on their anxiety and related psychological or social problems conflicts with the experiential primacy of their somatic distress. In either case, the assumption that they have been adequately reassured may not be justified, as features of the clinical encounter may aggravate hypochondriacal concerns. The observation that many hypochondriacal patients respond well to systematic reassurance and reattribution training points to the limitations of their earlier encounters with physicians (Kellner, 1992; Warwick, 1992).

It is a short segue from the notion that symptoms are medically unexplained or amplified by patients' anxieties to the assumption that symptoms are caused by psychological factors. Given the epistemological constraints of the clinical setting, however, this assumption often is difficult to support with concrete data. The difficulty of ascertaining psychological causation was openly acknowledged in the DSM-III-R criteria for somatoform pain disorder, where there was a retreat from the causal imputations of psychogenic pain to the judgment that pain simply persists too long or is too intense. DSM-IV pain disorder reinstates a judgment of whether pain is entirely or partially due to medical or psychological factors as a diagnostic qualifier, but this faces the same epistemological difficulties. Melzack and Wall (1983) have noted the low correlation between size of tissue injury and severity of pain. Indeed, such observations are basic to their theory of pain that emphasizes the ability of central cognitive-evaluative processes to regulate somatic pain no matter what its origin. This problem is compounded by the fact that observers are not able to reliably discriminate individual differences in style of expression or coping with pain from actual pain experience (Poole & Craig, 1992). In practice, any distinction between psychogenic and organic pain reflects patients' style of self-presentation and credibility as well as the larger functioning of the hospital ward or health care team as a system in which the patient is made to carry the brunt of diagnostic uncertainty and treatment failure.

In DSM-II, conversion disorder was classified as hysterical neurosis, conversion type and characterized by involuntary psychogenic loss or disorder of function involving the special senses or voluntary motor system. This definition was broadened in DSM-III to include any symptom that involved a loss of, or alteration in sensory or motor function, attributed to an expression of a psychological conflict or need.

It has proved to be difficult to operationalize and of limited use in discriminating conversion symptoms from symptoms that ultimately prove to have organic causation (Cloninger, 1987; Watson & Buranen, 1979b).

Neither "medically explained," "exaggerated distress," nor psychogenic causation, then, are easy criteria to apply, and these diagnostic judgments remain liable to clinician bias and other extraneous factors (Kirmayer, 1988). It may be more useful, therefore, to approach somatoform disorders in terms of psychosocial factors than shape the reporting of all distress—although whether these will prove sufficient to explain the extreme variants that form the prototypical definitions of the *DSM* remains to be seen.

DSM-IV stipulates that to receive a diagnosis of somatoform disorder, symptoms must not be attributable to another psychiatric disorder. In many cases, however, symptoms of somatoform disorder are clearly secondary to another antecedent or underlying psychiatric disorder. Somatic symptoms commonly accompany mood and anxiety disorders. Pain, fatigue, and a wide range of other vegetative symptoms are among the most frequent symptoms of major depression. Palpitations, feelings of faintness or dizziness, and other symptoms of autonomic hyperarousal are cardinal signs of panic disorder and other anxiety disorders. Hypochondriacal worry and disease conviction also are common in depression and anxiety disorders. It has been claimed that many somatizing patients have masked depressions in which the emotional and cognitive symptoms are muted, hidden, or denied. More commonly, the emotional distress is quite evident, but patients insist that it is secondary to their original somatic illness. A somatoform diagnosis serves to acknowledge the prominence of physical symptoms and patients' own somatic causal attributions.

All symptoms should be treated as having both physiological and psychosocial dimensions and should be investigated and treated at multiple levels. This integrative approach avoids the danger that, in labeling symptoms as psychogenic, clinicians will no longer search for or discount evidence of underlying organic disease that requires medical attention.

Case Study 5

A 22-year-old Laotian man who had immigrated to Canada 4 years earlier was brought to the hospital emergency room by his brothers and mother. Several hours earlier, while comfortably watching TV and experiencing no distress, he had the sudden onset of pain in his lower back, radiating forward through his buttocks. This was followed by a paralysis affecting all four limbs. His trunk was unaffected, and he had no difficulty breathing. In the emergency room, he appeared to be in little distress, answering the doctor's questions in good humor and apparently only mildly worried about his dramatic symptoms. His physical examination was inconsistent. He had some power in his extremities, though deep tendon reflexes could not be elicited. He stated that these symptoms had occurred several times in the last year and always subsided after a few hours. He had stopped work several months earlier and was living with his parents because of fear of recurrent symptoms. A psychiatric consultation was requested to rule out conversion disorder.

(continued)

The psychiatric consultant was unable to elicit any history of emotional trauma or stress that might account for the acute onset of symptoms. He considered the impact of migration and the possibility of a poor social adjustment but felt this was too remote to account for increasing symptoms over the last year. He attempted hypnosis to assess the availability of dissociative mechanisms for symptom production, but while the patient relaxed and appeared to enjoy the experience, his paralysis persisted.

On hearing the history of the symptoms, an astute neurologist made the diagnosis of familial periodic hypokalemic paralysis (Stedwell, Allen, & Binder, 1992). The diagnosis was confirmed by the finding of a low serum potassium level, which returned to normal as the patient's paralysis spontaneously resolved over the next few hours.

The determination that symptoms are medically unexplained can involve extensive investigation to rule out occult or obscure diseases. Many chronic illnesses, like asthma or hypothyroidism, have systemic effects resulting in fatigue and other somatic symptoms. The manifestations and course of these diseases have a high degree of individual variability, and often it remains uncertain whether patients' somatic symptoms are caused by a pathophysiological process. Table 12.2 lists

Table 12.2

Diseases That May Be Mistaken for Conversion
Symptoms (see Jefferson & Marshall, 1981)

Basilar artery migraine

Brain tumors

Creutzfeldt-Jakob disease

Diabetic neuropathy

Drug-induced dystonic reactions

Endocrine disorders (e.g., Addison's disease)

Hypokalemic periodic paralysis

Multiple sclerosis

Myasthenia gravis

Temporal lobe epilepsy

Torsion dystonia

Toxic neuropathy

Porphyria

Sensory seizures

Spinal cord tumors

Parkinson's disease

Wilson disease

some of the many uncommon diseases that give rise to symptoms that are readily mistaken for conversion symptoms. In some cases, laboratory tests or diagnostic maneuvers can elicit physical signs that distinguish between conversion and organic disease.

Psychological factors contributing to somatic distress should be assessed whatever the evidence for or against organic disease. From the illness behavior perspective, the same cognitive and social factors that affect functional illness also influence the symptoms and course of organic illness. The principal difference is the social response to illness based on whether it is viewed as medically validated or remains ambiguous. This underscores the fact that the making of a diagnosis is itself an intervention. Diagnostic terms carry personal and social meanings that have immediate implications for the patient's wellness, self-esteem, interpretation of subsequent sensations, and potential stigmatization. Diagnostic labels may also function as metaphors that influence subsequent illness experience, coping, and self-image (Kirmayer, 1994).

PSYCHOLOGICAL AND BIOLOGICAL ASSESSMENT

Assessment of patients with somatoform disorders occurs in the context of outpatient or hospital management, disability or compensation evaluation, and research. Depending on context, the goals of assessment include (1) to rule out coexisting medical disorders; (2) to make a psychiatric diagnosis that can guide clinical treatment planning and intervention; (3) to determine the level and types of symptoms, illness impact, and disability; (4) to predict outcome or prognosis; and (5) to assess mediating processes relevant to research or clinical intervention. The diagnosis of a somatoform disorder does not indicate the specific symptoms, their meaning, and impact for the patient or their interaction with other psychological, medical, and social problems. Assessment must go well beyond the mere establishment of a diagnosis to include a clinically rich and useful picture of the person's pathology, resources, and lifeworld (see Table 12.3).

Establishing a collaborative relationship with somatizing patients can pose special challenges (Bass & Benjamin, 1993; McDaniel, Campbell, & Seaburn, 1989). Patients who fear their own emotional vulnerability or who have experienced rejection and stigmatization by doctors, employers, and others may vigorously resist any implication that their problems are psychological in nature (Looper & Kirmayer, 2004). This may reflect both psychological defensiveness and an effort to avoid further stigmatization and negation of the seriousness of their symptoms. The clinician can offer himself or herself as a consultant who is expert in assessing the psychosocial factors that can aggravate any physical illness and in teaching strategies to improve coping with illness. The clinician cannot arbitrate the ontological distinction between "real" organic disease and "imaginary" psychological disorder but must focus instead on factors that maintain symptoms and that are relevant to treatment. It is important to start from the assumption that all pain and other somatic symptoms are "real," regardless of the relative contribution of physiological and psychological, or peripheral and central, processes. Even pain from identifiable physical lesions is always the outcome of psychological processes (Merskey, 1991). What is at stake in the psychological assessment and diagnosis of somatic symptoms is the identification, for each individual in a specific life context,

Table 12.3

An Outline for the Assessment of Somatizing Patients

Medical comorbidity

Psychiatric comorbidity

Symptom characteristics

    Type

        Location

        Intensity

        Sensory qualities

    Temporal pattern

        Frequency

        Duration

        Contours of onset and resolution

Amplifying factors

    Attention

        Body focus

        Self-focus (introspectiveness)

        Hypnotizability

    Cognition

        Symptom attributions

        Perception of vulnerability and risk

        Catastrophizing thoughts

Coping strategies

Symptom context

    Recent life events

    Chronic stressors

    Marital and family adjustment

    Economic situation

    Work satisfaction

    Social supports

---

of factors that exacerbate or maintain symptoms and that may be modified to reduce suffering and disability.

Situating the evaluation process in a medical setting may help avoid some of the implicit message that the patients' problems are essentially psychological. In general, somatizing patients are not adverse to considering a psychosocial dimension to their problem but rightly reject the implication that their problems are entirely psychological or "all in their head." Frequently, as patients see that the clinician is interested in the details of their somatic symptoms, they will volunteer information about emotional distress, social problems, and psychological issues. Sometimes this opening does not occur until the clinician has succeeded in helping the patient to reduce symptoms. Wickramasekera (1989) argues for a more frontal approach in which the links between emotional distress and conflict and somatic symptoms are directly demonstrated to patients with biofeedback monitoring during a stress-inducing interview in the clinician's office.

Assessment usually begins with the collection of detailed information on the presenting symptoms as well as their intensity, quality, temporal characteristics, and impact on the patient's life. Using the symptoms as a focus, it is possible to collect detailed information about other aspects of psychological and social functioning, which are introduced in terms of their possible impact on somatic distress, or as areas of functioning where somatic illness may be having disruptive effects. It is often useful to obtain a symptom diary in which the patient records each occurrence of major symptoms; their characteristics; the situations or context in which they occur; the associated cognitive, emotional, and behavioral responses; and the responses of others. This diary involves a form of self-monitoring that may have immediate therapeutic effects and sets the stage for subsequent cognitive and family interventions.

Although for most clinical purposes simple visual analog scales suffice (McDowell, 2006, pp. 477–483), a number of self-report or interview-based measures assess the intensity and quality of specific somatic symptoms including pain (Melzack, 1975), nausea (Melzack, Rosberger, Hollingsworth, & Thirlwell, 1985), and fatigue (Smets, Garssen, Bonke, & De Haes, 1995). These provide sensitive indicators of level of distress as well as various qualitative dimensions and can be used to monitor treatment progress.

INTERACTIONAL PROCESSES IN THE CLINICAL SETTING

Most clinical management of somatoform disorders takes place in primary medical care settings. Surveys of primary care physicians indicate that somatoform disorders comprise a significant part of their clinical practice but that physicians are not well trained to manage these patients (Reid, Whooley, Crayford, & Hotopf, 2001; Wileman, May, & Chew-Graham, 2002). Recent qualitative studies have examined interactional processes of the patient-physician encounter. These suggest that the mind-body dualism intrinsic to the theory and practice of Western medicine is present in the dialogue of clinical consultations, and that expectations of incompatible attitudes on the behalf of both patient and physician are unnecessarily perpetuated. Physicians tend to view somatizing patients as having inappropriate symptoms that are manifestations of emotional or social distress, anticipate that they will not be open to psychosocial explanations, and presume that they will insist on medical investigation. In contrast, a study of audiotaped interactions found that virtually all patients with somatoform symptoms provided opportunities to explore the psychological aspects of their symptoms but that primary care physicians did not respond to these cues (Salmon, Dowrick, Ring, & Humphris, 2004, 2005). Only a minority of somatizing patients in another study requested somatic interventions such as medication prescriptions and physical investigations (Ring, Dowrick, Humphris, & Salmon, 2004). An important goal of assessment and ongoing management is to construct a meaningful narrative regarding the otherwise unexplained symptoms. Many medically unexplained symptoms are, in fact, culturally explained, but patients may be reluctant to discuss their social predicaments with clinicians they perceive as uninterested or ill equipped to be of help (Kirmayer, Groleau, Looper, & Dao, 2004). Establishing the validity of their physical suffering is an essential starting point for patients with somatoform problems. The challenge for physicians is to acknowledge and validate the experience of patients with unexplained symptoms and to develop a satisfactory explanatory model of physical distress.

PSYCHIATRIC DIAGNOSIS

A number of screening interviews and self-report measures for SD have been devised based on the assumption that common nonspecific somatic symptoms are more likely to be an indication of underlying psychiatric disorder than of organic medical illness, particularly when symptoms involve many different functional physiological systems (Kroenke, Spitzer, & Williams, 2002). *DSM-IV* introduced a simplified set of criteria for SD that were validated in a field trial (Yutsy et al., 1995). Clinical screening based on these criteria first ascertains whether patients have a lifetime history of at least four separate pain complaints; if not, the diagnosis of SD can be excluded. Otherwise, the clinician proceeds to inquire about gastrointestinal, sexual, or reproductive symptoms and conversion symptoms. If at least one of each is identified, the patient meets *DSM-IV* criteria for SD.

A variety of structured diagnostic interviews have been devised to assess psychiatric diagnoses in community and clinical populations by standardized criteria. The Diagnostic Interview Schedule (DIS) has been the most widely used instrument of this type (Robins, Helzer, & Orvaschel, 1985). Despite this wide use, the DIS has been criticized by many authors (Bass & Murphy, 1990). Robins (1982) found low concordance between psychiatrist and lay interviewers for the diagnosis of SD using the DIS, and a sensitivity of only 41%. The DIS asks about lifetime occurrence of symptoms, and the patient's memory may be poor for details of remote illnesses. As well, some patients suffering with somatoform disorders may conceal information in the fear that the physicians will not take their current symptoms seriously. Nonphysician interviewers may have difficulty recognizing SD because they are less able to reject implausible medical explanations offered by patients.

The Composite International Diagnostic Interview (CIDI) is a standardized diagnostic instrument based on the DIS that assesses mental disorders according to both *DSM-III-R* and *ICD-10* criteria (Robins et al., 1989). The CIDI assesses more somatoform disorders than the DIS, including SD, conversion disorder, somatoform pain disorder, and hypochondriasis. It is available in 16 languages and incorporates some efforts to make distinctions relevant to cross-cultural diagnosis. The CIDI has been used in a cross-national study of somatoform disorders (Janca, Isaac, Bennett, & Tacchini, 1995).

Barsky and colleagues (1992) developed the Structured Diagnostic Interview for Hypochondriasis (SDIH), a clinician-administered diagnostic interview for hypochondriasis modeled on the Structured Clinical Interview for *DSM-III-R* (Spitzer, Williams, Gibbon, & First, 1990). In a sample of general medical clinic patients, the SDIH had an interrater agreement on the diagnosis of 96%, and there was high concordance between the interview and the Whiteley Index of Hypochondriasis (Pilowsky, 1967) and physicians' ratings of patients as hypochondriacal. Similar findings were reported by Noyes and colleagues (1993). A seven-item version of the

Whiteley Index has also shown promise as a screening tool for both hypochondriasis and other somatoform disorders in primary care (Fink et al., 1999).

Pope and Hudson (1991) developed a structured interview modeled on the SCID to diagnose several common functional somatic syndromes that the authors hypothesized were variant forms of affective spectrum disorder. Although these authors have not published psychometric characteristics of their interview, they have used it to examine the overlap between functional syndromes and their relationship to major depression (Hudson, Goldenberg, Pope, Keck, & Schlesinger, 1992). Robbins and colleagues (Kirmayer, Robbins, Taillefer, & Helzer, 1995) developed the Diagnostic Interview for Functional Syndromes (DIFS), modeled on the DIS for use by trained lay interviewers to estimate the prevalence of the three most common functional syndromes by currently accepted criteria: fibromyalgia, irritable bowel, and chronic fatigue syndromes. However, there was substantial discrepancy between clinician and interview-based diagnoses. This may reflect inconsistencies in clinicians' diagnostic practices and the waxing and waning of symptoms in functional syndromes, as well as inherent limitations of the instrument.

Several instruments have been developed for the assessment of patients with BDD. Jorgensen, Castle, Roberts, and Groth-Marnat (2001) and Phillips and colleagues (Phillips, Kim, & Hudson, 1995; Phillips, 2005) developed the Body Dysmorphic Disorder Questionnaire for use in psychiatric settings. Dufresne, Philips, Vittorio, and Wilkel (2001) developed a brief self-report questionnaire for use in settings such as dermatology clinics. The Dysmorphic Concern Questionnaire (DCQ; Jorgensen et al., 2001) identifies body-related symptoms in patients who present with depression, obsessive-compulsive disorder, social phobia, or BDD, based on the Body Dysmorphic Disorder Questionnaire (Phillips, Kim, & Hudson, 1995), to screen for BDD in dermatology settings. The Overvalued Ideas Scale (OVIS) is an 11-item clinician-administered scale that measures the severity of overvalued ideation (Neziroglu, McKay, Yaryura-Tobias, Stevens, & Todaro, 1999), which may be predictive of treatment outcome in obsessive-compulsive and BDD patients.

The Irritable Bowel Syndrome Misconception Scale (IBS-MS; Dancey, Fox, & Devins, 1999) is a 17-item questionnaire that measures misconceptions held by people with irritable bowel syndrome. It can be used to evaluate the changes in illness-related knowledge gained during intervention programs.

ASSOCIATED FACTORS: PERSONALITY, AMPLIFICATION, AND COPING

Determination of the intensity, duration, and quality of specific symptoms allows diagnosis of somatoform disorders and other possibly comorbid conditions by standardized criteria. However, *DSM-IV* diagnosis is only one aspect of the clinical evaluation. In addition to diagnosis, the clinical assessment of patients with SDs requires attention to illness cognitions and coping skills, somatic amplification, attributional biases, and related personality traits as well as the family system, work, and larger social contexts of suffering. These domains can be explored with clinical interviews that start from the nature of somatic symptoms and inquire about the patients' cognitive response as well as their impact on others.

Psychological testing using standard instruments must be adapted to the experience of patients with predominately somatic symptomatology. Test results may be subject to physiogenic invalidity—misinterpreting symptoms that arise from the disturbed physiology of disease as evidence of psychopathology.

Neuropsychological testing has limited utility but should be considered where there is a history or signs suggestive of dementia or other organic mental disorder. On formal cognitive testing, chronic fatigue syndrome patients have mild cognitive impairments that usually are correlated with depressive symptomatology and cannot account for the magnitude of their subjective complaints (Cope, Pernet, Kendall, & David, 1995; DeLuca, Johnson, Beldowicz, & Natelson, 1995; Krupp, Sliwinski, Masur, Friedberg, & Coyle, 1994; McDonald, Cope, & David, 1993).

The MMPI in both its original and second-generation versions (MMPI-2) generates several scales relevant to the assessment of somatizing patients (Hathaway & McKinley, 1989). The hypochondriasis scale consists of 32 items, all of which deal with somatic preoccupation or general physical functioning. The standard interpretation of the MMPI suggests that patients with high scores on hypochondriasis have excessive bodily concern; may have conversion disorder or somatic delusions; are likely to be diagnosed as having somatoform, somatoform pain, depressive, or anxiety disorders; are not good candidates for psychotherapy; and tend to be critical of therapists and may terminate therapy prematurely when therapists suggest psychological reasons for symptoms. The MMPI does not provide an adequate assessment of hypochondriacal beliefs for which more specialized instruments are needed.

The 60-item MMPI hysteria scale identifies individuals who tend to react to stress by demonstrating physical symptoms such as headaches, stomach discomfort, chest pains, weakness, and somatic symptoms that do not fit the pattern of any known organic disorder. The typical high scorer is said to be someone who avoids responsibility through the development of physical symptoms and is self-centered, narcissistic and egocentric, psychologically immature, and resistant to psychological interpretations. The hysteria scale has been divided into two subscales: items that primarily address denial of psychological problems and items relating to admission of physical problems (McGrath & O'Malley, 1986).

In addition to individual scale scores, the MMPI yields profiles based on multiple scales. A high score on both hypochondriasis and hysteria scales may indicate the presence of a somatoform disorder, particularly if the score on the depression scale is low (the so-called conversion V pattern). With few exceptions, however, more recent studies with the MMPI have shown that it is not able to reliably distinguish patients with symptoms caused by organic disease from those with medically unexplained symptoms (Blakely et al., 1991; Kim, Hsu, Williams, Weaver, & Zinsmeister, 1996; Pincus, Callahan, Bradley, Vaughn, & Wolfe, 1986). MMPI profile patterns also have not been shown to consistently predict treatment outcome among chronic pain patients (Chapman & Pemberton, 1994). Patients' specific beliefs regarding pain are better predictors of satisfaction and response to treatment (Deyo & Diehl, 1988). This points to the need for more specific inventories that assess cognitions involved in coping with somatic distress (DeGood & Shutty, 1992).

The Whiteley Index (WI) is a self-report measure of hypochondriacal beliefs (Pilowsky, 1967). It contains 14 items tapping three factors: (1) *bodily preoccupation* (e.g., "Are you bothered by many pains and aches?"), (2) *disease phobia* (e.g., "If a disease is brought to your attention [through radio, television, newspapers or someone you know], do you worry about getting it yourself?"), and (3) *conviction of the presence of disease with nonresponse to reassurance* (e.g., "If you feel ill and someone tells you that you are looking better, do you become annoyed?"). It has good test-retest reliability and internal consistency. The WI has been widely used in studies of hypochondriasis and provides a useful screening measure (Pilowsky, 1990). Although it might be thought to measure illness worry rather than hypochondriasis, in fact it has a low correlation with estimates of the severity of disease and seems to reflect patient characteristics more than disease burden (Robbins & Kirmayer, 1996).

Subsequently, Pilowsky and colleagues (Pilowsky, Murrell, & Gordon, 1979; Pilowsky & Spence, 1983; Pilowsky, Spence, Cobb, & Katsikitis, 1984) developed the Illness Behavior Questionnaire (IBQ) to study the association to assess forms of abnormal illness behavior (Pilowsky, 1978). The IBQ is a 62-item self-report instrument measuring patients' attitudes, ideas, affects, and attributions in relation to illness. It generates scores on seven factors of illness behavior, including general hypochondriasis, disease conviction, and denial. While there is a lack of information regarding the IBQ's internal and test-retest reliability (Bradley, Prokop, Gentry, Van der Heide, & Prieto, 1981), an interview form of the questionnaire has been shown to have adequate interrater reliability, with a mean percentage of agreement of 88% (Pilowsky & Spence, 1983).

Several studies have shown that patients with diverse chronic pain syndromes or pain symptoms without organic cause have elevated scores on relevant IBQ scales (Bradley, McDonald Haule, & Jaworski, 1992). However, a study of outpatients, visiting a gastroenterology clinic, whose primary complaint was upper abdominal pain found that among the patients with no organic cause for their pain, only patients with a psychiatric diagnosis had indications of abnormal illness behavior on the IBQ (Colgan, Creed, & Klass, 1988). Other studies have found little difference between patients with chronic fatigue syndrome and those with multiple sclerosis (Trigwell, Hatcher, Johnson, Stanley, & House, 1995). Despite its questionable use to discriminate somatoform disorders from other medical conditions, the IBQ remains a useful clinical and research tool to systematically assess a range of important illness cognitions.

The IBQ measures beliefs and attitudes rather than actual behaviors. One of the few attempts to develop an instrument that taps illness behavior is the Illness Behavior Inventory (IBI), developed by Turkat and Pettegrew (1983). The IBI is a 20-item self-report questionnaire assessing two dimensions of illness-related behaviors: work-related illness behavior (9 items pertaining to work and activity when feeling ill; e.g., "I work fewer hours when I'm ill") and social illness behavior (11 items concerning illness behaviors in social situations; e.g., "Most people who know me are aware that I take medication"). It has good internal consistency and concurrent validity with the McGill Pain Questionnaire (Melzack, 1975) but has been little used in subsequent research.

The Illness Attitude Scale (IAS) is a 21-item self-report questionnaire measuring seven components of hypochondriasis, including generic worry about illness, concern about pain, health beliefs, and bodily preoccupation (Kellner, Abbott, Winslow, & Pathak, 1987). The IAS reflects the authors' hypothesis that the most distinctive characteristic of hypochondriasis is not that patients worry about health but that their fears are not eliminated by a satisfactory medical examination and they are resistant to medical reassurance (Fava & Grandi, 1991). The IAS differentiates between patients with *DSM-III* hypochondriasis and various other clinical groups (Hitchcock & Mathews, 1992).

The Multidimensional Inventory of Hypochondriacal Traits is a recent self-report instrument designed to capture cognitive, behavioral, perceptual, and affective dimensions of the clinical syndrome (Longley, Watson, & Noyes, 2005). Interestingly, all of the dimensions have strong interpersonal components based on the individual's perception and experience of others.

Instruments also have been devised for the assessment of body image. For example, the Body Dysmorphic Disorder Examination assesses self-consciousness, preoccupation with appearance, overvalued ideas about the importance of appearance to self-worth, and body image avoidance and checking behaviors (Rosen, Reiter, & Orosan, 1995a). The Yale-Brown Obsessive Compulsive Scale has also been modified for the diagnostic assessment of the severity of symptoms of BDD (Phillips et al., 1997).

The assessment of symptom and illness meanings and attributions follows standard cognitive therapy strategies developed for work with anxiety and depressive disorders (Salkovskis, 1989; Sharpe, Peveler, & Mayou, 1992; Warwick, 1995). Assessment involves eliciting automatic thoughts and images, exploring cognitive and behavioral coping strategies, and testing alternative thoughts and behaviors. This type of assessment is typically woven into ongoing treatment.

THE SOCIAL CONTEXT OF ILLNESS

Assessment of the social context of illness should be a routine part of the assessment of all individual psychopathology. In addition to recent life events, chronic stressors, and social supports, couple and family interviews may reveal crucial interactions that are aggravating or maintaining symptoms—or uncover important resources to aid the clinician in devising treatment strategies (Griffith & Griffith, 1994; McDaniel et al., 1989; Rolland, 1987). The perceptions and responses of family members to patients with chronic pain and somatic syndromes may be crucial for understanding their persistence and identifying strategies for intervention (Cordingley, Wearden, Appleby, & Fisher, 2001; Sharp & Nicholas, 2000). *DSM-IV* provides an outline for a cultural formulation in Appendix I that should be part of the assessment of all patients with somatoform disorders. This draws attention to the impact of cultural dimensions of the individual's identity, illness explanations, social supports, and stressors as well as the relationship with the clinician. When there is significant cultural distance between patient and clinician, other family and community members, culture brokers, and anthropologists can be consulted to explore the local meanings of the symptoms and appropriate treatment approaches (Kirmayer et al., 2003).

GENDER AND CULTURAL ISSUES

As discussed earlier in this chapter, SD is about nine times more common among women than men in the general population of North America, and women are more likely to report the range of somatic symptoms (Kroenke & Spitzer, 1998). Similarly, the most common forms of undifferentiated somatoform disorder (e.g., the functional somatic syndromes of fibromyalgia, irritable bowel, and chronic fatigue) are diagnosed from two to nine times more frequently among women than among men (Toner, 1995). In contrast, hypochondriasis is equally represented across the genders, and somatized presentations of depression and anxiety may actually be proportionately more common among men (Kirmayer & Robbins, 1991b).

Potential explanations for these gender differences in prevalence include (1) a higher prevalence of related psychiatric disorders among women (i.e., mood and anxiety disorders) that secondarily give rise to somatoform disorders, (2) differences in illness behavior and help seeking, (3) differential exposure to sexual and physical abuse, (4) social stresses and psychological conflicts associated with gender roles, (5) hormonal or other physiological differences, and (6) gender bias in the diagnostic process (Toner, 1995; Wool & Barsky, 1994).

1. The prevalence of major depression (Nolen-Hoeksma, 1995) and several anxiety disorders (Yonkers & Gurguis, 1995) is higher among women than among men. As noted previously, patients with somatoform disorders often have underlying mood or anxiety disorders that may account, in part, for their symptoms. A higher prevalence of these disorders among women could give rise to part of the gender difference in prevalence of somatoform disorders. However, many patients with somatoform disorders do not have identifiable mood or anxiety disorders. Further, the gender difference in somatoform disorders is much greater than that for mood or anxiety, suggesting that other factors must be involved.
2. Women may have a greater tendency to focus on their bodies, and hence notice and report more symptoms (Pennebaker & Watson, 1991). In addition, women may be more likely to seek help because they are more willing than men to admit distress and acknowledge the need for assistance (Verbrugge, 1985). In some circumstances, women may be more able to seek help because they are less constrained than men by full-time employment. More commonly, however, women face considerable barriers to help seeking because of heavy work and family responsibilities. Indeed, Ginsburg and Brown (1982) found that many women with postpartum depression presented their babies to the pediatrician for minor somatic complaints in a sort of "somatization by proxy," both because they could not justify taking time for themselves to seek help and because others around them normalized their seriously depressed mood as ordinary "baby blues."
3. A number of recent studies have demonstrated high prevalences of sexual or physical abuse among women with somatoform disorders including irritable bowel and other functional gastrointestinal disorders as well as chronic pelvic pain (Walker et al., 1988; Walker, Gelfand, Gelfand, & Katon, 1995). Women are generally more likely than men to experience sexual and physical abuse, and although somatization is only one possible outcome (Mayer, 2007), this could account for some of the differential prevalence. Childhood and domestic violence are common contributors to a wide range of somatic and psychological forms of distress.

4. Gender roles may subject women to increased social stressors, causing elevated levels of both emotional and somatic distress (Verbrugge, 1985). Women may face narrow standards and rigid expectations for physical attractiveness and reproductive fitness that make them preoccupied with their bodies and prone to somatoform disorders (Cash & Pruzinsky, 1990).

5. Physiological differences between men and women may result in differential rates and patterns of functional somatic symptoms. Female sex hormones have effects on smooth muscle throughout the gut and other organ systems and may contribute directly to a higher prevalence of irritable bowel syndrome among women (Talley, 1991). The menstrual cycle itself may be associated with a wide range of somatic symptoms and with the intensification of preexisting functional somatic symptoms to a level that prompts help seeking and clinical attention, although perception of menstrual symptoms is itself influenced by other psychological factors (Whitehead, Busch, Heller, & Costa, 1986).

6. Finally, there may be gender bias in the diagnostic process itself, whereby clinicians are more likely to attribute symptoms to psychosocial causes for women than for men (Kirmayer, 1988). Such a gender bias has been found for the diagnosis of histrionic personality (Chodoff, 1982; Fernbach, Winstead, & Derlega, 1989; Warner, 1978; Winstead, 1984), although the diagnostic criteria themselves are not obviously gender biased, at least when applied by a standardized diagnostic interview (Nestadt et al., 1990). To the extent that women are more forthcoming about psychosocial problems and emotions in the clinician-patient interaction, clinicians may be more likely to view women as emotionally distressed, histrionic, or both. Women may be more likely, then, to have their medically unexplained or functional symptoms explicitly labeled as a somatoform disorder (Slavney, Teitelbaum, & Chase, 1985).

Although somatoform disorders are common worldwide, they show great variation in form and prevalence across geographical regions and ethnocultural groups (Hsu & Folstein, 1997; Kirmayer, 1984). Indeed, the gender ratio itself differs markedly across cultures, giving some evidence of the importance of sociocultural factors in shaping illness experience. A review of cultural aspects of the somatoform disorders for *DSM-IV* suggested three major issues for existing nosology: (1) the overlap between somatoform, affective, and anxiety disorders; (2) cultural variations in symptomatology; and (3) the use of somatic symptoms as idioms of distress (Kirmayer & Weiss, 1997).

Most basically, cross-cultural work challenges the separation of affective, anxiety, dissociative, and somatic categories in the *DSM*. The requirement that patients with somatoform disorders not have another disorder that explains their symptoms seems overly restrictive given that somatic symptoms may be such a prominent part of depressive and anxiety disorders. Further, syndromes resembling depression or anxiety but without prominent mood symptoms are common. Neurasthenia may represent an example of this overlap that is not well captured by existing nosology (Ware & Weiss, 1994).

A wealth of clinical observations and anthropological fieldwork demonstrates that there are many culture-specific symptoms. For example, feelings of heat in the head or body are common in equatorial regions, as are "peppery" feelings and the sensations of "worms crawling in the head." In South Asia, men may complain of losing semen in the urine. There have been several attempts to develop expanded symptom inventories with items tapping culture-specific somatic symptoms, but these have not been widely used (Ebigbo, 1982; Mumford et al., 1991). Some of the symptoms that appear culture specific may, in fact, occur in other places but lack salience in terms of local illness categories and so are rarely noticed or reported.

The preferential use of a bodily idiom to express suffering has been linked to cognitive factors in symptom expression, as well as to social, familial, and cultural responses to distress (Angel & Thoits, 1987; Kirmayer, 1984; Kleinman, 1986). In Appendix I, *DSM-IV-TR* lists a variety of cultural idioms of distress with prominent somatic symptoms, including: *ataques de nervios, bilis* or *colera, brain fag, dhat, falling out* or *blacking out, hwa-byung, koro, nervios, shenjing shuairuo,* and *shenkui.* Many of these terms refer to illness causes or explanations rather than to discrete syndromes. They direct attention to the links between social circumstances and somatic distress. They are tied to ethnophysiological notions about how the body works and to local ways of talking about everyday problems. Worldwide, sociosomatics is a more common mode of illness explanation than psychosomatics—that is, people see the connections between difficult social situations and consequent illness, and put more emphasis on this link than on an individual's psychological characteristics (Groleau & Kirmayer, 2004). Within a somatic cultural idiom of distress, bodily symptoms may serve to communicate one's plight to others (Kirmayer, Dao, & Smith, 1998; Kirmayer & Young, 1998).

Anthropological research suggests several potential ways in which symptoms may have meaning (Table 12.4). Symptoms may be direct indices of underlying disease or physiological disturbance, occurring as one manifestation of abnormalities in structure or process. To the extent that this meaning is available to the patient, it may play a role in exacerbating illness worry and somatic distress.

Symptoms may also be indices of underlying psychopathology, as when, for example, conversion symptoms are taken to indicate dissociative pathology. The classical psychoanalytic interpretation of somatic symptoms understood them as symbolic expressions of underlying (unconscious) conflicts that they either represented through analogy or displaced. More recent clinical experience suggests that

Table 12.4
Levels of Potential Meaning of Somatic Symptoms

1. Index of disease or physiological disorder
2. Index of psychopathology
3. Symbolic representation of psychological conflict
4. Representation of illness model
5. Metaphor for experience
6. Cultural idiom of distress
7. Act of positioning in a local world
8. Form of social commentary or protest

symptoms more often are related to available illness models in the individual's local world (Slavney, 1990). Prototypes in individuals' own experience, the experience of their family or friends, or examples present through mass media provide templates for symptom experience.

Somatic symptoms may also have meaning as metaphors for other domains of experience. These may be idiosyncratic to the individual or drawn from common cultural idioms. These communicative meanings of symptoms may be conscious and explicit or hidden and implicit to patients and their entourage. The meaning of symptoms as communication can change over time and even in the span of a single interview as trust is established and the patient is led to reflect on his or her experience (Groleau & Kirmayer, 2004).

Finally, symptoms may function as moves in a local system of power, serving to position the individual and providing more or less explicit social commentary, criticism, or protest. For example, in many families, a woman who suffers persistent physical complaints may be able to command more resources for help and gain more control over her time and activities than one who tries to criticize her spouse directly.

These meanings are not intrinsic to the somatic symptoms but arise from how they are used by patients, their families, and others. In fact, the epistemological limitations of the clinical situation are such that the meaning of symptoms remains largely indeterminate (Kirmayer, 1994). The interpretation of a symptom as having symbolic meaning or as a rhetorical strategy on the part of a patient should always be made because it will be helpful to the patient rather than simply because it gives the clinician a satisfying feeling of closure or the license to blame the patient for the limitations of current therapeutics.

SUMMARY

The *DSM-IV* category of somatoform disorder implies that persistent complaint of somatic distress in the absence of a medical explanation represents a distinctive form of psychopathology. Somatic symptoms, however, can arise from a wide range of physiological perturbations, as well as being a normal concomitant of emotional distress. Milder forms of somatoform disorders, then, do not represent a distinctive type of psychopathology. More severe forms (e.g., somatization disorder) may reflect the generalized effects of intense emotional distress, as well as other psychological and social factors that contribute to chronicity and disability.

While the *DSM-IV* somatoform disorder diagnoses have some utility for research purposes, they may be misleading in clinical contexts: They reify patterns of illness behavior that cut across other psychiatric disorders as discrete conditions; they situate interactional problems inside the person and so promote biological and psychological reductionism; they ignore the social context of suffering and so point away from exactly those social contingencies that explain the onset of symptoms and that hold clues to their alleviation.

An approach in terms of dimensions of illness cognition and behavior may be more fruitful in terms of assessing the psychological factors that may contribute to somatic distress and help seeking. In this view, there are three basic forms of somatization: (1) functional somatic symptoms that arise from a wide range of different physiological and psychological mechanisms including autonomic dysregulation, hyperventilation, cognitive-attentional amplification, and dissociation (this category includes undifferentiated somatoform disorder and conversion disorder); (2) hypochondriacal illness worry that has similar roots to those of other anxiety disorders including panic and generalized anxiety disorder with pathologizing attributions and catastrophizing cognitions that specifically invoke the threat of disease or deformity (dysmorphophobia also fits this model); and (3) somatic presentations of depression, anxiety, and other psychiatric disorders or psychosocial distress that reflect patients' efforts to avoid the stigma of psychiatric illness and present the doctor with an appropriate somatic complaint.

A broader social focus on family, work, disability, and health care systems may provide explanations for persistent distress and functional impairment that appear inexplicable at purely physiological or even psychological levels. From this perspective, symptoms have potential meanings that may be taken up by patients, their families, and others in ways that either reinforce illness or serve to further invalidate the afflicted person. To the extent that patients must struggle to prove the reality of their suffering to skeptical physicians and incredulous family and friends, they may be forced into a rigid position that exacerbates their illness. For this reason, we have emphasized the importance of understanding the physical and social roots of somatic distress as an entrée into the lifeworld of the patient.

REFERENCES

Abbey, S. E., & Garfinkel, P. E. (1991). Neurasthenia and chronic fatigue syndrome: The role of culture in the making of a diagnosis. *American Journal of Psychiatry, 148,* 1638–1646.

Agreus, L., Svardsudd, K., Nyren, O., & Tibblin, G. (1994). The epidemiology of abdominal symptoms: Prevalence and demographic characteristics in a Swedish adult population. A report from the Abdominal Symptom Study. *Scandinavian Journal of Gastroenterology, 29*(2), 102–109.

Akagi, H., & House, A. (2001). The epidemiology of hysterical conversion. In P. W. Halligan, C. M. Bass, & J. C. Marshall (Eds.), *Contemporary approaches to the study of hysteria: Clinical and theoretical perspectives.* Oxford, England: Oxford University Press.

Alper, K., Devinsky, O., Perrine, K., Vazquez, B., & Luciano, D. (1993). Nonepileptic seizures and childhood sexual and physical abuse. *Neurology, 43*(10), 1950–1953.

American Psychiatric Association. (1994). *Diagnostic and statistical manual of mental disorders* (4th ed.). Washington, DC: Author.

Angel, R., & Thoits, P. (1987). The impact of culture on the cognitive structure of illness. *Culture, Medicine, and Psychiatry, 11,* 465–494.

Arkes, H. R., & Harkness, A. R. (1980). Effect of making a diagnosis on subsequent recognition of symptoms. *Journal of Experimental Psychology, 6,* 568–575.

Arnow, B. A., Hunkeler, E. M., Blasey, C. M., Lee, J., Constantino, M. J., Fireman, B., Kraemer, H. C., Dea, R., Robinson, R., & Hayward, C. (2006). Comorbid depression, chronic pain, and disability in primary care. *Psychosomatic Medicine, 68*(2), 262–268.

Aronson, K. R., Barrett, L. F., & Quigley, K. S. (2001). Feeling your body or feeling badly. Evidence for the limited validity of the Somatosensory Amplification Scale as an index of somatic sensitivity. *Journal of Psychosomatic Research, 51,* 387–394.

Axelrod, S., Noonan, M., & Atanacio, B. (1980). On the laterality of psychogenic somatic symptoms. *Journal of Nervous and Mental Disease, 168*(9), 517–528.

Barsky, A. J. (1992). Amplification, somatization, and the somatoform disorders. *Psychosomatics, 33*(1), 28–34.

Barsky, A. J. (1996). Hypochondriasis: Medical management and psychiatric treatment. *Psychosomatics, 37*(1), 48–56.

Barsky, A. J., & Borus, J. F. (1995). Somatization and medicalization in the era of managed care. *Journal of the American Medical Association, 274*(24), 1931–1934.

Barsky, A. J., & Borus, J. F. (1999). Functional somatic syndromes. *Annals of Internal Medicine, 130,* 910–921.

Barsky, A. J., Cleary, P. D., & Klerman, G. L. (1992). Determinants of perceived health status of medical outpatients. *Social Science and Medicine, 10,* 1147–1154.

Barsky, A. J., Cleary, P. D., Sarnie, M. K., & Klerman, G. L. (1993). The course of transient hypochondriasis. *American Journal of Psychiatry, 150*(3), 484–488.

Barsky, A. J., Cleary, P. D., Wyshak, G., Spitzer, R. L., Williams, J. B. W., & Klerman, G. L. (1992). A structured diagnostic interview for hypochondriasis: A proposed criterion standard. *Journal of Nervous and Mental Disease, 180*(1), 20–27.

Barsky, A. J., Goodson, J. D., Lane, R. S., & Cleary, P. D. (1988). The amplification of somatic symptoms. *Psychosomatic Medicine, 50,* 510–519.

Barsky, A. J., & Klerman, G. L. (1983). Overview: Hypochondriasis, bodily complaints and somatic styles. *American Journal of Psychiatry, 140*(3), 273–283.

Barsky, A. J., Orav, E. J., & Bates, D. W. (2005). Somatization increases medical utilization and costs independent of psychiatric and medical comorbidity. *Archives of General Psychiatry, 62*(8), 903–910.

Barsky, A. J., Wyshak, G., & Klerman, G. L. (1990a). The Somatosensory Amplification Scale and its relationship to hypochondriasis. *Journal of Psychiatry Research, 24*(4), 323–334.

Barsky, A. J., Wyshak, G., & Klerman, G. L. (1990b). Transient hypochondriasis. *Archives of General Psychiatry, 47*(8), 746–753.

Barsky, A. J., Wyshak, G., & Klerman, G. L. (1992). Psychiatric comorbidity in DSM-III-R hypochondriasis. *Archives of General Psychiatry, 49,* 101–108.

Barsky, A. J., Wyshak, G., Klerman, G. L., & Latham, K. S. (1990). The prevalence of hypochondriasis in medical outpatients. *Social Psychiatry and Psychiatric Epidemiology, 25,* 89–94.

Bass, C. (1992). Chest pain and breathlessness: Relationship to psychiatric illness. *American Journal of Medicine, 92*(Suppl. 1A), 12–15.

Bass, C., & Benjamin, S. (1993). The management of chronic somatisation. *British Journal of Psychiatry, 162,* 472–480.

Bass, C. M., & Murphy, M. R. (1990). Somatization disorder: Critique of the concept and suggestions for further research. In C. M. Bass & R. H. Cawley (Eds.), *Somatization: Physical symptoms and psychological illness* (pp. 301–332). Oxford, England: Blackwell Scientific.

Beitman, B. D., Mukerji, V., Flaker, G., & Basha, I. M. (1988). Panic disorder, cardiology patients, and atypical chest pain. *Psychiatric Clinics of North America, 11*(2), 387–397.

Benini, A., & DeLeo, J. A. (1999). Rene Descartes' physiology of pain. *Spine, 24*(20), 2115–2119.

Benjamin, S., & Eminson, D. M. (1992). Abnormal illness behavior: Childhood experiences and long-term consequences. *International Review of Psychiatry, 4,* 55–70.

Bennett, R. M. (1981). Fibrositis: Misnomer for a common rheumatic disorder. *Western Journal of Medicine, 134,* 405–413.

Binzer, M., & Kullgren, G. (1998). Motor conversion disorder: A prospective 2- to 5-year follow-up study. *Psychosomatics, 39,* 519–527.

Blakely, A. A., Howard, R. C., Sosich, R. M., Murdoch, J. C., Menkes, D. B., & Spears, G. F. (1991). Psychiatric symptoms, personality and ways of coping in chronic fatigue syndrome. *Psychological Medicine, 21*(2), 347–362.

Blanchard, E. B. (1992). Psychological treatment of benign headache disorders. *Journal of Consulting and Clinical Psychology, 60*(4), 537–551.

Bliss, E. L. (1984). Hysteria and hypnosis. *Journal of Nervous and Mental Disease, 172*(4), 203–206.

Block, A. R., Kremer, E. F., & Gaylor, M. (1980). Behavioral treatment of chronic pain: The spouse as a discriminative cue for pain behavior. *Pain, 9*(2), 243–252.

Blumer, D., & Heilbronn, M. (1982). Chronic pain as a variant of depressive disease: The pain-prone disorder. *Journal of Nervous and Mental Disease, 170*(7), 381–406.

Bohman, M., Cloninger, C. R., von Knorring, A.-L., & Sigvardsson, S. (1984). An adoption study of somatoform disorders. III. Cross-fostering analysis and genetic relationship to alcoholism and criminality. *Archives of General Psychiatry, 41,* 863–871.

Bohne, A., Keuthen, N. J., Wilhelm, S., Deckersbach, T., & Jenike, M. A. (2002). Prevalence of symptoms of body dysmorphic disorder and its correlates: A cross-cultural comparison. *Psychosomatics, 43*(6), 486–490.

Bonanno, G. A., & Singer, J. L. (1990). Repressive personality style: Theoretical and methodological implications for health and pathology. In J. L. Singer (Ed.), *Repression and dissociation: Implications for personality theory, psychopathology, and health* (pp. 435–470). Chicago: University of Chicago Press.

Bradley, L. A., McDonald Haule, J., & Jaworski, T. M. (1992). Assessment of psychological status using interviews and self-report instruments. In D. C. Turk & R. Melzack (Eds.), *Handbook of pain assessment* (pp. 193–213). London: Guilford Press.

Bradley, L. A., Prokop, C. K., Gentry, W. D., Van der Heide, L. H., & Prieto, E. J. (1981). Assessment of chronic pain. In C. K. Prokop & L. A. Bradley (Eds.), *Medical psychology: Contributions to behavioral medicine* (pp. 91–117). New York: Academic Press.

Bridges, K., Goldberg, D., Evams, B., & Sharpe, T. (1991). Determinants of somatization in primary care. *Psychological Medicine, 21,* 473–483.

Brown, G. K. (1990). A causal analysis of chronic pain and depression. *Journal of Abnormal Psychology, 99*(2), 127–137.

Brown, R. J. (2004). Psychological mechanisms of medically unexplained symptoms: An integrative conceptual model. *Psychological Bulletin, 130*(5), 793–812.

Brown, R. J., Schrag, A., & Trimble, M. R. (2005). Dissociation, childhood interpersonal trauma, and family functioning in patients with somatization disorder. *American Journal of Psychiatry, 162*(5), 899–905.

Cash, T. F., & Pruzinsky, T. (Eds.). (1990). *Body images: Development, deviance and change.* New York: Guilford Press.

Chapman, S. L., & Pemberton, J. S. (1994). Prediction of treatment outcome from clinically derived MMPI clusters in rehabilitation for chronic low back pain. *Clinical Journal of Pain, 10*(4), 267–276.

Chodoff, P. (1982). Hysteria and women. *American Journal of Psychiatry, 139,* 545–551.

Cioffi, D. (1991). Beyond attentional strategies: A cognitive-perceptual model of somatic interpretation. *Psychological Bulletin, 109*(1), 25–41.

Cloninger, C. R. (1987). Diagnosis of somatoform disorders: A critique of DSM-III. In G. L. Tischler (Ed.), *Diagnosis and classification in psychiatry: A critical appraisal of DSM-III.* New York: Cambridge University Press.

Cloninger, C. R., Martin, R. L., Guze, S. B., & Clayton, P. J. (1986). A prospective follow-up and family study of somatization in men and women. *American Journal of Psychiatry, 143*(7), 873–878.

Cloninger, C. R., Sigvardsson, S., von Knorring, A.-L., & Bohman, M. (1984). An adoption study of somatoform disorders. II. Identification of two discrete somatoform disorders. *Archives of General Psychiatry, 41,* 863–871.

Cohen, K., Auld, F., & Brooker, H. (1994). Is alexithymia related to psychosomatic disorder and somatizing? *Journal of Psychosomatic Research, 38*(2), 119–127.

Colgan, S., Creed, F., & Klass, H. (1988). Symptom complaints, psychiatric disorder and abnormal illness behavior in patients with upper abdominal pain. *Psychological Medicine, 18,* 887–892.

Cope, H., David, A., Pelosi, A., & Mann, A. (1994). Predictors of chronic "postviral" fatigue. *Lancet, 344,* 864–868.

Cope, H., Pernet, A., Kendall, B., & David, A. (1995). Cognitive functioning and magnetic resonance imaging in chronic fatigue. *British Journal of Psychiatry, 167,* 86–94.

Cordingley, L., Wearden, A. J., Appleby, L., & Fisher, L. (2001). The Family Response Questionnaire: A new scale to assess the responses of family members to people with chronic fatigue syndrome. *Journal of Psychosomatic Research, 51,* 417–424.

Cororve, M. B., & Gleaves, D. H. (2001). Body dysmorphic disorder: A review of conceptualizations, assessment, and treatment strategies. *Clinical Psychology Review, 21*(6), 949–970.

Coryell, W., & Norten, S. (1981). Briquet's syndrome (somatization disorder) and primary depression: Comparison of background and outcome. *Comprehensive Psychiatry, 22*(3), 249–255.

Couprie, W., Wijdicks, E. F., Rooijmans, H. G., & van Gijn, J. (1995). Outcome in conversion disorder: A follow up study. *Journal of Neurology, Neurosurgery and Psychiatry, 58*(6), 750–752.

Cox, B. J., Borger, S. C., Asmundson, G. J. G., & Taylor, S. (2000). Dimensions of hypochondriasis and the five-factor model of personality. *Personality and Individual Differences, 29*(1), 99–108.

Craig, T. K., Bialas, I., Hodson, S., & Cox, A. D. (2004). Intergenerational transmission of somatization behaviour: 2. Observations of joint attention and bids for attention. *Psychological Medicine, 34*(2), 199–209.

Craig, T. K. J., Drake, H., Mills, K., & Boardman, A. P. (1994). The South London Somatisation Study: II. Influence of stressful life events, and secondary gain. *British Journal of Psychiatry, 165,* 248–258.

Crane, C., & Martin, M. (2004). Illness-related parenting in mothers with functional gastrointestinal symptoms. *American Journal of Gastroenterology, 99*(4), 694–702.

Creed, F., & Barsky, A. (2004). A systematic review of the epidemiology of somatisation disorder and hypochondriasis. *Journal of Psychosomatic Research, 56*(4), 391–408.

Crimlisk, H. L., Bhatia, K., Cope, H., David, A., Marsden, C. D., & Ron, M. A. (1998). Slater revisited: 6 year follow up study of patients with medically unexplained motor symptoms. *British Medical Journal, 316,* 582–586.

Dancey, C. P., Fox, R., & Devins, G. M. (1999). The measurement of irritable bowel syndrome (IBS)-related misconceptions in people with IBS. *Journal of Psychosomatic Research, 47*(3), 269–276.

Dantzer, R. (2005). Somatization: A psychoneuroimmune perspective. *Psychoneuroendocrinology, 30*(10), 947–952.

Deary, I. J. (1999). A taxonomy of medically unexplained symptoms. *Journal of Psychosomatic Research, 47*(1), 51–59.

DeGood, D. E., & Shutty, M. S. J. (1992). Assessment of pain beliefs, coping, and self-efficacy. In D. C. Turk & R. Melzack (Eds.), *Handbook of pain assessment* (pp. 214–234). New York: Guilford Press.

De Gucht, V., Fischler, B., & Heiser, W. (2004). Personality and affect as determinants of medically unexplained symptoms in primary care: A follow-up study. *Journal of Psychosomatic Research, 56*(3), 279–285.

DeLuca, J., Johnson, S. K., Beldowicz, D., & Natelson, B. H. (1995). Neuropsychological impairments in chronic fatigue syndrome, multiple sclerosis, and depression. *Journal of Neurology, Neurosurgery and Psychiatry, 58*(1), 38–43.

Deyo, R. A., & Diehl, A. K. (1988). Psychosocial predictors of disability in patients with low back pain. *Journal of Rheumatology, 15,* 1557–1564.

Dickinson, W. P., Dickinson, L. M., deGruy, F. V., Candib, L. M., Main, D. S., Libby, A.M., & Rost, K. (2003). The somatization in primary care study: A tale of three diagnoses. *General Hospital Psychiatry, 25*(1), 1–7.

Dinan, T. G., Quigley, E. M., Ahmed, S. M., Scully, P., O'Brien, S., O'Mahony, L., O'Mahony, S., Shanahan, F., & Keeling, P. W. (2006). Hypothalamic-pituitary-gut axis dysregulation in irritable bowel syndrome: Plasma cytokines as a potential biomarker? *Gastroenterology, 130*(2), 304–311.

Dufresne, R. G., Philips, K. A., Vittorio, C. C., &Wilkel, C. S. (2001). A screening questionnaire for body dysmorphic disorder in a cosmetic dermatologic surgery practice. *Dermatologic Surgery, 27*(5), 457–462.

Dworkin, R. H., Hartstein, G., Rosner, H. L., Walther, R. R., Sweeney, E. W., & Brand, L. (1992). A high-risk method for studying psychosocial antecedents of chronic pain: The prospective investigation of herpes zoster. *Journal of Abnormal Psychology, 101*(1), 200–205.

Dworkin, S. F., Von Korff, M., & LeResche, L. (1990). Multiple pains and psychiatric disturbance: An epidemiologic investigation. *Archives of General Psychiatry, 47,* 239–244.

Ebigbo, P. O. (1982). Development of a culture specific (Nigeria) screening scale of somatic complaints indicating psychiatric disturbance. *Culture, Medicine and Psychiatry, 6,* 29–43.

Eifert, G. (1991). Cardiophobia: A paradigmatic behavioral model of heart-focused anxiety and non-anginal chest pain. *Behavior Research and Therapy, 30*(4), 329–345.

Engel, G. E. (1959). "Psychogenic" pain and the pain-prone patient. *American Journal of Medicine, 26,* 899–918.

Escobar, J. L., Rubio-Stipec, M., Canino, G., & Karno, M. (1989). Somatic Symptom Index (SSI): A new and abridged somatization construct. *Journal of Nervous and Mental Disease, 177*(3), 140–146.

Faravelli, C., Salvatori, S., Galassi, F., Aiazzi, L., Drei, C., & Cabras, P. (1997). Epidemiology of somatoform disorders: A community survey in Florence. *Social Psychiatry and Psychiatric Epidemiology, 32,* 24–29.

Fava, G. A., & Grandi, S. (1991). Differential diagnosis of hypochondriacal fears and beliefs. *Psychotherapy and Psychosomatics, 55*(2–4), 114–119.

Felten, S. Y., Madden, K. S., Bellinger, D. L., Kruszewska, B., Moynihan, J. A., & Felten, D. L. (1998). The role of the sympathetic nervous system in the modulation of immune responses. *Advances in Pharmacology, 42,* 583–587.

Fernbach, B. E., Winstead, B. A., & Derlega, V. J. (1989). Sex differences in diagnosis and treatment recommendations for antisocial personality and somatization disorders. *Journal of Social and Clinical Psychology, 8*(3), 238–255.

Fields, H. L. (2000). Pain modulation: Expectation, opioid analgesia and virtual pain. *Progress in Brain Research, 122,* 245–253.

Fink, P., Ewald, H., Jensen, J., Sorensen, L., Engberg, M., Holm, M., & Munk-Jorgensen, P. (1999). Screening for somatization and hypochondriasis in primary care and neurological patients: A seven-item scale for hypochondraisis and somatization. *Journal of Psychosomatic Research, 46*(3), 261–273.

Fink, P., Ornbol, E., Toft, T., Sparle, K. C., Frostholm, L., & Olesen, F. (2004). A new, empirically established hypochondriasis diagnosis. *American Journal of Psychiatry, 161*(9), 1680–1691.

Fishbain, D. A., & Goldberg, M. (1991). The misdiagnosis of conversion disorder in a psychiatric emergency service. *General Hospital Psychiatry, 13*(3), 177–181.

Fitts, S. N., Gibson, P., Redding, C. A., & Deister, P. J. (1989). Body dysmorphic disorder: Implications for its validity as a DSM-III-R disorder. *Psychological Reports, 64,* 655–658.

Fleshner, M., Campisi, J., Amiri, L., & Diamond, D. M. (2004). Cat exposure induces both intra- and extracellular Hsp72: The role of adrenal hormones. *Psychoneuroendocrinology, 29*(9), 1142–1152.

Fletcher, C. M. (2006). Environmental sensitivity: Equivocal illness in the context of place. *Transcultural Psychiatry, 43*(1), 86–195.

Fochtmann, L. J. (1995). Intractable sneezing as a conversion symptom. *Psychosomatics, 36*(2), 103–112.

Gaab, J., Engert, V., Heitz, V., Schad, T., Schurmeyer, T. H., & Ehlert, U. (2004). Associations between neuroendocrine responses to the Insulin Tolerance Test and patient characteristics in chronic fatigue syndrome. *Journal of Psychosomatic Research, 56*(4), 419–424.

Ginsburg, S., & Brown, G. W. (1982). No time for depression: A study of help-seeking among mothers of preschool children. In D. Mechanic (Ed.), *Symptoms, illness behavior, and help-seeking* (pp. 87–114). New York: Neale Watson Academic.

Göthe, C.-J., Molin, C., & Nilsson, C. G. (1995). The environmental somatization syndrome. *Psychosomatics, 36*(1), 1–11.

Grabe, H. J., Meyer, C., Hapke, U., Rumpf, H. J., Freyberger, H. J., Dilling, H., & John, U. (2003). Specific somatoform disorder in the general population. *Psychosomatics, 44*(4), 304–311.

Griffith, J. L., & Griffith, M. E. (1994). *The body speaks: Therapeutic dialogues for mind-body problems.* New York: Basic Books.

Groleau, D., & Kirmayer, L. J. (2004). Sociosomatic theory in Vietnamese immigrants' narratives of distress. *Anthropology and Medicine, 11*(2), 117–133.

Gureje, O., Simon, G. E., Ustun, T. B., & Goldberg, D. P. (1997). Somatization in cross-cultural perspective: A world health organization study in primary care. *American Journal of Psychiatry, 154,* 989–995.

Guze, S. B., Woodruff, R. A., & Clayton, P. J. (1971). A study of conversion symptoms in psychiatric outpatients. *American Journal of Psychiatry, 128*(5), 643–646.

Hall, W., & Morrow, L. (1988). "Repetition strain injury": An Australian epidemic of upper limb pain. *Social Science and Medicine, 27*(6), 645–649.

Halligan, P. W., Bass, C., & Marshall, J. C. (Eds.). (2001). *Contemporary approaches to the study of hysteria: Clinical and theoretical perspectives.* Oxford, England: Oxford University Press.

Hansell, S., & Mechanic, D. (1986). The socialization of introspection and illness behavior. In S. McHugh & T. M. Vallis (Eds.), *Illness behavior* (pp. 253–260). New York: Plenum.

Hathaway, S. R., & McKinley, J. C. (1989). *Minnesota Multiphasic Personality Inventory—2: Manual for administration.* Minneapolis: University of Minnesota Press.

Hendryx, M. S., Haviland, M. G., Gibbons, R. D., & Clark, D. C. (1992). An application of item response theory to alexithymia assessment among abstinent alcoholics. *Journal of Personality Assessment, 58*(3), 506–515.

Hendryx, M. S., Haviland, M. G., & Shaw, D. G. (1991). Dimensions of alexithymia and their relationships to anxiety and depression. *Journal of Personality Assessment, 56*(2), 227–237.

Hitchcock, P. B., & Mathews, A. (1992). Intepretation of bodily symptoms in hypochondriasis. *Behavior Research and Therapy, 30*(3), 223–234.

Hollander, E., Neville, D., Frenkel, M., Josephson, S., & Liebowitz, M. R. (1992). Body dysmorphic disorder: Diagnostic issues and related disorders. *Psychosomatics, 33*(2), 156–165.

Honkalampi, K., Hintikka, J., Tanskanen, A., Lehtonen, J., & Viinamaki, H. (2000). Depression is strongly associated with alexithymia in the general population. *Journal of Psychosomatic Research, 48,* 99–104.

Houtveen, J. H., Rietveld, S., & de Geus, E. J. (2003). Exaggerated perception of normal physiological responses to stress and hypercapnia in young women with numerous functional somatic symptoms. *Journal of Psychosomatic Research, 55*(6), 481–490.

Hsu, L. K. G., & Folstein, M. F. (1997). Somatoform disorders in Caucasian and Chinese Americans. *Journal of Nervous and Mental Disease, 185*(6), 382–387.

Hudson, J. I., Goldenberg, D. L., Pope, H. G., Jr., Keck, P. E., Jr., & Schlesinger, L. (1992). Co-morbidity of fibromyalgia with medical and psychiatric disorders. *American Journal of Medicine, 92,* 363–367.

Hyler, S. E., & Spitzer, R. L. (1978). Hysteria split asunder. *American Journal of Psychiatry, 135*(12), 1500–1503.

Janca, A., Isaac, M., Bennett, L. A., & Tacchini, G. (1995). Somatoform disorders in different cultures—a mail questionnaire survey. *Social Psychiatry and Psychiatric Epidemiology, 30,* 44–48.

Jefferson, J. W., & Marshall, J. R. (1981). *Neuropsychiatric features of medical disorders.* New York: Plenum.

Jones, M. P., Roth, L. M., & Crowell, M. D. (2005). Symptom reporting by functional dyspeptics during the water load test. American Journal of Gastroenterology, 100(6), 1334–1339.

Jorgensen, L., Castle, D., Roberts, C., & Groth-Marnat, G. (2001). A clinical validation of the Dysmorphic Concern Questionnaire. *Australian and New Zealand Journal of Psychiatry, 35,* 124–128.

Kapoor, W. N., Fortunato, M., Hanusa, B. H., & Schulberg, H. C. (1995). Psychiatric illnesses in patients with syncope. *American Journal of Medicine, 99*(5), 505–512.

Karoly, P., & Lecci, L. (1993). Hypochondriasis and somatization in college women: A personal projects analysis. *Health Psychology, 12*(2), 103–109.

Kashner, T. M., Rost, K., Cohen, B., Anderson, M., & Smith, G. R. (1995). Enhancing the health of somatization disorder patients: Effectiveness of short-term group therapy. *Psychosomatics, 36,* 462–470.

Katon, W., Lin, E., Van Korff, M., Russo, J., Lipscomb, P., & Bush, T. (1991). Somatization: A spectrum of severity. *American Journal of Psychiatry, 148,* 34–40.

Katon, W. J., Ries, R. K., Bokan, J. A., & Kleinman, A. (1980). Hyperemesis gravidarum: A biopsychosocial perspective. *International Journal of Psychiatry in Medicine, 10*(2), 151–162.

Katon, W. J., & Walker, E. A. (1998). Medically unexplained symptoms in primary care. *Journal of Clinical Psychiatry* (Suppl. 20), 15–21.

Kauhanen, J., Kaplan, G. A., Julkunen, J., Wilson, T. W., & Salonen, J. T. (1993). Social factors in alexithymia. *Comprehensive Psychiatry, 34*(5), 330–335.

Kelley, K. W., Bluthe, R. M., Dantzer, R., Zhou, J. H., Shen, W. H., Johnson, R. W., & Broussard, S. R. (2003). Cytokine-induced sickness behavior. *Brain Behavior and Immunology, 17*(Suppl. 1), S112–S118.

Kellner, R. (1992). The case for reassurance. *International Review of Psychiatry, 4,* 71–80.

Kellner, R., Abbott, P., Winslow, W. W., & Pathak, D. (1987). Fears, beliefs, and attitudes in DSM-III hypochondriasis. *Journal of Nervous and Mental Disease, 175*(1), 20–25.

Kent, D. A., Tomasson, K., & Coryell, W. (1995). Course and outcome of conversion and somatization disorders. *Psychosomatics, 36,* 138–144.

Kihlstrom, J. F. (1992). Dissociation and conversion disorders. In D. J. Stein, J. Young, & F. L. Orlando (Eds.), *Cognitive science and clinical disorders* (pp. 247–270). New York: Academic Press.

Kim, C. H., Hsu, J. J., Williams, D. E., Weaver, A. L., & Zinsmeister, A. R. (1996). A prospective psychological evaluation of patients with dysphagia of various etiologies. *Dysphagia, 11*(1), 34–40.

Kirkwood, C. R., Clure, H. R., Brodsky, R., Gould, G. H., Knaak, R., Metcalf, M., & Romeo, S. (1982). The diagnostic content of family practice: 50 most common diagnoses recorded in the WAMI community practices. *Journal of Family Practice, 15*(3), 485–492.

Kirmayer, L. J. (1984). Culture, affect and somatization. *Transcultural Psychiatric Research Review, 21*(3 & 4), 159–188 & 237–262.

Kirmayer, L. J. (1986). Somatization and the social construction of illness experience. In S. McHugh & T. M. Vallis (Eds.), *Illness behavior: A multidisciplinary perspective* (pp. 111–133). New York: Plenum.

Kirmayer, L. J. (1987). Languages of suffering and healing: Alexithymia as a social and cultural process. *Transcultural Psychiatric Research Review, 24,* 119–136.

Kirmayer, L. J. (1988). Mind and body as metaphors: Hidden values in biomedicine. In M. Lock & D. Gordon (Eds.), *Biomedicine examined* (pp. 57–92). Dordrecht, The Netherlands: Kluwer.

Kirmayer, L. J. (1994). Improvisation and authority in illness meaning. *Culture, Medicine and Psychiatry, 18*(2), 183–214.

Kirmayer, L. J. (1999). Rhetorics of the body: Medically unexplained symptoms in sociocultural perspective. In Y. Ono, A. Janca, M. Asai, & N. Sartorius (Eds.), *Somatoform disorders—a worldwide perspective* (pp. 271–286). Tokyo: Springer-Verlag.

Kirmayer, L. J. (2000). Broken narratives: Clinical encounters and the poetics of illness experience. In C. Mattingly & L. Garro (Eds.), *Narrative and the cultural construction of illness and healing* (pp. 153–180). Berkeley: University of California Press.

Kirmayer, L. J., Dao, T. H. T., & Smith, A. (1998). Somatization and psychologization: Understanding cultural idioms of distress. In S. Okpaku (Ed.), *Clinical methods in transcultural psychiatry* (pp. 233–265). Washington, DC: American Psychiatric Press.

Kirmayer, L. J., Groleau, D., Guzder, J., Blake, C., & Jarvis, E. (2003). Cultural consultation: A model of mental health service for multicultural societies. *Canadian Journal of Psychiatry, 48*(2), 145–153.

Kirmayer, L. J., Groleau, D., Looper, K. J., & Dao, M. D. (2004). Explaining medically unexplained symptoms. *Canadian Journal of Psychiatry, 49*(10), 663–672.

Kirmayer, L. J., & Robbins, J. M. (1991a). Functional somatic syndromes. In L. J. Kirmayer & J. M. Robbins (Eds.), *Current concepts of somatization: Research and clinical perspectives* (pp. 79–106). Washington, DC: American Psychiatric Press.

Kirmayer, L. J., & Robbins, J. M. (1991b). Three forms of somatization in primary care: Prevalence, co-occurrence and sociodemographic characteristics. *Journal of Nervous and Mental Disease, 179*(11), 647–655.

Kirmayer, L. J., & Robbins, J. M. (1993). Cognitive and social correlates of the Toronto Alexithymia Scale. *Psychosomatics, 34*(1), 41–52.

Kirmayer, L. J., & Robbins, J. M. (1996). Patients who somatize in primary care: A longitudinal study of cognitive and social characteristics. *Psychological Medicine 26* (5), 937–951.

Kirmayer, L. J., Robbins, J. M., Dworkind, M., & Yaffe, M. (1993). Somatization and the recognition of depression and anxiety in primary care. *American Journal of Psychiatry, 150*(5), 734–741.

Kirmayer, L. J., Robbins, J. M., & Paris, J. (1994). Somatoform disorders: Personality and the social matrix of somatic distress. *Journal of Abnormal Psychology, 103*(1), 125–136.

Kirmayer, L. J., Robbins, J. M., Taillefer, S., & Helzer, J. (1995). *Development of a structured diagnostic interview for functional somatic syndromes* (Working Paper 5). Culture & Mental Health Research Unit, Department of Psychiatry, Sir Mortimer B. Davis—Jewish General Hospital, Montréal.

Kirmayer, L. J., and R. Santhanam (2001). The anthropology of hysteria. In P. W. Halligan, C. Bass, and J. C. Marshall (Eds.), *Contemporary approaches to the study of hysteria: Clinical and theoretical perspectives* (pp. 251–270). Oxford, England: Oxford University Press.

Kirmayer, L. J., & Weiss, M. G. (1997). Cultural considerations on somatoform disorders. In T. A. Widiger, A. J. Frances, H. A. Pincus, R. Ross, M. B. First, & W. W. Davis (Eds.), *DSM-IV Sourcebook* (Vol. 3, pp. 933–941). Washington: American Psychiatric Press.

Kirmayer, L. J., & Young, A. (1998). Culture and somatization: Clinical, epidemiological, and ethnographic perspectives. *Psychosomatic Medicine, 60*(4), 420–430.

Kleinman, A. (1986). *Social origins of distress and disease.* New Haven, CT: Yale University Press.

Kleinman, A., Brodwin, P. E., Good, B. J., & Good, M. J. D. (1992). Pain as a human experience: An introduction. In M. J. D. Good, P. E. Brodwin, B. J. Good, & A. Kleinman (Eds.), *Pain as human experience: Anthropological perspectives* (pp. 1–28). Berkeley: University of California Press.

Kolk, A. M., Hanewald, G. J., Schagen, S., & Gijsbers van Wijk, C. M. (2002). Predicting medically unexplained physical symptoms and health care utilization. A symptom-perception approach. *Journal of Psychosomatic Research, 52*(1), 35–44.

Kolk, A. M., Hanewald, G. J., Schagen, S., & Gijsbers van Wijk, C. M. (2003). A symptom perception approach to common physical symptoms. *Social Science and Medicine, 57*(12), 2343–2354.

Kolk, A. M., Schagen, S., & Hanewald, G. J. (2004). Multiple medically unexplained physical symptoms and health care utilization: Outcome of psychological intervention and patient-related predictors of change *Journal of Psychosomatic Research, 57*(4), 379–389.

Kooiman, C. G., Bolk, J. H., Brand, R., Trijsburg, R. W., & Rooijmans, H. G. (2000). Is alexithymia a risk factor for unexplained physical symptoms in general medical outpatients? *Psychosomatic Medicine, 62*(6), 768–778.

Kooiman, C. G., Bolk, J. H., Rooijmans, H. G., & Trijsburg, R. W. (2004). Alexithymia does not predict the persistence of medically unexplained physical symptoms. *Psychosomatic Medicine, 66*(2), 224–232.

Kooiman, C. G., Spinhoven, P., & Trijsburg, R. W. (2002). The assessment of alexithymia: A critical review of the literature and a psychometric study of the Toronto Alexithymia Scale-20. *Journal of Psychosomatic Research, 53*(6), 1083–1090.

Kroenke, K., & Mangelsdorff, A. D. (1989). Common symptoms in ambulatory care: Incidence, evaluation, therapy, and outcome. *American Journal of Medicine, 86*(3), 262–266.

Kroenke, K., O'Malley, P., Jackson, J., Tomkins, G., Santoro, J., & Balden, E. (2002). Efficacy of antidepressants for somatization and symptom syndromes: A critical review. *Psychosomatic Medicine, 64*(1), 98–99.

Kroenke, K., & Price, R. K., (1993). Symptoms in the community: Prevalence, classification, and psychiatric comorbidity. *Archives of Internal Medicine, 153,* 2474–2480.

Kroenke, K., & Spitzer, R. L. (1998). Gender differences in the reporting of physical and somatoform symptoms. *Psychosomatic Medicine, 60,* 150–155.

Kroenke, K., Spitzer, R. L., deGruy, F. V., Hahn, S. R., Linzer, M., Williams, J. B., Brody, D., & Davies, M. (1997). Multisomatoform disorder. An alternative to undifferentiated somatoform disorder for the somatizing patient in primary care. *Archives of General Psychiatry, 54,* 352–358.

Kroenke, K., Spitzer, R. L., & Williams, J. B. (2002). The PHQ-15: Validity of a new measure for evaluating the severity of somatic symptoms. *Psychosomatic Medicine, 64*(2), 258–266.

Krupp, L. B., Sliwinski, M., Masur, D. M., Friedberg, F., & Coyle, P. K. (1994). Cognitive functioning and depression in patients with chronic fatigue syndrome and multiple sclerosis. *Archives of Neurology, 51*(7), 705–710.

Kuczmierczyk, A., Labrum, A. H., & Johnson, C. C. (1995). The relationship between mood, somatization, and alexithymia in premenstrual syndrome. *Psychosomatics, 36,* 26–32.

Kwan, C. L., Diamant, N. E., Mikula, K., & Davis, K. D. (2005). Characteristics of rectal perception are altered in irritable bowel syndrome. *Pain, 113*(1–2), 160–171.

Lackner, J. M., Gudleski, G. D., & Blanchard, E. B. (2004). Beyond abuse: The association among parenting style, abdominal pain, and somatization in IBS patients. *Behavior Research and Therapy, 42*(1), 41–56.

Lacy, T. J., & McManis, S. E. (1994). Psychogenic stridor. *General Hospital Psychiatry, 16,* 213–223.

Lazarus, R., & Folkman, S. (1984). *Stress, appraisal and coping.* New York: Springer.

Leff, J. (1988). *Psychiatry around the globe: A transcultural view.* London: Gaskell.

Lidbeck, J. (2003). Group therapy for somatization disorders in primary care: maintenance of treatment goals of short cognitive-behavioural treatment one-and-a-half-year follow-up. *Acta Psychiatrica Scandinavica, 107*(6), 449–456.

Lishman, W. A. (1988). Physiogenesis and psychogenesis in the "post-concussional syndrome." *British Journal of Psychiatry, 153,* 460–469.

Longley, S. L., Watson, D., & Noyes, R., Jr. (2005). Assessment of the hypochondriasis domain: The multidimensional inventory of hypochondriacal traits (MIHT). *Psychological Assessment, 17*(1), 3–14.

Looper, K., & Kirmayer, L. (2001). Hypochondriacal concerns in a community population. *Psychological Medicine, 31,* 577–584.

Looper, K., & Kirmayer, L. (2002). Behavioral medicine approaches to somatoform disorders. *Journal of Consulting and Clinical Psychology, 70*(3), 810–827.

Looper, K. J., & Kirmayer, L. J. (2004). Perceived stigma in functional somatic syndromes and comparable medical conditions. *Journal of Psychosomatic Research, 57*(4), 373–378.

Lundh, L. G., & Simonsson-Sarnecki, M. (2001). Alexithymia, emotion and somatic complaints. *Journal of Personality, 69,* 483–510.

Magni, G., Caldieron, C., Rigatti-Luchini, S., & Merskey, H. (1990). Chronic musculoskeletal pain and depressive symptoms in the general population. An analysis of the 1st National Health and Nutrition Examination Survey data. *Pain, 43,* 299–307.

Magni, G., Marchetti, M., Moreschi, C., Merskey, H., & Rigatti Luchini, S. (1993). Chronic musculoskeletal pain and depressive symptoms in the National Health and Nutrition Examination I. Epidemiologic follow-up study. *Pain, 53,* 163–168.

Magni, G., Moreschi, C., Rigatti Luchini, S., & Merskey, H. (1994). Prospective study on the relationship between depressive symptoms and chronic musculoskeletal pain. *Pain, 56,* 289–297.

Martin, R. L. (1996). Conversion disorder, proposed autonomic arousal disorder, and pseudocyesis. In T. A. Widiger, A. J. Frances, H. A. Pincus, R. Ross, M. B. First, & W. W. Davis (Eds.), *DSM-IV Sourcebook* (Vol. 2, pp. 893–914). Washington, DC: American Psychiatric Press.

Mayer, E. (2007). Somatic manifestations of trauma. In L. J. Kirmayer, R. Lemelson & M. Barad (Eds.), *Understanding trauma: Biological, psychological and cultural perspectives* (pp. 142-170). New York: Cambridge University Press.

Mayou, R., Kirmayer, L. J., Simon, G., Kroenke, K., & Sharpe, M. (2005). Somatoform disorders: Time for a new approach in DSM-V. *American Journal of Psychiatry, 162*(5), 847–855.

McCauley, J., Kern, D. E., Kolodner, K., Dill, L., Schroeder, A. F., Dechant, H. K., Ryden, J., Bass, E. B., & Derogatis, L. R. (1995). The battering syndrome: Prevalence and clinical characteristics of domestic violence in primary care internal medicine practices. *Annals of Internal Medicine, 123*(10), 737 ff.

McDaniel, S. H., Campbell, T., & Seaburn, D. (1989). Somatic fixation in patients and physicians: A biopsychosocial approach. *Family Systems Medicine, 7*(1), 5–16.

McDaniel, S. H., Hepworth, J., & Doherty, W. J. (1992). *Medical family therapy.* New York: Basic Books.

McDonald, E., Cope, H., & David, A. (1993). Cognitive impairment in patients with chronic fatigue: A preliminary study. *Journal of Neurology, Neurosurgery and Psychiatry, 56*(7), 812–815.

McDowell, I. (2006). *Measuring health: A guide to rating scales and questionnaires.* Oxford, England: Oxford University Press.

McEwen, B. S. (2000). Protective and damaging effects of stress mediators: Central role of the brain. *Progress in Brain Research, 122,* 25–34.

McGrath, R. E., & O'Malley, W. B. (1986). The assessment of denial and physical complaints: The validity of the Hy Scale and associated MMPI signs. *Journal of Clinical Psychology, 42*(5), 754–760.

McKay, M., & Farrington, J. (1995). Vulvodynia: Chronic vulvar pain syndromes. In A. Stoudemire & B. S. Fogel (Eds.), *Medical-psychiatric practice* (Vol. 3, pp. 381–414). Washington, DC: American Psychiatric Press.

McLeod, C. C., Budd, M. A., & McClelland, D. C. (1997). Treatment of somatization in primary care. *General Hospital Psychiatry, 19,* 251–258.

Meana, M., & Binik, Y. M. (1994). Painful coitus: A review of female dyspareunia. *Journal of Nervous and Mental Disease, 182*(5), 264–272.

Mechanic, D. (1972). Social psychologic factors affecting the presentation of bodily complaints. *New England Journal of Medicine, 286*(21), 1133–1139.

Mechanic, D. (1979). Development of psychological distress among young adults. *Archives of General Psychiatry, 36,* 1233–1239.

Melzack, R. (1975). The McGill Pain Questionnaire: Major properties and scoring methods. *Pain, 1,* 277–299.

Melzack, R., Rosberger, Z., Hollingsworth, M. L., & Thirlwell, M. (1985). New approaches to measuring nausea. *Canadian Medical Association Journal, 133,* 755–759.

Melzack, R., & Wall, P. (1983). *The challenge of pain.* New York: Basic Books.

Merskey, H. (1991). The definition of pain. *European Psychiatry, 6,* 153–159.

Merskey, H. (1993). The classification of fibromyalgia and myofascial pain. In H. Vaerøy & H. Merskey (Eds.), *Progress in fibromyalgia and myofascial pain* (pp. 191–194). New York: Elsevier.

Morrison, J. (1989). Childhood sexual histories of women with somatization disorder. *American Journal of Psychiatry, 146,* 239–241.

Mumford, D. B., Bavington, J. T., Bhatnagar, K. S., Hussain, Y., Mirza, S., & Naeaghi, M. M. (1991). The Bradford Somatic Inventory: A multi-ethnic inventory of somatic symptoms reported by anxious and depressed patients in Britain and the Indo-Pakistan subcontinent. *British Journal of Psychiatry, 158,* 379–386.

Nandi, D. N., Mukherjee, S. P., Boral, G. C., Banerjee, G., Ghosh, A., Sarkar, S., & Ajmany, S. (1980). Socio-economic status and mental morbidity in certain tribes and castes in India—a cross-cultural study. *British Journal of Psychiatry, 136,* 73–85.

Nestadt, G., Romanoski, A. J., Chahal, R., Merchant, A., Folstein, M. F., Gruenbeg, E. M., & McHugh, P. R. (1990). An epidemiological study of histrionic personality disorder. *Psychological Medicine, 20*(2), 413–422.

Neziroglu, F., McKay, D., Yaryura-Tobias, J. A., Stevens, K. P., & Todaro, J. (1999). The Overvalued Ideas Scale: Development, reliability and validity in obsessive-compulsive disorder. *Behavior Research and Therapy, 37,* 881–902.

Nolen-Hoeksma, S. (1995). Epidemiology and theories of gender differences in unipolar depression. In M. V. Seeman (Ed.), *Gender and psychopathology* (pp. 63–87). Washington, DC: American Psychiatric Press.

Noyes, R., Jr., Hartz, A. J., Dobbeling, C. C., Malis, R. W., Happel, R. L., Werner, L. A., & Yagla, S. J. (2000). Illness fears in the general population. *Psychosomatic Medicine, 62,* 318–325.

Noyes, R., Jr., Kathol, R. G., Fisher, M. M., Philips, B. M., Suelzer, M. T., & Holt, C. S. (1993). The validity of DSM-III-R hypochondriasis. *Archives of General Psychiatry, 50,* 961–970.

Noyes, R., Jr., Kathol, R. G., Fisher, M. M., Phillips, B. M., Suelzer, M. T., & Woodman, C. L. (1994a). Psychiatric comorbidity among patients with hypochondriasis. *General Hospital Psychiatry, 16,* 78–87.

Noyes, R., Jr., Kathol, R. G., Fisher, M. M., Phillips, B. M., Suelzer, M. T., & Woodman, C. L. (1994b). One-year follow-up of medical outpatients with hypochondriasis. *Psychosomatics, 35,* 533–545.

Noyes, R., Jr., Stuart, S. P., Langbehn, D. R., Happel, R. L., Longley, S. L., & Muller, B. A. (2003). Test of an interpersonal model of hypochondriasis. *Psychosomatic Medicine, 65*(2), 292–300.

O'Connor, K. P., Hallam, R., Beyts, J., & Hinclife, R. (1988). Dizziness: Behavioral, subjective and organic aspects. *Journal of Psychosomatic Research, 32*(3), 291–302.

Otto, M. W., Wilhelm, S., Cohen, L. S., & Harlow, B. L. (2001). Prevalence of body dysmorphic disorder in a community sample of women. *American Journal of Psychiatry, 158,* 2061–2063.

Pawlikowska, T., Chalder, T., Hirsch, S. R., Wallace, P., Wright, D. J., & Wessely, S. C. (1994). Population based study of fatigue and psychological distress. *British Medical Journal, 308*(6931), 763–766.

Pennebaker, J. W. (1982). *The psychology of physical symptoms.* New York: Springer.

Pennebaker, J. W. (1990). *Opening up: The healing power of confiding in others.* New York: William Morrow.

Pennebaker, J. W. (Ed.). (1995). *Emotion, disclosure, and health.* Washington, DC: American Psychological Association.

Pennebaker, J. W., & Watson, D. (1991). The psychology of somatic symptoms. In L. J. Kirmayer & J. M. Robbins (Eds.), *Current concepts of somatization* (pp. 21–35). Washington, DC: American Psychiatric Press.

Petrovic, P., Kalso, E., Petersson, K. M., & Ingvar, M. (2002). Placebo and opioid analgesia— imaging a shared neuronal network. *Science, 295*(5560), 1737–1740.

Phillips, K. A. (2005). *The broken mirror: Understanding and treating body dysmorphic disorder* (Rev. and expanded ed.). New York: Oxford University Press.

Phillips, K. A., Hollander, E., Rasmussen, S. A., Aronowitz, B. R., DeCaria, C., & Goodman, W. K. (1997). A severity rating scale for body dysmorphic disorder: Development, reliability, and validity of a modified version of the Yale-Brown Obsessive Compulsive Scale. *Psychopharmacology Bulletin, 33*(1), 17–22.

Phillips, K. A., Kim, J. M., & Hudson, J. I. (1995). Body image disturbance in body dysmorphic disorder and eating disorders. Obsessions or delusions? *Psychiatric Clinics of North America, 18*(2), 317–334.

Phillips, K. A., & McElroy, S. L. (1993). Insight, overvalued ideation, and delusional thinking in body dysmorphic disorder: Theoretical and treatment implications. *Journal of Nervous and Mental Disease, 181*, 699–702.

Phillips, K. A., McElroy, S. L., Keck, P. E., Pope, H. G., & Hudson, J. L. (1993). Body dysmorphic disorder: 30 cases of imagined ugliness. *American Journal of Psychiatry, 150*, 302–309.

Pilowsky, I. (1967). Dimensions of hypochondriasis. *British Journal of Psychiatry, 113*, 89–93.

Pilowsky, I. (1978). A general classification of abnormal illness behaviors. *British Journal of Medical Psychology, 51*, 131–137.

Pilowsky, I. (1990). The concept of abnormal illness behavior. *Psychosomatics, 31*(2), 207–213.

Pilowsky, I., Murrell, G. C., & Gordon, A. (1979). The development of a screening method for abnormal illness behavior. *Journal of Psychosomatic Research, 23*, 203–207.

Pilowsky, I., & Spence, N. D. (1983). *Manual for the Illness Behavior Questionnaire (IBQ)*. Adelaide, South Australia: University of Adelaide.

Pilowsky, I., Spence, N. D., Cobb, J., & Katsikitis, M. (1984). The illness behavior questionnaire as an aid to clinical assessment. *General Hospital Psychiatry, 6*, 123–130.

Pincus, T., Callahan, L. F., Bradley, L. A., Vaughn, W. K., & Wolfe, F. (1986). Elevated MMPI scores for hypochondriasis, depression, and hysteria in patients with rheumatoid arthritis reflect disease rather than psychological status. *Arthritis and Rheumatism, 29*(12), 1456–1466.

Poole, G. D., & Craig, K. D. (1992). Judgments of genuine, suppressed, and faked facial expressions of pain. *Journal of Personality and Social Psychology, 63*(5), 797–805.

Pope, H. G., Jr., & Hudson, J. I. (1991). A supplemental interview for forms of "affective spectrum disorder." *International Journal of Psychiatry in Medicine, 21*(3), 205–232.

Powell, R., Dolan, R., & Wessely, S. (1990). Attributions and self-esteem in depression and chronic fatigue syndromes. *Journal of Psychosomatic Research, 34*(6), 665–673.

Putnam, F. W., Guroff, J. J., Silberman, E. K., Barban, L., & Post, R. M. (1986). The clinical phenomenology of multiple personality disorder. *Journal of Clinical Psychiatry, 47*(6), 285.

Rada, R. T., Meyer, G. G., & Kellner, R. (1978). Visual conversion reaction in children and adults. *Journal of Nervous and Mental Disease, 166*(8), 580–587.

Raguram, R., Weiss, M. G., Channabasavanna, S. M., & Devins, G. M. (1996). Stigma, depression, and somatization in South India. *American Journal of Psychiatry, 153*, 1043–1049.

Ratliff, T. L., Klutke, C. G., & McDougall, E. M. (1994). The etiology of interstitial cystitis. *Urologic Clinics of North America, 21*(1), 21–30.

Reid, S., Whooley, D., Crayford, T., & Hotopf, M. (2001). Medically unexplained symptoms—GPs' attitudes towards their cause and management. *Family Practice, 18*(5), 519–523.

Rief, W., Hessel, A., & Braehler, E. (2001). Somatization symptoms and hypochondriacal features in the general population. *Psychosomatic Medicine, 63,* 595–602.

Rief, W., Hiller, W., Geissner, E., & Fichter, M. M. (1995). A two-year follow-up study of patients with somatoform disorders. *Psychosomatics, 36,* 376–386.

Rietveld, S., & Houtveen, J. H. (2004). Acquired sensitivity to relevant physiological activity in patients with chronic health problems. *Behaviour Research & Therapy, 42*(2), 137–153.

Ring, A., Dowrick, C., Humphris, G., & Salmon, P. (2004). Do patients with unexplained physical symptoms pressurise general practitioners for somatic treatment? A qualitative study. *British Medical Journal, 328,* 1057–1060.

Ringel, Y., & Drossman, D. A. (1999). From gut to brain and back—a new perspective into functional gastrointestinal disorders. *Journal of Psychosomatic Research, 47*(3), 205–210.

Robbins, J. M., & Kirmayer, L. J. (1986). Illness cognition, symptom reporting and somatization in primary care. In S. McHugh & T. M. Vallis (Eds.), *Illness behavior: A multidisciplinary model* (pp. 283–302). New York: Plenum.

Robbins, J. M., & Kirmayer, L. J. (1991a). Attributions of common somatic symptoms. *Psychological Medicine, 21,* 1029–1045.

Robbins, J. M., & Kirmayer, L. J. (1991b). Cognitive and social factors in somatization. In L. J. Kirmayer & J. M. Robbins (Eds.), *Current concepts of somatization: Research and clinical perspectives* (pp. 107–141). Washington, DC: American Psychiatric Press.

Robbins, J. M., & Kirmayer, L. J. (1996). Transient and persistent hypochondriacal worry. *Psychological Medicine, 26*(3), 575–589.

Robbins, J., Kirmayer, L., & Hemami, S. (1997). Latent variable models of functional somatic distress. *Journal of Nervous and Mental Disease, 185,* 606–615.

Robins, L. N. (1982). Validity of the Diagnostic Interview Schedule, Version II: DSM-III diagnoses. *Psychological Medicine, 12,* 855–870.

Robins, L. N., Helzer, J. E., & Orvaschel, H. (1985). The Diagnostic Interview Schedule. In W. W. Eaton & L. G. Kessler (Eds.), *Epidemiologic field methods in psychiatry* (pp. 143–170). Orlando, FL: Academic Press.

Robins, L. N., & Regier, D. (1991). *Psychiatric disorders in America: The Epidemiologic Catchment Area Study.* New York: Free Press.

Robins, L. N., Wing, J., Wittchen, H.-U., Helzer, J. E., Babor, T. F., Burke, J., Farmer, A., Jablinsky, A., Pickens, R., Regier, D. A., Sartorius, N., & Towle, L. H. (1989). The Composite International Diagnostic Interview: An epidemiologic instrument suitable for use in conjunction with different diagnostic systems and in different cultures. *Archives of General Psychiatry, 45,* 1069–1077.

Rolland, J. S. (1987). Chronic illness and the life cycle: A conceptual framework. *Family Process, 26*(2), 203–222.

Romano, J. M., & Turner, J. A. (1985). Chronic pain and depression: Does the literature support a relationship? *Psychological Bulletin, 97,* 18–34.

Rosen, J. C., Reiter, J., & Orosan, P. (1995a). Assessment of body image in eating disorders with the body dysmorphic disorder examination. *Behavior Research and Therapy, 33*(1), 77–84.

Rosen, J. C., Reiter, J., & Orosan, P. (1995b). Cognitive-behavioral body image therapy for body dysmorphic disorder. *Journal of Consulting and Clinical Psychology, 63*(2), 263–269 (published erratum appears in *Journal of Consulting and Clinical Psychology, 63*(3), 437).

Rost, K., Kashner, T. M., & Smith, G. R., Jr. (1994). Effectiveness of psychiatric intervention with somatization disorder patients: Improved outcomes at reduced cost. *General Hospital Psychiatry, 16,* 381–387.

Sackeim, H. A., Nordlie, J. W., & Gur, R. C. (1979). A model of hysterical and hypnotic blindness: Cognition, motivation, and awareness. *Journal of Abnormal Psychology, 88*(5), 474–489.

Salkovskis, P. M. (1989). Somatic problems. In K. Hawton, P. M. Salkovskis, J. Kirk, & D. M. Clark (Eds.), *Cognitive behavior therapy for psychiatric problems* (pp. 235–276). Oxford, England: Oxford University Press.

Salmon, P., Al-Marzooqi, S. M., Baker, G., & Reilly, J. (2003). Childhood family dysfunction and associated abuse in patients with nonepileptic seizures: Towards a causal model. *Psychosomatic Medicine, 65*(4), 695–700.

Salmon, P., Dowrick, C. F., Ring, A., & Humphris, G. M. (2004). Voiced but unheard agendas: Qualitative analysis of the psychosocial cues that patients with unexplained symptoms present to general practitioners. *British Journal of General Practice, 54*(500), 171–176.

Salmon, P., Dowrick, C. F., Ring, A., & Humphris, G. M. (2005). What do general practice patients want when they present medically unexplained symptoms, and why do their doctors feel pressurized? *Journal of Psychosomatic Research, 59,* 255–262.

Savard, G. (1990). Convulsive pseudoseizures: A review of current concepts. *Behavioral Neurology, 3*(3), 133–141.

Schwartz, G. E. (1990). Psychobiology of repression and health: A systems approach. In J. L. Singer (Ed.), *Repression and dissociation: Implications for personality theory, psychopathology, and health* (pp. 405–434). Chicago: University of Chicago Press.

Sensky, T., MacLeod, A. K., & Rigby, M. F. (1993). Causal attributions about somatic sensations among frequent general practice attenders. *Psychological Medicine, 26*(3), 641–646.

Sharp, T. J., & Nicholas, M. K. (2000). Assessing the significant others of chronic pain patients: The psychometric properties of significant other questionnaires. *Pain, 88,* 135–144.

Sharpe, M., & Bass, C. (1992). Pathophysiological mechanisms in somatization. *International Review of Psychiatry, 4,* 81–97.

Sharpe, M., Hawton, K., Simkin, S., Surawy, C., Hackmann, A., Klimes, I., Peto, T., Warrell, D., & Seagroatt, V. (1996). Cognitive behavior therapy for the chronic fatigue syndrome: A randomised controlled trial. *British Medical Journal, 312,* 22–26.

Sharpe, M. J., Peveler, R., & Mayou, R. (1992). The psychological treatment of patients with functional somatic symptoms: A practical guide. *Journal of Psychosomatic Research, 36*(6), 515–529.

Shedler, J., Mayman, M., & Manis, M. (1993). The illusion of mental health. *American Psychologist, 48*(11), 1117–1131.

Shorter, E. (1994). *From the mind into the body: The cultural origins of psychosomatic symptoms.* New York: Free Press.

Sifneos, P. E. (1973). The prevalence of "alexithymic" characteristics in psychosomatic patients. *Psychotherapy and Psychosomatics, 22,* 255–262.

Sigvardsson, S., Bohman, M., von Knorring, A. L., & Cloninger, C. R. (1986). Symptom patterns and causes of somatization in men: I. Differentiation of two discrete disorders. *Genetic Epidemiology, 3*(3), 153–169.

Simeon, D., Hollander, E., Stein, D. J., Cohen, L., & Aronowitz, B. (1995). Body dysmorphic disorder in the DSM-IV field trial for obsessive-compulsive disorder. *American Journal of Psychiatry, 152*(8), 1207–1209.

Simon, G., Gater, R., Kisely, S., & Piccinelly, M. (1996). Somatic symptoms of distress: An international primary care study. *Psychosomatic Medicine, 58,* 481–488.

Simon, G. E., Gureje, O., & Claudio, F. (2001). Course of hypochondriasis in an international primary care study. *General Hospital Psychiatry, 23,* 51–55.

Simon, G. E., Katon, W. J., & Sparks, P. J. (1990). Allergic to life: Psychological factors in environmental illness. *American Journal of Psychiatry, 147*(7), 901–908.

Simon, G. E., & Von Korff, M. (1991). Somatization and psychiatric disorder in the NIMH Epidemiologic Catchement Area study. *American Journal of Psychiatry, 148*(11), 1494–1500.

Sinclair, D. S. (1988). Repetitive strain syndrome: An Australian experience. *Journal of Rheumatology, 15*(11), 1729–1730.

Singh, S. P., & Lee, A. S. (1997). Conversion disorders in Nottingham: Alive, but not kicking. *Journal of Psychosomatic Research, 43,* 425–430.

Slater, E. (1965). Diagnosis of "hysteria." *British Medical Journal, 1*(5447), 1395–1399.

Slavney, P. R. (1990). *Perspectives on hysteria.* Baltimore: Johns Hopkins University Press.

Slavney, P. R. (1994). Pseudoseizures, sexual abuse, and hermeneutic reasoning. *Comprehensive Psychiatry, 35*(6), 471–477.

Slavney, P. R., Teitelbaum, M. L., & Chase, G. A. (1985). Referral for medically unexplained somatic complaints: The role of histrionic traits. *Psychosomatics, 26*(2), 103–109.

Small, G. W. (1986). Pseudocyesis: An overview. *Canadian Journal of Psychiatry, 31,* 452–457.

Smets, E. M., Garssen, B., Bonke, B., & De Haes, J. C. (1995). The Multidimensional Fatigue Inventory (MFI) psychometric qualities of an instrument to assess fatigue. *Journal of Psychosomatic Research, 39*(3), 315–325.

Smith, C. G., Clarke, D. M., Handrinos, D., Dunsis, A., & McKenzie, D. P. (2000). Consultation-liaison psychiatrists' management of somatoform disorders. *Psychosomatics, 41,* 481–489.

Smith, G. R., Golding, J. M., Kashner, T. M., & Rost, K. (1991). Antisocial personality disorder in primary care patients with somatization disorder. *Comprehensive Psychiatry, 32*(4), 367–372.

Smith, G. R., Monson, R. A., & Ray, D. C. (1986a). Psychiatric consultation in somatization disorder: A randomized controlled study. *New England Journal of Medicine, 314,* 1407–1413.

Smith, G. R., Monson, R. A., & Ray, D. C. (1986b). Patients with multiple unexplained symptoms: Their characteristics, functional health, and health care utilization. *Archives of Internal Medicine, 146,* 69–72.

Smith, G. R., Jr., Rost, K., & Kashner, M. (1995). A trial of the effect of a standardized psychiatric consultation on health outcomes and costs in somatizing patients. *Archives of General Psychiatry, 52,* 238–243.

Speckens, A. E., Van Hemert, A. M., Bolk, J. H., Rooijmans, H. G. M., & Hengeveld, M. W. (1996). Unexplained physical symptoms: Outcome, utilization of medical care and associated factors. *Psychological Medicine, 26,* 745–752.

Speckens, A. E., van Hemert, A. M., Spinhoven, P., Hawton, K. E., Bolk, J. H., & Rooijmans, H. G. (1995). Cognitive behavioral therapy for medically unexplained physical symptoms: A randomised controlled trial. *British Medical Journal, 311*(7016), 1328–1332.

Spitzer, R. L., Williams, J. B. W., Gibbon, M., & First, M. B. (1990). *Structured Clinical Interview for DSM-III-R—non-patient edition.* Washington, DC: American Psychiatric Press.

Starcevic, V. (1990). Relationship between hypochondriasis and obsessive compulsive disorder: Close relatives separated by nosological schemes? *American Journal Psychotherapy, 44*(3), 340.

Starkman, M. N., Marshall, J. C., La Ferla, J., & Kelch, R. P. (1985). Pseudocyesis: Psychologic and neuroendocrine interrelationships. *Psychosomatic Medicine, 47*(1), 46–57.

Stedwell, R. E., Allen, K. M., & Binder, L. S. (1992). Hypokalemic paralyses: A review of the etiologies, pathophysiology, presentation, and therapy. *American Journal of Emergency Medicine, 10*(2), 143–148.

Stefansson, J. D., Messina, J. A., & Meyerowitz, S. (1976). Hysterical neurosis, conversion type: Clinical and epidemiological considerations. *Acta Psychiatrica Scandinavica, 53,* 119–138.

Stern, J., Murphy, M., & Bass, C. (1993). Personality disorders in patients with somatisation disorder: A controlled study. *British Journal of Psychiatry, 363,* 785–789.

Sullivan, M. D., Katon, W., Dobie, R., Sakai, C., Russo, J., & Harrop-Griffiths, J. (1988). Disabling tinnitus: Association with affective disorder. *General Hospital Psychiatry, 10,* 285–291.

Sumathipala, A., Hewege, S., Hanwella, T., & Mann, A. H. (2000). Randomized controlled trial of cognitive behavior therapy for repeated consultations for medically unexplained complaints: A feasibility study in Sri Lanka. *Psychological Medicine, 30,* 747–757.

Swartz, M., Landerman, R., Blazer, D., & George, L. (1989). Somatization symptoms in the community: A rural/urban comparison. *Psychosomatics 30*(1), 44–53.

Swartz, M., Landerman, R., George, L. K., Blazer, D. G., & Escobar, J. (1991). Somatization disorder. In L. N. Robins & D. A. Regier (Eds.), *Psychiatric disorders in America: The Epidemiologic Catchment Area Study* (pp. 220–257). New York: Free Press.

Talley, N. J. (1991). Diagnosing an irritable bowel: Does sex matter? *Gastroenterology, 110,* 834–837.

Taylor, G. J., Bagby, R. M., Ryan, D. P., & Parker, J. D. A. (1990). Validation of the alexithymia construct: A measurement-based approach. *Canadian Journal of Psychiatry, 35,* 290–297.

Thieme, K., Turk, D. C., & Flor, H. (2004). Comorbid depression and anxiety in fibromyalgia syndrome: Relationship to somatic and psychosocial variables. *Psychosomatic Medicine, 66*(6), 837–844.

Thompson, W. G., & Pigeon-Reesor, H. (1990). The irritable bowel syndrome. *Seminars in Gastrointestinal Disease, 1*(1), 57–73.

Tomasson, K., Dent, D., & Coryell, W. (1991). Somatization and conversion disorders: Comorbidity and demographics at presentation. *Acta Psychiatrica Scandinavica, 84,* 288–293.

Toner, B. B. (1995). Gender differences in somatoform disorders. In M. V. Seeman (Ed.), *Gender and psychopathology* (pp. 287–310). Washington. DC: American Psychiatric Press.

Toone, B. K. (1990). Disorders of hysterical conversion. In C. M. Bass & R. H. Cawley (Eds.), *Somatization: Physical symptoms and psychological illness* (pp. 207–234). Oxford, England: Blackwell Scientific.

Trigwell, P., Hatcher, S., Johnson, M., Stanley, P., & House, A. (1995). "Abnormal" illness behavior in chronic fatigue syndrome and multiple sclerosis. *British Medical Journal, 311*(6996), 15–18.

Turk, D. C., & Melzack, R. (Eds.) (1992). *Handbook of pain assessment.* New York: Guilford.

Turkat, I. D., & Pettegrew, L. S. (1983). Development and validation of the Illness Behavior Inventory. *Journal of Behavioral Assessment, 5*(1), 35–47.

Van Houdenhove, B., & Joostens, P. (1995). Burning mouth syndrome: Successful treatment with combined psychotherapy and pharmacotherapy. *General Hospital Psychiatry, 17,* 385–388.

Veale, D., Boocock, A., Gournay, K., Dryden, W., Shah, F., Willson, R., & Walburn, J. (1996). Body dysmorphic disorder, a survey of fifty cases. *British Journal of Psychiatry, 169,* 196–201.

Verbrugge, L. M. (1985). Gender and health: An update on hypotheses and evidence. *Journal of Health and Social Behavior, 26,* 156–182.

Verhaak, P. F. M., & Tijhuis, M. A. R. (1994). The somatizing patient in general practice. *International Journal of Psychiatry in Medicine, 24*(2), 157–177.

Vollmer-Conna, U., Fazou, C., Cameron, B., Li, H., Brennan, C., Luck, L., Davenport, T., Wakefield, D., Hickie, I., & Lloyd, A. (2004). Production of pro-inflammatory cytokines correlates with the symptoms of acute sickness behavior in humans. *Psychological Medicine, 34*(7), 1289–1297.

Von Korff, M., Dworkin, S. F., LeResche, L., & Kruger, A. (1990). An epidemiologic comparison of pain complaints. *Pain, 32,* 173–183.

Von Korff, M., Wagner, E. H., Dworkin, S. F., & Saunders, K. W. (1991). Chronic pain and use of ambulatory health care. *Psychosomatic Medicine, 53,* 61–79.

Wahlund, K., List, T., & Ohrbach, R. (2005). The relationship between somatic and emotional stimuli: A comparison between adolescents with temporomandibular disorders (TMD) and a control group. *European Journal of Pain, 9*(2), 219–227.

Waldinger, R. J., Schulz, M. S., Barsky, A. J., & Ahern, D. K. (2006). Mapping the road from childhood trauma to adult somatization: The role of attachment. *Psychosomatic Medicine, 68*(1), 129–135.

Walker, E. A., Gelfand, A. N., Gelfand, M. D., & Katon, W. J. (1995). Psychiatric diagnoses, sexual and physical victimization, and disability in patients with irritable bowel syndrome or inflammatory bowel disease. *Psychological Medicine, 25,* 1259–1267.

Walker, E. A., Gelfand, A. N., Gelfand, M. D., Koss, M. P., & Katon, W. J. (1995). Medical and psychiatric symptoms in female gastroenterology clinic patients with histories of sexual victimization. *General Hospital Psychiatry, 17,* 85–92.

Walker, E. A., Katon, W. J., Hansom, J., Harrop-Griffiths, J., Holm, L., Jones, M. L., Hickok, L., & Jemelka, R. P. (1992). Medical and psychiatric symptoms in women with childhood sexual abuse. *Psychosomatic Medicine, 54,* 658–664.

Walker, E. A., Katon, W. J., Harrop-Griffiths, J., Holm, L., Russo, J., & Hickok, L. R. (1988). Relationship of chronic pelvic pain to psychiatric diagnosis and childhood sexual abuse. *American Journal of Psychiatry, 145,* 75–80.

Walker, E. A., Katon, W. J., Neraas, K., Jemelka, R. P., & Massoth, D. (1992). Dissociation in women with chronic pelvic pain. *American Journal of Psychiatry, 149*(4), 534–537.

Waller, E., & Scheidt, C. E. (2004). Somatoform disorders as disorders of affect regulation: a study comparing the TAS-20 with non-self-report measures of alexithymia. *Journal of Psychosomatic Research, 57*(3), 239–247.

Waller, E., Scheidt, C. E., & Hartmann, A. (2004). Attachment representation and illness behavior in somatoform disorders. *Journal of Nervous and Mental Disease, 192*(3), 200–209.

Ware, N. C., & Weiss, M. G. (1994). Neurasthenia and the social construction of psychiatric knowledge. *Transcultural Psychiatric Research Review, 31*(2), 101–124.

Warner, R. (1978). The diagnosis of antisocial and hysterical personality disorders: An example of sex bias. *Journal of Nervous and Mental Disease, 166,* 839–845.

Warwick, H. (1992). Provision of appropriate and effective reassurance. *International Review of Psychiatry, 4,* 76–80.

Warwick, H. (1995). Assessment of hypochondriasis. *Behavior Research and Therapy, 33*(7), 845–853.

Warwick, H. C., & Salkovskis, P. M. (1990). Hypochondriasis. *Behavior Research and Therapy, 28,* 105–117.

Watson, C. G., & Buranen, C. (1979a). The frequencies of conversion reaction symptoms. *Journal of Abnormal Psychology, 88*(2), 209–211.

Watson, C. G., & Buranen, C. (1979b). The frequency and identification of false positive conversion reactions. *Journal of Nervous and Mental Disease, 167,* 243–247.

Watt, M. C., Stewart, S. H., & Cox, B. J. (1998). A retrospective study of the learning history origins of anxiety sensitivity. *Behavior Research and Therapy, 36*(5), 505–525.

Watts, C. A. H., Cawte, E. C., & Kuenssberg, E. V. (1964). Survey of mental illness in general practice. *British Medical Journal, 2,* 1351–1359.

Wessely, S. (1994). Neurasthenia and chronic fatigue: Theory and practice in Britain and America. *Transcultural Psychiatric Research Review, 31*(2), 173–208.

Wessely, S., Nimnuan, C., & Sharpe, M. (1999). Functional somatic syndromes: One or many? *Lancet, 354,* 936–939.

Wessely, S., & Sharpe, M. (1995). Chronic fatigue, chronic fatigue syndrome, and fibromyalgia. In R. Mayou, C. Bass, & M. Sharpe (Eds.), *Treatment of functional somatic symptoms* (pp. 285–312). Oxford, England: Oxford University Press.

Westermeyer, J., Bouafuely, M., Neider, J., & Callies, A. (1989). Somatization among refugees: An epidemiologic study. *Psychosomatics, 30,* 34–43.

Wetzel, R. D., Guze, S. B., Cloninger, C. R., & Martin, R. L. (1994). Briquet's syndrome (hysteria) is both a somatoform and a "psychoform" illness: A Minnesota Multiphasic Personality Inventory study. *Psychosomatic Medicine, 56*(6), 564–569.

Whitehead, W. E., Busch, C. M., Heller, B. R., & Costa, P. T. (1986). Social learning influences on menstrual symptoms and illness behavior. *Health Psychology, 5,* 13–23.

Whitehead, W. E., Crowell, M. D., Heller, B. R., Robinson, J. C., Schuster, M. M., & Horn, S. (1994). Modeling and reinforcement of the sick role during childhood predicts adult illness behavior. *Psychosomatic Medicine, 56,* 541–550.

Wickramasekera, I. (1989). Enabling the somatizing patient to exit the somatic closet: A high risk model. *Psychotherapy, 26*(4), 530–544.

Wickramasekera, I. (1995). Somatization: Concepts, data, and predictions from the high risk model of threat perception. *Journal of Nervous and Mental Disease, 183*(1), 15–23.

Wileman, L., May, C., & Chew-Graham, C. A. (2002). Medically unexplained symptoms and the problem of power in the primary care consultation: A qualitative study. *Family Practice, 19*(2), 178–182.

Wilhelmsen, I., Haug, T. T., Ursin, H., & Berstad, A. (1995). Discriminant analysis of factors distinguishing patients with functional symptoms from patients with duodenal ulcer. Significance of somatization. *Digestive Diseases and Sciences, 40*(5), 1105–1111.

Wilkinson, S. R. (1988). *The child's world of illness: The development of health and illness behavior.* Cambridge, England: Cambridge University Press.

Williams, D. T., Spiegel, H., & Mostofsky, D. I. (1978). Neurogenic and hysterical seizures: Differential diagnostic and therapeutic considerations. *American Journal of Psychiatry, 135*(1), 82–86.

Winstead, B. A. (1984). Hysteria. In C. S. Widom (Ed.), *Sex roles and psychopathology* (pp. 73–100). New York: Plenum.

Wise, T. N., & Mann, L. S. (1994). The relationship between somatosensory amplification, alexithymia and neuroticism. *Journal of Psychosomatic Research, 38,* 515–521.

Wise, T. N., Mann, L. S., Mitchell, J. D., Hryniak, M., & Hill, B. (1990). Secondary alexithymia: An empirical validation. *Comprehensive Psychiatry, 31*(4), 284–285.

Wool, C. A., & Barsky, A. J. (1994). Do women somatize more than men? Gender differences in somatization. *Psychosomatics, 35*(5), 445–452.

World Health Organization. (1992). *The ICD-10 classification of mental and behavioral disorders: Clinical descriptions and diagnostic guidelines.* Geneva, Switzerland: World Health Organization.

Yonkers, K. A., & Gurguis, G. (1995). Gender differences in the prevalence and expression of anxiety disorders. In M. V. Seeman (Ed.), *Gender and psychopathology* (pp. 113–130). Washington, DC: American Psychiatric Press.

Yutsy, S. H., Cloninger, C. R., Guze, S. B., Pribor, E. F., Martin, R. L., Kathol, R. G., Smith, G. R., & Strain, J. J. (1995). DSM-IV field trial: Testing a new proposal for somatization disorder. *American Journal of Psychiatry, 152*(1), 97–101.

CHAPTER 13

Dissociative Disorders

ETZEL CARDEÑA AND DAVID H. GLEAVES

I felt totally estranged from all things and people ... I felt dazed and
detached from what was going on all around me.
Survivor from the 1989 San Francisco/Bay Area earthquake
(Cardeña, unpublished data)

DESCRIPTION OF THE DISORDERS

Few categories of psychopathology are as controversial as the dissociative
disorders (DDs). Detractors find some of them, particularly dissociative
identity disorder, suspect, if not outright iatrogenic; supporters maintain
that the disregard of dissociation diagnoses has condemned many patients to
inadequate diagnosis and treatment. Leaving aside for a moment this debate,
it is undeniable that the study of dissociation and DD has grown exponentially
in the last couple of decades, after considerable neglect since the turn of the
century (e.g., Hilgard, 1994; D. Spiegel & Cardeña, 1991). Besides a specialized
journal, the *Journal of Trauma & Dissociation,* and a professional society, the
International Society for the Study of Dissociation (ISSD), a number of volumes
have been dedicated to clinical and theoretical issues, including several comprehensive anthologies (e.g., Cohen, Berzoff, & Elin, 1995; Lynn & Rhue, 1994;
Michelson & Ray, 1996; D. Spiegel, 1994).

The rise of systematic research on dissociation has been fostered by recent
cognitive (e.g., Freyd & DePrince, 2001) and neural-developmental models
(Forrest, 2001) consistent with dissociative theories and by the development of
specific measures of dissociation, including paper-and-pencil questionnaires
of dissociative traits (e.g., Dissociative Experiences Scale [DES], Carlson & Putnam, 1993; Questionnaire of Experiences of Dissociation, Riley, 1988) and states
(e.g., Stanford Acute Stress Reaction Questionnaire, see Cardeña, Koopman,

Classen, Waelde, & Spiegel, 2000; Peritraumatic Dissociative Experiences Questionnaire, Marmar et al., 1994). A mental status examination (Loewenstein, 1991a) and structured clinical interviews also have been developed (e.g., Structured Clinical Interview of Dissociative Disorders [SCID-D], Steinberg, 1993; Dissociative Disorders Interview Schedule [DDIS], Ross, 1991; see Cardeña & Weiner, 2004, for a review of these and other measures).

Despite these developments, there is no consensus on what dissociation actually means. Although in simple terms, it refers to a lack of integration of psychological processes that normally should be integrated, the term has been used for different phenomena, such as the activation of behavioral subroutines (e.g., driving while focusing on a conversation), a lack of mental contents (e.g., "blanking out"), the recollection of forgotten traumatic memories, experiences in which the phenomenal self seems to be located outside the physical body (i.e., out-of-body experiences), the partial independence of explicit and implicit forms of memory, the apparently painless piercing of flesh in some rituals, and intrusive and realistic memories (flashbacks), among others. Dissociation has been used as a descriptive term or as a hypothetical construct, sometimes synonymous with repression, sometimes as a distinct defense mechanism.

Erdelyi (1994) subsumed the notion of the unconscious under the idea of dissociation, which he defined as the discrepancy between two indicators of information (e.g., conscious experience of calmness concurrent with physiological indicators of distress) or as memories that, while inaccessible at one point, may be later recovered. Besides this use (compartmentalization of experience), Cardeña (1994) also pointed out that other uses of the term include an alteration of consciousness characterized by detachment from the self or the environment and a purposeful mechanism of defense to ward off the emotional impact of traumatic events and memories. The clinical implications of the two descriptive concepts of dissociation (compartmentalization of psychological processes and experiential detachment) have been elaborated by Holmes and colleagues (2005).

Repression and dissociation frequently have been used to refer to the same manifestations such as the inability to remember a traumatic event. Some authors differentiate repression as a defense mechanism to ward off internal pressures and dissociation as an alteration in consciousness to deflect the overwhelming impact of ongoing trauma. This distinction, although problematic and not consensually accepted, does make some reference to the historical fact that Pierre Janet, who developed the concept of dissociation, saw it as a lack of integration produced by the impact of trauma on a psychologically deficient system, whereas Freud saw it more as the product of conflict among psychological structures. Dissociation can be used as a descriptive term to encompass disorders centered on the lack of integration among psychological processes such as the sense of self and/or the environment (e.g., depersonalization), emotions (e.g., emotional behaviors without the related feeling), physical sensations and agency (e.g., conversion disorders), memory (e.g., dissociative amnesia), and identity (e.g., dissociative identity disorder; Butler, Duran, Jasiukaitis, Koopman, & Spiegel, 1996; Cardeña, 1997). Converging research suggests that there are five moderately intercorrelated dimensions of dissociation: disengagement, identity dissociation, emotional constriction, memory disturbance, and depersonalization/derealization (Briere, Weathers, & Runtz, 2005). Janet also made a useful distinction between positive symptoms (exaggerations or additions to normal processes such as flashbacks in posttraumatic stress disorder [PTSD]) and negative symptoms (diminution of normal processes, such as lack of memory for personal information; Janet, 1907/1965).

The concept of dissociation, according to the *Diagnostic and Statistical Manual of Mental Disorders* (*DSM-IV-TR;* American Psychiatric Association [APA], 2000) is narrower and, arguably, descriptive rather than explanatory. In contrast, other authors use the term to describe a hypothetical mental process that gives rise to the DD (e.g., Nemiah, 1989). The *DSM-IV-TR* defines DDs as being characterized by a "disruption in the usually integrated functions of consciousness, memory, identity, or perception of the environment" (APA, 2000, p. 519) that is distressing or impairs basic areas of functioning. To qualify as dissociative, such discrepancies cannot be the product of malingering or other forms of conscious deception, and they cannot be directly caused by a medical condition. The effort to conceptualize dissociative disorders according to their observable characteristics follows the move of the *DSM* taxonomy from a psychodynamic characterization in its first two editions to the more descriptive model adopted later. However, some changes in the nosology have been controversial. Foremost among them, conversion and related somatoform disorders were moved from the dissociative category to the somatoform category. Critics of this taxonomic change have invoked historical, conceptual, and empirical arguments. Many of the cases of "hysteria" described at the turn of the century involved concurrent somatoform and dissociative phenomena such as conversion paralysis and dissociated identities (Kihlstrom, 1994). Conceptually, dissociation as a discrepancy or lack of integration between behaviors, experiences, and conscious experience would fit the nature of the somatoform disorders in which experiences of pain, motor, visceral, and sensory dysfunctions are present in the absence of pathophysiology. Furthermore, a substantial comorbidity of somatoform disorders with traumatic history and dissociative symptomatology has been replicated in various studies (e.g., Cardeña & Nijenhuis, 2000; Nijenhuis, 2000; Pribor, Yutzi, Dean, & Wetzel, 1993; Saxe et al., 1994).

One should bear in mind that dissociative experiences are associated with various medical conditions and biological factors, including damage to the central nervous system, prescription and nonprescription drugs, and seizure disorders (Good, 1993). Some authors use the term dissociation to address neurologically based conditions such as blindsight, in which there is a discrepancy between conscious experience and behavior (Farthing, 1992). However, the dissociative disorders refer strictly to conditions with a sociocultural/psychological etiology rather than a neurological one. For instance, the *DSM-IV* distinguishes between the presumed psychological etiology of dissociative amnesia and the biological etiology of alcohol amnestic syndrome. This distinction may be somewhat lost now, because some of these disorders were renamed in the last edition; for instance, psychogenic amnesia became dissociative amnesia. The presumption of a psychological etiology does not, of course, imply absence of biological underpinnings to these conditions (APA, 2000; P. Brown, 1994).

Even in the strict province of psychological conditions, other clarifications must be made. Dissociative phenomena, though they may be present as part of a clinical condition, are also experienced by normal individuals and may be associated with hypnosis, rituals, artistic activities, or personal development practices such as meditation (Cardeña, 1997). Dissociative experiences in general have been viewed as occurring on a continuum of severity (e.g., Braun, 1993), but Waller, Putnam, and Carlson (1996) found that, whereas some dissociative phenomena (i.e., absorption) overlap in clinical and nonclinical populations, others seem to distinguish non-pathological from pathological conditions (e.g., severe depersonalization, chronic amnesia). Thus, types of dissociative experiences that occur in the general population may be qualitatively different from those experienced by people with DD. Besides the general issues of distress and dysfunction, other dimensions such as controllability, recurrence, and organization of the experience help distinguish pathological from nonpathological manifestations. The previous considerations refer mostly to Western industrialized culture and do not address the fact that cultural beliefs and practices can pathologize or normalize diverse gaps in experience (Kirmayer, 1994), an issue discussed in a later section that discusses dissociative trance disorder.

The *DSM-IV* does not assume that dissociative disorders develop as the result of a defense mechanism invoked to cope with ongoing trauma, but it nonetheless asserts that these disorders are typically linked to traumatic events. In an important prospective, longitudinal study, Diseth (2006) has shown that a necessary but traumatic medical treatment (chronic anal dilation among children patients with anorectal anomalies or Hirschprung disease) was a strong and significant predictor of dissociative symptoms among adolescents and adults. Some researchers have argued that the clinical conditions most similar to the DDs are the posttraumatic diagnoses (acute stress disorder and PTSD) and that all of these conditions might be classified under the same category (e.g., Barlow & Durand, 2001; Cardeña, Butler, & Spiegel, 2003). Nonetheless, although traumatic events are related to DD, they are not a sufficient cause for these conditions. Other risk factors proposed include repeated exposure to trauma in an inescapable situation, at least among children (Terr, 1991), especially when brought about by a parental figure (Freyd, DePrince, & Zurbriggen, 2001). There is also evidence that the deleterious effects of reported sexual abuse are statistically independent from the effects of a general negative family context (Nelson et al., 2002). Recent research also provides growing evidence that disturbed forms of early attachment (especially avoidant and disorganized) predict pathological dissociation (e.g., Ogawa, Sroufe, Weinfield, Carlson, & Egeland, 1997).

An inborn disposition to dissociate has been proposed as a diathesis for the DDs (e.g., Braun, 1993; Butler et al., 1996). Consistent with this proposal, two studies have found substantial evidence for genetic and non–shared environment contributions to dissociation (Becker-Blease et al., 2004; Jang, Paris, Zweig-Frank, & Livesley, 1998), although an earlier study had not found evidence for the heritability of dissociation (Waller & Ross, 1997). We may speculate that the contribution of non–shared environment may refer to the traumatic events and failures of attachment mentioned previously. There is also consistent evidence for heritability of the related phenomena of hypnotizability (Morgan, 1973) and absorption (Tellegen et al., 1988).

The diagnoses of acute stress disorder (ASD), initially proposed as brief reactive dissociative disorder (Spiegel & Cardeña, 1991), and PTSD also involve substantial dissociative symptomatology; but they are discussed in chapter 11, Anxiety Disorders (see also Cardeña et al., 2003). Dissociative symptoms also may occur in the context of other conditions, including somatoform and panic disorders, psychosis, and some severe types of depression. Whether to assign one of these diagnoses a dissociative disorder or a dual diagnosis depends on the constellation and presentation of symptoms.

The following sections address DD in adults, by far the most studied group. The dissociative disorders are usually manifested in early to middle adulthood. Nonetheless, reports of childhood DD can be traced at least to the eighteenth century. Their assessment is particularly difficult because some manifestations (e.g., spontaneous staring spells, imaginary companions) are normal in some age groups. Putnam (1997) and Silberg (1998) provide authoritative introductions to the diagnosis and treatment of DD in children and adolescents.

EPIDEMIOLOGY

Epidemiological studies have rarely used instruments that evaluate DD directly (e.g., Kessler et al., 1994). Mezzich, Fabrega, Coffman, and Haley (1989) reported that these disorders, using *DSM-I* criteria, were rare in a psychiatric population. However, the assessment instrument that they used did not systematically inquire about dissociative experiences and only defined them as a "narrowing of consciousness" (Mezzich, Dow, Rich, Costello, & Himmelhoch, 1981, p. 471). In a review of studies using systematic measures, Gleaves (1996) found that the rate of DD among various clinical populations ranged from a low of 10% among obsessive-compulsive disorder patients to a high of 88% among women in treatment for severe sexual abuse. DDs also may be common among persons with personality disorders (Johnson, Cohen, Kasen, & Brook, 2006).

Ross (1991) evaluated systematically the epidemiology of DD in clinical and nonclinical samples. Using *DSM-III-R* criteria (which differ in some important ways from the current *DSM-IV-TR* criteria; Cardeña, Lewis-Fernández, Beahr, Pakianathan, & Spiegel, 1996), he found that approximately 21% of psychiatric patients also fulfilled criteria for DDs (5% to 14% fulfilled criteria for dissociative identity disorder). In a nonclinical Canadian sample ($N = 454$), Ross reported the following rates: 7% dissociative amnesia, 3.1 dissociative identity disorder (DID), 2.4 depersonalization disorder, 0.2% dissociative fugue, 0.2% of dissociative disorders not otherwise specified (11.2% a dissociative disorder of some type). The 3.1% prevalence of DID in the general population seems very high, but Ross commented that it included high-functioning individuals, and the *DSM-III-R* criteria he used did not include the requirements for amnesia or for the symptoms to be clinically distressing or to produce maladjustment. Ross's description of a pathological type of DID in about 1% of his sample is likely to be closer to the actual prevalence of this condition. In fact, Johnson et al. (2006) reported a DID prevalence of 1.5% in their community sample.

In a more recent study in an inpatient setting, Ross, Duffy, and Ellason (2002) found a lifetime prevalence of some type of DD of 41%, 44.5%, and 27% using structured interviews, semistructured interviews, or a masked clinician, respectively. However, there was not a single instance of dissociative fugue, and the diagnostic reliability for dissociative amnesia and depersonalization disorder were not adequate. In what is probably the most sound epidemiological study so far, there was a 29% prevalence of DD among a group of outpatients attending a nonspecialized inner-city center in New York (Foote, Smolin, Kaplan, Legatt, & Lipschitz, 2006). The authors explain the higher percentage by noting that their sample included a high number of clients reporting early physical and/or sexual abuse, and that their interview evaluation included all participants instead of eliminating some a priori through a screening questionnaire. The authors did not find a case of dissociative fugue, in accordance with the Ross et al. (2002) study and with previous calls to subsume dissociative fugue under dissociative amnesia (e.g., Cardeña, 1994). Studies in México (Robles-García, Garibay-Rico, Páez-Agraz, 2006), Turkey (Tutkun et al., 1998), and the Netherlands (Friedl & Draijer, 2000) also have found substantial rates of DD in clinical samples: 38%, 10%, and 8%, respectively.

DEMOGRAPHIC VARIABLES

Studies in the United States and Europe (see Vanderlinden, van der Hart, & Varga, 1996) suggest that, at least among nonclinical populations, dissociativity reaches its peak somewhere in early adolescence and then gradually declines with age. It is of interest that hypnotizability has a similar age distribution (Hilgard, 1968).

There is scant information on the impact of socioeconomic status or ethnicity on the incidence of dissociative pathology. Some researchers report that dissociative symptoms (not necessarily disorders) were more common among minorities, but when socioeconomic status was controlled, that difference disappeared (Zatzick, Marmar, Weiss, & Metzler, 1994). Nor have European studies found that ethnicity affects dissociativity (Vanderlinden et al., 1996), but an important caveat is that these studies have been conducted mostly in Western industrialized societies. Dissociative phenomena and disorders seem to have a different presentation in some societies (see later discussion). With respect to the so-called culture-bound syndromes with a dissociative component, both pathological spirit possession and *ataque de nervios* are predominantly found among women of lower socioeconomic status, while amok, berserk, and similar "assault" conditions are mostly found among men (Lewis-Fernández, 1994; Simons & Hughes, 1985).

Other than for some culture-bound syndromes and DID, there are no consistent findings about the gender distribution of other DDs (e.g., Vanderlinden et al., 1996). Some proponents of a strong skeptic position affirm that DID is mostly a condition of affluent U.S. White women, but research shows that this condition is found in other countries (e.g., Coons, Bowman, Kluft, & Milstein, 1991). Further, in the United States, DID does not affect only either White or affluent women (or men). For instance, Coons, Bowman, and Milstein (1988) described 50 cases, 40 of which came from a state psychiatric hospital and were patients who could not afford private care. The largest occupational level (28%) of these clients was clerical/sales/technician (P. M. Coons, personal communication, 1996). Similarly, Ross, Joshi, and Currie (1991) found that, in a large representative sample of Canadians, socioeconomic status was unrelated to the distribution of reported dissociative experiences.

What remains true is that, at least in the United States, DID is found at much higher rates among women than among men. As Kluft (1996) maintains, however, the 9-to-1 ratio of women to men found in many studies may be excessive because some men with DID end up incarcerated and are not assessed in epidemiological studies (see Lewis, Yeager, Swica, Pincus, & Lewis, 1997).

Depersonalization Disorder

Case Study 1

Frank, a 20-year-old college student, visited his student counseling center with a presenting problem that he described as a "freaked-out feeling." He described that, often while studying in his room, he would begin to feel somewhat disconnected from his body, as if he could barely feel his arms, face, or body. If he got up to walk around, he would become more distressed because it felt as if his feet were not touching the floor. He reported that he first became aware of the problem one night when he had stayed up late studying and drinking several cups of coffee, but the problems did not occur only while taking some sort of drug. Frank found the experiences very distressful (although they never led to episodes of panic), and they began to interfere with his academic functioning. His initial suspicion was that there was something physically wrong with him (such as a neurological problem), and, before going to the student counseling service, he had gone to the medical clinic. He was referred to the counseling service after no physical cause could be determined.

The therapist recognized that Frank was experiencing both depersonalization and derealization. In assessing the problem, it became clear that the episodes were generally associated with stress, lack of sleep, and Frank keeping his mind focused on one target (such as staring at a book) for a long period. It was as if he were putting himself into a hypnotic state. However, because of hypersensitivity to unexpected bodily sensations—interpreted as a loss of control—he found the experience very frightening, and his heightened fear led to increased depersonalization. In treatment, Frank acquired stress management skills and learned to break up his study habits to avoid inducing depersonalization while studying. However, the therapist also incorporated exercises to directly induce depersonalization (as is sometimes done in treating panic disorder) to desensitize him to the experiences and the bodily sensations.

Feeling estranged from bodily or psychological processes is not that unusual, although it is not a common topic of conversation. Poets (e.g., Trakl, Villaurrutia) have written about these experiences. Perhaps the most extreme form is autoscopy, in which an individual encounters a self-image outside the body. The experience of a "double" of oneself was studied by psychoanalyst Otto Rank and described by various writers (Poe and Dostoevsky, among others). Researchers have distinguished among various alterations of the self such as out-of-body experiences, autoscopy, and depersonalization proper (Gabbard, Twemlow, & Jones, 1982).

DSM-IV-TR (APA, 2000) defines depersonalization as persistent or recurrent experiences of feeling detached from one's mental processes or body, without loss of reality testing. It involves a perception or experience in which the usual sense of one's reality is temporarily lost or altered. The individual may experience a sense of being unreal, of being dead or unfeeling. Five types of depersonalization have been proposed: inauthenticity, self-negation, self-objectification, derealization, and body detachment (where self-objectification was more closely related to psychological disorganization than the other types) (Jacobs & Bovasso, 1992). Because only students participated in that study, it is unknown to what extent this finding would generalize to depersonalization disorder. The terms *depersonalization* and *derealization* are often used interchangeably. However, they describe different concepts. Whereas depersonalization involves detachment from or a sense of unreality about the self, in derealization this sense of detachment or unreality refers to the external world. Experiencers may describe feeling as if they were seeing the world "through a fog ... as if it were a dream," or as if they were watching a film. However, it is rare to find a case of chronic depersonalization without derealization, or vice versa.

Depersonalization experiences are distinguished from psychotic ones in that the former describe experiences of experiential detachment with intact reality testing, whereas psychotic episodes involve delusional beliefs. A depersonalized individual may feel like a robot or as if body movements are mechanical; people with psychosis, on the other hand, may hold delusional beliefs that they may have actual mechanical implants, are turning into metal, or that their relatives are impostors (i.e., *l'illusion des sosies,* Reed, 1972).

A literature review found that the four most common features of depersonalization were:

1. An altered sense of self (e.g., "My body doesn't belong to me").
2. A precipitating event (e.g., an accident, marijuana use).
3. A sense of unreality or a dream-like state (e.g., "Nothing seems real"; "I'm not real").
4. Sensory alterations (e.g., "Colors are less vibrant"; "Voices sound strange"; Kubin, Pakianathan, Cardeña, & Spiegel, 1989).

Depersonalization disorder should be distinguished from isolated or transient symptoms. The disorder involves depersonalization as the predominant disturbance with recurrent and chronic episodes that cause distress or maladjustment. Depression and anxiety are frequently present in depersonalization syndrome, and there is evidence that early emotional abuse is an important risk factor for this condition (Simeon, Guralnik, Schmeidler, Sirof, & Knutelska, 2000).

Isolated depersonalization symptoms may be the third most common psychiatric symptom, present in about 40% of psychiatric patients (Steinberg, 1990). Depersonalization symptoms are frequent in other dissociative disorders and in panic disorder. When depersonalization occurs exclusively in the presence of another psychological disorder, the latter is the superordinate diagnosis. Because depersonalization symptoms co-occur often with anxiety, the construct of depersonalization disorder has been questioned, but empirical work has upheld its validity (Simeon et al., 1997).

Depersonalization episodes are not uncommon among nonclinical populations and frequently occur during or shortly after a traumatic event (Cardeña & Spiegel, 1993; Koopman, Classen, Cardeña, & Spiegel, 1995; Noyes & Kletti, 1977). They also can occur as a by-product of meditation (Lazarus, 1976) or psychedelic drug ingestion, and some hypnotic suggestions are specifically geared to produce a sense of disconnection with the individual's movements or sensations (Cardeña & Spiegel, 1991). In a survey of more than 1,000 nonclinical adults, Aderibigbe, Bloch, and Walker (2001) reported prevalence rates of 19.1% for depersonalization, 14.4% for derealization, and 23.4% for either experience. However, a much smaller percentage of the population will meet the full criteria for depersonalization disorder. In Johnson et al.'s (2006) sample of 658 adults, only 0.8% appeared to meet them.

The diagnosis is difficult because patients may not report depersonalization initially, but rather may complain of depression, general anxiety, or fear of becoming insane. They may lack the language to describe how they feel, or they may confuse their experiences with incipient psychosis. Because of this communication problem, clinicians should consider using direct queries about whether the individual may have chronic episodes of disconnections with the body or emotions, out-of-body experiences, sensations of the world being unreal at times, and so on, besides inquiring about other dissociative phenomena such as episodes of amnesia or alterations of consciousness.

Differential diagnoses include other conditions in which depersonalization is one—but not the central—symptom (e.g., DID, panic disorder, depression, obsessive-compulsive disorder, and hypochondriasis). Other conditions to rule out include schizophrenia, borderline personality disorder, substance abuse disorders, medical conditions, and medication side effects. Diagnosticians should be particularly careful to rule out seizure disorders, particularly temporal lobe epilepsy, which often include depersonalization episodes (Litwin & Cardeña, 2000).

To remedy the lack of systematic research on the disorder, Simeon and collaborators have initiated a program of research on depersonalization. Their findings about depersonalization include: (1) Related attentional and memory problems (Guralnik, Schmeidler, & Simeon, 2000); (2) Functional abnormalities in cortical areas associated with sensory integration and body schema (Simeon et al., 2000); and (3) Hypothalamic-pituitary-adrenal dysregulation (Simeon, Guralnik, Knutelska, Hollander, & Schmeidler, 2001).

Dissociative Amnesia

Case Study 2

A soldier in his early 20s was found in the bathroom of an airport, with his pants down (and no evidence of sexual assault, but see Kaszniak, Nussbaum, Berren, & Santiago, 1988) and without his wallet or any recollection of his name, family, where he came from, or where he was going. He also showed various signs of anxiety, including heavy stuttering. Initially, he did not recognize his family or his girlfriend, but after he was taken to a military hospital and started treatment with medications and hypnosis, his anxiety symptoms started to subside and he began to recognize his relatives and girlfriend. He was eventually dismissed from the military and went back to his family's home, where he seemed to respond to and enjoy the care he was receiving. His memories continued coming back, although a follow-up 6 months after the incident still found him amnesic for the precipitating event. Analysis of his personality strongly suggested immaturity, although this is not necessarily generalizable to other individuals with dissociative amnesia.

This disorder is important for its own sake and because it serves as the basis for two other DDs: dissociative fugue and dissociative identity disorder.

According to the *DSM-IV* (APA, 2000), dissociative (previously called psychogenic) amnesia is characterized by one or more instances of amnesia for important personal information that cannot be explained by ordinary forgetfulness, the common developmental amnesia for the first years of life, or an organic condition.

The distinction between psychogenic amnesia and that caused by a neurological condition is critical for diagnosis. Fortunately, the two conditions typically have different presentations. In the case of dissociative amnesia after a traumatic event, loss of memory is typically retrograde in the sense that the patient does not remember all or part of the trauma or previous events, and he or she usually has no problem with learning new material or remembering what occurred after the trauma. Such presentation is in sharp contrast with a number of organic amnesias (e.g., various dementias, alcohol amnestic syndrome) in which the amnesia is anterograde; that is, the patient is unable to remember events occurring after the onset of amnesia, although he or she may preserve older memories and may show implicit, but not explicit, memory for new material. Generally, dissociative amnesia involves loss of explicit/declarative (autobiographical knowledge) memory rather than nondeclarative (general knowledge, feelings, sensations, conditioning, and habits) memory. A second distinction is that dissociative amnesia is believed to be, at least potentially, a reversible memory impairment. In contrast, explicit memories for neurologically based amnesias are typically inaccessible, or whatever recovery occurs is very gradual and incomplete.

Dissociative amnesia is closely related to severe stress or exposure to trauma, including experiences of combat, natural disaster, being the victim of violence, or childhood abuse. Legal problems, financial disaster, severe marital problems, depression, and suicide attempts have also triggered this disorder (Coons & Milstein, 1992; Kopelman, 1987; Loewenstein, 1991b).

The precipitating event(s) for dissociative amnesia, although usually traumatic (APA, 2000), can be complex and involve idiosyncratic elements. In the case study, the only obvious external event before the amnesia episode was the impending sale of the soldier's childhood home (which seemed to have a greater personal impact for him than for most individuals), but forgotten fantasies about that event or about something else might have played an equal or more important role. In a Gulf War veteran with PTSD, hearing a cannon shot made him slide under a parked car. Even weeks after the incident, he had no memory of the period from the moment of the shooting to the time when other soldiers got him out from under the car. Not uncharacteristically, he did not respond to his colleagues for a few minutes.

The presentation of amnesia can vary according to the frequency of episodes, the extent of amnesia, and temporal parameters. As to frequency, patients can have one or very few episodes of amnesia or have a chronic condition. Coons and Milstein (1992) described a group of patients, typically with reported history of early abuse, with chronic forms of amnesia. These recurrent episodes usually involved one or more of the following: episodes of "missing time," unexplainable forgetfulness, chronic amnesia for periods that should be remembered (e.g., not remembering any event that occurred when the individual was 13–15 years of age), and so on.

Episodes of amnesia can be generalized, localized, selective, or systematized. Most cases (76% in Coons & Milstein, 1992) involve forms of amnesia other than the generalized type. Generalized or global amnesia involves amnesia for all or most personal information, including name, personal history, and identity of relatives and friends. Localized amnesia refers to forgetting what transpired during a certain period, although the individual remembers previous and subsequent events (e.g., an individual involved in an automobile accident, who did not suffer neurological damage, may nonetheless not remember anything that occurred some minutes before and after the accident). With selective amnesia, the individual may recall some but not all features of a specified event or circumstance (e.g., a victim of a violent armed robbery may have forgotten the incident or some central elements of it.). Systematized amnesia involves an inability to remember certain categories of experiences. For example, following the tragic death of a sibling, an individual may be unable to recall memories containing the lost sibling. The controversial type of amnesia in which an individual is unable to remember a series of sexually abusive experiences but retains memories of other events falls into the systematized amnesia category, assuming that the individual did not meet the diagnostic criteria for a more severe dissociative disorder. Sometimes the concepts of systematized and selective amnesia are used interchangeably, although they differ along the lines just described. In any case, typically, dissociative amnesia is organized according to emotional rather than temporal parameters (Schacter, Wang, Tulving, & Freedman, 1982).

Depression, anxiety, episodes of depersonalization, and trance (i.e., apparent unawareness of or unresponsiveness to one's surroundings) frequently predate or are associated with dissociative amnesia. In people with a history of early and chronic abuse, a more complex syndrome that may also include relationship problems, PTSD symptoms, self-injurious behavior, substance abuse, sexual problems, and various other symptoms may be present (see Cardeña et al., 2003, for a review).

When dissociative amnesia is not chronic and follows a traumatic event, the prognosis is usually good. Once the client is in a safe environment, therapy can gradually bring a complete or substantial recovery of the memories in a matter of days or weeks; there also can be spontaneous recovery of material without therapeutic intervention. Chronic and recurrent episodes of amnesia, on the other hand, are much more complex, may require therapy, and have a less certain outcome.

Differential diagnoses of this condition include other dissociative disorders that are superordinate to amnesia (dissociative fugue, DID, ASD, PTSD, and somatization disorder). Other diagnoses to consider include various medical conditions that can produce amnesia, among them transient global amnesia, a brief amnestic episode involving confusion and typically caused by transient vascular insufficiency (Rollinson, 1978); amnestic alcohol or Korsakoff's syndrome; head injury; epilepsy; dementia; stroke; postoperative amnesia; postinfectious amnesia; and anoxic amnesia (Benson, 1978; Keller & Shaywitz, 1986; Kopelman, 1987). Dissociative amnesia must be differentiated also from that produced by various drugs, foremost alcohol blackouts and the amnesia produced by "date rape" drugs such as rohypnol. In a legal context, clinicians should also consider the possibility of malingering.

Usually, presentation of the amnesia (e.g., selective, retrograde, associated with depression or anxiety) and the surrounding circumstances (e.g., precipitating trauma or severe stress without head injury) give an indication of the likely diagnosis (Sivec & Lynn, 1995). A detailed clinical history and laboratory analyses can usually rule out other possibilities. The clinician has to be mindful that amnesia may not be a presenting problem. Among the reasons for this are that the individuals may have amnesia for the amnestic episodes—that is, they may be aware of suddenly finding themselves in a place without knowing how they got there but may later forget that this event occurred, or they may assume that these episodes of "forgetfulness" are shared by everybody else. Assessment for this and other DDs may include one or more of the questionnaires and clinical interviews mentioned previously. At the very least, if the clinician suspects amnesia, a number of areas should be investigated, including memory gaps in everyday life, failure to give an account of salient episodes from late childhood onward, finding items that recently have been bought but for which the client has no memory, and so on. (cf. Loewenstein, 1991a).

Although the earlier reports of dissociative amnesia and fugue concentrated on male soldiers in time of war, more recent work (e.g., Coons & Milstein, 1992) has reported a preponderance of females, and, as with the other DDs, dissociative amnesia seems to affect young adults more than other groups.

As with the other dissociative disorders, at present there are no biological techniques to evaluate dissociative amnesia, although cognitive procedures are being developed to distinguish real from simulated amnesia (e.g., Kopelman, Christensen, Puffett, & Stanhope, 1994). Given the possibility of simulated, or otherwise nongenuine, amnesia, there is some skepticism (e.g., Loftus, 1993) concerning reports of apparently recovered memories, particularly concerning early abuse, which could be interpreted as denying the existence of dissociative amnesia. Although a full coverage of these issues is beyond the scope of this chapter, there is good reason to question the view that false memories about substantial matters are easily or commonly produced by psychotherapists (D. Brown, 1995; Gleaves, Smith, Butler, & Spiegel, 2004). More importantly, evidence for the reality of dissociative amnesia has accumulated for decades and in contexts independent of therapy or early abuse, including combat trauma, torture, traumatic loss, and crime (e.g., van der Hart & Nijenhuis, 1995). D. Brown, Scheflin, and Whitfield (1999) reviewed the clinical research in this area and concluded: "In just this past decade alone, 68 research studies have been conducted on naturally occurring dissociative or traumatic amnesia for childhood sexual abuse. Not a single one of the 68 data-based studies failed to find it" (p. 126).

At this stage, the debate should no longer be on whether most recovered memories are completely accurate or inaccurate—untenable positions given the evidence—but on the individual and social characteristics that facilitate or hinder accurate retrieval. Even in less controversial examples than early abuse, an evaluation of the validity of the amnesia is likely to be more complex than has been usually considered. For instance, Kopelman and collaborators (1994) thoroughly studied a case of functional retrograde amnesia in which there was a probable mixture of actual amnesia and simulation. The authors proposed that dissociative amnesia involves different levels of awareness for different memories, in accord with early Freudian and current models of memory and cognition, rather than a simple conscious-nonconscious dichotomy. Amnesia may fluctuate in time, and cognitive (Schooler, 1994) and neurophysiological (Bremner, Krystal, Southwick, & Charney, 1995) mechanisms may explain both dissociative amnesia and the recovery of the forgotten material. Finally, the external validity of some recovered memories does not in any way negate the reality of confabulation and suggestive influences on memory (Loftus, 1993). Both phenomena show the malleability of memory and the effect of suggestive influences (self- or other-generated) on forgetfulness of matters that did occur or remembrance of matters that did not occur (Butler & Spiegel, 1997).

Dissociative Fugue
Case Study 3

Marta, a middle-aged single mother, arrived at a health clinic in rural Mexico. While interviewing her, it became clear that she was unable to be still or remain seated; during the rare moments when she sat, she kept on fidgeting. She was lucid and could give a coherent account of her life. Some months before arriving at the clinic, a man had attempted to rape one of her nieces. He was caught by the child's relatives, who nearly hanged him from a roof beam. A few days later, Marta left her home for a short while, and when she came back, she noticed that the door was open. The thought that one of her daughters had been raped immediately came to her mind (although nothing had actually happened), and the next thing she remembers is walking by Mexico City's cathedral, hundreds of miles from her hometown, with no recollection of how she had gotten there and feeling confused about herself. She was referred to a medical center, where a physician prescribed neuroleptics. When seen by a psychiatrist and the first author, she was taking four types of neuroleptics. Her restlessness was neuroleptic-induced akathisia; when her medications were tapered down, the symptoms disappeared. The other symptoms are indicative of dissociative fugue.

Dissociative fugue is defined by the sudden wandering away from a place of residence or employment, amnesia for the past, and confusion about personal identity or adoption of a new identity. It is not surprising that generalized amnesia and personal confusion would be associated with leaving one's customary surroundings, so dissociative fugue may be considered an extreme case of generalized amnesia.

Before the *DSM-IV*, the diagnosis of dissociative fugue was circumscribed to individuals who changed their identity for another one. This form was probably immortalized by William James's description of the Reverend Ansel Bourne, who left his hometown and adopted a new name and profession, only to "wake up" at a later point to the knowledge of his previous identity (James, 1890/1923; see also Kenny, 1986). It is relatively common to read in newspapers of modern-day "Bournes." More recent studies show that it is by far more common to find a presentation in which the individual is, at least initially, confused about his or her identity (Loewenstein, 1991b; Riether & Stoudemire, 1988); nonetheless, an undetected and unresolved case of identity confusion may resolve into a new identity.

The nature of the confusion of identity is not clear at present, but some authors have described it as an alteration of consciousness. William James (1890/1923) saw fugue as a long-lasting "trance"; Stengel (1941, p. 255, in Loewenstein, 1991b) defined it as "states of altered or narrowed consciousness with the impulse to wander." These definitions are consistent with Pierre Janet's view of dissociation as involving a focusing and narrowing of consciousness (van der Kolk & van der Hart, 1989). Supportive of this notion, nonclinical groups exposed to the 1989 Bay Area earthquake reported that their attention was significantly narrower and more focused during the earthquake week than it was 4 months afterward (Cardeña & Spiegel, 1993), a finding consistent with laboratory studies (e.g., Christianson & Loftus, 1987). Some authors propose other constructs such as strategic self-presentation and a culturally prescribed "idiom of distress" (Kenny, 1986; Spanos, 1994), but these concepts are not incompatible with an alteration of consciousness.

As in the case of dissociative amnesia, traumatic events and severe stress are the common precipitants of this condition. Early references to dissociative amnesia and fugue centered on soldiers at time of war. Grinker and Spiegel (1945, p. 372) wrote that "the psychotic reactions seen mostly in ground troops were due to a negation of reality by the process of dissociation." Although the aftereffects of war continue to produce dissociative symptomatology, most fugue patients in hospitals today are civilians fleeing the terrors of urban life.

Loewenstein (1991b) maintains that, in nomadic modern societies, some patients have a "nonclassic" presentation in which they do not complain of fugue unless queried about it. He maintains that, in urban settings, isolated or abused individuals may have episodes of fugue without anyone noticing, much less bringing this fact to official agencies. Some may become homeless; others, particularly teenagers having a fugue episode after abuse, may be easily lured or forced into illegal activities. For these reasons, accurate estimates of the prevalence of fugue are difficult to obtain.

The symptoms associated with dissociative fugue are the same as those for dissociative amnesia. If the fugue is part of a DID, the *DSM* nosology makes the latter a superordinate diagnosis. Differential diagnoses of fugue include complex partial seizure involving postictal episodes of aimless wandering, amnesia, and disorientation, also known as poriomania (Mayeux, Alexander, Benson, Brandt, & Rosen, 1979). Episodes of poriomania tend to be short-lived, usually a matter of minutes, in contrast to the longer duration of a fugue; and, as compared with poriomanias, fugues may respond to hypnosis and similar techniques (Sivec & Lynn, 1995). Other diagnoses to consider are manic or schizophrenic episodes accompanied by traveling, organic, nonepileptic factors such as brain tumors, and alcohol and drug-related loss of memory and wandering (cf. Akhtar & Brenner, 1979). Generally, the characteristic symptoms of other diagnoses (e.g., the grandiosity and impulsivity in mania) can easily differentiate the conditions. Nonetheless, clinicians unfamiliar with the dissociative disorders may conclude that they are dealing with a psychosis, as in the case study.

Dissociative Identity Disorder

Case Study 4

Joan, a 30-year-old married mother of two, presented for treatment of a sexual dysfunction that was reportedly affecting her marriage. Although Joan reported also having problems with depression dating back to childhood, she denied other problems. Because of the presenting problem, Joan's therapist asked that Joan's spouse come in for an information-gathering session and to discuss possible sex therapy. During the first discussion with Joan's spouse, it became clear that Joan had a variety of problems that she had not disclosed during the initial assessment. Most striking to her husband were her memory problems. He described how frequently she would do things and then not remember having done them. He also described sometimes finding her in a terrified state, hiding in her closet or under the bed, acting as if she did not recognize him during these times. Joan's husband also reported that Joan had grown up in a violent, abusive family and that several of Joan's siblings reported having been severely abused, both physically and sexually.

Joan was very frightened about discussing many of these problems with the therapist because she felt they meant that she was "crazy." However, when reassured by the therapist and supported by her husband, she described striking episodes of amnesia lasting for hours, days, or even weeks. She described having no memory of a variety of significant events in her life, including the birth of her two children, her marriage, her sexual experiences, and several events from her childhood and adolescence. Joan also described frequent episodes of depersonalization and derealization, nightmares, and flashbacks; she also disclosed that she frequently heard voices coming from within her head. She described that some of the voices sounded angry and others comforting. She perceived the voices as coming from other people inside her head, and the voices expressed a belief that they were different people. It became clear that these voices were of the alter identities that sometimes took control of Joan's functioning. These "alters" also seemed to remember the events (both recent and remote) that Joan could not otherwise remember.

The therapist arrived at primary diagnoses of DID and PTSD. The sexual problems and depression were seen as secondary features of the DID and comorbid PTSD, and it was decided to not directly target these problems until progress had been made on the primary problems. In the early phases of treatment, Joan's therapist worked on improving Joan's overall level of functioning, first orienting her to the fact that she was one individual, working to reduce internal conflict and restore continuity of memory. In the middle and later phases of the treatment, Joan and her therapist directed their efforts toward processing memories of the childhood physical and sexual abuse that she had experienced. As this work progressed, the perceived separateness of the alter identities diminished, other dissociative experiences decreased in frequency, and Joan developed a cohesive memory for her life. Joan's sexual aversion, as well as her depression, also began to dissipate.

The possibility that two or more streams of consciousness or identity states coexist in one body has intrigued scientists and writers for centuries. At the beginning of the twentieth century, William James, Morton Prince, Pierre Janet, and other eminent clinicians studied this phenomenon. Although long regarded as an exotic and extremely rare curiosity, this condition has been systematically studied in recent years.

Dissociative identity disorder is the current label for what was formerly called multiple personality disorder. According to the *DSM-IV-TR* (APA, 2000), its defining features are the presence in the person of two or more distinct identities or personality states with enduring patterns of perceiving, relating to, and thinking about the environment and the self, which recurrently take control of the individual.

The other essential feature is psychogenic amnesia. In the case of DID, the issue of amnesia is more complex than in pure dissociative amnesia because an alter may claim to have memory for events of which another alter is amnesic.

A core set of features of DID may be as essential as the diagnostic criteria. They include chronic depersonalization and derealization, a variety of memory disturbances, identity alteration and confusion, and experiences of auditory hallucinations perceived as coming from inside the individual's head (Boon & Draijer, 1993; Gleaves, May, & Cardeña, 2001; Steinberg, Cicchetti, Buchanan, Rakfeldt, & Rounsaville, 1994). Some researchers have argued that the *DSM* criteria should be revised to focus on these features, and an issue of the *Journal of Trauma & Dissociation* was devoted to this topic (see Dell, 2001, and commentaries).

The *DSM-IV* made more changes to the diagnostic criteria of this condition than to those of any other dissociative disorder (Cardeña et al., 1996). There were two main reasons for changing the name from multiple personality disorder to dissociative identity disorder. First, the older term emphasized the concept of "many" personalities, whereas the current view is that the main problem of these individuals does not involve having a number of personalities, but failing to have the sort of complex, multifaceted, but unified, personality that most of us have. That is, the many aspects of personality—acquiescent or aggressive, playful or serious—are not integrated in these people, but remain as isolated and personalized nuclei. The International Society for the Study of Trauma and Dissociation (2005) states it this way: "The DID patient is a single person who experiences himself/herself as having separate self-states or alternate identities, each of which has relative psychological autonomy from one another."

Another reason for the name change is that the term personality refers to the characteristic pattern of thoughts, feelings, moods, and behaviors of the whole individual. From this perspective, the fact that DID patients consistently switch between different identities, behavior styles, and so on, constitutes their characteristic personality. This is also the main reason that the current phraseology of the *DSM* refers to "distinct identities or personality states" rather than to personalities. Other phrasing changes in diagnostic criteria clarified that, although alters may be personalized by the individual, they are not to be considered as having an objective, independent existence.

The *DSM-IV* adopted the criterion of amnesia, which had been considered but not adopted for the *DSM-III-R* (APA, 1987). The rationale then had been that, although amnesia may indeed be an essential characteristic of the condition, individuals might fail to report this symptom because they might not remember their own amnesic episodes, or for other reasons (Kluft, Steinberg, & Spitzer, 1988). Analysis of various publications and datasets revealed, however, that an increase in false negative diagnoses with the re-adoption of the new criterion is very unlikely because amnesia was a symptom in all DID patients who had been systematically evaluated (Cardeña et al., 1996). These data confirmed that amnesia is a central component of the condition (see Dorahy, 2001, for a review of memory functioning in DID).

DID is generally considered the most severe of the dissociative disorders, and it is the most thoroughly researched. Initially, only a few authors accounted for most of the research in this area, but there has been a steady growth in the number of contributors to the field. Although acceptance of the diagnosis among psychologists and psychiatrists is considerable at least in the United States (Dunn,

Paolo, Ryan, & van Fleet, 1994), DID remains the most controversial of all DDs. Two issues have been vigorously debated in the mental health field: first, the etiology/reality of the phenomenon and, second, its diagnostic validity. Currently, the two primary positions on the etiology of DID are the posttraumatic and iatrogenic perspectives.

Proponents of the posttraumatic, or traumatogenic, model (e.g., Gleaves, 1996; Kluft, 1985) suggest that DID is a form of developmental psychopathology that occurs as a response to overwhelming childhood trauma within a diathesis-stress model, in which a disposition to use dissociative skills, including hypnotic ability, interacts with early trauma and attachment disturbances. The *DSM-IV-TR* (APA, 2000, p. 528) maintains that DID is more common among first-degree biological relatives, but there is no current information on whether this relationship is caused by genetic or environmental factors or, more likely, an interaction of both (see earlier sections).

In contrast with the posttraumatic model, proponents of the iatrogenesis (sometimes referred to as sociocognitive) position (e.g., Piper & Merskey, 2004; Spanos, 1994) maintain that DID is an artifact of psychotherapy and/or the popular media. There is some variability among this camp with positions ranging from those who think that the condition is mostly or completely iatrogenic (e.g., Aldridge-Morris, 1989), produced by naive therapists and the media, to those who state that the condition is not necessarily iatrogenic but is molded by cultural expectations and social roles and strategies (e.g., Spanos, 1994). Proponents of the iatrogenic explanation point out that DID patients show significantly higher hypnotizability than other clinical groups and normal individuals (Frischholz, Lipman, Braun, & Sachs, 1992) and are thus prone to follow manifest or subtle suggestions provided by hypnotists probing for possible hidden personalities or alters. Two studies (Putnam, Guroff, Silberman, Barban, & Post, 1986; Ross, Norton, & Fraser, 1989) have answered this objection by showing that neither the use of hypnosis nor other proposed therapist characteristics can account for the majority of DID diagnoses. Also, if DID patients were just following clinicians' suggestions, they would present with other conditions, because the vast majority have previously received other diagnoses (Coons et al., 1988; Putnam et al., 1986; Ross, Norton, & Wozney, 1989).

Although more research is needed, the available evidence generally supports the posttraumatic conceptualization for most cases. People with DID almost invariably report a history of childhood trauma, with some research demonstrating independent corroboration through medical and legal records or other means (Coons, 1994; Coons & Milstein, 1986; Hornstein & Putnam, 1992). This does not mean, of course, that all reports, or all details of every report, are valid or accurate, but it shows that at least a significant proportion of DID patients have verifiable histories of abuse. Most or all people with DID also have comorbid PTSD, and many of the symptoms of PTSD are dissociative (see Cardeña, Butler, & Spiegel, 2003). Accumulating data on the psychobiology of chronic trauma support the posttraumatic formulation (Forrest, 2001; Vermetten, Schmahl, Lindner, Loewenstein, & Bremner, 2006). Interalter amnesia is both complex and not consistent with a simple malingering hypothesis (Eich, Macaulay, Loewenstein, & Patrice, 1997). Studies using brain imaging technology support the validity for the concept of switching between alters (Tsai, Condie, Wu, & Chang, 1999) and the diagnosis as a whole (Sar, Unal, Kiziltan, Kundakci, & Ozturk, 2001).

Gleaves (1996) proposed that most, if not all, of the assumptions of the iatrogenesis/sociocognitive model are inaccurate and misrepresent the psychopathology, assessment, and treatment of DID. Perhaps the greatest misconception is equating DID with the concept of multiple identity enactment (e.g., Spanos, 1994). As noted previously, DID is characterized by a chronic pattern of dissociative experiences including amnesia, depersonalization, and derealization. The identity disturbance is better understood as a perception of having separate selves, rather than as having different individuals coexisting in the same body. People with DID also appear to actively conceal what they perceive to be a set of separate selves.

DID may be more frequently diagnosed in North America than in other places, but there is considerable evidence for its existence in other countries (e.g., Boon & Draijer, 1991; Coons et al., 1991; Leonard, Brann, & Tiller, 2005; Martínez-Taboas, 1991; Tutkun, Yargic, & Sar, 1995). An alternative explanation to iatrogenesis is that clinicians in the United States only recently have become aware of the characteristics and method of evaluation of DID, and other countries are lagging behind. For instance, when the first author taught a course in Spain on DD, three clinicians without previous knowledge of dissociation independently described clients from their practices who were almost textbook descriptions of DID but had received other diagnoses. That DID, as well as our nonpathological sense of self, is mediated by cultural notions of self, identity, personal consistency, and so on (e.g., Kirmayer, 1994) is a different issue from whether DID is an iatrogenic condition.

The high hypnotic susceptibility of DID patients, coupled with the possible incompetent use of hypnosis or other suggestive techniques by some practitioners, raises the possibility of iatrogenesis. The empirical support for the traumatogenic theory does not preclude the likelihood that therapist suggestion or malingering are causal factors in a few cases (Ross, 1997), but this is the case for all disorders, not only DID. There are serious problems with the iatrogenesis model, and even the model's proponents admit that there is "a paucity of data" to support it (Lilienfeld et al., 1999, p. 36). Similarly, Brown, Frischolz, and Scheflin (1999) concluded that "these sparse data fail to meet a minimal standard of scientific evidence justifying the claim that a major psychiatric diagnosis like dissociative identity disorder per se can be produced through suggestive influences in therapy" (p. 549). The absence of empirical studies by some of the critics seems to be substituted by their intemperate tone (e.g., Piper & Merskey, 2004).

As to the second area of controversy—that of diagnostic validity—some researchers and clinicians regard the phenomenology as genuine (i.e., not iatrogenic), but symptomatic of other disorders, and not an independent diagnostic entity (North, Ryall, Ricci, & Wetzel, 1993). Fahy (1988), for example, described DID as "an intriguing symptom of a wide range of psychological disturbances" (p. 603). Ross (1997) reviewed much of the data on this issue and concluded that, "although the data are not definitive, the burden of proof lies on extreme disbelievers to establish through scientific studies that DID is not valid and reliable, since the existing data point to the opposite conclusion" (p. 79). More recently, after reviewing three different guidelines to establish diagnostic validity, Gleaves, May, and Cardeña (2001) concluded that considerable converging evidence supports the validity of the diagnosis and its inclusion in the *DSM*. They demonstrated that the reliability and validity data for DID were generally equal to or better than those for most well-accepted diagnoses. Data suggest that DID can be quite reliably discriminated from other conditions with which it is sometimes allegedly confused (schizophrenia, borderline personality disorder, and seizure disorder). Consistent with the posttraumatic model of the disorder's etiology, the greatest degree of diagnostic overlap may be with PTSD, especially so-called complex PTSD (Cardeña et al., 2003).

The clinical presentation of people with DID can vary widely. Even among DID patients, there is a wide range of symptom severity and level of adaptation, with some individuals being able to perform adequately in various areas of functioning (Kluft, 1994). Symptom presentation can vary across time in the same patient, sometimes fulfilling all the criteria for DID, sometimes fulfilling criteria only for DDNOS (dissociative disorders not otherwise specified; see later discussion). Besides the "textbook" presentation, Kluft (1991) provides an extensive list of variants, including epochal or sequential (i.e., switches are rare), latent (alters are manifested only at times of stress), posttraumatic DID, and others.

Until some years ago, individuals with DID usually received, on average, about four previous diagnoses (e.g., depression and other affective disorders, personality disorders, and schizophrenia) before the final DID diagnosis (Coons et al., 1988; Putnam et al., 1986). This may be explained by the substantial comorbidity between DID and depression and affective liability (including self-injury attempts); anxiety, conversion, and other somatoform disorders (headaches are almost always found among people with DIDs); personality disorders (especially avoidant and borderline personality disorders); and substance abuse and eating disorders (see Cardeña & Spiegel, 1996, for a review). Individuals with DID report some Schneiderian first-rank symptoms such as auditory hallucinations, but they typically have adequate reality testing outside of specific events such as fugues or flashbacks and do not present the negative symptoms of schizophrenia.

Because DID patients are multisymptomatic and often have previous diagnoses, a thorough evaluation is essential. A careful differential diagnosis of DID should rule out other DDs (DID is the superordinate diagnosis), dissociative symptoms produced by epilepsy, psychotic states, some personality disorders, transient effects of medications and drugs, malingering and factitious disorder, somatoform disorders, depression, and sexual disorders such as gender identity disorder (Cardeña & Spiegel, 1996; Coons & Milstein, 1994; Ross, 1997).

In most cases, thorough assessment with a systematic interview and one or more of the instruments mentioned previously can provide enough information for a diagnosis. Although a questionnaire such as the DES can provide valuable information, more thorough clinical interviews such as the SCID-D or DDIS are recommended (Foote et al., 2006). The Guidelines for Treating Dissociative Identity Disorder in Adults of ISSTD (2005) explicitly warn against using such techniques as amytal interviews except in emergency situations. Even then, caution should be exercised not to provide leading or suggestive questions. Considering the high suggestibility of these patients, this caution is warranted.

The course and prognosis of treatment depends on symptom severity and the psychological fragility of the patient. A wide variety of therapy trajectories is possible, even while maintaining a number of therapy variables constant (Kluft, 1994); nonetheless, it is widely accepted that therapy for these patients typically takes many years (Putnam & Loewenstein, 1993).

Dissociative Disorders Not Otherwise Specified

Case Study 5

A young Brazilian man described that he became possessed by spirits from the Afro-Brazilian pantheon that would take over his body and voice, and make him act in a style that was uncharacteristic of him. Unless someone told him what he had done, he could not remember what had transpired during these episodes. He was very distressed about it, because he could not control the episodes and they sometimes happened while he was at his job. The local Candomblé priest recommended that he be initiated into that religion. After a number of rituals and instruction, the young man had spirit possession experiences only in the midst of carefully arranged ritual settings.

The dissociative disorders not otherwise specified include dissociative pathologies of consciousness, identity, or memory that do not fulfill the criteria of the DDs described so far. A substantial proportion of dissociative patients fall under this category. In a large general psychiatric sample ($N = 11,292$), Mezzich et al. (1989) found most (57%) dissociative disorder diagnoses to be atypical (a previous designation for DDNOS). This figure is close to the 60% obtained by Saxe and collaborators (1993) in a subgroup of general psychiatric patients reporting clinical levels of dissociation. In the community study by Johnson et al. (2006), DDNOS was the most prevalent DD, and it was the second most prevalent (after dissociative amnesia) in the study by Foote and collaborators (2006).

Lynn and Rhue (1988), H. Spiegel (1974), and Hartmann (1984), respectively, have described subgroups of high fantasizers, hypnotic "virtuosos," and "thin boundaried" individuals who are vulnerable to distressing fantasies, excessive suggestibility, and uncontrolled loss of boundaries, which increase their risk for psychopathology. Uncontrolled and disorganized fluctuations of consciousness seem to increase the risk of pathology in this and other cultures (Cardeña, 1992), but clinicians should bear in mind that the mere presence of unusual experiences does not imply psychological dysfunction (Cardeña, Lynn, & Krippner, 2000).

What little evidence is available suggests that the majority of dissociative patients in other cultures have presentations different from the ones described so far (Cardeña et al., 1996; Saxena & Prasad, 1989). Social, political, gender, and cultural variables must be considered to understand these syndromes (Littlewood, 1998).

The *DSM-IV* contains the following examples of DDNOS:

1. Cases similar to DID that do not fulfill all its criteria; for instance, an individual presenting with two or more identities but without amnesia. The instances of identity alteration without amnesia, and typically with a greater integration of personality, have been called ego states. Coons (1992) has described different personality states associated with gender identity disorder.
2. Derealization without depersonalization; for example, sensing the self as normal, but the world as not quite real or as diffuse. This example is specific to adults; children without any pathology might blur the distinction between fantasy and consensual reality.

3. Dissociative states in individuals who have been subjected to chronic forms of coercion, suggestion, "brainwashing," and so on. West and Martin (1994) have described the presentation of captivity and cult victims. Among the phenomena they describe are having an emotionally and intellectually restricted "pseudo-identity," which, at least temporarily, substitutes for the previous identity; episodes of unawareness and disorientation; emotional unresponsiveness and lack of motivation; and so on. There is suggestive evidence of high dissociation scores among some members of a cult that originally prescribed sex with minors (Stewart, Cain, & Cardeña, 2001).
4. Dissociative trance disorder (see next section).
5. Loss of consciousness, being stuporous, or being comatose without a medical reason. For instance, a medically unexplained epidemic of fainting among Bhutanese refugees was found to be significantly related to recent and early loss (Van Ommeren et al., 2001). Similar epidemics have been observed in Western countries.
6. Ganser's syndrome or the giving of approximate answers (e.g., "a car has three wheels"), that cannot be explained by dementia, psychosis, or malingering. Ganser's syndrome is often accompanied by other alterations of consciousness such as time alteration. The *DSM-IV* considers dissociative amnesia and fugue as superordinate diagnoses to Ganser's syndrome.

The assessment of DDNOS is the same as that for the other dissociative disorders, and its prognosis depends on factors such as the severity of the disorder and its chronicity and history. Differential diagnoses should include dissociative-like phenomena occurring as the by-product of medication (e.g., Finestone & Manly, 1994) and seizure or other medical conditions (cf. Cardeña et al., 1996; Good, 1993). As with the other dissociative disorders, DDNOS can be diagnosed only when there is evidence of clinical levels of distress or maladjustment.

One of the examples of DDNOS is dissociative trance disorder, which includes trance or spirit possession phenomena. Cardeña, Lewis-Fernández, and colleagues (Cardeña et al., 1996) proposed that dissociative trance disorder be removed from the list of DDNOS and considered a dissociative disorder in its own right. This action would enhance the cross-cultural applicability of the *DSM* taxonomy, because there is evidence that many, if not most, of the dissociative manifestations in other cultures might fall under this rubric. Although we do not yet have a cross-cultural comparative database for other cultures, there are indications that they often differ in important ways from the criteria used by the *DSM-IV*. For instance, Saxena and Prasad (1989) reported that 90% of clinic outpatients in India with a *DSM-I* dissociative diagnosis had atypical dissociative disorder (an earlier version of DDNOS); many of those patients specifically complained of distressing or maladjusting forms of spirit possession. Alterations of consciousness that could be defined as spirit possession or trance are frequently a common aspect of cultural and religious practices in many parts of the world (Bourguignon, 1976), and the proposal for a dissociative trance disorder explicitly excludes culturally accepted practices and experiences from the disorder. In fact, a review of recent studies on spirit possession and related phenomena finds that most practitioners of spirit possession within ecstatic religions seem to be psychologically healthy (Cardeña, in press; see also Negro, 2002). The *DSM-IV* included the proposal of a dissociative trance disorder in an appendix for further study.

The word *trance* has been used in many, often inconsistent, ways. In the *DSM-IV*, it is defined as a consciousness state characterized by a narrow focus of consciousness and/or stereotypical behaviors experienced as alien to the subject. The notion of trance entails a diminution of the temporal, spatial, and memory context for the self—or what Shor (1959) called "generalized reality orientation"—and a decrease in reflective awareness (Cardeña & Spiegel, 1991). Examples of trance include a patient who suddenly becomes unaware of and/or unresponsive to the therapist (either because he or she has no apparent mental contents or because he or she is fully absorbed in a memory or a fantasy) and a patient who starts writing lines on a paper and becomes temporarily unable to stop scribbling on the paper. Although amnesia has been mentioned as a central component of most DDs, lack of reflective consciousness and control of behavior are often seen in the clinical context and are central to modern views of dissociation (Hilgard, 1994; Nijenhuis, 2000; Woody & Bowers, 1994).

Spirit possession is defined by the *DSM-IV* as an alteration of identity and consciousness characterized by the replacement of the individual's usual identity by a different one, commonly believed to be that of an ancestor or some form of noncorporeal being; it is typically accompanied by amnesia. Spirit possession in this sense is different from the belief that illnesses or other occurrences are caused by metaphysical forces. It might be tempting to conclude that spirit possession is just a metaphysical explanation for what we call DID, but, at this point, such conclusion would require further research. In contrast with DID, dysfunctional spirit possession has not been unequivocally associated with a history of early abuse, the possessing entity is experienced as external to the individual and generally conforms to a specific religious pantheon, and the disorder seems to be more reactive to a current stressor and less chronic than DID.

Examples of culture-bound pathological manifestations with a central dissociative component include:

- Cases of long-lasting, dysfunctional, and uncontrolled spirit possession involving identity substitution, harming or self-harming acts, amnesia, and so on.
- *Ataque de nervios,* a condition characterized by dysphoric feelings after exposure to trauma, somatic complaints and paresthesias, unawareness of surroundings, and partial or total amnesia for the event.
- Latah and other startle syndromes in which the victim, after a sudden fright, may start mimicking others without apparent control.
- Amok, berserk, and similar phenomena in which, after being humiliated, the experiencer may brood for a while, have a narrow focus of consciousness, and then go on an apparently automatic killing rampage until he or she is stopped (cf. Simons & Hughes, 1985).

Assessment of general dissociative alterations in Western culture may be done through the instruments mentioned, but an evaluation of dissociative manifestations in someone from another culture or subculture requires that clinicians be conversant with the semantic network of disease and health of that group and be able to find a common language. As the APA states (1995, p. 76), diagnostic evaluation "must be sensitive to the patient's ethnicity and place of birth, gender, social class, sexual orientation, and religious/spiritual beliefs," a principle that is even more crucial in the evaluation of complex experiential and behavioral phenomena.

There is no systematic database on which to evaluate the prognosis of dissociative trance disorder, but we have considerable anthropological literature on the efficacy of indigenous treatment for some of these manifestations.

SUMMARY

This chapter gives an overview of dissociative disorders. Considering the brief span in which systematic research on dissociation and the DDs has been conducted, it is likely that our conception of, and diagnostic criteria for, these disorders will change—although, as a whole, recent studies of methodological and technological sophistication seem to be mostly confirming earlier clinical observations. This chapter has skimmed the surface in areas such as consideration of cultural variations. The dissociative disorders have been mired in controversy for a number of years, but empirical investigation has been gradually replacing uninformed speculation, and the onus is now on the critics of the DDs to provide data supporting their position. It is now established, for example, that traumatic events and attachment dysfunctions are commonly associated with dissociative phenomena and symptomatology, that DDs are much more common than was once thought, and that DDs can be present at an early age. Many other areas remain open for debate: for example, what personal characteristics predispose individuals to react to trauma with dissociativity rather than with other symptoms? What is the nature of DID alters? What neurophysiological and perceptual processes underlie dissociative experiences?

Whatever the outcome of these debates, we now have psychometrically sound instruments to measure dissociative experiences and disorders, but many more theoretical and empirical developments need to occur before we can state that we have really gone beyond the conceptualization of brilliant observers and thinkers such as Sigmund Freud, Pierre Janet, and William James. It seems that the dissociative disorders, in some shape or another, are here to stay.

REFERENCES

Aderibigbe, Y. A., Bloch, R. M., & Walker, W. R. (2001). Prevalence of depersonalization and derealization experiences in a rural population. *Social Psychiatry and Psychiatric Epidemiology, 36,* 63–69.

Akhtar, S., & Brenner, I. (1979). Differential diagnosis of fugue-like states. *Journal of Clinical Psychiatry, 9,* 381–385.

Aldridge-Morris, R. (1989). *Multiple personality: An exercise in deception.* Hillside, NJ: Erlbaum.

American Psychiatric Association. (1987). *Diagnostic and statistical manual of mental disorders* (3rd ed., rev). Washington, DC: Author.

American Psychiatric Association. (1995). Practice guidelines for psychiatric evaluation of adults. *American Journal of Psychiatry, 152*(Suppl. 1), 67–80.

American Psychiatric Association. (2000). *Diagnostic and statistical manual of mental disorders* (4th ed., text rev.). Washington, DC: Author.

Barlow, D. H., & Durand, V. M. (2001). *Abnormal psychology: An integrative approach.* Stamford, CT: Wadsworth/Thomson Learning.

Becker-Blease, K. A., Deater-Deckard, K., Eley, T., Freyd, J. J., Stevenson, J., & Plomin, R. (2004). A genetic analysis of individual differences in dissociative behaviors in childhood and adolescence. *Journal of Child Psychology and Psychiatry, 45,* 522–532.

Benson, D. F. (1978). Amnesia. *Southern Medical Journal, 71,* 1221–1227.

Boon, S., & Draijer, N. (1991). Diagnosing dissociative disorders in the Netherlands: A pilot study with the Structured Clinical Interview for the DSM-III-R Dissociative Disorders. *American Journal of Psychiatry, 148,* 458–462.

Boon, S., & Draijer, N. (1993). *Multiple personality disorder in the Netherlands: A study on reliability and validity of the diagnosis.* Amsterdam: Swets & Zeitlinger.

Bourguignon, E. (1976). *Possession.* San Francisco: Chandler.

Braun, B. G. (1993). Multiple personality disorder and posttraumatic stress disorder. In J. P. Wilson & B. Raphael (Eds.), *International handbook of traumatic stress syndromes* (pp. 35–47). New York: Plenum.

Bremner, J. D., Krystal, J. H., Southwick, S. M., & Charney, D. S. (1995). Functional neuro-anatomical correlates of the effects of stress on memory. *Journal of Traumatic Stress, 8,* 527–553.

Briere, J., Weathers, F. W., & Runtz, M. (2005). Is dissociation a multidimensional construct? Data from the Multiscale Dissociation Inventory. *Journal of Traumatic Stress, 18,* 221–231.

Brown, D. (1995). Pseudo-memories, the standard of science and the standard of care in trauma treatment. *American Journal of Clinical Hypnosis, 37,* 1–24.

Brown, D., Frischolz, E. J., & Scheflin, A. W. (1999). Iatrogenic dissociative identity disorder: An evaluation of the scientific evidence. *Journal of Psychiatry and Law, 27,* 549–637.

Brown, D., Scheflin, A. W., & Whitfield, C. L. (1999). Recovered memories: The current weight of the evidence in science and in the courts. *Journal of Psychiatry and Law, 27,* 5–156.

Brown, P. (1994). Toward a psychobiological model of dissociation and posttraumatic stress disorder. In S. J. Lynn & J. Rhue (Eds.), *Dissociation: Clinical and theoretical perspectives* (pp. 94–122). New York: Guilford Press.

Butler, L. D., Duran, E. E., Jasiukaitis, P., Koopman, C., & Spiegel, D. (1996). Hypnotizability and traumatic experience: A diathesis-stress model of dissociative symptomatology. *American Journal of Psychiatry, 153,* 42–63.

Butler, L. D., & Spiegel, D. (1997). Trauma and memory. In L. J. Dickstein, M. B. Riba, & J. O. Oldham (Eds.), *Review of psychiatry* (Vol. 16, pp. 1113–1153). Washington, DC: American Psychiatric Press.

Cardeña, E. (1992). Trance and possession as dissociative disorders. *Transcultural Psychiatric Research Review, 29,* 287–300.

Cardeña, E. (1994). The domain of dissociation. In S. J. Lynn & J. Rhue (Eds.), *Dissociation: Clinical and theoretical perspectives* (pp. 15–31). New York: Guilford Press.

Cardeña, E. (1997). The etiologies of dissociation. In S. Powers & S. Krippner (Eds.), *Broken images, broken selves* (pp. 61–87). New York: Brunner/Mazel.

Cardeña, E. (in press). Anomalous identity experiences: Mediumship, spirit possession, and dissociative identity disorder (DID, MPD). In *The study of mediumship: Interdisciplinary perspectives.* New York: Parapsychology Foundation.

Cardeña, E., Butler, L., & Spiegel, D. (2003). Stress disorders. In G. Stricker & T. Widiger (Eds.), *Handbook of psychology* (pp. 229–249). New York: Wiley.

Cardeña, E., Koopman, C., Classen, C., Waelde, L., & Spiegel, D. (2000). Psychometric properties of the Stanford Acute Stress Reaction Questionnaire (SASRQ): A valid and reliable measure of acute stress reactions. *Journal of Traumatic Stress, 13,* 719–734.

Cardeña, E., Lewis-Fernández, R., Beahr, D., Pakianathan, I., & Spiegel, D. (1996). Dissociative disorders. In T. A. Widiger, A. J. Frances, H. J. Pincus, R. Ross, M. B. First, & W. W. Davis (Eds.), *Sourcebook for the DSM-IV* (Vol. 2, pp. 973–1005). Washington, DC: American Psychiatric Press.

Cardeña, E., Lynn, S. J., & Krippner, S. (2000). *Varieties of anomalous experience.* Washington, DC: American Psychological Association.

Cardeña, E., & Nijenhuis, E. (Eds.). (2000). Special issue on somatoform dissociation. *Journal of Trauma and Dissociation, 1*(4).

Cardeña, E., & Spiegel, D. (1991). Suggestibility, absorption, and dissociation: An integrative model of hypnosis. In J. F. Schumaker (Ed.), *Human suggestibility: Advances in theory, research and application* (pp. 93–107). New York: Routledge.

Cardeña, E., & Spiegel D. (1993). Dissociative reactions to the Bay Area earthquake. *American Journal of Psychiatry, 150,* 474–478.

Cardeña, E., & Spiegel, D. (1996). Diagnostic issues, criteria and comorbidity of dissociative disorders. In L. Michelson & W. Ray (Eds.), *Handbook of dissociation: Theoretical, empirical and clinical perspectives* (pp. 227–250). New York: Plenum.

Cardeña, E., & Weiner, L. (2004). Evaluation of dissociation across the lifespan. *Psychotherapy, 41,* 496–508.

Carlson, E. B., & Putnam, F. W. (1993). An update on the Dissociative Experiences Scale. *Dissociation, 6,* 16–27.

Christianson, S. A., & Loftus, E. F. (1987). Memory for traumatic events. *Applied Cognitive Psychology, 1,* 225–239.

Cohen, L., Berzoff, J., & Elin, M. (Eds.). (1995). *Dissociative identity disorder.* Northvale, NJ: Aronson.

Coons, P. M. (1992). Dissociative disorders not otherwise specified: A clinical investigation of 50 cases with suggestions for typology and treatment. *Dissociation, 5,* 187–195.

Coons, P. M. (1994). Confirmation of childhood abuse in child and adolescent cases of multiple personality and dissociative disorder not otherwise specified. *Journal of Nervous and Mental Diseases, 182,* 461–464.

Coons, P. M., Bowman, E. S., Kluft, R. P., & Milstein, V. (1991). The cross-cultural occurrence of MPD: Additional cases from a recent survey. *Dissociation, 4,* 124–128.

Coons, P. M., Bowman, E. S., & Milstein, V. (1988). Multiple personality disorder: A clinical investigation of 50 cases. *Journal of Nervous and Mental Disorders, 176,* 519–527.

Coons, P. M., & Milstein, V. (1986). Psychosexual disturbances in multiple personality: Characteristics, etiology and treatment. *Journal of Clinical Psychiatry, 47,* 106–110.

Coons, P. M., & Milstein, V. (1992). Psychogenic amnesia: A clinical investigation of 25 cases. *Dissociation, 5,* 73–79.

Coons, P. M., & Milstein, V. (1994). Factitious or malingered multiple personality disorder: Eleven cases. *Dissociation, 7,* 81–85.

Dell, P. F. (2001). Why the diagnostic criteria for dissociative identity disorder should be changed. *Journal of Trauma and Dissociation, 2,* 7–37.

Diseth, T. H. (2006). Dissociation following traumatic medical treatment procedures in childhood: A longitudinal follow-up. *Development and Psychopathology, 18,* 233–251.

Dorahy, M. J. (2001). Dissociative identity disorder and memory dysfunction: The current state of experimental research and its future directions. *Clinical Psychology Review, 21,* 771–795.

Dunn, G. E., Paolo, A.M., Ryan, J. J., & van Fleet, J. N. (1994). Belief in the existence of multiple personality disorder among psychologists and psychiatrists. *Journal of Clinical Psychology, 50,* 454–457.

Eich, E., Macaulay, D., Loewenstein, R., & Patrice, H. (1997). Memory, amnesia, and dissociative identity disorder. *Psychological Science, 8,* 417–422.

Erdelyi, M. E. (1994). Dissociation, defense, and the unconscious. In D. Spiegel (Ed.), *Dissociation: Culture, mind, and body* (pp. 3–20). Washington, DC: American Psychiatric Press.

Fahy, T. (1988). The diagnosis of multiple personality disorder: A critical review. *British Journal of Psychiatry, 153,* 597–606.

Farthing, G. W. (1992). *The psychology of consciousness.* Englewood Cliffs, NJ: Prentice-Hall.

Finestone, D. H., & Manly, D. T. (1994). Dissociation precipitated by propranolol. *Psychosomatics, 35,* 83–87.

Foote, B., Smolin, Y., Kaplan, M., Legatt, M. E., & Lipschitz, D. (2006). Prevalence of dissociative disorders in psychiatric outpatients. *American Journal of Psychiatry, 163,* 623–629.

Forrest, K. A. (2001). Toward an etiology of dissociative identity disorder: A neurodevelopmental approach. *Consciousness and Cognition, 10,* 259–293.

Freyd, J. J., & DePrince, A. P. (2001). *Trauma and cognitive science: A meeting of minds, science, and human experience.* New York: Haworth Press.

Freyd, J. J., DePrince, A. P., & Zurbriggen, E. L. (2001). Self-reported memory for abuse depends upon victim-perpetrator relationship. *Journal of Trauma and Dissociation, 2*(5), 5–16.

Friedl, M. C., & Draijer, N. (2000). Dissociative disorders in Dutch psychiatric inpatients. *American Journal of Psychiatry, 157*(6), 1012–1013.

Frischholz, E. J., Lipman, L. S., Braun, B. G., & Sachs, R. G. (1992). Psychopathology, hypnotizability, and dissociation. *American Journal of Psychiatry, 149,* 1521–1525.

Gabbard, G. O., Twemlow, S. W., & Jones, F. C. (1982). Differential diagnosis of altered mind/body perception. *Psychiatry, 45,* 361–369.

Gleaves, D. H. (1996). The sociocognitive model of dissociative identity disorder: A reexamination of the evidence. *Psychological Bulletin, 120,* 42–59.

Gleaves, D. H., May, M. C., & Cardeña, E. (2001). An examination of the diagnostic validity of dissociative identity disorder. *Clinical Psychology Review, 21,* 577–608.

Gleaves, D. H., Smith, S. M., Butler, L. D., & Spiegel, D. (2004). False and recovered memories in the laboratory and clinic: A review of experimental and clinical evidence. *Clinical Psychology: Science and Practice, 11,* 3–28.

Good, M. I. (1993). The concept of an organic dissociative disorder: What is the evidence? *Harvard Review of Psychiatry, 1,* 145–157.

Grinker, R. R., & Spiegel, J. P. (1945). *Men under stress.* Philadelphia: Blakiston.

Guralnik, O., Schmeidler, J., & Simeon, D. (2000). Feeling unreal: Cognitive processes in depersonalization. *American Journal of Psychiatry, 157,* 103–109.

Hartmann, E. (1984). *The nightmare.* New York: Basic Books.

Hilgard, E. R. (1968). *The experience of hypnosis.* New York: Harcourt, Brace & World.

Hilgard, E. R. (1994). Neodissociation theory. In S. J. Lynn & J. Rhue (Eds.), *Dissociation: Clinical and theoretical perspectives* (pp. 32–51). New York: Guilford Press.

Holmes, E. A., Brown, R. J., Mansell, W., Fearon, R. P., Hunter, E. C., Frasquilho, F., & Oakley, D. A. (2005). Are there two qualitatively distinct forms of dissociation? A review and some clinical implications. *Clinical Psychological Review, 25,* 1–23.

Hornstein, N. L., & Putnam, F. W. (1992). Clinical phenomenology of child and adolescent dissociative disorders. *Journal of the American Academy of Child and Adolescent Psychiatry, 31,* 1077–1085.

International Society for the Study of Trauma and Dissociation. (2005). Guidelines for treating dissociative identity disorder (multiple personality disorder) in adults. Retrieved November 29, 2006, from www.issd.org/indexpage/treatguide1.htm.

Jacobs, J. R., & Bovasso, G. B. (1992). Toward the clarification of the construct of depersonalization and its association with affective and cognitive dysfunctions. *Journal of Personality Assessment, 59,* 352–365.

James, W. (1923). *Principles of psychology.* New York: Holt. (Original work published 1890)

Janet, P. (1965). *The major symptoms of hysteria* (2nd ed.). New York: Hafner. (Original work published 1907)

Jang, K. L., Paris, J., Zweig-Frank, H., & Livesley, W. J. (1998). Twin study of dissociative experience. *Journal of Nervous and Mental Diseases, 186,* 345–351.

Johnson, J. G., Cohen, P., Kasen, S., & Brook, J. S. (2006). Dissociative disorders among adults in the community, impaired functioning, and axis I and comorbidity. *Journal of Psychiatric Research, 40,* 131–140.

Kaszniak, A. W., Nussbaum, P. D., Berren, M. R., & Santiago, J. (1988). Amnesia as a consequence of male rape: A case report. *Journal of Abnormal Psychology, 97,* 100–104.

Keller, R., & Shaywitz, B. A. (1986). Amnesia or fugue state: A diagnostic dilemma. *Developmental and Behavioral Pediatrics, 7,* 131–132.

Kenny, M. (1986). *The passion of Ansel Bourne: Multiple personality in American culture.* Washington, DC: Smithsonian Institution Press.

Kessler, R. C., McGonagle, K. A., Zhao, S., Nelson, C. B., Hughes, M., Eshleman, S., et al. (1994). Lifetime and 12-month prevalence of DSM-III-R psychiatric disorders in the United States. *Archives of General Psychiatry, 51,* 8–19.

Kihlstrom, J. F. (1994). One hundred years of hysteria. In S. J. Lynn & J. W. Rhue (Eds.), *Dissociation: Clinical and theoretical perspectives* (pp. 365–394). New York: Guilford Press.

Kirmayer, L. J. (1994). Pacing the void: Social and cultural dimensions of dissociation. In D. Spiegel (Ed.), *Dissociation: Culture, mind, and body* (pp. 91–122). Washington, DC: American Psychiatric Press.

Kluft, R. P. (1985). The natural history of multiple personality disorder. In R. P. Kluft (Ed.), *Childhood antecedents of multiple personality disorder* (pp. 197–238). Washington, DC: American Psychiatric Press.

Kluft, R. P. (1991). Clinical presentations of multiple personality disorder. *Psychiatric Clinics of North America, 14,* 605–629.

Kluft, R. P. (1994). Treatment trajectories in multiple personality disorder. *Dissociation, 7,* 63–76.

Kluft, R. P. (1996). Dissociative identity disorder. In L. K. Michelson & W. J. Ray (Eds.), *Handbook of dissociation: Theoretical, empirical and clinical perspectives* (pp. 337–366). New York: Plenum.

Kluft, R. P., Steinberg, M., & Spitzer, R. L. (1988). DSM-III-R revisions in the dissociative disorders: Exploration of their derivation and rationale. *Dissociation, 1,* 39–46.

Koopman, C., Classen, C., Cardeña, E., & Spiegel, D. (1995). When disaster strikes, acute stress disorder may follow. *Journal of Traumatic Stress, 8,* 29–46.

Kopelman, M. D. (1987). Amnesia: Organic and psychogenic. *British Journal of Psychiatry, 150,* 428–442.

Kopelman, M. D., Christensen, H., Puffett, A., & Stanhope, N. (1994). The great escape: A neuropsychological study of psychogenic amnesia. *Neuropsychologia, 32,* 675–691.

Kubin, M., Pakianathan, I., Cardeña, E., & Spiegel, D. (1989). *Depersonalization disorder.* Unpublished manuscript, Stanford University, Stanford, CA.

Lazarus, A. (1976). Psychiatric problems precipitated by transcendental meditation. *Psychological Reports, 10,* 39–74.

Leonard, D., Brann, S., & Tiller, J. (2005). Dissociative disorders: Pathways to diagnosis, clinician attitudes and their impact. *Australian and New Zealand Journal of Psychiatry, 39,* 940–946.

Lewis, D. O., Yeager, C. A., Swica, Y., Pincus, J. H., & Lewis, M. (1997). Objective documentation of child abuse and dissociation in 12 murderers with dissociative identity disorder. *American Journal of Psychiatry, 154,* 1703–1710.

Lewis-Fernández, R. (1994). Culture and dissociation: A comparison of ataque de nervios among Puerto Ricans and possession syndrome in India. In D. Spiegel (Ed.), *Dissociation: Culture, mind, and body* (pp. 123–167). Washington, DC: American Psychiatric Press.

Lilienfeld, S. O., Lynn, S. J., Kirsch, I., Chaves, J. F., Sarbin, T. R., Ganaway, G. K., et al. (1999). Dissociative identity disorder and the sociocognitive model: Recalling the lessons of the past. *Psychological Bulletin, 125,* 507–523.

Littlewood, R. (1998). Mental illness as ritual theatre. *Performance Research, 3,* 41–52.

Litwin, R., & Cardeña, E. (2000). Demographic and seizure variables, but not hypnotizability or dissociation, differentiated psychogenic from organic seizures. *Journal of Trauma and Dissociation, 1,* 99–122.

Loewenstein, R. J. (1991a). An office mental status examination for chronic complex dissociative symptoms and dissociative identity disorder. *Psychiatric Clinics of North America, 14,* 567–604.

Loewenstein, R. J. (1991b). Psychogenic amnesia and psychogenic fugue: A comprehensive review. In A. Tasman & S. M. Goldfinger (Eds.), *Review of psychiatry* (Vol. 10, pp. 189–222). Washington, DC: American Psychiatric Press.

Loftus, E. F. (1993). The reality of repressed memories. *American Psychologist, 48,* 518–537.

Lynn, S. J., & Rhue, J. W. (1988). Fantasy proneness: Hypnosis, developmental antecedents, and psychopathology. *American Psychologist, 43,* 35–44.

Lynn, S. J., & Rhue, J. W. (1994). *Dissociation: Clinical and theoretical perspectives.* New York: Guilford Press.

Marmar, C. R., Weiss, D. S., Schlenger, W. E., Fairbank, J. A., Jordan, B. K., Kulka, R. A., et al. (1994). Peritraumatic dissociation and posttraumatic stress in male Vietnam theater veterans. *American Journal of Psychiatry, 151,* 902–907.

Martínez-Taboas, A. (1991). Multiple personality in Puerto Rico: Analysis of fifteen cases. *Dissociation, 4,* 189–192.

Mayeux, R., Alexander, M. P., Benson, F., Brandt, J., & Rosen, J. (1979). Poriomania. *Neurology, 29,* 1616–1619.

Mezzich, J. E., Dow, J. T., Rich, C. L., Costello, A. J., & Himmelhoch, J. M. (1981). Developing an efficient clinical information system for a comprehensive psychiatric institute: Initial evaluation form. *Behavior Research Methods and Instrumentation, 13,* 464–478.

Mezzich, J. E., Fabrega, H., Coffman, G. A., & Haley, R. (1989). DSM-I disorders in a large sample of psychiatric patients: Frequency and specificity of diagnoses. *American Journal of Psychiatry, 146,* 212–219.

Michelson, L. K., & Ray, W. J. (Eds.) (1996). *Handbook of dissociation: Theoretical, empirical and clinical perspectives.* New York: Plenum.

Morgan, A. H. (1973). The heritability of hypnotic susceptibility in twins. *Journal of Abnormal Psychology, 82,* 55–61.

Negro, P. J. (2002). Do religious mediumship dissociative experiences conform to the sociocognitive theory of dissociation? *Journal of Trauma and Dissociation, 3,* 51–73.

Nelson, E. C., Heath, A. C., Madden, P. A., Cooper, M. L., Dinwiddle, S. H., Bucholz, K., et al. (2002). Association between self-reported childhood sexual abuse and adverse psychosocial outcomes. *Archives of General Psychiatry, 59,* 139–145.

Nemiah, J. C. (1989). Dissociative disorders (hysterical neuroses, dissociative type). In H. I. Kaplan & B. J. Sadock (Eds.), *Comprehensive textbook of psychiatry* (5th ed, pp. 1028–1044). Baltimore: Williams & Wilkins.

Nijenhuis, E. R. S. (2000). Somatoform dissociation: Major symptoms of dissociative disorders. *Journal of Trauma and Dissociation, 1*(4), 7–32.

North, C. S., Ryall, J. M., Ricci, D. A., & Wetzel, R. D. (1993). *Multiple personalities, multiple disorders: Psychiatric classification and media influence.* New York: Oxford University Press.

Noyes, R., & Kletti, R. (1977). Depersonalization in response to life-threatening danger. *Comprehensive Psychiatry, 18,* 375–384.

Ogawa, J. R., Sroufe, L. A., Weinfield, N. S., Carlson, E. A., & Egeland, B. (1997). Development and the fragmented self: Longitudinal study of dissociative symptomatology in a nonclinical sample. *Development and Psychopathology, 9,* 855–879.

Piper, A., & Merskey, H. (2004). The persistence of folly: A critical examination of dissociative identity disorder. Part 1. The excesses of an improbable concept. *Canadian Journal of Psychiatry, 49,* 592–600.

Pribor, E. E., Yutzi, S. H., Dean, T. J., & Wetzel, R. D. (1993). Briquet's syndrome, dissociation, and abuse. *American Journal of Psychiatry, 150,* 1507–1511.

Putnam, F. W. (1997). *Dissociation in children and adolescents: A developmental approach.* New York: Guilford Press.

Putnam, F. W., Guroff, J. J., Silberman, E. K., Barban, L., & Post, R. M. (1986). The clinical phenomenology of multiple personality disorder: Review of 100 recent cases. *Journal of Clinical Psychiatry, 47,* 285–293.

Putnam, F. W., & Loewenstein, R. J. (1993). Treatment of multiple personality disorder: A survey of current practices. *American Journal of Psychiatry, 150,* 1048–1052.

Reed, G. (1972). *The psychology of anomalous experience.* London: Hutchinson University.

Riether, A. M., & Stoudemire, A. (1988). Psychogenic fugue states: A review. *Southern Medical Journal, 81,* 568–571.

Riley, K. C. (1988). Measurement of dissociation. *Journal of Nervous and Mental Diseases, 176,* 449–450.

Robles-García, R., Garibay-Rico, S. E., & Páez-Agraz, F. (2006). Evaluación de trastornos disociativos en población psiquiátrica mexicana: Prevalencia, comorbilidad y características psicométricas de la escala de experiencias disociativas (Evaluation of dissociative disorders in a Mexican psychiatric population: Prevalence, comorbidity, and psychometric characteristics of the scale of dissociative experiences). *Salud Mental, 29,* 38–43.

Rollinson, R. D. (1978). Transient global amnesia: A review of 213 cases from the literature. *Australian and New Zealand Journal of Medicine, 8,* 547–549.

Ross, C. A. (1991). Epidemiology of multiple personality and dissociation. *Psychiatric Clinics of North America, 14,* 503–517.

Ross, C. A. (1997). The validity and reliability of dissociative identity disorder. In L. Cohen, J. Berzoff, & M. Elin (Eds.), *Dissociative identity disorder* (pp. 65–84). Northvale, NJ: Aronson.

Ross, C. A., Duffy, C. M., & Ellason, J. W. (2002). Prevalence, reliability and validity of dissociative disorders in an inpatient setting. *Journal of Trauma and Dissociation, 3,* 7–17.

Ross, C. A., Joshi, S., & Currie, R. (1991). Dissociative experiences in the general population: A factor analysis. *Hospital and Community Psychiatry, 42,* 297–301.

Ross, C. A., Norton, G. R., & Fraser, G. A. (1989). Evidence against the iatrogenesis of multiple personality disorder. *Dissociation, 2,* 61–65.

Ross, C. A., Norton, G. R., & Wozney, K. (1989). Multiple personality disorder: An analysis of 236 cases. *Canadian Journal of Psychiatry, 34,* 413–418.

Sar, V., Unal, S. N., Kiziltan, E., Kundakci, T., & Ozturk, E. (2001). HMPAO SPECT study of regional cerebral blood flow in dissociative identity disorder. *Journal of Trauma and Dissociation, 2,* 5–25.

Saxe, G. N., Chinman, G., Berkowitz, R., Hall, K., Lieberg, G., Schwartz, J., et al. (1994). Somatization in patients with dissociative disorders. *American Journal of Psychiatry, 151,* 1329–1334.

Saxe, G. N., van der Kolk, B. A., Berkowitz, R., Chinman, G., Hall, K., Lieberg, G., et al. (1993). Dissociative disorders in psychiatric patients. *American Journal of Psychiatry, 150,* 1037–1042.

Saxena, S., & Prasad, K.V. (1989). DSM-I subclassification of dissociative disorders applied to psychiatric outpatients in India. *American Journal of Psychiatry, 146,* 261–262.

Schacter, D. L., Wang, P. L., Tulving, E., & Freedman, M. (1982). Functional retrograde amnesia: A quantitative case study. *Neuropsychologia, 20,* 523–532.

Schooler, J. W. (1994). Seeking the core: The issues and evidence surrounding recovered accounts of sexual trauma. *Consciousness and Cognition, 3,* 452–469.

Shor, R. E. (1959). Hypnosis and the concept of the generalized reality-orientation. *American Journal of Psychotherapy, 13,* 582–602.

Silberg, J. L. (Ed.) (1998). *The dissociative child.* Lutherville, MD: Sidran Press.

Simeon, D., Gross, S., Guralnik, O., Stein, D., Schmeidler, J., & Hollander, E. (1997). Feeling unreal: 30 cases of DSM-III-R depersonalization disorder. *American Journal of Psychiatry, 154,* 1107–1113.

Simeon, D., Guralnik, O., Knutelska, M., Hollander, E., & Schmeidler, J. (2001). Hypothalamic-pituitary-adrenal axis dysregulation in depersonalization disorder. *Neuropsychopharmacology, 5,* 793–795.

Simeon, D., Guralnik, O., Schmeidler, J., Sirof, B., & Knutelska, M. (2000). The role of childhood interpersonal trauma in depersonalization disorder. *American Journal of Psychiatry, 157,* 1027–1033.

Simons, R. C., & Hughes, C. C. (Eds.) (1985). *The culture bound syndromes.* Dordrecht, The Netherlands: Reidel.

Sivec, H. J., & Lynn, S. J. (1995). Dissociative and neuropsychological symptoms: The question of differential diagnosis. *Clinical Psychology Review, 15,* 297–316.

Spanos, N. P. (1994). Multiple identity enactments and multiple personality disorder: A sociocognitive perspective. *Psychological Bulletin, 116,* 143–165.

Spiegel, D. (Ed.). (1994). *Dissociation: Culture, mind, and body.* Washington, DC: American Psychiatric Press.

Spiegel, D., & Cardeña, E. (1991). Disintegrated experience: The dissociative disorders revisited. *Journal of Abnormal Psychology, 100,* 366–378.

Spiegel, H. (1974). The grade 5 syndrome: The highly hypnotizable person. *International Journal of Clinical and Experimental Hypnosis, 22,* 303–319.

Steinberg, M. (1990). The spectrum of depersonalization: Assessment and treatment. In A. Tasman & S. M. Goldfinger (Eds.), *Review of psychiatry* (Vol. 10, pp. 223–247). Washington, DC: American Psychiatric Press.

Steinberg, M. (1993). *The structured clinical interview for DSM-IV dissociative disorders.* Washington, DC: American Psychiatric Press.

Steinberg, M., Cicchetti, D., Buchanan, J., Rakfeldt, J., & Rounsaville, B. (1994). Distinguishing between multiple personality disorder (dissociative identity disorder) and schizophrenia using the Structured Clinical Interview for DSM-IV Dissociative Disorders. *Journal of Nervous and Mental Diseases, 182,* 495–502.

Stewart, A., Cain, R., & Cardeña, E. (2001, August). *Psychological profile of second generation "Children of God" cult (ex)members: An exploratory study.* Paper presented at the 103rd annual meeting of the American Psychological Association, San Francisco, CA.

Tellegen, A., Lykken, D. T., Bouchard, T. J., Wilcox, K. J., Segal, N. L., & Rich S. (1988). Personality similarity in twins reared apart and together. *Journal of Personality and Social Psychology, 54,* 1031–1039.

Terr, L. C. (1991). Childhood traumas: An outline and overview. *American Journal of Psychiatry, 148,* 10–20.

Tsai, G. E., Condie, D., Wu, M. T., & Chang, I. W. (1999). Functional magnetic resonance imaging of personality switches in a woman with dissociative identity disorder. *Harvard Review of Psychiatry, 7,* 119–122.

Tutkun, H., Sar, V., Yargic, L., Ozpulat, T., Yanik, M., & Kiziltan, E. (1998). Frequency of dissociative disorders among psychiatric inpatients in a Turkish university clinic. *American Journal of Psychiatry, 155,* 800–805.

Tutkun, H., Yargic, L. I., & Sar, V. (1995). Dissociative identity disorder: A clinical investigation of 20 cases in Turkey. *Dissociation, 8,* 3–9.

van der Hart, O., & Nijenhuis, E. (1995). Amnesia for traumatic experiences. *Hypnos, 22,* 73–86.

van der Kolk, B. A., & van der Hart, O. (1989). Pierre Janet and the breakdown of adaptation in psychological trauma. *American Journal of Psychiatry, 146,* 1530–1540.

Vanderlinden, J., van der Hart, O., & Varga, K. (1996). European studies of dissociation. In L. K. Michelson & W. J. Ray (Eds.), *Handbook of dissociation: Theoretical, empirical and clinical perspectives* (pp. 25–49). New York: Plenum.

Van Ommeren, M. V., Sharma, B., Komproe, I., Sharma, G. K., Cardeña, E., de Jong, J. T., et al. (2001). Trauma and loss as determinants of medically unexplained epidemic illness in a Bhutanese refugee camp. *Psychological Medicine, 31,* 1259–1267.

Vermetten, E., Schmahl, C., Lindner, S., Loewenstein, R. J., & Bremner, J. D. (2006). Hyppocampal and amygdalar volumes in dissociative identity disorder. *American Journal of Psychiatry, 163,* 630–636.

Waller, N. G., Putnam, F. W., & Carlson, E. B. (1996). Types of dissociation and dissociative types: A taxometric analysis of dissociative experiences. *Psychological Methods, 1,* 300–321.

Waller, N. G., & Ross, C. A. (1997). The prevalence and biometric structure of pathological dissociation in the general population: Taxometric and behavior genetic findings. *Journal of Abnormal Psychology, 106,* 499–510.

West, L. J., & Martin, P. R. (1994). Pseudo-identity and the treatment of personality change in victims of captivity and cults. In S. J. Lynn & J. Rhue (Eds.), *Dissociation: Clinical and theoretical perspectives* (pp. 268–288). New York: Guilford Press.

Woody, E. Z., & Bowers, K. S. (1994). A frontal assault on dissociated control. In S. J. Lynn & J. Rhue (Eds.), *Dissociation: Clinical and theoretical perspectives* (pp. 52–79). New York: Guilford Press.

Zatzick, D. F., Marmar, C. R., Weiss, D. S., & Metzler, T. (1994). Does trauma-linked dissociation vary across ethnic groups? *Journal of Nervous and Mental Diseases, 182,* 576–582.

CHAPTER 14

Sexual and Gender Identity Disorders

LORI A. BROTTO AND CAROLIN KLEIN

With the availability of oral treatments for male sexual dysfunction (e.g., sildenafil, vardenafil, and tadalafil), there has been a boom in scientific interest in sexual dysfunction and its treatment. Since the approval of Viagra® (sildenafil) in 1998 in the United States, there have been at least 3,000 publications on pharmacological treatments for male sexual dysfunction and approximately 500 publications on such treatments for female sexual dysfunction. With this pharmacological interest, the field of sexual dysfunction more broadly has seen an increase in research, including studies focused on functional magnetic resonance imaging (fMRI), cross-cultural issues, qualitative methods, and testing of herbal remedies.

Sexual disorders are classified according to the *Diagnostic and Statistical Manual of Mental Disorders,* text revision (*DSM-IV-TR;* American Psychiatric Association [APA], 2000) into three groups: (1) sexual dysfunctions, which characterize sexual problems related to the sexual response cycle or pain; (2) paraphilias, which are recurrent, sexually arousing fantasies, urges, or behaviors involving nonconventional or nonconsenting persons or objects; and (3) gender identity disorder, which involves strong discomfort with one's own sex and a desire to be the other sex (APA, 2000). In this chapter, we organize our remarks about each of these three categories according to the more broad headings of epidemiology, diagnosis and assessment, and treatment, separately for men and women.

SEXUAL DYSFUNCTIONS

Disorders of sexual dysfunction are divided in the *DSM-IV-TR* according to problems in desire, arousal, orgasm, or pain. This classification system is based on Masters and Johnson's four-stage Human Sexual Response Cycle (Masters & Johnson, 1966), which was based on observations of 700 men and women studied in the authors' St. Louis clinic. Based on arousal patterns, they formulated a model of sexual stimulation that proceeds through a linear sequence: excitement, plateau, orgasm, and resolution. The noted psychotherapist, Helen Singer Kaplan, added a desire phase to the response cycle (Kaplan, 1979), and this was incorporated into the *DSM* taxonomy. The disorders of sexual pain were not a component of Masters and Johnson's cycle; however, their prevalence in the general population necessitated their inclusion in the taxonomy.

This four-category system has been commonplace since *DSM-III* in 1980. However, given numerous criticisms about this linear response cycle—particularly when conceptualizing women's sexual problems—there have been recent attempts to refine the model. Concerns about the lack of generalizability of this sexual response cycle for women include: (1) it is based on the sexual response patterns of men; (2) it assumes a linear progression from desire to arousal to orgasm; however, healthy sexual experiences can progress in any order, and this sequence is not necessary for sexual satisfaction; (3) many experiences considered to be normal parts of female sexual response (e.g., fantasizing) are not reported by all women; and (4) characteristics of the original sample are considered biased (Hill & Preston, 1996; Klusmann, 2002; Lunde, Larsen, Fog, & Garde, 1991; Regan & Berscheid, 1996). Thus, alternative conceptualizations have been offered. For example, the Definitions Committee sponsored by the American Foundation for Urologic Diseases was an international panel of experts in the area of women's sexual dysfunction (Basson et al., 2003) who retained the four categories but improved and/or deleted criteria based on the evidence-based literature. The suggestions from this committee will be discussed for each sexual dysfunction.

An alternative system for classifying sexual dysfunctions as "problems" was proposed by the New View Task Force, led by sexologist Leonore Tiefer. The resultant "New View Document" (Kaschak & Tiefer, 2002; Tiefer, 2001) was a radical departure from the *DSM* classification system and suggested that sexual problems in women have been overdiagnosed and medicalized and that the designating of "dysfunctions" is unhelpful. This alternate system removes the emphasis on biological components of sexual complaints and posits that sexual problems can be due to sociocultural, political, or economic factors; partner and relationship status; psychological factors; or medical factors.

There have been notable paradigm shifts over time in sex research, with numerous publications on the psychological and sociocultural aspects of sexual disorders emanating from the mid- to late twentieth century. More recently, however, there has been an imbalance in the amount of scientific attention devoted to refining and developing psychological interventions; instead, many recent publications focus on medical and physiological treatments. In this chapter, we adopt a biopsychosocial approach to discussing sexual dysfunctions its application to the etiological, assessment, and treatment domains.

We now turn to the specific sexual dysfunctions in men and women. The *DSM-IV-TR* (APA, 2000) divides these into the following six diagnoses: (1) sexual desire disorders, (2) sexual arousal disorders, (3) orgasmic disorders, (4) sexual pain disorders, (5) sexual dysfunction due to a general medical condition, and (6) sexual dysfunction not otherwise specified. In addition, each sexual dysfunction diagnosis has a number of specifiers, including: lifelong (i.e., the person has always had the problem) versus acquired (i.e., the problem is new in onset); generalized (i.e., the problem exists in all sexual situations and with all partners) versus situational (i.e., the problem occurs in only select situations or with certain partners); and whether the dysfunction is due to psychological factors or to combined psychological and biological factors. This method of diagnostic subtyping is helpful in that it provides insight into possible etiological factors involved and therefore may guide treatment (Maurice, 1999).

EPIDEMIOLOGY

Alfred Kinsey's *Sexual Behavior in the Human Male* (1948) and *Sexual Behavior in the Human Female* (1953), which compiled information gathered from in-depth interviews on a variety of sexual attitudes and practices in 5,300 American men and 5,940 women, set the stage for sex research over the next fifty years. Only very recently has there been a survey that surpassed the numbers accumulated by Kinsey (Laumann et al., 2005). There have been numerous attempts to document the prevalence of sexual practices and difficulties using randomized study designs. One of the most frequently cited such studies is the National Health and Social Life Survey (NHSLS), a population-based study of 3,159 American men and women between the ages of 18 and 59 identified from random telephone digit dialing (Laumann, Gagnon, Michael, & Michaels, 1994). With an impressive 79% response rate, researchers conducted face-to-face interviews and collected brief questionnaire data. Using multivariate techniques to estimate the relative risk of sexual difficulties for men and women who had at least one sexual partner over the past year, the authors assessed (1) lack of sexual desire, (2) arousal difficulties, (3) problems achieving climax or ejaculation, (4) anxiety about sexual performance, (5) climaxing or ejaculating too quickly, (6) pain during intercourse, and (7) not finding sex pleasurable. In addition, the authors examined the role of various demographic variables, including age, marital status, education, and race/ethnicity. They also examined a number of risk factors, including sexual experiences, alcohol use, sexually transmitted diseases, presence of urinary tract symptoms, circumcision, health status, and experience of emotional or stress-related problems.

The NHSLS reported the total prevalence for sexual difficulties in women was 43% and in men was 31% (Laumann, Paik, & Rosen, 1999). The prevalence of each type of sexual difficulty in men and women are presented in Tables 14.1 and 14.2, respectively. Being married and having a higher educational level were each associated with significantly lower rates of sexual difficulties in men and women. Differences according to ethnic status were more prominent for women than for men; African American women reported lower levels of sexual desire and pleasure than White women, but White women were more likely to have sexual pain than African American women. In contrast, both groups had higher rates of sexual difficulty than Hispanic women. Emotional or stress-related problems were strongly associated with sexual difficulties for women, whereas physical health-related problems were more predictive of sexual dysfunction in men only. A decline in social status was related to an increased risk for all types of sexual difficulty for women but only with erectile dysfunction in men. Quality of life significantly predicted sexual difficulties, however more strongly for women than for men (Laumann et al., 1999).

A similar large-scale randomized survey on adults aged 18 to 74 was conducted using individuals of Swedish descent (Fugl-Meyer & Sjogren Fugl-Meyer, 1999). Two features of the Swedish study that set it apart from the NHSLS were that it included individuals of old age (up to age 74) and that it inquired about the extent to which sexual difficulties (which the authors termed "disabilities") were experienced as

Table 14.1

Prevalence (%) of Sexual Difficulties According to Age in Men Aged 18 to 19 (*n* = 1,249) in the National Health and Social Life Survey (Laumann, Paik, & Rosen, 1999)

Sexual Difficulty	Age			
	18–29	30–39	40–49	50–59
Lack of interest in sex	14	13	15	17
Unable to achieve orgasm	7	7	9	9
Climax too early	30	32	28	31
Sex not pleasurable	10	8	9	6
Anxious about performance	19	17	19	14
Trouble maintaining or achieving an erection	7	9	11	18

Table 14.2

Prevalence (%) of Sexual Difficulties According to Age in Women Aged 18 to 19 (*n* = 1,486) in the National Health and Social Life Survey (Laumann, Paik, & Rosen, 1999)

Sexual Difficulty	Age			
	18–29	30–39	40–49	50–59
Lack of interest in sex	32	32	30	27
Unable to achieve orgasm	26	28	22	23
Experienced pain during sex	21	15	13	8
Sex not pleasurable	27	24	17	17
Anxious about performance	16	11	11	6
Trouble lubricating	19	18	21	27

problematic. Moreover, the response rate was 59%, slightly lower than that of the NHSLS. Sexual disabilities were reported by 47% of the 1,335 women and 23% of the 1,475 men; however, anywhere from 38% to 69% of those who reported the difficulty also experienced it as problematic. Rates of sexual disabilities were higher among women than among men, and sexual difficulties among partners were highly comorbid. For example, among men with erectile dysfunction, 60% of the female partners had low sexual desire and 44% had arousal complaints (Sjogren Fugl-Meyer & Fugl-Meyer, 2002).

More recently, Pfizer Inc. funded a Global Study of Sexual Attitudes and Behaviors (GSSAB), which surveyed 13,882 women and 13,618 men from 29 countries (Laumann et al., 2005). The study collected information on (a) the prevalence of sexual concerns in men and women aged 40 to 80 using a combination of interview and touch-telephone responses, and (b) correlates of sexual difficulties. The results from this study will be discussed in the specific sections of each sexual dysfunction.

In response to growing concern over the medicalization of women's sexuality and a tendency to "diagnose dysfunction" for economic reasons (Tiefer, 2002), there has been criticism of the 43% figure cited from the NHSLS. In part, this debate is centered on the notion that a sexual difficulty is not necessarily a "dysfunction" if such a large proportion of the population experience it. Thus, Bancroft and colleagues assessed the prevalence of sexual difficulties in women and the extent to which these difficulties were associated with distress about their sexual relationship and with distress about their own sexuality (Bancroft, Loftus, & Long, 2003). The authors also explored determinants of sexual distress in women. Based on a national probability sample of 987 American women between the ages of 20 and 65, sexual distress was associated with poor mental health, whereas poor physical health was only associated with distress about a woman's own sexuality. Interestingly, neither lubrication problems, nor genital pain, nor orgasm predicted sexual distress. Bancroft et al. (2003) concluded that only 24% of the sample (almost half that reported by the NHSLS) experienced a distressful sexual problem and that without an assessment of perceived difficulty, the findings from the NHSLS are likely inflated.

DESCRIPTION OF THE DISORDERS

HYPOACTIVE SEXUAL DESIRE DISORDER

Hypoactive sexual desire disorder (HSDD) is defined as "persistently or recurrently deficient (or absent) sexual fantasies and desire for sexual activity" (APA, 2000). Citing the NHSLS findings, low desire occurs in approximately 15% of men aged 19 to 59 and in approximately 30% of women aged 19 to 59 (Laumann et al., 1999). Although the diagnostic criteria do not differentiate HSDD in men and women, we will discuss the phenomenon separately by gender, given its differential experience and expression (Baumeister, Catanese, & Vohs, 2001).

In men, Maurice (2005) operationalized low sexual desire as: (1) reduced thoughts, fantasies, and sexual dreams; (2) reduced sexual behavior with a partner; and (3) reduced sexual behavior through masturbation. In the NHSLS study, low desire in men was associated with never being married, poor health, general unhappiness, having less than a high school education, and poverty (Laumann et al., 1999). Moreover, men in the 50 to 59 age category were three times as likely to experience low desire as men in the 18 to 29 age category. Across cultures, there is a higher prevalence of HSSD among men from the Middle East (21.6%) and Southeast Asia (28.0%) compared to European and North American and South American men (Laumann et al., 2005).

HSDD in women has been the focus of much media attention, given the promising findings of testosterone for women's complaints of absent desire. The prevalence of low sexual desire in American and Swedish women ranges from 27% to 34% of the population (Fugl-Meyer & Sjogren Fugl-Meyer, 1999; Laumann et al., 1999). Among women seeking routine gynecologic care, 87% report low sexual interest (Nusbaum, Gamble, Skinner, & Heiman, 2000), but less than 10% report low sexual interest when a distress criterion is used (Bancroft et al., 2003). HSDD is reported by 43% of women from the Middle East and Southeast Asia (Laumann et al., 2005). The case presented on pages 513–514 describes the loss of sexual desire in a woman in a long-term relationship—a very common presentation in the clinical setting.

SEXUAL AVERSION DISORDER

Although it is classified as a sexual desire disorder, little data exist concerning sexual aversion disorder (SAD). Defined as "persistent or recurrent extreme aversion to, and avoidance of, all (or almost all) genital sexual contact with a sexual partner" (APA, 2000). The aversion and subsequent avoidance are highly distressing and considered a marked anxiety response focusing either directly on genital sexual contact or on other nongenital aspects of sexual expression such as kissing or hugging (Katz, Gipson, Kearl, & Kriskovich, 1989). A person with SAD may experience panic attacks that lead to impairment in his or her interpersonal relations as well as avoidance of all potential sexual encounters. The prevalence of SAD is unknown given that individuals avoid sexual encounters and are therefore infrequently seen in sexual therapy clinics.

SEXUAL AROUSAL DISORDERS

Erectile Dysfunction   Arousal disorders are diagnosed according to impairments in the physical genital response. In men, erectile dysfunction (ED) is defined as "persistent or recurrent inability to attain, or to maintain until completion of sexual activity, an adequate erection," which causes distress (APA, 2000). According to the NHSLS, the prevalence of ED is 7% in men aged 18 to 29 and 18% in men aged 50 to 59 (Laumann et al., 1999); in the Swedish cohort study, ED was reported by 24% of men aged 66 to 74 (Fugl-Meyer & Sjogren Fugl-Meyer, 1999). Rates of ED are higher among men seeking treatment in an outpatient setting. Among 1,352 Polish men seeking routine outpatient care, 43% met the criteria for ED (Haczynsk et al., 2006). In another survey of older men, 58% of those aged 75 to 79 had ED (Monga, Bettencourt, & Barrett-Connor, 2002). There are also cross-cultural differences in ED prevalence, with rates that were double in East Asia (27.1%) and Southeast Asia (28.1%) compared to Western countries (Laumann et al., 2005).

Female Sexual Arousal Disorder   In women, the prevalence of sexual arousal difficulties, defined as "persistent or recurrent inability to attain, or to maintain until completion of the sexual activity an adequate lubrication, swelling response of sexual excitement" (APA, 2000), is approximately 12% to 21% in U.S. and Swedish populations (Fugl-Meyer & Sjogren Fugl-Meyer, 1999; Laumann et al., 1999); rates were much higher in Southeast Asia (34.2%) and East Asia (37.9%; Laumann et al., 2005). In the gynecologic setting, as many as 75% of women seeking routine care complain of inadequate genital lubrication (Nusbaum et al., 2000). In the clinical setting, however, arousal complaints that are independent of desire and/or orgasm complaints rarely occur, leading to the suggestion that female sexual arousal disorder (FSAD) may not be a truly independent sexual disorder (Segraves & Segraves, 1991). Instead, others have argued that there may be subtypes of FSAD that reflect various combinations of purely subjective (i.e., mental or psychological) versus physiological arousal difficulties (Basson, 2002b). The importance of separately assessing subjective and physiological aspects of arousal in women is essential given the finding that these processes are often desynchronous (Rosen & Beck, 1988). Genital arousal (experienced as lubrication, swelling, and pulsing) may not provide a strong afferent feedback to affect subjective arousal and, moreover, in

Table 14.3

Definitions of Subjective Sexual Arousal Disorder, Genital Sexual Arousal Disorder, and Combined Sexual Arousal Disorder, According to the New Definitions Committee (Basson et al., 2003)

Disorder	Description
Subjective Sexual Arousal Disorder	Absence of or markedly diminished feelings of sexual arousal (sexual excitement and sexual pleasure) from any type of sexual stimulation. Vaginal lubrication or other signs of physical response still occurs.
Genital Sexual Arousal Disorder	Complaints of absent or impaired genital sexual arousal. Self-report may include minimal vulval swelling or vaginal lubrication from any type of sexual stimulation and reduced sexual sensations from caressing genitalia. Subjective sexual excitement still occurs from nongenital stimuli.
Combined Sexual Arousal Disorder	Absence of or markedly diminished feelings of sexual arousal (sexual excitement and sexual pleasure) from any type of sexual stimulation as well as complaints of absent or impaired genital sexual arousal (vulval swelling, lubrication).

some women may be experienced as unpleasant (Laan, Everaerd, van der Velde, & Geer, 1995). Instead, indirect evidence of genital arousal through manual, oral, or vibratory stimulation may confirm the presence of genital arousal and be experienced as rewarding for some women (Basson, 2002b). Among some women with FSAD—specifically, those who experience an impairment in genital arousal only—this second level confirmation is also absent. Given that women's sexual arousal appears to be much more complex than genital lubrication alone, the Definitions Committee has suggested that three subtypes of FSAD be differentiated (Basson et al., 2003). The criteria for subjective sexual arousal disorder, genital sexual arousal disorder, and combined sexual arousal disorder are listed in Table 14.3.

Recently, a new category, persistent sexual arousal disorder (PSAS), has been proposed as "spontaneous intrusive and unwanted genital arousal in the absence of sexual interest and desire" (Basson et al., 2003; Leiblum, Brown, Wan, & Rawlinson, 2005; Leiblum & Nathan, 2001). Women with PSAS experience persistent and unwanted genital arousal that is often only temporarily relieved by orgasm. A recent Internet study of 103 women complaining of symptoms of PSAS endorsed frequent distress and other associated features (Leiblum et al., 2005) and represents the first attempt to collect data on this provisional new diagnosis. Research on its etiology and treatments is being conducted, but results are yet to be published.

ORGASMIC DISORDERS

The orgasm disorders in men include premature ejaculation (PE) and male orgasmic disorder—the former defined as ejaculation too early and the latter as ejaculation later than the individual wishes it. Given their different prevalence, etiology, and treatments, they are discussed separately.

Premature Ejaculation   The *DSM-IV-TR* defines PE, also known as rapid ejaculation, as "persistent or recurrent ejaculation with minimal sexual stimulation before, on, or shortly after penetration and before the person wishes it" (APA, 2000). Men with PE report lack of control over ejaculation and fewer than the desired number of thrusts during intercourse (Rowland et al., 2004). Moreover, men with PE report fulfilling a partner's needs as being very important to their own rating of sexual satisfaction (Rowland et al., 2004), highlighting the impact of this disorder on the partner. When determining a diagnosis, factors affecting duration of the excitement phase, such as age, novelty of the sexual partner or situation, and recent frequency of sexual activity should be considered. According to the NHSLS, PE affects approximately 30% of men aged 18 to 59 (Laumann et al., 1999), making it the most prevalent male sexual dysfunction. Rates are relatively uniform around the world except in the Middle East, where the rate is approximately 12.4% (Laumann et al., 2005). However, controversy about what defines "too early" has led to differing prevalence rates, as the national probability study in Sweden found a prevalence of only 9% (Fugl-Meyer & Sjogren Fugl-Meyer, 1999).

Male Orgasmic Disorder   Male orgasmic disorders, also known as delayed or retarded ejaculation (RE), is defined as "persistent or recurrent delay in, or absence of, orgasm following a normal sexual excitement phase during sexual activity that the clinician, taking into account the person's age, judges to be adequate in focus, intensity, and duration." RE is much less frequent than PE. Prevalence of RE in men aged 19 to 59 is 8% in the NHSLS (Laumann et al., 1999), 2% in the Swedish probability study (Fugl-Meyer & Sjogren Fugl-Meyer, 1999), and 21.1% in Southeast Asia (Laumann et al., 2005). Some have argued that RE is not a true disorder because penetration for a prolonged period of time enhances the potential for the woman's pleasure. However, RE is clinically distressing for the man, leading to frustration and sometimes pain.

Female Orgasmic Disorder   Orgasm in women has received extensive attention over the past century. For example, Freud proposed that only vaginal orgasms (not clitoral orgasms) were associated with sexual maturity. A recent study of 575 women suggested that the primary differentiation between clitoral versus vaginal orgasms was in the stimulation applied and not in the subjective experience of the orgasm (Lehmann, Rosemeier, & Grüsser-Sinopoli, 2004). The existence of the G-spot has been another topic of intense study, despite the fact that this anatomical location in the anterior wall of the vagina is still not conclusively linked to orgasm in women (Hines, 2001). Lack of orgasm is a common complaint that deserves careful assessment to avoid overdiagnosis. The *DSM-IV-TR* defines female orgasmic disorder (FOD) as "persistent or recurrent delay in, or absence of, orgasm following a normal sexual excitement phase.... The diagnosis ... should be based on the clinician's judgment that orgasmic capacity is less than would be reasonable for age, sexual experience, and adequacy of sexual stimulation" (APA, 2000).

The prevalence in Swedish and American probability samples is 22% and 25%, respectively (Fugl-Meyer & Sjogren Fugl-Meyer, 1999; Laumann et al., 1999). The highest prevalence was reported in the youngest age cohort (NHSLS), and this was attributed to lack of sexual skill and high partner turnover. Thus, one might speculate that young women complaining of anorgasmia might be reassured that this is a skill that develops over time within a stable relationship. Rates of anorgasmia are also culturally determined, with the highest prevalence (41.2%) reported among women in Southeast Asia (Laumann et al., 2005).

Sexual Pain Disorders

Based on Masters and Johnson's Human Sexual Response Cycle of desire, arousal, and orgasm as a basis for classification of sexual dysfunctions, one may wonder why the sexual pain disorders are indicated in the *DSM-IV-TR*. In fact, pain elicited from sexual activity is a common complaint, affecting approximately 14% of American women (Laumann et al., 1999), and is a common sexual complaint expressed by 72% of women during routine gynecologic examinations (Nusbaum et al., 2000). Rates approximate 30% in women from East and Southeast Asia (Laumann et al., 2005). A disorder commonly associated with genital pain in women is vaginismus, affecting approximately 1% of Swedish women (Fugl-Meyer & Sjogren Fugl-Meyer, 1999). Compared to research on the etiology of and treatments for sexual pain disorders in women, less has been published on sexual pain in men. As such, there is an imbalance in the amount of information in the following sections.

Dyspareunia in Men   Estimates of the prevalence of male dyspareunia are sparse but appear to affect 3% to 5% of men in Western countries and 10% to 12% of men in the Middle East and Southeast Asia (Laumann et al., 2005). A study of 404 gay men reported a prevalence rate of approximately 14% for anodyspareunia (pain from receptive anal sex; Damon & Rosser, 2005), with the majority experiencing it lifelong. A significant proportion of men found it highly distressing, and, as a result, it led to avoidance of sexual activity or restricting activity to insertive anal sex.

Dyspareunia in Women   The *DSM-IV-TR* classification of dyspareunia as "recurrent or persistent genital pain associated with sexual intercourse" (APA, 2000) has been challenged by the Definitions Committee. A new description has been suggested: "persistent or recurrent pain with attempted or complete vaginal entry and/or penile vaginal intercourse" (Basson et al., 2003) with the focus on *attempted* intercourse because many women with dyspareunia are unsuccessful with actual penetration. Vulvodynia is another term commonly used to describe chronic vulvar pain or discomfort that can take place without direct stimulation. In contrast, vulvar vestibulitis syndrome (VVS) is the most common cause of dyspareunia and is diagnosed when there is severe pain upon direct stimulation of the vulvar vestibule.

Vaginismus   Vaginismus is characterized by the unwanted involuntary spasm of the vaginal muscles that prevents intercourse, and it is defined by the New Definitions Committee as "the persistent or recurrent difficulties of the woman to allow vaginal entry of a penis, a finger, and/or any object, despite the woman's expressed wish to do so. There is often (phobic) avoidance and anticipation or fear of pain" (Basson et al., 2003). The problem affects 1% to 6% of women (Weijmar Schultz &

Van de Wiel, 2005) and is highly comorbid with dyspareunia. In fact, given their high degree of comorbidity, it is often difficult to differentiate vaginismus from dyspareunia (de Kruiff, Ter Kuile, Weijenborg, & Van Lankveld, 2000), and vaginismus should be diagnosed only when structural (physical) abnormalities have been ruled out or addressed. The following case illustrates a woman with comorbid vaginismus and dyspareunia in more detail.

Case Studies

Hypoactive Sexual Desire Disorder

Jane is a 43-year-old White heterosexual woman. She and her husband, Frank, have been married for 19 years and have two children aged 15 and 12. They presented to the sexual health clinic with complaints of "lost libido," and Frank was very interested in inquiring about the testosterone patch. They met with the clinical psychologist, who conducted a detailed biopsychosocial assessment, first with the couple together, during which she inquired about the sexual complaint and the couple's patterns of sexual behavior. The second part of the assessment took place with Jane and Frank separately, during which the therapist inquired about family social and psychiatric history, early sexual experiences, masturbation and fantasy, and medical health. Jane reported that she no longer thought about sexual intercourse and was often resistant to Frank's invitations for sexual activity. She masturbated approximately twice per month; this was enjoyable for her and led to orgasmic release. She denied any history of past sexual abuse and reported a few sexual relationships prior to meeting Frank 22 years earlier. She denied any loss of desire in these early sexual experiences. Her health was excellent, she was still menstruating regularly, and although she had experienced periods of depression throughout her life, she was currently not depressed. Jane maintained that she loved Frank very much but worried about the future of the relationship given her lack of desire and her belief that "normal relationships need sex in order to survive." During the interview with Frank, it was obvious that Jane's low desire was highly distressing to him. He had been in a number of relationships prior to his marriage that ended due to the couple's sexual difficulties. He worked as a corporate lawyer and was away from home at least 14 hours per day. He appeared anxious during the interview and had some perfectionistic traits when describing his ideal life. He admitted, privately, that his own ejaculation difficulties are a concern for him. Specifically, he ejaculated within 1 minute of penetration during intercourse, and this usually led to early discontinuation of the sexual encounter. He had successfully tried medical treatments for premature ejaculation 20 years earlier and felt that the problem was relatively under control until about 5 years ago, when his promotion at work led to a dramatic increase in stress and his workload. Frank wondered if his premature ejaculation was related to his wife's low desire or if this was a symptom of perimenopause that might require hormone replacement. On the basis of these detailed interviews, the therapist

(continued)

diagnosed Jane with acquired hypoactive sexual desire disorder and Frank with lifelong premature ejaculation. Given the relationships between Jane's low desire, Frank's premature ejaculation, early discontinuation of intercourse, and Jane's being unsatisfied with the sexual encounter, an obvious treatment goal will be to address both sexual conditions while simultaneously teaching the couple sexual skills for maintaining their intimacy. Testosterone therapy was not considered a first-line treatment approach in this situation.

Dyspareunia

Lily is a 25-year-old East Asian university graduate student who was referred to the sexual health clinic for complaints of not being able to have intercourse with her boyfriend of 2 years. She had seen a gynecologist who attempted to perform a genital examination, but Lily found this very anxiety provoking and therefore asked the physician to discontinue the examination. She told the therapist that she had never been able to have a Pap smear and that she had attempted to insert a tampon once at the age of 15 without success and it felt as if "a wall would go up in my vagina" preventing anything from being inserted. She has been in one previous long-term relationship that involved oral sex but not vaginal intercourse. Lily ended that relationship after 2 years because she felt guilty about "depriving" her boyfriend of intercourse. She has engaged in oral sex with her current boyfriend and feels that they have an excellent and intimate relationship, apart from the problem of not being able to have intercourse. Lily described an authoritarian father and a shy and private mother. She did not talk about sexuality with her parents, and when she began her relationship with her first boyfriend at the age of 17, she kept this hidden from her parents for fear that her father would order her to end the relationship. Although Lily is in excellent health, she reported a history of yeast infections beginning at the age of 17 and continuing today. These infections are painful and lead her to avoid sexual activity. Moreover, when her doctor attempted to examine her during her first infection, she became highly distressed at the pain and recalls it vividly. Her mood is euthymic and she is slightly anxious and experiences uncued panic attacks three times per year. She is very distressed about her inability to have intercourse given that she is very much in love with her boyfriend, and she is worried about the relationship ending like the first one. The therapist discussed the diagnoses of dyspareunia and vaginismus with Lily, and she appeared to relate to the features of both disorders. Lily was informed that to make an accurate diagnosis of vulvar vestibulitis syndrome—one of the most frequent causes of dyspareunia, which is commonly associated with yeast infections—a knowledgeable gynecologist must perform a cotton swab test on her vulva, and the therapist provided Lily with a referral for this. In addition, the therapist would work with her on her anxiety and vaginismus, which could be conceptualized as a learned response to anticipation of pain.

DIAGNOSIS, ASSESSMENT, AND ETIOLOGY

HYPOACTIVE SEXUAL DESIRE DISORDER IN MEN

An accurate diagnosis of HSDD in men requires a physical examination, a laboratory examination, and a psychosexual history. A large-scale study of men with erectile dysfunction and HSDD found that psychological and biological factors contributed equally in accounting for men's low desire (Corona et al., 2004). A physical examination is necessary for diagnosis, particularly if the problem is acquired and generalized because it may be a symptom of a larger disease or syndrome. Some common diseases that are associated with low desire in men are hypothyroidism and hypogonadism (Maurice, 2005). Other medical factors (e.g., cardiovascular disease, cancers) may also dampen sexual desire in men through any combination of biological or psychological means. Many psychiatric medications (e.g., antipsychotics, benzodiazepines, antidepressants), medical drugs (e.g., cardiovascular, cancer, antiseizure), and illicit or recreational drugs (e.g., marijuana, nicotine, alcohol, methadone) have effects on sexual desire and should be carefully assessed.

A laboratory examination of testosterone and prolactin can be very helpful for understanding etiology and guiding treatment. Testosterone is secreted from the testes (and, to a lesser degree, from the adrenal glands) in response to hypothalamic release of gonadotropin releasing hormone and pituitary gland release of leutinizing hormone. Testosterone that is free, bound to albumin, and that which is bound to sex hormone binding globulin (SHBG) should be measured first thing in the morning. As men age, SHBG levels increase, thereby decreasing the level of free testosterone. Reductions in testosterone can reduce sexual desire and erections because both processes are androgen dependent. Reductions in testosterone as a result of chemical castration (as in the case of treatment for sex offenders) can also reduce sexual desire. As well, there is a normal age-related decline in testosterone such that bioavailable testosterone begins to decline in men in their 30s and 40s and continues to decline for the remainder of their lives (Seidman, 2003).

Prolactin is another hormone that, when elevated, is associated with reduced levels of sexual desire (Morales et al., 2004). Causes of elevated prolactin levels can include antipsychotic medication use or a prolactin-secreting tumor. A syndrome known as androgen deficiency in the aging male (ADAM) or partial ADAM has been suggested in favor of andropause, given the difficulty in determining whether the androgen decline is a cause of or is a result from other coexisting health-related changes with age (Morales, Heaton, & Carson, 2000). Clinical correlates of ADAM include fatigue, depression, reduced sex drive, erectile dysfunction, and changes in mood and cognition.

Determining the onset and context of the low desire in men is essential and guides the adoption of a psychological or a medical approach to treatment. Other factors that must be assessed include the presence of another sexual difficulty in the man (Schiavi, 1999; Segraves and Segraves, 1991) or in his partner (Sjogren Fugl-Meyer & Fugl-Meyer, 2002), significant relationship distress, aging factors, poor health, and infrequent sex (Laumann et al., 2005), depressive disorders, and problems in sexual self-esteem (Beutel et al., 2005).

The issue of "misdirected sexual desire" in gay men deserves some comment. Sandfort and de Keizer (2001) reviewed all of the studies published on the sexual difficulties experienced by gay men and found the prevalence of low desire to be

25% in men without HIV/AIDS. Although sexual desire may be satisfactory for an individual of the desired gender, a man who is ashamed or insecure about his own sexual orientation may have low desire if he feels compelled to remain in a hetero-sexual relationship (Sandfort & de Keizer, 2001).

Hypoactive Sexual Desire Disorder in Women

The *DSM-IV-TR* criterion for HSDD of reduced sexual fantasies and lack of sponta-neous thinking about sexual activity has been criticized, because spontaneous sexual thoughts and fantasies are rarely a feature of women's desire experiences (Regan & Berscheid, 1996). More recent models of women's sexual desire propose that sexual desire, particularly in long-term relationships, is more likely to be experienced *after* sexual arousal is accessed such that if arousal does not occur, desire to continue the sexual experience is dampened (Basson, 2002a; 2003; 2004). Although empirical sup-port for this model is only beginning to mount, the model has proven effective in the clinical setting for guiding the management of low desire in women (Basson, 2001). The recognition that "responsive desire" might be more accessible than "spontane-ous desire," particularly for women in long-term relationships, has resulted in the suggested revision of the traditional *DSM* linear focus of sexual response and en-couraged the American Foundation for Urologic Diseases Definitions Committee (Basson et al., 2003) to redefine sexual interest/desire disorder for women as:

> absent or diminished feelings of sexual interest or desire, absent sexual thoughts or fantasies and a lack of responsive desire. Motivations (here de-fined as reasons/incentives) for attempting to become sexually aroused are scarce or absent. The lack of sexual interest is considered to be beyond a nor-mative lessening with lifecycle and relationship duration.

Thus, absence of spontaneous sexual desire is not considered evidence of a dys-function according to this definition. Given that responsive sexual desire occurs in response to sexual arousal, in the assessment, clinicians should take into account the context; the types and intensities of stimuli used by the woman and her part-ner; her mood, fears, distractions; and any other factors that might affect her ability to experience arousal (i.e., her arousability). Thus, a comprehensive assessment of sexual desire usually focuses on sexual arousal and explores the reasons for the lack of motivation for sexual activity, the sexual context and stimuli employed, and what factors make the experience dissatisfying (Basson, 2005).

Psychosocial factors that can impact women's sexual desire include fear of vulner-ability, guilt or shame regarding sexual activity, prior negative sexual experiences or abuse, distractions, and excessive need for control (Basson, 2005). Depressed mood, low self-esteem, and guilt are also contributing factors with 27% to 62% of women with low desire also meeting criteria for a depressive disorder (Hartmann, Heiser, Ruffer-Hesse, & Kloth, 2002; Phillips & Slaughter, 2000; Schreiner-Engel & Schiavi, 1986). Interestingly, a few studies have found the opposite relationship, such that depressed mood is associated with increased frequency of masturbation (Cyranowski et al., 2004; Frohlich & Meston, 2002)—one potential index of sexual desire. Interpersonal factors can trigger in HSDD so that an inappropriate context or insufficient sexual stimulation that prevents arousal becomes the primary focus in treatment. Low expectations about the future of the relationship and the belief that aging reduces sexual desire both contributed significantly to HSDD (Laumann et al., 2005). Other interpersonal factors found to affect women's desire are lack of privacy, fear of STDs, fear of performance failure, fear of sexual pain, minimal emotional closeness, and lack of trust in the relationship (Basson, 2005).

Biological events that can dampen desire include fatigue (Basson, 2005), anxiety (Trudel, Landry, & Larose, 1997), antidepressant medications (Kennedy, Dickens, Eisfeld, & Bagby, 1999), endocrinological diseases such as renal failure (Peng et al., 2005), hypothyroidism (Davis, Guay, Shifren, & Mazer, 2004), and low androgen levels resulting from bilateral ovary removal (BSO; Sherwin & Gelfand, 1987) or from pituitary disease (Hulter & Lundberg, 1994). Excitatory neurotransmitters involved include dopamine, norepinephrine, oxytocin, and serotonin acting via the 1A or 2C receptors, whereas the neurotransmitters prolactin, GABA, and serotonin acting via most other receptor types are considered inhibitory for sexual desire. The study of androgens in women's sexual desire has led to the general conclusion that androgens are necessary for desire. However, it is unclear whether the mechanisms of action are via one of the androgen receptors or through aromatization to estradiol. Moreover, studies that have attempted to correlate women's desire with testosterone levels have been inconclusive (Burger, Dudley, Cui, Dennerstein, & Hopper, 2000; Davis, Davison, Donath, & Bell, 2005; Santoro et al., 2005), and there are no existing normative ranges of testosterone values that correspond to sexual function status.

ERECTILE DYSFUNCTION

A basic understanding of the anatomy and physiology of erection is necessary to properly evaluate ED. There are no bones in the penis, and erection is entirely mediated by blood flow. The urethra, through which both urine and the ejaculate passes, is surrounded by erectile tissue called the *corpus spongiosum,* which runs the entire length of the penis around the urethra. Other erectile components are the two *corpora cavernosa,* which are composed of numerous cavernosal arteries. When the penis is unaroused, or flaccid, these arteries contract, thereby preventing an inflow of blood. When a man becomes aroused, smooth muscles of the penis relax, these cavernosal arteries relax, and there is an inflow of blood. The veins leaving the penis are squeezed shut from the pressure, thereby maintaining blood flow in the penis and causing an erection. Specific chemical factors found to influence the physiology of erection are intracellular free calcium, nitric oxide (both local and neural), hyperpolarizing factor, cyclic guanosine monophosphate-dependent protein kinase, and phosphodiesterate type 5 (Saenz de Tejada et al., 2004)—the latter of which has been the target in developing oral medications for ED (discussed later). Vigorous pharmaceutical efforts aimed at improving ED in men are based largely on the accurate identification of these factors and the pathways involved in erection.

There are two mechanisms involved in producing an erection. The first involves processing of sexual stimuli in the brain involving neurotransmitters mentioned previously. The second mechanism involves a balance of parasympathetic with sympathetic nervous system input. Direct stimulation of the penis leads to parasympathetic nervous system input to the spinal cord, specifically spinal nerves S2 through S4. In the spinal cord, the message forms a reflex arc and elicits the erection (Wylie & MacInnes, 2005). Input from the sympathetic nervous system, particularly at levels T11 through L2 and especially at times of stress, is involved in detumescence, or loss of erection.

It is important to determine the extent to which an erectile dysfunction includes a psychological versus a biological or organic etiology. Anxiety or stress may lead to an overactive sympathetic nervous system that can both increase smooth muscle tone and interfere with signals from the sacral spinal cord. Thus, performance anxiety is a major treatment target for men with ED. Inquiries about morning erections allow determination of the degree to which the problem is situational (i.e., with only certain partners or in certain situations) versus generalized (i.e., present in all contexts). A complete loss of morning erections indicates a possible vascular or neurological component, and the man is best treated by a qualified urologist. Rate of onset of ED can help indicate etiology. Radical genital or pelvic surgeries may result in a sudden loss of erectile function, such as the case with prostate cancer surgery (Bolt, Evans, & Marshall, 1987). Alternatively, no prior difficulties with erectile function followed by one failure to reach an erection and subsequent concern about further attempts are likely to be maintained by performance anxiety. This example also highlights the fact that factors maintaining a sexual dysfunction may not be different than those that precipitate its onset.

The assessment should include interviewing the man's partner, whether male or female, to gain a sense of the interpersonal context that might contribute to ED. Lack of attraction to one's partner, mistrust, communication problems, and difficulties in providing adequate sexual stimulation may all contribute to ED and may be the focus of psychological therapy. Major depressive disorder, whether independent of or secondary to relationship discord, has been strongly associated with ED (Araujo, Durante, Feldman, Goldstein, & McKinley, 1998). Distinguishing ED that is secondary to the depression versus ED that is a result of antidepressant use (Ferguson, 2001) will affect management of the disorder. Finally, the NHSLS found that a childhood history of sexual abuse was significantly related to ED (Laumann et al., 1999).

An assessment of medical status—in particular, the diagnosis of diabetes, other endocrinological conditions, heart disease, and obesity—is integral to guiding appropriate treatment. Because androgens and prolactin are of particular concern with ED (Morales et al., 2004), any medical condition, whether primary or secondary to stress, drugs, or a tumor, requires hormonal assessment. Among men treated for diabetes, the prevalence of ED is 28% (Feldman, Goldstein, Hatzichristou, Krane, & McKinlay, 1994), given that there are both vascular and neurological aspects of diabetes than can affect erectile function. Other conditions that affect vascular function and can trigger ED include smoking, hypertension, cardiovascular disease, coronary heart disease, and hyperlipidemia. ED prevalence was significantly associated with history of vascular or prostate disease (Laumann et al., 2005). It is not surprising that any medical concern that affects blood vessel damage will likely negatively impact erectile function. Surgical contributors, particularly radical prostatectomy, is strongly linked to ED (Stanford et al., 2000), especially if the procedure did not involve nerve-sparing techniques. Finally, a thorough assessment of recreational and medicinal drug use is warranted because these commonly cause ED.

FEMALE SEXUAL AROUSAL DISORDER

The delineation of the three types of FSAD mentioned in Table 14.3 is essential for thoughtful and effective diagnosis and management of female sexual arousal disorder. Only women with genital arousal complaints, specifically, are likely to have vascular or other medical etiology (Goldstein & Berman, 1988) that might warrant the use of a pharmacological intervention (Basson, 2002b). Unfortunately, at this time, there are neither epidemiological data nor other empirical data available to further describe these subgroups.

PREMATURE EJACULATION

Assessment of PE in clinical trials has adopted a stop-watch technique in which the duration of time between penetration and ejaculation is monitored, usually by the man's female partner. This additional layer of performance anxiety may artificially inflate the man's dysfunction and render this technique suboptimal for PE. Also confounding accurate assessment of prevalence is the fact that it may be a highly embarrassing condition (Symonds, Roblin, Hart, & Althof, 2003) that prevents inquiry by clinicians and/or admission by men who suffer from it. Furthermore, prevalence rates differ depending on the operational definition of "rapid" (Grenier & Byers, 2001). Thus, a multifaceted approach is recommended that encompasses behavior, affect, self-efficacy, and degree of severity.

PE's precise etiology is unknown; however, a combination of psychological, biological, and behavioral components likely contribute. Much of the research is based on rodent studies in which serotonergic disruption is the primary etiological factor. Stimulation of 5-HT_{1A} receptors in rats leads to rapid ejaculation, whereas hyposensitivity at the 5-HT_{2C} receptor shortens ejaculation time (Waldinger, 2002). Studies in rodents have led Waldinger, a leading authority on PE, to formulate the Ejaculation Threshold Hypothesis, which posits that men with PE have a lower ejaculatory setpoint (threshold) due to low serotonin neurotransmission. Therefore, men with PE tolerate only a very low amount of sexual arousal prior to ejaculation (Waldinger, 2005). There is also evidence of a genetic predisposition to PE; 71% of first-degree relatives of men with PE also have the condition (Waldinger, Rietschel, Nothen, Hengeveld, & Olivier, 1998). Previous speculation that PE was associated with abnormal hormonal levels has not been empirically supported.

Acquired and/or situational PE may indicate a more psychological etiology related to anxiety, early sexual experiences, low frequency of sexual activity, or poor ejaculatory control techniques. The possibility that performance anxiety leads to loss of ejaculatory control was proposed by Masters and Johnson (1970) and became the basis for their sensate focus exercises that aimed to decrease anxiety while simultaneously teaching the man to experience arousal. Moreover, case studies document a beneficial effect of anxiolytic medication on PE (Segraves, 1987). However, more recent research does not support the role of anxiety in PE in the clinical or laboratory setting (Strassberg, Kelly, Carroll, & Kircher, 1987), and instead suggests that high anxiety, if present, may be the consequence, rather than the cause. Masters and Johnson (1970) also speculated that haste in one's first sexual experience due to fear of dissatisfying a partner may condition a man to ejaculate quickly. Although this theory makes sense intuitively, it has only been tested and supported in a small case series (Williams, 1984). It has also been speculated that men with PE have fewer sexual intercourse experiences than men without PE (Spiess, Geer, O'Donohue, 1984), which may reinforce performance anxiety and decrease ejaculatory control. However, men may simply avoid sexual encounters because of PE. It is possible that men with good ejaculatory control learn techniques for deferring ejaculation until desired and that they unconsciously use these techniques in all future sexual experiences (Zilbergeld, 1978). For example, thought distraction, pelvic floor muscle contraction, and altering the mechanics of pelvic thrusting may all delay ejaculation until the man wishes it.

Sociodemographic variables related to PE include lower education (but only in Central and South America and the Middle East) and financial stressors (but only in the Middle East), as found in the GSSAB (Laumann et al., 2005). PE has an impact on the man's partner given that the defining criterion is that ejaculation takes place before, on, or shortly after penetration *with a partner.* Two recent studies have explored the impact of PE on a man's partner. Based on qualitative interviews, 50% of men reported that PE resulted in distressing effects on either finding new relationships or not satisfying a current partner (Symonds et al., 2003). Byers and Grenier (2003) found that women rated the ejaculatory latency as being much shorter than the men with PE rated it and admitted that a partner's PE reduced her sexual satisfaction. Moreover, among Swedish men with PE, 50% of the female partners met criteria for anorgasmia and 54% met criteria for hypoactive sexual desire (Fugl-Meyer & Sjogren Fugl-Meyer, 1999), suggesting that the man's PE has a significant negative impact on a woman's sexual response. Given these findings, ideal treatment of PE will include the man's partner.

Retarded Ejaculation (Male Orgasmic Disorder)

During the assessment distinction between lifelong (primary) versus acquired (secondary) retarded ejaculation (RE), and generalized versus situational RE may point to important etiological factors. Psychological contributory factors include fear, anxiety, hostility, and relationship factors (Waldinger, 2005); however, these factors have not been consistently supported. A recent chart review suggests that idiosyncratic masturbatory style (e.g., using rapid stimulation or pressure in a manner that is not easily duplicated by partnered sexual activity) as well as using a variant sexual fantasy (e.g., fantasy about sadomasochism) act as predisposing factors for RE (Perelman, 2006b). Organic factors related to genetics also have a likely role in the etiology of RE (Waldinger, 2005). In rodent studies, aberrations in the serotonergic system such as hyperactivity at the 5-HT_{2C} receptor and hypoactivity at the 5-HT_{1A} receptor have been found to be related to delayed ejaculation. Although these findings pave the way for pharmacological interventions, to date there are no FDA-approved treatments for RE.

Other biological factors linked to RE include treatment with selective serotonin reuptake inhibitor (SSRI) antidepressants, androgen deficiency with aging and/or hypogonadism, and any injury to the lumbar sympathetic ganglia (i.e., such as from multiple sclerosis). Age and prostate disease are highly associated with RE (Laumann et al., 2005). In addition, alcohol use is commonly associated with delayed ejaculation and may trigger a sexual difficulty that is subsequently maintained by psychological factors related to performance anxiety.

Female Orgasmic Disorder

Due to dissatisfaction with the *DSM-IV-TR* criteria that led to the possibility that many cases of arousal disorder were mistakenly diagnosed as female orgasmic disorder (FOD) because of insufficient sexual stimulation, the New Definitions Committee proposed a new criterion for women's orgasmic disorder (Basson et al., 2003): "Despite the self-report of high sexual arousal/excitement, there is either lack of orgasm, markedly diminished intensity of orgasmic sensations, or marked delay of orgasm from any kind of stimulation." This definition highlights the necessity of adequate arousal preceding the anorgasmia for the diagnosis to be met. If there is insufficient arousal leading to anorgasmia, on the other hand, the diagnosis is simply FSAD.

Another important differential diagnostic feature is the extent to which the FOD is situational or generalized. By definition, orgasm via masturbation of the clitoris in a woman who is anorgasmic with intercourse does fulfill the criteria for FOD. Although Freud argued that orgasm arising from clitoral stimulation was a sign of immaturity, many more women are orgasmic with clitoral as opposed to vaginal stimulation (Lehmann et al., 2004).

The same organic factors implicated in retarded ejaculation in men have been associated with FOD in women (e.g., neurologic injury, SSRI use, alcohol use). Psychological factors associated with anorgasmia include lower educational levels, high religiosity, and sex guilt (Laumann et al., 1999). Although sexual abuse is sometimes associated with anorgasmia, other studies have failed to find such a relationship. There does not appear to be a correlation between relationship satisfaction and orgasmic ability, given that many women are sexually satisfied with their partners despite not consistently or, perhaps, ever attaining orgasm with intercourse (Basson, 2004). However, women who had a dim outlook on the future of their relationship tend to have more anorgasmic symptoms (Laumann et al., 2005).

Dyspareunia

In men, psychological factors play a primary role in the etiology of dyspareunia compared to organic factors and led the authors of one study to conclude that ano-dyspareunia in men deserves a place in the *DSM* taxonomy (Damon & Rosser, 2005). Apart from this research in gay men, there are no other data on the assessment or etiology of dyspareunia in men.

In women, an accurate assessment begins with a genital examination by an experienced gynecologist. The vestibule is considered part of the external female genitalia and extends from the labia minora to the hymen, and it contains both the vaginal and the urethral orifices. Common causes for genital pain include skin (dermatologic) infections, sexually transmitted infections, and trauma. The specific diagnosis of vulvar vestibulitis syndrome is made with a cotton swab test in which the vestibule is palpated with a Q-tip and the woman reports areas of particular tenderness or pain. In addition, the assessment involves looking for erythema (redness) in the area of the vestibule (Friedrich, 1987). This assessment should include determination of the qualities of pain (location, intensity, characteristics). Because the pain may evoke distressing emotions, the clinician must be sensitive to the woman's emotional state and only conduct the genital exam after sufficient explanation and preparation. Because VVS is the most common cause of dyspareunia, its etiology, evaluation, and treatment are presented here.

Pelvic or vulvar surgeries, chemotherapy, or radiation are associated with dyspareunia (Amsterdam, Carter, & Krychman, 2006), as are menopausal changes due to loss of estrogen and subsequent loss of vaginal tissue elasticity. In VVS specifically, biological etiological factors include yeast infections, use of oral contraceptives, early menarche, a genetic predisposition, human papilloma virus, and urethral conditions or infections (Pukall, Payne, Kao, Khalife, & Binik, 2005). Recently, fMRI assessment documented a more general hypersensitivity to touch and pain in women with VVS compared to unaffected women (Pukall, Strigo et al., 2005). Such sophisticated assessment measures enhance the etiological understanding of VVS and have promise in finding an effective intervention.

Although psychological factors are not considered primary in dyspareunia, personality and psychiatric symptoms can exacerbate pain as well as pain-induced affect. Potential psychological factors correlated with VVS include anxiety, depression, low self-esteem, harm avoidance, somatization, shyness, and pain catastrophization (as summarized in Pukall, Payne, et al., 2005). Anxiety is a prominent feature in women with VVS because anticipated pain prior to intercourse attempts leads many women to either fear or avoid sexual experiences. Not surprisingly, most women with VVS note that the condition significantly interferes with their relationship (Bergeron, Bouchard, Fortier, Binik, & Khalife, 1997).

VAGINISMUS

Given the frequent avoidance of gynecologic examinations in women with vaginismus, it often takes many sessions, reassurance, and rapport building before the gynecologist can perform an examination to assess structural abnormalities. Moreover, the vaginal muscle spasm is an unreliable characteristic of vaginismus that is diagnosed very differently among different health care providers (Reissing, Binik, Khalife, Cohen & Amsel, 2004). Physiotherapists obtain the greatest diagnostic accuracy based on measures of vaginal spasm.

Weijmar Schultz and van de Wiel (2005) summarize eight major etiological theories for vaginismus, and we will discuss four of the most empirically supported views here. Behavioral theory views the vaginal muscle spasm as a conditioned reaction occurring during a single episode of sexual intercourse (e.g., as in the case of sexual assault with forced penetration) or over repeated trials (e.g., as in the case of voluntary intercourse in a woman with dyspareunia). The fear of pain and the subsequent avoidance of any genital contact maintain the phobic anxiety in vaginismus, and this is the focus of treatment.

A physiological view (Weijmar Schultz & van de Wiel, 2005) considers vaginismus as a pelvic floor dysfunction and not as a sexual dysfunction. Because conditioning is the likely mechanism behind the overactive pelvic floor muscles in this theory, physiotherapy with biofeedback is the most logical treatment approach. This is described in detail by Rosenbaum (2003), who advocates a complementary approach between pelvic floor physiotherapists, gynecologists, and sex therapists in the treatment of vaginismus.

The interactional view (Weijmar Schultz & van de Wiel, 2005) suggests that vaginismus maintains balance between partners. Although empirical data are sparse, it is not uncommon in the clinical setting for male partners to be passive, dependent, anxious, and lacking in self-confidence. There is also evidence that these partners suffer from sexual dysfunction themselves (Lamont, 1978); therefore, the vaginismus serves to maintain balance in the sexless relationship. In this case, couples therapy is suggested (possibly as an adjunct to other treatments) although efficacy rates are not available. In general, therapists tend to exclude the partner from treatment of vaginismus, and this omission has been suggested to slow treatment progress (Weijmar Schultz & van de Wiel, 2005).

A multidimensional view of vaginismus is most explanatory when there is co-morbid dyspareunia (Weijmar Schultz & van de Wiel, 2005). In this view, treatment is individualized and combines attention to the pelvic floor and mucous mem-branes, sex therapy (with a partner), and physiotherapy. This view strongly dis-courages the understanding of vaginismus in any unidimensional manner, such as solely being a disorder of the pelvic floor, a pain disorder, a vestibulum disorder, or a psychological dysfunction.

TREATMENT

As implied in the section on etiology, there has been a shift in the past decade toward much research attention focused on finding effective pharmacological treatments. As a result, there has been a recent dearth of randomized controlled trials of psychological treatments, and much of the efficacy data for psychologi-cal treatments are based on studies conducted in the 1970s and 1980s. However, psychological treatments are efficacious and necessary (Heiman, 2002) and there is an urgent call for integrating the talents of mental health providers into phar-macological treatments administered by physicians (e.g., Perelman, 2006a).

HYPOACTIVE SEXUAL DESIRE DISORDER IN MEN

Treatment for HSDD in men and women largely depends on presumed etiol-ogy and can involve any combination of psychotherapy (either alone or with the partner), medications, and hormonal therapy. Psychotherapy may involve explo-ration of interpersonal issues, including anger, trust, exploration of an affair, and feelings of attractiveness. Treatment might also encourage men to use fantasies, erotic stimuli, and include forms of sexual activity besides intercourse. Unfor-tunately, there are no published results of controlled studies on the efficacy of psychological treatment without concomitant medication treatment for HSDD in men. However, an uncontrolled study that focused on developing emotional aspects while increasing sexual repertoire found a significant improvement in performance and sexual identity with no significant increase in sexual desire (McCabe, 1992).

Among the pharmacological treatments for HSSD, bupropion (marketed as the antidepressant Wellbutrin®) is a norepinephrine and dopamine agonist with an efficacy rate of approximately 86% in nondepressed men (Crenshaw, Goldbert, & Stern, 1987). Testosterone replacement has been the primary hormonal treatment and is administered as an injection, a patch, or as a gel. In a double-blind com-parison of testosterone treatment for men with HSDD versus men with erec-tile dysfunction, 30% of the men in the HSDD group responded (O'Carroll & Bancroft, 1984). However, the small sample size ($n = 10$) limits the study's gen-eralizability. In a recent meta-analysis of the effects of testosterone on sexual dysfunction in men with heterogeneous sexual complaints, it was found that tes-tosterone treatment improved sexual desire among men with clinically low levels of testosterone but not in men with normal levels (Isidori et al., 2005). If testoster-one treatment is considered in men with low desire, close consultation with an endocrinologist is essential because of possible negative side effects on prostate size and gynecomastia.

HYPOACTIVE SEXUAL DESIRE DISORDER IN WOMEN

Because testosterone administration significantly improves sexual desire in men (Isidori et al., 2005) and in nonhuman primates (see Wallen, 2005, for a review), much research has focused on finding an effective dose and method of administration of testosterone for improving women's sexual desire. Administration of a testosterone patch to women with surgical menopause from hysterectomy and BSO and who had been receiving estrogen replacement (Shifren et al., 2000) found that, despite a very high placebo response and no difference between the 150 microgram/day dose and placebo, the 300 microgram/day dose resulted in significantly higher rates of intercourse frequency and pleasure from orgasm (Shifren et al., 2000). There were no significant group differences on level of sexual desire, however. Five published randomized, placebo-controlled trials investigating a transdermal testosterone patch for improving desire in postmenopausal women receiving estrogen replacement all found a benefit for sexual desire (Braunstein et al., 2005; Buster et al., 2005; Davis et al, 2006; Kroll et al., 2004; Simon et al., 2005). The advantage of a patch is that it delivers continuous, low-dose levels of testosterone and may reduce unwanted side effects such as hair growth, acne, and supraphysiological levels of testosterone (Chu & Lobo, 2004). However, given a concern over the lack of long-term safety data, particularly regarding the possible link between testosterone and breast cancer (Tworoger et al., 2005), the testosterone patch currently does not have FDA regulatory approval and therefore continues to be prescribed off-label until sufficient long-term safety data are accrued.

The synthetic hormone, tibolone, which has estrogenic, androgenic, and progestogenic effects while not stimulating the uterus lining is licensed for the treatment of menopausal symptoms in Europe. In a randomized double-blind study of postmenopausal women free of sexual complaints, tibolone was found to significantly increase sexual desire, the frequency of sexual fantasies, and sexual arousability relative to control (Laan, van Lunsen, & Everaerd, 2001). At the time of this writing (December 2006), tibolone was under consideration for FDA approval in the United States.

Relatively less research has focused on the efficacy of nonhormonal pharmacological treatments for low desire in women. However, bupropion, effective in men with HSDD, also significantly improved sexual response in women in one placebo-controlled randomized trial (Segraves, Clayton, Croft, Wolf, & Warnock, 2004). The melanocortin agonist, PT-141 (bremelanotide), has been found to stimulate proceptive approach behaviors in female rats (Pfaus, Shadiack, Van Soest, Tse, & Molinoff, 2004) and is currently the subject of clinical investigations in women when administered intranasally. Preliminary data suggest that bremelanotide may significantly enhance sexual desire and perceived genital arousal among women (Perelman et al., 2006), but larger-scale randomized trials are required.

No published empirical studies have documented the efficacy of psychodynamic or systemic treatments for low desire, despite the rich clinical literature supporting these treatments among individuals and couples (Schnarch, 2000; Verhulst & Heiman, 1988). Similarly, multi-element treatments that incorporate cognitive and behavioral procedures with systemic approaches have been used effectively, especially for difficult-to-treat couples (Pridal & LoPiccolo, 2000). However, these types of treatments have not been subjected to randomized controlled trials.

There is moderate support from a number of controlled trials for cognitive behavioral therapy (CBT) directed at low desire. For example, behavioral treatment administered over 15 to 20 weekly sessions significantly improved initiation of sexual activity, sexual satisfaction, and increased frequency of sexual activity (Schover & LoPiccolo, 1982). A 12-session behavioral treatment for low desire modified from a Masters and Johnson approach led to significant improvements in intercourse ability. However, there was a marked attrition rate of 37% (Hawton, 1995). In the most recent, and only, study to include a control group, Trudel and colleagues compared the effects of CBT to a wait-list control group in 74 couples in which women met the criteria for HSDD (Trudel et al., 2001). Treatment included psychoeducation, skills and emotional training, and couple assignments in a group format. After 12 weeks, 74% of the women no longer met the diagnostic criteria, and this stabilized to 64% after a 1-year follow-up evaluation. In addition to significantly improved sexual desire, women experienced an improvement in quality of marital life and perception of sexual arousal. Others have found that CBT addressing a different aspect of the sexual response cycle—namely, orgasm—is effective in increasing sexual desire in women (Hurlbert, 1993), providing additional evidence that components of sexual response are highly correlated. A number of studies including both members of the couple that tested the efficacy of marital therapy for women's low desire have also found promising effects on sexual desire (Fish, Busby, & Killian, 1994; MacPhee, Johnson, & Van der Veer, 1995); however, these studies await randomized testing against a control group.

SEXUAL AVERSION DISORDER

Systematic desensitization has been found efficacious in two published case studies of women with SAD (Finch, 2001; Kingsberg & Janata, 2003), although, in general, SAD is less responsive to behavioral treatment than is HSDD (Schover & LoPiccolo, 1982). We were unable to locate any published efficacy studies on the treatment of SAD in men.

ERECTILE DYSFUNCTION

With the approval of sildenafil citrate (Viagra®) in the United States in 1998, treatment for ED is vastly different than it was decade ago. Sildenafil is a phosphodiesterase type-5 (PDE5) inhibitor and is a front-line treatment for ED. More recent PDE5 inhibitors that have been approved include tadalafil (Cialis®) and vardenafil (Levitra®). All work by inhibiting the action of PDE5, a molecule in the corpus cavernosum of the penis, which is involved in detumescence (loss of erection). Since its approval in 1998, sildenafil has been the focus of almost two thousand published studies in various subgroups of men with ED ranging in age from 19 to 87 years. The drug, which is available in 20-, 50-, or 100-mg doses, is taken 1 hour before planned sexual activity with a low-fat meal and must be combined with subjective or mechanical sexual stimulation. Its effectiveness ranges from 43% for men with radical prostatectomy to 59% for men with diabetes and 84% for men with ED due to psychological causes (Osterloh & Riley, 2002). Up to 33% of men who use these drugs experience mild side effects, including headaches, facial flushing, rhinitis, and visual disturbances. More serious side effects, such as priapism (sustained erection), occur in a small proportion of men. An important contraindication to the use of any of the PDE5 inhibitors is concomitant use of any form of nitrate treatment (including sublingual sprays and nitrates used recreationally), because both classes of medications act as blood pressure hypotensives.

Tadalafil is a newer PDE5 inhibitor with a 17.5-hour half-life and is touted as the "weekend drug" that promotes greater sexual spontaneity—an important factor for some couples. An analysis of 2,100 men taking tadalafil from 10 to 20 mg found that the drug was significantly more effective than placebo among all subgroups of men studied, including those with diabetes, hypertension, cardiovascular disease, hyperlipidemia, depression, and benign prostatic hyperplasia, and across ethno-cultural groups (Lewis et al., 2005).

Vardenafil is another PDE5 inhibitor with greater affinity for PDE5 than PDE6, resulting in fewer visual side effects than sildenafil. Vardenafil has been found to be particularly effective for two difficult-to-treat groups: men with diabetes and men with post-radical prostatectomy. Over 70% of men in both groups responded to vardenafil with improved erections (Brock et al., 2001; Goldstein, Fischer, Taylor, & Thibonnier, 2002). Ongoing clinical trials exploring the efficacy of vardenafil, tadalafil, and sildenafil in more specialized subgroups of men are underway. Finally, testosterone therapy, both alone (Isidori et al., 2005) and with a PDE5 inhibitor (Shabsigh, 2005), is also effective in the treatment of erectile dysfunction.

Before approval of the PDE5 inhibitors, injectable and intraurethral treatments were considered the mainstay of ED treatment. Traditionally reserved for men with an organic basis to their ED, these techniques involve intracavernosal injection of alprostadil (prostaglandin E1) directly into the penis, and, unlike the oral medications, sexual stimulation is not required to produce an erection. Although found to be highly effective in 87% of men (Linet & Ogrinc, 1996), the side effects of penile pain or prolonged erections make compliance a concern. Alprostadil also can be delivered directly into the urethra as MUSE (medicated urethral system for erection). This mode of delivery is favorable for men who cannot tolerate oral medications or injections. Approximately 70% of men respond positively to MUSE (Padma-Nathan et al., 1997), which requires some training from a sexual health clinician for proper insertion.

Vacuum constriction devices (VCDs) and constriction rings are also available for ED and do not require administration or ingestion of a medication, which might be necessary for some groups of men with medical contraindications. A VCD is a tube that is placed over the flaccid penis and a vacuum draws blood into the penis either manually or with a battery-operated motor. A constriction ring is then typically placed over the base of the penis to sustain the erection for intercourse. Although very effective for men who cannot tolerate medical forms of ED treatment, it does require a certain degree of manual dexterity and is not suitable for men with sickle cell disease, leukemia, or those who use anticoagulation treatments (Wylie & MacInnes, 2005).

Psychological interpretation is essential for couples in which relationship discord and communication difficulties are related to ED, although there are few data on the efficacy of psychological therapies for men with ED. In a randomized comparison of 12 biweekly sessions of rational-emotive therapy versus a wait-list control group, men with ED responded with significantly more successful intercourse attempts and reduced sexual anxiety (Munjack et al., 1984); however, these beneficial effects were not maintained 9 months later. More recently, combination treatments have been explored (see Perelman, 2005, for a review) in recognition that emotional or other psychological factors can interfere with the success of medical treatments (Kaplan, 1990). There have been multiple case reports of men benefiting from combined oral medications plus cognitive behavioral therapies for ED (McCarthy, 1998; Perelman, 2002; Segraves, 1999). Addition of a one-session group psychoeducational intervention, comprised of behavioral skills and motivational enhancement, led to significantly improved patient satisfaction, confidence in sexual ability, and improved sexual communication in men receiving sildenafil compared to a waitlist control group (Phelps, Jain, & Monga, 2004). Perelman (2006a) has described the Sexual Tipping Point™ model of combined treatment for male sexual dysfunction. In it, he argues that, by optimally combining cognitive behavioral treatments with pharmacologic interventions, medication dosages may be titrated downward and efficacy may be enhanced. Given the widespread success of the oral medications for ED, we expect to see more publications in the future comparing medication with and without psychological therapy using the Tipping Point™ model.

FEMALE SEXUAL AROUSAL DISORDER

Given the mentioned high degree of comorbidity between arousal and desire and orgasm complaints, there are no published trials testing the efficacy of a psychological intervention for FSAD alone. Numerous investigations of pharmacologic treatments have been undertaken, particularly for women with genital sexual arousal disorder. One uncontrolled trial examined a psychoeducational intervention that combined behavioral skills training, cognitive challenging of maladaptive thoughts, relationship exercises, and mindfulness techniques for women with FSAD secondary to gynecologic cancer (Brotto et al., 2006). This three-session intervention led to significantly improved reports of genital and subjective sexual arousal and to physiological sexual arousal measured with a vaginal photoplethysmograph. Because a control group was not included in this trial, replication using a larger sample and including a control group is necessary to generalize the findings.

Among women with genital sexual arousal disorder, a number of pharmacological studies find variable degrees of efficacy. The dopaminergic agonist, apomorphine SL, significantly improved sexual arousal, desire, orgasm, satisfaction, and enjoyment when taken daily at 2- to 3-mg doses but not when used "as needed" (Caruso et al., 2004). Phentolamine mesylate, an antagonist at the α-1 and α-2 receptors, commonly used in the treatment of ED, significantly improved self-reported lubrication and tingling sensations, with no effect on physiological sexual arousal, subjective pleasure, or arousal in postmenopausal women when administered orally (Rosen, Phillips, Gendrano, & Ferguson, 1999). In a much larger, double-blind replication of the study, vaginally applied phentolamine significantly increased physiological arousal in postmenopausal women receiving hormone replacement (Rubio-Aurioles et al., 2002). Although prostaglandins have been used to treat ED for decades, their results are not as promising for women with FSAD. The prostaglandin E_1, alprostadil, only marginally increased satisfaction with sexual arousal while not significantly affecting arousal success rates or sexual distress in premenopausal women with FSAD (Padma-Nathan et al., 2003).

With the remarkable success of the PDE5 inhibitors for men, it is not surprising that there has been a race to determine efficacy for women's sexual arousal complaints. However, studies using sildenafil have found conflicting results. A large double-blind study of sildenafil found no benefit for women with mixed sexual complaints (Basson, McInnes, Smith, Hodgson, & Koppiker, 2002). When a more diagnostically homogeneous group of women with specific genital sexual arousal concerns was examined, results were more promising in both premenopausal women (Caruso, Intelisano, Lupo, & Agnello, 2001) and estrogen-replete postmenopausal women (Basson & Brotto, 2003; Berman, Berman, Toler, Gill, & Haughie, 2003). There are no published investigations of either vardenafil or tadalafil in women with FSAD, although such trials are likely underway.

Currently, there is one product approved by the FDA for the treatment of FSAD. The EROS-CTD™ is a small, handheld, battery-operated clitoral therapy device that is placed over the clitoris and increases blood flow through a gentle suction. The EROS-CTD™ was found to significantly improve all measures of sexual response and satisfaction in women with FSAD (Billups et al., 2001) and in women with arousal complaints secondary to radiation therapy for cervical cancer (Schroder et al., 2005). The lack of a control condition and the fact that women had to use the device several times per week for the duration of the study make it difficult to ascertain whether these positive effects were due to the suction per se or to nonspecific attentional factors.

PREMATURE EJACULATION

Once a thorough assessment of PE has ruled out physiological obstacles to ejaculatory control, clinicians may attempt a behavioral and/or pharmacological treatment approach. Seman's "stop-squeeze" technique, which was later adopted by Masters and Johnson, and Kaplan's "stop-pause" technique remain highly efficacious behavioral treatments in PE. The stop-squeeze method requires the man to provide direct feedback to his partner for when the ejaculatory urge nears. The couple discontinues sexual stimulation and the partner applies pressure to the glans of the penis until the urge is reduced (Masters & Johnson, 1970; Semans, 1956). The man may practice the technique on his own during masturbation before generalizing it to the partner. The efficacy of the stop-squeeze technique is approximately 60% (Metz, Pryor, Nesvacil, Abuzzahab, & Koznar, 1997). The stop-pause approach (Kaplan, 1989) is thought to better simulate the natural behaviors during intercourse and essentially involves a reduction in penile stimulation as the man nears ejaculatory inevitability. He resumes sexual stimulation once he feels control over his ejaculation. Although early studies by Masters and Johnson and Kaplan find efficacy rates nearing 100%, more recent controlled trials found the stop-pause technique to be effective for approximately 64% of men (Hawton, Catalan, Martin, & Fagg, 1986). Numerous adaptations of these behavioral techniques have been suggested, such as including various breathing techniques, adding a stage of ejaculatory control training with oral sex, and the addition of psychoeducation.

In an uncontrolled trial, there was significant improvement in PE by using a self-administered psychological treatment (Trudel & Proulx, 1987). In another uncontrolled study, 15 to 20 sessions of pelvic floor rehabilitation led to complete cure of PE in 61% of men (Giuseppe & Nicastro, 1996). Although evidence of a psychogenic etiology in PE is not strong, the efficacy of these behavioral techniques is excellent and they remain one of the first-line treatments in PE.

Based on the hypothesis that a low ejaculatory setpoint due to low serotonin neurotransmission may underlie some forms of PE, selective serotonin reuptake inhibitors have become a mainstay in pharmacological treatment of PE. One of the negative side effects of SSRIs is delayed orgasm in men and women. SSRIs may be administered daily or on an as-needed basis. Across several dozen trials examining the efficacy of SSRIs in PE, a recent meta-analysis of daily SSRI use showed paroxetine (Paxil®) to have the greatest efficacy in delaying ejaculation (Kara et al., 1996). Clomipramine (Anafranil®), sertraline (Zoloft®), and fluoxetine (Prozac®) all have reported efficacy. When used on an as-needed basis, clomipramine, taken 4 to 6 hours prior to intercourse is most efficacious (Strassberg, de Gouveia Brazao, Rowland, Tan, & Slob, 1999). Most recently, the SSRI dapoxetine, which has a rapid onset of action and is quickly cleared after intercourse, has shown excellent efficacy in the treatment of PE without several of the unwanted side effects of other SSRIs (Andersson, Mulhall, & Wyllie, 2006). The FDA did not approve this medication for the treatment of PE, stating that there were insufficient data to support its efficacy.

Another pharmacological treatment for PE involves the use of topical local anesthetics applied to the penis. For example, lidocaine and/or prilocaine as a cream, gel, or spray has been found effective for treating PE in about 85% of men (Xin, Choi, Lee, & Choi, 1997). More recently, the PDE5 inhibitors have been tested for efficacy with PE; however, double-blind trials find that they do not increase the efficacy of a topical anesthetic cream (Atan et al., 2006). The Sexual Tipping Point™ model for ED has also been applied to PE and argues that the most elegant treatment of PE would integrate a pharmacologic with a psychological treatment (Perelman, 2006a). Indeed, a comparison of behavior therapy with and without sildenafil shows the combination to significantly delay time to ejaculation (Tang, Ma, Zhao, Liu, & Chen, 2004).

RETARDED EJACULATION (MALE ORGASMIC DISORDER)

Relative to treatments for PE, much less has been published on efficacious treatments for retarded ejaculation. In cases of an organic etiology, amelioration of the underlying biological factors is an important first line of treatment. This may include switching the patient to a different antidepressant, androgen administration, or other attempts to control diabetic neuropathy. Kaplan (1974) described a behavioral treatment in which a male partner with situational RE is asked to masturbate in front of his female partner on the other side of the room and subsequently masturbate while moving progressively closer and closer to her. Eventually he continues the action with his penis close to the vagina and finally attempts penetration with simultaneous penile manipulation with the goal of ejaculation inside the vagina. Efficacy rates for this behavioral treatment do not exist; however, it has been found to be useful in the clinical setting for a large number of men. In addition, individual or couples therapy may be warranted if there are interpersonal factors perpetuating the RE. This is particularly true for men with situational RE who have good ejaculatory control during masturbation but experience anxiety or other distracting emotions when in a partnered sexual situation.

FEMALE ORGASMIC DISORDER

Both psychological and pharmacological treatments are efficacious for female orgasmic disorder. Behavioral treatments initially developed and tested by Masters and Johnson (1970) were demonstrated to be highly effective and remain in widespread use today. For example, directed masturbation exercises are designed to teach women to focus on sexually erotic cues, not focus on distracting nonsexual cues, and apply graded stimulation to the clitoris in an effort to become orgasmic with masturbation. Because effects of a partner on sexual anxiety, awkwardness in sexual communication, and insufficient genital arousal by a partner are removed, a woman is able to focus on eliciting sexual stimulation that is effective for her. Heiman and LoPiccolo (1987) have authored *Becoming Orgasmic: A Sexual Growth Program for Women,* an excellent self-help book for women that details the steps and exercises involved in directed masturbation. Women with FOD may work through the book independently or with therapist guidance. It has been translated into nine languages and remains one of the most widely used behavioral treatments for FOD with an approximate 90% efficacy rate.

In addition to directed masturbation, anxiety reduction is another important intervention for FOD. Because anxiety may act as a cognitive distraction, thereby distracting the woman from sexual cues, and/or it may lead the woman to engage in spectatoring—a process of self-monitoring—anxiety reduction is often a target in treatment. Systematic desensitization, used with anxiety disorders, pairs muscle relaxation with the simultaneous presentation of sexual anxiety-evoking stimuli. Sensate focus is another technique that involves the partner touching the woman, as she guides his touch with words focuses on relaxation (Masters & Johnson, 1970). Moreover, comparable effects are achieved when treatment is administered independently, in a group or in a self-help format (Libman et al., 1984), suggesting that more cost-effective methods may be considered in the treatment of FOD.

The coital alignment technique (CAT) is another behavioral method designed to improve orgasmic ability with intercourse. In CAT, the man is in the superior position and shifts forward such that the base of his penis makes direct contact with the woman's clitoris. This ensures that penetration is accompanied by constant clitoral stimulation and results in improved coital orgasmic ability in approximately 56% of women (Hurlbert & Apt, 1995). Other behavioral techniques found to be helpful adjuncts include kegel exercises (described in the section on vaginismus), sex education, assertiveness, and communication skills—although considerably less research exists for these treatments as compared to directed masturbation and anxiety reduction.

A number of placebo-controlled studies have examined the efficacy of pharmacologic treatments for FOD. For example, pre- and postmenopausal women with low arousal and anorgasmia showed significant improvements with sildenafil (Basson & Brotto, 2003; Caruso et al., 2001). Studies on transdermal testosterone treatment for women with low desire have shown conflicting findings with either an improvement (Buster et al., 2005) or no effect (Braunstein et al., 2005) on orgasmic function.

Among women with SSRI-induced anorgasmia, Ashton and Weinstein (2006) describe a case series of three women who acquired anorgasmia secondary to SSRI use. All women had complete reversal of the anorgasmia with the PDE5 inhibitor tadalafil. Double-blind replications are necessary, however, to determine the extent to which the improvement is due to expectancy versus a true drug effect. In a double-blind trial, 47 mg of buspirone resulted in marginal improvement in orgasmic function among women taking citalopram or paroxetine (Landen, Eriksson, Agren, & Fahlen, 1999). A number of other pharmacologic agents have been tried in the treatment of SSRI-induced anorgasmia (e.g., sublingual apomorphine, ephedrine, gingko biloba, yohimbine, and mirtazepine) without notable effects on orgasmic ability.

The EROS-CTD™, mentioned earlier as a treatment for FSAD, has been found to significantly improve orgasmic ability in women with FOD (Berman et al., 2003; Billups, et al., 2001). Again, however, the extent to which these positive effects might be obtained by using a much less expensive vibrator is a possibility.

DYSPAREUNIA

There are four general categories of treatment for VVS, the most common cause of dyspareunia: medical, psychological, physical, and surgical. Among the medical treatments for VVS, first-line suggestions include hygiene modification and sitz baths. If ineffective, then topical treatments in the form of anesthetics or cortico-steroids, oral treatments in the form of low-dose antidepressants (e.g., amitrip-tyline, nortriptyline), anticonvulsants (e.g., tegretol, neurontin), corticosteroids or antifungals, and injectable treatments (e.g., interferon) are available with variable degrees of efficacy. There is a lack of randomized double-blind and prospective studies assessing these treatments, so precise efficacy rates are not known. It is not uncommon for women to try many different forms and dosages of medical treat-ments before experiencing any relief from VVS.

Psychologists often work with the treating gynecologist, and this multidisci-plinary approach is highly effective and acceptable to women. Among the psycho-logical treatments, CBT has received the most empirical support, including the use of group CBT protocol for women with VVS that adopts a pain control strategy as its primary target and includes kegel exercises, vaginal dilatation, relaxation, and cognitive challenging (Bergeron & Binik, 1998).

Physiotherapy with pelvic floor biofeedback also has been effective in the treat-ment of VVS (Bergeron et al., 2002) and is based on the idea that pelvic floor hyper-tonicity can exacerbate pain. The technique involves reducing hypertonicity of the pelvic floor muscles and is also an effective treatment for vaginismus (described later). Physiotherapy involves direct vaginal/genital massage and stimulation of trigger points by an experienced pelvic floor physiotherapist. Biofeedback is also incorporated and involves placement of a single-user electromyograph (EMG) sensor in or around the vagina, and by measuring pelvic floor muscle tension and projecting it onto a screen for the patient to view, she is taught to reduce muscle tension, thereby decreasing genital pain.

Surgery is usually a treatment of last resort for women who have tried some com-bination of these treatments, despite the fact that it is considered a minor proce-dure that can be completed in day surgery. Vestibulectomy involves excision of the hymen and sensitive areas of the vestibule, and occasionally mobilization of vaginal mucosa to cover the excised area. Recent studies demonstrate a highly effective improvement rate of 73% to 90% (Gaunt, Good, & Stanhope, 2003; Lavy, Lev-Sagie, Hamani, Zacut, & Ben-Chetrit, 2005); however, there is a lower efficacy rate for women with acquired VVS and a higher rate of recurrence following vestibulec-tomy compared to women with lifelong VVS (Rettenmaier, Brown, & Micha, 2003).

In the only published head-to-head comparison of 12-week group CBT, pelvic floor physiotherapy, and vestibulectomy, 78 women were randomized to group and followed for a 2-year period (Bergeron et al., 2001). All groups experienced a sig-nificant reduction in pain at post-treatment and at a 6-month follow-up evaluation, with the vestibulectomy group showing the most improvement (Bergeron et al., 2001). All groups also significantly improved on measures of psychological and sexual function. A 2.5-year follow-up of the study found continued improvement in all three groups with no significant treatment differences in pain from intercourse, sexual functioning, or intercourse frequency, suggesting that CBT is as effective as surgery for the treatment of VVS (Bergeron, 2003).

VAGINISMUS

Weijmar Schultz and Van de Wiel (2005) describe, in detail, the important components of treatment for vaginismus from a multidisciplinary view. They note that providing information to women about the characteristics of, physical aspects of, and treatments for vaginismus is a necessary starting point. They also acknowledge that a physical examination is necessary to rule out other physical contributors to the muscle tightening during which women are invited to play an active role by watching with a mirror and guiding the speculum insertion. Pain measurement is another important component of the assessment, as is assessment of pelvic floor strength.

Additional interventions depend on the etiological view that one adopts. According to the behavioral view, treatment of vaginismus involves a reconditioning of the body's response to feared objects such as the penis, a speculum, or a tampon, much like the treatment approach for other specific phobias. Using a systematic desensitization approach, the woman is asked to create a hierarchy of feared objects that she will then progressively work through to insert vaginally over the course of treatment. Simultaneously, the woman is taught to engage in activity incompatible with tension or anxiety, such as relaxation and diaphragmatic breathing. Highly useful as an object of insertion is the vaginal dilator (or insert or accommodator) shown in Figure 14.1 (Laurel Prescriptions, Vancouver, Canada), which can be made of wax, plastic, silicone, or other nonirritating substance. Dilators can be included in the fear hierarchy and involve insertion for a fixed period of time (e.g., 10 to 15 minutes) by either the woman or her partner while simultaneously relaxing. If the woman has a reluctance, fear, or lack of awareness of her own anatomy, treatment is best initiated with a phase of self-exploration using a handheld mirror and an anatomical diagram of the vulva. The cognitive elements of therapy involve challenging irrational thoughts such as "I am too small," "intercourse will always hurt," or "there is something abnormal about me." Research examining the efficacy of this behavioral approach combined with cognitive elements found it to be highly effective for nearly all women in reducing vaginismus, anxiety, and improving the couple relationship (Kabakci & Batur, 2003).

SUMMARY OF SEXUAL DYSFUNCTIONS

Clearly, there is a large degree of heterogeneity in the diagnostic features, presumed etiologies, and treatments of the sexual dysfunctions in men and women. Despite this, these complaints tend to be highly comorbid within an individual and between partners in a couple. Thus, it is essential that a comprehensive biopsychosocial assessment of both partners—assessing all aspects of sexual response, satisfaction, and distress—be undertaken for an accurate diagnosis and

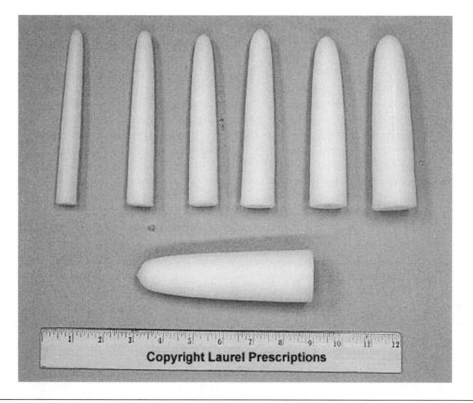

Figure 14.1   Wax vaginal inserts used in the treatment of vaginismus (Laurel Prescriptions, Vancouver, Canada).

therefore optimal treatment to be decided upon. The field of sexual medicine is rapidly expanding with several national and international society meetings across the globe. The interested reader is encouraged to explore the web site of the Kinsey Institute at www.kinseyinstitute.org for a list of sexuality-related meetings and training opportunities.

GENDER IDENTITY DISORDER

Gender identity disorder (GID), originally termed transsexualism, was first defined by professionals during the 1950s and described individuals who had a desire to be of the opposite sex. Initially, individuals with this disorder were often described as being "trapped" in the body of the opposite sex as the case below illustrates (Denny, 2004). Other terms that have been used somewhat synonymously with GID and transsexualism are transgenderism and gender dysphoria. However, while transsexualism and GID refer to the diagnostic names given to the disorder by the American Psychiatric Association (1980; 2000), gender dysphoria refers more generally to feelings of dissatisfaction with one's biological sex and may be present in individuals who do not meet specific diagnostic criteria.

Similarly, transgenderism is a newer term that also encompasses individuals who experience gender dysphoria but do not necessarily meet diagnostic criteria for GID. The term transsexualism also reflects a more recent conceptualization of GID, not as a mental disorder but rather as a natural variant along the continuum of human variability (Denny, 2004).

Another term that has at times been confused with GID is transvestic fetishism, discussed in more detail in the section on paraphilias. The two terms are not synonymous, although they can co-occur. Specifically, while GID refers to strong and persistent *dissatisfaction* with one's biological sex and simultaneous strong and persistent *cross-gender identification,* transvestic fetishism refers to strong and persistent *sexual arousal* involving cross-dressing.

Case Study

James is a 35-year-old single White man who was referred to the gender identity clinic by his family doctor for concerns about "wishing he was not a male." James presented to his first appointment with the psychiatrist with some visible signs of feminization such as gynecomastia (breast growth). He reported to have been taking oral contraceptive pills that he purchased "from a friend" over the past year. He stated that he has never felt like a man and feels that he is a woman trapped in a man's body. He grew up in a middle-upper-class family with an older sister, and, as such, he was exposed to stereotypical girls' toys and clothing. In private, he would go into his sister's closet, put her clothes on, and feel a sense of relief. Although he strongly detested his male genital parts, he did not share his feelings with his parents for fear that they would laugh at him. He experimented with a few relationships with women during his twenties, and has had sexual intercourse with ejaculation, but reported that these relationships felt "fake" given that he often wished he was his female partner with a vagina. At the age of 28, he moved to a new city thinking that this was what he needed to overcome his depressed mood and uncertain sense of self, but he realized, instead, that his desire to be a woman intensified as he did not feel the constraints of concealing his identity concerns from his parents. He began to network with other individuals who were questioning their identity, and at the age of 33 he realized that he was a transsexual and desired to have sex reassignment surgery. He has spoken to his family physician about this on a few occasions, but has never been formally evaluated nor diagnosed with GID. In addition, he reported "wanting to get the transition started quickly" and, as such, was obtaining hormones through illegal means. During the assessment, the psychiatrist diagnosed James with gender identity disorder and suggested that he see the clinic's endocrinologist, who would be able to ensure that James's hormonal regimen was effective and safe. James was relieved to begin the transition process but knew that there was a long road ahead before he would be considered for surgery.

EPIDEMIOLOGY

Although no epidemiological studies on the prevalence of GID are available, there are some preliminary data. Based on data from smaller European countries, approximately 1 in 30,000 males and 1 in 100,000 females experience the disorder as indicated by the *DSM-IV-TR*. These numbers are consistent with those reported by the Harry Benjamin International Gender Dysphoria Association (HBIGDA; Meyer et al., 2001) which notes rates of 1 in 37,000 for males and 1 in 107,000 for females.

Thus, GID is more commonly diagnosed in males than in females; however, it is unclear whether the diagnosis is truly more prevalent in males or whether these numbers are an artifact of diagnoses more commonly being made in the former than in the latter. As Bradley and Zucker (1997) point out, the sex difference in diagnoses of GID may be due to a greater acceptance when girls behave in cross-gender ways than when boys do the same, a phenomenon that may mask true prevalence rates.

COURSE AND PROGNOSIS

Childhood onset of GID usually begins between the ages of 2 and 4 years (American Psychiatric Association, 2000). However, few individuals who are diagnosed with GID in childhood continue meeting diagnostic criteria or having symptoms of the disorder in adolescence and adulthood. Instead, approximately 75% of males with childhood GID later report homosexual or bisexual orientations without further GID symptoms, and most of the remaining 25% report heterosexual orientations as adults, also without any GID symptomatology (APA, 2000). Corresponding numbers for females are unknown.

For men with adult onset GID, the course appears more gradual, is generally chronic, and is more often preceded by, or concurrent with, a diagnosis of transvestic fetishism. The *DSM-IV-TR* lists four specifiers that can be given with a diagnosis of GID: (1) sexually attracted to males; (2) sexually attracted to females; (3) sexually attracted to both; and (4) sexually attracted to neither (APA, 2000). While all four specifiers are used with males, females with the disorder tend to be sexually attracted only to females.

DIAGNOSTIC CONSIDERATIONS

Transsexualism was first introduced in the third edition of the *DSM* (*DSM-III*; American Psychiatric Association, 1980). Since its inception, the diagnostic criteria have evolved somewhat requiring individuals to show, over a period of at least 2 years, persistent interest in changing their gender and living socially as the opposite sex.

The current criteria for GID require both a strong and persistent cross-gender identification and persistent discomfort with one's assigned sex (Criterion A and B, respectively; APA, 2000). In addition, the individual cannot have a concomitant physical intersex condition such as congenital adrenal hyperplasia (Criterion C), and the symptoms must cause clinically significant distress or impairment (Criterion D). With respect to Criterion A, the cross-gender identification cannot be due to a desire for any social or cultural advantages held by the opposite sex.

The *DSM-IV-TR* (APA, 2000) also specifies how Criterion A and B are manifested in children. Children must show at least four of the following five characteristics: (1) repeatedly stating a desire to be of the opposite sex or stating that one is of the opposite sex; (2) cross-dressing in clothing stereotypical of the opposite sex; (3) strong and persistent fantasies of being the opposite sex or preferences for cross-sex roles in make-believe play; (4) a strong desire to participate in games and activities of the opposite sex; and (5) a strong preference for playmates of the opposite sex. To meet Criterion B, boys must show at least one of the following four characteristics: (1) expressions of disgust with respect to their penis or testes; (2) statements that their penis will disappear; (3) statements that it would be better not to have a penis; and (4) aversion toward rough-and-tumble play as well as toys, games, and activities considered to be stereotypically male. Similarly, to meet Criterion B, girls must show at least one of the following four characteristics: (1) rejection toward urinating while sitting; (2) assertions that they either already have or will grow a penis; (3) statements about not wanting to grow breasts or menstruate; and (4) marked aversion toward feminine clothing.

Adolescents and adults meeting criteria for GID may not only have the desire to be the other sex and to be treated as such, but may also try to pass as, or become, the opposite sex by cross-dressing and changing primary and secondary sex characteristics through hormones and surgery. Intense gender dysphoria, together with the stigmatization by friends, family, and others, often lead to feelings of guilt, shame, and low self-esteem (Schaefer & Wheeler, 2004). Many with GID also have comorbid psychiatric symptoms including anxiety, depression, personality disorders, and psychotic disorders (à Campo, Nijman, Merckelbach, & Evers, 2003; Cole, O'Boyle, Emory, & Meyer, 1997; Hepp, Kraemer, Schnyder, Miller, & Delsignore, 2005); however, these psychiatric conditions are generally not the cause of GID (Cole et al., 1997; Langer & Martin, 2004; Meyer, 2004). Rather, psychiatric symptoms likely result from the stigmatization, rejection, and emotional abuse these individuals experience (Denny, 2004; Sadowski & Gaffney, 1998) or as psychiatric conditions unrelated to, and independent of, GID (Hepp et al., 2005).

PSYCHOLOGICAL AND BIOLOGICAL ASSESSMENT

Assessment and diagnosis of GID relies completely on the client's self-report. The role of the assessing clinician is not only to make an accurate diagnosis with regard to GID but also to assess for comorbid psychiatric conditions that may be contributing to the individual's distress and symptomatology (Meyer et al., 2001). In children and adolescents presenting with gender dysphoria, the Standards of Care by the HBIGDA state that, in addition to comprehensive psycho-diagnostic and psychiatric evaluation, assessments should include a family evaluation to assess for unresolved issues in the child's or adolescent's life (Meyer et al., 2001). Although diagnostic criteria indicate that the symptoms cannot be due to a concurrent intersex condition, tests to confirm this are not generally undertaken during the diagnostic assessment phase.

Because the diagnosis relies solely on self-report, it is possible that individuals presenting with this disorder may have coached themselves on the diagnostic criteria and presentation of symptoms, or may be exaggerating their symptoms, in order to be eligible for sex reassignment surgery (Michel, Mormont, & Legros, 2001). However, Seil (2004) points out that, although clinicians may hear very similar stories from clients presenting with this disorder, they need to realize "that the course of [GID] varies little in substance from one person to another within each subgroup of patients" (p. 102).

TREATMENT

Since 1979, the HBIGDA has outlined and published Standards of Care for clinicians working with those with GID that provide comprehensive guidelines for treatment of GID (whether psychological, hormonal, or surgical). These standards include "lasting personal comfort with the gendered self in order to maximize overall psychological well-being and self-fulfillment" (Meyer et al., 2001, p. 2), whereas, in the past, intervention often focused on making the individual more like their biological sex. For example, past treatments have included various behavioral therapies targeted toward changing the individual's social and sexual behaviors to be more stereotypically masculine or feminine, including behavioral modification of vocal characteristics, sexual fantasies, patterns of sexual arousal, and even movements and posture (Barlow, Abel, & Blanchard, 1979). In contrast, current treatment, as outlined by the Standards of Care (Meyer et al., 2001), includes three principal elements comprising a "triadic therapy." These elements include living as the desired gender, hormone therapy, and sex reassignment surgery—although not all individuals will desire, or complete, all three steps.

The Standards of Care (Meyer et al., 2001) assert that living as the desired gender should occur for at least 2 years (full-time) before any genital surgeries are performed. This step involves adopting the new gender role to become aware of the effects this change has on interpersonal, familial, economic, and vocational areas of life, and is considered to be crucial in the transition from one gender to the other.

Hormone therapy involves the administration of testosterone to biological females who desire to become male and estrogens to biological males who want to become female. Hormonal administration leads to the reduction of secondary sex characteristics of the natal sex and the development of secondary sex characteristics of the desired sex. These include such features as facial and body hair, breasts, vocal pitch, testicular and clitoral size, and weight distribution throughout the body. Hormone therapy can be an important component of treatment, often improving quality of life for the individual and thereby limiting the presence of other psychiatric difficulties (Meyer et al., 2001). However, it is also noted that it may take up to 2 years of uninterrupted treatment to see the maximal effects of this intervention.

Sex reassignment surgery is often the final step in the treatment of individuals with GID, although, as mentioned, not all individuals desire surgery. Sex reassignment surgery can take a number of forms. For biological males, these include orchiedectomy (castration), penectomy (surgical removal of the penis), clitoroplasty and labioplasty (formation of a clitoris and labia, respectively), and the creation of a "neovagina" (an artificial vagina). For biological females, the surgical techniques can include hysterectomy, BSO, vaginectomy (removal of the vagina), metaidoioplasty (construction of a microphallus using the skin of the clitoris), scrotoplasty (formation of a scrotum), urethroplasty (plastic surgery of the urethra), placement of testicular prostheses, and the creation of a neophallus (an artificial penis). Increasingly, doctors are performing these surgeries with special attention to preserving sexual function in order to improve the quality of life for these individuals (Freundt, Toolenaar, Jeekel, Drogendijk, & Huikeshoven, 1994; Lawrence, 2003).

One final recommended component of treatment of GID is ongoing psychotherapy before, during, and after each of these steps. The goals of psychotherapy are to educate the client about the various options for treatment, help the client set realistic vocational and interpersonal goals, and help the client recognize and work through any conflicts that prevent stability in his or her life (Meyer et al., 2001).

GENDER IDENTITY DISORDER SUMMARY

Understanding of GID has vastly expanded since its earliest *DSM* descriptions, and the number of multidisciplinary gender identity clinics offering assessment and treatment services to individuals with GID has grown. Hormonal, psychological, and surgical treatments have been well described and offer adequate support for many individuals with GID. However, given that a number of individuals with GID keep their distress hidden for a significant period of time and may therefore miss early opportunities for support, efforts must be placed toward the earliest possible opportunity for supporting individuals with gender identity confusion to minimize their distress.

DESCRIPTION OF THE PARAPHILIAS

The paraphilias, as defined in the *DSM-IV-TR* (APA, 2000), refer to sexual disorders of "recurrent, intense sexual urges, fantasies, or behaviors that involve unusual objects, activities, or situations and cause clinically significant distress or impairment in social, occupational, or other important areas of functioning" (p. 535). The paraphilias tend to fall into one of three types, involving sexual arousal toward non-human objects, sexual arousal toward children or other nonconsenting individuals, or sexual arousal related to the suffering or humiliation of oneself or others.

The term *paraphilia* was coined by Stekel in 1923 and translates into love (*philia*) beyond the usual (*para;* Money, 1984). Although paraphilias are often associated with sexual offending, the two terms are not synonymous. As Krueger and Kaplan (2001) point out, paraphilias are considered to refer to a type of mental disorder. In contrast, "sexual offender" is a legal term to denote individuals who have been convicted of a sexual offense. Many sexual offenders meet diagnostic criteria for one or more paraphilias, and some individuals diagnosed with a paraphilia have committed sexual offenses; thus, the two are by no means mutually exclusive (McElroy et al., 1999).

However, because of this association, much research is based on samples of convicted sexual offenders, which leads to three major confounds in understanding the paraphilias. First, many sexual offenders were never formally diagnosed. Second, the generalizability of these samples to all individuals with paraphilias is suspect, because it is likely that individuals convicted of a sexual offense represent the more severe end of the paraphilic spectrum. Third, the veracity of the self-reports by sexual offenders needs to be considered because these individuals often have high motivations to appear less "deviant" in their sexual interests and so may under- and overreport certain fantasies and experiences.

EXHIBITIONISM

Exhibitionism, involving recurrent and intense sexually arousing fantasies, sexual urges, or behaviors of exposing one's genitals to an unsuspecting stranger over a period of at least 6 months, is the most commonly reported paraphilia (Murphy, 1997). Exhibiting may consist of either showing the genitals to or actively masturbating in front of a stranger. To meet *DSM-IV-TR* criteria, the individual must either have acted on the sexual urges or fantasies or have experienced marked distress or interpersonal difficulty as a result of them (APA, 2000).

Although primarily a disorder of men, female exhibitionism has been reported (Federoff, Fishell, & Federoff, 1999; Freund, 1990; Grob, 1985; Hooshmand & Brawley, 1969). The majority of victims of exhibitionism are females, including both children and adolescents. Often, it is the victim's shock that is sexually arousing to the perpetrator, and in most cases there is no other contact.

Exhibitionists are a heterogeneous group whose education, intelligence, and socioeconomic status does not differ from the general population (Blair & Lanyon, 1981). Initial investigations found high rates of personality pathology in exhibitionists, particularly shy and nonassertive personalities (Ellis & Brancale, 1956), but later studies utilizing more standardized assessment instruments did not find abnormal or specific personality patterns (Langevin, Paitich, Freeman, Mann, & Handy, 1978; Langevin et al., 1979; Smukler & Schiebel, 1975) nor did they find that psychopathology symptoms differed from other sexual or nonsexual offenders (Murphy, Haynes, & Worley, 1991; Murphy & Peters, 1992). Moreover, the majority of exhibitionists are married or in common-law relationships and they enjoy nonpathological sexual relationships with their partners (Langevin & Lang, 1987; Maletzky, 1991).

In comparison to those with other paraphilias, Cox and Maletzky (1980) found that exhibitionists are least likely to see their behavior as harmful to their victims—a factor likely to influence both motivations for, and success of, treatment. Relatedly, they are more likely to underreport or minimize their exhibitionistic and other paraphilic fantasies and behaviors (McConaghy, 1993; McConaghy, Blaszcyzynski, & Kidson, 1988). Freund and Blanchard (1986) and Langevin and Lang (1987) found that of all individuals with paraphilias, exhibitionists were most likely to have committed other sexual offenses.

FETISHISM

Fetishism involves recurrent sexual arousal (fantasies, urges, or behaviors) toward nonliving objects that are present for at least 6 months and are accompanied by clinically significant distress or impairment in at least one area of functioning (APA, 2000). Further, the objects are not limited to female clothing used in cross-dressing or to devices specifically designed for tactile genital stimulation, such as vibrators.

Fetish objects can take a number of forms, including clothing (particularly underwear and stockings), footwear, certain fabrics or materials such as rubber and leather, diapers, and gloves. Sexual arousal may take the form of looking at, fondling, smelling, licking or sucking, cutting, burning, stealing, or seeing someone else dressed in the fetish objects (Chalkley & Powell, 1983). As with exhibitionism, fetishism is largely a disorder found in men, although a few reports in women have been published (Zavitzianos, 1971).

FROTTEURISM

Frotteurism is characterized by sexual arousal involving touching and rubbing against nonconsenting individuals. The sexual urges, fantasies, or behaviors must be recurrent over at least a 6-month period (Criterion A). However, unlike fetishism but similar to exhibitionism, clinically significant distress or impairment is not a requirement for the diagnosis if the individual has acted on the urges (Criterion B). Although numerous researchers (e.g., Freund, 1990; Freund, Seto, & Kuban, 1997) include both touching and rubbing under the definition of frotteurism, others have differentiated frotteurism from toucherism (e.g., Adams & McAnulty, 1993), the latter referring to sexual arousal from touching exclusively with the hands, rather than touching with, for example, the groin.

Frotteurism generally takes place in crowded places, such as on public transportation or on busy sidewalks where escape for the frotteur is feasible (APA, 2000). Moreover, while engaging in frotteuristic activities, the frotteur "usually fantasizes an exclusive, caring relationship with the victim" (p. 570). Very little published data exist on frotteurism. For example, Krueger and Kaplan (1997) found only 17 studies published on the topic between 1966 and 1997 on Psychlit and Medline. Our own search from 1997 to 2005 yielded an additional nine publications. The first and only case of frotteurism in a female was reported in 1999 (Fedoroff et al., 1999), and, as such, frotteurism appears to mainly occur in men. Krueger and Kaplan (1997) note that "men who engage in frotteurism have large numbers of victims, are not often arrested, and, when apprehended, do not serve long sentences" (p. 145).

PEDOPHILIA

Pedophilia, a term often incorrectly used interchangeably with child molestation, refers to a disorder involving sexual arousal toward a prepubescent child. To meet criteria, the sexual urges, fantasies, or behaviors must be recurrent over a period of at least 6 months, and the individual must either have experienced consequent distress or interpersonal difficulty or have acted on the urges. Moreover, the individual must be at least 16 years of age and at least 5 years older than the prepubescent target of arousal; therefore, a diagnosis is not made if the individual is in late adolescence and in an ongoing consensual relationship with a pre-adolescent aged 12 or 13 years.

Pedophile and child molester are not interchangeable terms, although they can overlap. Similar to the terms paraphilia and sexual offender discussed at the beginning of this section, pedophilia describes the diagnostic term for a type of mental disorder. In contrast, child molester is a broad term that refers to any individual who has engaged in sexual activity with a prepubescent or pubescent child. As Barbaree and Seto (1997) point out, some pedophiles who have recurrent fantasies or urges but have never acted on them would not be considered child molesters; conversely, individuals who have engaged in sexual activity with a minor once or even on occasion, but do not experience recurrent fantasies, urges, or behaviors over a 6-month period would not be diagnosed with pedophilia.

Compared to other paraphilias, an extensive literature exists for pedophilia (although much is based on child molesters who were never formally diagnosed). For example, a relatively high proportion of convicted child molesters experienced sexual abuse as children (50% versus 20% in non–sex offenders; Dhawan & Marshall, 1996), as well as nonsexual abuse and neglect (Davidson, 1983; Finkelhor, 1979, 1984;

Marshall, Hudson, & Hodkinson, 1993). However, child molesters do not suffer from higher rates of psychopathology or personality disturbances than nonmolesters (Abel, Rouleau, & Cunningham-Rathner, 1986; Mohr, Turner, & Jerry, 1964).

Finkelhor (1984) proposed that child molesters may suffer from a lack of empathy that disinhibits any restrictions the individual would otherwise have against offending. This finding has been supported (Fernandez, Marshall, Lightbody, & O'Sullivan, 1999); however, empathy toward adults and children in general (not their victims) was no different from that of nonoffenders (Fernandez et al., 1999; Marshall, Hudson, Jones & Fernandez, 1995). Thus, child molesters may push away empathic feelings toward their victims, enabling them to carry out the sexual activities, but they do not suffer from any pervasive empathy deficits—results that have implications for treatment, particularly treatment involving empathy training.

Individuals with pedophilia may be sexually aroused to girls, boys, both girls and boys, and even to both adults and children (APA, 2000). Further, sexual arousal may be specific to children of particular age ranges. While pedophilia involving girl victims has been reported more frequently than pedophilia with boy victims, the average number of victims is higher in pedophiles attracted to boys than in pedophiles attracted to girls (Abel & Osborn, 1992). In addition, the rate of recidivism of male-preferential pedophilia is higher than that of female-preferential pedophilia (Abel & Osborn, 1992; Maletzky, 1993). Although originally believed to be a disorder of males, data are emerging to reveal the existence of child sexual molestation by women (Cavanaugh-Johnson, 1988; Johnson & Shrier, 1987; Knopp & Lackey, 1987; Lane, 1991; Matthews, Matthews, & Speltz, 1989).

SEXUAL MASOCHISM

Sexual arousal in response to being humiliated, bound, or beaten characterizes sexual masochism. The individual must experience this sexual arousal in the form of fantasies, urges, or behaviors over a minimum of 6 months and must suffer consequent distress or impairment in at least one important area of functioning. Further, the sexual arousal must be in response to actual, not simulated, humiliation, bondage, or beatings.

Although pain through being slapped, spanked, or whipped is considered sexually arousing by most sexual masochists (Baumeister, 1989; Moser & Levitt, 1987), many sexual masochists use little or no pain (Baumeister & Butler, 1997), instead becoming aroused through loss of control by being bound or becoming aroused by carrying out humiliating acts such as wearing diapers, licking their partner's shoes, or having to display themselves while naked. Other masochistic activities include the use of electrical shocks, piercing (infibulation), being urinated or defecated on, being subjected to verbal abuse, self-mutilation, and oxygen deprivation (hypoxyphilia). Although many sexual masochists appear to practice these activities with safety in mind—by, for example, prearranging a signal with their partners to indicate when to stop (Scott, 1983; Weinberg & Kamel, 1983)—masochistic behaviors can lead to serious injuries and death. This is particularly true for activities involving oxygen deprivation such as hanging or the use of ligatures, plastic bags, scarves, and chemicals.

The ratio of men to women who meet criteria for this disorder is much smaller than that of the other paraphilias, with approximately 20 men having the disorder for every woman (APA, 2000). Interestingly, sexual masochism seems to be fairly modern compared to the other paraphilias and also appears to be limited to Western cultures (Baumeister, 1989). Further, it is significantly correlated with socioeconomic status, being more common in those of higher income. These findings have been corroborated by the demographics of those involved in S&M (sadism and masochism) organizations (Moser & Levitt, 1987; Scott, 1983; Spengler, 1977).

Gender differences in the preferences for various masochistic activities reveal that pain is the preferred form of masochism for women. However, women prefer less severe forms of pain than men (Baumeister, 1989). Women also prefer humiliation more than men. However, being forced to be a slave and anal penetration have been found to be somewhat equally enjoyed by both sexes (Baumeister, 1989).

Some investigators have examined whether masochistic individuals enjoy pain, humiliation, and/or loss of control outside of sexual activity. There appears to be no relationship between sexual masochism and nonsexual forms of masochism such as self-defeating behaviors or enjoyment of painful behaviors such as going to the dentist (Baumeister, 1989; 1991; Baumeister & Scher, 1988; Berglas & Baumeister, 1993; Friedman, 1991; Grossman, 1986; Scott, 1983; Weinberg, Williams, & Moser, 1984). In fact, in line with the correlation between sexual masochism and socioeconomic status, research has found that sexual masochists are well-adjusted individuals who are often quite successful and above norms on measures of mental health (Cowan, 1982; Moser & Levitt, 1987; Scott, 1983; Spengler, 1977).

Sexual Sadism

Sexual sadism, in some ways the complementary opposite of sexual masochism, involves recurrent sexual arousal over a 6-month period in response to fantasies, urges, or behaviors involving the psychological or physical suffering of another. The urges or fantasies must have been carried out, must be distressing, or must cause interpersonal difficulty to meet diagnostic criteria.

As with sexual masochism, many individuals with sexual sadism engage in this behavior consensually and take precautions to ensure their behavior does not pass a certain threshold of pain or injury. However, sexual sadism can lead to serious injury or death, particularly when individuals with sexual sadism have a co-morbid diagnosis of antisocial personality disorder (APA, 2000). Although the lay public often associates torture and cruelty to sexual sadism, it should be noted that these violent behaviors are not always accompanied by sexual arousal (Dietz, Hazelwood, & Warren, 1990; Hazelwood, Dietz, & Warren, 1992). As with all of the paraphilias, sexual sadism is more common in men than in women.

Transvestic Fetishism

Specific to heterosexual men, transvestic fetishism is a disorder involving at least 6 months of recurrent sexual arousal associated with wearing women's clothing (cross-dressing) and accompanied by significant distress or impairment. Of all of the disorders in the *DSM-IV-TR*, this is the only one for which the diagnostic criteria specify both the gender and sexual orientation of the individual. Transvestic fetishism must be distinguished from transvestic *behavior,* the former involving sexual arousal in response to cross-dressing and the latter not. As discussed in the section on GIDs, transvestic *behavior* is one sign of gender dysphoria.

Although individuals with transvestic fetishism may experience gender dysphoria, many are happy with their gender and only cross-dress in sexual situations. In fact, studies that have examined the childhood and adolescent behaviors of men with transvestic fetishism have found their behaviors to be in line with those of other heterosexual men and unlike the childhood and adolescent behaviors often seen in homosexual men and in male-to-female transsexuals (Buhrich & McConaghy, 1985; Doorn, Poortinga, & Verschoor, 1994; Zucker & Bradley, 1995). Similarly, as adults, men with transvestic fetishism have masculine occupations and hobbies (Chung & Harmon, 1994).

The *DSM-IV-TR* states that, in many individuals, "sexual arousal is produced by the accompanying thought or image of the person as a female (referred to as 'autogynephilia'). These images can range from being a woman with female genitalia to that of a view of the self fully dressed as a woman with no real attention to genitalia" (APA, 2000, p. 574). The fact that the *DSM-IV-TR* limits the diagnosis to heterosexual men is currently at issue because homosexual men have been known to endorse sexual arousal to cross-dressing as well (Blanchard & Collins, 1993).

Voyeurism

Voyeurism refers to recurrent, intense sexual arousal, as demonstrated by fantasies, urges, or behaviors of seeing an unsuspecting person who is either naked, in the process of undressing, or engaging in sexual activity. Criterion B for this disorder is similar to that for all of the paraphilias, requiring that the behavior cause significant distress or interpersonal difficulty or be present in the form of voyeuristic activity.

Abel et al. (1986) and Marshall and Eccles (1991) examined interpersonal skills and sexual functioning in voyeurs and found that these individuals have deficits in social and assertiveness skills as well as sexual knowledge, and that they also have higher rates of sexual dysfunctions and difficulties with intimacy than nonvoyeurs. However, approximately half are involved in marital relationships (Gebhard, Gagnon, Pomeroy, & Christenson, 1965).

Paraphilia Not Otherwise Specified

The diagnosis of paraphilia not otherwise specified is given to those paraphilias that do not meet the criteria for any of the eight specified above. These include paraphilias such as necrophilia (sexual activity with corpses), zoophilia (sexual arousal involving activity with animals), coprophilia (sexual arousal involving activity with feces), klismaphelia (sexual arousal involving enemas), and urophilia (sexual arousal involving urination). Very little is known about these paraphilias because they appear to occur relatively infrequently.

EPIDEMIOLOGY

The incidence and prevalence of the paraphilias is unknown due to their secretive and often illegal nature. Therefore, frequency estimates are generally based on small, nonrepresentative samples, most often involving convicted sexual offenders. However, this research is useful in deriving a preliminary indication of the occurrence of this group of disorders.

With respect to its prevalence, studies have found that exhibitionism accounts for between one-third and two-thirds of all sexual offenses reported to police in Canada, the United States, and Europe (Arieff & Rotman, 1942; East, 1924; Ellis & Brancale, 1956; Gebhard et al., 1965; Mohr et al., 1964; Smukler & Shiebel, 1975; Taylor, 1947). Similarly, Abel and Rouleau (1990) found that 25% of offenders in their outpatient clinics had a history of exhibitionism.

Among 60 college males, 2% admitted to a history of exhibiting (Templeman & Stinnett, 1991). Although estimates have varied, up to 20% of women may have been the victims of exhibitionism (Kaplan & Krueger, 1997; Meyer, 1995). Abel and Rouleau (1990) found that the 142 participants who admitted to exhibitionistic behavior reported a total of 72,074 victims, corroborating the high number of victims.

Fetishism is a rare condition (APA, 2000). Chalkley and Powell (1983) reported that 0.8% of patients seen in three psychiatric hospitals over a period of 20 years met criteria, and Curren (1954) found only 5 out of 4,000 clients seen in private practice had a primary diagnosis of fetishism.

As Mason (1997) notes, clinicians likely see only a small minority of the total number of individuals with fetishistic interests considering the wide proliferation of organizations and materials catering to these individuals. Nevertheless, it is unlikely that the majority of these individuals meet *DSM-IV* criteria for fetishism, given that many do not experience distress or impairment.

Abel et al. (1987) interviewed 561 nonincarcerated paraphiliacs and found that 62 (11%) had a primary diagnosis of frotteurism, leading them to conclude that frottage is not the uncommon paraphilic act it has otherwise been touted to be. Higher rates were found by Templeman and Stinnett (1991), who asked 60 college-aged men about frotteuristic activities and found that 35% indicated that they had engaged in frottage.

Although a substantial amount of research has been conducted on pedophilia, its prevalence is also unknown. In one community sample of 501 women in the southern United States, 55% reported at least one incident of sexual abuse (including touching, kissing, showing one's genitals, masturbation, and oral and vaginal intercourse) prior to the age of 14 (Kilpatrick, 1992). However, these numbers likely underestimate its true prevalence, because it is suspected that most cases of child abuse are not reported (McConaghy, 1998).

Baumeister (1989) estimated that between 5% and 10% of the population have engaged in some form of masochistic activities based on a literature review of findings from other studies. He further hypothesized that double this number have had fantasies about sexual masochism but that less than 1% of the population likely engages in masochistic sexual activities on a regular basis.

Several studies shed light on the extent of sexual sadism in the population. Hunt (1974) surveyed both men and women on their sexual experiences and found that 5% of men and 2% of women endorsed becoming sexually aroused to inflicting pain on others. Crepault and Couture (1980) assessed rates of sexually sadistic fantasies in a community sample of men and found that 11% had fantasies of beating up a woman and 15% had fantasies of humiliating a woman. Arndt, Foehl, and Good (1985) found that half of their sample of men and one-third of their sample of women indicated having had prior fantasies of tying up their partners.

With respect to voyeurism, 12.9% of adults seeking outpatient treatment at a clinic were voyeurs, and the corresponding percentage for adolescents was 13.9% (Abel, 1989). Among male college students, 42% had engaged in voyeuristic activities and

53% had some sort of interest in voyeurism (Templeman & Stinnett, 1991). Meyer (1995) posited that up to 20% of women have been targeted by voyeurs. No data on the prevalence of transvestic fetishism exist.

It is not uncommon for individuals to meet diagnostic criteria for more than one paraphilia; only 10.4% of 561 nonincarcerated paraphiliacs had only one paraphilia (Abel, Becker, Cunningham-Rathner, Mittelman, & Rouleau, 1988; Abel et al., 1987). Further, having one paraphilic disorder increases the probability of having another (Langevin, 1983).

COURSE AND PROGNOSIS

In individuals meeting the *DSM-IV-TR* criteria for exhibitionism, symptoms usually appear in adolescence, although Mohr, Turner, and Jerry (1964) found a bimodal age of onset in the mid-teens and mid-20s. Charges and convictions tend to occur most frequently in early adulthood (Berah & Meyers, 1983; Gebhard et al., 1965; Mohr et al., 1964), and, as with many of the paraphilias and sexual offenses, onset appears to decrease steadily and markedly after age 40 (Murphy, 1997).

Many individuals with fetishism recall interest in the fetish objects as children followed by sexual arousal toward the objects after puberty (McConaghy, 1993). The course of fetishism is chronic (Gosselin & Wilson, 1980).

Frotteurism begins in adolescence, with the majority of frotteuristic activities being carried out between ages 15 and 25, whereupon its frequency is thought to decline. Similarly, pedophilia is believed to begin in adolescence; however, like fetishism, the course of this disorder is considered chronic (APA, 2000).

The age of onset of voyeurism is generally before age 15 according to the *DSM-IV-TR* (APA, 2000), although Abel, Osborn, and Twigg (1993) found the age of onset to be 18 in a sample of 133 voyeurs.

Unlike many of the other paraphilias, sexual masochism has been found to first occur across ages, from childhood to adulthood (see Moser & Levitt, 1987; Spengler, 1977). In most men, sadism first presents in adolescence (Breslow, Evans, & Langley, 1985; Spengler, 1977) and appears to begin without precipitating events or introductions by others (Breslow et al., 1985). However, in women the disorder seems to take somewhat longer to manifest and is often precipitated by the encouragement of male partners (Scott, 1983). In the majority of cases, the severity of sadistic acts increases over the course of the disorder (APA, 2000).

The relationship between sexual sadism and sexual masochism is apparent not only in their complementary roles, but also in the finding that many sexually sadistic individuals began as sexual masochists (Baumeister, 1989; Scott, 1983). Furthermore, sadistic and masochistic fantasies often co-occur in the same individual (Arndt et al., 1985), and approximately 30% of self-reported sadists alternated in their sexual relationships between playing the dominant, sadistic role and playing the submissive, masochistic role (Spengler, 1977). Abel and colleagues (1988) found that 18% of their sample of sexual sadists was also masochistic.

Transvestic fetishism appears to begin with a childhood or early adolescent interest in women's clothing, followed by cross-dressing (Zucker & Bradley, 1995). This cross-dressing is then followed by sexual arousal and orgasm (Zucker & Blanchard, 1997).

PSYCHOLOGICAL AND BIOLOGICAL ASSESSMENT

A number of assessment techniques are at the disposal of individuals with paraphilias to assist them in determining sexual preferences and behaviors. These
assessment tools include various questionnaires and self-report measures and
objective, physiological measures such as the plethysmograph, the polygraph,
and measures of visual reaction time. Two challenges inherent in measuring
paraphilic interests are (1) the fact that sexuality is typically a private matter that
many individuals are uncomfortable discussing and the fact that certain sexual
interests may be subject to public stigmatization, therefore leading to denial
or underreporting of them; and (2) the ethical aspects of assessment whereby
some techniques are invasive and/or involve the presentation of sexual stimuli,
which may be disturbing to the individual being assessed. Care must be taken
to ensure that not only ethical issues are given consideration but also that the
benefits outweigh the risks, particularly in the assessment of minors. Furthermore, all of these techniques suffer from problems with reliability, validity, and
vulnerability to dissimulation, and, as a result, no one technique should be used
in isolation.

Self-Report Measures

One of the most widely used self-report measures is the Clarke Sexual History
Questionnaire for Males (Paitich, Langevin, Freeman, Mann, & Handy, 1977), a 190-
item sexual history questionnaire that assesses a wide range of sexual experiences, including paraphilic experiences and their frequency and age of onset. The
Multiphasic Sex Inventory (Nichols & Molinder, 1984; 1992) contains numerous
scales assessing paraphilic sexual preferences, sexual knowledge, sexual dysfunction, and validity of the responses. The Wilson Sex Fantasy Questionnaire (Wilson,
1978) is another standardized, commonly used instrument. All of these measures
have the potential for biased or dishonest responses.

Even though personality often does not distinguish those with and without
paraphilias, some measures of personality—such as the Minnesota Multiphasic
Personality Inventory, second edition (Butcher, Dahlstrom, Graham, Tellegen, &
Kraemmer, 1989)—are commonly administered to individuals with paraphilias.
The card sort technique contains rating scales composed of pictorial or written
sexual stimuli that individuals are asked to view or read and then rate according to
the extent to which the stimuli are found to be sexually arousing. Examples include
the Sexual Interest Card Sort Questionnaire (Holland, Zolondek, Abel, Jordan, &
Becker, 2000) and Laws's (1986) Sexual Deviance Card Sort. Clinicians can also develop their own card sorts specific to what they know about a client, or they can
ask their clients to record their daily sexual fantasies and urges and then rate the
degree of sexual arousal to each of these (Maletzky, 1997).

A review by Schiavi, Derogatis, Kuriansky, O'Connor, and Sharpe (1979) that
looked at over 50 self-report instruments used with sexual offenders found little
evidence for the validity of these measures. However, their usefulness may lie in
their ability to be used in conjunction with historical information gathered about
the individual to look for inconsistencies (Kaplan & Krueger, 1997). Further, as
Maletzky (1997) notes, "[w]hile extrapolation from other studies of paraphilias
leads to the conclusion that self-reports are undoubtedly biased (Abel & Rouleau,
1990), the offender's perceptions of his crimes are always of interest" (p. 44).

PSYCHOPHYSIOLOGICAL ASSESSMENT TECHNIQUES

Because of the difficulties with self-report, many clinicians and researchers depend on objective measures. Of these, phallometric assessment is considered to be the best technique with regard to reliability, validity, and the ability to prevent dissimulation (Quinsey, 1988; Quinsey & Earls, 1990; Seto, 2001). The technique, used extensively in clinical and correctional settings across North America for diagnostic, treatment, and risk assessment purposes, involves the psychophysiological recording of sexual arousal through a device that measures either volumetric or circumferential changes in penile tumescence in response to sexual stimuli. The stimuli can take various forms, such as videos, audiotapes, photographs, and written text. Consistent increases in penile tumescence to specific sexual stimuli relative to other sexual and nonsexual stimuli are considered to indicate sexual preferences for those stimuli (Freund, 1963). The use of stimuli depicting individuals of all ages and both sexes engaged in various sexual and nonsexual activities reliably discriminates sexual from nonsexual offenders, including child molesters and non–child molesters (Barbaree & Marshall, 1989; Freund & Blanchard, 1989); rapists and nonrapists (Harris, Rice, Chaplin, & Quinsey, 1999; Lalumiere & Quinsey, 1994); men who admit to sadistic fantasies, cross-dress, or expose their genitals in public from men who do not (Freund, Seto, & Kuban, 1996; Marshall, Payne, Barbaree, & Eccles, 1991; Seto & Kuban, 1996); and incest offenders and nonoffenders (Barsetti, Earls, & Lalumiere, 1998; Chaplin, Rice, & Harris, 1995). Phallometry also has high predictive power for sexual and violent recidivism (Malcolm, Andrews, & Quinsey, 1993; Rice, Harris, & Quinsey, 1990; Seto, 2001), similar to that of psychopathy diagnoses and criminal history (Hanson & Bussiere, 1998). To date, sexual interests, as measured through phallometric testing, are considered to be the most consistently identifiable distinguishing characteristics of sexual offenders compared to general psychopathology, empathy, and social skills (Quinsey & Lalumiere, 1996; Seto & Lalumiere, 2001).

Phallometric testing is not without its criticisms. For example, group discrimination is not perfect, with the distributions of phallometric scores overlapping between sex offenders and nonoffenders (Seto, 2001). Further, while the specificity of phallometry is very high (i.e., the test is able to accurately identify men who have not committed a sexual offense as nondeviant 90% to 97.5% of the time), the sensitivity of the test (i.e., the ability of the test to identify men who have committed a sexual offense as deviant), appears to only be between 44% and 50% (Freund & Watson, 1991; Lalumiere & Quinsey, 1993). This finding is likely due to the ability of some individuals to control their physiological arousal levels in response to deviant stimuli. In addition, in 21% of participants assessed with phallometric testing, no clear diagnosis with respect to paraphillic sexual preferences was possible (Freund & Blanchard, 1989).

Further, a lack of standardization in stimuli, testing procedures, and data analysis has resulted in considerable variability in procedures, data interpretation, and results across phallometric laboratories (Howes, 1995), making it difficult to evaluate the technical adequacy of different phallometric studies, replicate experiments, and account for discrepancies between studies (Schouten & Simon, 1992). There are also ethical concerns because sexual stimuli that depict violent sexual behavior or sexual images of children are usually presented. Finally, although phallometric testing is much less susceptible to response bias or dissimulation than self-report, it has been found that some participants can alter their physiological responses in a socially desirable direction (see Freund, Watson, & Rienzo, 1988, for a review; Lalumiere & Earls, 1992), an issue that has an impact on the procedure's sensitivity. Further, the ability of participants to control, or alter, their physiological responses seems to increase with subsequent testing (Quinsey, Rice, & Harris, 1995), suggesting that multiple assessments give participants the opportunity to learn how to alter their responses so they appear less sexually deviant than they actually are (Lalumiere & Harris, 1998).

The polygraph (also known as the "lie detector") is another psychophysiological assessment technique used with individuals who have been accused or convicted of a sexual offense. However, unlike the plethysmograph, which is used to assess current sexual interests as well as to make subsequent predictions about future risks, the polygraph is used with sexual offenders to assess past sexual behaviors and deceitfulness in admitting to them by measuring galvanic skin response, heart rate, blood pressure, and respiration. Changes in these indices of arousal are associated with involuntary responses to fear. The technique is based on the assumption that when people lie, they fear that their lie will be discovered, leading to measurable increases in physiological arousal. Therefore, by asking examinees questions to which they may have motivations to lie (such as questions related to sexual offending), examiners can monitor increases in physiological arousal to these questions and make deductions about past behaviors and deceitfulness by the physiological profiles. As Branaman and Gallagher (2005) point out, the validity of the polygraph largely depends on the types of questions asked during the assessment. This has led to much caution with using the test, because the implications of incorrectly identifying someone as having committed sexual offenses are numerous and by no means inconsequential. Further, those skeptical of this instrument have also voiced concerns that some individuals may feel coerced into admitting to offenses they never committed (Cross & Saxe, 1992; 2001).

Because of the error rates and these concerns, the polygraph is not generally admissible in court. Nevertheless, many treatment providers have found the instrument useful for getting offenders to disclose behaviors they previously denied (Ahlmeyer, Heil, McKee, & English, 2000; English, Jones, Pasini-Hill, Patrick, & Cooley-Towell, 2000) and as a measure of change with treatment (see Kokish, 2003; Kokish, Levenson, & Blasingame, 2005).

Another objective assessment technique is visual reaction time (also referred to as viewing time). Similar to phallometric testing, this technique involves showing pictures of various sexual and nonsexual stimuli. Participants are informed that the technique assesses sexual interests through their self-reported ratings of sexual attractiveness to each picture. However, participants are not informed that the main element of the technique actually involves the unobtrusive recording of the length of time that they view each stimuli (i.e., unlike phallometric testing, in which each stimuli is presented for a set period of time, this technique allows participants to control how long they view each stimuli). The technique is based on the finding that individuals will view images they find sexually stimulating longer than those they do not (Lang, Searles, Lauerman, & Adesso, 1980; Quinsey, Rice, Harris, & Reid, 1993). Visual reaction time shows similar reliability and validity as phallometric testing (Abel, Huffman, Warberg, & Holland, 1998; Letourneau, 2002), with the added advantages of greater efficiency, less intrusiveness, and less technological complexity than phallometry (Abel et al., 1998; Harris, Rice, Quinsey, & Chaplin, 1996). Because the technique is less intrusive and thus less ethically controversial, it has also been researched with adolescent sexual offenders with promising results (Abel et al., 2004).

ETIOLOGICAL CONSIDERATIONS

Numerous theories have been proposed to explain how the paraphilias develop; however, empirical evidence is either lacking or contradictory, and, as a result, no individual theory has been able to satisfactorily explain the development of most cases. Nevertheless, the theories provide some insight into current thinking about how paraphilic sexual disorders develop and the rationale behind the development of various treatment approaches discussed in the next section.

NEUROLOGICAL DEFICITS

Cases in which individuals developed paraphilic interests following brain injuries and degenerative brain diseases led practitioners to hypothesize that the paraphilias may be caused by certain neurological abnormalities, particularly temporal lobe and limbic area abnormalities. In keeping with this hypothesis, many case studies have been published that implicate abnormalities in these areas of the brain with various paraphilias (e.g., Blumer, 1970; Blumer & Walker, 1967; Hucker et al., 1988; Langevin et al., 1989; see Langevin, 1990, for a review). For example, Huws, Shubsachs, and Taylor (1991) described the case of a man who developed a foot fetish following the onset of multiple sclerosis, which resulted in damage to the temporal regions of the brain. Langevin et al. (1989) found that the rate of exhibitionism was higher among individuals with developmental disabilities than among normal males. And Gratzer and Bradford (1995) found that 55% of sadists in their sample showed neurological deficits, again mainly in the temporal regions.

However, these findings are not uniform, and they fail to account for a large number of individuals with paraphilias. For example, Hucker et al. (1988) used computed tomography and magnetic resonance imaging to look for brain abnormalities in exhibitionists, but most of the exhibitionists lacked any evidence of neurological deficits, outcomes replicated by O'Carroll (1989) and Tarter, Hegadus, Alterman, and Katz-Garris (1983). Numerous studies have found that temporal lobe disorders are associated with hyposexuality, not hypersexuality (Miller, Darby, Swartz, Yener, & Mena, 1995; Rosenblum, 1974).

SOCIAL THEORIES

The belief that negative and disruptive early childhood and family functioning may lead to paraphilias comes from research indicating high rates of childhood abuse (both sexual and nonsexual), neglect, and disturbed family relations in paraphiliacs (Awad, Saunders, & Levene, 1984; Davidson, 1983; Marshall et al., 1993; Saunders, Awad, & White, 1986). Marshall and colleagues (1993) suggest that these negative experiences serve as templates for future relationships, leading to distrust or ambivalence with appropriate partners and teaching the child to be abusive toward those he or she can dominate. However, these findings fail to account for the many individuals who have experienced abuse and dysfunctional family relationships who do not go on to develop paraphilias, and, conversely, the many individuals with paraphilias who have no history of familial instability or victimization (Murphy, Haynes, & Page, 1992; Murphy & Smith, 1996).

BEHAVIORAL AND COGNITIVE-BEHAVIORAL THEORIES

The behavioral and cognitive-behavioral theories of paraphilias have garnered much attention from and support by psychologists and have shaped many of the psychotherapies currently used to treat the paraphilias. Behavioral theories posit that paraphilias develop through operant or classical conditioning in which the object of paraphilic attention becomes paired with sexual arousal, resulting in abnormal arousal patterns. In essence, sexual arousal becomes the conditioned response to the paraphilic target and is reinforced through masturbation and orgasm.

Research by Rachman and colleagues (Rachman, 1966; Rachman & Hodgson, 1968) demonstrated that sexual arousal can in fact be conditioned; they conditioned a sexual response to a picture of a pair of boots by pairing the picture of the boots with photographs of nude adult women. However, the responses were easily extinguished, leading others to argue that the behavioral theory is not sufficient on its own to explain the maintenance of such behaviors throughout an individual's life (Bancroft, 1989). More recent cognitive-behavioral theories have emphasized the role of cognitions, including minimization and denial of harm, which disinhibit individuals to act on their initial paraphilic interests and serve to maintain and justify their fantasies, urges, or behaviors over time.

TREATMENT

Treatment of the paraphilias consists of a number of techniques, the most common of which are behavioral, cognitive, and pharmacological approaches. Because of ethical and methodological limitations in conducting empirical investigations of treatment efficacy with offenders (such as randomly assigning convicted offenders to a no-treatment control group) and because most have extremely low base rates leading to difficulties with acquiring adequate sample sizes, efficacy rates for the treatment of sexual offenders has not been conclusive, with some professionals arguing that there currently is no empirical basis indicating that treatment for sex offenders is superior than placebo (Furby, Weinrott, & Blackshaw, 1989). However, others argue that, even if treatment is no more effective than placebo for reducing recidivism, it can have other desirable effects such as teaching social skills, fostering honesty and openness, and enhancing empathy for victims.

Further, studies conducted on the efficacy of the various treatments are difficult to compare due to differences in outcome measures (i.e., some studies have used sexual recidivism while others have used general recidivism; some have used phallometry or other measures of sexual interest), length of follow-up (ranging anywhere from 6 months to 10 years), sample characteristics (e.g., incarcerated offenders versus outpatient or voluntary patients), and various definitions and inclusion criteria (i.e., those meeting *DSM* criteria for a paraphilia versus those having been convicted of a sexual offense). As a result, efficacy rates of the various treatments are be reported here.

BEHAVIORAL INTERVENTIONS

Behavior therapy views maladaptive behaviors as stemming from maladaptive learning. As a result, this behavioral approach focuses on replacing unhealthy behaviors with new, healthier ones. With sex offenders, behavioral interventions generally fall into one of two categories: counterconditioning and aversive conditioning.

Counterconditioning is a technique based on classical conditioning principles, which involve replacing negative conditioned responses with positive ones. In the case of treatment with sex offenders, this translates into replacing paraphilic with nonparaphilic sexual interests and occurs through a variety of specific techniques. One counterconditioning technique is *plethysmographic biofeedback,* during which the plethysmograph is attached to a light or sound source that is activated whenever the client experiences physiological arousal, thereby providing feedback to the client. Often the lights or sounds vary such that higher levels of arousal activate more lights or louder sounds. The goal for clients is to try to prevent their arousal levels from activating lights or sounds in the higher ranges when the stimuli are deviant but to maintain them in the higher ranges when the stimuli are nondeviant.

A second counterconditioning technique is *orgasmic* or *masturbatory reconditioning* (Johnston, Hudson, & Marshall, 1992; Laws & Marshall, 1991). In this technique, clients are instructed to masturbate to their paraphilic fantasies until shortly before reaching the point of orgasm, at which time they are told to switch their fantasies to nonparaphilic ones. Over the course of treatment, clients are instructed to make this change progressively earlier during masturbation until paraphilic fantasies have been completely replaced. If clients are unable to maintain their arousal with the switch, they may return to their deviant fantasies as long as they do not achieve orgasm; orgasm may only be associated with nonparaphilic fantasies. To ensure that clients are in fact switching their fantasies during the technique, often they will be asked to describe their fantasies aloud and record them on tape for their therapists (Maletzky, 1997).

In aversive conditioning, the undesirable behavior (in this case arousal to paraphilic stimuli) is repeatedly paired with an unpleasant stimulus such that over repeated pairings, the behavior becomes associated with unpleasant feelings and therefore diminishes. With sex offenders, aversive conditioning can take a variety of forms. Originally, unpleasant but nonharmful electrical shocks were used, so that as soon as the client began to become aroused to deviant stimuli, a shock was administered (MacCulloch & Feldman, 1967; MacCulloch, Waddington, & Sambrooks, 1978). Now, other unpleasant stimuli are often used, such as foul odors including ammonia, the smell of cadavers, and rotting meat (Laws, 2001).

Aversive conditioning can also be conducted through *covert sensitization,* which involves having clients relax and then visualizing themselves carrying out the sexually arousing paraphilic behavior. Once the client is visualizing the behavior, an aversive image or thought is introduced; for example, imagining being discovered by spouses or family members or thinking about aversive things such as feces or vomit (Levin, Barry, Gambaro, Wofinsohn, & Smith, 1977). As with electrical shock, continued pairing leads to the expectation that the deviant arousal will be associated with these negative images and thoughts. As Maletzky (1997) points out, covert sensitization is widely used in treatment programs involving a behavioral component because the technique is easy and economical to implement and is considered by many to be more humane than electrical shocks. Maletzky and George (1973) developed *assisted covert sensitization,* which builds upon covert sensitization by introducing a foul odor at the same time that aversive thoughts and images are introduced into the imagery. In this way, although the imagery is imaginal, the aversion includes a real component.

A more controversial but effective aversive conditioning technique originally designed specifically for use with exhibitionists but employed with other paraphilics as well is *aversive behavior rehearsal*. In this technique, the exhibitionist exposes to consenting staff; however, staff members give no response while the client exposes, generally leading the client to feel embarrassed and ashamed rather than the usual sexual arousal experienced by the look of shock on victims' faces. However, this technique is hindered by ethical issues, including gaining consent from clients and problems with finding staff who are willing to participate in the procedure (Maletzky, 1997).

Finally, *satiation* is an aversive conditioning technique that involves masturbation to nondeviant fantasies until orgasm. Immediately following orgasm, the client is instructed to masturbate again for 30 to 60 minutes, however this time to deviant fantasies. Because it is unsatisfying for men to masturbate immediately following orgasm, the unpleasant feelings associated with this become paired with the deviant fantasies. Laws (1995) has even found that verbal satiation, involving repetition of the same deviant fantasies over and over again, also produces boredom and fatigue, similarly leading to unpleasant feelings being paired with the deviant fantasies.

Cognitive Approaches

Cognitive therapy assumes that faulty thought patterns lead to maladaptive behavior. Therefore, treatment focuses on changing thoughts to solve psychological and behavioral difficulties. Two common cognitive techniques are *cognitive restructuring* and *empathy training*. In cognitive restructuring, the goal is to challenge and reduce clients' cognitive distortions, such as beliefs by some pedophiles that the victim enjoyed the sexual activity or that the victim initiated it. Once the cognitive distortions are identified, treatment focuses on understanding how these faulty cognitions lead to the harmful behaviors.

Empathy training involves helping offenders recognize the harm their actions have on their victims. After being able to identify the harm induced by the behaviors, clients are guided toward putting themselves in the shoes of their victims in an effort to help them build empathy toward their victims. Approximately 94% of treatment programs for sex offenders in North America include empathy training in their programming (Knopp, Freeman-Longo, & Stevenson, 1992).

Biological Interventions

Because surgical castration is no longer considered ethical with paraphiliacs, current biological interventions consist of pharmacological manipulation with either antiandrogens or SSRIs. Of the antiandrogens, medroxyprogesterone acetate is used in the United States and cyproterone acetate is used in Canada and Europe. Both of these medications reduce circulating testosterone levels, found to significantly reduce sexual drive (Wincze, Bansal, & Malamud, 1986). However, because these medications can lead to undesirable side effects, in general they are only prescribed to those clients for whom psychotherapy appears ineffective. The SSRIs are used because of their side effect of reducing sexual drive due to increasing serotonin concentrations in the synaptic cleft. These drugs are preferred over the antiandrogens because they are associated with fewer and less-severe side effects. However, the administration of either type of medication is accompanied by numerous ethical and legal implications because they are most often administered under duress, as part of an offender's parole or probation conditions (Demsky, 1984). For a more detailed review of the pharmacological interventions, their mechanisms of action, and their specific effects, see Rösler and Witztum (2000) and Krueger and Kaplan (2002).

SUMMARY

Often associated with sexual deviance and sexual offending, the paraphilias are one of the most controversial groups of disorders in the *DSM*. This controversy stems from disagreements over such issues as whether the paraphilias should be categorized as mental disorders or instead be seen simply as variants of human sexuality; arguments over why certain sexual behaviors are included under the paraphilias (such as fetishism) while others are not (such as rape); and arguments over the specific diagnostic criteria for each of the paraphilias. This controversy is furthered by the limited amount of sound empirical research—particularly epidemiological research—with individuals with these conditions. However, assessment and treatment of the paraphilias have advanced significantly toward more effective, efficient, and ethical techniques, and we look forward to having some of the more "diagnostic conundrum" issues addressed in the future.

REFERENCES

Abel, G. G. (1989). Paraphilias. In H. I. Kaplan & B. J. Sadock (Eds.), *Comprehensive textbook of psychiatry* (Vol. 1, 5th ed., pp. 1069–1085). Baltimore: Williams & Wilkins.

Abel, G. G., Becker, J. V., Cunningham-Rathner, J., Mittelman, M., & Rouleau, J. L. (1988). Multiple paraphilic diagnoses among sex offenders. *Bulletin of the American Academy of Psychiatry and the Law, 16,* 153–168.

Abel, G. G., Becker, J. V., Mittelman, M., Cunningham-Rathner, J., Rouleau, J. L., & Murphy, W. D. (1987). Self-reported sex crimes of nonincarcerated paraphiliacs. *Journal of Interpersonal Violence, 2,* 3–25.

Abel, G. G., Huffman, J., Warberg, B., & Holland, C. L. (1998). Visual reaction time and plethysmography as measures of sexual interest in child molesters. *Sexual Abuse: A Journal of Research and Treatment, 10,* 81–95.

Abel, G. G., Jordan, A., Rouleau, J. L., Emerick, R., Barboza-Whitehead, S., & Osborn, C. (2004). Use of visual reaction time to assess male adolescents who molest children. *Sexual Abuse: A Journal of Research and Treatment, 16,* 255–265.

Abel, G. G., & Osborn, C. (1992). The paraphilias: The extent and nature of sexually deviant and criminal behavior. *Clinical Forensic Psychiatry, 15,* 675–687.

Abel, G., Osborn, C., & Twigg, D. (1993). Sexual assault through the life span: Adult offenders with juvenile histories. In H. E. Barbaree, W. Marshall, & S. M. Hudson (Eds.), *The juvenile sex offender* (pp. 104–117). New York: Guilford Press.

Abel, G. G., & Rouleau, J. L. (1990). The nature and extent of sexual assault. In W. L. Marshall, D. R. Laws, & H. E. Barbaree (Eds.), *Handbook of sexual assault: Issues, theories, and treatment of the offender* (pp. 9–21). New York: Plenum.

Abel, G. G., Rouleau, J. L., & Cunningham-Rathner, J. (1986). Sexually aggressive behavior. In W. J. Curran, A. L. McGarry, & S. Shah (Eds.), *Forensic psychiatry and psychology* (pp. 289–313). Philadelphia: F.A. Davis Co.

à Campo, J., Nijman, H., Merckelbach, H., & Evers, C. (2003). Psychiatric comorbidity of gender identity disorders: A survey among Dutch psychiatrists. *American Journal of Psychiatry, 160,* 1332–1336.

Adams, H. E., & McAnulty, R. D. (1993). Sexual disorders: The paraphilias. In P. B. Sutker & H. E. Adams (Eds.), *Comprehensive handbook of psychopathology* (2nd ed., pp. 563–579). New York: Plenum.

Ahlmeyer, S., Heil, P., McKee, B., & English, K. (2000). The impact of polygraphy on admissions of victims and offenses in adult sex offenders. *Sexual Abuse: A Journal of Research and Treatment, 2,* 123–138.

American Psychiatric Association. (1980). *Diagnostic and statistical manual of mental disorders* (3rd ed.). Washington, DC: Author.

American Psychiatric Association (2000). *Diagnostic and statistical manual of mental disorders, fourth edition, text revision.* Washington, DC: Author, 574.

Amsterdam, A., Carter, L., & Krychman, M. (2006). Prevalence of psychiatric illness in women in an oncology sexual health population: A retrospective pilot study. *Journal of Sexual Medicine, 3,* 292–295.

Andersson, K. E., Mulhall, J. P., & Wyllie, M. G. (2006). Pharmacokinetic and pharmacodynamic features of dapoxetine, a novel drug for "on-demand" treatment of premature ejaculation. *BJU International, 97,* 311–315.

Araujo, A. B., Durante, R., Feldman, H. A., Goldstein, I., & McKinley, J. B. (1998). The relationship between depressive symptoms and male erectile dysfunction: Cross-sectional results from the Massachusetts Male Aging Study. *Psychosomatic Medicine, 60,* 458–465.

Arieff, A. J., & Rotman, D. B. (1942). One hundred cases of indecent exposure. *Journal of Nervous and Mental Disease, 96,* 523–528.

Arndt, W., Foehl, J., & Good, F. (1985). Specific sexual fantasy themes: A multidimensional study. *Journal of Personality and Social Psychology, 48,* 472–480.

Ashton, A. K., & Weinstein, W. (2006). Tadalafil reversal of sexual dysfunction caused by serotonin enhancing medications in women. *Journal of Sex and Marital Therapy, 32,* 1–3.

Atan, A., Basar, M. M., Tuncel, A., Ferhat, M., Agras, K., & Tekdogan, U. (2006). Comparison of efficacy of sildenafil-only, sildenafil plus topical EMLA cream, and topical EMLA-cream-only in treatment of premature ejaculation. *Urology, 67,* 388–391.

Awad, G., Saunders, E., & Levene, J. (1984). A clinical study of male adolescent sex offenders. *International Journal of Offender Therapy and Comparative Criminology, 20,* 105–116.

Bancroft, J. (1989). *Human sexuality and its problems* (2nd ed.). Edinburgh, Scotland: Churchill Livingstone.

Bancroft, J., Loftus, J., & Long J. S. (2003). Distress about sex: A national survey of women in heterosexual relationships. *Archives of Sexual Behavior, 32,* 193–208.

Barbaree, H. E., & Marshall, W. L. (1989). Erectile responses among heterosexual child molesters, father-daughter incest offenders, and matched non-offenders: Five distinct age preference profiles. *Canadian Journal of Behavioural Science, 21,* 70–82.

Barbaree, H. E., & Seto, M. C. (1997). Pedophilia: Assessment and treatment. In D. R. Laws & W. O'Donohue (Eds.), *Sexual deviance: Theory, assessment, and treatment* (pp. 175–193). New York: Guilford Press.

Barlow, D. H., Abel, G. G., & Blanchard, E. B. (1979). Gender identity change in transsexuals: Follow-up and replications. *Archives of General Psychiatry, 36,* 1001–1007.

Barsetti, I., Earls, C. M., & Lalumiere, M. L. (1998). The differentiation of intrafamilial and extrafamilial heterosexual child molesters. *Journal of Interpersonal Violence, 13,* 275–286.

Basson, R. (2001). Using a different model for female sexual response to address women's problematic low sexual desire. *Journal of Sex and Marital Therapy, 27,* 395–403.

Basson, R. (2002a). Women's sexual desire—disordered or misunderstood? *Journal of Sex and Marital Therapy, 28,* 17–28.

Basson, R. (2002b). A model of women's sexual arousal. *Journal of Sex and Marital Therapy, 28,* 1–10.

Basson, R. (2003). Biopsychosocial models of women's sexual response: Applications to management of "desire disorders." *Sexual and Relationship Therapy, 18,* 107–115.

Basson, R. (2004). Pharmacotherapy for sexual dysfunction in women. *Expert Opinion in Pharmacotherapy, 5,* 1045–1059.

Basson, R. (2005). Female hypoactive sexual desire disorder. In R. Balon & R. T. Segraves (Eds.), *Handbook of sexual dysfunction* (pp. 43–65). Boca Raton, FL: Taylor & Francis.

Basson, R., & Brotto, L. A. (2003). Sexual psychophysiology and effects of sildenafil citrate in oestrogenised women with acquired genital arousal disorder and impaired orgasm: A randomised controlled trial. *British Journal of Obstetrics and Gynaecology, 110,* 1014–1024.

Basson, R., Leiblum, S. L., Brotto, L. A., Derogatis, L., Fourcroy, J., Fugl-Meyer, K., Graziottin, A., Heiman, J. R., Laan, E., Meston, C., Schover, L., van Lankveld, J., & Weijmar Schultz, W. C. M. (2003). Definitions of women's sexual dysfunctions reconsidered: Advocating expansion and revision. *Journal of Psychosomatic Obstetrics and Gynaecology, 24,* 221–229.

Basson, R., McInnes, R., Smith, M. D., Hodgson, G., & Koppiker, N. (2002). Efficacy and safety of sildenafil citrate in women with sexual dysfunction associated with female sexual arousal disorder. *Journal of Women's Health and Gender-Based Medicine, 11,* 367–377.

Baumeister, R. F. (1989). *Masochism and the self.* Hillsdale, NJ: Erlbaum.

Baumeister, R. F. (1991). *Escaping the self: Alcoholism, spirituality, masochism, and other flights from the burden of selfhood.* New York: Basic Books.

Baumeister, R. F., & Butler, J. L. (1997). Sexual masochism: Deviance without pathology. In D. R. Laws & W. O'Donohue (Eds.), *Sexual deviance: Theory, assessment, and treatment* (pp. 225–239). New York: Guilford Press.

Baumeister, R. F., Catanese, K. R., & Vohs, K. D. (2001). Is there a gender difference in strength of sex drive? Theoretical views, conceptual distinctions, and a review of relevant evidence. *Personality and Social Psychology Review, 5,* 242–273.

Baumeister, R. F., & Scher, S. J. (1988). Self-defeating behavior patterns among normal individuals: Review and analysis of common self-destructive tendencies. *Psychological Bulletin, 104,* 3–22.

Berah, E. F., & Meyers, R. G. (1983). The offense records of a sample of convicted exhibitionists. *Bulletin of the American Academy of Psychiatry and the Law, 11,* 365–369.

Bergeron, S. (2003, April). *Surgical and behavioral treatments for vulvar vestibulitis: 2.5-year follow-up and predictors of treatment outcome.* Paper presented at the conference on Vulvodynia: Toward Understanding a Pain Syndrome, National Institutes of Health, Bethesda, MD.

Bergeron, S., & Binik, Y. M. (1998). *Treatment manual for cognitive-behavioural group therapy with women suffering from vulvar vestibulitis syndrome.* Unpublished treatment manual, McGill University, Montreal, Canada.

Bergeron, S., Binik, Y. M., Khalife, S., Pagidas, K., Glazer, H. I., Meana, M., & Amsel, R. (2001). A randomized comparison of group cognitive behavioural therapy, surface electromyographic biofeedback, and vestibulectomy in the treatment of dyspareunia resulting from vulvar vestibulitis. *Pain, 91,* 297–306.

Bergeron, S., Bouchard, C., Fortier, M., Binik, Y. M., & Khalife, S. (1997). The surgical treatment of vulvar vestibulitis syndrome: A follow-up study. *Journal of Sex and Marital Therapy, 23,* 317–325.

Bergeron, S., Brown, C., Lord, M. J, Oala, M., Binik, Y. M., & Khalife, S. (2002). Physical therapy for vulvar vestibulitis syndrome: A retrospective study. *Journal of Sex and Marital Therapy, 28,* 183–192.

Berglas, S. C., & Baumeister, R. F. (1993). *Your own worst enemy: Understanding the paradox of self-defeating behavior.* New York: Basic Books.

Berman, J. R., Berman, L. A., Toler, S. M., Gill, J., Haughie, S., & Sildenafil Study Group. (2003). Safety and efficacy of sildenafil citrate for the treatment of female sexual arousal disorder: A double-blind, placebo controlled study. *Journal of Urology, 170,* 2333–2338.

Beutel, M. E., Wiltink, J., Hauck, E. W., Auch, D., Behre, H. M., Brahler, E., Weidner, W., & Hypogonadism Investigator Group. (2005). Correlations between hormones, physical, and affective parameters in aging urologic outpatients. *European Urology, 47,* 749–755.

Billups, K. L., Berman, L., Berman, J., Metz, M. E., Glennon, M. E., & Goldstein, I. (2001). A new non-pharmacological vacuum therapy for female sexual dysfunction. *Journal of Sex and Marital Therapy, 27,* 435–441.

Blair, C. D., & Lanyon, R. I. (1981). Exhibitionism: Etiology and treatment. *Psychological Bulletin, 89,* 439–463.

Blanchard, R., & Collins, P. (1993). Men with sexual interest in transvestites, transsexuals and she-males. *Journal of Nervous and Mental Disease, 181,* 570–575.

Blumer, D. (1970). Changes of sexual behavior related to temporal lobe disorders in man. *Journal of Sex Research, 6,* 173–180.

Blumer, D., & Walker, A. E. (1967). The neural basis of sexual behavior. In D. F. Benson & D. Blumer (Eds.), *Psychiatric aspects of neurologic disease* (pp. 199–217). New York: Grune & Stratton.

Bolt, J. W., Evans, C., & Marshall, V. R. (1987). Sexual dysfunction after prostatectomy. *British Journal of Urology, 59,* 319–322.

Bradley, S. J., & Zucker, K. J. (1997). Gender identity disorder: A review of the past 10 years. *Journal of the American Academy of Child and Adolescent Psychiatry, 36,* 872–880.

Branaman, T. F., & Gallagher, S. N. (2005). Polygraph testing in sex offender treatment: A review of limitations. *American Journal of Forensic Psychology, 23,* 45–64.

Braunstein, G. D., Sundwall, D. A., Katz, M., Shifren, J. L., Buster, J. E., Simon, J. A., Bachman, G., Aguirre, O. A., Lucas, J. D., Rodenberg, C., Buch, A., & Watts, N. B. (2005). Safety and efficacy of a testosterone patch for the treatment of hypoactive sexual desire disorder in surgically menopausal women: A randomized, placebo-controlled trial. *Archives of Internal Medicine, 165,* 1682–1689.

Breslow, N., Evans, N., & Langley, J. (1985). On the prevalence and roles of females in sado-masochistic sub-culture: Report of an empirical study. *Archives of Sexual Medicine, 14,* 303–317.

Brock, G., Iglesias, J., Toulouse, K., Ferguson, K. M., Pullman, W. E., & Anglin, G. (2001). Efficacy and safety of tadalafil (IC351) treatment for ED. Paper presented at the 16th Congress of the European Association of Urology.

Brotto, L. A., Heiman, J. R., Goff, B., Greer, B., Lentz, G. M., Swisher, E., Tamimi, H., & van Blaricom, A. (2006). *Feasibility study of a psychoeducational intervention targeting sexual dysfunction following gynecologic cancer.* Manuscript under review.

Buhrich, N., & McConaghy, N. (1985). Preadult feminine behaviors of male transvestites. *Archives of Sexual Behavior, 14,* 413–419.

Burger, H. G., Dudley, E. C., Cui, J., Dennerstein, L., & Hopper, J. L. (2000). A prospective longitudinal study of serum testosterone, dehydroepiandrosterone sulfate, and sex hormone-binding globulin levels through the menopause transition. *Journal of Clinical Endocrinology and Metabolism, 85,* 2832–2838.

Buster, J. E., Kingsberg, S. A., Aguirre, O., Brown, C., Breaux, J. G., Buch, A., Rodenberg, C. A., Wekselman, K., & Casson, P. (2005). Testosterone patch for low sexual desire in surgically menopausal women: A randomized trial. *Obstetrics & Gynecology, 105,* 944–952.

Butcher, J. N., Dahlstrom, W. G., Graham, J. R., Tellegen, A., & Kraemmer, B. (1989). *MMPI-2: Minnesota Multiphasic Personality Inventory-2: Manual for administration and scoring.* Minneapolis: University of Minnesota Press.

Byers, E. S., & Grenier, G. (2003). Premature or rapid ejaculation: Heterosexual couples' perceptions of men's ejaculatory behaviour. *Archives of Sexual Behavior, 32,* 261–270.

Caruso, S., Agnello, C., Intelisano, G., Farina, M., Di Mari, L., & Cianci, A. (2004). Placebo-controlled study on efficacy and safety of daily apomorphine SL intake in premenopausal women affected by hypoactive sexual desire disorder and sexual arousal disorder. *Urology, 63,* 955–959.

Caruso, S., Intelisano, G., Lupo, L., & Agnello, C. (2001). Premenopausal women affected by sexual arousal disorder treated with sildenafil: A double-blind, cross-over, placebo-controlled study. *British Journal of Obstetrics and Gynaecology, 108,* 623–628.

Cavanaugh-Johnson, T. (1988). Child perpetrators: Children who molest children. *Child Abuse and Neglect, 12,* 219–229.

Chalkley, A. J., & Powell, G. E. (1983). The clinical description of forty-eight cases of sexual fetishism. *British Journal of Psychiatry, 142,* 292–295.

Chaplin, T. C., Rice, M. E., & Harris, G. T. (1995). Salient victim suffering and the sexual responses of child molesters. *Journal of Consulting and Clinical Psychology, 63,* 249–255.

Chu, M. C., & Lobo, R. A. (2004). Formulations and use of androgens in women. *Mayo Clinic Proceedings, 79,* S3–S7.

Chung, Y. B., & Harmon, L. W. (1994). The career interests and aspirations of gay men: How sex-role orientation is related. *Journal of Vocational Behavior, 45,* 223–239.

Cole, C. M., O'Boyle, M., Emory, L. E., & Meyer, W. J. (1997). Comorbidity of gender dysphoria and other major psychiatric diagnoses. *Archives of Sexual Behavior, 26,* 13–26.

Corona, G., Mannucci, E., Petrone, L., Giommi, R., Mansani, R., Fei, L., Forti, G., & Maggi, M. (2004). Psycho-biological correlates of hypoactive sexual desire in patients with erectile dysfunction. *International Journal of Impotence Research, 16,* 275–281.

Cowan, L. (1982). *Masochism: A Jungian view.* Dallas, TX: Spring.

Cox, D. J., & Maletzky, B. M. (1980). Victims of exhibitionism. In D. J. Cox & R. J. Daitzman (Eds.), *Exhibitionism: Description, assessment and treatment* (pp. 289–293). New York: Garland.

Crenshaw, T. L., Golbert, J. P., & Stern, W. C. (1987). Pharmacologic modification of psychosexual dysfunction. *Journal of Sex and Marital Therapy, 13,* 239–252.

Crepault, E., & Couture, M. (1980). Men's erotic fantasies. *Archives of Sexual Behavior, 9,* 565–581.

Cross, T. P., & Saxe, L. (1992). A critique of the validity of polygraph testing in child sexual abuse cases. *Journal of Child Sexual Abuse, 1,* 19–33.

Cross, T. P., & Saxe, L. (2001). Polygraph testing and sexual abuse: The lure of the magic lasso. *Child Maltreatment, 6,* 195–206.

Curren, D. (1954). Sexual perversion. *Practitioner, 172,* 440–445.

Cyranowski, J. M., Bromberger, J., Youk, A., Matthews, K., Kravitz, H., & Powell, L. H. (2004). Lifetime depression and sexual function in women at midlife. *Archives of Sexual Behavior, 33,* 539–548.

Damon, W., & Rosser, B. R. (2005). Anodyspareunia in men who have sex with men: Prevalence, predictors, consequences and the development of DSM diagnostic criteria. *Journal of Sex and Marital Therapy, 31,* 129–141.

Davidson, A. T. (1983). Sexual exploitation of children: A call to action. *Journal of the National Medical Association, 75,* 925–927.

Davis, S. R., Davison, S. L., Donath, S., & Bell, R. J. (2005). Circulating androgen levels in self-reported sexual function in women. *Journal of the American Medical Association, 294,* 91–96.

Davis, S. R., Guay, A. T., Shifren, J. L., & Mazer, N. A. (2004). Endocrine aspects of female sexual dysfunction. *Journal of Sexual Medicine, 1,* 82–86.

Davis, S. R., van der Mooren, M. J., van Lunsen, R. H. W., Lopes, P., Ribot, C., Rees, M., et al. (2006). Efficacy and safety of a testosterone patch for the treatment of hypoactive sexual desire disorder in surgically menopausal women: A randomized placebo control trial. *Menopause, 13,* 389–396.

de Kruiff, M. E., Ter Kuile, M. M., Weijenborg, P. T., & Van Lankveld, J. J. (2000). Vaginismus and dyspareunia: Is there a difference in clinical presentation? *Journal of Psychosomatic Obstetrics and Gynaecology, 21,* 149–155.

Demsky, L. S. (1984). The use of depo-provera in the treatment of sex offenders. *Journal of Legal Medicine, 5,* 295–322.

Denny, D. (2004). Changing models of transsexualism. *Journal of Gay and Lesbian Psychotherapy, 8,* 25–40.

Dhawan, S., & Marshall, W. L. (1996). Sexual abuse histories of sexual offenders. *Sexual Abuse: A Journal of Research and Treatment, 8,* 7–15.

Dietz, P. E., Hazelwood, R. R., & Warren, J. (1990). The sexually sadistic criminal and his offenses. *Bulletin of the American Academy of Psychiatry and the Law, 18,* 163–178.

Doorn, C. D., Poortinga, J., & Verschoor, A. M. (1994). Cross-gender identity in transvestites and male transsexuals. *Archives of Sexual Behavior, 23,* 185–201.

East, W. N. (1924). Observations on exhibitionism. *Lancet, 2,* 370–375.

Ellis, A., & Brancale, R. (1956). *The psychology of sex offenders.* Springfield, IL: Thomas.

English, K., Jones, L., Pasini-Hill, D., Patrick, D., & Cooley-Towell, S. (2000). *The value of polygraph testing in sex offender treatment.* Washington, DC: National Institute of Justice.

Feldman, H. A., Goldstein, I., Hatzichristou, D. G., Krane, R. J., & McKinlay, J. B. (1994). Impotence and its medical and psychosocial correlates: Results of the Massachusetts Male Aging Study. *Journal of Urology, 151,* 54–61.

Federoff, J. P., Fishell, A., & Federoff, B. (1999). A case series of women evaluated for paraphilic sexual disorders. *Canadian Journal of Human Sexuality, 8,* 127–140.

Ferguson, J. M. (2001). The effects of antidepressants on sexual functioning in depressed patients: A review. *Journal of Clinical Psychiatry, 62*(Suppl. 3), 22–34.

Fernandez, Y. M., Marshall, W. L., Lightbody, S., & O'Sullivan, C. (1999). The child molester empathy measure: Description and examination of its reliability and validity. *Sexual Abuse: A Journal of Research and Treatment, 11,* 17–32.

Finch, S. (2001). Sexual aversion disorder treated with behavioural desensitization. *Canadian Journal of Psychiatry, 46,* 563–564.

Finkelhor, D. (1979). *Sexually victimized children.* New York: Free Press.

Finkelhor, D. (1984). *Child sexual abuse: New theory and research.* New York: Free Press.

Fish, L. S., Busby, D., & Killian, K. (1994). Structural couple therapy in the treatment of inhibited sexual desire. *American Journal of Family Therapy, 22,* 113–125.

Freund, K. (1963). A laboratory method for diagnosing predominance of homo- or hetero erotic interest in the male. *Behaviour Research and Therapy, 1,* 85–93.

Freund, K. (1990). Courtship disorders. In W. L. Marshall, D. R. Laws, & H. E. Barbaree (Eds.), *Handbook of sexual assault: Issues, theories, and treatment of the offender* (pp. 195–207). New York: Plenum.

Freund, K., & Blanchard, R. (1986). The concept of courtship disorder. *Journal of Sex and Marital Therapy, 12,* 79–92.

Freund, K., & Blanchard, R. (1989). Phallometric diagnosis of pedophilia. *Journal of Consulting and Clinical Psychology, 57,* 100–105.

Freund, K., Seto, M. C., & Kuban, M. (1996). Two types of fetishism. *Behaviour Research and Therapy, 34,* 687–694.

Freund, K., Seto, M. C., & Kuban, M. (1997). Frotteurism: The theory of courtship disorder. In D. R. Laws & W. O'Donohue (Eds.), *Sexual deviance: Theory, assessment, and treatment* (pp. 111–130). New York: Guilford Press.

Freund, K., & Watson, R. J. (1991). Assessment of the sensitivity and specificity of a phallometric test: An update of phallometric diagnosis of pedophilia. *Psychological Assessment, 3,* 254–260.

Freund, K., Watson, R., & Reinzo, D. (1988). Signs of feigning in the phallometric test. *Behaviour Research and Therapy, 26,* 105–112.

Freundt, I., Toolenaar, T. A. M., Jeekel, H., Drogendijk, A. C., & Huikeshoven, F. J. M. (1994). Prolapse of the sigmoid neovagina: Report of three cases. *Obstetrics and Gynecology, 83,* 876–879.

Friedman, R. C. (1991). The depressed masochistic patient: Diagnostic and management considerations. *Journal of the American Academy of Psychoanalysis, 19,* 9–30.

Friedrich, E. G. (1987). Vulvar vestibulitis syndrome. *Journal of Reproductive Medicine, 32,* 110–114.

Frolich, P., & Meston. C. (2002). Sexual functioning and self-reported depressive symptoms among college women. *Journal of Sex Research, 39,* 321–325.

Fugl-Meyer, A. R., & Sjogren Fugl-Meyer, K. (1999). Sexual disabilities, problems and satisfaction in 18–74 year old Swedes. *Scandinavian Journal of Sexology, 2,* 79–105.

Furby, L., Weinrott, M. R., & Blackshaw, L. (1989). Sex offender recidivism: A review. *Psychological Bulletin, 105,* 3–30.

Gaunt, G., Good, A., & Stanhope, C. R. (2003). Vestibulectomy for vulvar vestibulitis. *Journal of Reproductive Medicine, 48,* 591–595.

Gebhard, P. H., Gagnon, J. H., Pomeroy, W. B., & Christenson, C. V. (1965). *Sex offenders: An analysis of types.* New York: Harper & Row.

Giuseppe, L., & Nicastro, A. (1996). A new treatment for premature ejaculation: The rehabilitation of the pelvic floor. *Journal of Sex and Marital Therapy, 22,* 22–26.

Goldstein, I., & Berman, J. R. (1998). Vasculogenic female sexual dysfunction: Vaginal engorgement and clitoral erectile insufficiency syndromes. *International Journal of Impotence Research, 10*(Suppl. 2), S84–S90.

Goldstein, I., Fischer, J., Taylor, T., & Thibonnier, M. (2002, June). Influence of HbA1c on the efficacy and safety of vardenafil for the treatment of erectile dysfunction in men with diabetes. Paper presentend at the American Diabetes Association 62nd Scientific Session, San Francisco, CA.

Gosselin, C., & Wilson, G. (1980). *Sexual variations.* London: Faber & Faber.

Gratzer, T., & Bradford, J. M. W. (1995). Offender and offense characteristics of sexual sadists: A comparative study. *Journal of Forensic Sciences, 40,* 450–455.

Grenier, G., & Byers, E. S. (2001). Operationalizing early or premature ejaculation. *Journal of Sex Research, 38,* 369–378.

Grob, C. S. (1985). Single case study: Female exhibitionism. *Journal of Nervous and Mental Disease, 173,* 253–256.

Grossman, W. I. (1986). Notes on masochism: A discussion of the history and development of a psychoanalytic concept. *Psychoanalytic Quarterly, 55,* 379–413.

Haczynski, J., Lew-Starowicz, Z., Darewicz, B., Krajka, K., Piotrowicz, R., & Ciesielska, B. (in press). The prevalence of erectile dysfunction in men visiting outpatient clinics. *International Journal of Impotence Research, 18,* 578.

Hanson, P. K., & Bussiere, M. T. (1998). Predicting relapse: A meta-analysis of sexual offender recidivism studies. *Journal of Consulting and Clinical Psychology, 66,* 348–362.

Harris, G. T., Rice, M. E., Chaplin, T. C., & Quinsey, V. L. (1999). Dissimulation in phallometric testing of rapists' sexual preferences. *Archives of Sexual Behavior, 28,* 223–232.

Harris, G. T., Rice, M. E., Quinsey, V. L., & Chaplin, T. C. (1996). Viewing time as a measure of sexual interest among child molesters and normal heterosexual men. *Behaviour Research Therapy, 34,* 389–394.

Hartmann, U., Heiser, K., Ruffer-Hesse, C., & Kloth, G. (2002). Female sexual desire disorders: Subtypes, classification, personality factors and new directions for treatment. *World Journal of Urology, 20,* 79–88.

Hawton, K. (1995). Treatment of sexual dysfunctions by sex therapy and other approaches. *British Journal of Psychiatry, 16,* 307–314.

Hawton, K., Catalan, J., Martin, P., & Fagg, J. (1986). Long-term outcome of sex therapy. *Behavioral Research and Therapy, 24,* 665–675.

Hazelwood, R. R., Dietz, P. E., & Warren, J. (1992). The criminal sexual sadist. *FBI Law Enforcement Bulletin, 61,* 12–20.

Heiman, J. R. (2002). Psychologic treatments for female sexual dysfunction: Are they effective and do we need them? *Archives of Sexual Behavior, 31,* 445–450.

Heiman, J. R., & LoPiccolo, J. (1987). *Becoming orgasmic: A sexual and personal growth program for women* (rev. and expanded ed.). New York: Simon & Schuster.

Hepp, U., Kraemer, B., Schnyder, U., Miller, N., & Delsignore, A. (2005). Psychiatriccomorbidity in gender identity disorder. *Journal of Psychosomatic Research, 58,* 259–261.

Hill, C. A., & Preston, L. K. (1996). Individual differences in the experience of sexual motivation: Theory and measurement of dispositional sexual motives. *Journal of Sex Research, 33,* 27–45.

Hines, T. M. (2001). The G-spot: A modern gynecologic myth. *American Journal of Obstetrics and Gynecology, 185,* 359–362.

Holland, L. A., Zolondek, S. C., Abel, G. G., Jordan, A. D., & Becker, J. V. (2000). Psychometric analysis of the Sexual Interest Cardsort Questionnaire. *Sexual Abuse: A Journal of Research and Treatment, 12,* 107–122.

Hooshmand, H., & Brawley, B. W. (1969). Temporal lobe seizures and exhibitionism. *Neurology, 19,* 1119–1124.

Howes, R. J. (1995). A survey of plethysmographic assessment in North America. *Sexual Abuse: A Journal of Research and Treatment, 7,* 9–24.

Hucker, S., Langevin, R., Dickey, R., Handy, L., Chambers, J., Wright, S., et al. (1988). Cerebral damage and dysfunction in sexually aggressive men. *Annals of Sex Research, 1,* 33–47.

Hulter, B., & Lundberg, P. O. (1994). Sexual function in women with hypothalamo-pituitary disorders. *Archives of Sexual Behavior, 23,* 171–183.

Hunt, M. (1974). *Sexual behavior in the 1970's.* New York: Playboy Press.

Hurlbert, D. F. (1993). A comparative study using orgasm consistency training in the treatment of women reporting hypoactive sexual desire. *Journal of Sex and Marital Therapy, 19,* 41–55.

Hurlbert, D. F., & Apt, C. (1995). The coital alignment technique and direct masturbation: A comparison study on female orgasm. *Journal of Sex and Marital Therapy, 21,* 21–29.

Huws, R., Shubsachs, A. P., & Taylor, P. J. (1991). Hypersexuality, fetishism, and multiple sclerosis. *British Journal of Psychiatry, 158,* 280–281.

Isidori, A. M., Giannetta, E., Gianfrilli, D., Greco, E. A., Bonifacio, V., Aversa, A., Isidori, A., Fabbri, A., & Lenzi, A. (2005). Effects of testosterone on sexual function in men: Results of a meta-analysis. *Clinical Endocrinology (Oxford), 63,* 381–394.

Johnson, R. L., & Shrier, D. (1987). Past sexual victimization by females of male patients in an adolescent medicine clinic population. *American Journal of Psychiatry, 144,* 650–652.

Johnston, P., Hudson, S. M., & Marshall, W. L. (1992). The effects of masturbatory reconditioning with nonfamilial child molesters. *Behaviour Research and Therapy, 30,* 559–561.

Kabakci, E., & Batur, S. (2003). Who benefits from cognitive behavioural therapy for vaginismus? *Journal of Sex and Marital Therapy, 29,* 277–288.

Kaplan, H. S. (1974). Retarded ejaculation. In H. S. Kaplan (Ed.), *The new sex therapy* (pp. 316–338). New York: Brunner Mazel.

Kaplan, H. S. (1979). *Disorders of sexual desire.* New York: Brunner Mazel.

Kaplan, H. S. (1989). *Premature ejaculation: Overcoming early ejaculation.* New York: Brunner Mazel.

Kaplan, H. S. (1990). The combined use of sex therapy and intrapenile injections in the treatment of impotence. *Journal of Sex and Marital Therapy, 16,* 195–207.

Kaplan, M. S., & Krueger, R. B. (1997). Voyeurism: Psychopathology and theory. In D. R. Laws & W. O'Donohue (Eds.), *Sexual deviance: Theory, assessment, and treatment* (pp. 297–310). New York: Guilford Press.

Kara, H., Aydin, S., Yucel, M., Agargun, M. Y., Odabas, O., & Yilmaz, Y. (1996). The efficacy of fluoextine in the treatment of premature ejaculation: A double-blind placebo controlled study. *Journal of Urology, 156,* 1631–1632.

Kaschak, E., & Tiefer, L. (2002). *A new view of women's sexual problems.* Binghamton, NY: Haworth Press.

Katz, R. C., Gipson, M. T., Kearl, A., & Kriskovich, M. (1989). Assessing sexual aversion in college students. *Journal of Sex and Marital Therapy, 15,* 135–140.

Kennedy, S. H., Dickens, S. E., Eisfeld, B. S., & Bagby, R. M. (1999). Sexual dysfunction before antidepressant therapy in major depression. *Journal of Affective Disorders, 56,* 201–208.

Kilpatrick, A. C. (1992). *Long-range effects of child and adolescent sexual experiences.* Hillsdale, NJ: Erlbaum.

Kingsberg, S. A., & Janata, J. W. (2003). The sexual aversions. In S. B. Levine, C. B. Risen, & S. E. Althof (Eds.), *Handbook of clinical sexuality for mental health professionals* (pp. 153–165). New York: Brunner-Routledge.

Kinsey, A. C., Pomeroy, W. B., & Martin, C. E. (1948). *Sexual behavior in the human male.* Philadelphia: W. B. Saunders.

Kinsey, A. C., Pomeroy, W. B., Martin, C. E., & Gebhard, P. H. (1953). *Sexual behavior in the human female.* Philadelphia: W. B. Saunders.

Klusmann, D. (2002). Sexual motivation and the duration of partnership. *Archives of Sexual Behavior, 31,* 275–287.

Knopp, F. H., Freeman-Longo, R., & Stevenson, W. (1992). *Nationwide survey of juvenile and adult sex offender treatment programs.* Orwell, VT: Safer Society Press.

Knopp, F. H., & Lackey, L. B. (1987). *Female sexual abusers: A summary of data from forty four treatment providers.* Orwell, VT: Safer Society Press.

Kokish, R. (2003). The current role of post-conviction sex offender polygraph testing in sex offender treatment. *Journal of Child Sexual Abuse, 12,* 175–194.

Kokish, R., Levenson, J. S., & Blasingame, G. D. (2005). Post-conviction sex offender polygraph examination: Client-reported perceptions of utility and accuracy. *Sexual Abuse: A Journal of Research and Treatment, 17,* 211–221.

Kroll, R., Davis, S., Moreau, M., Waldbaum, A., Shifren, J., & Wekselman, K. (2004). Testosterone transdermal patch (TTP) significantly improved sexual function in naturally menopausal women in a large phase III study. *Fertility and Sterility, 82*(Suppl. 2), S77–S78.

Krueger, R. B., & Kaplan, M. S. (1997). Frotteurism: Assessment and treatment. In D. R. Laws & W. O'Donohue (Eds.), *Sexual deviance: Theory, assessment, and treatment* (pp. 131–151). New York: Guilford Press.

Krueger, R. B., & Kaplan, M. S. (2001). The paraphilic and hypersexual disorders: An overview. *Journal of Psychiatric Practice, 7,* 391–403.

Krueger, R. B., & Kaplan, M. S. (2002). Behavioral and psychopharmacological treatment of the paraphilic and hypersexual disorders. *Journal of Psychiatric Practice, 8,* 21–32.

Laan, E., Everaerd, W., van der Velde, J., & Geer, J. H. (1995). Determinants of subjective experience of sexual arousal in women: Feedback from genital arousal and erotic stimulus content. *Psychophysiology, 32,* 444–451.

Laan, E., van Lunsen, R. H., & Everaerd, W. (2001). The effects of tibolone on vaginal blood flow, sexual desire and arousability in postmenopausal women. *Climacteric, 4,* 28–41.

Lalumiere, M. L., & Earls, C. M. (1992). Voluntary control of penile responses as a function of stimulus duration and instructions. *Behavioral Assessment, 14,* 121–132.

Lalumiere, M. L., & Harris, G. T. (1998). Common questions regarding the use of phallometric testing with sexual offenders. *Sexual Abuse: A Journal of Research and Treatment, 10,* 227–237.

Lalumiere, M. L., & Quinsey, V. L. (1993). The sensitivity of phallometric measures with rapists. *Annals of Sex Research, 6,* 123–138.

Lalumiere, M. L., & Quinsey, V. L. (1994). The discriminability of rapists from non-sex offenders using phallometric measures: A meta-analysis. *Criminal Justice and Behavior, 21,* 150–175.

Lamont, J. A. (1978). Vaginismus. *American Journal of Obstetrics and Gynecology, 131,* 632–636.

Landen, M., Eriksson, E., Agren, H., & Fahlen, T. (1999). Effect of buspirone on sexual dysfunction in depressed patients treated with selective serotonin reuptake inhibitors. *Journal of Clinical Psychopharmacology, 19,* 268–271.

Lane, S. (1991). The sexual abuse cycle. In G. D. Ryan & S. L. Lane (Eds.), *Juvenile sexual offending: Causes, consequences, and correction* (pp. 103–141). Lexington, MA: Lexington Books.

Lang, A. R., Searles, J., Lauerman, R., & Adesso, V. (1980). Expectancy, alcohol, and sex guilt as determinants of interest in and reaction to sexual stimuli. *Journal of Abnormal Psychology, 95,* 150–158.

Langer, S. J., & Martin, J. I. (2004). How dresses can make you mentally ill: Examining gender identity disorder in children. *Child and Adolescent Social Work Journal, 21,* 5–23.

Langevin, R. (1983). *Sexual strands: Understanding and treating sexual anomalies in men.* Hillsdale, NJ: Erlbaum.

Langevin, R. (1990). Sexual anomalies and the brain. In W. L. Marshall, D. R. Laws, & H. E. Barbaree (Eds.), *Handbook of sexual assault: Issues, theories, and treatment of the offender* (pp. 103–113). New York: Plenum.

Langevin, R., & Lang, R. A., (1987). The courtship disorders. In G. O. Wilson (Ed.), *Variant sexuality: Research and theory* (pp. 202–228). London: Croom Helm.

Langevin, R., Lang, R. A., Wortzman, G., Frenzel, R. R., & Wright, P. (1989). An examination of brain damage and dysfunction in genital exhibitionists. *Annals of Sex Research, 2,* 77–87.

Langevin, R., Paitich, D., Freeman, R., Mann, K., & Handy, L. (1978). Personality characteristics and sexual anomalies in males. *Canadian Journal of Behavioural Science, 10,* 222–238.

Langevin, R., Paitich, D., Ramsey, G., Anderson, C., Kamrad, J., Pope, S., et al. (1979). Experimental studies of the etiology of genital exhibitionism. *Archives of Sexual Behavior, 8,* 307–331.

Laumann, E. O., Gagnon, J. H., Michael, R. T., & Michaels, S. (1994). *The social organization of sexuality: Sexual practices in the United States.* Chicago: University of Chicago Press.

Laumann, E. O., Nicolosi, A., Glasser, D. B., Paik, A., Gingell, C., Moreira, E., Wang, T., & GSSAB Investigators' Group. (2005). Sexual problems among women and men aged 40–80 y: Prevalence and correlates identified in the Global Study of Sexual Attitudes and Behaviors. *International Journal of Impotence Research, 17,* 39–57.

Laumann E. O., Paik, A., & Rosen, R. C. (1999). Sexual dysfunction in the United States. *Journal of the American Medical Association, 281,* 537–544.

Lavy, Y., Lev-Sagie, A., Hamani, Y., Zacut, D., & Ben-Chetrit, A. (2005). Modified vulvar vestibulectomy: Simple and effective surgery for the treatment of vulvar vestibulitis. *European Journal of Obstetric & Gynecology and Reproductive Biology, 120,* 91–95.

Lawrence, A. A. (2003). Factors associated with satisfaction or regret following male-to-female sex reassignment surgery. *Archives of Sexual Behavior, 32,* 299–315.

Laws, D. R. (1986). *Sexual Deviance Card Sort.* Unpublished manuscript, Florida Mental Health Institute, Tampa.

Laws, D. R. (1995). Verbal satiation: Notes on procedure, with speculations on its mechanism of effect. *Sexual Abuse: A Journal of Research and Treatment, 7,* 155–166.

Laws, D. R. (2001). Olfactory aversion: Notes on procedure, with speculations on its mechanism of effect. *Sexual Abuse: A Journal of Research and Treatment, 13,* 275–287.

Laws, D. R., & Marshall, W. L. (1991). Masturbatory reconditioning: An evaluative review. *Advances in Behaviour Research and Therapy, 13,* 13–25.

Lehmann, A., Rosemeier, H., & Grüsser-Sinopoli, S. M. (2004). Female orgasm: Clitoral or vaginal? *Sexuologie, 10,* 128–133.

Leiblum, S. R., Brown, C., Wan, J., & Rawlinson, L. (2005). Persistent sexual arousal syndrome: A descriptive study. *Journal of Sex and Marital Therapy, 2,* 331–337.

Leiblum, S. R., & Nathan, S. G. (2001). Persistent sexual arousal syndrome: A newly discovered pattern of female sexuality. *Journal of Sex and Marital Therapy, 24,* 365–380.

Letourneau, E. J. (2002). A comparison of objective measures of sexual arousal and interest: Visual reaction time and penile plethysmography. *Sexual Abuse: A Journal of Research and Treatment, 14,* 207–223.

Levin, S. M., Barry, S. M., Gambaro, S., Wofinsohn, L., & Smith, A. (1977). Variations of covert sensitization in the treatment of pedophilic behavior: A case study. *Journal of Consulting and Clinical Psychology, 45,* 896–907.

Lewis, R. W., Sadovsky, R., Eardley, I., O'Leary, M., Seftel, A., Wang, W. C., Shen, W., Walker, D. J., Wong, D. G., & Ahuja, S. (2005). The efficacy of tadalafil in clinical populations. *Journal of Sexual Medicine, 2,* 517–531.

Libman, E., Fichten, C. S., Brender, W., Burstein, R., Cohen, J., & Binik, Y. M. (1984). A comparison of three therapeutic formats in the treatment of secondary orgasmic dysfunction. *Journal of Sex and Marital Therapy, 10,* 147–159.

Linet, O. I., & Ogrinc, F. G. (1996). Efficacy and safety of intracavernosal alprostadil in men with erectile dysfunction. *New England Journal of Medicine, 334,* 873–877.

Lunde, I., Larsen, G. K., Fog, E., & Garde, K. (1991). Sexual desire, orgasm, and sexual fantasies: A study of 625 Danish women born in 1910, 1936 and 1958. *Journal of Sex Education and Therapy, 17,* 111–115.

MacCulloch, M. J., & Feldman, M. P. (1967). Personality and the treatment of homosexuality. *Acta Psychiatrica Scandinavica, 43,* 300–317.

MacCulloch, M. J., Waddington, J. L., & Sambrooks, J. E. (1978). Avoidance latencies reliably reflect sexual attitude change during aversion therapy for homosexuality. *Behavior Therapy, 9,* 562–577.

MacPhee, D. C., Johnson, S. M., & Van der Veer, M. M. (1995). Low sexual desire in women: The effects of marital therapy. *Journal of Sex and Marital Therapy, 21,* 159–182.

Malcolm, P. B., Andrews, D. A., & Quinsey, V. L. (1993). Discriminant and predictive validity of phallometrically measured sexual age and gender preference. *Journal of Interpersonal Violence, 8,* 486–501.

Maletzky, B. M. (1991). *Treating the sexual offender.* Newbury Park, CA: Sage.

Maletzky, B. M. (1993). Factors associated with success and failure in the behavioral and cognitive treatment of sexual offenders. *Annals of Sex Research, 6,* 241–258.

Maletzky, B. M. (1997). Exhibitionism: Assessment and treatment. In D. R. Laws & W. O'Donohue (Eds.), *Sexual deviance: Theory, assessment, and treatment* (pp. 40–74). New York: Guilford Press.

Maletzky, B. M., & George, F. S. (1973). The treatment of homosexuality by "assisted" covert sensitization. *Behaviour Research and Therapy, 11,* 655–657.

Marshall, W. L., & Eccles, A. (1991). Issues in clinical practice with sex offenders. *Journal of Interpersonal Violence, 6,* 68–93.

Marshall, W. L., Hudson, S. M., & Hodkinson, S. (1993). The importance of attachment bonds in the development of juvenile sex offending. In H. E. Barbaree, W. L. Marshall, & S. M. Hudson (Eds.), *The juvenile sex offender* (pp. 164–181). New York: Guilford Press.

Marshall, W. L., Hudson, S. M., Jones, R., & Fernandez, Y. M. (1995). Empathy in sex offenders. *Clinical Psychology Review, 15,* 99–113.

Marshall, W. L., Payne, K., Barbaree, H. E., & Eccles, A. (1991). Exhibitionists: Sexual preferences for exposing. *Behaviour Research and Therapy, 29,* 37–40.

Mason, F. L. (1997). Fetishism: Psychopathology and theory. In D. R. Laws & W. O'Donohue (Eds.), *Sexual deviance: Theory, assessment, and treatment* (pp. 75–91). New York: Guildford Press.

Masters, W. H., & Johnson, V. E. (1966). *Human sexual response.* Boston: Little, Brown.

Masters, W. H., & Johnson, V. E. (1970). *Human sexual inadequacy.* Boston: Little, Brown.

Matthews, R., Matthews, J. K., & Speltz, K. (1989). *Female sex offenders: An exploratory study.* Orwell, VT: Safer Society Press.

Maurice, W. L. (1999). *Sexual medicine in primary care.* St. Louis, MO: Mosby.

Maurice, W. L. (2005). Male hypoactive sexual desire disorder. In R. Balon & R. T. Segraves (Eds.), *Handbook of sexual dysfunction* (pp. 67–109). Boca Raton, FL: Taylor & Francis.

McCabe, M. P. (1992). A program for the treatment of inhibited sexual desire in males. *Psychotherapy, 29,* 288–296.

McCarthy, B. W. (1998). Integrating sildenafil into cognitive-behavioral couple's sex therapy. *Journal of Sex Education and Therapy, 23,* 302–308.

McConaghy, N. (1993). *Sexual behavior: Problems and management.* New York: Plenum.

McConaghy, N. (1998). Pedophilia: A review of the evidence. *Australian and New Zealand Journal of Psychiatry, 32,* 252–265.

McConaghy, N., Blaszcyzynski, A., & Kidson, W. (1988). Treatment of sex offenders with imaginal desensitization and/or medroxyprogesterone. *Acta Psychiatrica Scandinavica, 77,* 199–206.

McElroy, S. L., Soutullo, C. A., Taylor, P. Jr., Nelson, E. B., Beckman, D. A., Brusman, L. A., Ombaba, J. M., Strakowski, S. M., Keck, P. E. Jr. (1999). Psychiatric features of 36 men convicted of sexual offenses. *Journal of Clinical Psychiatry, 60,* 414–420.

Metz, M. E., Pryor, J. L., Nesvacil, L. J., Abuzzahab, F. Sr., & Koznar, J. (1997). Premature ejaculation: A psychophysiological review. *Journal of Sex and Marital Therapy, 23,* 3–23.

Meyer, J. K. (1995). Paraphilias. In H. I. Kaplan & B. J. Sadock (Eds.), *Comprehensive textbook of psychiatry VI* (Vol. 1, 6th ed., pp. 1334–1347). Baltimore: Williams & Wilkins.

Meyer, W. J. III. (2004). Psychiatric comorbidity of gender identity disorders: A survey among Dutch psychiatrists: Comment. *American Journal of Psychiatry, 161,* 934–935.

Meyer, W. III., Bockting, W. O., Cohen-Kettenis, P., Coleman, E., DiCeglie, D., Devor, H., et al. (2001). The Harry Benjamin International Gender Dysphoria Association's Standards of Care for Gender Identity Disorders, Sixth Version. *Journal of Psychology and Human Sexuality, 13,* 1–30.

Michel, A., Mormont, C., & Legros, J. J. (2001). A psycho-endocrinological overview of transsexualism. *European Journal of Endocrinology, 145,* 365–376.

Miller, B. L., Darby, A. L., Swartz, J. R., Yener, G. G., & Mena, I. (1995). Dietary changes, compulsions and sexual behavior in frontotemporal degeneration. *Dementia, 6,* 195–199.

Mohr, J. W., Turner, R. E., & Jerry, M. B. (1964). *Pedophilia and exhibitionism.* Toronto, Canada: University of Toronto Press.

Money, J. (1984). Paraphilias: Phenomenology and classification. *American Journal of Psychotherapy, 38,* 164–179.

Monga, M., Bettencourt, R., & Barrett-Connor, E. (2002). Community-based study of erectile dysfunction and sildenafil use: The Rancho Bernardo study. *Urology, 59,* 753–757.

Morales, A., Buvat, J., Gooren, L. J., Guay, A. T., Kaufman, J.-M., Tan, H. M., & Torres, L. O. (2004). Endocrine aspects of sexual dysfunction in men. *Journal of Sexual Medicine, 1,* 69–81.

Morales, A., Heaton, J. P. W., & Carson, C. C. III. (2000). Andropause: A misnomer for a true clinical entity. *Journal of Urology, 163,* 705–712.

Moser, C., & Levitt, E. E. (1987). An exploratory-descriptive study of a sadomasochistically oriented sample. *Journal of Sex Research, 23,* 322–337.

Munjack, D. J., Schlaks, A., Sanchez, V. C., Usigli, R., Zulueta, A., & Leonard, M. (1984). Rational-emotive therapy in the treatment of erectile failure: An initial study. *Sexual and Marital Therapy, 10,* 170–175.

Murphy, W. D. (1997). Exhibitionism: Psychopathology and theory. In D. R. Laws & W. O'Donohue (Eds.), *Sexual deviance: Theory, assessment, and treatment* (pp. 22–39). New York: Guilford Press.

Murphy, W. D., Haynes, M. R., & Page, I. J. (1992). Adolescent sex offenders. In W. O'Donohue & J. H. Geer (Eds.), *The sexual abuse of children: Clinical issues* (Vol. 2, pp. 395–429). Hillsdale, NJ: Erlbaum.

Murphy, W. D., Haynes, M. R., & Worley, P. J. (1991). Assessment of adult sexual interest. In C. R. Hollin & K. Howells (Eds.), *Clinical approaches to sex offenders and their victims* (pp. 77–92). West Sussex, England: Wiley.

Murphy, W. D., & Peters, J. M. (1992). Profiling child sexual abusers: Psychological considerations. *Criminal Justice and Behavior, 19,* 24–37.

Murphy, W. D., & Smith, T. A. (1996). Sex offenders against children: Empirical and clinical issues. In J. Briere, L. Berliner, J. A. Bulkley, C. Jenny, & T. Reid (Eds.), *The APSAC handbook on child maltreatment* (pp. 175–191). Thousand Oaks, CA: Sage.

Nichols, H. R., & Molinder, I. (1984). *The Multiphasic Sex Inventory manual.* Tacoma, WA: Author.

Nichols, H. R., & Molinder, I. (1992). *The Multiphasic Sex Inventory manual.* Tacoma, WA: Author.

Nusbaum, M. R., Gamble, G., Skinner, B., & Heiman, J. (2000). The high prevalence of sexual concerns among women seeking routine gynecological care. *Journal of Family Practice, 49,* 229–232.

O'Carroll, R. (1989). A neuropsychological study of sexual deviation. *Sexual and Marital Therapy, 4,* 59–63.

O'Carroll, R., & Bancroft, J. (1984). Testosterone therapy for low sexual interest and erectile dysfunction in men: A controlled study. *British Journal of Psychiatry, 145,* 146–151.

Osterloh, I. H., & Riley, A. (2002). Clinical update on sildenafil citrate. *British Journal of Clinical Pharmacology, 53,* 219–223.

Padma-Nathan, H., Brown, C., Fendl, J., Salem, S., Yeager, J., & Harningr, R. (2003). Efficacy and safety of topical alprostadil cream for the treatment of female sexual arousal disorder (FSAD): A double-blind, multicenter, randomized, and placebo-controlled clinical trial. *Journal of Sex and Marital Therapy, 29,* 329–344.

Padma-Nathan, H., Hellstrom, W. J., Kaiser, F. E., Labasky, R. F., Lue, T. F., Nolten, W. E., Norwood, P. C., Peterson, C. A., Shabsigh, R., & Tam, P. Y. (1997). Treatment of men with erectile dysfunction with transurethral alprostadil: Medicated Urethral System for Erection (MUSE) Study Group. *New England Journal of Medicine, 336,* 1–7.

Paitich, D., Langevin, R., Freeman, R., Mann, K., & Handy, L. (1977). The Clarke Sexual History Questionnaire: A clinical sex history questionnaire for males. *Archives of Sexual Behavior, 6,* 421–435.

Peng, Y. S., Chiang, C. K., Kao, T. W., Hung, K. Y., Chiang, S. S., Yang, C. S., Huang, Y. C., Wu, K. D., Wu, M. S., Lien, Y. R., Yang, C. C., Tsai, D. M., Chen, P. Y., Liao, C. S., Tsai, T. J., & Chen, W. Y. (2005). Sexual dysfunction in female hemodialysis patients: A multicenter study. *Kidney International, 68,* 760–765.

Perelman, M. A. (2002). FSD partner issues: Expanding sex therapy with sildenafil. *Journal of Sex and Marital Therapy, 28*(Suppl. 1), 195–204.

Perelman, M. A. (2005). Combination therapy for sexual dysfunction: Integrating sex therapy and pharmacology. In R. Balon & R. T. Segraves (Eds.), *Handbook of sexual dysfunction* (pp. 13–41). Boca Raton, FL: Taylor & Francis.

Perelman, M. A. (2006a). A new combination treatment for premature ejaculation: A sex therapist's perspective. *Journal of Sexual Medicine, 3,* 1004–1012.

Perelman, M. A. (2006b). *Masturbation is a key variable in the treatment of retarded ejaculation by health care professionals.* Poster session presented at the annual meeting of the International Society for the Study of Women's Sexual Health, Lisbon, Portugal.

Perelman, M. A., Diamond, L. E., Earle, D. C., Heiman, J. R., Rosen, R. C., & Harning, R. (2006). *The potential role of bremelanotide (PT-141) as a pharmacologic intervention for FSD.* Poster session presented at the annual meeting of the International Society for the Study of Women's Sexual Health, Lisbon, Portugal.

Pfaus, J. G., Shadiack A., Van Soest, T., Tse, M., & Molinoff, P. (2004). Selective facilitation of sexual solicitation in the female rat by a melanocortin receptor agonist. *Proceedings of the National Academy of Sciences of the United States of America, 101,* 10201–10204.

Phelps, J. S., Jain, A., & Monga, M. (2004). The psychoedPlusMed approach to erectile dysfunction treatment: The impact of combining a psychoeducational intervention with sildenafil. *Journal of Sex and Marital Therapy, 30,* 305–341.

Phillips, L. Jr., & Slaughter, J. R. (2000). Depression and sexual desire. *American Family Physician, 62,* 782–786.

Pridal C. G., & LoPiccolo, J. (2000). Multi-element treatment of desire disorders: Integration of cognitive, behavioral, and systemic therapy. In S. R. Leiblum & R. C. Rosen (Eds.), *Principles and practice of sex therapy* (pp. 57–81). New York: Guilford Press.

Pukall, C. F., Payne, K. A., Kao, A., Khalife, S., & Binik, Y. M. (2005). In R. Balon & R. T. Segraves (Eds.), *Handbook of sexual dysfunction* (pp. 249–272). Boca Raton, FL: Taylor & Francis.

Pukall, C. F., Strigo, I. A., Binik, Y. M., Amsel, R., Khalife, S., & Bushnell, M. C. (2005). Neural correlates of painful genital touch in women with vulvar vestibulitis syndrome. *Pain, 115,* 118–117.

Quinsey, V. L. (1988). Assessments of the treatability of forensic patients. *Behavioral Sciences and the Law, 6,* 443–452.

Quinsey, V. L., & Earls, C. M. (1990). The modification of sexual preferences. In W. L. Marshall, D. R. Laws, & H. E. Barbaree (Eds.), *Handbook of sexual assault: Issues, theories, and treatment of the offender* (pp. 343–361). New York: Plenum.

Quinsey, V. L., & Lalumiere, M. L. (1996). *Assessment of sexual offenders against children.* Newbury Park, CA: Sage.

Quinsey, V. L., Rice, M. E., & Harris, G. T. (1995). The actuarial prediction of sexual recidivism. *Journal of Interpersonal Violence, 10,* 85–105.

Quinsey, V. L., Rice, M. E., Harris, G. T., & Reid, K. S. (1993). The phylogenetic and ontogenetic development of sexual age preferences in males: Conceptual and measurement issues. In H. E. Barbaree, W. L. Marshall, & S. M. Hudson (Eds.), *The juvenile sex offender* (pp. 143–163). New York: Guilford Press.

Rachman, S. (1966). Sexual fetishism: An experimental analogue. *Psychological Record, 16,* 293–296.

Rachman, S., & Hodgson, R. J. (1968). Experimentally-induced "sexual fetishism": Replication and development. *Psychological Record, 18,* 25–27.

Regan, P., & Berscheid, C. E. (1996). Belief about the state, goals, and objects of sexual desire. *Journal of Sex and Marital Therapy, 22,* 110–120.

Reissing, E. D., Binik, Y. M., Khalife, S., Cohen, D., & Amsel, R. (2004). Vaginal spasm, pain, and behavior: An empirical investigation of the diagnosis of vaginismus. *Archives of Sexual Behavior, 33,* 5–17.

Rettenmaier, M. A., Brown, J. V., & Micha, J. P. (2003). Modified vestibulectomy is inadequate treatment for secondary vulvar vestibulitis. *Journal of Gynecologic Surgery, 19,* 13–17.

Rice, M. E., Harris, G. T., & Quinsey, V. L. (1990). A follow-up of rapists assessed in a maximum security psychiatric facility. *Journal of Interpersonal Violence, 5,* 435–448.

Rosen, R. C., & Beck, J. G. (1988). *Patterns of sexual arousal: Psychophysiological processes and clinical applications.* New York: Guilford Press.

Rosen, R. C., Phillips, N. A., Gendrano, N. C. III, & Ferguson, D. M. (1999). Oral phentolamine and female sexual arousal disorder: A pilot study. *Journal of Sex and Marital Therapy, 25,* 137–144.

Rosenbaum, T. Y. (2003). Physiotherapy treatment of sexual pain disorders. *Journal of Sex and Marital Therapy, 31,* 329–340.

Rosenblum, J. A. (1974). Human sexuality and the cerebral cortex. *Diseases of the Nervous System, 35,* 268–271.

Rösler, A., & Witztum, E. (2000). Pharmacotherapy of paraphilias in the next millennium. *Behavioral Sciences and the Law, 18,* 43–56.

Rowland, D., Perelman, M., Althof, S., Barada, J., McCullough, A., Bull, S., Jamieson, C., & Ho, K. (2004). Self-reported premature ejaculation and aspects of sexual functioning and satisfaction. *Journal of Sexual Medicine, 1,* 225–232.

Rubio-Aurioles, E., Lopez, M., Lipezker, M., Lara, C., Ramirez, A., Rampazzo, C., Hurtado de Mendoza, M. T., Lowrey, F., Loehr, L. A., & Lammers, P. (2002). Phentolamine mesylate in postmenopausal women with female sexual arousal disorder: A psychophysiological study. *Journal of Sex and Marital Therapy, 28*(Suppl. 1), 205–215.

Sadowski, H., & Gaffney, B. (1998). Gender identity disorder, depression, and suicidal risk. In D. DiCeglie (Ed.), *A stranger in my own body: Atypical gender identity development and mental health* (pp. 126–136). London: Karnac Books.

Saenz de Tejada, I., Angulo, J., Cellek, S., Gonzalez-Cadavid, N., Heaton, J., Pickard, R., & Simonsen, U. (2004). Physiology of erectile function. *Journal of Sexual Medicine, 1,* 254–265.

Sandfort, T. G., & de Keizer, M. (2001). Sexual problems in gay men: An overview of empirical research. *Annual Review of Sex Research, 12,* 93–120.

Santoro, N., Torrens, J., Crawford, S., Allsworth, J. E., Finkelstein, J. S., Gold, E. B., Korenman, S., Lasley, W. L., Luborsky, J. L., McConnell, D., Sowers, M. F., & Weiss, G. (2005). Correlates of circulating androgens in mid-life women: The study of women's health across the nation. *Journal of Clinical Endocrinology and Metabolism, 90,* 4836–4845.

Saunders, E., Awad, G. A., & White, G. (1986). Male adolescent sexual offenders: The offender and the offense. *Canadian Journal of Psychiatry, 31,* 542–549.

Schaefer, L. C., & Wheeler, C. C. (2004). Guilt in cross gender identity conditions: Presentations and treatment. *Journal of Gay and Lesbian Psychotherapy, 8,* 117–127.

Schiavi, R. C. (1999). *Aging and male sexuality.* Cambridge, England: Cambridge University Press.

Schiavi, R. C., Derogatis, L. R., Kuriansky, J., O'Connor, D., & Sharpe, L. (1979). The assessment of sexual function and marital interaction. *Journal of Sex and Marital Therapy, 5,* 169–224.

Schnarch, D. (2000). Desire problems: A systemic perspective. In S. R. Leiblum & R. C. Rosen (Eds.), *Principles and practice of sex therapy* (pp. 17–56). New York: Guilford Press.

Schouten, P. G. W., & Simon, W. T. (1992). Validity of phallometric measures with sex offenders: Comments on the Quinsey, Laws, and Hall debate. *Journal of Consulting and Clinical Psychology, 60,* 812–814.

Schover, L. R., & LoPiccolo, J. (1982). Treatment effectiveness for dysfunctions of sexual desire. *Journal of Sex and Marital Therapy, 8,* 179–197.

Schreiner-Engel, P., & Schiavi, R. C. (1986). Lifetime psychopathology in individuals with low sexual desire. *Journal of Nervous and Mental Disorders, 174,* 646–651.

Schroder, M., Mell, L. K., Hurteau, J. A., Collins, Y. C., Rotmensch, J., Waggoner, S. E., Yamada, S. D., Small, W. Jr., & Mundt, A. J. (2005). Clitoral therapy device for treatment of sexual dysfunction in irradiated cervical cancer patients. *International Journal of Radiation Oncology Biology, and Physics, 61,* 1078–1086.

Scott, G. G. (1983). *Dominant women, submissive men.* New York: Praeger.

Segraves, R. T. (1987). Treatment of early ejaculation with lorazepam. *American Journal of Psychiatry, 144,* 1240.

Segraves, R. T. (1999). Case report, two additional uses for sildenafil in psychiatric patients. *Journal of Sex and Marital Therapy, 25,* 265–266.

Segraves, R. T., Clayton, A., Croft, H., Wolf, A., & Warnock, J. (2004). Bupropion sustained release for the treatment of hypoactive sexual desire disorder in premenopausal women. *Journal of Clinical Psychopharmacology, 24,* 339–342.

Segraves, K. B., & Segraves, R. T. (1991). Hypoactive sexual desire disorder: Prevalence and comorbidity in 906 subjects. *Journal of Sex and Marital Therapy, 17,* 55–58.

Seidman, S. N. (2003). Testosterone deficiency and mood in aging men: Pathogenic and therapeutic interactions. *Journal of Clinical Psychiatry, 4,* 14–20.

Seil, D. (2004). The diagnosis and treatment of transgendered patients. *Journal of Gay and Lesbian Psychotherapy, 8,* 99–116.

Semans, J. H. (1956). Premature ejaculation. *Southern Medical Journal, 49,* 353–358.

Seto, M. C. (2001). The value of phallometry in the assessment of male sex offenders. *Journal of Forensic Psychology Practice, 1,* 65–75.

Seto, M. C., & Kuban, M. (1996). Criterion-related validity of a phallometric test for paraphilic rape and sadism. *Behaviour Research and Therapy, 34,* 175–183.

Seto, M. C., & Lalumiere, M. L. (2001). A brief screening scale to identify pedophilic interests among child molesters. *Sexual Abuse: A Journal of Research and Treatment, 13,* 15–25.

Shabsigh, R. (2005). Testosterone therapy in erectile dysfunction and hypogonadism. *Journal of Sexual Medicine, 2,* 785–792.

Sherwin, B. B., & Gelfand, M. M. (1987). The role of androgen in the maintenance of sexual functioning in oophorectomized women. *Psychosomatic Medicine, 49,* 397–409.

Shifren, J. L., Braunstein, G. D., Simon, J. A., Casson, P. R., Buster, J. E., Redmond, G. P., Burki, R. E., Ginsburg, E. S., Rosen, R. C., Leiblum, S. R., Caramelli, K. E., & Mazer, N. A. (2000). Transdermal testosterone treatment in women with impaired sexual function after oophorectomy. *New England Journal of Medicine, 343,* 682–688.

Simon, J., Braunstein, G., Nachtigall, L., Utian, W., Katz, M., Miller, S., Waldbaum, A., Bouchard, C., Derzko, C., Buch, A., Rodenberg, C., Lucas, J., & Davis, S. (2005). Testosterone patch increases sexual activity and desire in surgically menopausal women with hypoactive sexual desire disorder. *Journal of Clinical Endocrinology and Metabolism, 90,* 5226–5233.

Sjogren Fugl-Meyer, K., & Fugl-Meyer, A. R. (2002). Sexual disabilities are not singularities. *International Journal of Impotence Research, 14,* 487–493.

Smukler, A. J., & Schiebel, D. (1975). Personality characteristics of exhibitionists. *Diseases of the Nervous System, 36,* 600–603.

Spengler, A. (1977). Manifest sadomasochism of males: Results of an empirical study. *Archives of Sexual Behavior, 6,* 441–456.

Spiess, W. F., Geer, J. H., & O'Donohue, W. T. (1984). Premature ejaculation: Investigation of factors in ejaculatory latency. *Journal of Abnormal Psychology, 93,* 242–245.

Stanford, J. L., Feng, Z., Hamilton, A. S., Gilliland, F. D., Stephenson, R. A., Eley, J. W., Albertson, P. C., Harlan, L. C., & Potosky, A. L. (2000). Urinary and sexual function after radical prostatectomy for clinically localized prostate cancer: The prostate cancer outcomes study. *Journal of the American Medical Association, 283,* 354–360.

Stekel, W. (1923). Der Fetischismus dargestellt für Ärzte und Kriminalogen. *Störungen des Trieb- und Affektlebens* (die parapathischen Erkrankungen). Berlin: Urban & Schwarzenberg.

Strassberg, D. S., de Gouveia Brazao, C. A., Rowland, D. L., Tan, P., & Slob, A. K. (1999). Clomipramine in the treatment of rapid (premature) ejaculation. *Journal of Sex and Marital Therapy, 25,* 89–101.

Strassberg, D. S., Kelly, M. P., Carroll, C., & Kircher, J. C. (1987). The psychophysiological nature of premature ejaculation. *Archives of Sexual Behavior, 16,* 327–336.

Symonds, T., Roblin, D., Hart, K., & Althof, S. (2003). How does premature ejaculation impact a man's life? *Journal of Sex and Marital Therapy, 29,* 361–370.

Tang, W., Ma, L., Zhao, L., Liu, Y., & Chen, Z. (2004). Clinical efficacy of Viagra with behavior therapy against premature ejaculation. *Zhonghua Nan Ke Xue, 10,* 366–370.

Tarter, R. E., Hegadus, A. M., Alterman, A. I., & Katz-Garris, L. (1983). Cognitive capacities of juvenile, violent, nonviolent, and sexual offenders. *Journal of Nervous and Mental Disease, 171,* 564–567.

Taylor, F. H. (1947). Observations on some cases of exhibitionism. *Journal of Mental Science, 93,* 631–638.

Templeman, T. L., & Stinnett, R. D. (1991). Patterns of sexual arousal and history in a "normal" sample of young men. *Archives of Sexual Behavior, 20,* 137–150.

Tiefer, L. (2001). A new view of women's sexual problems: Why new? Why now? *Journal of Sex Research, 38,* 89–96.

Tiefer, L. (2002). Sexual behaviour and its medicalisation. Many (especially economic) forces promote medicalisation. *British Medical Journal, 325,* 45.

Trudel, G., Landry, L., & Larose, Y. (1997). Low sexual desire: The role of anxiety, depression and marital adjustment. *Sexual and Marital Therapy, 12,* 95–99.

Trudel, G., Marchand, A., Ravart, M., Aubin, S., Turgeon, L., & Fortier, P. (2001). The effect of a cognitive behavioral group treatment program on hypoactive sexual desire in women. *Sexual and Relationship Therapy, 16,* 145–164.

Trudel, G., & Proulx, S. (1987). Treatment of premature ejaculation by bibliotherapy: An experimental study. *Sex & Marital Therapy, 2,* 163–167.

Tworoger, S. S., Missmer, S. A., Barbieri, R. L., Willett, W. C., Colditz, G. A., & Hankinson, R. G. (2005). Plasma sex hormone concentrations and subsequent risk of breast cancer among women using postmenopausal hormones. *Journal of the National Cancer Institute, 97,* 595–602.

Verhulst, J., & Heiman, J. (1988). A systems perspective on sexual desire. In S. Leiblum & R. Rosen (Eds.), *Sexual desire disorders* (pp. 243–270). New York: Guilford Press.

Waldinger, M. D. (2002). The neurobiological approach to early ejaculation. *Journal of Urology, 168,* 2359–2367.

Waldinger, M. D. (2005). Male ejaculation and orgasmic disorders. In R. Balon & R. T. Segraves (Eds.), *Handbook of sexual dysfunction* (pp. 215–248). Boca Raton, FL: Taylor & Francis.

Waldinger, M. D., Rietschel, M., Nothen, M. M., Hengeveld, M. W., & Olivier, B. (1998). Familial occurrence of primary premature ejaculation. *Psychiatric Genetics, 8,* 37–40.

Wallen, K. (2005). Hormonal influences on sexually differentiated behavior in nonhuman primates. *Frontiers in Neuroendocrinology, 26,* 7–26.

Weijmar Schultz, W. C. M., & Van de Wiel, H. B. M. (2005). Vaginismus. In R. Balon & R. T. Segraves (Eds.), *Handbook of sexual dysfunction* (pp. 43–65). Boca Raton, FL: Taylor & Francis.

Weinberg, T., & Kamel, W. L. (Eds.). (1983). *S and M: Studies in sadomasochism.* Buffalo, NY: Prometheus.

Weinberg, T. S., Williams, C. J., & Moser, C. (1984). The social constituents of sadomasochism. *Social Problems, 31,* 379–389.

Williams, W. (1984). Secondary early ejaculation. *Australian New Zealand Journal of Psychiatry, 18,* 333.

Wilson, G. (1978). *The secrets of sexual fantasy.* London: Dent.

Wincze, J. P., Bansal, S., & Malamud, M. (1986). Effects of medroxyprogesterone acetate on subjective arousal, arousal to erotic stimulation, and nocturnal penile tumescence in male sex offenders. *Archives of Sexual Behavior, 15,* 293–305.

Wylie, K., & MacInnes, I. (2005). Erectile dysfunction. In R. Balon & R. T. Segraves (Eds.), *Handbook of sexual dysfunction* (pp. 155–191). Boca Raton, FL: Taylor & Francis.

Xin, Z. C., Choi, Y. D., Lee, S. H., & Choi, H. K. (1997). Efficacy of a topical agent SS-cream in the treatment of premature ejaculation: Preliminary clinical studies. *Yonsei Medical Journal, 38,* 91–95.

Zavitzianos, G. (1971). Fetishism and exhibitionism in the female and their relationship to psychopathology and kleptomania. *International Journal of Psycho-Analysis, 52,* 297–305.

Zilbergeld, B. (1978). *Male sexuality.* Toronto, Canada: Bantam.

Zucker, K. J., & Blanchard, R. (1997). Transvestic fetishism: Psychopathology and theory. In D. R. Laws & W. O'Donohue (Eds.), *Sexual deviance: Theory, assessment, and treatment* (pp. 253–279). New York: Guilford Press.

Zucker, K. J., & Bradley, S. J. (1995). *Gender identity disorder and psychosexual problems in children and adolescents.* New York: Guilford Press.

CHAPTER 15

Eating Disorders

J. KEVIN THOMPSON, MEGAN ROEHRIG, AND BILL N. KINDER

DESCRIPTION OF THE DISORDERS

ating disorders are some of the most common and debilitative psychological disorders, especially for young girls and women (Striegel-Moore & Smolak, 2001; Thompson & Smolak, 2001). The medical and psychological complications of eating dysfunction are numerous and lead it to have the highest mortality rate of any psychiatric disorder (Fairburn, Cooper, Doll, Norman, & O'Conner, 2000). Research efforts focused on understanding eating disorders have increased dramatically in recent years. In this chapter, we report on the latest diagnostic, assessment, and etiological developments.

There are four categories of eating disorders currently listed in the fourth edition of the *Diagnostic and Statistical Manual of Mental Disorders* (*DSM-IV-TR;* American Psychiatric Association [APA], 2000): anorexia nervosa, bulimia nervosa, eating disorder not otherwise specified, and binge-eating disorder. Binge-eating disorder is included in an appendix of "criteria sets and axes provided for further study"; however, it is reviewed in this chapter for two reasons: It will likely be included as a formal eating disorder category in the next revision of the *DSM,* and the disorder has been the subject of intense empirical study in recent years.

ANOREXIA NERVOSA

Any description of anorexia nervosa should begin with the most obvious and critical feature of the disorder, which is the weight status of the individual. The *DSM-IV-TR* quantifies this criterion as a body weight of "85% of that expected"(APA, 2000, p. 583). Reference to average weight charts for adults or expected weight gain during growth periods (pediatric charts) is often used to assist in this assessment. Typically, individuals who present with the clinical picture of anorexia nervosa have a much lower body weight than 85% of that expected. A clinical picture of emaciation or cachexia is often easily observable, and such malnourishment in the absence of any medical or physiological disturbance directs the clinician to a consideration of a diagnosis of anorexia nervosa. Walsh and Garner (1997) also emphasize that a rigid adherence to the weight criterion may not be advisable if the patient meets all other criteria for diagnosis, yet misses the weight cutoff (i.e., weighing 90% of that expected).

Individuals with this disorder also usually report an extreme dissatisfaction or disparagement of their appearance, insisting that they are not underweight and expressing a desire to maintain their current weight status or even lose more weight. Such a disturbance of the body image may manifest in subjective dissatisfaction, behavioral avoidance (for instance, of evaluating oneself in a mirror or attending social functions), disturbed cognitions ("Everyone notices my fat stomach"), and, possibly, perceptual overestimation of body size (Thompson, Heinberg, Altabe, & Tantleff-Dunn, 1999). An intense fear of gaining weight, often referred to as a "pursuit of thinness," is also very characteristic and may be indicated by symptoms such as avoidance of highly caloric foods, excessive exercise, and presence of purgative activities (laxative use, diuretics, self-induced vomiting). Purgative activities are commonly thought to be confined to the diagnosis of bulimia nervosa; however, the DSM-IV-TR notes that such behaviors may occur during the time period when an individual meets the weight criteria of anorexia nervosa. Such individuals should receive the subtype specification of *binge-eating/purging type* (APA, 2000, p. 585). Individuals who maintain their low weight status without reliance on purgative methods are classified as *restricting* subtype.

Because of the intense biological disruption engendered by excessive weight loss and caloric restriction, many individuals with anorexia nervosa experience a severe disruption of normal menstrual cycle functioning. The DSM-IV-TR requires absence of three consecutive menstrual periods for a diagnosis of anorexia nervosa; however, this criterion is perhaps the most problematic and controversial of the four criteria. Menstrual functioning is sometimes disrupted and irregular with anorexia nervosa, but amenorrhea does not eventuate. In addition, the criterion is not appropriate or applicable to men. However, the *International Classification of Diseases* (World Health Organization, 1992) criteria include evidence of testosterone function alterations in men by indications of loss of sexual potency or interest. For these reasons, many researchers do not require that patients meet this criterion for inclusion in research studies, and its relevance for clinical psychotherapy and/or pharmacological management is debatable.

BULIMIA NERVOSA

This disorder is most easily contrasted with anorexia nervosa in terms of the amount of food consumed. Whereas individuals with anorexia nervosa greatly restrict intake and, even in the case of the binge-purge subtype, typically do not consume excessively large quantities of food, individuals with bulimia nervosa may eat vast quantities of food. The food is normally eaten in a short period of time with psychological concomitants of a sense of distress and a feeling of lack of control over the binging behavior. There is often a sense that once eating begins, it is impossible to stop until finished. Most often, such binges are followed by severe self-disparagement and a sense that something must be done to undo the potential damage of ingesting such a large number of calories. Therefore, commonly, a variety of purgative methods is employed, including self-induced vomiting, laxatives, diuretics, enemas, purgative-inducing medications, fasting, and excessive exercise.

As with anorexia nervosa, there are two subtypes; in the case of bulimia nervosa, the categories are *purging* type and *nonpurging* type. The distinction is in the type of compensatory procedure that the individual uses to "handle" excessive food intake so that excessive calories are not stored as fat and lead to weight gain. In the purging type, the individual self-induces vomiting, uses diuretics or laxatives, or performs enemas. In the nonpurging type, other types of compensatory, yet nonpurging, behaviors are used, such as fasting or excessive exercise. Body image disturbance is also evident in individuals with bulimia nervosa, and body shape and weight are inextricably linked with their self-esteem.

BINGE-EATING DISORDER

This disorder was recently added to the *DSM*, yet was assigned to a section for disorders in need of further study. It has features in common with bulimia nervosa— the description of the criterion for recurrent binge eating is identical to that for bulimia nervosa. However, the frequency requirement is different—for a diagnosis of bulimia nervosa, the binge eating occurs at least twice a week for 3 months, but for binge-eating disorder, the criterion is 2 days a week for 6 months. Of greater importance is the essential defining feature that distinguishes between the two eating disorders: to be diagnosed with binge-eating disorder, the individual does not use any compensatory behaviors (purging or nonpurging) as a consequence of binging. In addition, there is no body image disturbance criterion for binge-eating disorder, whereas there is for bulimia nervosa. A fourth difference between the two disorders is the chance to rate the occurrence of five different binge-associated features for binge-eating disorder, with three of the options required for diagnosis.

EATING DISORDER NOT OTHERWISE SPECIFIED (EDNOS)

The EDNOS category is used typically for cases in which one or more of the required criteria are not met, yet there is evidence that the individual's level of eating disturbance meets a degree of severity that warrants clinical attention. Examples might be someone who engages in compensatory behaviors, yet the "binge" consists of small amounts of food that would not meet the *DSM-IV* definition of "an amount of food that is definitely larger than most people would eat during a similar period of time and under similar circumstances" (APA, 2000, p. 594). Another example might be an individual who chews and spits out, but does not swallow, large amounts of food. The case study below explores some such behaviors.

Case Study

Case Identification and Presenting Complaints

Ms. T. was a 17-year-old White college freshman who was referred to therapy by her father. At the time of initial assessment she weighed 85 pounds, distributed on a 5'5" frame. She reported no problem with binge eating or self-induced vomiting; however, she used laxatives occasionally (once a week) to relieve a "feeling of constipation." She exercised approximately 1 hour each

(continued)

day, reported a fear of obesity, and weighed herself several times a day. Her meals consisted primarily of vegetables, fruits, and cottage cheese.

History

She reported that her problem began approximately 4 years previously, when her sister left home to get married. At this time she began to lose weight and was hospitalized. Treatment with a behavior modification program followed, and she gained to within a normal weight range for her age. However, after discharge, she gradually began to lose weight again. Shortly thereafter, she saw a psychiatrist, who prescribed Tagamet for stomach problems, a medication she continued to take. She had most recently been seen by her school counselor. Her weight had fluctuated from 80 to 100 pounds during the 4 years from onset of dieting to the current assessment.

She reported that her mother was quiet, dependent, prone to stomach problems, and currently seeing a psychiatrist. She described a poor relationship with her father, noting a disdain for his drinking and relating an inability to talk with him. She reported a history of family conflicts about her weight. When Ms. T. was 10, her father stated that she was "too fat" and required her mother to seek medical assistance for her problems. She reported that family arguments often took place at the dinner table, causing her to lose her appetite. Recently, her father almost denied her permission to enter college because of her weight status. She stated that her desire to maintain weight following earlier treatment was challenged by her father, who insisted that she gain weight. She maintained that this attitude contributed to her continued weight loss. She reported considerable difficulty expressing feelings to others and noted that she felt totally dependent on her parents.

She also noted considerable stress at school, despite having no difficulty with academics. At her parents urging, she joined a sorority but now had reservations about the decision. She said that sorority-mates constantly commented on her weight, which disturbed her, but she failed to reply, not knowing how to handle the situation. She also reported dissatisfaction with the sorority's focus on appearance and social demands. She reported that a commonality between home and school life was a lack of independence, stating "someone is always telling me what to do." In addition, she reported that her new friends, in repeating an old theme of focusing on her weight, were trying to change her in a manner similar to that of her father. She indicated increasing feelings of confusion, withdrawal, depression, and "being out of control" (Thompson & Williams, 1987, pp. 246–247).

Assessment

Assessment included a focus on the initial interview and additional measures to document the presence of *DSM* criteria and associated features of eating disturbance. The MMPI, Eating Attitudes Test, Eating Disorder Inventory, and Zung Depression Inventory were administered. Additionally, the patient self-monitored eating behaviors and thoughts/emotions associated with such behaviors. She met the weight criteria for anorexia nervosa and also met the other required symptoms for diagnosis. She scored in the moderately depressed range on the Zung inventory, but in the subclinical range on all scales of the MMPI. Her body dissatisfaction scores on a subscale of the Eating Disorder Inventory indicated moderate levels of body dissatisfaction with weight-relevant body sites (waist, hips, thighs). Self-monitoring corroborated self-report in that interpersonal situations and mealtimes were associated with considerable emotional distress and disturbed food-related cognitions.

This case illustrates several of the formative experiences and related features that are often present in individuals with an eating disorder. Ms. T.'s focus on appearance apparently began at an early age, most likely fostered by her father's feeling that she needed to lose weight. Her feelings of dependency and lack of control may have been fostered by the decision to take her to a variety of physicians because of her inability to control her weight. She felt an early lack of acceptance by her family because of her overweight status. Eating, or not eating (which occurred later) became the central focus of her family interactions and a defining feature of her personality. Mealtimes were associated with stress and family discord, leading to emotional upset and stomach problems, producing a conditioned aversion to meals and food. At an early age, she learned to evaluate herself in terms of body size and appearance. Interpersonal interactions, with family and peers, often centered on food and appearance, rather than a broader array of social and interpersonal topics. After losing a substantial amount of weight, in fact, reaching an anorexic weight status, it became increasingly difficult to eat reasonable amounts of food due to a feeling of fullness and constipation. Such feelings led to greater food avoidance and excessive exercise.

EPIDEMIOLOGY

Considerable effort has gone into the analysis of issues related to the epidemiology of eating disorders. Not only is there some debate as to the actual prevalence of the well-established eating disorders of anorexia nervosa and bulimia nervosa, but there are minimal data on the prevalence of binge-eating disorder. Additionally, researchers have begun to address, yet not fully determine, whether eating disorders are increasing in prevalence. Also, research on the prevalence of eating disorders among children and adolescents offers unique challenges.

The *DSM-IV-TR* puts the prevalence rate for anorexia nervosa at approximately 0.5% and between 1% and 3% for bulimia nervosa (APA, 2000). These numbers generally have been supported by research studies and other reviews of prevalence and incidence statistics (Hoek & Van Hoeken, 2003; Lucas, Beard, O'Fallon, & Kurland, 1988; Nielson, 2001; Pawluck & Gorey, 1998; Walters & Kendler, 1995; Williamson, Zucker, Martin, & Smeets, 2001). However, there is some variability across studies and populations. A recent review of epidemiological studies published between 2003 and 2005 reported that point prevalence rates of anorexia nervosa in females ranged from 0 to 1.5, and lifetime prevalence rates ranged from 0.6 to 4.0; whereas point prevalence rates of bulimia nervosa in females ranged from 0.37 to 3.0, and lifetime prevalence ranged from 1.2 to 5.9 (Striegel-Moore, Franko, & Ach, in press). The data for binge-eating disorder are far less conclusive, and it appears that the incidence may be between 1% and 3% (Hoek & Van Hoeken, 2003; Striegel-Moore et al., 2000; Varnado et al., 1997). Striegel-Moore and colleagues (in press) reported point prevalence rates for binge-eating disorder ranged from 0.4 to 0.7, with life-time prevalence rates ranging between 0.6 and 2.7, although these rates may be an underestimate of true prevalence rates because the samples utilized consisted of young adults.

Gender differences for anorexia nervosa and bulimia nervosa are prominent (Jacobi, Hayward, de Zwann, Kraemer, & Agras, 2004), and full-syndrome anorexia nervosa and bulimia nervosa are rare in males (Striegel-Moore et al., in press). Generally, women outnumber men by a 10-to-1 ratio; however, this ratio may be significantly less for anorexia nervosa and bulimia nervosa at the younger ages and for all ages with reference to binge-eating disorder (Nielson, 2001). Pawluck and Gorey (1998) found that the rate for females aged 13 to 19 was five times greater than that for other age groups, and Hoek and Van Hoeken (2003) concluded that, although eating disorders are relatively rare in the general population, they are quite common in adolescent girls and young women.

Statistics for children and adolescents indicate that the rate for anorexia nervosa and bulimia nervosa may be a bit lower than that found for adults (Thompson & Smolak, 2001), and the rate of binge-eating disorder much lower, perhaps around 1% (Rosenvinge, Sundgot-Borgen, & Boerresen, 1999). A review of recent epide-miological studies suggests that rates of anorexia nervosa do not appear to be in-creasing in adolescents; however, risk for bulimia nervosa may now be highest in 10- to 19-year-olds (Bryant-Waugh, in press).

Interestingly, many prevalence rate studies do not include the category of eating disorder not otherwise specified, which may add another 50% of possible clinically relevant treatment cases (Nicholls, Chater, & Lask, 2000). These cases, which may also be referred to as "partial syndrome" or "subthreshold" eating disorders, may dramatically increase numbers of individuals considered "eating disturbed." For instance, Shisslak, Crago, and Estes (1995), in a review of studies of adolescents, found a prevalence rate of partial syndrome that ranged from 1.78% to 13.3%. In one of the most comprehensive examinations of prevalence, adolescent girls were followed for more than 10 years and were assessed periodically for the presence of eating disorders (Lewinsohn, 2001). By age 24, 1.4% had anorexia nervosa and 2.8% had bulimia nervosa. Additionally, 4.4% met criteria for a partial syndrome.

CLINICAL PICTURE

The clinical presentation of someone with an eating disorder may manifest in many ways, especially given the recent addition of binge-eating disorder to the research and clinical arena. The "classic" case of the restricting anorexic who is re-sistant to treatment and has little insight into her "distorted" body image is one vignette often sensationalized by media, yet this might be a good place to begin, for it offers a distinct clinical picture that allows for a clear differentiation with bulimia nervosa and binge-eating disorder. Such individuals typically have an early onset, possibly in the late adolescent years, and have never had a normal menstrual cycle or even have primary amenorrhea (never having experienced a menstrual period). The food restriction is severe, and these individuals may consume significantly less than 1,000 calories a day, for an extended period of time. Weight is significantly below average, perhaps at a level of 50% to 60% of expected. Treatment is met with much resistance and even subterfuge, such as hiding ankle weights or other heavy objects under clothing to increase observed weight during weighings. The denial of illness that characterizes the lack of insight includes either a perceptual inability or psychological denial of the emaciated body. Perfectionistic and obsessive-compulsive features are paramount and may consist of excessive and obligatory exercise patterns, rigid adherence to daily routines, and food hoarding. In fact, a preoccupation with food may include such activities as preparing food for others and conversations that center on food. This seemingly paradoxical behavior (for someone who doesn't eat and is afraid of weight gain) might be explained by the central control issue that food is for a patient with an eating disorder: what better way to illustrate one's control of eating than by preparing food for others and organizing one's life around food, yet not eating it?

This classic picture of the restrictor subtype can be contrasted with a similar, perhaps stereotypical, view of the individual with bulimia nervosa. Such an individual is usually of normal or average weight, or only slightly overweight, yet is extremely distressed by her weight status. Food restriction may have been attempted and, in fact, may have been successful at some point, but now the individual is in a cycle of overeating and compensating, either via purging or non-purging means. Overeating, according to the *DSM-IV* definition, is definitely a binge: studies indicate that some individuals may consume over 10,000 calories a day. Binging creates a physical sensation of discomfort, along with a psychological state of extreme anxiety and depression. Getting rid of the food is essential to restore some level of equilibrium. This strategy is generally followed by temporary relief, the return of hunger (due to the lack of satiety), and another attempt at restriction to reduce body weight. Hunger and perhaps unrealistic restriction of food intake set the stage for an eventual failure—that is, eating a forbidden food or too much of some food, leading to another binge. Interpreting any variation from planned restriction a failure, many patients consider even small intakes of forbidden foods a violation of their planned abstinence, and feel the relief that they can now eat all they want, having already decided that compensatory activities will be necessary (additionally, overeating with significant water intake, makes self-induced vomiting easier to achieve).

The typical individual with bulimia nervosa does not evidence resistance to treatment, denial, and lack of insight into her problem that is often found with the restricting anorexic. Such individuals are very disturbed by the food intake patterns that they have developed, and depression is a common comorbid feature. In addition, there exists a great deal of shame and guilt associated with the depression. In contrast to anorexics' subjective sense that they are in control and would prefer to be left alone, bulimics prototypically feel out of control and in desperate need of someone to help them handle their problem.

These general vignettes are oversimplifications of the full range of manifestations of individuals with eating disorders. Perhaps 30% to 40% of the individuals who meet the diagnosis of anorexia nervosa also binge and purge, necessitating an assignment to the binge-eating/purging type. These patients may be at an "anorexic" weight, but their distress, depression, and feeling out of control are more like that of the bulimic case described earlier than the restrictor anorexic. In fact, except for the weight criterion, the individual would receive assignment to the *DSM* category for bulimia nervosa. Additionally, body image disturbance is a required criterion for both anorexia nervosa and bulimia nervosa, and this core characteristic has been found empirically to exist in both disorders.

The clinical picture of people with binge-eating disorder is very similar to that of people with bulimia nervosa. As noted, the diagnostic criteria are quite similar between the two conditions. There is a difference in the frequency-duration criterion regarding binge eating; however, this does not affect the clinical presentation of binging. An additional list of binge related features is required for binge eating disorder (i.e., feeling embarrassed, disgusted, or depressed regarding the binge); however, these features are also present in individuals with bulimia nervosa. The primary *DSM*-related difference is in the requirement that individuals with binge-eating disorder may not engage in any compensatory behaviors. Therefore, the presence of purging and nonpurging compensation (i.e., vomiting, excessive exercise, laxatives, and so on) indicates the bulimia nervosa diagnosis. There is also no weight criterion for distinguishing bulimia nervosa from binge-eating disorder, so these individuals may present similarly in this regard. Interestingly, evidence suggests that individuals with binge-eating disorder may, on average, be heavier than persons with bulimia nervosa (Johnson & Torgrud, 1996). Perhaps this is a consequence of not engaging in compensatory methods.

COURSE AND PROGNOSIS

Eating disorders have the highest mortality rate of any psychiatric disorder (Fairburn et al., 2000) and also have one of the highest rates of hospitalization and suicidality (Newman et al., 1996). Mortality rates vary but appear to be much higher for individuals with anorexia nervosa. Estimates for anorexia nervosa cluster around 5% to 6% (Agras, 2001; Herzog et al., 2000; Sullivan, 1995), with about half of the deaths attributable to suicide and the rest related to physical complications of the disorder. The rate for bulimia nervosa may be closer to 0.5% to 1% or a bit higher (e.g., Agras, 2001; Nielson, 2001). On the positive side, however, Steinhausen (1995) reviewed the treatment outcome literature from the 1950s to the 1980s and found that about one-third of cases of anorexia nervosa improved, one-fifth had a chronic course, and two-fifths recovered. Ten-year follow-up studies also indicate that approximately 60% of individuals with bulimia nervosa are in full or partial remission (Herzog et al., 1999). Furthermore, a 12-year, longitudinal study of bulimia nervosa patients of the purging subtype found that, at the 12-year follow-up assessment, 70.1% did not meet *DSM* criteria for an eating disorder, 13.2% met *DSM* criteria for EDNOS, 10.1% continued with the diagnosis of bulimia nervosa with purging, and 2% of the sample had died (Fichter & Quadflieg, 2004).

Much less is known about the course of binge-eating disorder. Fairburn, Cooper, Doll, Norman, and O'Connor (2000) followed two cohorts of individuals with either bulimia nervosa or binge-eating disorder prospectively for a period of 5 years. At follow-up, 9% of the original binge-eating disorder sample still had the disorder, and 15% of the original bulimia nervosa group continued to meet criteria for bulimia nervosa. Some of the individuals in the initial groups had developed a different eating disorder at the time of the follow-up. For instance, 7% of the original bulimia nervosa sample met criteria for binge-eating disorder, and 32% met EDNOS criteria. For the binge-eating sample, at 5-year follow-up, 12% met EDNOS criteria, and 3% had bulimia nervosa.

Another interesting aspect of the course of eating disorders is the finding that perhaps 25% to 30% of individuals who seek treatment for bulimia nervosa report a previous history of anorexia nervosa (Klump, Kaye, & Strober, 2001). Herzog and colleagues, in a 7.5-year prospective study, found that 16% of women with restricting anorexia nervosa developed bulimia nervosa, and 7% of women with bulimia nervosa developed anorexia nervosa (Herzog et al., 1999). Tozzi et al. (2005) examined this phenomenon in a multisite sample of patients with eating disorders who had "crossed over" to another eating disorder diagnosis—specifically, anorexia nervosa to bulimia nervosa or bulimia nervosa to anorexia nervosa—and found that the changes in symptoms had occurred by the fifth year of illness in the vast majority of cases. Such findings question the temporal stability of the diagnostic categories, as well as whether a categorical or dimensional model best characterizes eating disturbance (Anderson & Williamson, 2002; Herzog & Delinsky, 2001).

It will be important to further evaluate the course for individuals with eating disorders in future studies. Many individuals with binge-eating disorder are also obese; therefore, morbidity and mortality rates might be expected to be higher than in the general population. Excessive weight is associated with a multitude of physical complications (Pomeroy, 1996); such issues plus the disordered eating patterns indicate that individuals with binge-eating disorder may need to be followed carefully from a clinical perspective.

DIAGNOSTIC CONSIDERATIONS

As with many *DSM* categories, there is continuing debate about the utility and accuracy of the current system. Frequency and duration criteria for the binge eating in bulimia nervosa ("twice a week for 3 months") and binge-eating disorder ("2 days a week for 6 months") are often criticized as being somewhat arbitrary. Striegel-Moore, Wilson, Wilfley, Elder, and Brownell (1998) found that individuals with binge-eating disorder who met all criteria except the ones just mentioned were similar psychologically and behaviorally to individuals who met all criteria. Individuals with bulimia nervosa who binge once a week do not seem to differ substantially from those who meet the binge criterion (Sullivan, Bulik, & Kendler, 1998; Walsh et al., 1997). Defining what constitutes a *binge* is also a problem that has produced some concern among researchers. *DSM* criteria require an "objective" binge, yet many individuals define even small amounts of food as a subjective binge, leading them to engage in compensatory methods. Some researchers suggest that the loss of control or dysphoria associated with the binge should be used in defining it (Beglin & Fairburn, 1992; Telch & Agras, 1996).

The amenorrhea criterion for anorexia nervosa is also problematic, given that it is a physical sequalae of starvation and lower body fat/weight, and not generally seen as a cause of either the psychology or physiology of the disorder. Watson and Andersen (2003) compared patients in treatment who met all *DSM* criteria for anorexia nervosa to those who met all the criteria except amenorrhea and/or were above the 85% expected weight. They found few differences between the two groups in terms of treatment response and duration and concluded that amenorrhea may not be a useful diagnostic criterion. In addition, some women, even at low weights, do not experience menstrual flow disruption (Cachelin & Maher, 1998), and birth control pills can be used to regulate menses in underweight patients (Bulik, Reba, Siega-Riz, & Reichborn-Kjennrud, 2005).

The body image criterion, required for the diagnosis of anorexia nervosa and bulimia nervosa but not binge-eating disorder, is also a topic of dissension among researchers. Research suggests that shape concerns are present in binge-eating disorder, yet there is no criterion related to body image in the *DSM-IV* criteria. Also, wording of the criteria for anorexia nervosa is more extensive than that for bulimia nervosa, despite there being little evidence that distinguishes the types of disturbance between the two eating disorders (Thompson, 1996).

Bulik, Sullivan, and Kendler (2000) also addressed the current classification system problems. They criticized development of the current *DSM* categorization schemes because of the reliance on clinical samples for data evaluation, noting that only a subset of women seek treatment and that referral bias may be a factor. They sought to evaluate a nonbiased sample by using an epidemiological methodology, assessing via interview 2,163 female twins from a population-based registry. Using latent class analysis, they developed an empirically based categorization of eating disorders. Interestingly, they found that a six-class solution fit the data best, with three of the classes resembling the extant categories (anorexia nervosa, bulimia nervosa, binge-eating disorder). However, they also found potential separate classifications—one based on "distorted eating attitudes without low body weight" and two classes with "low weight without the psychological features of eating disorders" (Bulik et al., 2000, p. 886).

Taxometric analysis, which statistically tests whether symptoms are best described as categorical or dimensional, has recently been applied to eating disorders in a series of preliminary studies. Williamson, Gleaves, and Stewart (2005) reviewed these studies and suggest that these preliminary taxometric studies indicate that neither the categorical nor the dimensional model fully captures the range of eating-disordered symptomatology. Rather, binge eating appears to be qualitatively different from normal overeating, whereas restriction appears to occur on a continuum from anorexia nervosa restricting subtype to normalcy.

DUAL DIAGNOSIS

Another important issue with respect to diagnostic considerations is the possible co-occurrence of other Axis I disorders or Axis II personality disorders. A variety of disorders are comorbid with anorexia nervosa. Depression meeting *DSM* criteria may be present in one-third of cases, and lifetime diagnosis of major depression may reach 60% (Agras, 2001). Symptoms of depression contemporaneous with a diagnosis of anorexia nervosa may be present in an even higher percentage of cases (Williamson et al., 2001). Anxiety disorders—particularly obsessive-compulsive disorder and social phobia—also commonly occur in individuals with anorexia nervosa, with lifetime prevalence data ranging from 20% to 65% (Kaye et al., 2004; Williamson et al., 2001; Wonderlich & Mitchell, 1997). Onset of the anxiety disorder typically occurs in childhood and precedes the development of the eating disorder (Kaye et al., 2004). A secondary diagnosis of personality disorder may approach 50% (Agras, 2001), with such disorders as obsessive-compulsive personality disorder being the most common in the anorexia nervosa restricting subtype and borderline personality disorder being the most common in the anorexia nervosa binge/purge subtype (Sansone, Levitt, & Sansone, 2005).

Depression is also commonly a feature of bulimia nervosa. Agras (2001) noted that about 20% of patients with bulimia nervosa may have current major depression and half may develop major depression at some point concurrent with the eating disorder. Patients with bulimia nervosa appear to have comorbid anxiety disorders at a rate similar to those with anorexia nervosa—with the exception of posttraumatic stress disorder, which was found to occur three times more frequently in patients with bulimia nervosa than in patients with anorexia nervosa (Kaye et al., 2004). Half of patients with bulimia nervosa may experience current anxiety disorders and perhaps two-thirds develop such disorders during the course of their eating disorder (Williamson et al., 2001). Estimates of the comorbidity of personality disorders vary widely from study to study; however, Dennis and Sansone (1997) found an average prevalence rate of 34%. In particular, borderline personality disorder has been found to co-occur most with bulimia nervosa, with rates ranging from 2% to 47% (Sansone et al., 2005; Wonderlich, 1995). Substance abuse may be evident in 25% of cases (Agras, 2001).

Binge-eating disorder is also associated with a current diagnosis of Major Depression in approximately 40% to 50% of cases (Williamson et al., 2001). Personality disorders—including histrionic, borderline, and avoidant—may affect one-third or more of cases (Yanovski, Nelson, Dubbert, & Spitzer, 1993). A recent study identified obsessive-compulsive personality disorder as the most common comorbid personality disorder with binge-eating disorder (Sansone et al., 2005). Alcohol abuse may affect one-third of individuals with binge-eating disorder (Eldredge & Agras, 1996).

Methodological issues are of concern when considering comorbidity. The drastic weight loss and compromised biological status of individuals with anorexia nervosa may contribute to the symptomatology of depression. Obsessive-compulsive characteristics may follow, rather than precede, many of the characteristic symptoms of anorexia nervosa (food preoccupation, hoarding, etc.). Axis II diagnoses for individuals with bulimia nervosa are also problematic—borderline is often diagnosed; however, the criterion of impulsivity for borderline notes eating disturbance as one possible facet. This type of conceptual overlap between the two disorders results in potential criterion contamination. Coprevalence of disorders certainly has clinical significance; however, it explains little about specific mechanisms or the directionality of causality. Clearly, future research should address such issues (Westen & Harnden-Fischer, 2001).

PSYCHOLOGICAL AND BIOLOGICAL ASSESSMENT

Any comprehensive assessment of eating disorders includes a broad array of strategies to determine the biological, physiological, behavioral, cognitive, and affective components of the presenting picture. We begin with some of the basic physical assessment methods that should be undertaken, usually by a physician, to understand the biological and physiological aspects of the eating disorder (see also Hill & Pomeroy, 2001; Pomeroy, 1996).

Biological Assessment

An initial physical exam may reveal abnormalities in various body systems, such as the cardiovascular, hematologic, gastrointestinal, renal, endocrine, and skeletal systems, as well as indicate avenues for laboratory testing. Such an exam might yield information concerning the current state of inanition and hydration and might also include dental, dermatological, and gynecological evaluations. A history should also accompany the exam; it might focus on issues such as weight/dieting, menstrual history, chemical abuse and dependency, and any purgative activity (vomiting, diuretics, laxatives, etc.).

Specific medical complications may be associated with dysfunction of different systems. In terms of the potential cardiovascular problems, tachycardia, hypotension, ventricular arrhythmias, and cardiac failure are possibilities. Arrhythmias may develop, often due to electrolyte problems, and these may be fatal. In the case of bulimic patients who use ipecac to induce vomiting, irreversible myocardial damage may eventuate.

Dermatological assessment may reveal carotenodermia (yellowing skin due to excessive carotene intake) and lanugo hair (emergence of soft, light-colored hair in nontraditional places such as the face and back). Russell's sign, which is a distinct change in the skin over the dorsum of the hand caused by trauma during self-induced vomiting, may be present in some cases. Dental assessment may reveal decalcification of the surfaces of the teeth, as well as possible gum problems.

Gastrointestinal evaluation often finds esophageal complications, such as dismotility. Decreased stomach motility may also present, giving substance to patient complaints of increased fullness and abdominal pain, even on consuming small amounts of food. Transit time in the small intestine may be delayed. Rectal impaction is a potential sequelae of these problems; it is exacerbated by a low volume of liquid intake. Pancreatic problems may also emerge, often as a consequence of refeeding. Parotid gland enlargement may occur, possibly related to a high level of binge eating and purging, high carbohydrate intake, malnutrition, and/or alkalosis. Such enlargement is easily visible because the parotid glands are located bilaterally next to the ear.

A variety of laboratory tests may reveal problems in these and other bodily systems. Decrease in bone density is a characteristic dysfunction of the skeletal system. Endocrine problems are multifold. Disruption of the primary hypothalamic pituitary gonadotropin axis leads to problems with gonadal growth and function, hypothalamic pituitary adrenal axis overstimulation leads to heightened cortisol activity, and thyroid function may be severely depressed. Renal function may be altered drastically given the vomiting, diuretic, and laxative abuses that often occur in individuals with eating disorders.

PSYCHOLOGICAL ASSESSMENT

Psychological assessment should be multifaceted, including a focus on discrete eating behaviors, along with a broader evaluation of symptoms necessary for a diagnosis (see Anderson & Paulosky, 2004; Netemeyer & Williamson, 2001; Williamson, 1990; Williamson, Anderson, & Gleaves, 1996). Several questionnaire measures and structured interviews have been developed specifically for the assessment of eating disorders.

The Eating Disorder Examination (EDE) is perhaps the most widely used structured interview. It focuses on the evaluation of symptoms of anorexia nervosa and bulimia nervosa and has been revised 12 times (Fairburn & Cooper, 1993). It yields scores on four subscales: restraint, eating concern, shape concern, and weight concern. The EDE was also found to be appropriate for the assessment of binge eating disorder (Grilo, Masheb, & Williamson, 2001). The Structured Interview for

Anorexia and Bulimic Disorders assesses a range of symptoms related to eating disorders and addresses six factors: body image; general psychopathology; measures to counteract weight gain, fasting, and substance abuse; sexuality and social integration; bulimic symptoms; and atypical binges (Fichter, Herpertz, Quadflieg, & Herpertz-Dahlmann, 1998). The Interview for Diagnosis of Eating Disorders IV was designed to address the specific diagnosis of anorexia nervosa, bulimia nervosa, and binge-eating disorder, along the lines of *DSM-IV* criteria (Kutlesic, Williamson, Gleaves, Barbin, & Murphy-Eberenz, 1998; Williamson, 1990).

In addition, many questionnaire measures can be used for assessing the full clinical picture of one or more eating disorders or for evaluating a more specific component of the disorder. The Eating Disorder Inventory, now in its third edition (EDI-3), is probably the most widely used self-report index; it has 12 nonoverlapping subscales, 3 of which are specific to eating disorders (drive for thinness, body dissatisfaction, and bulimia) while the other 9 are general psychological functioning indices relevant to eating disorders (Garner, 2005). Other questionnaire measures that have received considerable use in research and clinical settings include the Eating Attitudes Test, the Dutch Eating Behavior Questionnaire, the Children's Eating Attitudes Test, the Kid's Eating Disorder Survey, the Bulimia Test-Revised, the Dietary Intent Scale, the Dieting and Body Image Questionnaire, the Children's Eating Behavior Inventory, Mize's Cognitive Distortions Questionnaire, and the Bulimic Cognitive Distortions Scale (see Anderson & Paulosky, 2004; Netemeyer & Williamson, 2001; Williamson, 1990; Williamson et al., 1996, for a detailed examination of these and other measures).

There are also some innovative approaches that should be considered for the measurement of self-report levels of eating symptoms. For instance, Anderson, Williamson, Duchmann, Gleaves, and Barbin (1999) developed the Multiaxial Assessment of Eating Disorders as a brief self-report measure, ideally suited for measuring treatment outcome. It has six subscales: binge eating, purgative behavior, avoidance of forbidden foods, restrictive eating, fear of fatness, and depression. It has excellent psychometric characteristics, including criterion validity (Martin, Williamson, & Thaw, 2000). Stice, Rizvi, and Telch (2000) also describe a 22-item self-report measure, the Eating Disorder Diagnostic Scale (EDDS), which has excellent psychometric characteristics. In particular, Stice et al. found excellent agreement between the diagnoses of eating disorders from structured interviews and those from the EDDS (99% for anorexia nervosa; 96% for bulimia nervosa; 93% for binge-eating disorder).

Self-monitoring of eating-disordered behaviors and associated cognitive and affective components is also an important aspect of assessment (Williamson et al., 2001). Forms might include sections for the recording of amounts and types of food, purgative activity, environmental circumstances, associated cognitions and feelings, and pre- and post-eating behaviors (see Williamson et al., 1996). Test meals have also been advocated for the determination of binge-eating level. For instance, Anderson, Williamson, Johnson, and Grieve (2001) evaluated individuals with binge-eating disorder, obese nonbinge-eaters, and control participants in a laboratory setting designed to increase the potential of binge eating. Individuals with binge-eating disorder ate more and felt more psychologically out of control of their eating behaviors.

Measurement of body image disturbance, a central feature of all eating disorders, should also be a core aspect of assessment plans. Some of the more widely used measures include the Multidimensional Body Self-Relations Questionnaire, the Body Dysmorphic Disorder Examination, the Body Shape Questionnaire, the Body Image Avoidance Questionnaire, and several others developed by Cash and colleagues (www.body-images.com) and Thompson and colleagues (Thompson et al., 1999; Thompson & Gardner, 2002; Thompson, Roehrig, Cafri, & Heinberg, 2005; Thompson & van den Berg, 2002; www.bodyimagedisturbance.org).

ETIOLOGICAL CONSIDERATIONS

FAMILIAL AND GENETIC

Familial approaches typically indict the parents and, possibly, siblings as agents in the onset and perpetuation of eating disorders. From the early days of research on eating disorders, it was noted that families play a central role in understanding eating disorders; families were sometimes kept apart from patients during assessment and treatment (Gull, 1874/1964). Family therapy was one of the earliest and most utilized methods of intervention (Minuchin, Rosman, & Baker, 1978). As noted by Steinberg and Phares (2001), several avenues of family effect have been noted, including level of family functioning, communication patterns within the family, parental modeling of eating patterns, psychological functioning of the parents, and specific feedback (i.e., weight-related criticism or teasing) to the child regarding some aspect of appearance.

Several studies have addressed family functioning. Humphrey (1994) found greater rigidity and dependency for families with a restricting anorexic child when compared to families that had either a child with bulimia nervosa or a child of anorexic weight who also had bulimic characteristics. Horesh et al. (1996) found, in a sample of adolescent girls with binge-eating disorder, significant relations between disturbed eating patterns and parental overprotection and pressures. In a direct comparison of individuals with bulimia nervosa and obese binge eaters, Friedman, Wilfley, Welch, and Kunce (1997) found that troubled family functioning was higher for the bulimia nervosa group. Low levels of family cohesion have been found to be associated with abnormal eating behavior in adolescents (Steinhausen, Gavez, & Metzke, 2005). In terms of parental functioning, there is little evidence that parents of children with eating disorders, when compared to control groups of parents with children who have no eating disorders and parents who have an obese child, have elevated levels of psychopathology (Steinberg & Phares, 2001).

However, mothers with eating disorders may have a negative effect on their children. Strober, Lampert, Morrell, Burroughs, and Jacobs (1990) found that daughters with a mother who has anorexia nervosa were five times more likely to develop an eating disorder than daughters without a mother who suffers from an eating disorder. Stein, Wooley, Cooper, and Fairburn (1994) found that mothers with eating disorders were also more negative toward infants during feeding times than mothers in a control group. Mothers with a current or past history of an eating disorder may have unrealistic expectations about their child's eating behavior and weight, and recent work suggests that these mothers report feeling extremely concerned about the influence their eating disorder has on their child's eating behavior, physical activity, body image, and self-esteem (Mazzeo, Zucker, Gerke, Mitchell, & Bulik, 2005).

The role of parental attitudes, modeling, and direct feedback in the development of eating disorders has received a great deal of attention (Steinberg & Phares, 2001). Such influences may begin early in life, possibly by the time girls are 5 years of age. In a series of studies, 5-year-old girls' attitudes toward dieting and their own weight concerns were found to be related to mothers' weight concerns and dieting behaviors (Abramovitz & Birch, 2000; Carper, Fisher, & Birch, 2000; Davison, Markey, & Birch, 2000). Leung, Schwartzman, and Steiger (1996), using covariance structure modeling, found a direct relationship between family preoccupation with appearance and the child's level of body dissatisfaction and eating problems. Perceived pressure to be thin from the family has been found to be a significant predictor of bulimic behaviors in college women (Young, Clopton, & Bleckley, 2004).

Direct communications may take the form of comments, teasing, or criticism regarding a child's appearance or eating behaviors. Rieves and Cash (1996), in a study of the sources of teasing, identified high levels for mothers (30%), fathers (24%), and siblings (sisters 36%, brothers 79%). Schwartz, Phares, Tantleff-Dunn, and Thompson (1999) asked college students to recall teasing experiences from mothers and fathers, and related the responses to current body image dissatisfaction. For women, but not men, higher levels of teasing were associated with dissatisfaction.

Familial influences on eating disorders have also been examined from a genetic perspective, and it is now generally accepted that a considerable amount of variance in eating disorders is due to a genetic influence. Within the past decade, a great deal of research began to work toward identifying genes or alleles that are associated with eating disorder risk. Researchers have examined genetic influences on full-syndrome eating disorders and have more recently stressed the importance of also examining the role of genetics at the symptom level (Mazzeo, Slof-Op't, van Furth, & Bulik, in press). Bulik, Sullivan, Wade, and Kendler (2000) offer a concise guide to the methodology and findings for the extremely complicated issue of genetic versus environmental contributions to eating disorders. They note that limitations of the existing research, primarily insufficient sample sizes, make it difficult to draw conclusions about the contribution of genetic and environmental factors to anorexia nervosa. However, there is a reasonable database for bulimia nervosa, suggesting that additive genetic effects and unique environmental factors play a role in liability. In their review of twin studies, Klump et al. (2001) concluded that 58% to 76% of the variance in anorexia nervosa was due to genetic factors, and 54% to 83% of the variance in bulimia nervosa was due to genetic factors. They also found that eating-disturbed symptoms were heritable: 32% to 72% of factors such as body dissatisfaction, eating and weight concerns, and weight preoccupation were heritable, as were 46% to 72% of dietary restraint, binge eating, and vomiting.

Recent research suggests several promising genetic pathways at the syndrome level. Serotonin (5-HT) has been implicated in the pathophysiology of eating disorders—particularly for anorexia nervosa—and researchers have examined the role of genes that regulate serotonin as well as those that transport serotonin (Mazzeo et al., in press). Several studies have identified the 5-HT2A receptor gene—specifically, the G-143AA polymorphism in the promoter region—in the etiology of anorexia nervosa (Klump & Gobrogge, 2005). 5-HTTLPR, a serotonin transporter, has also been found to be associated with anorexia nervosa in recent studies and with bulimia nervosa in one study (see Mazzeo et al., in press, for an excellent review). Additionally, promising evidence exists that the serotonin receptor HTR1D and the opiod delta receptor OPRD1 may be associated with anorexia nervosa, and regions on chromosomes 1, 10, and 14 appear to play a role in a range of eating pathologies (Klump & Gobrogge, 2005; Mazzeo et al., in press).

Symptom-level studies have also examined the genetic pathways involved in eating disordered symptoms. Body image disturbance is an essential symptom of eating disorders, and a study by Reichborn-Kjennerud et al. (2004) examined the heritability of "undue influence of weight on self-evaluation" (*DSM-IV-TR* body image-disturbance criteria for anorexia nervosa and bulimia nervosa) in a sample of 8,045 same-sex and opposite-sex Norwegian twins between the ages of 18 and 31. Their results suggest that shared environmental factors accounted for 31% of the variance in body image disturbance, whereas 69% of the variance was attributed to nonshared or common environmental factors. Keski-Rahkonen et al. (2005) found significant gender differences in the heritability of drive for thinness and body dissatisfaction in a study of 4,667 Finnish twins ages 22 to 27, with moderate to high levels of heritability in women but no heritability in men. Interestingly, pubertal status appears to be a significant factor in gene activation, and, based on their research with prepubescent and postpubescent girls, Klump and colleagues found that symptom-level eating disorder genes appear to activate during puberty (Klump, McGue, & Iacono, 2003).

Much more research needs to be conducted in this area, particularly in the domain of common factors for body image disturbance such as the media, peers, and parents (Heinberg & Thompson, 2006; Schmidt, 2004). One of the most exciting and ambitious enterprises in this area is an international multisite collaborative project designed to map the genetic loci of anorexia nervosa (Kaye et al., 2000). This is a much-needed development in the field, given that more than 200 genes that contribute to appetite, hunger, satiety, and other aspects of energy balance have been identified (Yager, 2000).

LEARNING AND MODELING

Relevant to learning and modeling are the data reviewed previously that indicate the role of parents as etiological agents. However, research has demonstrated that media and peer influences may also be powerful modeling and didactic agents that contribute to level of eating disturbance (Keery, van den Berg, 2004; Shroff & Thompson, in press; Thompson et al., 1999). Weight concern, the acceptability of dieting, the normative nature of being dissatisfied with looks, and the details of weight control strategies are a few of the areas wherein media, parents, and peers exert an influence. The media have often been spotlighted because of the omnipresent nature of a seemingly inexhaustible array of impossibly thin and beautiful models and celebrities. Countless studies have documented the presence of thinness in these images and the associated endless parade of magazine articles that focus on dieting and appearance management (Thompson & Heinberg, 1999). Research in the area of internalization of media images has indicated that women who incorporate or "buy into" the images and messages to the point of desiring thinness or modifying behavior to achieve the perfect "look" are at a much greater risk to develop eating disturbances (Thompson & Stice, 2001). A meta-analysis of the influence of sociocultural factors concluded that thin-ideal internalization and perceived pressure to be thin are strongly related to body dissatisfaction, which is a robust risk factor for disturbed eating (Cafri, Yamamiya, Brannick, & Thompson, 2005).

Peers and parents also may model behaviors that connote an imperative to the friend or child of the importance of appearance and thinness (Smolak & Levine, 2001). For instance, teasing or negative appearance-related comments have received remarkably consistent support as a factor in level of eating disturbance (Thompson, Coovert, Richards, Johnson, & Cattarin, 1995; Wertheim, Koerner, & Paxton, 2001). Comments also may manifest not in teasing or disparagement, but in simple encouragement to modify weight. Significant relationships have been found between parental comments and a daughter's desire to lose weight as well as body esteem scores (Thelen & Cormier, 1995; Smolak, Levine, & Schermer, 1999). Parents may also express concern about their own weight that may serve to model such attitudes to offspring. Smolak et al. (1999) found that a mother's complaints about her weight and weight loss attempts were related to the daughter's body esteem scores. Vander Wal and Thelen (2000) found that parental modeling of weight and shape concerns and daughters' perception of parental influence to lose or control weight were significant predictors of body image disturbance. Other studies have found that direct (e.g., teasing) and indirect (e.g., modeling, investment in appearance) peer and parental influences are important contributors to body dissatisfaction and eating concerns (Field et al., 2001; Keery et al., 2004; Smolak & Levine, 2001; Vander Wal & Thelen, 2000).

LIFE EVENTS

Life events, a relatively heterogeneous category of influences, have the power to radically affect an individual's psychological and, possibly, physical status, leading to body image and eating problems. Common experiences such as a family move to a different city or state, loss of a loved one, and a physical illness can initiate change in eating patterns that may evolve into an eating disorder. Negative comments in the form of criticism or teasing about one's appearance or weight, as noted earlier, also have been associated with the onset of eating and shape-related problems. Perhaps the most often cited and researched life events involve traumatic experiences related to sexual abuse.

Connors (2001) offers an excellent review of the confusing and controversial area of sexual abuse, concluding that it "constitutes a significant risk factor for the development of body image and eating problems" (p. 160). Her review encompasses a wide range of studies, from childhood through early adulthood. She concludes that many factors affect the connection between abuse and its effect on eating symptomatology, including familiarity of the perpetrator, level of physical contact, and level of negative reaction at the time of the abuse (the most consistent finding may be that level of negative reaction predicts level of eating pathology). Family factors that may moderate the effect of abuse on eating include such family variables as unreliability of parents, reduced expressiveness and warmth, and family chaos (Hastings & Kern, 1994; Malinckrodt, McCreary, & Robertson, 1995; Smolak, Levine, & Sullins, 1990). A comprehensive review of the eating-disorder risk factor literature by Jacobi and colleagues (2004) found that sexual abuse is a common risk factor for the development of disturbed eating but that it has not been found to be a specific risk factor for any one of the three eating-disorder diagnoses. Stice (2002), however, concluded in a recent meta-analysis that there is not yet enough prospective research to determine whether sexual abuse is a risk factor for eating disorders.

These conflicting findings are likely due in part to methodological issues. One of the many methodological issues in this area is the definition of *abuse,* which varies drastically across studies. For instance, some studies require sexual penetration or forced sexual activities as essential for defining sexual abuse, while others use a general definition related to touching in a place that was not welcome or doing something sexual that should not have been done. Weiner and Thompson (1997) identified two types of sexual abuse via factor analysis: overt and covert. Overt sexual abuse consisted of explicit sexual violations of one's body, while covert sexual abuse was defined as a variety of more subtle, yet offensive, activities (such as sexually related staring, verbal harassment about sexual development, inappropriate parental sharing of sexually related information). In regression analyses, covert sexual abuse was found to explain variance in eating problems and body dissatisfaction beyond that accounted for by overt sexual abuse.

GENDER AND RACIAL-ETHNIC

Gender and racial-ethnic factors have been found to play a large role, historically, in helping researchers and clinicians understand dispositional factors in eating disorders (Thompson, 1996). *Gender* has typically been viewed as synonymous with biological sex (male, female); however, gender also can connote socialization and social roles (i.e., masculine and feminine). Racial-ethnic etiological factors, additionally, need to consider within- and between-country ethnic comparisons, as well as the identification of respondents with racial-ethnic background or culture.

Feminist theorists and other researchers often focus on the nature of the gender role adopted by the individual and/or promoted by the society (Gilbert & Thompson, 1996; Smolak & Murnen, 2001). One such component is the traditional feminine gender role, consisting of the traits of passivity, need for approval, dependence, and focus on interpersonal relationships. Research is not conclusive about whether the adoption of such a gender role is central to the development of an eating disorder; however, Murnen and Smolak (1998), using meta-analysis, found that high femininity was associated with increased risk for eating problems and high masculinity was related to a decreased risk. They noted, however, that effect sizes, indicating the degree of association, were quite small. Smolak and Murnen (2001) detail several components of women's "lived experiences" that they think contribute to eating disorders: a culture of thinness, sexual harassment and abuse, and societal limitations on achievement, which function to "focus girls on a good body as the key to success and . . . limit girls' voices" (p. 96).

Men present with the eating disorders of anorexia nervosa and bulimia nervosa much less frequently than women—only about 10% of cases are men. However, the sex ratio is roughly equivalent for binge-eating disorder. The societal ideal of thinness for women is paralleled by a relatively intense pressure on men to achieve a muscular ideal (Anderson, 1995; Cafri et al., 2005; Thompson et al., 1999: Thompson & Cafri, in press). Men in certain avocations may be at elevated risk to develop an eating disorder. For instance, athletes who are wrestlers, bodybuilders, jockeys, or gymnasts have size and/or weight imperatives that may induce extreme forms of weight control. Homosexuality also appears to be associated with an elevated risk, with perhaps 20% or more of men with eating disorders stating this sexual orientation (Anderson, 1995). However, research on a randomly selected sample of heterosexual and gay men found few differences in eating disturbance or body image, even when groups were further categorized by exercise status (bodybuilders vs. sedentary controls; Boroughs & Thompson, 2002).

Considerable research has evaluated the ethnic differences that exist in eating disorders and related disturbances, such as body dissatisfaction. Although the data are still sketchy and no large-scale epidemiological study has been conducted, it is clear that "no ethnic group is completely immune to developing an eating disorder" (Smolak & Striegel-Moore, 2001, p. 114). Shaw, Ramirez, Trost, Randall, and Stice (2004) found few differences between ethnic groups on eating-disordered symptoms and risk factors for eating disorders, suggesting that sociocultural influences for thinness have become so widespread that all ethnic groups are affected; however, greater level of acculturation to Western society appears to be related to higher rates of eating-disordered symptoms (Jacobi et al., 2004). Much of the available research is limited, however, because researchers have typically looked at individual symptoms, such as dieting level or body dissatisfaction, rather than a comprehensive assessment and diagnosis of eating disorders.

Biological and Physiological

As noted earlier in the section on physical assessment, a variety of metabolic, endocrine, and other physiological changes accompanies eating disorders. The challenge for any biological or physiological theory of eating disorders is to illustrate that physical changes predict or precede the onset of eating-disordered symptoms. A recent review of neurobiological functioning in eating disorders highlights three promising pathways that may be associated with eating disorders: the neurotransmitter serotonin, the adipokine leptin, and the gut-related peptide ghrelin (Jimerson & Wolfe, in press).

Kaye and colleagues (2005) have noted that serotonin (5-HT) dysregulation likely plays a role in the pathology of eating disorders, because (1) evidence suggests that serotonin is associated with feeding, mood, and impulse control; (2) pharmacological treatments that affect serotonin levels have been found to have some efficacy in the treatment of eating disorders; and (3) serotonin disturbances appear to persist beyond recovery from the eating disorder, suggesting that 5-HT dysregulation may be a trait associated with eating disorders (Kaye, Bailer, Frank, Wagner, & Henry, 2005a). Research has consistently demonstrated reduced serotonin functioning in anorexia nervosa—specifically, low levels of CSF 5-HIAA (a metabolite of serotonin)—although it is unclear whether this finding is associated with the eating disorder or the nutritional deprivation characteristic of anorexics (Jimerson & Wolfe, in press). Further support for the role of 5-HT comes from studies in which patients with anorexia nervosa have been found to have a blunted plasma prolactin response to 5-HT drugs and reduced 3-H imapramine binding (Kaye et al., 2005b).

Serotonin also has been implicated in bulimia nervosa (Jimerson & Wolfe, in press; Kaye et al., 2005b; Pirke, 1995). Decreased levels of the serotonin metabolite 5-hydroxyindoleacetic acid in cerebrospinal fluid have been found in patients with bulimia nervosa (Jimerson & Wolfe, in press). Additionally, bulimia nervosa is associated with blunted prolactin response to 5-HT receptor agonists m-chlorophynelpiperazine, 5-hydroxytrytophan, and dlfenfluramine (Kaye et al., 2005b). Dysregulation of serotonin has been found to persist in recovered bulimics (Jimerson & Wolfe, in press). A review of the neurobiological literature suggests that serotonin neuronal pathways may create neurobiological vulnerabilities that may then interact with environmental stressors, leading to eating-disordered symptoms (Kaye et al., 2005a).

Since its discovery in 1994, leptin has been found to play a significant role in energy homeostasis. Leptin, which comes from the Greek root *leptos,* meaning thin, inhibits ingestive behavior and stimulates energy expenditure through interactions with specific receptors in the central nervous system (Calandra, Musso, & Musso, 2003; Kishi & Elmquist, 2005). Serum leptin levels have been found to correlate with weight and percentage body fat in normal-weight and obese individuals (Jimerson & Wolfe, in press). A recent review of the role of leptin in eating disorders suggests that patients with bulimia nervosa tend to have lower leptin levels than body mass index–matched control subjects; however, some studies have found no differences between patients with bulimia nervosa and control participants (Monteleone, DiLieto, Castaldo, & Maj, 2004). Lowered leptin levels appear more robust in patients with severe symptomatology, which may account for the inconsistent results in the literature (Jimerson & Wolfe, in press; Monteleone, Martiadis, Colurcio, & Maj, 2002). Patients with anorexia nervosa also have been found to have decreased levels of leptin compared to healthy-weight control participants (Monteleone et al., 2004); however, this finding may be a result of chronic malnutrition (Jimerson & Wolfe, in press). Leptin levels increase in weight-restored anorexics but may not reach levels equivalent to normal subjects (Satoh et al., 2003).

The gut-related peptide ghrelin has received substantial attention for its role in eating. Ghrelin is synthesized and released by endocrine cells in the stomach and is thought to stimulate hunger and meal initiation (Geary, 2004). Research has found that ghrelin levels progressively increase prior to meals and decrease after meals in normal subjects (Geary, 2004). Additionally, ghrelin levels are higher in normal-weight individuals than in obese individuals (Fassino et al., 2005). Recent research suggests that dysfunctional ghrelin regulation may be associated with binge eating (Jimerson & Wolfe, in press). Studies have found increased ghrelin levels in patients with bulimia nervosa despite normal body mass index (Fassino et al., 2005). Additionally, ghrelin levels do not appear to decrease after meals sufficiently in bulimia nervosa patients as compared to control subjects, which could play a role in the binge–purge cycle (Jimerson & Wolfe, in press). Ghrelin levels have been found to be elevated in individuals with anorexia nervosa when compared with control subjects; however, ghrelin approaches normal levels after weight restoration (Jimerson & Wolfe, in press).

Smolak and Murnen (2001) note several methodological issues that should be considered with regard to biological factors. First, prospective studies are lacking—studies have compared clinical versus nonclinical cases in which the eating disorder has already developed. Often, the assumption is that any current biological finding preexisted the eating pathology, which is debatable. Second, comparisons between recovered patients and nonclinical control participants are also suspect. Any biochemical differences may not reflect causes of eating disorders, but perhaps the long-term effects of eating pathology on biochemistry (even in recovered cases). Third, it is crucial to equate comparison groups on other psychiatric disorders—such as depression, substance abuse, and personality disorders—which may have unique biochemical associates. Finally, the behavior of dieting, alone, may produce a variety of biochemical changes (e.g., serotonin; Walsh, Oldman, Franklin, Fairburn, & Cowen, 1995) that may be mistaken for precursors to restricting behavior.

INTEGRATIVE APPROACHES

Multivariate approaches perhaps offer the most comprehensive and accurate strategy for evaluating etiology and maintenance of eating disorders (Stice, 2001). For instance, Levine and Smolak (1996) developed a cumulative stressor model that proposes that three developmental processes (weight gain from puberty, dating, and academic demands) interact with the societal imperative for a thin ideal to produce dieting and eating disturbance. According to Stice and colleagues' dual-pathway model (Stice, 2001), perceived pressure to be thin and thin-ideal internalization both have direct impact on body dissatisfaction, which is then hypothesized to lead to bulimic symptoms through two pathways: dieting and negative affect. Dieting is also hypothesized to have a direct effect on negative affect. The dual-pathway model has been supported in cross-sectional (Stice, Nemeroff & Shaw, 1996) and prospective studies (Stice, 2001).

Another multivariate model of eating-disordered symptoms posits that the interaction between perfectionism and perceived weight status is necessary for the development of bulimic symptoms (Joiner, Heatherton, Rudd, & Schmidt, 1997; Vohs, Bardone, Joiner, Abramson, & Heatherton, 1999). Joiner and colleagues (1997) tested this model in a cross-sectional study and found support for their hypothesis that women who were high on perfectionism and perceived themselves as overweight (regardless of actual weight status) reported greater levels of bulimic pathology. Vohs et al. (1999) conducted a prospective test of this model on 342 adolescent girls. In addition to examining the interaction between perfectionism and perceived weight status, Vohs et al. hypothesized that self-esteem would moderate this interaction, resulting in a three-way interaction between perfectionism, perceived weight status, and self-esteem. Thus, they posited that perfectionists who perceive themselves as overweight will report a growth in bulimic pathology only if they have low self-esteem. Results supported this hypothesis. Perfectionism, perceived weight status as overweight, and low self-esteem prospectively predicted growth in bulimic symptoms over a 9-month period. An independent, prospective test of this model in a sample of adolescent girls, however, did not replicate Vohs and colleagues' findings (Shaw, Stice, & Springer, 2004).

Thompson et al. (1999) proposed a tripartite influence model that enlists three formative factors (peers, parents, and media) in the development of body dissatisfaction and eating disturbances. The tripartite model suggests that two factors —internalization of the thin ideal and appearance comparison—mediate this relationship between influence and disturbance. In one cross-sectional test of this model, Keery, van den Berg, and Thompson (2004) found that peer, parental, and media influences had both direct and indirect effects (via internalization and appearance comparison) on body dissatisfaction and eating disturbance in a sample of adolescent girls. This study was replicated by Shroff and Thompson (in press). The tripartite model also has received empirical support in a cross-section study of college women (van den Berg, Thompson, Obremski-Brandon, & Coovert, 2002). The tripartite model of influence is a promising etiological theory; however, no prospective studies to date have provided a test of this model.

SUMMARY

Great advancements have been made in the investigation of many facets of eating disorders over the past few years. Many measures are now available for the assessment of multiple characteristics of anorexia nervosa, bulimia nervosa, and binge-eating disorder. Research continues to address the accuracy and utility of the current diagnostic systems. Exploration of the complex etiological factors involved has given rise to an explosion of interest in putative risk factors. To date, tremendous progress has been made in capturing the clinical picture of the various eating disorders, constructing classification systems, evaluating course and prognosis, and developing multifactorial theoretical models. Perhaps the greatest challenge for future researchers is not the ability to detect relative genetic and environmental causation, but to use this information to inform diagnostic, measurement, treatment, and prevention strategies.

REFERENCES

Abramovitz, B. A., & Birch, L. L. (2000). Five-year-old girls' ideas about dieting are predicted by mothers' dieting. *Journal of the American Dietetic Association, 100,* 1157–1163.

Agras, W. S. (2001). The consequences and cost of the eating disorders. *Psychiatric Clinics of North America, 24,* 371–379.

American Psychiatric Association. (2000). *Diagnostic and Statistical Manual of Mental Disorders* (4th ed., text revision). Washington, DC: Author.

Andersen, A. E. (1995). Eating disorders in males. In K. D. Brownell & C. G. Fairburn (Eds.), *Eating disorders and obesity: A comprehensive handbook* (pp. 177–182). New York: Guilford Press.

Anderson, D. A., & Paulosky, C. A. (2004). Psychological assessment of eating disorders and related features. In J. K. Thompson (Ed.), *Handbook of eating disorders and obesity* (pp. 112–129). Washington, DC: American Psychological Association.

Anderson, D. A., & Williamson, D. A. (2002). Outcome measurement in eating disorders. In W. W. Ishack, T. Burt, & L. Sedeser (Eds.), *Outcome measurement in clinical psychiatry: A critical review* (pp. 284–301). Washington, DC: American Psychiatric Press.

Anderson, D. A., Williamson, D. A., Duchmann, E. G., Gleaves, D. H., & Barbin, J. M. (1999). Development and validation of a multifactorial treatment outcome measure for eating disorders. *Assessment, 6,* 7–20.

Anderson, D. A., Williamson, D. A., Johnson, W. G., & Grieve, C. O. (2001). Validity of test meals for determining binge eating. *Eating Behaviors, 2,* 105–112.

Beglin, S. J., & Fairburn, C. G. (1992). What is meant by the term "binge"? *American Journal of Psychiatry, 149,* 123–124.

Boroughs, M., & Thompson, J. K. (2002). Body image and eating disturbances in men: The moderating effects of exercise status and sexual orientation. *International Journal of Eating Disorders, 31,* 307–311.

Bryant-Waugh, R. J. (in press). Eating disorders in children and adolescents. In S. Wonderlich, J. E. Mitchell, M. de Zwann, & H. Steiger (Eds.), *Annual review of eating disorders part 2–2006* (pp. 129–142). Oxford, England: Radcliffe.

Bulik, C. M., Reba, L., Siega-Riz, A. M., & Reichborn-Kjennrud, T. (2005). Anorexia nervosa: Definition, epidemiology, and cycle of risk. *International Journal of Eating Disorders, 37*(Suppl.), S2–S9.

Bulik, C. M., Sullivan, P. F., & Kendler, K. S. (2000). An empirical study of the classification of eating disorders. *American Journal of Psychiatry, 157,* 886–895.

Bulik, C. M., Sullivan, P. F., Wade, T. D., & Kendler, K. S. (2000). Twin studies of eating disorders: A review. *International Journal of Eating Disorders, 27,* 1–20.

Cachelin, F. M., & Maher, B. A. (1998). Is amenorrhea a critical criterion for anorexia nervosa? *Journal of Psychosomatic Research, 44,* 435–440.

Cafri, G., Thompson, J. K., Ricciardelli, L., McCabe, M., Smolak, L., & Yesalis, C. (2005). Pursuit of the muscular ideal: Physical and psychological consequences and putative risk factors. *Clinical Psychology Review, 25,* 215–239.

Cafri, G., Yamamiya, Y., Brannick, M., & Thompson, J. K. (2005). The influence of sociocultural factors on body image: A meta-analysis. *Clinical Psychology: Science and Practice, 12,* 421–433.

Calandra, C., Musso, F., & Musso, R. (2003). The role of leptin in the etiopathogenesis of anorexia nervosa and bulimia. *Eating and Weight Disorders, 8,* 130–137.

Carper, J. L., Fisher, J. O., & Birch, L. L. (2000). Young girls' emerging dietary restraint and disinhibition are related to parental control in child feeding. *Appetite, 35,* 121–129.

Connors, M. E. (2001). Relationship of sexual abuse to body image and eating problems. In J. K. Thompson & L. Smolak (Eds.), *Body image, eating disorders, and obesity in youth: Assessment, prevention, and treatment* (pp. 149–167). Washington, DC: American Psychological Association.

Davison, K. K., Markey, C. N., & Birch, L. L. (2000). Etiology of body dissatisfaction and weight concerns among 5-year-old girls. *Appetite, 35,* 143–151.

Dennis, A. B., & Sansone, R. A. (1997). Treatment of patients' personality disorders. In D. M. Garner & P. E. Garfinkel (Eds.), *Handbook of treatment for eating disorders* (2nd ed., pp. 437–439). New York: Guilford Press.

Eldredge, K. L., & Agras, W. S. (1996). Weight and shape overconcern and emotional eating in binge eating disorder. *International Journal of Eating Disorders, 19,* 73–82.

Fairburn, C. G., & Cooper, Z. (1993). The Eating Disorder Examination (12th ed.). In C. G. Fairburn & G. T. Wilson (Eds.), *Binge eating: Nature, assessment and treatment* (pp. 317–360). New York: Guilford Press.

Fairburn, C. G., Cooper, Z., Doll, H. A., Norman, P., & O'Connor, M. (2000). The natural course of bulimia nervosa and binge eating disorder in young women. *Archives of General Psychiatry, 57,* 659–665.

Fassino, S., Daga, G. A., Mondelli, V., Piero, A., Broglio, F., Picu, A., et al. (2005). Hormonal and metabolic responses to acute ghrelin administration in patients with bulimia nervosa. *Psychoneuroendocrinology, 30,* 534–540.

Fichter, M. M., Herpertz, S., Quadflieg, N., & Herpertz-Dahlmann, B. (1998). Structured interview for anorexic and bulimic disorders for *DSM-IV* and *ICD-10:* Updated (third) revision. *International Journal of Eating Disorders, 24,* 227–249.

Fichter, M. M., & Quadflieg, N. (2004). Twelve-year course and outcome of bulimia nervosa. *Psychological Medicine, 34,* 1395–1406.

Field, A. E., Camargo, C. A., Taylor, C. B., Berkey, C. S., Roberts, S. B., & Colditz, G. A. (2001). Peer, parent, and media influences on the development of weight concerns and frequent dieting among preadolescent and adolescent girls and boys. *Pediatrics, 107,* 54–60.

Friedman, M. A., Wilfley, D. E., Welch, R. R., & Kunce, J. T. (1997). Self-directed hostility and family functioning in normal-weight bulimics and overweight binge eaters. *International Journal of Eating Disorders, 22,* 367–375.

Garner, D. M. (2005). *Eating Disorder Inventory-3.* Lutz, FL: Psychological Assessment Resources.

Geary, N. (2004). Endocrine controls of eating: CCK, leptin, and ghrelin. *Physiology & Behavior, 18,* 719–733.

Gilbert, S., & Thompson, J. K. (1996). Feminist explanations of the development of eating disorders: Common themes, research findings, and methodological issues. *Clinical Psychology: Science and Practice, 3,* 183–202.

Grilo, C. M., Masheb, R. M., & Wilson, G. T. (2001). A comparison of different methods for assessing the features of eating disorders in patients with binge eating disorder. *Journal of Consulting and Clinical Psychology, 69,* 317–322.

Gull, W. W. (1964). Anorexia nervosa. In R. M. Kaufman & M. Heiman (Eds.), *Evolution of psychosomatic concepts anorexia nervosa: A paradigm*. New York: International Universities Press. (Original work published 1874)

Hastings, T., & Kern, J. M. (1994). Relationships between bulimia, childhood sexual abuse, and family environment. *International Journal of Eating Disorders, 15,* 103–111.

Heinberg, L. J., & Thompson, J. K. (2006). Body Image. In S. Wonderlich, J. E., Mitchell, M. deZwaan, & H. Steiger (Eds.) *Annual Review of Eating Disorders: Part 2—2006*. Oxford, England: Radcliffe Publishing Ltd.

Herzog, D. B., & Delinsky, S. S. (2001). Classification of eating disorders. In R. Striegel-Moore & L. Smolak (Eds.), *Eating disorders: Innovative directions in research and practice* (pp. 31–50). Washington, DC: American Psychological Association.

Herzog, D. B., Dorer, D. J., Keel, P. K., Selwyn, S. E., Ekeblade, E. R., Flores, A. T., et al. (1999). Recovery and relapse in anorexia and bulimia nervosa: A 7.5-year follow-up study. *Journal of the American Academy of Child and Adolescent Psychiatry, 38,* 829–837.

Herzog, D. B., Greenwood, D. N., Dorer, D. J., Flores, A. T., Ekeblade, E. R., Richards, A., et al. (2000). Mortality in eating disorders: A descriptive study. *International Journal of Eating Disorders, 28,* 20–26.

Hill, K., & Pomeroy, C. (2001). Assessment of physical status of children and adolescents with eating disorders and obesity. In J. K. Thompson & L. Smolak (Eds.), *Body image, eating disorders, and obesity in youth: Assessment, prevention and treatment* (pp. 171–191). Washington, DC: American Psychological Association.

Hoek, H. W., & van Hoeken, D. (2003). Review of the prevalence and incidence of eating disorders. *International Journal of Eating Disorders, 34,* 383–396.

Horesh, N., Apter, A., Ishai, J., Danziger, Y., Miculincer, M., Stein, D., et al. (1996). Abnormal psychosocial situations and eating disorders in adolescence. *Journal of the American Academy of Child and Adolescent Psychiatry, 35,* 921–927.

Humphrey, L. L. (1994). Family relationships. In K. A. Halmi (Ed.), *Psychobiology and treatment of anorexia nervosa and bulimia nervosa* (pp. 263–282). Washington DC: American Psychiatric Press.

Jacobi, C., Hayward, C., de Zwann, M., Kraemer, H. C., & Agras, W. S. (2004). Coming to terms with risk factors for eating disorders: Application of risk terminology and suggestions for a general taxonomy. *Psychological Bulletin, 130,* 19–65.

Jimerson, D. C., & Wolfe, B. E. (in press). Psychobiology of eating disorders. In S. Wonderlich, J. E. Mitchell, M. de Zwann, & H. Steiger (Eds.), *Annual review of eating disorders part 2–2006* (pp. 1–16). Oxford, England: Radcliffe.

Johnson, W. G., & Torgrud, L. J. (1996). Assessment and treatment of binge eating disorder. In J. K. Thompson (Ed.), *Body image, eating disorders and obesity: An integrative guide for assessment and treatment* (pp. 321–343). Washington, DC: American Psychological Association.

Joiner, T. E., Heatherton, T. F., Rudd, M. D., & Schmidt, N. B. (1997). Perfectionism, perceived weight status, and bulimic symptoms: Two studies testing a diathesis-stress model. *Journal of Abnormal Psychology, 106,* 145–153.

Kaye, W. H., Bailer, U. F., Frank, G. K., Wagner, A., & Henry, S. E. (2005a). Brain imaging of serotonin after recovery from anorexia and bulimia nervosa. *Physiology & Behavior, 86,* 15–17.

Kaye, W. H., Devlin, B., Barbarich, N., Bulik, C. M., Thornton, L., Bacanu, S. A., et al. (2004). Genetic analysis of bulimia nervosa: Methods and sample description. *International Journal of Eating Disorders, 35,* 556–570.

Kaye, W. H., Frank, G. K., Bailer, U. F., Henry, S. E., Meltzer, C. C., Price, J. C., et al. (2005b). Serotonin alterations in anorexia and bulimia nervosa: New insights from imaging studies. *Physiology & Behavior, 85,* 73–81.

Kaye, W. H., Lilenfield, L. R., Berretini, W. H., Strober, M., Devlin, B., Klump, K., et al. (2000). A genome-wide search for susceptibility loci for anorexia nervosa: Methods and sample description. *Biological Psychiatry, 47,* 794–803.

Keery, H., van den Berg, P., & Thompson, J. K. (2004). An evaluation of the tripartite influence model of body dissatisfaction and eating disturbance with adolescent girls. *Body Image, 1,* 237–251.

Keski-Rahkonen, A., Bulik, C. M., Neale, B. M., Rose, R. J., Rissanen, A., & Kaprio, J. (2005). Body dissatisfaction and drive for thinness in young adult twins. *International Journal of Eating Disorders, 37,* 188–199.

Kishi, T., & Elmquist, J. K. (2005). Body weight is regulated by the brain: A link between feeding and emotion. *Molecular Psychiatry, 10,* 132–146.

Klump, K. L., & Gobrogge, K. L. (2005). A review and primer of molecular genetic studies of anorexia nervosa. *International Journal of Eating Disorders, 37*(Suppl.), S43–S48.

Klump, K. L., Kaye, W. H., & Strober, M. (2001). The evolving genetic foundations of eating disorders. *Psychiatric Clinics of North America, 24,* 215–225.

Klump, K. L., McGue, M., & Iacono, W. G. (2003). Differential heritability of eating attitudes and behaviors in prepubertal versus pubertal twins. *International Journal of Eating Disorders, 33,* 287–292.

Kutlesic, V., Williamson, D. A., Gleaves, D. H., Barbin, J. M., & Murphy-Eberenz, K. P. (1998). The Interview for the Diagnosis of Eating Disorders IV: Application to *DSM-IV* diagnostic criteria. *Psychological Assessment, 10,* 41–48.

Leung, F., Schwartzmann, A., & Steiger, H. (1996). Testing a dual-process family model in understanding the development of eating pathology: A structural equation modeling analysis. *International Journal of Eating Disorders, 20,* 367–375.

Levine, M. P., & Smolak, L. (1996). Media as a context for the development of disordered eating. In L. Smolak, M. P. Levine, & R. Striegel-Moore (Eds.), *The developmental psychopathology of eating disorders* (pp. 235–237). Mahwah, NJ: Erlbaum.

Lewinsohn, P. M. (2001, December). *The role of epidemiology in prevention science.* Paper presented at the Eating Disorders' Research Society, Albuquerque, NM.

Lucas, A. R., Beard, C. M., O'Fallon, W. M., & Kurland, L. T. (1998). Anorexia nervosa in Rochester, Minnesota: A 45-year study. *Mayo Clinic Proceedings, 63,* 433–442.

Malinckrodt, B., McCreary, B. A., & Robertson, A. K. (1995). Co-occurrence of eating disorders and incest: The role of attachment, family environment, and social competencies. *Journal of Counseling Psychology, 42,* 178–186.

Martin, C. K., Williamson, D. A., & Thaw, J. M. (2000). Criterion validity of the multiaxial assessment of eating disorders symptoms. *International Journal of Eating Disorders, 28,* 303–310.

Mazzeo, S. E., Slof-Op't, M. C. T., van Furth, E. F., & Bulik, C. M. (in press). Genetics of eating disorders. In S. Wonderlich, J. E. Mitchell, M. de Zwann, & H. Steiger (Eds.), *Annual review of eating disorders part 2–2006* (pp. 17–34). Oxford, England: Radcliffe.

Mazzeo, S. E., Zucker, N. L., Gerke, C. K., Mitchell, K. S., & Bulik, C. M. (2005). Parenting concerns of women with histories of eating disorders. *International Journal of Eating Disorders, 37*(Suppl.), S77–S79.

Minuchin, S., Rosman, B. L., & Baker, L. (1978). *Psychosomatic families: Anorexia nervosa in context.* Cambridge, MA: Harvard University Press.

Monteleone, P., DiLieto, A., Castaldo, E., & Maj, M. (2004). Leptin functioning in eating disorders. *CNS Spectrums, 9,* 523–529.

Monteleone, P., Martiadis, V., Colurcio, B., & Maj, M. (2002). Leptin secretion is related to chronicity and severity of the illness in bulimia nervosa. *Psychosomatic Medicine, 64,* 874–879.

Murnen, S., & Smolak, L. (1998). Femininity, masculinity, and disordered eating: A meta-analytic approach. *International Journal of Eating Disorders, 22,* 231–242.

Netemeyer, S. B., & Williamson, D. A. (2001). Assessment of eating disturbance in children and adolescents with eating disorders and obesity. In J. K. Thompson & L. Smolak (Eds.), *Body image, eating disorders, and obesity in youth: Assessment, prevention and treatment* (pp. 215–233). Washington, DC: American Psychological Association.

Newman, D. L., Moffitt, T. E., Caspi, A., Magdol, L., Silva, P. A., & Stanton, W. R. (1996). Psychiatric disorder in a birth cohort of young adults: Prevalence, comorbidity, clinical significance, and new case incidence from ages 11 to 21. *Journal of Consulting and Clinical Psychology, 64,* 552–562.

Nicholls, D., Chater, R., & Lask, B. (2000). Children into *DSM* don't go: A comparison of classification systems for eating disorders in childhood and early adolescence. *International Journal of Eating Disorders, 28,* 317–324.

Nielson, S. (2001). Epidemiology and mortality of eating disorders. *Psychiatric Clinics of North America, 24,* 201–214.

Pawluck, D. E., & Gorey, K. M. (1998). Secular trends in the incidence of anorexia nervosa: Integrative review of population-based studies. *International Journal of Eating Disorders, 23,* 347–352.

Pirke, K. M. (1995). Physiology of bulimia nervosa. In K. D. Brownell & C. G. Fairburn (Eds.), *Eating disorders and obesity: A comprehensive handbook* (pp. 261–265). New York: Guilford Press.

Pomeroy, C. (1996). Anorexia nervosa, bulimia nervosa, and binge eating disorder: Assessment of physical status. In J. K. Thompson (Ed.), *Body image, eating disorders and obesity: An integrative guide for assessment and treatment* (pp. 177–203). Washington, DC: American Psychological Association.

Reichborn-Kjennerud, T., Bulik, C. M., Kendler, K., Roysamb, E., Tambs, K., Torgersen, S., et al. (2004). Undue influence of weight on self-evaluation: A population-based twin study of gender difference. *International Journal of Eating Disorders, 35,* 123–132.

Rieves, L., & Cash, T. F. (1996). Social developmental factors and women's body-image attitudes. *Journal of Social Behavior and Personality, 11,* 63–78.

Rosenvinge, J. H., Sundgot-Borgen, S., & Borresen, R. (1999). The prevalence of psychological correlates of anorexia nervosa, bulimia nervosa, and binge eating among 15-year-old students: A controlled epidemiological study. *European Eating Disorders Review, 7,* 382–391.

Sansone, R. A., Levitt, J. L., & Sansone, L. A. (2005). The prevalence of personality disorders among those with eating disorders. *Eating Disorders: The Journal of Treatment and Prevention, 13,* 7–21.

Satoh, Y., Shimizu, T., Lee, T., Nishizawa, K., Iijima, M., & Yamashiro, Y. (2003). Resting energy expenditure and plasma leptin levels in adolescent girls with anorexia nervosa. *International Journal of Eating Disorders, 34,* 156–161.

Schwartz, D. J., Phares, V., Tantleff-Dunn, S., & Thompson, J. K. (1999). Body image, psychological functioning, and parental feedback regarding physical appearance. *International Journal of Eating Disorders, 25,* 339–343.

Shaw, H., Ramirez, L., Trost, A., Randall, P., & Stice, E. (2004). Body image and eating disturbances across ethnic groups: More similarities than differences. *Psychology of Addictive Behaviors, 18,* 12–18.

Shaw, H. E., Stice, E., & Springer, D. W. (2004). Perfectionism, body dissatisfaction, and self-esteem in predicting bulimic symptomatology: Lack of replication. *International Journal of Eating Disorders, 36,* 41–47.

Shisslak, C. M., Crago, M., & Esters, L. S. (1995). The spectrum of eating disturbances. *International Journal of Eating Disorders, 18,* 1209–1219.

Smolak, L., & Levine, M. P. (2001). Body image in children. In J. K. Thompson & L. Smolak (Eds.), *Body image, eating disorders, and obesity in youth: Assessment, prevention and treatment* (pp. 41–66). Washington, DC: American Psychological Association.

Smolak, L., Levine, M. P., & Schermer, F. (1999). Parental input and weight concerns among elementary school children. *International Journal of Eating Disorders, 25,* 263–272.

Smolak, L., Levine, M. P., & Sullins, E. (1990). Are child sexual experiences related to eating-disordered attitudes and behaviors in a college sample? *International Journal of Eating Disorders, 9,* 167–178.

Smolak, L., & Murnen, S. K. (2001). Gender and eating problems. In R. H. Striegel-Moore & L. Smolak (Eds.), *Eating disorders: Innovative directions in research and practice* (pp. 91–110). Washington, DC: American Psychological Association.

Smolak, L., & Striegel-Moore, R. (2001). Challenging the myth of the golden girl: Ethnicity and eating disorders. In R. H. Striegel-Moore & L. Smolak (Eds.), *Eating disorders: Innovative directions in research and practice* (pp. 111–132). Washington, DC: American Psychological Association.

Steinberg, A. B., & Phares, V. (2001). Family functioning, body image, and eating disturbances. In J. K. Thompson & L. Smolak (Eds.), *Body image, eating disorders, and obesity in youth: Assessment, prevention and treatment* (pp. 127–147). Washington, DC: American Psychological Association.

Steinhausen, H. C. (1995). The course and outcome of anorexia nervosa. In K. D. Brownell & C. G. Fairburn (Eds.), *Eating disorders and obesity: A comprehensive handbook* (pp. 234–237). New York: Guilford Press.

Steinhausen, H. C., Gavez, S., & Metzke, C. W. (2005). Psychosocial correlates, outcome, and stability of abnormal adolescent eating behavior in community samples of young people. *International Journal of Eating Disorders, 37,* 119–126.

Stice, E. (2001). A prospective test of the dual-pathway model of bulimic pathology: Mediating effects of dieting and negative affect. *Journal of Abnormal Psychology, 110,* 124–135.

Stice, E. (2002). Risk and maintenance factors for eating pathology: A meta-analytic review. *Psychological Bulletin, 128,* 825–848.

Stice, E., Nemeroff, C., & Shaw, H. E. (1996). Test of the dual pathway model of bulimia nervosa: Evidence for dietary restraint and affect regulation mechanisms. *Journal of Social and Clinical Psychology, 15,* 340–363.

Stice, E., Rizvi, S. L., & Telch, C. F. (2000). Developmental and validation of the Eating Disorder Diagnostic Scale: A brief self-report measure of anorexia, bulimia, and binge-eating disorder. *Psychological Assessment, 22,* 123–131.

Striegel-Moore, R. H., Dohm, F. A., Solomon, E. E., Fairburn, C. G., Pike, K. M., & Wilfley, D. E. (2000). Subthreshold binge eating disorder. *International Journal of Eating Disorders, 27,* 270–278.

Striegel-Moore, R. H., Franko, D. L., & Ach, E. L. (in press). Epidemiology of eating disorders. In S. Wonderlich, J. E. Mitchell, M. de Zwann, & H. Steiger (Eds.), *Annual review of eating disorders part 2–2006* (pp. 65–78). Oxford, England: Radcliffe.

Striegel-Moore, R. H., & Smolak, L. (Eds.). (2001). *Eating disorders: Innovative directions in research and practice.* Washington, DC: American Psychological Association.

Striegel-Moore, R. H., Wilson, G. T., Wilfley, D. E., Elder, K. A., & Brownell, K. D. (1998). Binge eating in an obese community sample. *International Journal of Eating Disorders, 23,* 27–37.

Strober, M., Lampert, C., Morrell, W., Burroughs, J., & Jacobs, C. (1990). A controlled family study of anorexia nervosa: Evidence of familial aggregation and lack of shared transmission with affective disorders. *International Journal of Eating Disorders, 9,* 239–253.

Sullivan, P. F. (1995). Mortality in anorexia nervosa. *American Journal of Psychiatry, 152,* 1073–1074.

Sullivan, P. F., Bulik, C. M., & Kendler, K. S. (1998). The epidemiology of bulimia nervosa: Symptoms, syndromes and diagnostic thresholds. *Psychological Medicine, 28,* 599–610.

Telch, C. F., & Agras, W. S. (1996). Do emotional states influence binge eating in the obese? *International Journal of Eating Disorders, 20,* 271–280.

Thelen, M., & Cormier, J. (1995). Desire to be thinner and weight control among children and their parents. *Behavior Therapy, 26,* 85–99.

Thompson, J. K. (Ed.). (1996). *Body image, eating disorders, and obesity: An integrative guide for assessment and treatment.* Washington, DC: American Psychological Association.

Thompson, J. K., & Cafri, G. (in press). *The muscular ideal.* Washington, DC: American Psychological Association.

Thompson, J. K., Coovert, M. D., Richards, K. J., Johnson, S., & Cattarin, J. (1995). Development of body image, eating disturbance, and general psychological functioning in female adolescents: Covariance structure modeling and longitudinal investigations. *International Journal of Eating Disorders, 18,* 221–236.

Thompson, J. K., & Gardner, R. M. (2002). Assessment of perceptual body image in adolescents and adults. In T. F. Cash & T. Pruzinsky (Eds.), *Body images: A handbook* (pp. 135–141). New York: Guilford Press.

Thompson, J. K., & Heinberg, L. J. (1999). The media's influence on body image disturbance and eating disorders: We've reviled them, now can we rehabilitate them? *Journal of Social Issues, 55,* 339–353.

Thompson, J. K., Heinberg, L. J., Altabe, M. N., & Tantleff-Dunn, S. (1999). *Exacting beauty: Theory, assessment and treatment of body image disturbance.* Washington, DC: American Psychological Association.

Thompson, J. K., Roehrig, M., Cafri, G., & Heinberg, L. J. (2005). Assessment of body image disturbance. In J. E. Mitchell & C. B. Peterson (Eds.), *Assessment of eating disorders* (pp. 175–202). New York: Guilford Press.

Thompson, J. K., & Smolak, L. (Eds.). (2001). *Body image, eating disorders, and obesity in youth: Assessment, prevention and treatment.* Washington, DC: American Psychological Association.

Thompson, J. K., & Stice, E. (2001). Internalization of the thin-ideal: Mounting evidence for a new risk factor for body image disturbance and eating pathology. *Current Directions in Psychological Science, 11,* 181–183.

Thompson, J. K., & van den Berg, P. (2002). Assessment of body image attitudes in adolescents and adults. In T. F. Cash & T. Pruzinsky (Eds.), *Body images: A handbook* (pp. 142–154). New York: Guilford Press.

Thompson, J. K., & Williams, D. E. (1987). An interpersonally based cognitive-behavioral psychotherapy. In M. Hersen, R. M. Eisler, & P. M. Miller (Eds.), *Progress in behavior modification* (Vol. 21, pp. 230–258). Newbury Park, CA: Sage.

Tozzi, F., Thornton, L. M., Klump, K. L., Fichter, M. M., Halmi, K. A., Kaplan, A. S., et al. (2005). Symptom fluctuation in eating disorders: Correlates of diagnostic crossover. *American Journal of Psychiatry, 162,* 732–740.

van den Berg, P., Thompson, J. K., Obremski-Brandon, K., & Coovert, M. (2002). The tripartite influence model of body image and eating disturbance: A covariance structure modeling investigation testing the mediational role of appearance comparison. *Journal of Psychosomatic Research, 53,* 1007–1020.

Vander Wal, J. S., & Thelen, M. H. (2000). Predictors of body image dissatisfaction in elementary-age school girls. *Eating Behaviors, 1,* 105–122.

Varnado, P. J., Williamson, D. A., Bentz, G. G., Ryan, D. H., Rhodes, S. K., O'Neil, P. M., et al. (1997). Prevalence of binge eating disorder in obese adults seeking weight loss treatment. *Eating and Weight Related Disorders, 2,* 117–124.

Vohs, K. D., Bardone, A. M., Joiner, T. E., Abramson, L. Y., & Heatherton, T. F. (1999). Perfectionism, perceived weight status, and self-esteem interact to predict bulimic symptoms: A model of bulimic symptom development. *Journal of Abnormal Psychology, 108,* 695–700.

Walsh, B. T., & Garner, D. M. (1997). Diagnostic issues. In D. M. Garner & P. E. Garfinkel (Eds.), *Handbook of treatment for eating disorders* (pp. 25–33). New York: Guilford Press.

Walsh, B. T., Oldman, A., Franklin, M., Fairburn, C. G., & Cowen, P. (1995). Dieting decreases plasma tryptohan and increases prolactin response to d-fenfluramine in women but not in men. *Journal of Affective Disorders, 33,* 89–97.

Walsh, B. T., Wilson, G. T., Loeb, K. L., Devlin, M. J., Pike, K. M., Roose, S. P., et al. (1997). *American Journal of Psychiatry, 154,* 523–531.

Walters, E. E., & Kendler, K. S. (1995). Anorexia nervosa and anorexia-like syndromes in a population-based female twin sample. *American Journal of Psychiatry, 152,* 64–71.

Watson, T. L. & Andersen, A. E. (2003). A critical examination of the amenorrhea and weight criteria for diagnosing anorexia nervosa. *Acta Psychiatrica Scandinavica, 108,* 175–182.

Weiner, K., & Thompson, J. K. (1997). Overt and covert sexual abuse: Relationship to body image and eating disturbance. *International Journal of Eating Disorders, 22,* 273–284.

Wertheim, E. H., Koerner, J., & Paxton, S. J. (2001). Longitudinal predictors of restrictive eating and bulimic tendencies in three different age groups of adolescent girls. *Journal of Youth and Adolescence, 30,* 69–81.

Westen, D., & Harnden-Fischer, J. (2001). Personality profiles in eating disorders: Rethinking the distinction between Axis I and Axis II. *American Journal of Psychiatry, 158,* 547–562.

Williamson, D. A. (1990). *Assessment of eating disorders: Obesity, anorexia, and bulimia nervosa.* New York: Pergamon Press.

Williamson, D. A., Anderson, D. A., & Gleaves, D. H. (1996). Anorexia nervosa and bulimia nervosa: Structured interview methodologies and psychological assessment. In J. K. Thompson (Ed.), *Body image, eating disorders and obesity: An integrative guide for assessment and treatment* (pp. 205–233). Washington, DC: American Psychological Association.

Williamson, D. A., Gleaves, D. H., & Stewart, T. M. (2005). Categorical versus dimensional models of eating disorders: An examination of the evidence. *International Journal of Eating Disorders, 37,* 1–10.

Williamson, D. A., Zucker, N. L., Martin, C. K., & Smeets, M. A. M. (2001). Etiology and management of eating disorders. In P. B. Sutker & H. E. Adams (Eds.), *Comprehensive handbook of psychopathology* (3rd ed., pp. 641–670). New York: Kluwer Academic/Plenum.

Wonderlich, S. A. (1995). Personality and eating disorders. In K. D. Brownell & C. G. Fairburn (Eds.), *Eating disorders and obesity: A comprehensive handbook* (pp. 171–176). New York: Guilford Press.

Wonderlich, S. A., & Mitchell, J. E. (1997). Eating disorders and comorbidity: Empirical, conceptual, and clinical implications. *Psychopharmacology Bulletin, 33,* 381–390.

World Health Organization. (1992). *The ICD-10 classification of mental and behavioral disorders: Clinical descriptions and diagnostic guidelines.* Geneva, Switzerland: Author.

Yager, J. (2000). Weight perspectives: Contemporary challenges in obesity and eating disorders. *American Journal of Psychiatry, 157,* 851–853.

Yanovski, S. Z., Nelson, J. E., Dubbert, B. K., & Spitzer, R. L. (1993). Association of binge eating disorder and psychiatric comorbidity in obese subjects. *American Journal of Psychiatry, 150,* 1472–1479.

Young, E. A., Clopton, J. R., & Bleckley, M. K. (2004). Perfectionism, low self-esteem, and family factors as predictors of bulimic behavior. *Eating Behaviors, 5,* 273–283.

CHAPTER 16

Sleep Disorders

CHARLES M. MORIN AND JACK D. EDINGER

S leep disorders are common and debilitating conditions that contribute to emotional distress, social and occupational dysfunction, increased risks for injury, and, in some instances, serious medical illnesses. Despite their prevalence and clinical significance, sleep disorders have traditionally received relatively little attention in health provider training programs. This chapter is designed to familiarize readers with those sleep disorders most likely to be encountered in their practices. Specifically, this chapter reviews the diagnostic classification, clinical characteristics, course, and prognosis of various sleep disorders and explores the epidemiology of sleep pathology in modern society. In addition, etiological factors involved in the development of sleep disorders are considered, and methods for assessing patients' sleep complaints are described.

CLASSIFICATION

Three different nosologies are available for sleep disorder classification: the *International Classification of Sleep Disorders-2nd Edition: Diagnostic and Coding Manual* (*ICSD-2*; American Academy of Sleep Medicine [AASM], 2005), the Sleep Disorders sections of the *International Classification of Diseases* (*ICD*; World Health Organization, 1993, 1994), and the *Diagnostic and Statistical Manual of Mental Disorders* (*DSM-IV-TR*; American Psychiatric Association [APA], 2000). The ICSD-2 delineates clinical features and diagnostic criteria for more than 80 highly specific sleep disorders. Although traditional versions of the *ICD* offer a far less complex sleep disorder classification system, future versions are likely to adopt the ICSD-2 classification scheme. Given the level of detail and specificity, the ICSD-2 system is arguably best suited for sleep specialists. In contrast, the *DSM-IV-TR* nosology includes fewer and more global diagnostic categories. Whereas there is some overlap between the more detailed ICSD-2 and global *DSM-IV-TR* systems, psychologists and other mental health practitioners are generally more familiar and comfortable with the latter of these nosologies. Thus, only the sleep disorders classification scheme provided in the *DSM-IV-TR* is considered at length herein.

As illustrated in Table 16.1, the *DSM-IV-TR* delineates a variety of discrete diagnostic sleep disorders that are grouped into four broad categories on the basis of their presumed etiologies. *Primary sleep disorders* include various sleep-wake disturbances arising from abnormalities in the biological sleep-wake system and complicated by such factors as conditioned arousal at bedtime, poor sleep hygiene practices, and the development of secondary medical illnesses. Included within this broad category are several *dyssomnias* arising from abnormalities in the timing, amount, or quality of sleep and *parasomnias* characterized by abnormal events (e.g., nightmares) or unusual behaviors (e.g., sleepwalking) occurring during sleep. In contrast, *sleep disorders related to another mental disorder* involve a prominent sleep complaint attributable to a coexisting mental disorder such as a mood or anxiety disorder. Similarly, *sleep disorders due to a general medical condition* include disturbances arising directly from the effects (pain, seizures, etc.) of an active medical illness. Finally, *substance-induced sleep disorders* are presumed to arise from inappropriate use of or withdrawal from medications, illicit drugs, stimulants, or alcohol.

Table 16.1
DSM-IV-TR Sleep Disorders Classification

I. Primary sleep disorders
    A. Dyssomnias
        1. Primary insomnia
        2. Narcolepsy
        3. Breathing-related sleep disorders
        4. Primary hypersomnia
        5. Circadian rhythm sleep disorders
        6. Dyssomnia not otherwise specified
    B. Parasomnias
        1. Nightmare disorder
        2. Sleep terror disorder
        3. Sleepwalking disorder
        4. Other parasomnias
II. Sleep disorders related to another mental disorder
    A. Insomnia related to another mental disorder
    B. Hypersomnia related to another mental disorder
III. Sleep disorder related to a general medical condition
    A. Insomnia type
    B. Hypersomnia type
    C. Parasomnia type
    D. Mixed type
IV. Substance-induced sleep disorder*
    A. Insomnia type
    B. Hypersomnia type
    C. Parasomnia type
    D. Mixed type

*Note: The additional specifier *with onset during intoxication* should be used with substance-induced sleep disorders if sleep-related symptoms develop during intoxification with the substance; the specifier *with onset during withdrawal* should be used when the sleep symptoms develop during or shortly after withdrawal from the substance.

Of the various sleep disorders listed in Table 16.1, only those classified as primary sleep disorders may occur in the absence of a coexisting psychiatric, medical, or substance use problem. Moreover, even when a psychiatric, medical, or substance abuse disorder is also present, primary sleep disorders are viewed as having etiologies independent of such comorbid conditions. In contrast, the remaining diagnoses are assigned only as co-diagnoses among individuals who present a prominent sleep-wake complaint that warrants separate clinical attention. For example, a patient who presents a clinically prominent complaint of insomnia that is determined to arise from a recurrent major depressive disorder would be assigned both a diagnosis of major depressive disorder-recurrent and a diagnosis of insomnia related to another mental disorder. The ensuing discussion describes the various diagnostic subgroups listed in Table 16.1. Inasmuch as readers are likely to have less knowledge of the primary sleep disorder subtypes, more extensive descriptions of these disorders are provided.

DESCRIPTION OF THE DISORDERS

DYSSOMNIAS

Primary Insomnia   Primary insomnia, characterized by difficulty initiating or maintaining sleep or persistent poor-quality sleep, is a relatively common form of sleep disturbance that cannot be attributed to an underlying psychiatric, medical, or substance abuse problem. However, the diagnosis of primary insomnia does not necessarily imply a total absence of psychiatric or medical disorders but rather a sleep disturbance that is viewed as independent of any other coexisting conditions. Indeed, individuals suffering from primary insomnia often complain of mild anxiety, mood disturbances, concentration or memory dysfunction, somatic concerns, and general malaise, but such clinical findings are viewed as common symptoms rather than as causes of their sleep disturbances.

The development and persistence of this condition has been ascribed to myriad psychological, behavioral, and physiological anomalies. As suggested by some writers (Hauri, 2000; Hauri & Fisher, 1986; Spielman, Conroy & Glovinsky, 2003; Stepanski, 2000), primary insomnia, like many other forms of sleep disturbance, arises from a special confluence of endogenous *predisposing characteristics,* sleep-disruptive *precipitating events,* and *perpetuating behaviors or circumstances.* Vulnerabilities, such as proneness to worry, repression of disturbing emotion, physiological hyperarousal, or innate propensity toward light, fragmented sleep—or all of the above—may predispose certain individuals to a primary sleep disturbance. Among such individuals, insomnia may develop given sufficient stress or disruption from a precipitating event (e.g., loss of a loved one, undergoing a painful medical procedure, frequent disruption of sleep-wake schedule). Subsequently, primary insomnia persists when conditioned environmental cues and maladaptive habits serve to perpetuate sleep disturbance long after the initial precipitating circumstances are resolved.

Many primary insomnia sufferers report intense preoccupation with sleep, heightened arousal as bedtime approaches, and excessive, albeit unproductive, sleep efforts (Espie, 2002; Hauri, 2000). This pattern is demonstrated by the following case study.

Case Study

Ms. P. was a 71-year-old married woman who presented to a sleep disorders clinic with a 6-month history of insomnia. She noted her sleep difficulty had begun during a time when she was worried about her husband's medical status. Although her husband's medical condition eventually was resolved, her insomnia persisted and had worsened over time. At the time of her initial sleep clinic visit, she reported that she had developed a marked aversion to thoughts of her bedtime. Indeed, she noted that her anxiety level typically rose each day as her usual bedtime approached. Reportedly, she typically had great difficulty initiating sleep and, as a result, had resorted to frequent use of prescription sleeping pills to remedy her problem. However, on many occasions she continued to have increased anxiety about sleep and a less-than-desirable night's sleep despite the use of prescribed sleep aids. A full work-up, including a medical exam by her primary physician and psychological screening assessment by a sleep clinician revealed no medical or psychiatric cause of her sleep difficulty. As part of the assessment, Ms. P. also completed self-report measures of anxiety and depression and kept a daily sleep diary for a period of 2 weeks before initiating treatment. Although she appeared to have developed some psychological dependence on her sleep medication, this dependence appeared secondary to what was viewed as her primary insomnia problem.

Patients such as Ms. P. usually describe bedtime as the worst time of day. A vicious cycle often emerges for such patients in which repetitive unsuccessful sleep attempts reinforce their sleep-related anxiety, which, in turn, contributes to continued sleep difficulty. Through repetitive association with unsuccessful sleep efforts, the bedroom environment and presleep rituals often become cues or stimuli for poor sleep. Moreover, in some cases, formerly benign habits, such as watching television, eating, or reading in bed may reduce the stimulus value of the bed and bedroom for sleep and may further enhance the sleep problem. As a result, it is not unusual for primary insomnia sufferers to report improved sleep in novel settings where conditioned environmental cues are absent and usual presleep rituals are obviated.

Narcolepsy   Narcolepsy is a relatively rare sleep disorder arising from environmental influences acting on specific hereditary factors. Characteristically, this condition results in moderate to severe daytime dysfunction. Classic narcolepsy is defined by a tetrad of symptoms: (1) *excessive daytime sleepiness* and unintended sleep episodes occurring during situations (e.g., driving, at work, during conversations) when those without sleep disorders typically are able to remain awake; (2) *cataplexy,* which consists of an abrupt and reversible decrease or loss of muscle tone (without loss of consciousness) precipitated by such emotions as laughter, anger, surprise, or exhilaration; (3) *sleep paralysis,* which involves awakening from nocturnal sleep with an inability to move; and (4) *hypnagogic hallucinations* consisting of vivid images and dreams, usually just as sleep develops but sometimes intruding into wakefulness (Guilleminault & Fromherz, 2005).

Individuals with narcolepsy complain of frequent overwhelming episodes throughout the day during which they feel compelled to sleep despite having obtained a seemingly adequate amount of sleep during the previous night. Although daytime naps can be momentarily restorative, excessive sleepiness may return shortly thereafter. As the syndrome progresses, naps may lose their restorative value, and even nocturnal sleep may become disturbed (Guilleminault & Fromherz, 2005; Parkes, 1985).

Breathing-Related Sleep Disorders   A variety of breathing-related sleep disorders (BRSDs) may produce significant nocturnal sleep disruption and result in sleep-wake complaints. Patients suffering form *obstructive sleep apnea* experience repetitive partial (hypopneas) or complete (apneas) obstructions of their upper airways during sleep despite continued diaphragmatic effort to breathe. Other patients who suffer from *upper airway resistance syndrome* may show repeated arousals in association with far more subtle periods of reduced patency in the upper airway. In contrast, patients suffering from *central sleep apnea* experience sleep disruption as a result of repeated events during which both airflow and respiratory efforts cease. Finally, patients with *central alveolar hypoventilation syndrome* experience sleep-related worsening of their daytime proneness to hypoventilate. Whatever their exact form, such BRSDs lead to repeated arousals from sleep (to restart normal breathing) and consequent diminution in sleep's quality and restorative value.

Although some patients with BRSDs complain of insomnia, most report excessive daytime sleepiness and unintentional sleep episodes occurring while watching television, reading, or driving. Additional symptoms may include loud snoring, gasping for breath during sleep, frequent dull headaches upon awakening, and *automatic behaviors* (i.e., carrying out activities without, at the moment, being aware of one's actions). BRSDs may result in such psychological consequents as dysphoria, irritability, concentration difficulties, and memory dysfunction. In addition, they may produce serious medical consequences, including hypertension, cardiac arrhythmias and arrest, cerebral vascular infarction (stroke), sexual dysfunction, and nocturnal enuresis (Bassetti, Aldrich, Chervin, & Quint, 1996; Guilleminault & Bassiri, 2005; Nieto et al., 2000; Somers & Javaheri, 2005). The pathological daytime sleepiness of patients with BRSDs places them at significantly increased risk for serious daytime mishaps such as traffic accidents (Horstmann, Hess, Bassetti, Gugger, & Mathis, 2000; Teran-Santos, Jimenez-Gomez, & Cordero-Guevara, 1999).

Primary Hypersomnia   Primary hypersomnia is a sleep-wake disorder characterized by excessive daytime sleepiness that cannot be attributed to a BRSD; presence of narcolepsy; or a medical, psychiatric, or substance abuse problem. Individuals with this condition present complaints of severe daytime drowsiness that interferes with work performance, social functioning, and general quality of life. Daytime somnolence leads to frequent naps that are not refreshing. Nocturnal sleep time is usually greater than 6 hours but in some patients may be more than 10 hours on a nightly basis (Bassetti, Pelayo, & Guilleminault, 2005). Unlike patients with a BRSD or narcolepsy, patients with primary hypersomnia show no sleep paralysis, cataplexy, or respiratory impairment during sleep. Nonetheless, their awakenings in the morning are often difficult and accompanied by excessive grogginess or *sleep drunkenness* (Bassetti et al., 2005). Like patients with BRSDs or narcolepsy, patients suffering from primary hypersomnia usually require referral to sleep specialists for proper diagnosis and management.

Circadian Rhythm Sleep Disorders   Individuals with circadian rhythm sleep disorders (CRSDs) experience persistent or recurrent sleep-wake difficulties as a result of a mismatch between their endogenous, circadian sleep-wake rhythms and the sleep-wake schedules imposed on them by their educational pursuits, work settings, or social demands. Alterations of the usual sleep-wake pattern due to jet lag, rotating shift work, or social and recreational pursuits may all lead to CRSDs. In some individuals, CRSDs are intermittent or recurrent as a function of frequently changing work or travel schedules. For others, aberrant bedtimes may, over a period of time, lead to a persistent shift (either advance or delay) in the underlying circadian mechanisms that regulate the timing of sleep.

These individuals typically complain that their sleep is disrupted or does not occur at a time that is consistent with their desired sleep-wake schedule. In addition, they often report insomnia during their preferred sleep periods and excessive sleepiness during the times they choose to be awake. Among individuals engaged in rotating shift work, alterations in chosen sleep-wake schedules between workdays and days off may perpetuate the sleep-wake complaints. In other cases, the person may obtain a normal amount of sleep if it is allowed to occur spontaneously and not at a time chosen in response to actual or perceived external demands (AASM, 2005; Reid & Zee, 2005). Whatever the cause, such individuals usually require interventions designed to resynchronize their endogenous and exogenous sleep-wake rhythms.

PARASOMNIAS

Nightmare Disorder   Nightmare disorder is characterized by repeated awakenings from nocturnal sleep or daytime naps precipitated by disturbing dreams. Typically such dreams involve threats to the individual's physical, psychological, or emotional well-being. Upon awakening, the individual appears fully alert, oriented, and cognizant of the arousing dream's content. Although anxiety and depressed mood may develop as secondary features of the nightmares, such emotional symptoms do not meet criteria for a psychiatric disorder. Moreover, inasmuch as nightmares are common to children, college students, and many noncomplaining normal adults (Nielsen & Zadra, 2005), nightmare disorder is diagnosed only when recurrent disturbing dreams cause impairment of emotional, social, or occupational functioning (APA, 2000).

Individuals with nightmare disorder complain of repeated disturbing dreams that arouse them from their sleep. Since nightmares arise during rapid eye movement (REM) sleep, individuals with nightmare disorder typically report nightmare-induced awakenings during the latter half of the night, when REM episodes typically become longer and more vivid. Careful interview also usually reveals dream content that reflects a recurrent theme reflective of underlying conflicts, characteristic fears, neuroticism, or openness/sensitivity to emotional intrusions (Berquier & Ashton, 1992; Hartmann, Elkin & Garg, 1991; Kales, Soldatos, Caldwell, Charney, et al., 1980). For example, individuals with obsessive-compulsive traits often report recurrent nightmares during which they find themselves unable to finish an important assignment despite their persistent efforts to do so.

Case Study

Ms. R. was a 45-year-old successful businesswoman who presented to the sleep center with a complaint of frequent disturbing dreams. In particular, she reported being bothered by a recurrent dream that often awakened her and left her feeling anxious. The theme of this dream centered on her trying to arrive on time for an important job interview. The dream typically began with her leaving home with the intent to arrive for the interview on time. However, she noted that she typically would be running late and, hence, felt uncertain about whether she would arrive for the interview on time. As the dream typically progressed, she arrived at a building where the interview was to take place and encountered a male doorkeeper standing beside the building entry, which looked very much like a garage door. At that point she would request entry to the building and the doorkeeper would set in motion an apparatus that looked like a mechanical mouse. This "mouse" would then travel slowly up the wall beside the door until it reached the unlocking mechanism. At that point, the mouse inserted itself into this mechanism and the door opened. The patient reported that she then would typically enter the building and walk down a hallway until she encountered a very similar locked door and another doorkeeper who again had to engage the maddeningly slow mechanical mouse to unlock the door. Once this second door opened she entered another hallway only to eventually encounter yet another door that had to be opened in similar fashion by an attendant. This process typically repeated several times during the dream, and with each new door encountered, Ms. R. noted increased anxiety and fear that she would be late for her interview. Typically the dream would culminate with her going through a final door and finding herself back outside of the building right back where she started. At this point in the dream she would awaken feeling anxious and frustrated. In addition to assessment of her sleep complaint, the evaluation revealed no significant symptomatology of either anxiety or depression. The patient was asked to keep a daily diary of her nightmares, noting the frequency, intensity, and content of disturbing dreams. This material was subsequently used for an exposure-based intervention.

In addition, individuals with nightmare disorder usually complain of anxiety and sleep disturbance caused by the nightmares as well as resultant disruption of their normal day-to-day functioning. The preceding case study exemplifies the nature of this condition.

Sleepwalking and Sleep Terror Disorders   In approximately 1 out of every 100 patients presenting to sleep centers, aberrant nocturnal behaviors disrupt normal sleep (Punjabi, Welch, & Strohl, 2000). Among the more common of these are sleepwalking and sleep terrors. Both phenomena occur early in the sleep period and appear to represent incomplete arousals from the deepest stages of sleep known as slow-wave sleep. Individuals with *sleepwalking disorder* arise from bed in a stuporous state and amble about their homes but may also walk out of doors. Typically, such sleepwalking episodes involve behaviors such as using the bathroom, eating, talking, or walking aimlessly about the home. In contrast, individuals with *sleep terror disorder* display episodes during which they suddenly emit a shrill scream, usually after sitting up in bed. Because neither of these conditions is associated with REM sleep, the affected individual usually does not report dream content in association with the event. Moreover, the patient is usually difficult to arouse from the episode and may have no recall of the event the next morning. Since more slow-wave sleep occurs in younger age groups, these events are observed most commonly in children, although they also may develop in adults. At a minimum, such events cause the individual embarrassment and may contribute to avoidance of certain situations (e.g., going on trips, overnight visits to friends' homes). At worst, both sleepwalking and sleep terror episodes may result in injury to the affected individual or to a bed partner. In some cases, acts of violence such as striking out at others may occur during these events, and rare instances of homicide during sleep-walking episodes have been reported (Broughton et al., 1994). Of course, referral to a specialty sleep disorders clinic would be indicated whenever historical information suggests such parasomnias pose risks to the affected individual or others.

SLEEP DISORDERS RELATED TO ANOTHER MENTAL DISORDER

Sleep-wake complaints are extremely common among a range of psychiatric disorders (Benca, 2005; Nofzinger, Buysse, Reynolds, & Kupfer, 1993). However, a small subset of individuals with psychiatric disorders either minimizes the importance of other symptoms or reports disturbances of sleep and wakefulness as the most salient concerns. In such cases, the diagnosis of sleep disorder related to another mental condition would be assigned in addition to the diagnosis for the contributing psychiatric condition.

Several clinical case series (Buysse et al., 1994; Coleman et al., 1982; Edinger et al., 1989; Mendelson, 1997; Tan, Kales, Kales, Soldatos, & Bixler, 1984) have shown that mood disorders are more prevalent than other psychiatric conditions among patient groups who present to sleep disorders centers. Among such groups, those suffering from depression typically complain of insomnia characterized by sleep-onset difficulty; early morning awakenings; and nonrefreshing, fragmented sleep. Nocturnal sleep recordings generally corroborate these difficulties. In addition, they show a reduced latency to the onset of the first REM period, an increase in the number of eye movements during REM episodes (particularly early in the night), a reduction in deep or slow-wave sleep, and an increase in both lighter sleep stages and arousals (Reynolds & Kupfer, 1987). However, many of these sleep aberrations may be observed in other psychiatric disorders as well (Benca, Obermeyer, Thisted, & Gillin, 1992). Conversely, patients with bipolar disorder show a cyclic pattern of insomnia and hypersomnia corresponding to their manic-depressive swings, but such individuals most often complain of hypersomnia and fatigue during their depressive periods. Finally, individuals with atypical mood disorders (e.g., seasonal depression) complain of hypersomnia, which is manifested by extended nocturnal sleep periods, frequent napping, and feelings of fatigue and lethargy (Benca, 2005; Walsh, Moss, & Sugerman, 1994).

Anxiety disorders also frequently contribute to sleep disturbances, but proportionately account for a lower percentage of sleep disorder diagnoses than do the mood disorders among those who present to sleep centers (Buysse et al., 1994; Tan et al., 1984). Nonetheless, general population surveys suggest that insomnia associated with anxiety disorders may be slightly more prevalent than insomnias associated with depressive conditions (Ohayon, Caulet, & Lemoine, 1998). Most commonly, individuals with anxiety disorders complain of difficulty initiating or maintaining sleep and less commonly report early morning awakening or complain solely that their sleep is not restorative (Ohayon et al., 1998). Among individuals with phobic or obsessive-compulsive disorders, sleep disturbance may emerge in response to troublesome stimuli or situations, whereas those with generalized anxiety disorders and posttraumatic stress disorders may experience a more pervasive and unrelenting insomnia problem (Walsh et al., 1994). Alternatively, some patients with panic disorder complain of sleep disturbances caused by nocturnal panic attacks occurring during non-REM sleep (Hauri, Friedman, & Ravaris, 1989; Mellman & Uhde, 1989).

In addition to mood and anxiety disorders, a number of other psychiatric conditions may give rise to a sleep-wake complaint. Insomnia is not uncommon among individuals with somatoform disorders, likely because of their tendencies to somatize emotional or psychological conflicts (Walsh et al., 1994). In contrast, insomnia arises among some Axis II personality disorders as a result of their chaotic lifestyles and irregular sleep schedules. Insomnia and *night wandering* commonly accompany dementia as a result of associated anomalies in the biological sleep-wake system (Bliwise, 1993). Finally, marked sleep disturbance is common to schizophrenia and other psychoses, but individuals with such disorders rarely report sleep difficulties as their primary or sole complaint.

SLEEP DISORDER DUE TO A GENERAL MEDICAL CONDITION

Sleep-wake disturbances arise in the context of medical disorders that are too numerous to consider here. However, most such medical conditions do not warrant a separate sleep disorder diagnosis, because sleep complaints do not dominate their clinical presentation. Nevertheless, a subset of patients with medical conditions complain of sleep difficulties to such a degree that such complaints warrant separate clinical attention. A diagnosis of sleep disorder due to a general medical condition is made in such cases.

Individuals with sleep disorders due to a general medical condition may suffer from an insomnia type, hypersomnia type, parasomnia type, or a mixture (mixed type) of these forms of sleep-wake disturbances. Insomnia may arise from a variety of medical conditions, including vascular headaches, cerebrovascular disease, hyperthyroidism, chronic bronchitis, degenerative neurological conditions, and pain accompanying various chronic medical disorders (Lavigne, McMillan, & Zucconi, 2005). In contrast, conditions such as hypothyroidism, viral encephalitis, and chronic fatigue syndrome may result in hypersomnia complaints. Among patients with medically based parasomnias, those with sleep-related epileptic seizures constitute the largest subgroup. Regardless of their presenting sleep difficulties, individuals with a medically based sleep disorder usually require intervention for their contributing medical conditions in order to realize sleep-wake improvements.

SUBSTANCE-INDUCED SLEEP DISORDER

A variety of medications, illicit drugs, and other substances in common use may contribute to sleep-wake disturbances. Many of these substances produce insomnia, hypersomnia, parasomnias, or a mixture of these symptoms, either while in use or during periods of withdrawal and abstinence. When such sleep-wake disturbances are presented as a predominant clinical complaint, a diagnosis of substance-induced sleep disorder would be warranted as a co-diagnosis in addition to the *DSM-IV-TR* diagnosis of the substance abuse problem. Most commonly, such a diagnosis would be associated with excessive use of alcohol, sedative hypnotic medications, and stimulants.

Approximately 10% of men and 3% to 5% of women develop significant alcohol dependence/abuse problems (Gillin, Drummond, Clark, & Moore, 2005; Schuckit & Irwin, 1988). Various factors may contribute to alcohol dependence, but chronic sleep difficulties may lead many to rely on alcohol as a hypnotic aid. Survey data suggest that 2% to 5% of those between 18 and 45 years of age routinely use alcohol by itself or with other sleep aids to combat insomnia (Johnson, Roehrs, Roth, & Breslau, 1998). Alcohol ingestion may facilitate sleep onset but usually leads to sleep maintenance difficulties due to sleep fragmentation caused by metabolic withdrawal effects occurring amid the sleep period. Also, heavy alcohol consumption may result in variety of parasomnias, such as bedwetting, sleep terrors, and sleepwalking. Moreover, given alcohol's pronounced suppressant effects on REM sleep, vivid, disturbing dreams may emerge during alcohol withdrawal due to a *REM rebound effect.* Among chronic alcohol abusers, insomnia may persist through even extended periods of abstinence and is the primary catalyst for relapse (Brower, Aldrich, & Hall, 1998).

Like alcohol, sedating prescription medications and sedative-hypnotics in particular may contribute to a substance-induced sleep disorder. Although most sedating medications used as sleep aids are effective for transient sleep disturbances, some such medications lose their effectiveness with continued use. Individuals who frequently use sedating medications for sleep often experience a return of their insomnia as they become tolerant to such drugs. In turn, hypersomnia complaints may emerge among those who increase medication dosages to reestablish drug efficacy. In addition, abrupt withdrawal of some sedating medications with short half-lives may lead to a period of *rebound insomnia* during which sleep disturbances worsen (Gillin et al., 2005). Clinical observations suggest that such withdrawal effects often contribute to loss of self-efficacy in regard to sleep and encourage many individuals to continue use of hypnotics long after such drugs lose their effectiveness.

In contrast, stimulants such as amphetamines, cocaine, caffeine, and nicotine increase daytime alertness and may disrupt nighttime sleep. As a result, insomnia complaints may arise during periods of use. Conversely, complaints of hypersomnia may emerge during periods of withdrawal and abstinence. However, paradoxical symptoms, such as insomnia during nicotine withdrawal and hypersomnia during periods of heavy caffeine use, also have been observed (Gillin et al., 2005; Regestein, 1989). Whatever their exact characteristics, stimulant-related sleep disorders often may persist for prolonged periods given the addictive properties of many of the substances that perpetuate them.

EPIDEMIOLOGY

PREVALENCE

Various surveys have suggested high prevalence of intermittent and chronic sleep-wake complaints in industrialized societies. For example, insomnia is reported as an intermittent problem for approximately one-third of the adult population in industrialized countries, whereas 8% to 18% of those surveyed report chronic sleep difficulties with associated daytime impairment (Mellinger, Balter, & Uhlenhuth, 1985; Morin, LeBlanc, Daley, Grégoire, & Mérette, 2006; National Sleep Foundation, 2005; Ohayon, 2002; Weissman, Greenwald, Nino-Murcia, & Dement, 1997). Women are twice as likely to present insomnia complaints than men, and middle-aged and older adults are more prone to this form of sleep difficulty than younger age groups. Both general population (e.g., Ohayon et al., 1998) and sleep clinic–based (e.g., Buysse et al., 1994) studies suggest that insomnia associated with psychiatric disorders is more prevalent than primary insomnia, and both of these forms of insomnia are more common than circadian rhythm sleep disorders and substance-induced insomnia problems.

Somewhat less prevalent but still relatively common are hypersomnia complaints. Survey results vary but generally suggest that excessive daytime sleepiness affects 5% to 15% of the adult populations in Western nations (Partinen & Hublin, 2005). Sleep apnea sufferers likely account for the largest subgroup of these individuals, as most population studies suggest that between 1% and 4% of adults (Partinen & Hublin, 2005) suffer from this condition. Narcolepsy is a much less prevalent disorder that occurs in 50 out of 100,000 individuals, a rate similar to the occurrence of Parkinson's disease. However, genetic factors seemingly cause variation in population prevalence rates. For instance, the Japanese appear to have the highest vulnerability for this disease, with prevalence estimates of up to 160 per 100,000 individuals (Honda, 1979; Partinen & Hublin, 2005). Primary hypersomnia is relatively rare; reports from sleep centers show this diagnosis is assigned only about one-tenth as often as a diagnosis of narcolepsy (Billard & Dauvilliers, 2001). The population prevalence of primary hypersomnia remains unknown in part because this diagnosis is derived by exclusion of many other medical, psychiatric, and sleep disorder diagnoses that are difficult to assess by common epidemiological survey methodology.

Less is known about the prevalence of parasomnias, but limited data suggest prevalence of 3% to 9% for frequent nightmares and 0.1% to 1.0% for sleepwalking among adults. Among children, 2% to 11% are bothered by frequent nightmares, whereas sleepwalking occurs in 1% to 3% on a regular basis. Finally, sleep terrors hit a peak prevalence in children between the ages of 5 and 7 years old but occur at a rate of less than 1% in the adult population (Lugaresi, Zucconi, & Bixler, 1987; Partinen & Hublin, 2005).

PSYCHOLOGICAL, BEHAVIORAL, AND MEDICAL CONSEQUENCES

Sleep disorders may impart significant psychological, behavioral, and medical morbidity to those who suffer from such conditions. Several studies have suggested that the presence of insomnia, in the absence of psychiatric and medical disease, increases significantly the risk for the subsequent onset of major depressive illness and other psychiatric disorders, even many years after the insomnia is first identified (Chang, Ford, Mead, Cooper-Patrick, & Klag, 1997; Weissman et al., 1997). Other studies have suggested that those who suffer from insomnia report a reduced quality of life, a greater propensity for work-related accidents, and higher alcohol consumption than those without sleep complaints (Johnson et al., 1998; Johnson & Spinweber, 1983; Katz & McHorney, 2002; Zammit, Weiner, Damato,

Sillup, & McMillan, 1999). Moreover, both primary insomnia and insomnia complicated by comorbid conditions enhance utilization of the health care system and lead to work absenteeism (Simon & VonKorff, 1997; Weissman et al., 1997).

Like insomnia, hypersomnia complaints, in the absence of other psychiatric symptoms, increase the risk for subsequent depressive disorders (Ford & Kamerow, 1989; Lugaresi et al., 1987). In addition, several studies have implicated BRSDs in the development of such serious medical conditions as hypertension, cardiac arrhythmias, myocardial infarction, stroke, cognitive decline, and some forms of dementia, all of which increase the risk of mortality (Foley et al., 2001; Ohayon & Vecchierini, 2002; Partinen & Hublin, 2005). Traffic fatalities also are more common among those who suffer from chronic hypersomnia (Horstmann et al., 2000; Teran-Santos et al., 1999), particularly in those who suffer from BRSDs. However, the exact rate of accidents due to all causes of excessive sleepiness is difficult to ascertain because sleepiness as a causal factor is difficult—if not impossible—to ascertain after the accident occurs. One study found that a driver's falling asleep behind the wheel caused 27% of all traffic accidents, and such occurrences accounted for 83% of all observed fatalities (Findley, Unverzadt, & Suratt, 1988).

Circadian rhythm disorders, like many other sleep disorders, may impart considerable morbidity to affected individuals. Circadian disturbances caused by frequent exposure to jet lag or shift work can lead to gastrointestinal or cardiac disorders (Arendt, Stone, & Skene, 2005; Knutsson, 1989). Furthermore, adverse effects on mood and mental well-being may arise from chronic sleep disruption due to shift work and other causes of circadian disorders (National Commission on Sleep Disorders Research, 1993). Along with their potential contribution to driver errors, improper sleep scheduling and resultant sleep loss have been implicated in serious air-travel and maritime accidents as well as in accidents in the workplace (National Transportation Safety Board, 1990; Rosekind, 2005). Hence, the sleep disorders discussed here may contribute to significant psychological, behavioral, and medical disorders that result in serious consequences for the affected individuals.

COURSE AND PROGNOSIS

Insomnia can begin at any time during the course of the life span, but onset of the first episode is more common in young adulthood (Morin, 1993). It is often triggered by stressful life events, with the most common precipitants involving separation or divorce, death of a loved one, occupational stress, and interpersonal conflicts (Bastien, Vallières, & Morin, 2004; Healy et al., 1981; Vollrath, Wicki, & Angst, 1989). In a small subset of cases, insomnia begins in childhood, in the absence of psychological or medical problems, and persists throughout adulthood (Hauri & Olmstead, 1980). Insomnia is a frequent problem among women during menopause and often persists after other symptoms (e.g., hot flashes) have resolved. The first episode of insomnia also can occur in late life, although it must be distinguished from normal age-related changes in sleep patterns and from sleep disturbances due to medical problems or prescribed medications (Lichstein & Morin, 2000).

For most insomnia sufferers, sleep difficulties are transient, lasting a few days and resolving themselves once the initial precipitating event has subsided. Its course also may be intermittent, with repeated brief episodes of sleep difficulties following a close association with the occurrence of stressful events (Vollrath et al., 1989). Even when insomnia has developed a chronic course, typically there is extensive night-to-night variability in sleep patterns, with an occasional restful night's sleep intertwined with several nights of poor sleep (Vallières, Ivers, Bastien, Beaulieu-Bonneau, & Morin, 2005). The subtype of insomnia (i.e., sleep onset, maintenance, or mixed insomnia) also may change over time (Hohagen et al., 1994).

There are several hypothetical risk factors for insomnia (e.g., female gender; advancing age, emotional factors), and a past history of insomnia increases the risk for future episodes of sleep difficulties (Klink, Quan, Kaltenborn, & Lebowitz, 1992). This pattern of recurrence is present in both primary insomniacs and in patients whose sleep difficulties are associated with affective or anxiety disorders (Vollrath et al., 1989). The prognosis for insomnia varies extensively across individuals and is probably mediated by psychological factors. It can also be complicated by prolonged use of hypnotic drugs (Morin & Espie, 2003).

In narcolepsy, primary symptoms of excessive daytime sleepiness and irresistible sleep attacks usually develop during late adolescence. While the onset of the syndrome may occur at any time between childhood and the fifth decade of life, accurate diagnosis is often made when an individual has already experienced symptomatology for many years. Cataplexy, sleep paralysis, and hypnagogic hallucinations almost always follow rather than precede onset of daytime sleepiness, and some features may not develop at all. Although drug therapy can provide some relief for sleep attacks and cataplexy, narcolepsy is a lifelong disorder. Excessive daytime sleepiness may worsen over time, and nighttime sleep can become impaired as a result of stimulant medications used to stay awake during the day. Other symptoms may decrease or fluctuate in intensity over the life span (Billard, Dauvilliers, & Carlander, 1998).

The most common form of BRSD, obstructive sleep apnea, can occur at any age. It is, however; much more prevalent among middle-aged obese men (Guilleminault & Bassiri, 2005). When left untreated, its course is usually progressive and, in most severe cases, it can lead to significant daytime impairments (sleepiness, memory and concentration difficulties) and severe medical complications (e.g., hypertension, heart failures). Onset of primary hypersomnia usually occurs between ages 15 and 30, and symptoms develop gradually over several weeks or months.

CRSDs due to jet lag and shift work have a recurrent course that is directly linked to the frequency of traveling or schedule change (Arendt et al., 2005; Rosekind, 2005). Following a transmeridian flight, it takes approximately 1 day for each time zone crossed for the circadian rhythm to become resynchronized with local time. Likewise, after a week of work on the night shift, it takes up to 10 days to become fully reacclimated to working in the daytime and sleeping at night. Adjustment to frequent changes in sleep schedules becomes more difficult with advancing age. Shift workers tend to consume more stimulants to stay awake and more hypnotics to sleep than workers who have regular day shifts. Working on night shifts for several years may increase risk of sleep difficulties when returning to a regular daytime shift.

Most parasomnias occur first in childhood. Sleep terror and sleepwalking have a typical onset between ages 5 and 12 and tend to resolve spontaneously by mid-adolescence, suggesting a developmental course to these conditions. Their persistence, and especially onset, in adulthood have been associated with greater likelihood of concomitant psychopathology (Kales, Kales, et al., 1980; Kales, Soldatos, Caldwell, Kales, et al., 1980). Sleepwalking is more common than sleep terrors, but their co-occurrence is frequent. In some individuals, both conditions may develop at the same time, whereas in others they may develop at different times. Following sleep deprivation, there is an increase in the amount of deep sleep during the recovery period. As such, sleep deprivation can increase incidence of sleep terror and sleepwalking, which originate from deep sleep (stages 3 to 4). Fever and sleeping in an unfamiliar environment also have been associated with higher risks for these parasomnias. Nightmares can occur at any age, but their first occurrence is usually between 3 and 5 years of age. Frequency and course of nightmares are highly variable. Stressful life events (e.g., natural disasters, violence) can trigger nightmares in both children and adults, although they can also be isolated phenomena, independent of anxiety (Wood & Bootzin, 1990).

Sleep pathologies due to mental, medical, or substance abuse disorder tend to closely parallel the temporal course of the underlying disorder. Conditioning factors may contribute to or perpetuate a sleep problem, especially insomnia, even after the underlying condition has resolved. For example, sleep disturbances associated with major depression may persist long after the depression has lifted (Rush et al., 1986). Likewise, sleep difficulties associated with chronic use of benzodiazepines or with alcohol abuse may continue even after complete withdrawal from the substance (Morin et al., 2004).

DIAGNOSTIC CONSIDERATIONS

This section outlines the most important issues to consider in making a differential diagnosis. After outlining the main clinical features of four broad categories of sleep-wake complaints, we review the distinguishing features leading to specific sleep disorder diagnoses.

INSOMNIA

The clinical features of insomnia involve a subjective complaint of difficulty initiating or maintaining sleep or of nonrestorative sleep that causes significant distress or impairments in social or occupational functioning (APA, 2000). The *DSM-IV-TR* does not provide specific operational criteria to define insomnia severity. In clinical research, however, insomnia is often operationalized as a sleep-onset latency or wake after sleep onset (or both) greater than 30 minutes per night for more than three nights per week (Morin & Espie, 2003), with a corresponding sleep efficiency (ratio of time asleep to time spent in bed) of less than 85%. Sleep duration alone is not always useful to diagnose insomnia because of individual differences in sleep needs. Some people function well with as little as 5 to 6 hours of sleep and would not necessarily complain of insomnia; conversely, others needing 9 to 10 hours may complain of inadequate sleep when they sleep for only 7 or 8 hours. Thus, the patient's subjective complaint is crucial in establishing a diagnosis of primary or secondary insomnia. Associated features of insomnia often include complaints of daytime fatigue, cognitive impairments (attention, memory, concentration), social discomfort, and mood disturbances (Edinger et al., 2004).

Although numerous factors can produce a subjective complaint of insomnia (e.g., emotional, medical, environmental), the main differential diagnosis is usually between primary insomnia and insomnia related to another mental disorder. This distinction is not always easily made. A high rate of comorbidity exists between sleep and psychiatric disorders in general, and more specifically between insomnia, depression, and anxiety conditions (Billard, Partinen, Roth, & Shapiro, 1994; Ford & Kamerow, 1989; Morin & Ware, 1996; National Institutes of Health [NIH], 2005; Ohayon et al., 1998). A difficult issue in the diagnosis of insomnia is that sleep disturbance is a common feature of several psychiatric disorders, and problems falling asleep and staying asleep observed in primary insomnia are also often linked to anxiety disorders and mood disorders (Bélanger, Morin, Langlois, & Ladouceur, 2004; Benca et al., 1992; Harvey, Schmidt, Scarna, Semler, & Goodwin, 2005). Nonetheless, many individuals present insomnia with concurrent features of anxiety, depression, or both, who do not meet criteria for a psychiatric disorder. In the presence of coexisting insomnia and anxiety or depression, it is important to clarify the relative onset and temporal course of each disorder, although this distinction is not always easily made (McCrae & Lichstein, 2001; NIH, 2005). The diagnosis of primary insomnia is made when its onset and course are independent of a mental disorder. Conversely, a diagnosis of insomnia associated with psycho-pathology is indicated when onset of the sleep problem coincides with, and its sub-sequent course occurs exclusively with psychopathology. Data from clinical case series suggest that between 35% and 44% of patients presenting to a sleep clinic with a primary complaint of insomnia receive a diagnosis of insomnia related to another mental disorder (AASM, 2005; Buysse et al., 1994; Coleman et al., 1982).

Insomnia also can result from another sleep disorder. Restless legs syndrome, a condition characterized by an unpleasant and creeping sensation in the calves, can produce severe sleep-onset insomnia. Periodic limb movement is a related condition characterized by repetitive leg twitches that can produce sleep main-tenance difficulties. Some breathing-related sleep disorders, especially central sleep apnea, can also produce difficulties maintaining sleep. Obstructive sleep apnea more typically leads to a complaint of excessive daytime sleepiness. A pa-tient's clinical history combined with daily monitoring of sleep-wake schedules is usually sufficient to determine whether insomnia is related to an underlying circadian rhythm disorder. Some parasomnias, especially nightmares, can cause awakenings, but the main diagnostic focus is the nightmare. Insomnia also can arise from various medical conditions (e.g., hyperthyroidism, pain, congestive heart failure, pulmonary disease) or from use or withdrawal of prescribed medications (e.g., steroids, bronchodilators), sedative-hypnotics, alcohol, or illicit stimulants (e.g., cocaine). In those instances, the primary diagnosis would be, respectively, a sleep disorder associated with a medical condition or a substance-induced sleep disorder (AASM, 2005).

HYPERSOMNIA

The main sleep disorders with a predominant complaint of excessive daytime sleepiness are narcolepsy, BRSD (e.g., sleep apnea), and primary hypersomnia. The differential diagnosis among these conditions is based on the patient's his-tory, clinical features, nocturnal sleep recordings, and measurement of daytime sleepiness. The first diagnostic consideration with a complaint of excessive daytime sleepiness is whether a person is allowing enough time for sleep. This possibility is suggested when a person reports fewer than 6 or 7 hours of sleep per night and by evidence of adequate daytime alertness when sleep duration is extended to 8 or 9 hours. Such presentation is more likely among chronically sleep-deprived indi-viduals with highly demanding occupational and family schedules. When time is

Table 16.2

Symptoms Associated with Sleep Apnea, Narcolepsy, and Primary Hypersomnia

Symptom	Apnea	Narcolepsy	Primary Hypersomnia
Snoring	+	−	−
Breathing lapses	+	−	−
Sleep attacks	−	+	−
Cataplexy	−	+	−
Hypnagogic hallucinations	−	+	−
Sleep paralysis	−	+	−
Restless sleep	+	+	−
Excessive daytime sleepiness	+	+	+
Sleep drunkenness	+	−	+
Automatic behaviors	+	+	+

available to catch up on sleep, such as on weekends, daytime alertness is much improved. Conversely, individuals with narcolepsy, BRSD, and primary hypersomnia experience daytime sleepiness regardless of the amount of nocturnal sleep they obtain. Several additional symptoms help to distinguish among those conditions (see Table 16.2).

The most prominent symptoms in BRSD, especially obstructive sleep apnea, include loud snoring and pauses in breathing (Guilleminault & Bassiri, 2005). These symptoms are typically witnessed by a bed partner. In narcolepsy, the main clinical features are repeated and irresistible sleep attacks throughout the day with or without accompanying symptoms of cataplexy, hypnagogic hallucinations, and sleep paralysis (Billard et al., 1998). A short latency to REM sleep is a diagnostic feature of narcolepsy. In both apnea and narcolepsy, sleep continuity is impaired and the proportion of time spent in stages 3 to 4 sleep is significantly reduced. Conversely, nocturnal sleep is usually long, deep, and undisrupted in primary hypersomnia. This latter diagnosis is often made by default, in the absence of other classic symptoms. Daytime napping is refreshing in narcoleptics but not in patients with apnea or primary hypersomnia. Sleep drunkenness, which is characterized by difficult arousal and disorientation, is more often associated with primary hypersomnia and apnea than with narcolepsy. Automatic behaviors may be present in all disorders associated with hypersomnia. Onset of the disorder can provide additional clues for the differential diagnosis; narcolepsy typically occurs early in life (i.e., late adolescence), whereas sleep apnea is much more prevalent among middle-aged obese men. Patients suspected of sleep apnea, narcolepsy, or primary hypersomnia should always be referred to a sleep disorders center for nocturnal polysomnography and daytime multiple sleep-latency tests, two assessment procedures (described below) essential to confirm these diagnoses.

Several additional factors should be considered in the differential diagnosis of hypersomnia. In shift workers, a complaint of excessive sleepiness is typically due to the underlying desynchronization of circadian rhythms. Hypersomnia also may occur in the context of another mental disorder. This is more common in major affective disorder, especially in bipolar patients. Hypersomnia is usually part of the depressive phase, whereas insomnia is predominant during the manic phase. Several medical conditions (e.g., hypothyroidism and chronic fatigue syndrome) and prescribed drugs (e.g., antihypertensives) may cause hypersomnia. Use of or withdrawal from substances (e.g., alcohol and sedative-hypnotics) also can impair daytime wakefulness. Individuals with primary insomnia often report fatigue and tiredness, but they are not necessarily sleepy during the day. When there is evidence of daytime sleepiness, insomnia is more likely to be associated with another medical (pain) or sleep disorder (apnea).

CIRCADIAN RHYTHM SLEEP DISORDERS

Most circadian rhythm sleep disorders can produce insomnia, hypersomnia, or a combination of both. The main feature distinguishing CRSDs from other sleep disorders is a poor timing of sleep and wake episodes with reference to the desired schedule. In shift work and jet lag, sleep and wakefulness are compromised by frequently changing schedules or traveling across several time zones. Insomnia due to a delayed sleep phase is characterized by intractable difficulty falling asleep until early in the morning (e.g., 3:00 A.M.). There is usually no difficulty staying asleep once sleep has been achieved. More common in younger people, particularly college students, this condition is presumed to arise from an endogenous delay in the biological clock (Arendt et al., 2005; Rosekind, 2005), but it may be exacerbated by irregular sleep schedules and a natural tendency to stay up late. The main differential diagnosis is with primary sleep-onset insomnia, which is more strongly associated with sleep-anticipatory anxiety and concomitant psychological symptomatology. In the phase advance syndrome, the presenting complaint involves a compelling difficulty in staying awake during the evening (e.g., after 8:00 or 9:00 P.M.), followed by early morning awakening (e.g., 4:00 A.M.). Total sleep duration is not shortened. More frequent in older adults, this condition must be distinguished from early morning awakening, which is a common form of sleep maintenance insomnia in both depression and in late life. Duration of the previous sleep episode must be considered instead of relying exclusively on the actual clock time of the final awakening. In true early morning awakening, the final awakening is premature regardless of bedtime on the previous night.

PARASOMNIAS

The main differential diagnosis among parasomnias involves sleep terrors and nightmares. The former is characterized by a piercing scream, confusion, excessive autonomic arousal, and partial awakening. There is no recollection of disturbing dreams or of the incident upon awakening in the morning. In contrast, nightmares trigger a full awakening, followed by a quick return to consciousness and vivid recall of a disturbing dream. The timing of the abnormal or distressful event is critical to make an accurate diagnosis. Sleep terrors originate from stage 3 to 4 sleep, which occur almost exclusively in the first third of the night, whereas nightmares arise from REM sleep, which is more predominant and more intense in the last third of the night. The distinction between sleepwalking and sleep terrors is more difficult. These conditions often occur together and are considered by some as manifestations of the same arousal disorder with varying intensity (Kales, Kales et al., 1980; Kales, Soldatos, Caldwell, Charney, et al., 1980). Parasomnias do not always lead to a complaint of insomnia or hypersomnia, although in the most severe forms, either of these difficulties may be present.

Because parasomnias may accompany other primary sleep disorders such as narcolepsy and breathing-related sleep disorders, those conditions should be excluded before a diagnosis of parasomnia is made. Nightmares are a common symptom of posttraumatic stress disorder (Ross, Ball, Sullivan, & Caroll, 1989) and major depressive episodes, so it is important to exclude such psychiatric conditions from consideration as well. Nocturnal panic attack may present similar features to sleep terrors and nightmares. Unlike in sleep terror, nocturnal panic attack leads to a full awakening, and, unlike nightmares, there is no recollection of disturbing dreams (Hauri, Friedman, & Ravaris, 1989; Mellman & Uhde, 1989). A seizure disorder is the most common medical condition producing symptoms similar to those of parasomnias. Finally, the introduction of certain medications (L-dopa compounds and certain antihypertensive drugs) and the withdrawal of others (antidepressants and benzodiazepines) may lead to transient increases in nightmare activity, but such occurrences are not indicative of a nightmare disorder.

PSYCHOLOGICAL AND BIOLOGICAL ASSESSMENT

Accurate diagnosis of sleep disorders rests on thorough evaluation. This principle applies to all psychiatric disorders but is even more relevant to sleep disorders because sleep is affected by a host of psychological, medical, pharmacological, and circadian factors. The differential diagnosis of sleep disorders requires a multifaceted evaluation involving a clinical interview, psychological and physical examinations, daily sleep monitoring, and, for some disorders, more specialized diagnostic procedures.

CLINICAL HISTORY

A detailed clinical history is the most important diagnostic tool for evaluation of sleep disorders. The clinical history should elicit type of complaint (insomnia, hypersomnia, unusual behaviors during sleep), chronology, and course; exacerbating and alleviating factors; and responses to previous treatments. In particular, it is important to inquire about life events, psychological disorders, substance use, and medical illnesses at the time of onset of the sleep problem to help establish its etiology. Several interviews are available to gather this information in a structured format. The *Structured Interview for Sleep Disorders* (Schramm et al., 1993), designed according to *DSM-III-R* criteria, is helpful to establish a preliminary differential diagnosis among the different sleep disorders. The *Insomnia Interview Schedule* (Morin, 1993) is more specifically geared for patients with a suspected diagnosis of insomnia. Spielman and Anderson (1999) developed the *CCNY Interview for Insomnia*, which enables the interviewer to rate symptomatology in relation to the different ICSD diagnoses, while considering psychological, social, and physiological etiology of sleep disturbances. Espie (2000) has outlined a plan for conducting a sleep history assessment specifically with older adults.

Determining whether the course of the symptomatology has been chronic or intermittent is crucial in the diagnosis of some disorders. For instance, patients with narcolepsy have persistent daytime sleepiness, whereas patients with hypersomnia related to depression have more intermittent symptoms. Duration and course of insomnia can be transient, intermittent, or chronic; these distinctions can have important implications for diagnosis and treatment planning. For example, transient insomnia may require an intervention that focuses directly on precipitating conditions, whereas chronic insomnia will almost always require an intervention that also targets perpetuating factors (e.g., maladaptive sleep habits and dysfunctional cognitions; see Morin & Espie, 2003). In light of the high comorbidity between sleep disturbances and psychiatric disorders, the history should identify relative onset and course of each condition in order to establish whether the sleep disorder is primary or secondary.

A careful functional analysis of exacerbating and alleviating factors also can be quite useful diagnostically. For insomnia patients, detailed analysis of the following factors is crucial: sleeping environment; evening activities leading up to bedtime; patient's cognitions at bedtime or in the middle of the night; perceived impact of sleep disruptions on mood, performance, and relationships; coping strategies; and secondary gains. Interviewing the bed partner can yield valuable diagnostic information about a patient suspected of sleep apnea or some forms of parasomnia. Patients may be unaware of their own snoring or breathing pauses in their sleep, and they may deny or underestimate their degree of daytime sleepiness. Patients suffering from sleepwalking or sleep terrors typically have no recollection of such events, and the bed partner (or parents) are an important source of clinical information.

DAILY SELF-MONITORING

Prospective daily sleep diary monitoring is extremely useful for establishing a diagnosis of some sleep disorders, especially for insomnia (Buysse, Ancoli-Israel, Edinger, Lichstein, & Morin, 2006). A typical sleep diary includes entries for bedtime, arising time, sleep latency, number and duration of awakenings, sleep duration, naps, use of sleep aids, and various indices of sleep quality and daytime functioning (Morin & Espie, 2003). These data provide information about a patient's sleep habits and schedules, the nature of the sleep problem, and its frequency and intensity, all of which may vary considerably from the patient's global and retrospective report during a clinical interview. Despite some discrepancies between subjective and objective measurements of sleep parameters, daily morning estimates of specific sleep parameters represent a useful index of insomnia (Coates et al., 1982). The sleep diary is a practical and economical assessment tool for prospectively tracking sleep patterns over long periods of time in the patient's home. Self-monitoring is also helpful for establishing a baseline prior to initiating treatment and for monitoring progress as the intervention unfolds. Because of the extensive night-to-night variability in sleep patterns of insomnia sufferers, it is recommended that baseline data for at least 1 or 2 weeks be obtained (Buysse et al., 2006). Self-monitoring can be helpful not only for elucidating insomnia complaints, but also for diagnosing circadian rhythm sleep disorders and for distinguishing daytime sleepiness due to insufficient sleep from that due to other sleep pathologies. Recording the timing of unusual events in sleep can assist the clinician in differentiating between a sleep terror or a nightmare.

PSYCHOLOGICAL ASSESSMENT

Clinical indications for psychological assessment vary according to the suspected sleep disorders. Although any sleep disorder can be associated with comorbid psychopathology, and chronic sleep disturbances of any kind can produce psychological symptoms, such findings are less probable when the presenting complaint is hypersomnia or the suspected diagnosis is circadian rhythm sleep disorders. Psychopathology is rare among children with parasomnias, whereas its incidence is more variable among adults. Psychological assessment should be an integral component in the evaluation of insomnia. At the very least, a screening assessment is indicated because insomnia is frequently associated with psychopathology, and even when formal criteria for specific psychiatric disorders are not met, symptoms of anxiety and depression are common among patients with insomnia complaints (Sateia, Doghramji, Hauri, & Morin, 2000).

Although the Minnesota Multiphasic Personality Inventory has been extensively used to document the rate of psychopathology and predict the outcome among insomnia patients (Edinger, Stout, & Hoelscher; 1988), a more cost-effective approach is to use brief screening instruments that target specific psychological features (e.g., emotional distress, anxiety, and depression) most commonly associated with insomnia complaints. Instruments such as the Brief Symptom Inventory, the Beck Depression Inventory, and the State-Trait Anxiety Inventory can yield valuable screening data. As with all self-report measures, these instruments are subject to bias resulting from denial or exaggeration of symptoms and should never be used in isolation to make a diagnosis. Psychometric screening should always be complemented by a more in-depth clinical interview.

Numerous other self-report measures tapping various dimensions of insomnia can yield useful information (see Table 16.3). Some instruments are used as global measures of quality (Pittsburgh Sleep Quality Index; Buysse, Reynolds, Monk, Berman, & Kupfer, 1989), satisfaction (Coyle & Watts, 1991), or impairment of sleep (Morin, 1993). Other scales are designed to evaluate mediating factors of insomnia, such as state (Pre-Sleep Arousal Scale; Nicassio, Mendlowitz, Fussell, & Petras, 1985) and trait arousal (Arousal Predisposition Scale; Coren, 1988), dysfunctional sleep cognitions (Beliefs and Attitudes about Sleep Scale; Morin, 1994), self-monitoring of perceived sleep-related threats (Neitzert Semler & Harvey, 2004), sleep-incompatible activities (Sleep-Behavior Self-Rating Scale; Kazarian, Howe, & Csapo, 1979), and sleep hygiene principles (Sleep Hygiene Awareness and Practice Scale; Lacks & Rotert, 1986). Measures of fatigue, daytime performance, and quality of life also can be quite useful for evaluating the impact of insomnia. All these measures are particularly useful for designing individually tailored insomnia interventions and assessing their outcome.

Three self-report measures can provide useful screening data on daytime sleepiness: the Epworth Sleepiness Scale (Johns, 1991), a global and retrospective measure assessing the likelihood (on a 4-point scale) of falling asleep in several situations (e.g., watching TV, riding in a car); the Stanford Sleepiness Scale (Hoddes, Zarcone, Smythe, Phillips, & Dement, 1973), a 7-point Likert-type scale measuring subjective sleepiness at a specific moment in time; and the Karolinska Sleepiness Scale (Akerstedt & Gillberg, 1990), also a Likert-type (9-point) rating scale. As with any self-report measure, the score from these sleepiness scales cannot be taken in isolation as evidence of a sleep disorder; however, when the clinical history is positive for other symptoms, a high score should be confirmed with more objective measures.

Behavioral Assessment Device

Of several behavioral assessment devices available to monitor sleep, wrist actigraphy is increasingly being used for ambulatory data collection. This activity-based

Table 16.3
Self-Report Measures of Insomnia and Associated Features

Measure	Authors
Pittsburgh Sleep Quality Index	Buysse, Reynolds, Monk, Berman, and Kupfer (1989)
Insomnia Severity Index	Morin (1993)
Sleep Satisfaction Questionnaire	Coyle and Watts (1991)
Pre-Sleep Arousal Scale	Nicassio, Mendlowitz, Fussell, and Petras (1985)
Arousal Predisposition Scale	Coren (1988)
Dysfunctional Beliefs and Attitudes about Sleep Scale	Morin (1994)
Sleep-Behavior Self-Rating Scale	Kazarian, Howe, and Csapo (1979)
Sleep Hygiene Awareness and Practice Scale	Lacks and Rotert (1986)
Sleep Associated Monitoring Index	Neitzert Semler and Harvey (2004)
Stanford Sleepiness Scale	Hoddes, Zarcone, Smythe, Phillips, and Dement (1973)
Epworth Sleepiness Scale	Johns (1991)
Karolinska Sleepiness Scale	Akersdedt and Gillberg (1990)

monitoring system uses a microprocessor to record and store wrist activity along with actual clock time. Data are processed through microcomputer software, and an algorithm is used to estimate sleep and wake states based on wrist activity. It is a useful tool for detecting sleep and monitoring sleep-wake schedules in normal, healthy populations, but it is less reliable for detecting disturbed sleep. It is reliable for estimating global sleep parameters (e.g., total sleep time, total wake time, time spent in bed), but less reliable for estimating more discrete sleep parameters such as the time required to fall asleep or the time awake at night. Wrist actigraphy can be used for monitoring compliance with some behavioral treatment procedures (e.g., restriction of time spent in bed). Overall, it is a useful adjunct for monitoring sleep-wake schedules and circadian patterns, but it is not recommended for the routine evaluation or diagnosis of any sleep disorder, including insomnia (Littner et al., 2003; Sadeh, Hauri, Kripke, & Lavie, 1995).

SLEEP LABORATORY EVALUATION

Polysomnography   Nocturnal polysomnography (PSG) involves monitoring of electroencephalogram, electro-oculogram, and electromyogram readings. These three parameters are sufficient to distinguish sleep and wake states and to quantify the proportion of time spent in various stages of sleep. Several additional variables such as respiration, oxygen saturation, and leg movements are usually monitored to detect other sleep-related abnormalities (e.g., breathing pauses and leg twitches) not recognized by the sleeping person and that may be present among individuals with insomnia complaints. A PSG evaluation is essential for the diagnosis of sleep apnea, narcolepsy, and periodic limb movements. It can also yield useful data to quantify the severity of sleep disturbances, which can be particularly important given the discrepancies between subjective complaints and objective findings. Although it has become fairly standard practice to use PSG in insomnia research, its use in clinical practice is not considered essential when insomnia is the suspected diagnosis (Buysse et al., 2006; Littner et al., 2002). The high cost of PSG remains a major deterrent to its routine use. Most insurance companies do not cover the cost of a sleep study for a suspected diagnosis of insomnia, whereas they reimburse for sleep apnea and narcolepsy. Standard PSG evaluation is usually conducted in a sleep laboratory, but it is also possible to conduct unattended sleep monitoring in the patient's home—a method that yields more naturalistic sleep data, particularly for those with insomnia complaints.

Multiple Sleep Latency Test (MSLT)   Assessment of daytime sleepiness should be an integral component of the evaluation process when daytime alertness is compromised by a sleep disorder. The MSLT is a daytime assessment procedure in which a person is offered five or six 20-minute nap opportunities at 2-hour intervals throughout the day. Latency to sleep onset provides an objective measure of physiological sleepiness. Individuals who are well rested and without sleep disorders take 10 minutes or more to fall asleep or do not fall asleep at all. A mean sleep latency of less than 5 minutes is considered pathological and is associated with increased risks of falling asleep at inappropriate times or places, such as while driving. The MSLT is also a diagnostic test for narcolepsy in that patients with this condition enter REM sleep in two or more of the scheduled naps whereas normal sleepers rarely get into REM sleep during daytime naps. The MSLT is performed almost exclusively on patients with a presenting complaint of excessive daytime sleepiness. Although insomnia patients may complain about daytime tiredness, typically they do not display pathological sleepiness on the MSLT.

Combining nocturnal PSG and daytime MSLT provides the most comprehensive assessment of sleep disorder. These two procedures are recognized as the "gold standards" in assessing sleep and its disorders. These evaluation procedures are clinically indicated when the presenting complaint is excessive daytime sleepiness and when symptoms suggestive of BRSD, narcolepsy, and periodic limb movements are present (Littner et al., 2003). The diagnosis of insomnia, particularly sleep-onset insomnia in younger patients, can be established fairly reliably through careful clinical evaluation complemented by daily sleep diaries. A clinician can always initiate treatment, and if the patient is unresponsive, a PSG evaluation can still be conducted to screen for another disorder that was missed during the clinical evaluation. A sleep study may have a higher yield of diagnostically useful information in older patients, especially those with a subjective complaint of sleep maintenance insomnia, because this segment of the population is at increased risk for several sleep pathologies (Edinger et al., 1989; Lichstein & Morin, 2000). Patients with circadian rhythm sleep disorders usually do not require PSG evaluation. These disorders can be reliably diagnosed by clinical history, sleep diary monitoring, and, possibly, with ambulatory monitoring of rest-activity cycles using wrist actigraphy. PSG is usually not indicated for patients with parasomnias such as sleepwalking, sleep terrors, or nightmares. Because these conditions rarely occur on a nightly basis, a single night of sleep monitoring is unlikely to capture the disorder. However, PSG may be warranted if other disorders (e.g., seizures) are suspected.

ETIOLOGICAL CONSIDERATIONS

FAMILIAL AND GENETIC

Familial and genetic factors may predispose some individuals to the development of certain sleep disorders (Dauvilliers, Maret, & Tafti, 2005). For instance, individuals suffering from a sleep disorder often report a positive family history for a similar condition. Twin studies indicate that monozygotic twins have a higher concordance of sleep habits and sleep difficulties than dizygotic twins (Heath, Kendler, Eaves, & Martin, 1990). Although some evidence suggests that the complaint of insomnia runs in families (Bastien & Morin, 2000; Dauvilliers, Morin, et al., 2005), it is unclear whether this is strictly due to genetic predisposition, influence of familial and social learning factors, or a combination of both. Narcolepsy is the only sleep disorder for which there is strong evidence of genetic transmission (Guilleminault & Fromherz, 2005). Studies of human leukocyte antigens have traced two antigens (DR2 and DQwl) in 90% to 100% of narcoleptic patients. These antigens are also present in up to 35% of nonnarcoleptic individuals as well as in other autoimmune diseases (e.g., lupus and multiple sclerosis). Nonetheless, first-degree relatives of a narcoleptic proband are eight times more likely to have a disorder of excessive daytime sleepiness than are individuals in the general population. A familial predisposition has also been suggested for other sleep disorders such as sleep terrors and sleepwalking (Kales, Soldatos, Bixler, et al., 1980). Risk of sleepwalking increases to 45% when one parent is affected and to 60% when both are affected. Prevalence of these conditions is up to 10 times greater in first-degree relatives of an affected individual than in the general population. The association of nightmares to familial and genetic factors has not been documented.

Except for narcolepsy, relatively few studies have examined the role of familial and genetic factors as predisposing factors to sleep disorders. It may be that hereditary factors predispose some individuals to develop sleep disorders, but the actual manifestation of the disorder may be influenced by psychological and environmental factors as well.

LEARNING AND MODELING

Primary insomnia is the sleep disorder with the strongest learning component. In an earlier section of this chapter, the role of conditioning factors was outlined in both the development and maintenance of insomnia. Briefly, insomnia may initially be precipitated by a variety of stressful life events, but a negative association is established between sleeplessness and temporal (bedtime) and environmental (bed/bedroom) stimuli previously associated with sleep. This conditioning process may develop more rapidly among individuals already predisposed to insomnia. Over time, the combination of maladaptive sleep habits (e.g., daytime napping, excessive amounts of time spent in bed) and sleep-related cognitions (e.g., unrealistic sleep expectations, fear of the consequences of insomnia, sleep-related monitoring) contribute to perpetuate sleep disturbances (Espie, 2002; Harvey, 2005; Morin & Espie, 2003). For instance, primary insomnia sufferers are prone to many sleep-disruptive practices that initially may emerge as a means of combating their sleep disturbances. For example, poor sleep at night may lead to daytime napping or sleeping late on weekends in efforts to catch up on lost sleep. Alternatively, such individuals may lie in bed for protracted periods trying to *force* sleep only to find themselves becoming more and more awake. Such practices are particularly common among middle-aged and older adults due to an increase in sleep fragmentation and shortening of their natural biological sleep-wake rhythm due to aging (Bliwise, 1993; Edinger, Wohlgemuth, Radtke, Marsh, & Quillian, 2001). In addition, other practices, such as routinely engaging in physically or mentally stimulating activities shortly before bed or failing to adhere to a regular sleep-wake schedule, may emerge as a function of life-style choices or perceived social obligations and also contribute to sleep difficulty. Dysfunctional sleep cognitions, such as unrealistic expectations and amplification of the consequences of insomnia, can exacerbate or perpetuate what might otherwise have been a transient sleep problem (Edinger et al., 2000; Morin & Espie, 2003).

Although the role of behavioral and cognitive factors is more clearly established in primary insomnia, these factors are most likely involved in all forms of chronic insomnia, whether primary or secondary (McCrae & Lichstein, 2001; NIH, 2005). Likewise, learning factors might be involved in other forms of chronic sleep disturbances such as nightmares.

LIFE EVENTS

The role of life events in the etiology of sleep disorders is more clearly documented for insomnia, a condition with a stronger psychological component, than for any other disorders. One study by Healy and colleagues (1981) found that individuals with insomnia reported more stressful life events in the year preceding the onset of their insomnia than in the following year. The precipitating events of insomnia are often related to work, family, and health (Bastien et al., 2004). A longitudinal study (Vollrath et al., 1989) has also confirmed the role of stressful life events in the onset or exacerbation of insomnia. Although there is no evidence that sleep disorders such as sleep apnea are associated with life events, one study found that narcolepsy, a disorder with a predominant biological origin, was associated with environmental factors (e.g., stressful life events, change in sleep schedule) in about half of the narcoleptic patients surveyed (Orellana et al., 1994). Among the different forms of parasomnias, nightmares and night terrors are the only conditions that have been associated with major life events such as combat experience, sexual aggression, and natural disasters (Nielsen & Zadra, 2005).

GENDER AND RACIAL-ETHNIC

Insomnia complaints are twice as common among women as among men, and such complaints increase across the life span. The nature of insomnia complaints also changes with aging. Sleep-onset insomnia is more common among younger people, whereas difficulties maintaining sleep, such as nocturnal or early morning awakenings, are more prevalent in middle-aged and older people. Although women report more sleep difficulties, their sleep pattern is apparently better preserved with aging. Among noncomplaining older adults, men display more sleep pathologies than women (Reynolds et al., 1985). BRSDs also increase with aging, but, unlike insomnia, obstructive sleep apnea is much more prevalent in men than in women. After menopause, women may have a higher predisposition to some forms of sleep apnea. Some limited data suggest that in adults, nightmares are more common in women, whereas in children, sleep terrors are more frequent in boys (Kales, Kales et al., 1980; Kales, Soldatos, Caldwell, Charney et al., 1980). There are no data on age, gender, or cultural differences in circadian rhythm sleep disorders. However, older adults may have more difficulties adjusting to schedule changes. Aside from a suspected higher incidence of isolated sleep paralysis in African Americans and a higher predisposition for narcolepsy among Japanese, there is no other evidence of racial or ethnic differences in any of the sleep disorders.

Biological and Physiological

A biological component is probably involved in the etiology of all sleep disorders, even among those with a predominant psychological etiology. For instance, in primary insomnia, there is increased physiological arousal (e.g., heart rate, body temperature, metabolic rate, cerebral glucose) both before sleep onset and during the sleep period, relative to baseline and to normal control sleepers (Bonnet & Arand, 1995; Nofzinger et al., 2004). People with insomnia display more fast (beta) brainwave activity before sleep onset and during sleep, reflecting some cognitive hyperactivity relative to noncomplaining good sleepers (Merica, Blois, & Gaillard, 1998; Perlis, Smith, Andrews, Orff, & Giles, 2001). Although it is unclear whether hyperarousal is causal, a covariation, or even the consequence of insomnia, it is likely to contribute to sleep disturbances at least in some people complaining of insomnia.

Most sleep disorders associated with a subjective complaint of excessive daytime sleepiness have a predominantly biological origin. Sleep apnea is primarily the result of a physical/anatomical obstruction in the upper-airway area causing breathing impairment during sleep. Although the etiology of narcolepsy is unknown, increasing evidence suggests that it is primarily a neurological disorder involving brain structures that control the regulation of REM sleep and play an important role in reducing the production of a neuropeptive called hypocretin (Guilleminault & Fromherz, 2005).

All circadian rhythm disorders share a chronobiological component, in which some physiological parameters (body temperature, melatonin secretion) that are normally regulated by a circadian rhythm (e.g., light-darkness) become out of phase with the desired sleep period. For example, in shift work, a person has to stay awake at night when his or her biological clock is ready to go to sleep. In jet lag, a mismatch between the internal circadian sleep propensity and the new required sleep-wake schedule often hampers the sleep of individuals who travel across time zones. While some circadian disorders have an intrinsic chronobiological origin, other forms of sleep disturbances resulting from a rotating or night shift are generally caused by scheduling factors imposed by societal or occupational obligations.

Parasomnias are disorders of arousal involving unusual behaviors during sleep. Most of these disorders are more prevalent in childhood and are manifestations of abnormal or excessive activation of the central nervous system, involving changes in autonomic or skeletal muscle activity (AASM, 2005). Sleepwalking and night terrors are disorders of arousal occurring mostly during the transition from deep sleep to lighter sleep. These parasomnias, which involve a dissociative state during which there is a lack of awareness of the environment accompanied by automatic behaviors, are predominantly explained by a hyperactivation of electrophysiological activity of the brain during sleep. While infrequent nightmares are considered normal phenomena, an increase in dopaminergic or noradrenergic activity may increase the frequency of these episodes.

SUMMARY

Sleep disorders are extremely prevalent in the general population and even more so in patients with psychiatric and medical disorders. Consequences of sleep disorders are numerous, impairing daytime functioning, diminishing quality of life, and even posing significant health and public safety hazards. Increasing evidence suggests that sleep disturbances may increase vulnerability to psychiatric disorders and, perhaps, prevent or delay recovery from such disorders (see Billard et al., 1994; Morin & Ware, 1996). Unless a systematic inquiry about sleep-wake complaints is integrated in a clinical evaluation, many sleep disorders go unrecognized and remain untreated. A detailed sleep history is often sufficient to make a preliminary diagnosis. When a more medically based sleep disorder (e.g., sleep apnea or narcolepsy) is suspected, referral to a sleep disorders center is essential to confirm the diagnosis and initiate appropriate treatment. Mental health practitioners are more likely to encounter patients with a primary sleep disorder such as insomnia or sleep complaints co-occurring with psychopathology. An accurate differential diagnosis has important implications for treatment planning. When sleep disturbance is a core symptom of underlying psychopathology, treatment should focus on the basic psychopathology. If, on the other hand, the sleep disorder is primary, treatment should be primarily sleep focused. At times, sleep and psychological symptomatology coexist without clear evidence of a specific cause-effect relationship. In such a case, multifocused interventions targeting both symptom clusters may be required to optimize treatment outcome.

REFERENCES

Akerstedt, T., & Gillberg, M. (1990). Subjective and objective sleepiness in the active individual. *International Journal of Neuroscience, 52,* 29–37.

American Academy of Sleep Medicine. (2005). *International classification of sleep disorders (ICSD): Diagnostic and coding manual* (2nd ed.). Westchester, IL: Author.

American Psychiatric Association. (2000). *Diagnostic and statistical manual of mental disorders* (4th ed.). Washington, DC: Author.

Arendt, J., Stone, B., & Skene, D. J. (2005). Sleep disruption in jetlag and other circadian rhythm-related disorders. In M. H. Kryger, T. Roth, & W. C. Dement (Eds.), *Principles and practice of sleep medicine* (4th ed., pp. 659–672). Philadelphia: Elsevier Saunders.

Bassetti, C., Aldrich, M., Chervin, R., & Quint, D. (1996). Sleep apnea in the acute phase of TIA and stroke. *Neurology, 47,* 1167–1173.

Bassetti, C. L., Pelayo, R., & Guilleminault, C. (2005). Idiopathic hypersomnia. In M. H. Kryger, T. Roth, & W. C. Dement (Eds.), *Principles and practice of sleep medicine* (4th ed., pp. 791–800). Philadelphia: Elsevier Saunders.

Bastien, C. H., & Morin, C. M. (2000). Familial incidence of insomnia. *Journal of Sleep Research, 9,* 49–54.

Bastien, C. H., Vallières, A., & Morin, C. M. (2004). Precipitating factors of insomnia. *Behavioral Sleep Medicine, 2,* 50–62.

Bélanger, L., Morin, C. M., Langlois, F., & Ladouceur, R. (2004). Insomnia and generalized anxiety disorder: Effects of cognitive-behavior therapy for generalized anxiety disorders on insomnia symptoms. *Journal of Anxiety Disorders, 18,* 561–571.

Benca, R. M. (2005). Mood disorders. In M. H. Kryger, T. Roth, & W. C. Dement (Eds.), *Principles and practice of sleep medicine* (4th ed., pp. 1311–1326). Philadelphia: Elsevier Saunders.

Benca, R. M., Obermeyer, W. H., Thisted, R. A, & Gillin, J. C. (1992). Sleep and psychiatric disorders: A meta analysis. *Archives of General Psychiatry, 49,* 651–668.

Berquier, A., & Ashton, R. (1992). Characteristics of the frequent nightmare sufferer. *Journal of Abnormal Psychology, 101,* 246–250.

Billard, M., & Dauvilliers, Y. (2001). Idiopathic hypersomnia. *Sleep Medicine Reviews, 5,* 351–360.

Billard, M., Dauvilliers, Y., & Carlander, B. (1998). La narcolepsie. In M. Billard (Ed.), *Le sommeil normal et pathologique* (2nd ed., pp. 278–292). Paris: Masson.

Billard, M., Partinen, M., Roth, T., & Shapiro, C. (1994). Sleep and psychiatric disorders. *Journal of Psychosomatic Research, 38*(Suppl. 1), 1–2.

Bliwise, D. L. (1993). Sleep in normal aging and dementia. *Sleep, 16,* 40–81.

Bonnet, M. H., & Arand, D. L. (1995). 24-hour metabolic rate in insomniacs and matched normal sleepers. *Sleep, 18,* 581–588.

Broughton, R., Billings, R., Cartwright, R., Doucette, D., Edmeads, J., Edwardh, M., Ervin, F., Orchard, B., Hill, R., & Turrell, G. (1994). Homicidal somnambulism: A case report. *Sleep, 17,* 253–264.

Brower, K. J., Aldrich, M. S., & Hall, J. M. (1998). Polysomnographic and subjective sleep predictors of alcoholic relapse. *Alcohol Clinical and Experimental Research, 22,* 1864–1871.

Buysse, D. J., Ancoli-Israel, S., Edinger, J. E., Lichstein, K. L., & Morin, C. M. (2006). Recommendations for a standard research assessment of insomnia. *Sleep, 29,* 1155–1173.

Buysse, D. J., Reynolds, C. F., Kupfer, D. J., Thorpy, M. J., Bixler, E., Manfredi, R., Kales, A., Vgontzas, A., Stepanski, E., Roth, T., Hauri, P., & Mesiano, D. (1994). Clinical diagnoses in 216 insomnia patients using the International Classification of Sleep Disorders (ICSD), DSM-IV, and ICD-10 categories: A report from the APA/NIMH DSM-IV field trial. *Sleep, 17,* 630–637.

Buysse, D. J., Reynolds, C. F., Monk, T. H., Berman, S. R., & Kupfer, D. J. (1989). The Pittsburgh Sleep Quality Index: A new instrument for psychiatric practice and research. *Psychiatry Research, 28,* 193–213.

Chang, P. P., Ford, D. E., Mead, L. A., Cooper-Patrick, L., & Klag, M. J. (1997). Insomnia in young men and subsequent depression. The Johns Hopkins Precursors Study. *American Journal of Epidemiology, 146,* 105–114.

Coates, T. J., Killen, J. D., George, J., Marchine, F., Silverman, S., & Thoresen, C. (1982). Estimating sleep parameters: A multitrait multimethod analysis. *Journal of Consulting and Clinical Psychology 50,* 345–352.

Coleman, R. M., Roffwarg, H. P., Kennedy, S. J., Guilleminault, C., Cinque, J., Cohn, M. A., Karacan, I., Kupfer, D. J., Lemmi, H., Miles, L. E., Orr, W. C., Phillips, E. R., Roth, T., Sassin, J. F., Schmidt, H. S., Weitzman, E. D., & Dement, W. C. (1982). Sleep-wake disorders based on a polysomnographic diagnosis. A national cooperative study. *Journal of the American Medical Association, 247,* 997–1003.

Coren, S. (1988). Prediction of insomnia from arousability predisposition scores: Scale development and cross-validation. *Behaviour Research and Therapy, 26,* 415–420.

Coyle, K., & Watts, F. N. (1991). The factorial structure of sleep dissatisfaction. *Behaviour Research and Therapy, 29,* 513–520.

Dauvilliers, Y., Maret, S., & Tafti, M. (2005). Genetics of normal and pathological sleep in humans. *Sleep Medicine Reviews, 9,* 91–100.

Dauvilliers, Y., Morin, C., Cervena, K., Carlander, B., Touchon, J., Besset, A., & Billiard, M. (2005). Family studies in insomnia. *Journal of Psychosomatic Research, 58,* 271–278.

Edinger, J. E., Bonnet, M. H., Bootzin, R. R., Doghramji, K., Dorsey, C. M., Espie, C. A., Jamieson, A. O., McCall, W. V., Morin, C. M., & Stepanski, E. J. (2004). Derivation of research diagnostic criteria for insomnia: Report of an American Academy of Sleep Medicine work group. *Sleep, 27,* 1567–1596.

Edinger, J. D., Fins, A. I., Glenn, D. M., Sullivan, R. J. Jr., Bastian, L. A., Marsh, G. R., Dailey, D., Hope, T. V., Young, M., Shaw, E., & Vasilas, D. (2000). Insomnia and the eye of the beholder: Are there clinical markers of objective sleep disturbances among adults with and without insomnia complaints? *Journal of Consulting and Clinical Psychology, 68,* 586–593.

Edinger, J. D., Hoelscher, T. J., Webb, M. D., Marsh, G. R., Radtke, R. A., & Erwin, C. W. (1989). Polysomnographic assessment of DIMS: Empirical evaluation of its diagnostic value. *Sleep, 12,* 315–322.

Edinger, J. D., Stout, A. L., & Hoelscher, T. J. (1988). Cluster analysis of insomniacs' MMPI profiles: Relation of subtypes to sleep history and treatment outcome. *Psychosomatic Medicine, 50,* 77–87.

Edinger, J. D., Wohlgemuth, W. K., Radtke, R. A., Marsh, G. R., & Quillian, R. E. (2001). Efficacy of cognitive-behavioral therapy for treating primary sleep-maintenance insomnia: A randomized controlled trial. *Journal of the American Medical Association, 285,* 1856–1864.

Espie, C. A. (2000). Assessment and differential diagnosis. In K. L. Lichstein & C. M. Morin (Eds.), *Treatment of late-life insomnia* (pp. 81–108). Thousand Oaks, CA: Sage.

Espie, C. A. (2002). Insomnia: Conceptual issues in the development persistence and treatment of sleep disorder in adults. *Annual Review of Psychology, 53,* 215–243.

Findley, L. J., Unverzadt, M., & Suratt, P. (1988). Automobile accidents in patients with obstructive sleep apnea. *American Review of Respiratory Disease, 138,* 337–340.

Foley, D., Monjan, A., Masaki, K., Ross, W., Havlik, R., White, L., & Launer, L. (2001). Daytime sleepiness is associated with 3-year incident dementia and cognitive decline in older Japanese-American men. *Journal of the American Geriatrics Society, 49,* 1628–1632.

Ford, D. E., & Kamerow, D. B. (1989). Epidemiologic study of sleep disturbances and psychiatric disorders: An opportunity for prevention? *Journal of the American Medical Association, 262,* 1479–1484.

Gillin, J. C., Drummond, S. P. A., Clark, C. P., & Moore, P. (2005). Medication and substance abuse. In M. H. Kryger, T. Roth, & W. C. Dement (Eds.), *Principles and practice of sleep medicine* (4th ed., pp. 1345–1358). Philadelphia: Elsevier Saunders.

Guilleminault, C., & Bassiri, A. (2005). Clinical features and evaluation of obstructive sleep apnea-hypopnea syndrome and upper airway resistance syndrome. In M. H. Kryger, T. Roth, & W. C. Dement (Eds.), *Principles and practice of sleep medicine* (4th ed., pp. 1043–1052). Philadelphia: Elsevier Saunders.

Guilleminault, C., & Fromherz, A. (2005). Narcolepsy: Diagnosis and management. In M. H. Kryger, T. Roth, & W. C. Dement (Eds.), *Principles and practice of sleep medicine* (4th ed., pp. 780–790). Philadelphia: Elsevier Saunders.

Hartmann, E., Elkin, R., & Garg, M. (1991). Personality and dreaming: The dreams of people with very thick and thin boundaries. *Dreaming, 1,* 311–324.

Harvey, A. G. (2005). A cognitive theory of and therapy for chronic insomnia. *Journal of Cognitive Psychotherapy. An International Quarterly, 19,* 41–60.

Harvey, A. G., Schmidt, D. A. F., Scarna, A., Semler, C. N., & Goodwin, G. M. (2005). Sleep-related functioning in euthymic patients with bipolar disorder, patients with insomnia, and subjects without sleep problems. *American Journal of Psychiatry, 162,* 50–57.

Hauri, P. J. (2000). Primary insomnia. In M. H. Kryger, T. Roth, & W. C., Dement (Eds.), *Principles and practice of sleep medicine* (3rd ed., pp. 633–639). Philadelphia: Saunders.

Hauri. P. J., & Fisher, J. (1986). Persistent psychophysiological (learned) insomnia. *Sleep, 9,* 38–53.

Hauri, P. J., Friedman, M., & Ravaris, C. L. (1989). Sleep in patients with nocturnal panic attacks. *Sleep, 12,* 323–337.

Hauri. P. J., & Olmstead, E. M. (1980). Childhood-onset insomnia. *Sleep, 3,* 59–65.

Healy, E. S., Kales, A., Monroe, L. J., Bixler, E. O., Chamberlin, K., & Soldatos, C. R. (1981). Onset of insomnia: Role of life-stress events. *Psychosomatic Medicine, 43,* 439–451.

Heath. A. C., Kendler, K. S., Eaves, L. J., & Martin, N. G. (1990). Evidence for genetic influences on sleep disturbance and sleep pattern in twins. *Sleep, 13,* 318–335.

Hoddes, E., Zarcone, V., Smythe, H., Phillips, R., & Dement, W. C. (1973). Quantification of sleepiness: A new approach. *Psychophysiology, 10,* 431–436.

Hohagen, F., Kappler, C., Schramm, E., Riemann, D., Weyerer, S., & Berger, M. (1994). Sleep onset insomnia, sleep maintaining insomnia and insomnia with early morning awakening: Temporal stability of subtypes in a longitudinal study on general practice attenders. *Sleep, 17,* 551–554.

Honda, Y. (1979). Census of narcolepsy, cataplexy and sleep life among teenagers in Fujisawa City. *Sleep Research, 8,* 191.

Horstmann, S., Hess, C. W., Bassetti, C., Gugger, M., & Mathis, J. (2000). Sleepiness-related accidents in sleep apnea patients. *Sleep, 23,* 383–389.

Johns, M. W. (1991). A new method for measuring daytime sleepiness: The Epworth Sleepiness Scale. *Sleep, 14,* 540–545.

Johnson, E. O., Roehrs, T., Roth, T., & Breslau, N. (1998) Epidemiology of alcohol and medication as aids to sleep in early adulthood. *Sleep, 21,* 178–186.

Johnson L. C., & Spinweber, C. L. (1983). Quality of sleep and performance in the Navy: A longitudinal study of good and poor sleepers. In C. Guilleminault & E. Lugaresi (Eds.), *Sleep/wake disorders: Natural history, epidemiology, and long-term evolution* (pp. 13–28). New York: Raven Press.

Kales, J. D., Kales, A., Soldatos, C. R., Caldwell, A. B., Charney, D. S., & Martin, E. D. (1980). Night terrors: Clinical characteristics and personality patterns. *Archives of General Psychiatry, 37,* 1413–1417.

Kales, A., Soldatos, C. R., Bixler, E. O., Ladda, R. L., Charney, D. S., Weber, G., & Schweitzer, P. K. (1980). Hereditary factors in sleepwalking and night terrors. *British Journal of Psychiatry, 137,* 111–118.

Kales, A., Soldatos, C. R., Caldwell, A. B., Charney, D. S., Kales, J. D., Markel, D., & Cadieux, R. (1980). Nightmares: Clinical characteristics and personality patterns. *American Journal of Psychiatry, 137,* 1197–1201.

Kales, A., Soldatos, C. R., Caldwell, A. B., Kales. J. D., Humphrey, F. J., Charney, D. S., & Schweitzer, P. K. (1980). Somnambulism: Clinical characteristics and personality patterns. *Archives of General Psychiatry, 37,* 1406–1410.

Katz, D. A., & McHorney, C. A. (2002). The relationship between insomnia and health-related quality of life in patients with chronic illness. *Journal of Family Practice, 51,* 229–235.

Kazarian, S. S., Howe, M. G., & Csapo, K. G. (1979). Development of the sleep behavior self-rating scale. *Behavior Therapy, 10,* 412–417.

Klink, M. E., Quan, S. F., Kaltenborn, W. T., & Lebowitz, M. D. (1992). Risk factors associated with complaints of insomnia in a general adult population: Influence of previous complaints of insomnia. *Archives of Internal Medicine, 152,* 1572–1575.

Knutsson, A. (1989). Shift work and coronary heart disease. *Scandinavian Journal of Sociology, 44,* 1–36.

Lacks, P., & Rotert, M. (1986). Knowledge and practice of sleep hygiene techniques in insomniacs and poor sleepers. *Behaviour Research and Therapy, 24,* 365–368.

Lavigne, G. J., McMillan, D., & Zucconi, M. (2005). Pain and sleep. In M. H. Kryger, T. Roth, & W. C. Dement (Eds.), *Principles and practice of sleep medicine* (4th ed., pp. 1246–1255). Philadelphia: Elsevier Saunders.

Lichstein K. L., & Morin, C. M. (Eds.). (2000). *Treatment of late-life insomnia.* Thousand Oaks, CA: Sage.

Littner, M., Hirshkowitz, M., Kramer, M., Kapen, S., Anderson, W. M., Bailey, D., Berry, R. B., Davila, D., Johnson, S., Kushida, C., Loube, D. I., Wise, M., & Woodson, B. T. (2002). Practice parameters for using polysomnography to evaluate insomnia: An update. *Sleep, 26,* 754–760.

Littner, M., Kushida, C. A., Anderson, W. M., Bailey, D., Berry, R. B., Davila, D. G., Hirshkowitz, M., Kapen, S., Kramer, M., Loube, D., Wise, M., & Johnson, S. F. (2003). Practice parameters for the role of actigraphy in the study of sleep and circadian rhythms: An update for 2002. *Sleep, 26,* 337–341.

Lugaresi, E., Zucconi, M., & Bixler, E. O. (1987). Epidemiology of sleep disorders. *Psychiatric Annals, 17,* 446–453.

McCrae, C., & Lichstein, K. L. (2001). Secondary insomnia: Diagnostic challenges and intervention opportunities. *Sleep Medicine Review, 5,* 47–61.

Mellinger, C. D., Balter, M. B., & Uhlenhuth, E. H. (1985). Insomnia and its treatment. *Archives of General Psychiatry, 42,* 225–232.

Mellman, T. A., & Uhde, T. W. (1989). Electroencephalographic sleep in panic disorder: A focus on sleep-related panic attacks. *Archives of General Psychiatry, 46,* 178–184.

Mendelson, W. B. (1997). 1700 patients later: The experience of a sleep disorders center. *Cleveland Clinic Journal of Medicine, 64,* 46–51.

Merica, H., Blois, R., & Gaillard, J. M. (1998). Spectral characteristics of sleep EEG in chronic insomnia. *European Journal of Neurosciences, 10,* 1826–1834.

Morin, C. M. (1993). *Insomnia: Psychological assessment and management.* New York: Guilford Press.

Morin, C. M. (1994). Dysfunctional beliefs and attitudes about sleep: Preliminary scale development and description. *Behavior Therapist, 17,* 163–164.

Morin, C. M., Bastien, C. H., Guay, B., Radouco-Thomas, M., Leblanc, J., & Vallières, A. (2004). Randomized clinical trial of supervised tapering and cognitive-behavior therapy to facilitate benzodiazepine discontinuation in older adults with chronic insomnia. *American Journal of Psychiatry, 161,* 332–342.

Morin, C. M., & Espie, C. A. (2003). *Insomnia: A clinical guide to assessment and treatment.* New York: Kluwer Academic/Plenum.

Morin, C. M., LeBlanc, M., Daley, M., Grégoire, J. P., & Mérette, C. (2006). Epidemiology of insomnia: Prevalence, self-help treatments and consultations initiated, and determinants of help-seeking behaviors. *Sleep Medicine, 7,* 123–130.

Morin, C. M., & Ware, C. (1996). Sleep and psychopathology. *Applied and Preventive Psychology, 5,* 211–224.

National Commission on Sleep Disorders Research. (1993). *Wake up America: A national sleep alert.* Washington, DC: Author.

National Institutes of Health. (2005). Manifestations and management of chronic insomnia in adults. State of the Science Conference Statement. *Sleep, 28,* 1049–1057.

National Sleep Foundation. (2005). *Sleep in America poll.* Washington, DC: Author.

National Transportation Safety Board. (1990). Marine accident report—Grounding of the U.S. Tankship EXXON VALDEZ on Bligh Reef, Prince William Sound, near Valdez, Alaska, March 24, 1989 (No. NTSB/Mar-90/04). Washington, DC: Author.

Neitzert Semler, C., & Harvey, A. G. (2004). Monitoring of sleep-related threat in primary insomnia: Development and validation of the sleep associated monitoring inventory (SAMI). *Psychosomatic Medicine, 66,* 242–250.

Nicassio, P. M., Mendlowitz, D. R., Fussell, J. J., & Petras, L. (1985). The phenomenology of the presleep state: The development of the presleep arousal scale. *Behaviour Research and Therapy, 23,* 263–271.

Nielsen, T. A., & Zadra, A. (2005). Nightmares and other common dream disorders. In M. H. Kryger, T. Roth, & W. C. Dement (Eds.), *Principles and practice of sleep medicine* (4th ed., pp. 926–935). Philadelphia: Elsevier Saunders.

Nieto, F. J., Young, T. B., Lind, B. K., Shahar, E., Samet, J. M., Redline, S., D'Agostino, R. B., Newman, A. B., Lebowitz, M. D., & Pickering, T. G. (2000). Association of sleep-disordered breathing, sleep apnea, and hypertension in a large community-based study. *Journal of the American Medical Association, 283,* 1829–1836.

Nofzinger, E. A., Buysse, D. J., Germain, A., Price, J. C., Miewald, J. M., & Kupfer, D. J. (2004). Functional neuroimaging evidence for hyperarousal in insomnia. *American Journal of Psychiatry, 161,* 2126–2128.

Nofzinger, E. A., Buysse, D. J, Reynolds, C. F., & Kupfer, D. J. (1993). Sleep disorders related to another mental disorder (nonsubstance/primary): A DSM-IV literature review. *Journal of Clinical Psychiatry, 54,* 244–255.

Ohayon, M. M. (2002). Epidemiology of insomnia: What we know and what we still need to learn. *Sleep Medicine Reviews, 6,* 97–111.

Ohayon, M. M., Caulet, M., & Lemoine, P. (1998). Comorbidity of mental and insomnia disorders in the general population. *Comprehensive Psychiatry, 39,* 185–197.

Ohayon, M., & Vecchierini, M. (2002). Daytime sleepiness and cognitive impairment in the elderly population. *Archives of Internal Medicine, 162,* 201–208.

Orellana, C., Villemin, E., Tafti, M., Carlander, B., Besset, A., & Billard, M. (1994). Life events in the year preceding the onset of narcolepsy. *Sleep, 17,* S50–S53.

Parkes, J. D. (1985). *Sleep and its disorders.* London: Saunders.

Partinen, M., & Hublin, C. (2005). Epidemiology of sleep disorders. In M. H. Kryger, T. Roth, & W. C. Dement (Eds.), *Principles and practice of sleep medicine* (4th ed., pp. 626–647). Philadelphia: Elsevier Saunders.

Perlis, M. L., Smith, M. T., Andrews, P. J., Orff, H., & Giles, D. E. (2001). Beta/gamma EEG activity in patients with primary and secondary insomnia and good sleeper controls. *Sleep, 24,* 110–117.

Punjabi, N. M., Welch, D., & Strohl, K. (2000). Sleep disorders in regional sleep centers: A national cooperative study. *Sleep, 23,* 471–480.

Regestein, Q. R. (1989). Pathologic sleepiness induced by caffeine. *American Journal of Medicine, 87,* 586–588.

Reid, K. J., & Zee, P. C. (2005). Circadian disorders of the sleep-wake cycle. In M. H. Kryger, T. Roth, & W. C. Dement (Eds.), *Principles and practice of sleep medicine* (4th ed., pp. 691–701). Philadelphia: Elsevier Saunders.

Reynolds, C. F., & Kupfer, D. J. (1987). Sleep research in affective illness: State of the art circa 1987. *Sleep, 10,* 199–215.

Reynolds, C. F, Kupfer, D. J., Taska, L. S., Hoch, C. C., Sewitch, D. W., & Spiker, D. G. (1985). The sleep of healthy seniors: A revisit. *Sleep, 8,* 20–29.

Rosekind, M. R. (2005). Managing work schedules: An alertness and safety perspective. In M. H. Kryger, T. Roth, & W. C. Dement (Eds.), *Principles and practice of sleep medicine* (4th ed., pp. 680–690). Philadelphia: Elsevier Saunders.

Ross, R. J., Ball, W. A., Sullivan, K. A., & Caroll, S. N. (1989). Sleep disturbance as the hallmark of posttraumatic stress disorder. *American Journal of Psychiatry, 146,* 697–707.

Rush, A. J., Erman, M. K., Giles, D. E., Schlesser, M. A., Carpenter, G., Vasavada, N., & Roffwarg, H. P. (1986). Polysomnographic findings in recently drug-free and clinically remitted depressed patients. *Archives of General Psychiatry, 43,* 878–884.

Sadeh, A., Hauri, P., Kripke, D. F., & Lavie, P. (1995). The role of actigraphy in the evaluation of sleep disorders. *Sleep, 18,* 288–302.

Sateia, M., Doghramji, K., Hauri, P., & Morin, C. M. (2000). Evaluation of chronic insomnia. *Sleep, 23,* 243–308.

Schramm, E., Hohagen, F., Grasshoff, U., Rieman, D., Hujak, G., Weeb, H.-G., & Berger, M. (1993). Test-retest reliability and validity of the structured interview for sleep disorders according to DSM-III-R. *American Journal of Psychiatry, 150,* 867–872.

Schuckit, M. A., & Irwin, M. (1988). Diagnosis of alcoholism. *Medical Clinics of North America, 72,* 1133–1153.

Simon, G. E., & VonKorff, M. (1997). Prevalence, burden, and treatment of insomnia in primary care. *American Journal of Psychiatry, 154,* 1417–1423.

Somers, V. K., & Javaheri, S. (2005). Cardiovascular effects of sleep-related breathing disorders. In M. H. Kryger, T. Roth, & W. C. Dement (Eds.), *Principles and practice of sleep medicine* (4th ed., pp. 1180–1191). Philadelphia: Elsevier Saunders.

Spielman, A. J., & Anderson, M. W. (1999). The clinical interview and treatment planning as a guide to understanding the nature of insomnia: The CCNY Interview for Insomnia. In S. Chokroverty (Ed.), *Sleep disorders medicine: Basic science, technical considerations and clinical aspects* (2nd ed., pp. 385–426). Boston: Butterworth-Heinemann.

Spielman, A. J., Conroy, D., & Glovinsky, P. B. (2003). Evaluation of insomnia. In M. L. Perlis & K. L. Lichstein (Eds.), *Treating sleep disorders: Principles and practice of behavioral sleep medicine* (pp. 190–213). Hoboken, NJ: Wiley.

Stepanski, E. J. (2000). Behavioral therapy for insomnia. In M. H. Kryger, T. Roth, & W. C. Dement (Eds.), *Principles and practice of sleep medicine* (3rd ed., pp. 647–656). Philadelphia: Saunders.

Tan, T., Kales, J. D., Kales, A., Soldatos, C. R., & Bixler, E. O. (1984). Biopsychobehavioral correlates of insomnia: IV. Diagnoses based on DSM-III. *American Journal of Psychiatry, 141,* 356–362.

Teran-Santos, J., Jimenez-Gomez, A., & Cordero-Guevara, J. (1999). The association between sleep apnea and the risk for traffic accidents. *New England Journal of Medicine, 340,* 847–851.

Vallières, A., Ivers, H., Bastien, C. H., Beaulieu-Bonneau, S., & Morin, C. M. (2005). Variability and predictability in sleep patterns of chronic insomniacs. *Journal of Sleep Research, 14,* 447–453.

Vollrath, M., Wicki, W., & Angst, J. (1989). The Zurich study: VIII. Insomnia: Association with depression, anxiety, somatic syndromes, and course of insomnia. *European Archives of Psychiatry and Neurological Sciences, 239,* 113–124.

Walsh, J. K., Moss, K. L., & Sugerman, J. (1994). Insomnia in adult psychiatric disorders. In M. H. Kryger, T. Roth, & W. C. Dement (Eds.), *Principles and practice of sleep medicine* (2nd ed., pp. 500–508). Philadelphia: Saunders.

Weissman, M. M., Greenwald, S., Nino-Murcia, G., & Dement W. C. (1997). The morbidity of insomnia uncomplicated by psychiatric disorders. *General Hospital Psychiatry, 19,* 245–250.

Wood, J. M., & Bootzin, R. R. (1990). The prevalence of nightmares and their independence from anxiety. *Journal of Abnormal Psychology, 99,* 64–68.

World Health Organization. (1994). *ICD-9-CM: International classification of diseases, clinical modification* (4th ed., 9th rev.). Salt Lake City, UT: Medicode.

World Health Organization. (1993). *The ICD-10 classification of mental and behavioural disorders.* Geneva, Switzerland: Author.

Zammit, G. R., Weiner, J., Damato, N., Sillup, G. P., & McMillan, C. A. (1999). Quality of life in people with insomnia. *Sleep, 22*(Suppl. 2), 379–385.

CHAPTER 17

Personality Disorders

EMILY B. ANSELL AND CARLOS M. GRILO

DESCRIPTION OF THE DISORDERS

A personality disorder (PD) is defined in the *Diagnostic and Statistical Manual of Mental Disorders* (4th edition, text revision; *DSM-IV-TR*) as "an enduring pattern of inner experience and behavior that deviates markedly from the expectations of the individual's culture, is pervasive and inflexible, has an onset in adolescence or early adulthood, is stable over time, and leads to distress or impairment" (American Psychiatric Association [APA], 2000, p. 685; see Table 17.1). The construct of PD has evolved considerably during the past few decades (see Skodol, 1997, for an ontogeny of the *DSM* system; see Oldham, 2005, for a historical review). Substantial changes have occurred in both the types of specific PD diagnoses over time as well as their criteria. One central tenet that continues to be viewed as the hallmark of PDs is that they reflect stable or persistent maladaptive patterns. The *DSM-IV-TR* specifies that the "enduring pattern" can be manifested by problems in at least two of the following areas: cognition, affectivity, interpersonal functioning, or impulse control. Recent research has revealed that personality disorders are more prevalent than originally thought, with more than 1 in 10 adults meeting criteria for at least one PD (Torgersen, 2005b; Torgersen, Kringlen, & Cramer; 2001), and that they represent important public health problems insofar as they are associated with substantial psychosocial morbidity (Skodol et al., 2002). This chapter provides an overview of PDs. We briefly describe each personality disorder in terms of its diagnostic features as well as typical clinical presentation. In addition, we selectively provide an overview of emerging research on the assessment and conceptualization of PDs as well as recent important findings regarding their course, outcome, and impact.

Personality disorders are not merely "difficult" personalities. Although it is sometimes difficult to determine the extent to which a difficult personality type or an abnormal character trait is distinct from impairment, this is an important and necessary consideration from a clinical perspective. PDs, like other forms

Table 17.1

General Diagnostic Criteria for a Personality Disorder (APA, 2000)

A. An enduring pattern of inner experience and behavior that deviates markedly from the expectations of the individual's culture. This pattern is manifested in two (or more) of the following areas:

1) Cognition (i.e., ways of perceiving and interpreting self, other people, and events)

2) Affectivity (i.e., the range, intensity, lability, and appropriateness of emotional response)

3) Interpersonal functioning

4) Impulse control

B. The enduring pattern is inflexible and pervasive across a broad range of personal and social situations.

C. The enduring pattern leads to clinically significant distress or impairment in social, occupational, or other important areas of functioning.

D. The pattern is stable and of long duration, and its onset can be traced back at least to adolescence or early adulthood.

E. The enduring pattern is not better accounted for as a manifestation or consequence of another mental disorder.

F. The enduring pattern is not due to the direct physiological effects of a substance (e.g., a drug abuse, a medication) or a general medical condition (e.g., head trauma).

of psychiatric problems, can have strong stigmas associated with the diagnosis. Therefore, it is critical to consider the functional significance and impairment level before imparting a diagnostic label. One of the primary distinctions between adaptive and maladaptive expressions of personality, character, or any behavior is the impact on the individual's functioning. Skodol et al. (2002) examined the functional impairment in four PD groups (schizotypal, borderline, avoidant, and obsessive-compulsive personality disorders) as compared to Axis I diagnosis of major depressive disorder (MDD). Schizotypal and borderline PDs exhibited significantly more functional impairment than MDD or obsessive-compulsive personality disorder.

Thus, despite previous emphasis on Axis I disorders such as MDD as primary contributors to psychiatric and psychosocial dysfunction (Murray & Lopez, 1996), Axis II diagnoses appear to contribute comparably, if not more, to overall psychosocial function. Skodol et al. (2002, p. 280) noted, "Personality disorders appear likely to be a significant health problem, and more work is needed to document the persistence of functional impairment in patients with personality disorders and its costs to patients, their families, and society." Torgersen (2005b) affirmed these findings by identifying a negative relationship between the number of criteria met for a PD and the overall quality of life experienced by the individual as well as a positive relationship between the number of PD criteria and dysfunction. Grant et al. (2004) also found evidence in a large epidemiological study that PDs were significant predictors of emotional disability and impairment in social and role functioning.

CATEGORICAL VERSUS DIMENSIONAL APPROACHES

Long-standing debate regarding the conceptual and empirical advantages of dimensional versus categorical models of personality disorders (Frances, 1982; Grilo & McGlashan, 1999; Grilo, McGlashan, & Oldham, 1998; Livesley, Jackson, & Schroeder, 1992; Loranger et al., 1994; Trull & Durrett, 2005; Widiger, 1992) has accompanied the *DSM* categorical classification system. Ongoing research has provided support that important aspects of the structure of PDs are dimensional (Trull & Durrett, 2005; Wiggins & Pincus, 2002), and emerging assessment of dimensional models of PDs incorporate normal and abnormal conceptualizations of personality functioning. Normal personality traits are those experiences and attributes that espouse one's individuality. Differential standing on personality traits influences patterns of thoughts, feelings, and behaviors (McCrae & Costa, 1987, 1990). Abnormal personality represents the extent to which these individual differences have evolved into relatively enduring patterns with maladaptive expression and impact on psychosocial functioning, well-being, and interpersonal relationships. Although the field is increasingly open to dimensional approaches for conceptualizing PDs, there is yet no consensus on the best model, components, or assessment methods. At a global level, the most influential dimensional models attempt to incorporate personality trait models into an understanding of disorder and dysfunction (e.g., Clark, 1999, 2005; Cloninger, Svrakic, & Przybeck, 1993; Costa & McCrae, 1992; Costa & Widiger, 2002; Wiggins, 1996).

In support of the importance of dimensional models, we note that longitudinal studies of PDs have reported moderate levels of stability for dimensional scores for most PDs and that the stability coefficients tend to be higher than for categorical or diagnostic stability (Ferro, Klein, Schwartz, Kasch, & Leader, 1998; Grilo, Shea, et al., 2004; Johnson et al., 1997; Klein & Shih 1998; Loranger et al., 1991, 1994). In support of categorical models, we emphasize the great clinical utility that a categorical construct can have as a basic starting point for diagnosis and case formulation. It is important to not lose sight of this basic issue and potential integrative solution. Essentially, categorical constructs may be most useful for describing clinical disorders, while dimensional approaches may best assess the underlying structure of personality. A simple example of a public health message from a different field clearly illustrates this difference. In diagnosing diabetes, glucose control, a dimensional construct, has been statistically examined to determine clear guidelines for health professionals and patients regarding prediabetic or diabetic diagnostic categories and treatment. So, too, may the dimensional structure of personality be statistically examined to identify areas of disorder and dysfunction within the current categorical system.

As progress is made toward a *DSM-V* format for personality disorders, a dimensional approach to personality disorder is gaining support and additional proponents (see Trull & Durrett, 2005; Widiger & Simonsen, 2005; Widiger, Simonsen, Krueger, Livesley, & Verheul, 2005). Although there are a variety of competing (and partly overlapping) dimensional models of personality/character and its dysfunction/disorder, space constraints for this review chapter do not allow for consideration of all of the major models. Thus, we briefly describe one of the most influential dimensional models—the five-factor model (FFM) of personality—and apply its concepts in an attempt to complement our description of the categorical PD diagnoses.

Table 17.2

NEO Personality Inventory (NEO-PI-R) Traits and Facets (Costa & McCrae, 1992)

Trait	Facets
Neuroticism	Anxiousness, Angry Hostility, Depression, Self-Consciousness, Impulsiveness, Vulnerability
Extraversion	Warmth, Gregariousness, Assertiveness, Activity, Excitement Seeking, Positive Emotions
Openness to experience	Fantasy, Aesthetic, Feelings, Actions, Ideas, Values
Agreeableness	Trust, Straightforwardness, Altruism, Compliance, Modesty, Tendermindedness
Conscientiousness	Competence, Order, Dutifulness, Achievement Striving, Self-Discipline, Deliberation

Five-Factor Model (FFM)   Using the conceptualization of the FFM presented within the NEO-PI-R (Costa & McCrae, 1992), clinicians can identify personality traits associated with being extremely high or extremely low on the following five factors: Neuroticism (N), Extraversion (E), Openness (O), Agreeableness (A), and Conscientiousness (C) (see Table 17.2). Widiger, Costa, and McCrae (2002) propose a four-step process to determine whether an individual's profile of personality traits as determined with respect to the five domains and 30 facets of the FFM leads to identifiable problems, difficulties, or impairments. Through these steps, it can be determined whether an individual's profile matches a constellation of FFM traits and whether impairments secondary to each of the traits results in clinical significance sufficient for a particular PD diagnosis. Stability of these FFM traits is greater than stability of *DSM* diagnoses across longitudinal follow-up (Warner et al., 2004). While deliberation continues over the most suitable path for incorporating dimensional models into the traditional categorical *DSM* system, the integration of both approaches potentially enriches the understanding and assessment of PD diagnoses. Given the benefits of understanding PDs in both systems, descriptions are provided for each specific PD diagnoses using identified domains and facets of the traits considered prototypic for that PD.

SPECIFIC PERSONALITY DISORDERS

The *DSM-IV* organizes personality disorders into three descriptive clusters: the odd and eccentric *Cluster A;* the dramatic, emotional, and erratic *Cluster B;* and the anxious and fearful *Cluster C.* These clusters, derived partly from empirical and clinical traditions (see Fabrega, Ulrich, Pilkonis, & Mezzich, 1991; Gunderson et al., 2000; Sanislow et al., 2002) are limited in their empirical relevance to understanding PDs and assessment. For example, studies of diagnostic co-occurrence of PDs consistently reveal high rates of co-occurrence across clusters at both the diagnostic level (Becker et al., 2000) and criterion level (Grilo, McGlashan, Morey, Gunderson, Skodol, Shea, et al., 2001). The clusters, however, continue to be used as an organizing concept descriptively.

In addition, the diagnosis of personality disorder not otherwise specified (PD NOS; APA, 1994) is a commonly used diagnosis that can capture the presence of several criteria across several PD constructs without fully meeting criteria for any one PD. This is appropriate when important areas of functioning are impaired by character pathology but the individual does not fit any of the *DSM-IV* classifications (APA, 1994). PD NOS is not uncommon and is associated with severe impairment (Johnson et al., 2005). When PD NOS is considered in epidemiological investigations, rates of PD diagnosis in outpatient settings increase from 31.4% to 45.4% (Zimmerman, Rothschild, & Chelminksi, 2005).

CLUSTER A: ODD AND ECCENTRIC

Paranoid, schizoid, and schizotypal PDs encompass the cluster most associated with Axis I diagnoses of psychosis. Camisa and colleagues (2005) distinguished schizophrenia spectrum patients from Cluster A PDs by the presence of more severe social withdrawal and maladjustment in the Axis I disorders. Cluster A PDs were best distinguished from nonclinical populations by the presence of odd or novel ideation and decreased levels of conscientiousness.

PARANOID PERSONALITY DISORDER

A person who expects harm and is on a mission to detect evidence of impending attacks, without sufficient basis or by ignoring logical alternatives.

Behavioral: Vigilance
Intrapsychic: Overwhelming Fear
Interpersonal: Hostility

The *DSM-IV* diagnostic criteria for paranoid personality disorder (PPD; APA, 1994) include having "pervasive distrust and suspiciousness of others" as indicated by suspicion without sufficient basis that others are attempting to exploit, harm, or deceive him or her; preoccupation with unjustified doubts about loyalty or trustworthiness of friends and associates; reluctance to confide in others due to unwarranted fears that the information confided will be used against him or her; the perception of hidden demeaning or threatening meanings in benign remarks or events; bears grudges against those who have slighted, insulted, or injured him or her; perceives attacks on his or her reputation or character that are not apparent to others and that are reacted to quickly and with anger; and has recurrent suspicions that a sexual partner or spouse is unfaithful without justification. Although many individuals may be suspicious of others, the crux of the diagnosis is that these beliefs are unjustified in their content or extremity. The PPD diagnoses is prototypically described within the NEO-PI-R five-factor model of personality by high levels on the Neuroticism facet of Angry-Hostility and low levels on the three Agreeableness facets of Trust, Straightforwardness, and Compliance.

Previous estimates for the prevalence of PPD were in the range of 0.5% to 2.5% for the general population, 2% to 10% for outpatient psychiatric populations and 10% to 30% among inpatient psychiatric populations (APA, 2000). More recent epidemiological studies put prevalence rates in the general population between 2% and 4% (Grant et al., 2004; Torgersen et al., 2001) and prevalence in an outpatient psychiatric setting at around 4% (Zimmerman et al., 2005).

Clinical Presentation   Individuals with paranoid personality disorder are keen observers with outstanding attention to detail (Millon & Davis, 2000). These observational skills are used to identify details consistent with the cognitive schema that others are out to demean, betray, harm, or criticize him or her. These beliefs are unmitigated by alternative explanations or evidence that contradicts the individual's belief system. Hypersensitive to criticism, every interaction is carefully monitored for small signs of criticism, deception, or impending attacks. When people with PPDs perceive these signs, they are likely to react with considerable defensiveness and argumentativeness. Therapeutic work may be particularly difficult with these individuals because of their refusal to confide in others. Open-ended questions may be perceived as attempts to obtain information that could be used against them. Refusing to confide in others protects individuals with PPD from putting themselves in the "line of fire" and also isolates them from contemplating reasonable explanations for subtle criticisms. Every remark, action, and interaction is taken personally, and resulting behaviors are seen as justified retribution for such insidious but subtle attacks.

The internal world of an individual with PPD is overrun with fears of physical harm and emotional mortification accompanied by feelings of shame and guilt (Tomkins, 1963). These unacknowledged feelings of shame and guilt are adamantly defended against through denial and projection (McWilliams, 1994). While they overtly view themselves as righteous and mistreated (Beck & Freeman, 1990), they covertly view themselves as inferior and vulnerable (Shapiro, 1965). They respond to their subsequent shame by denying their own feelings of inferiority and vulnerability and projecting these negative feelings on to others as a way to decrease their own anxiety and distress. The subtle indicators of criticism, deception, or impending harm are magnified by the projected negative feelings, making the angry retaliation justified in the mind of the person with PPD.

Those with PPD anticipate hostile behavior from others, which results in them identifying many "false positives" (Horowitz, 2004). Hidden meanings are read into benign acts, innocent mistakes, and casual remarks. Compliments, humorous anecdotes, and other acts generated to create connection with the person who has PPD are viewed as attempts to take control through manipulation, coercion, or criticism. When individuals with PPD confront others, they elicit the hostility that they believe existed in the first place, and this confirms their suspicions of others' malice and critical intent (Benjamin, 1996; Horowitz, 2004). They have considerable difficulty collaborating with others, whether it is at work or home, and they are particularly reactive to individuals in positions of authority.

> The individual with PPD suspects malice at every turn. He or she will often react with anger, argumentativeness, fault finding, sarcasm, or criticism when signs of hostility (real or imagined) are identified. This anger and hostility is more likely to be expressed toward others than toward oneself, which may result in frequent legal disputes and court involvement (McWilliams, 1994). Individuals with PPD are often successful in finding hidden signs of malice due to their keen attention to details (Millon & Davis, 2000). However, this attention to detail does not extend to evidence that contradicts beliefs that others intend to harm them. Unlike Axis I psychosis or delusional disorders, these individuals have nonspecific interpersonal fears of being harmed, criticized,

or subtly demeaned. These fears are pervasive, unlike the transient stress-related paranoid ideation associated with borderline personality disorder.

By maintaining control, autonomy, and internal isolation, people with PPD are able to protect themselves from the perceived threats. The strong desire for control and autonomy is motivated by a fear for one's own safety and the belief that he or she will inevitably be cheated, deceived, exploited, betrayed, persecuted, or in some way harmed by others (Benjamin, 1996; Horowitz, 2004; Sperry, 2003). (See Case Study 1.)

Etiology   The developmental path of PPD predominantly involves environmental responses of criticism, blame, and hostility. Benjamin (1996) links this diagnosis to caregivers who treated the individual with PPD in a sadistic, degrading, or humiliating manner, imposing the belief that he or she was fundamentally bad. This process began in infancy, restricting the individual's ability to trust and promoting the belief that hateful criticism and abuse would result from interpersonal interactions. This leads to an anxious withdrawal from interactions that are later compensated for with rage and peremptory behaviors seeking to protect the individual from impending harm (Benjamin, 1996). Besides research examining links between psychotic spectrum Axis I disorders and Cluster A PDs, there is a dearth of research examining possible biological components leading to this specific personality disorder.

Case Study 1

One PPD client was asked by a new receptionist in his therapist's clinic whether he was there for the anxiety research study. The bristled client asked in an angry tone whether receptionists were now licensed to make clinical diagnoses. Despite an apology and explanation from the receptionist that it was her first week on the job, the patient perseverated throughout his session on the hidden meanings behind the comment, the potential disregard for his confidentiality, and his plans to register a complaint about the receptionist: How dare the receptionist suggest he looked anxious! Had this person read his files? Why would she attack him in this way? The perceived threat eventually expanded to others in his immediate interpersonal field: Neutral responses in the session were perceived as confirmation of his fears that he was being criticized and deceived. Denials were perceived as outright lies, and empathic responses were received as intrusive and condescending. He denied all feelings of embarrassment or shame in response to the statement by the receptionist. The patient suggested that his therapist must be quite embarrassed given that he had discovered the unprofessionalism of her staff. He stated that she must be quite ashamed of her outright lies and denials. He came to the conclusion that his therapist must agree he was too anxious and was trying to enroll him in the research study without his permission. His anger toward the therapist escalated, he left the session early, cancelled all remaining sessions, and informed the clinic director that his lawyer would "be in touch."

Schizoid Personality Disorder

Pervasively disinterested and detached from all relationships, including those with family.

Behavioral: The bland and lethargic loner
Intrapsychic: Comfort with emptiness
Interpersonal: The lover of distance

The *DSM-IV* diagnostic criteria for schizoid personality disorder (SPD; APA, 1994) include a pattern of detachment and restricted range of emotion as demonstrated by at least four of the following characteristics: neither desires nor enjoys close relationships, including family; chooses solitary activities; has little interest in sexual experiences; takes little pleasure in any activities; lacks friends or confidants; is indifferent to praise or criticism; and displays emotional detachment or flattened affect. The crux of the SPD diagnosis is the indifference to relationships and activities. While some individuals with avoidant personality will report not enjoying close relationships and choosing solitary activities, further probing generally reveals a fear of being humiliated, embarrassed, or criticized. People with SPD report no such fears. Just as there is indifference to praise or enjoyment, there is indifference to criticism or anger. The SPD diagnoses is prototypically described within the NEO-PI-R five-factor model of personality by low levels on the Openness facet of Feelings and low levels on the three Extraversion facets of Warmth, Gregariousness, and Positive Emotions.

Previous estimates for the prevalence of SPD indicate that it is a clinical rarity. Among psychiatric populations, its occurrence is estimated at around 1% (Stone, 1993). More recent epidemiological studies put prevalence rates in the general population between 1% and 3% (Grant et al., 2004; Torgersen et al., 2001) and prevalence in an outpatient psychiatric setting at around 1% (Zimmerman et al., 2005). The lack of general distress and preference for solitude may explain the low prevalence rates in clinical populations. The low rates may be due to the particular personality characteristics that make this individual less likely to volunteer for or comply with recruitment studies. However, contact between people with SPD and mental health professionals may take an alternative route than typical clinical outlets. Rouff (2000) diagnosed SPD in 14% of a homeless population sample and determined that the presence of schizoid personality characteristics predicted the total amount of time spent homeless.

Clinical Presentation   The individual with SPD prefers solitary activities and isolation. This is not because of social anxiety or paranoia, but instead due to an inner emptiness and blanket indifference toward others. Behavior will frequently disregard social convention and lack spontaneity. They frequently exhibit an apathetic and indecisive stance. The individual with SPD reports no strong emotional experiences and minimal reciprocity in facial expressions or body language. If complaints of mood or anxiety are made, they are typically expressed without the accompanying emotional states (Sperry, 2003). Characteristic behaviors of individuals with SPD include long silences and limited verbal exchanges (Othmer & Othmer, 2002).

Individuals with SPD are unmotivated by internal needs to engage with the external world. Instead, they withdraw from the external world, choosing to watch from the safety of the internal world (McWilliams, 1994). Attachment to others is experienced as overwhelming and engulfing to people with SPD, and solace and safety are found by walling off the internal world. They believe they are emotionally self-sufficient. This well-defended, unemotional demeanor differs from the coldness seen with antisocial personality disorder. Those with SPD reflect an internal emptiness and lack of awareness of others' feelings, not the awareness but conscious indifference toward others' feelings that is seen in psychopaths. With little ability for introspection, their inner world appears humorless and cold.

The *philobat,* or lover of distance, is how Balint (1945) described the style of the schizoid personality. This aloof, inattentive individual lacks the appropriate social skills for or interest in engaging others to facilitate relationships. There is little or no interest in emotional or physical intimacy, rapport building is strained, and the ability to empathize is nonexistent. The individual with SPD may refer to close friends, but further probing will reveal limited involvement in the relationships. While others may complain that the person with SPD does not take expected or appropriate steps to develop a relationship, he or she will express confusion over the necessity of these steps or the need for increased intimacy. However, the person with SPD may have the minimal social abilities to be able to maintain the more formal distance necessary for a work environment.

It is frequently difficult to determine the level of distress that an individual with SPD is experiencing because of his or her limited expression of emotions. Interpersonal reciprocity is not expressed; particularly reciprocity associated with communal activities or that evokes warmth (Horowitz, 2004). These individuals' repellence of others wards off the potentially intrusive intimacy that relationships foster. These clients are difficult to engage in treatment, likely because of the fear that they will become engulfed by a therapeutic relationship. As Sperry (2003) notes, a treatment alliance will be demonstrated by a willingness to explore therapeutic topics, reveal inner feelings, or by simply attending the sessions. Although this is likely to feel dismissive to a therapist, the person with SPD is likely to experience this engagement as a heightened level of attachment.

Etiology   Research exploring the etiological aspects of SPD suggests that there are links between SPD and Asperger syndrome, autism, and pervasive developmental disorder not otherwise specified (Wolff, 2000). These connections may account for the vastly empty internal world experienced by those with SPD. Some form of genetic predisposition is believed to contribute to SPD (Torgersen, 1984). Environmental factors that may contribute to SPD include rigid, unemotional responsiveness; indifference; and fragmented communication patterns (Sperry, 2003). Individuals with SPD are believed to be undersocialized and severely deficient in interpersonal or coping skills.

Schizotypal Personality Disorder

Odd or peculiar beliefs, appearance, or demeanor accompanied by social anxiety from paranoid fears.

Behavioral: Eccentricities
Intrapsychic: Odd beliefs and unusual perceptions
Interpersonal: Suspicious and apprehensive

The *DSM-IV* diagnostic criteria for schizotypal personality disorder (STPD; APA, 1994) include a pattern of interpersonal discomfort accompanied by social deficits; discomfort with close relationships; and eccentricities in behavior, thought, and perceptions as demonstrated by five or more of the following characteristics: ideas of reference, magical thinking, unusual perceptual experiences, odd thinking or speech, suspiciousness, inappropriate or constricted affect, behavior or appearance that is odd or peculiar, a lack of close friends other than first-degree relatives, and excessive social anxiety that is associated with paranoid fears rather than negative evaluations of the self. The crux of the STPD diagnosis is the existence of social discomfort, paranoid fears, and eccentricity independent of an Axis I psychosis diagnosis. The STPD diagnoses is prototypically described within the NEO-PI-R five-factor model of personality by high levels of the Neuroticism facets of Anxiety and Self-consciousness; high levels of the Openness facets of Fantasy, Actions and Ideas; low levels of the Extraversion facets of Warmth, Gregariousness, and Positive Emotions; and low levels of the Agreeableness facet of Trust.

Previous estimates for the prevalence of STPD in the general population were approximately 3% (APA, 1994) and approximately 9% in an outpatient clinical sample (Morey, 1988). More recent epidemiological studies put prevalence rates in the general population at less than 1% (Torgersen et al., 2001) and prevalence in an outpatient psychiatric setting at less than 1% (Zimmerman et al., 2005). The psychosocial functioning of individuals with STPD is believed to be very poor and may account for the relative low prevalence of the disorder in outpatient settings.

Clinical Presentation   Erratic or bizarre manner; peculiar speech that is overelaborate or vague; ruminative or cognitive slippage that is not incoherent; unusual perceptual experiences that do not meet threshold for psychosis; and other unusual experiences such as superstitiousness, telepathy, and clairvoyance are the eccentricities that characterize people with STPD. These behaviors are not attributable to an Axis I diagnoses but are associated with severely impaired psychosocial functioning.

Emotions may be constricted or inappropriate when expressed. This differs from the emotional constriction found in SPD and is associated with emotional avoidance. The thoughts of people with STPD are scattered and ruminative although they maintain a sense of control by claiming to have special cognitive powers (superstition, telepathy, clairvoyance). Individuals with STPD will frequently believe they are responsible for external situations when it is not the case, and they use "undoing" as a defense mechanism to control the uncontrollable (Sperry, 2003).

The social anxiety experienced by the individual with STPD is characterized by the presence of paranoid fears and suspiciousness, unlike the negative self-appraisals that characterize avoidant personality disorder. Individuals with STPD believe that others have malicious intent, and this belief does not diminish with familiarity. The social isolation further distances them from threatening interpersonal and emotional experiences, resulting in hypersensitive individuals who are apprehensive to truly engage with others. This interpersonal response is self-insulating and limits opportunities for the individuals to develop social skills or experience interactions that disconfirm the paranoid beliefs. The person with STPD is likely to be a loner but without the indifference to criticism or praise exhibited by the schizoid personality. If an individual with STPD marries, the relationship is likely to end in divorce due to the superficial relatedness and general mistrust. Examination of the components underlying schizotypy suggests that there may be two dimensions: one associated with psychosis proneness and an underdeveloped character and the second associated with a creative and mature character that is open to unusual and divergent feelings, thoughts, and behaviors (Daneluzzo, Stratta, & Rossi, 2005).

Etiology   A familial or genetic predisposition is believed to link STPD to schizophrenic spectrum disorders (Battaglia & Torgersen, 1996; Kendler, 1993; Kendler et al., 1991), although little is known of biogenic factors or the interplay with environment. Horowitz (2004) suggests that the oddities in children with STPD are reinforced when they are shunned and rejected by others, thus increasing their social anxiety and suspicion. An alternative pathogenic hypothesis suggests that the child was severely abused, limited in autonomy development and peer interactions while caregivers modeled illogical formulations of reality, leading the adult with STPD to claim an unusual ability of knowing or controlling events combined with paranoid withdrawal from others (Benjamin, 1996). Other hypotheses suggest that the infant's needs were met—but without sufficient emotional intimacy or warmth—and that subsequent childhood development was hindered by punitive criticism, fragmented communications, and humiliation by peers (Sperry, 2003).

CLUSTER B: DRAMATIC, EMOTIONAL, OR ERRATIC

Cluster B is comprised of antisocial, borderline, histrionic, and narcissistic personality disorders and are commonly described as the dramatic, emotional, or erratic subset of personality disorders. Cluster B PDs are characterized by impulsivity, lack of self-control, and substance abuse (Casillas & Clark; 2002; Taylor, 2005).

ANTISOCIAL PERSONALITY DISORDER

The control or manipulation of others without remorse, shame, or regard for the rights or feelings of others.

Behavioral: Aggressive and controlling
Intrapsychic: Focus on one's own needs
Interpersonal: Manipulation through charm, deceit or coercion

The *DSM-IV* diagnostic criteria for antisocial personality disorder (ASPD; APA, 1994) identify a pattern of deceit and manipulation, including a disregard for the rights of others that begins in childhood or early adolescence and is indicated by three or more of the following characteristics: failure to conform to social norms by repeatedly performing unlawful acts, deceitfulness, impulsivity, aggressiveness, reckless disregard for the safety of self or others, irresponsibility in work behavior or financial obligations, and lack of remorse. The crux of the ASPD diagnosis is the establishment of this pattern of externalizing behaviors prior to age 15 as indicated by conduct disorder. ASPD is the only PD diagnosis that requires a history of conduct disorder in childhood or adolescence. Conduct disorder is a pattern of behavior closely related to antisocial personality phenomenon exhibited by aggressive conduct toward people or animals, nonaggressive conduct that causes property loss or damage, deceitfulness or theft, and serious violations of rules. The ASPD diagnoses is prototypically described within the NEO-PI-R five-factor model of personality by high levels on the Extraversion facets of Angry-Hostility and Excitement-Seeking; low levels on the Agreeableness facets of Straightforwardness, Altruism, Compliance, and Tendermindedness; and low levels on the Conscientiousness facets of Dutifulness, Self-Discipline, and Deliberation.

Previous estimates for the prevalence of ASPD were in the range of 3% for males and 1% for females in the general population with much higher prevalence rates in forensic populations (APA, 1994). More recent epidemiological studies put prevalence rates in the general population between 1% and 4% (Grant et al., 2004; Torgersen et al., 2001) and prevalence in an outpatient psychiatric setting at around 3% to 4% (Zimmerman et al., 2005).

Clinical Presentation   The individual with ASPD enjoys defying social conventions by breaking laws, taking risks, and seeking excitement and sensation. This behavior is typically carried out with a recklessness and impulsiveness that is consistent with an overall failure to plan ahead and failure to accept responsibility for one's actions. The individual with ASPD will have considerable difficulty maintaining long-term monogamous relationships and will not accept the responsibilities that the role of parent or guardian entails. Work and financial obligations are similarly overlooked, and a criminal history is possible. They are deceitful and cunning and exhibit a superficial charm and glibness that belies their selfish motivations (Horowitz, 2004).

Individuals with ASPD have very low tolerance for boredom, depression, or frustration. They rarely, if ever, experience shame or guilt in response to their manipulation or coercion of others. They enjoy the expressions of aggression and lack remorse for the consequences of their actions. This unburdened state differs from the lack of shame reported by individuals with narcissistic personality disorder, who covertly are overwhelmed by their feelings of shame. People with ASPD are interpersonally sensitive enough to be aware of situations where it is socially appropriate to express guilt or remorse, particularly when it furthers their position. However, these feelings are likely to be shallow and transient and will dissipate once they have successfully manipulated or deceived others. While individuals with ASPD may experience dysphoria and irritability, particularly when challenged or frustrated, they will rarely seek treatment independently. It is usually through coercion by others, typically legal influences, that these individuals enter mental health treatment.

The interpersonal style of individuals with ASPD entails repeated betrayals of trust and a pervasive lack of empathy. There is a general disregard for social standards and rules and no regard for the impact of their actions on others. This is not due to a limited awareness of others' feelings since these individuals are exceptionally interpersonally perceptive. Instead, there is limited motivation to share in the emotional experience of other individuals. They can be described as slick, manipulative, calculating, or as a con-artist. They have superficial relationships with few, if any, lasting ties; the relationships that are maintained typically serve a purpose for the self. Although they are initially viewed as exceptionally charming, those that know individuals with ASPD well describe them as cold, callous, and contemptuous (Horowitz, 2004).

There is considerable overlap between the construct of the psychopath and ASPD. In general, psychopathy predicts ASPD, but ASPD does not predict psychopathy—suggesting that psychopathy exists in a subset of individuals meeting criteria for ASPD. The Hare Psychopathy Checklist–Revised version (Hare, 1991) is a widely used tool in the assessment of psychopathy. This measure provides a two-factor structure: interpersonal and affective features and socially deviant features that reliably identify the unique personality constellation that psychopaths present. Psychopathy is linked to recidivism (Serin & Amos, 1995), violence (Douglas, Ogloff, Nicholls, & Grant, 1999), and malingering (Gacono et al., 1995) in forensic populations and is therefore particularly useful in assessing the malignancy of an individual with ASPD.

Etiology   Research on externalizing disorders (conduct disorder, adult antisocial behavior, alcohol dependence, and drug dependence) suggests that a highly heritable general vulnerability contributes to transmission of the group of externalizing disorders (Hicks, Krueger, Iacono, McGue, & Patrick, 2004). However, results also suggest disorder-specific effects are closely related to environmental factors. Developmental explanations include a history of caregiver hostility, deficient adult role models, and reinforcement of vindictive behaviors (Sperry, 2003). A history of childhood abuse, including harsh and neglectful caregiving, is believed to result in the adult individual with ASPD neglecting others' needs and feelings (Benjamin, 1996). Some suggest that individuals with ASPD exhibited difficult temperaments in childhood, eliciting hostile reactions in caregivers and reinforcing withdrawal from others (Sperry, 2003). Developmental examinations of ASPD suggest that children who are repeatedly rejected by their normative peer group and who are more involved in deviant peer groups are more likely to develop antisocial personality disorders (van Lier, Vitaro, Wanner, Vuijk, & Crijnen, 2005).

BORDERLINE PERSONALITY DISORDER

Instability in affect and identity accompanied by fears of rejection or abandonment by others.

> Behavioral: Impulsively self-damaging
> Intrapsychic: Emptiness and anger
> Interpersonal: Excessive reactivity to real or imagined abandonment

The *DSM-IV* diagnostic criteria for borderline personality disorder (BPD; APA, 1994) include a pattern of instability in relationships, identity, and affect accompanied by impulsivity as demonstrated by five or more of the following characteristics: frantic efforts to avoid real or imagined abandonment; unstable and intense relationships that alternate between extreme idealization and devaluation; persistent unstable self-image; impulsivity in at least two areas that are self-damaging; recurrent suicidal behavior, gestures, threats, or self-mutilation; affective instability; chronic emptiness; inappropriate or intense anger; or transient, stress-related paranoid ideation or dissociative symptoms. Recent studies have examined the diagnostic efficiency of the BPD criteria and have documented the varying predictive utility of the individual criteria (Becker et al., 2002; Grilo, Becker, Anez, McGlashan, 2004). Factor analyses of BPD criteria have suggested the presence of three homogeneous components: disturbed relatedness, behavioral dysregulation, and affective dysregulation (Sanislow, Grilo, & McGlashan, 2000; Sanislow et al., 2002).

There has been long-standing debate about whether BPD can be or should be diagnosed during adolescence. Milder versions of identity diffusion, impulsivity, and affective instability are associated with normal early adolescent psychological development; therefore, clinicians have emphasized the difficulties in disentangling such development storms from pathological functioning. Empirical research on the construct of BPD in adolescents has documented its somewhat more diffuse presence at both the criterion level (Becker et al., 1999) and the diagnostic level (Becker et al., 2002, 2006) and its limited stability over time (Grilo, Becker, Edell, & McGlashan, 2001), although it appears to be prospectively predictive of general psychosocial impairment (Levy et al., 1999). The BPD diagnoses is prototypically described within the NEO-PI-R five-factor model of personality by high levels on the Neuroticism facets of Anxiety, Angry-Hostility, Depression, Impulsiveness, and Vulnerability; low levels on the Agreeableness facets of Trust and Compliance; and low levels on the Conscientiousness facet of Competence.

Previous estimates for the prevalence of BPD were approximately 2% of the general population, 10% of outpatient psychiatric populations, and 20% of inpatient psychiatric populations (APA, 1994). More recent epidemiological studies put prevalence rates in the general population around 1% (Samuels et al., 2002; Torgersen et al., 2001) and prevalence in an outpatient psychiatric setting at around 9% (Zimmerman et al., 2005).

Clinical Presentation   The individual with BPD lacks a clear and coherent understanding of the self with frequent vacillations between good and bad images of self and others. When faced with being alone, the individual with BPD experiences profound feelings of emptiness, abandonment, or rejection and views the self disparagingly: as bad, defective, evil, unlovable, or unwanted. Extreme lability or affective dysregulation is a hallmark of the emotional experience of those with BPD (Gunderson, 1984; Livesley, Jang, Jackson, & Vernon, 1993). The mood shifts from euthymic to dysphoric are easily triggered—particularly by interpersonal events related to abandonment or rejection—and last a few hours to a few days. The predominant internal experiences are of profound internal emptiness. A young man in treatment vividly described his experience of emptiness and solitude as if he were standing at the top of a great precipice looking into a dark and deep void. He felt helpless, overwhelmed, and profoundly anxious as he was certain he would plummet into the vast depths of nothingness unless he was "rescued" by a loved one.

Cognitively, people with BPD are rigid, abstract, and dichotomous thinkers (Beck & Freeman, 1990; Millon, 1987) who believe they are powerless to change their circumstances. Beck and Freeman (1990) describe three basic assumptions made by individuals with BPD that further entrench their maladaptive stance: "I am powerless and vulnerable," "I am inherently unacceptable," and "The world is dangerous and malevolent." When under stress, individuals with BPD are prone to experience episodes of dissociation, paranoid ideation, or "micropsychotic episodes."

A history of attachment failures results in separation anxiety and frantic efforts to avoid real or imagined abandonment. Signs of abandonment are reacted to as if it is imminent and life-threatening (Millon & Davis, 1996). Those with BPD will quickly and easily develop close relationships and negotiate these interactions through alternating idealizing and devaluing of others. This diffi-culty in negotiating relationships is exacerbated by the uncertainty of identity, internal emptiness, and fear of enmeshment versus fear of utter isolation. This conflict results in rocky relationships marked by repeated break-ups and just as frequent make-ups.

The individual with BPD exhibits a hyper-responsiveness to rejection and aban-donment that frequently leads to a variety of reckless behaviors: suicidal gestures, self-mutilation, physical altercations, eating-disordered behaviors, alcohol or drug abuse, shopping sprees, or brief sexual encounters. Fears of abandonment and lone-liness may elicit repeated phone calls to family, friends, or acquaintances at inap-propriate times. The individual with BPD also exhibits intense and uncontrollable anger or rage that may result in heated arguments, yelling, or physical confronta-tions. Excessive aggression is particularly likely to occur in response to frustra-tion and may be linked to temperament (Kernberg, 1976). Borderline features and personality disorder are also associated with increased utilization of psychological treatment, psychopharmacological treatment, and the number of outpatient health visits (Bagge, Stepp, & Trull, 2005; Bender et al., 2001, 2006). See Case Study 2.

Case Study 2

A woman presented for a diagnostic interview with a history of relationship problems and a suicide attempt involving an overdose of psychiatric medi-cations. She reported significant interpersonal stressors during the previous year, including being bullied by a fellow coworker, being unfaithful to her fiancé, ending her engagement on her wedding day, ending a relationship with a good friend, and difficulty in her relationship with her grown son. She met criteria for posttraumatic stress disorder related to childhood sex-ual abuse. She reported feeling angry most of the time, had frequent mood changes that lasted only a few hours and were typically triggered by minor interpersonal events, and experienced an overwhelming internal emptiness. She felt she had a sense of who she was but that this identity was unsteady and that she vacillated in her feelings toward herself: at times she felt okay about herself, and at other times felt she was "quite horrible." She reported a vague paranoid ideation that occurred occasionally and was more preva-lent during times of stress. During these periods she would feel picked on by coworkers, family, and friends and would interpret casual remarks as subtle put-downs directed at her. She lives with her boyfriend and her son. She de-scribed the relationship with the boyfriend as "having its ups and downs." Over the previous year, she had been unfaithful several times during her engagement to her boyfriend and eventually terminated their engagement the hour before their wedding was to take place. She reports ongoing fears that he will abandon her and she will frequently plead with him to take days off from work to be with her. When he refuses, she threatens to kill herself if he leaves. She reported frequent arguments in which she would lose her temper and really scream ("approximately 250 times in the last year"), sev-eral threats to harm other people, and three occurrences of acting on these

(continued)

threats. She had a history of alcohol abuse and engaged in reckless behaviors while intoxicated, including impulsive sexual encounters and driving under the influence. Her suicide attempt followed an argument over the telephone with her then-fiancé regarding financial matters. Her last words to him were "you'll be sorry" before hanging up. She took an overdose of psychiatric medications accompanied by a significant amount of alcohol before driving away in her car. She reported a handful of additional suicidal gestures over the previous year and 11 previous suicide attempts.

BPD is one of the most lethal psychiatric disorders with 10% completing suicide (Gunderson & Ridolfi, 2001; Paris & Zweig-Frank, 2001). Individuals who make highly lethal attempts are more likely to have a co-morbid major depressive disorder, antisocial personality disorder, and family histories of substance abuse (Soloff, Fabio, Kelly, Malone, & Mann, 2005). Diagnostic factors preceding suicide attempts include a worsening of major depressive disorder and substance use disorders (Yen et al., 2003). While worsening of depression precedes the suicide attempt, it is the affective instability criterion that most strongly predicts suicidal behaviors (Yen et al., 2004).

Etiology Research on the underlying biological contributors to BPD suggest that there is an association between the reduction of serotonin and impulsive aggression that is due, in part, to individual genetic differences (Skodol, Siever, et al., 2002). Examination of twins and family probands suggests that there are multiple underlying genetic dimensions that contribute to the diagnosis of BPD (Livesley, Jang, & Vernon, 1998), and no single dimension of "borderlineness" (Skodol, Siever, et al., 2002) accounts for the expression of BPD traits or diagnosis. Instead, research indicates that a complex interaction of environmental and genetic factors likely contributes to the presence of BPD. One environmental factor hypothesized to contribute to BPD has been pathological child experiences leading to trauma as indicated by a co-occurring diagnosis of posttraumatic stress disorder (PTSD). Co-morbid PTSD with a BPD diagnosis contributes to lower overall functioning and increased hospitalizations (Zlotnick et al., 2003), although the occurrence of childhood trauma is not restricted to borderline personality pathology (Goodman, New, & Siever, 2004). Alternatively, childhood trauma, neglect, and abuse are linked more broadly to all personality pathologies (Bierer et al., 2003; Golier et al., 2003), while certain BPD criteria are linked to a history of psychological trauma, particularly dissociation (Brodsky, Cloitre, & Dulit, 1995; Goodman & Yehuda, 2002).

A biosocial theory of BPD posited by Linehan (1993) suggests that BPD is a dysfunction in the emotion regulation system that results from a combination of biological predisposition and environmental factors. Environmental factors that facilitate the development of BPD in Linehan's theory include an invalidating environment in which the "communication of private experiences is met by erratic, inappropriate, and extreme responses" (p. 49). In this model, the individual with BPD, predisposed to emotional vulnerability, fails to learn how to identify, modulate, and appropriately express emotions, thereby facilitating maladaptive responses to emotions as adults.

HISTRIONIC PERSONALITY DISORDER

Vague and dramatic presentation that elicits attention and caregiving.

Behavioral: Seductive and capricious
Intrapsychic: Shallow and impressionistic
Interpersonal: A social butterfly

The *DSM-IV* diagnostic criteria for histrionic personality disorder (HPD; APA, 1994) include a pattern of excessive emotionality and attention seeking as demonstrated by five or more of the following characteristics: feeling discomfort and unappreciated when not the center of attention; interactions that utilize inappropriate seductive or provocative behaviors; superficial and rapidly changing expressions of emotion; using one's physical appearance to attract and maintain others' attention; a style of speech that is excessively impressionistic and lacking in detail; dramatic, theatrical, or exaggerated expressions of emotion; suggestible; and a tendency to consider relationships as more intimate than they actually are. Historically derived from hysteria, individuals with HPD exhibit an exaggerated emotionality accompanied by diffuse vagueness to their expressions. The HPD diagnosis is prototypically described within the NEO-PI-R five-factor model of personality by high levels on the Neuroticism facets of Depression and Self-Consciousness; high levels on the Extraversion facets of Warmth, Gregariousness, Excitement-Seeking, and Positive Emotions; high levels on the Openness facets of Fantasy and Feelings; and high levels on the Agreeableness facet of Trust.

Previous estimates for the prevalence of HPD were in the range of 2% to 3% for the general population, and 10% to 15% among psychiatric populations (APA, 1994). More recent epidemiological studies put prevalence rates in the general population around 2% (Grant et al., 2004; Torgersen et al., 2001) and prevalence in an outpatient psychiatric setting at around 1% (Zimmerman et al., 2005). The lower prevalence rate in psychiatric settings may be understood in the context of the culturally adaptive qualities associated with the sex role stereotypes found in individuals with HPD.

Clinical Presentation   People with HPD are hedonistic, unmethodical, charming, labile, capricious, and superficial and exhibit a tendency to exaggerate to gain attention (Millon, 1990; Sperry, 2003; Stone, 1993). These individuals are not detail oriented, and novel stimuli—whether in the environment or associated with other people—will easily capture their attention. This characteristic attentional style offers a potential explanation of the shallow and vague interactional style found in those with HPD. As the individual with HPD focuses on the object of attention, a peripheral stimulus upstages and displaces the original object, which accounts for the lively, spontaneous but flighty presentation seen in HPD. However, this distractibility limits the ability of the person with HPD to attend long enough to integrate a deep, coherent, or complex description of an object or experience. Thus, later recollections or emotional expressions are notable for their shallow and impressionistic qualities (Horowitz, 2004; Shapiro, 1965). Short-term goals, commitments, and promises are easily forgotten, and long-term goals and life direction are not present (Horowitz, 2004). People with HPD have difficulty reflecting on anything and instead use intensified emotions and exaggerated displays of feelings as defenses against cognitive processing of intrapsychic conflicts (Easser & Lesser, 1989). They rely more on colorful language and hyperbole and less on reason.

Individuals with HPD will make great efforts to look their best and grab the attention of others by being exhibitionistic or flirtatious. This need to be the center of attention results in a charming interpersonal style that also functions to manipulate important others. As noted by Benjamin (1996), people with HPD force the delivery of love. This exaggerated desire to connect to others results in a lack of interpersonal boundaries, a surrendering of their separateness, and the appearance of extreme neediness (Horowitz, 2004). Physical attractiveness and sexuality often are viewed as means to engage the attention and care of others with a depreciation of self-efficacy and competence. The need for constant attention frequently alienates friends, particularly when the use of sexually provocative behavior is directed toward friends' partners. Others are further alienated by the apparent "phony" quality exhibited by people with HPD in relationships. When ignored, individuals with HPD are likely to be angry, not because it is a threat to their self-esteem, but because it is experienced as a threat to their dependency on others. When isolated from others, they are likely to feel empty, lonely, depressed, or anxious. It is this dysphoria that is likely to motivate people with HPD to seek treatment. In treatment, they are likely to focus more on gaining the attention and approval of the therapist than on developing a meaningful therapeutic relationship. HPD is frequently associated with Axis I diagnoses of conversion or somatization disorders.

Etiology   The development of HPD illustrates a complicated interaction of biological predispositions and environmental responses. The temperament of extraversion and emotional expressiveness that underlie the character of an individual with HPD are recognized as having biological components (Millon & Davis, 1996). In addition, the characteristic attentional style (Shapiro, 1965) discussed previously contributes to the overall presentation of HPD. These factors interact with a lack of caregiver attention during formative years that led the child to develop strategies of attention-grabbing presentation and shallow interaction that would elicit attention and connection (Benjamin, 1996; Horowitz, 2004).

NARCISSISTIC PERSONALITY DISORDER

The use of grandiosity, entitlement, or exploitation to maintain self-esteem.

Behavioral: Arrogance and superiority
Intrapsychic: Anger, shame, and envy
Interpersonal: Lack of empathy

The *DSM-IV* diagnostic criteria for narcissistic personality disorder (NPD; APA, 1994) include a pattern in fantasy or behavior of grandiosity, need for admiration, and lack of empathy as indicated by five or more of the following characteristics: a grandiose sense of self-importance; preoccupation with fantasies of unlimited success, power, beauty, intellect, or ideal love; believes self is special and unique so can only be understood by or associated with other special or high-status people; requires excessive admiration; has a sense of entitlement; is interpersonally exploitative; lacks empathy; is envious of others or believes others are envious of him or her; and shows arrogant, haughty attitudes or behaviors. The crux of the NPD diagnosis is the focus on the enhancement of self-esteem through a myriad of behaviors, emotions, and interpersonal exchanges. The NPD diagnosis is prototypically described within the NEO-PI-R five-factor model of personality by high levels on the Neuroticism facets of Angry-Hostility and Self-Consciousness; high levels on the Openness facet of Fantasy; high levels on the Conscientiousness facet of Achievement Striving; and low levels on the Agreeableness facets of Altruism, Modesty, and Tendermindedness.

The prevalence of NPD was previously estimated at less than 1% for the general population and 2% to 16% in clinical populations (APA, 1994). More recent epidemiological studies put prevalence rates in the general population at slightly less than 1% (Torgersen et al., 2001) and prevalence in an outpatient psychiatric setting at around 2% (Zimmerman et al., 2005).

Clinical Presentation Individuals with NPD appear conceited, boastful, and snobbish. Their self-centeredness, tendency to dominate conversation, and admiration seeking frequently alienate others. The appearance of superiority, pomposity, and arrogance contrasts the thin-skinned sensitivity to criticism that marks the NPD. Individuals with NPD may try to hide their sensitivity to rejection, criticism, or defeat and the subsequent deteriorating effects on their self-esteem. Their attempts to elicit admiration from others are done in service to their self-esteem. Impatient when demands go unmet, they are focused on goals of superior power, wealth, or ability.

The narcissist's self is viewed as fragmented and fragile, precariously dependent on relationships and behaviors to maintain self-esteem. The self is hypersensitive to the smallest criticism or failure, and the person with NPD may distort facts or engage in self-deception to preserve the illusion of success and competence. Rage is the common response to criticism or failure and allows the individual with NPD to avoid experiencing overwhelming shame and dysphoria. Individuals with NPD use others to maintain self-esteem through entitlement or exploitation. They vacillate between overidealization and devaluation of others, depending on the purpose that the others can serve. Their expectation of others is sometimes outside the realm of possibility or reality and leaves them feeling vulnerable. This is frequently responded to with dismissal of the needed others. Limited empathic responses are characteristic of those with NPD, although empathic response may be exhibited through a masochistic giving of oneself for a broader good. While seemingly altruistic, the motive behind the demonstration is the narcissist's ability to increase self-esteem through self-aggrandizing sacrifice for others. Depression frequently follows these masochistic sacrifices when others do not perceive or laud the narcissist's sacrifice.

Western culture accepts the disinhibited self-centeredness that NPD exhibits (Sperry, 2003; Stone, 1993), which may be one of the reasons narcissistic traits are so common but do not elicit sufficient dysfunction to meet *DSM* criteria. Alternatively, Stone (1993) states, "the number of persons exhibiting significant narcissistic traits, even short of 'NPD,' but enough to cause difficulty in interpersonal life is clearly very great" (p. 259). Alternative conceptualizations of narcissism identify a covert, shy, or vulnerable narcissist in addition to the *DSM* depiction of the overt, arrogant, or grandiose narcissist (Akhtar, 1997; Cooper, 1998; Dickinson & Pincus,

2003; Ronningstam, 2005; Wink, 1991). This vulnerable conceptualization of NPD shares common maladaptive qualities of narcissism (e.g., rage, entitlement, and limited empathy) but lacks the adaptive qualities of narcissism (assertiveness, self-confidence, and ambition) found in the grandiose conceptualization and may be an example of narcissistic traits associated with psychosocial dysfunction that do not meet *DSM* criteria for NPD.

Etiology   NPD has traditionally been viewed as a product of overindulgent parenting styles or absence of attuned parental responses (Beck & Freeman, 1990; Kernberg, 1998; Kohut, 1972; Millon, 1996; Ronningstam, 2005). These parenting styles typically include either overindulgence, eliciting a sense of developmentally inappropriate entitlement in the child, or a failure to empathically mirror the child's affect or meet the needs of the child. However, additional evidence suggests a genetic influence may be at play in determining the character of NPD (Torgersen et al., 2000). These inherited aspects include hypersensitivity, aggression, low frustration tolerance, and problems in affect regulation (Ronningstam, 2005; Schore, 1994).

CLUSTER C: ANXIOUS AND FEARFUL

Avoidant, dependent, and obsessive-compulsive personality disorders comprise the anxious and fearful group referred to as Cluster C. The common thread in this group is an underlying anxiety, particularly regarding relations with others (Nordahl & Stiles, 2000).

AVOIDANT PERSONALITY DISORDER

Social withdrawal due to fear of being embarrassed, criticized, or rejected.

> Behavioral: Shy and guarded
> Intrapsychic: Feelings of inadequacy
> Interpersonal: Reticent but longing

The *DSM-IV* diagnostic criteria for avoidant personality disorder (AVPD; APA, 1994) include a pattern of social inhibition, feelings of inadequacy, and hypersensitivity to negative evaluation as evidenced by four or more of the following characteristics: avoids occupational activities that involve interpersonal contact due to fears of criticism, disapproval, or rejection; is unwilling to develop relationships unless certain of being liked; is restrained in intimate relationships due to fears of being shamed or ridiculed; is preoccupied with being criticized or rejected; is inhibited in new interpersonal situations due to feelings of inadequacy; views self as socially inept, unappealing, or inferior; is reluctant to take personal risks or engage in new activities because they may result in embarrassment. The crux of the AVPD diagnosis is the avoidance of interactions due to the fear of impending embarrassment, criticism, or rejection. Unlike most other personality disorders, factor analysis of AVPD has revealed a relatively homogeneous and coherent construct (Grilo, 2004a). The AVPD diagnoses is prototypically described within the NEO-PI-R five-factor model of personality by high levels on the Neuroticism facets of Anxiety, Depression, Self-Consciousness, and Vulnerability and low levels on the Extraversion facets of Gregariousness, Assertiveness, and Excitement-Seeking.

Previous estimates for the prevalence of AVPD were in the range of 0.5% to 1.0% for the general population and 10% for outpatient psychiatric populations (APA, 1994). More recent epidemiological studies put prevalence rates in the general population between 2% and 5% (Grant et al., 2004; Torgersen et al., 2001) and prevalence in an outpatient psychiatric setting at around 15% (Zimmerman et al., 2005).

Clinical Presentation   Individuals with AVPD present as aloof, apprehensive, and guarded. Attempts to engage them will be met with monosyllabic responses and little eye contact. This avoidance is not due to paranoid ideation as found in Cluster A personality disorders; rather, it is a result of the fear of humiliating oneself in front of others. The belief of individuals with AVPD that they are lacking in social skills or are personally unappealing leads to the active avoidance of social and public appearances. While individuals with AVPD may be socially skilled, the certainty of inadequacy and subsequent ridicule makes it unlikely that they will put themselves in situations where these skills may be used. They may report a fear that they will blush or start crying in the course of attending a social event. This overwhelming fear of criticism or rejection may make it difficult for those with AVPD to share these beliefs with a clinician. However, many individuals with AVPD feel more comfortable describing their fears and sensitivities after they have been made to feel safe and accepted. The inner world of the individual with AVPD is dominated by intense fears of embarrassment and rejection and associated self-criticisms such as "I am inferior," and "I am incompetent" (Beck & Freeman, 1990). Thus, people with AVPD maintain interpersonal distance because they expect to be seen as socially unacceptable.

The individual with AVPD fears rejection and therefore restricts activities to avoid rejection; the resulting anxiety and depression from restricting activities reinforces the negative self-evaluation and increases fears of rejection. Although individuals with AVPD fear others' rejection, they also wish for love and acceptance and can experience great loneliness (Benjamin, 1996; Sperry, 2003). Those with AVPD will scan social interactions for clues that they are being accepted or rejected and will misinterpret neutral interpersonal stimuli as negative or critical (Benjamin, 1996). Others must pass tests set in place by people with AVPD to prove they are unlikely to criticize or reject them. See Case Study 3.

Case Study 3

A young woman with a history of significant interpersonal problems and depression was interviewed over the telephone. Despite living close to the interviewer's office, she refused to enter the building for fear that someone would see her and ask what she was doing there. When asked open-ended questions, she gave monosyllabic answers that were vague and unrevealing of her inner world. When asked for details or examples, there would be long silences, uncomfortable shifting of the telephone, and requests for the interviewer to hold on while she checked whether family members had returned home before responding. She held a job but avoided any interpersonal contacts at work and reported no friends. The lack of friends was a difficult point

(continued)

for her to discuss and an area she desperately wanted improvement in but feared taking any steps to change her situation. She also experienced considerable shame over the implication of what the lack of friends meant about her. Despite having a full-time job, she continued to live at home with her parents, with whom she reported a "good" but not close relationship. She believed they were disappointed in her and her life. She reported having several hobbies that she fully enjoyed but were distinctly limited in social contact (i.e., writing, photography, and walking). She firmly believed she lacked social skills, despite conversing in a very appropriate and polite manner, and was convinced that people would inevitably criticize or reject her in social situations. She reported she could tell right away that people were judging her and was reluctant to interact with others due to fears of not being liked. She felt overwhelmingly awkward and tense in new social situations because of her belief that she was inadequate. She would not share her feelings with anyone, even with her own family, for fear that she would be made fun of. As mentioned previously, she avoided meetings at work that might involve an interaction because she feared she would be rejected by coworkers. Despite her obvious intellectual strengths, she would not pursue new career opportunities or schooling for fear that admissions officials would think her application was "a joke" and she would embarrass herself. When questioned about symptoms of a self-reported recent depression, she shut down and gave no responses to inquires. She attempted to muffle her sobs by covering the telephone receiver and then asked for a break in the interview. During the second interview, she apologized profusely for having to end the first interview and feared it would negatively impact her ability to continue with the interviewer. When this was denied, she seemed very surprised but slightly more open and willing to discuss her fears that treaters might view her as "crazy."

Etiology   Anxiety and vigilance found in AVPD is believed to be linked to biogenetic tendencies toward a lowered autonomic arousal threshold (Millon & Davis, 1996). Shyness is also believed to be genetically linked and may interact with environmental factors to develop into the maladaptive personality characteristics found in AVPD (Kagan, Reznick, & Snidman, 1988). Environmental factors that may contribute to this disorder include parental or peer rejection and/or ridicule (Benjamin, 1996; Sperry, 2003). Benjamin (1996) postulates that relentless parental control may have been invoked during the development of the individual with AVPD to construct an impressive and memorable social image. This image was destroyed by visible flaws in the individual with AVPD, which led to humiliation and embarrassment.

DEPENDENT PERSONALITY DISORDER

Excessive fears of autonomy and extensive need to be taken care of by more competent others.

Behavioral: Defers excessively and inappropriately
Intrapsychic: The self is weak and ineffectual
Interpersonal: Cultivating relationships that provide protection and support

The *DSM-IV* diagnostic criteria for dependent personality disorder (DPD; APA, 1994) include an excessive need to be taken care of, expressed through submissive and clinging behaviors, and fears of separation as demonstrated by five or more of the following characteristics: difficulty making everyday decisions without an excessive amount of advice or reassurance from others; needs others to assume responsibility for major areas of his or her life; difficulty expressing disagreement with others due to fears that support or approval will be withdrawn; difficulty initiating projects or carrying out tasks autonomously; going to excessive lengths to obtain nurturance and support from others, including volunteering for unpleasant or aversive tasks; feeling discomfort or helplessness when alone due to excessive fears of being unable to take care of oneself; urgent seeking of a new relationship to provide care and support when a previous relationship ends; unrealistic fears of or preoccupation with being left to take care of oneself. The crux of the DPD diagnosis is the submissive, reactive, and clinging behavior. The DPD diagnoses is prototypically described within the NEO-PI-R five-factor model of personality by low levels on the Extraversion facet of Assertiveness; high levels on the Neuroticism facets of Anxiety, Self-Consciousness, and Vulnerability; high levels on the Extraversion facet of Warmth; and high levels on the Agreeableness facets of Trust, Altruism, Compliance, and Modesty.

Prevalence rates for DPD are generally unknown, although *DSM-IV-TR* reports it is one of the most frequently reported personality disorders encountered in outpatient clinics (APA, 2000). However, research suggests that outpatient prevalence rates vary between 0% and 7% (Mezzich, Fabrega, & Coffman, 1987; Poldrugo & Forti, 1988). Studies on inpatient rates suggest a much higher prevalence rate, between 15% and 25%, which fits with theoretical understanding of the strong need for care among those with DPD (Jackson et al., 1991; Oldham et al., 1995). More recent epidemiological studies put prevalence rates in the general population between 0.5% and 1.5% (Grant et al., 2004; Torgersen et al., 2001) and prevalence in an outpatient psychiatric setting at around 1.4% (Zimmerman et al., 2005). These low prevalence rates seem contrary to *DSM* assertions that DPD is one of the most prevalent PDs in outpatient settings. One possible explanation is that current diagnostic criteria are "underinclusive and overly conservative" (Bornstein, 1997, p. 178). Bornstein (1997) suggests that several changes must be made to DPD criteria in order for the disorder's symptoms to match contemporary empirical research findings. These changes include emphasis on the self-view of individuals with DPD as weak and ineffectual and the view of others as powerful and competent and the use of a variety of active and passive behaviors to cultivate relationships that will provide protection, support, and security over the long run.

Clinical Presentation   Individuals with DPD are focused entirely on obtaining and maintaining relationships with more competent and powerful others that will compensate for the self-view as weak, incompetent, and inadequate. To that end, those with DPD present with the least troublesome behaviors (Benjamin, 1996). Individuals with DPD feel they have no choice but to be overcompliant with others and volunteer for activities that are unpleasant or demeaning, all for the sake of winning approval and care. This can present as neglect of outside interests with primary focus on the attachment to the needed other. The individual with DPD will actively avoid being alone and will collapse or frantically and actively seek assistance when forced into autonomy.

Overtly, people with DPD are very agreeable individuals who appear to trust others excessively and at times inappropriately. They may agree with others on points that they inherently disagree with to ensure care for the incompetent self. This self-sacrifice and overcompliance is done to ensure the affection and support of the vitally needed other (Stone, 1993). Problems can arise when the clinginess of the person with DPD alienates others. However, the passive dependent and submissive individual with DPD will stick with relationships through thick and thin. They fear autonomy due to feelings of inadequacy and self-doubt. If left on their own, individuals with DPD believe they will be unable to survive. The response to autonomy is to increasingly attach and subvert to ensure that the attachment remains and caregiving continues.

The internal life of the person with DPD is filled with extensive anxiety and feelings of incompetence, which fits with the frequent Axis I co-morbidities. Individuals with mood or anxiety disorders demonstrate poorer outcomes when this psychopathology is accompanied by dependency traits (Bornstein, 1993; Overholser, 1992). DPD is associated with depression (Overholser, 1991), eating disorders (Tisdale, Pendelton, & Marler, 1990; Wonderlich, Swift, Slotnick, & Goodman, 1990), somatic complaints (Greenberg & Bornstein, 1988), and somatization disorder (Hayward & King, 1990; Rost, Akins, Brown, & Smith, 1992). There appears to be small to moderate overlap of DPD with anxiety disorders (Ng & Bornstein, 2005), although the direction of causality between DPD and Axis I anxiety is unclear (McLaughlin & Mennin, 2005).

Etiology   Developmental factors suggest that authoritarian parenting styles are associated with dependency traits. While individuals with DPD have learned to trust others for care, they were restricted from normal developmental challenges that promote autonomy, frequently having all needs immediately and completely met. When these individuals did make attempts at autonomy, they were met with responses of subtle abandonment, rejection, or were viewed as ungrateful or disloyal (Benjamin, 1996; Sperry, 2003). These responses restricted the development of self-efficacy and appropriate autonomy (Coyne & Whiffen, 1995; Whiffen & Sasseville, 1991). Peers may have responded to these individuals with rejection, teasing, and other remarks on their dependence and incompetence, thereby reinforcing the views conveyed by caregivers that the person with DPD is in dire need of constant care. Recent research suggests that depression in early adolescent girls may influence the development of dependency and self-criticism, reinforcing these personality styles over time (Shahar, Blatt, Zuroff, Kuperminc, & Leadbeater, 2004). Infantile temperament may be an additional variable that interacts with parenting style to further elicit overprotective and authoritarian responses to the individual child (Millon, 1996).

OBSESSIVE-COMPULSIVE PERSONALITY DISORDER

Perfectionism and control that interfere with efficiency, task completion, and social interactions.

Behavioral: Stubbornly perfectionistic
Intrapsychic: Self-critical
Interpersonal: Inflexible control

The *DSM-IV* diagnostic criteria for obsessive-compulsive personality disorder (OCPD; APA, 1994) include a preoccupation with orderliness, perfectionism, and mental and interpersonal control as evidenced by four or more of the following characteristics: preoccupation with details, rules, lists, schedules, and organization to the extent that the major point of the activity is lost; perfectionism that interferes with task completion; excessive devotion to work to the exclusion of leisure activities; is overconscientious, scrupulous, or inflexible about morality, ethics, or values; inability to discard worn-out or worthless objects that have no real or sentimental value; reluctance to delegate tasks; a miserly spending style toward self and others; and rigidity and stubbornness. The crux of the OCPD diagnosis is rigidity and control with which the individual approaches all tasks and situations. A recent factor analysis reveals three components that may reflect distinct interpersonal, intrapersonal, and behavioral features (Grilo, 2004b). These findings are generally consistent with contemporary clinical views emphasizing the behaviors as exaggerated attempts at interpersonal and intrapersonal control (Pollak, 1979, 1995). The OCPD diagnoses is prototypically described within the NEO-PI-R five-factor model of personality by high levels on the Extraversion facet of Assertiveness; high levels on the Conscientiousness facets of Competence, Order, Dutifulness, and Achievement Striving; low levels on the Openness facet of Values; and low levels on the Agreeableness facet of Compliance.

Previous estimates for the prevalence of OCPD were approximately 1% in the general population and 3% to 10% in outpatient psychiatric populations (APA, 2000). More recent epidemiological studies put prevalence rates in the general population between 2% and 8% (Grant et al., 2004; Torgersen et al., 2001) and prevalence in an outpatient psychiatric setting between 8% and 9% (Zimmerman et al., 2005).

Clinical Presentation   The presentation of the individual with OCPD is quite different from characteristics associated with an Axis I diagnosis of obsessive-compulsive disorder (OCD). The perfectionism of individuals with OCPD can lead to procrastination, inefficiency, and failure to complete tasks. They may pay inordinate attention to unnecessary or less important details and lose sight of the forest for the trees. Their perfectionistic need to avoid making mistakes leads to hypervigilance for possible errors, as well as detail-focused behavior. The conscientiousness and high standards of individuals with OCPD can impede decision making. Frequently described as workaholics, these individuals focus excessively on achievement and productivity and are reluctant to take vacations or weekends off from work. There is considerable difficulty letting go of a task if criteria for perfection are not clearly achieved (Horowitz, 2004). The high ideals and sense of morality can lead to inordinate deference to authority or rules (Benjamin, 1996).

The compliance with high standards exhibited by individuals with OCPD compensates for their perceived inner flaws. While righteously competent and focused on perfection through self-control, this stance, when directed toward the self, is likely to result in self-criticism, excessive dwelling on personal flaws, and beliefs of personal unworthiness. In general, discussions of emotions are avoided with particular aversion to expressions of warmth. Individuals with OCPD are adept at using intellectualization and rationalization to avoid emotional expression. However, they may be more comfortable in expressing anger or frustration than other emotions. They will frequently focus on concrete problems and disregard attempts by others to discuss personal distress. Expressions of empathy and concern are therefore regarded as irrelevant and may impede development of a therapeutic alliance. Cognitive processes are dominated by dichotomous thinking and cata-strophizing (Beck & Freeman, 1990).

Individuals with OCPD are preoccupied with accomplishments and interper-sonal agency to the detriment of their relationships. They are motivated to be per-fect and, thus, to be respected by others (Horowitz, 2004). They are very dependable but also interpersonally difficult due to their rigidity and control. They may turn their perfectionistic focus on others, resulting in judgmental attitudes and critical comments, particularly when others do not submit to the same pursuit of perfec-tion. The individual with OCPD may be reluctant to delegate tasks to others out of concern that others will do things "incorrectly." "Incorrectly" is frequently in any manner different than the modus operandi of the person with OCPD and is irre-spective of the potential benefits or efficiencies provided by a creative or alterna-tive approach. Interpersonally, these individuals may appear antagonistic in their pursuit of agentic goals and offend or exasperate others in the process. Interest-ingly, the focus on achievement and work productivity leads those with OCPD to present as higher functioning than their distress and diagnosis may indicate. This striving for perfection allows them to maintain occupational success even when emotional and interpersonal functioning is severely impaired.

Etiology   Those with OCPD frequently exhibit a preoccupied attachment style (Sperry, 2003). As children, these individuals were punished for failing to be perfect and received no rewards for success. Affection and emotions were to be controlled and remain unexpressed (Benjamin, 1996). Individuals with OCPD expect others to judge and criticize them in the same way that caregivers did during their develop-ment. Therefore, individuals with OCPD judge others by the same strict standards and self-criticize in the same manner as the caregivers who once criticized them (Horowitz, 2004).

ASSESSMENT

Assessment of any diagnostic entity involves careful consideration and integra-tion from several sources. This is particularly true of personality disorders in which symptoms permeate interpersonal, intrapsychic, and behavioral fields. Standardized assessment procedures not only increase reliability and validity but also compensate for problems with missed diagnoses (Zimmerman & Mattia, 1999). The assessment process interacts with the treatment or research goals of the procedure. Therefore, conceptual and clinical issues should be carefully considered when determining the assessment tools. As in many areas of psy-chopathology, measures employ formats as varied as diagnostic interviews to self-report questionnaires and vary in the focus of diagnostic criteria and the theoretical approach to the disorder. However, these theoretical differences do not necessarily result in different diagnoses when different approaches are used (see Wiggins, 2003, for a case demonstration of this principle and a theoretically integrative approach to personality assessment).

Diagnostic Interviews   Diagnostic interviews can be performed in unstructured, structured, or semi-structured forms. Unstructured interviews have been criticized for their lack of standardization and poor reliability in making diagnoses. Although structured interviews provide the highest reliability, they lack the flexibility for follow-up questions that are frequently necessary for determining complex diagnoses such as personality disorders. Semistructured interviews offer the empirical benefits of a standardized interview format while allowing the interviewer to bypass unnecessary portions or clarify responses through additional avenues and follow-up questions. Although semistructured interviews offer an appealing balance of standardization and flexibility that has proved useful to research settings, it is clear that this assessment process is very different from the way personality disorder diagnoses are made in clinical practice (Westen, 1997). The use of standardized methods of personality disorder assessment can promote more valid and reliable diagnoses and uncover personality disorders that might inhibit progress in the treatment of Axis I disorders (McDermut & Zimmerman, 1997; McDermut & Zimmerman, 2005; Zimmerman & Mattia, 1999). The following are several commonly used diagnostic interviews aimed at diagnosing a wide range of personality disorders.

The Diagnostic Interview for *DSM-IV* Personality Disorders (Zanarini et al., 1996) consists of 398 items designed to assess the 10 *DSM-IV* PD diagnoses as well as 2 *DSM-IV* appendix PDs identified for further study: negativistic and depressive personality disorders. Items correspond to *DSM* criteria, and questions focus on the presence of thoughts, feelings, and behaviors within the previous 2 years. The International Personality Disorders Examination (Loranger, 1999) is a 537-question semistructured interview that evaluates personality according to *DSM-IV* criteria as well as the *ICD-10* criteria. The interview assesses criteria across the realms of work, self, interpersonal relationships, affects, reality testing, and impulse control. Personality disorders assessed include paranoid, schizoid, dissocial, emotionally unstable-impulsive, emotionally unstable-borderline, histrionic, anankastic, anxious, and dependent. The Personality Disorder Interview–IV (Widiger et al., 1995) assesses the 10 *DSM-IV* personality disorders as well as 2 appendix diagnoses: depressive and negativistic PD. The criteria are rated if they are present and characteristic for much of the subject's adult life (since age 18). The Structured Clinical Interview for *DSM-IV* Axis II Personality Disorders (SCID-II; First et al., 1997) is a 119-item semistructured interview with items directly corresponding to the *DSM-IV* criteria. The SCID-II evaluates the presence of the criteria for the past 5 years. The interview is preceded by the 119-item SCID-II personality questionnaire, and interviewers follow up on items endorsed on the screening instrument. The Structured Interview for *DSM-IV* Personality Disorders (SIDP-IV; Pfohl, Blum, & Zimmerman, 1997) is a 101-item semistructured interview that assesses the 10 *DSM-IV* personality disorders along with 3 of the proposed appendix PDs: depressive, self-defeating, and negativistic. For a diagnosis to be made, the criteria must have been present for the majority of the time over the preceding 5 years. The Structured Interview for the Five-Factor Model of Personality (Trull & Widiger, 1997) is a 120-item interview designed to assess adaptive and maladaptive traits and corresponds to the personality domains of the five-factor model of personality reviewed earlier. Twenty-four questions assess the six facets of each of the five traits of the model.

Self-Report Questionnaires   The administration of self-report or self-administered questionnaires is useful in identifying personality pathology. Questionnaires also provide alternatives when the administration of a diagnostic interview is logistically precluded. Self-report measures also may provide different types of information not necessarily obtained through diagnostic interviewing that can incrementally enhance the interviewer's diagnosis. The following are several self-report questionnaires aimed at measuring domains typically considered relevant to PD diagnoses.

The Dimensional Assessment of Personality Pathology (Livesley & Jackson, 2000) is a 290-item questionnaire that assesses 18 dimensions of personality traits, related behaviors, and interpersonal problems. Reponses are given on a Likert-type scale ranging from 1 (very unlike me) to 5 (very like me). The Inventory of Interpersonal Problems (IIP; Horowitz, Rosenberg, Baer, Ureno, & Villasenor, 1988) consists of 127 interpersonal problem statements involving inhibition ("It is hard for me to . . .) or excess ("I . . . too much). Respondents indicate the extent to which each statement is problematic for them on a 5-point Likert scale ranging from 0 (not at all) to 4 (extremely). A 64-item version (Alden, Wiggins, & Pincus, 1990) was constructed to correspond to the interpersonal circle model (Kiesler, 1983; Leary, 1957; Wiggins, 1982) and was subsequently standardized (IIP-64; Horowitz, Alden, Wiggins, & Pincus, 2000). The Millon Clinical Multiaxial Inventory–III (Millon, Davis, & Millon, 1997) is a 175-item true-false questionnaire that assesses a range of psychopathology including personality. This questionnaire operationalizes Millon's theory of psychopathology and includes aggressive, self-defeating, depressive, and negativistic PDs in addition to those found in the *DSM-IV.* The Minnesota Multiphasic Personality Inventory–2 (Butcher et al., 2001) consists of 567 true-false items aimed at assessing a wide range of psychopathology. No specific scales are designed to diagnose the *DSM-IV* PDs; however, interpretive strategies do provide information on general personality patterns and maladaptive components (Graham, 2000). The NEO Personality Inventory–Revised (NEO-PI-R; Costa & McCrae, 1992) is a 240-item questionnaire designed to assess the five-factor model of personality discussed previously. The Personality Assessment Inventory (Morey, 1991) is a 344-item questionnaire that provides ratings of clinical syndromes and personality features. Respondents rate each item on a 4-point Likert-type scale. The Personality Diagnostic Questionnaire–4+ (Hyler, 1994) is a 99-item true-false questionnaire designed to assess the symptoms and criteria of the 10 *DSM-IV* PDs and 2 appendix PDs. The Schedule for Nonadaptive and Adaptive Personality (Clark, 1993) contains 375 true-false items derived to assess 15 temperament and trait dimensions. It also contains 12 diagnostic scales congruent with personality disorder constructs.

Several of the above questionnaires also exist as informant versions, or formats designed for a respondent who is not the subject of the diagnosis but is very familiar with the subject. Informant reports offer the benefits of corroborating self-reports from a collateral source who can inform the assessor of behaviors that were denied, minimized, or distorted by the subject. An alternative reporter to an informant is the subject's clinician, an informant equipped with clinical knowledge. The Shedler-Westen Assessment Procedure (Westen & Shedler, 1998) is a 200-item clinician-rated questionnaire designed to assess the *DSM-IV* personality disorder criteria as well as PD symptoms, defense mechanisms, and adaptive personality traits.

Biological Assessment   A growing area in PD research is the examination of brain imaging in PD subgroups to infer cognitive and processing correlates of the observable dysfunction. A potential benefit of this research is to identify brain imaging patterns that can accurately assess and discriminate PD diagnoses (Driessen et al., 2004).

Problems exist in some of the research due to technical and methodological challenges of brain imaging procedures that are compounded when dealing with PD patient groups (Nahas, Molnar, & George, 2005). Some of these difficulties include controlling for co-morbidities, medications, and small sample sizes. STPD, BPD, and ASPD have been the focus of several investigations examining brain correlates of these disorders, and similar patterns have been identified across studies. Two recent reviews summarize findings of neuroimaging in PD subject groups (McCloskey, Phan, & Coccaro, 2005; Nahas et al., 2005). Patients with STPD have demonstrated structural abnormalities in the thalamus and basal ganglia (Byne et al., 2001; Downhill et al., 2001). Functional abnormalities in patients with STPD include altered frontal activation, deficits in temporal and nonlimbic subcortical areas, and altered striatal dopamine release (Bushsbaum et al., 1997, 2002; Shihabuddin et al., 2001). Patients with BPD diagnoses demonstrate decreased hippocampal volume, diminished response to serotonergic stimulation, aberrant functioning in the cingulated cortex, and increased amygdale activation to general emotional stimuli (Donegan et al., 2003; Drieseen et al., 2004, Herpertz et al., 2001; Soloff et al., 2000). Patients with ASPD diagnoses have demonstrated decreased limbic and increased prefrontal activation to emotional or abstract stimuli and increased corpus collosum volume (Intrator et al., 1997; Kiehl et al., 2001; Raine et al., 2003). Functional magnetic resonance imaging studies examining the neurological correlates of empathy have proposed associations to the amygdala, anterior and posterior cingulated, and medial prefrontal cortex (Völlm et al., 2006), and Blair (2003) has suggested that a developmental impairment in the amygdala leads to difficulties in empathy found in patients with ASPD.

COURSE AND PROGNOSIS

RISK FACTORS

Longitudinal and epidemiological research has examined the factors that put individuals most at risk for developing PDs, and recent reports from several major research programs have contributed much to our understanding. Some support for demographic, temperamental, and environment risk factors has been noted. Torgersen and colleagues (2001) identified several factors that increased probability for meeting criteria for a personality disorder: Native American or Black ethnicity; being a young adult; having low socioeconomic status; and being divorced, separated, widowed, or never married. PDs were diagnosed more frequently among single individuals from lower socioeconomic classes who were living in urban settings. Experiences involving abuse, neglect, and maladaptive parenting styles during early childhood and early adolescence predict the onset of PDs in adolescence in adulthood (Cohen, Crawford, Johnson, & Kasen, 2005). Environment factors identified by Cohen and colleagues (2005) as predicting PD symptoms include parenting and parent-child relationships, low-closeness to caregivers, power assertive punishment, maternal control through guilt, and having been the result of an unwanted pregnancy. Difficult temperaments (Cloninger et al., 1993; Paris, 2000; Siever & Davis, 1991) with early disruptive externalizing behavioral patterns also appear to put youngsters at risk for developing PDs (Myers et al., 1998). Some evidence exists for other early temperamental features as risk factors for specific PDs, such as shyness for AVPD (Rettew et al., 2003).

Developmental Onset

Establishing the long-standing nature of the maladaptive pattern is viewed as necessary in both *DSM-IV* and *ICD-10* diagnostic criteria for personality disorders. However, longitudinal research suggests this may not necessarily reflect the course of personality disorders. PD symptoms are highest in early adolescence and decline steadily during the period from age 9 to age 27, although relative standing to same-age peers in personality pathology stays approximately the same (Johnson et al., 2000). Additionally, predictive validity of PDs diagnosed in adolescence is only modest. Becker and Grilo (2005), in their review of the BPD literature in adolescents, concluded that, while BPD is associated with concurrent psychological distress, the diagnosis is only moderately predictive of having an adult diagnosis of BPD. However, it seems that an early diagnosis of BPD is related to general maladaptive personality traits and psychosocial impairment in adults.

A related point, stressed by Widiger (2003), is that PDs need to be more clearly conceptualized and carefully characterized as having an early onset. As noted earlier, the validity of PDs in adolescents remains controversial (Krueger & Carlson, 2001). It can be argued, for example, that determining early onset of PDs is impossible because adolescence is a period of profound changes and flux in personality and identity. A recent critical review of the longitudinal literature on personality traits throughout the life span revealed that personality traits are less stable during childhood and adolescence than they are throughout adulthood (Roberts & DelVecchio, 2000). Roberts and DelVecchio's (2000) meta-analysis of data from 152 longitudinal studies of personality traits revealed that rank-order consistency for personality traits increased steadily throughout the life span; test-retest correlations (over 6.7-year time intervals) increased from .31 (during childhood) to .54 (during college) to .64 (at age 30) to a high of .74 (at ages 50 to 70).

Nonetheless, if childhood precursors of PDs could be identified (as in the case of conduct disorder for antisocial PD), they could become part of the diagnostic criteria and create some degree of longitudinal continuity in the diagnostic system. Myers et al. (1998), for example, found that early onset (before 10 years of age) of conduct disorder problems predicted subsequent antisocial PD. More generally, temperamental vulnerabilities or precursors to PDs have been posited as central in several models of PDs (e.g., Cloninger et al., 1991; Siever & Davis 1991). Specific temperamental features evident in childhood have been noted to be precursors for diverse PDs (Paris, 2000; Rettew et al., 2003; Wolff et al., 1991) as well as for differences in interpersonal functioning (Newman, Caspi, Moffitt, & Silva, 1997) in adulthood. For example, studies have noted early odd and withdrawn patterns for schizotypal PD in adults (Wolff et al., 1991) and shyness for avoidant PD (Rettew et al., 2003). More generally, although the degree of stability for personality traits is higher throughout adulthood than throughout childhood and adolescence (Roberts & DelVecchio, 2000), longitudinal analyses of personality data have revealed that the transition from adolescence to adulthood is characterized by greater personality continuity than change (Roberts et al., 2001).

Stability, Course, and Impact: Findings from Recent Major Longitudinal Studies of Personality Disorders

Earlier critical reviews of the research literature pertaining to the stability, course, and impact of the *DSM-III-R* (and earlier) concluded that "personality disorders demonstrate only moderate stability and that, although personality disorders are generally associated with negative outcomes, they can improve over time and can benefit from specific treatments" (Grilo & McGlashan, 1999, p. 157; Grilo, McGlashan, & Oldham, 1998). Those conclusions, which were in sharp contrast to prevailing clinical lore, were tempered somewhat by significant methodological limitations in the literature, as noted by the authors.

Since then, important findings have emerged from three prospective longitudinal multiwave studies, funded by the National Institutes of Health during the 1990s, examining the course of adult PDs. Two of these studies were naturalistic studies of clinical groups: the multisite Collaborative Longitudinal Study of Personality Disorders (CLPS; Gunderson et al., 2000), which focused primarily on four PDs and a comparison group of major depressive disorder, and the McLean Study of Adult Development (MSAD; Zanarini et al., 2003), which focused on BPD while making use of a mixed comparison group of "other" PDs. The third study—the Children in the Community Study (Brook et al., 2002; Cohen & Cohen, 1996)—is a community-based prospective longitudinal study of personality, psychopathology, and psychosocial functioning of children and their mothers that has continued through the children's entry into adulthood. These three ongoing studies are complementary and have corrected, to varying degrees, many of the conceptual and methodological limitations of previous research summarized by Grilo and McGlashan (1999).

A special 2005 issue of the *Journal of Personality Disorders* provides detailed overviews of the major findings from each of these research programs (Cohen et al., 2005; Skodol et al., 2005; Zanarini et al., 2005). The special issue provides cogent commentaries by several leading PD experts who attempt to place these important findings within the major issues facing the field. These studies have contributed much to our understanding of the stability, course, and impact of PDs. Several misconceptions concerning the seriousness of PDs, the diagnostic applicability of PDs, prognosis, and social costs have been rectified by these studies (Krueger & Tackett, 2005), elucidating the importance of diagnosing PDs, the potential for improvement, and the differential impact on functioning of PDs. Here we provide a brief overview of the major findings.

The CLPS (Gunderson et al., 2000) has examined the nature, course, and impact of four personality disorders (STPD, BPD, OCPD, and AVPD) and has made use of MDD (a well-characterized Axis I problem) as a comparison group for context. CLPS has reported on different aspects of the stability of categorical and dimensional approaches to PDs (Grilo, Shea, Sanislow, Skodol, Gunderson et al., 2004; Shea et al., 2003) using prospective data obtained for 668 patients. Based on the traditional test-retest approach, blinded repeated administration of a semistructured interview conducted 24 months after baseline revealed "remission" rates (based solely on falling below *DSM-IV* diagnostic thresholds) ranging from 50% (AVPD) to 61% (STPD). Grilo, Shea, Sanislow et al. (2004) also used life table survival analyses to compare the time to remission for the four PD groups and for the MDD comparison group. Based on data over 24 months of prospective follow-along, remission rates for the PD groups were as follows: 33% for STPD, 42% for BPD, 47% for AVPD, and 55% for OCPD. These remission rates for PDs were significantly less than the remission rate (roughly 90%) for MDD without PD. This represents the first convincing empirical demonstration of the central tenet that PDs are characterized by a greater degree of stability than the hypothesized episodic course of Axis I psychiatric disorders. Readers are referred to Shea and Yen (2003) for a broader discussion of the issue of stability in Axis I versus Axis II disorders. CLPS also provided complementary analyses using dimensional approaches for 12-month (Shea et al., 2002) and 24-month

(Grilo, Shea, Sanislow et al., 2004) follow-ups. Grilo, Shea, Sanislow, et al. (2004) reported that PD patients are consistent in terms of their rank order of PD criteria (i.e., that individual differences in PD features are stable), but that they fluctuate in the severity of PD features over time. Interestingly, the range of the stability coefficients reported by Grilo, Shea, Sanislow, et al. (2004) for these clinical entities were similar to those reported by Lenzenweger (1999) for a nonclinical sample of college students.

As detailed in the overall review by Skodol (2005) of the CLPS findings to date, a series of published reports have documented that the course of PDs is more stable than the course of Axis I disorders, and meaningful improvements in PDs occur over time. However, PDs exhibit high treatment utilization (Bender et al., 2006), are associated with continued psychosocial dysfunction (Skodol et al., 2005; Skodol, Gunderson, et al., 2002; Skodol, Pagano, et al., 2005), and prognostically substantially dampen recovery from some psychiatric problems such as MDD (Grilo et al., 2005) but not other problems such as eating disorders (Grilo et al., 2003). Importantly, emerging findings suggest that personality traits may underlie personality disorders (Warner et al., 2004), and this may explain the greater stability of dimensional models of PDs. These traits are the foundation for intermittently expressed behaviors that result in meeting criteria for PDs. Therefore, a hybrid model of traits and maladaptive behaviors may be a more appropriate model for understanding PDs (McGlashan et al., 2005).

In the MSAD longitudinal examination of BPD, Zanarini and colleagues (2005) confirmed that improvements and remissions are more common in BPD than originally thought (about 74%). Importantly, analyses performed over 6 years of prospective follow-along revealed that BPD remissions are stable, and reoccurrences of PD diagnosis are surprisingly rare (approximately 6%). The MSAD study also suggests a distinction between acute symptoms associated with suicidal ideation or gestures and temperamental symptoms that were long-standing and associated with decreased functioning. Unexpectedly, completed suicide rates were lower than anticipated in the BPD population (4% versus an expected 10%). Improvements in the psychosocial functioning of individuals with BPD continued even after diagnostic criteria had remitted, suggesting the potential for an increasingly positive outcome from a debilitating disorder.

A theme that emerges from the longitudinal studies is that comorbidity with PD diagnoses increases the severity of psychopathology and decreases overall functioning. Diagnostic criteria for personality disorders must be considered in the context of any co-morbid Axis I diagnoses as well as co-morbid Axis II diagnoses. "Diagnosing a co-occurring personality disorder in psychiatric patients with an Axis I disorder is clinically important because of their association with the duration, recurrence, and outcome of Axis I disorders"(Zimmerman et al., 2005, p. 1911).

Another issue in the study of personality disorders concerns the aging process. Considerable research suggests that personality remains relatively stable through adulthood (Heatherton & Weinberger, 1994; Roberts & DelVecchio, 2000) and is highly stable after age 50 (Roberts & DelVecchio, 2000). Little is known, however, about PDs in older persons (Abrams et al., 1998). A 12-year follow-up of individuals with PDs as part of the Nottingham Study of Neurotic Disorders (Seivewright, Tyrer, & Johnson, 2002) documented substantial changes in PD trait scores based on blind administration of a semistructured interview. Seivewright and colleagues (2002) reported that Cluster B PD diagnoses (antisocial, histrionic) showed significant improvements, while Cluster A and Cluster C disorders appeared to worsen with age. While the Seivewright et al. (2002) findings are limited somewhat by the 2-point cross-sectional assessment (little is known about the intervening period), Tyrer, Strauss, and Cicchetti (1983) previously reported good reliability (weighted kappa of .64) for this diagnostic interview over a 3-year test-retest period. These findings somewhat echo the results of the seminal Chestnut Lodge follow-up studies (McGlashan, 1986a, 1986b) that suggested, in BPD and STPD, decreases in impulsivity and interpersonal instability with age, and increased avoidance with age. There exist other reports of diminished impulsivity with increasing age in BPD (Paris & Zweig-Frank, 2001; Stevensen et al., 2003), although this was not observed in a recent prospective analysis of individual BPD criteria (McGlashan et al., 2005).

TREATMENT

Reviews of psychotherapy studies examining PD populations suggest that PDs can and do improve with treatment (Perry & Bond, 2000; Perry et al., 1999; Roth & Fonagy, 2005; Sanislow & McGlashan, 1998; Shea, 1993; Target, 1998). Duration of therapy is positively related to improved outcomes of PD symptoms (Perry & Bond, 2000). However, dropouts from treatment in PD populations are substantially high (Gunderson et al., 1989; Perry et al., 1999; Skodol et al., 1983). Therapeutic alliance is a vital component in predicting good outcome from treatment for PD populations (Bender, 2005a, 2005b). A variety of pharmacological (mostly symptom-focused methods) and diverse psychological approaches are currently used to treat PDs, including psychoanalysis, psychodynamic approaches, schema therapy, dialectical behavior therapy, interpersonal therapy, supportive psychotherapy, and group psychotherapy. These various clinical methods differ in the extent of rigorous investigation, and clear evidence-based guidelines await continued research. Because space constraints here limit thorough reviews of each method, readers are referred to in-depth overviews covering techniques and research related to each treatment (see Appelbaum, 2005; Gabbard, 2000, 2005; Gunderson, 2000; Markowitz, 2005; Piper & Ogrodniczuk, 2005; Stanley & Brodsky, 2005; Stone, 2000; Tyrer & Davidson, 2000; Yeomans, Clarkin, & Levy, 2005; Young & Klosko, 2005).

SUMMARY

An individual's character is understood by the experiences and attributes that espouse one's individuality. These personality traits, when moderated by environmental circumstance, can elicit a maladaptive enduring pattern that affects psychosocial functioning, well-being, and relationships functioning. When this occurs, an individual's personality is considered to be disordered. Research has established the substantial impact personality disorders have on psychiatric health and overall functioning. While diagnostic quandaries remain in the identification of specific disorders, the overall dysfunction of emotional, interpersonal, and cognitive functioning found in PD diagnosis is quite clear: functioning in some PDs is more impaired than Axis I disorders. Personality disorders are not less important than Axis I disorders in determining mental health, nor are they less treatable. Careful assessment of personality pathology can not only inform treatment strategies, it can also elucidate course and severity of co-occurring Axis I disorders.

REFERENCES

Abrams, R. C., Spielman, L. A., Alexopoulos, G. S., & Klausner, E. (1998). Personality disorder symptoms and functioning in elderly depressed patients. *American Journal of Geriatric Psychiatry, 6,* 24–30.

Akhtar, S. (1997). *The shy narcissist.* Paper presented at the 150th American Psychiatric Association annual meeting, San Diego, CA.

Alden, L. E., Wiggins, J. S., & Pincus, A. L. (1990). Construction of circumplex scales for the Inventory of Interpersonal Problems. *Journal of Personality Assessment, 55,* 521–536.

American Psychiatric Association. (1994). *Diagnostic and statistical manual of mental disorders* (4th ed.). Washington, DC: Author.

American Psychiatric Association. (2000). *Diagnostic and statistical manual of mental disorders,* text revision (4th ed.). Washington, DC: Author.

Appelbaum, A. H. (2005). Supportive Psychotherapy. In J. M. Oldham, A. E. Skodol, & D. S. Bender (Eds.). *Textbook of personality disorders* (pp. 335–346). Washington, DC: American Psychiatric Publishing.

Bagge, C. L., Stepp, S. D., & Trull, T. J. (2005). Borderline personality disorder features and utilization of treatment over two years. *Journal of Personality Disorders, 19*(4), 420–439.

Balint, M. (1945). Friendly expanses—Horrid empty spaces. *International Journal of Psycho-Analysis, 36,* 225–241.

Battaglia, M., & Torgersen, S. (1996). Schizotypal disorder: At the crossroads of genetics and nosology. *Acta Psychiatrica Scandinavica, 94*(5), 303–310.

Beck, A. T., & Freeman, A. F. (1990). *Cognitive therapy of personality disorders.* New York: Guilford Press.

Becker, D. F., & Grilo, C. M. (2005). Validation studies of the borderline personality disorder construct in adolescents: Implications for theory and practice. *Annals of the American Society for Adolescent Psychiatry, 29,* 217–235.

Becker, D. F., Grilo, C. M., Edell, W. S., & McGlashan, T. H. (2000). Comorbidity of borderline personality disorder with other personality disorders in hospitalized adolescents and adults. *American Journal of Psychiatry, 157*(12), 2011–2016.

Becker, D. F., Grilo, C. M., Edell, W. S., & McGlashan, T. H. (2002). Diagnostic efficiency of borderline personality disorder criteria in hospitalized adolescents: Comparison with hospitalized adults. *American Journal of Psychiatry, 159*(12), 2042–2047.

Becker, D. F., Grilo, C. M., Morey, L. C., Walker, M. L., Edell, W. S., & McGlashan, T. H. (1999). Applicability of personality disorder criteria to hospitalized adolescents: Evaluation of internal consistency and criterion overlap. *Journal of the American Academy of Child and Adolescent Psychiatry, 38*(2), 200–205.

Becker, D. F., McGlashan, T. H., & Grilo, C. M. (2006). Exploratory factor analysis of borderline personality disorder criteria in hospitalized adolescents. *Comprehensive Psychiatry, 47*(2), 99–105.

Bender, D. S. (2005). The therapeutic alliance in the treatment of personality disorders. *Journal of Psychiatric Practice, 11,* 73–87.

Bender, D. S. (2005). Therapeutic Alliance. In J. M. Oldham, A. E. Skodol, & D. S. Bender (Eds.). *Textbook of personality disorders* (pp. 405–420). Washington, DC: American Psychiatric Publishing.

Bender, D. S., Dolan, R. T., Skodol, A. E., Sanislow, C. A., Dyck, I. R., McGlashan, T. H., et al. (2001). Treatment utilization by patients with personality disorders. *American Journal of Psychiatry, 158*(2), 295–302.

Bender, D. S., Skodol, A. E., Pagano, M. E., Dyck, I. R., Grilo, C. M., Shea, M. T., et al. (2006). Brief reports: Prospective assessment of treatment use by patients with personality disorders. *Psychiatric Services, 57*(2), 254–257.

Benjamin, L. S. (1996). *Interpersonal diagnosis and treatment of personality disorders* (2nd ed.). New York: Guilford Press.

Bierer, L. M., Yehuda, R., Schmeidler, J., Mitropoulou, V., New, A. S., Silverman, J. M., et al. (2003). Abuse and neglect in childhood: Relationship to personality disorder diagnoses. *CNS Spectrums, 8*(10), 737–754.

Blair, R. J. (2003). Neurobiological basis of psychopathy. *British Journal of Psychiatry, 182,* 5–7.

Bornstein, R. F. (1993). *The dependent personality.* New York: Guilford Press.

Bornstein, R. F. (1997). Dependent personality disorder in the DSM-IV and beyond. *Clinical Psychology: Science and Practice, 4*(2), 175–187.

Brodsky, B. S., Cloitre, M., & Dulit, R. A. (1995). Relationship of dissociation to self-mutilation and childhood abuse in borderline personality disorder. *American Journal of Psychiatry, 152*(12), 1788–1792.

Brook, D. W., Brook, J. S., Zhang, C., Cohen, P., & Whiteman, M. (2002). Drug use and the risk of major depressive disorder, alcohol dependence, and substance use disorders. *Archives of General Psychiatry, 59,* 1039–1044.

Bushsbaum, M. C., Nenadic, I., Hazlett, E., et al. (2002). Differential metabolic rates in prefrontal and temporal Brodmann areas in schizophrenia and schizotypal personality disorder. *Schizophrenia Research, 54,* 141–150.

Bushsbaum, M. C., Trestman, R. I., Hazlett, E., et al. (1997). Regional cerebral blood flow during the Wisconsin Card Sort Test in schizotypal personality disorder. *Schizophrenia Research, 27,* 21–28.

Butcher, J. N., Graham, J. R., Ben-Porath, Y. S., Tellegen, A., Dahlstrom, W. G., & Kaemmer, B. (2001). *The Minnesota Multiphasic Personality Inventory-2 (MMPI-2): Manual for administration, scoring, and interpretation* (rev. ed.). Minneapolis: University of Minnesota Press.

Byne, W., Bushsbaum, M. C., Kemether, E., et al. (2001). Magnetic resonance imaging of the thalamic mediodorsal nucleus and pulvinar in schizophrenia and schizotypal personality disorder. *Archives of General Psychiatry, 58,* 141–150.

Camisa, K. M., Bockbrader, M. A., Lysaker, P., Rae, L. L., Brenner, C. A., & O'Donnell, B. F. (2005). Personality traits in schizophrenia and related personality disorders. *Psychiatry Research, 133*(1), 23–33.

Casillas, A., & Clark, L. A. (2002). Dependency, impulsivity, and self-harm: Traits hypothesized to underlie the association between cluster B personality and substance use disorders. *Journal of Personality Disorders, 16,* 424–436.

Clark, L. A. (1993). *Manual for the schedule for nonadaptive and adaptive personality.* Minneapolis: University of Minnesota Press.

Clark, L. A. (1999). Dimensional approaches to personality disorder assessment and diagnosis. In C. R. Cloninger (Ed.), *Personality and psychopathology* (pp. 219–244). Washington, DC: American Psychiatric Association.

Clark, L. A. (2005). Temperament as a unifying basis for personality and psychopathology. *Journal of Abnormal Psychology, 114*(4), 505–521.

Cloninger, C. R., Przybeck, T. R., & Svrakic D. M. (1991). The Tridimensional Personality Questionnaire: U.S. normative data. *Psychological Reports, 69,* 1047–1057.

Cloninger, C. R., Svrakic, D. M., & Przybeck, T. R. (1993). A psychobiological model of temperament and character. *Archives of General Psychiatry, 50*(12), 975–990.

Cohen, P. & Cohen, J. (1996). *Life values and adolescent mental health.* Mahwah, NJ: Lawrence Erlbaum Associates.

Cohen, P., Crawford, T. N., Johnson, J. G., & Kasen, S. (2005). The Children in the Community study of developmental course of personality disorder. *Journal of Personality Disorders, 19*(5), 466–486.

Cooper, A. M. (1998). Further developments of the diagnosis of narcissistic personality disorder. In E. Ronningstam (Ed.), *Disorders of narcissism: Diagnostic, clinical, and empirical implications* (pp. 53–74). Washington, DC: American Psychiatric Press.

Costa, P. T., & McCrae, R. R. (1992). *Revised NEO Personality Inventory (NEO PI-R) and NEO Five Factor Inventory Professional Manual.* Odessa, FL: Psychological Assessment Resources.

Costa, P. T., & Widiger, T. A. (Eds.). (2002). *Personality disorders and the five-factor model of personality* (2nd ed.). Washington, DC: American Psychological Association.

Coyne, J. C., & Whiffen, V. E. (1995). Issues in personality as diathesus for depression: The case of sociotropy-dependency and autonomy-self-criticism. *Psychological Bulletin, 118,* 358–378.

Daneluzzo, E., Stratta, P., & Rossi, A. (2005). The contribution of temperament and character to schizotypy multidimensionality. *Comprehensive Psychiatry, 46*(1), 50–55.

Dickinson, K. A., & Pincus, A. L. (2003). Interpersonal analysis of grandiose and vulnerable narcissism. *Journal of Personality Disorders, 17,* 188–207.

Donegan, N. H., Sanislow, C. A., Blumberg, H. P., Fulbright, R. K., Lacadie, C., Skudlarski, P., et al. (2003). Amygdala hyperreactivity in borderline personality disorder: Implications for emotional dysregulation. *Biological Psychiatry, 54*(11), 1284–1293.

Douglas, K. S., Ogloff, J. R. P., Nicholls, T. L., & Grant, I. (1999). Assessing risk for violence among psychiatric patients: The HCR-20 violence risk assessment scheme and the Psychopathy Checklist: Screening Version. *Journal of Consulting and Clinical Psychology, 67*(6), 917–930.

Downhill, J. E. J., Bushsbaum, M. C., Hazlett, E., et al. (2001). Temporal lobe volume determined by magnetic resonance imaging in schizotypal personality disorder and schizophrenia. *Schizophrenia Research, 48,* 187–199.

Driessen, M., Beblo, T., Mertens, M., et al. (2004). Posttraumatic stress disorder and fMRI activation patterns of traumatic memory in patients with borderline personality disorder. *Biological Psychiatry, 55,* 603–611.

Easser, B. R., & Lesser, S. R. (1989). Transference resistance in hysterical character neurosis: Technical considerations. In R. F. Lax (Ed.), *Essential papers on character neurosis and treatment* (pp. 249–260). New York: New York University Press.

Fabrega, H., Ulrich, R., Pilkonis, P., & Mezzich, J. (1991). On the homogeneity of personality disorder clusters. *Comprehensive Psychiatry, 32,* 373–386.

Ferro, T., Klein, D. N., Schwartz, J. E., Kasch, K. L., & Leader, J. B. (1998). 30-month stability of personality disorder diagnoses in depressed outpatients. *American Journal of Psychiatry, 155,* 653–659.

First, M. B., Gibbon, R. L., Spitzer, R. L., et al. (1997). *Structured Clinical Interview for DSM-IV Axis II Personality Disorders (SCID-II).* Washington, DC: American Psychiatric Press.

Frances, A. (1982). Categorical and dimensional systems of personality diagnosis: A comparison. *Comprehensive Psychiatry, 23,* 516–527.

Gabbard, G. O. (2000). Combining medication with psychotherapy in the treatment of personality disorders. In J. M. Oldham & M. B. Riba (Series Eds) & J. G. Gunderson & G. O. Gabbard (Vol. Eds.), *Psychotherapy of Personality Disorders: Vol. 19* (pp. 65–94). Washington, DC: American Psychiatric Press.

Gabbard, G. O. (2005). Psychoanalysis. In J. M. Oldham, A. E. Skodol, & D. S. Bender (Eds.), *Textbook of personality disorders* (pp. 257–274). Washington, DC: American Psychiatric Publishing.

Gacono, C. B., Meloy, J. R., Sheppard, K., Speth, E., et al. (1995). A clinical investigation of malingering and psychopathy in hospitalized insanity acquittees. *Bulletin of the American Academy of Psychiatry & the Law, 23,* 387–397.

Golier, J. A., Yehuda, R., Bierer, L. M., Mitropoulou, V., New, A. S., Schmeidler, J., et al. (2003). The relationship of borderline personality disorder to posttraumatic stress disorder and traumatic events. *American Journal of Psychiatry, 160*(11), 2018–2024.

Goodman, M., New, A., & Siever, L. (2004). Trauma, genes, and the neurobiology of personality disorders. *Annals of the New York Academy of Science, 1032,* 104–116.

Goodman, M., & Yehuda, R. (2002). The relationship between psychological trauma and borderline personality disorder. *Psychiatric Annals, 32,* 337–345.

Graham, J. R. (2000). *The MMPI-2: Assessing personality and psychopathology* (3rd ed.). New York: Oxford University Press.

Grant, B. F., Hasin, D. S., Stinson, F. S., Dawson, D. A., Chou, S. P., Ruan, W. J., et al. (2004). Prevalence, correlates, and disability of personality disorders in the United States: Results from the National Epidemiologic Survey on alcohol and related conditions. *Journal of Clinical Psychiatry, 65,* 948–958.

Greenberg, R. P., & Bornstein, R. F. (1988). The dependent personality: I. Risk for physical disorders. *Journal of Personality Disorders, 2,* 126–135.

Grilo, C. M. (2004a). Factorial structure and diagnostic efficiency of DSM-IV criteria for avoidant personality disorder in patients with binge eating disorder. *Behaviour Research Therapy, 42*(10), 1149–1162.

Grilo, C. M. (2004b). Factor structure of DSM-IV criteria for obsessive compulsive personality disorder in patients with binge eating disorder. *Acta Psychiatrica Scandinavica, 109*(1), 64–69.

Grilo, C. M., Becker, D. F., Anez, L. M., & McGlashan, T. H. (2004). Diagnostic efficiency of DSM-IV criteria for borderline personality disorder: An evaluation in Hispanic men and women with substance use disorders. *Journal of Consulting and Clinical Psychology, 72*(1), 126–131.

Grilo, C. M., Becker, D. F., Edell, W. S., & McGlashan, T. H. (2001). Stability and change of DSM-III-R personality disorder dimensions in adolescents followed up 2 years after psychiatric hospitalization. *Comprehensive Psychiatry, 42*(5), 364–368.

Grilo, C. M., & McGlashan, T. H. (1999). Stability and course of personality disorders. *Current Opinion in Psychiatry, 12,* 157–162.

Grilo, C. M., McGlashan, T. H., Morey, L. C., Gunderson, J. G., Skodol, A. E., Shea, M. T., et al. (2001). Internal consistency, intercriterion overlap and diagnostic efficiency of criteria sets for DSM-IV schizotypal, borderline, avoidant and obsessive-compulsive personality disorders. *Acta Psychiatrica Scandinavica, 104*(4), 264–272.

Grilo, C. M., McGlashan, T. H., & Oldham, J. M. (1998). Course and stability of personality disorders. *Journal of Practical Psychiatry and Behavioral Health, 4,* 61–75.

Grilo, C. M., Shea, M. T., Sanislow, C. A., Skodol, A. E., Gunderson, J. G., Stout, R. L., Pagano, M. E., Yen, S., Morey, L. C., Zanarini, M. C., & McGlashan, T. H. (2004). Two-year stability and change of schizotypal, borderline, avoidant, and obsessive-compulsive personality disorders. *Journal of Consulting and Clinical Psychology, 72*(5), 767–775.

Grilo, C. M., Sanislow, C. A., Shea, M. T., Skodol, A. E., Stout, R. L., Gunderson, J. G., Yen, S., Bender, D. S., Pagano, M. E., Zanarini, M. C., Morey, L. C., & McGlashan, T. H. (2005). Two-year prospective naturalistic study of remission from major depressive disorder as a function of personality disorder comorbidity. *Journal of Consulting and Clinical Psychology, 73,* 78–85.

Grilo, C. M., Sanislow, C. A., Shea, M. T., Skodol, A. E., Stout, R. L., Pagano, M. E., Yen, S., & McGlashan, T. H. (2003). The natural course of bulimia nervosa and eating disorder not otherwise specified is not influenced by personality disorders. *International Journal of Eating Disorders, 34,* 319–330.

Grilo, C. M., Skodol, A. E., Gunderson, J. G., Sanislow, C. A., Stout, R. L., Shea, M. T., et al. (2004). Longitudinal diagnostic efficiency of DSM-IV criteria for obsessive-compulsive personality disorder: A 2-year prospective study. *Acta Psychiatrica Scandinavica, 110*(1), 64–68.

Gunderson, J. G. (1984). *Borderline personality disorder.* Washington, DC: American Psychiatric Press.

Gunderson, J. G. (2000). Psychodynamic psychotherapy for borderline personality disorder. In J. M. Oldham & M. B. Riba (Series Eds) & J. G. Gunderson & G. O. Gabbard (Vol. Eds.), *Psychotherapy of Personality Disorders: Vol 19.* (pp. 33–64). Washington, DC: American Psychiatric Press.

Gunderson, J. G., Frank, A. F., Ronningstam, E. F., Wachter, S., Lynch, V. J., & Wolf, P. J. (1989). Early discontinuance of borderline patients from psychotherapy. *Journal of Nervous and Mental Disease, 177,* 38–42.

Gunderson, J. G., Shea, M. T., Skodol, A. E., McGlashan, T. H., Morey, L. C., Stout, R. L., et al. (2000). The Collaborative Longitudinal Personality Disorders Study: Development, aims, design, and sample characteristics. *Journal of Personality Disorders, 14*(4), 300–315.

Hare, R. D. (1991). *The Hare psychopathy checklist—Revised manual.* Toronto, Canada: Multi-Health Systems.

Hayward, C., & King, R. (1990). Somatization and personality disorder traits in nonclinical volunteers. *Journal of Personality Disorders, 4,* 402–406.

Heatherton, T. F., & Weinberger, J. L. (Eds.). (1994). *Can personality change?* Washington, DC: American Psychological Press.

Herpertz, S. C., Dietrich, T. M., Wenning, B., et al. (2001). Evidence of abnormal amygdala functioning in borderline personality disorder: A functional MRI study. *Biological Psychiatry, 50,* 292–298.

Hicks, B. M., Krueger, R. F., Iacono, W. G., McGue, M., & Patrick, C. J. (2004). Family transmission and heritability of externalizing disorders: A twin-family study. *Archives of General Psychiatry, 61*(9), 922–928.

Horowitz, L. M. (2004). *Interpersonal foundations of psychopathology.* Washington, DC: American Psychological Association.

Horowitz, L. M., Alden, L. E., Wiggins, J. S., & Pincus, A. L. (2000). *Inventory of Interpersonal Problems: IIP-64.* San Antonio, TX: Harcourt Assessment.

Horowitz, L. M., Rosenberg, S. E., Baer, B. A., Ureno, G., & Villasenor, V. S. (1988). The Inventory of Interpersonal Problems: Psychometric properties and clinical applications. *Journal of Consulting and Clinical Psychology, 56,* 885–892.

Hyler, S. E. (1994). *Personality Diagnostic Questionnaire-4 (PDQ-4).* New York: New York State Psychiatric Institute.

Intrator, J., Hare, R., Stritzke, P., Brichtswein, K., Dorfman, D., Harpur, T., et al. (1997). A brain imaging (single photon emission computerized tomography) study of semantic and affective processing in psychopaths. *Biological Psychiatry, 42,* 96–103.

Jackson, H. J., Whiteside, H. L., Bates, G. W., Bell, R., Rudd, R. P., & Edwards, J. (1991). Diagnosing personality disorders in psychiatric inpatients. *Acta Psychiatrica Scandinavica, 83*(3), 206–213.

Johnson, J. G., Cohen, P., Kasen, S., Skodol, A. E., Hamagami, F., & Brook, J. S. (2000). Age-related change in personality disorder trait levels between early adolescence and adulthood: A community-based longitudinal investigation. *Acta Psychiatrica Scandinavica, 102*(4), 265–275.

Johnson, J. G., First, M. B., Cohen, P., Skodol, A. E., Kasen, S., & Brook, J. S. (2005). Adverse outcomes associated with personality disorder not otherwise specified in a community sample. *American Journal of Psychiatry, 162,* 1926–1932.

Johnson, J. G., Williams, J. B., Rabkin, J. G., Goetz, R. R., Remien, R. H., & Lipsitz, J. D. (1997). Stability and change in personality disorder symptomatology: Findings from a longitudinal study of HIV+ and HIV- men. *Journal of Abnormal Psychology, 106,* 154–158.

Kagan, J., Reznick, J. S., & Snidman, N. (1988). Biological bases of childhood shyness. *Science, 240*(4849), 167–171.

Kendler, K. S. (1993). Twin studies of psychiatric illness: Current status and future directions. *Archives of General Psychiatry, 50*(11), 905–915.

Kendler, K. S., Ochs, A. L., Gorman, A. M., Hewitt, J. K., Ross, D. E., & Mirsky, A. F. (1991). The structure of schizotypy: A pilot multitrait twin study. *Psychiatry Research, 36*(1), 19–36.

Kernberg, O. (1976). *Object relations theory and clinical psychoanalysis.* New York: Jason Aronson.

Kernberg, O. (1998). Pathological narcissism and narcissistic personality disorder: Theoretical background and diagnostic classifications. In E. Ronningstam (Ed.), *Disorders of narcissism: Diagnostic, clinical and empirical implications* (pp. 29–51). Washington, DC: American Psychiatric Press.

Kiehl, K. A., Smith, A. M., Hare, R. D., et al. (2001). Limbic abnormalities in affective processing by criminal psychopaths as revealed by functional magnetic resonance imaging. *Biological Psychiatry, 50,* 677–684.

Kiesler, D. J. (1983). The 1982 Interpersonal Circle: A taxonomy for complementarity in human transactions. *Psychological Review, 90*(3), 185–214.

Klein, D. N., & Shih, J. H. (1998). Depressive personality: associations with DSM-III-R mood and personality disorders and negative and positive affectivity, 30-month stability, and prediction of course of Axis I depressive disorders. *Journal of Abnormal Psychology, 107,* 319–327.

Kohut, H. (1972). Thoughts on narcissism and narcissistic rage. *The Psychoanalytic Study of the Child, 23,* 86–113.

Krueger, R. F., & Carlson, S. R. (2001). Personality disorders in children and adolescents. *Current Psychiatry Reports, 3,* 46–51.

Krueger, R. F., & Tackett, J. L. (2005). Progress and innovation: Personality disorders and the vanguard of psychopathology research. *Journal of Personality Disorders, 19,* 540–546.

Leary, T. (1957). *Interpersonal diagnosis of personality: A functional theory and methodology for personality evaluation.* New York: Ronald Press.

Levy, K. N., Becker, D. F., Grilo, C. M., Mattanah, J. J., Garnet, K. E., Quinlan, D. M., et al. (1999). Concurrent and predictive validity of the personality disorder diagnosis in adolescent inpatients. *American Journal of Psychiatry, 156*(10), 1522–1528.

Linehan, M. (1993). *Cognitive-behavioral treatment of borderline personality disorder.* New York: Guilford Press.

Livesley, W. J., & Jackson, D. N. (2000). *Dimensional Assessment of Personality Problems.* Port Huron, MI: Sigma Assessment Systems.

Livesley, W. J., Jackson, D. N., & Schroeder, M. L. (1992). Factorial structure of traits delineating personality disorders in clinical and general population samples. *Journal of Abnormal Psychology, 101,* 432–440.

Livesley, W. J., Jang, K. L., Jackson, D. N., & Vernon, P. A. (1993). Genetic and environmental contributions to dimensions of personality disorder. *American Journal of Psychiatry, 150*(12), 1826–1831.

Livesley, W. J., Jang, K. L., & Vernon, P. A. (1998). Phenotypic and genetic structure of traits delineating personality disorder. *Archives of General Psychiatry, 55*(10), 941–948.

Loranger, A. W. (1999). *International Personality Disorders Examination Manual.* Odessa, FL: Psychological Assessment Resources.

Loranger, A. W., Lenzenweger, M. F., Gartner, A. F., Susman, V. L., Herzig, J., Zammit, G. K., Gartner, J. D., Abrams, R. C., & Young, R. C. (1991). Trait-state artifacts and the diagnosis of personality disorders. *Archives of General Psychiatry, 48,* 720–728.

Loranger, A. W., Sartorius, N., Andreoli, A., Berger, P., et al. (1994). The International Personality Disorder Examination: The World Health Organization/Alcohol, Drug Abuse, and Mental Health Administration international pilot study of personality disorders. *Archives of General Psychiatry, 51,* 215–224.

Markowitz, J. C. (2005). Interpersonal therapy. In J. M. Oldham, A. E. Skodol, & D. S. Bender (Eds.), *Textbook of personality disorders* (pp. 321–334). Washington, DC: American Psychiatric Publishing.

McCloskey, M. S., Phan, K. L., & Coccaro, E. F. (2005). Neuroimaging and personality disorders. *Current Psychiatry Reports, 7*(1), 65–72.

McCrae, R. R., & Costa, P. T. (1987). Validation of the five-factor model of personality across instruments and observers. *Journal of Personality and Social Psychology, 52,* 81–90.

McCrae, R. R., & Costa, P. T. (1990). *Personality in adulthood.* New York: Guilford Press.

McDermut, W., & Zimmerman, M. (1997). The effect of personality disorders on outcome in the treatment of depression. In A. J. Rush (Ed.), *Mood and anxiety disorders* (pp. 321–338). Philadelphia: Current Science.

McDermut, W., & Zimmerman, M. (2005). Assessment instruments and standardized evaluation. In J. M. Oldham, A. E. Skodol, & D. S. Bender (Eds.), *Textbook of personality disorders* (pp. 623–640). Washington, DC: American Psychiatric Press.

McGlashan, T. H. (1986a). The Chestnut Lodge Follow-up Study, Part III: Long-term outcome of borderline personalities. *Archives of General Psychiatry, 42,* 20–30.

McGlashan, T. H. (1986b). The Chestnut Lodge Follow-up Study, Part VI: Schizotypal personality disorder. *Archives of General Psychiatry, 43,* 329–334.

McGlashan, T. H., Grilo, C. M., Sanislow, C. A., Ralevski, E., Morey, L. C., Gunderson, J. G., et al. (2005). Two-year prevalence and stability of individual DSM-IV criteria for schizotypal, borderline, avoidant, and obsessive-compulsive personality disorders: Toward a hybrid model of axis II disorders. *American Journal of Psychiatry, 162*(5), 883–889.

McLaughlin, K. M., & Mennin, D. S. (2005). Clarifying the temporal relationship between dependent personality disorder and anxiety disorders. *Clinical Psychology: Science and Practice, 12,* 1–4.

McWilliams, N. (1994). *Psychoanalytic diagnosis: Understanding personality structure in the clinical process.* New York: Guilford Press.

Mezzich, J. E., Fabrega, H. Jr., & Coffman, G. A. (1987). Multiaxial characterization of depressive patients. *Journal of Nervous and Mental Disease, 175*(6), 339–346.

Millon, T. (1987). On the genesis and prevalence of the borderline personality disorder: A social learning thesis. *Journal of Personality Disorders, 1,* 354–372.

Millon, T. (1990). *Toward a new personology: An evolutionary model.* Oxford, England: Wiley.

Millon, T., & Davis, R. D. (1996). *Disorders of personality* (2nd ed.). New York: Wiley.

Millon, T., & Davis, R. D. (2000). *Personality disorders in modern life.* New York: Wiley.

Millon, T., Davis, R., & Millon, C. (1997). *Manual for the MCMI-III.* Minneapolis, MN: National Computer Systems.

Morey, L. C. (1988). The categorical representation of personality disorder: A cluster analysis of DSM-III-R personality features. *Journal of Abnormal Psychology, 97*(3), 314–321.

Morey, L. C. (1991). *Personality Assessment Inventory Professional Manual.* Odessa, FL: Psychological Assessment Resources.

Murray, C. J. L., & Lopez, A. D. (Eds.). (1996). *The global burden of disease: A comprehensive assessment of mortality and disability from diseases, injuries, and risk factors in 1990 and projected to 2020* (Vol. 1). Cambridge, MA: Harvard School of Public Health on behalf of World Health Organization and World Bank.

Myers, M. G., Stewart, D. G., & Brown, S. A. (1998). Progression from conduct disorder to antisocial personality disorder following treatment for adolescent substance abuse. *American Journal of Psychiatry, 155,* 479–485.

Nahas, Z., Molnar, C., & George, M. S. (2005). Brain imaging. In J. M. Oldham, A. E. Skodol, & D. S. Bender (Eds.), *Textbook of personality disorders* (pp. 623–640). Washington, DC: American Psychiatric Press.

Newman, D. L., Caspi, A., Moffitt, T. E., & Silva, P. A. (1997). Antecedents of adult interpersonal functioning: Effects of individual differences in age 3 temperament. *Developmental Psychology, 33,* 206–217.

Ng, H. M., & Bornstein, R. F. (2005). Comorbidity of dependent personality disorder and anxiety disorders: A meta-analytic review. *Clinical Psychology: Science and Practice, 12*(4), 395–406.

Nordahl, H. M., & Stiles, T. C. (2000). The specificity of cognitive personality dimensions in cluster C personality disorders. *Behavioural and Cognitive Psychotherapy, 28,* 235–246.

Oldham, J. M. (2005). Personality disorders: Recent history and future directions. In J. M. Oldham, A. E. Skodol, & D. Bender (Eds.), *Textbook of personality disorders* (pp. 3–16). Washington, DC: American Psychiatric Press.

Oldham, J. M., Skodol, A. E., Kellman, H. D., Hyler, S. E., Doidge, N., Rosnick, L., et al. (1995). Comorbidity of axis I and axis II disorders. *American Journal of Psychiatry, 152*(4), 571–578.

Othmer, E., & Othmer, S. (2002). *The clinical interview using DSM-IV-TR: Vol. 2: The difficult patient.* Washington, DC: American Psychiatric Press.

Overholser, J. C. (1991). Categorical assessment of the dependent personality disorder in depressed inpatients. *Journal of Personality Disorders, 5,* 243–255.

Overholser, J. C. (1992). Interpersonal dependency and social loss. *Personality and Individual Differences, 13,* 17–23.

Paris, J. (2000) Childhood precursors of borderline personality disorder. *The Psychiatric Clinics of North America, 23,* 77–88.

Paris, J., & Zweig-Frank, H. (2001). The 27-year follow-up of patients with borderline personality disorder. *Comprehensive Psychiatry, 42,* 482–487.

Perry, J. C., Banon, L., & Ianni, F. (1999). The effectiveness of psychotherapy for personality disorders. *American Journal of Psychiatry, 156,* 1312–1321.

Perry, J. C., & Bond M. (2000). Empirical studies of psychotherapy for personality disorders. In J. M. Oldham & M. B. Riba (Series Eds.) & J. G. Gunderson & G. O. Gabbard (Vol. Eds.), *Psychotherapy of Personality Disorders: Vol 19.* (pp. 1–31). Washington, DC: American Psychiatric Press.

Pfohl, B., Blum, N., & Zimmerman, M. (1997). *Structured Interview for DSM-IV Personality.* Washington, DC: American Psychiatric Press.

Piper, W. E., & Ogrodniczuk, J. S. (2005). Group Treatment. In J. M. Oldham, A. E. Skodol, & D. S. Bender (Eds.), *Textbook of personality disorders* (pp. 347–358). Washington, DC: American Psychiatric Publishing.

Poldrugo, F., & Forti, B. (1988). Personality disorders and alcoholism treatment outcome. *Drug and Alcohol Dependence, 21*(3), 171–176.

Pollak, J. M. (1979). Obsessive-compulsive personality: A review. *Psychological Bulletin, 86,* 225–241.

Pollak, J. M. (1995). Commentary on obsessive-compulsive personality disorder. In W. Livesley (Ed.), *The DSM-IV personality disorders* (pp. 277–283). New York: Guilford Press.

Raine, A., Lencz, T., Taylor, K., et al. (2003). Corpus callosum abnormalities in psychopathic antisocial individuals. *Archives of General Psychiatry, 60,* 1134–1142.

Rasmussen, P. R. (2005). The paranoid prototype. In *Personality-guided cognitive-behavioral therapy* (pp. 49–71). Washington, DC: American Psychological Association.

Rettew, D. C., Zanarini, M. C., Yen, S., Grilo, C. M., Skodol, A. E., Shea, M. T., McGlashan, T. H., Morey, L. C., Culhane, M. A., & Gunderson, J. G. (2003) Childhood antecedents of avoidant personality disorder: A retrospective study. *Journal of the American Academy of Child and Adolescent Psychiatry, 42,* 1122–1130.

Roberts, B. W., Caspi, A., & Moffitt, T. E. (2001). The kids are alright: growth and stability in personality development from adolescence to adulthood. *Journal of Personality and Social Psychology, 81,* 670–683.

Roberts, B. W., & DelVecchio, W. F. (2000). The rank-order consistency of personality traits from childhood to old age: A quantitative review of longitudinal studies. *Psychological Bulletin, 126,* 3–25.

Ronningstam, E. (2005). *Identifying and understanding the narcissistic personality.* New York: Oxford University Press.

Rost, K. M., Akins, R. N., Brown, F. W., & Smith, G. R. (1992). The comorbidity of DSM-II-R personality disorders in somatization disorder. *General Hospital Psychiatry, 14,* 322–326.

Roth, A., & Fonagy, P. (2004). *What works for whom? A critical review of psychotherapy research* (2nd ed.). New York: Guilford.

Rouff, L. (2000). Schizoid personality traits among the homeless mentally ill: A quantitative and qualitative report. *Journal of Social Distress & the Homeless, 9,* 127–141.

Samuels, J., Eaton, W. W., Bienvenu, O. J. III, Brown, C. H., Costa, P. T. Jr., & Nestadt, G. (2002). Prevalence and correlates of personality disorders in a community sample. *British Journal of Psychiatry, 180,* 536–542.

Sanislow, C. A., Grilo, C. M., & McGlashan, T. H. (2000). Factor analysis of the DSM-III-R borderline personality disorder criteria in psychiatric inpatients. *American Journal of Psychiatry, 157*(10), 1629–1633.

Sanislow, C. A., & McGlashan, T. H. (1998). Treatment outcome of personality disorders. *Canadian Journal of Psychiatry, 43*(3), 237–250.

Sanislow, C. A., Morey, L. C., Grilo, C. M., Gunderson, J. G., Shea, M. T., Skodol, A. E., et al. (2002). Confirmatory factor analysis of DSM-IV borderline, schizotypal, avoidant and obsessive-compulsive personality disorders: Findings from the Collaborative Longitudinal Personality Disorders Study. *Acta Psychiatrica Scandinavica, 105*(1), 28–36.

Schore, A. (1994). *Affect regulation and the origin of the self.* Hillsdale, NJ: Erlbaum.

Seivewright, H., Tyrer, P., & Johnson, T. (2002). Change in personality status in neurotic disorders. *Lancet, 359,* 2253–2254.

Serin, R. C., & Amos, N. L. (1995). The role of psychopathy in the assessment of dangerousness. *International Journal of Law and Psychiatry, 18,* 231–238.

Shahar, G., Blatt, S. J., Zuroff, D. C., Kuperminc, G. P., & Leadbeater, B. J. (2004). Reciprocal relations between depressive symptoms and self-criticism (but not dependency) among early adolescent girls (but not boys). *Cognitive Therapy and Research, 28,* 85–103.

Shapiro, D. (1965). *Neurotic styles.* New York: Basic Books.

Shea, M. T. (1993). Psychosocial treatment of personality disorders. *Journal of Personality Disorders* (Suppl. 1), 167–180.

Shea, M. T., Stout, R., Gunderson, J., Morey, L. C., Grilo, C. M., McGlashan, T., Skodol, A. E., Dolan-Sewell, R., Dyck, I., Zanarini, M. C., & Keller, M. B. (2002). Short-term diagnostic stability of schizotypal, borderline, avoidant, and obsessive-compulsive personality disorders. *American Journal of Psychiatry, 159,* 2036–2041.

Shea, M. T., & Yen, S. (2003). Stability as a distinction between Axis I and Axis II disorders. *Journal of Personality Disorders, 17,* 373–386.

Shihabuddin, L., Bushsbaum, M. C., Hazlett, E., et al. (2001). Striatal size and relative glucose metabolic rate in schizotypal personality disorder and schizophrenia. *Archives of General Psychiatry, 58,* 877–884.

Siever, L. J., & Davis, K. L. (1991). A psychobiological perspective on the personality disorders. *American Journal of Psychiatry, 148,* 1647–1658.

Skodol, A. E. (1997). Classification, assessment, and differential diagnosis of personality disorders. *Journal of Practical Psychiatry and Behavioral Health, 3,* 261–274.

Skodol, A. E., Buckley, P., & Charles, E. (1983). Is there a characteristic pattern to the treatment history of clinic outpatients with borderline personality? *Journal of Nervous and Mental Disease, 171,* 405–410.

Skodol, A. E., Gunderson, J. G., McGlashan, T. H., Dyck, I. R., Stout, R. L., Bender, D. S., et al. (2002). Functional impairment in patients with schizotypal, borderline, avoidant, or obsessive-compulsive personality disorder. *American Journal of Psychiatry, 159*(2), 276–283.

Skodol, A. E., Gunderson, J. G., Shea, M. T., McGlashan, T. H., Morey, L. C., Sanislow, C. A., et al. (2005). The Collaborative Longitudinal Personality Disorders Study (CLPS): Overview and implications. *Journal of Personality Disorders, 19*(5), 487–504.

Skodol, A. E., Gunderson, J. G., Shea, M. T., McGlashan ,T. H., Morey, L. C., Sanislow, C. A., Bender, D. S., Grilo, C. M., Zanarini, M. C., Yen, S., Pagano, M. E., & Stout, R. L. (2005). The Collaborative Longitudinal Personality Disorders Study (CLPS): Overview and implications. *Journal of Personality Disorder, 19,* 487–504.

Skodol, A. E., Pagano, M. E., Bender, D. S., Shea, M. T., Gunderson, J. G., Yen, S., Stout, R. L., Morey, L. C., Sanislow, C. A., Grilo, C. M., Zanarini, M. C., & McGlashan, T. H. (2005). Stability of functional impairment in patients with schizotypal, borderline, avoidant, or obsessive-compulsive personality disorder over two years. *Psychological Medicine, 35,* 443–451.

Skodol, A. E., Siever, L. J., Livesley, W. J., Gunderson, J. G., Pfohl, B., & Widiger, T. A. (2002). The borderline diagnosis II: Biology, genetics, and clinical course. *Biological Psychiatry, 51*(12), 951–963.

Soloff, P. H., Fabio, A., Kelly, T. M., Malone, K. M., & Mann, J. J. (2005). High-lethality status in patients with borderline personality disorder. *Journal of Personality Disorders, 19*(4), 386–399.

Soloff, P. H., Meltzer, C. C., Greer, P. J., et al. (2000). A fenfluramine-activated FDG-PET study of borderline personality disorder. *Biological Psychiatry, 47,* 540–547.

Sperry, L. (2003). *Handbook of diagnosis and treatment of DSM-IV personality disorders* (rev. ed.). New York: Brunner-Routledge.

Stanley, B., & Brodsky, B. S. (2005). Dialectical Behavior Therapy. In J. M. Oldham, A. E. Skodol, & D. S. Bender (Eds.), *Textbook of personality disorders* (pp. 307–320). Washington, DC: American Psychiatric Publishing.

Stevenson, J., Meares R., & Comerford, A. (2003). Diminished impulsivity in older patients with borderline personality disorder. *American Journal of Psychiatry, 160,* 165–166.

Stone, M. H. (1993). *Abnormalities of personality: Within and beyond the realm of treatment.* New York: Norton.

Stone, M. H. (2000). Gradations of antisociality and responsivity to psychosocial therapies. In J. M. Oldham & M. B. Riba (Series Eds.) & J. G. Gunderson & G. O. Gabbard (Vol. Eds.), *Psychotherapy of Personality Disorders: Vol 19* (pp. 95–130). Washington, DC: American Psychiatric Press.

Target, M. (1998). Outcome research on the psychosocial treatment of personality disorders. *Bulletin of the Menninger Clinic, 62,* 215–230.

Taylor, J. (2005). Substance use disorders and cluster B personality disorders: Physiological, cognitive, and environmental correlates in a college sample. *American Journal of Drug and Alcohol Abuse, 31,* 515–535.

Tisdale, M. J., Pendleton, L., & Marler, M. (1990). MCMI characteristics of DSM-III-R bulimics. *Journal of Personality Assessment, 55*(3–4), 477–483.

Tomkins, S. S. (1963). *Affect, imagery, consciousness: Vol. 2. The negative affects.* New York: Springer.

Torgersen, S. (1984). Genetic and nosological aspects of schizotypal and borderline personality disorders. A twin study. *Archives of General Psychiatry, 41*(6), 546–554.

Torgersen, S. (2005a). Behavioral genetics of personality. *Current Psychiatry Reports, 7*(1), 51–56.

Torgersen, S. (2005b). Epidemiology. In J. M. Oldham, A. E. Skodol, & D. Bender (Eds.), *Textbook of personality disorders* (pp. 129–141). Washington, DC: American Psychiatric Press.

Torgersen, S., Kringlen, E., & Cramer, V. (2001). The prevalence of personality disorders in a community sample. *Archives of General Psychiatry, 58*(6), 590–596.

Torgersen, S., Lygren, S., Oien, P. A., Skre, I., Onstad, S., Edvardsen, J., et al. (2000). A twin study of personality disorders. *Comprehensive Psychiatry, 41*(6), 416–425.

Trull, T. J., & Durrett, C. A. (2005). Categorical and dimensional models of personality disorders. *Annual Review of Clinical Psychology, 1,* 355–380.

Trull, T. J., & Widiger, T. A. (1997). *Structured Interview for the Five-Factor Model of Personality.* Odessa, FL: Psychological Assessment Resources.

Tyrer, P., & Davidson, K. (2000). Cognitive therapy for personality disorders. In J. M. Oldham & M. B. Riba (Series Eds.) & J. G. Gunderson & G. O. Gabbard (Vol. Eds.), *Psychotherapy of Personality Disorders: Vol 19* (pp. 131–150). Washington, DC: American Psychiatric Press.

Tyrer, P., Strauss, J., & Cicchetti, D. (1983). Temporal reliability of personality in psychiatric patients. *Psychological Medicine, 13,* 393–398.

van Lier, P. A., Vitaro, F., Wanner, B., Vuijk, P., & Crijnen, A. A. (2005). Gender differences in developmental links among antisocial behavior, friends' antisocial behavior, and peer rejection in childhood: Results from two cultures. *Child Development, 76*(4), 841–855.

Völlm, B. A., Taylor, A. N., Richardson, P., Corcoran, R., Stirling, J., McKie, S., et al. (2006). Neuronal correlates of theory of mind and empathy: A functional magnetic resonance imaging study in a nonverbal task. *Neuroimage, 29*(1), 90–98.

Warner, M. B., Morey, L. C., Finch, J. F., Gunderson, J. G., Skodol, A. E., Sanislow, C. A., et al. (2004). The longitudinal relationship of personality traits and disorders. *Journal of Abnormal Psychology, 113*(2), 217–227.

Westen, D. (1997). Divergences between clinical research methods for assessing personality disorders: Implications for research and the evolution of Axis II. *American Journal of Psychiatry, 154,* 895–903.

Westen, D., & Shedler, J. (1998). Refining the measurement of Axis II: A Q-sort procedure for assessing personality pathology. *Assessment, 5,* 333–353.

Whiffen, V. E., & Sasseville, T. M. (1991). Dependency, self-criticism, and recollections of parenting: Sex differences and the role of depressive affect. *Journal of Social & Clinical Psychology, 10,* 121–133.

Widiger, T. A. (1992). Categorical versus dimensional classification: Implications from and for research. *Journal of Personality Disorders, 6,* 287–300.

Widiger, T. A. (2003). Personality disorder and Axis I psychopathology: the problematic boundary of Axis I and Axis II. *Journal of Personality Disorders, 17,* 90–108.

Widiger, T. A., Costa, P. T., & McCrae, R. R. (2002). A proposal for Axis II: Diagnosing personality disorder using the five-factor model. In P. T. Costa & T. A. Widiger (Eds.), *Personality disorders and the five-factor model of personality* (2nd ed., pp. 431–456). Washington, DC: American Psychological Association.

Widiger, T. A., Mangine, S., Corbitt, E. M., et al. (1995). *Personality Disorder Interview-IV: A Semi-structured interview for the assessment of personality disorders, professional manual.* Odessa, FL: Psychological Assessment Resources.

Widiger, T. A., & Simonsen, E. (2005). Alternative dimensional models of personality disorder: Finding a common ground. *Journal of Personality Disorders, 19*(2), 110–130.

Widiger, T. A., Simonsen, E., Krueger, R., Livesley, W. J., & Verheul, R. (2005). Personality disorder research agenda for the DSM-V. *Journal of Personality Disorders, 19*(3), 315–338.

Wiggins, J. S. (1982). Circumplex models of interpersonal behavior. In L. Wheeler (Ed.), *Review of personality and social psychology* (Vol. 1, pp. 265–294). Beverly Hills, CA: Sage.

Wiggins, J. S. (Ed.). (1996). *The five-factor model of personality: Theoretical perspectives.* New York: Guilford Press.

Wiggins, J. S. (2003). *Paradigms of personality assessment.* New York: Guilford Press.

Wiggins, J. S., & Pincus, A. L. (2002). Personality structure and the structure of personality disorders. In P. T. Costa & T. A. Widiger (Eds.), *Personality disorders and the five-factor model of personality* (2nd ed., pp. 103–124). Washington, DC: American Psychological Association.

Wink, P. (1991). Two faces of narcissism. *Journal of Personality and Social Psychology, 61,* 590–597.

Wolff, S. (2000). Schizoid personality in childhood and Asperger syndrome. In A. Klin, F. R. Volkmar, & S. S. Sparrow (Eds.), *Asperger syndrome* (pp. 278–305). New York: Guilford Press.

Wolff, S., Townshend, R., McGuire, R. J., & Weeks, D. J. (1991). Schizoid personality in childhood and adult life. II: adult adjustment and the continuity with schizotypal personality disorder. *British Journal of Psychiatry, 159,* 620–629.

Wonderlich, S. S., Swift, W. J., Slotnick, H. B., & Goodman, S. (1990). DSM-III-R personality disorders in eating disorder subtypes. *International Journal of Eating Disorders, 9,* 607–616.

Yen, S., Shea, M. T., Pagano, M., Sanislow, C. A., Grilo, C. M., McGlashan, T. H., et al. (2003). Axis I and axis II disorders as predictors of prospective suicide attempts: Findings from the collaborative longitudinal personality disorders study. *Journal of Abnormal Psychology, 112*(3), 375–381.

Yen, S., Shea, M. T., Sanislow, C. A., Grilo, C. M., Skodol, A. E., Gunderson, J. G., et al. (2004). Borderline personality disorder criteria associated with prospectively observed suicidal behavior. *American Journal of Psychiatry, 161*(7), 1296–1298.

Yeomans, F. E., Clarkin, J. F., & Levy, K. N. (2005). Psychodynamic psychotherapies. In J. M. Oldham, A. E. Skodol, & D. S. Bender (Eds.), *Textbook of personality disorders* (pp. 275–288). Washington, DC: American Psychiatric Publishing..

Young, J., & Klosko, J. (2005). Schema therapy. In J. M. Oldham, A. E. Skodol, & D. S. Bender (Eds.), *Textbook of personality disorders.* (pp. 289–306) Washington, DC: American Psychiatric Publishing.

Zanarini, M. C., Frankenburg, F. R., Hennen, J., Reich, D. B., & Silk, K. R. (2005). The McLean Study of Adult Development (MSAD). *Journal of Personality Disorders, 19,* 505–523.

Zanarini, M. C., Frankenburg, F. R., Hennen, J., & Silk, K. R. (2003). The longitudinal course of borderline psychopathology: 6-year prospective follow-up of the phenomenology of borderline personality disorder. *American Journal of Psychiatry, 160,* 274–283.

Zanarini, M. C., Frankenburg, F. R., Sickel, A. E., et al. (1996). *Diagnostic interview for DSM-IV personality disorders.* Boston: Laboratory for the Study of Adult Development, McLean Hospital and the Department of Psychiatry, Harvard University.

Zimmerman, M., & Mattia, J. I. (1999). Psychiatric diagnoses in clinical practice: Is comorbidity being missed? *Comprehensive Psychiatry, 40,* 182–191.

Zimmerman, M., Rothschild, L., & Chelminski, I. (2005). The prevalence of DSM-IV personality disorders in psychiatric outpatients. *American Journal of Psychiatry, 162*(10), 1911–1918.

Zlotnick, C., Johnson, D. M., Yen, S., Battle, C. L., Sanislow, C. A., Skodol, A. E., et al. (2003). Clinical features and impairment in women with borderline personality disorder (BPD) with posttraumatic stress disorder (PTSD), BPD without PTSD, and other personality disorders with PTSD. *Journal of Nervous and Mental Disease, 191*(11), 706–713.

Author Index

Aalto-Setalae, T., 349
Aarsland, D., 141
Aasland, O. G., 178, 213
Abbey, S. E., 413, 437
Abbott, R., 327, 328
Abel, G. G., 537, 541, 543, 544, 545, 546, 548
Aboud, A., 47
Abramovitz, B. A., 585
Abrams, B. I., 45
Abrams, D. B., 36, 168, 218
Abrams, K., 63, 174, 212
Abrams, R. C., 664
Abramson, L. Y., 295, 305, 306, 307, 591
Abreau, J. M., 110
Abukmeil, S. S., 255
Abuzzahab, F., 528
Ach, E. L., 575
à Campo, J., 536
Acosta, F. X., 261
Acton, G. S., 14, 18
Adams, C. M., 334
Adams, G. L., 240, 261
Adams, S. D., 238
Addington, J., 224
Aderibigbe, Y. A., 480
Ades, J., 333
Adesso, V., 548
Adler, A., 324
Aggarwal, J., 234
Agnello, C., 528
Agras, W. S., 351, 370, 375, 576, 578, 579, 580, 581
Agrawal, S., 178, 181
Agren, H., 530

Agresta, J., 258
Aguilar-Gaxiola, S., 294
Aguirre-Molina, M., 186
Ahern, D. K., 433
Ahern, F. M., 172
Ahlmeyer, S., 548
Ahn, C. W., 41, 43
Ahrens, C., 54
Aidroos, N., 44
Aikins, D., 361
Akagi, H., 417, 418, 421
Akerstedt, T., 620, 621
Akhtar, S., 486, 651
Akiskal, H. G., 366
Akiskal, H. S., 42, 45, 294, 318, 323, 328, 329, 331
Alan, W., 143
Alarcon, R. D., 4, 19
Albus, M., 364
Alda, M., 331
Aldeman, N. E., 333
Alden, L. E., 660
Alderete, E., 294
Aldrich, M. S., 605, 610
Aldridge-Morris, R., 489
Alessi, S. M., 222
Alexander, M. P., 486
Alhes, T. A., 363
Ali, R., 215, 218
Allan, T., 362, 363
Allen, B. A., 168
Allen, J. P., 104, 175, 177, 178
Allen, K. A., 224
Allen, K. M., 440

Allen, M. H., 320, 321, 323
Allik, J., 20
Allness, D. J., 248
Alloy, L. B., 295, 305, 306, 307, 324
Al-Marzooqi, S. M., 432
Almeida, O., 244
Almi, C. R., 136
Alper, J. S., 5
Alper, K., 432
Alphs, L. D., 44
Altabe, M. N., 572
Altenor, A., 306
Alterman, A. I., 44, 142, 549
Althof, S., 519
Altman, E., 248
Altshuler, L. L., 41, 45, 322, 323, 333, 334
Alvir, J. M. J., 255
Amador, X. F., 241, 252
Amaro, H., 224
Ambrosini, P. J., 331
American Psychiatric Association, 3, 4, 5, 6, 7, 8, 10, 12, 13, 15, 16, 22, 35, 78, 87, 89, 90, 107, 111, 125, 126, 138, 169, 170, 173, 177, 201, 211, 235, 244, 246, 249, 286, 317, 349, 350, 351, 352, 353, 354, 379, 475, 479, 482, 487, 488, 489, 494, 504, 505, 508, 509, 511, 512, 535, 536, 538, 539, 540, 541, 542, 543, 544, 545, 571, 572, 573,

American Psychiatric
  Association *(continued)*
  575, 601, 606, 614, 633,
  634, 637, 640, 642, 643,
  644, 645, 646, 649, 650,
  651, 652, 653, 655, 657
American Psychological
  Association, 102, 103,
  106
Amies, P. L., 357, 358
Amir, M., 379
Amir, N., 368
Amodeo, M., 225
Amos, N. L., 645
Amrein, R., 361
Amsel, R., 522
Amsterdam, A., 521
Anand, A., 332
Ananth, J., 41
Anastasopoulou, E., 43
Ancoli-Israel, S., 619
Anders, T. F., 51
Andersch, S., 359
Anderson, B., 324, 325,
  326
Anderson, D. A., 579,
  582, 583, 588
Anderson, M. A., 157,
  425
Anderson, N. B., 238
Anderson, P. L., 365
Andersson, K. E., 529
Andersson, L., 181
Andrade, L., 366
Andreasen, N. C., 23,
  245, 251, 252, 255, 263,
  320, 331
Andreoli, A., 96
Andrew, B., 297
Andrew, C., 333
Andrews, B., 324
Andrews, C. M., 181
Andrews, D. A., 547
Andrews, G., 4, 19, 362,
  364, 374
Andrews, P. J., 625
Anez, L. M., 645
Anglin, M. D., 186, 210,
  211, 224

Angold, A., 293
Angst, F., 322
Angst, J., 7, 322, 328
Anguelova, M., 333
Anisman, H., 297
Anker, M., 237
Annis, H. A., 175
Annon, K., 186
Annon, T. A., 186
Ansel, M., 239
Anthony, E. J., 329
Anthony, J. C., 174, 204,
  221, 222, 224, 330
Anthony, W., 322
Anton, R. F., 176, 185
Anton, S. F., 42
Antoni, G., 126
Antony, M. M., 86, 98,
  364, 367, 368
Apfel, R. J., 259
Appelbaum. P. S., 47,
  239
Appelo, M. T., 253
Appleby, L., 248, 448
Applewhaite, G., 242
Apt, C., 530
Arana, G., 330, 331
Arand, D. L., 625
Araujo, A. B., 518
Arbona, C., 116
Ardila, A., 103
Areán, P. A., 106, 298,
  300, 302, 307
Arendt, J., 612, 613, 617
Arendt, M., 42
Argyle, N., 240
Arieff, A. J., 544
Armor, D. J., 173
Armour-Thomas, E.,
  107
Armstrong, M. A., 181
Arndt, S. O., 251, 255, 330
Arnold, B. R., 105
Arnold, R., 225
Arnow, B. A., 427
Arns, P. G., 46
Aro, H., 238
Aro, S., 238
Aronowitz, B. R., 419

Arredondo, P., 102, 112,
  113
Arseneault, L., 242
Asberg, M., 301
Ascher, J. A., 326
Asghar, S. A., 326
Ashikaga, T., 245
Ashley, M. J., 171
Ashton, A. K., 530
Ashton, M. C., 19, 20
Ashton, R., 606
Asmundson, G. J., 44,
  426
Astin, M. C., 363
Atan, A., 529
Atanacio, B., 422
Atkins, R. N., 656
Atkinson, J. H., 144, 158
Atkinson, R. M., 173
Aubert, J. L., 13
AuBuchon, P. G., 364
Auld, F., 431
Ausén, B., 126
Avants, S. K., 225
Avenevoli, S., 299, 320
Avison, W. R., 245
Awad, G. A., 549
Awward, E., 215
Axelrod, S., 422
Axelson, D., 323
Azeni, H., 48, 50
Azocar, F., 106, 307
Azorin, J. M., 333
Azrin, N. H., 242

Babor, T. F., 175, 176,
  178, 212, 213, 215, 368
Bachman, J. G., 204
Back, S., 44, 45
Bacon, S. D., 166, 167
Baddeley, A., 127
Badger, G. J., 222
Badner, J. A., 332
Baer, B. A., 660
Baer, L., 351, 367
Baethge, C., 41
Bagby, R. M., 431, 571
Bagge, C. L., 647
Baigent, M. F., 173, 174

Bailer, U. F., 589
Bailey, A., 51
Baird, A., 36
Baiyewu, O., 212
Baker, G., 432
Baker, S. C., 172
Baker, T. B., 180, 183
Balden, E., 424
Baldessarini, R. J., 41, 322, 326
Baldwin, D., 361
Bale, E., 19
Balint, M., 641
Ball, D. E., 234
Ball, R., 302
Ball, W. A., 618
Ballenger, J. C., 350, 360, 361
Balogh, R., 60
Balter, M. B., 144, 611
Bancroft, J., 508, 523, 550
Bandura, A., 183, 375
Banken, J. A., 54
Bansal, S., 552
Baraona, E., 185
Barban, L., 428, 489
Barbato, L. M., 361
Barbee, J. G., 35, 44, 60
Barber, J. P., 44
Barbin, 583
Barbini, B., 325
Barch, D. M., 239, 252
Bardone, A. M., 591
Bargh, J. A., 5
Barker, J., 168
Barker, S., 251
Barletta, J., 126
Barlow, D. H., 98, 351, 357, 360, 361, 362, 363, 364, 365, 366, 367, 368, 370, 378, 476, 537
Barnaby, B., 47
Barnes, G. M., 171
Baron, I. S., 136
Barraclough, B., 240, 322
Barreira, P. J., 50
Barret, J. E., 378
Barrett, A., 116

Barrett, J. E., 297
Barrett, L. F., 428
Barrett-Connor, E., 509
Barrner, H., 181
Barry, K. L., 172, 178
Barry, S. M., 551
Barsetti, I., 547
Barsky, A. J., 410, 412, 415, 416, 417, 418, 419, 421, 425, 426, 428, 429, 433, 444, 449
Bartels, S. J., 241, 244
Barth, J. T., 157
Bartholow, B. D., 185
Barzega, G., 378
Basco, M. R., 368
Basha, I. M., 427
Baskin, D., 261
Basoglu, M., 364
Bass, C. M., 414, 420, 425, 426, 437, 441, 444
Bassetti, C. L., 605
Bassiri, A., 605, 613, 615
Basson, R., 505, 509, 510, 512, 516, 517, 519, 521, 528, 530
Bastien, C. H., 612, 613, 623, 624
Basu, D., 46
Bates, D. W., 410
Bates, M. E., 179
Bateson, G., 256
Bathija, J., 60
Batson, S. C., 242
Battaglia, M., 640
Battjes, R. J., 175
Batur, S., 532
Bauer, M. S., 41, 321, 327, 330, 331, 335
Baumeister, R. F., 508, 541, 542, 544, 545
Bauwens, F., 324
Baxter, L. R., 370, 383
Bayart, D., 329
Baysinger, C. M., 381
Beam-Goulet, J., 50
Bear, D., 12
Beard, C. M., 575
Bearh, D., 477

Beaudett, M. S., 174
Beauliu-Bonneau, S., 613
Bebbington, P. E., 47, 48, 295, 296, 307
Beck, A. T., 16, 179, 288, 295, 301, 302, 322, 361, 362, 368, 376, 620, 638, 646, 652, 653, 658
Beck, J. G., 509
Becker, D. F., 636, 645, 646, 662
Becker, J. B., 332
Becker, J. V., 546
Becker, T. M., 185
Becker-Blease, K. A., 476
Beckham, J. C., 353
Beckman, L. J., 171
Beech, H. R., 352
Beekman, A. T., 349
Beers, S. R., 125, 137, 148
Begleiter, H., 142
Beglin, S. J., 579
Behrendt, B., 259
Beidel, D. C., 11, 12, 350, 351, 352, 357, 358, 359, 360, 361, 362, 363, 364, 365, 367, 368, 373, 374, 377, 379, 381, 382, 385
Beitman, B. D., 42, 52, 58, 427
Beldowicz, D., 446
Bell, C. B., 18
Bell, C. C., 380
Bell, M. D., 253
Bell, R. J., 517
Bellack, A. S., 35, 41, 46, 51, 60, 239, 253, 351, 369, 370
Bellinger, D. L., 434
Bellivier, F., 331, 333
Bellodi, L., 325
Beloch, E., 360
Benabarre, A., 41, 327
Benazzi, F., 328, 329
Benca, R. M., 608, 615
Ben-Chetrit, A., 531

Bender, D. S., 647, 664, 665
Benedetti, F., 325
Benini, A., 434
Benjamin, J., 361
Benjamin, L. S., 16, 18, 92, 638, 639, 643, 645, 650, 653, 654, 655, 656, 658
Benjamin, S., 425, 432, 441
Benkelfat, C., 333
Bennett, L. A., 444
Bennett, M. E., 51, 241, 253
Bennett, R. M., 414
Benson, D. F., 483, 486
Benson, P., 221
Benson, T. A., 222
Bentall, R. P., 234, 240, 324, 327, 328
Benton, A. L., 131, 135, 149, 157
Bentsen, K. D., 181
Berah, E. F., 545
Berenbaum, H., 251
Beresford, T., 41
Berg, R. A., 135
Berger, P., 96
Bergeron, S., 522, 531, 532
Berglas, S. C., 542
Berglund, M., 174, 175
Berglund, P., 39, 40, 292, 293
Bergman, H., 214
Bergner, R. M., 4, 9, 10
Bergström, M., 126
Beringer, I., 331, 334
Berkson, J., 35
Bernadt, M. R., 180
Bernstein, A. D., 181
Bernstein, D., 53
Berquier, A., 606
Berreira, P. J., 50
Berren, M. R., 481
Berrenberg, J. L., 325
Berrettini, W. H., 167, 332

Berscheid, 505, 516
Berstad, A., 413
Berthier, M. L., 298
Bertini, N., 331
Berzoff, J., 473
Bettencourt, R., 509
Beutler, L. E., 98
Bhangoo, R. K., 329
Bhui, K., 114
Biafora, F., 186
Bialas, I., 432
Bibb, J. L., 42
Bickel, M., 322
Bickel, W. K., 7, 222
Biederman, J., 329, 331
Bien, T. H., 36, 167, 172, 177
Bienvenu, O. J., 358, 359, 379
Bierer, L. M., 648
Biever, J., 370
Bifulco, A. T., 307
Bigelow, G. E., 43, 224
Bigelow, L. B., 239
Biggs, J. T., 381
Biglan, A., 370
Bihari, B., 142
Bilder, L. S., 440
Billard, M., 611, 613, 615, 616, 626
Billups, K. L., 528, 531
Binder, R. L., 47
Bindman, J., 47
Binghan, S. F., 42, 43, 44
Binik, Y. M., 413, 522, 531
Binkoff, J. A., 168
Binzer, M., 425
Bioty, S. M., 253
Birch, L. L., 585
Birchwood, M., 239, 240, 254, 258
Bird, L., 239
Birmaher, B., 323, 326, 329, 331
Birnbaum, H. G., 234
Bisserbe, J. C., 354, 358
Biuckians, A., 328
Bixler, E. O., 608, 611, 623

Black, D. B., 371
Black, D. W., 359
Black, J., 181
Blacker, D., 13, 18
Blackshaw, L., 550
Blackwood, D. H., 328
Blaine, J. D., 44, 212, 215
Blair, C. D., 539
Blair, R. J., 661
Blake, D. D., 369
Blakely, A. A., 446
Blanchard, E. B., 351, 353, 369, 413, 432, 537, 539, 543, 545, 547
Blanchard, J. J., 35, 54, 58, 60, 174
Bland, R. C., 352
Blashfield, R. K., 19, 55
Blasingame, G. D., 548
Blass, J. P., 142, 160
Blaszcyzynski, A., 539
Blatt, S. J., 656
Blazer, D. G., 38, 39, 210, 293, 353, 378, 379, 416, 418
Bleckley, M. K., 585
Blendell, K. A., 363
Bleuler, E., 256
Bliss, E. L., 428
Bliwise, D. L., 609, 624
Bloch, R. M., 480
Block, A. R., 436
Blois, R., 625
Blomqvist, G., 126
Blomqvist, J., 168
Blonk, R., 369
Blow, F. C., 172
Bluestone, H., 261
Blum, K., 213, 220
Blum, N., 93, 94, 371, 659
Blumberg, H. P., 334
Blumenthal, D., 49
Blumer, D., 427, 549
Blundell, M. L., 359
Boardman, A. P., 432
Bobes, J., 361
Boedicker, A. E., 224
Boerresen, R., 576

Bogardis, J., 177
Bogetto, F., 378
Bogojevic, G., 365
Bohman, M., 143, 167, 421, 427
Bohne, A., 419
Bokan, J. A., 413
Bolduc, P. L., 298
Bolhofner, K., 330
Bolk, J. H., 431
Boller, F., 151
Bolt, J. W., 517
Bona, J. R., 286, 308
Bonanno, G. A., 431
Bond, G. R., 54, 245, 249, 252
Bonilla, E., 157
Bonin, M. F., 44
Bonke, B., 443
Bonnet, M. H., 625
Boodoo, G., 24
Boon, 488, 490
Booth, B. M., 46
Bootzin, R. R., 614
Bor, D. H., 36
Borchardt, C., 63, 174, 212
Borden, J. W., 366, 367
Boreat, F., 361
Borg, S., 181
Borgeois, M. L., 328
Borger, S. C., 426
Boring, E. G., 127, 128
Borkovec, T. D., 357, 363, 368
Bornstein, R. A., 144, 158
Bornstein, R. F., 655, 656
Borrelli, B., 36
Borroughs, J., 326
Borum, R., 47, 242
Borus, J. F., 412, 415, 421
Bostwick, J. M., 240
Bottelender, R., 321
Bouchard, T. J., 24
Boudewyns, P., 362
Bourguignon, E., 493
Bourne, M. L., 322, 326
Boutagy, J., 185

Bouvard, M., 372
Bovasso, G. B., 480
Bowden, C. L., 46, 320, 321, 323, 326, 335
Bowen, R. C., 44
Bowers, K. S., 494
Bowers, M. B., 255
Bowler, A. E., 238, 263
Bowman, E. S., 478
Boyd, J. W., 36
Boydell, J., 238
Boyer, P., 354, 358
Boykin, A. W., 24
Bracha, H. S., 239
Bradizza, C. M., 46
Bradley, B. P., 223
Bradley, F., 215
Bradley, L. A., 446, 447
Bradley, S. J., 535, 543
Brady, E. U., 239
Brady, K. T., 44, 45, 47, 49, 52, 330, 331
Braff, D., 239
Braga, R. J., 240, 243
Braiker, H. B., 173
Brammer, M. J., 333
Branaman, T. F., 548
Brancale, R., 539, 544
Brand, R., 431
Brandon, T. H., 180
Brandsma, L., 367, 368
Brandt, J., 486
Brann, S., 490
Brannan, S. K., 10, 333, 334
Brannick, M., 586
Braun, B. G., 476, 489
Braunstein, D. G., 524, 530
Braverman, E. R., 213, 220
Brawley, B. W., 539
Breier, A., 240, 241, 245, 359, 366
Brekke, J. S., 239
Bremmer, M. A., 349
Bremner, J. D., 383
Brennan, P. A., 242
Brenner, I., 486

Brent, D., 331
Breslau, N., 42, 60, 243, 259
Breslin, F. C., 178
Breslow, N., 545
Brewerton, T. D., 52, 261
Brewin, C. R., 377
Bride, B. E., 224
Bridges, K., 424, 430
Briere, J., 474
Briggs, G., 263
Bright, J., 327
Broadhead, W. E., 294, 295
Broca, P., 128
Brodaty, H., 298
Brodsky, A., 41
Brodsky, B. S., 648, 665
Brodwin, B. J., 437
Brodwin, P. E., 437
Brody, A. L., 370, 384
Brody, L., 374
Brody, N., 24
Bromet, E. J., 55, 240, 243
Brook, D. W., 663
Brook, J. S., 330, 331, 477
Brooker, H., 431
Brookheimer, S. Y., 333, 334
Brooks, G. W., 245
Broome, K. M., 225
Brooner, R. K., 43, 224
Brotto, L. A., 527, 528, 530
Broughton, R., 608
Brower, K. J., 610
Brown, B. S., 210
Brown, C., 321, 510
Brown, D., 484, 490
Brown, F. W., 656
Brown, G. G., 155, 179, 255, 334
Brown, G. K., 322, 324, 427
Brown, G. M., 60
Brown, G. W., 323, 378, 449
Brown, J., 176, 531

Brown, P. J., 45, 475
Brown, R. A., 53, 204
Brown, R. J., 47, 428, 432
Brown, S. A., 174
Brown, S. L., 213
Brown, T. A., 11, 357, 358, 364, 365, 367, 368, 369, 370
Brown, V. B., 51
Browne, S., 47
Brownell, K. D., 579
Bruce, M. L., 238, 261
Bruce, S. E., 361
Bruch, M. A., 363
Brugha, T., 295, 296, 307
Brune, M., 240
Brunello, N., 52
Brunette, M. F., 51, 60, 241, 248, 259
Bruno, Z., 105
Bryant-Waugh, R. J., 576
Bryer, J. B., 214
Buchanan, J., 488
Buchanan, R. W., 239, 241, 245, 255, 263
Buchheim, P., 96
Bucholz, K. K., 38, 53, 86, 87, 182
Buckley, M. E., 330
Buckminster, S., 363
Budd, M. A., 425
Budde, D., 42
Budman, S. H., 215
Budney, A. J., 222
Buhrich, N., 543
Bukstein, O. G., 174
Bulik, C. M., 351, 579, 580, 584, 585
Bullmore, E. T., 334
Bunney, W. E., 58
Buono, R. J., 167
Buranen, C., 421, 425, 439
Burge, J., 36
Burger, H. G., 323, 517
Burglass, M. E., 175
Burke, J. D., 293
Burke, K. C., 293
Burks, J. S., 141

Burlig, T. A., 175
Burmeister, M., 20
Burn, D., 141
Burnam, A., 49
Burnam, M. A., 297
Burns, B. J., 47, 255, 261, 294, 295
Burns, G. L., 370
Burns, L., 43
Burr, R., 59, 174, 212, 224
Burroughs, J., 584
Burton, W. N., 296
Busby, D., 525
Busch, C. M., 450
Bushsbaum, M. C., 661
Bussiere, M. T., 547
Buster, J. E., 524, 530
Busto, U. E., 43
Butau, T., 215
Butcher, J. N., 105, 214, 546, 660
Butcher, J. N., 545, 660
Butler, A. C., 361
Butler, G., 362, 363
Butler, J. L., 541
Butler, L. D., 12
Butler, L. D., 474, 476, 484, 489
Butler, S. F., 215
Butterfield, M. I., 353
Butters, N., 154
Butzlaff, R. L., 245, 254, 257, 259, 324
Buysse, D. J., 608, 611, 615, 619, 620, 621, 622
Byers, E. S., 519, 520
Bystritsky, A., 362

Caap-Ahlgren, M., 298
Cabrol, S., 372
Cachelin, F. M., 579
Caddell, J., 362
Caetano, R., 171, 173
Caetano, S. C., 334
Cafri, G., 584, 586, 588
Cahalan, D., 167, 171, 173
Cai, G., 359
Cain, R., 493

Caine, E. D., 8, 156
Calabrese, J. R., 46, 318, 320, 321, 323, 326, 329, 330, 331, 335
Calandra, C., 590
Calder, A. J., 334
Calderone, G. E., 15
Caldieron, C., 418
Caldwell, A. B., 606, 613, 618, 625
Calhoun, K. S., 351
Caligiuri, M. P., 334
Callahan, L. F., 446
Cameron, O. G., 358
Camp, P., 294, 297
Campbell, L. A., 11, 368
Campbell, T., 441
Campori, C., 325
Cancro, R., 381
Cannon, M., 332
Cantor-Graae, E., 238
Cao, X., 212
Caplan, R. D., 296
Carbonell, S. I., 106, 114
Cardeña, E., 7, 12, 473, 474, 475, 476, 477, 478, 480, 481, 483, 485, 488, 489, 490, 491, 492, 493, 494
Cardenas, A., 19
Cardno, A., 257
Carey, G., 220
Carey, K. B., 179
Carey, K. B., 49, 56, 175, 222
Carey, M. P., 49
Carey, R., 366
Carlander, B., 613
Carlen, P. L., 179
Carlson, E. A., 476
Carlson, E. B., 473, 476
Carlson, G. A., 240, 329
Carlson, R. G., 42
Carlson, S. R., 213
Carmen, E., 242
Caroll, S. N., 615
Caron, C., 10
Carpena, M. P., 204
Carpenter, D., 327

Carpenter, K. M., 215
Carpenter, W. T. J., 44
Carper, J. L., 585
Carr, K. D., 186
Carr, L. G., 167
Carrieri, K., 58
Carroll, K. M., 42, 175, 183
Carroll, M. E., 221, 222
Carson, C. C., 515
Carson, J. E., 41
Carter, B. L., 223
Carter, C. W., 255
Carter, R. E., 47, 49
Caruso, S., 527, 528, 530
Carver, C., 325
Cascardi, M., 242, 260
Cash, T. F., 450, 584, 585
Cashel, M., 90
Casillas, A., 643
Caspi, A., 20, 46, 56, 57, 242, 257, 662
Cassano, G. B., 331
Cassisi, J., 238
Castaldo, E., 590
Castaneda, R., 35, 41
Castillo-Canez, I., 110
Castle, D. J., 364, 445
Casto, S., 330, 331
Castonguay, L. G., 98
Catalan, J., 528
Catanese, K. R., 508
Cate, T., 333
Caton, C. L., 50
Cattarin, J., 587
Caudill, B. D., 183
Caulet, M., 609
Cavalieri, T. A., 302
Cavanaugh, J. L., 45
Cavanaugh-Johnson, T., 541
Caveness, W. F., 134
Caviness, V. S., 334
Cawte, E. C., 417
Ceci, S. J., 24
Center for Disease Control, 353
Cermak, L. S., 154
Cerney, J. A., 362

Cernovsky, Z. Z., 47
Chadwick, P., 239, 240, 258
Chalkley, A. J., 362, 539, 544
Chambers, R. A., 61
Chambers, W. J., 331
Chambless, D. L., 42, 363, 366, 369, 377, 381
Chan, T., 9, 12
Chang, G., 110
Chang, I. W., 489
Chang, K. D., 322, 331, 333
Chang, P. P., 611
Channabasavanna, S. M., 96, 352, 378
Chaplin, T. C., 547
Chapman, J. E., 361
Chapman, L. J., 329
Chapman, S. L., 446
Charney, D. S., 329, 332, 359, 366, 484, 606, 618, 625
Chase, G. A., 450
Chater, R., 576
Chatterji, S., 212
Chauhan, R. V., 107
Chauncey, D. L., 97
Checkley, G. E., 49
Cheine, M., 240
Chelminski, I., 637
Chen, C. M., 60, 171
Chen, T. J. H., 213, 220
Chen, Z., 529
Chengappa, K. N., 41
Chervin, R., 605
Chesluk, D., 248
Cheung, F. K., 261
Chew-Graham, C. A., 443
Chiappetta, L., 323
Chiaroni, P., 333
Chichester, C. S., 44
Chilcoat, H. D., 60, 259, 366
Child Psychiatric Workgroup on Bipolar Disorder, 326

Chiu, H., 141
Chiu, W. T., 40, 318, 320, 330
Chiu, Y. F., 47
Choi, H. K., 529
Choi, Y. D., 529
Chorot, P., 379
Chorpita, B. F., 368
Chou, C. P., 210
Chou, P. S., 168
Chou, S. P., 36, 37, 38, 39, 48
Chouinard, G., 361
Chrestman, K. R., 45
Christensen, H., 364
Christenson, C. V., 543
Christianson, S. A., 485
Christoffersen, P., 181
Chu, M. C., 524
Chu, M. P., 329
Chue, P., 244
Chui, T. L., 102, 112
Chung, Y. B., 543
Cicchetti, D., 488, 665
Ciechanowski, P., 297
Cioffi, D., 428
Ciompi, L., 246
Cipani, E., 258
Cipywnyk, D., 44
Claridge, G. C., 306
Clark, C. P., 610
Clark, D. A., 362, 370, 377
Clark, D. B., 174, 221
Clark, D. C., 431
Clark, D. M., 370
Clark, J. C., 368
Clark, K., 238
Clark, L. A., 3, 7, 10, 11, 18, 21, 635, 643, 660
Clark, P. D., 35, 44, 60
Clark, R. E., 50, 238
Clark, V. R., 238
Clark, W. B., 172
Clarke, D. M., 416
Clarkin, J. F., 22, 327
Clary, C. M., 361
Classen, C., 474, 480
Claudio, F., 418

Clay, C., 258
Clayton, A., 524
Clayton, P. J., 331, 417, 427
Cleary, P. D., 419, 428, 429
Cleary, S. D., 221
Cleghorn, J. M., 60
Cloitre, M., 648
Cloninger, C. R., 11, 18, 143, 167, 420, 421, 425, 427, 439, 635, 661, 662
Clopton, J. R., 585
Cloud, W., 168
Clum. G., 361, 362, 363
Coates, T. J., 619
Coccaro, E. F., 661
Cochran, S. D., 327
Cochrane, R., 254
Cockerham, M. S., 215
Coe, D., 251
Coffey, S. F., 44, 45
Coffman, G. A., 477, 655
Cohen, A. N., 324
Cohen, B., 425
Cohen, D., 522
Cohen, J. D., 239, 252, 255
Cohen, K., 431
Cohen, L., 47, 419, 473
Cohen, M. S., 60, 332
Cohen, P., 330, 331, 477, 661, 663
Cohen-Mansfield, J., 141
Coid, B., 96
Cole, C. M., 536
Cole, M., 151
Cole, S. W., 9, 12
Coleman, R. M., 608, 615
Coles, M. E., 368
Collins, E. D., 222
Collins, M. E., 212
Collins, M. W., 135
Collins, P., 543
Collins, R. L., 171, 183, 186
Colliver, J. A., 242

Colom, F., 41, 327
Colombo, C., 325
Columbus, M., 177
Colurcio, B., 590
Comas-Díaz, L., 261
Combs, D. R., 238, 240, 241, 261
Comer, S. D., 222
Comes, M., 327
Comings, D. E., 213, 220
Compton, P., 215
Compton, W. M., 37, 39, 44, 86, 87, 88, 212, 224
Comstock, C., 48
Comtois, K. A., 51
Condie, E., 489
Conger, A. J., 370
Conger, J. C., 370
Conigliaro, J., 321
Conneally, P. M., 157
Connelly, A., 136
Connor, K. M., 384
Connors, G. J., 175, 176, 180
Connors, M. E., 587
Conover, S., 235
Conrod, P. J., 42, 61
Conroy, D., 603
Constantine, M. G., 114
Constantino, G., 109
Conte, H. R., 60
Conti, D. J., 296
Contreras, S., 106
Convit, A., 179
Conway, C. G., 5
Cook, E. H., 308
Cook, M., 375, 376
Cook, R. F., 181
Cooley, M. R., 362, 369
Cooley-Quille, M. R., 361, 381
Cooley-Towell, S., 548
Coolidge, F. L., 81, 83, 85, 92
Cooney, N. L., 214, 218
Coons, P. M., 478, 482, 484, 489, 490, 491, 492
Cooper, A. M., 651
Cooper, J. E., 237

Cooper, M. L., 184
Cooper, N., 362
Cooper, Z., 571, 578, 582, 584
Cooper-Patrick, L., 611
Coovert, M. D., 587, 591
Cope, H., 429, 446
Copeland, L. A., 172
Coplan, J. D., 384
Copolov, D. L., 239
Coppock, H. W., 221
Copstake, S., 254
Corbella, B., 327
Corbitt, E. M., 96
Cordero-Guevara, J., 605
Cordingley, L., 448
Coren, S., 620, 621
Cormier, J., 587
Corominas, J., 327
Corona, G., 515
Correia, C. J., 56, 179, 222
Corrigan, J. M., 49
Corrigan, P. M., 240, 242, 262
Corse, S. J., 248
Corty, E., 45, 247
Coryell, W. D. S., 42, 45, 294, 298, 318, 320, 322, 323, 331, 421, 425, 432
Costa, J. F., 45
Costa, P. T., 14, 17, 18, 20, 21, 22, 23, 450, 635, 636, 660
Costello, A., 373
Costello, E., 363
Costello, F., 299
Cottler, L. B., 44, 86, 87, 88, 212, 224, 334
Cotton, P. G., 240
Cournos, F., 49
Couture, M., 544
Coverdale, J. H., 259
Cowan, L., 542
Cowley, D. S., 46, 47
Cox, B. J., 358, 368, 426, 432
Cox, B. M., 174

Cox, D. J., 539
Cox, G. B., 48
Coyle, K., 620, 621
Coyle, P. K., 446
Coyne, J. C., 15, 18, 656
Craddock, N., 258
Crago, M., 15, 576
Craig, R. J., 84
Craig, T. J., 55, 114
Craig, T. K. J., 432, 433
Craine, L. S., 242
Cramer, D., 306
Cramer, V., 633
Crane, C., 432
Craney, J. L., 330
Crapanzano, M. S., 35, 44, 60
Craske, M. G., 361, 362, 363, 364, 370
Craughan, J. L., 216
Crawford, T. N., 661
Crawley, J. N., 240
Crayford, T., 443
Creed, F., 415, 416, 417, 418
Crenshaw, T. L., 523
Crepault, E., 544
Crijnen, A. A., 645
Crimlisk, H. L., 425
Crino, R., 362
Critchley, M., 134
Crits-Cristoph, P., 43, 44
Crockett, L. J., 105
Croes, E. A., 333
Croft, H., 524
Crofts, N., 49
Cross, T. P., 548
Cross-National Collaborative Panic Study Second Phase Investigation, 361
Croughan, J., 87
Crowe, R. R., 53
Crowell, M. D., 427
Crowther, J., 380
Cruley, K. A., 54
Crum, R. C., 330
Crum, R. M., 224
Crystal, J. D., 62

Csapo, K. G., 620, 621
Csikszentmihalya, M., 296
Cuellar, A., 323, 324, 332
Cuesta, M. J., 18
Cuffel, B. J., 46
Cui, J., 517
Cummings, J. L., 45
Cunningham, J. A., 168, 179
Cunningham, P. J., 49
Cunningham-Rathner, J., 541, 545
Curran, J. P., 369
Currie, R., 478
Curtis, G. C., 351, 358, 361, 367, 379
Cuthbert, B., 18
Cuthbertson, B., 45
Cutting, J., 239
Cyranowski, J. M., 331, 516
Czobor, P., 242

Dahl, A., 96
Dahl, R. E., 320
Dahlstrom, W. G., 545
Dalack, G. W., 36
Daley, M., 611
Daley, S. E., 324
Dalh, J. P., 167
Damato, N., 611
Damon, W., 512, 521
Dana, R. H., 101, 102, 106, 107, 113, 114
Dancey, C. P., 445
Dancu, C. V., 358, 368
Daneluzzo, E., 643
D'Angelo, N., 42, 43
Danielsen, B. H., 51
Danielson, C. K., 329
Danielyan, A., 321
Dansky, B. S., 44, 45
Dantzer, R., 433
Dao, M. D., 444
Dao, T. H. T., 431, 451
Darakjian, J., 215
D'Arcy, C., 44
Darkes, J., 183

Dassa, D., 333
Dauvilliers, Y., 611, 613, 623
David, A. S., 242, 252, 429, 446
Davidson, A. T., 540, 549
Davidson, J. R., 13, 52, 296, 353, 359, 360, 361, 363, 369, 376, 384
Davidson, K., 665
Davidson, M., 239
Davidson, R., 178, 333
Davies, A. D. M., 179
Davies, R. K., 331
Davies-Netzley, S., 242
Davis, C. G., 37, 38, 42
Davis, C. G., 58
Davis, C. W., 43
Davis, D. D., 16
Davis, J. M., 45
Davis, K. D., 427
Davis, K. L., 661, 662
Davis, M., 181, 204
Davis, P., 329
Davis, R. D., 638, 646, 650, 654, 660
Davis, S. R., 517, 524
Davis, T. M., 44
Davis, W. W., 6, 8
Davison, K. K., 585
Davison, S. L., 517
Dawkins, M. P., 186
Dawson, D. A., 36, 37, 38, 39, 48, 167, 168, 170, 171, 173, 221
Dawson, M. E., 245, 258
Deahl, M., 52
Deakin, J. F. W., 223
Dean, R. S., 131
Dean, T. J., 475
Dean, W., 242
Deary, I. J., 421
de Asis, J., 334
DeBeurs, E., 363, 369
Debnat, M. L., 126
De Boeck, P., 14, 18
de Cacerda, R. B., 215
Deckersbach, T., 419
De Clercq, B., 20

de Corral, P., 362
Deeg, D. J., 349
Deeks, J. J., 240
de Flores, T., 306
De Fruyt, F., 20
DeGirolomo, J., 242
de Gouveia Brazao, C. A., 529
de Groot, M., 298
De Gucht, V., 431
De Haes, J. C., 443
Deister, P. J., 419
de Keizer, M., 515, 516
Dekker, J., 238
Dekosky, S. T., 126
de Kruiff, M. E., 513
De La Fuente, J. R., 178, 213
Delaney, H. D., 175
DelBello, M. P., 43, 174, 321, 330
Del Boca, F. K., 54, 176, 183
DeLeo, J. A., 434
de Lima, M. S., 204
Delinsky, S. S., 579
Delizio, R. D., 381
Dell, P. F., 488
DeLoof, C., 378
Delprato, D. J., 375
Delsignore, A., 536
DeLuca, J., 446
Delucchi, K. L., 44
DelVecchio, W. F., 20, 662, 664
Dembling, B., 50
Dement, W. C., 611, 620, 621
DeMet, E. M., 45
Demler, O., 39, 40, 50, 292, 293, 318, 320, 330
Demsky, L. S., 553
den Boer, J. A., 361
Dence, C. S., 126
Denicoff, K. D., 41, 322, 323
Dennis, A. B., 581
Denny, D., 533, 534, 536
DePaulo, J. R., 47

DePress, J. A., 357
DePrince, A. P., 473, 476
DePue, J., 36
Depue, R. A., 318, 329
De Raad, B., 17, 21
Dermatis, H., 49, 50
Derogatis, L. R., 179
DeSisto, M. J., 245
De Soto, C. B., 173
De Soto, J. L., 173
DeVeaugh-Geiss, J., 326
Devereaux, B., 382
Devins, G. M., 445
Devinsky, O., 432
de Wit, H., 184
de Zwann, M., 576
Dhawan, S., 540
Dhawan, V., 334
Diamond, P. L., 239
Diamond, R., 157
Dibble, E., 58
Dickens, S. E., 517
Dickey, B., 48, 50
Dickinson, K. A., 651
Dickinson, W. P., 617
Dickson, D., 141
DiClemente, C. C., 175, 217
Dicurzio, S., 44
Diehl, S. R., 256
Diekstra, R. F. W., 96
Dienes, K., 333
Dietz, P. E., 542
Dignan, M. A., 214
Dikeos, D. G., 305
DiLieto, A., 590
Dilts, S. L., 181, 248
Dimitrova, A., 333
Dinan, T. G., 434
DiNardo, P. A., 351, 367, 368
Dingemans, P. M., 45
Dion, G., 322
di Padova, C., 185
Direnfeld, D. M., 358
Diseth, T. H., 476
Dixie-Bell, D. D., 380
Dixon, L. B., 41, 46, 50, 60, 248, 254

Dockens, W., 221
Dodrill, C. B., 146
Dogramji, K., 620
Doherty, W. J., 434
Dohrenwend, B. R., 238
Dolan, R. T., 358, 430
Dolder, C. R., 47
Dolinsky, Z. S., 175
Doll, H. A., 571, 578
Dominguez, B., 50
Donath, S., 517
Donegan, N. H., 661
Dongier, M., 42, 61
Donham, R., 222
Donovan, D. M., 175
Donovan, P., 295, 305, 306, 307
Doorn, C. D., 543
Dorward, J., 368
Douaihy, A., 50
Dougherty, D. M., 325
Douglas, K. S., 645
Douglas, M. S., 239, 253, 259
Dow, J. T., 477
Dow, M. G., 370
Downey, G., 257
Downhill, J. E. J., 661
Downing, R. W., 360, 361
Dowrick, C. F., 443
Doyle, G. A., 167
Doyle, T., 220
Draguns, J. G., 108, 110
Draijer, N., 478, 488, 490
Drake, H., 432
Drake, R. E., 44, 46, 51, 54, 57, 58, 59, 60, 174, 240, 241, 245, 248, 249, 252
Dramaix, M., 324
Drevets, W. C., 10, 333, 334
Driessen, M., 660
Driscoll, A. K., 105
Drogendijk, A. C., 538
Drossman, D. A., 434
Druley, K. A., 41
Drummond, C., 47
Drumond, S. P. A., 610

Druss, B. G., 296
Dubbert, B. K., 581
Dubois, B., 141
Duchmann, E. G., 583
Duda, J. E., 141
Dudley, E. C., 517
Duffy, C. M., 477
Duffy, P., 332
Dufour, M. C., 36, 37, 38, 39, 48
Dufresne, R. G., 445
Dugas, M. J., 354
Dulit, R. A., 648
DuMars, L. A., 332
Dunbar, G., 178
Duncan, A. A., 62
Dunn, G. E., 488
Dunner, D. L., 331
Dunsis, A., 417
Dupree, L. W., 173
Duran, E. E., 474
Durand, V. M., 476
Durante, R., 518
Durbin, J., 59, 174, 212, 224
Durham, R., 362, 363
Durrant, J. D., 383
Durrett, C. A., 18, 635
Dutton, M. A., 51, 242, 243
Dworkin, R. J., 261, 418, 424, 426
Dyce, J. A., 20
Dyck, D. G., 257
Dyson, V., 248
D'Zurilla, T. J., 305

Eagle, P. F., 50
Earl, N. L., 326
Earleywine, M., 169
Easser, B. R., 650
East, W. N., 544
Eaton, W. W., 238, 240, 349, 351, 358, 359, 366, 379, 515
Eaves, L. J., 167, 220, 365, 374, 623
Ebener, P., 42
Eberson, S. C., 334

Ebigbo, P. O., 451
Eccles, A., 543, 547
Echeburua, E., 362, 363
Echemendia, R. J., 115
Eckblad, M., 329
Ecker, C., 333
Eckert, S. L., 239
Edell, W. S., 646
Edinger, J. D., 608, 620, 622, 624
Edinger, J. E., 614, 619
Edlund, M. J., 174
Edwards, B., 240
Edwards, J., 240
Eerly, G. S., 368
Egeland, B., 476
Eghøje, K., 181
Ehlers, A., 370
Ehlers, C. L., 325
Eich, E., 325
Eidelberg, D., 334
Eifert, G., 413
Eisen, J. L., 42, 44, 365
Eisen, S. A., 220
Eisenberg, H. M., 135
Eisenberger, N., 333, 334
Eisfeld, B. S., 517
Eisler, R. M., 369
Eisner, L. R., 333
Elder, K. A., 579
Elder, P., 321
Eldredge, K. L., 581
Eley, T. C., 378, 379
El-Guebaly, N., 224
Elias, M. F., 139
Elinson, L., 7
Elkin, R., 606
Ellason, J. W., 477
Ellenbogen, M., 322, 332
Ellicott, A., 323
Ellingstad, T. P., 168
Ellis, A., 539, 544
Ellis, C. G., 96
Elmquist, J. K., 590
Emery, G., 376
Eminson, D. M., 432
Emmelkamp, P. M. G., 351, 367

Emmerich, S., 334
Emory, L. E., 536
Endicott, J., 41, 42, 44, 45, 46, 88, 89, 173, 294, 298, 318, 320, 322, 323, 331, 368
Endler, N. S., 174
Engberg, M., 242
Engel, G. E., 427
Engle, J. D., 242
Engler, H., 126
English, K., 548
Englund, S. A., 305
Epstein, E. E., 182, 183
Epstein, J., 10, 334
Epstein, L. H., 382
Epstein, N., 179
Erdelyi, M. E., 474
Erdlen, D. L., 44
Erdlen, F. R., 44
Eriksson, A., 375
Eriksson, E., 530
Ernberg, G., 237
Ernest, A., 186
Escobar, J., 110
Escobar, J., 110, 416, 417
Eshleman, S., 34, 36, 37, 39, 292, 299
Espie, C. A., 603, 613, 614, 618, 619, 623, 624
Essali, A., 240
Essock, S., 239, 252
Estes, L. S., 15, 576
Estrada, S., 126
Estroff, S. E., 260
Etain, B., 331
Evams, B., 424
Evans, C., 517
Evans, D. L., 52
Evans, D. R., 41
Evans, J. D., 251, 261
Evans, L. A., 261
Evans, N., 545
Everaerd, W., 510, 524
Everitt, B., 242
Evers, C., 536
Ewusi-Mensah, I., 181

Fabio, A., 648

Fabrega, H., 41, 43, 477, 636, 655

Faedda, G. L., 326

Fagan, A. M., 126

Fagergren, P., 62

Fagg, J., 297, 528

Fagiolini, A., 322, 327, 331

Fahlen, T., 530

Fahy, T., 490

Fairbank, J. A., 362

Fairbrother, N., 363

Fairburn, C. G., 571, 578, 579, 582, 584, 590

Falck, R. S., 42

Falk, B., 81, 85

Fallon, B., 53

Falloon, I. R. H., 363

Falsetti, S., 368

Fals-Stewart, W., 182, 218

Fannon, D., 255

Faraone, S. V., 23, 257, 329, 331

Faravelli, C., 378, 379, 417, 418

Farmer, A. E., 256

Farmer, M. E., 15, 36, 37, 55, 174, 212, 330

Farr, S. P., 179

Farrel, A. D., 370

Farrell, M., 215, 218

Farrington, J., 413

Fassino, S., 590

Fatemi, S. H., 318, 323

Faucher, B., 322, 332

Faure, M., 361

Fava, G. A., 359, 361, 362

Fava, M., 335, 366

Fawcett, J., 322

Federoff, B., 539

Federoff, J. P., 539

Feldman, H. A., 141, 518

Feldman, M. E., 353

Feldman, M. P., 551

Felix, A., 50

Felt, S. M., 49

Felten, S.Y., 434

Fenigstein, A., 261

Fennell, M., 362, 363

Fennig, S., 55

Fenton, W. S., 239, 244, 252

Ferguson, B., 96

Ferguson, F., 225

Ferguson, M. J., 5

Fergusson, D. M., 213, 382

Ferman, J., 35, 41

Fernandez, K., 215

Fernandez, S., 106

Fernandez, Y. M., 541

Ferrari, P., 329

Ferraro, T. N., 167

Ferro, T., 635

Fertig, J., 180

Fertuck, E., 239

Feske, U., 331, 363

Fichter, M. M., 424, 578, 583

Field, A. E., 587

Field, C. D., 248

Field, M., 223

Field, P., 180

Fields, H. L., 434

Fieve, R. R., 301

Figueria, I. L., 240

Figueroa, R. A., 112

Fillmore, K. M., 171, 173

Finch, J. F., 22

Finch, S., 525

Findley, L. J., 612

Findling, R. L., 321, 326, 329

Fineberg, N. A., 363

Finegeld, D., 168

Finestone, D. H., 493

Fingarette, H., 167

Fingerhut, R., 324

Fink, M., 360

Fink, P. J., 260, 423, 445

Finkelhor, D., 540, 541

Finlay-Jones, F., 378

Finney, J. W., 54, 173

First, M. B., 3, 4, 6, 7, 8, 10, 11, 13, 14, 16, 18,

90, 91, 92, 93, 215, 247, 320, 331, 368, 444, 659

Fischer, E. P., 46

Fischler, B., 431

Fischman, M. W., 222

Fish, L. S., 525

Fishbain, D. A., 413

Fishell, A., 539

Fisher, W. H., 50

Fishman, R., 320

Fiszbein, A., 252

Fitts, S. N., 419

Flaherty, J. A., 43

Flaker, G., 427

Flatow, L., 45

Flaum, M., 251, 255

Fleck, D. E., 330

Fleming, M. F., 178, 214

Fletcher, B., 225

Fletcher-Janzen, E., 101, 103

Flett, G. L., 15, 18

Flor, H., 427

Flor-Henry, P., 244

Florin, I., 372

Flourens, M. J. P., 128

Flynn, C., 331

Foa, E. B., 13, 362, 364, 368, 369, 385

Fochtmann, L. J., 240, 413

Foerg, F. E., 222

Fog, E., 505

Fogel, D., 578

Foley, D., 612

Folkman, S., 428

Folnegoic-Smalc, V., 46

Folnegovic, Z., 46

Folsom, D. P., 47, 51

Folstein, M. F., 450

Fong, G. W., 334

Fonseca, M., 334

Fontaine, R., 361

Fontana, A., 47

Foote, B., 477, 491, 492

Foote, J., 53

Forbes, C., 47

Ford, D. E., 611

Forde, D. R., 15, 357

Forman, E. M., 361
Forman, R. F., 215
Formigoni, M. L. O. S., 215
Forneris, C. A., 353
Forrest, K. A., 473, 489
Forti, B., 655
Fortier, M., 522
Fossey, M., 46
Foster, C. L., 238, 360
Fowles, D. C., 13
Fox, J. W., 238
Fox, P. T., 10
Fox, R., 445
Foy, D. W., 370
Franc, Z., 360
France, R., 296
Frances, A. J., 5, 6, 7, 8, 10, 11, 13, 14, 16, 41, 60, 383, 635
Francis, G., 372
Franco, S., 60
Frangou, S., 333
Frank, A., 44
Frank, E., 321, 322, 324, 325, 326, 327, 330, 331, 335
Frank, L. R., 334
Frank, R. G., 174
Franken, I. H. A., 223
Frankenburg, F. R., 97
Franklin, G. M., 141
Franklin, M. E., 385, 590
Franko, D. L., 575
Fraser, G. A., 489
Frazier, J. A., 331, 334
Fredrikson, M., 375
Freedman, M., 483
Freeman, A. F., 16, 638, 646, 652, 653, 658
Freeman, D. H., 240, 241
Freeman, R. C., 181, 539, 546
Freeman-Longo, R., 552
Freeston, M. H., 358, 361
Freitas, T. T., 218
Frenkel, M., 424
Fresco, D. M., 324

Frese, F., 239, 252
Freund, B. V., 369
Freund, K., 539, 540, 547, 548
Freundt, I., 538
Frey, L., 115
Freyd, J. J., 473, 476
Frezza, M., 185
Friedl, M. C., 478
Friedman, M. A., 584, 609, 618
Friedman, R. C., 542
Friedman, S., 377, 381
Friedrich, E. G., 521
Frisch, A., 305
Frischholz, E. J., 489
Fristad, M. A., 326, 327, 328
Frohlich, P., 516
Fromherz, A., 604, 605, 623, 625
Fromm-Reichmann, F., 256
Frone, M. R., 184
Frueh, B. C., 362
Frye, M. A., 41, 45, 322, 323
Fu, S. S., 111
Fugl-Meyer, A. R., 506, 507, 508, 509, 511, 512, 515, 520
Fujino, D. C., 261
Fulwiler, C., 47
Fung, D., 381
Furby, L., 550
Furman, J. M., 383
Fussell, J. J., 620, 621
Fyer, A. J., 360, 361, 371, 383

Gabb, J., 433
Gabbard, G. O., 479, 665
Gacono, C. B., 645
Gadian, D. G., 136
Gadish, D., 42, 43
Gaffney, B., 536
Gagnon, J. H., 506, 543
Gaillard, J. M., 625

Galanter, M., 35, 41, 49, 50
Gale, T. M., 363
Gallagher, S. N., 548
Gallardo-Cooper, M., 113
Galletly, C. A., 248
Gamache, G., 254
Gamal, R., 41
Gambaro, S., 551
Gamble, G., 248, 508
Gamma, A., 322
Gammon, G. D., 372
Ganguli, M., 294
Ganju, V. K., 242
Gara, M., 110
Garb, H. N., 112, 115, 320
Garbin, M. G., 179
Garcia, L., 306
Garcia, P., 47, 51, 110
Garde, K., 505
Gardner, C. O., 221
Garety, P. A., 240, 241, 258
Garfinkel, 413, 437
Garg, M., 606
Garibay-Rico, S. E., 478
Garner, D. M., 572, 583
Garnick, D. W., 48
Garno, J. L., 54, 330
Garratt, L. S., 244
Garrett, J. L., 62
Garrity, T. F., 184
Garssen, B., 443
Gaskin, J., 179
Gaspari, J. P., 43
Gasquoine, P. G., 112, 115
Gastaut, H., 145
Gastfiend, D. R., 36, 44
Gasto, C., 41, 327
Gates, C., 240
Gatz, M., 301
Gaunt, G., 531
Gauthier, S., 141
Gavazzi, S. M., 327, 328
Gavez, S., 584
Gavin, D. R., 168

Gawin, F., 42
Gay, N. W., 241
Gaylor, M., 436
Gaynes, B. N., 294, 295
Gearon, J. S., 51
Geary, N., 590
Gebhard, P. H., 543, 544, 545
Geddes, J. R., 263
Geer, J. H., 510, 519
Geissner, E., 424
Gelder, M. G., 357, 358, 362, 363, 377
Gelernter, C. S., 43, 58
Gelfand, A. N., 432, 449
Gelfand, M. D., 432, 449
Gelfand, M. M., 517
Geller, B., 330, 331
Geltman, D., 110
Gendel, M. H., 181
Gendrano, N. C., 527
Genevrois, C., 324
George, E. L., 327
George, F. S., 551
George, L. J., 353, 378, 416, 418
George, M. S., 661
George, T. P., 36
Georgieva, L., 333
Gerardi, R. J., 42
Gerber-Werder, R., 322
Gerdeman, B., 151
Gerke, C. K., 584
Germanson, T., 42, 44
Gerre Sullivan, J., 294
Gershon, E. S., 58, 332
Gershon, S., 41
Gervin, M., 47
Geschwind, N., 128
Gettings, B., 223
Geyer, M. A., 333
Ghaemi, S. N., 326
Ghaziuddin, N., 309
Ghosh, D., 20
Giachello, A. L. M., 186
Giampietro, V., 333
Gianoulakis, C., 186, 187

Gibbon, M., 90, 91, 92, 93, 215, 247, 320, 331, 368, 382, 431, 444
Gibbons, J., 382
Gibbons, R. D., 431
Gibson, G. E., 142, 160
Gibson, G. S., 181
Gibson, P., 419
Gil, A. G., 185, 186
Gilbert, S., 588
Gilbert, W. M., 51
Giles, D. E., 625
Gill, J., 528
Gill, K., 45
Gill, M. K., 323
Gillberg, M., 620, 621
Gilliland, F. D., 185
Gillin, J. C., 608, 610
Gilmer, T. P., 47, 51
Gilvarry, C., 19, 238
Gima, K., 54
Gingerich, S., 258
Ginsburg, P. B., 49
Gioia, G. A., 136
Giordano, L. A., 222
Gipson, M. T., 509
Giraldo, C., 19
Gitlin, M. J., 323
Giudicelli, S., 333
Giuliano, A. J., 157
Giuseppe, L., 528
Gladsjo, J. A., 239
Gladstone, G., 382
Glahn, D., 334
Glaser, F. B., 42, 44
Glaser, S. R., 370
Gleaves, D. H., 418, 477, 484, 488, 489, 490, 580, 582, 583
Glenn, S. W., 54
Glick, I., 327
Glicklich, J., 383
Glover, G., 238
Glovinsky, P. B., 603
Glynn, S. M., 235, 255, 256, 257, 260, 262, 362
Gobrogge, K. L., 585
Godoy, J. F., 258
Goerre, S., 234

Goethe, K. E., 135
Goff, D. C., 351
Gogus, A., 212
Goikolea, J. M., 327
Goiny, M., 62
Goisman, R. M., 359, 360
Gold, J. M., 239, 252
Gold, R., 217
Goldapple, K., 333
Goldberg, D., 18, 416, 424
Goldberg, J. F., 54, 220, 320, 321, 322, 323, 326, 330
Goldberg, M., 413
Goldberg, T. E., 239, 252
Goldbert, J. P., 523
Golden, B., 322
Goldenberg, D. L., 445
Goldenberg, I., 359, 361
Goldin, L. R., 58
Golding, J. M., 51, 420
Goldman, H. H., 55, 235
Goldman, M. S., 183
Goldner, E. M., 237, 294
Goldring, E., 87
Goldstein, A. J., 377
Goldstein, G., 125, 137, 139, 142, 148
Goldstein, I., 518, 519, 526
Goldstein, J. M., 244
Goldstein, K., 129
Goldstein, M., 36, 323, 327
Goldstein, R. B., 371, 372
Golier, J. A., 648
Golinelli, D., 364
Golshan, S., 51
Gomberg, E. S. L., 185
Gomez-Maqueo, E. L., 105, 106
Gonzales, M., 110
Gonzalez, F., 19
Gonzalez, M., 324
González-Wippler, M., 261

Good, A., 531
Good, B. J., 102, 112, 437
Good, C. B., 321
Good, F., 544
Good, M. I., 475, 493
Good, M. J. D., 437
Goodman, A., 44
Goodman, L. A., 51, 259, 260
Goodman, M., 648
Goodman, S., 656
Goodman, W. K., 361, 369, 371, 384
Goodnick, P., 324
Goodson, J. D., 429
Goodwin, D. W., 142
Goodwin, F. K., 36, 37, 41, 47, 60, 174, 263, 320, 330
Gopaul-McNicol, S., 107
Gordon, J. R., 173, 178
Gorenstein, E., 5, 8
Gorey, K. M., 575, 576
Gorman, J. M., 241, 360, 383, 384
Gorrindo, T., 330, 331
Gorwood, P., 333
Gosselin, C., 545
Gothe, C. J., 413
Gottesman, I. I., 49, 220, 256, 257
Gould, R., 363
Grabe, H. J., 416, 417
Grace, A. A., 263
Gracely, E. J., 366
Graham, J. R., 545, 660
Grande, T. P., 34
Granfield, R., 168
Granstrand, C., 181
Grant, B. F., 36, 37, 38, 39, 42, 43, 44, 48, 168, 170, 171, 173, 174, 212, 221, 634, 637, 640, 644, 649, 653, 655, 657
Grant, I., 144, 158, 645
Grant, M., 178, 213
Gray, B. A., 261
Grayson, C., 296

Grazioli, R., 306
Greden, J. F., 240
Green, A. I., 173, 174, 175, 179
Green, M. F., 137, 239, 240, 242, 252
Greenberg, P. E., 360
Greenberg, R. P., 656
Greenburg, B. D., 11
Greene, P. L., 326
Greener, J., 225
Greenhouse, W. J., 324
Greenstein, R., 248
Greenwald, A. G., 223
Greenwald, S., 611
Grégoire, J. P., 611
Greist, J., 364
Grella, C. E., 44, 51, 210
Grenier, G., 519, 520
Gretchen, D., 107
Grieve, C. O., 583
Griez, E. J., 378
Griffin, M. L., 42
Griffith, A. N., 260
Griffith, J. M., 46
Grills, C., 186
Grilo, C. M., 22, 582, 635, 636, 645, 646, 652, 657, 662, 663, 664
Grinker, R. R., 486
Grisham, J. R., 11, 322
Grissom, G., 216
Grisson, T., 47
Grob, C. S., 539
Grochocinski, V. J., 321, 327, 331
Groleau, D., 443, 451, 452
Groome, C. S., 49
Gross, J. J., 5
Grossman, H., 47
Grossman, J. M., 49
Grossman, L. S., 45, 245, 246, 322
Grossman, R. G., 157
Grossman, W. I., 542
Groth-Marnat, G., 445
Grubb, H. J., 373
Gruber, J. L., 334

Grunebaum, H., 259
Grüsser-Sinopoli, S. M., 511
Guay, A. T., 517
Gudleski, G. D., 432
Gugger, M., 605
Guido, J. R., 49
Guilleminault, C., 604, 605, 613, 616, 623, 625
Gull, W. W., 584
Gunderson, J. G., 18, 22, 97, 324, 636, 646, 648, 663, 664, 665
Gunnarsdottir, E. D., 299
Guralnik, O., 480, 481
Gureje, O., 416, 418
Gurguis, G., 449
Guroff, J. J., 428, 489
Guroff, J. J., 58, 428, 489
Gursky, D. M., 377
Gurvits, T. V., 383
Gusella, J. F., 157
Guth, D., 302
Guze, S. B., 14, 142, 417, 420, 427
Gynther, L. M., 220
Gyulai, L., 323

Haas, G. L., 41, 60, 244, 321
Haczynsk, J., 509
Haddock, G., 252
Hadzi-Pavlovic, D., 364
Haellstroem, T., 359
Hafner, H., 240, 243, 244
Haggard, P., 322, 326
Haigler, E. D., 21, 22
Hakkaart-an Roijen, L., 320
Halari, R., 244
Haley, J., 256
Haley, R., 477
Halford, W. K., 254
Hall, J. M., 610
Hall, W., 217
Halliday, G., 141
Halligan, C. M., 425
Halpern, D. F., 24

Halstead, W. C., 129
Hamani, Y., 531
Hamburger, S. D., 137
Hamilton, M., 179, 369
Hamilton, N., 51
Hammen, C., 323, 324
Hamovit, J., 58
Han, C., 221
Han, X., 321
Hand, I., 362
Handel, M. H., 259
Handelsman, L., 53
Handrinos, D., 417
Handy, L., 539, 546
Hanewald, G. J., 436
Hanna, G. H., 371
Hansell, S., 427
Hanson, L., 359
Hanson, P. K., 547
Hantouche, E. G., 329
Hanwella, T., 425
Harding, C. M., 50, 245, 246
Hare, R. D., 645
Harford, T. C., 36, 37, 38, 39, 43, 48, 171
Hargreaves, W. A., 50
Harkness, K., 323
Harmon, L. W., 543
Harnden-Fischer, J., 581
Harpin, R. E., 363
Harris, E. C., 322
Harris, G. T., 547, 548
Harris, M. J., 51, 239, 240, 242, 244, 245, 251, 258, 260
Harris, T. R., 184, 185
Harrison, N., 328
Harrison, P. J., 258
Harrow, M., 240, 245, 246, 322
Hart, K., 519
Hart, R., 248
Hartmann, A., 433
Hartmann, E., 492, 606
Hartmann, U., 516
Harvey, A. G., 615, 620, 621, 624

Hasin, D. S., 41, 42, 43, 44, 45, 46, 173, 212, 215
Haslam, N., 23
Hassler, A., 181
Hassman, H., 360, 361
Hastings, T., 587
Hatch, M., 381
Hatcher, S., 447
Hatfield, A. B., 257
Hathaway, S. R., 446
Hatzichristou, D. G., 518
Haug, T. T., 413
Hauger, R., 41
Haughie, S., 528
Hauri, P. J., 603, 609, 612, 618, 620, 621
Havassy, B. E., 46, 55
Haviland, M. G., 431
Haw, C., 240
Hawkins, J. M., 322, 326
Hawthorne, W., 51
Hawton, K. E., 240, 297, 525, 528
Hayhurst, H., 327, 328
Haynes, M. R., 539, 549
Hays, P. A., 44, 104
Hays, R., 297
Hayton, B., 379
Hayward, C., 374, 382, 576, 656
Hayward, P., 242, 327
Haywood, T. W., 45
Hazelton, B. C., 239
Hazelwood, R. R., 542
Hazen, A. L., 15
Headlee, C. P., 221
Healy, E. S., 612, 624
Heath, A. C., 182, 365, 374, 623
Heather, N., 172, 217
Heatherton, T. F., 591, 664
Heaton, J. P., 515
Heaton, R. K., 127, 141, 145, 239, 252
Heerlein, A., 324
Heffron, N. E., 141
Hegedus, A. M., 142, 216, 221

Hegel, M. T., 363
Heil, S. H., 221, 222
Heilbronn, M., 427
Heilman, K. M., 147, 156
Heiman, J. R., 508, 523, 524, 530
Heimberg, R. G., 351, 363, 370
Heinberg, J. L., 572, 584, 586
Heinrichs, D. W., 44
Heinrichs, R. W., 239
Heinssen, R. K., 253
Heintz, G. C., 35, 44, 60
Heinz, A., 213
Heir, R., 376
Heiser, K., 516
Heiser, N., 377
Heiser, W., 431
Hellander, M., 326
Heller, B. R., 450
Heller, T. L., 323
Helzer, J. E., 7, 14, 37, 48, 87, 216, 444, 445
Hemami, S., 416
Hendershot, C. S., 167
Hendricks, A. M., 48
Hendrickse, W., 46
Hendriks, V. M., 223
Hendryx, M. S., 431
Hengeveld, M. W., 519
Heninger, G. R., 332, 359, 366
Henk, H., 364
Henn, F. A., 62
Hennen, J., 41
Henry, C., 331
Henry, J. M., 333
Henry, R. M., 324
Henry, S. E., 589
Henson, C. E., 242, 243
Hepp, U., 536
Hepworth, J., 434
Herald, C., 242
Herbener, E. S., 245, 246
Herbert, J. D., 351, 367, 368
Herbert, M. R., 334
Herd, D., 171, 186

Herman, D. S., 368
Herman, R., 49
Hermansen, L., 142
Herpertz, S. C., 583, 661
Herpertz-Dahlmann, B., 583
Hersen, M., 92, 369, 370, 373
Herz, L. R., 42, 43
Herzog, D. B., 578, 579
Hess, C. W., 605
Hesselbrock, M. A., 172
Hesselbrock, M. N., 42, 43, 182, 183, 185
Hesselbrock, V. M., 42, 53, 58, 182, 183, 185
Hesselink, J. R., 144, 158
Hettema, J., 374
Hewege, S., 425
Heyman, R. A., 141
Hicks, B. M., 213, 645
Hicks, T. V., 364
Hiday, V. A., 47
Higgins, S. T., 7, 221, 222
Higuchi, S., 333
Hildreth, C., 380
Hilgard, E. R., 473, 478, 494
Hill, B., 432
Hill, C. A., 505
Hill, C. L., 112, 115
Hill, E. M., 42
Hill, K., 481, 581
Hill, N., 105
Hill, S. Y., 142, 143, 171
Hillegers, M. H., 323, 329
Hiller, W., 424
Hilton, M. E., 170, 171
Himle, J. A., 42
Himmelhoch, J. M., 331, 477
Himmelstein, D. U., 36
Hines, T. M., 511
Hirsch, M., 331
Hirschfeld, R. M. A., 46, 94, 328, 331
Hirschinger, N. B., 248
Hirshfeld, D. R., 374, 382

Hiss, H., 362
Hlastala, S. A., 324, 326
Hobbes, J., 185
Hoberman, H. M., 295
Hocking, J. S., 49
Hoddes, E., 620, 621
Hodge, S. M., 334
Hodges, L., 365
Hodgings, D., 168
Hodgins, D. C., 224
Hodgins, S., 242, 322, 332
Hodgson, G., 528
Hodgson, R. J., 178, 368
Hodkinson, S., 541
Hodson, S., 432
Hoehn-Saric, R., 361
Hoek, H. W., 575, 576
Hoelscher, T. J., 620
Hofann, S. G., 362
Hoff, R. A., 50
Hoffart, A., 361
Hoffman, E. K., 143
Hoffman, N. G., 43
Hofstede, G., 108
Hogan, M. E., 295, 305, 306, 307
Hohagen, F., 613
Holaway, R. M., 363
Holder, J. M., 213, 220
Holford, T. R., 320
Holland, C. L., 548
Holland, J. C., 298
Holland, L. A., 545
Hollander, E., 384, 419, 423, 481
Hollingshead, A. B., 238
Hollingsworth, M. L., 443
Hollon, S. D., 7
Holmes, P. V., 62
Holt, C. S., 351, 363
Holt, D., 126
Holtzman, D. M., 126
Holzer, C. E., 242
Hommer, D., 334
Hompland, M., 326
Honda, Y., 611
Honig, A., 333

Hoogduin, C., 364
Hooley, J. M., 245, 254, 257, 259, 324
Hooshmand, H., 539
Hope, D. A., 351, 363
Horan, W. P., 174
Horesh, N., 379, 584
Horgan, C., 48
Hornstein, N. L., 489
Hornyak, R., 301
Horowitz, L. M., 638, 639, 641, 643, 644, 649, 650, 657, 658, 660
Horstmann, S., 605, 612
Horwath, E., 372
Horwood, L. J., 213, 382
Hotopf, M., 443
Houck, P. R., 321, 322, 327, 331
Hough, R. L., 51, 242, 261, 294
House, A., 417, 418, 421, 447
Houtveen, J. H., 427
Howanitz, E., 60
Howard, G. S., 5
Howard, R., 244
Howe, M. G., 620, 621
Howes, R. J., 547
Howland, R. H., 332
Hoybye, G., 181
Hoyer, J., 354, 359, 379
Hryniak, M., 432
Hser, Y. I., 210, 224
Hsiao, J. K., 238
Hsieh, S. C., 186
Hsu, L., 237, 294
Hu, L. T., 261
Huang, B., 168, 170
Huang, G., 126
Huang, Y., 224
Huba, G. L., 51
Hublin, C., 611
Hucker, S., 549
Hudson, J. I., 419, 424, 445
Hudson, L., 334
Hudson, S. M., 541, 551
Huffman, J., 548

Hufford, D., 380
Hugdahl, K., 374, 375
Hughes, A., 363
Hughes, C. C., 478, 494
Hughes, D., 353, 378
Hughes, I. C. T., 257, 377
Hughes, J. R., 7
Hughes, M., 34, 36, 37, 39, 221, 292, 299
Hughs, T., 254
Hugo, F. J., 383, 384
Hui, C. H., 105
Huikeshoven, F. J. M., 538
Hull, J. W., 239, 327
Hulter, B., 517
Hultman, O., 181
Humber, K., 239
Hume, J. H., 326
Humphrey, L. L., 584
Humphreys, I., 362
Humphris, G. M., 443
Hunt, G., 168
Hunt, J., 323
Hunter, S. B., 42
Hurd, Y. L., 62
Hurlbert, D. F., 530
Hurlburg, M. S., 242
Hurlbut, S. C., 174
Hurwicz, M. L., 301
Huska, J. A., 368
Hutchings, P. S., 242
Hutchinson, G., 109
Hutchinson, M., 329
Huws, R., 549
Hwang, S., 327
Hyde, T. S., 372
Hyer, L., 362
Hyler, S. E., 410, 660
Hyman, K., 181
Hyman, S. E., 5
Hynes, G., 174

Iacono, W. G., 213, 221, 586, 645
Iannone, V. N., 239
Ingram, R. E., 106
Ingvar, M., 434
Innis, R. B., 333

Insel, T. R., 371, 384, 385
Inskip, H. M., 240
Institute of Medicine, 167, 170, 175
Intelisano, G., 528
International Late-Onset Schizophrenia Group, 244
International Society for the Study of Trauma and Dissociation, 488, 491
Intoccia, V., 19
Intrator, J., 661
Iqbal, Z., 240
Irwin, M., 610
Isaac, M., 444
Isenberg, N., 10, 334
Isidori, A. M., 523, 524, 526
Israel, A. C., 11
Isralowitz, R., 215
Issacowitz, D. M., 295
Ivers, H., 613
Iwamsas, G. Y., 308
Iyengar, S., 320, 323

Jablensky, A., 237, 260
Jackel, L., 370
Jackson, D. N., 635, 646
Jackson, H. F., 234
Jackson, H. J., 240, 256, 665
Jackson, J. S., 4, 19, 424
Jackson, R. L., 90
Jackson-Triche, M. E., 294
Jacob, R. G., 334, 350, 354, 361, 363, 364, 367, 369, 383
Jacob, T., 256
Jacobi, C., 576, 587, 589
Jacobs, C., 584
Jacobs, J. R., 480
Jacobsberg, L. B., 96
Jacobsen, S. E., 212
Jacobson, A., 51, 242
Jahn, H., 186
Jain, A., 527

Jamerson, J. E., 17
James, W., 485
Jamison, K. R., 41, 47, 60, 263, 320, 322, 323
Jamison, R. N., 215
Janata, J. W., 525
Janca, A., 44, 444
Janet, P., 475
Jang, K. L., 20, 21, 476, 646, 648
Jasiukaitis, P., 474
Javaheri, S., 605
Jaworski, T. M., 447
Jeekel, H., 538
Jefferson, J. W., 364, 440
Jellinek, E. M., 166, 172
Jemelka, R. P., 432
Jenike, M. A., 351, 367, 419
Jenkins, E. J., 380
Jensvold, M. F., 185
Jerabek, P. A., 10
Jerrell, J. M., 225
Jerry, M. B., 541, 545
Jervis, G. A., 144
Jeste, D. V., 47, 51, 239
Jimenez, J. M., 258
Jimenez-Gomez, A., 605
Jimerson, D. C., 589, 590
Jin, R., 39, 40, 292, 293
Jindal, R., 332
Jobe, T. H., 245, 246
Jodar, I., 306
Joe, G. W., 210, 225
Johanson, C. E., 222
John, K., 293
Johns, M. W., 620
Johnson, C. C., 413
Johnson, D., 136
Johnson, E. O., 220, 221, 610, 611
Johnson, J. G., 477, 481, 492, 635, 637, 661, 662
Johnson, J. L., 46
Johnson, L. C., 611
Johnson, L. D., 204
Johnson, M. O., 382, 447
Johnson, R. C., 9, 12
Johnson, R. L., 541

Johnson, S., 47, 48, 238, 322, 323, 324, 325, 326, 332, 334, 446, 525
Johnson, T., 327, 328, 664
Johnson, V., 184, 504, 519, 528, 529, 530
Johnson, W. G., 578, 583, 587
Johnstone, B. M., 184
Joiner, T. E., 591
Jones, B. E., 251, 261
Jones, B. M., 185
Jones, D. R., 50
Jones, F. C., 479
Jones, J., 102
Jones, L., 548
Jones, M. K., 185
Jones, M. P., 427
Jones, R., 541
Jones, W., 362
Jones-Hick, L., 302
Jono, R. T., 242
Joober, R., 244
Joostens, P., 413
Jordan, A. D., 546
Jorenby, D. E., 183
Jorgensen, L., 445
Josephson, S., 424
Joshi, S., 478
Joyal, C. C., 47
Joyce, P. R., 43
Joynt, R. J., 131
Judd, F. K., 49
Judd, L. L., 36, 37, 174, 294, 320, 323, 328, 330
Julien, R. M., 204
Junginger, J., 251
Junker, C., 168

Kabakci, E., 532
Kadden, R. M., 175, 218, 368
Kadlec, K. E., 181
Kaelber, C. T., 15, 55
Kagan, J., 374, 382, 654
Kahler, C. W., 53, 204, 214
Kahn, R. J., 350
Kahn, R. S., 263

Kaiser, G., 362
Kales, A., 606, 608, 613, 618, 623, 625
Kales, J. D., 606, 608, 613, 618, 623, 625
Kalichman, S. C., 49
Kalivas, P. W., 5, 332
Kallqvist, A., 181
Kalso, E., 434
Kaltenborn, W. T., 613
Kamal, M., 41
Kamel, W. L., 541
Kamerow, D. B., 612, 615
Kanba, S., 333
Kandel, D. B., 204
Kane, H. S., 47
Kane, J. M., 240
Kaniasty, K., 353
Kanner, L., 137
Kao, A., 522
Kapci, E. G., 306
Kaplan, G. A., 431
Kaplan, H. L., 181
Kaplan, H. S., 505, 527, 528, 529
Kaplan, K., 37, 39
Kaplan, M., 477, 538, 540, 544, 546, 553
Kaplan, R. D., 60
Kaprio, J., 167
Karayiogou, M., 359
Karimi, A., 255
Karkowski, L. M., 318
Karmali, M., 47
Karoly, P., 429
Karson, C. N., 239
Kasch, K. L., 635
Kaschak, E., 505
Kaschka, W. P., 332
Kasen, S., 477, 661
Kashner, T. M., 420, 425
Kaskutas, L. A., 171
Kaszniak, A., 481
Kathol, R. G., 383
Katon, W. J., 413, 415, 432, 449
Katz, D. A., 611
Katz, L. J., 137, 148

Katz, L. S., 45
Katz, R. C., 509
Katzelnick, D., 364
Katz-Garris, L., 549
Kaufman, E., 175
Kaufman, J., 331
Kauhanen, J., 431
Kawachi, I., 298
Kay, S. R., 244, 252, 255
Kaye, W. H., 579, 580, 581, 586, 589
Kazarian, S. S., 620, 621
Kazdin, A. E., 373
Keane, T. M., 42, 362, 368
Kearl, A., 509
Keck, P. E., 41, 45, 321, 322, 323, 326, 332, 419, 445
Keddie, A., 175
Kedem, P., 379
Kee, K., 35, 41, 46
Keefe, R. S. E., 238, 239, 252
Keegan, D., 44
Keener, J. J., 42, 43
Keery, H., 586, 587, 591
Kehoe, C. E., 35, 44, 60
Keifer, F., 186
Keightley, M., 333, 334
Keijsers, G., 364
Keith, S. J., 36, 37, 174, 237, 330, 331
Keitner, G. I., 297, 307
Keller, M. B., 22, 42, 45, 294, 298, 318, 320, 322, 323, 331, 351, 358, 359, 361, 378
Keller, M. D., 46
Keller, R., 483
Kelley, K. W., 433
Kellner, R., 413, 438, 447
Kelly, L., 47
Kelly, M. P., 519
Kelly, R. H., 51
Kelly, T. M., 648
Kemp, R., 242
Kemper, P., 49
Kemperman, I., 334

Kendall, B., 446
Kendell, R. E., 4, 19
Kendell. R. C., 3, 10, 14
Kendler, K. S., 4, 10, 11, 13, 17, 19, 34, 36, 37, 38, 39, 58, 221, 292, 299, 318, 365, 374, 575, 579, 580, 585, 623, 643
Kennedy, C. J., 144, 158
Kennedy, D. N., 333
Kennedy, J. L., 333
Kennedy, S. H., 517
Kenny, M., 485, 486
Kent, D. A., 424, 425
Kern, J. M., 370, 587
Kern, R. S., 239, 252
Kernberg, O., 647, 652
Kerr, N., 327
Keshavan, M. S., 255, 371
Keskimaki, I., 238
Keski-Rahkonen, A., 586
Kessing, L. V., 297
Kessler, R. C., 15, 34, 36, 37, 38, 39, 40, 52, 55, 58, 174, 210, 212, 216, 221, 224, 234, 238, 292, 293, 296, 299, 318, 320, 330, 349, 351, 356, 360, 374, 379, 477
Ketter, T. A., 320, 321, 322, 323, 331, 335
Keuthen, N. J., 36, 419
Key, C. R., 185
Keys, D. J., 358
Khalife, S., 522
Khalsa, H. M., 41
Khan, A., 358
Khanna, S., 352, 378
Khantzian, E. J., 43
Kidorf, M., 43, 224
Kidson, W., 539
Kiehl, K. A., 661
Kihlstrom, J. F., 428, 475
Kilbourne, A. M., 321
Killeen, T. K., 52
Killen, J. D., 374
Killian, K., 525
Kilpatrick, A. C., 544

Kilpatrick, D. G., 45, 353, 368
Kim, C. H., 413, 446
Kim, E. Y., 324, 331
Kim, J. M., 300, 424, 445
Kindermann, S. S., 255, 327, 328, 334
King, D. W., 353
King, H. E., 139
King, L. A., 353
King, M. P., 167
King, R., 656
King, V. L., 43, 224
Kingsberg, S. A., 525
Kinsey, A. C., 506
Kirch, D. G., 263
Kirisci, L., 50
Kirksey, W. A., 370
Kirkwood, C. R., 415
Kirmayer, L. J., 379, 380, 381, 410, 411, 415, 418, 419, 420, 421, 424, 425, 427, 429, 430, 431, 432, 436, 437, 439, 441, 444, 445, 447, 448, 449, 450, 451, 452, 476, 490
Kirov, G., 242, 333
Kirsch, I., 5
Kishi, T., 590
Kissin, B., 142
Kizer, A., 324
Kiziltan, E., 489
Klag, M. J., 611
Klamen, D., 43
Klassen, A. D., 173
Klatsky, A. L., 181
Kleber, H. D., 42, 43, 54
Klein, D. E., 358
Klein, D. F., 4, 8, 9, 60, 248, 350, 360, 383, 384
Klein, D. N., 18, 297, 305, 320, 329, 330, 635
Klein, D. R., 360
Kleindienst, N., 321
Kleinman, A. M., 260, 413, 437, 451
Kleinman, R. M., 329

Klerman, G. L., 288, 293, 322, 331, 418, 419, 425, 428, 429
Kletti, R., 480
Klingemann, H. K., 168
Klinger, E., 365
Klink, M. E., 613
Klosko, J. S., 362, 363, 370, 665
Kloth, G., 516
Klove, H., 145
Kluft, R. P., 478, 488, 489, 491
Klump, K. L., 579, 585, 586
Klunk, W. E., 126
Klusmann, D., 505
Kmetz, G. F., 326
Knapp, M., 234
Knapp, W. P., 44
Knauper, B., 15
Knauper, B., 55
Knight, G. P., 105
Knopik, V. S., 182
Knopp, F. H., 541, 552
Knutelska, M., 480, 481
Knutson, B., 9, 12, 334
Knutsson, A., 612
Ko, G., 263
Kobak, K., 364
Kochman, F. J., 329
Kocsis, J. H., 54, 330, 334
Koele, P., 363, 369
Koenig, H. G., 293, 302
Koerner, J., 587
Kogan, J., 330, 331
Kohn, L. T., 49
Koivisto, P., 126
Kokish, R., 548
Kokkevi, A., 43
Kolada, J. L., 352
Koleva, S., 333
Kolk, A. M., 436
Kolody, B., 294
Konarski, J. Z., 328
Kooiman, C. G., 431
Koopman, C., 473, 474, 480

Kopelman, M. D., 482, 483, 484
Kopelowicz, A., 239
Koppiker, N., 368, 528
Kordon, A., 364
Koretz, D., 40
Korfine, L., 18
Korn, M. L., 213
Korten, A., 237
Koss, M. P., 432
Kostelnik, B., 331
Kosten, T. R., 54
Kostogianni, C., 43
Kotler, M., 379
Kouzis, A. C., 48
Koverola, C., 383
Kowatch, R. A., 321, 326
Kozak, M. J., 362, 368
Kozaric-Kovacic, D., 46
Kozlowski, L. T., 173
Koznar, J., 528
Kraaimaat, F., 362
Kraemer, B., 536
Kraemer, G. U., 381
Kraemer, H. C., 18, 239, 252, 374, 576
Kraemmer, B., 545
Kraeplin, E., 23, 256
Krakow, D. S., 49
Kramer, J., 53
Kramer, M. S., 250
Krames, L., 15, 18
Krane, R. J., 518
Kranier-Fox, R., 383
Kranzler, H. R., 54, 173, 174, 175, 176, 179, 247, 368
Krauss, S. P., 329
Kravitz, H. M., 45
Kremer, E. F., 436
Kring, A. M., 244
Kringlen, E., 633
Kripke, D. F., 621
Krippner, S., 492
Krishnan, B., 187
Krishnan, K. R. R., 10
Krishnan, R., 296
Kriskovich, M., 509
Kristensson, H., 180

Kroenke, K., 301, 302, 415, 417, 424, 434, 436, 444, 449
Kroll, R., 524
Kromelis, M., 326
Krueger, R. B., 538, 540, 544, 546, 553
Krueger, R. F., 10, 11, 18, 21, 55, 56, 57, 213, 635, 645, 662, 663
Kruger, A., 418
Kruger, S., 333
Krupp, L. B., 445
Krychman, M., 521
Krystal, J. H., 18, 61, 484
Kuban, M., 540, 547
Kubin, M., 480
Kubzansky, L. D., 298
Kucera, J., 240
Kuck, J., 239
Kuczenski, R., 333
Kuczmierczyk, A., 413
Kuenssberg, E. V., 417
Kuipers, E., 47, 48, 241, 258
Kujawa, M., 318, 323
Kukleta, M., 360
Kulka, R. A., 353
Kullgren, G., 425
Kunce, J. T., 584
Kundakci, T., 489
Kung, F. Y., 49
Kunovac, J. L., 294
Kuperminc, G. P., 656
Kupfer, D. J., 4, 41, 321, 322, 324, 325, 326, 327, 331, 335, 608, 620, 621
Kupka, R. W., 41, 45, 322, 323
Kurland, L. T., 575
Kushner, H., 216
Kushner, M. G., 42, 52, 58, 63, 174, 212
Kushner, S. F., 241, 255
Kusumakar, V., 326
Kutlesic, V., 583
Kwan, K. K., 115

Laan, E., 510, 524
Labouvie, E., 43, 174
LaBrie, J., 169
Labrum, A. H., 413
Lackey, L. B., 541
Lackner, J. M., 432
Lacks, P., 620, 621
Lacy, T. J., 413
Ladd, C., 384
Ladouceur, R., 354, 358, 363, 615
Lalumiere, M. L., 547, 548
Lam, D. H., 255, 327
Lam, R. W., 325
Lambert, D., 44
Lambert, M. T., 46, 50
Lamparski, D., 370
Lampert, C., 326
Lancaster, J. L., 10
Lance, C. E., 105
Lancrenon, S., 329
Landau, S., 334
Landen, M., 530
Lander, S., 333
Landerman, R., 416, 418
Landmark, J., 47
Landry, L., 517
Lane, R., 333, 334
Lang, A. J., 361
Lang, E., 178
Lang, P. J., 357
Lang, R. A., 539, 548
Lange, A., 363, 369
Langenbucher, J., 43, 174
Langevin, R., 539, 545, 546, 549
Langley, J., 242
Langlois, F., 358, 615
Långström, B., 126
Lanyon, R. I., 539
LaPalme, M., 332
Laporte, D. L., 44
Larco, J. P., 47
Larkin, C., 47
LaRoche, C., 332
Larose, Y., 516
Larossa, G. N., 126

Larsen, G. K., 505
Larson, J., 296
Lashley, K. S., 130
Lask, B., 576
Lasser, K., 36
Last, C. G., 370, 373
Latham, K. S., 418
Lating, J. M., 368
Lauerman, R., 548
Laumann, E. O., 506, 507, 508, 509, 511, 512, 515, 517, 518, 520, 521
Lavie, P., 621
Lavigne, G. J., 609
Lavori, P. W., 45, 298, 323, 331, 335
Lavy, Y., 531
Lawford, B. R., 220, 221
Lawlor, B., 141
Lawrence, A. A., 538
Lawrence, J. S., 370
Lawrence, N. S., 333
Lawrie, S. M., 255, 263
Laws, D. R., 441, 546, 552
Lazarus, A., 480
Lazarus, R., 428
Leadbeater, B. J., 656
Leader, J. B., 635
Leaf, P. J., 48, 174, 320
Leaf, R. J., 238, 261
Leal, D., 50
LeBlanc, M., 611
Lebowitz, B., 335
Lebowitz, M. D., 613
Leboyer, M., 331, 333
Lecci, L., 429
Leckman, A. L., 175
Leckman, J. F., 41, 58, 371, 372
Lecrubier, Y., 354, 358
Lee, C. S., 49
Lee, D. J., 185
Lee, K., 19, 20
Lee, R., 221
Lee, S. H., 529
Lee, S. Y., 126
Le Fauve, C. E., 173, 174, 175, 179

Leff, J., 240, 254, 418
Lefley, H. P., 257, 260
Legatt, M. E., 477
Legros, J. J., 536
Lehman, A. F., 45, 46, 247, 248, 255, 511, 521
Lehman, C. L., 11, 361, 362, 368
Lehmann, A., 511, 521
Leibenluft, E., 321, 325, 329, 330, 331
Leiblum, S. R., 510
Leigh, G. L., 176, 180
Lemoine, P., 609
Lencz, T., 239
Lennox, R., 334
Lenoir, M. E., 45
Lenox, M. S., 326
Lenzenweger, M. F., 18, 664
Leo, G. I., 174, 177
Leon, A. C., 42, 45, 54, 294, 318, 320, 323, 330
Leonard, D. M., 302, 490
Leonard, H., 323, 384, 385
LePage, J. P., 50
Lepine, J. P., 354, 358, 372
LeResche, L., 418, 426
Leslie, D., 238
Lesnick, L. A., 221
Lesser, I. M., 366, 381
Lesser, S. R., 650
Letourneau, E. J., 548
Leung, A., 244
Leung, F., 585
Levav, I., 238
Levene, J., 549
Levenson, J. S., 548
Leventhal, R. M., 358
Leverich, G. S., 41, 45, 322, 323, 331
Levin, H. S., 135, 157
Levin, S. M., 551
Levine, J., 41, 180
Levine, J. B., 16
Levine, M. P., 586, 587, 591

Levinson, D. F., 35, 41, 46, 250
Levitt, E. E., 541, 542, 545
Levitt, J. L., 580
Levitt, M. M., 250
Lev-Sagie, A., 531
Levy, K. N., 646, 665
Levy, R., 244
Lewin, M., 370
Lewine, R., 238
Lewinsohn, P. M., 204, 295, 320, 330, 576
Lewis, C., 41
Lewis, D. A., 45
Lewis, D. O., 478
Lewis, M., 478
Lewis-Fernández, R., 12, 477, 478, 493
Lezak, M. D., 179
Li, D., 361
Li, J., 262
Li, L. C., 112, 115
Liberman, R. P., 239, 242, 245, 252, 253, 258, 259, 260
Lichstein, K. L., 612, 615, 619, 622, 624
Lidbeck, J., 425
Liddell, A., 358
Liddle, P. F., 238, 255
Lieb, R., 373
Lieber, C. S., 185
Lieberman, J. A., 238, 240, 243, 255, 263
Liebowitz, M. R., 12, 358, 360, 361, 363, 365, 369, 379
Liese, B. S., 42, 43, 44
Lightbody, S., 541
Lilienfeld, S. O., 9, 11, 112, 115, 490
Lim, K. O., 255
Lin, K. M., 184
Lin, N., 220
Lincoln, E. C., 260
Lindamer, L., 47, 51
Lindenmayer, J., 244
Lindner, S., 489

Lindsay, M., 362
Linehan, M. M., 16, 648
Linet, O. I., 526
Link, B. G., 238
Links, P. S., 18
Linszen, D. H., 45
Liotti, M., 10
Lipinski, J. F., 249
Lipman, L. S., 489
Lippa, C., 141
Lipschitz, D. S., 242, 477
Lipton, D. S., 181
Lishman, W. A., 413
Liskow, B., 43
List, T., 427
Litten, R. Z., 173, 174, 175, 179, 180
Littlewood, R., 492
Littner, M., 621, 622
Litwin, E. M., 378
Litwin, R., 481
Litz, B. T., 368
Liu, J., 38, 39
Liu, W. T., 172
Liu, Y., 529
Livesley, W. J., 12, 16, 19, 20, 21, 476, 635, 646, 648, 660
Lloyd, G. G., 363
Lo, T., 260
Lo, W. H., 260
Lobo, R. A., 524
Locke, B. Z., 36, 37, 174, 330
Locke, D. C., 102
Loehlin, J. C., 24
Loennqvist, J., 349
Loewenstein, R. J., 474, 482, 484, 485, 486, 489, 491
Loftus, E. F., 484, 485
Loftus, J., 508
Lohoff, F. W., 167
Lohr, J. B., 239, 333, 334
Long, J. S., 508
Longabaugh, R., 175, 216
Longley, S. L., 448
Longshore, D., 186
Lonnqvist, J. K., 56

Looper, K., 418, 424, 432, 441, 444
Lopez, A. D., 234, 634
Lopez, L. S., 333
Lopez, O. L., 141
LoPiccolo, J., 524, 525, 530
Lopresti, B. J., 126
Loranger, A. W., 94, 95, 96, 635, 659
Lorea, C. F., 204
Loring, M., 261
Lotrich, F. E., 333
Lousberg, H., 378
Loveday, W. A. L., 174
Lovell, M. R., 135
Lowenstein, G., 222
Lozano, B. L., 324, 325
Lubar, J. O., 213, 220
Lubar, J. R., 213, 220
Lubinski, D., 24
Lubman, D. I., 223
Luborsky, L., 54
Lucas, A. R., 575
Lucerini, S., 52
Luchins, D., 248
Luciano, D., 432
Luckenbaugh, D. A., 45, 323
Ludman, E. J., 327
Lugaresi, E., 611, 612
Lundberg, P. O., 517
Lunde, I., 505
Lundgren, L. M., 225
Lundh, L. G., 431
Lupo, L., 528
Lupson, V., 334
Luria, A. R., 129, 152
Lusiardo, M., 263
Lussier, J. P., 221, 222
Lydiard, R. B., 330, 331, 350, 361
Lye, T. C., 134, 158
Lynam, D. R., 17, 22, 23
Lynn, J., 473, 492
Lynn, S. J., 5, 483, 486, 492
Lynskey, M. T., 41, 43, 213

Lyon, H. M., 324
Lyons, J., 174
Lyons, J. A., 42
Lyons, M. J., 220, 358

Ma, L., 529
MacCarthy, B., 295, 296, 307
Macciardi, F., 19
MacDonald, R., 178
Mach, R. H., 126
Machado, J. C., 141
Macias, C., 50
MacInnes, I., 517, 526
Mackinaw-Koons, B., 327, 328
MacKinnon, A., 239
MacKinnon, D. F., 47
MacLean, D. G., 242
MacLeod, A. K., 429
MacPhee, D. C., 525
MacPherson, L., 167
Madden, K. S., 434
Madden, P. A. F., 182
Madsen, C. H., 370
Maes, L., 308
Maes, M., 308
Magaña, C. B., 254
Magee, W. J., 349, 351, 358, 360, 379
Mager, D., 44, 212
Maglione, M. A., 210
Magni, G., 418, 426, 427
Magnusson, P., 181
Magruder, K. M., 15
Magura, S., 53, 181
Maher, B. A., 579
Maher, J. J., 181
Mahurin, R. K., 10, 239, 333, 334
Maidenberg, E., 362
Maier, W., 354
Maina, G., 378
Maisto, S. A., 176, 180, 248
Maj, M., 590
Malamud, M., 552
Malatesta, V. J., 364
Malcarne, V. L., 106

Malchy, L., 45
Malcolm, P. B., 547
Malcom, R., 330, 331
Maletzky, B. M., 539, 541, 546, 551, 552
Malgady, R. G., 109
Malhi, G., 382
Malinckrodt, B., 587
Malison, R. T., 18, 333
Malkoff-Schwartz, S., 324, 325, 326
Malla, A. K., 240, 243, 244
Mallinger, A. G., 327, 331
Malone, K. M., 648
Malthiery, Y., 333
Mamiya, L. H., 260
Mancill, R. B., 11
Mancini, C., 360
Mancuso, D. M., 359
Mandell, W., 173
Mangalore, R., 234
Mangine, S., 96
Manis, M., 430
Manki, H., 333
Manley, C., 238
Manley, S., 181
Manly, D. T., 493
Mann, A., 425, 429
Manschreck, T. C., 251
Marangell, L. B., 323, 335
Marazziti, D., 361
March, J., 385
Marchetti, M., 418
Marchione, K., 370
Marchione, N., 370
Marcos, L. R., 381
Marcotte, D., 225, 239
Mardekian, J., 361
Marder, S. R., 239, 240, 252
Marengo, J., 245
Maret, S., 623
Margolese, H. C., 45
Margolin, A., 225
Margraf, J., 370, 372
Marin, G., 105, 106
Marino, L., 9
Marion, B., 34

Markey, C. N., 585
Markides, K. S., 185
Markon, K. E., 10, 11, 18, 21
Marks, I. M., 358, 362, 368
Marlatt, G. A., 167, 173, 178, 183
Marler, M., 656
Marmar, C. R., 44, 474, 478
Marracos, R. P., 240, 243
Marriotta, M. J., 370
Marsch, L. A., 222
Marsden, J., 215, 218
Marsh, A., 181
Marsh, G. R., 624
Marshall, G. N., 105
Marshall, J., 47, 48, 421, 425, 440
Marshall, L. E., 384
Marshall, V. R., 518
Marshall, W. L., 540, 541, 543, 547, 549, 551
Martiadis, V., 590
Martin, C. C., 10, 372
Martin, C. K., 575, 583
Martin, J. B., 157
Martin, M., 432
Martin, N. G., 182, 365, 623
Martin, P. R., 493, 528
Martin, R. L., 420, 421, 427
Martines, K. A., 214
Martinez, D., 334
Martinez-Aran, A., 41, 327
Martínez-Taboas, A., 490
Marttunen, M., 349
Marusic, A., 46
Marwaha, S., 238
Marx, E. M., 306
Marzuk, P. M., 47
Masalehdan, A., 322
Masand, P. S., 294
Maser, J. D., 11, 42, 45, 294, 318, 322, 323

Masheb, R. M., 582
Masi, G., 331
Masini, C. V., 62
Mason, F. L., 544
Massoth, D., 432
Masters, W. H., 504, 519, 528, 529, 530
Masterton, T., 212
Mathis, C. A., 126
Mathis, J., 605
Matsuda, K. T., 381
Mattes, J. A., 250
Matthews, C. G., 145
Matthews, J. K., 541
Mattia, J. I., 658, 659
Mattick, R. P., 364, 368, 368
Mattoo, S. J., 46
Mattson, M. E., 175
Matus, Y. E., 105
Maurice, W. L., 506, 508, 515
Mavissakalian, M., 366, 367, 369
Mavreas, V., 212
May, A., 261
May, C., 443
Mayberg, H. S., 10, 333, 334
Mayer, E., 449
Mayeux, R., 486
Mayman, M., 430
Maynard, C., 48
Mayo, J. A., 45
Mazel, R., 294
Mazer, N. A., 517
Mazure, C. M., 255
Mazzeo, S. E., 584, 585
McAllister-Williams, R. H., 326
McBride, P. A., 334
McCabe, M. P., 523
McCarthy, E., 327
McCaul, M. E., 225
McCaulay, D., 325
McClarty, B., 383
McClellan, J., 329
McCloskey, M. S., 661
McCloud, A., 47

McClure, R. J., 255
McConaghy, N., 539, 543, 544, 545
McCormick, D., 36
McCormick, R. V., 245
McCrae, C., 615, 624
McCrae, R. R., 14, 17, 18, 20, 21, 635, 636, 660
McCreary, B. A., 587
McCrone, P., 48
McCusker, C. G., 223
McCutchen, J. A., 144, 158
McDaniel, S. H., 436, 441, 448
McDavis, R. J., 102, 112
McDermut, W., 659
McDonald, C., 255, 332
McDougle, C. J., 361
McDowell, I., 443
McElroy, S. L., 41, 45, 322, 323, 326, 419, 538
McEvoy, J. P., 238, 241
McEvoy, L., 37
McFall, R. M., 47, 370
McFarland, B. H., 326
McGhee, D. E., 223
McGinnis, S., 10
McGlashan, T. H., 22, 244, 635, 636, 645, 646, 663, 664, 665
McGlynn, F. D., 369, 375
McGonagle, K. A., 34, 36, 37, 38, 39, 174, 210, 292, 293, 299
McGrath, D., 178
McGrath, E., 7
McGrath, R. E., 446
McGue, M., 182, 213, 221, 586, 645
McGuffin, P., 256, 331, 332
McGurk, S. R., 234
McHorney, C. A., 611
McHugo, G. J., 50, 54, 249
McInnis, M. G., 47
McIntyre, R. S., 328
McKay, D., 445

McKay, J. R., 176
McKay, M., 413
McKee, B., 548
McKeith, I., 141
McKenna, T., 214
McKenzie, D. P., 417
McKenzie, K., 109, 238
McKibbon, C. L., 254
McKinley, J. B., 518
McKinley, J. C., 446
McKinnon, K., 49
McLean, P. D., 362
McLellan, A. T., 41, 54, 216, 248
McLeod, C. C., 425
McLeod, D. R., 361
McMahon, F. J., 47
McMahon, R. P., 239
McManis, S. E., 413
McMillan, C. A., 612
McMillan, D., 609
McMurray, J., 301
McNab, C. E., 370
McNally, R. J., 358, 359, 375, 377, 378
McNiel, D. E., 47
McQueen, L. E., 7
McRee, B., 215
McWilliams, N., 638, 640
Mead, L. A., 611
Meador-Woodruff, J. H., 36
Meagher, S. E., 214
Meana, M., 413
Mechanic, D., 262, 427, 430
Mednick, S. A., 242
Meehl, P. E., 18
Melchert, T. P., 54
Melchior, L. A., 51
Meller, P. J., 101
Mellinger, C. D., 611
Mellman, T. A., 609, 618
Meloy, M. J., 334
Meltzer, H. Y., 322
Melzack, R., 427, 438, 443, 447
Mena, I., 549
Mendelson, W. B., 608

Mendlewicz, J., 52, 324
Mendlowicz, M. V., 240, 243
Mendlowitz, D. R., 620, 621
Menezes, P. R., 47, 48
Menkes, D. B., 332
Mennin, D., 331, 333
Merali, A., 297
Mercante, D. E., 359
Mercer, J. R., 112
Mercer-McFadden, C., 54, 249
Merckelbach, H., 536
Mérette, C., 611
Merica, H., 625
Merikangas, K. R., 36, 37, 38, 39, 40, 41, 43, 58, 63, 174, 292, 293, 299, 372
Merluzzi, T. V., 370
Merriam, A. E., 255, 263
Merskey, H., 47, 414, 418, 489, 490
Mervielde, I., 20
Meston, C., 516
Mesulam, M. M., 129
Metcalf, C. E., 49
Metz, C. W., 584
Metz, M. E., 528
Metzger, D., 216
Metzger, R. L., 368
Metzke, C. W., 584
Metzler, T., 478
Meyer, B., 324, 325
Meyer, G. G., 413
Meyer, J. K., 544, 545
Meyer, J. M., 220
Meyer, R. E., 18, 42, 43, 175
Meyer, T. J., 368
Meyer, W., 353, 536, 537, 538
Meyers, J. K., 11, 42, 43, 212
Meyers, R. G., 545
Mezzich, J. E., 41, 43, 477, 492, 636, 655
Michael, A., 325

Michael, C. O., 238
Michael, J. L., 42
Michael, R. T., 506
Michaels, S., 506
Michel, A., 536
Michelson, L. K., 370, 473
Mick, E., 329
Midanik, L., 173
Miele, G. M., 6, 8, 215
Mijch, A. M., 49
Miklowitz, D. J., 320, 321, 322, 323, 324, 327, 328, 331, 335
Miles, D. R., 167, 213, 220
Miles, K. M., 58, 244
Millepiedi, S., 331
Miller, A. L., 239
Miller, B. L., 549
Miller, E. N., 158
Miller, I. W., 297, 303, 324
Miller, J. D., 22, 23
Miller, K. J., 43, 174
Miller, M., 41, 368
Miller, N. S., 43, 536
Miller, P. M., 369
Miller, R. E., 139
Miller, W. R., 167, 172, 175, 177, 179, 180, 216, 217, 218
Millon, C., 660
Millon, T., 214, 638, 646, 649, 650, 652, 654, 656, 660
Mills, K., 432
Mills, T., 242
Milstein, V., 478, 482, 484, 489, 491
Mineka, S., 11, 375, 376
Miner, C. H., 53
Minichiello, W. E., 358, 367
Minks-Brown, C., 59, 174, 212, 224
Minshew, N. J., 137
Minsky, S., 110
Mintun, M. A., 126

Mintz, J., 239, 323, 327, 332
Mintzer, J., 141
Minuchin, S., 583
Miotto, K., 215
Mirabella, R., 362
Miranda, J., 106, 298, 302, 307
Mirin, S. M., 42
Mirsky, A. F., 146
Mishkin, M., 136
Mishler, E. G., 256
Miskien, T., 110
Mitchell, J. D., 432
Mitchell, J. E., 580
Mitchell, K. S., 584
Mitchell, P., 382
Mittelman, M., 545
Miyahara, S., 320, 321, 323, 330, 331
Miyamoto, S., 255, 258
Moak, D. H., 173, 174, 175, 179, 185
Modesto-Lowe, V., 173, 174, 175, 179
Moeller, F. G., 325
Moffitt, T. E., 46, 56, 57, 242, 662
Mogg, K., 223
Moggi, F., 168
Mohamed, S., 240
Mohamud, S., 114
Mohr, J. W., 541, 544, 545
Mohr, P., 242
Moilanen, I., 167
Molin, C., 413
Molina, C. W., 186
Molinder, I., 546
Moller, H., 321, 328
Moller, M. B., 383
Molnar, C., 661
Mombour, W., 96
Monahan, J., 47, 242
Monastra, V. J., 213, 220
Money, J., 538
Monga, M., 509, 527
Monk, T. H., 325, 327
Monoaghan, E., 326

Monroe, S. M., 318, 323
Monson, R. A., 420, 437
Monteiro, M. G., 52, 62, 215, 218
Monteleone, P., 590
Montero, I., 262
Montgomery, D., 370
Montgomery, P., 326
Montgomery, S. A., 301, 361
Monti, P. M., 168, 218
Montoya, I. D., 215
Moore, E. A., 9, 12
Moore, H., 263
Moore, J. D., 286, 308
Moore, P., 610
Moore, R. D., 225
Moore, T. M., 214, 370
Moos, B. S., 254
Moos, R. H., 54, 173, 254
Morales, A., 515, 518
Morales-Dorta, J., 261
Moreci, P., 331
Moreschi, C., 418, 427
Morey, L. C., 22, 636, 642, 660
Morgan, A. H., 476
Morgan, M. Y., 185
Morgell, R., 181
Morgenstern, J., 43, 174
Morin, C. M., 611, 612, 613, 614, 615, 618, 619, 620, 621, 622, 623, 624, 626
Mormont, C., 536
Morrell, W., 326, 584
Morris, E. F., 107
Morris, J. C., 126
Morris, T. L., 358
Morrison, J., 432
Morrison, R. L., 35, 41, 46, 244, 252, 253
Morriss, R., 327, 328
Morrow, L. A., 125
Morton, W. A., 44
Moss, K. L., 608
Mostofsky, D. I., 428
Moulis, M., 234

Mouren-Simeoni, M., 372
Mowbray, C. T., 212
Mowrer, O. H., 375
Mowry, B. J., 250
Mucci, M., 331
Mudar, P., 184
Mueller, T. I., 42, 45, 294, 318, 320, 323
Muenz, L. R., 44
Mueser, K. T., 35, 41, 46, 51, 54, 57, 58, 59, 60, 174, 234, 239, 253, 370
Mufson, L., 372
Muglia, P., 333
Muir, W., 328
Mukerji, V., 427
Mulder, R., 212
Mulhall, J. P., 529
Mullins-Sweatt, S. N., 17, 19, 20, 21
Mulsant, B. H., 294, 298
Mulvey, E. P., 47
Mumford, D. B., 451
Mumford, J., 180
Munchau, N., 362
Mundo, E., 333
Mundy, E., 331
Munjack, D. J., 526
Munk-Jorgensen, P., 42, 238
Munoz, R. F., 5, 7, 106, 289, 307
Murakami, S. R., 172
Muramatsu, T., 333
Murdock, T. B., 362
Murnen, S. K., 588, 590
Murphy, C., 36
Murphy, D., 178, 361, 384
Murphy, F. C., 325
Murphy, H. B. M., 260
Murphy, M. T., 370, 420, 444
Murphy, W. D., 539, 545, 549
Murphy-Eberenz, K. P., 583
Murray, C. J. L., 234, 634

Murray, R. M., 19, 109, 180, 238, 332
Murrin, M., 242
Musso, F., 590
Musso, R., 590
Myers, C. P., 45, 46, 247, 248
Myers, J. K., 318
Myers, M. G., 167, 661
Myou, R., 436, 448
Myrick, H., 47, 49
Myslobodsky, M. S., 146
Mystkowski, J. L., 361

Nace, E. P., 43
Nahas, Z., 661
Najavitis, L. M., 44, 45, 49
Nakajima, S., 251
Naranjo, C. A., 181
Narrow, W. E., 15, 237
Nasrallah, H. A., 145, 158
Natelson, B. H., 446
Nathan, P. E., 111
Nathan, S. G., 510
National Commission on Sleep Disorders Research, 612
National Institute of Mental Health, 318
National Institute on Alcohol Abuse and Alcoholism, 170, 171, 172, 176
National Institute on Drug Abuse, 171
National Institutes of Health, 294
National Sleep Foundation, 611
National Transportation Safety Board, 612
Naveh, G., 238
Nay, W. T., 368
Nayak, D., 250
Naylor, M. W., 329
Naylor, S. L., 157, 329
Nbdimie, O. K., 50

Neal, A. M., 186, 379
Neal-Barnett, A., 380
Neale, J. M., 32
Neale, M. C., 11, 13, 220, 221, 374
Negrete, J. C., 44, 45
Negro, P. J., 493
Neighbors, B. D., 221
Neighbors, H. W., 186, 380
Neils, J., 151
Neiman, J., 179
Neisser, U., 24
Neiswanger, K., 305
Neitzert Semler, C., 620, 621
Nelson, C. B., 34, 36, 37, 38, 39, 174, 224, 292, 299, 330
Nelson, E. C., 182
Nelson, L. M., 141
Nelson, M., 261
Nelson-Jones, R., 115
Nemeroff, C., 384, 591
Nemiah, J. C., 475
Neraas, K., 432
Nesse, R. M., 358
Nestadt, G., 359, 371, 450
Nesvacil, L. J., 528
Netemeyer, S. B., 582, 583
Neuchterlein, K. H., 239, 252
New, A. S., 648
Newcomb, M. D., 204
Newel, R., 51
Newman, D. L., 46, 56, 57, 578, 662
Newman, L., 240
Newman, M. G., 362, 368
Newman, S. C., 352
Neziroglu, F., 368, 445
Nezu, A. M., 296
Nezworski, M. T., 112, 115
Ng, H. M., 656
Nguyen, T. D., 261

Niaura, R. S., 36, 168
Nicastro, A., 528
Nicholas, M. K., 448
Nicholls, D., 576
Nicholls, T. L., 645
Nichols, D. S., 105, 106
Nichols, H. R., 546
Nichols, J. R., 221
Nickel, E. J., 43
Nickelsburg, M. J., 334
Nickless, C. J., 175
Niculescu, A. B., 333
Nidecker, M., 51
Nielsen, T. A., 606, 624
Nielson, S., 575, 576, 578
Nierenberg, A. A., 46, 323, 330, 331, 335
Nieto, F. J., 605
Nijenhuis, E. R., 475, 484, 494
Nijman, H., 536
Nikolov, I., 333
Nilsson, C. G., 413
Nimnuan, C., 416
Nino-Murcia, G., 611
Nishith, P., 224, 363
Nitschke, J. B., 333
Noble, E. P., 220, 221
Noda, A., 18
Nofzinger, E. A., 608, 625
Noguchi, T., 251
Nolan, K. A., 242
Nolan, W. A., 45
Nolen, W. A., 41, 320, 322, 323, 329
Nolen-Hoeksema, S., 293, 296, 449
Noll, D. C., 255
Noll, J. A., 176
Noonan, M., 422
Noordsy, D. L., 174
Nordahl, H. M., 652
Nordberg, A., 126
Nordentoft, M., 240
Noriega-Dmitri, R., 370
Norman, P., 571, 578
Norman, R. M., 244
Normand, S. T., 50

Norquist, G. S., 15, 55
Norris, F. H., 353
Norten, S., 432
North, C. S., 86, 87, 490
Norton, G. R., 44, 358, 368, 489
Norton, R. G., 174
Nothen, M. M., 519
Nowakowska, C., 322
Nowinski, J., 172
Noyes, R., 357, 359, 366, 371, 372, 418, 422, 433, 444, 448, 480
Nuechterlein, K. H., 245, 258, 323
Nurnberger, J. I., 53, 58
Nusbaum, M. R., 508, 509, 512
Nussbaum, P. D., 157, 481
Nutting, A., 220, 221

Obermeyer, W. H., 608
O'Boyle, M., 536
Obremski-Brandon, K., 591
O'Brien, B. E., 45
O'Brien, C. P., 54
O'Brien, G. T., 370
O'Brien, J., 141
O'Calleghan, E., 47, 238
Ocampo, K. A., 105
O'Carroll, R., 523, 549
O'Connell, R. A., 45
O'Connor, B. P., 20, 22
O'Connor, D., 546
O'Connor, K. P., 413
OConnor, M., 578
O'Donnell, D., 331
O'Donnell, W. E., 173
O'Donohue, W. T., 519
O'Donovan, M. C., 258
Oei, T. P. S., 174
O'Fallon, W. M., 575
O'Farrell, T. J., 180, 182, 218
Office of Applied Studies, 210

Office of National Drug Control Policy, 201
Offord, D. R., 18
Ogawa, J. R., 476
Ogden, C. A., 333
Ogloff, J. R. P., 645
Ogrinc, F. G., 526
O'Hara, R., 18
Ohayon, M. M., 609, 611, 612, 615
Ohman, A., 375
Ohrbach, R., 427
Ojehagen, A., 174, 175
Öjesjö, L., 210
Okazaki, S., 103, 106
O'Keane, V., 304
Oldham, J. M., 22, 94, 633, 635, 655, 663
Oldman, A., 590
Oldridge, M. L., 257
O'Leary, D., 299
Oliveau, D., 351
Oliveto, A. H., 7
Olivier, B., 519
Olmstead, E. M., 612
Olofsson, A., 181
Olson, D. R., 17
Olsson, E., 181
Olvera, R. L., 334
O'Malley, P. M., 204, 424
O'Malley, W. B., 446
Omu, N., 47
O'Neill, K., 43
Ono, Y., 96
Operskalski, B., 327
Opler, L. A., 50, 252, 255
Orav, E. J., 410
Orellana, C., 624
Orff, H., 625
Orford, J., 168, 175
Orholm, M., 181
Orlando, M., 105
Ormel, J., 323, 329
Orosan, P., 426, 448
Ortiz, V., 381
Orvaschel, H., 320, 373, 444
Osborn, C., 541, 545

Osher, F. C., 46, 60, 174, 245
Oslin, D. W., 167
Ostacher, M. J., 46, 323
Ostafin, D. B., 223
O'Sullivan, C., 541
Othmer, E., 42, 43, 44, 640
Othmer, S., 640
Ottina, K., 157
Otto, M. W., 46, 323, 330, 331, 335, 359, 363, 364, 365, 418
Ouimette, P. C., 45, 54
Overall, J. E., 252
Overholser, J. C., 656
Overstreet, D. H., 62
Owen, M. J., 256, 258, 333
Owen, R. R., 46
Ozarow, B. J., 369
Ozturk, E., 489

Paavola, P., 47
Pack Brown, S., 102
Paddock, S., 42, 49
Padgett, D. K., 261
Padilla, J., 105, 106
Padma-Nathan, H., 526, 527
Paez, P., 331
Páez-Agraz, F., 478
Pagano, M. E., 664
Page, A. C., 20, 21, 357
Page, I. J., 549
Pages, K. P., 46, 47
Paik, A., 506, 507
Paitich, D., 539, 546
Pakianathan, I., 12, 477, 480
Pal, H., 215
Palacios, S., 51
Palfai, T. P., 223
Pallanti, S., 378, 379
Palmer, B. W., 239, 240
Palmstierna, T., 214
Pandina, R. J., 184
Pankratz, V. S., 240
Paolo, A. M., 489

Para, M. F., 145, 158
Paradis, C., 381
Paramon, G., 327
Pardini, J. F., 135
Pardoen, D., 324
Paris, J., 427, 476, 648, 661, 662, 665
Park, N., 296
Parker, G., 382
Parker, J. D. A., 431
Parkes, J. D., 605
Parra, F., 260
Parr-Davis, G., 327
Parrish, R. T., 358
Parron, D. L., 115
Parrott, B., 238
Parsons, E. B., 261
Parsons, O. A., 54, 142, 179
Partinen, M., 611, 612
Partonen, T., 56
Pasini-Hill, D., 548
Patel N. C., 321
Patel, J., 323
Pato, M. T., 361
Patrice, H., 489
Patrick, C. J., 213, 261, 645
Patrick, D., 548
Patterson, D., 324, 325, 326
Patterson, M. B., 34
Patterson, T. L., 254
Pattison, E. M., 166, 167
Pattison, P. E., 240
Patton, G. K., 363
Paulosky, C. A., 582, 583
Pauls, D. L., 41, 58, 371
Paulsen, J. S., 239, 251
Paulus, M. P., 333
Pavuluri, M. N., 329
Pawlikowska, T., 416
Pawluck, D.E., 575, 576
Paxton, S. J., 587
Paykel, E., 325, 327, 328
Payne, J., 240, 243, 244
Payne, K. A., 522, 547
Pazzaglia, P. J., 325
Peabody, C. G., 242

Pedersen, E., 169
Pedraza, M., 168
Peele, R., 16
Peele, S., 5, 168
Pelayo, R., 605
Pelosi, A., 429
Pelton, S., 296
Pemberton, J. S., 446
Pendelton, L., 656
Penick, E. C., 42, 43, 44
Penn, D. L., 238, 240, 241, 243, 253, 261, 262
Pennebaker, J. W., 426, 427, 431, 449
Penninkilampi-Kerola, V., 167
Peralta, V., 18
Perelman, M. A., 520, 523, 524, 526, 527, 529
Perez, M., 258
Perez-Arce, P., 186
Perez-Stable, E. J., 105, 106
Perkins, D. O., 238, 240, 243
Perkonnigg, A., 34
Perlin, M. L., 143, 625
Perlis, R. H., 323
Perloff, R., 24
Perlstein, W. M., 255
Pernet, A., 446
Perrine, K., 432
Perry, A., 327
Perugi, G., 328, 329, 331, 359
Perugini, M., 17, 21
Peters, J. M., 539
Peters, L. A., 212, 223
Peters, R., 216
Peterson, C., 296
Peterson, E. L., 42
Peterson, R. A., 377
Petersson, B., 180
Petersson, K. M., 434
Petras, L., 620, 621
Petronis, A., 333
Petronis, K. R., 204, 222
Petrovic, P., 434
Pettegrew, J. W., 255

Pettit, A. R., 286, 296
Peziosi, T. J., 298
Pfohl, B., 93, 94, 659
Phalet, K., 114
Pham, M., 325
Phan, K. L., 661
Phares, V., 584, 585
Phelps, G., 180
Phelps, J. S., 527
Phillips, K. A., 11, 324, 419, 423, 424, 445, 448
Phillips, L., 516, 527
Phillips, M. L., 333, 334
Phillips, R., 620, 621
Phillips, S. D., 245, 262
Pickens, R. W., 167, 220, 221, 225
Pickering, R. P., 36, 37, 38, 39, 48
Pidlubney, S., 44
Pigeon-Reesor, H., 413
Pigott, T. A., 384
Pigrim, H., 362
Pihl, R. O., 42, 61
Pilgrim, D., 234
Pilkonis, P., 41, 43
Pilowsky, I., 429, 444, 446, 447
Pincus, A. L., 635, 653, 660
Pincus, H. A., 6, 7, 8, 10, 11, 13, 14, 16, 286, 296, 321
Pincus, J. H., 478
Pincus, T., 446
Pine, D. S., 329, 330, 331
Pinkham, A., 240
Piper, A., 489, 490
Piper, W. E., 665
Pitschel-Walz, G., 254
Pizzagalli, D., 333
Planells, R., 333
Platman, S. R., 301
Playfer, J., 141
Pliszka, S., 334
Plotsky, P., 384
Plum, T. B., 212
Plutchik, R., 60, 301
Podell, K., 135

Pohorecky, L. A., 184
Poland, R. E., 381
Polcin, D. L., 54
Poldrugo, F., 47, 655
Polich, J. M., 173
Policy, S. I. F. H., 170
Polinsky, M. L., 210
Pollack, M. H., 46, 330, 331, 359, 361, 363, 365, 366
Pollio, C., 323
Pollock. B. G., 333
Pols, H., 378
Pomeroy, C., 579, 581
Pomeroy, W. B., 543
Ponterotto, J. G., 101, 107, 116
Poortinga, J., 543
Pope, H. G., 249, 419, 445
Porjesz, B., 142
Portera, L., 54, 330
Posner, S. F., 105, 106, 114
Post, R. M., 41, 45, 322, 323, 328, 331
Posternak. M. A., 318
Potash, J. B., 47
Potter, J., 295, 296, 307
Potter, W. Z., 323
Powell, B. J., 42, 43, 44, 261
Powell, G. E., 544
Powell, R., 430
Powers, K. I., 211
Pozzato, G., 185
Prasad, K. V., 492, 493
Prescott, C. A., 11, 221, 374
Preston, K. L., 219
Preston, L. K., 505
Pribor, E. E., 475
Price, J. C., 126
Price, L. H., 11, 361, 365, 369
Price, R. H., 212
Price, R. K., 417, 434
Pridal, C. G., 524
Prien, R. F., 323

Primuaux, S. D., 62
Prior, M., 248
Prochaska, J. O., 217
Proenza, M. A., 333, 334
Prosser, D., 48
Proulx, S., 528
Prusoff, B. A., 41, 42, 58, 293, 372
Pruzinsky, T., 357, 450
Pryor, J. L., 528
Pryzbeck, T. R., 37, 48, 635
Puffett, A., 484
Puig-Antich, J., 331
Pukall, C. F., 522
Pull, C., 96, 212
Punjabi, N. M., 607
Purdon, C. L., 370
Putkonen, A., 47
Putnam, F. W., 428, 473, 476, 477, 489, 491
Puzantian, V., 366

Qin, P., 240
Quadflieg, N., 578, 583
Quan, S. F., 613
Quattrocki, E., 36
Quian, Y., 305
Quigley, B. M., 183
Quigley, K. S., 428
Quigley, L. A., 55, 183
Quillian, R. E., 624
Quinlivan, R., 245
Quinsey, V. L., 547, 548
Quint, D., 605

Rabinowitz, J., 351
Rabins, P. V., 244
Racagni, G., 52
Racenstein, J. M., 240
Rachman, S. J., 368, 369, 375, 376, 377, 550
Rada, R. T., 413
Radloff, L. S., 301
Radtke, R. A., 624
Rae, D. S., 15, 36, 37, 55, 174, 212, 237, 293, 330
Raimo, E. B., 62
Raine, A., 239, 661

Raistrick, D., 178
Rajendra, P. N., 378
Rakfeldt, J., 488
Ralph, R., 44
Raman, A. C., 260
Ramirez, L., 589
Ramsey, S. E., 53
Randall, B. A., 105
Randall, C. L., 44, 105, 173, 174, 175, 179
Randall, P., 589
Rankin, H., 180
Rankin, J. G., 171
Rao, U., 331
Rapaport, M. H., 361
Rapee, R. M., 361, 370, 378
Raskind, M., 47
Rasmussen, S. A., 11, 42, 44, 359, 365, 371, 374
Ratcliff, K. S., 87, 212
Rauch, S. L., 333, 334
Ravaris, C. L., 363, 609, 618
Rawlings, R., 263
Rawlinson, L., 510
Ray, L. A., 185, 420, 437
Rayner, R., 375
Rea, M. M., 327
Read, J. P., 53
Reba, L., 579
Rebach, H., 225
Redding, C. A., 419
Redlick, F. C., 238
Reece, S., 381
Reed, D., 253
Reed, G., 480
Reed, V., 34, 349, 379
Regan, P., 505, 516
Regeer, E. J., 320
Regestein, Q. R., 610
Regier, D. A., 15, 36, 37, 55, 94, 96, 171, 174, 212, 237, 241, 292, 293, 330, 366, 416
Regier, D. E., 4
Rehm, L. P., 7
Reich, J. H., 18, 359, 366

Reich, L. H., 331
Reich, T., 320
Reichart, C. G., 323, 329
Reichborn-Kjennrud, T., 579, 586
Reichler, R. J., 372
Reid, K. J., 606
Reid, K. S., 548
Reid, S., 443
Reid, W., 141
Reif, S., 44
Reilly, J., 432
Reilly, M. P., 222
Reilly-Harrington, N. A., 323, 324
Reinares, M., 41, 327
Reiss, A., 333
Reiss, D., 18
Reiss, S., 368, 377
Reissing, E. D., 522
Reiter, J., 426, 448
Reitner, S. R., 36
Rennenberg, B., 366
Renteria, L., 112, 113
Resick, P. A., 363, 368
Resnick, H. S., 368
Rettew, D. C., 661, 662
Reus, V. H., 9, 12
Reynolds, C. F., 608, 620, 621, 624
Reynolds, C. R., 101, 103
Reynolds, S., 7, 10, 11
Reznick, J. S., 382, 654
Rhedin, A., 181
Rheingold, A., 367, 368
Rhue, J. W., 473, 492
Ricci, D. A., 490
Rice, A. S., 42, 43, 44
Rice, J. A., 45, 294, 320, 323
Rice, M. E., 547, 548
Rich, C. L., 477
Rich, M. E., 333
Richards, J. A., 327, 328
Richardson, B., 242
Richardson, M. A., 204
Richman, D. D., 144, 158
Richter, P., 324
Rickels, K., 350, 360, 361

Ricketts, S. K., 50, 334
Ridgely, M. S., 44, 55
Ridley, C. R., 112, 115
Riedel, W. J., 333
Rief, W., 416, 417, 418, 424
Rieger, B. P., 116
Rieker, P. P., 242
Rienzo, D., 548
Ries, R. K., 46, 47, 51, 320
Riesco, N., 306
Riether, 485
Rietschel, M., 519
Rietveld, S., 427
Rieves, L., 585
Rigatti-Luchini, S., 418, 427
Rigby, M. F., 429
Riggs, D. S., 362
Rihmer, A., 328, 329
Riley, A., 525
Riley, K. C., 473
Rimmo, P. A., 375
Ring, A., 443
Ringel, Y., 434
Ripp, K., 248
Riso, L. P., 18
Rivas-Vazquez, R. A., 361
Rizvi, S. L., 583
Robbins, J. M., 415, 418, 419, 421, 424, 425, 427, 429, 430, 431, 436, 445, 447, 449
Robbins, L. H., 37
Robbins, P. C., 47
Robbins, T. W., 325
Roberson-Nay, R., 382
Roberts, A., 363
Roberts, B. W., 20, 662, 664
Roberts, C., 445
Robertson, A. K., 587
Robins, E., 88
Robins, L. N., 86, 87, 171, 216, 237, 239, 379, 416, 444
Robinson, E., 357

Robinson, T. E., 332
Robles-García, R., 478
Roblin, D., 519
Robson, P., 362, 363
Rochussen, J. R., 41
Rodebaugh, T. A., 363
Rodrigo, G., 263
Roehrig, M., 584
Roehrs, T., 610
Rogers, R., 80, 81, 82, 83, 84, 85, 86, 90, 325
Rogers, W., 294, 297
Rohde, P., 204
Rohsenow, D. J., 168, 218
Roll, J. M., 222
Rolland, J. S., 448
Rollinson, R. D., 483
Rollnick, S., 172, 179, 180, 217
Romach, M. K., 43
Roman, L., 186
Romanelli, S., 239
Romano, J. M., 427
Romelsjö, A., 181
Ronfeldt, H., 44
Ronningstam, E. F., 652
Rooijmans, H. G., 424, 431
Room, R., 171, 173, 212
Roosa, M., 105
Rosberger, Z., 443
Rose, D. T., 295, 305, 306, 307
Rose, R. J., 167
Rose, S. M., 242
Rosekind, M. R., 612, 613, 617
Rosemeier, H., 511
Rosen, J. C., 426, 448, 486
Rosen, R. C., 506, 507, 509, 527
Rosenbaum, J. F., 359, 374
Rosenbaum, M., 295, 335
Rosenberg, D., 371
Rosenberg, S. D., 58, 248, 249, 260, 261

Rosenberg, S. E., 660
Rosenblum, A., 53
Rosenburg, S., 51
Rosenfeld, N., 322
Rosenheck, R. A., 47, 50, 238, 296
Rosenstein, L. D., 152
Rosenthal, I., 366
Rosenthal, N. E., 325
Rosenthal, R. N., 53
Rosenvinge, J. H., 576
Rösler, A., 553
Rosman, B. L., 584
Ross, C. A., 242, 474, 476, 477, 478, 489, 490, 491
Ross, H. E., 42, 44
Ross, J., 360
Ross, R. J., 618
Rosser, B. R., 512, 521
Rossi, A., 299, 643
Rosso, M. L., 320
Rost, K., 420, 425, 656
Rotert, M., 620, 621
Roth, L. H., 47, 239
Roth, L. M., 427
Roth, T., 610, 615
Roth, W. T., 362, 370
Rothbaum, B. O., 353, 362, 365
Rothschild, L., 637
Rotman, D. B., 544
Rouff, L., 640
Rouillon, F., 331
Rouleau, J. L., 541, 544, 545, 546
Rounsaville, B. J., 4, 19, 42, 43, 54, 175, 368, 488
Rourke, B. P., 155
Rourke, K., 86, 87
Rowan-Szal, G. R., 225
Rowe, M., 370
Rowland, D. L., 511, 529
Roy-Byrne, P. P., 46, 47, 350
Roysicar, G., 115
Ruan, W. J., 168, 170
Rubinsztein, J. S., 325
Rubio-Stipee, M., 215

Rucci, P., 331
Rudd, G. D., 326
Rudd, M. D., 591
Rudorder, M., 335
Ruffer-Hesse, C., 516
Ruggero, C., 324
Rumsey, J. M., 137
Runtz, M., 474
Ruscio, A. M., 18
Ruscio, J., 18
Rush, A. J., 13, 40, 41, 322, 323, 614
Russakoff, L. M., 94
Russell, M., 171, 184
Russell, S. T., 105
Russo, J. E., 46, 47
Ruthazer, R., 47
Rutherford, J., 305
Rutter, C., 327
Rutter, M., 10, 23
Ryall, J. M., 490
Ryan, C. E., 297
Ryan, D. P., 431
Ryan, J. J., 489
Ryan, N. D., 320, 323, 331
Rychtarik, R., 175

Saab, F., 333, 334
Sabshin, M., 5
Sachs, G. S., 46, 320, 321, 323, 326, 330, 331, 335, 359
Sachs, R. G., 489
Sack, D. A., 325
Sadeh, A., 621
Sadowski, H., 536
Saenz de Tejada, I., 517
Safer, D. J., 41
Safferman, A. Z., 255
Saha, S., 238
Saha, T., 170
Sahakian, B. J., 325
Sakaguchi, A. Y., 157
Salaberria, K., 363
Saladin, M. E., 44, 45
Salaspuro, M., 180
Saleem, R., 322
Salem, J. E., 244

Salkovskis, P. M., 368, 370, 377, 426, 429, 436, 448
Salloum, I. M., 41, 46, 50, 173, 174, 175, 179
Salmon, P., 432, 443
Salokangas, R. K. R., 238
Salvatore, P., 41
Salzman, C., 361
Salzman, D. G., 363
Samele, C., 238
Samet, J. M., 185
Sammons, M. T., 251
Samson, J. A., 298
Samuel, D. B., 3, 7, 17, 18, 80
Samuels, J., 359, 646
Sanchez, J., 6, 102
Sanchez, M., 384
Sandberg, D. A., 47
Sandell, J., 126
Sanderson, C. J., 19, 22
Sandfort, T. G., 515, 516
Sandin, B., 379
Sandrow, D., 325
Sands, J. R., 240
Sandy, J. M., 221
Sanger, T. M., 240
Sanislow, C. A., 22, 645, 663, 664, 665
Sankis, L., 4, 5, 9
Sansone, L. A., 580
Sansone, R. A., 580, 581
Santander, J., 324
Sante, M., 379
Santiago, J., 481
Santiago-Rivera, A. L., 113
Santor, D. A., 18
Santoro, J., 424
Santoro, N., 517
Santosa, C. M., 322
Sar, V., 489, 490
Sarasua, B., 362
Sarnie, M. K., 419
Sartorius, N., 94, 96, 212, 237
Sasseville, T. M., 656

Sateia, M., 620
Sato, T., 321
Satoh, Y., 590
Satz, P., 130, 158
Saucedo, C. F., 179
Saulsman, L. M., 20, 21
Saunders, E., 549
Saunders, J. B., 178, 181, 212, 213, 238
Saunders, K. W., 426
Saunders, W. B., 360
Savard, G., 413, 422
Savitcheva, I., 126
Sax, K. W., 322, 326, 332
Saxe, G. N., 475
Saxe, L., 548
Saxena, S., 370, 371, 492, 493
Sayed-Tabatabaei, F. A., 333
Sayers, S. L., 253
Sayette, M. A., 183, 184
Scarna, A., 615
Sceery, W., 58
Schaap, C., 364
Schacter, D. L., 483
Schaefer, L. C., 536
Schaeffer, K. W., 142
Schagen, S., 436
Schatz, P., 135
Schaub, A., 259
Scheerer, M., 129
Scheftner, W., 322
Scheibe, G., 364
Scheidt, C. E., 431, 433
Schein, R. L., 302
Schenker, S., 185
Schermer, F., 587
Schers, H. J., 294
Schettler, P. J., 320, 323
Schiavi, R. C., 515, 516, 546
Schick, M., 186
Schiebel, D., 539
Schlesinger, H. J., 261
Schlosser, S., 359
Schlyter, F., 214
Schmahl, C., 489
Schmeidler, J., 480, 481

Schmidt, C. W., 43, 224
Schmidt, D. A. F., 615
Schmidt, L., 180
Schmidt, N. B., 586, 591
Schmitt, A. L., 50
Schmitt, J. A. J., 333
Schmitz, M., 49
Schnarch, D., 524
Schneck, C. D., 320, 321, 323
Schneider, S., 372
Schneier, F. R., 60, 363
Schnyder, U., 536
Schock, K., 258
Scholing, A., 366
Schonfeld, L., 173
Schore, A., 652
Schork, N. J., 333
Schouten, P. G. W., 547
Schover, L., 525
Schrag, A., 432
Schramke, C. J., 141
Schreiner-Engel, P., 516
Schroder, M., 528
Schroeder, M. L., 21, 635
Schroeder-Hartwig, K., 362
Schubert, D. S. P., 34
Schuckit, M. A., 42, 52, 53, 62, 175, 182, 247, 610
Schul, Y., 296
Schulenberg, J. E., 204, 224, 330
Schuller, R., 177
Schulman, A., 306
Schulsinger, F., 142, 242
Schultz, L., 42
Schultz, W., 220
Schur, B. E., 173
Schuster, C. R., 219, 221
Schwartz, C. E., 366, 373
Schwartz, D. J., 585
Schwartz, J. E., 635
Schwartz, J. L. K., 223, 370
Schwartz, J. M., 374
Schwartz, S., 238

Schwartzman, A., 585
Schwarwachter, I., 361
Schweitzer, R. D., 254
Schweizer, E., 360, 361
Sciuto, G., 366
Scnwartz, G. E., 431
Scott, G., 541, 542, 545
Scott, H., 47, 48
Scott, J. A., 322, 327, 328
Scott, P., 329
Seaburn, D., 441
Searles, H., 256
Searles, J., 548
Sedler, M. J., 251
Seeley, J. R., 204, 320, 330
Seeman, M.V., 244
Segal, D. L., 81, 83, 85, 92
Segraves, K. B., 509, 515
Segraves, R.T., 509, 515, 519, 524, 527
Seibyl, J. P., 332
Seidman, L. J., 334
Seil, D., 536
Seivewright, H., 664, 665
Self, D. W., 61
Seligman, M. E., 295, 296, 306, 375
Sellers, E. M., 43, 181
Sellman, J. D., 43
Sellwood, W., 381
Selten, J. P., 238
Semans, J. H., 528
Seminowicz, S., 333
Semler, C. N., 615, 620, 621
Sen, S., 20
Seneca, N., 332
Sensky, T., 429
Serin, R. C., 645
Serreti, A., 19
Sethuraman, G., 326
Seto, M. C., 540, 547
Setters, M. J., 332
Sevy, S., 239
Shabsigh, R., 526
Shad, M., 321
Shadick, R., 357

Shaffer, H., 175
Shafran, R., 377
Shah, A. R., 126
Shahar, G., 656
Shalev, A.Y., 52
Sham, P., 238, 327, 332
Shapiro, C., 615
Shapiro, L. J., 364, 638, 649, 650
Sharan, P., 46
Sharma, A., 221
Sharpe, L., 546
Sharpe, M., 416, 424, 426, 436, 437, 448
Sharpe, T., 424
Sharpley, M., 109
Shaw, D. G., 431
Shaw, H. E., 589, 591
Shaw, P. M., 357
Shaw, S. R., 45
Shaywitz, B. A., 483
Shea, M. T., 18, 22, 635, 636, 663, 664, 665
Shea, T., 54, 55
Shear, M. K., 331, 360, 383
Shedler, J., 16, 92, 430, 660
Sheehan, D.V., 302, 303, 304, 358
Sheehan, K. E., 358
Sheikh, J. I., 361
Sheline,Y. I., 309
Shelly, C., 142
Shelton, M. D., 320, 321, 323
Shelton, R. C., 297
Shemansky, W. J., 125
Shen, S., 143
Shen,Y. L., 105
Shenfield, G. M., 185
Sher, K. J., 42, 52, 54, 55, 57, 58, 59, 174, 185, 212, 224
Sherman, J. E., 183
Sherrill, J. T., 324, 325, 326
Sherrington, J. M., 297, 298

Sherwin, B. B., 517
Sherwood, A. R., 174
Sheu, W. J., 177
Shi, L., 234
Shields, J., 257
Shifren, J. L., 517, 524
Shih, J. H., 635
Shihabuddin, L., 661
Shillingford, J. A., 174
Shin, I. S., 300
Shinar, O., 221
Shiner, R. L., 20
Shisslak, C. M., 15, 576
Shopshire, M. S., 55
Shor, R. E., 494
Shores, E. A., 134, 158
Short, R., 257
Shorter, E., 437
Shoulson, I., 157
Shrier, D., 541
Shrout, P. E., 50, 238
Shubsachs, A. P., 549
Shute, P. A., 180
Sickel, A. E., 97
Siddiqi, Q., 181
Siegal, H. A., 42
Siega-Riz, A. M., 579
Siegel, L., 324, 325, 326
Siever, L. J., 648, 661, 662
Sifneos, P. E., 431
Sigmon, A., 294, 295
Sigmon, S. C., 222
Sigvardsson, S., 143, 167, 421, 427
Sihvo, S., 56
Silberg, J. L., 167, 477
Silberman, E. K., 428, 489
Silbersweig, D. A., 10, 334
Sillup, G. P., 612
Silva, J. A., 10
Silva, P. A., 46, 56, 57, 662
Silver, E., 47
Silverman, K., 219, 222
Silverstein, S., 240

Simeon, D., 419, 480, 481
Simeonova, D. J., 322, 333
Simon, G. E., 327, 413, 416, 417, 418, 430, 436, 612
Simon, J., 234, 524
Simon, N. M., 46, 330, 331
Simon, R. C., 478, 494
Simon, W. T., 547
Simoneau, T. L., 322, 327
Simons, A. D., 288, 323
Simonsen, E., 635
Simonsson-Sarnecki, M., 431
Simpson, D. D., 210, 225
Simpson, S. G., 47
Sinclair, J., 240
Singareddy, R., 383, 384, 385
Singer, J. L., 431
Singh, H., 35, 41, 46
Singh, J., 46
Singh, K. N., 168
Singh, S. P., 417
Siris, S. G., 60
Sirof, B., 480
Sitharthan, T., 178
Sjogren Fugl-Meyer, K., 506, 507, 508, 509, 511, 512, 515, 520
Skene, D. J., 612
Skilbeck, W. M., 261
Skinner, B., 508
Skinner, C., 332
Skinner, H. A., 168, 169, 176, 177, 178, 180, 214
Skinner, J. B., 184
Sklar, S. M., 179
Skodol, A. E., 11, 13, 16, 22, 238, 633, 634, 648, 663, 664, 665
Slater, E., 425
Slaughter, J. R., 516
Slavny, P. R., 420, 422, 450, 452
Sledge, W. H., 296
Slob, A. K., 529

Slof-Op't, M. C. T., 585
Slotnick, H. B., 656
Slutske, W. S., 182
Small, G. W., 421
Small, J., 324
Smart, R. G., 168, 170
Smeets, M. A. M., 575
Smeets, R., 212
Smeraldi, E., 19, 325, 384
Smets, E. M., 443
Smith, A., 431, 451, 551
Smith, B., 180, 181
Smith, C. G., 417, 425
Smith, D., 297, 328
Smith, G. R., 420, 425, 437, 656
Smith, G. T., 5, 18
Smith, I., 216
Smith, L., 378
Smith, M., 184, 381, 528, 625
Smith, R. J., 157
Smith, S., 365, 484
Smith, T. A., 549
Smith, T. E., 239
Smolak, L., 571, 576, 586, 587, 588, 589, 590, 591
Smolin, Y., 477
Smoot, T. M., 326
Smukler, A. J., 539, 544
Smyth, H., 620, 621
Snidman, N., 373, 382, 654
Snowden, L. R., 108, 261
Snyder, K. S., 323
Soares, J. C., 334
Sobcazk, S., 333
Sobell, L. C., 166, 167, 168, 169, 170, 172, 173, 174, 175, 176, 177, 178, 179, 180, 181
Sobell, M. B., 166, 167, 168, 169, 170, 172, 173, 174, 175, 176, 177, 178, 179, 180, 181
Sobin, C., 359, 367
Sokoll, R., 186
Sokolow, L., 174

Sokolski, K. N., 45
Soldatos, C. R., 606, 608, 613, 618, 623, 625
Soloff, P. H., 648, 661
Solomon, A., 112, 115
Solomon, D., 42, 45, 318, 323
Somers, J. M., 237, 294
Somers, V. K., 605
Sommerfield, C., 362
Sonne, S. C., 44, 45
Sorensen, J. L., 186
Sørensen, T. I., 181
Soriano, F., 110
Southwick, S. M., 484
Soyka, M., 47
Spanagel, R., 62
Spanos, N. P., 486, 489, 490
Sparks, P. J., 413
Sparks, R., 116
Spaulding, W. D., 240, 253
Speckens, A. E., 424, 425
Spector, S. A., 144, 158
Speechley, K. N., 245
Speltz, K., 541
Spencer, T., 329, 331
Spengler, A., 542, 545
Spengler, R. M., 116
Sperry, L., 639, 640, 641, 642, 632, 645, 649, 651, 653, 654, 656, 658
Spiegel, D., 7, 12, 473, 474, 476, 477, 480, 484, 485, 486, 489, 491, 492, 494
Spiegel, H., 428
Spielberger, C. D., 368
Spielman, A. J., 603, 618
Spiess, W. F., 519
Spinhoven, P., 431
Spinner, M. L., 126
Spinweber, C. L., 611
Spitzer, R. L., 4, 6, 7, 8, 9, 11, 12, 13, 16, 88, 89, 90, 91, 92, 215, 247, 301, 302, 320, 331, 368, 410, 444, 449, 488, 581

Spragg, S. D. S., 221
Spreen, O., 137
Sprenkel, D. G., 141
Spring, B., 258
Springer, D. W., 591
Sprock. J., 16
Sptiznagel, E. L., 44
Sroufe, L. A., 476
Stadler, H., 102
Staley, J. K., 333
Staner, L., 324
Stanford, J. L., 518
Stang, P. E., 238, 360
Stanhope, C. R., 531
Stanhope, N., 484
Stanley, M. A., 357, 361, 362, 364, 367, 368, 377
Stanley, B., 665
Stanley, P., 447
Stansfeld, S. A., 114
Stanton, S. P., 332
Starcevic, V., 365, 422
Starkman, M. N., 413, 421
Starkstein, S. E., 298
Startup, M., 324
Stasiewicz, P. R., 46
Statham, D., 182
Statler-Cowen, T., 363
Steadman, H. J., 47, 242
Stedwell, R. E., 440
Steen, T. A., 296
Steer, R. A., 179, 302, 322, 368
Steffens, D. C., 10
Steiger, H., 585
Stein, M. B., 15, 351, 357, 361, 383, 384
Steinberg, A. B., 584
Steinberg, D. L., 295, 305, 306, 307
Steinberg, K., 176
Steinberg, M., 474, 480, 488
Steiner, H., 331
Steinhauer, S. R., 125, 142, 143

Steinhausen, H. C., 578, 584
Steketee, G., 358, 359, 364, 368, 369
Stemberger, R. I., 351
Stepanski, E. J., 603
STEP-BD Investigators, 46, 330, 331
Stephan, C., 333
Stephanis, N., 43
Stepp, S. D., 647
Stern, E., 10, 334
Stern, G. S., 325
Sternberg, R. J., 24
Sternberger, L. G., 370
Stevens, K. P., 445
Stevenson, J., 378, 379
Stevenson, W., 552
Stewart, A. L., 105, 106, 493
Stewart, G., 374
Stewart, R., 300
Stewart, S. H., 42, 61, 364, 432
Stewart, T. M., 580
Stiasny, S., 42, 44
Stice, E., 583, 586, 587, 589, 590, 591
Stiles, T. C., 652
Stinnett, R. D., 544, 545
Stinson, F. S., 37, 39, 168, 170
Stipec, M. R., 212
St. Lawrence, J. S., 370
Stockmeier, C. A., 332, 333
Stockwell, T., 178
Stogner, K. S., 62
Stone, A., 248
Stone, B., 612
Stone, M. H., 640, 649, 651, 656, 665
Stone, W. S., 23
Stopa, L., 370
Stoudemire, A., 485
Stout, R. L., 22, 620
Stover, E., 239, 252
St. Peter, R. F., 49

Strakowski, S. M., 43, 174, 242, 321, 322, 326, 330, 332
Strang, J., 181, 218
Strassberg, D. S., 529
Stratigeas, B., 242
Stratta, P., 643
Straus, R., 184
Strauss, A., 129
Strauss, J. S., 241, 245
Strecker, E. A., 329
Streeten, D. H. P., 139
Streiner, D., 360
Strickland, T. L., 101, 103
Striegel-Moore, R. H., 571, 575, 576, 579, 589
Strigo, I. A., 522
Strober, M., 323, 326, 579, 584
Strohl, K., 607
Strong, C. M., 322
Stroup, S., 238
Strouse, R. C., 49
Stuart, G. L., 53, 214
Stuart, R. B., 102
Stuening, E. L., 235
Stueve, A., 238
Sturt, E., 295, 296, 307
Stuyt, E. B., 50
Substance Abuse and Mental Health Administration, 169, 172, 176, 180, 201, 203, 210, 214, 222, 225
Suddarth, R. L., 327
Sue, D. C., 102, 262
Sue, D. W., 102, 112, 262
Sue, S., 103, 106, 261
Sugden, R., 49
Sugerman, J., 608
Sullins, E., 587
Sullivan, C. N., 324
Sullivan, K. A., 618
Sullivan, M. D., 413
Sullivan, P. F., 578, 579, 580, 585
Sullivan, T. P., 49
Sumathipala, A., 425

Summerfeldt, L. J., 86
Sundgot-Borgen, S., 576
Suomi, S. I., 381
Suomi, S. J., 381
Suppes, T., 41, 45, 322, 323, 326
Suratt, P., 612
Surguladze, S., 333
Susman, V. L., 94
Susser, E., 235, 263
Sutton, L., 240
Sutton, S., 217
Suy, E., 308
Suzuki, L. A., 101
Svanborg, P., 301
Svikis, D., 215, 225
Svrakic, D. M., 635
Swales, P. J., 361
Swann, A. C., 325, 326
Swanson, J. W., 47, 242
Swartz, A., 45
Swartz, H. A., 327
Swartz, J. R., 549
Swartz, M. S., 38, 39, 47, 210, 238, 416, 418, 419, 424
Swayze, I. I., 255
Swedo, S. E., 385
Sweeney, J., 41, 60
Swendsen, J. D., 41, 58, 63, 174, 306, 323
Swica, Y., 478
Swift, W. J., 656
Swinson, R. P., 174, 358
Switzer, G. E., 242
Sylvester, C. E., 372
Sylvester, D., 351
Symonds, L., 255
Symonds, T., 519, 520
Syzmanski, K., 185
Szechtman, B., 60
Szechtman, H., 60

Tabrizi, M. A., 331
Tacchini, G., 444
Tackett, J. L., 663
Tafti, M., 623
Taillefer, S., 445
Takai, N., 238

Takeuchi, D. T., 238, 261
Talbot, F., 354
Talley, N. J., 450
Tam, T. W., 173
Tan, T., 608
Tanaka-Matsumi, J., 108, 110
Tandon, R., 240
Tanenberg-Karant, M., 55, 240
Tang, W., 529
Tantleff-Dunn, S., 572, 585
Tanzi, R. E., 157
Targum, S. D., 384
Tarke, H., 110
Tarrier, N., 327, 362, 381
Tarter, R. E., 137, 142, 216, 549
Tashman, N. A., 295, 305, 306, 307
Task Force on DSM-IV, 12
Tasman, A., 260
Tassinari, R., 363
Tatten, T., 19, 238
Tauber, R., 252
Tay, L. K., 331
Taylor, C., 180, 362, 370, 374
Taylor, G. J., 431
Taylor, J. R., 61, 643
Taylor, P. J., 549
Taylor, S., 363, 369
Taylor, T. R., 112, 526, 544
Teague, G. B., 174
Teesson, M., 43
Teichner, G., 242
Teitelbaum, M. L., 450
Tekell, J. L., 10
Telch, C. F., 579, 583
Tellegen, A., 476, 546
Telles, C., 262
Tempier, R., 45
Templeman, T. L., 544, 545
ten Have, M., 320
Tennen, H., 368

Teran-Santos, J., 605, 612
Terkelsen, K. G., 256
Terpin, M., 185
Terpstra, J., 9, 12
Terr, L. C., 476
Terrazas, A., 263
Terry, D. J., 306
Teruga, C., 224
Tervo, K. E., 382
Tessler, R., 254
Test, M. A., 47, 248
Testa, S., 370
Teuber, H. L., 130
Thase, M. E., 41, 44, 46, 288, 297, 323, 327, 330, 331, 332, 335
Thavundayil, J., 187
Thaw, J. M., 583
Thelen, M. H., 587
Thevos, A. J., 44
Thibonnier, M., 526
Thieme, K., 427
Thirlwell, M., 443
Thisted, E. A., 608
Thoennes, N., 242
Thomas, G. V., 96
Thomas, H. V., 263
Thomas, J., 325
Thomas, M. R., 320, 321, 323
Thomas, S. E., 44
Thomas, V. H., 54
Thomas-Lohrman, S., 253
Thompson, B., 380
Thompson, D. S., 141
Thompson, J. K., 572, 574, 580, 584, 585, 586, 587, 588, 591
Thompson, J. W., 45
Thompson, L., 571, 576
Thompson, S. C., 49
Thompson, T., 221
Thompson, W., 327, 413
Thordarson, D. S., 377
Thornicroft, G., 47, 48
Thornton, L. M., 303, 304

Thyer, B. A., 358
Tiefer, L., 505, 508
Tienari, P., 257
Tiffany, S. T., 223
Tiihonen, J., 47
Tijhuis, M. A. R., 430
Tilfors, M., 384
Tiller, J., 490
Tillman, R., 330
Tilly, S., 6, 8
Timmerman, M. A., 47, 49
Tinkcom, M., 175
Tipp, J. E., 53
Tisdale, M. J., 656
Tjaden, P., 242
Todman, M., 258
Todorov, C., 361
Tohen, M., 41, 242, 244, 322, 326, 331
Toler, S. M., 528
Tollefson, G. D., 240
Tomasson, K., 54
Tomkins, G., 424
Tomkins, S. S., 638
Tompson, M., 327
Toncheva, D., 333
Tondo, L., 326
Toneatto, T., 174, 175, 177, 179, 180, 181
Toner, B. B., 449
Toni, C., 331
Tonigan, J. S., 167, 172, 177, 216, 217, 218
Toolenaar, T. A. M., 538
Toomey, R., 220
Toone, B. K., 413, 417, 421
Toporek, R., 102
Torchia, M. G., 383
Torgersen, S., 374, 633, 634, 637, 640, 641, 642, 643, 644, 646, 649, 651, 652, 653, 655, 657, 661
Torgrud, L. J., 578
Torrent, C., 327
Torrey, E. F., 235, 237, 238

Towbin, K. E., 329
Townsend, J., 333, 334
Townsend, M. H., 359
Townsley, R. M., 351
Townsley, R. N., 12
Tozzi, F., 579
Trabert, W., 362
Tracy, A., 324
Trauer, T., 239
Trautman, K. D., 215
Treece, C., 43
Trell, E., 180
Tress, K., 240
Triandis, H. C., 105
Triebwasser, J., 324
Triffleman, E. G., 44
Trijsburg, R. W., 431
Trimble, M. R., 432
Trinder, H., 370
Trivedi, M., 384, 385
Trost, A., 589
Trower, P., 240
Trudel, G., 369, 517, 525, 528
True, W., 220
Trull, T. J., 4, 5, 14, 17, 18, 22, 23, 54, 55, 57, 59, 174, 185, 212, 224, 635, 647, 659
Trumbetta, S. L., 259
Tsai, G. E., 489
Tsuang, M. T., 13, 18, 23, 220, 257, 331, 359
Tsvetkova, R., 333
Tu, W., 42
Tucker, J. A., 167
Tugrul, K. C., 326
Tulving, E., 483
Turecki, G., 333
Turk, D. C., 427
Turner, C. E., 180
Turner, J. A., 541
Turner, N. E., 179
Turner, R. A., 9, 11, 12
Turner, R. E., 545
Turner, S. M., 12, 186, 350, 351, 352, 354, 357, 358, 359, 360, 361, 362, 364, 365, 367, 369, 370,

373, 374, 377, 379, 380, 381, 382, 383, 385
Turvey, C., 42, 45, 320
Tutkun, H., 478, 490
Tuulio-Henriksson, A., 349
Twemlow, S. W., 479
Twentyman, C. T., 370
Twigg, D., 545
Tworoger, S. S., 524
Tyrer, P., 664, 665
Tyrrell, G., 255

Uhde, T. W., 366, 383, 384, 385, 609, 618
Uhlenhuth, E. H., 611
Ulmer, A., 263
Unal, S. N., 489
Unnewehr, S., 372
Unutzer, J., 51, 327
Unverzadt, M., 612
Uomoto, J. M., 114
Upadhyaya, V. H., 326
Urbina, S., 24
Ureno, G., 660
Urmann, C. F., 51
Ursin, H., 413
U.S. Department of Health and Human Services, 108, 109, 113, 186
Üstün, B., 16, 212, 216
Uttaro, T., 262

Vaccarino, V. R., 106
Vaglum, P., 54
Vaillant, G. E., 5
Valdes, M., 306
Valenstein, E., 147, 156, 241
Valeri, S., 323
Valiente, R., 379
Valle, R., 294
Vallières, A., 612, 613
Van Amerigan, M., 360
van Balcom, A. J., 349, 363
Van Broeckhoven, C., 333

van Dam-Baggen, R., 362
van den Berg, P., 586, 591
Vandenberg, R. J., 105
VandenBos, G. P., 7
van den Bosch, W. J., 294
Van den Bree, M. B. M., 220, 221
Van Den Brink, W., 212
Van den Bulke, D., 331
van den Hoogen, H. J., 294
van der Ende, J., 329
van der Hart, O., 478, 484, 485
van der Kolk, B. A., 361, 485
Vanderlinden, J., 478
VanderSpek, R., 176
Van der Veer, M. M., 525
Vander Wal, J. S., 587
Vandewater, S., 41
Van de Wiel, H. B. M., 513, 522, 523, 532
Van Duijn, C. M., 333
Van Dyck, R., 363, 369
Van Eerdewegh, M., 320
van elzen, C., 366
van er Velde, J., 510
Van Etten, M. L., 222
van Fleet, J. N., 489
van Furth, E. F., 585
Van Gorp, W. G., 158
Van Hasselt, V. B., 92
Van Hoeken, D., 575, 576
Van Horn, E., 19
Van Houdenhove, B., 413
Van Lakveld, J. J., 513
Van Leeuwen, K., 20
van Lier, P. A., 645
Van Ommeren, M. V., 493
Van Os, J., 19, 238, 332
Van Paesschen, W. P., 136

Van Pragg, H. M., 213, 255
van Ryn, M., 111
Van Valkenberg, C., 366
van Vliet, I. M., 361
van Weel-Baumgarten, E. M., 294
van Wijk, C. M., 436
Varga, K., 478
Vargha-Kahdem, F., 136
Varghese, F. N., 254
Vasile, R., 359
Vaughn, C., 254
Vaughn, W. K., 446
Vazquez, B., 432
Vecchierini, M., 612
Veenstra-VanderWeele, J., 308
Vega, W. A., 110, 185, 186, 294
Velasquez, R. J., 110
Velligan, D. I., 239
Vendetti, J., 215
Vengeliene, V., 62
Venturello, S., 378
Verbrugge, L. M., 449, 450
Verduin, M. L., 47, 49
Verebey, K., 180
Verhaak, P. F. M., 430
Verheul, R., 7, 16, 17, 635
Verhoeff, P., 332
Verhulst, F. C., 323, 329
Vermetten, E., 489
Vermilyea, B. B., 351
Vermilyea, J. A., 351
Vernon, P. A., 20, 21, 646, 648
Verschoor, A. M., 543
Versiani, M., 361
Vidaver, R., 58
Vieta, E., 41, 327
Vieth, A., 185
Viinamaki, H., 296
Vijver, F., 114
Villasenor, V. S., 660
Vinokur, A., 296
Virdin, L. M., 105
Visscher, B., 158

Vitagliano, H. L., 351
Vitaliano, P. P., 257
Vitaro, F., 645
Vittorio, C. G., 445
Vogeltanz, N. D., 184, 185
Vogler, V. P., 220
Vohs, K. D., 508, 591
Volicer, L., 42, 43
Volkow, N. C., 5
Vollebergh, W., 320
Völlm, B. A., 661
Vollmayr, B., 62
Vollrath, M., 612, 613, 624
Volpicelli, J. R., 306
von Knorring, A. L., 421
Von Korff, M., 418, 426, 430, 612
Vrasti, R., 212
Vredenburg, K., 15, 18
Vuijk, P., 645

Wade, J. H., 239, 253
Wade, T. D., 585
Wagner, E. F., 186
Wagner, H. R., 47, 242, 294, 295
Wagner, K. D., 326
Wahlbeck, K., 240
Wahlund, K., 427
Wakefield, J. C., 4, 5, 8, 9
Walde, L., 474
Waldinger, M. D., 519, 520
Waldinger, R. J., 433
Waldman, I. D., 11
Walker, A. E., 134, 549
Walker, E. A., 413, 415, 432, 449
Walker, E. F., 243, 257
Walker, J. R., 15, 357
Walker, V. J., 352
Walker, W. R., 480
Wall, A., 126
Wall, C., 383
Wall, P., 438
Wall, T. L., 167
Wallace, C. J., 252
Wallace, M. R., 157

Wallach, M. A., 44, 46, 57, 58, 59, 60
Wallen, K., 524
Waller, E., 431, 433
Waller, N. G., 18, 476
Wallisch, L. S., 248
Wals, M., 323, 329
Walsh, B. T., 572, 579, 590
Walsh, D., 13
Walsh, J. A., 104
Walsh, J. K., 608, 609
Walters, E. E., 39, 40, 292, 293, 318, 320, 330, 575
Wan, J., 510
Wang, J., 42
Wang, M., 262
Wang, P. L., 483
Wang, P. S., 40
Wang, P. W., 322
Wang, Y., 126
Wanner, J., 238
Waraich, P., 237, 294
Warberg, B., 548
Ware, C., 615, 626
Ware, N. C., 450
Warfa, N., 114
Warner, K. L., 331
Warner, L. A., 174, 221, 224, 330
Warner, M. B., 22, 23, 174, 636, 664
Warner, R., 450
Warner, V., 372
Warnock, J., 524
Warren, J., 542
Warshaw, M. G., 45, 358
Warwick, H., 426, 436, 438, 448
Waternaux, C. M., 322, 331
Watkins, E. R., 327
Watkins, K. E., 42, 49, 136
Watkins, P. C., 157
Watkins, S., 305
Watson, C. G., 421, 425, 439

Watson, D., 7, 10, 11, 18, 21, 426, 448, 449
Watson, I. B., 374
Watson, R. J., 547, 548
Watson, T. L., 579
Watt, M. C., 432
Watts, C. A. H., 417
Watts, F. N., 620, 621
Waxler, N. E., 256
Weakland, J., 256
Wearden, A. J., 448
Weathers, F. W., 368, 474
Weaver, A. L., 446
Weaver, T. L., 363
Webb, C., 254
Weed, N. C., 214
Weeks, J. M., 221
Wegner, D. M., 5
Wehr, T. A., 325
Weiden, P., 41, 60
Weidenman, M., 185
Weigenborg, P. T., 513
Weijmar Schultz, W. C. M., 512, 522, 523, 532
Weiller, E., 354, 358
Weinberg, T. S., 541, 542
Weinberg, W. A., 326
Weinberger, D. R., 239, 252
Weinberger, J. L., 664
Weiner, J., 611
Weiner, K., 588
Weiner, L., 474
Weinfield, N. S., 476
Weinraub, M., 306
Weinrott, M. R., 550
Weinstein, W., 530
Weisner, C., 180
Weiss, D. S., 478
Weiss, K. A., 239
Weiss, M. G., 450
Weiss, R. D., 42, 44, 45, 46, 49, 330, 331
Weissman, M. M., 41, 42, 43, 54, 58, 293, 318, 320, 371, 372, 471, 611, 612
Welch, D., 607

Welch, K. B., 298, 306
Welch, P. R., 584
Welch, S., 218
Wells, C. E., 156
Wells, K. B., 294, 297
Welte, J. W., 171, 174
Wentzel, A., 363
Wenzel, S. L., 42
Werner, H., 129
Werry, J., 329
Wertheim, E. H., 587
Wessberg, H. W., 370
Wessely, S. C., 412, 415, 421, 430, 436, 437
West, A. R., 263
West, L. J., 493
West, S. A., 322, 326
Westen, D., 16, 92, 581, 659, 660
Westenberg, H. G., 361
Westerberg, V. S., 218
Westermeyer, J., 224
Westra, H., 364
Westreich, L. M., 49, 50
Wetton, S., 254
Wetzel, R. D., 420, 475, 490
Wexler, N. S., 157
Whaley, A. L., 109, 115, 261
Wheatley, T., 5
Wheeler, C. C., 536
Whiffen, V. E., 656
Whitacre, C. C., 145, 158
Whitaker, A., 240
White, G., 549
White, I., 19
White, T., 334
Whitehead, W. E., 413, 432, 450
Whitehouse, W. G., 295, 305, 306, 307, 324
Whitfield, J. B., 182
Whooley, D., 443
Wicki, W., 612
Wickramaratne, P., 293, 320, 372
Widiger, T. A., 3, 4, 5, 6, 7, 8, 9, 10, 11, 12, 14,

16, 17, 18, 19, 20, 21, 22, 23, 54, 55, 80, 92, 96, 635, 636, 659, 662
Wiedmann, K., 186
Wiggins, J. S., 635, 658, 660
Wiita, B., 361
Wikblad, O., 181
Wikler, A., 183
Wilber, C. H., 42, 43
Wileman, A., 443
Wilens, T. E., 329
Wilfley, D. E., 579, 584
Wilhelm, K., 382
Wilhelm, S., 365, 418, 419
Wilhelmsen, I., 413
Wilk, C. M., 239
Wilkel, C. S., 445
Wilkinson, D. A., 174, 179
Wilkinson, S. R., 432
Willenbring, M., 55
Williams, A. M., 333
Williams, C. J., 542
Williams, D. E., 446, 574
Williams, D. R., 238
Williams, D. T., 428
Williams, J. B. W., 4, 6, 7, 8, 11, 12, 13, 16, 90, 91, 92, 215, 247, 301, 302, 306, 320, 331, 368, 444
Williams, M., 181, 331
Williams, R., 181
Williams, W., 519
Williams. K. E., 381
Williamson, D. A., 320, 331, 575, 579, 580, 581, 582, 583
Williford, W. O., 41
Willner, P., 327, 332
Wills, T. A., 221
Wilner, P., 327
Wilsnack, R. W., 171, 173, 184, 185
Wilsnack, S. C., 171, 173, 184, 185
Wilson, G., 545, 546, 579
Wilson, J. L., 225

Wilson, M., 14, 18
Wilson, T. W., 431
Wincze, J. P., 552
Winett, C., 324
Wingerson, D. K., 46
Wink, P., 652
Winokur, G., 42, 45, 142
Winslow, J. T., 371, 385
Winslow, W. W., 447
Winstead, B. A., 6
Winter, L. B., 302
Winters, K. C., 323, 324, 325, 332
Wise, T. N., 429, 432
Wisiewski, S. R., 46
Wisner, K. L., 18
Wisniewski, S. R., 320, 321, 323, 330, 331, 335
Wittchen, H., 34, 36, 37, 39, 292, 299, 349, 351, 354, 359, 360, 379
Witztum, E., 553
Wixted, J. T., 252, 253
Wlazlo, A., 362
Wodak, A. D., 181
Wofinsohn, L., 551
Wohlgemuth, W. K., 624
Wolf, A. W., 34, 524
Wolfe, B. E., 589, 590
Wolfe, F., 446
Wolfe, J., 42, 45, 353
Wolff, K., 218
Wolff, P., 364, 374, 382
Wolff, S., 641, 662
Wolford, G., 58
Wolkow, R. M., 361
Wolkowitz, O. M., 9, 12, 239
Wonderlich, J. E., 580, 581
Wonderlich, S. S., 656
Wong, T. M., 103, 114
Wood, J. M., 112, 115, 614
Wood, P. S., 44
Wood, T. D., 238
Woodman, C. L., 359
Woods, S. W., 360

Woody, E. Z., 494
Woody, G. E., 54, 174, 179
Woody, S., 369, 377
Wool, C. A., 449
Woolhandler, S., 36
Workman-Daniels, K. L., 42
World Health Organization, 212, 416, 572, 601
Worley, P. J., 539
Wormworth, J. A., 21
Woysville, M. J., 318, 323
Wozney, K., 489
Wozniak, J., 329, 331
Wright, A., 238
Wright, I. C., 255
Wright, K., 327
Wu, E. Q., 234
Wu, L., 48
Wu, M. T., 489
Wunder, J., 46
Wykes, T., 295, 296, 307
Wylie, K., 517, 526
Wyllie, M. G., 529
Wyshak, G., 418, 425, 429

Xia, Z., 172
Xie, H., 60
Xin, Z. C., 529
Xiong, W., 262

Yadalam, K. G., 35, 41, 46
Yaeger, A., 221
Yager, J., 586
Yagla, S. J., 359
Yale, S., 241
Yamada, N., 251
Yamamiya, Y., 586
Yamamoto, J., 261, 381
Yan, L. J., 324
Yang, H., 361
Yanovski, S. Z., 581
Yap, L., 363
Yarnall, K. S., 294, 295

Yarnold, P. R., 35, 41, 46, 60, 241, 370
Yaryura-Tobias, J. A., 445
Yatham, L. N., 326
Yeager, C. A., 478
Yehuda, R., 385, 648
Yen, S., 648, 663
Yener, G. G., 549
Yesavage, J. A., 301
Yi, H., 171
Yohman, J. R., 142
Yong, L., 97
Yonkers, K. A., 449
Yoon, J. S., 300
Young, A. B., 157, 379, 451
Young, E. A., 585
Young, J. L., 255, 260, 665
Young, R., 220, 221
Youngstrom, E. A., 321, 329
Yu, E. S. H., 172
Yurgelun-Todd, D., 36
Yutsy, S. H., 443, 444
Yutzi, S. H., 475

Zachar, P., 15, 24
Zacut, D., 531
Zadra, A., 606, 624
Zaider, T. I., 363

Zalcman, S., 239, 252
Zammit, G. R., 611
Zanarini, M. C., 22, 97, 368, 659, 663, 664
Zandbergen, J., 378
Zane, N. W. S., 261
Zanelli, J., 332
Zanis, D., 248
Zarac, A., 322, 332
Zarcone, V., 620, 621
Zatzick, D. F., 51, 478
Zavitzianos, G., 539
Zechmester, J. S., 324
Zee, P. C., 606
Zeller, P. J., 294
Zellner, A., 62
Zezza, N., 143
Zhang, A. Y., 108
Zhang, H., 323
Zhang, M., 172, 262
Zhang, W., 360
Zhao, L., 529
Zhao, S., 34, 36, 37, 39, 292, 299
Ziedonis, D. M., 36
Ziegler, V. E., 381
Ziff, D. C., 175
Zilbergeld, B., 520
Zilberman, D., 212
Zimering, R., 362
Zimmerman, B., 331

Zimmerman, M., 93, 94, 637, 640, 642, 644, 649, 651, 653, 655, 657, 658, 659, 664
Zimmerman, R. S., 186
Zinbarg, R., 375, 376
Zinsmeister, A. R., 446
Zisook, S., 239, 361
Zitma, F. G., 294
Zito, W. S., 253
Zlotnick, C., 297
Zoghbi, S. S., 332
Zohar, J., 52, 361, 384
Zohar-Kadouch, R., 361, 384
Zolondek, S. C., 546
Zorrilla, L. E., 334
Zubenko, G. S., 298
Zubin, J., 258
Zubizarreta, I., 362
Zucconi, M., 609, 611
Zucker, B., 365
Zucker, K. J., 543, 545
Zucker, N. L., 575, 584
Zung, W. W., 301
Zurbin, J., 142, 143
Zurbriggen, E. L., 476
Zuroff, D. C., 656
Zweben, A., 175, 214
Zweig-Frank, H., 476, 648, 665

Subject Index

Acute stress disorder. *See* Anxiety disorders
Addiction Potential Scale, 214
Addiction Research Foundation, 168
Addiction Severity Index, 202, 216, 218
Addiction Severity Inventory, 248
Age-related cognitive decline, 8. *See also* specific disorders
Agnosia. *See* Perceptual disorders
Agoraphobia. *See* Anxiety disorders
AIDS dementia, 125, 144
Alcohol Dependence Scale, 168–169, 178
Alcoholics Anonymous, 166–167, 172
Alcohol, Smoking, and Substance Involvement Screening Test (ASSIST), 215
Alcohol use disorders, 141–143
  addiction, 166–168, 169
  assessment of, 168–169, 176–182, 187
    methods of, 177–182
  biological factors of, 186–187
  clinical treatment of, 172
  comorbidity with, 179
  course of, 172–173
  diagnosis of, 173–175
  epidemiology, 170–172
  etiology of, 182–187
  gender and, 184–185
  minority groups and, 185–186
  prevalence of use, 170
Alcohol Use Disorders Identification Test (AUDIT), 178, 213
Alexia. *See* Perceptual disorders

Alzheimer's disease, 140–141. *See also* Brain damage
  Diagnosis, 126
Amnesia. *See* Brain damage; Dissociative disorders
Amphetamine use disorders, 204
Anorexia nervosa. *See* Eating disorders
Antidepressants, 9–10
Antisocial personality disorder. *See* Personality disorders
Anxiety disorders, 349–386
  acute stress disorder, 12–13, 353, 476
  agoraphobia, 350–351
  behavioral theories of, 374–37
  biology of, 381–385
  characteristics of, 357–358
  cognitive theories of, 376–378
  course of, 359–360
  diagnosis of, 365–367
  ethnic minorities, 379–381
  etiology of, 371–386
  generalized anxiety disorder, 353–354, 355
  medical conditions, due to, 354
  obsessive-compulsive disorder, 352, 356
  onset, 358–359
  panic attacks, 349–350
  panic disorder, 350, 355–356, 476
  posttraumatic stress disorder, 12–13, 37, 352–353, 355, 475, 476, 482
  prevalence of, 356
  social phobia, 11–12, 351, 355
  specific phobia, 351–352
  substance use and, 354

Anxiety disorders (*continued*)
  toxic exposure and, 354
  Treatment of, 360–365, 386
Anxiolytics, 10
Aphasia, 128,131. *See also*
    Communicative disorders
Apraxia. *See* Motility disorders
Arousal Predisposition Scale, 621
Ataque de nervios. See Dissociative
    disorders
Attention-deficit/hyperactivity
    disorder, 6, 11
Avoidant personality disorder. *See*
    Personality disorders

Beck Anxiety Inventory (BAI), 179
Beck Depression Inventory (BDI), 179,
    301, 302, 620
Binge eating disorder, 7. *See also*
    Eating disorders
Bipolar disorder, 317–335
  assessment of, 320
  course, 322–328
  description of, 319–320
  diagnosis of, 328–329, 334–335
    in children, 329–330
    methods for, 331
  dual diagnosis of, 330–331
  epidemiology of, 320–321
  in ethnic minorities, 321
  etiology, 317, 324–325, 331–334
  functional impairment in,
    322
  gender factors, 321
  heritability of, 331–332
  neuropsychology of, 332–334
  onset, 320
  phenomenology of, 321
  prevalence, 293, 320
  psychosocial factors, 323–325
  sleep and, 325–326
  subtypes of, 318
  suicide and, 321–322
  symptomatology, 317–318
  treatment of, 326–328, 335
Body dysmorphic disorder. *See*
    Somatoform disorders
Body Dysmorphic Disorder
    Examination, 448, 584

Body Dysmorphic Disorder
    Questionnaire, 445
Body Image Avoidance Questionnaire,
    584
Body Shape Questionnaire, 584
Borderline personality disorder. *See*
    Personality disorders
Brain damage, 126–130. *See also*
    specific disorders
  alcoholism, 137, 141–143, 160
  Alzheimer's disease, 140–141, 160
  amnesia, 153–154, 483
  bacterial infections and, 144
  course of, 158–160
  delirium, 143
  dementia, 139–141, 151–153
  diagnosis, 154–157
  early life malformations and,
    136–137
  epidemiology, 157–158
  genetic influences in, 160–161
  localization of, 127–132
  multiple sclerosis, 139–141
  phenylketonuria, 143
  Pick's disease, 140
  prognosis, 158–160
  Tay-Sach's disease, 143, 161
  toxins and, 143–145
  vascular diseases, 137–139, 161, 483
Brain tumor, 135–136
Breath alcohol tests, 180–181
Breathing-related sleep disorders.
    See Sleep disorders
Brief Psychiatric Rating Scale (BPRS),
    252
Brief Situational Confidence
    Questionnaire (BSCQ-39), 178
Brief Symptom Inventory, 620
Bulimia nervosa. *See* Eating disorders
Bulimia Test-Revised, 583
Bulimic Cognitive Distortions Scale,
    583

Caffeine, 170
CAGE mnemonic, 214
Camberwell Family Interview, 254
Cannabinoids, 205. *See also* Marijuana
    use disorders; Substance use
    disorders

Carbon monoxide testing, 181–182
Center for Epidemiological
    Studies-Depression
    Scale (CES-D), 301
Children's Eating Attitudes Test,
    583
Children's Eating Behavior Inventory,
    583
Circadian rhythm sleep disorders.
    See Sleep disorders
Clarke Sexual History Questionnaire,
    546
CNS depressants, 205. *See also* Alcohol
    use disorders; Substance use
    disorders
Cocaine use disorders
    dependence, 203
    diagnosis of, 211
    epidemiology, 203
    treatment, 202–203, 210
Communicative disorders, 147–148
Composite International Diagnostic
    Interview-Second Edition, 216,
    302–303, 444
Conduct disorder, 11
Conversion disorder. *See* Somatoform
    disorders
Creutzfeldt-Jakob disease, 141, 144
Culture. *See* Multicultural clients

Dartmouth Assessment of Lifestyle
    Instrument (DALI), 248
Delirium, 125,143. *See also* Brain
    damage
Delusional disorder, 250–251
Dementia. *See* Brain damage
Dependent personality disorder. *See*
    Personality disorders
Depression. *See* Depressive disorders
Depressive disorders, 286–309.
    See also Bipolar disorder;
    Mood disorders
    age factors, 293
    assessment of, 300–304
    biology of, 308–309
    cancer, 298
    cerebrovascular disease, 298
    classification, 286
    conceptualizations of, 289

coronary heart disease, 298
    course of, 297
    description of, 290–292, 295–296
    diabetes, 298
    diagnosis of, 289–290, 298–300
    dissociation in, 476
    due to general medical conditions,
        289
    dysthymia, 288–289, 291, 304
    in elderly, 300
    epidemiology of, 292
    etiology of, 304–309
    gender factors, 293
    grief and, 299
    hyperthyroidism, 298
    hypothyroidism, 298
    major depressive disorder, 287–288,
        290–291, 304
    with medical illnesses, 298–299
    minor depressive disorder, 289
    in minorities, 294, 307–308
    myocardial infarction, 298
    not otherwise specified, 289, 291–292,
        304
    in nursing facilities, 294
    Parkinson's disease and, 298
    postpsychotic depressive disorder of
        schizophrenia, 289
    premenstrual dysphoric disorder,
        289
    prevalence of, 292–294
    prognosis of, 297–298
    recurrent brief disorder, 289
    stroke and, 298
    substance abuse and, 299
    superimposed on psychotic or
        delusional disorders, 289
    symptomatology, 286–287
Depressive personality disorder, 11
Diagnosis. *See* Dual diagnosis; specific
    disorders
    categorical model, 3, 14–24, 635
    comorbidity, 10, 34
    dimensional model, 14–24, 635
    multicultural, 111–113
    not otherwise specified, 11
Diagnostic Interview for *DSM-IV*
    Personality Disorders-IV,
    86, 97, 659

Diagnostic Interview for Functional
    Syndromes, 445
Diagnostic Interview Schedule for
    DSM-IV, 86–88, 216, 417, 444
Dietary Intent Scale, 583
Dieting and Body Image
    Questionnaire, 583
Dimensional Assessment of
    Personality Pathology, 660
Disconnection syndrome, 128
Dissociative anesthetic drugs, 206
Dissociative disorders, 473–495
    assessment of, 473–474, 484
    characteristics of, 478
    conceptualization of, 474–475
    culture-bound syndromes in,
        478, 494
    depersonalization disorder,
        479–481
    derealization, 479–480
    diagnosis of, 475–476, 479
    differential diagnosis of, 481, 483
    dissociative amnesia, 481–482
    dissociative fugue, 482, 485–486
    dissociative identity disorder, 478,
        481, 486–491
    dissociative trance disorder,
        493–494
    drug use and, 483
    epidemiology of, 477
    malingering of, 483
    not otherwise specified, 492–495
    recovered memories and, 484
    trauma and, 484
Dissociative Disorders Interview
    Schedule, 474
Dissociative Experiences Scale, 473
Dissociative identity disorder. *See*
    Dissociative disorders
Down syndrome, 136
Drinker Inventory of Consequences,
    216
Drug Abuse Screening Test, 168–169
Drug-Taking Confidence
    Questionnaire-8 (DTCQ-8), 179
Drug Use Disorder Identification Test
    (DUDIT), 213–214
Drug Use Screening Inventory (DUSI),
    216

Dual diagnosis, 34–64
    anxiety disorders and, 42, 44, 45
    assessment of, 52–54
    bidirectional model of, 63–64
    clinical studies of, 40–44
    common factors models of, 58–59
    eating disorders and, 580–581
    epidemiology of, 35–44
    genetics and, 58
    homelessness and, 50–51
    legal problems and, 50
    life functioning and, 44–46
    personality disorders and, 43, 54, 55
    physical illness and, 49–50
    prevalence, 36–39, 41
    psychopathology research of,
        55–57
    secondary psychiatric disorder
        model of, 62–63
    service utilization with, 47–49
    severity, 40
    substance-induced disorders,
        52–54, 62–63
    substance use disorders and,
        42–43
    treatment compliance and, 46–47
    treatment outcomes with, 54–57
    violence and, 46–47
    women's issues and, 51–52
Dutch Eating Behavior Questionnaire,
    583
Dyscontrol, 4–5
Dysfunctional Beliefs and Attitudes
    About Sleep Scale, 621
Dysmorphic Concern Questionnaire,
    445
Dyspareunia. *See* Sexual dysfunction
Dyssomnias. *See* Sleep disorders
Dysthymic disorder. *See* Depressive
    disorders

Eating Attitudes Test, 574, 583
Eating Disorder Diagnostic Scale,
    583
Eating Disorder Inventory, 574–575,
    583
Eating disorders, 571–592
    anorexia nervosa, 5, 11, 571–572,
        573–575

assessment of, 581–584
binge-eating disorder, 573
bulimia nervosa, 5, 11, 572–573
characteristics of, 576–578
course of, 578–579
diagnosis of, 579–581
epidemiology of, 575–576
etiology of, 584–591
gender factors of, 588–589
not otherwise specified, 573
Entactogens, 206–207. *See also*
Substance use disorders
Epidemiological Catchment Area
Study, 36–38, 292
Epilepsy, 145–146, 483
Epworth Sleepiness Scale, 621
Erectile dysfunction. *See* Sexual
dysfunction
Ethnic minorities. *See* Multicultural
clients
Exhibitionism. *See* Paraphilias
Expressed emotion (EE), 254, 257

Family Experiences Interview
Schedule, 254
Female orgasmic disorder. *See* Sexual
dysfunction
Fetal alcohol syndrome, 137
Fetishism. *See* Paraphilias
Fibromyalgia, 412
Five-factor model, 17–23, 636
Frontotemporal dementia, 141
Frotteurism. *See* Paraphilias

Gambling, pathological, 5
Ganser's syndrome, 493. *See also*
Dissociative disorders
Gender dysphoria, 533–534
Gender identity disorder, 533–538
assessment of, 536–537
course of, 535
diagnosis of, 535–536
epidemiology of, 535
treatment of, 537–538
Generalized anxiety disorder.
See Anxiety disorders
Geriatric Depression Scale, 301
Guided Self-Change Clinic, 168–169
Gulf War Syndrome, 125–126

Hair analysis, 181, 219
Hallucinogens, 207. *See also*
Hallucinogen use disorders;
Substance use disorders
Hallucinogen use disorders, 203
Hamilton Rating Scale for Depression,
179
Head trauma, 133–135
Histrionic personality disorder. *See*
Personality disorders
Human Immunodeficiency Virus,
49–50, 224
Huntington's Disease, 125, 133, 140, 160.
See also Brain damage
Hypersomnia. *See* Sleep disorders
Hypoactive sexual desire disorder. *See*
Sexual dysfunction
Hypochondriasis. *See* Somatoform
disorders

Impairment, 5–8
Inhalants, 208. *See also* Inhalant use
disorders; Substance use
disorders
Inhalant use disorders, 204
Illness Attitude Scale, 447–448
Illness Behavior Questionnaire, 447
Insomnia, 6. *See also* Sleep disorders
Insomnia Interview Schedule, 618
Insomnia Severity Index, 621
Intelligence, 15, 24
Assessment in multicultural clients,
112–113
Intermittent explosive disorder, 5
International Classification of
Diseases, Tenth Revision,
211–212, 292, 414–415
International Personality Disorder
Examination (IPDE), 86, 94–96,
659
International Society for the Study of
Dissociation, 473
Interview for Diagnosis of Eating
Disorders, 583
Inventory of Interpersonal Problems,
660
Irritable bowel syndrome, 412
Irritable Bowel Syndrome
Misconception Scale, 445

Karolinska Sleepiness Scale, 621
Kiddie Schedule for Affective
    Disorders and Schizophrenia
    (KSADS), 331
Kid's Eating Disorder Survey, 583
Kleptomania, 5
Korsakoff's syndrome, 160, 483

Learning theory, 183
Lewy body dementia, 141
Lifetime Drinking History, 177
Liver function tests, 181

Manic-depression. *See* Bipolar
    disorder
Male orgasmic disorder. *See* Sexual
    dysfunction
Marijuana use disorders, 203–204. *See
    also* Substance use disorders
Maryland Assessment of Social
    Competence (MASC), 253
Mental retardation, 15, 129, 136
Millon Clinical Multiaxial Inventory,
    Third Edition (MCMI-III),
    214, 660
Mini-International Neuropsychiatric
    Interview, 302–304
Minnesota Multiphasic Personality
    Inventory, 446, 546, 574–575,
    620, 660
Mize's Cognitive Distortions
    Questionnaire, 583
Mood disorders. *See also* Depressive
    disorders; Dual diagnosis
  anxiety,
  bipolar disorders, 11, 37
  comorbidity
    with schizophrenia, 249–250
    with substance use disorders,
      212
  depression, 7, 10,
  mixed anxiety-depression, 7, 11
Montgomery Asberg Depression
    Rating Scale, 301
Motility disorders, 149–151
Multiaxial Assessment of Eating
    Disorders, 583
Multicultural clients
  alcohol use and, 171–172, 185

assessment, 103–107, 114, 117
  of intelligence, 112–113
  clinician bias of, 115
  competency, 102–103, 116–117
  considerations, 103–104, 115–116
  diagnosis of, 111–113
  language and, 109
  somatization, 108–109
  Spanish-speaking populations,
    112–113
  stereotypes of, 110–111, 115
  substance use disorders and, 225
  symptomatology, 109–110, 115
Multidimensional Body Self-Relations
    Questionnaire, 583
Multidimensional Inventory of
    Hypochondriacal Traits, 448
Multiple sclerosis. *See* Brain damage
Multiple Sleep Latency Test, 622
Multiphasic Sex Inventory, 546

Narcissistic personality disorder.
    See Personality disorders
Narcolepsy. *See* Sleep disorders
Narcotics Anonymous, 216
National Comorbidity Survey (NCS),
    36–40, 292
National Epidemiologic Survey on
    Alcohol and Related Condition
    (NESARC), 37, 39
National Institute of Mental Health
    Collaborative Program on the
    Psychobiology of Depression, 42
National Institute of Mental Health
    Collaborative Study of
    Depression, 41, 45
National Institute of Mental Health
    Life Charting method, 331
National Institute of Mental Health-
    Measurement and Treatment
    Research to Improve
    Cognition in Schizophrenia,
    252
National Longitudinal Alcohol
    Epidemiology Study (NLAES),
    36–39
National Survey of Veterans, 50
NEO-Personality Inventory-Revised,
    21–22, 636, 660

Neuropsychology
  of brain damage, 126–132
  of alcohol use, 179
Nightmares. *See* Sleep disorders
Nine-Item Patient Health
  Questionnaire, 301

Obsessive-compulsive disorder. *See*
  Anxiety disorders
Obsessive-compulsive personality
  disorder. *See* Personality
  disorders
Opiate use disorders
  diagnosis of, 211
  epidemiology of, 203
  treatment, 210
Opioid analgesics, 208. *See also* Opiate
  use disorders
Oppositional defiant disorder, 6, 11
Orgasmic disorders. *See* Sexual
  dysfunction
Overvalued Ideas Scale, 445

Pain disorder. *See* Somatoform
  disorders
Panic attacks. *See* Anxiety disorders
Panic disorder. *See* Anxiety disorders
Paranoid personality disorder. *See*
  Personality disorders
Paraphilias, 538–553
  assessment of, 546–548
  course of, 545
  description of, 538
  epidemiology of, 543–545
  etiological theories of, 548–550
  exhibitionism, 539, 545
  fetishism, 534, 539, 542–543, 545
  frotteurism, 540, 545
  not otherwise specified, 543
  pedophilia, 540–541
  sexual masochism, 541–542, 545
  sexual sadism, 542, 545
  treatment of, 550–553
  voyeurism, 543, 545
Parasomnias. *See* Sleep disorders
Parkinson's disease, 141
Pathology, 8–10
Pedophilia, 5. *See also* Paraphilias
Perceptual disorders, 149–151

Peritraumatic Dissociative Experiences
  Questionnaire, 474
Personality Assessment Inventory, 660
Personality Diagnostic
  Questionnaire–4+, 660
Personality Disorder Interview–IV
  (PDI-IV), 86, 96, 659
Personality disorders, 633–666
  antisocial personality disorder, 5, 37,
    643–645
  assessment of, 658–661
  avoidant personality disorder,
    652–654
  borderline personality disorder,
    645–648
  classification of, 636
  course of, 662–665
  dependent personality disorder,
    654–656
  diagnosis of, 17–23, 634–635
  histrionic personality disorder,
    649–650
  narcissistic personality disorder,
    650–652
  obsessive-compulsive personality
    disorder, 656–658
  onset of, 662
  paranoid personality disorder,
    637–640
  risk factors for, 661
  schizoid personality disorder,
    640–641
  schizotypal personality disorder,
    641–643
  treatment of, 665
Pervasive developmental disorders, 126
Phenylketonuria, 143
Pittsburgh Sleep Quality Index,
  620, 621
Polysomnography, 621–622
Positive and Negative Syndrome Scale,
  (PANNS), 252
Postpsychotic disorder of
  schizophrenia, 11
Posttraumatic stress disorder. *See*
  Anxiety disorders
Premature ejaculation. *See* Sexual
  dysfunction
Premenstrual dysmorphic disorder, 6

Prescription Drug Use Questionnaire (PDUQ), 215
Pre-Sleep Arousal Scale, 621
Primary Care Evaluation of Mental Disorders, 302
Profile of Mood States, 301
Psychosis, 476. *See also* Schizophrenia
Psychotic Rating Scale, 252

Quantity-frequency methods, 177
Questionnaire of Experiences Scale, 473
Quick Inventory of Depressive Symptomatology Self Report (QIDS-SR), 40

Readiness to Change Questionnaire, 217
Research Diagnostic Criteria, 88–89

Schedule for Affective Disorders and Schizophrenia (SADS), 86, 88–90
Schedule for Nonadaptive and Adaptive Personality, 660
Schizoaffective disorder, 13, 249–250
Schizoid personality disorder. *See* Personality disorders
Schizophrenia, 37, 61, 234–264
    assessment
        biological, 255–256
        of family, 254–255
        psychological, 251–254
    in childhood, 244
    comorbidity
        with delusional disorder, 250–251
        with mood disorders, 249–250
        with substance use disorders, 212, 247–249
    course of, 243–246
    cultural factors in, 260–262
    description of, 235–237
    diagnosis of, 246–247
    epidemiology of, 237–238
    etiology of, 256–263
    gender factors, 259–260
    misdiagnosis of, 112
    onset, 244

symptomatology of, 238–243
treatment, 234, 255–256
vulnerability for, 137
Schizotypal personality disorder. *See* Personality disorders
SCID. *See* Structured Clinical Interview for *DSM-IV*
Seizures. *See* Epilepsy
Self-monitoring, 177
Semi-structured interviews, 78–97
    advantages of, 81–83, 85–86
    and axis I disorders, 86–92
    and axis II disorders, 92–97
    disadvantages of, 81, 83–86
    nature of, 72–79, 81
    reliability and validity of, 81–83, 84–85
Severity of Alcohol Dependence Questionnaire (SADQ), 178
Sexual arousal disorders. *See* Sexual dysfunction
Sexual aversion disorder. *See* Sexual dysfunction
Sexual Deviance Card Sort, 546
Sexual dysfunction, 504–533
    assessment of, 515–523
    classification, 504–506
    diagnosis of, 515–523
    epidemiology of, 506–508
    hypoactive sexual desire disorder, 508, 513–514, 515–517, 523–525
    orgasmic disorders, 510–512, 519–521, 528–531
    sexual arousal disorders, 509–510, 517–519, 525–528
    sexual aversion disorder, 509, 525
    sexual pain disorders, 512–513, 514, 521–523, 531–533
    treatment of, 523–532
Sexual Interest Card Sort Questionnaire, 546
Sexual masochism. *See* Paraphilias
Sexual sadism. *See* Paraphilias
Shedler-Western Assessment Procedure, 660
Short Alcohol Dependence Data Questionnaire (SADD), 178
Simple Screening Instrument for Substance Abuse (SSI-SA), 214

Situational Confidence Questionnaire
(SCQ-39), 178
Sleep Associated Monitoring Index,
621
Sleep-Behavior Self-Rating Scale,
621
Sleep disorders, 601–626
assessment of, 618–622
classification of, 601–603
course of, 612–614
diagnosis of, 614–618
due to general medical conditions,
609
dyssomnias, 603–606, 611–612, 613,
614–617
epidemiology of, 610–612
etiology of, 623–625
parasomnias, 606–608, 611, 617–618
related to other mental disorders,
608–609
substance induced, 609–610
Sleep Hygiene Awareness and
Practice Scale, 621
Sleep Satisfaction Questionnaire, 621
Sleep terrors. *See* Sleep disorders
Sleepwalking. *See* Sleep disorders
Social anxiety disorder. *See* Anxiety
disorders
Social Functioning Scale, 254
Social phobia. *See* Anxiety disorders
Somatization, 424. *See also* Somatoform
disorders
multicultural issues and, 108–109
Somatoform disorders, 410–453
assessment of, 441–452
body dysmorphic disorder, 414,
418–419, 423–424, 445
characteristics of, 411–415, 419, 476
chronic illness and, 440–441
comorbidity of, 416, 426–427
conceptualization of, 410–411,
452–453
conversion disorder, 412–413,
417–418, 421–422, 425, 438–439
course of, 424–426
cultural meanings of, 448–452
diagnosis of, 410, 437–441, 444
epidemiology of, 415–419
etiology of, 426–437

cognitive factors in, 428–430
emotional factors in, 430–432
integrative model for, 434–437
psychophysiological processes in,
433–434
psychosocial factors in, 432–433
somatic amplification and,
427–428, 429
gender differences in, 448–450
hypochondriasis, 414, 418, 422–423,
425–426, 428, 438
multisomatoform disorder, 417
not otherwise specified, 414, 417,
419
pain disorder, 414, 418, 438
somatization disorder, 411–412,
419–420
undifferentiated somatoform
disorder, 412, 417, 420–421
Somatosensory Amplification Scale,
428
Spanish-speaking populations,
112–113
Specific phobia. *See* Anxiety disorders
Stages of Change Readiness and
Treatment Eagerness Scale
(SOCRATES), 203, 217
Stanford Acute Stress Reaction
Questionnaire, 473
Stanford Sleepiness Scale, 621
State-Trait Anxiety Inventory, 620
Stimulants, 209. *See also* Amphetamine
use disorders; Substance use
disorders
Structured Clinical Interview for
DSM-IV Axis I Disorders
(SCID-I), 86, 90–92, 202, 215,
247, 251, 302–303, 331, 444–445
Structured Clinical Interview for
DSM-IV Axis II Personality
Disorders (SCID-II), 86,
92–93, 659
Structured Clinical Interview of
Dissociative Disorders, 474
Structured Diagnostic Interview for
Hypochondriasis, 444
Structured Interview for *DSM-IV*
Personality (SIDP-IV), 86,
93–94, 659

Structured Interview for Sleep Disorders, 618
Structured Interview for the Five-Factor Model of Personality, 659
Structured interviews, 78–97
    advantages of, 81–83, 85–86
    and axis I disorders, 86–92
    and axis II disorders, 92–97
    disadvantages of, 81, 83–86
    nature of, 72–81
    reliability and validity of, 81–83, 84–85
Substance Dependence Severity Scale (SDSS), 215–216
Substance-induced sleep disorders. See Sleep disorders
Substance use disorders, 5, 201. See also Dual diagnosis; specific disorders
    in adolescents, 204
    assessment of, 213–216
        functional analysis, 217
        motivation, 217
        posttreatment measures, 218–219
        screening measures, 213–215
        treatment planning, 216–218
    comorbidity with, 212–213
        with depression, 299
    course of, 204–211
    diagnosis of, 211–213, 215–216
    drug classes, 204
    epidemiology of, 203–204
    etiology of, 220–225
        gender issues in, 204, 224
        in schizophrenia, 247–249
        treatment, 210
Symptom Checklist-90, 179

Tay-Sach's disease, 143
Timeline Followback assessment, 169, 177, 218
Trail Making Test, 179
Transgenderism, 534
Transsexualism. See Gender identity disorder
Transvestic fetishism, 5, 6. See also Paraphilias

Undifferentiated somatoform disorder. See Somatoform disorders
University of Rhode Island Change Assessment (URICA), 217
Urinalysis, 181, 219

Vaginismus. See Sexual dysfunction
Vascular diseases, 137–139
Voyeurism. See Paraphilias

Wechsler Adult Intelligence Scale, 112–113, 179
Whiteley Index of Hypochrondriasis, 444–445, 446–447
Wilson Sex Fantasy Questionnaire, 546

Yale-Brown Obsessive Compulsive Scale, 448

Zung Depression Scale, 301, 574–575